39TH ANNUAL EDITION

PHOTOGRAPHER'S
MARKET 2016

·······

Mary Burzlaff Bostic, Editor

NORTH LIGHT BOOKS
CINCINNATI, OHIO

artistsmarketonline.com

Publisher and Community Leader, Fine Art Community: Jamie Markle
Content Director, North Light Books: Mona Clough
Market Books Assistant, North Light Books: Keeyana Avery

Artist's Market Online website: artistsmarketonline.com
Artist's Network website: artistsnetwork.com
North Light Shop website: northlightshop.com

Other fine North Light Books are available from your local bookstore, art supply store or online
supplier. Visit our website at fwcommunity.com.

Distributed in Canada by Fraser Direct
100 Armstrong Avenue
Georgetown, ON, Canada L7G 5S4

Distributed in the U.K. and Europe by F&W Media International, LTD
Brunel House, Forde Close, Newton Abbot, Devon, TQ12 4PU, UK
Tel: (+44) 1626 323200, Fax: (+44) 1626 323319
E-mail: enquiries@fwmedia.com

Distributed in Australia by Capricorn Link
P.O. Box 704
S. Windsor NSW, 2756 Australia
Tel: (02) 4560-1600, Fax: (02) 4577-5288
E-mail: books@capricornlink.com.au

ISSN: 0147-247X
ISBN-13: 978-1-4403-4264-6
ISBN-10: 1-4403-4264-4

Cover design by Geoffrey Raker
Interior layout by Zach Nicholas and Geoffrey Raker
Interior design by Claudean Wheeler
Production coordinated by Debbie Thomas

Attention Booksellers: This is an annual directory of F+W, a Content + eCommerce Company.
Return deadline for this edition is December 31, 2016.

fw
a content + ecommerce company

CONTENTS

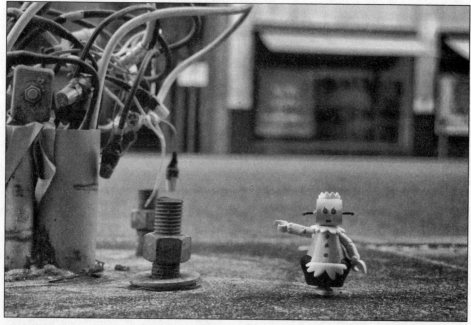

© Chad Moore

ARTICLES & INTERVIEWS

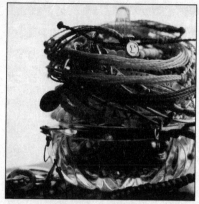

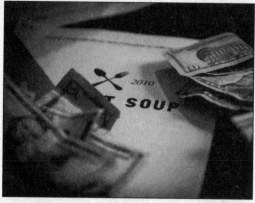

© Lucrecer Braxton   © David Lewinski

MARKETS

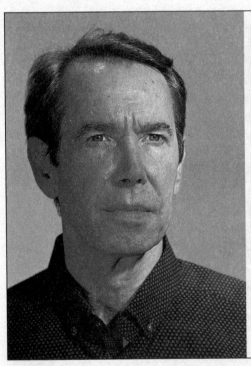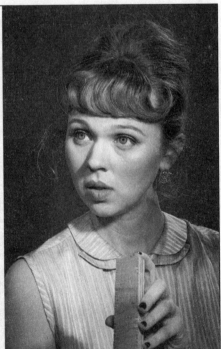

© Jeff Brown

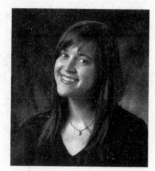

FROM
THE
EDITOR

Love it or hate it, dealing with money is a key component of running a successful photography business. While your passion for shooting is why you became a photographer, competently handling your income and outgo allows you to keep doing what you love.

If handling money isn't your strength, we're here to help. This edition of *Photographer's Market* includes articles on pricing your work, selling without begging, obtaining micro funding for your business, and options for accepting payment from your clients.

You'll also find features on a variety of topics to help keep your business running smoothly and inspiring interviews with three successful photographers. And, as always, we've included more than 1,500 individually verified market contacts (complete with payment information!). So, what's holding you back?

Keep creating and good luck!

Mary Burzlaff Bostic

Mary Burzlaff Bostic
photomarket@fwmedia.com
www.artistsmarketonline.com

P.S. Don't forget to register at **Artist's Market Online, which you get FREE for a year with the purchase of this book**. With your free 1-year subscription, you'll be able to search market contacts, track your submissions, read up on the latest market news, and much more. Use the activation code from the front insert to access your free subscription today.

HOW TO USE THIS BOOK

The first thing you'll notice about most of the listings in this book is the group of symbols that appears before the name of each company. Scanning the listings for symbols can help you quickly locate markets that meet certain criteria. (You'll find a quick-reference key to the symbols as well as a sample listing on the back inside cover of the book.) Here's what each symbol stands for:

- ✚ This photo buyer is new to this edition of the book.
- ✪ This photo buyer is located in Canada.
- ✿ This photo buyer is located outside the U.S. and Canada.
- ◎ This photo buyer uses only images created on assignment.
- ⊟ This photo buyer uses only stock images.

COMPLAINT PROCEDURE

If you feel you have not been treated fairly by a company listed in *Photographer's Market*, we advise you to take the following steps:

- First, try to contact the listing. Sometimes one phone call, e-mail, or letter can quickly clear up the matter.
- Document all your correspondence with the listing. If you write to us with a complaint, provide the details of your submission, the date of your first contact with the listing, and the nature of your subsequent correspondence.
- We will enter your letter into our files.
- The number and severity of complaints will be considered in our decision whether to delete the listing from the next edition.

◐ This photo buyer accepts submissions in digital format.

✿ This photo buyer uses film or other audiovisual media.

☝ This art fair is a juried event; a juror or committee of jurors views applicants' work and selects those whose work fits within the guidelines of the event.

Pay Scale

We asked photo buyers to indicate their general pay scale based on what they typically pay for a single image. Their answers are signified by a series of dollar signs before each listing. Scanning for dollar signs can help you quickly identify which markets pay at the top of the scale. However, not every photo buyer answered this question, so don't mistake a missing dollar sign as an indication of low pay rates. Also keep in mind that many photo buyers are willing to negotiate.

     $ Pays $1–150

     $$ Pays $151–750

     $$$ Pays $751–1,500

     $$$$ Pays more than $1,500

Openness

We also asked photo buyers to indicate their level of openness to freelance photography. Looking for these symbols can help you identify buyers who are willing to work with newcomers, as well as prestigious buyers who publish only top-notch photography.

○ Encourages beginning or unpublished photographers to submit work for consideration; publishes new photographers. May pay only in copies or have a low pay rate.

◑ Accepts outstanding work from beginning and established photographers; expects a high level of professionalism from all photographers who make contact.

● Hard to break into; publishes mostly previously published photographers.

⊘ May pay at the top of the scale. Closed to unsolicited submissions.

Subheads

Each listing is broken down into sections to make it easier to locate specific information (see sample listing on the back inside cover of this book). In the first section of each listing you'll find mailing addresses, phone numbers, e-mail and website addresses, and the name of the person you should contact. You'll also find general information about photo buyers, including when their business was established and their publishing philosophy. Each listing will include one or more of the following subheads:

Needs. Here you'll find specific subjects each photo buyer is seeking. (Use the subject index at the end of the book to help you narrow your search.) You'll also find the average

FREQUENTLY ASKED QUESTIONS

1 How do companies get listed in the book?

No company pays to be included—all listings are free. Every company has to fill out a detailed questionnaire about their photo needs. All questionnaires are screened to make sure the companies meet our requirements. Each year we contact every company in the book and ask them to update their information.

2 Why aren't other companies I know about listed in this book?

We may have sent those companies a questionnaire, but they never returned it. Or if they did return a questionnaire, we may have decided not to include them based on our requirements.

3 Some publishers say they accept photos with or without a manuscript. What does that mean?

Essentially, the word *manuscript* means a written article that will be published by a magazine. Some magazines will consider publishing your photos only if they accompany a written article. Other publishers will consider publishing your photos alone, without a manuscript.

4 I sent a CD with large digital files to a photo buyer who said she wanted to see my work. I have not heard from her, and I am afraid that my photos will be used without my permission and without payment. What should I do?

Do not send large, printable files (300 dpi or larger) unless you are sure the photo buyer is going to use them, and you know what you will be paid for their usage and what rights the photo buyer is requesting. If a photo buyer shows interest in seeing your work in digital format, send small JPEGs at first so they can "review" them—i.e., determine if the subject matter and technical quality of your photos meet their requirements. Until you know for sure that the photo buyer is going to license your photos and you have some kind of agreement, do not send high-resolution files. The exception to this rule would be if you have dealt with the photo buyer before or perhaps know someone who has. Some companies receive a large volume of submissions, so sometimes you must be patient. It's a good idea to give any company listed in this book a call before you submit anything and be sure nothing has changed since we contacted them to gather or update information. This is true whether you submit slides, prints, or digital images.

5 A company says they want to publish my photographs, but first they will need a fee from me. Is this a standard business practice?

No, it is not a standard business practice. You should never have to pay to have your photos reviewed or to have your photos accepted for publication. If you suspect that a company may not be reputable, do some research before you submit anything or pay their fees. The exception to this rule is contests. It is not unusual for some contests listed in this book to have entry fees (usually minimal—between five and twenty dollars).

number of freelance photos a buyer uses each year, which will help you gauge your chances of publication.

Audiovisual Needs. If you create images for media such as filmstrips or overhead transparencies, or you shoot videotape or motion picture film, look here for photo buyers' specific needs in these areas.

Specs. Look here to see in what format the photo buyer prefers to receive accepted images. Many photo buyers will accept both digital and film (slides, transparencies, prints) formats. However, many photo buyers are reporting that they accept digital images only, so make sure you can provide the format the photo buyer requires before you send samples.

Exhibits. This subhead appears only in the Galleries section of the book. Like the Needs subhead, you'll find information here about the specific subjects and types of photography a gallery shows.

Making Contact & Terms. When you're ready to make contact with a photo buyer, look here to find out exactly what they want to see in your submission. You'll also find what the buyer usually pays and what rights they expect in exchange. In the Stock section, this subhead is divided into two parts, Payment & Terms and Making Contact, because this information is often lengthy and complicated.

Handles. This subhead appears only in the Photo Representatives section. Some reps also represent illustrators, fine artists, stylists, make-up artists, etc., in addition to photographers. The term *handles* refers to the various types of *talent* they represent.

Tips. Look here for advice and information directly from photo buyers in their own words.

HOW TO START SELLING YOUR WORK

///

If this is your first edition of *Photographer's Market*, you're probably feeling a little overwhelmed by all the information in this book. Before you start flipping through the listings, read the eleven steps below to learn how to get the most out of this book and your selling efforts.

1. Be honest with yourself. Are the photographs you make of the same quality as those you see published in magazines and newspapers? If the answer is yes, you may be able to sell your photos.

2. Get someone else to be honest with you. Do you know a professional photographer who would critique your work for you? Other ways to get opinions about your work: join a local camera club or other photo organization; attend a stock seminar led by a professional photographer; attend a regional or national photo conference or a workshop where they offer daily critiques.

- You'll find workshop and seminar listings in the Markets section.
- You'll find a list of photographic organizations in the Resources section.
- Check your local camera store for information about camera clubs in your area.

3. Get organized. Create a list of subjects you have photographed and organize your images into subject groups. Make sure you can quickly find specific images and keep track of any sample images you send out. You can use database software on your home computer to help you keep track of your images.

Other resources:

- *Photo Portfolio Success* by John Kaplan (Writer's Digest Books)
- *Sell and Re-Sell Your Photos* by Rohn Engh (Writer's Digest Books)

- *The Photographer's Market Guide to Building Your Photography Business* by Vik Orenstein (Writer's Digest Books)

4. Consider the format. Are your pictures color snapshots, black-and-white prints, color slides, or digital captures? The format of your work will determine, in part, which markets you can approach. Below are some general guidelines for where you can market various photo formats. Always check the listings in this book for specific format information.

- **digital**—nearly all newspapers, magazines, stock agencies, ad agencies, book and greeting card publishers
- **black-and-white prints**—some galleries, art fairs, private collectors, literary/art magazines, trade magazines, newspapers, book publishers
- **color prints**—some newsletters, very small trade or club magazines
- **large color prints**—some galleries, art fairs, private collectors
- **color slides (35mm)**—a few magazines, newspapers, some greeting card and calendar publishers, a very few book publishers, textbook publishers, stock agencies
- **color transparencies (2¼×2¼ and 4×5)**—a few magazines, book publishers, calendar publishers, ad agencies, stock agencies. Many of these photo buyers have begun to accept only digital photos, especially stock agencies.

5. Do you want to sell stock images or accept assignments? A stock image is a photograph you create on your own and then sell to a publisher. An assignment is a photograph created at the request of a specific buyer. Many of the listings in *Photographer's Market* are interested in both stock and assignment work.

⮡ Listings that are interested only in stock photography are marked with this symbol.

◉ Listings that are interested only in assignment photography are marked with this symbol.

6. Start researching. Generate a list of the publishers that might buy your images—check the newsstand, go to the library, search the Web, read the listings in this book. Don't forget to look at greeting cards, stationery, calendars, and CD covers. Anything you see with a photograph on it, from a billboard advertisement to a cereal box, is a potential market.

7. Check the publisher's guidelines. Do you know exactly how the publisher you choose wants to be approached? Check the listings in this book first. If you don't know the format, subject, and number of images a publisher wants in a submission, you should check their website first. Often, guidelines are posted there. Or you can send a short letter with a self-addressed, stamped envelope (SASE) or e-mail asking those questions. A quick call to the receptionist might also yield the answers.

8. Check out the market. Get in the habit of reading industry magazines.

9. Prepare yourself. Before you send your first submission, make sure you know how to respond when a publisher agrees to buy your work.

Pay Rates

Most magazines and newspapers will tell you what they pay, and you can accept or decline. However, you should become familiar with typical pay rates. Ask other photographers what they charge—preferably ones you know well or who are not in direct competition with you. Many will be willing to tell you to prevent you from devaluing the market by undercharging.

Other resources:

- *Pricing Photography: The Complete Guide to Assignment & Stock Prices* by Michal Heron and David MacTavish (Allworth Press)
- *fotoQuote*, a software package that is updated each year to list typical stock photo and assignment prices, (800)679-0202, www.cradocfotosoftware.com
- *Negotiating Stock Photo Prices* by Jim Pickerell (www.jimpickerell.com)

Copyright

You should always include a copyright notice on any slide, print, or digital image you send out. While you automatically own the copyright to your work the instant it is created, the notice affords extra protection. The proper format for a copyright notice includes the word or symbol for copyright, the date and your name: © 2016 Jane Photographer. To fully protect your copyright and recover damages from infringers, you must register your copyright with the Copyright Office in Washington DC.

Rights

In most cases, you will not actually be selling your photographs, but rather, the rights to publish them. If a publisher wants to buy your images outright, you will lose the right to resell those images in any form or even display them in your portfolio. Most publishers will buy one-time rights and/or first rights.

Resource:

- *Legal Guide for the Visual Artist* by Tad Crawford (Allworth Press)

Contracts

Formal contract or not, you should always agree to any terms of sale in writing. This could be as simple as sending a follow-up letter restating the agreement and asking for confirmation, once you agree to terms over the phone. You should always keep copies of any correspondence in case of a future dispute or misunderstanding.

Resource:

- *Business and Legal Forms for Photographers* by Tad Crawford (Allworth Press)

10. Prepare your submission. The number one rule when mailing submissions is: "Follow the directions." Always address letters to specific photo buyers. Always include a SASE of sufficient size and with sufficient postage for your work to be safely returned to you. Never send originals when you are first approaching a potential buyer. Try to include something in your submission that the potential buyer can keep on file, such as a tearsheet and your résumé. In fact, photo buyers prefer that you send something they don't have to return to you. Plus, it saves you the time and expense of preparing a SASE.

Resource:

- *Photo Portfolio Success* by John Kaplan (Writer's Digest Books)

11. Continue to promote yourself and your work. After you've made that first sale (and even before), it is important to promote yourself. Success in selling your work depends in part on how well and how often you let photo buyers know what you have to offer. This is known as self-promotion. There are several ways to promote yourself and your work. You can send postcards or other printed material through the mail, send an e-mail with an image and a link to your website, and upload your images to a website that is dedicated to showcasing your work and your photographic services.

RUNNING YOUR BUSINESS

Photography is an art that requires a host of skills, some that can be learned and some that are innate. To make money from your photography, the one skill you can't do without is business savvy. Thankfully, this skill can be learned. We'll cover:

- Submitting Your Work
- Digital Submission Guidelines
- Using Essential Business Forms
- Stock List
- Charging for Your Work
- Figuring Small Business Taxes
- Self-Promotion
- Organizing & Labeling Your Images
- Protecting Your Copyright

SUBMITTING YOUR WORK

Editors, art directors, and other photo buyers are busy people. Many spend only 10 percent of their work time actually choosing photographs for publication. The rest of their time is spent making and returning phone calls, arranging shoots, coordinating production, and doing a host of other unglamorous tasks that make publication possible. They want to discover new talent, and you may even have the exact image they're looking for, but if you don't follow a market's submission instructions to the letter, you have little chance of acceptance.

To learn the dos and don'ts of photography submissions, read each market's listing carefully and make sure to send only what they ask for. Don't send prints if they want only digital files. Don't send color if they want only black and white. Check their website or send for guidelines whenever they are available to get the most complete and up-to-date submission advice. When in doubt, follow these ten rules when sending your work to a potential buyer:

1. Don't forget your SASE. Always include a self-addressed, stamped envelope whether you want your submission back or not. Make sure your SASE is big enough, has enough packaging, and has enough postage to ensure the safe return of your work.

2. Don't over-package. Never make a submission difficult to open and file. Don't tape down all the loose corners. Don't send anything too large to fit in a standard file.

3. Don't send originals. Try not to send things you must have back. Never, ever send originals unsolicited.

4. Label everything. Put a label directly on the slide mount or print you are submitting. Include your name, address, and phone number, as well as the name or number of the image. Your slides and prints will almost certainly get separated from your letter.

5. Do your research. Always research the places to which you want to sell your work. Request sample issues of magazines, visit galleries, examine ads, look at websites, etc. Make sure your work is appropriate before you send it out. A blind mailing is a waste of postage and a waste of time for both you and the art buyer.

6. Follow directions. Always request submission guidelines. Include a SASE for reply. Follow *all* the directions exactly, even if you think they're silly.

7. Include a business letter. Always include a cover letter, no more than one page, that lets the potential buyer know you are familiar with their company, what your photography background is (briefly), and where you've sold work before (if it pertains to what you're trying to do now). If you send an e-mail, follow the same protocol as you would for a business cover letter and include the same information.

8. Send to a person, not a title. Send submissions to a specific person at a company. When you address a cover letter to Dear Sir or Madam, it shows you know nothing about the company you want to buy your work.

9. Don't forget to follow through. Follow up major submissions with postcard samples several times a year.

10. Have something to leave behind. If you're lucky enough to score a portfolio review, always have a sample of your work to leave with the art director. Make it small enough to fit in a file but big enough not to get lost. Always include your contact information directly on the leave-behind.

DIGITAL SUBMISSION GUIDELINES

Today, almost every publisher of photographs prefers digital images. Some still accept "analog" images (slides and prints) as well as digital images, but most accept only digital images. There are a few who still do not accept digital images at all, but their number is rapidly decreasing. Follow each buyer's size and format guidelines carefully.

STARTING A BUSINESS

To learn more about starting a business:

- Take a course at a local college. Many community colleges offer short-term evening and weekend courses on topics like creating a business plan or finding financial assistance to start a small business.

- Contact the Small Business Administration at (800)827-5722 or check out their website at www.sba.gov. The U.S. Small Business Administration was created by Congress in 1953 to help America's entrepreneurs form successful small enterprises. Today, SBA's program offices in every state offer financing, training, and advocacy for small firms.

- Contact the Small Business Development Center at (202)205-6766. The SBDC offers free or low-cost advice, seminars, and workshops for small business owners.

- Read a book. Try *Commercial Photography Handbook: Business Techniques for Professional Digital Photographers* by Kirk Tuck (Amhearst Media) or *The Business of Studio Photography* by Edward R. Lilley (Allworth Press). The business section of your local library will also have many general books about starting a small business.

Previews

Photo buyers need to see a preview of an image before they can decide if it will fit their needs. In the past, photographers mailed slides or prints to prospective photo buyers so they could review them, determine their quality, and decide whether the subject matter was something they could use. Or photographers sent a self-promotion mailer, often a postcard with one or more representative images of their work. Today, preview images can be e-mailed to prospective photo buyers, or they can be viewed on a photographer's website. This eliminates the hassle and expense of sending slides through the mail and wondering if you'll ever get them back.

The important thing about digital preview images is size. They should be no larger than 3×5 inches at 72 dpi. E-mailing larger files to someone who just wants a peek at your work could greatly inconvenience them if they have to wait a long time for the files to open or if their e-mail system cannot handle larger files. If photo buyers are interested in using your photographs, they will definitely want a larger, high-resolution file later, but don't overload their systems and their patience in the beginning with large files. Another option is sending a CD with preview images. This is not as efficient as e-mail or a website since the photo buyer has to put the CD in the computer and view the images one by one. If you send a CD, be sure to include a printout of thumbnail images; if the photo buyer does not have time to put the CD in the computer and view the images, she can at least glance at the printed thumbnails. CDs and DVDs are probably best reserved for high-resolution photos you know the photo buyer wants and has requested from you.

Size & Quality

Size and quality might be the two most important aspects of your digital submission. If the quality is not there, photo buyers will not be interested in buying your image regardless of its subject matter. Find out what the photo buyer needs. If you scan your slides or prints, make sure your scanning quality is excellent: no dirt, dust, or scratches. If the file size is too small, they will not be able to do much with it either. A resolution of 72 dpi is fine for previews, but if a photo buyer wants to publish your images, they will want larger, high-resolution files. While each photo buyer may have different needs, there are some general guidelines to follow. Often digital images that are destined for print media need to be 300 dpi and the same size as the final printed image will be (or preferably a little larger). For example, for a full-page photo in a magazine, the digital file might be 8×10 inches at 300 dpi. However, always check with the photo buyer who will ultimately be publishing the photo. Many magazines, book publishers, and stock photo agencies post digital submission guidelines on their websites or will provide copies to photographers if they ask. Photo buyers are usually happy to inform photographers of their digital guidelines since they don't want to receive images they won't be able to use due to poor quality.

Note: Many of the listings in this book that accept digital images state the dpi they require for final submissions. They may also state the size they need in terms of megabytes (MB). See subhead Specs in each listing.

Formats

When you know that a photo buyer is definitely going to use your photos, you will then need to submit a high-resolution digital file (as opposed to the low-resolution 72 dpi JPEGs used for previews). Photo buyers often ask for digital images to be saved as JPEGs or TIFFs. Again, make sure you know what format they prefer. Some photo buyers will want you to send them a CD or DVD with the high-resolution images saved on it. Most photo buyers appreciate having a printout of thumbnail images to review in addition to the CD. Some may allow you to e-mail images directly to them, but keep in mind that anything larger than 9 megabytes is usually too large to e-mail. Get the permission of the photo buyer before you attempt to send anything that large via e-mail.

Another option is FTP (file transfer protocol). It allows files to be transferred over the Internet from one computer to another. This option is becoming more prevalent.
Note: Most of the listings in this book that accept digital images state the format they require for final digital submissions. See subhead Specs in each listing.

Color Space

Another thing you'll need to find out from the photo buyer is what color space they want photos to be saved in. RGB (red, green, blue) is a very common one. You might also encounter

CMYK (cyan, magenta, yellow, black). Grayscale is for photos that will be printed without any color (black and white). Again, check with the photo buyer to find out what color space they require.

USING ESSENTIAL BUSINESS FORMS

Using carefully crafted business forms will not only make you look more professional in the eyes of your clients, it will make bills easier to collect while protecting your copyright. Forms from delivery memos to invoices can be created on a home computer with minimal design skills and printed in duplicate at most quick-print centers. When producing detailed contracts, remember that proper wording is imperative. You want to protect your copyright and, at the same time, be fair to clients. Therefore, it's a good idea to have a lawyer examine your forms before using them.

The following forms are useful when selling stock photography as well as when shooting on assignment:

Delivery Memo

This document should be mailed to potential clients along with a cover letter when any submission is made. A delivery memo provides an accurate count of the images that are enclosed, and it provides rules for usage. The front of the form should include a description of the images or assignment, the kind of media in which the images can be used, the price for such usage, and the terms and conditions of paying for that usage. Ask clients to sign and return a copy of this form if they agree to the terms you've spelled out.

FORMS FOR PHOTOGRAPHERS

Where to learn more about forms for photographers:
- Editorial Photographers (EP), www.editorialphoto.com
- *Business and Legal Forms for Photographers* by Tad Crawford (Allworth Press)
- *Legal Guide for the Visual Artist* by Tad Crawford (Allworth Press)
- *ASMP Professional Business Practices in Photography* (Allworth Press)
- The American Society of Media Photographers offers traveling business seminars that cover issues from forms to pricing to collecting unpaid bills. Write to them at 14 Washington Rd., Suite 502, Princeton Junction NJ 08550 for a schedule of upcoming business seminars, or visit www.asmp.org.
- The Volunteer Lawyers for the Arts, 1 E. 53rd St., 6th Floor, New York NY 10022, (212)319-2910. The VLA is a nonprofit organization, based in New York City, dedicated to providing all artists, including photographers, with sound legal advice.

PROPERTY RELEASE

In consideration of $_____ and/or _____
_____, receipt of which is acknowledged, I being the legal owner of or having the right to permit the taking and use of photographs of certain property designated as _____, do hereby give _____, his/her assigns, licensees, and legal representatives the irrevocable right to use this image in all forms and media and in all manners, including composite or distorted representations, for advertising, trade, or any other lawful purposes, and I waive any rights to inspect or approve the finished product, including written copy that may be created in connection therewith.

Short description of photographs: _____
_____
_____

Additional information: _____

I am of full age. I have read this release and fully understand its contents.

Please Print:

Name _____

Address _____

City _____ State _____ Zip Code _____

Sample property release

Terms & Conditions

This form often appears on the back of the delivery memo, but be aware that conditions on the front of a form have more legal weight than those on the back. Your terms and conditions should outline in detail all aspects of usage for an assignment or stock image. Include copyright information, client liability, and a sales agreement. Also, be sure to include conditions covering the alteration of your images, the transfer of rights, and digital storage. The more specific your terms and conditions are to the individual client, the more legally binding they will be. If you create your forms on your computer, seriously consider altering your standard contract to suit each assignment or other photography sale.

Invoice

This is the form you want to send more than any of the others, because mailing it means you have made a sale. The invoice should provide clients with your mailing address, an explanation of usage, and the amount due. Be sure to include a reasonable due date for payment, usually thirty days. You should also include your Employer Identification Number or Social Security number.

Model/Property Releases

Get into the habit of obtaining releases from anyone you photograph. The releases increase the sales potential for images and can protect you from liability. A model release is a short form, signed by the person(s) in a photo, that allows you to sell the image for commercial purposes. The property release does the same thing for photos of personal property. When photographing children, remember that a parent or guardian must sign before the release is legally binding. In exchange for signed releases, some photographers give their subjects copies of the photos; others pay the models. You may choose the system that works best for you, but keep in mind that a legally binding contract must involve consideration, the exchange of something of value. Once you obtain a release, keep it in a permanent file.

You do not need a release if the image is being sold editorially. However, magazines now require such forms in order to protect themselves, especially when an image is used as a photo illustration instead of as a straight documentary shot. You always need a release for advertising purposes or for purposes of trade and promotion. In works of art, you need a release only if the subject is recognizable. When traveling in a foreign country, it is a good idea to carry releases written in that country's language. To translate releases into a foreign language, check with an embassy or a college language professor.

STOCK LIST

Some market listings in this book ask for a stock list, so it is a good idea to have one on hand. Your stock list should be as detailed and specific as possible. Include all the subjects you have in your photo files, breaking them into logical categories and subcategories.

CHARGING FOR YOUR WORK

No matter how many books you read about what photos are worth and how much you should charge, no one else can set your fees for you. If you let someone try, you'll be setting yourself up for financial ruin. Figuring out what to charge for your work is a complex task that will require a lot of time and effort. But the more time you spend finding out how much you need to charge, the more successful you'll be at targeting your work to the right markets and getting the money you need to keep your business, and your life, going.

MODEL RELEASE

In consideration of $ _____ and/or _____, receipt of which is acknowledged, I, _____, do hereby give _____, his/her assigns, licensees, and legal representatives the irrevocable right to use my image in all forms and media and in all manners, including composite or distorted representations, for advertising, trade, or any other lawful purposes, and I waive any rights to inspect or approve the finished product, including written copy that may be created in connection therewith. The following name may be used in reference to these photographs:

My real name, or _____

Short description of photographs: _____

_____

Additional information: _____

Please print:

Name _____

Address _____

City _____ State _____ Zip code _____

Country _____

CONSENT

(If model is under the age of 18) I am the parent or guardian of the minor named above and have the legal authority to execute the above release. I approve the foregoing and waive any rights in the premises.

Please print:

Name _____

Address _____

City _____ State _____ Zip code _____

Country _____

Signature _____

Witness _____ Date _____

Sample model release

STOCK LIST

INSECTS
Ants
Aphids
Bees
Beetles
Butterflies
Grasshoppers
Moths
Termites
Wasps

PROFESSIONS
Bee Keeper
Biologist
Firefighter
Nurse
Police Officer
Truck Driver
Waitress
Welder

LANDMARKS
Asia
  Angkor Wat
  Great Wall of China

Europe
  Big Ben
  Eiffel Tower
  Louvre
  Stonehenge

United States
  Empire State Building
  Grand Canyon
  Liberty Bell
  Mt. Rushmore
  Statue of Liberty

TRANSPORTATION
Airplanes and helicopters
Roads
  Country roads
  Dirt roads
  Interstate highways
  Two-lane highways

WEATHER
Clouds
  Cumulus
  Cirrus
  Nimbus
  Stratus
Flooding
Lightning
Snow and Blizzards
Storm Chasers
Rainbows
Tornadoes
Tornado Damage

Sample stock list

Keep in mind that what you charge for an image may be completely different from what a photographer down the street charges. There is nothing wrong with this if you've calculated your prices carefully. Perhaps the other photographer works in a basement on old equipment and you have a brand new, state-of-the-art studio. You'd better be charging more. Why the disparity? For one thing, you have a much higher overhead, the continuing costs of running your business. You're also probably delivering a higher-quality product and are more able to meet client requests quickly. So how do you determine just how much you need to charge in order to make ends meet?

Setting Your Break-Even Rate

All photographers, before negotiating assignments, should consider their break-even rate—the amount of money they need to make in order to keep their studios open. To arrive at the actual price you'll quote to a client, you should add on to your base rate things like usage, your experience, how quickly you can deliver the image, and what kind of prices the market will bear.

Start by estimating your business expenses. These expenses may include rent (office, studio), gas and electric, insurance (equipment), phone, fax, Internet service, office supplies, postage, stationery, self-promotions/portfolio, photo equipment, computer, staff salaries and taxes. Expenses like film and processing will be charged to your clients.

Next, figure your personal expenses, which will include food, clothing, medical, car and home insurance, gas, repairs and other car expenses, entertainment, retirement savings and investments, etc.

PRICING INFORMATION

Where to find more information about pricing:

- *Pricing Photography: The Complete Guide to Assignment and Stock Prices* by Michal Heron and David MacTavish (Allworth Press)
- *ASMP Professional Business Practices in Photography* (Allworth Press)
- fotoQuote, a software package produced by the Cradoc Corporation, is a customizable, annually updated database of stock photo prices for markets from ad agencies to calendar companies. The software also includes negotiating advice and scripted telephone conversations. Call (800)679-0202, or visit www.cradocfotosoftware.com for ordering information.
- Stock Photo Price Calculator, a website that suggests fees for advertising, corporate and editorial stock, photographersindex.com/stockprice.htm.
- Editorial Photographers (EP), www.editorialphoto.com.

Before you divide your annual expenses by the 365 days in the year, remember you won't be shooting billable assignments every day. A better way to calculate your base fee is by billable weeks. Assume that at least one day a week is going to be spent conducting office business and marketing your work. This amounts to approximately ten weeks. Add in days for vacation and sick time, perhaps three weeks, and add another week for workshops and seminars. This totals fourteen weeks of non-billable time and thirty-eight billable weeks throughout the year.

Now estimate the number of assignments/sales you expect to complete each week and multiply that number by thirty-eight. This will give you a total for your yearly assignments/sales. Finally, divide the total overhead and administrative expenses by the total number of assignments. This will give you an average price per assignment, your break-even or base rate.

As an example, let's say your expenses come to $65,000 per year (this includes $35,000 of personal expenses). If you complete two assignments each week for thirty-eight weeks, your average price per assignment must be about $855. This is what you should charge to break even on each job. But, don't forget, you want to make money.

Establishing Usage Fees

Too often, photographers shortchange themselves in negotiations because they do not understand how the images in question will be used. Instead, they allow clients to set prices and prefer to accept lower fees rather than lose sales. Unfortunately, those photographers who shortchange themselves are actually bringing down prices throughout the industry. Clients realize if they shop around they can find photographers willing to shoot assignments at very low rates.

There are ways to combat low prices, however. First, educate yourself about a client's line of work. This type of professionalism helps during negotiations because it shows buyers that you are serious about your work. The added knowledge also gives you an advantage when negotiating fees because photographers are not expected to understand a client's profession.

For example, if most of your clients are in the advertising field, acquire advertising rate cards for magazines so you know what a client pays for ad space. You can also find print ad rates in the *Standard Rate and Data Service* directory at the library. Knowing what a client is willing to pay for ad space and considering the importance of your image to the ad will give you a better idea of what the image is really worth to the client.

For editorial assignments, fees may be more difficult to negotiate because most magazines have set page rates. They may make exceptions, however, if you have experience or if the assignment is particularly difficult or time-consuming. If a magazine's page rate is still too low to meet your break-even price, consider asking for extra tearsheets and copies of the issue in which your work appears. These pieces can be used in your portfolio and as mailers, and the savings they represent in printing costs may make up for the discrepancy between the page rate and your break-even price.

There are still more ways to negotiate sales. Some clients, such as gift and paper product manufacturers, prefer to pay royalties each time a product is sold. Special markets, such as galleries and stock agencies, typically charge photographers a commission of 20 to 50 percent for displaying or representing their images. In these markets, payment on sales comes from the purchase of prints by gallery patrons, or from fees on the rental of photos by clients of stock agencies. Pricing formulas should be developed by looking at your costs and the current price levels in those markets, as well as on the basis of submission fees, commissions, and other administrative costs charged to you.

Bidding for Jobs

As you build your business, you will likely encounter another aspect of pricing and negotiating that can be very difficult. Like it or not, clients often ask photographers to supply bids for jobs. In some cases, the bidding process is merely procedural and the assignment will go to the photographer who can best complete it. In other instances, the photographer who submits the lowest bid will earn the job. When asked to submit a bid, it is imperative that you find out which bidding process is being used. Putting together an accurate estimate takes time, and you do not want to waste your efforts if your bid is being sought merely to meet some budget quota.

If you decide to bid on a job, it's important to consider your costs carefully. You do not want to bid too much on projects and repeatedly get turned down, but you also don't want to bid too low and forfeit income. When a potential client calls to ask for a bid, consider these dos and don'ts:

1. Always keep a list of questions by the telephone so you can refer to it when bids are requested. The answers to the questions should give you a solid understanding of the project and help you reach a price estimate.

2. Never quote a price during the initial conversation, even if the caller pushes for a ballpark figure. An on-the-spot estimate can only hurt you in the negotiating process.

3. Immediately find out what the client intends to do with the photos, and ask who will own copyrights to the images after they are produced. It is important to note that many clients believe if they hire you for a job, they'll own all the rights to the images you create. If they insist on buying all rights, make sure the price they pay is worth the complete loss of the images.

4. If it is an annual project, ask who completed the job last time, then contact that photographer to see what he charged.

5. Find out who you are bidding against and contact those people to make sure you received the same information about the job. While agreeing to charge the same price is illegal, sharing information about reaching a price is not.

6. Talk to photographers not bidding on the project and ask them what they would charge.

7. Finally, consider all aspects of the shoot, including preparation time, fees for assistants and stylists, rental equipment, and other materials costs. Don't leave anything out.

FIGURING SMALL BUSINESS TAXES

Whether you make occasional sales from your work or you derive your entire income from your photography skills, it's a good idea to consult with a tax professional. If you are just starting out, an accountant can give you solid advice about organizing your financial records. If you are an established professional, an accountant can double-check your system and maybe find a few extra deductions. When consulting with a tax professional, it is best to see someone who is familiar with the needs and concerns of small business people, particularly photographers. You can also conduct your own tax research by contacting the Internal Revenue Service.

Self-Employment Tax

As a freelancer it's important to be aware of tax rates on self-employment income. All income you receive over $400 without taxes being taken out by an employer qualifies as self-

---

TAX INFORMATION

To learn more about taxes, contact the IRS. There are free booklets available that provide specific information, such as allowable deductions and tax rate structure:

- Tax Guide for Small Business, 334
- Travel, Entertainment, Gift, and Car Expenses, 463
- Tax Withholding and Estimated Tax, 505
- Business Expenses, 535
- Accounting Periods and Methods, 538
- Business Use of Your Home, 587

To order any of these booklets, phone the IRS at (800)829-3676. IRS forms and publications, as well as answers to questions and links to help, are available on the Internet at www.irs.gov.

employment income. Normally, when you are employed by someone else, the employer shares responsibility for the taxes due. However, when you are self-employed, you must pay the entire amount yourself.

Freelancers frequently overlook self-employment taxes and fail to set aside a sufficient amount of money. They also tend to forget state and local taxes. If the volume of your photo sales reaches a point where it becomes a substantial percentage of your income, then you are required to pay estimated tax on a quarterly basis. This requires you to project the amount of money you expect to generate in a three-month period. However burdensome this may be in the short run, it works to your advantage in that you plan for and stay current with the various taxes you are required to pay. Read IRS Publication 505 (Tax Withholding and Estimated Tax).

Deductions

Many deductions can be claimed by self-employed photographers. It's in your best interest to be aware of them. Examples of 100-percent-deductible claims include production costs of résumé, business cards and brochures; photographer's rep commissions; membership dues; costs of purchasing portfolio materials; education/business-related magazines and books; insurance; and legal and professional services.

Additional deductions can be taken if your office or studio is home-based. The catch here is that your work area must be used only on a professional basis; your office can't double as a family room after hours. The IRS also wants to see evidence that you use the work space on a regular basis via established business hours and proof that you've actively marketed your work. If you can satisfy these criteria, then a percentage of mortgage interests, real estate taxes, rent, maintenance costs, utilities, and homeowner's insurance, plus office furniture and equipment, can be claimed on your tax form at year's end.

In the past, to qualify for a home-office deduction, the space you worked in had to be "the most important, consequential, or influential location" you used to conduct your business. This meant that if you had a separate studio location for shooting but did scheduling, billing, and record keeping in your home office, you could not claim a deduction. However, as of 1999, your home office will qualify for a deduction if you "use it exclusively and regularly for administrative or management activities of your trade or business and you have no other fixed location where you conduct substantial administrative or management activities of your trade or business." Read IRS Publication 587 (Business Use of Your Home) for more details.

If you are working out of your home, keep separate records and bank accounts for personal and business finances, as well as a separate business phone. Since the IRS can audit tax records as far back as seven years, it's vital to keep all paperwork related to your business. This includes invoices, vouchers, expenditures and sales receipts, canceled checks, deposit slips, register tapes, and business ledger entries for this period. The burden of proof will be on you if the IRS questions any deductions claimed. To maintain professional status in the eyes of the IRS, you will need to show a profit for three years out of a five-year period.

Sales Tax

Sales taxes are complicated and need special consideration. For instance, if you work in more than one state, use models or work with reps in one or more states, or work in one state and store equipment in another, you may be required to pay sales tax in each of the states that apply. In particular, if you work with an out-of-state stock photo agency that has clients over a wide geographic area, you should explore your tax liability with a tax professional.

As with all taxes, sales taxes must be reported and paid on a timely basis to avoid audits and/or penalties. In regard to sales tax, you should:

- Always register your business at the tax offices with jurisdiction in your city and state.
- Always charge and collect sales tax on the full amount of the invoice unless an exemption applies.
- If an exemption applies because of resale, you must provide a copy of the customer's resale certificate. If an exemption applies because of other conditions, such as selling one-time reproduction rights or working for a tax-exempt, nonprofit organization, you must also provide documentation.

SELF-PROMOTION

There are basically three ways to acquaint photo buyers with your work: through the mail, over the Internet, or in person. No one way is better or more effective than another. They each serve an individual function and should be used in concert to increase your visibility and, with a little luck, your sales.

IDEAS FOR GREAT SELF-PROMOTION

Where to find ideas for great self-promotion:
- *HOW* magazine's self-promotion annual (October issue)
- *Photo District News*, magazine's self-promotion issue (October issue)
- *The Photographer's Guide to Marketing & Self-Promotion* by Maria Piscopo (Allworth Press)
- *The Business of Photography: Principles and Practices* by Mary Virginia Swanson, available at www.mvswanson.com

Self-Promotion Mailers

When you are just starting to get your name out there and want to begin generating assignments and stock sales, it's time to design a self-promotion campaign. This is your chance to do your best, most creative work and package it in an unforgettable way to get the attention of busy photo buyers. Self-promotions traditionally are sample images printed on card stock and sent through the mail to potential clients. If the image you choose is strong and you carefully target your mailing, a traditional self-promotion can work.

But don't be afraid to go out on a limb here. You want to show just how amazing and creative you are, and you want the photo buyer to hang on to your sample for as long as possible. Why not make it impossible to throw away? Instead of a simple postcard, maybe you could send a small, usable notepad with one of your images at the top, or a calendar the photo buyer can hang up and use all year. If you target your mailing carefully, this kind of special promotion needn't be expensive.

If you're worried that a single image can't do justice to your unique style, you have two options. One way to get multiple images in front of photo buyers without sending an overwhelming package is to design a campaign of promotions that builds from a single image to a small group of related photos. Make the images tell a story and indicate that there are more to follow. If you are computer savvy, the other way to showcase a sampling of your work is to point photo buyers to an online portfolio of your best work. Send a single sample that includes your Internet address, and ask buyers to take a look.

Websites

Websites are steadily becoming more important in the photographer's self-promotion repertory. If you have a good collection of digital photographs—whether they have been scanned from film or are from a digital camera—you should consider creating a website to showcase samples of your work, provide information about the type of work you do, and display your contact information. The website does not have to be elaborate or contain every photograph you've ever taken. In fact, it is best if you edit your work very carefully and choose only the best images to display on your website. The benefit of having a website is that it makes it so easy for photo buyers to see your work. You can send e-mails to targeted photo buyers and include a link to your website. Many photo buyers report that this is how they prefer to be contacted. Of course, your URL should also be included on any print materials, such as postcards, brochures, business cards, and stationery. Some photographers even include their URL in their credit line.

Portfolio Presentations

Once you've actually made contact with potential buyers and piqued their interest, they'll want to see a larger selection of your work—your portfolio. Once again, there's more than one way to get this sampling of images in front of buyers. Portfolios can be digital—stored on a disk or CD-ROM, or posted on the Internet. They can take the form of a large box or binder and require a special visit and presentation by you. Or they can come in a small binder and be sent through the mail. Whichever ways you choose to showcase your best work, you should always have more than one portfolio, and each should be customized for potential clients.

Keep in mind that your portfolios should contain your best work (dupes only). Never put originals in anything that will be out of your hands for more than a few minutes. Also, don't include more than twenty images. If you try to show too many pieces, you'll overwhelm the buyer, and any image that is less than your best will detract from the impact of your strongest work. Finally, be sure to show only work a buyer is likely to use. It won't do any good to show a shoe manufacturer your shots of farm animals or a clothing company your food pictures. For more detailed information on the various types of portfolios and how to select which photos to include and which ones to leave out, see *Photo Portfolio Success* by John Kaplan (Writer's Digest Books).

Do You Need a Résumé?

Some of the listings in this book say to submit a résumé with samples. If you are a freelancer, a résumé may not always be necessary. Sometimes a stock list or a list of your clients may suffice and may be all the photo buyer is really looking for. If you do include a résumé, limit the details to your photographic experience and credits. If you are applying for a position teaching photography or for a full-time photography position at a studio, corporation, newspaper, etc., you will need the résumé. Galleries that want to show your work may also want to see a résumé, but, again, confine the details of your life to significant photographic achievements.

ORGANIZING & LABELING YOUR IMAGES

It will be very difficult for you to make sales of your work if you aren't able to locate a particular image in your files when a buyer needs it. It is imperative that you find a way to organize your images—a way that can adapt to a growing file of images. There are probably as many ways to catalog photographs as there are photographers. However, most photogra-

IMAGE ORGANIZATION & STORAGE

To learn more about selecting, organizing, labeling, and storing images, see:
- *Photo Portfolio Success* by John Kaplan (Writer's Digest Books)
- *Sell & Re-Sell Your Photos* by Rohn Engh, 5th edition (Writer's Digest Books)

phers begin by placing their photographs into large, general categories such as landscapes, wildlife, countries, cities, etc. They then break these down further into subcategories. If you specialize in a particular subject—birds, for instance—you may want to break the bird category down further into cardinal, eagle, robin, osprey, etc. Find a coding system that works for your particular set of photographs. For example, nature and travel photographer William Manning says, "I might have slide pages for Washington, DC (WDC), Kentucky (KY), or Italy (ITY). I divide my mammal subcategory into African wildlife (AWL), North American wildlife (NAW), zoo animals (ZOO)."

After you figure out a coding system that works for you, find a method for naming your digital files or captioning your slides. Images with complete information often prompt sales; photo editors appreciate having as much information as possible. Always remember to include your name and the copyright symbol © on each image. If you're working with slides, computer software can make this job a lot easier. Programs such as Caption Writer (www.hindsightltd.com) allow photographers to easily create and print labels for their slides.

The computer also makes managing your photo files much easier. Programs such as fotoBiz (www.cradocfotosoftware.com) and StockView (www.hindsightltd.com) are popular with freelance assignment and stock photographers. FotoBiz has an image log and is capable of creating labels. It can also track your images and allows you to create documents such as delivery memos and invoices. StockView also tracks your images, has labeling options, and can create business documents.

PROTECTING YOUR COPYRIGHT

There is one major misconception about copyright: Many photographers don't realize that once you create a photo, it becomes yours. You (or your heirs) own the copyright, regardless of whether you register it for the duration of your lifetime plus seventy years.

The fact that an image is automatically copyrighted does not mean that it shouldn't be registered. Quite the contrary. You cannot even file a copyright infringement suit until you've registered your work. Also, without timely registration of your images, you can only recover actual damages—money lost as a result of sales by the infringer plus any profits the infringer earned. For example, recovering $2,000 for an ad sale can be minimal when weighed against the expense of hiring a copyright attorney. Often this deters photographers from filing lawsuits if they haven't registered their work. They know that the attorney's fees will be more than the actual damages recovered, and, therefore, infringers go unpunished.

Registration allows you to recover certain damages to which you otherwise would not be legally entitled. For instance, attorney fees and court costs can be recovered. So too can statutory damages—awards based on how deliberate and harmful the infringement was.

PROTECTING YOUR COPYRIGHT

How to learn more about protecting your copyright:

- Call the United States Copyright Office at (202)707-3000 or check out their website, www.copyright.gov, for answers to frequently asked questions.
- American Society of Media Photographers (ASMP), www.asmp.org
- Editorial Photographers (EP), www.editorialphoto.com
- *Legal Guide for the Visual Artist* by Tad Crawford, Allworth Press
- Society of Photographers and Artists Representatives (SPAR), www.spar.org

---

Statutory damages can run as high as $100,000. These are the fees that make registration so important.

In order to recover these fees, there are rules regarding registration that you must follow. The rules have to do with the timeliness of your registration in relation to the infringement:

- **Unpublished images** must be registered before the infringement takes place.
- **Published images** must be registered within three months of the first date of publication or before the infringement began.

The process of registering your work is simple. Visit the United States Copyright Office's website at www.copyright.gov to file electronically. Registration costs $35, but you can register photographs in large quantities for that fee. For bulk registration, your images must be organized under one title, for example, "The works of John Photographer, 2013–2016." It's still possible to register with paper forms, but this method requires a higher filing fee ($65). To request paper forms, contact the Library of Congress, Copyright Office-COPUBS, 101 Independence Avenue SE, Washington, DC 20559-6304, (202)707-9100, and ask for Form VA (works of visual art).

The Copyright Notice

Another way to protect your copyright is to mark each image with a copyright notice. This informs everyone reviewing your work that you own the copyright. It may seem basic, but in court this can be very important. In a lawsuit, one avenue of defense for an infringer is "innocent infringement"—basically the "I didn't know" argument. By placing a copyright notice on your images, you negate this defense for an infringer.

The copyright notice basically consists of three elements: the symbol, the year of first publication, and the copyright holder's name. Here's an example of a copyright notice for an image published in 2016: © 2016 John Q. Photographer. Instead of the symbol ©, you can use the word "Copyright" or simply "Copr." However, most foreign countries prefer © as a common designation.

Also consider adding the notation "All rights reserved" after your copyright notice. This phrase is not necessary in the U.S. since all rights are automatically reserved, but it is recommended in other parts of the world.

Know Your Rights

The digital era is making copyright protection more difficult. As this technology grows, more and more clients will want digital versions of your photos. Don't be alarmed, just be careful. Your clients don't want to steal your work. When you negotiate the usage of your work, consider adding to your contract a phrase that limits the rights of buyers who want digital versions of your photos. You might want them to guarantee that images will be removed from their computer files once the work appears in print. You might say it's okay to perform limited digital manipulation and then specify what can be done. The important thing is to discuss what the client intends to do and spell it out in writing.

It's essential not only to know your rights under the copyright law, but also to make sure that every photo buyer you deal with understands them. The following list of typical image rights should help you in your dealings with clients:

- **One-time rights.** These photos are leased or licensed on a one-time basis; one fee is paid for one use.
- **First rights.** This is generally the same as purchase of one-time rights, though the photo buyer is paying a bit more for the privilege of being the first to use the image. He may use it only once unless other rights are negotiated.
- **Serial rights.** The photographer has sold the right to use the photo in a periodical. This shouldn't be confused with using the photo in "installments." Most magazines will want to be sure the photo won't be running in a competing publication.
- **Exclusive rights.** Exclusive rights guarantee the buyer's exclusive right to use the photo in his particular market or for a particular product. A greeting card company, for example, may purchase these rights to an image with the stipulation that it not be sold to a competing company for a certain time period. The photographer, however, may retain rights to sell the image to other markets. Conditions should always be put in writing to avoid any misunderstandings.
- **Electronic rights.** These rights allow a buyer to place your work on electronic media such as CD-ROMs or websites. Often these rights are requested with print rights.
- **Promotion rights.** Such rights allow a publisher to use a photo for promotion of a publication in which the photo appears. The photographer should be paid for promotional use in addition to the rights first sold to reproduce the image. Another

form of this—agency promotion rights—is common among stock photo agencies. Likewise, the terms of this need to be negotiated separately.

- **Work for hire.** Under the Copyright Act of 1976, section 101, a "work for hire" is defined as "(1) a work prepared by an employee within the scope of his or her employment; or (2) a work … specially ordered or commissioned for use as a contribution to a collective, as part of a motion picture or audiovisual work or as a supplementary work … if the parties expressly agree in a written instrument signed by them that the work shall be considered a work made for hire."

- **All rights.** This involves selling or assigning all rights to a photo for a specified period of time. This differs from work for hire, which always means the photographer permanently surrenders all rights to a photo and any claims to royalties or other future compensation. Terms for all rights, including time period of usage and compensation, should only be negotiated and confirmed in a written agreement with the client.

It is understandable for a client not to want a photo to appear in a competitor's ad. Skillful negotiation usually can result in an agreement between the photographer and the client that says the images will not be sold to a competitor, but could be sold to other industries, possibly offering regional exclusivity for a stated time period.

BREAKING IN

Starting a New Business

....

by Vik Orenstein

Your very first step in starting your new business should be to go to the U.S. Small Business Administration website: www.sba.gov. They have a wealth of information on every aspect of small business from the planning stage on through to your exit strategy.

Your next step should be to enter "starting a small business" along with the name of your state in your search engine. Most states have free guides to setting up small businesses, along with other resources including such things as low-interest loans. When searching, look specifically for government sites and avoid sponsored sites (the ones that appear at the top of the page highlighted in yellow boxes that run down the right side of the page). Sponsored sites will often charge you for information you can get free from your Department of Commerce.

Generally, the first thing you'll apply for will be your state business tax I.D. number. This number will allow you to purchase anything you resell without paying sales tax, as your client will pay the sales tax to you after they receive their goods, and you will then pay it to the state.

UNDERSTAND SALES TAX

You can wind up paying too much sales tax if you don't have a business tax I.D. number, or if you don't use it. This was perhaps the second most expensive mistake of my business career. I purchased film, paper, chemicals and other supplies from several local pro photo stores in Minneapolis. These supplies went into the making of my portraits, which were sold to my clients, the end users. I wasn't required to pay sales tax on these items. But as usual I wasn't paying attention, so I paid the tax anyway. Eventually, one of my vendors suggested I fill out a resale tax-exempt certificate and stop paying unnecessary taxes. That guy saved me tons of money.

So, if you haven't already, file with your state for a business tax-exempt number. Then contact all of your vendors and ask for resale tax-exempt certificates. The vendors will keep these certificates on file so you can purchase items for resale without paying sales tax.

Commercial and architectural photographers often find themselves in the vendor's role when dealing with ad agency clients (who resell photos to their end users). Be sure you keep resale tax-exempt certificates on file for them. Otherwise, if you are ever audited, you may have to pay a fine even if they hold tax-exempt status.

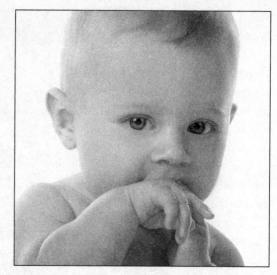

A high-key portrait by Chris Darbonne.

UNDERSTAND USE TAX

I've made a lot of mistakes in my fifteen years in business, most of them of the, "Oops, oh well, life goes on," variety. But my most expensive—and therefore most memorable—mistake involved a little thing called "use tax." On the form that I fill out every month when I pay my sales tax, there is a line for "use tax purchases." I had no idea what it meant, so I blissfully assumed it didn't apply to me. For years I left the line blank. Then one day, I got a call from the Minnesota Department of Revenue: I was being audited by the sales tax division. No problem, I thought. I charged my clients and paid the state the proper sales taxes. That was when I found out what "use tax" is. When you purchase merchandise from out-of-state sources by phone, Internet or mail, they don't charge you sales tax because you are supposed to pay the sales tax in your home state. That's a use tax. (Use tax is figured at the same rate as your regular state sales tax.)

For years I'd been buying almost all my equipment, art supplies, props and other miscellaneous items via mail order, from companies in other states. These purchases over the course of those years totaled in the tens of thousands of dollars. Once the tax I owed, plus the penalties, were tabulated, that little oversight wound up costing me thousands of dollars.

And it didn't stop there. I also did business with a local printer who created all my printed material. Some of the material—holiday cards, for instance—was resold to my clients, so I wasn't required to pay sales tax to the printer for those. The end user, my client, paid that. But this printer also did my stationery and some promotional pieces—items of which I was the end user—and therefore I should have paid the sales tax on these. But he assumed it was all for resale and never charged me sales tax, and I never paid any attention to his invoices. (I'm a photographer, not a businessperson, remember?) So there was another boatload of sales tax and penalties for me to pay.

Commercial photographers can also wind up in trouble when they don't charge their clients sales tax if the client is the end user. What is the moral of this story? Pay the state and charge your clients sales tax as required by law. Don't assume any lines on any forms don't apply to you. If you don't understand something, check with the appropriate government agency and have it explained. Yes, you will spend a lot of

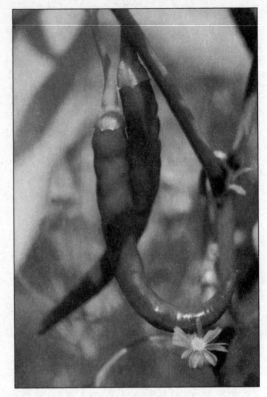

A botanical image by Maria Mosolova.

time getting to know your search engine or on the telephone on hold. But it'll save you money in the long run.

HAVE A RECORD-KEEPING SYSTEM THAT WORKS FOR YOU

I don't know anybody who ever says, "Oh, goodie, I get to organize my files now!" And photographers are probably more challenged in this arena than most. So you need to give yourself a lot of help.

- **Use visual cues.** You're a very visual person, remember? So use visual cues, such as color and tab placement, to make it easier on yourself. For example, I put all my vendor invoices in blue files and put their tabs all the way to the right. My leases, rental invoices and everything else that pertains to my spaces are in blue files, with their tabs all the way to the left. Banking-related documents: red file, center tab. And so on.

- **Be consistent.** Always keep your files in the same place. This might sound basic to some of you, but you'd be amazed at what some of the offices of photographers can look like. They're working on a file, so they take it to their desk or their couch or their copier, set it down to go do something else, leaving it there. Pretty soon something else gets laid on top of it, and something on top of that, and so forth, and suddenly the file is MIA. Depending on the depth of the stack, you might not find that file again until you retire and hold a going-out-of-business sale. So my rule of thumb is this: Always keep your files in the same drawers of the same filing cabinets when you're not using them. After you use them, put them back.

- **Keep it in plain sight.** I subscribe to the old adage "out of sight, out of mind." So I keep everything that needs to be filed in an "in" tray on my desk, where I can't ignore it.

- **Schedule a regular time to file and enter records.** If you stay current with your record keeping and filing, you'll avoid those nasty pileups that take days to sort out, and you'll never lose a file. I file once a week, every Friday evening before I leave the office. Once a day would be better. I record credit card batches, sales logs, framing logs, etc., every day. It's a lot like flossing. It's easier to remember to do it if you make it an everyday habit. And it's essential to your business.

- **Keep ledgers and logs.** Whether you keep your ledgers and logs on computer or the old-fashioned way—written in books—or a combination of the two, you should always keep your information absolutely up to date. This means when you make a credit card transaction, you should record it immediately if not sooner. It's a real bear to go backwards from your batch receipts and re-create the day's transactions. When you get your report from your credit card server at the end of the month, reconcile it the same day you receive it. Bank statements—same thing. The longer you wait to update your logs, the longer you will have to spend entering the information once you get around to it.

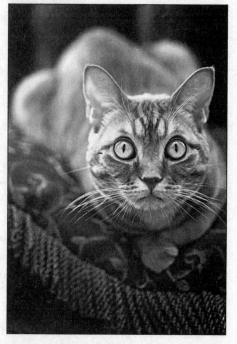

A pet portrait by Michelle Frick.

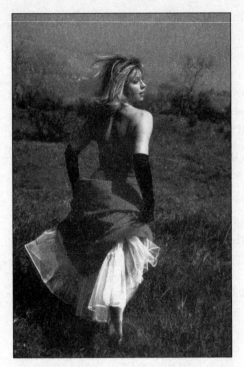

A portrait by Stephanie Adams.

And I always have redundant systems built into my record keeping. The client's name and phone number go into the computer on the mailing list, onto her invoice and next to her appointments in our schedule book. Credit card transactions are recorded in a credit card transaction log and in the client log. It takes a little longer, but it saves time when there is a question regarding a payment and you need to go back and look it up.

THE TAX MAN COMETH

Paying your income taxes is a whole new experience when you're self-employed. Kiss those handy little 1040 forms good-bye. You've entered the world of itemizing, of depreciation, of mysterious column A's that you add to column B's and subtract from column C's. The first year of my business I was determined to do my own taxes. I sat down with the form for a short while before I put my tail between my legs and ran whining to a CPA who specializes in small businesses. I felt silly going to a professional accountant for my piddly little $38,000 gross studio, but, boy, am I glad I did.

My accountant, Jim Orenstein (no relation), was able not only do my taxes but to act as an advisor on such issues as disability and life insurance, whether or not to incorporate, and when and how to expand. He gave me the heads-up when my net income hit the level at which I had to start paying my personal income taxes on a quarterly instead of a yearly basis.

He told me all about the dirty little secret that is self-employment tax. One of the more unpleasant surprises intrepid small business owners encounter is that on top of your regular taxes—which seem like enough, thank you—the government claims an additional 7 percent on earnings up to about $87,000. Ouch! Cruel as it seems, there is a reason behind this. What many of us don't realize until we become employers (of ourselves or others) is that while the government is happily making off with a portion of the employee's earnings, the employer is also paying employment tax. So when you're both the employee and the employer, you get hit with a double whammy.

The moral of this story? You can live without an accountant. But why suffer?

CHOOSING A VENUE

You've budgeted for your studio space in your business plan, and now it's time to choose a door on which to hang your shingle. Whether you rent on an as-needed basis from another photographer or sign the lease yourself, the location where you set up shop will go a long way toward establishing your image in your clients' minds. Think about the identity you want to project: Do you

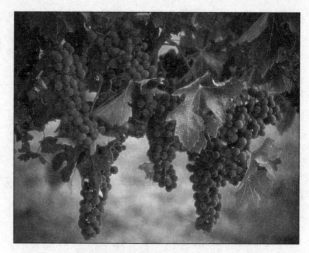

A vineyard shot by Connie Cooper-Edwards.

want to be a trendy, artsy, edgy warehouse habitué? A suburban office park straight shooter? A downtown or uptown girl or guy? If your studio is a retail business, do you want to project upscale boutique chic or shopping mall sass?

Your work can be artistic and editorial as all get out, but if your studio is in a suburban office park, your venue will be undermining your message. On the other hand, if you're a photographer who shoots good, old standard catalog shots and solid mainstream product images, an office park might be just the place for you. Choose a location that complements your message, your story.

You also need to consider accessibility. Are you going to need to get big wheel monster trucks into your shooting bay? Or will you be shooting nothing larger than an earring? Will your clients have to park far away, and will they be willing to pay to park? Or do you need a building with free adjacent parking? If your studio is on an upper level, is there a freight elevator? Or will you be hauling equipment, sets and props up and down in the passenger elevator? Will you need access to your studio on weekends and after hours? These are all issues you need to resolve before you enter into any agreement or sign a lease.

If you rent as needed from another photographer, will there always be a shooting bay available to you? How far in advance will you need to reserve the studio? Or will you have standing days for which you pay whether or not you shoot on those days?

Working From Home

There are pros and cons to operating your studio, office, or darkroom out of your home. The biggest pro, obviously, is that it doesn't cost you anything—assuming that you would have the home in any case. The drawbacks are twofold: It's harder to project a professional image when you bring clients into your residence; and it's darned hard to know when to stop working.

"You just work all the time," says Bob Dale, who ran a studio from his home for eight years before leasing a retail space. "I'd be in my pajamas and slippers sitting at my desk masking negs at midnight."

If you do choose to work from your home, ideally any

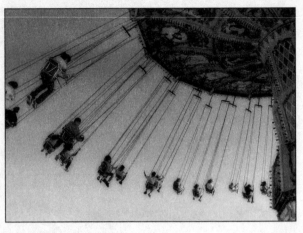

Swingers by Donna Pagakis.

area to which you bring clients should be completely separate from your living area, with a separate entrance if at all possible.

And don't take liberties with that fabled "home office deduction" on your income taxes. You can't just slap your laptop down on your dining room table and deduct that space as an office. For a room to qualify as home office space, it has to be separated from living spaces by a door that closes. The room must be dedicated solely to business use. If you do laundry in there or watch TV, it's no go. You should strictly adhere to the rules governing the deduction. So many people have been tempted to cheat in this area that simply claiming a home office deduction raises little red flags at the IRS and increases the likelihood you'll be audited.

Sharing Space

Since fixed overhead is the bane of small businesses everywhere, and rent will probably be your biggest fixed expense provided you don't have employees, sharing space either with another photographer or with someone in a complimentary business seems like the next best thing, cost-wise, to working from home. But it, too, has its pros and cons. Obviously, reducing your rent by half or more is a big plus. But having "studio mates" and "office mates" can be a lot like having roommates—or worse yet, spouses! There's the basic *Odd Couple* trap—one of you is a neatnick and one of you is a slob. Or one of you subscribes to the "what's yours is mine and what's mine is mine" theory of equipment sharing. Or one of you starts poaching the other one's clients.

Another complication is that the image or identity of your office mate's business will reflect on you and your business. This can be a drawback if your buddy's image isn't as high-end or as professional as yours.

If you do decide to share space, get an agreement in writing as to what you'll do in the event of a breakup. It doesn't need to be in legalese, but it should spell out who will be responsible for the obligations of the remainder of the lease (if any) and who will get to keep the space and any shared property. You also might want to have a written agreement divvying up the cleaning and maintenance duties. Or better yet, take some of that money you're saving by splitting the rent and spend it on a cleaning service.

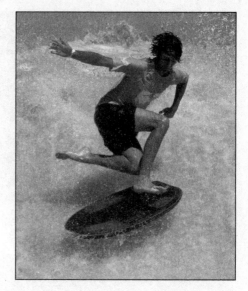

Fierce Competitor by Donna Pagakis.

Renting as Needed

The first two years I was in business, I rented a studio on an as-needed basis from an established fashion photographer. At first the arrangement worked out spectacularly; he was a slob and I was a slob, so we were compatible on the cleaning front. At first I only needed to shoot on Saturdays, and he only shot Monday through Friday, so there was no disagreement. But as my business grew, I started needing more shooting days. The day rate I was paying him for the use of his space was 20 percent of his monthly rent. So if I shot more than five days in a given month, which began to happen more and more often, I was paying him more than what it would have cost me to have my own space in the same building. And then his busy season kicked in, and suddenly the studio wasn't available to me when I needed it. So after two years, we parted ways.

Would I do it again? In a heartbeat! It was the only way I could have a whole warehouse studio to use without the big risk inherent in signing a lease. But my advice to anyone considering such an arrangement—from either end—would be to have an agreement to revisit your "terms of engagement" every three to six months, with the option for either party to end or alter the relationship at that time.

Partnering

Taking on a business partner can be, in my opinion, a great idea, but very few photographers ever try. I think we're all just a bit blind to the importance of the business aspect of our work, and we think if we can shoot, the rest will take care of itself. Just as in any business, the photographer should only partner with someone who has something to offer that the photographer does not himself possess: capital, sales experience, business experience, clients, etc.

Of course, a partnership is in many ways like a marriage, so you'll want to be sure you like and trust anyone you plan to go into business with. And there's always the possibility that the partnership could end before the business does, so you'll be wise to have a prenup, i.e., a "buy/sell" agreement that spells out who gets to buy whom out in the event of a split, and what the terms will be.

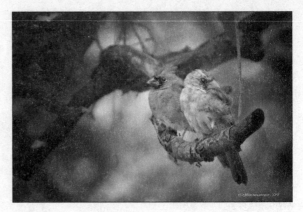

Cardinals by Judy Kennamer.

LEASE AGREEMENTS

It can be very scary the first time you sign a lease for a studio space. Most property companies require a minimum of a three- to five-year commitment. There's usually a page in the agreement that says the exact amount you'll owe for the life of the lease, and I guarantee you the number will be higher than you can count on your fingers and toes.

Beware of the personal guarantee. If you have incorporated your business, you probably did so to avoid personal liability in the event that the business fails and you can't pay your creditors. But landlords know this, and they don't want to leave you any outs. So most of them will ask you to sign a personal guarantee that insures you will pay the remaining rent as per the terms of your lease even if your corporation, or entity, is dissolved. If your business is new there may be no way around this. But if your business has a sound history, you may be able to avoid it. One way you might eliminate the personal guarantee is to offer to pay a two- to three-month deposit instead. This way, the landlord is covered for the time it may take to lease your space in the event you can't fulfill your contract, and you aren't on the hook for up to five years of rent.

Most commercial spaces are rented by the square foot and by CAM (common area maintenance) charges. Rent is rent; when you are quoted a price per square foot, that is exactly what you will pay. But CAM charges are different. At the beginning of the year, the landlord projects what the CAM charges will be for the next twelve-month period and bills you accordingly. If his projections are off and the actual cost of maintaining the building is lower than he anticipated, you will receive a refund at the end of the year. But if his projections are low, and it costs more than he projected to maintain the property, you'll get a bill at the end of the year. I've been hit for as much as $3,500 in CAM adjustments, and I can tell you, it's a rude surprise.

There are many factors that can make the CAM charges go up: snow removal, gas or electrical prices, special assessments and unplanned repairs such as reroofing. Even the occupancy rate of the property will affect how much your CAM charges are because the more tenants there are to spread the cost among, the lower the cost is per tenant.

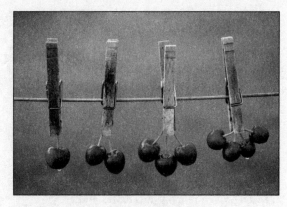

Four Cherries by Susana Heide-Theissen.

Before you sign a lease, be sure to add it all up. Take a look at the landlord's projected and actual budgets for the last three to five years. Have his projections been relatively accurate? Ask how old the mechanicals are, and the roof and any other pertinent items. Is he anticipating any repairs in the near future? The more information you have, the less risk you'll assume.

BUYING AN EXISTING STUDIO

Rather than starting from scratch, some photographers opt to purchase an existing studio from a shooter who is retiring or going out of business.

The benefits of this are that you can get a client list, a complete setup (including photographic equipment, backdrops, props, and office equipment), and take over a space that probably needs little or no remodeling or construction (also referred to as build-out) all in one fell swoop.

There are drawbacks, too. There might not be as much value in the studio as there appears to be at first blush. Buying a photographic studio can be a little like buying a private practice from a dentist or a lawyer. Without Dr. Livingstone, D.D.S., there is no Livingstone Dental Clinic, even if there is an office, a chair, a client list and a drill. That's because when Dr. Livingstone leaves, his clients just might leave, too. Businesses are built on relationships, remember, and Dr. Livingstone's patients have a relationship with him, not with his office. And not with you.

It can be a workable arrangement if you don't pay too much for the business, and if the retiring photographer stays on and works with you for a year or two, part-time, to smooth the transition and help you win the trust of his clients.

BUYING A FRANCHISE

Buying a franchise can be a safer bet. A franchise is like a business in a box—the planning and product development and name selection and logo—everything down to the minutiae is already in place. Just add your time, money and talent! Before a business is offered as a franchise it has to have a working model that's proven reliably successful and repeatable. For example, suppose you want to open a bagel shop. You could go into business as Anita's Bagel Bakery and try to break into your market with no name recognition and untried business plan, or you can buy a Bruegger's Bagels franchise and open your doors with instant name recognition and a successful business plan. As a franchisee you'll have the advantage of a proven guide for every aspect of operation and a product that you know can be sold. You also get comprehensive training up front.

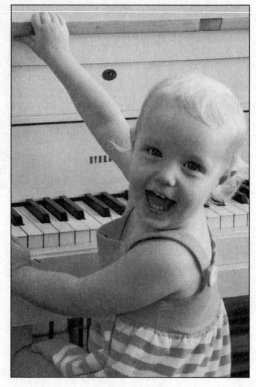

A location portrait by Kathy Locke.

But like any other avenue into the world of business, this one has its drawbacks. It can be expensive to start up, and the company takes 5 to 10 percent of your gross for a minimum of seven years. The very benefits that make you want to buy in—those proven systems—may dampen your entrepreneurial spirit once you've got some experience and you want to try out some systems of your own.

CONTRACTORS, EMPLOYEES, NEPOTISM, AND DOING IT YOURSELF

When you're just starting out it's wise to keep your fixed overhead to a minimum. There are various ways to do this.

You can hire independent contractors on an as-needed basis. You just have to make sure they actually are contractors, and not employees, or you could wind up paying some stiff penalties. There are a couple of big indicators that a person is a contractor and not an employee. The person does the same job for other clients besides you. Examples of this would

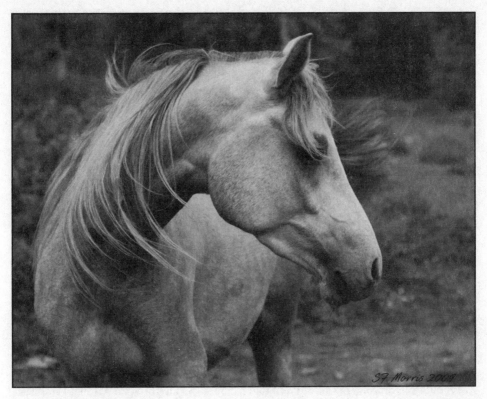

Profile by Sharon Morris.

be a housekeeper who cleans homes for various clients, a photo assistant who works for more than one photographer or a bookkeeper who works for other clients in addition to you. Another, stronger, indicator is whether the person is hired on a per job basis. You've got a big shoot coming up for MegaHuge, Inc., that's going to last two weeks. You hire the assistant for that job only. After the job is done you part ways.

While you don't have to file W-4's or take withholding for contractors, you do have to file a 1099 if they earn over $600 from you for the year.

Nepotism, the practice of hiring one's friends and relatives, can be an arrangement that works out like a dream—or your worst nightmare. When family is involved, there's a greater likelihood that you could wind up taking advantage of them as your employees or that they could take advantage of you as their employer. "Oh, I can get Auntie Frances to answer the phone for minimum wage, she'll just enjoy being able to get out and about, and talk to people," you think. Whereas Auntie Frances is thinking, "Oh, I can work for Stanley and he won't mind if I come in late when traffic is bad or the weather is nice or my gout is acting up."

It's also more difficult to tell friends and family when they're doing something wrong. When an ordinary contractor or employee botches an order, it's relatively easy to say, "You know this Parsons wedding order you sent in? You ordered 1,620 five-by-sevens instead of 57 sixteen-by-twenties and your mistake cost us $9,400." It's harder to say that to your mom.

That said, I have to admit that my mother worked full-time for me for six years and continues to work part-time. My cousin and close friend work for me full-time and at various times my sister has helped out on a temporary basis. My motto, for those who have good communications skills, is, "A little nepotism never hurt a nepit."

"Well, I'm not afraid of hard work," you're thinking. "I'll just save a whole wad of cash if I do everything myself. Who needs contractors and employees?" And when your business is new, that may well

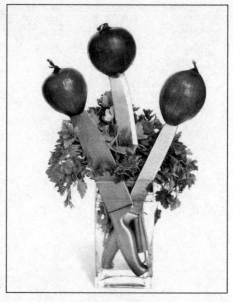

Onions by Susana Heide-Theissen.

be the case. But after a certain amount of growth—and that amount will vary from business to business—it is actually counterproductive to do everything yourself. After my business was about two years old, my accountant told me not to do anything myself that I could get someone else to do for $20 an hour or less. This is somewhat of an oversimplification, but his point is this: Your time is valuable. If you own a growing business, the time you take emptying your wastebasket or balancing your check register is time away from refining your marketing message or developing new products or spending quality time with clients—all things that you must do! You can't afford to delegate these tasks. You need to learn to set a value and ability level on each task and delegate the least valuable and least challenging ones. Otherwise you'll be working hard, but not working smart, and your business will suffer. Sure, it might seem like a large or an unnecessary expense to hire a cleaning service or a bookkeeper when you can do these things yourself, but like the old cliché says, your time is money. So plan on delegating some of your duties at some point down the road.

When do you make the leap from doing it yourself or using contractors to hiring a permanent employee? Employees come with a much bigger commitment than contractors; you need to give them benefits and promise them a certain level of employment, and if you can't deliver on your promises and you lay them off, you have to pay them unemployment benefits. (Frequently you wind up paying unemployment compensation even if you justifiably fire them.) You pay worker's compensation insurance, Social Security and Medicare deductions for them, and unemployment insurance. In return, they give you their talents and, most importantly, their time.

I take my commitment to my employees very seriously. By taking the opportunity to work for me, they are passing up opportunities to work elsewhere. There are few things harder then telling an employee they don't have a job anymore, even when the dismissal is justified and necessary.

I went from contractors to employees when my studio met the following criteria: It had realized at least 20 percent growth every year for four years; it became more practical to hire people who would stay around for a while instead of having to repeatedly find and train new contractors; and the workload became too large year round for me to handle alone.

I have discovered over the years that one excellent employee can accomplish ten times more than a merely adequate one—and those excellent workers are worth keeping around.

PROTECTING YOUR NAME

If you are using your own name as your business name, you don't have to worry about trademarking it. Your name is yours to use. The downside of that is that anyone else whose name it is can use it, too. So if your name is Stanley Kowalski and your studio is called Stanley Kowalski Photography, and the guy down the street is named Stanley Kowalski, too, and he calls himself Stanley Kowalski Photography, there's nothing you can do about it. This could be especially troublesome if, say, you shoot high-end editorial fashion and he shoots cheesy boudoir photos for ads that appear in the back of swinger magazines. You could lose clients if they confuse the two of you, and there would still be nothing you could do about it.

While you don't have to trademark or service mark your own name, you do need to reserve your domain name as soon as possible. Since it is, after all, the World Wide Web, there's a good chance that some other Stanley has already purchased your name of choice. You may be forced to use Stanley J. Kowalski Photography or even Stanley James Kowalski Photo.

THE REASONS MOST SMALL BUSINESSES FAIL

I hate to bring up an ugly word like failure when you're just getting started, but the fact is that roughly 80 percent of all new businesses fail. I'm not trying to be pessimistic or even cautionary, just pragmatic. I believe that if you're aware in advance of the reasons others before you have failed, you'll be able to avoid repeating them yourself.

- **A lack of knowledge.** Failure can result when the new business owner hasn't done his research. Not just research into his market as it exists in the present, but the history of the market and the names of all the major players. Knowing where your colleagues have been will help you steer yourself where you want to go.

- **A lack of passion.** No matter that you try to have realistic expectations going into your new business venture; no matter that you've intentionally taken off those rose-colored glasses to face the glare of reality; no matter how well you try to prepare yourself, starting up your own studio is going to be harder than you think. Really. So unless you have that big fire in your belly, unless you love creating images so much that you wax rhapsodic just thinking about it, don't bother. Because you will find the sacrifices too great and the rewards too few, and you'll go sprinting back to that "real" job before you can say "Bruce Weber and Annie Leibovitz."

- **That little four letter word: fear.** Human beings are funny animals. We fear failure. We fear success. And in either case, that fear can make us abandon ship.

- **Lack of adaptability.** The market changes. Technology changes. Fashions, styles and trends change. Your maturity level (and that of your studio) changes. The economy changes. Your financial needs change. All this requires you to adapt. Just as in Darwinian theory, it's survival of the fittest—evolve or become extinct.

- **Quitting too soon.** Giving up and giving in—it's horrible and wonderful at the same time. The faint of heart ride the cash flow roller coaster and the first time there's no money in the till, they assume the worst! "I'm not profitable, I'm operating in the red, I'm failing, I have to cut my losses!" and they jump ship. But the fact is, cash flow and profit are two different issues. It commonly takes new businesses about two years to become profitable. If that seems like too much uncertainty to you, stick with your day job.

- **Working hard, but not working smart.** Some of us bind anxiety by being busy. We think if we're in constant motion we're moving ahead, when in fact we're only spinning our wheels. Sometimes the best thing you can do for your business (and for yourself) is to take some time off, go sit still and clear your head, set your subconscious to percolate on your studio's biggest priorities and get some recreation. You'll be more productive when you go back to work, you'll work smarter and you won't be as likely to suffer from burnout or make bad decisions.

THE MYTH OF BUSINESS-CHALLENGED PHOTOGRAPHERS

All right, I'll admit that I am one of the culprits who has bought into the "I'm a photographer, not a business person" myth. I actually like to think I'm bad at business—it makes me feel more artistic. But as my less artistic, more business-oriented friends point out, I must be good at business or I wouldn't still be here after twenty-one years. Erica Stoller, owner and operator of ESTO Photographic, Inc., said it best: "Photographers clearly have a visual bias, but I'm often surprised at how well they deal with the written word (a skill important in every profession). And how good their instincts are for business. But there's a strange cultural divide: art versus business. In fact, business arrangements can be creative and not all that difficult." Erica posits that the trouble comes in when the photographer/business owner is wearing both hats at once because "… it is hard to concentrate on one job while thinking about the last job and worrying about the next."

I agree with Erica—the too-many-hats syndrome is an affliction I think most entrepreneurs suffer from, whether in professions commonly regarded as creative or not. But how do you ease the burden? Erica recommends having someone who makes your arrangements for you: someone who negotiates fees, sets up jobs, and who "… has the [emotional] distance to present your work with enthusiasm and some hyperbole and who, if the going gets rough, can say no."

For those working alone, Erica emphasizes that it's important to create a system or protocol that allows you to move forward without reinventing the framework for each assignment. A standardized approach to bids and estimates can be useful, and forms for this purpose can be found on the Internet and from associations like the ASMP (American Society of Media Photographers).

KEY INGREDIENTS FOR SUCCESS

There is no recipe for success. However, there are some essential ingredients. Since I've told you some of the things that can help you fail, it's only fair I highlight some of the things that can help contribute to your success.

- **Adaptability.** Imagine you started out shooting family portraits in 1988. Direct color, white on white was big. It was so big you didn't take out your canvas backdrop for four years. You even named your studio Blanc de Blanc (not a particularly good name choice, since not everyone speaks French). You never thought you'd have to shoot anything else ever again. You set your sights on coasting into retirement as a one-trick pony. But business dropped off and you studied your market to see what everybody else was up to. It appeared that black-and-white fine art prints were enjoying a resurgence. You told yourself that you are adaptable, you can learn how to change with the market—and you did just that. You did it before you needed to take out a loan just to keep the doors open, and before you became a dinosaur. You changed your business name, but not too much: Blanc Avec Negra, perhaps. You went back to school, or back to the darkroom, or back to square one—whatever it takes to learn how to make top-quality black-and-white art prints. And business picked up again. You have adapted. And you didn't have to rise out of your own ashes.
- **Common sense.** Over the years I've learned that common sense is a real premium. If you have it, you're in the minority. If it goes without saying that you pay your bills on time, keep adequate records, answer your phone, return all your calls, provide the best product you know how at an appropriate price and view every client as a

person as well as a source of income, you can parlay this unique sensibility into a successful career.

- **Talent.** Talent is important. It is necessary. If you don't have talent, you won't be able to deliver a satisfactory product, and you'll never have a repeat client. Talent is the yin to your good business practice's yang.

- **A gut you can trust.** Common wisdom is usually right, but sometimes it's wrong. You need to know what common wisdom holds. Check it against your gut and decide whether to follow the pack or to break away and do something new. That's how markets evolve. For instance, common wisdom states that one should be a generalist, then one day someone stands up and decides to specialize. The rest of us hold our breath, watching him and waiting for him to fail. But he doesn't fail— he laughs all the way to the bank. Then the rest of us think, heck, we'll specialize, too. New and better ways of doing business are born. Trusting your gut can give you a reference point, so you can decide whether to take a risk and veer off course or stick to the path.

- **Creative problem solving.** We become photographers because we want to do something that's creative, but then we often forget to apply our creativity to our business operations. Cash flow, record keeping, client relationships, sales and marketing are all areas that seem dry and boring until we look at the problems they present in a new way and create solutions to these problems. By bringing our creativity not just to the making of our images but to the making of our businesses, we'll not only be poised for success, we'll enjoy every aspect of our profession.

It can be daunting. Entities, tax-exempt numbers, choosing and protecting a name, and leasing space is just the beginning. This is not exactly the stuff you had in mind when you were dreaming of becoming a photographer. But the very trait that makes you want to make images creatively can be applied to your business endeavors to bring your financial goals to fruition. It seems that creativity is not, after all, a handicap for a photographer running his own business, but a necessity.

Vik Orenstein is a photographer, writer and teacher. She founded KidCapers Portraits in 1988, followed by Tiny Acorn Portraits in 1994. In addition to her work creating portraits of children, she has photographed children for such commercial clients as Nikon, Pentax, Microsoft, and 3M. Vik teaches several photography courses at BetterPhoto.com.

Excerpted from *The Photographer's Market Guide to Building Your Photography Business* © 2010 by Vik Orenstein. Used with the kind permission of Writer's Digest Books, an imprint of F+W, a Content + eCommerce Company.

ART OF BUSINESS

Work Your Art

....

by Jen Cushman

///

There's a rampant stereotype that creatives make poor business people. The archetype of the starving artist is so entrenched in our culture; it's one of the most popular recurring themes in literature and filmmaking. It may be romantic to watch a movie about a tortured, sensitive creative, but it's not so pleasant to see in real life. It's also a cop-out. It's easier to perpetuate this myth than it is to do the hard work it takes to create a successful photography-based business.

What separates the aesthetics of photography from the business of photography is money. While business and passion make great bedfellows, money and emotions often run at odds. As creatives, we use our emotions as fuel to birth our imagery. Because we pour so much of ourselves into our work, it's difficult to separate the process of making a photograph from the end product—the piece itself—and to see that piece as a commodity to be sold.

It's much easier to throw in the towel and let someone else handle the dirty money stuff than it is to buck up and learn viable business and marketing skills. But your ability to make a living from your work is in your hands, no one else's. Yes, you can get an agent or sales rep or a marketing guru, but good people can be costly. You first have to make money to spend money, and you can do it. You. All by yourself.

You may have to spend more time reading business and marketing advice books than you do taking photos. You may feel stressed as weeks fly by while you're designing business cards or creating a mailing list, writing a blog, or setting up a website. It's all good. Every time you feel stressed, remind yourself that you're working to bust the myth of the starving artist. You're showing yourself and the world that being a creative professional also means having business savvy. The world needs artists and makers, and we need to remind the world that being a photographer is a viable profession.

Your ability to make a living off your photography is in your hands, no one else's.

Q: I'm successful at selling my work at craft fairs and festivals. I travel across the country and do lots of shows. It seems like at every show there are always one or two customers who like my work and really want to own a particular piece, but they always want to haggle on the price. Everything about these people screams that they have the cash to pay for it, but they just want a deal. What would you do?

A: Ahh, the deal seekers. These are the people who have money because they have the confidence to ask for what they want. But deal seekers are different from bargain hunters. Bargain hunters will choose Photograph A over Photograph B because of the $10 difference in the price tag, and are willing to settle for any photograph of yours instead of the piece. Deal seekers are people who want Photograph A, but want it for the same price as Photograph B. They know that if you put a range of prices on your work to sell them—a smart marketing move on your part, by the way—everything you sell is potentially up for negotiation. Also, don't forget there are people in this world who truly enjoy the art of negotiation.

Here are a couple of helpful business tips: First, figure out if this potential customer is really a bargain hunter or a deal seeker. If you've got a bargain hunter, start talk-

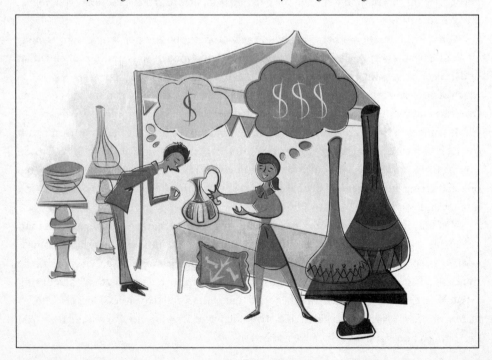

ing about your work in a general way, and lead them to pieces in a lower price range. Feel flattered that your work is appreciated, and, depending on the level of enthusiasm, you will most likely make a sale. If this potential customer is a deal seeker, then your encounter can be as much about how you play the game as the value of the piece itself. Start talking about the piece and why it's one of your favorites, too. Ask the person what he sees in it, and what draws him to it. Is it the story? The color? Does it trigger a good memory? Once you engage in conversation, your intuition will kick in and you'll be able to decide if the deal hunter truly feels a connection with your piece, and could potentially be a repeat customer. Then you'll know whether to cut

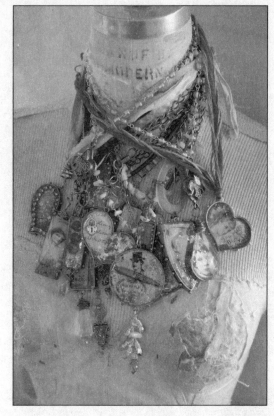

Jewelry and photos by Jen Cushman.

a slight deal, or hold firm on your price. Whatever you decide, own it. Don't second-guess yourself. It's your work and you decide its market value.

Q: I teach classes in my home studio, so teaching is part of my DNA. How do I begin teaching at retreats or conferences?

A: There are good photographers and then there are good teachers, but they do not always go hand-in-hand. In my experience, the best teachers are the ones who deep down want their students to be successful, and feel as though it's part of their calling to see them thrive. It's terrific that you want to inspire others to succeed.

Building a successful teaching career is not as simple as hopping a plane to your next gig. Think of it more long term, like ripples on a pond.

If you're teaching in your home studio, how about branching out into your community? Approach a local photography store or gallery and talk to the owners or managers. Be respectful of their time and ask for an appointment, rather than ambushing them with your portfolio. Show up to the appointment as if it were a job interview (because

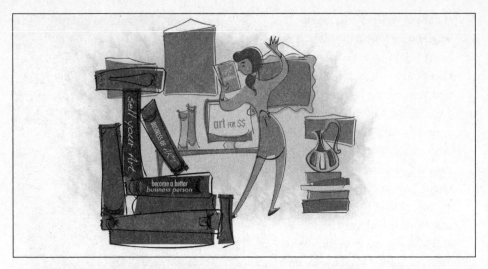

it is) and be ready to discuss your ideas. Approach it as a collaboration; they want to offer services to their customers, and you want to be of service.

In the end, successful classes are all about an exchange of positive energy and new ideas. Build your confidence and clientele first in your community and you'll soon find opportunities coming your way for bigger gigs. I'm a believer in being a big fish in your small pond first before jumping too soon to another pond where you might wind up feeling like bait.

Jen Cushman is a former journalist who found mixed-media art 14 years ago and never looked back. She's the author of *Making Metal Jewelry; How to Stamp, Forge, Fold and Form Metal Jewelry Designs* and *Explore, Create, Resinate: Mixed Media Techniques Using ICE Resin*. Jen writes the Mixed-Media Metalsmith column for *Cloth Paper Scissors* and teaches at CREATE Mixed-Media Retreats and at other national and international venues. She's also Vice President/Partner of Susan Lenart Kazmer LLC/ICE Resin. jencushman.com and jencushman.wordpress.com

Adapted from the winter 2015 issue of *Artists & Makers*. Used with the kind permission of *Artist's & Makers*, a publication of F+W, a Content + eCommerce Company.

SELLING WITHOUT BEGGING

....

by David C. Baker

Forget cold-calling—reel in the clients you really want with these six practical techniques.

The problem is clear: You need more business. Not because you aren't busy, but because then you could be choosier about which clients you work with. But if there's one thing firm owners and entrepreneurs hate, it has to be selling themselves to prospects. Selling feels uncomfortable, needy, and it also seems like something we probably shouldn't have to do, right? If our work is great, shouldn't it sell itself?

I want to help you by explaining some ways to attract more business without begging for it. First, I'm going to assume that you're really talented. That's an important assumption. Unless you're an expert in something where there aren't a lot of other experts, clients will find you interchangeable, and when they have a lot of choices, they'll dive down to the cheapest option. Second, you need work, but you don't want to harm your carefully earned position as an expert. That means you need thoughtfully chosen and very effective methods of finding new clients. Here are six ways to reach prospects while keeping your expert status.

1. Send a Letter by Express Mail.

In the past, any letter you sent blended into all the other letters that a prospective client received, and so you had to resort to flashy and expensive brochures instead. But now, nobody gets letters, so they stand out. They're also quick and cheap, which makes them an even better choice.

Sit down and write a really good one, highlighting what helps you stand out from the crowd. Make it punchy (i.e., confident), but keep it short. About two-thirds of a page is ideal.

Next, find about 50 prospects to send it to. You might start with clients who work at a competitor to a client you just lost because those are the ones most likely to be intrigued by the chance to hire you. Then, concentrate on the companies where you know someone or have something that you could mention in the letter. Or maybe think of a place with a mission or work that ignites so much passion in you that the prospect will be drawn to that enthusiasm.

Now here's the trick: Send it by FedEx Express Saver or USPS Priority Mail to fifty contacts. First, no one throws a letter away that's delivered by an express service. Second, it's easier to get past a gatekeeper if you can say that you're calling to follow up on an express shipment. "May I ask what this is about, please?" now has a good answer: "I'm calling to follow up on a FedEx that I sent to her last week." Expect at least one nice project from this technique.

2. Put Paid Advertising on LinkedIn.

LinkedIn has become the digital water cooler among the next generation of decision-makers, and it's surprisingly easy to post messages on the bulletin board hanging above that water cooler. This often underutilized tool is a breeding ground for professionals looking to connect with practitioners who possess the skills they need for a particular project.

Once your profile is established, you need to promote your services and skills. Under your profile picture, use the pull-down menu to manage your "Advertising." Then select "Create New Campaign." From there, you can choose to create an ad or sponsor your content. If you've written a blog post that you think might get some traction with just a little help, choose that route. The content you've written that's most likely to help you get work is the kind that has a clear point of view. So don't aim to softly inform your readers, but rather aim to take a stand on something so that your prospect is almost required to agree or disagree with you. (Not everyone agrees with experts.)

Either way, target your promotion using these rules of thumb. Set aside about $25/week, and agree to pay $1–$2/click. LinkedIn will push you to pay more, but resist—you'll get plenty of clicks without dishing out more cash.

Think about how succinctly you can word your ad, because you get only 75 characters. Use an image (like your logo or a piece of compelling work you've done) to create a visual hook. Be sure to "collect leads"—it doesn't cost any more—so that prospects can request more information right then and there, delivering the request to your inbox.

Target the ad to your specific industry, and narrow your audience further by selecting an age range, seniority ranking (such as a job title) and geography. And here's the kicker: You can make the ad appear only to those who work for the specific companies you're targeting. Think about correlating this campaign with the express mail strategy, so prospects will receive your letter and then see your ad on LinkedIn and request more information. You'll get 10–20 leads per week with this method, and you can expect to have a conversation with at least one of them.

3. Host a Webinar.

Online education webinars are very effective tools because they don't require travel, they can be watched on demand and there's none of the financial risk that comes from holding a seminar. Mostly, there's no risk of failure. Let's dive into this last point a bit more, as it's the secret sauce to this tool.

Contrast a webinar with a speaking engagement. For the latter, you'll spend months landing one and preparing for it. That big day will come—but what if you end up with three people in attendance? First of all, those numbers don't work. Most important, it looks like you've failed. The few people there look around and then wonder how much of an expert you really are. But now think of a webinar, where you can choose to hide the list of attendees from your prospects. Unless you tell them otherwise, they'll assume that there are dozens of others who are listening and learning.

I'd recommend you use GoToWebinar for this and keep it short: about 40 minutes long, using the rest of the hour for a question-and-answer session, in which attendees will type their questions into a box within the program. Have someone help you as a "guest presenter," pitching the questions to you: "John, we have a question from Lucy, who wants to know what elements are most interesting to teenage buyers these days." Write a few questions out for yourself in case the audience is slow to ask them. That will help you avoid awkward pauses.

GoToWebinar also allows you to record your presentation, syncing the slides with your voice. When you finish the webinar, it'll convert the recording into a file you can post. That will be even more content for your website, and it will give prospects a way to learn more about how you think. You can even transcribe your presentation at sites like www.rev.com and then post it as a downloadable PDF.

Practice, practice, practice, though, because talking to a "nonexistent audience"—which is what it feels like—can be very disorienting at first. One key is to over-deliver enthusiasm while you work hard to picture one very engaged attendee. Slow down, too, because there's something about doing a webinar that will tempt you to speak rapidly. Who do you invite? Round people up through your letter, your ad or a list—which is what we'll cover next.

4. Buy a List.

If you already have a subscriber list with at least 8,000 names of people who have opted-in to receive your e-mails, that should do it. Any quantity below that should grow on a net basis from e-mailing to e-mailing, but reaching a critical mass of that size organically will take too long if you need some quick hits, and that's when you buy a list. Keep in mind that the more data fields that come with each record, the better, but what matters most is getting a current e-mail address.

There are three places to look for good e-mail addresses for your own marketing purposes, and you want to do a search in this order. First, check with any associations that might gather your prospects. *The Encyclopedia of Associations* is a good place to double-check your knowledge and see if you've overlooked any. That source will also indicate how many members each association has and whether or not they make their list available for purchase.

The second place to check is www.thelistinc.com, a professional research service in Atlanta that does the hard work for you, verifying each name on the lists they sell every four months. Call them up and see if they can help. The third place is www.data.com, a more generalized list broker where you can buy from scratch, or just have them fill in any missing data for partial records you already have.

Once you get a list, set up your own marketing automation platform, ideally using software or a service such as Pardot, HubSpot or Act-On. But you can keep it simpler and cheaper with an e-mail marketing provider. My favorite is Campaign Monitor or MailChimp, but there are many viable platforms. There are no issues with the legality of this approach, either. The CAN-SPAM Act merely requires that there be a reasonable expectation that the recipient would be interested in what you send them and that there is a simple means to unsubscribe. From a best practices standpoint, avoid selling and give the recipient value instead. That means avoiding anything that might be construed as a newsletter. Prospects don't care about case studies or seeing work you're doing. Talk about what interests them and leave yourself out of the conversation.

When it comes to getting along with your e-mail marketing provider, remember to avoid doing things that will make them hate you. For example, when you do things that blacklist their e-mail servers, it affects their entire client base. And they won't hesitate to dump you on the street, regardless of whether your action violates any law.

Once your list has significant mass, and if you're doing this right, expect an unsubscribe rate of less than 0.5% per mailing, no more than one spam complaint per 4,000 records addressed, a soft bounce rate of less than 4% and an open rate of at least 30%.

5. Be Interviewed as an Expert.
Scour the free Help a Reporter Out website (www.helpareporter.com) and make yourself available for expert interviews. The signal-to-noise ratio is a little distracting, though, and you might be better off spending a little money and subscribing to the ProfNet service. It's Help a Reporter Out on steroids. It's curated, simpler, and collects more serious journalists.

If you have a good profile and your answers are well-written, you can expect one interview per month, based on about four times that many responses. Each day you'll receive 150–300 interview requests through several e-mails. Quickly eliminate the ones that don't apply to your focus and isolate one or two that might be worth contacting. Don't spend any more than 30 minutes in total every week. Prospects will learn about you in a respected, peer-reviewed manner, and some of them will reach out for help to this expert they've just learned about.

6. Write a Short E-Book.

Apple has a product called QuickReads, and Amazon has matched it with their Kindle Singles. The two products are nearly identical: 5,000–30,000 words, with a mandated low price. It's a wonderful tool in selling your services because it gives you a reason to contact a prospect by including a gift certificate to the book. Regardless of whether or not they read it, they'll be left with a suitable impression.

The topic should be something you'd expect from an expert, and not poorly disguised self-promotion. (However, the cover can be an opportunity to showcase your design skills.) Give away great thinking that isn't personalized for the prospect, and then charge big fees when you do apply your experience to a specific client. If you're starting from scratch, you should be able to write 5,000 words in one week. Chances are, though, you already have that much content in the can and it just needs some skillful editing.

There you have it. You need new clients, you need them quick, and you don't want to beg. So, pick two or three of these six suggestions and get busy. I bet you're pretty good at landing work once you get a chance to talk to a prospect, right? You just need more opportunity, and this list is designed to give you just that.

David C. Baker has been an author, speaker and adviser to the creative community for 20 years, and has worked closely with nearly 800 firms. His blog is read by 20,000 designers. www.recourses. com

Excerpted from the November 2014 issue of *HOW* magazine. Used with the kind permission of *HOW* magazine, a publication of F+W, a Content + eCommerce Company. Visit www.howdesign. com to subscribe.

MICRO FUNDING FOR MACRO DREAMS

....

by Sean J. Miller

///

Micro grants and grass-roots funding programs are helping artists and makers achieve success.

Amy Peterson and Diana Russell walked into the Jam Handy building in Detroit, Michigan, last summer ready to pitch an idea to potential investors. The friends wanted to start a jewelry business called Rebel Nell, and employ women transitioning from homelessness. "We wanted the jewelry to be teachable," Peterson says, "and we wanted to have complete creative input from the women so they could be really, truly the designers."

As more creatives look for ways to turn their passions into profit, they're also looking for viable ways to finance their dreams. Today, getting a business loan or seed money to launch something like a small artisan jewelry company isn't as difficult as it used to be, thanks to a growing cultural shift toward appreciation of local and small over global and corporate. That appreciation isn't just happening among consumers, but among lenders and investors as well.

But a small creative enterprise is a different animal when it comes to capital, says Stephen Marotta, a researcher at Portland State University in Oregon. "It isn't like in the past when you drew up a business plan, went into a bank, and either came out with a smile on your face or pounded your fists in the sand."

Sure, you can fund your business by building a Kickstarter campaign or dipping into your 401(k), or begging mom and dad for a loan. Among other options now available are programs such as the partnership of ArtHome and Project Enterprise in New York City. This innovative setup offers business training and a peer-lending program for local, low-income artists, with loans ranging from $1,500 to $12,000.

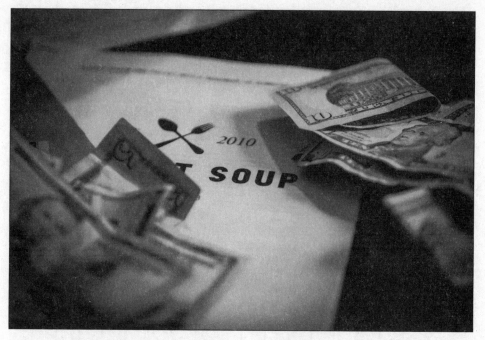

"It's not just about getting access to capital, it's also about getting a plan for a sustainable business," says Esther Robinson, founder of ArtHome. Photo by David Lewinski.

In the case of Peterson and Russell, without a small business track record the pair wasn't able to approach traditional funding sources like banks, foundations, or government agencies. Detroit, though, is one of the cities at the forefront of a shift away from the traditional funding model for artisans, artists, and social entrepreneurs.

Detroit SOUP, for example, offers micro grants for local creative and community projects. The money comes from fundraising dinners that Detroit SOUP hosts. But there's no high ticket price here—for just $5 guests can judge presenters and award a grant. Peterson and Russell pitched their company at a July 2013 dinner, keeping their presentation light and making people laugh. When it came time to vote on the awardee, Rebel Nell received almost $1,500.

Peterson and Russell used the money to buy silver—the base metal for their jewelry— and then sold their first pieces for a $6,500 profit at a local market. "That money is really what we credit for being the catalyst for starting Rebel Nell," Peterson says.

Amy Kaherl, Detroit SOUP's director, said the group has awarded more than $75,000 to artists, craftspeople, and social entrepreneurs since it was founded five years ago. The micro grants range from $700 to $3,000, depending on the attendance at the dinner.

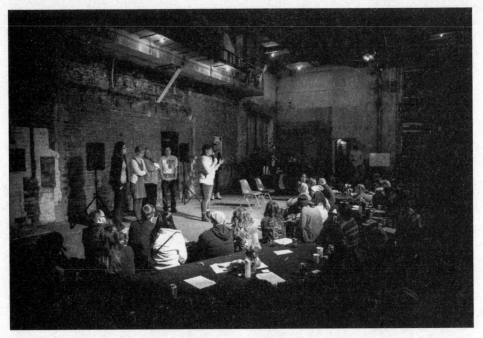

At Detroit SOUP, a pitch is attended by potential investors. Photo by David Lewinski.

"This is for people who have ideas but need some initial funding," says Kaherl. "There are only two rules: [The business] has to be within the city, and you cannot use technology to present."

The concept for Detroit SOUP originated in Chicago and is now spreading around the country and internationally. Kaherl says she's helped similar organizations get off the ground in cities such as Columbus, Ohio; Dublin, Ireland; and London, England.

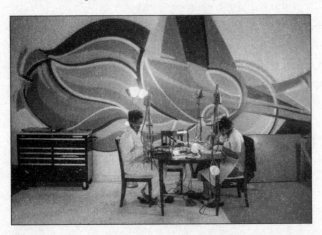

Women work on jewelry designs at Rebel Nell. Photo by Sebastian Sullen.

Marotta, the researcher who has been exploring funding sources in Portland's artisan economy, says he's beginning to see creatives benefit from the kind of angel investors that launched Silicon Valley start-ups. He recently attended a small gathering of artisans to which an angel investor also came. "It's kind of like a loan officer going out into the community," he says.

As the artisan economy offers options to corporate-driven consumerism, it's also driving the creation of alternatives to traditional banking practices. Crowd funding lenders such as Kiva Zip put lenders and borrowers in direct contact. Moreover, loans are interest free up to $5,000.

To be sure, money may solve some of an artist's problems, but not all. In many cases they need the financial literacy and industrial acumen necessary to grow and expand an enterprise.

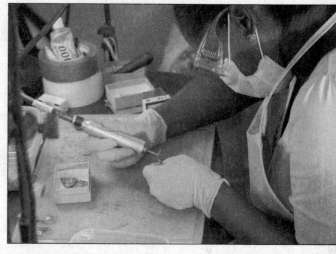

Photo by Sebastian Sullen.

"You really do need a business plan that has research and thought behind it," says Esther Robinson, founder of ArtHome, an entrepreneurial non-profit that works with artists and artisans.

ArtHome runs a program that matches the personal savings of low-income artists up to $2,000, but requires participants to take business classes. "It's not just about getting access to capital, it's also about getting a plan for a sustainable business," she says. For many participants there are "translation issues" when it comes to turning art into commerce. "There's somewhat of a disconnect with the language of commerce," she says.

A savings program is meant to help creatives overcome one of the greatest challenges their businesses may face: variable income. "You need to learn how to save if your work is seasonal," Robinson says.

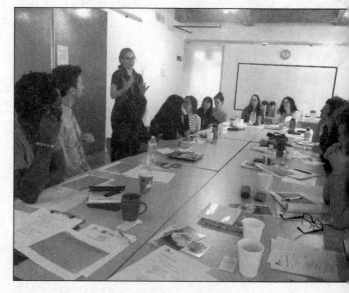

ArtHome founder Esther Robinson leads a personal finance bootcamp. Photo by Michelle Proffit.

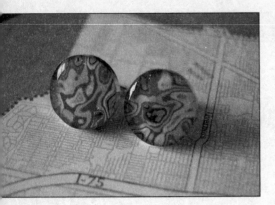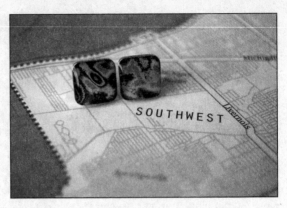

The jewelry Rebel Nell produces is made from repurposed graffiti. Photos by Amy Peterson.

Don't be surprised, Marotta says, if larger corporations start moving in on the micro financing trend, especially since it doesn't take much to fund an artisanal start up. "We've done some preliminary research on a maker's collective in East Portland, Oregon. A good chunk of them [operate] below $20,000," he says. "But there's collective power in these small numbers."

Back in Detroit, Peterson and Russell are ready for a busy holiday season. They plan to hire two more women by the end of the year to add to their three-person team of creative designers. "In the big scheme of loans and grants it's not that much," Peterson says of the $1,500 they received from SOUP. "But to us, that was the most important money we received, because at the time we were just an idea. It was a wonderful confirmation."

Sean J. Miller is a journalist and playwright based in Los Angeles, CA.

Excerpted from the winter 2015 issue of *Artists & Makers*. Used with the kind permission of *Artists & Makers*, a publication of F+W, a Content + eCommerce Company.

CALCULATOR MAGIC

Pricing Your Work

....

by Vik Orenstein

Within the different specialties of photography, there are very different fee structures and methods for pricing work, but photographers in every discipline share one characteristic: We have all, at one time or another in our careers, charged too little for our work, or we've given up usage rights and copyrights for little or no compensation.

To be fair, it's not just photographers who have trouble exacting their fees. I think its common among entrepreneurs and self-employed people across the board. I have a psychologist friend who jokes that she's going to teach a seminar for other psychologists that will consist of nothing but three days of repeating the same phrase over and over: "That'll be $200, please."

Fine art/commercial photographer Doug Beasley says, "It's somewhat arbitrary. I make up a number. Sometimes I check it against the ASMP (American Society for Media Photographers) guides and it's usually pretty close to what their standard is. I simplify the process—figuring out usage can be so complicated. I give away more rights than I should, but I'd rather live that way than live in fear of being ripped off."

Fashion/commercial shooter Lee Stanford credits part of the success and growth of his business to his ability to become savvier about charging for usage and setting his prices. "I used to give away too much. Now I go by the industry standard, and no one flinches. I think clients expect to pay for good work, and they don't appreciate you any more if you give it away than if you charge a fair price."

Though usage fees don't often come into play in my portrait business, there are gray areas when a portrait client wants to use a portrait for a business application, or a business owner asks to sneak in a few portraits of her kids during a commercial shoot. Early in my career, I just swallowed my tongue—and the monetary losses—and allowed my clients any little favor, even if it violated my copyright. But now I, too, go by the book.

HOW TO SET YOUR FEE STRUCTURE

Fee structure and pricing are entirely different animals. Fee structure refers to what the client pays for and when he pays it. For instance, this is the fee structure for one of my studios: The sitting fee is required at the time of the booking; the cost of the sitting is determined by the number of subjects; the sitting fee covers expenses (the client doesn't pay extra for film, processing, proofs or anything else); the portraits are payable 50 percent upon placement of the initial order and 50 percent upon delivery.

That's my fee structure. Notice that there aren't any dollar amounts in there—that would be my price list.

Fee structures vary markedly from one area of specialty to the next. My fee structure is fairly standard for portrait studios. But a standard commercial shooter's fee structure would go something like this: A

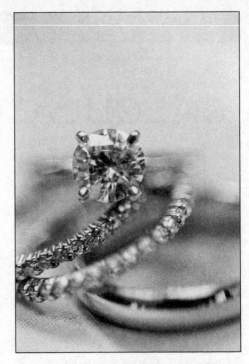

Most clients want to receive their digital files along with any photo albums, photo books and prints they order, so photographers like Hilary Bullock tend to charge an up front fee that includes the shooting fee, a photo book, and DVDs of part or all of the images.

commercial photographer charges a standard day rate. The client pays the photographer's fee by the eight-hour day—usually there is a half day minimum; the day rate will fluctuate based on the usage of the photos (higher exposure usage results in higher shooting fees); the client pays for materials and expenses, usually with a 15 percent markup.

You can see that a commercial photographer's fee structure is decidedly different from a portrait photographer's. Each different area of specialty will have its own little quirks in its way of billing for services.

You need to find out what the standard is for your specialty in your geographic location, and use it with integrity.

PRICE STRUCTURE

Your price structure refers to what you charge for your products and services. Here's the price structure for one of my studios: The basic sitting fee starts at $145; a black-and-white 5" × 7"

(13cm × 18cm) portrait costs $89; a hand-painted 20" × 24" (51cm × 61cm) costs $850, and so forth. A commercial shooter's price structure might look something like this: A basic day rate is $2,500 for limited usage; higher exposure usage doubles the day rate to $5,000; travel time is billed at 50 percent of the day rate.

How do you know how to price your work when you're just starting out? First, you want to find out what your industry and market standards are. That is, what are other photographers who work in your city charging in your area of specialty?

Professional Organizations

One way to get up to speed fast is to join a professional organization like the one Doug Beasley mentioned earlier—American Society for Media Photographers. Not only do members receive a wealth of information on all aspects of the business, including how to figure usage charges, they also hold monthly meetings on issues like

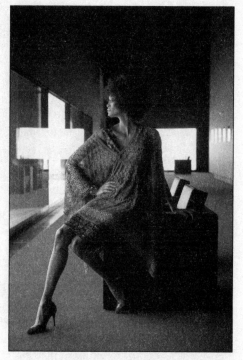

Fashion photographers like Lee Stanford generally charge a day rate that averages from $1,200 to $8,000 depending on your market. Editing/retouching and archiving may be built into the day rate or may be charged separately.

this very topic. If you attend these meetings, you can network with the people in the business, find out what they're charging and get a feel for the pulse of your market.

If you're a portrait photographer, you might consider joining Professional Photographers of America (PPA). They have a beautiful monthly magazine that covers all aspects of the portrait photography business, including creative, technical and business.

Apprenticeships, Internships and Assistant Work

Of course one of your goals, if you do an apprenticeship or work as an assistant, is to learn this aspect of the business. Remember the advice of our seasoned photographers: Don't just learn how to set up lights when you assist—learn it all. When you work with an established photographer you get to see the how they put a price on their work, when they flex on a fee and when their fee is nonnegotiable.

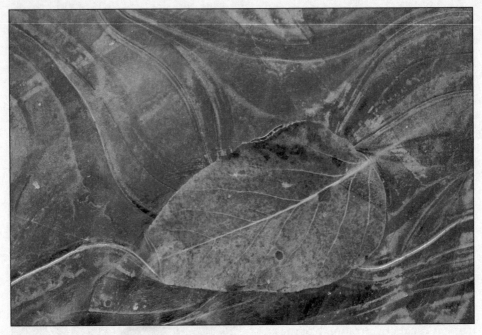

This macro nature image by Brenda Tharp could sell as stock and/or as decorative or fine art prints. The same image can be resold, so it's possible for a single successful image to make a lot of money for the photographer.

Informational Interviews

Informational interviews can be instructive in setting up your payment structure. You can also phone a few shooters and/or their reps and inquire about their basic day rate. Some may give you this information up front. Others may hesitate to make a blanket statement, preferring to make bids on a job-by-job basis.

Pick Up the Phone or Cruise the Web

Often photographers in portrait or wedding photography list their fee structures and prices on their websites. If they don't, try e-mailing them or calling on the phone to ask for pricing details.

Whatever you do, level with the businesses you approach. Sometimes people who are learning the market with the intention of starting up their own shop call my studio and are afraid to tell us they are our would-be competitors, so they pretend they're potential clients.

Generally we can spot them right away, and this approach makes my coworkers and me feel extremely disrespected. We are more than happy to send out information to anyone so there's no need to invent stories. Our pricing is public record—it's no secret.

Speaking of secrets, some shooters, even seasoned established professionals, "secret shop" the competition from time to time. This is an especially common practice for national chains. I guess they like to see what we little guys are up to.

I have personally been shopped by three local photographers and one national studio, Lifetouch Inc. (They revealed their shopping trip to me and shared their impressions with me.)

I have never employed this practice, although I have been tempted. It is intriguing to find out how other people work.

BARGAIN BASEMENT, CARRIAGE TRADE, AND EVERYTHING IN BETWEEN

Once you've discovered what the range is for prices in your market, you need to decide where within that range you want to position yourself.

Let's say you're an architectural photographer in Minneapolis. There are established shooters—people whose names you see on photo credits in local magazines—whose day rates range from $1,200 to $2,000 for editorial work, with the average falling around $1,600.

"I'm new," you think, "I'm just breaking in, so I should come in under the market, let's say at $800 or $900 per day, just until I get established." But that could be a bad idea for several reasons.

PERCEIVED VALUE

If your billing rate is below market, potential clients will think your work is below market quality. This is because your prices tell the client how to perceive the value of your work.

It's different when you're selling a television, for instance. The television has an established value; it sells for $500 at a big electronics store. If the television goes on sale for $425, the consumer will be ecstatic! He'll know he's getting a great deal because he is getting a television that's worth $500 for $75 less. Your work has no established value, other than what you charge for it. Your clients have no other way to appraise it, unlike the television.

"The client is probably not looking for the cheapest deal," says Pam Schmidt, a former photographer's rep turned art buyer. "Usually they want someone whose estimate falls somewhere in the middle. Low-ball bids give the impression the work will be poor quality, and high-end bidders just aren't for everyone. There are clients who are simply price shopping—they're not concerned about quality, they just want a deal. But in my experience, you really don't want to be working with those guys. They want more for their dime than a regular client wants for their dollar, and they're really aggravating."

So where should a newbie position herself on the pricing ladder?

"Somewhere on the lower end of the middle—using your example range, I'd say just under the $1,600 mark. Don't go for the low end, or not only will your perceived value be less but you'll be competing with a huge pool of shooters. Remember, it's crowded at the bottom. And don't go for the high end, because you can't justify that—at least, not yet—and you'll take yourself out of the running for a lot of jobs," says Pam.

It's different for retail studios because their location gives them a certain perceived value, a niche. For instance, my Tiny Acorn Studios offer a hand-colored 8" × 10" (20cm × 25cm) portrait starting at $79—much below what you'd expect to pay. But because the studios are located in high-end boutique-style shopping areas, the product doesn't strike our clients as cheap, it strikes them as a boutique product at a shopping mall price.

Perceived value as it affects your market position is an important factor to consider when pricing your work, but there are many other concerns to add to your equation, too.

COGS, FIXED OVERHEAD, AND YOUR TIME

All your expenses including start-up, COGS (cost of goods sold), fixed overhead, pass-through and your own time, need to inform your pricing decisions. You have to charge what you need to stay in business, or you won't be in business for long. I hear from many people who say, "Oh, I'd just be doing this anyway as a hobby, so if I just mark up the costs of my prints a little bit, I'll be fine." But as fledgling wedding photographer Stacey King discovered, that isn't often the case.

"When I first started shooting weddings, I thought I was really going to rake it in just by charging my clients $20 per hour and a 100 percent markup on my prints," Stacey says. "I thought I was going to make an outrageous fortune. I felt so magnanimous I was throwing in extra shots for free—after all, heck, digital capture is free, right? But when I revisited my first three jobs, I realized that not only wasn't I making any money, I was losing it! I had forgotten to figure in things like gas and mileage, recovering my initial investment in equipment, the costs I had to eat when brides ordered shots they didn't pay for, my dedicated business phone line, office supplies … you name it. It all seemed so insignificant at the time, but oh, baby, does it add up!"

Price Point Appeal

There's a whole psychology to pricing that could be the topic of several books all by itself. For some reason, $19.99 sounds cheaper than an even twenty. And 10 percent off gets just as many people excited as 15 percent off—but up the ante to 20 percent and watch them come out in droves. Two sweaters for the price of one doesn't bring out as many shoppers as "Buy one, buy the second one for a nickel." I don't pretend to understand it. Sometimes the human animal is just a mystery.

I never worried about price point appeal when I opened up KidCapers Portraits. I was running on caffeine and blissful ignorance. But six years later, when I opened my first Tiny Acorn Studio, I had a specific price point in mind that I thought would be especially attrac-

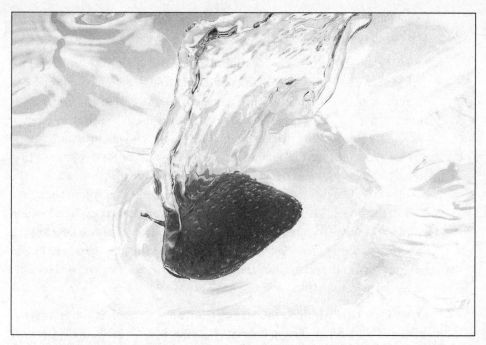

Leo Kim sells his macro food images as 3" × 3" (8cm × 8cm) prints in classic gallery frames for about $20. He also sells them for stock through various agencies.

tive to my client base: I wanted to offer a hand-colored 8" × 10" (20cm × 25cm) for $49. That sounded like such a deal! A hand-painted portrait for under $50? Amazing! So I went at the whole pricing process backwards—instead of figuring out my COGS, fixed overhead and time, and basing my prices on that, I noodled my expenses around to fit.

OH THE DRAMA OF IT

Given that money is a very sensitive, emotional issue for many of us—photographers as well as clients—how can we make these transactions easier on everybody?

- **Give all the bad news up front.** Hiding or downplaying costs may get you a client, but it will never keep one. It'll be easier to collect your fees and you'll stay on good terms when the job is done if you give your client all the bad news up front. Reveal all fees that the client might incur in the process of his shoot. For instance, at all my studios there is an extra charge for the painting of additional figures in a portrait. Each subject after the first costs an additional amount. So, if the basic cost of an 8" × 10" (20cm × 25cm) is $50, and each additional subject is a $15 painting fee, then an 8" × 10" (20cm × 25cm) with three kids in it would cost $80: $50+$15+$15. We tell our clients about the additional painting charge before they book their photo session. It's also stated boldly on our price lists and in our promotional material. This way the client never gets any rude surprises—and neither do we.

- **Know the difference between bids and estimates.** In order to be considered for a job in such photographic specialties as commercial or architectural shooting, when the photographer is in essence acting as a contractor for the client, he will be required to give either a bid or an estimate of how much he will charge for the job. A bid is generally "written in granite." Here's a sample bid situation: *Winsome Woman Magazine* needs six outline shots for their May issue. Stanley Kowalski figures out what he thinks his time and expenses will be to do the job (if he's smart he adds 10 percent on top of that, because, after all, surprises happen), and he agrees to shoot the job for that amount. That's it—if it rains and he gets stuck on location with a trailer full of rental equipment and damp talent, tough cookies. He eats the extra costs—he may even wind up taking a loss on the job. But if he gets lucky and gets the job done in half the time and half the material costs, he still gets paid the amount of his original bid.

- **An estimate is a little different.** Stanley figures it will take him two full days to shoot at $1,600 a day. Archiving and post processing will run $450. Any bad weather days will cost $800. So Stanley's estimate for the job is $4,080, give or take a rain day. Technically, because this is an estimate and not a bid, Stanley is allowed to have his final bill come in at up to $4,488, or 10 percent more than his original estimate. Conversely, if Stanley gets the shots he needs in only one day and half the material costs, he should only charge the client $2,040.

- **Get it in writing.** Never make a deal on a handshake. No matter how good intentions are, misunderstandings can and do crop up even with clients with whom you share a long, happy relationship. Having a written agreement doesn't imply that you think your clients are going to try to cheat you, anymore than the person who takes out a life insurance policy thinks he's going to die prematurely. It's simply insurance. Just create your estimate or bid on paper with the parameters of the job and the terms of payment clearly explained. Sign and date the document, and ask the client to sign and date it upon acceptance.

- **Bill for partial payment up front.** Believe it or not, this practice benefits the client as well as you. Obviously, it helps you insure that you'll receive at least partial payment, and it also helps you cover your expenses up front. But it also helps your clients with budgeting when the payments are spread out over time. It's human nature to put off until tomorrow what you can pay today, but when the final bill comes, it can be a nasty reality. Paying bills is sort of like childbirth—after it's over, we forget the pain. So if a client pays you $500 up front for a $1,000 job, he forgets the ouch from that first $500. And after the job is done, and he gets his final $500 bill, it hurts less than that $1,000 would have.

DON'T APOLOGIZE

I don't know many people who feel comfortable asking for money on their own behalf. It's almost always uncomfortable. But whatever you do, don't apologize! Don't shirk or cower, or say, "I'm sorry, the bill is $450." It goes back to perceived value: If the client thinks you don't believe you deserve your fee, he won't, either. You did an honest job, and you collect your honest fee. Period.

DON'T GIVE AWAY THE INTELLECTUAL PROPERTY FARM

It's always been difficult to protect intellectual property, and never more so than now. While more and more photographers are

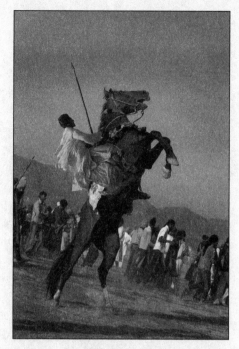

Jim Zuckerman sells editorial travel images such as this one through stock agencies.

giving away their copyrights, it's more important than ever not to join the pack. Not only will you be losing money on the reuse of the images you give away, you'll be devaluing the quality of your work (your images could be reproduced shoddily and nonetheless they will still represent your work), and you'll be devaluing your own image (you'll be perceived as a bargain basement shooter and clients who are looking for the best photographers won't hire you).

Stick to your guns when it comes to retaining the rights to your images rather than offering complete buyouts. It can be hard during periods of bad economy and when your market is crowded, but in the long run, everyone will be better off.

WHEN A CLIENT VIOLATES YOUR COPYRIGHT

Don't assume that every copyright infringement is intentional—sometimes it results in a lack of knowledge on the part of the client, and sometimes, as when the client is a large corporation, it's a simple case of one hand not knowing what the other hand is doing.

If a client violates your copyright agreement, what should you do? I recommend taking action but giving the client the benefit of the doubt. When you approach them the first time, leave your big guns at home. Take the position, "I know this was an oversight/accident/misunderstanding, but …" Be prepared to tell the client exactly what compensation you require, and explain how you arrived at your figure. Most of the time, whether the violation was intentional or accidental, the client is willing to comply.

If you meet with an uncooperative response, the next step would be a little chat with your lawyer.

Not all fee violations are as obvious as copyright infringement. Sometimes clients carry away the photographer's profits a few crumbs at a time, like ants at a picnic. One big way they do this is by squeezing extra shots into a job after you've already arrived at a price. It used to happen to me all the time when I shot commercial jobs. I was hired to shoot twenty-five cutout shots of kids and the client shows up toting thirty-five assorted play tables, sandboxes and art easels, and says, "Gee, we forgot to have the product photographer shoot these, can you just sneak these in between the kids shots?" The correct answer to this question is, "Sure, we can work those into the schedule! The shoot will go an extra four hours, so that'll run another half day." But they're standing there with the furniture they've lugged all the way up the freight elevator, smiling at me hopefully and I know they want me to "just throw it in" and they know I know, so it's a standoff.

Another little profit crumb gets carried away when a job that was supposed to run regionally suddenly turns out to be national. Or a job that you shot for one local store gets picked up by one of the store's vendors and used all over the country. Often these infringements are carried out in markets that the photographer never sees, and you never find out. I don't know of any way to keep tabs on all the markets in the world. If you do find out, you should first approach the offender and request remuneration. In the unlikely event that the request is denied, the next step is legal action. If this is the case, you should consult an intellectual property law attorney. Many people give up at this point, intimidated by the financial and emotional cost of a legal action. But if you follow through, you'll be doing a great service to your fellows in the industry.

RAISING PRICES

Many businesses have formulas they use to figure out when and how much to increase prices. I had one vendor that raised prices 10 percent uniformly, across the board, every year. It had nothing to do with actual inflation, their COGS or the economic environment—they just did their 10 percent increase each year, come hell or high water.

In some years inflation is nominal and the consumer index drops, so many businesses hold off on price increases temporarily. On the other hand, the cost of medical insurance, worker's comp and rent in some areas have skyrocketed. So what's a photographer to do? When and how much should she raise her prices?

A slow, steady increase is best. I made the mistake of going six years without a price increase. I'd like to tell you it was part of a brilliant marketing scheme, but the fact is, I was simply not paying attention. My COGS and fixed overhead were going up every year, but my business was growing every year, too, so my income was increasing even though my margins were dropping. Then suddenly, I woke up and smelled the coffee. My trusty accountant told me, "You know, Vik, you should be hanging on to more of this money you're bringing in." So I checked around my market to see what my competitors were charging and raised my prices about 20 percent overall.

That seemed like a great solution until a long-standing client came in and threw a fit. She felt betrayed. "How could you do this? I've been coming here forever!" she said.

At first I just wanted her to leave my studio and never come back. But after some contemplation I realized she was actually doing me a favor. I realized that if she felt this way, there were probably other clients feeling this way, too, only they weren't telling me about it. They were just ticked off and maybe they were even taking their business elsewhere. My solution was to honor the old prices for old clients for one year. That way I could have my much-needed price increase, but my old clients felt pampered and appreciated. And now I keep my eye on my margins, so I make small increases when necessary instead of big ones when the situation is about to turn ugly.

I wouldn't recommend raising prices just because another year has gone by, but don't wait until you're just doing damage control.

The bottom line on pricing your services is this: Always do an honest job for honest pay. Learn what your industry standards are and position yourself within those standards according to your ability and experience level, taking into consideration your costs and the realities of your market. Don't let your emotions get in the way of collecting fair fees.

Ibarionex Perello says it very well: "You need to charge enough for your work to get your clients to give over their complete and total trust in you. Not only that, but the less you charge, the harder you'll work, because your clients will respect you less. You may think you should charge less than market value because of what you don't know. But you should charge based on what you do know."

Don't give away your copyrights. Intellectual property is still property—you wouldn't give away your house after all! And keep your price increases slow and steady. Do all this, and your clients will respect you, and you'll respect yourself.

Vik Orenstein is a photographer, writer and teacher. She founded KidCapers Portraits in 1988, followed by Tiny Acorn Portraits in 1994. In addition to her work creating portraits of children, she has photographed children for such commercial clients as Nikon, Pentax, Microsoft, and 3M. Vik teaches several photography courses at BetterPhoto.com.

Excerpted from *The Photographer's Market Guide to Building Your Photography Business* © 2010 by Vik Orenstein. Used with the kind permission of Writer's Digest Books, an imprint of F+W, a Content + eCommerce Company.

PAYMENT OPTIONS

How to Accept Payment for Your Work

by Daniel Grant

At Sam's Club, members have a range of options to pay for their purchases, from cash and checks to credit and debit cards and even food stamps. Wal-Mart adds PayPal to the mix, and the California Department of Motor Vehicles notes its willingness to accept money orders and e-checks. A buyer comes into your studio or booth ready to make a purchase: What are you willing to accept?

Perhaps, the best answer is most of the above. "You want to make it as easy as possible for people to pay you," said Dr. William Osgood, director of The Knowledge Institute in Exeter, New Hampshire, which provides counseling for small business development. Let's consider the advantages and disadvantages of some of the payment options available.

Cash

Cash has obvious advantages. Unlike checks and credit card payments, it doesn't need any time to "clear," and there is no 2–4 percent service percent for the vendor to pay to a middleman, as exist with credit cards and PayPal. In fact, vendors might have reason to encourage prospective buyers to pay in cash by offering a small discount. Still, as a practical matter, most people do not carry large amounts of cash on them for the same reason that vendors might be reluctant to be paid with large amounts of cash—they make themselves a potential target for thieves.

Money orders and certified checks are as close to actual cash as one may get, and some people use them to pay for purchases through the mail. A benefit of these types of payment for the buyer is that they do not contain any personal information (home address or telephone number). For the vendor, the benefit is a type of check that cannot bounce. Both money orders and certified checks are available through post offices and banks, and the principal

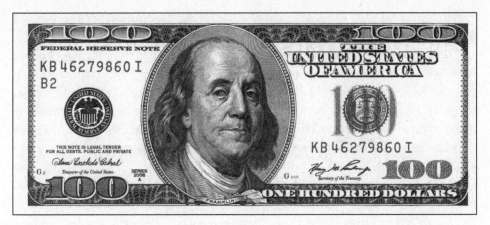

Cash may be king, but you and your customers may not want to keep large sums on hand.

difference between them is that money orders are written for specific amounts—say, $200 or $1,000—while certified checks may be for any amount (e.g., $126.27). There have been rare instances of counterfeit postal money orders, and they may not be accepted if damaged in the mail (e.g., if the routing number on the bottom of the money order cannot be read by a processing machine). The process of getting the bank or post office to issue a replacement is neither quick nor assured. In any case, it is very unlikely that someone entering your booth or studio will pay for anything by this method.

Personal Checks

Personal checks continue to be an option, although a declining number of people pay for their purchases this way these days due to the ubiquity of credit cards. The benefit of a personal check is that, just like cash, they do not require the vendor to concede some percent of the payment to a middleman. Hanging over a check, however, is the potential that the buyer's bank account has insufficient funds, which would be discovered only after the purchased object has been taken and the check has been returned (five to ten business days later). A number of craftspeople in Minnesota had this experience when an elderly woman attended a number of crafts fairs, purchasing items with checks that did not clear. As one jeweler wrote on the ArtFairInsiders forum page, "I live in Florida and, after spending considerably more time on it than the amount was worth, have found that I can't attempt to collect on it without returning to Minnesota and taking her to conciliation court, where the filing fee is far higher than the amount of the check." Her comment named the individual, recommending that others not accept checks from her.

Publicly outing someone who writes bad checks may help the next person who interacts with her or make you feel slightly avenged, or it may open you up to a charge of defamation and the likely loss of this person as a future customer. Perhaps there was no scam intended, since the elderly woman might be suffering from dementia or her direct deposit Social Security check was late.

There are other recourses for artists and craftspeople, including requiring those wishing to pay with a check to provide a telephone number (if it isn't preprinted on the check) and present a driver's license (write down the license number on the back of the check) in order to confirm his or her address and identity. If the check is returned, you will have a means of contacting the buyer to explain the problem and get it resolved amicably. If a telephone call doesn't work, artists might send a certified letter that restates what was requested over the phone, or contact the customer's bank to see if his or her account now has sufficient funds to cover the check—the bank may agree to collect the amount from that person's account following the next deposit, transferring the money to you. Another option is taking the individual to court or hiring a collection agency. Two final options include not delivering the purchased item until the check has cleared or not taking checks at all.

Debit Cards and E-Checks

Debit cards tend to be accepted at most of the same places that take credit cards, and the main difference between them and credit cards is where the money comes from. Using a credit card is a form of borrowing money, while debit cards draw directly from the purchaser's bank account. Vendors who receive authorization to accept debit cards can find out immediately if the buyer has the money to pay for the purchase, and the bank would put a hold on that amount of money in the account. Presumably, that should protect buyers and sellers, since no one would be able to spend money he or she doesn't have in the bank. The only problem in the system is that the process of transferring money from one bank account to the other may take a few days, during which time the "hold" has elapsed and the buyer may no longer have sufficient funds to cover the purchase. That doesn't happen often, but it has occurred.

E-checks are a paperless form of payment made online or over the telephone and are becoming more popular among people who don't have credit cards or are reluctant to use them. Similar to a debit card, the e-check taps one's checking account directly. Buyers supply the name of their bank, the name on their account, the account number and routing number, as well as the amount of the purchase. And the advantage for vendors is that payment is assured (otherwise, the check bounces immediately). The only drawback for vendors is that, similar to accepting credit cards, they must apply to and be accepted by an e-check processing service, paying an initial set-up fee ($100 is standard), monthly user fees ($20) and transaction fees, and there may be other optional or required fees, such as fraud detection and a chargeback fund. Vendors also may be required to purchase special payment processors.

Credit Cards

There are many different types of credit cards, including MasterCard and Visa, that are bank-issued and underwritten by these companies. Discover and Capital One as well as Diner's Club and American Express are charge cards. To accept charge cards as payment, vendors must obtain a merchant services account,

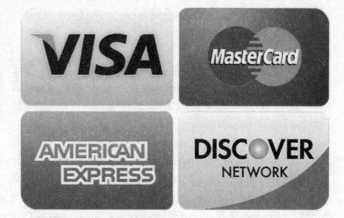

Visa and MasterCard are credit cards, while Discover and American Express are charge cards.

which involves a range of set-up fees, the acquisition of a credit card terminal, transaction fees (the percentage of the purchase price that the company takes, plus a flat per-purchase cost), authorization fees (a charge for each time the company authorizes a transaction), statement fees, annual or monthly fees (the cost of having an account), monthly minimum fees (an additional cost if the amount of charges does not reach a certain amount) and charge-back fees (for reimbursing the buyer if there is a return).

American Express and Discover tend to be accepted by fewer businesses than MasterCard and Visa because the transaction fees are higher, sometimes as much as 4 percent as compared to the 1–2.5 percent that the bank-issued cards generally charge, which cuts down on a vendor's profits. Those merchants simply have to hope that the buyer has more than one type of card or some other way of paying.

Online Payments

PayPal (and other, similar companies) has become a popular way for consumers to make purchases online, though, just as with every other option, there are benefits and drawbacks. The largest benefit is that it is easy for buyers to use; paying for items with their credit cards or e-checks, and setting up a PayPal payment option on a vendor's website (with buttons for single purchases or a shopping cart) is quick and uncomplicated. What's more, customers may be familiar with PayPal already through purchases from eBay or Amazon, which adds to their comfort level.

There are no set-up fees for vendors setting up merchant accounts with PayPal, but it takes four business days for funds to be deposited into one's account, which is a bit slow. Vendors still may find the costs of being a PayPal merchant to be high, with monthly fees of up to $30 and transaction fees of 2.9 percent in addition to 30 cents for debit and credit card purchases. Even more costly are returns with chargeback fees of $20 (and PayPal will still retain its 2.9 percent transaction fee). As with many other online services, contacting an actual person at PayPal's customer service department about problems you may be experiencing is not easy.

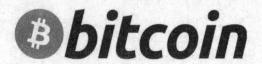

Bitcoin is now accepted at a variety of online retailers including Etsy and Overstock.com.

With both e-checks and PayPal, the monthly costs of being able to use these payment systems may begin to bite if buyers don't want to make purchases in this way, or they do so rarely. Spending hundreds of dollars per year to enable just a few small sales may make the convenience unprofitable.

Bitcoin

In its short history of existence, the nontangible Internet currency bitcoin has earned an uneven reputation, but increasingly this "cryptocurrency" has gained legitimacy and is being used in a variety of online stores, such as at Etsy and Overstock.com. Will artwork and other collectibles be next? Perhaps. Burning Man, the nonprofit summer arts festival based in California, began accepting bitcoin donations in late 2014, and a number of online exhibition sites (cointemporary.com, btcartgallery.com, bitdazzle.com/art, art4bitcoin.net and bitpremier.com/4-fine-art-antiques) accept this form of currency.

So far, artists who have had their work displayed on bitcoin-accepting online galleries have not been disappointed at the experience, even if nothing has sold. "I like the idea of trading in bitcoins as it has parallels with the speculative nature of the art market," said Marita Fraser, a Viennese artist who showed a 2014 painting titled *O.T.* (priced at 3.5 bitcoin) on Cointemporary. She concluded, "I see trading art in bitcoins as an interesting experiment, and an art project within itself, which calls into question the value of things in the world and different kinds of exchange." On the other hand, British sketch artist Oli Witcomb claimed that he has sold two drawings on art4bitcoin.net, and "I've had a few donations."

Bitcoin, which was first created in 2009, is referred to as a cryptocurrency, a form of money based not on the value of gold or other currencies but on computer code that controls the creation of new units and their transfer from one computer user to another. Banks and governments are not involved in the production or movement of new bitcoin (the U.S. Treasury refers to bitcoin as a "decentralized currency"), and "payments are processed almost instantly, with close to zero fees," according to Valentin Ruhry, one of Cointemporary's directors. Online exchange agencies convert bitcoin to dollars or other currencies on the basis of the current exchange rate, which has ranged from $160 to $1,200 per bitcoin.

The volatility in the exchange rate and the fact that banks have declined deposits of bitcoin into accounts has been discouraging for Orlando, Florida painter Alex Vera, whose payment for a single sale is "still stored in my digital wallet." However, he noted that "bitcoin could make huge gains again in value and would pay off once it is accepted everywhere."

The mainstream art-selling businesses have tended to shy away from bitcoin. However, the tech world has become more comfortable with bitcoin's legitimacy. In December 2014, Microsoft began to accept bitcoin for buyers of Windows Phone, Xbox Music, Xbox Video, apps, games and other company products, following a similar move by both Apple and Dell in June 2014. The King's College, a liberal arts Christian college in Manhattan's financial district, began accepting bitcoin as tuition in 2013.

The subject of money often makes artists uneasy. How much should they charge for their work? Should they offer or agree to discounts? And then, when the sale is about to take place, comes the issue of what kind of money to accept. Every form of currency brings with it some form of anxiety, and artists should select the option that makes them feel most secure and satisfies their buyers.

Daniel Grant is the author of several books including *The Business of Being an Artist* and *The Fine Artist's Career Guide* (Skyhorse Publishing).

TAKING & MAKING STOCK PHOTOS

....

by Rohn Engh

The stock photo as we know it today has evolved from a documentary snapshot to a subtle and sophisticated art form. This evolution can be traced in magazines such as *National Geographic* that have existed for one hundred years. Following the progression in bound *National Geographic* volumes at the library can be entertaining as well as informative.

As we learn in zoology class, ontogeny recapitulates phylogeny (the stages in the development of the individual mirror those of the species). A photographer entering the field undergoes the same sort of progression. She begins by taking simplistic photographs, similar to the early photo illustrations, and gradually incorporates new ideas and technical knowledge that enable her to produce better and more interesting pictures, until, if she endures, she eventually turns out fine photo illustrations—editorial stock photos. This evolution is a valuable learning experience for the photographer, but it can be accelerated. Here's how.

Many photographers are conditioned to take photographs that reflect the world, somewhat as a mirror does. A documentary photographer takes a picture: He simply records things the way they were at that moment.

However, to limit photography to mirrorlike documentation is to restrict knowledge and understanding.

Stock photography opens up a vast new field of interpretive endeavor. The fact that stock photos are in a large measure workaday pictures doesn't preclude innovative and creative treatment of them. Photo illustration allows a photographer to make photographs. The stock photographer creates a situation as it could be, or as it should be, or distills the essence of a scene or event. As we all know, painters rarely paint their landscapes true to nature. To limit their illustrations to exact duplications of nature would be to confine their creativity and their viewers' enjoyment. They rearrange the elements in their paintings to achieve a composition of wholeness and meaning that didn't exist earlier. Similarly, jazz musicians improvise on the melody and rhythm of a familiar tune not because they wish to seem clever or self-consciously different, but because they wish to discover, for themselves and their listeners, new meaning in the music. Photographs, like other expressive media, can offer fresh insights and deeper understanding. A photograph can become a microscope or a telescope for the viewer to see into or beyond what is being photographed.

All of this, of course, does not apply to photojournalism or documentary photography. It would be dishonest and unethical to alter or shape a news photograph to misrepresent a scene or subject. The line between photo illustration (stock photography) and photojournalism can be thin. Photojournalist W. Eugene Smith was criticized for moving the bed away from the wall for a better camera angle in some of his photographs of a midwife for *Life Magazine*.

Stock photographers often confront ethical questions when it comes to such improvisation. For example, if you photograph a teenager whose blemishes are here today but gone tomorrow, do you leave them in the picture or retouch them out? Which is the truer interpretation? Are the blemishes inappropriate if you're illustrating the winners in a student government activity or a science fair? Should they remain if you're illustrating nutritional deficiencies or youth gangs? Or should the blemishes remain no matter what the context?

The answers are ultimately left to you, the stock photographer. It might appear to photography purists that allowing free rein to interpretive photography could lead to a lack of respect for the truth. However, before the arrival of the photograph and the photographer, pictorial illustrations came in the form of etchings, cartoons, drawings, and paintings. We accepted the artists' interpretations and managed to survive.

In photo illustration work, then, you are frequently and legitimately *making* a picture, not *taking* it. For example, you see something happen, you feel it was significant, and you would like to photograph it. You have two alternatives:

1. You can hope it happens again in your lifetime.
2. While you're still on the scene, you can attempt to re-create it, "improving" it (stripping it of distracting elements).

THE WAY THE PROS DO IT

Trends are an important factor for some of your editorial stock photo clients. Here are two clues on how to keep up. Check out the new book categories at popular stores like Barnes & Noble. They've already done the market research for you by bringing out books that will match current trends. Secondly, attend trendy events like film festivals and observe what's currently hip in the way of clothing styles.

In stock photography, you can also create scenes that never happened, but could happen. On an assignment to photograph a child's visit to a toy factory, for example, I realized my little model wasn't at all intrigued by the assembly-line production. The bits and pieces didn't look like toys yet, the pounding and banging of the machinery was hurting his ears, the paint smell was disagreeable—yet I needed to illustrate a small boy's excitement at seeing toys being manufactured. In desperation, I wadded up a piece of bubble gum (when working with kids, always have a supply of goodies handy) and stuck it on one of the panels of a toy truck as it moved toward the next assembly stage. I stood on a ladder above the moving belt and asked my model to point out the bubble gum as it came into view. He did so with enthusiasm, and I snapped a picture of a delighted youngster pointing at a toy truck on an assembly line. In stock photography, it is true, you may bring elements together that never happened. You are, in effect, contriving. However, you can keep your illustrations authentic by selecting situations that could happen and then reenacting them in a way that appears unposed.

Danger Ahead: Trite Pictures

There's a trap waiting for the photographer who is new to stock photography. Although I continually remind you that workaday pictures are the most marketable, that kind of subject matter can fall into the trite category—if you let it. Corny pictures are easy to produce. Beware of the temptation to take pictures that are trite, cute, or clichéd.

"There's nothing new!" you're probably saying.

Stop. Think about the pictures in your portfolio, print notebook, or recent slide show. If you were to eliminate (1) dramatic silhouettes, (2) sunset scenes, (3) postcard scenes of mountains and clouds, (4) portraits of old men, (5) the father lovingly holding his daughter, and (6) experimental abstract shots, how many pictures do you have left?

I don't want to imply that the previous subjects are always trite. We have all seen these subjects treated with compassion, depth, and a sense of beauty. Many of them can qualify as standard excellent pictures. However, the more photographs we see of these familiar subjects, the less charity we have available for them in our appreciation bank.

The tendency to take trite pictures is almost a disease among photographers—even veterans. Because we see trite pictures every day in the local, regional, and national publications, we become conditioned to the status quo. Photographers find an easy way to take a school portrait, a commercial or architectural shot, or a standard stock photograph, and they gradually lock themselves into an effortless routine that stifles creativity.

Photography, especially photo illustration, has become a vibrant communication vehicle in our daily lives. The public expects not only to be entertained, but also to be informed by photos; people don't take well to stock photographs that, like old news or old jokes, are mere repeats. People want new insights and angles, and thought-provoking interpretations of everyday subjects. As Don Hewitt, the late producer of CBS-TV's *60 Minutes*, said, "Show me something I don't already know!"

How to Avoid Making Trite Photos

Let's say a publisher has assigned you to produce a photo essay on "The Circus." Take a scratch pad and jot down ten picture situations that come to mind. Don't read further until you've jotted down at least ten. . . .

That was easy, wasn't it? Well, if it was, I'll bet you've listed ten trite ideas. Producing untrite pictures takes thought.

Before you rush out and snap away hundreds of photos on a subject that every man, woman and child is familiar with, take at least a half hour to sketch out some picture possibilities. This brief exercise will save you hours of location and computer time spent on pictures that a publisher would probably reject. It will also eliminate those blinders we often inadvertently wear when we arrive at a picture-taking locale and become immersed in the scope and immediacy of the situation. Objectivity is easier to retain if you have a pre-planned sketch of what you want to photograph before you get there. By the same token, don't go overboard and lock yourself into a plan that has no room for spontaneity and innovation sparked by on-the-scene elements. Always be ready to discover and adjust to new picture possibilities.

Let's take our circus example. These shots are not new to us: the clown in his dressing room; the elephant's trunk appearing through the window of the circus moving van; the tightrope walker silhouetted by spotlight against the tent's ceiling; the roustabouts taking a well-earned coffee break; the trainer at work with his chimpanzees; the cleanup crew the day after. We've all seen these pictures over and over again. Maybe the documentary photographer can be satisfied with such pictures, but not the stock photographer or the photobuyer who strives to provide fresh insights, even on such a familiar subject as the circus.

What do we want to see in your essay on the circus? The answer will take thought, timing, and preparation on your part. Imagination, luck, and persistence will be important, too. You've got to zig when other photographers zag. You've got to anticipate. Most importantly, you've got to show us the circus as we never imagined it could be. (Don't interpret this as license to shoot obscure, experimental, weird-angle pictures in an effort to be different. That would be equally trite.)

What nontrite pictures, then, will you shoot at the circus? For starters, let's see an extreme closeup of one of the acrobats straining at push-ups, showing the effort and dedication it takes behind the scenes to produce a quality performance come showtime. How about a mother with toddler in arms happily finding a seat ringside? Or a stocky father lifting his three-year-old up to touch the bar of the trapeze? How about a backstage shot of a roustabout pumping air into the tire of the goofy mobile while the chimpanzee driver waits nearby? As a stock photographer, you must remember that readers of publications are people and that people love to watch and learn about other people. You will record how spectators at the circus relate to the performers (with admiration?); to the animals (with amazement, fear, or pity?); to the atmosphere generated by the circus (with awe?); to each other (with friendship?). You will include symbols of the circus in your pictures—a trapeze, a cage, a tent—but you'll keep these low-key, to serve only as incidental elements to establish the circus atmosphere.

In most cases, you will want to apply the principle of making a picture rather than taking one. You can reenact or improve picture possibilities by asking the cooperation of spectators or performers. To a clown: "Would you mind taking a bite of that cotton candy again?" To a teenager: "Could I ask you to do that again—over by the zebras?"

To see a refreshing photographic insight into the circus, look up an archive copy of the January 1986 issue of *American Photographer* (now *American Photo*) at your library, and turn to the feature by Susan Felter on page 58.

Photography is visual, and you can escape the plague of triteness by constantly visualizing picture-taking possibilities. Most successful photographers use this secret, so why not try it out yourself? In free moments, even days before you actually perform your assignment (circus, annual report, political convention, and so on), visualize the hundreds of picture-taking possibilities that will probably come up. Eliminate the trite, the corny, and the too cute. Concentrate on innovative possibilities that are practical and realistic. (This process will save you on-the-scene time, too.) If you visualize, you'll arrive at your assignment well prepared. Most important, you will have worked all the tempting trite pictures out of your system, and you'll be able to concentrate on a fresh approach to your subject matter.

Are trite pictures salable? Like trite paintings, songs, and handicrafts, they are. There also are directories, websites, and catalogs devoted to displaying trite stock photos, and books devoted to making trite photographs—*but not this one*. If, after reading this admonition against trite pictures, you find some culprits in your stock photo file, send them to a stock photo agency. Veteran photographers are familiar with stock agencies' need to provide standard trites to their (mostly commercial) clientele. One photographer friend says "I market the best pictures myself, and I dump my clichés on my agency, which can use all I can send." While agency cliché sales do come in, for any one photographer the checks are "every now and then." You don't want to depend on them to pay the rent.

Rohn Engh, accomplished stock photographer, publisher, author, has had an enormous influence on the business of stock photography for more than three decades. His best-selling book, *Sell & Re-Sell Your Photos*, is considered by both veteran photographers and newcomers to be the premiere desktop guide on marketing principles for the stock photographer. Engh worked out of his 80-acre farm in rural Wisconsin, where he and his wife lived and raised two sons.

HOW TO MANAGE MODELS

....

by Rohn Engh

Marketable stock photos are very often pictures of people doing things. How well the people in your pictures perform can determine the success of your photos. The commercial service photographer usually has the convenience of working with professional models. In contrast, most of your models in stock photography will be regular folks rather than professionals, and it's up to you to make sure they feel comfortable and are cooperative.

You will encounter many of your models spontaneously in the course of your routine shooting. For the most part, children, teenagers, and adults will willingly cooperate with you for the fun or novelty of being photographed or being involved in the action. People often are intrigued that their picture might be published.

Before you begin photographing your on-the-spot models, let them know who you are and why you want to photograph them. Take the time to make them feel at ease.

Often their first question will be, "What's this photograph going to be used for?" Give your models a direct answer: "For a book. If this photo is selected for publication, you'll appear in a school textbook." Or "For a magazine [name]." Or "For my photograph files. I'm a stock photographer and have a library of pictures that I sell to magazines and books." Give some examples of where the picture might be used.

Control the Conversation

If it seems appropriate, explain the mood you're trying to capture in your pictures. Control the conversation throughout the whole picture-taking session to trigger naturally the kind of expressions you're aiming for. Don't let the conversation slip into a subject that is contrary to the mood you are trying to create. For example, if your picture calls for a happy mood, steer the conversation away from war, taxes, or the fire that took so many lives last week or the twenty-car pileup on the freeway this morning. However, if your picture calls for somberness, guide the conversation to something difficult or puzzling (not necessarily sad—serious expressions can be interpreted as sad).

How to Get the Most From Your Models

Sometimes, to elicit the right kind of expressions from a nonprofessional model, you'll need to go a few steps further and become an actor—occasionally to the point of giving an award-winning performance as a clown, demagogue, or saint.

After a while, you'll find that in working with people for your pictures, you've developed a technique of gentle persuasion. You become adept at moving the conversation along the lines you want it to go.

Be as selective as the situation allows in your choice of models. Don't choose the model because she is a neighbor, relative or friend. You'll make your task easier if you choose a model whose natural style or demeanor comes close to the expression you're aiming for—a serious thinker for sadness or weary expressions; a clear-eyed, upbeat individual for happy shots; and so on. Here are some tips on how this works in practice:

Happiness. Don't ask for a smile. Instead, maneuver the conversation to some magic question that always get smiles.

SENIORS: "Do you have any grandchildren?"

ADULTS: "How's your golf [bowling, tennis] game?" Or "Been anywhere fun on vacation lately?"

TEENAGERS: Teenagers usually won't allow themselves to be categorized. I've found it best to learn the teenager's interests first (sports, music, movies, and so on), and then ask questions in those areas. Don't attempt to speak their language. They'll only become more suspicious of you.

PRETEENS: "Who's your best friend?"

SMALL CHILDREN: "What's your dog's [cat's, fish's] name?"

BABIES: If you make strange noises, you'll usually be rewarded with a smile (from everyone!).

Sorrow. Some people (Abraham Lincoln, for example) look sad naturally. You can induce a sad-looking expression by asking a model to look tired. Another method is to catch him "between expressions," which can appear pensive and sad-looking.

Intimacy. Shoot from a three-quarter view with a long lens. This will bring two people closer. Ask your models to look at each other's eyebrows. Unless they are pros, models who do not know each other will feel self-conscious, and your resulting pictures will look stilted. For your intimate pictures, choose models who know each other.

Overcoming shyness. Use a long lens when your model is shy about being photographed. Teenagers are often self-conscious when asked to be photographed. If you need a single shot, ask the shy teen to be photographed with a friend. Then use a telephoto lens to capture a single portrait of the person. "Don't take my picture," shy people will often say. To accomplish your mission, try taking a picture of what they are doing. If people truly do not want their photograph taken, you should respect this.

Children are good models and can be diverted in ways that will enhance picture content. They tend to participate more fully than teenagers or adults. A good technique is to get your kid models involved in guessing games with you (the type of games we offer our children on long, boring car rides). Kids become animated when they like what they're doing. Children, like pets, are fast, though, and when photographing these subjects, you have to be alert and on your toes.

Pictures of people sell. Photo editors know that we're human, that nothing touches us more than a picture of someone feeling something we identify with—be it anger, humor, pensiveness, bewilderment, or delight. Thus, when you aim your camera at your models with photo illustration in mind, you've got to adjust your thinking from the cosmetic approach usually employed when taking pictures of people. Your customer is not the portrait client or the bride or Aunt Harriet, but a photobuyer. Photo editors are not interested in how pretty or handsome you have made your subject appear, but in what emotion, what spontaneity, what insight into the human condition you have captured.

Should You Pay Your Models?

If you're shooting on speculation for inventory for your stock photo file, many of your on-the-spot models will be satisfied with a copy of the published picture (tearsheet) if and when it is published. Other nonprofessional models are willing to cooperate just for fun or for the experience, especially if you're a beginner yourself. Still others are happy to have copies of the photographs. Give them your card, and have them write to you for the pictures. If you do promise photographs, and they contact you for them, follow through. You'll find, though, that the majority of people don't get around to writing for the pictures.

Monetary payment is in order for nonprofessional models when you're shooting a commercial assignment as a service photographer. A good rule of thumb is to budget a minimum of 5 percent and a maximum of 10 percent of the fee you're receiving for the picture to pay your model(s). Seal the transaction with a signed model release.

Other Model Sources

A good source of models is your local community theater. Amateur actors always need portraits for their portfolios. You can trade them some portrait shots for their posing (in natural settings, of course) for your people-picture needs (e.g., people talking, engaged in some activity, expressing fear, sadness, loneliness, joy, and so on).

You can try to find models in the drama departments at your local university, community college, and high school.

Check also with local families and neighbors in need of family portraits. I will often sketch out photo illustration ideas and have the members of the family act out the photo illustration situations. In return for their modeling services (about an hour's work), I supply them with a family portrait.

When Is a Model Release Necessary?

It is the usage, not the picture, that determines whether or not a model release is needed.

If the photograph you take might be used commercially (basically for advertising), you will need a model release (you may also need a property release). If the photograph will only be used editorially, you will not need a model release in ninety-nine out of one hundred situations.

Generally speaking, commercial usage is when a photograph is used in an advertisement and/or to endorse a product or service. Editorial usage is when a photograph is used to illustrate an article in a magazine, newspaper, or book.

If you don't want the intrusion or the administration of releases for each photo, a general rule many stock photographers (and some service photographers) follow is to use photogenic neighbors, friends, and relatives as models. If you need a model release for a particular photo later, you know where to find the models to obtain it.

Occasionally I get a model release request for a picture I took a decade ago. I consult my model file-card box and usually find that I received a blanket model release for an entire family when I originally took the picture. To obtain a blanket release, I had both parents fill out and sign the release and asked them to list their (minor) children.

What if I don't have a release? Because the model was usually a neighbor, friend, or relative, I often can track them down for the release.

In the early stages of my stock photography career, I obtained model releases on every occasion. I have since turned this completely around and now almost never get one. Experience has shown me that this administrative disruption of the mood or atmosphere of my picture-taking session isn't necessary. Model releases are not required when a picture is used for educational or informational purposes. Since my personal market list consists of magazine and book publishers, I rarely get a release request from an editor. However, since your market list is different from mine, you will know how extensive you'll want your model release system to be.

Rohn Engh, accomplished stock photographer, publisher, author, has had an enormous influence on the business of stock photography for more than three decades. His best-selling book, *Sell & Re-Sell Your Photos*, is considered by both veteran photographers and newcomers to be the premiere desktop guide on marketing principles for the stock photographer. Engh worked out of his 80-acre farm in rural Wisconsin, where he and his wife lived and raised two sons.

SLOW DOWN TO GO FAST

by Peleg Top

Tackling everything at lightning speed can actually stifle a designer's most valuable asset: her creativity. Learn how going slower will help you achieve a clear mind and put you on the path to true productivity.

I suspect that at the start of your day, the first thing you do is reach for your phone. You might even do this before you get out of bed. From the moment your eyes open, the input begins. E-mail, Facebook, Twitter, texting, newsfeed—all pouring in like an electronic fire-hose aimed at your brain. From daybreak to sunset, it's a nonstop, get-it-done overload. It started in the 1980s when FedEx changed everything by introducing overnight delivery. Soon thereafter, fax machines came along, followed by e-mail and now smartphones. We've been spoiled. We're used to immediate results and, in return, we've lost our patience. We don't like waiting and when we have to, it causes anxiety and stress.

While technology brought convenience to our lives, it also brought a whole new set of expectations that soon became the status quo. Our world has become addicted to speed and impatience. Clients expect projects completed in ridiculous time frames and demand creative people to generate ideas instantaneously. Our over-connectivity has led to an avalanche of information that requires us to absorb far more than we ever did before. We've become a nation of anxious people who are always worried about what's next—so much so that we forget to look at what's in front of us.

And for creative people, it's even harder not to get distracted. We have many interests and options to choose from. Slowing down to actually experience life in its depth becomes the biggest challenge we face. Besides, "slow" in our society often means "lazy," "slacker" or plain "dumb"—and those are the last things we want to be known as. We keep cramming things into our lives, always searching for the combination that will provide us the most pleasure, and we distract ourselves from the tough questions (the slow questions) about what's really important: our values, beliefs, big-picture plans, goals and how to achieve them. Not to mention how this pace stifles creativity.

The No. 1 question I hear from creative business leaders isn't "Why are we running so fast?" It's "How do we keep up and stay ahead in this fast-paced world?" The answer is simple. We think that moving fast will help us keep up. But this only works when we do it with precision and purpose. And in order to so do, we have to slow down.

....

To move quickly with precision and purpose, however, slowing down is precisely what we need to do. Instead of running at full speed in all directions, we need to pause, think, focus and then run in the right direction.

....

Stop Multitasking

At first glance, "slow down to go fast" doesn't seem to make much sense. Our brains tell us that if we pause even for a moment, we'll fall further behind. So we go at it with more grit than ever. In order to move quickly with precision and purpose, however, slowing down is precisely what we need to do. Instead of running at full speed in all directions, we need to pause, think, focus and then run in the right direction.

But most creatives (and, really, most people) don't take the time to discern the "right" direction for themselves. We just start running. We say "yes" to too many things, fearing we'll miss out on whatever surprise is waiting around the corner. We mistake being busy for being productive. We pretend to be masterful multitaskers, thinking we'll get more done in less time if we do it all at once.

The truth is, multitasking is only slowing us down further—and not in a good way. Multitasking, as most people understand it, is a myth that makes overly scheduled and stressed-out people feel efficient. The lie is that you can actually do two or more tasks at the same time with full focus and attention, but in reality, what you're doing is serial tasking. You're shifting from one task to another to another in rapid succession. You think you're doing these tasks simultaneously. But you're not. Are you actually savoring that microwave dinner while you're reading e-mail? Not really.

Doing everything at once is neither effective nor efficient. You're expending more brain power switching from one thing to another, which only adds to feeling rushed and incomplete. It can't be done. Choose a single task, and slow down. Start one project and stay present with it until you complete it, and watch how much faster you'll get your to-do list done.

Be Mindful in Order to Be Present

If your creativity seems to suffer and you're having difficulty coming up with new ideas, then slow down. Don't panic and step on the gas; ease up instead. Slowing down can be a tremendous source of creativity, which exists in the present moment. You can't find it anywhere else. Taking our time ultimately helps us become more mindful. When we're mindful, we're able to create our best.

Here's an example of how putting this into practice helped me. Seven years ago, I spent a year in cooking school learning to be a chef. It was a creative experiment. I had no intention of starting a culinary career but rather wanted to awaken my creative spirit, which had become dormant and was missing from my life. I learned to chop and bake and broil, but the most important lesson I learned was about pacing myself.

On our first day of class, we were immediately shown the location of the first-aid kit. "Each of you will most likely have a serious kitchen accident during the course of the year," said the head chef, "unless you learn to slow down and be present."

And the head chef was right. As the year progressed, nearly every student experienced serious knife cuts, burns, slips and falls. Moving too fast led to first aid time-outs or, worse, no chance of getting the day's dish finished on time.

But safety concerns aside, in order for me to connect to my creativity in cooking school, I had to learn to be present and focused. I became more aware of how I handled myself. If I used my knife carefully, I'd avoid accidents. Not to mention, my dishes would turn out well, and I'd managed to get everything done ahead of the deadline, with enough time for dishwashing.

Practice a Slower Pace

The way I initially showed up in the kitchen was a reflection of how I was showing up in the rest of my life. I was distracted and not present. Now, I'm able to see that same malaise everywhere. Nearly everyone I know is suffering in this age of distraction, never catching up and always feeling like they're falling behind. It doesn't have to be that way. We've come to accept distractions as a way of life. But life isn't the problem; we are. We're simply moving too fast.

Slowing down allows us to create in an intentional way and not react from fear, which is generally the root cause of our speed. Slowing down takes practice and mindfulness. It's a way of being that requires focus, attention and work. To start this mindful pace, consider these tips for creating a slower life:

BENEFITS OF SLOWING DOWN

There are lots of reasons to slow down. Here's just a few to give you an idea of why it's important to live a slower lifestyle:

1. **Better focus.** When you slow down, you focus better. Give yourself the time to complete just one task. With just one thing you have to do, you are less likely to procrastinate by doing other, less important tasks.

2. **Deeper insight.** Rushing produces shallowness, because you never have time to dig beneath the surface. Slow down and dive into deeper waters.

3. **Better appreciation.** When you slow down you notice more and pay attention to things you normally pass by. You can appreciate what you have, what you're doing and who you're with.

4. **Better communication.** Slowing down will help you choose your words carefully. Your written and oral communication will be more intentional and present and not come from a reactive place.

5. **Less stress.** Rushing produces anxiety and higher stress levels. You run the risk of becoming physically and emotionally exhausted, which causes high levels of anxiety and stress. Slowing down can help you manage and release stress as well as calm your body.

6. **Better creativity.** If your mind is constantly bombarded with new information it will be hard to find room for creative thinking. Our creative mind flows when we are relaxed, centered and open.

Disconnect. Set aside time to turn off your devices and e-mail alerts. Schedule a break where you don't take or make phone calls, when you're just creating, connecting with a friend, reading a book or simply taking a walk. And if you're brave, go an entire weekend disconnected. I promise, you'll be OK.

Practice mindfulness. Learn to live in the present rather than thinking so much about the future or the past. When you eat, fully appreciate your food. If you're with someone, be with them entirely. When you're walking, appreciate your surroundings, no matter where you are.

Eliminate commitments. Say "no" more often to non-essential commitments. Every "yes" is taking up space in your life, so slow down and reflect on every commitment and invitation you receive. Before you say "yes," make sure it isn't taking you away from your more important commitments.

Do less. Rename your to-do list as the much more gentle "All that I have to do today is …" list. Design a less stressful day that allows you to work in a natural, easy-going manner.

Single task. This is the opposite of multitasking. Focus on one thing at a time. When you feel the urge to switch to other tasks, pause, breathe and pull yourself back.

Slowing down can be a liberating experience for you, your business, your creativity and even your personal life. For example, Matt Steel, principal at Grain in St. Louis, put this advice into practice. After getting to a point of near-complete exhaustion and burnout, slowing down turned his life around. "The quality and variety of our design work has grown," Steel says. "We spend more time with our families. We have lives. We close the shop at 2 P.M. on Fridays and still manage to get things done on time. Our business is growing at a sustainable pace. We're far from perfect, but I wouldn't change a thing."

Take a close look at how you function throughout your day. Are you rushing around everywhere without ample time to do anything because you "don't have enough hours in the day"? Become the master of your own time, and watch your life change. Your days will start feeling longer and more satisfying, as you'll live a more intentional and present life. You'll begin to enjoy every moment of every day because you'll be present to witness them. And, surprise, you'll even get more done and find your creativity flowing.

Peleg Top is a leadership development coach and a business mentor to creative entrepreneurs worldwide. He teaches business owners how to create a profitable company while living an artistic, well-balanced life. www.PelegTop.com

Excerpted from the May 2014 issue of *HOW* magazine. Used with the kind permission of *HOW* magazine, a publication of F+W, a Content + eCommerce Company. Visit www.howdesign.com to subscribe.

LUCRECER BRAXTON

Inspiring the Everyday Photographer

....

by Deb Heneghan

"I believe everyone can take amazing pictures regardless of the type of camera you use or your skill level. If you are looking to grow as a photographer or to gain a little inspiration along your photography journey, then this is the place for you, and I am glad to have you here."

—Lucrecer Braxton, blogger/photographer

A portrait and still-life photographer in Cincinnati, Lucrecer (Lu-cree-sha) Braxton started blogging about ten years ago. She inspires amateur photographers (and likely some professionals) to be creative and tell their stories with photos. She encourages the faint of heart and hopes to help them become the self-confident photographers they aspire to be.

While Braxton has a website (Lucrecer.com) and is on Instagram, Twitter, Google+, Flickr and Pinterest, blogging is her favorite social media tool. She explains, "Blogs have allowed me to reach more people with my message that everyone can take a great picture with practice. Increasing frequency in posting can grow your following, but relevant content increases shares and thus brings new readers to my blogs." Braxton's blogs have led to keynote speaker and workshop leader engagements on writing, photography, and art.

#SHOOTEVERYDAMNDAY

Braxton kicked off 2015 with a new blog, "Shoot Every Damn Day!," where she invites followers to take a photo every day for 365 days. She provides tips to take better photos and learn the basics of photography. She also posts daily themes at the beginning of each month to help participants think out of the box when looking for their daily photo. For more information, to see the photos from the 365 daily photo challenge or to join the 2016 challenge, visit her blog at www.shoot everydamnday.com.

Braxton, who also participates in the daily challenge, sees it as a fun way to take great pictures and grow creatively while helping others find their "inner photographer." It's not easy to find the time to do something new on a daily basis—to create a new habit takes time. The challenge connects her to other photographers and having others join the effort is inspirational for everyone involved, including Braxton. She has tried to do this on her own and not succeeded in past years. The group effort makes a difference.

"There is no pressure, no guilt for missing a day," she says. "You just move on to the next day. But the camaraderie, knowing you are not doing it alone, helps keep you fired up and dedicated to the challenge." Braxton loves to cruise the photos on Instagram or Flickr, but she warns her blog followers "not to get caught up in comparing their photos to others, but to simply see them and then find the blessings and value in your own life and then create your own pictures."

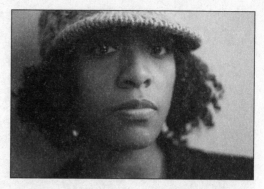

Lucrecer Braxton, portrait and still-life photographer, loves the self-portrait. She advises amateur photographers to take lots of self-portraits before leaping into taking portraits of others.

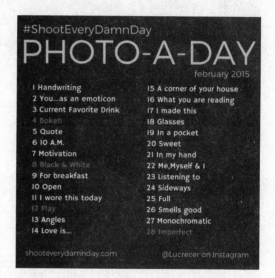

#ShootEveryDamnDay
PHOTO-A-DAY
february 2015

1 Handwriting	15 A corner of your house
2 You...as an emoticon	16 What you are reading
3 Current Favorite Drink	17 I made this
4 Bokeh	18 Glasses
5 Quote	19 In a pocket
6 10 A.M.	20 Sweet
7 Motivation	21 In my hand
8 Black & White	22 Me,Myself & I
9 For breakfast	23 Listening to
10 Open	24 Sideways
11 I wore this today	25 Full
12 Play	26 Smells good
13 Angles	27 Monochromatic
14 Love is...	28 Imperfect

shooteverydamnday.com   @Lucrecer on Instagram

Here are Braxton's February photo prompts. Prompts 4, 8, 12, and 28 repeat each month.

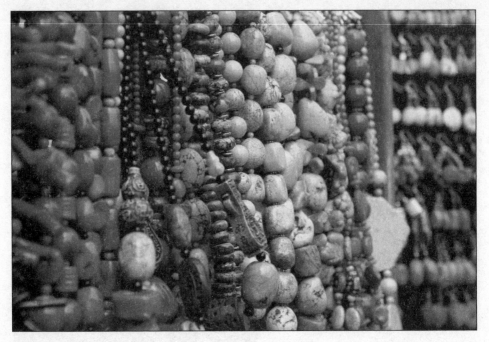

Step in close for a different perspective.

"What seems ordinary and routine to you—be it waiting at a bus stop, putting on your kids' boots, or stargazing out of your kitchen window—can be extraordinary to someone else looking at your photo," Braxton said.

Remember, when three people take the same picture, you get three perspectives and three very different pictures.

TEACHING THE "CHALLENGED PHOTOGRAPHER" WITH THEMES AND BLOG POSTS

Daily themes, such as, black-and-white photos, self-portraits or phone photos only, are a few of the themes Braxton employs to help develop various aspects of photography skills throughout the photo challenge. She also posts the theme-related articles to her blog and her website.

Braxton welcomes comments on assignments and loves to respond to questions. Below is an excerpt from one of her early 2015 blog posts.

Why Black-and-White Photography is Simply Beautiful

"Have fun with black and white … My first experience with photography was with black-and-white film. I was excited about it and a little terrified. … When I make a conscious decision to shoot an image knowing the end result will be black and white, I compose my picture

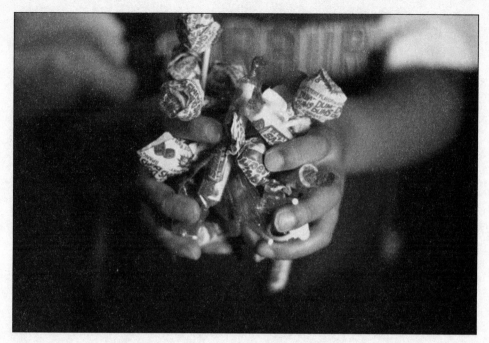

Play with your aperture and achieve an aesthetic blur, known as Bokeh, from your lens.

differently. Colors no longer become a distraction. Instead, my focus is on the relationship of my subject to my background. Textures matter. The light matters. I get to choose what the viewer focuses on. . . . What do you think about exploring black-and-white photography as one of our monthly challenges? It could be a fun experiment."

BRAXTON'S CHALLENGE TIPS: PLAN FOR SUCCESS

- **Shoot at the same time every day.** Set an alarm on your smartphone to remind you to take a picture at the same time every day.
- **Plan ahead.** It's okay to look ahead for the prompts and plan a creative shot. If you know you are going to shoot at the same time every day, it gives you time to get your props or people together before you compose your photo.
- **Make it a habit.** Do your best to shoot for 21 days in a row. I hear habits are easier to establish if you do them for 21 days consistently. So, if you shoot at the same time every day and plan your shot ahead of time, you are well on your way to making picture-taking a habit.

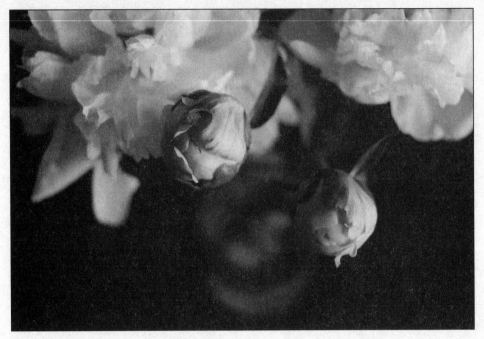

The simple beauty of a flower. Notice the reflection in the background.

A Month of Portraits Theme

Visit Braxton's website and you will see her passion for the self-portrait. She encourages her readers to take lots of self-portraits to become comfortable with this aspect of photography before leaping into taking portraits of others.

The portrait can indeed be one of the most difficult photo assignments for any photographer. "There are some people who refuse to give up control, and it shows in their pictures," says Braxton. "They look stiff and overly posed. There's not much you can do about that."

Braxton continues, "I am in constant conversation when I take portraits. I want the subject to be comfortable, and I want the pose to be natural. Since they are trusting me to take a great picture of them, it is my job to know how to put them in the most flattering pose and to bring out their personality."

Braxton has written several helpful articles on portraits. Her portrait guide, available on her website, offers helpful tips on shooting self-portraits, children, women, and men.

Camera-Phone-Only Photos Theme

If you shoot a lot with your digital single-lens reflex (DSLR) or point-and-shoot, Braxton suggests switching it up for a week or a month, if you dare, and shoot only with your camera phone. If you are primarily a camera phone user, pick up another kind of camera and experiment.

"I love the images I get from my mirrorless and DSLR cameras, but I don't always have them with me," says Braxton. "Camera phones can limit the way you can shoot, but you can be very creative with them, too. This is simply another way to learn to see differently."

"I have my smartphone with me 95 percent of the time, more than my point-and-shoot or my DSLR or mirrorless cameras," Braxton says. "That being the case, I have had to

BRAXTON'S 5 TIPS TO TAKE YOUR PHOTOGRAPHY TO THE NEXT LEVEL

Professional photographers are not the only people who can take great pictures. You can, too. With a little practice and the following tips, you will be well on your way to creating better than average photos.

Expensive cameras don't make you a better photographer. The best camera to shoot with is the one you have with you when you are ready to capture a moment. Be it your camera phone, point-and-shoot, mirrorless or DSLR, they all do the same thing. They make pictures. You are the one who gives your photos life and vision. Learn how to use the device you currently own really well, then upgrade to a better camera.

Carry your camera with you every day. There is nothing worse than missing a great shot, milestone, or moment because you left your camera at home. Make it a habit to carry your camera with you everywhere you go. I cannot tell you how many times I have missed an amazing sunset or cloud formation because I didn't have a camera with me. This is hands down one of the most important things you can do to improve your photographic eye.

Photograph the simple things in your life. Great photography stories are built on your small, daily rituals and familiar surroundings. Look at your home and your yard for inspiration. If you always shoot the flowers in your yard in color, consider photographing them in black and white and focus on composition and angles. How about taking pictures inside your home from the perspective of an ant? What used to be uninteresting and ordinary is actually the best thing you can do to grow your photographic skills. If you can master the everyday, you can master any kind of photography style.

Let Flickr and Instagram be your inspiration. Flickr and Instagram are treasure troves of photography inspiration. If you are not sure what kind of photography you are interested in pursuing, check out all the great pictures professional and amateur photographers are sharing on a daily basis. Here are a few Instagram accounts I am loving right now: houselarsbuilt, kidsandthecity, lotuscarroll, annebecca, and trytheworld.

Learn the Rule of Thirds, then break the rule. To understand the Rule of Thirds, imagine your image is divided in nine equal parts horizontally and vertically. The idea behind this is you place points of interest where the lines intersect. Now, you will create lovely images by following the Rule of Thirds, but you will also create killer photos when you break the Rule of Thirds. Experimentation is what photography is all about.

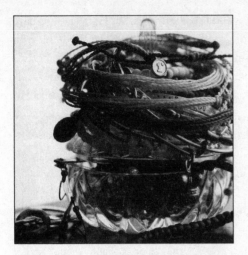

Think black and white. Varying textures give this photo an interesting perspective.

learn to be creative with the camera phone. It has some limited capabilities, which force you to think about the composition of your image differently. I suggest shooting from multiple angles or getting two steps closer to your subject, then taking the picture. Shoot in only black and white for a week and work on composition instead of technically perfect images. Be willing to experiment and make mistakes. That is how you learn."

Braxton's blog posts can also be easily found as articles on her webpage. She offers tips for taking photos of kids, flowers, men, women and food. She reviews apps and cameras, offers selfie pointers, discusses point-and-shoot versus DSLR cameras, offers tips for great conference photos and playing with your aperture to achieve the best aesthetic quality of blur (known as Bokeh) from your lens.

The reference page on Lucrecer.com is quite extensive and includes helpful resources for photographers, artists and designers. They are not endorsements, but resources Braxton uses.

OPENING DOORS TO PROFESSIONAL OPPORTUNITIES

One of Braxton's favorite things to do is share her love of photography and storytelling. She leads creative photography and blogging workshops throughout the year.

ABOUT LUCRECER BRAXTON

Braxton is an award-winning art director, communication, marketing professional, and project manager experienced with corporate identity, traditional and multimedia advertising, annual reports, and photographic direction.

She was born in Georgia and has lived in Montana, Florida, England, and now Ohio. She has a Bachelor of Arts in Advertising Graphics from Central State University in Wilberforce, Ohio, and an extensive background in graphic design, marketing communications, public relations, art, design, writing, and social media.

Braxton is available for speaking engagements, photography, and writing assignments. Contact her at lucrecerb@yahoo.com.

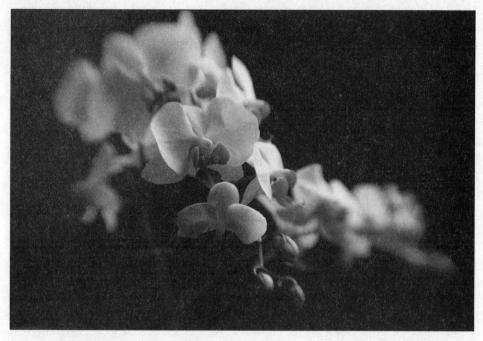

There is nothing worse than missing a great shot, milestone or moment because you left your camera at home.

Public speaking opportunities came Braxton's way through her blogs. "I was blogging at Life Is the Art in 2008 and was approached by BlogHer to be a part of a panel about positive posting and inspirational blogging," she explains. "That led to other speaking opportunities about crafting, portrait photography, and taking your photography to the next level. My goal in all my workshops is for people to walk away with actionable tips that help them take great pictures."

"Following a photography presentation, a few attendees approached me and shared their insecurities about their photos, and they believed they needed better equipment to take better pictures," recalls Braxton. "I am a believer that great equipment can make for a better picture, but the equipment is a tool. If you use only your expensive camera on auto, does that make you a better photographer? No! Practice and experimenting makes you a better photographer. My site, Shoot Every Damn Day, is inspiration for the everyday photographer. Our lives should be our main inspiration. The blessing and curse of platforms like Instagram and Flickr is that you have endless access to pictures that make you feel great or horrible about your own work and great or horrible about your life."

Braxton's final word: Practice, experiment, have fun, and join the "challenge" in 2016.

Deb Heneghan is a freelance writer and photographer based in Kentucky.

CHAD MOORE

More Than Piffle

....

by Luke McLaughlin

Despite having a full-time job, a wife, and three kids, Chad Moore has created a thriving small business selling his photographs. In fact, it is perhaps because of his job, wife, and kids that he has been successful. Moore got his start as an artist, a term that he still hesitates to use to describe himself, when his wife, Chesney, was organizing a charity art fundraiser for her interior design organization. They had just had their first child, Kate, and Moore used the camera they had purchased to take high-quality family photos to create still lifes of some of Kate's toys in the urban environment of downtown Birmingham, Alabama.

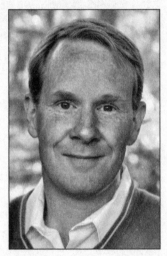

Chad Moore has created a growing business selling his photographs at art festivals in his spare time.

Pictures of Toys

Moore got his inspiration from a shot in a magazine, a picture that included a toy figure but not as the main subject of the image. He explains, "I saw a picture in a magazine of this diner scene. It was in this cool shade of blue, and in the forefront of the picture, it wasn't the focal point of the picture, but there was this honey bear with the little cone top that you snip off. So I decided to do a 'Honey Bear on Holiday' series around Birmingham." Moore created a triptych based on this idea and entered it into the fundraiser. A bidding war ensued on the piece.

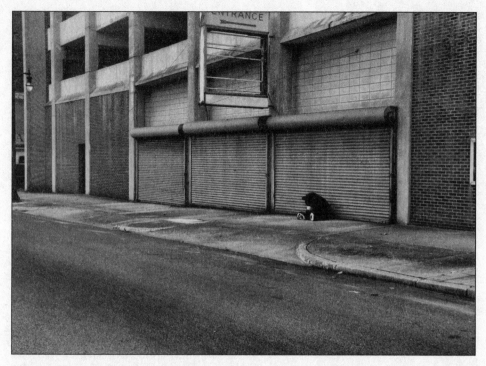

Closed on Sundays. Moore started out creating a series of images of his daughter's toys in urban locations in Birmingham, Alabama, for a charity auction.

Though his debut was successful, it took him another year before he tried again. "A full year went by and the art fundraiser comes up again," explains Moore, "and by this time Kate was born, so there was a bunch of stuffed animals and cutesy little pink things. Living downtown, there is a homeless population, and so I did a 'Bunny, Life on the Streets' triptych."

Moore continued to develop slowly, waiting another year for his third work, also for the same fundraiser. After his third success, he knew he was on to something, but still found it a bit difficult to explain to people what he was doing. He notes, "My biggest problem is when people talk to me and say 'I heard you are an artist doing photography. What do you shoot?' and I am like, 'Children's toys.'" He decided to entitle his body of work Piffle Pics and slowly began to enter his work into festivals and eventually into an art gallery.

Percentages

Even though his work is featured in a gallery and he has an online shop, Moore still makes the vast majority of his profits from selling his work at art fairs. Part of the reason is that you retain all art fair sale profits after paying the cost of entering and setting up a booth at a fair, while most galleries take a large percentage of the sale price. Depending on your pricing, you have to sell many more photographs at a gallery than you would at a fair to make the

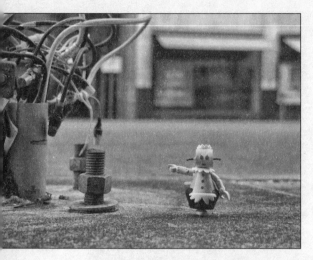

He Looks Nothing Like His Profile Pic. Moore decided that if his work was accepted to a Red Cross charity event he would enter his work into an art festival.

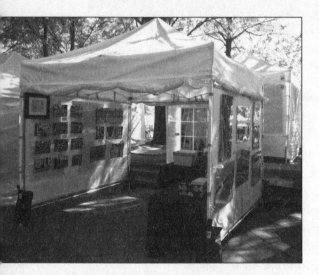

Moore uses large prints to make his work stand out in often-crowded festivals.

same profit yourself. The smaller your profit margin, the more volume you would have to sell through a gallery to make the same profit as you would at a fair or through your own online store. Moore estimates that 80 percent of his profits are from art festivals, 10–15 percent is through the gallery, and 5–10 percent is online. "The online I don't really publicize other than the business cards that I hand out at art festivals," explains Moore, "but it is a nice ancillary income." The online presence is also an easy way to distribute a portfolio of his work.

Festivals

Moore advises artists who are going to their first festival to be ready to hand out a lot of business cards. He explains, "I go through so many business cards at an art festival. It's incredible. I don't know what people do with them. But they take all of them." Once Moore had to improvise and write his e-mail and web addresses on a slip of paper and have people photograph it with their smartphone. Moore uses business cards with a different image on each side accompanying his web and e-mail addresses.

Moore advises talking to other artists who sell something similar to your work to get an idea of where you should price things. He says that at his first fair he had things priced just a little too high. He says that you can judge by customers' reactions when they see the price.

The formula that has worked for Moore is to show large pieces on the wall that he doesn't rely on selling, but that bring people into the booth. After they see the larger work, they often buy a smaller print that is more affordable. He sells a high volume of the smaller works. For Moore, this is a safer strategy than selling

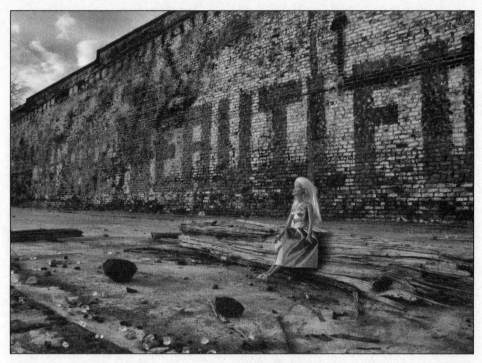

And So Am I. Moore says that if the price is right, people will often buy a piece they like even if they had no plan to buy art at a festival.

a lower volume of more expensive work. He says that a lot of artists just have big pieces and expect to sell only one or two things a show. He feels that this is a risky strategy especially when you are starting out. He explains, "There are a lot of other artists who just have the big pieces and they sell one or two things a show, and they are great. Whereas, for me, I sell volume, and I am moving product all day." One individual purchase isn't going to make or break Moore's business.

Moore sells some of the large prints but says that they are probably only 5 percent of what he sells at a show. It is essential to have the larger pieces, however, Moore explains: "They are the ones that people see as they walk through the sea of booths. They need something to grab their attention to make them walk into yours." Moore says to choose your best images and make them as big as possible so that when people see them they make a big first impression.

Moore believes that pricing thresholds play a big part in whether or not people go through with a purchase. "A lot of people don't want to spend too much and there is a certain threshold," says Moore. Pricing is key and it is good to try to figure out the important price thresholds in your market. He has found that about $200 is a high price threshold. There are people that will spend up to $200, and then there are people who will spend over $200, and from that point it almost doesn't matter if it is $250 or $400 to those buyers. Moore says that a lot of people are willing to spend a smaller amount of money even if they didn't intend to spend any in the first place. He explains, "There are the people who have fifty bucks or seventy-five dollars that they are willing to spend or even weren't thinking about spending but now they see something they really want." Moore says that these people are happy to spend twenty-five or forty dollars on a small piece that they love.

Galleries

Though they keep part of the profit, Moore thinks that galleries provide photographers with a lot of value. The gallery that represents Moore places his work in local restaurants and businesses. Having his work in these public places mean that people are already familiar with his work when they see him at a fair. He observes, "I will be at an art festival and someone will be like, 'Oh, I've seen your work before.'" This familiarity gives his work credibility. People know that Moore is an artist, whether he is willing to admit it or not.

Websites

Moore says that when you are starting out on the web you need to be sure that your shop is geared toward the type of photography that you sell. There are a lot of photography website companies that ship the prints directly to the client, which works more for wedding and event photographers but doesn't work for his business model. If you are selling signed art prints, you need to actually have your hands on the print before it is shipped. At first Moore's website was not set up for the kind of prints that he sells, so customers would have to e-mail him if they were interested and then he would have to figure out how to complete the transaction. Now he is able to take orders through his site and send the signed prints out himself. "Now there is no hurdle to go through. You can order online really simply, and it shows up," explains Moore. This makes it easier for people to buy his work and he has seen an increase in sales that far outweighs the additional cost for his website.

Business Background

In addition to his part-time art business, Moore is a full-time businessperson and salesperson in a small business that sells high-design office furniture. Moore developed his business skills in an environment where if someone needs something quickly, he has to deliver it that day or the next day or he will lose that business. He is therefore very quick to respond. This has earned him a reputation for reliability in the art world as well. He says that the owner of his gallery has told him that his response when she needs something done or a commissioned piece completed is refreshing compared to the flaky reputation that artists often have.

In addition, he says that office furniture is a surprisingly visual field. He is surrounded by really well composed images of furniture and advertising. "Office furniture you don't initially think of as being sexy, but it is high-design office furniture. I am surrounded by

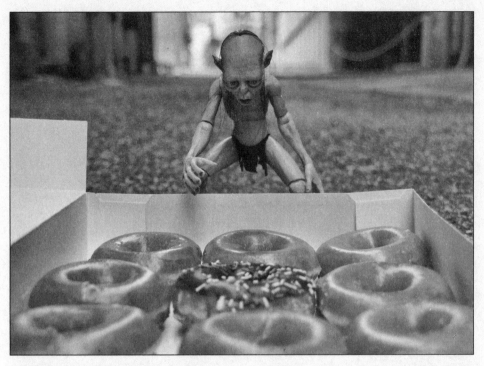

One Ring to Rule Them All. Moore uses the design sense that he has absorbed working in the high-design furniture business to create images that people want.

really well-composed images of the furniture and advertising. The advertising and marketing that I am exposed to pretty much daily … helps me as far as composition, how I frame a shot," he says. Moore thinks that artists can pick up tips from the composition and style of commercial images that they see every day.

Making It Easy

Moore stresses the importance of making things easy on himself. He orders pre-cut mat kits and orders his prints online and then assembles them himself. Even this assembly could be outsourced if he needed to, but for now he can easily put them together in his free time. He explains, "I put the kids to sleep, put on a movie, and put prints together."

If there is something that is taking up too much of your time, Moore says that there are often alternatives. At first Moore had framed prints of his work, but cleaning the glass and preventing breakages was time-consuming and tedious. He found the modern alternative of printing large prints on aluminum sheets meant that he did not need to frame his work. Now he can order a piece online, and it is ready to hang when it arrives and is easy to transport, set up, and take down at festivals.

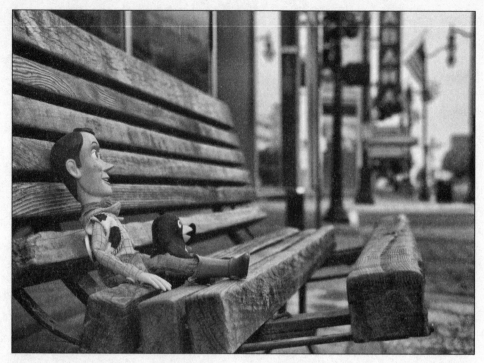

Shelved. In order to make his photography business fit in with his full-time job and family, Moore uses easy-to-hang prints and pre-cut mats to save time.

Avoiding Mistakes

Moore says that he has never really had a bad festival. He says that in addition to his business experience, his unique work is one of the big reasons for his success. He explains, "Multiple people, especially festival organizers, have said to me 'Your work is different.'" Moore advises taking a look at the work that other people are trying to sell at the festivals that you would like to enter to make sure that you have a niche. "Go through an art festival and you will see a lot that is the same. And then you are competing against someone who is doing exactly the same thing as you or very similar."

Moore believes another important strategy is to have a consistent body of work. He advises, "You don't want to throw together a bunch of different styles. If you create a certain line of photography or paintings or whatever, and then completely switch to something else and have it in the same booth, it confuses people." He says that you want to have a certain look all the way through your work so that when people can come in and quickly determine what your art is about and whether it interests them.

Engagement

Moore says that you don't want to pressure people or make them feel uncomfortable. He says to engage with people, but don't talk their heads off. He usually says, "Hi, how are you doing? Let me know if you need some help." Or he may point something out that they might not have noticed, but he tries not to talk too much. Moore's hands-off sales technique is informed by his own experience as a visitor to art festivals. He says that he has been at festivals where artists have rushed up to him, saying things like, "Let me talk to you about my process," and it felt very uncomfortable. "What if you don't care about the work or the process or just want to look for yourself?" he explains. You might be eager and excited to talk to people about your work, but it is really important to let people make up their own mind and interpret the work for themselves.

Selling your work is about striking the right balance and making the customers comfortable and interested enough to pull out their wallets. Although it isn't a pressure sales job, he does advocate having price breaks. He says you could offer five prints for the price of four, for example. If a customer is considering two or three anyway, she could spend just a little more and get two additional prints. Once people are willing to buy something, they might be willing to spend a bit more to get a better deal. The key is to make it easy for people to actually decide to buy something in the first place.

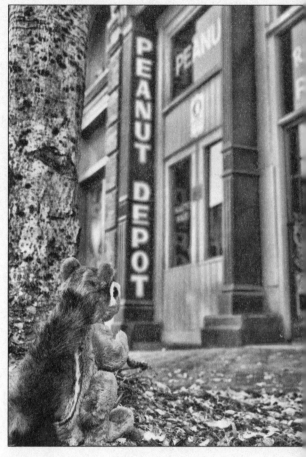

Ambush. Moore says that making it easy for people to buy your work will result in a lot more sales.

Point of Sale

Moore says that point-of-sale card readers have made it much easier to complete transactions. People might not have enough cash on them to buy the work, but, with a card reader, people can buy a piece that they like even if they didn't come with the intent to spend that much money. "The first few art festivals that I did, those did not exist," Moore explains,

"You had to create an account with a bank and pay a monthly fee. The card readers have been amazing. There are people who go to art festivals not to buy art, and are just strolling around and then they see something and they are like, 'Ooh, that would be great.'" With your own card reader, you can add this large group of festival visitors to your list of potential customers. "The trick is to get them to come into your booth. If they don't come into your booth, they aren't going to buy anything," Moore says. With unique and interesting work at the right price and with the right sales tools, you can have a successful business selling your photography at art fairs.

Luke McLaughlin is an American writer based in Oxford, England. Find out more about what he is working on at lucasmclaughlin.com.

JEFF BROWN

Unnatural Light Photography

....

by Luke McLaughlin

New York-based photographer Jeff Brown is known for his dynamic and dramatic portraits of businesspeople, important politicians, and celebrities as well as ordinary everyday people. He brings his signature hard-edged colorful style to the covers of magazines such as *Bloomberg Businessweek*, *Fast Company*, and the *New York Times Magazine*, but until he took a black-and-white photography course at a community college, he had never considered photography as a career. Before coming to New York to study photography, Jeff Brown took pictures in his grandparents' backyards and made a portfolio of street photography that got him into Parsons in New York.

But when he arrived in New York, he realized that the city that he had seen in the work of Garry Winogrand, Lee Friedlander, and Robert Frank looked different. Too modern, too dirty, and not in the gritty way that had made it look so cool in the work of those who had inspired him. So he turned to the studio. He would set up lights and call people to ask if they were free to model for him. It was something that he knew he could do and be OK with. Brown feels that New York City forced him to take pictures of people in the studio.

Finding a Niche, Finding a Style

In a competitive world where everyone carries a camera built into their phones, it is hard to stand out. Brown says you need to work to find your own style. He observes, "As much as you can, you have to try to make something that looks different on purpose." Many photographers are obsessed with creating color-balanced photographs using a neutral white balance, but Brown uses color gels on hot lights to create a different look. "Sometimes I use different colors to make the pictures look different or exciting," Brown explains. "If you look at paintings, they are awesome and use weird colors. You don't look at a painting and

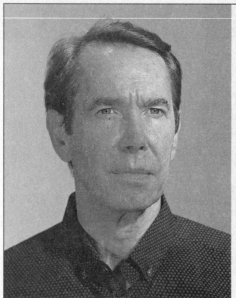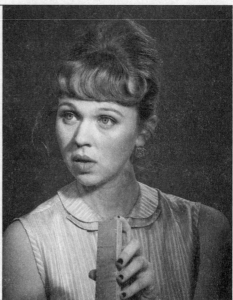

Brown creates striking portraits with an unconventional use of lighting and color.

say, 'That color is wrong' or 'Where's the graycard, bro?'" Brown clarifies that he is not saying that his pictures are like paintings, but he thinks the obsession with color neutral photographs is unnecessary. "It's weird to look at a photograph that is so color neutral," says Brown. He thinks it gets boring.

The Shadow

In addition to changing the color of an image with gels, Brown likes to use hard lights that create hard shadows rather than the flattering soft light from softboxes and umbrellas. He uses these shadows to create drama, to add a graphic line to the image, and to show that the lights are there and that the lighting isn't natural. "I like the shadow because it lets you know that you are making a photograph," Brown explains. "With a lot of photographs, they try to wash away the photograph and make it look 'real,' but the idea that you need to make a photograph look as real as real life is strange to me. I don't like it." The reality presented in photographs made with huge soft lights is very flattering, but it makes normal people look imperfect in comparison. Brown uses the shadow to show that his images aren't trying to look natural.

Getting Started

After high school, Brown took classes at American River College, a community college in Sacramento, California. One of his friends had decided to get a good camera to shoot snow-

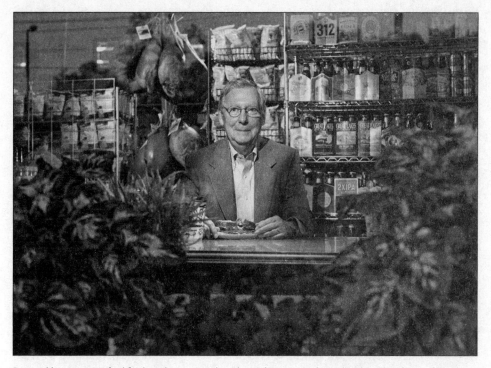

Brown likes to get a feel for how he can work with a subject in order to let them be themselves in front of the camera.

boarding photographs and had contacted a professional photographer, who had advised him on which camera to buy. Brown decided to buy his own camera. He recalls, "So I said, 'Shoot, man, I'll get a camera and shoot skateboarding.'" He decided to sign up for a black-and-white photography class the next semester. He had fun, so the next semester he decided to take the second photography class that was offered. His teacher had been a teacher in up-state New York and near the end of the second semester she asked him what he planned on doing after community college. He didn't know. She asked him if he had considered pho-tography. He hadn't. She said he should, so he visited some schools and that was it.

In a way, Brown fell into photography, but he had always taken pictures. He worked on his high school newspaper and remembers, "I took pictures for my sections, and I took pic-tures of friends in junior high and high school. It was lingering, but it was never something I thought I would do it until I met Jodie Fisher at American River College." It turned out to be a life-changing meeting, because before too long, Brown was on his way to New York to begin his career in photography.

Getting Comfortable

When starting to photograph a new subject, Brown says that you need to first get them to relax. He observes, "You need to make the subject comfortable with the fact that you are doing this job. You also need to make them comfortable with you or someone working with you on the shoot." Brown has enjoyed working with his friend Lalindra "Lalli" Wickramasinghe. He explains, "I'm not the best at [putting people at ease] and Lalli is."

If you are not working alone, get to know the strengths of the people you are working with. You don't have to do everything yourself. Brown got a first-hand demonstration of Wickramasinghe's communication skills when he was photographing longshoremen. The longshoremen were intimidating and tried to pick on Wickramasinghe, who was wearing an Oakland Raiders T-shirt, but, before they knew it, Lalli had made friends with them and they were smoking a cigarette together. "I will just let him go. He knows about everything and can just start talking with anyone. If you get through to someone and get them talking about what they like, then they immediately forget what is happening with the photo shoot," says Brown.

Brown says that if someone seems like they are going to ham it up a little, then let them. He recalls, "I was shooting a professor at Duke University, and he said, 'Can I do my own thing?' and I said, 'I'd love it if you do,' and then he starts posing and it was great. The same thing happened when I was shooting Jeff Koons." Part of capturing a portrait comes from your knowledge of the subject, but it is important to let them express themselves. "See what's possible," Brown advises. If the subject is comfortable, that makes it a lot easier.

Every Person Is Different

Brown has learned that you need to work very differently with people who are used to the camera than with people who are shyer. He says that someone like Senator Mitch McConnell is used to being in the public eye all of the time and is used to posing for photographs, but another government official with less public exposure might hate photo shoots because he is not used to them.

Brown says you need to match your directions to the skills and abilities of the model and the subject. "If it's an actress, you can say, 'This is how you feel,' and they will know what to do, but you can't just go up to someone [without acting abilities] and expect that," he explains. When he was starting out he shot a lot of e-commerce with very new models. At the beginning he thought he had to direct the models but afterwards he learned from the art director that if they don't know what they are doing, you are not expected to teach them on the job.

If you are working with subjects who aren't used to acting or modelling for the camera, Brown says that you can try to get them to imagine something they are familiar with. "You can tell someone to think about something that they are familiar with to get a particular

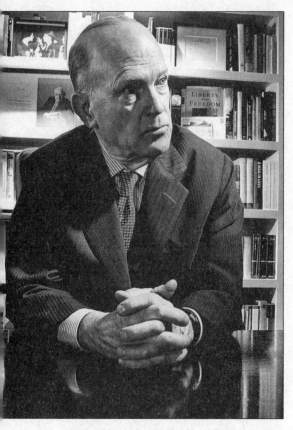

Brown tried to capture a bit of literary agent Andrew Wylie's notorious reputation in this dramatic portrait.

reaction. Different situations ask for different things," he explains.

When he was asked to photograph the literary agent Andrew Wylie, Brown did a bit of research and learned the Wylie was notorious for poaching talented clients. Wylie's roster is loaded with talent, including the photographer Annie Liebovitz. The magazine that commissioned the photograph simply asked for a photograph of him in his office, but the shot ended up capturing the reputation that he is famous for. "He was a bit of a ham in a very serious way," Brown explains. "When you get his vibe, you can take something from that, which is cool." The magazine wanted the photograph in black and white. This, combined with the dramatic lighting that Brown specializes in, resulted in a compelling picture. "I think that picture nailed what his reputation is," Brown says.

Working in a Team

While some assignments are as simple as a black-and-white photograph of an agent in his office, many are more complicated and require a photographer to work as part of a team. Brown was assigned to photograph two shots directed by Angela Campos that were planned from start to finish. "It was a man and a woman. The husband is on a business trip and the wife is at home. The wife calls the husband, the husband doesn't have time for her in the story. It's implied that he is cheating on her, and she is at home really sad," Brown explains. Campos art directed and styled the shoot and worked closely with Brown to make sure the shot was perfect. Each element in the shot was carefully selected and positioned so that the images tell the whole story.

Color

Brown developed his use of color while working with photo director Alis Atwell for *Bloomberg Businessweek*. He says that his use of hot lights lends a warm tone to his photographs anyway, but for a food assignment taking a photograph of a whole raw fish, Atwell suggest-

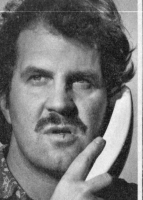
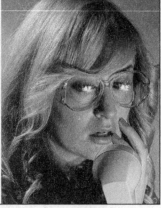

Some of Browns assignments are more to capture a story rather than a portrait.

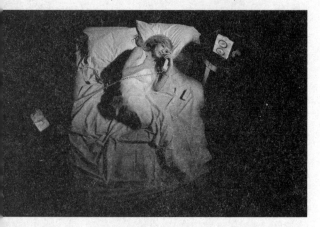

These images, telling a story of a late-night telephone call were carefully directed by Angela Campos.

ed making the photographs more colorful. Brown added a gel to the lighting and this colorful fish photo led him into using colorful gels in his portraits as well. The effects when adding color to your images can be unpredictable. "Some of the shots for that food [shoot] were disgusting," Brown laughs.

Portraits Without Faces

The first time that Brown worked with Atwell, he was photographing a portrait for an article entitled "A French Bistro Fit for a Queen" about Keith McNally's restaurant Balthazar opening up in London. "They got a woman who looks like Queen Elizabeth and did her up that way," says Brown. "As we were working on it, we just kept raising the menu. At first we had the menu lower down, but then we thought, 'The mouth isn't right,' so we moved it up to cover her mouth. Then we were like, 'That doesn't really look like her' and moved it up again. Then I thought, 'I don't really like the nose,' and we moved it up. And then *Boom*. Now we can believe it's the queen because her face is hidden."

Brown says that leaving things out of an image makes the brain ask more questions. Brown also likes the idea of obscurity. "Hopefully you get a second look out of it," he says. "What you try to do is make the second look." He continued the theme of portraits without faces in an assignment for a profile of the emoticon company Line for *Fast Company*'s "Most Innovative Companies 2015" feature. Brown says, "I hate emoticons, so it was perfect for me." He ended up shooting an image of people at a bar with huge emoticon masks under a wash of bright colored gels.

Distrust

Brown enjoys working with Atwell and feels that they have a similar sense of humor and a similar distrust of photography. "With Alis, we are kind of on the same page. She is trying to push an idea, which is cool," he says. One problem that Brown has with photography is that a normal-looking person in a photograph is considered "abnormal" for a picture in a magazine. One of his favorite assignments for far has been an assignment for the *New York Times Magazine*. They sent Brown to ten different bars to shoot portraits of people at bars over the course of three days. A girl that Brown went to school with worked at one of the bars. It was fall or early winter, and Brown photographed her playing ping-pong on a table outside of the bar. "So she is outside, a normal girl, in normal clothes for that time of year, playing ping-pong. That's kind of weird for a picture. A normal looking person. What a horrible idea. That's why I kind of hate photography," Brown says with a smile. The *New York Times Magazine* ran the photograph with the headline, "Here Comes an Irregular."

A Second Look

Brown thinks that the fact that a normal person is considered strange in a magazine is a crazy thing. He claims, "People say, 'Why didn't you get a stylist?'" if a person in a shot looks too much like a normal person or the hair or clothes aren't styled. On one assignment he was photographing Vanessa Kerry for a magazine. He recalls, "She brought some clothes, but in a photo sense they looked terrible." The magazine hadn't provided a particular outfit for Kerry, and although she brought several outfits, they weren't really what the magazine had in mind. The world

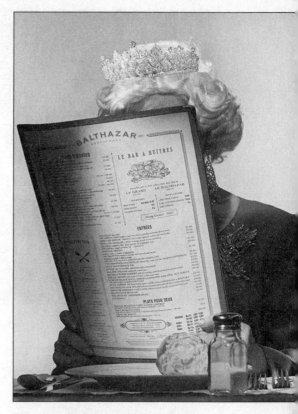

Sometimes leaving something out can be more convincing and more interesting than trying to include all of the information in a photograph.

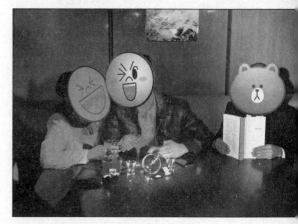

Brown likes the idea of obscuring the faces of the subject.

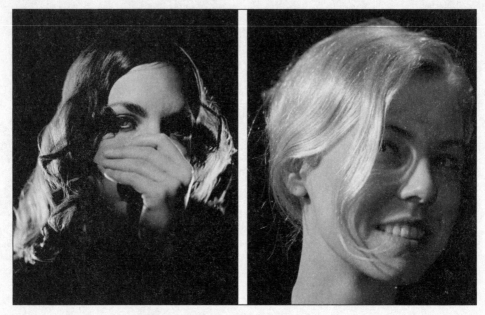

Brown is happy to ignore prevailing ideas of how a perfect photograph is supposed to look.

depicted in a picture isn't the real world. Brown explains, "You see pictures and think, 'Why isn't that in the right place?' Well, because what is? I guess I want to make something humorous if I can. If things aren't 'right,' then I'm okay with it." Brown deals with this discomfort with the unreality of photography by accentuating it and pointing it out. He changes the color, adds a hard shadow, pushes the pose just a little too much, and hopes to make the viewer take that second look.

Luke McLaughlin is an American writer based in Oxford, England. Find out more about what he is working on at lucasmclaughlin.com.

CONSUMER PUBLICATIONS

Research is the key to selling any kind of photography. If you want your work to appear in a consumer publication, you're in luck. Magazines are the easiest market to research because they're available on newsstands and at the library and at your doctor's office and . . . you get the picture. So, do your homework. Before you send your query or cover letter and samples, and before you drop off your portfolio on the prescribed day, look at a copy of the magazine. The library is a good place to see sample copies because they're free, and there will be at least a year's worth of back issues right on the shelf.

Once you've read a few issues and feel confident your work is appropriate for a particular magazine, it's time to hit the keyboard. Most first submissions take the form of a query or cover letter and samples. So, what kind of letter do you send? That depends on what kind of work you're selling. If you simply want to let an editor know you're available for assignments or have a list of stock images appropriate for the publication, send a cover letter, a short business letter that introduces you and your work and tells the editor why your photos are right for the magazine. If you have an idea for a photo essay or plan to provide the text and photos for an article, you should send a query letter, a one- to one-and-a-half-page letter explaining your story or essay idea and why you're qualified to shoot it. You can send your query letter through the U.S. postal system, or you can e-mail it along with a few JPEG samples of your work. Check the listing for the magazine to see how they prefer to be contacted initially.

Both kinds of letters can include a brief list of publication credits and any other relevant information about yourself. Both also should include a sample of your work—a tearsheet, a slide or a printed piece, but never an original negative. Be sure your sample photo is of something the magazine might publish. It will be difficult for the editor of a biking magazine to appreciate your skills if you send a sample of your fashion work.

If your letter piques the interest of an editor, she may want to see more. If you live near the editorial office, you might be able to schedule an appointment to show your portfolio in person. Or you can inquire about the drop-off policy—many magazines have a day or two each week when artists can leave their portfolios for art directors to review. If you're in Wichita and the magazine is in New York, you'll have to send your portfolio through the mail. Consider using FedEx or UPS; both have tracking services that can locate your book if it gets waylaid on its journey. If the publication accepts images in a digital format (most do these days), you can send more samples of your work via e-mail or on a CD—whatever the publication prefers. Make sure you ask first. Better yet, if you have a website, you can provide the photo buyer with the link.

To make your search for markets easier, consult the Subject Index. The index is divided into topics, and markets are listed according to the types of photographs they want to see.

⊖ ○ 4-WHEEL ATV ACTION

25233 Anza Dr., Valencia CA 91355. (661)295-1910. **Fax:** (661)295-1278. **E-mail:** atv@hi-torque.com. **Website:** www.4wheelatv.com. **Contact:** Joe Kosch, editor-at-large (joeatvaction@yahoo.com); Tim Tolleson, editor (timt@hi-torque.com). Estab. 1986. Circ. 65,000. Monthly magazine. Emphasizing all-terrain vehicles and anything closely related to them.

NEEDS Buys 4 photos from freelancers/issue; 50 photos/year. Needs photos of adventure, events, hobbies, sports. "We are interested only in ATVs and UTVs and very closely related ride-on machines with more than two wheels—no cars, trucks, buggies or motorcycles. We're looking for scenic riding areas with ATVs or UTVs in every shot, plus unusual or great looking ATVs." Reviews photos with or without a manuscript. Model/property release preferred. Photo captions preferred; include location, names.

SPECS Uses 8×10 glossy color prints; 35mm transparencies. Accepts images in digital format. Send via ZIP, e-mail as JPEG files at 300 dpi.

MAKING CONTACT & TERMS Send query letter with photocopies or e-mail JPEGs. Does not keep samples on file; cannot return material. Responds only if interested; send nonreturnable samples. Simultaneous submissions and previously published work OK. Pays $50-100 for color cover; $15-25 for color inside. Credit line given. Buys one-time rights, first rights; negotiable.

TIPS *"4-Wheel ATV Action* offers a good opportunity for amateur but serious photographers to get a credit line in a national publication."

⊖ ◑ 540 RIDER

TMB Publications, P.O. Box 1156, Lake Oswego OR 97035. (503)236-2524. **Fax:** (503)620-3800. **E-mail:** dank@youthrunner.com. **Website:** www.540rider. com. **Contact:** Dan Kesterson, publisher. Estab. 2002. Circ. 100,000. Quarterly. Emphasizes action sports for youth: snowboarding, skateboarding and other board sports. Features high school teams, results, events, training, "and kids that just like to ride." Sample copy available with 8×10 SASE and 75¢ first-class postage. Photo guidelines available by e-mail request or online.

NEEDS Buys 10-20 photos from freelancers/issue; 40-80 photos/year. Needs photos of sports. Reviews photos with or without a manuscript. Model/property release preferred. Photo captions preferred.

SPECS Accepts images in digital format only. Send via CD as TIFF files at 300 dpi.

MAKING CONTACT & TERMS Send query via e-mail. Provide self-promotion piece to be kept on file for possible future assignments. Responds only if interested; send nonreturnable samples. Simultaneous submissions OK. Pays $25 minimum for b&w and color covers and inside photos. Pays on publication. Credit line given. Buys all rights.

TIPS "Send an e-mail ahead of time to discuss. Send us stuff that even you don't like, because we just might like it."

◐ ⊖ ◑ AAA MIDWEST TRAVELER

AAA Auto Club of Missouri, 12901 N. 40 Dr., St. Louis MO 63141. (314)523-7350, ext. 6301. **Fax:** (314)523-6982. **E-mail:** dreinhardt@aaamissouri.com. **Website:** www.aaa.com/traveler. **Contact:** Deborah Reinhardt, managing editor. Estab. 1901. Circ. 500,000. Bimonthly. Emphasizes travel and driving safety. Readers are members of the Auto Club of Missouri. Sample copy and photo guidelines free with SASE (use large manila envelope) or online.

NEEDS Buys 3-5 photos/issue. "We use four-color photos inside to accompany specific articles. Our magazine covers topics of general interest, historical (of Midwest regional interest), profile, travel, car care and driving tips. Our covers are full-color photos mainly corresponding to an article inside. Except for cover shots, we use freelance photos only to accompany specific articles." Model release preferred. Photo captions required.

SPECS Accepts images in digital format. Send via ZIP as TIFF files at minimum of 300 dpi.

MAKING CONTACT & TERMS Send query letter with résumé of credits and list of stock photo subjects. Does not keep samples on file; include SASE for return of material. Responds in 1 month. Simultaneous submissions and previously published work OK. Pays $400 for color cover; $75-200 for color inside. **Pays on acceptance.** Credit line given. Buys first, second and electronic rights.

TIPS "Send an 8½×11 SASE for sample copies and study the type of covers and inside work we use. Photo needs driven by an editorial calendar/schedule. Write to request a copy and include SASE."

⊖ ◑ ADIRONDACK LIFE

P.O. Box 410, Rt. 9N, Jay NY 12941-0410. (518)946-2191. **Fax:** (518)946-7461. **E-mail:** aledit@adirondack life.com; astoltie@adirondacklife.com; alprod@adirondacklife.com. **Website:** www.adirondacklife.com. **Contact:** Annie Stoltie, editor; Kelly Hofschneider, photo editor. Estab. 1970. Circ. 50,000.

NEEDS Photos of environmental, landscapes/scenics, wildlife. Reviews photos with or without a manuscript.

SPECS Accepts color transparencies of any size; b&w prints no larger than 8×10. Digital images output to paper may be submitted.

MAKING CONTACT & TERMS Pays $400 maximum for color cover. Pays $150 maximum for b&w or color inside. Credit line given.

ADVENTURE CYCLIST

Adventure Cycling Association, Box 8308, Missoula MT 59807. (406)721-1776, ext. 222. **Fax:** (406)721-8754. **E-mail:** magazine@adventurecycling.org. **Website:** www.adventurecycling.org/adventure-cyclist. **Contact:** Greg Siple, art director; Michael Deme, editor. Estab. 1975. Circ. 45,500.

NEEDS People riding bicycles, cultural, detail, architectural, people historic, vertical, horizontal. Identification of subjects, model releases required.

SPECS Reviews color transparencies and digital files.

TIPS Sample copy and photo guidelines free with 9×12 SAE and 4 first-class stamps. Guidelines also available on website at www.adventurecycling.org/adventure-cyclist/adventure-cyclist-submissions

ADVOCATE, PKA'S PUBLICATION

1881 Little Westkill Rd., Prattsville NY 12468. (518)299-3103. **E-mail:** advoad@localnet.com. **Website:** advocatepka.weebly.com; www.facebook.com/Advocate/PKAPublications; www.facebook.com/GaitedHorseAssociation. **Contact:** Patricia Keller, publisher. Estab. 1987. Circ. 7,000.

NEEDS Equine is of strong interest but looks at many different types and styles.

SPECS Accepts print photos in b&w and color, no larger than 8×10.

⃝ AFRICAN AMERICAN GOLFER'S DIGEST

80 Wall St., Suite 720, New York NY 10005. (212)571-6559. **E-mail:** debertcook@aol.com. **Website:** www.africanamericangolfersdigest.com. **Contact:** Debert Cook, managing editor. Estab. 2003. Circ. 20,000. Quarterly. Emphasizes golf lifestyle, health, travel destinations, golfer profiles, golf equipment reviews. Editorial content focuses on the "interests of our mar-

ket demographic of African Americans and categories of high interest to them—historical, artistic, musical, educational (higher learning), automotive, sports, fashion, entertainment." Sample copy available for $6.

NEEDS Photos of golf, golfers, automobiles, entertainment, health/fitness/beauty, sports. Interested in lifestyle.

SPECS Accepts images in digital format. Send JPEG or GIF files, 4×6 at 300 dpi.

TIPS Reviews photos with or without a ms.

🌐 ⓘ ◑ AFRICAN PILOT

Wavelengths 10 (Pty) Ltd., 6 Barbeque Heights, 9 Dytchley Rd., Barbeque Downs, Midrand 1684 South Africa. +27 11 466-8524. **Fax:** +27 11 466 8496. **E-mail:** editor@africanpilot.co.za. **Website:** www.africanpilot.co.za. **Contact:** Athol Franz, editor. Estab. 2001. Circ. 7,000+ online; 6,600+ print. "*African Pilot* is southern Africa's premier monthly aviation magazine. It publishes a high-quality magazine that is well known and respected within the aviation community of southern Africa. The magazine offers a number of benefits to readers and advertisers, including a weekly e-mail Aviation News, annual service guide, aviation training supplement, executive wall calendar and an extensive website. The monthly aviation magazine is also available online as an exact replica of the paper edition, but where all major advertising pages are hyperlinked to the advertisers website. The magazine offers clean layouts with outstanding photography and reflects editorial professionalism as well as a responsible approach to journalism. The magazine offers a complete and tailored promotional solution for all aviation businesses operating in the African region."

MAKING CONTACT & TERMS Send e-mail with samples. Samples are kept on file. Portfolio not required. Credit line given.

TIPS "*African Pilot* is an African aviation specific publication, and, therefore, preference is given to articles, illustrations, and photographs that have an African theme. The entire magazine is online in exactly the same format as the printed copy for the viewing of our style and quality. Contact me for specific details on our publishing requirements for work to be submitted. Articles together with a selection of about 10 thumbnail pictures to be submitted so that a decision can be made on the relevance of the article and what pictures are available to be used to illustrate the article. If we decide to go ahead with the article, we will request high-resolution images from the portfolio already submitted as thumbnails."

AKRON LIFE

Baker Media Group, 1653 Merriman Rd., Suite 116, Akron OH 44313. (330)253-0056. **Fax:** (330)253-5868. **E-mail:** info@bakermediagroup.com; editor@bakermediagroup.com; acymerman@bakermediagroup.com. **Website:** www.akronlife.com. **Contact:** Abby Cymerman, managing editor. Estab. 2002. Circ. 15,000. "*Akron Life* is a monthly lifestyles publication committed to providing information that enhances and enriches the experience of living in or visiting Akron and the surrounding region of Summit, Portage, Medina and Stark counties. Each colorful, thoughtfully designed issue profiles interesting places, personalities and events in the arts, sports, entertainment, business, politics and social scene. We cover issues important to the Greater Akron area and significant trends affecting the lives of those who live here."
NEEDS Essays, general interest, historical, how-to, humor, interview, photo feature, travel. Query with published clips.

🆂 🅾 ALABAMA LIVING

Alabama Rural Electric Association, 340 TechnaCenter Dr., Montgomery AL 36117. (800)410-2737. **Website:** www.alabamaliving.com. **Contact:** Lenore Vickrey, editor; Michael Cornelison, art director. Estab. 1948. Circ. 400,000.
NEEDS Needs photos of Alabama specific scenes, particularly seasonal. Special photo needs include vertical scenic cover shots. Photo captions preferred; include place and date.
SPECS Accepts images in digital format. Send via CD, ZIP as EPS, JPEG files at 400 dpi.
MAKING CONTACT & TERMS Send query letter with stock list or transparencies ("dupes are fine") in negative sleeves. Keeps samples on file; include SASE for return of material. Responds in 1 month. Simultaneous submissions and previously published work OK "if previously published out-of-state."

ALARM

Alarm Press, 900 N. Franklin St., Suite 300, Chicago IL 60610. (312)341-1290. **E-mail:** info@alarmpress.com. **Website:** www.alarmpress.com/alarm-magazine. Published 6 times/year. "It does one thing, and it does it very well: it publishes the best new music and art. From our headquarters in a small Chicago office, along with a cast of contributing writers spread across

the country, we listen to thousands of CDs, view hundreds of gallery openings, and attend lectures and live concerts in order to present inspirational artists who are fueled by an honest and contagious obsession with their art."
MAKING CONTACT & TERMS Submit by e-mail with the subject line "ALARM Magazine Submissions." "Please send your work as part of the body of an e-mail; we cannot accept attachments." Alternatively, submissions may be sent by regular mail to Submissions Dept. "*ALARM* is not responsible for the return, loss of, or damage to unsolicited manuscripts, unsolicited artwork, or any other unsolicited materials. Those submitting manuscripts, artwork, or any other materials should not send originals." Art event listings should be e-mailed to artlistings@alarmpress.com.

🆂 🆂 🆂 ALASKA

301 Arctic Slope Ave., Suite 300, Anchorage AK 99518-3035. **E-mail:** editor@alaskamagazine.com. **Website:** www.alaskamagazine.com. **Contact:** Michelle Theall, editor; Corrynn Cochran, photo editor. Estab. 1935. Circ. 180,000. *Alaska* actively solicits photo-feature ideas having in-depth treatments of single subjects. The ideal photo essay would tell a story of a subject while having compelling content with vibrant color and contrast, and would include both the macro and the micro. Buys 500 photos/year, supplied mainly by freelancers. Photo captions required.
NEEDS Photographic submissions must be high-res digital images that are sharp and properly exposed. Please note: slides, transparencies, and prints will not be accepted. Also, no digital composites, please. Historical b&w prints for which negatives are not available can be submitted in any size. All photo submissions will be carefully packaged before being returned. *Alaska* assumes no responsibility for unsolicited photographs.
SPECS Images made with a digital camera of 5 megapixels or better are acceptable. Images may be submitted on CD, DVD, or flash drive. Photo manipulations of any kind must be clearly noted and defined. Digital composites will not be accepted.
MAKING CONTACT & TERMS Send carefully edited, captioned submission of 35mm, 2¼ ×2¼, or 4×5 transparencies. Include SASE for return of material. Also accepts images in digital format; check guide-

lines before submitting. Responds in 1 month. Send submissions to Alaska Magazine Photo Submissions.

ALTERNATIVES JOURNAL

200 University Ave. W., Waterloo Ontario N2L 3G1, Canada. (519)888-4505. **Fax:** (519)746-0292. **E-mail:** editor@alternativesjournal.ca; marcia@alternativesjournal.ca. **Website:** www.alternativesjournal.ca. **Contact:** Laura McDonald, managing editor; Nik Harron, creative director; Marcia Ruby, publisher. Estab. 1971. Circ. 5,000. Bimonthly. Emphasizes environmental issues. Readers are activists, academics, professionals, policy makers. Sample copy free with 9×12 SASE and 2 first-class stamps.

"*Alternatives* is a nonprofit organization whose contributors are all volunteer. We are only able to give a small stipend to artists and photographers. This in no way should reflect the value of the work. It symbolizes our thanks for their contribution to *Alternatives*."

NEEDS Buys 4-8 photos from freelancers/issue; 48-96 photos/year. Subjects vary widely depending on theme of each issue. "Strong action photos or topical environmental issues are needed—preferably with people. We also print animal shots. We look for positive solutions to problems and prefer to illustrate the solutions rather than the problems. Freelancers need a good background understanding of environmental issues." Check website for upcoming themes. Reviews photos with or without a ms. Photo captions preferred; include who, when, where, environmental significance of shot.

SPECS Accepts images in digital format. Send via CD, e-mail as JPEG files at 300 dpi. "E-mail your web address/electronic portfolio." Simultaneous submissions and previously published work OK. Pays on publication. Buys one-time rights; negotiable.

TIPS "You need to know the significance of your subject before you can powerfully present its visual perspective."

$ O AMC OUTDOORS

Appalachian Mountain Club, 5 Joy St., Boston MA 02108. (617)523-0636. **Fax:** (617)523-0722. **E-mail:** amcpublications@outdoors.org. **Website:** www.outdoors.org. Estab. 1908. Circ. 70,000. Published 6 times/year. "Our 94,000 members do more than just read about the outdoors; they get out and play. More than just another regional magazine, *AMC Outdoors* provides information on hundreds of AMC-sponsored adventure and education programs. With award-winning editorial, advice on Northeast destinations and trip planning, recommendations and reviews of the latest gear, AMC chapter news and more, *AMC Outdoors* is the primary source of information about the Northeast outdoors for most of our members." Photo guidelines available at www.outdoors.org/publications/outdoors/contributor-guidelines.cfm.

NEEDS Buys 6-12 photos from freelancers/issue; 75 photos/year. Needs photos of adventure, environmental, landscapes/scenics, wildlife, health/fitness/beauty, sports, travel. Other specific photo needs: people, including older adults (50+ years), being active outdoors. "We seek powerful outdoor images from the Northeast US, or non-location-specific action shots (hiking, skiing, snowshoeing, paddling, cycling, etc.). Our needs vary from issue to issue, based on content, but are often tied to the season."

SPECS Uses color prints or 35mm slides. Prefers images in digital format. Send via CD or e-mail as TIFF, JPEG files at 300 dpi. Low-res OK for review of digital photos.

MAKING CONTACT & TERMS Previously published work OK. Pays $300 (negotiable) for color cover; $50-100 (negotiable) for color inside. Pays on publication. Credit line given.

TIPS "We do not run images from other parts of the US or from outside the US unless the landscape background is 'generic.' Most of our readers live and play in the Northeast, are intimately familiar with the region in which they live, and enjoy seeing the area and activities reflected in living color in the pages of their magazines."

$$ AMERICAN ANGLER

735 Broad St., Augusta GA 30904. (706)828-3971. **E-mail:** benjaminromans@gmail.com; wayne.knight@morris.com. **Website:** www.americanangler.com. **Contact:** Ben Romans, editor; Wayne Knight, art director. Estab. 1976. Circ. 32,000. Bimonthly. Covers fly fishing. "More how-to than where-to, but we need shots from all over. More domestic than foreign. More trout, salmon and steelhead than bass or saltwater." Photo guidelines available on website. Buys 10 photos from freelancers/issue; 60 photos/year. "Most of our photos come from writers of articles."

NEEDS Photos that convey "the spirit, essence and exhilaration of fly fishing. Always need good fish-behavioral stuff—spawning, rising, riseforms, etc."

SPECS Prefers slides or digital images via CD or e-mail at 300 dpi; must be very sharp with good contrast.

MAKING CONTACT & TERMS "We prefer to work from e-mailed queries whenever possible, and you should send an e-mail outlining your article before submitting a manuscript. A query can save you the frustration and disappointment of making a futile submission, and it allows us to fine-tune an idea to suit our editorial needs. We read and respond to all queries, but expect at least a six-week wait for that response. Be patient, please. But squeak gently if you don't hear from us within 6-8 weeks. Send query letter with samples, brochure, stock photo list, tearsheets. Provide résumé, business card, self-promotion piece or tearsheets to be kept on file for possible future assignments. Portfolio review by prior arrangement. Query deadline: 6-10 months prior to cover date. Submission deadline: 5 months prior to cover date. Responds in 6 weeks to queries; 1 month to samples. Simultaneous submissions considered only with notification, and previously published work OK but "only for inside 'editorial' use—not for covers, prominent feature openers, etc."

TIPS "We don't want the same old shots: grip and grin, angler casting, angler with bent rod, fish being released. Sure, we need them, but there's a lot more to fly fishing. Don't send us photos that look exactly like the ones you see in most fishing magazines. Think like a storyteller. Let me know where the photos were taken, at what time of year, and anything else that's pertinent to a fly fisher."

AMERICAN ARCHAEOLOGY

The Archaeological Conservancy, 1717 Girard Blvd., NE, Albuquerque NM 87106. (505)266-9668. **Fax:** (505)266-0311. **E-mail:** tacmag@nm.net. **Website:** www.americanarchaeology.org. **Contact:** Michael Bawaya, editor; Vicki Singer, art director. Estab. 1997. Circ. 35,000. Quarterly. "We're a popular archaeology magazine. Our readers are very interested in this science. Our features cover important digs, prominent archaeologists, and most any aspect of the science. We only cover North America." Sample copies available.

SPECS Uses 35mm, 2¼×2¼, 4×5 transparencies. Accepts images in digital format.

MAKING CONTACT & TERMS Prefer digital submissions at 300 dpi or higher. Send query letter with résumé, photocopies and tearsheets. Provide résumé, business card, self-promotion piece to be kept on file for possible future assignments. Responds in 2 months to queries. Previously published work OK.

TIPS "Read our magazine. Include accurate and detailed captions."

AMERICAN FITNESS

15250 Ventura Blvd., Suite 200, Sherman Oaks CA 91403. (800)446-2322, ext. 200. **E-mail:** americanfitness@afaa.com. **Website:** www.afaa.com. **Contact:** Meg Jordan, editor. Estab. 1983. Circ. 42,900. Buys 20-40 photos from freelancers/issue; 120-240 photos/year. Assigns 90% of work. Payment is issued post-publication. Send query letter with samples, list of stock photo subjects; include SASE for return of material. Responds in 2 weeks. Simultaneous submissions and previously published work OK. Pays $10-35 for b&w or color photo; $50 for text/photo package. Pays 4-6 weeks after publication. Credit line given. Buys first North American serial rights.

NEEDS Action photography of runners, aerobic classes, swimmers, bicyclists, speedwalkers, in-liners, volleyball players, etc. Also needs food choices, babies/children/teens, celebrities, couples, multicultural, families, parents, senior fitness, people enjoying recreation, cities/urban, rural, adventure, entertainment, events, hobbies, humor, performing arts, sports, travel, medicine, product shots/still life, science. Interested in alternative process, fashion/glamour, seasonal. Model release required.

SPECS Uses b&w prints; 35mm, 2¼×2¼ transparencies. Cover: color slides, transparencies (2" preferred size) or high-res 300 dpi, TIFF, or PDF files of at least 8.75×11.5. Interior/editorial: color slides, transparencies or high-res 300 dpi, TIFF, PDF, or JPEG files; glossy print.

TIPS "Over-40 sports leagues, youth fitness, family fitness and senior fitness are hot trends. Wants high-quality, professional photos of people participating in high-energy activities—anything that conveys the essence of a fabulous fitness lifestyle. Also accepts highly stylized studio shots to run as lead artwork for feature stories. Since we don't have a big art budget, freelancers usually submit spin-off projects from their larger photo assignments."

$ ⊕ THE AMERICAN GARDENER

7931 E. Boulevard Dr., Alexandria VA 22308-1300. (703)768-5700. **Fax:** (703)768-7533. **E-mail:** editor@ahs.org; myee@ahs.org. **Website:** www.ahs.org. **Contact:** Mary Yee, art director. Estab. 1922. Circ. 20,000. Bimonthly. "This is the official publication of the American Horticultural Society (AHS), a national, nonprofit, membership organization for gardeners, founded in 1922." Sample copy available for $5. Photo guidelines free with SASE or via e-mail request. Uses 35-50 photos/issue. Reviews photos with or without a manuscript. "Lists of plant species for which photographs are needed are sent out to a selected list of photographers approximately 10 weeks before publication. We currently have about 20 photographers on that list. Most of them have photo libraries representing thousands of species. Before adding photographers to our list, we need to determine both the quality and quantity of their collections. Therefore, we ask all photographers to submit digital samples of their work and a list indicating the types and number of plants in their collection. After reviewing both, we may decide to add the photographer to our photo call for a trial period of 6 issues (1 year)."

NEEDS Photos of plants, gardens, landscapes.

SPECS Digital images—high-res JPEG or TIFF files with a minimum size of 5×7 at 300 dpi—should be submitted on a CD or posted to an online photo gallery.

MAKING CONTACT & TERMS Send query letter with samples, stock list via mail or e-mail. Will contact for portfolio review if interested.

$$ AMERICAN HUNTER

National Rifle Association of America, 11250 Waples Mill Rd., Fairfax VA 22030-9400. (800)672-3888. **E-mail:** publications@nrahq.org; americanhunter@nrahq.org. **Website:** www.americanhunter.org. **Contact:** Editor-in-Chief. Circ. 1,000,000. Monthly magazine of the National Rifle Association. "*American Hunter* contains articles dealing with various sport hunting and related activities both at home and abroad. With the encouragement of the sport as a prime game management tool, emphasis is on technique, sportsmanship, and safety. In each issue hunting equipment and firearms are evaluated, legislative happenings affecting the sport are reported, lore and legend are retold, and the business of the Association is recorded in the Official Journal section." Uses wildlife shots and hunting action scenes. Seeks general hunting stories on North American and African game.

SPECS Send via CD as TIFF, GIF, or RAW files at 300 dpi. Vertical format required for cover.

MAKING CONTACT & TERMS Sample copy and photo guidelines free with 9×12 SASE. Send material by mail for consideration; include SASE for return of material.

TIPS "Most successful photographers maintain a file in our offices so editors can select photos to fill holes when needed. We keep files on most North American big game, small game, waterfowl, upland birds, and some exotics. We need live hunting shots as well as profiles and portraits in all settings. Many times there is not enough time to call photographers for special needs. This practice puts your name in front of the editors more often and increases the chances of sales."

AMERICAN MOTORCYCLIST

American Motorcyclist Association, 13515 Yarmouth Dr., Pickerington OH 43147. (614)856-1900. **E-mail:** submissions@ama-cycle.org. **Website:** www.americanmotorcyclist.com. **Contact:** Grant Parsons, director of communications; James Holter, managing editor. Estab. 1947. Circ. 200,000. Monthly magazine. Emphasizes people involved in, and events dealing with, all aspects of motorcycling. Readers are "enthusiastic motorcyclists, investing considerable time in road riding or all aspects of the sport."

NEEDS "The cover shot is tied in with the main story or theme of that issue and generally needs to be submitted with accompanying manuscript. Show us experience in motorcycling photography, and suggest your ability to meet our editorial needs and complement our philosophy."

SPECS Prefers images in digital format. Send via CD as TIFF, GIF, JPEG files at 300 dpi.

MAKING CONTACT & TERMS Send query letter with samples to be kept on file for possible future assignments. Responds in 3 weeks.

$ ⊕ ◐ AMERICAN TURF MONTHLY

747 Middle Neck Rd., Great Neck NY 11024. (516)773-4075. **Fax:** (516)773-2944. **E-mail:** jcorbett@americanturf.com; editor@americanturf.com. **Website:** www.americanturf.com. **Contact:** Joe Girardi, editor. Estab. 1946. Circ. 30,000. Monthly magazine. Covers Thoroughbred horse racing, especially aimed at horseplayers and handicappers.

NEEDS Buys 10 photos from freelancers/issue; 120 photos/year. Needs photos of celebrities, racing action, horses, owners, trainers, jockeys. Reviews photos with or without a manuscript. Photo captions preferred; include who, what, where.

SPECS Uses glossy color prints. Accepts images in digital format. Send via CD, floppy disk, ZIP as TIFF, JPEG files at 300 dpi.

MAKING CONTACT & TERMS Send query letter with CD, prints. Provide business card to be kept on file for possible future assignments. Responds only if interested; send nonreturnable samples.

TIPS "Like horses and horse racing."

ANCHOR NEWS

75 Maritime Dr., Manitowoc WI 54220. (920)684-0218; (866)724-2356. **Fax:** (920)684-0219. **E-mail:** nbishop@wisconsinmaritime.org; museum@wisconsinmaritime.org. **Website:** www.wisconsinmaritime.org. **Contact:** Norma Bishop, executive director. Circ. 1,100. Quarterly publication of the Wisconsin Maritime Museum. Emphasizes Great Lakes maritime history. Readers include learned and lay readers interested in Great Lakes history. Sample copy available with 9×12 SASE and $3 postage. Photo guidelines free with SASE.

NEEDS Uses 8-10 photos/issue; infrequently supplied by freelance photographers. Needs historic/nostalgic; personal experience; Great Lakes environmental issues, including aquatic invasive species and other topics of interest to environmental educators; and general interest articles on Great Lakes maritime topics. How-to and technical pieces and model ships and shipbuilding are OK. Special needs include historic photography or photos that show current historic trends of the Great Lakes; photos of waterfront development, bulk carriers, sailors, recreational boating, etc. Model release required. Photo captions required.

SPECS Accepts images in digital format. Send via CD, e-mail as JPEG files at 300 dpi minimum.

MAKING CONTACT & TERMS Send 4×5 or 8×10 glossy b&w prints by mail for consideration; include SASE for return of material. Simultaneous submissions and previously published work OK. Pays in copies on publication. Credit line given. Buys first North American serial rights.

TIPS "Besides historic photographs, I see a growing interest in underwater archaeology, especially on the Great Lakes, and underwater exploration—also on the Great Lakes. Sharp, clear photographs are a must. Our publication deals with a wide variety of subjects; however, we take a historical slant with our publication. Therefore, photos should be related to a historical topic in some respect. Also, there are current trends in Great Lakes shipping. A query is most helpful. This will let the photographer know exactly what we are looking for and will help save a lot of time and wasted effort."

ANIMAL TRAILS MAGAZINE

E-mail: animaltrails@yahoo.com. **Website:** animaltrailsmagazine.doodlekit.com. **Contact:** Shannon Bridget Murphy. Quarterly. "*Animal Trails* is an anchor for memories that are made as a result of experiences with animals. Through writing, photography and illustrations animals are given a voice."

NEEDS Photos of environmental, landscapes/scenics, wildlife, architecture, cities/urban, gardening, interiors/decorating, pets, religious, rural, performing arts, agriculture, product shots/still life—as related to animals. Interested in alternative process, avant garde, documentary, fashion/glamour, fine art, historical/vintage, seasonal. Reviews photos with or without a ms. Model/property release preferred.

SPECS Uses glossy or matte color and b&w prints.

MAKING CONTACT & TERMS Send query letter via e-mail or online form at website. Provide résumé, business card, self-promotion piece to be kept on file for possible future assignments. "A photograph or two is requested but not required. Illustrations and artwork are also accepted." Responds within 1 month to queries; 1 week to portfolios. Simultaneous submissions and previously published work OK. **Pays on acceptance.** Credit line given. Buys one-time rights, first rights; negotiable.

APERTURE

547 W. 27th St., 4th Floor, New York NY 10001. (212)505-5555. **E-mail:** magazine@aperture.org. **Website:** www.aperture.org. **Contact:** Michael Famighetti, managing editor. Circ. 18,500. Quarterly. Emphasizes fine-art and contemporary photography, as well as social reportage. Readers include photographers, artists, collectors, writers. "Published by the the not-for-profit Aperture Foundation, which also publishes books, produces exhibitions, and has a gallery and bookstore in New York City."

NEEDS Uses about 60 photos/issue; biannual portfolio review. Model release required. Photo captions required.

MAKING CONTACT & TERMS To submit work, enter the annual Aperture Portfolio Prize competition "developed to bring work by emerging photographers to a wider audience. The next Portfolio Prize should be open for submissions in the fall. You can also enter your photobook in the First PhotoBook or PhotoBook of the Year categories of the Paris Photo-Aperture Foundation PhotoBook Awards. The next photobook competition should be open for submissions in the summer."

TIPS "We are a nonprofit foundation. Do not send unsolicited materials as they cannot be returned."

APOGEE PHOTO MAGAZINE

Jacksonville FL (904)619-2010. **E-mail:** mmeier@apogeephoto.com; general.information@apogeephoto.com. **Website:** apogeephoto.com. **Contact:** Marla Meier, editorial director. A free online monthly magazine designed to inform, educate and entertain photographers of all ages and levels.

NEEDS Digital photography, photo technique articles, product reviews, business and marketing, nature and wildlife photography, photographer profiles/interviews and all other photography-related articles.

TIPS "Please do a search by subject before submitting your article to see if your article covers a new subject or brings a new perspective on a particular subject or theme."

$ ◐ APPALACHIAN TRAIL JOURNEYS

P.O. Box 807, Harpers Ferry WV 25425. (304)535-6331. **Fax:** (304)535-2667. **E-mail:** jfolgar@appalachiantrail.org. **Website:** www.appalachiantrail.org. Estab. 2005. Circ. 45,000. Bimonthly publication of the Appalachian Trail Conservancy. Uses only photos related to the Appalachian Trail. Readers are conservationists, hikers. Photo guidelines available on website.

NEEDS Buys 4-5 photos from freelancers/issue in addition to 2- to 4-page "Vistas" spread each issue; 50-60 photos/year. Most frequent need is for candids of hikers enjoying the trail. Photo captions and release required.

SPECS Accepts high-res digital images (300 dpi). Uses 35mm transparencies.

MAKING CONTACT & TERMS Send query letter with ideas by mail, e-mail. Duplicate slides preferred over originals for query. Responds in 3 weeks. Simultaneous submissions and previously published work OK. Pays on publication. Pays $300 for cover; variable for inside. Credit line given. Rights negotiable.

APPALOOSA JOURNAL

2720 West Pullman Rd., Moscow ID 83843. (208)882-5578. **Fax:** (208)882-8150. **E-mail:** editor@appaloosajournal.com; designer2@appaloosajournal.com. **Website:** www.appaloosajournal.com. **Contact:** Dana Russell, editor; John Langston, art director. Estab. 1946. Circ. 25,000.

NEEDS Photos for cover, and to accompany features and articles. Specifically wants photographs of high-quality Appaloosa horses, especially in winter scenes. Model release required. Photo captions required.

SPECS Uses glossy color prints; 35mm transparencies; digital images 300 dpi at 5×7 or larger, depending on use. Send query letter with résumé, slides, prints, or e-mail as PDF or GIF. Keeps samples on file. Responds only if interested; send nonreturnable samples. Simultaneous submissions OK.

MAKING CONTACT & TERMS "Send a letter introducing yourself and briefly explaining your work. If you have inflexible preset fees, be upfront and include that information."

TIPS "Be patient. We are located at the headquarters; although an image might not work for the magazine, it might work for other printed materials. Work has a better chance of being used if allowed to keep on file. If work must be returned promptly, please specify. Otherwise, we will keep it for other departments' consideration."

ARCHAEOLOGY

Archaeological Institute of America, 36-36 33rd St., Long Island NY 11106. (718)472-3050. **Fax:** (718)472-3051. **E-mail:** cvalentino@archaeology.org; editorial@archaeology.org. **Website:** www.archaeology.org. **Contact:** Editor-in-chief. Estab. 1948. Circ. 750,000. *ARCHAEOLOGY* combines worldwide archaeological findings with photography, specially rendered maps, drawings, and charts. Covers current excavations and recent discoveries, and includes personality profiles, technology updates, adventure, travel and studies of ancient cultures.

● ARIZONA WILDLIFE VIEWS

5000 W. Carefree Hwy., Phoenix AZ 85086. (800)777-0015. **E-mail:** awv@azgfd.gov; hrayment@azgfd.gov. **Website:** www.azgfd.gov/magazine. **Contact:** Heidi Rayment. Circ. 22,000. Bimonthly official magazine of the Arizona Game and Fish Department. "*Arizona Wildlife Views* is a general interest magazine about Arizona wildlife, wildlife management and outdoor recreation (specifically hunting, fishing, wildlife watching, boating and off-highway vehicle recreation). We publish material that conforms to the mission and policies of the Arizona Game and Fish Department. Topics also include habitat issues and historical articles about wildlife and wildlife management."

NEEDS Photos of sports, environmental, landscapes/scenics, wildlife in Arizona. Reviews photos with or without a manuscript. Model release required only if the subject matter is of a delicate or sensitive nature. Captions required.

SPECS "We prefer and primarily use professional-quality 35mm and larger color transparencies. Submitted transparencies must be numbered, identified by artist, and an inventory list must accompany each shipment. The highest resolution digital images are occasionally used." Send JPEG or GIF files. See new information for photographers online at website.

MAKING CONTACT & TERMS Before contacting, please read the appropriate submission guidelines: www.azgfd.gov/i_e/pubs/contributorguidelines.shtml. "Half of the written content of *Arizona Wildlife Views* magazine is generated by freelance writers and photographers. Payment is made upon publication. We prefer queries by e-mail. Sample copies are available on request. The magazine does not accept responsibility for any submissions. It is the artist's responsibility to insure his work." Pays $400 for front cover; $350 for back cover; $250 for inside half-page or larger; $150 for inside smaller than half-page. Pays following publication. Credit line given. Buys one-time rights.

TIPS "Unsolicited material without proper identification will be returned immediately."

⊕ ARMY MAGAZINE

Association of the US Army, 2425 Wilson Blvd., Arlington VA 22201. (800)336-4570. **E-mail:** armymag@ausa.org. **Website:** www.ausa.org/publications/army magazine. **Contact:** Rick Maze, editor-in-chief. Estab. 1950. Circ. 65,000.

MAKING CONTACT & TERMS Reviews prints and high resolution digital photos. Pays $50-100 for 8×10 b&w glossy prints; $50-350 for 8×10 color glossy prints and 35mm and high-resolution (300 dip JPEGs) digital photos. Captions required. Buys all rights.

⊗ ASTRONOMY

Kalmbach Publishing, 21027 Crossroads Circle, P.O. Box 1612, Waukesha WI 53187-1612. (800)533-6644. **Fax:** (262)798-6468. **Website:** www.astronomy.com. **Contact:** LuAnn Williams Belter, art director. Estab. 1973. Circ. 108,000. Monthly magazine. Emphasizes astronomy, science and hobby. Median reader: 52 years old, 86% male. Submission guidelines on website. Buys 70 images from freelancers/issue, 840 images/year.

NEEDS Send high-res digital files. Captions, photo details and identification of subjects required; model/property releases preferred. Pays $25/photo, $200 for cover image. Photos of astronomical images.

SPECS "If you are submitting digital images, please send TIFF or JPEG files to us via our FTP site. Send duplicate images by mail for consideration." Keeps samples on file. Responds in 1 month. Pays on publication. Credit line given.

ATLANTA HOMES AND LIFESTYLES

Network Communications, Inc., 1117 Perimeter Center West, Suite N118, Atlanta GA 30338. (404)252-6670. **E-mail:** editor@atlantahomesmag.com. **Website:** www.atlantahomesmag.com. **Contact:** Elizabeth Ralls, editor-in-chief; Elizabeth Anderson, art director. Estab. 1983. Circ. 30,000. Monthly magazine. Covers residential design (home and garden); food, wine, and entertaining; people, lifestyle subjects in the metro Atlanta area. Sample copy available online.

NEEDS Photos of homes (interior/exterior), people, decorating ideas, products, gardens. Model/property release required. Photo captions preferred.

SPECS Accepts images in digital format only.

MAKING CONTACT & TERMS Contact creative director to review portfolio. Provide résumé, business card, brochure, flyer, or tearsheets to be kept on file for possible future assignments. Responds in 2 months. Simultaneous submissions and previously published work OK. Pays $150-750/job. **Pays on acceptance.** Credit line given.

⊕ ATLANTA PARENT

2346 Perimeter Park Dr., Atlanta GA 30341. (770)454-7599. **E-mail:** editor@atlantaparent.com. **Website:** www.atlantaparent.com. **Contact:** Editor. Estab. 1983. "*Atlanta Parent* magazine has been a valuable resource for Atlanta families since 1983. It is the only magazine in the Atlanta area providing pertinent, local, and award-winning family-oriented articles and information. Atlanta parents rely on us for features that are timely, informative, and reader-friendly on important issues such as childcare, family life, education, adolescence, motherhood, health, and teens. Fun, easy, and inexpensive family activities and crafts as well as the humorous side of parenting are also important to our readers."

MAKING CONTACT & TERMS State availability of or send photos. Offers $10/photo. Buys one-time rights.

➕ 🔄 THE ATLANTIC SALMON JOURNAL

The Atlantic Salmon Federation, P.O. Box 5200, St. Andrews NB E5B 3S8, Canada. (514)457-8737. **Fax:** (506)529-1070. **E-mail:** savesalmon@asf.ca; martinsilverstone@videotron.ca. **Website:** www.asf.ca. **Contact:** Martin Silverstone, editor. Circ. 11,000.

🔄 AUTO RESTORER

BowTie, Inc., 3 Burroughs, Irvine CA 92618. (213)385-2222. **Fax:** (213)385-8565. **E-mail:** tkade@i5publishing.com. **Website:** www.autorestorermagazine.com. **Contact:** Ted Kade, editor. Estab. 1989. Circ. 60,000. Offers no additional payment for photos accepted with ms. "Interview the owner of a restored car. Present advice to others on how to do a similar restoration. Seek advice from experts. Go light on history and nonspecific details. Make it something that the magazine regularly uses. Do automotive how-tos."

NEEDS Photos of auto restoration projects and restored cars.

SPECS Prefers images in high-res digital format. Send via CD at 240 dpi with minimum width of 5 inches. Uses transparencies, mostly 35mm, 2¼×2¼.

MAKING CONTACT & TERMS Submit inquiry and portfolio for review. Provide résumé, business card, brochure, flyer, or tearsheets to be kept on file for possible future assignments. Responds in 1 month. Simultaneous submissions OK.

⚫ BABYTALK

Bonnier Corp., 460 N. Orlando Ave., Suite 200, Winter Park FL 32789. (407)628-4802. **Website:** www.babytalk.com. **Contact:** Donna Reiss, art director. Estab. 1937. Monthly magazine. Non-newsstand circulation of 2 million; distributed via subscription and through physicians' offices and retail outlets. Readers are new mothers and pregnant women. Sample copies available upon request.

MAKING CONTACT & TERMS Send query letter and printed samples; include URL for your website. After introductory mailing, send follow-up postcard every 3 months. Samples are kept on file. Responds only if interested. Portfolios not required. **Pays on acceptance.** Buys one-time rights, reprint rights, all rights, electronic rights. Finds freelancers through agents, artists' submissions, word of mouth and sourcebooks.

TIPS "Please, no calls or e-mails. Postcards or mailers are best. We don't look at portfolios unless we request them. Websites listed on mailers are great."

BACKPACKER MAGAZINE

Cruz Bay Publishing, Inc., Active Interest Media Co., 5720 Flatiron Pkwy., Boulder CO 80301. **E-mail:** gfullerton@backpacker.com (senior associate photo editor). **Website:** www.backpacker.com. Estab. 1973. Circ. 340,000.

MAKING CONTACT & TERMS Sometimes considers simultaneous submissions and previously published work. Pays $500-1,000 for color cover; $100-600 for color inside. Pays on publication. Credit line given. Rights negotiable.

🔄 BASEBALL

E-mail: shannonaswriter@yahoo.com. **Contact:** Shannon Bridget Murphy. Quarterly. Covers baseball. Photo guidelines available by e-mail request.

NEEDS Photos of baseball scenes featuring children and teens; photos of celebrities, couples, multicultural, families, parents, environmental, landscapes/scenics, wildlife, agriculture—as related to the sport of baseball. Interested in alternative process, avant garde, documentary, fine art, historical/vintage, seasonal. Reviews photos with or without a ms.

SPECS Uses glossy or matte color and b&w prints.

MAKING CONTACT & TERMS Send query letter via e-mail. "If possible, please do not include photographs in files if they are sent through e-mail. A disk with your photographs is acceptable. If you plan to send a disk, photographs or portfolio, please send an e-mail stating this." Provide résumé, business card, self-promotion piece to be kept on file for possible future assignments. "Photographs sent with CDs are requested but not required. Write to request guidelines for artwork and illustrations." Responds within 1 month to queries; 1 week to portfolios. Simultaneous submissions and previously published work OK.

Pays on acceptance. Credit line given. Buys one-time, first rights; negotiable.

🍁 ◎ BC OUTDOORS HUNTING AND SHOOTING

Outdoor Group Media, 7261 River Place, 201 A, Mission British Columbia V4S 0A2, Canada. (604)820-3400. **Fax:** (604)820-3477. **E-mail:** info@outdoorgroupmedia.com; mmitchell@outdoorgroupmedia.com; production@outdoorgroupmedia.com. **Website:** www.bcoutdoorsmagazine.com. **Contact:** Mike Mitchell, editor. Estab. 1945. Circ. 30,000.

NEEDS Buys 30-35 photos from freelancers/issue; 60-70 photos/year. Prefers images in digital format. Send via e-mail at 300 dpi. Send by mail for consideration actual 5×7 or 8×10 color prints; 35mm, 2¼×2¼, 4×5 or 8×10 color transparencies; color contact sheet. If color negative, send jumbo prints, then negatives only on request. E-mail high-res electronic images. Send query letter with list of stock photo subjects. Include SASE or IRC. Pays in Canadian currency. Simultaneous submissions not acceptable if competitor. Editor determines payments. Pays on publication. Credit line given. Buys one-time rights for inside shots; for covers, "we retain the right for subsequent promotional use."

🍁 BC OUTDOORS SPORT FISHING

Outdoor Group Media, 7261 River Place, 201 A, Mission British Columbia V4S 0AZ, Canada. (604)820-3400. **E-mail:** production@outdoorgroupmedia.com. **Website:** www.bcosportfishing.com. **Contact:** Paul Bielicky. Estab. 1945. Circ. 35,000. Published 7 times/year. Emphasizes fishing, both fresh and salt water. Sample copy available for $4.95 Canadian.

NEEDS Buys 30-35 photos from freelancers/issue; 180-210 photos/year. "Fishing (in our territory) is a big need—people in the act of catching or releasing fish. Family oriented. By far, most photos accompany manuscripts. We are always on the lookout for good covers—fishing, wildlife, recreational activities, people in the outdoors—of British Columbia, vertical and square format. Photos with manuscripts must, of course, illustrate the story. There should, as far as possible, be something happening. Photos generally dominate lead spread of each story. They are used in everything from double-page bleeds to thumbnails. Column needs basically supplied in-house." Model/property release preferred. Photo captions or at least full identification required.

SPECS Prefers images in digital format. Send via e-mail at 300 dpi.

MAKING CONTACT & TERMS *No unsolicited submissions.* Send by mail for consideration actual 5×7 or 8×10 color prints; 35mm, 2¼×2¼, 4×5 or 8×10 color transparencies; color contact sheet. If color negative, send jumbo prints, then negatives only on request. E-mail high-resolution electronic images. Send query letter with list of stock photo subjects. Include SASE or IRC. Pays in Canadian currency. Simultaneous submissions not acceptable if competitor. Editor determines payments. Pays on publication. Credit line given. Buys one-time rights for inside shots; for covers, "we retain the right for subsequent promotional use."

$ ◐ THE BEAR DELUXE MAGAZINE

Orlo, 240 N. Broadway, #112, Portland OR 97227. **E-mail:** bear@orlo.org. **Website:** www.orlo.org. **Contact:** Tom Webb, editor-in-chief; Kristin Rogers Brown, art director. Estab. 1993. Circ. 19,000. "*The Bear Deluxe Magazine* is a national independent environmental arts magazine publishing significant works of reporting, creative nonfiction, literature, visual art, and design. Based in the Pacific Northwest, it reaches across cultural and political divides to engage readers on vital issues effecting the environment. Published twice per year, *The Bear Deluxe* includes a wider array and a higher percentage of visual artwork and design than many other publications. Artwork is included both as editorial support and as standalone or independent art. It has included nationally recognized artists as well as emerging artists. As with any publication, artists are encouraged to review a sample copy for a clearer understanding of the magazine's approach. Unsolicited submissions and samples are accepted and encouraged. *The Bear Deluxe* has been recognized for both its editorial and design excellence."

MAKING CONTACT & TERMS "Send us your current work samples and a brief cover letter outlining your availability and turn-around time estimates. Let us know if you'd like to be considered for editorial illustration/photography or only for independent art. Send slides (not more than one sheet), prints, high-quality photocopies, or high-res scans (TIFF files please) on a ZIP drive or CD. If you submit via e-mail, send PDF format files only, or a URL address for us to visit. (Note on e-mail submissions and URL suggestions we prefer hard-copy work samples but will consider electronic submissions and links. We cannot, however, guarantee a response to electronic submissions.) Send SASE for the return of materials. No faxes. Assumes no liability for submitted work samples."

○ BELLINGHAM REVIEW

Mail Stop 9053, Western Washington University, Bellingham WA 98225. (360)650-4863. **E-mail:** belling ham.review@wwu.edu. **Website:** wwww.bhreview. org. **Contact:** Brenda Miller, editor-in-chief; Kaitlyn Teer, managing editor. Estab. 1977. Circ. 2,000. Annual nonprofit magazine. "Literature of palpable quality: poems, stories, and essays so beguiling they invite us to touch their essence. *Bellingham Review* hungers for a kind of writing that nudges the limits of form or executes traditional forms exquisitely."

NEEDS Babies/children/teens, couples, multicultural, families, parents, senior citizens, architecture, cities/urban, gardening, pets, rural, disasters, environment, landscapes, wildlife, adventure, event.

MAKING CONTACT & TERMS Send an e-mail with sample photographs. Accepts JPEG samples at 72 dpi. Samples not kept on file. Portfolio not required. Pays on publication.

THE BINNACLE

University of Maine at Machias, 116 O'Brien Ave., Machias ME 04654. **E-mail:** ummbinnacle@maine. edu. **Website:** www.umm.maine.edu/binnacle. Estab. 1957. Circ. 300. Semiannual alternative paper format covering general arts. "We publish an alternative format journal of literary and visual art. *The Binnacle* accepts submissions from the students, faculty, and staff of the University of Maine at Machias and from writers and artists anywhere in the world. Please submit photography and other works of visual art, both color and b&w."

SPECS Files in JPEG, GIF, or PSD are preferable; BMP or TIFF are normally fine.

MAKING CONTACT & TERMS "We prefer submissions of all types in electronic form. Digital images should be submitted via postal mail on a CD or posted on a website for our viewing. Please do not send these in attachments. Please include SASE if you would like the media returned."

● ❸ ● BIRD WATCHER'S DIGEST

P.O. Box 110, Marietta OH 45750. (740)373-5285; (800)879-2473. **E-mail:** editor@birdwatchersdigest. com; submissions@birdwatchersdigest.com. **Website:** www.birdwatchersdigest.com. **Contact:** Bill Thompson III, editor. Estab. 1978. Circ. 42,000. Bimonthly;

digest size. Emphasizes birds and bird watchers. "We use images to augment our magazine's content, so we often look for nontraditional shots of birds, including images capturing unusual behavior or settings. For our species profiles of birds we look for more traditional images: sharp, well-composed portraits of wild birds in their natural habitat." Readers are bird watchers/birders (backyard and field, veterans and novices). Sample copy available for $4.99. Photo guidelines available online.

NEEDS Buys 25-35 photos from freelancers/issue; 150-210 photos/year. Needs photos of North American species.

SPECS Accepts high-res (300 dpi) digital images via Dropbox or HighTail. See guidelines online.

● ❸ ◎ ● BIRD WATCHING

Bauer Active, Media House, Lynch Wood, Peterborough PE2 6EA, Wales. 01733 468 201. **E-mail:** trevor. ward@bauermedia.co.uk. **Website:** www.birdwatch ing.co.uk. **Contact:** Trevor Ward, art editor. Estab. 1986. Circ. 22,000. Monthly hobby magazine for bird watchers. Sample copy free with SASE (first-class postage/IRC).

NEEDS Photos of "wild birds photographed in the wild, mainly in action or showing interesting aspects of behavior. Also stunning landscape pictures in birding areas and images of people with binoculars, telescopes, etc." Also considers travel, hobby and gardening shots related to bird watching. Reviews photos with or without a manuscript. Photo captions preferred.

SPECS Uses 35mm, 2¼×2¼ transparencies. Accepts images in digital format. Send via CD, e-mail as TIFF, EPS, JPEG files at 200 dpi.

MAKING CONTACT & TERMS Provide résumé, business card, self-promotion piece or tearsheets to be kept on file for possible future assignments. Returns unsolicited material if SASE enclosed. Responds in 1 month. Simultaneous submissions OK. Pays on publication. Buys one-time rights.

TIPS "All photos are held on file here in the office once they have been selected. They are returned when used or a request for their return is made. Make sure all slides are well labeled: bird, name, date, place taken, photographer's name and address. Send sample of images to show full range of subject and photographic techniques."

⚙ ◎ ○ BLACKFLASH MAGAZINE

P.O. Box 7381, Station Main, Saskatoon Saskatchewan S7K 4J3, Canada. (306)374-5115. **E-mail:** letters@blackflash.ca; travis.cole@blackflash.ca. **Website:** www.blackflash.ca. **Contact:** Travis Cole, managing editor. Estab. 1983. Circ. 1,500. Canadian journal of photo-based and electronic arts published 3 times/year.

NEEDS Lens-based and new media contemporary fine art and electronic arts practitioners. Reviews photos with or without a manuscript.

SPECS Accepts images in digital format. Send via CD, ZIP, e-mail as TIFF, EPS, BMP, JPEG files at 300 dpi.

MAKING CONTACT & TERMS Send query letter with résumé, digital images. Does not keep samples on file; will return material with SASE only. Simultaneous submissions OK. Pays when copy has been proofed and edited. Credit line given. One-time rights for print and digital editions.

TIPS "We are continuously seeking out visual artists that work within the mediums of photography, experimental/expanded cinema and contemporary art. Please review our mandate and read our magazine prior to submitting."

⑤ ◑ BLUE RIDGE COUNTRY

Leisure Media360, 3424 Brambleton Ave., Roanoke VA 24018. (540)989-6138. **Fax:** (540)989-7603. **E-mail:** krheinheimer@leisuremedia360.com. **Website:** www.blueridgecountry.com. **Contact:** Kurt Rheinheimer, editor. Estab. 1988. Circ. 425,000. Bimonthly. Emphasizes outdoor scenics, recreation, travel destinations in 9-state Blue Ridge Mountain region. Photo guidelines available for SASE or on website.

○ "We're looking for feature photography and cover images, and we're connecting covers to the stories inside the magazine, so we're not just looking for general mountain scenics. We're looking for scenes with and without people, for outdoor recreation from soft to extreme. We can especially use more images from Kentucky, South Carolina and Alabama as well as our other coverage states: Virginia, West Virginia, Maryland, Georgia, Tennessee and North Carolina. For each issue's travel destinations and weekend getaways, we are looking for scenics, town shots, people, outdoor recreation, historical attractions, etc. All should be shot within the season they are to appear (green, autumn, winter)."

NEEDS Buys 20-40 photos from freelancers/issue; 100-300 photos/year. Photos of travel, scenics and wildlife. Seeking more scenics with people in them. Model release preferred. Photo captions required.

SPECS Accepts images in digital format. Send via CD, e-mail, or FTP (contact editor for information) at 300 dpi; low-res images OK for initial review, but accepted images must be high-res.

MAKING CONTACT & TERMS Send query letter with list of stock photo subjects, samples with caption info and SASE. Responds in 2 months.

BOWHUNTER

InterMedia Outdoors, 6385 Flank Dr., Suite 800, Harrisburg PA 17112. (717)695-8085. **Fax:** (717)545-2527. **E-mail:** curt.wells@imoutdoors.com. **Website:** www.bowhunter.com. Mark Olszewski, art director; Jeff Waring, publisher. **Contact:** Curt Wells, editor. Estab. 1971. Circ. 126,480. Published 9 times/year. Emphasizes bow and arrow hunting. Sample copy available for $2. Submission guidelines free with SASE.

NEEDS Buys 40-50 photos/year. Wants scenic (showing bowhunting) and wildlife (big and small game of North America) photos. "No cute animal shots or poses. We publish informative, entertaining bowhunting adventure, how-to and where-to-go articles."

SPECS Digital submissions should be 300 dpi in RAW, JPEG, or TIFF format; CMYK preferred, provided on CD or DVD named in a simple and logical system with accompanying contact sheet.

MAKING CONTACT & TERMS Send query letter with samples, SASE. Responds in 2 weeks to queries; 6 weeks to samples. Reviews high-res digital images. Reviews photos with or without a manuscript. Offers $50-300/photo. Pays $50-125 for b&w inside; $75-300 for color inside; $600 for cover, "occasionally more if photo warrants it." **Pays on acceptance.** Captions required. Credit line given. Buys one-time publication rights.

TIPS "Know bowhunting and/or wildlife and study several copies of our magazine before submitting any material. We're looking for better quality, and we're using more color on inside pages. Most purchased photos are of big game animals. Hunting scenes are second. In b&w we look for sharp, realistic light, good contrast. Color must be sharp; early or late light is best. We avoid anything that looks staged; we want natural settings, quality animals. Send only your best, and, if at all possible, let us hold those we indicate interest in. Very little is taken on assignment; most comes from our files or is part of the manuscript package. If your work is in our files, it will probably be used."

BOWHUNTING WORLD

Grand View Media Group, 6121 Baker Rd., Suite 101, Minnetonka MN 55345. (888)431-2877. **E-mail:** molis@grandviewmedia.com. **Website:** www.bowhuntingworld.com. **Contact:** Mark Olis. Estab. 1952. Circ. 95,000. Bimonthly magazine with 3 additional issues for bowhunting and archery enthusiasts who participate in the sport year-round.

BOYS' LIFE

Boy Scouts of America, P.O. Box 152079, 1325 W. Walnut Hill Ln., Irving TX 75015. **Website:** www.boyslife.org. **Contact:** Paula Murphey, senior editor; Clay Swartz, associate editor. Estab. 1911. Circ. 1.1 million. Photo guidelines free with SASE. Boy Scouts of America Magazine Division also publishes *Scouting* magazine. "Most photographs are from specific assignments that freelance photojournalists shoot for *Boys' Life*. Interested in all photographers, but do not send unsolicited images."

MAKING CONTACT & TERMS Send query letter with list of credits. Pays $500 base editorial day rate against placement fees, plus expenses. **Pays on acceptance.** Buys one-time rights.

TIPS "Learn and read our publications before submitting anything."

[+] BREW YOUR OWN

Battenkill Communications, 5515 Main St., Manchester Center VT 05255. (802)362-3981. **Fax:** (802)362-2377. **E-mail:** edit@byo.com. **Website:** www.byo.com. **Contact:** Betsy Parker, editor. Estab. 1995. Circ. 50,000. "Our mission is to provide practical information in an entertaining format. We try to capture the spirit and challenge of brewing while helping our readers brew the best beer they can."

MAKING CONTACT & TERMS Reviews contact sheets, transparencies, 5x7 prints, slides, and electronic images. Negotiates payment individually. Buys all rights.

✪ BRIARPATCH MAGAZINE

(306)525-2949. **E-mail:** editor@briarpatchmagazine.com. **Website:** www.briarpatchmagazine.com. **Contact:** Adrew Loewen, editor. Estab. 1973. Circ. 2,000. Published 6 times/year. Emphasizes Canadian politics, indigenous, labor, environment, women. Readers are socially progressive and politically engaged.

NEEDS Buys 5-20 photos from freelancers/issue; 30-120 photos/year. Photos of Canadian and international politics, labor, environment, women, peace and personalities. Model/property release preferred. Photo captions preferred; include names in photo.

SPECS Minimum 300 dpi color prints.

MAKING CONTACT & TERMS Send query letter with samples or link to online portfolio. Do not send slides. Provide résumé, business card, brochure, flyer, or tearsheets to be kept on file for possible future assignments. Include SASE for return of material. Responds in 1 month. Simultaneous submissions and previously published work OK. Pays a "very modest compensation." Credit line given. Buys one-time rights. Submission guidelines available online.

$ ◐ BRIDAL GUIDES MAGAZINE

E-mail: BridalGuides@yahoo.com. **Contact:** Shannon Bridget Murphy. Estab. 1998. Quarterly. Photo guidelines available by e-mail request.

NEEDS Buys 12 photos from freelancers/issue; 48-72 photos/year. Photos of babies/children/teens, celebrities, couples, multicultural, families, parents, cities/urban, environmental, landscapes/scenics, wildlife, architecture, gardening, interiors/decorating, pets, religious, rural, adventure, entertainment, events, food/drink, health/fitness, performing arts, travel, agriculture—as related to weddings. Interested in alternative process, avant garde, documentary, fashion/glamour, fine art, historical/vintage, seasonal. Also wants photos of weddings "and those who make it all happen, both behind and in front of the scene." Reviews photos with or without a manuscript. Model/property release preferred.

SPECS Uses glossy or matte color and b&w prints.

MAKING CONTACT & TERMS Send query letter via e-mail. "If possible, please do not include photographs in files if they are sent through e-mail. A disc with your photographs is acceptable. If you plan to send a disc, photographs or portfolio, please send an e-mail stating this." Provide résumé, business card or self-promotion piece to be kept on file for possible future assignments. A photograph or 2 sent with CD is requested but not required. Illustrations and artwork are also accepted. Write to request guidelines for artwork and illustrations. Responds within 1 month to queries; 1 week to portfolios. Simultaneous submissions and previously published work OK. **Pays on acceptance.** Credit line given. Buys one-time rights, first rights; negotiable.

THE BRIDGE BULLETIN

American Contract Bridge League, 6575 Windchase Dr., Horn Lake MS 38637-1523. (662)253-3156. **Fax:** (662)253-3187. **E-mail:** editor@acbl.org; brent.man ley@acbl.org. **Website:** www.acbl.org. Paul Linxwiler, managing editor. **Contact:** Brent Manley, editor. Estab. 1938. Circ. 155,000. Monthly association magazine for tournament/duplicate bridge players. Sample copies available. Buys 6-10 photos/year.

SPECS Prefers high-res digital images, color only.

MAKING CONTACT & TERMS Query by phone. Responds only if interested; send nonreturnable samples. Previously published work OK. Credit line given. Photos must relate to bridge. Call first.

⊕⊕ BUSINESS NH MAGAZINE

55 S. Commercial St., Manchester NH 03101. (603)626-6354. **Fax:** (603)626-6359. **E-mail:** hcope land@BusinessNHmagazine.com. **Website:** www. millyardcommunications.com. **Contact:** Heidi Copeland, publisher. Estab. 1983. Circ. 15,000. Monthly magazine. Covers business, politics, and people of New Hampshire. Readers are male and female top management, average age 45. Sample copy free with 9×12 SASE and 5 first-class stamps. Offers internships for photographers. Looks for "people in environment shots, interesting lighting, lots of creative interpretations, a definite personal style."

NEEDS Photos of couples, families, rural, entertainment, food/drink, health/fitness, performing arts, travel, business concepts, industry, science, technology/computers.

SPECS Uses 3-6 photos/issue. Accepts images in digital format.

MAKING CONTACT & TERMS Send via CD, ZIP as TIFF, JPEG files at 300 dpi. Arrange personal interview to show portfolio. Provide résumé, business card, brochure, flyer or tearsheets to be kept on file for possible future assignments. Responds in 3 weeks.

TIPS "If you're just starting out and want excellent statewide exposure to the leading executives in New Hampshire, you should talk to us. Send letter and samples, then arrange for a portfolio showing."

⊕⊕ CALLIOPE

30 Grove St., Suite C, Peterborough NH 03458-1454. (603)924-7209. **Fax:** (603)924-7380. **E-mail:** custom erservice@caruspub.com. **Website:** www.cobble stonepub.com. **Contact:** Rosalie Baker and Charles Baker, co-editors; Lou Waryncia, editorial director; Ann Dillon, art director. Estab. 1990. Circ. 13,000. Published 9 times/year (May/June, July/August, November/December). Emphasis on non-U.S. history. Readers are children ages 9-14. "To be considered for publication, photographs must relate to a specific theme. Writers are encouraged to submit available photos with their query or article." Sample copies available for $5.95 with 9×12 or larger SASE and 5 first-class stamps. Photo guidelines available on website or free with SASE.

NEEDS Contemporary shots of historical locations, buildings, artifacts, historical reenactments and costumes.

SPECS Uses b&w and color prints; 35mm transparencies.

MAKING CONTACT & TERMS "If you have photographs pertaining to any upcoming theme, please contact the editor by mail or fax, or send them with your query. You may also send images on speculation." Send query letter with stock photo list. Provide résumé, business card, brochure, flyer or tearsheets to be kept on file for possible future assignments. Responds within 5 months. Simultaneous submissions and previously published work OK.

TIPS "Given our young audience, we like to have pictures that include people, both young and old. Pictures must be dynamic to make history appealing. Submissions must relate to themes in each issue."

◐ ⊕ ◑ CANADA LUTHERAN

302-393 Portage Ave., Winnipeg Manitoba R3B 3H6, Canada. (204)984-9171; (204)984-9172. **Fax:** (204)984-9185. **E-mail:** editor@elcic.ca. **Website:** www.elcic.ca/clweb. **Contact:** Kenn Ward, editor. Estab. 1986. Circ. 8,000. Monthly publication of Evangelical Lutheran Church in Canada. Emphasizes faith/religious content, Lutheran denomination. Readers are members of the Evangelical Lutheran Church in Canada. Sample copy available for $5 Canadian (includes postage).

NEEDS Buys 1-2 photos from freelancers/issue; 12-24 photos/year. Photos of people in worship, at work/

play, diversity, advocacy, youth/young people, etc. Canadian sources preferred.

SPECS Accepts images in digital format. Send via CD, e-mail as JPEG at 300 dpi minimum.

MAKING CONTACT & TERMS Send sample prints and photo CDs by mail (include SASE for return of material) or send low-res images by e-mail. Pays on publication (in Canadian dollars). Credit line given. Buys one-time rights.

TIPS "Portfolio submissions welcome. We keep photographer contacts on file for approximately one year. "

☼ ⑤ ◎ ⊘ CANADIAN HOMES & COTTAGES

The In-Home Show, Ltd., 2650 Meadowvale Blvd., Unit 4, Mississauga Ontario L5N 6M5, Canada. (905)567-1440. **Fax:** (905)567-1442. **E-mail:** jnaisby@homesandcottages.com; editorial@homesandcottages.com. **Website:** www.homesandcottages.com. **Contact:** Janice E. Naisby, editor-in-chief. Estab. 1987. Circ. 92,340.

NEEDS Photos of landscapes/scenics, architecture, interiors/decorating. Does not keep samples on file; cannot return material.

MAKING CONTACT & TERMS Photo guidelines free with SASE. Responds only if interested; send non-returnable samples.

☼ ⑤ ◎ ❶ CANADIAN RODEO NEWS

272245 RR2, Airdrie Alberta T4A 2L5, Canada. (403)945-7393. **Fax:** (403)945-0936. **E-mail:** editor@rodeocanada.com. **Website:** www.rodeocanada.com. **Contact:** Darell Hartlen, editor. Estab. 1964. Circ. 4,000. Monthly tabloid. Promotes professional rodeo in Canada. Readers are male and female rodeo contestants and fans of all ages.

NEEDS Photos of professional rodeo action or profiles.

SPECS Uses color and b&w prints. Accepts images in digital format. Send via CD or e-mail as JPEG or TIFF files at 300 dpi.

MAKING CONTACT & TERMS Send low-res unsolicited photos by e-mail for consideration. Call to confirm if photos are usable. Keeps samples on file. Simultaneous submissions and previously published work OK. Pays on publication. Credit line given. Rights negotiable. Media/photographer release form available online.

TIPS "Photos must be from or pertain to professional rodeo in Canada. Phone to confirm if subject/material is suitable before submitting. *CRN* is very specific in subject."

☼ ⑤ CANADIAN YACHTING

538 Elizabeth St., Midland Ontario L4R 2A3, Canada. (705)527-7666. **E-mail:** aadams@kerrwil.com. **Website:** www.canadianyachting.ca. **Contact:** Andy Adams, managing editor. Estab. 1976. Circ. 26,000. Published 6 times per year. Emphasizes sailing and powerboats, destination features and lifestyle. Readers are mostly male, highly educated, high income, well read. Sample copy free upon request.

NEEDS Occasionally buys photos from freelancers; approx. 10 photos/year. Needs photos of all sailing/boating-related (keelboats, dinghies, racing, cruising, etc.). Model/property release preferred. Photo captions preferred.

MAKING CONTACT & TERMS Submit portfolio electronically for review with photo list. Responds in 1 month. Simultaneous submissions and previously published work OK. Pays 60 days after publication. Buys one-time rights.

❹ ⑤⑤ ❶ CANOE & KAYAK

GrindMedia, LLC, 236 Avenida Fabricante, Suite 201, San Clemente CA 92672. (425)827-6363. **E-mail:** aaron@canoekayak.com. **Website:** www.canoekayak.com. **Contact:** Aaron Schmidt. Estab. 1972. Circ. 70,000. Published 6 times a year, in March, May, June, July, August, December. Packed with destination reviews and features a different region of North America, paddling techniques, photography from seasoned canoeists and expert reviews of paddle and camping gear. It is the world's largest paddle sports publication. Emphasizes a variety of paddle sports, as well as how-to material and articles about equipment. For upscale canoe and kayak enthusiasts at all levels of ability. Also publishes special projects. Sample copy free with 9×12 SASE.

NEEDS Buys 25 photos from freelancers/issue; 150 photos/year. Photos of canoeing, kayaking, ocean touring, canoe sailing, fishing when compatible to the main activity, canoe camping but not rafting. No photos showing disregard for the environment, be it river or land; no photos showing gasoline-powered, multi-hp engines; no photos showing unskilled persons taking extraordinary risks to life, etc. Accompanying manuscripts for "editorial coverage striving for balanced representation of all interests in today's paddling activity. Those interests include paddling adventures (both close to home and far away), camping, fishing, flatwater, whitewater, ocean kayaking, poling, sailing, outdoor photography, how-to projects, instruction and historical perspective. Regular columns feature paddling techniques, conservation topics, safety, interviews, equipment reviews, book/movie reviews, new products and letters from readers." Photos only occasionally purchased without accompanying manuscript. Model release preferred "when potential for litigation." Property release required. Photo captions preferred.

SPECS Uses 5×7, 8×10 glossy b&w prints; 35mm, 2¼×2¼, 4×5 transparencies; color transparencies for cover; vertical format preferred. Accepts images in digital format. Send via CD, ZIP as TIFF, EPS, JPEG files at 300 dpi.

MAKING CONTACT & TERMS Include SASE for return of material. Responds in 1 month. Simultaneous submissions and previously published work OK, in noncompeting publications. Pays $500-700 for color cover; $75-200 for b&w inside; $75-350 for color inside. Captions, identification of subjects, model releases required. Pays on publication. Credit line given. Buys one-time rights, first serial rights and exclusive rights.

TIPS "We have a highly specialized subject, and readers don't want just any photo of the activity. We're particularly interested in photos showing paddlers' *faces*; the faces of people having a good time. We're after anything that highlights the paddling activity as a lifestyle and the urge to be outdoors." All photos should be "as natural as possible with authentic subjects. We receive a lot of submissions from photographers to whom canoeing and kayaking are quite novel activities. These photos are often clichéd and uninteresting. So consider the quality of your work carefully before submission if you are not familiar with the sport. We are always in search of fresh ways of looking at our sport. All paddlers must be wearing life vests/PFDs."

CAPE COD LIFE

13 Steeple St., Suite 204, P.O. Box 1439, Mashpee MA 02649. (508)419-7381. **Fax:** (508)477-1225. **Website:** www.capecodlife.com. **Contact:** Amanda McCole, art director; Patty Dysart, art director. Circ. 45,000. Emphasizes Cape Cod lifestyle. Also publishes *Cape Cod & Islands Home*. Readers are 55% female, 45% male, upper income, second home, vacation homeowners.

Sample copy available for $4.95, photo guidelines free, send SASE. Buys 30 photos from freelancers/issue; 180 photos/year.

NEEDS Needs "photos of Cape and island scenes, South shore, and South coast of MA, people, places, general interest of this area." Subjects include boating, beaches, celebrities, families, environmental, landscapes/scenics, wildlife, architecture, gardening, interiors/decorating, rural, adventure, events, travel. Interested in fine art, historical/vintage, seasonal. Reviews photos with or without a manuscript. Model release required; property release preferred. Photo captions required, include location.

SPECS Uses 35mm, 2¼×2¼, 4×5 transparencies. Accepts images in digital format. Send via e-mail or FTP as TIFF files at 300 dpi.

MAKING CONTACT & TERMS "Photographers should not drop by unannounced. We prefer photographers to mail portfolio, then follow up with a phone call 1-2 weeks later." Send unsolicited photos by mail for consideration. Keeps samples on file. Simultaneous submissions and previously published work OK. Pays $225 for color cover; $25-175 for b&w or color inside, depending on size. Pays 30 days after publication. Credit line given. Buys one-time rights, reprint rights for *Cape Cod Life* reprints, negotiable.

TIPS Write for photo guidelines. Photographers who do not have images of Cape Cod, Martha's Vineyard, Nantucket or the Elizabeth Islands should not submit. Looks for "clear, somewhat graphic slides. Show us scenes we've seen hundreds with a different twist and elements of surprise. Photographers should have a familiarity with the magazine and the region first. Prior to submitting, photographers should send a SASE to receive our guidelines. They can then submit works (via mail) and follow up with a brief phone call. We love to see images by professional-calibre photographers who are new to us, and prefer it if the photographer can leave images with us at least 2 months if possible."

✪ ⊖⊖ THE CAPILANO REVIEW

2055 Purcell Way, North Vancouver British Columbia V7J 3H5, Canada. (604)984-1712. **E-mail:** tcr@capilanou.ca. **Website:** www.thecapilanoreview.ca. **Contact:** Todd Nickel, managing editor. Estab. 1972. Circ. 800. Publishes an 8- to 16-page visual section by 1 or 2 artists/issue. "Read the magazine before submitting. *TCR* is an avant garde literary and visual arts publication that wants innovative work. We've previously published photography by Barrie Jones, Roy Kiyooka, Robert Keziere, Laiwan, and Colin Browne."

NEEDS Work that is new in concept and in execution.

MAKING CONTACT & TERMS Send an artist statement and list of exhibitions. Submit a group of photos with SASE (with Canadian postage or IRCs). "We do *not* accept submissions via e-mail or on disc."

CAPPER'S FARMER/GRIT

Ogden Publications, Inc., 1503 SW 42nd St., Topeka KS 66609-1265. (800)678-5779. **E-mail:** editor@cappersfarmer.com; editor@grit.com. **Website:** www.cappersfarmer.com; www.grit.com. **Contact:** Caleb Regan, managing editor. Estab. 1879. Circ. 250,000. Bimonthly. Emphasizes small-town life, country lifestyle, or small-scale farm-oriented material. Readership is national. Sample copy available for $6.

NEEDS Buys 24+ photos/year with accompanying stories and articles; 50% from freelancers. Needs, on a regular basis, photos of small-farm livestock, animals, farm labor, gardening, produce, and related images. "Be certain pictures are well composed, properly exposed, and pin sharp. Must be *shot* at high-res (no less than 300 dpi). No pictures that cannot be shown to any member of the family. No pictures that are out of focus or over- or under-exposed. No ribbon-cutting, check-passing, or hand-shaking pictures. Story subjects include all aspects of the smalll-scale or country lifestyle farm, such as livestock, farm dogs, barn cats, sowing and hoeing, small tractors, fences, etc." Photo captions required. "Any image that stands alone must be accompanied by 50-100 words of meaningful caption information."

SPECS Uses high-res digital images.

$ CAREERFOCUS

7300 W. 110th St., 7th Floor, Overland Park KS 66210. (913)317-2888. **Fax:** (913)317-1505. **E-mail:** michelle.webb@cpgcommunications.com. **Website:** www.cpgpublications.com/focus.php. **Contact:** N. Michelle Paige, executive editor. Estab. 1988. Circ. 250,000. Bimonthly. Emphasizes career development. Readers are male and female African-American and Hispanic professionals, ages 21-45. Sample copy free with 9×12 SASE and 4 first-class stamps. Photo guidelines available online.

NEEDS Uses approximately 40 photos/issue. Needs technology photos and shots of personalities; career people in computer, science, teaching, finance, engineering, law, law enforcement, government, high-tech, leisure. Model release preferred. Photo captions required; include name, date, place, why.

MAKING CONTACT & TERMS Send query letter via e-mail with résumé of credits and list of stock photo subjects. Keeps samples on file. Simultaneous submissions and previously published work OK. Responds in 1 month. Pays $10-50 for color photos; $5-25 for b&w photos. Pays on publication. Credit line given. Buys one-time rights.

TIPS "Freelancer must be familiar with our magazine to be able to submit appropriate manuscripts and photos."

$$ CARIBBEAN TRAVEL & LIFE

460 N. Orlando Ave., Suite 200, Winter Park FL 32789. (407)571-4704; (407)628-4802. **E-mail:** editor@caribbeantravelmag.com. **Website:** www.caribbeantravelmag.com. Estab. 1985. Circ. 150,000. Published 9 times/year. Emphasizes travel, culture and recreation in islands of Caribbean, Bahamas and Bermuda. Readers are male and female, frequent Caribbean travelers, ages 32-52. Sample copy available for $4.95. Photo guidelines free with SASE.

NEEDS Uses about 100 photos/issue; 90% supplied by freelance photographers: 10% assignment and 90% freelance stock. "We combine scenics with people shots. Where applicable, we show interiors, food shots, resorts, water sports, cultural events, shopping and wildlife/underwater shots. We want images that show intimacy between people and place. Provide thorough caption information. Don't submit stock that is mediocre."

SPECS Uses 4-color photography.

MAKING CONTACT & TERMS Query by mail or e-mail with list of stock photo subjects and tearsheets. Responds in 3 weeks. Pays after publication. Buys one-time rights. Does not pay shipping, research or holding fees.

TIPS Seeing trend toward "fewer but larger photos with more impact and drama. We are looking for particularly strong images of color and style, beautiful island scenics and people shots—images that are powerful enough to make the reader want to travel to the region; photos that show people doing things in the destinations we cover; originality in approach, composition, subject matter. Good composition, lighting and creative flair. Images that are evocative of a place, creating story mood. Good use of people.

Submit stock photography for specific story needs; if good enough can lead to possible assignments. Let us know exactly what coverage you have on a stock list so we can contact you when certain photo needs arise."

CARLSBAD MAGAZINE

Wheelhouse Media, P.O. Box 2089, Carlsbad CA 92018. (760)729-9099. **Fax:** (760)729-9011. **E-mail:** tim@wheelhousemedia.com. **Website:** www.click oncarlsbad.com. **Contact:** Tim Wrisley. Estab. 2004. Circ. 35,000. Photos of gardening, entertainment, events, performing arts. Interested in historical/vintage, lifestyle. "People, places, events, arts in Carlsbad, CA."

CARUS PUBLISHING COMPANY

30 Grove St., Suite C, Peterborough NH 03458. **Website:** www.cricketmag.com. Publishes *Babybug, Cicada, Click, Cricket, Ladybug, Muse, Spider,* and *ASK.* Carus Publishing owns Cobblestone Publishing, publisher of *AppleSeeds, Calliope, Cobblestone, Dig, Faces,* and *Odyssey.*

CHA

E-mail: editors@asiancha.com; j@asiancha.com; submissions@asiancha.com. **Website:** www.asiancha.com. **Contact:** Tammy Ho Lai-Ming, founding co-editor; Jeff Zroback, founding co-editor; Eddie Tay, reviews editor. Estab. 2007. "*Cha* is the first Hong Kong-based English online literary journal. It is dedicated to publishing quality poetry, fiction, creative non-fiction, reviews, photography and art. *Cha* has a strong focus on Asian-themed creative work and work done by Asian writers and artists. It also publishes established and emerging writers/artists from around the world. *Cha* is an affiliated organization of the Asia-Pacific Writing Partnership and is catalogued in the School of Oriental and African Studies (SOAS) Library, among other universities."

SPECS Submit all visual work in JPEG format.

MAKING CONTACT & TERMS Submit 1-5 pieces. Include a brief biography (no more than 100 words). "Simultaneous submissions are accepted, but notify us as soon as possible if your work is accepted for publication elsewhere."

CHARISMA

600 Rinehart Rd., Lake Mary FL 32746. (407)333-0600. **Fax:** (407)333-7100. **E-mail:** charisma@charismamedia.com; sean.roberts@charismamedia.com. **Website:** www.charismamedia.com. **Contact:**

Joe Deleon, magazine design director. Circ. 200,000. Monthly magazine. Emphasizes Christian life. General readership. Sample copy available for $2.50.

NEEDS Buys 3-4 photos from freelancers/issue; 36-48 photos/year. Needs editorial photos—appropriate for each article. Model release required. Photo captions preferred.

SPECS Accepts images in digital format. Send via CD as TIFF, JPEG, EPS files at 300 dpi. Low-res images accepted for sample submissions.

MAKING CONTACT & TERMS Send unsolicited photos by mail for consideration. Provide brochure, flyer or tearsheets to be kept on file for possible future assignments. Simultaneous submissions and previously published work OK. Cannot return material. Responds ASAP. Pays $650 for color cover; $150 for b&w inside; $50-150/hour or $400-750/day. Pays on publication. Credit line given. Buys all rights; negotiable.

TIPS In portfolio or samples, looking for "good color and composition with great technical ability."

CHEMICAL HERITAGE

Chemical Heritage Foundation (CHF), 315 Chestnut St., Philadelphia PA 19106. (215)925-2222. **E-mail:** editor@chemheritage.org. **Website:** www.chemheritage.org. Estab. 1982. Circ. 17,000. *Chemical Heritage* reports on the history of the chemical and molecular sciences and industries, on Chemical Heritage Foundation activities, and on other activities of interest to our readers.

MAKING CONTACT & TERMS Captions required. Buys one-time print and online rights.

CHESAPEAKE BAY MAGAZINE

1819 Bay Ridge Ave., Annapolis MD 21403. (410)263-2662, ext. 32. **Fax:** (410)267-6924. **E-mail:** editor@chesapeakeboating.net. **Website:** www.chesapeakeboating.net. **Contact:** Ann Levelle, managing editor; T.F. Sayles, editor. Estab. 1972. Circ. 46,000. "Interested in reviewing work from newer, lesser-known photographers."

Chesapeake Bay is CD-equipped and does corrections and manipulates photos in-house.

NEEDS Buys 27 photos from freelancers/issue; 324 photos/year. Needs photos that are Chesapeake Bay-related (must); "vertical powerboat shots are badly needed (color)." Special needs include "vertical 4-color slides showing boats and people on Bay."

SPECS Uses 35mm, 2¼×2¼, 4×5, 8×10 transparencies. Accepts images in digital format. Send via CD as TIFF files at 300 dpi, at least 8×10 (16×10 for spreads). "A proof sheet would be helpful."

MAKING CONTACT & TERMS Send query letter with samples or list of stock photo subjects. Responds only if interested. Simultaneous submissions OK.

TIPS "We prefer Kodachrome over Ektachrome. Looking for boating, bay and water-oriented subject matter. Qualities and abilities include fresh ideas, clarity, exciting angles and true color. We're using larger photos—more double-page spreads. Photos should be able to hold up to that degree of enlargement. When photographing boats on the Bay, keep safety in mind. People hanging off the boat, drinking, women 'perched' on the bow are a no-no! Children must be wearing life jackets on moving boats. We must have IDs for *all* people in close-up to medium-view images."

CHESS LIFE

P.O. Box 3967, Crossville TN 38557. (931)787-1234. **Fax:** (931)787-1200. **E-mail:** dlucas@uschess.org; fbutler@uschess.org. **Website:** www.uschess.org. **Contact:** Daniel Lucas, editor; Francesca "Frankie" Butler, art director. Estab. 1939. Circ. 85,000. Monthly publication of the US Chess Federation. Emphasizes news of all major national and international tournaments; includes historical articles, personality profiles, columns of instruction, occasional fiction, humor for the devoted fan of chess. Sample copy and photo guidelines via PDF.

NEEDS News photos from events around the country; shots for personality profiles.

SPECS Accepts prints or high-res digital images (digital preferred). Send digital images as JPEG or TIFF files at 300 dpi; e-mail for single-shot submission. Contact art director for further details on submission options and specifications.

MAKING CONTACT & TERMS Query with samples via e-mail (preferred). Responds in 1 month, "depending on when the deadline crunch occurs." Simultaneous submissions and previously published work OK.

TIPS Using "more color, and more illustrative photography. The photographer's name, address and date of the shoot should appear on the back of all photos. Also, name of persons in photograph and event should be identified." Looks for "clear images, good composition and contrast with a fresh approach to interest the viewer. Typical 'player sitting at chessboard' photos are not what we want. Increasing emphasis on strong portraits of chess personalities, especially Americans. Tournament photographs of winning players and key games are in high demand."

CHESS LIFE FOR KIDS

P.O. Box 3967, Crossville TN 38557. (732)252-8388; (931)787-1234. **E-mail:** gpetersen@uschess.org. **Website:** www.uschess.org. **Contact:** Glenn Petersen, editor. Estab. 2006. Circ. 9,000 print; 17,000 online. Bimonthly association magazine geared for the young reader, age 12 and under, interested in chess; fellow chess players; tournament results; and instruction. Sample copy available with SASE and first-class postage. Photo guidelines available via e-mail.

NEEDS Photos of babies/children/teens, celebrities, multicultural, families, senior citizens, events, humor. Some aspect of chess must be present: playing, watching, young/old contrast. Reviews photos with or without a manuscript. Property release is required. Captions required.

SPECS Accepts images in digital format. Send via ZIP or e-mail. Contact Frankie Butler at catseyephotography@mac.com for more information on digital specs. Uses glossy color prints.

MAKING CONTACT & TERMS E-mail query letter with link to photographer's website. Provide self-promotion piece to be kept on file. Responds in 1 week to queries and portfolios. Simultaneous submissions and previously published work OK. Pays $150 minimum/$300 maximum for color cover. Pays $35 for color inside. Pays on publication. Credit line given. Rights are negotiable. Will negotiate with a photographer unwilling to sell all rights.

TIPS "Read the magazine. What would appeal to *your* 10-year-old? Be original. We have plenty of people to shoot headshots and award ceremonies. And remember, you're competing against proud parents as well."

CHICKADEE

10 Lower Spadina Ave., Suite 400, Toronto Ontario M5V 2Z2, Canada. (416)340-2700, ext. 318. **Fax:** (416)340-9769. **E-mail:** owl@owlkids.com. **Website:** www.owlkids.com. **Contact:** Tracey Jacklin. Estab. 1979. Circ. 79,800. Published 10 times/year. A discovery magazine for children ages 6-9. Sample copy available for $4.95 with 9×12 SASE and $1.50 money order to cover postage. Photo guidelines available with SASE or via e-mail.

💬 *chickaDEE* has received Magazine of the Year, Parents' Choice, Silver Honor, Canadian Children's Book Centre Choice and several Distinguished Achievement awards from the Association of Educational Publishers.

NEEDS Photo stories, photo puzzles, children ages 6-10, multicultural, environmental, wildlife, pets, adventure, events, hobbies, humor, performing arts, sports, travel, science, technology, animals in their natural habitats. Interested in documentary, seasonal. Model/property release required. Photo captions required.

SPECS Prefers images in digital format. E-mail as JPEG files at 72 dpi; 300 dpi required for publication.

MAKING CONTACT & TERMS Previously published work OK. Credit line given. Buys one-time rights.

🍁 ◐ CHIRP

10 Lower Spadina Ave., Suite 400, Toronto Ontario M5V 2Z2, Canada. (416)340-2700, ext. 318. **Fax:** (416)340-9769. **E-mail:** owl@owlkids.com. **Website:** www.owlkids.com. **Contact:** Tracey Jacklin. Estab. 1997. Circ. 64,700. Published 10 times/year. A discovery magazine for children ages 3-6. Sample copy available for $4.95 with 9×12 SASE and $1.50 money order to cover postage. Photo guidelines available with SASE or via e-mail.

💬 *Chirp* has received Best New Magazine of the Year, Parents' Choice, Canadian Children's Book Centre Choice and Distinguished Achievement awards from the Association of Educational Publishers.

NEEDS Photo stories, photo puzzles, children ages 5-7, multicultural, environmental, wildlife, adventure, events, hobbies, humor, animals in their natural habitats. Interested in documentary, seasonal. Model/property release required. Photo captions required.

SPECS Prefers images in digital format. E-mail as TIFF, JPEG files at 72 dpi; 300 dpi required for publication.

MAKING CONTACT & TERMS Request photo packages before sending photos for review. Responds in 3 months. Previously published work OK. Credit line given. Buys one-time rights.

$ ◎ ◐ THE CHRONICLE OF THE HORSE

P.O. Box 46, Middleburg VA 20118. (540)687-6341. **Fax:** (540)687-3937. **E-mail:** slieser@chronofhorse.com; bethr@chronofhorse.com (feature stories); results@chronofhorse.com (news stories). **Website:** www.chronofhorse.com. **Contact:** Sara Lieser, managing editor; Beth Rasin, executive editor. Estab. 1937. Circ. 18,000. Weekly. Emphasizes English horse sports. Readers range from young to old. "Average reader is a college-educated female, middle-aged, well-off financially." Sample copy available for $2. Photo guidelines free with SASE or on website. Buys 10-20 photos from freelancers/issue.

NEEDS Photos from competitive events (horse shows, dressage, steeplechase, etc.) to go with news story or to accompany personality profile. "A few stand alone. Must be cute, beautiful or newsworthy. Reproduced in b&w." Prefers purchasing photos with accompanying manuscript.

SPECS Uses b&w and color prints, slides (reproduced b&w). Accepts images in digital format at 300 dpi.

MAKING CONTACT & TERMS "We do not want to see portfolio or samples. Contact us first, preferably by letter; include SASE for reply. Responds in 6 weeks.

TIPS "Know horse sports."

$ ◐ CHRONOGRAM

314 Wall St., Kingston NY 12401. (845)334-8600. **E-mail:** dperry@chronogram.com. **Website:** www.chronogram.com. **Contact:** David Perry, art director. Estab. 1993. Circ. 50,000. Monthly arts and culture magazine with a focus on green living and progressive community building in the Hudson Valley. Tends to hire regional photographers, or photographers who are showing work regionally. Sample copy available for $5. Photo guidelines available on website.

NEEDS Buys 16 photos from regional freelancers/issue; 192 photos/year. Interested in alternative process, avant garde, fashion/glamour, fine art, historical/vintage, artistic representations of anything. "Striking, minimalistic and good! Great covers!" Reviews photos with or without a manuscript. Model/property release preferred. Photo captions required; include title, date, artist, medium.

SPECS Prefers images in digital format. Send via CD as TIFF files at 300 dpi or larger at printed size.

MAKING CONTACT & TERMS E-mail sample work at 72 dpi or mail work with SASE for return. Provide self-promotion piece to be kept on file for possible future assignments. Responds only if interested; send nonreturnable samples. Credit line given. Buys one-time rights; negotiable.

TIPS "Colorful, edgy, great art! See our website—look at the back issues and our covers, and check out back issues and our covers before submitting."

○ CITY LIMITS

Community Service Society of New York, 31 E. 32nd St., 3rd Floor, New York NY 10016. (212)481-8484, ext. 313. **E-mail:** editor@citylimits.org. **Website:** www.citylimits.org. **Contact:** Jarrett Murphy, executive editor and publisher. Estab. 1976. "*City Limits* is an urban policy monthly offering intense journalistic coverage of New York City's low-income and working-class neighborhoods." Sample copy available for 8×11 SAE with $1.50 first-class postage. Photo guidelines available for SASE.

NEEDS Needs assigned portraits, photojournalism, action, ambush regarding stories about people in low-income neighborhoods, government or social service sector, babies/children/teens, families, parents, senior citizens, cities/urban. Interested in documentary. Reviews photos with or without a manuscript. Special photo needs: b&w photo essays about urban issues.

SPECS Uses 5×7 and larger b&w prints. Accepts images in digital format. Send via CD, ZIP, e-mail as TIFF, EPS, JPEG files at 600 dpi. Inside photos are b&w; cover is 4-color.

MAKING CONTACT & TERMS Send query letter with samples, tearsheets, self-promotion cards. Provide résumé, business card, self-promotion piece, or tearsheets to be kept on file for possible future assignments. Art director will contact photographer for portfolio review if interested. Portfolio should include b&w prints and tearsheets. Keeps samples on file; cannot return material. Responds only if interested; send nonreturnable samples. Simultaneous submissions and previously published work OK.

TIPS "We need good photojournalists who can capture the emotion of a scene. We offer huge pay for great photos."

CLEVELAND MAGAZINE

City Magazines, Inc., 1422 Euclid Ave., Suite 730, Cleveland OH 44115. (216)771-2833. **Fax:** (216)781-6318. **E-mail:** gleydura@clevelandmagazine.com; miller@clevelandmagazine.com. **Website:** www.clevelandmagazine.com. **Contact:** Kristen Miller, design director; Steve Gleydura, editor. Estab. 1972. Circ. 50,000. Monthly magazine. Emphasizes Cleveland, Ohio. General interest to upscale audience.

NEEDS Photos of architecture, business concepts, education, entertainment, environmental, events, food/drink, gardening, health/fitness, industry, interiors/decorating, landscapes/scenics, medicine, people (couples, families, local celebrities, multicultural, parents, senior citizens), performing arts, political, product shots/still life, sports, technology, travel, interested in documentary and fashion/glamour.

SPECS Prefers images in digital format.

MAKING CONTACT & TERMS Please provide self-promotions, JPEG samples or tearsheets via e-mail or mail to be kept on file for possible future assignments. We will respond if interested. Send via CD, e-mail as TIFF, JPEG files at 300 dpi. Also uses color and b&w prints.

⊕ CLIMBING

Cruz Bay Publishing, Inc., 2520 55th St., Suite 210, Boulder CO 80302. (303)625-1600. **Fax:** (303)440-3618. **E-mail:** sdavis@climbing.com; contribute@climbing.com. **Website:** www.climbing.com. Estab. 1970. Circ. 51,000. Provides features on rock climbing and mountaineering worldwide.

MAKING CONTACT & TERMS Reviews negatives, 35mm transparencies, prints, digital submissions on CD. Pays $25-800.

CLOUD RODEO

E-mail: editors@cloudrodeo.org; submit@cloudrodeo.org. **Website:** cloudrodeo.org. "We want your problems deploying a term liek nonelen. We want your isolated photographs of immense locomotives slogged down by the delirium of drunken yet pristine jungles. We want the one eye you caught on fire doing alchemy. The world you collapsed playing architect. We want what you think is too. We want you to anesthetize this aesthetic. Your Enfer, your Ciel, your Qu'importe. We want all your to to sound out."

SPECS "If you are sending us art, photography, audio, or any other medium, attach your work as a JPEG, TIFF, PDF, RTF, WPF, GIF, PNG, or MP3/MP4A file. If somehow your work can't be transmitted or best represented by these file types, shoot us an e-mail at submit@cloudrodeo.org, and we'll do our best to accommodate."

MAKING CONTACT & TERMS "Simultaneous submissions are encouraged provided you notify us if your work has found another cloud to call rodeo. Please send these notification e-mails as responses to your original submission. Please provide a little cover letter in the body of your e-mail even if it's just to say hi. We want to be able to say hi back. Please limit your submissions to 1 prose piece, 5 pieces of art, or 5 poems at a time. Should we publish your work, all we ask is for first electronic publishing rights. After that the rights will revert back to you, although your work will be archived on the site where it will be available for you to spam your friends with, which we encourage wholeheartedly."

TIPS "Let's get weird."

○ COAST&KAYAK MAGAZINE

Wild Coast Publishing, P.O. Box 24 Stn. A, Nanaimo British Columbia V9R 5K4, Canada. (360)406-4708; (866)984-6437. **Fax:** (866)654-1937. **E-mail:** editor@coastandkayak.com; kayak@coastandkayak.com. **Website:** www.coastandkayak.com. **Contact:** John Kimantas, editor. Estab. 1991. Circ. 65,000 print and electronic readers. Quarterly. Emphasizes safe, ecologically sensitive paddling. For sample copy, see downloadable PDF version online.

NEEDS Buys 10 photos from freelancers/issue ("usually only from authors"); 60 photos/year. Needs kayaking shots. Photos should have sea kayak in them. Reviews photos with or without a manuscript. Model/property release preferred. Photo captions preferred.

SPECS Prefers digital submissions, but only after query. Send as low-res for assessment.

MAKING CONTACT & TERMS Send query letter first. Provide business card or self-promotion piece to be kept on file for possible future assignments. Responds in 2 months to queries. Absolutely no simultaneous submissions or previously published work accepted. Pays $100-200 for color cover; $25-50 for inside. Pays on publication. Credit line given. Buys one-time print rights including electronic archive rights.

TIPS "Look at free downloadable version online and include kayak in picture wherever possible. Always need vertical shots for cover!"

$$ ◐ COBBLESTONE

Cobblestone Publishing, 30 Grove St., Suite C, Peterborough NH 03458. **Website:** www.cobblestonepub.com. **Contact:** Meg Chorlian. Circ. 15,000. Published 9 times/year, September-May. Emphasizes American history; each issue covers a specific theme. Writers are encouraged to submit available photos with their query or article. Readers are children ages 8-14, parents, teachers. Sample copy available for $6.95 plus $2.00 s&h. Photo guidelines free with SASE. Mail queries to Editorial Dept. "Reporting dates depend on how far ahead of the issue the photographer submits photos. We work on issues 6 months ahead of publication." Simultaneous submissions and previously published work OK. See guidelines on website at: www.cricketmag.com/24-Submission-Guidelines-for-COBBLESTONE-magazine-for-children-ages-9-14.

NEEDS Buys 10-20 photos from freelancers/issue; 90-180 photos/year. Photos of children, multicultural, landscapes/scenics, architecture, cities/urban, agriculture, industry, military. Interested in fine art, historical/vintage, reenacters. "We need photographs related to our specific themes (each issue is theme-related) and urge photographers to request our themes list."

SPECS Uses 8×10 glossy prints; 35mm, 2¼×2¼ transparencies. Accepts images in digital format.

MAKING CONTACT & TERMS Send via CD, SyQuest, ZIP as TIFF files at 300 dpi, saved at 8×10 size. Send query letter with samples or list of stock photo subjects; include SASE for return of material.

TIPS "Most photos are of historical subjects, but contemporary color images of, for example, a Civil War battlefield, are great to balance with historical images. However, the amount varies with each monthly theme. Please review our theme list and submit related images."

$ ◐ COLLECTIBLE AUTOMOBILE

7373 N. Cicero Ave., Lincolnwood IL 60712. (847)676-3470. **Fax:** (847)329-5690. **E-mail:** jbiel@pubint.com. **Contact:** John Biel, editor-in-chief. Estab. 1984. Bimonthly. "*CA* features profiles of collectible automobiles and their designers as well as articles on literature, scale models, and other topics of interest to automotive enthusiasts." Sample copy available for $8 and 10½×14 SASE with $3.50 first-class postage. Photo guidelines available with #10 SASE.

NEEDS "For digital photography, we require our files to have a minimum resolution of A) no less than 25MB in their uncompressed state or B) approximately 3,500-4,000 pixels on the largest side or C) 12-14" on the largest side at 300 dpi. Raw TIFF is best, but lightly compressed JPEGs are acceptable as well. For film shoots, 2-3 rolls of 35mm, 2-3 rolls of 2¼×2¼, and 4-8 4×5 exposures. Complete exterior views, interior and engine views, and close-up detail shots of the subject vehicle are required."

SPECS Uses 35mm, 2¼×2¼, 4×5 transparencies.

MAKING CONTACT & TERMS Send query letter with transparencies and stock list. Provide business card to be kept on file for possible future assignments. Responds only if interested; send nonreturnable samples. Previously published work OK. Pays bonus if image is used as cover photo; $300-350 plus costs for standard auto shoot. **Pays on acceptance.** Photography is credited on an article-by-article basis in an "Acknowledgments" section at the front of the magazine. Buys all intellectual and digital property rights.
TIPS "Read our magazine for good examples of the types of backgrounds, shot angles and overall quality that we are looking for."

$ COLLEGE PREVIEW

7300 W. 110th St., 7th Floor, Overland Park KS 66210. (913)317-2888. **E-mail:** michelle.webb@cpgcommunications.com; nmpaige@collegepreviewmagazine.com; editorial@collegepreviewmagazine.com. **Website:** www.collegepreviewmagazine.com. **Contact:** Michelle Paige, executive editor. Circ. 600,000. Quarterly. Emphasizes college and college-bound African-American and Hispanic students. Readers are African American, Hispanic, ages 16-24. Sample copy free with 9×12 SASE and 4 first-class stamps.
NEEDS Uses 30 photos/issue. Needs photos of students in class, at work, in interesting careers, on campus. Special photo needs include computers, military, law and law enforcement, business, aerospace and aviation, health care. Model/property release required. Photo captions required; include name, age, location, subject.
MAKING CONTACT & TERMS Send query letter with résumé of credits. Simultaneous submissions and previously published work OK. Pays $10-50 for color photos; $5-25 for b&w inside. Pays on publication. Buys first North American serial rights.

COMMUNITY OBSERVER

Ann Arbor Observer Co., 2390 Winewood, Ann Arbor MI 48103. (734)769-3175. **Fax:** (734)769-3375. **E-mail:** editor@arborweb.com. **Website:** www.washtenawguide.com. John Hilton, editor. Circ. 20,000. Quarterly. "*Community Observer* serves 3 historic communities facing rapid change. We provide an intelligent, informed perspective on the most important news and events in the communities we cover." Sample copy available for $2.
SPECS Uses contact sheets, negatives, transparencies, prints. Accepts images in digital format; GIF or JPEG files.
MAKING CONTACT & TERMS Negotiates payment individually. Pays on publication. Buys one-time rights.

CONDE NAST TRAVELER

4 Times Square, 14th Floor, New York NY 10036. (212)286-2860. **Fax:** (212)286-2258. **E-mail:** web@condenasttraveler.com; letters@condenasttraveler.com. **Website:** www.cntraveler.com. **Contact:** Laura Garvey and Maeve Nicholson, editorial assistants; Greg Ferro, managing editor. Estab. 1987. Circ. 800,000. Provides the experienced traveler with an array of diverse travel experiences encompassing art, architecture, fashion, culture, cuisine and shopping. This magazine has very specific needs and contacts a stock agency when seeking photos.

$ ◐ ○ CONSCIENCE

Catholics for Choice, 1436 U St. W, Suite 301, Washington DC 20009. (202)986-6093. **E-mail:** conscience@catholicsforchoice.org. **Website:** www.catholicsforchoice.org. **Contact:** Jon O'Brien, executive editor. Estab. 1980. Circ. 12,000. Quarterly news journal of Catholic opinion. "Conscience offers in-depth coverage of a range of topics, including contemporary politics, Catholicism, women's rights in society and in religions, US politics, reproductive rights, sexuality and gender, ethics and bioethics, feminist theology, social justice, church and state issues, and the role of religion in formulating public policy."
NEEDS Photos of multicultural, religious, Catholic-related news.
SPECS Uses glossy color and b&w prints. Accepts high-res digital images. Send as TIFF, JPEG files.
MAKING CONTACT & TERMS Send query letter with tearsheets. Responds only if interested; send nonreturnable samples. Simultaneous submissions and previously published work OK. Model/property release preferred. Photo captions preferred; include title, subject, photographer's name. Pays $300 maximum for color cover; $50 maximum for b&w inside. Pays on publication. Credit line given.

CONTEMPORARY BRIDE

North East Publishing, Inc., 150 South Maple Ave., #318, South Plainfield NJ 07080. (908)756-0123; (908)756-0030. **E-mail:** valerie@contemporarybride.com; gary@contemporarybride.com. **Website:** www.

contemporarybride.com. **Contact:** Gary Paris, publisher. Estab. 1994. Circ. 120,000. Biannual bridal magazine; 4-color publication with feature editorials, real weddings, latest fashion, honeymoon hot spots and style inspiration. Sample copy available for first-class postage.

NEEDS Reviews photos with accompanying manuscript only. Model/property release preferred. Photo captions preferred; include photo credits.

SPECS Accepts images in digital format. Send as high-res files at 300 dpi.

MAKING CONTACT & TERMS Send query letter with samples. Art director will contact photographer for portfolio review if interested. Keeps samples on file; cannot return material. Responds only if interested; send nonreturnable samples. Simultaneous submissions and previously published work OK. Payment negotiable. Buys all rights, electronic rights.

TIPS "Digital images preferred with a creative eye for all wedding-related photos. Give us the *best* presentation."

⑤ ❹ ○ CONTINENTAL NEWSTIME

Continental Features/Continental News Service, 501 W. Broadway, Plaza A, PMB #265, San Diego CA 92101-3802. (858)492-8696. **E-mail:** continental newsservice@yahoo.com. **Website:** www.continental newsservice.com. **Contact:** Gary P. Salamone, editor-in-chief. Estab. 1987.

NEEDS Buys variable number of photos from freelancers. Photos of public figures, US and foreign government officials/cabinet ministers, breaking/unreported/under-reported news. Reviews photos with or without a manuscript. Model/property release required. Photo captions required.

SPECS Uses 8×10 color and b&w prints.

MAKING CONTACT & TERMS Send query letter with résumé, photocopies, tearsheets, stock list. Provide résumé to be kept on file for possible future assignments. Responds only if interested in absence of SASE being received; send nonreturnable samples. Simultaneous submissions OK. Pays $10 minimum for b&w cover. Pays on publication. Credit line given. Buys one-time rights.

TIPS "Read our magazine to develop a better feel for our photo applications/uses and to satisfy our stated photo needs."

CONVERGENCE: AN ONLINE JOURNAL OF POETRY AND ART

E-mail: clinville@csus.edu. **Website:** www.conver gence-journal.com. **Contact:** Cynthia Linville, managing editor. Estab. 2003.

NEEDS Ethnic/multicultural, experimental, feminist, gay/lesbian.

MAKING CONTACT & TERMS Send up to 6 JPEGs no larger than 4MB each to clinville@csus.edu with "Convergence" in the subject line. Include full name, preferred e-mail address, and a 75-word bio (bios may be edited for length and clarity). A cover letter is not needed. Absolutely no simultaneous or previously published submissions. Acquires electronic rights.

TIPS "Work from a series or with a common theme has a greater chance of being accepted. Seasonally-themed work is appreciated (spring and summer for the January deadline, fall and winter for the June deadline)."

COONHOUND BLOODLINES

United Kennel Club, Inc., 100 E. Kilgore Rd., Kalamazoo MI 49002-5584. (269)343-9020. **Fax:** (269)343-7037. **E-mail:** vrand@ukcdogs.com. **Website:** www.ukcdogs.com. **Contact:** Vicki Rand, editor. Estab. 1925. Circ. 10,000.

MAKING CONTACT & TERMS Reviews contact sheets. Captions, identification of subjects required. Negotiates payment individually.

COSMOPOLITAN

Hearst Corp., 300 W. 57th St., New York NY 10019-3791. (212)649-2000. **E-mail:** cosmo@hearst.com; youtellcosmo@hearst.com. **Website:** www.cosmopolitan.com. Estab. 1886. Circ. 3 million. *Cosmopolitan* targets young women for whom beauty, fashion, fitness, career, relationships and personal growth are top priorities. It includes articles and columns on nutrition and food, travel, personal finance, home/lifestyle and celebrities. Query before submitting.

COUNTRY WOMAN

Reiman Publications, 5400 S. 60th St., Greendale WI 53129. (414)423-0100. **E-mail:** editors@coun trywomanmagazine.com. **Website:** www.country womanmagazine.com. **Contact:** Lori Lau Grzybowski, editor. Estab. 1970. Bimonthly. Supported entirely by subscriptions and accepts no outside advertising. Emphasizes rural life and a special quality of living to which country women can relate; at work or play, in sharing problems, etc. Sample copy available for $2. Photo guidelines free with SASE.

NEEDS Uses 75-100 photos/issue; most supplied by readers, rather than freelance photographers. "Covers are usually supplied by professional photographers; they are often seasonal in nature and generally feature a good-looking country woman (mid-range to close up, shown within her business setting or with a hobby, craft or others; static pose or active)." Photos purchased with or without accompanying manuscript. Also interested in unique or well-designed country homes and interiors. Some work assigned for interiors. Works 6 months in advance. "No poor-quality color prints, posed photos, etc." Photo captions required.

SPECS Prefers color transparencies, all sizes. Accepts images in digital format. Send via lightboxes, CD/DVD with printed thumbnails and caption sheet, or e-mail if first review selection is small (12 or less).

MAKING CONTACT & TERMS Send material by mail for consideration; include SASE. Provide brochure, calling card, letter of inquiry, price list, résumé and samples to be kept on file for possible future assignments. Responds in 3 months. Previously published work OK. "If the material you are submitting has been published previously, we ask that you please let us know. We accept color prints, slides or high-res digital photos. Digital images should be about 4×6 at a minimum resolution of 300 dpi and sent as JPEGs on a CD or via e-mail. We cannot use photos that are printed on an ink-jet printer. After you share a story and photos, please be patient. We receive a lot of mail, and it takes our small staff a while to catch up. We may hold your material for consideration in a future issue without informing you first, but we will let you know if we publish it. If we publish your material, we will send you a complimentary copy of the issue and any payment mentioned in the original solicitation upon publication, or at our normal contributor's rates." Pays $300-800 for text/photo package depending on quality of photos and number used; $300 minimum for front cover; $200 minimum for back cover; $100-300 for partial page inside, depending on size. No b&w photos used. **Pays on acceptance.** Buys one-time rights.

TIPS Prefers to see "rural scenics, in various seasons; include a variety of country women—from traditional farm and ranch women to the new baby-boomer, rural retiree; slides appropriately simple for use with poems or as accents to inspirational, reflective essays, etc."

CRUISING WORLD

The Sailing Co., 55 Hammarlund Way, Middletown RI 02842. (401)845-5100. **Fax:** (401)845-5180. **E-mail:** cw.manuscripts@gmail.com; elaine.lembo@cruisingworld.com. **Website:** www.cruisingworld.com. **Contact:** Elaine Lembo, deputy editor. Estab. 1974. Circ. 91,244. Emphasizes sailboat maintenance, sailing instruction and personal experience. For people interested in cruising under sail. Sample copy free with 9×12 SASE.

NEEDS Buys 25 photos/year. Needs "shots of cruising sailboats and their crews anywhere in the world. Shots of ideal cruising scenes. No identifiable racing shots, please." Also wants exotic images of cruising sailboats, people enjoying sailing, tropical images, different perspectives of sailing, good composition, bright colors. For covers, photos "must be of a cruising sailboat with strong human interest, and can be located anywhere in the world." Prefers vertical format. Allow space at top of photo for insertion of logo. Model release preferred; property release required. Photo captions required; include location, body of water, make and model of boat. See guidelines at www.cruisingworld.com/cruising-world-guidelines-for-writers-and-photographers.

SPECS Prefers images in digital format via CD.

MAKING CONTACT & TERMS "We look for good color balance, very sharp focus, the ability to capture sailing, good composition and action. Always looking for *cover shots*." Responds in 2 months. Pays $600 for color cover; $50-300 for color inside. Pays on publication. Credit line given. Buys all rights, but may reassign to photographer after publication; first North American serial rights; or one-time rights.

CYCLE CALIFORNIA! MAGAZINE

1702-L Meridian Ave. #289, San Jose CA 95125. (408)924-0270. **Fax:** (408)292-3005. **E-mail:** tcorral@cyclecalifornia.com; BMack@cyclecalifornia.com. **Website:** www.cyclecalifornia.com. **Contact:** Tracy L. Corral; Bob Mack, publisher. Estab. 1995. Circ. 32,000 print; 88,000 digital. Monthly magazine. Provides readers with a comprehensive source of bicycling information, emphasizing the bicycling life in northern California and northern Nevada; promotes bicycling in all its facets. "While we do not exclude writers from other parts of the country, articles should reflect a

Californian slant." Sample copy available with 9×12 SASE and $1.39 first-class postage. Photo guidelines available with SASE.

NEEDS Buys 3-5 photos from freelancers/issue; 45 photos/year. Needs photos of recreational bicycling, bicycle racing, triathlons, bicycle touring and adventure racing. Cover photos must be vertical format, color. All cyclists must be wearing a helmet if riding. Reviews photos with or without ms. Model release required; property release preferred. Photo captions preferred; include when and where photo is taken; if an event, include name, date and location of event; for nonevent photos, location is important.

SPECS High-res TIFF images preferred (2000×3000 pixel minimum). Cover photos are 7×9.

MAKING CONTACT & TERMS Send query letter with CD/disc or e-mail. Keeps usable images on file; include SASE for return of material. Responds in 3 weeks. Simultaneous submissions OK. Pays $125 for color cover; $50 for inside. Pays on publication.

TIPS "We are looking for photographic images that depict the fun of bicycle riding. Your submissions should show people enjoying the sport. Read the magazine to get a feel for what we do. Label images so we can tell what description goes with which image."

CYCLE WORLD

15255 Alton Pkwy., Irvine CA 92618. (760)707-0100. **E-mail:** hotshots@cycleworld.com. **Website:** www.cycleworld.com. **Contact:** Mark Hoyer, editor-in-chief. Circ. 300,000. Monthly magazine. Readers are active motorcyclists who are "affluent, educated and very perceptive."

NEEDS Buys 10 photos/issue. Wants "outstanding" photos relating to motorcycling. Prefers to buy photos with manuscripts. For "Slipstream" column, see instructions in a recent issue.

SPECS Prefers high-res digital images at 300 dpi or quality 35mm color transparencies.

MAKING CONTACT & TERMS Send photos for consideration; include SASE for return of material. Responds in 6 weeks. "Cover shots are generally done by the staff or on assignment." Pays on publication. Buys first publication rights.

TIPS "Editorial contributions are welcomed, but must be guaranteed exclusive to *Cycle World*. We are not responsible for the return of unsolicited material unless accompanied by SASE."

DANCE

E-mail: shannonaswriter@yahoo.com. **Contact:** Shannon Bridget Murphy. Quarterly. Features international dancers.

NEEDS Performing arts, product shots/still life as related to international dance for children and teens. Interested in alternative process, avant garde, documentary, fashion/glamour, fine art, historical/vintage, seasonal. Reviews photos with or without a manuscript. Model/property release preferred.

SPECS Uses glossy or matte color and b&w prints.

MAKING CONTACT & TERMS Send query letter via e-mail. Provide résumé, business card, self-promotion piece to be kept on file for possible future assignments. "Photographs sent along with CDs are requested but not required. Write to request guidelines for artwork and illustrations." Responds within 1 month to queries; 1 week to portfolios. Simultaneous submissions and previously published work OK. **Pays on acceptance.** Credit line given. Buys one-time rights, first rights; negotiable.

DEER & DEER HUNTING

F+W, a Content + eCommerce Company, 700 E. State St., Iola WI 54990. (715)445-2214. **E-mail:** Outdoors fw@gmail.com. **Website:** www.deeranddeerhunting.com. **Contact:** Dan Schmidt, editor-in-chief. Estab. 1977. Circ. 200,000. Published 10 times/year. Emphasizes white-tailed deer and deer hunting. Readers are "a cross-section of American deer hunters—bow, gun, camera." Sample copy and photo guidelines free with 9×12 SASE with 7 first-class stamps. Photo guidelines also available on website.

NEEDS Buys 20 photos from freelancers/issue; 180 photos/year. Photos of deer in natural settings. Model release preferred. Photo captions preferred.

SPECS Accepts images in digital format. Send contact sheet.

MAKING CONTACT & TERMS Send query letter with résumé of credits and samples. "If we judge your photos as being usable, we like to hold them in our file. Send originals—include SASE if you want them returned." Responds in 2-4 weeks. Pays $800 for color cover; $75-250 for color inside; $50 for b&w inside. Pays net 30 days of publication. Credit line given. Buys one-time rights.

TIPS Prefers to see "adequate selection of 35mm color transparencies; action shots of whitetail deer only, as opposed to portraits. We also need photos of deer hunters in action. We are currently using almost all color—very little b&w. Submit a limited number of quality photos rather than a multitude of marginal photos. Include your name on all entries. Cover shots must have room for masthead."

🌑 ❸ 🌓 DIGITAL PHOTO

Bauer Consumer Media, Media House, Lynch Wood, Peterborough PE2 6EA, United Kingdom. 44 1733 468 000. **E-mail:** dp@bauerconsumer.co.uk. **Website:** www.photoanswers.co.uk. Estab. 1997. Circ. 35,281. Monthly magazine. "UK's best-selling photography and imaging magazine."

NEEDS Stunning, digitally manipulated images of any subject and Photoshop or Elements step-by-step tutorials of any subject. Reviews photos with or without a manuscript. Model/property release preferred. Photo captions preferred.

SPECS Accepts images in digital format. Send via e-mail as JPEG.

MAKING CONTACT & TERMS Send e-mail with résumé, low-res tearsheets, low-res JPEGs. Responds in 1 month to queries. Rates negotiable, but typically 50 GBP per page. Pays on publication. Credit line given. Buys first rights.

TIPS "Study the magazine to check the type of images we use, and send a sample of images you think would be suitable. The broader your style, the better for general acceptance, while individual styles appeal to our Planet Photo section. Step-by-step technique pieces must be formatted to house style, so check magazine before submitting. Supply a contact sheet or thumbnail of all the images supplied in electronic form to make it easier for us to make a quick decision on the work."

DOWNBEAT

102 N. Haven Rd., Elmhurst IL 60126. (651)251-9682; (877)904-5299. **E-mail:** editor@downbeat.com. **Website:** www.downbeat.com. Estab. 1934. Circ. 90,000. Monthly magazine. Emphasizes jazz musicians. Sample copy available with SASE.

NEEDS Buys 20 photos from freelancers/issue; 240 photos/year. Needs photos of live music performers/posed musicians/equipment, primarily jazz and blues. Photo captions preferred.

SPECS Accepts images in digital format. "Do not send unsolicited high-res images via e-mail!"

MAKING CONTACT & TERMS Send 8×10 b&w prints; 35mm, 2¼×2¼, 4×5, 8×10 transparencies;

b&w or color contact sheets by mail. Unsolicited samples will not be returned unless accompanied by SASE. Provide résumé, business card, brochure, flyer or tearsheets to be kept on file for possible future assignments. Responds only when needed. Simultaneous submissions and previously published work OK. Pay rates vary by size. Credit line given. Buys one-time rights.

TIPS "We prefer live shots and interesting candids to studio work."

THE DRAKE MAGAZINE

P.O. Box 11546, Denver CO 80211. (720)638-3114. **E-mail:** info@drakemag.com. **Website:** www.drakemag.com. Estab. 1998. Quarterly. For flyfishing enthusiasts.

NEEDS Buys 50 photos from freelancers/issue. Needs creative flyfishing shots. Reviews photos with or without a ms.

SPECS Uses digital photos only.

MAKING CONTACT & TERMS Responds in 6 months to queries. Pays $200 minimum for color cover; $40 minimum for b&w inside. Pays on publication. Credit line given. Buys one-time rights.

TIPS "No 'grip and grins' for fishing photos. Think creative. Show me something new."

❸ ❸ DUCKS UNLIMITED MAGAZINE

One Waterfowl Way, Memphis TN 38120. (901)758-3864. **E-mail:** jhoffman@ducks.org. **Website:** www.ducks.org. **Contact:** John Hoffman, photo editor. Estab. 1937. Circ. 700,000. Bimonthly association magazine of Ducks Unlimited Inc., a nonprofit organization. Emphasizes waterfowl hunting and conservation. Readers are professional males, ages 40-50. Sample copy available for $3. Photo guidelines available on website-www.ducks.org, via e-mail or with SASE.

NEEDS Images of wild ducks and geese, waterfowling and scenic wetlands. Special photo needs include waterfowl hunters, dynamic shots of waterfowl interacting in natural habitat. Buys 84 photos from freelancers/issue; 504 photos/year

SPECS Accepts images in digital format. Send via CD as TIFF, JPEG, EPS files at 300 dpi; include thumbnails.

MAKING CONTACT & TERMS Responds in 1 month. Previously published work *will not be considered*. Pays on publication. Credit line given. Buys one-time rights "plus permission to reprint in our Mexican and Canadian publications."

⊕ $ EASTERN ART REPORT

(44)208-392-1122. **Website:** www.eapgroup.com. Estab. 1989. *EAR* has a worldwide readership—from scholars to connoisseurs—with varying knowledge of or interest in the historical, philosophical, practical, or theoretical aspects of Eastern art.

MAKING CONTACT & TERMS Reviews illustrations, electronic images of at least 300 dpi.

$ EASYRIDERS

P.O. Box 3000, Agoura Hills CA 91376. (818)889-8740. **E-mail:** davenichols@easyriders.net. **Website:** www.easyriders.com. **Contact:** Dave Nichols, editorial director. Estab. 1971. Monthly magazine. Emphasizes "motorcycles (Harley-Davidsons in particular), motorcycle women, bikers having fun." Readers are "adult men who own, or desire to own, custom motorcycles; the individualist—a rugged guy who enjoys riding a custom motorcycle and all the good times derived from it." Sample copy free. Photo guidelines free with SASE.

NEEDS Uses about 60 photos/issue; majority supplied by freelancers; 70% assigned. Photos of "motorcycle riding (rugged chopper riders), motorcycle women, good times had by bikers, etc." Model release required. Also interested in technical articles relating to Harley-Davidsons.

SPECS Prefers images in digital format ("raw from camera, no effects added").

MAKING CONTACT & TERMS Use online submission form. 3 megapixel, 300 dpi minimum. "Acceptable formats: TIFF, Photoshop (PSD), Kodak Photo CDs, JPEG. GIF format is NOT acceptable." Other terms for bike features with models to satisfaction of editors. Pays 30 days after publication. Credit line given. Buys all rights. All material must be exclusive.

TIPS Trend is toward "more action photos, bikes being photographed by photographers on bikes to create a feeling of motion." In samples, wants photos "clear, in-focus, eye-catching and showing some emotion. Read magazine before making submissions. Be critical of your own work. Check for sharpness. Also, label photos/slides clearly with name and address."

THE ELKS MAGAZINE

425 W. Diversey Pkwy., Chicago IL 60614. (773)755-4740. **E-mail:** magnews@elks.org. **Website:** www.elks.org/elksmag. **Contact:** Anna L. Idol, editor/publisher. Estab. 1922. Circ. 800,000.

NEEDS Buys 10 cover photos/year; mostly from stock photo houses; approximately 20 photos/month for interior use. Reviews photos with or without a manuscript.

SPECS Accepts high-res digital images.

MAKING CONTACT & TERMS Send query letter with samples. Does not keep samples on file; include SASE for return of material. Responds in 2 months to queries. Simultaneous submissions OK. Pays $475 for color cover. Pays on publication. Credit line given. Buys one-time rights.

TIPS "Artistry and technical excellence are as important as subject matter. We are now purchasing 90% of our photographs from photographic stock houses."

$$ ◐ ENTREPRENEUR

2445 McCabe Way, Suite 400, Irvine CA 92614. (949)261-2325. **Website:** www.entrepreneur.com. **Contact:** Richard R. Olson, design director; Megan Roy, creative director. Estab. 1977. Circ. 650,000. Monthly. Emphasizes business. Readers are existing and aspiring small business owners.

NEEDS Uses 40 photos/issue; 10% supplied by freelance photographers; 80% on assignment; 10% from stock. Needs people at work, home office, business situations. "I want to see colorful shots in all formats and styles." Model/property release preferred. Photo captions required; include names of subjects.

SPECS Accepts images in digital format and film. Send via ZIP, CD, e-mail as TIFF, EPS, JPEG files at 300 dpi.

MAKING CONTACT & TERMS All magazine queries should be e-mailed to: queries@entrepreneur.com. Responds in 6 weeks. No phone calls, please. Entrepreneur Media Inc. assumes no responsibility for unsolicited manuscripts or photos. Provide résumé, business card, brochure, flyer or tearsheets to be kept on file for possible future assignments. **Pays on acceptance.** Credit line given. Buys one-time North American rights; negotiable.

TIPS "I am looking for photographers who use the environment creatively; I do not like blank walls for backgrounds. Lighting is also important. I prefer medium-format for most shoots. I think photographers are going back to the basics—a good, clean shot, different angles and bright colors. I also like gelled lighting. I prefer examples of your work—promo cards and tearsheets—along with business cards and résumés."

◐ ⑨ ○ EOS MAGAZINE

Robert Scott Publishing, The Old Barn, Ball Lane, Tackley, Kidlington, Oxfordshire 0X5 3AG, United Kingdom. (44)(186)933-1741. **Fax:** (44)(186)933-1641. **E-mail:** editorial@eos-magazine.com. **Website:** www.eos-magazine.com. **Contact:** Robert Scott, editor. Estab. 1993. Circ. 20,000. Quarterly. For all users of Canon EOS cameras. Photo guidelines at www.eos-magazine-forum.com/forumdisplay.php?83-EOS-magazine-photo-requirements.

NEEDS Looking for quality stand-alone images as well as photos showing specific photographic techniques and comparison pictures. All images must be taken with EOS cameras but not necessarily with Canon lenses. Photo captions required; include technical details of photo equipment and techniques used.

SPECS Accepts images in digital format exclusively.

MAKING CONTACT & TERMS Pays on publication. Credit line given. Buys one-time rights.

◑ EVENT

Douglas College, P.O. Box 2503, New Westminster British Columbia V3L 5B2, Canada. (604)527-5293. **Fax:** (604)527-5095. **E-mail:** event@douglascollege.ca. **Website:** www.eventmags.com. Estab. 1971. Circ. 1,000. Published every 4 months. Emphasizes literature (short stories, reviews, poetry, creative nonfiction).

NEEDS Only publishes photography by B.C.-based artists. Buys approximately 3 photographs/year. Has featured photographs by Mark Mushet, Lee Hutzulak, and Anne de Haas. Assigns 50% of photographs to new and emerging photographers. Uses freelancers mainly for covers. "We look for art that is adaptable to a cover, particularly images that are self-sufficient and don't lead the reader to expect further artwork within the journal."

MAKING CONTACT & TERMS "Please send photography/artwork (no more than 10 images) to *EVENT*, along with SASE (Canadian postage, or IRCs, or USD $1) for return of your work. We also accept e-mail submissions of cover art. We recommend that you send low-res versions of your photography/art as small JPEG or PDF attachments. If we are interested, we will request high-res files. We do not buy the actual piece of art; we only pay for the use of the image." Simultaneous submissions OK. Pays $150 on publication. Credit line given. Buys one-time rights.

FACES

Cobblestone Publishing, 30 Grove St., Peterborough NH 03458. **E-mail:** ecarpentiere@caruspub.com. **Website:** www.cobblestonepub.com. **Contact:** Elizabeth Crooker Carpentiere. Estab. 1984. Circ. 15,000. Photo guidelines and themes available online.

NEEDS Uses about 30-35 photos/issue; 75% supplied by freelancers. "Photos (color) for text must relate to themes; cover photos (color) should also relate to themes." Themes online. Photos purchased with or without accompanying ms. Model release preferred. Photo captions preferred.

MAKING CONTACT & TERMS Query with stock photo list and/or samples. Responds in 1 month. Simultaneous submissions and previously published work OK. Pays $200-350 for color cover; $25-100 color inside. Pays on publication. Credit line given.

TIPS "Photographers should request our theme list. Most of the photographs we use are of people from other cultures. We look for an ability to capture people in action—at work or play. We primarily need photos showing people, young and old, taking part in ceremonies, rituals, customs and with artifacts and architecture particular to a given culture. Appropriate scenics and animal pictures are also needed. All submissions must relate to a specific future theme."

◑ ◑ ○ FAITH & FRIENDS

The Salvation Army, 2 Overlea Blvd., Toronto Ontario M4H 1P4, Canada. (416)422-6226. **Fax:** (416)422-6120. **E-mail:** faithandfriends@can.salvationarmy.org. **Website:** www.faithandfriends.ca. **Contact:** Ken Ramstead, editor. Circ. 50,000. Monthly. "Our mission: To show Jesus Christ at work in the lives of real people, and to provide spiritual resources for those who are new to the Christian faith."

NEEDS Photos of religion.

SPECS Accepts images in digital format. Send JPEG or GIF files. Uses prints.

MAKING CONTACT & TERMS Payment negotiated. Captions required. Buys one-time rights.

FAMILY MOTOR COACHING

8291 Clough Pike, Cincinnati OH 45244. (513)474-3622; (800)543-3622. **Fax:** (513)388-5286. **E-mail:** rgould@fmca.com; magazine@fmca.com. **Website:** www.fmca.com. **Contact:** Robbin Gould, editor. Estab. 1963. Circ. 140,000. Monthly publication of the Family Motor Coach Association. Emphasizes motor homes. Readers are members of national associa-

tion of motor home owners. Sample copy available for $3.99 ($5 if paying by credit card). Writer's/photographer's guidelines free with SASE or via e-mail.
NEEDS Buys 55-60 photos from freelancers/issue; 660-720 photos/year. Each issue includes varied subject matter—primarily needs photos depicting motor home travel, travel with scenic shots, couples, families, senior citizens, hobbies and how-to material. Photos purchased with accompanying manuscript only. Model release preferred. Photo captions required.
SPECS Accepts images in digital format. Send via CD as EPS, TIFF files at 300 dpi.
MAKING CONTACT & TERMS Send query letter with résumé of credits, samples, contact sheets; include SASE for return of material. Responds in 3 months. Pays $100 for color cover; $25-100 for b&w and color inside. $125-500 for text/photo package. **Pays on acceptance.** Credit line given if requested. Prefers first North American rights, but will consider one-time rights on photos *only*.
TIPS Photographers are "welcome to submit brochures or copies of their work. We'll keep them in mind should a freelance photography need arise."

⊕ FAMILY TREE MAGAZINE

F+W, a Content and eCommerce Company, 10151 Carver Rd., Suite 200, Blue Ash OH 45242. (513)531-2690. **Fax:** (513)891-7153. **E-mail:** ftmedit@fwpubs.com. **Website:** www.familytreemagazine.com. Estab. 1999. Circ. 75,000. "*Family Tree Magazine* is a special-interest consumer magazine that helps readers discover, preserve, and celebrate their family's history. We cover genealogy, ethnic heritage, genealogy websites and software, photography and photo preservation, and other ways that families connect with their past."
MAKING CONTACT & TERMS Captions required. Negotiates payment individually. Buys all rights.

FCA MAGAZINE

Fellowship of Christian Athletes, 8701 Leeds Rd., Kansas City MO 64129. (816)921-0909; (800)289-0909. **Fax:** (816)921-8755. **E-mail:** mag@fca.org. **Website:** www.fca.org/mag. **Contact:** Clay Meyer, editor; Matheau Casner, creative director. Estab. 1959. Circ. 75,000. Monthly association magazine featuring stories and testimonials of prominent athletes and coaches in sports who proclaim a relationship with Jesus Christ. Sample copy available for $1 and 9×12 SASE. Photo guidelines available at www.fca.org/mag/media-kit.

NEEDS Photos of sports. "We buy photos of persons being featured in our magazine. We don't buy photos without story being suggested first." Reviews photos with accompanying manuscript only. "All submitted stories must be connected to the FCA Ministry." Model release preferred; property release required. Photo captions preferred.
SPECS Uses glossy or matte color prints; 35mm, 2¼×2¼ transparencies. Accepts images in digital format. Send via CD, ZIP, e-mail as TIFF, JPEG files at 300 dpi.
MAKING CONTACT & TERMS Contact through e-mail with a list of types of sports photographs in stock. Do not send samples. Simultaneous submissions OK. Pays $150 maximum for color cover; $100 maximum for color inside. Pays on publication. Credit line given. Buys one-time rights.
TIPS "We would like to increase our supply of photographers who can do contract work."

ⓢ ◯ FELLOWSHIP

P.O. Box 271, Nyack NY 10960. (845)358-4601, ext. 35. **E-mail:** lkelly@forusa.org. **Website:** www.forusa.org. **Contact:** Linda Kelly, communications director. Estab. 1935. Circ. 5,000. Publication of the Fellowship of Reconciliation published 2 times/year. Emphasizes peace-making, social justice, nonviolent social change. Readers are interested in peace, justice, nonviolence and spirituality. Sample copy available for $7.50.
NEEDS Buys up to 2 photos from freelancers/issue. Needs stock photos of people, civil disobedience, demonstrations—Middle East, Latin America, Caribbean, prisons, anti-nuclear, children, gay/lesbian, human rights issues, Asia/Pacific. Captions required.
MAKING CONTACT & TERMS Provide résumé, business card, brochure, flyer or tearsheets to be kept on file for possible future assignments. "Call for specs." Responds in 4-6 weeks. Simultaneous submissions and previously published work OK. Pays $100 for color cover; $35 for b&w inside. Pays on publication. Credit line given. Buys one-time rights.
TIPS "You must want to make a contribution to peace movements. Money is simply token."

FIELD & STREAM

2 Park Ave., New York NY 10016. (212)779-5296. **Fax:** (212)779-5114. **E-mail:** fsletters@bonniercorp.com. **Website:** www.fieldandstream.com. Estab. 1895. Circ. 1,500,000. Broad-based monthly service maga-

zine published 11 times/year. Editorial content ranges from very basic "how it's done" filler stories that tell in pictures and words how an outdoor technique is accomplished or device is made, to feature articles of penetrating depth about national conservation, game management and resource management issues; also recreational hunting, fishing, travel, nature and outdoor equipment.

NEEDS Photos using action and a variety of subjects and angles in color and occasionally b&w. "We are always looking for cover photographs, in color, vertical or horizontal. Remember, a cover picture must have room for cover lines." Also looking for interesting photo essay ideas related to hunting and fishing. Query photo editor by e-mail. Needs photo information regarding subjects, the area, the nature of the activity and the point the picture makes. First Shots: these photos appear every month (2/issue). Prime space, 2-page spread. One-of-a-kind, dramatic, impactful images, capturing the action and excitement of hunting and fishing. Great beauty shots. Unique wildlife images. See recent issues.

MAKING CONTACT & TERMS Please do not submit images without reviewing past issues and having a strong understanding of our audience. Uses 35mm slides. Will also consider large-format photography. Accepts images in digital format. Send via CD, e-mail as JPEG files at 300 dpi. Submit photos by registered mail. Send slides in 8½×11 plastic sheets and pack slides and prints between cardboard. Include SASE for return of material. Drop portfolios at receptionist's desk, 9th floor. Buys first North American rights.

FINESCALE MODELER

Kalmbach Publishing Co., 21027 Crossroads Circle, P.O. Box 1612, Waukesha WI 53187-1612. (414)796-8776. **Website:** www.finescale.com. Circ. 60,000. Published 10 times/year. Emphasizes "how-to information for hobbyists who build non-operating scale models." Readers are "adult and juvenile hobbyists who build non-operating model aircraft, ships, tanks and military vehicles, cars and figures." Photo and submission guidelines free with SASE or online.

NEEDS Buys 10 photos from freelancers/issue; 100 photos/year. Needs "in-progress how-to photos illustrating a specific modeling technique; photos of full-size aircraft, cars, trucks, tanks and ships." Model release required. Photo captions required.

SPECS Prefers prints and transparencies; will accept digital images if submission guidelines are followed.

MAKING CONTACT & TERMS Provide résumé, business card, brochure, flyer or tearsheets to be kept on file for possible future assignments. "Will sometimes accept previously published work if copyright is clear. Pays for photos on publication, for text/photo package on acceptance. Credit line given. Buys all rights.

TIPS Looks for "sharp color prints or slides of model aircraft, ships, cars, trucks, tanks, figures and science-fiction subjects. In addition to photographic talent, must have comprehensive knowledge of objects photographed and provide complete caption material. Freelance photographers should provide a catalog stating subject, date, place, format, conditions of sale and desired credit line before attempting to sell us photos. We're most likely to purchase color photos of outstanding models of all types for our regular feature, 'Showcase.'"

FLORIDA SPORTSMAN

Wickstrom Communications, Intermedia Outdoors, 2700 S. Kanner Hwy., Stuart FL 34994. (772)219-7400. **Fax:** (772)219-6900. **E-mail:** editor@floridasportsman.com. **Website:** www.floridasportsman.com. **Contact:** Jeff Weakley, executive editor. Circ. 115,000. Edited for the boat owner and offshore, coastal, and fresh water fisherman. It provides a how, when, and where approach in its articles, which also includes occasional camping, diving, and hunting stories—plus ecology (in-depth articles and editorials attempting to protect Florida's wilderness, wetlands, and natural beauty).

SPECS Send high-res digital images on CD or via Dropbox.

MAKING CONTACT & TERMS Offers no additional payment for photos accepted with ms. Pays from $60-120 for supplemental photos, up to $750 for cover. Buys nonexclusive additional rights.

🟢 🟡 🔵 FLY ROD & REEL

P.O. Box 370, Camden ME 04843. (207)594-9544. **Fax:** (207)594-5144. **E-mail:** gthomas@flyrodreel.com; editor@flyrodreel.com. **Website:** www.flyrodreel.com. **Contact:** Greg Thomas, editor. Estab. 1979. Circ. 61,941. Quarterly. Emphasizes fly-fishing. Readers are primarily fly-fishers ages 30-60. Sample copy and photo guidelines free with SASE; photo guidelines also available via e-mail.

NEEDS Buys 15-20 photos from freelancers/issue; 90-120 photos/year. Needs "photos of fish, scenics (preferably with anglers in shot), equipment." Photo captions preferred; include location, name of model (if applicable).

SPECS Uses 35mm slides; 2¼×2¼, 4×5 transparencies.

MAKING CONTACT & TERMS Send query letter with list of stock photo subjects. Send unsolicited photos by mail for consideration; include SASE for return of material. Provide résumé, business card, brochure, flier or tearsheets to be kept on file for possible future assignments. Responds in 1 month. Pays $600-800 for color cover photo; $75 for b&w inside (seldom needed); $75-200 for color inside. Pays on publication. Credit line given. Buys one-time rights.

TIPS "Photos should avoid appearance of being too 'staged.' We look for bright color (especially on covers), and unusual, visually appealing settings. Trout and salmon are preferred for covers. Also looking for saltwater fly-fishing subjects. Ask for guidelines, then send 20 to 40 shots showing breadth of work."

✛ ⊛ FOGGED CLARITY

(231)670-7033. **E-mail:** editor@foggedclarity.com. **E-mail:** submissions@foggedclarity.com. **Website:** www.foggedclarity.com. **Contact:** Editors. Estab. 2008. Circ. between 15,000 and 22,000 visitors per month. "*Fogged Clarity* is an arts review that accepts submissions of poetry, fiction, nonfiction, music, visual art, and reviews of work in all mediums. We seek art that is stabbingly eloquent. Our print edition is released once every year, while new issues of our online journal come out at the beginning of every month. Artists maintain the copyrights to their work until they are monetarily compensated for said work. If your work is selected for our print edition and you consent to its publication, you will be compensated."

MAKING CONTACT & TERM Reviews GIF, JPEG, PNG, TIFF, PSD, AI, and PDF files, at least 700 pixels.

○ FOLIATE OAK LITERARY MAGAZINE

University of Arkansas-Monticello, P.O. Box 3460, Monticello AR 71656. (870)460-1247. **E-mail:** foliateoak@uamont.edu. **Website:** www.foliateoak.com. **Contact:** Online submission manager. Estab. 1973. Circ. 500. "We are a university general literary magazine publishing new and established artists." Has featured Terry Wright, Brett Svelik, Lucita Peek, David Swartz and Fariel Shafee. No samples kept on file.

NEEDS People, architecture, cities, gardening, landscapes, wildlife, environmental, natural disasters, adventure, humor, alternative, avant garde, documentary, erotic, fashion/glamour, fine art, historical, and lifestyle photographs. Photo captions are preferred.

MAKING CONTACT & TERMS Online submission manager must be used to submit all artwork.

TIPS "We are unable to pay our contributors but we love to support freelancers. We solicit work for our online magazine and our annual print anthology. Read submission guidelines online."

FOOD & WINE

(212)382-5600. **Fax:** (212)764-2177. **Website:** www.foodandwine.com. **Contact:** Mary Ellen Ward, managing editor. Circ. 964,000. Monthly. Emphasizes food and wine. Readers are "upscale people who cook, entertain, dine out and travel stylishly."

NEEDS Uses 25-30 photos/issue; 85% freelance photography on assignment basis, 15% freelance stock. "We look for editorial reportage specialists who do restaurants, food on location, and travel photography." Model release required. Photo captions required.

MAKING CONTACT & TERMS Drop off portfolio on Wednesday. Call for pickup. Submit fliers, tearsheets, etc., to be kept on file for future assignments and stock usage. **Pays on acceptance.** Credit line given. Buys one-time world rights.

FORTUNE

Time, Inc., 1271 Avenue of the Americas, New York NY 10020. (212)522-1212. **Fax:** (212)522-0810. **E-mail:** letters@fortune.com. **Website:** www.fortune.com. **Contact:** Eric Danetz, publisher; Michael Schneider, associate publisher. Circ. 1,066,000. Emphasizes analysis of news in the business world for management personnel.

MAKING CONTACT & TERMS Picture editor reviews photographers' portfolios on an overnight drop-off basis. Photos purchased on assignment only. Day rate on assignment (against space rate): $500; page rate for space: $400; minimum for b&w or color usage: $200.

⦿ ⦵ ⦿ ⦿ FRANCE MAGAZINE

Archant House, Oriel Rd., Cheltenham, Gloucestershire GL50 1BB, United Kingdom. +44 1242 216050. **E-mail:** editorial@francemag.com. **Website:** www.francemag.com. **Contact:** Art editor. Estab. 1990. Circ. 40,000. Monthly about France. Readers are male and female, ages 45 and over; people who holiday in France.

NEEDS Photos of France and French subjects: people, places, customs, curiosities, produce, towns, cities, countryside. Photo captions required; include location and as much information as is practical.

SPECS Uses 35mm, medium-format transparencies; high-quality digital.

MAKING CONTACT & TERMS "E-mail in the first instance with list of subjects. Please do not send digital images. We will add you to our photographer list and contact you on an ad-hoc basis for photographic requirements."

FT. MYERS MAGAZINE

15880 Summerlin Rd., Suite 189, Fort Myers FL 33908. (516)652-6072. **E-mail:** ftmyers@optonline.net. **Website:** www.ftmyersmagazine.com. Estab. 2001. Circ. 20,000. Bimonthly. Covers regional arts and living for educated, active, successful and creative residents of Lee and Collier counties (FL) and guests at resorts and hotels in Lee County.

NEEDS Buys 3-6 photos from freelancers/year. Photos of celebrities, architecture, gardening, interiors/decorating, medicine, product shots/still life, environmental, landscapes/scenics, wildlife, entertainment, events, food/drink, health/fitness/beauty, performing arts, sports, travel. Interested in alternative process, avant garde, documentary, fashion/glamour, fine art, historical/vintage. Also needs beaches, beach scenes/sunsets over beaches, boating/fishing, palm trees. Reviews photos with or without a ms. Model release required. Photo captions preferred; include description of image and photo credit.

SPECS Uses 4×5, 8×10 glossy or matte color and b&w prints; 35mm, 2×2, 4×5, 8×10 transparencies ("all are acceptable, but we prefer prints or digital"). Accepts images in digital format. Send via CD or e-mail (preferred) as TIFF, EPS, PICT, JPEG, PDF files (prefers TIFF or JPEG) at 300-600 dpi.

MAKING CONTACT & TERMS Send query letter via e-mail with digital images and stock list. Responds only if interested; send nonreturnable samples. Simultaneous submissions and previously published work OK. Pays $100 for b&w or color cover; $25-100 for b&w or color inside. Pays on publication. Credit line given. Buys one-time rights.

FUR-FISH-GAME

2878 E. Main St., Columbus OH 43209-9947. **E-mail:** ffgcox@ameritech.net. **Website:** www.furfishgame.com. **Contact:** Mitch Cox, editor. Estab. 1900. Circ. 118,000. Monthly. For outdoorsmen of all ages who are interested in hunting, fishing, trapping, dogs, camping, conservation, and related topics.

NEEDS Buys 4 photos from freelancers/issue; 50 photos/year. Photos of freshwater fish, wildlife, wilderness and rural scenes. Reviews photos with or without a ms. Photo captions required; include subject.

SPECS Reviews transparencies, color 5×7 or 8×10 prints, digital photos on CD only with thumbnail sheet of small images and a numbered caption sheet.

MAKING CONTACT & TERMS Send query letter "and nothing more." Does not keep samples on file; include SASE for return of material. Responds in 1 month to queries. Simultaneous submissions (but no previously published work) OK. Pays $35 minimum for b&w and color inside. Pays on publication. Credit line given. Buys first North American serial rights, print and digital publication one-time rights.

GAME & FISH

3330 Chastain Meadows Pkwy., NW, Suite 200, Kennesaw GA 30144. (770)953-9222. **Fax:** (678)279-7512. **E-mail:** ken.dunwoody@imoutdoors.com. **Website:** www.gameandfishmag.com. **Contact:** Ken Dunwoody, editorial director; Ron Sinfelt, photo editor; Allen Hansen, graphic artist. Estab. 1975. Circ. 570,000 for 28 state-specific magazines. Publishes several different monthly outdoors magazines: *Alabama Game & Fish, Arkansas Sportsman, California Game & Fish, Florida Game & Fish, Georgia Sportsman, Illinois Game & Fish, Indiana Game & Fish, Iowa Game & Fish, Kentucky Game & Fish, Michigan Sportsman, Minnesota Sportsman, Mississippi/Louisiana Game & Fish, New England Game & Fish, New York Game & Fish, North Carolina Game & Fish, Ohio Game & Fish, Oklahoma Game & Fish, Pennsylvania Game & Fish, Rocky Mountain Game & Fish, South Carolina Game & Fish, Tennessee Sportsman, Texas Sportsman, Washington-Oregon Game & Fish, West Virginia Game & Fish, Wisconsin Sportsman*, and *North American Whitetail*. All magazines are for experienced hunters and fishermen and provide information about where, when, and how to enjoy the best hunting and fishing in their particular state or region, as well as articles about game and fish management, conservation and environmental issues. Photo guidelines and current needs list free with SASE.

NEEDS 50% of photos supplied by freelance photographers; 5% assigned. Photos of live game animals/birds in natural environments and hunting scenes; game fish photos and fishing scenes. Photo captions required; include species identification and location. Number slides/prints.

SPECS Accepts images in digital format. Send via CD at 300 dpi with output of 8×12.

MAKING CONTACT & TERMS Send 5×7, 8×10 glossy b&w prints or 35mm transparencies (preferably Fujichrome, Kodachrome) with SASE for consideration. Responds in 1 month. Simultaneous submissions not accepted. Pays 60 days prior to publication. Tearsheet provided. Credit line given. Buys one-time rights.

TIPS "Send separate CD and proof sheet for each species, with digital submissions. We'll return photos we don't expect to use and hold remainder in-house so they're available for monthly photo selections. Please do not send dupes. Photos will be returned upon publication or at photographer's request."

GARDENING HOW-TO

12301 Whitewater Dr., Minnetonka MN 55343. **E-mail:** editors@gardeningclub.com. **Website:** www.gardeningclub.com. **Contact:** Jennifer Mahoney, art director. Estab. 1996. Circ. 400,000. Special interest magazine published 5 times/year. For the avid home gardener, from beginner to expert. Readers are 78% female, average age of 49. Sample copies available.

NEEDS Buys 50 photos from freelancers/issue; 450 photos/year. Needs photos related to all aspects of gardening, including plants, garden profiles, landscaping, hardscaping and more. Photos are typically requested as needed; profiles can be sent unsolicited. Photo captions preferred.

SPECS Images must be in digital format. Send via CD as TIFF, EPS, JPEG files at 300 dpi. "FTP site available for digital images."

MAKING CONTACT & TERMS Query art director. Provide self-promotion piece to be kept on file for possible future assignments. Responds only if interested; send nonreturnable samples. Previously published work may be considered. **Pays on acceptance.** Credit line given. Buys one-time rights, first rights, electronic rights; negotiable.

TIPS "Looking for well-lit, sharp, colorful photos and will send specific wants if interested in your work. Send a complete list of photos along with CD in package."

GEORGIA STRAIGHT

1701 W. Broadway, Vancouver British Columbia V6J 1Y3, Canada. (604)730-7000. **Fax:** (604)730-7010. **E-mail:** contact@straight.com; photos@straight.com. **Website:** www.straight.com. **Contact:** Charlie Smith, editor. Estab. 1967. Circ. 117,000. Weekly tabloid. Emphasizes entertainment. Readers are generally well-educated people, ages 20-45. Sample copy free with 10×12 SASE.

NEEDS Buys 3 photos from freelancers/issue; 364 photos/year. Needs photos of entertainment events and personalities. Photo captions essential.

MAKING CONTACT & TERMS Send query letter with list of stock photo subjects. Provide résumé, business card, brochure, flyer or tearsheets to be kept on file for possible future assignments. Responds in 1 month. Simultaneous submissions and previously published work OK. Include SASE for return of material. Pays on publication. Credit line given. Buys one-time rights.

TIPS "Almost all needs are for in-Vancouver assigned photos, except for high-quality portraits of film stars. We rarely use unsolicited photos, except for Vancouver photos for our content page."

GERMAN LIFE

Zeitgeist Publishing, Inc., 1068 National Hwy., LaVale MD 21502. (301)729-6190. **Fax:** (301)729-1720. **E-mail:** mslider@germanlife.com. **Website:** www.germanlife.com. **Contact:** Mark Slider. Estab. 1994. Circ. 40,000. Bimonthly. Focusing on history, culture, and travel relating to German-speaking Europe and German-American heritage. Sample copy available for $5.95.

MAKING CONTACT & TERMS Reviews color transparencies, 5×7 color or b&w prints, and digital images. Buys one-time rights.

GHOST TOWN

E-mail: shannonsdustytrails@yahoo.com. **Contact:** Shannon Bridget Murphy. Estab. 1998. Quarterly. Photo guidelines available by e-mail request.

NEEDS Buys 12 photos from freelancers/issue; 48-72 photos/year. Photos of babies/children/teens, celebrities, couples, multicultural, families, parents, disasters, environmental, landscapes/scenics, wildlife, architecture, cities/urban, education, gardening, interiors/decorating, pets, religious, rural, adventure, events, food/drink, sports, travel, agriculture, medicine, military, political, product shots/still life, science, technology—as they are related to archaeology and ghost towns. Interested in alternative process, avant garde, documentary, fashion/glamour, fine art, historical/vintage, seasonal. Wants photos of archaeology sites and excavations in progress of American ghost towns. "Would like photographs from ghost towns and western archaeological sites." Reviews photos with or without a manuscript. Model/property release preferred.

SPECS Uses glossy or matte color and b&w prints.

MAKING CONTACT & TERMS Send query letter via e-mail. "If possible, please do not include photographs in files if they are sent through e-mail. A CD sent with your photographs is acceptable." Provide résumé, business card or self-promotion piece to be kept on file for possible future assignments. "Photographs sent with CDs are requested but not required. Illustrations and artwork are also accepted." Responds within 1 month to queries; 1 week to portfolios. Simultaneous submissions and previously published work OK. **Pays on acceptance.** Credit line given. Buys one-time rights, first rights; negotiable.

GIRLS' LIFE

Monarch Publishing, 3 S. Frederick St., Suite 806, Baltimore MD 21202. (410)426-9600. **Fax:** (866)793-1531. **E-mail:** writeforGL@girlslife.com. **Website:** www.girlslife.com. **Contact:** Karen Bokram, founding editor and publisher; Jessica D'Argenio Waller, fashion editor; Chun Kim, art director. Estab. 1994. Circ. 2.16 million. Emphasizes advice, relationships, school, current news issues, entertainment, quizzes, fashion and beauty pertaining to preteen girls. Readers are preteen girls (ages 10-15). *Girls' Life* accepts unsolicited manuscripts on a speculative basis only. First, send an e-mail or letter query with detailed story ideas. No telephone solicitations, please. Guidelines available online.

NEEDS Buys 65 photos from freelancers/issue. Submit seasonal materials 3 months in advance. Uses 5×8, 8½×11 color and b&w prints; 35mm, 4×5 transparencies.

MAKING CONTACT & TERMS Send query letter with stock list. E-mail queries are responded to within 90 days. Works on assignment only. Keeps samples on file. Responds in 3 weeks. Simultaneous submissions and previously published work OK. Pays on usage. Credit line given. Please familiarize yourself with the voice and content of *Girls' Life* before submitting.

⊕ ↻ GOLF CANADA

Chill Media Inc., 482 S. Service Rd. E., Suite 103, Oakville Ontario L6J 2X6, Canada. (905)337-1886. **Fax:** (905)337-1887. **E-mail:** scotty@ichill.ca; alison@ichill.ca. **Website:** www.golfcanada.ca. Alison King, managing editor. **Contact:** Scott Stevenson, publisher. Estab. 1994. Circ. 159,000. Published 4 times/year. Covers Canadian golf. The official magazine of the Royal Canadian Golf Association, published to entertain and enlighten members about RCGA-related activities and to generally support and promote amateur golf in Canada.

GOLF TIPS

Werner Publishing Corp., 12121 Wilshire Blvd., 12th Floor, Los Angeles CA 90025-1176. (310)820-1500. **Fax:** (310)826-5008. **E-mail:** editors@golftipsmag.com. **Website:** www.golftipsmag.com. Estab. 1986. Circ. 300,000. Published 9 times/year. Readers are "hardcore golf enthusiasts." Sample copy free with SASE. Submission guidelines at www.golftipsmag.com/submissions.html.

NEEDS Buys 40 photos from freelancers/issue; 360 photos/year. Photos of golf instruction (usually pre-arranged, on-course), equipment; health/fitness, travel. Interested in alternative process, documentary, fashion/glamour. Reviews photos with accompanying ms only. Model/property release preferred. Photo captions required.

SPECS Uses prints; 35mm, 2¼×2¼, 4×5, 8×10 transparencies. Accepts images in digital format. Send via ZIP as TIFF files at 300 dpi.

MAKING CONTACT & TERMS Send query letter with résumé of credits. Submit portfolio for review. Cannot return material. Responds in 1 month. Pays $500-1,000 for b&w or color cover; $100-300 for b&w inside; $150-450 for color inside. Pays on publication. Buys one-time rights; negotiable.

GOOD HOUSEKEEPING

Hearst Corp., 300 W. 57th St., 28th Floor, New York NY 10019. (212)649-2200. **Website:** www.goodhousekeeping.com. Circ. 4,000,000. Articles focus on food, fitness, beauty, and childcare, drawing upon the resources of the Good Housekeeping Institute. Editorial includes human interest stories and articles that focus on social issues, money management, health news, and travel. Photos purchased mainly on assignment. *Query before submitting.*

♻ ⊙ GOSPEL HERALD

5 Lankin Blvd., Toronto Ontario M4J 4W7, Canada. (416)461-7406. **Fax:** (416)424-1850. **E-mail:** editorial@gospelherald.org. **Website:** www.gospelherald.org. **Contact:** Max Craddock, managing editor. Estab. 1936. Circ. 1,000.

GRACE ORMONDE WEDDING STYLE

Elegant Publishing, Inc., P.O. Box 89, Barrington RI 02806. (401)245-9726. **Fax:** (401)245-5371. **E-mail:** contact@weddingstylemagazine.com. **Website:** www. weddingstylemagazine.com. **Contact:** Human Resources. Estab. 1997. Circ. 400,000. Monthly. Covers weddings for the affluent bride.

GRAND RAPIDS FAMILY MAGAZINE

Gemini Publications, 549 Ottawa Ave. NW, Suite 201, Grand Rapids MI 49503-1444. (616)459-4545. **Fax:** (616)459-4800. **E-mail:** cvalade@geminipub.com. **Website:** www.grfamilymag.com. **Contact:** Carole Valade, editor. Circ. 30,000. Monthly. Covers local parenting issues. *Grand Rapids Family* seeks to inform, instruct, amuse, and entertain its readers and their families.

NEEDS Buys 20-50 photos from freelancers/issue; 240-600 photos/year. Needs photos of families, children, education, infants, play, etc. Model/property release required. Photo captions preferred; include who, what, where, when.

MAKING CONTACT & TERMS Send query letter with résumé of credits, stock list. Sometimes keeps samples on file; include SASE for return of material. Responds in 1 month, only if interested. Simultaneous submissions and previously published work OK. Pays $200 minimum for color cover; $35-75 for inside. Pays on publication. Credit line given. Buys one-time rights, all rights; negotiable.

TIPS "We are not interested in clip art variety photos. We want the honesty of photojournalism; photos that speak to the heart, that tell a story, that add to the story told."

GRAND RAPIDS MAGAZINE

Gemini Publications, 549 Ottawa Ave. NW, Suite 201, Grand Rapids MI 49503. (616)459-4545. **Fax:** (616)459-4800. **E-mail:** cvalade@geminipub.com. **Website:** www.grmag.com. Estab. 1964. Circ. 20,000.

Monthly magazine. Emphasizes community-related material of metro Grand Rapids area and West Michigan; local action and local people.

NEEDS Photos of animals, nature, scenic, travel, sport, fashion/beauty, photo essay/photo feature, fine art, documentary, human interest, celebrity/personality, humorous, wildlife, vibrant people shots and special effects/experimental. Wants, on a regular basis, West Michigan photo essays and travel-photo essays of any area in Michigan. Model release required. Photo captions required.

SPECS Prefers images in digital format. Send via CD at 300 dpi minimum. Also uses 2¼×2¼, 4×5 color transparencies for cover, vertical format required. "High-quality digital also acceptable."

MAKING CONTACT & TERMS Send material by mail for consideration; include SASE for return. Provide business card to be kept on file for possible future assignments; "only people on file with us are those we have met and personally reviewed." Arrange a personal interview to show portfolio. Responds in 3 weeks. Pays $35-100 for color photos; $100 minimum for cover. Buys one-time rights, exclusive product rights, all rights; negotiable.

TIPS "Most photography is by our local freelance photographers, so you should sell us on the unique nature of what you have to offer."

THE GREYHOUND REVIEW

P.O. Box 543, Abilene KS 67410. (785)263-4660. **E-mail:** nga@ngagreyhounds.com. **Website:** www.ngagreyhounds.com. Estab. 1911. Circ. 3,500. Monthly publication of The National Greyhound Association. Emphasizes Greyhound racing and breeding. Readers are Greyhound owners and breeders. Sample copy free with SASE and 11 first-class stamps.

NEEDS Buys 1 photo from freelancers/issue; 12 photos/year. Needs "anything pertinent to the Greyhound that would be of interest to Greyhound owners." Photo captions required.

MAKING CONTACT & TERMS Query via e-mail first. After response, send b&w or color prints and contact sheets by mail for consideration. Provide résumé, business card, brochure, flyer or tearsheets to be kept on file for possible future assignments. Can return unsolicited material if requested; include SASE for return of material. Responds in 1 month. Simultaneous submissions and previously published work OK. Pays $85 for color cover; $25-100 for color inside.

Pays on acceptance. Credit line given. Buys one-time and North American rights.

TIPS "We look for human-interest or action photos involving Greyhounds. No muzzles, please, unless the Greyhound is actually racing. When submitting photos for our cover, make sure there's plenty of cropping space on all margins around your photo's subject; full breeds on our cover are preferred."

GUERNICA MAGAZINE

112 W. 27th St., Suite 600, New York NY 10001. E-mail: editors@guernicamag.com; art@guernicamag.com; publisher@guernicamag.com. **Website:** www.guernicamag.com. **Contact:** See masthead online for specific editors. Estab. 2005. Biweekly. "*Guernica* is one of the Web's most acclaimed new magazines. *Guernica* is called a 'great online literary magazine' by *Esquire*. Contributors come from dozens of countries and write in nearly as many languages."

🖼️🅂 🄾 GUIDEPOSTS

P.O. Box 5814, Harlan IA 51593. (800)431-2344. E-mail: submissions@guidepostsmag.com. **Website:** www.guideposts.org. **Contact:** Kevin Eans, photo editor. Estab. 1945. Circ. 2.6 million. Monthly. True stories of hope and inspiration. Emphasizes tested methods for developing courage, strength and positive attitudes through faith in God.

NEEDS Uses 90% assignment, 10% stock on a story-by-story basis. Photos are mostly environmental portraiture, editorial reportage. Stock can be scenic, sports, fine art, mixed variety. Model release required.

SPECS Vertical for cover, horizontal or vertical for inside. Accepts images in digital format. Send via CD at 300 dpi.

MAKING CONTACT & TERMS Send photos or arrange a personal interview. Responds in 1 month. Simultaneous submissions OK. Pays by job or on a per-photo basis. **Pays on acceptance.** Credit line given. Buys one-time rights.

TIPS "I'm looking for photographs that show people in their environment; straight portraiture and people interacting. We're trying to appear more contemporary. We want to attract a younger audience and yet maintain a homey feel. For stock—scenics; graphic images in color. *Guideposts* is an 'inspirational' magazine. No violence, nudity, sex. No more than 20 images at a time. Write first and ask for a sample issue; this will give you a better idea of what we're looking for."

GUITAR WORLD

NewBay Media, LLC, 28 E. 28th St., 12th Floor, New York NY 10016. (212)378-0400. **Fax:** (212)281-4704. **E-mail:** soundingboard@guitarworld.com. **Website:** www.guitarworld.com. Circ. 150,000. Written for guitar players categorized as either professionals, semi-professionals or amateur players. Every issue offers broad-ranging interviews that cover technique, instruments, and lifestyles.

NEEDS Buys 20 photos from freelancers/issue; 240 photos/year. Photos of guitarists. Reviews photos with or without a manuscript. Property release preferred. Photo captions preferred.

SPECS Uses glossy or matte color and b&w prints; 35mm, 2¼×2¼ transparencies. Accepts images in digital format. Send via e-mail as TIFF, EPS, JPEG files at 300 dpi.

MAKING CONTACT & TERMS Send query letter with slides, prints, photocopies, tearsheets. Keeps samples on file. Responds in 2 weeks to queries. Previously published work OK. Pay rates vary by size. **Pays on acceptance.** Credit line given. Buys one-time rights.

HADASSAH MAGAZINE

50 W. 58th St., New York NY 10019. (212)688-0227. **Fax:** (212)446-9521. **E-mail:** magazine@hadassah.org. **Website:** www.hadassah.org/magazine. **Contact:** Elizabeth Barnea. Circ. 255,000. Bimonthly publication of the Hadassah Women's Zionist Organization of America. Emphasizes Jewish life, Israel. Readers are 85% females who travel and are interested in Jewish affairs, average age 59. Photo guidelines free with SASE.

NEEDS Uses 10 photos/issue; most supplied by freelancers. Photos of travel, Israel and general Jewish life. Photo captions preferred; include where, when, who and credit line.

SPECS Accepts images in digital format. Send via CD as JPEG files at 300 dpi. High-res, digital photos preferred.

MAKING CONTACT & TERMS Submit portfolio for review. Send unsolicited photos by e-mail for consideration. Keeps samples on file. Responds in 3 months. Payment depends on size and usage. Pays on publication. Credit line given. Buys one-time rights with web use.

TIPS "We frequently need travel photos, especially of places of Jewish interest."

◐ HAMILTON MAGAZINE

Town Media, Sun Media, 1074 Cooke Blvd., Burlington Ontario L7T 4A8, Canada. (905)634-8003. **Fax:** (905)634-7661. **E-mail:** marc.skulnick@sunmedia.ca; tm.info@sunmedia.ca. **Website:** www.hamilton magazine.com. **Contact:** Marc Skulnick, editor; Kate Sharrow, art director. Estab. 1978. "Our mandate: to entertain and inform by spotlighting the best of what our city and region have to offer. We invite readers to take part in a vibrant community by supplying them with authoritative and dynamic coverage of local culture, food, fashion, and design."

NEEDS Photos of cities/urban, entertainment, food/drink, health/fitness/beauty, fashion/glamour, lifestyle. Reviews photos with or without a manuscript. Captions required; include identification of subjects.

SPECS Accepts images in digital format. Send JPEG files at 8×10 at 300 dpi. Uses 8×10 prints.

MAKING CONTACT & TERMS Pays on publication. Credit line given.

HARPER'S MAGAZINE

666 Broadway, 11th Floor, New York NY 10012. (212)420-5720. **Fax:** (212)228-5889. **E-mail:** readings@harpers.org; scg@harpers.org. **Website:** www.harpers.org. **Contact:** Ellen Rosenbush, editor. Estab. 1850. Circ. 230,000. Monthly literary magazine. "The nation's oldest continually published magazine providing fiction, satire, political criticism, social criticism, essays." *Harper's Magazine* encourages national discussion on current and significant issues in a format that offers arresting facts and intelligent opinions.

NEEDS Buys 8-10 photos from freelancers/issue; 120 photos/year. Needs photos of human rights issues, environmental, political. Interested in alternative process, avant garde, documentary, fine art, historical/vintage. Model/property release preferred.

SPECS Uses any format. Accepts images in digital format. Send preferably via e-mail to scg@harpers.org or on CD; TIFF, EPS, JPEG files at 72 dpi (address to Assistant Art Director).

MAKING CONTACT & TERMS Send query letter with résumé, slides, prints, photocopies, tearsheets, transparencies. Provide self-promotion piece to be kept on file for possible future assignments. Responds in 1 week. Pays $200-800 for b&w/color cover; $250-400 for b&w/color inside. Pays on publication. Credit line given. Buys one-time rights; negotiable.

TIPS "*Harper's* is geared more toward fine art photos or artist's portfolios than to 'traditional' photo usages. For instance, we never do fashion, food, travel (unless it's for political commentary), lifestyles, or celebrity profiles. A good understanding of the magazine is crucial for photo submissions. We consider all styles and like experimental or nontraditional work. Please don't confuse us with *Harper's Bazaar!*"

◑ HEALING LIFESTYLES & SPAS MAGAZINE

JLD Publications, P.O. Box 271207, Louisville CO 80027. (303)917-7124. **Fax:** (303)926-4099. **E-mail:** melissa@healinglifestyles.com. **Website:** www.healinglifestyles.com. **Contact:** Melissa B. Williams, editorial director. Estab. 1997. *HL&S* is an online-only publication—a trusted leading social media platform for the spa/wellness industry, focusing on spas, retreats, therapies, food and beauty geared toward a mostly female audience, offering a more holistic and alternative approach to healthy living. Photo guidelines available with SASE.

NEEDS Buys 3 photos from freelancers/issue; 6-12 photos/year. Photos of multicultural, environmental, landscapes/scenics, adventure, health/fitness/beauty, food, yoga, travel. Reviews photos with or without a manuscript. Model/property release preferred. Photo captions required; include subject, location, etc.

SPECS Prefers images in digital format. Send via CD, ZIP, e-mail as TIFF, EPS, JPEG files at 300 dpi. Also uses 35mm or large-format transparencies.

MAKING CONTACT & TERMS Send query letter with résumé, prints, tearsheets. Provide résumé, business card, self-promotion piece to be kept on file for possible future assignments. Responds in 1 month. Responds only if interested; send nonreturnable samples. Simultaneous submissions OK. Pays on assignment. Credit line given. Buys one-time rights.

TIPS "We strongly prefer digital submissions, but will accept all formats. We're looking for something other than the typical resort/spa shots—everything from at-home spa treatments to far-off, exotic locations. We're also looking for reliable lifestyle photographers who can shoot yoga-inspired shots, healthy cuisine, ingredients, and spa modalities in an interesting and enlightening way."

◎ ○ HEARTLAND BOATING

The Waterways Journal, Inc., 319 N. Fourth St., Suite 650, St. Louis MO 63102. (314)241-4310. **Fax:** (314)241-

4207. **E-mail:** brad@heartlandboating.com. **Website:** www.heartlandboating.com. **Contact:** Brad Kovach, editor. Estab. 1989. Circ. 10,000. "*Heartland Boating*'s content is both informative and inspirational—describing boating life as the heartland boater knows it. The content reflects the challenge, joy, and excitement of our way of life afloat. We are devoted to both power and sailboating enthusiasts throughout middle America; houseboats are included. The focus is on the freshwater inland rivers and lakes of the heartland, primarily the waters of the Arkansas, Tennessee, Cumberland, Ohio, Missouri, Illinois, and Mississippi rivers, the Tennessee-Tombigbee Waterway, the Gulf Intracoastal Waterway, and the lakes along these waterways."

NEEDS Hobby or sports photos, primarily boating.

MAKING CONTACT & TERMS No follow-ups. Samples kept on file. Portfolio not required. Credit line given.

TIPS "Please read the magazine first. Our rates are low, but we do our best to take care of and promote our contributors."

HERITAGE RAILWAY MAGAZINE

P.O. Box 43, Horncastle, Lincolnshire LN9 6JR, United Kingdom. (44)(507)529529. **Fax:** (44)(507)529301. **Website:** www.heritagerailway.co.uk. **Contact:** Mr. Robin Jones, editor. Circ. 15,000. Monthly leisure magazine emphasizing preserved railways; covering heritage steam, diesel and electric trains with over 30 pages of news in each issue.

NEEDS Interested in railway preservation. Reviews photos with or without a manuscript. Photo captions required.

SPECS Uses glossy or matte color and b&w prints; 35mm, 2¼×2¼, 4×5, 8×10 transparencies. No digital images accepted.

MAKING CONTACT & TERMS Send query letter with slides, prints, transparencies. Query with online contact form. Does not keep samples on file; include SASE for return of material. Responds in 1 month to queries. Simultaneous submissions OK. Buys one-time rights.

HIGHLIGHTS FOR CHILDREN

803 Church St., Honesdale PA 18431. (570)253-1080. **Fax:** (570)251-7847. **Website:** www.highlights.com. **Contact:** Christine French Cully, editor-in-chief. Estab. 1946. Circ. approximately 1.5 million.

NEEDS "We will consider outstanding photo essays on subjects of high interest to children." Reviews photos with accompanying ms only. Wants no single photos without captions or accompanying ms.

SPECS Accepts images in digital format. Send via CD at 300 dpi. Also accepts transparencies of all sizes.

MAKING CONTACT & TERMS Send photo essays with SASE for consideration. Pays $50 minimum for color photos; $100 minimum for ms. Buys all rights.

TIPS "Tell a story that is exciting to children. We also need mystery photos, puzzles that use photography/collage, special effects, anything unusual that will visually and mentally challenge children."

HIGHWAYS

Affinity Group, Inc., 2575 Vista Del Mar Dr., Ventura CA 93001. (805)667-4100. **E-mail:** highways@goodsamclub.com. **Website:** www.goodsamclub.com/highways. Estab. 1966. Circ. 975,000. Monthly magazine covering recreational vehicle lifestyle. Sample copy free with 8½×11 SASE.

SPECS Accepts images in digital format. Send via CD or e-mail at 300 dpi.

MAKING CONTACT & TERMS Editorial director will contact photographer for portfolio review if interested. Pays $500 for cover; $75-350 for inside. Buys one-time rights.

HOME EDUCATION MAGAZINE

P.O. Box 1083, Tonasket WA 98855. (800)236-3278; (509)486-1351. **Fax:** (509)486-2753. **E-mail:** articles@homeedmag.com. **Website:** www.homeedmag.com. **Contact:** Jeanne Faulconer, articles editor. Estab. 1983. Circ. 120,000. Bimonthly. Emphasizes homeschooling. Readership includes parents, educators, researchers, media—anyone interested in homeschooling. Sample copy available for $6.50. Photo guidelines free with SASE or via e-mail.

NEEDS Number of photos used/issue varies based on availability; 50% supplied by freelance photographers. Photos of babies/children/teens, multicultural, families, parents, senior citizens, education. Special photo needs include homeschool personalities and leaders. Model/property release preferred. Photo captions preferred.

SPECS Uses color prints in normal print size. "Enlargements not necessary." Accepts images in digital format. Send via CD, ZIP, e-mail as TIFF files at 300 dpi.

MAKING CONTACT & TERMS Send unsolicited color prints by mail with SASE for consideration. Responds in 1 month. Pays $100 for color cover; $12.50 for color inside; $50-150 for photo/text package. Pays on publication. Credit line given. Buys first North American serial rights.

TIPS In photographer's samples, wants to see "sharp, clear photos of children doing things alone, in groups, or with parents. Know what we're about! We get too many submissions that are simply irrelevant to our publication."

HOOF BEATS

6130 S. Sunbury Rd., Westerville OH 43081-9309. **E-mail:** hoofbeats@ustrotting.com. **Website:** www.hoofbeatsmagazine.com. Estab. 1933. Circ. 10,000. Monthly publication of the US Trotting Association. Emphasizes harness racing. Readers are participants in the sport of harness racing. Sample copy free.

NEEDS Buys 6 photos from freelancers/issue; 72 photos/year. Needs "artistic or striking photos that feature harness horses for covers; other photos on specific horses and drivers by assignment only."

MAKING CONTACT & TERMS Send query letter with samples; include SASE for return of material. Responds in 3 weeks. Simultaneous submissions OK. Pays $150 minimum for color cover; $25-150 for b&w inside; $50-200 for color inside; freelance assignments negotiable. Pays on publication. Credit line given if requested. Buys one-time rights.

TIPS "We look for photos with unique perspective and that display unusual techniques or use of light. Send query letter first. Know the publication and its needs before submitting. Be sure to shoot pictures of harness horses only, not thoroughbred or riding horses. We always need good night racing action or creative photography."

HORSE ILLUSTRATED

I-5 Publishing, P.O. Box 12106, Lexington KY 40580. (800)546-7730. **E-mail:** horseillustrated@i5publishing.com. **Website:** www.horseillustrated.com. **Contact:** Elizabeth Moyer, editor. Estab. 1976. Circ. 160,660. Readers are "primarily adult horsewomen, ages 18-40, who ride and show mostly for pleasure, and who are very concerned about the well being of their horses. Editorial focus covers all breeds and all riding disciplines." Sample copy available for $4.99. Photo guidelines on website.

NEEDS Buys 30-50 photos from freelancers/issue. Needs stock photos of riding and horse care. "Photos must reflect safe, responsible horsekeeping practices. We prefer all riders to wear protective helmets; prefer people to be shown only in action shots (riding, grooming, treating, etc.). We like all riders—especially those jumping—to be wearing protective headgear."

SPECS Prefer digital images—high-res JPEGs on a CD with printout of thumbnails.

MAKING CONTACT & TERMS Send by mail for consideration. Responds in 2 months. Pays $250 for color cover; $65-250 for color inside. Credit line given. Buys one-time rights.

TIPS "Looks for clear, sharp color shots of horse care and training. Healthy horses, safe riding and care atmosphere is standard in our publication. Send SASE for a list of photography needs, photo guidelines, and to submit work. Photo guidelines are also available on our website."

🔲 💲 🔵 HUNGER MOUNTAIN

Vermont College of Fine Arts, 36 College St., Montpelier VT 05602. (802)828-8517. **E-mail:** hungermtn@vcfa.edu. **Website:** www.hungermtn.org. **Contact:** Miciah Bay Gault, editor. Estab. 2002. No unsolicited photos.

NEEDS Buys no more than 10 photos/year. Interested in avant garde, documentary, fine art, seasonal. Reviews photos with or without a manuscript.

MAKING CONTACT & TERMS Send query letter with résumé, slides, prints, tearsheets. Does not keep samples on file; include SASE for return of material. Responds in 3 months to queries and portfolios. Simultaneous submissions OK. Pays $30-45 for inside photos; cover negotiable. Pays on publication. Credit line given. Buys first rights.

⊕ HYDE PARK LIVING

(859)291-1412. **E-mail:** hydepark@livingmagazines.com. **Website:** www.livingmagazines.com. **Contact:** Grace DeGregorio. Estab. 1983. Circ. 6,800.

MAKING CONTACT & TERMS Reviews contact sheets, negatives, transparencies, prints, GIF/JPEG files. Captions, identification of subjects, model releases required. Negotiates payment individually. Buys all rights.

🔵 IMAGE BY DESIGN LICENSING

Suite 3, 107 Bancroft, Hitchin, Herts SG4 1NB, United Kingdom. 44(0) 1462 422244. **E-mail:** lucy@ibd-licensing.co.uk. **Website:** www.ibd-licensing.co.uk. **Contact:** Lucy Brenham. Agency specializing in art licensing. Serves fine artists, illustrators, and photographers. Interested in reviewing fine art, design, and photography.

MAKING CONTACT & TERMS Send a link to a website with résumé, bio, brochure of work, photocopies or digital images in low-res JPEG format.

TIPS Be aware of current trends.

⊕⊕ INDIANAPOLIS MONTHLY

Emmis Communications, 1 Emmis Plaza, 40 Monument Circle, Suite 100, Indianapolis IN 46204. (317)237-9288. **Fax:** (317)684-2080. **Website:** www.indianapolismonthly.com. **Contact:** Amanda Heckert, editor-in-chief. Estab. 1977. Circ. 50,000. "*Indianapolis Monthly* attracts and enlightens its upscale, well-educated readership with bright, lively editorial on subjects ranging from personalities to social issues, fashion to food. Its diverse content and attention to service make it the ultimate source by which the Indianapolis area lives." Sample copy available for $4.95 and 9×12 SASE.

NEEDS Buys 10-12 photos from freelancers/issue; 120-144 photos/year. Needs seasonal, human interest, humorous, regional; subjects must be Indiana- or Indianapolis-related. Model release preferred. Photo caption information required.

SPECS Glossy prints; transparencies, digital. Send via CD, e-mail as TIFF, EPS, JPEG files at 300 dpi at actual size.

MAKING CONTACT & TERMS Send query letter with samples, SASE. Responds in 1 month. Previously published work on occasion OK, if different market. Pays $300-1,200 for color cover; $75-350 for b&w inside; $75-350 for color inside. Pays on publication. Credit line given. Buys first North American serial rights.

TIPS "Read publication. Send photos similar to those you see published. If you see nothing like what you are considering submitting, it's unlikely we will be interested. We are always interested in photo essay queries if they are Indiana-specific."

⊕⊕ ⓞ INSIGHT MAGAZINE

55 W. Oak Ridge Dr., Hagerstown MD 21740. (301)393-4038. **E-mail:** insight@rhpa.org. **Website:** www.insightmagazine.org. Estab. 1970. Circ. 16,000. Weekly Seventh-Day Adventist teen magazine. "We print teens' true stories about God's involvement in their lives. All stories, if illustrated by a photo, must uphold moral and church organization standards while capturing a hip, teen style." Sample copy $2 and #10 SASE.

NEEDS Model/property release required. Photo captions preferred; include who, what, where, when.

MAKING CONTACT & TERMS "Send query letter with photo samples so we can evaluate style." Provide résumé, business card, self-promotion piece or tearsheets to be kept on file for possible future assignments. Responds only if interested; send nonreturnable samples. Simultaneous submissions and previously published work OK. Pays $200-300 for color cover; $200-400 for color inside. Pays 30-45 days after receiving invoice and contract. Credit line given. Buys first rights. Submission guidelines available online.

ⓞ INSTINCT MAGAZINE

11856 Balboa Blvd., #312, Granada Hills CA 91344. (818)284-4525. **E-mail:** editor@instinctmag.com. **Website:** instinctmagazine.com. **Contact:** Mike Wood, editor-in-chief. Estab. 1997. Circ. 115,000. Monthly gay men's magazine. "*Instinct* is geared towards a gay male audience. The slant of the magazine is humor mingled with entertainment, travel, and health and fitness." Sample copies available. Photo guidelines available via website.

NEEDS Buys 50-75 photos from freelancers/issue; 500-750 photos/year. Needs photos of celebrities, couples, cities/urban, entertainment, health/fitness, humor, travel. Interested in lifestyle, fashion/glamour. High emphasis on humorous and fashion photography. Reviews photos with or without a manuscript. Model release required; property release preferred. Photo captions preferred.

SPECS Uses 8×10 glossy color prints; 2¼×2¼ transparencies. Accepts images in digital format. Send via CD, Jaz, ZIP as TIFF files at least 300 dpi.

MAKING CONTACT & TERMS Portfolio may be dropped off every weekday. Provide résumé, business card, self-promotion piece to be kept on file for possible future assignments. Responds in 2 weeks. Simultaneous submissions OK. Payment negotiable. Pays on publication. Credit line given.

TIPS "Definitely read the magazine. Keep our editor updated about the progress or any problems with the shoot."

INTERVAL WORLD

P.O. Box 431920, Miami FL 33243-1920. (305)666-1861. **E-mail:** kimberly.dewees@intervalintl.com. **Website:** www.intervalworld.com. **Contact:** Kimberly Dewees, photo editor. Estab. 1982. Circ. 1,080,000. Quarterly publication of Interval International. Emphasizes vacation exchange and travel. Readers are members of the Interval International vacation exchange network.

NEEDS Uses 100 or more photos/issue. Needs photos of travel destinations, vacation activities. Model/property release required. Photo captions required; all relevant to full identification.

MAKING CONTACT & TERMS Send query letter with stock list. Provide business card, brochure, flyer or tearsheets to be kept on file for possible future assignments. Cannot return materials. Simultaneous submissions and previously published work OK. Payment negotiable. Pays on publication. Credit line given for editorial use. Buys one-time rights; negotiable.

TIPS Looking for beautiful scenics; family-oriented, fun travel shots; superior technical quality.

IN THE FRAY

113 Schumacher Dr., New Hyde Park NY 11040-3644. (347)850-3935. **E-mail:** art@inthefray.org. **Website:** www.inthefray.org. **Contact:** Benjamin Gottlieb, art director. Estab. 2001.

NEEDS Buys stock photos and offers assignments. Encourages beginning or unpublished photographers to submit work for consideration. Publishes new photographers, may only pay in copies or have a low pay rate. Buys 2 photos from freelancers/issue. 24 photos/year.

SPECS Accepts images in digital format. Send e-mail with JPEG samples at 72 dpi. Keeps samples on file, please provide business card to be kept on file for possible future assignments. Responds only if interested, send nonreturnable samples. Company will contact artist for portfolio review if interested.

MAKING CONTACT & TERMS Reviews photos with or without a manuscript. Photo captions are preferred. Finds freelancers through submissions, word-of-mouth and Internet. Payment range: $20-75. Paid on publication.

🟢 🔵 THE IOWAN MAGAZINE

300 Walnut, Suite 6, Des Moines IA 50309. (515)246-0402; (877)899-9977. **E-mail:** brussie@pioneermagazines.com. **Website:** www.iowan.com. **Contact:** Bobbie Russie, art director. Estab. 1952. Circ. 22,000. Bimonthly. Emphasizes "Iowa's people, places, events, nature and history." Readers are over age 40, college-educated, middle-to-upper income. Sample copy available for $4.50 plus shipping/handling; call the distribution center toll-free at (877)899-9977. Photo guidelines available on website or via e-mail.

NEEDS "We print only Iowa-related images from Iowa photographers, illustrators, and artists. Show us Iowa's residents, towns, environmental, landscape/scenics, wildlife, architecture, rural, entertainment, events, performing arts, travel." Interested in Iowa heritage, historical/vintage, seasonal. Accepts unsolicited stock photos related to above. Editorial stock photo needs available on website or via e-mail. Model/property release preferred. Photo captions required.

SPECS Digital format preferred, see website for details. Press resolution is 300 dpi at 9×12. "If electronic means are not available, mail protected prints with complete contact information and details of items enclosed. NOTE: *The Iowan* does not return any mailed materials."

MAKING CONTACT & TERMS Pays $50-150 for stock photo one-time use, depending on size printed; pays on publication.

🟢🟢 🔵 ISLANDS

Bonnier Corporation, 460 N. Orlando Ave., Suite 200, Winter Park FL 32789. (407)628-4802. **Fax:** (407)628-7061. **E-mail:** editor@islands.com. **Website:** www.islands.com. **Contact:** Lori Barbely, photo editor. Circ. 200,000. Published 8 times/year. "From Bora Bora to the Caribbean, Tahiti to Bali and beyond, *Islands* is your passport to the world's most extraordinary destinations. Each issue is filled with breathtaking photography and detailed first-hand accounts of the fascinating cultural experiences and tranquil, relaxing escapes unique to each vibrant locale."

NEEDS Buys 25 photos from freelancers/issue; 200 photos/year. Needs photos of island travel. Reviews photos with or without a manuscript. Model/property release preferred. Detailed captions required (please use metadata); include name, phone, address, subject information.

SPECS Only accepts images in digital format. Send via e-mail, web gallery, FTP site as JPEG files at 72 dpi (must have 300 dpi file available if image is selected for use). Film is not accepted.

MAKING CONTACT & TERMS Send query letter with tearsheets. Provide business card and self-promotion piece or tearsheets to be kept on file for possible future assignments. You will be contacted if additional information or a portfolio is desired. Simultaneous submissions OK. Pays $600-1,000 for color cover; $100-500 for inside. Pays 45 days after publication. Credit line given. Buys one-time rights. No phone calls.

ITALIAN AMERICA

219 E St. E, Washington DC 20002. (202)547-2900. **Fax:** (202)546-8168. **E-mail:** ddesanctis@osia.org. **Website:** www.osia.org. **Contact:** Dona De Sanctis, editor. Estab. 1996. Circ. 65,000. *Italian America* is the official publication of the Order Sons of Italy in America, the nation's oldest and largest organization of American men and women of Italian heritage. Italian America strives to provide timely information about OSIA, while reporting on individuals, institutions, issues and events of current or historical significance in the Italian-American community. Sample copy and photo guidelines free and available online

NEEDS Buys 5-10 photos from freelancers/issue, 25 photos/year. Needs photos of travel, history, personalities, anything Italian or Italian-American. Reviews photos with or without a manuscript. Special photo needs include travel in Italy. Model releases preferred. Photo captions required.

MAKING CONTACT & TERMS Accepts images in digital format. Send via CD, e-mail as TIFF, EPS, PICT, BMP, GIF or JPEG files at 400 dpi. Send query letter with tearsheets. Provide résumé, business card, self-promotion piece or tearsheets to be kept on file for possible future assignments. Art director will contact photographer for portfolio review if interested. Portfolio should include color tearsheets. Responds only if interested, send nonreturnable samples. Simultaneous submissions OK. Pays on publication. Credit line given. Buys one-time rights.

😊😊 JEWISH ACTION

Orthodox Union, 11 Broadway, New York NY 10004. (212)613-8146. **Fax:** (212)613-0646. **E-mail:** ja@ou.org. **Website:** www.ou.org/jewish_action. **Contact:** Nechama Carmel, editor; Rashel Zywica, assistant editor. Estab. 1986. Circ. 40,000. Quarterly. Covers a vibrant approach to Jewish issues, Orthodox lifestyle, and values. Sample copy available for $5 or on website.

NEEDS Buys 30 photos/year. Photos of Jewish lifestyle, landscapes and travel photos of Israel, and occasional photo essays of Jewish life. Reviews photos with or without a manuscript. Model/property release preferred. Photo captions required; include description of activity, where taken, when.

SPECS Uses color and b&w prints. Accepts images in digital format. Send CD, Jaz, ZIP as TIFF, GIF, JPEG files.

MAKING CONTACT & TERMS Send query letter with samples, brochure or stock photo list. Keeps samples on file. Responds in 2 months. Simultaneous submissions OK. Pays $250 maximum for b&w cover; $400 maximum for color cover; $100 maximum for b&w inside; $150 maximum for color inside. Pays within 6 weeks of publication. Credit line given. Buys one-time rights.

TIPS "Be aware that models must be clothed in keeping with Orthodox laws of modesty. Make sure to include identifying details. Don't send work depicting religion in general. We are specifically Orthodox Jewish."

🌐 JOURNEY MAGAZINE

AAA, 1745 114th Ave. SE, Bellevue WA 98004. (800)562-2582. **E-mail:** sueboylan@aaawin.com; robbhatt@aaawin.com. **Website:** www.aaajourney.com/magazine. **Contact:** Rob Bhatt, editor. Circ. 550,000. Bimonthly. For members of AAA Washington; reaches readers in Washington and northern Idaho.

🔘 "Photographers interested in submitting work to *Journey* magazine are encouraged to send a link to their website, along with a stock listing of regions and subjects of specialty for us to review. You are encouraged to familiarize yourself with *Journey* before sending in submissions. We review photographers' stock lists and samples and keep the names of potential contributors on file to contact as needed. We do not post our photo needs online or elsewhere. To be considered for an assignment, send links to journey@aaawin.com."

MAKING CONTACT & TERMS "We run all articles with high-quality photographs and illustrations. If you are a published photographer, let us know but please do not submit any photos unless requested. To be considered for an assignment, mail a query along with 3 samples of published work or send links to journey@aaawin.com."

💲💲 🌓 KANSAS!

1020 S. Kansas Ave, Suite 200, Topeka KS 66612-1354. (785)296-8478. **Fax:** (785)296-6988. **E-mail:** ksmag azine@sunflowerpub.com. **Website:** www.travelks. com/ks-mag/. **Contact:** Andrea Etzel. Estab. 1945. Circ. 45,000. Quarterly magazine published by the Travel & Tourism Development Division of the Kansas Department of Commerce. Emphasizes Kansas travel, scenery, arts, recreation, and people. Photo guidelines available on website.

NEEDS Buys 60-80 photos from freelancers/year. Subjects include animal, human interest, nature, seasonal, rural, scenic, sport, travel, wildlife, photo essay/photo feature, all from Kansas. No nudes, still life or fashion photos. Will review photographs with or without a ms. Model/property release mandatory.

SPECS Images must be digital at 300 dpi for 8×10.

MAKING CONTACT & TERMS Send material by mail for consideration. Previously published work is accepted if no longer under contract. Pays on acceptance. Credit line given. Buys one-time first North American reprint for 90 days or perpetual rights depending on assignment/gallery/cover/calendar.

TIPS Kansas-oriented material only. Prefers Kansas photographers. "Follow guidelines, submission dates specifically. Shoot a lot of seasonal scenics."

💲 🌓 KASHRUS MAGAZINE

The Kashrus Institute, P.O. Box 204, Brooklyn NY 11204. (718)336-8544. **E-mail:** editorial@kashrus magazine.com. **Website:** www.kashrusmagazine. com. **Contact:** Rabbi Wikler, editor. Estab. 1981. Circ. 10,000. "The periodical for the kosher consumer. We feature updates including mislabeled kosher products and recalls. Important for vegetarians, lactose intolerant and others with allergies."

NEEDS 25% freelance written. Prefers to work with published/established writers, but will work with new/ unpublished writers.

SPECS Uses 2¼×2¼, 3½×3½ or 7½×7½ matte b&w and color prints.

MAKING CONTACT & TERMS Send unsolicited photos by mail with SASE for consideration. Provide business card, brochure, flyer or tearsheets to be kept on file for possible future assignments. Responds in 1 week. Simultaneous submissions and previously published work OK. Pays $40-75 for b&w cover; $50-100 for color cover; $25-50 for b&w inside; $75-200/job; $50-200 for text for photo package. Pays part on acceptance, part on publication. Buys one-time rights, first North American serial rights, all rights; negotiable. Byline given. Submit seasonal materials 2 months in advance. Responds in 2 weeks.

TIPS "Seriously in need of new photo sources, but *call first* to see if your work is appropriate before submitting samples."

💲 ⭕ KENTUCKY MONTHLY

P.O. Box 559, Frankfort KY 40602-0559. (502)227-0053; (888)329-0053. **Fax:** (502)227-5009. **E-mail:** kymonthly@kentuckymonthly.com; steve@ken tuckymonthly.com. **Website:** www.kentuckymonthly. com. **Contact:** Stephen Vest, editor. Estab. 1998. Circ. 40,000. Monthly. Focuses on Kentucky and Kentucky-related stories. Sample copy available for $5.

NEEDS Buys average of 10-20 photos from freelancers/issue; 120-300 photos/year. Photos of celebrities, wildlife, entertainment, landscapes. Reviews photos with or without a manuscript. Model release required. Photo captions required.

SPECS Accepts images in digital format only. Send via CD, e-mail at 300 dpi, sized minimum of 4×6, larger preferred.

MAKING CONTACT & TERMS Send query letter. Provide self-promotion piece to be kept on file for possible future assignments. Responds in 1-3 months. Simultaneous submissions OK. Pays $25 minimum for inside photos. Pays the 15th of the month within 3 months of issue publication. Credit line given.

💲💲 ⚫ KNOWATLANTA

450 Northridge Pkwy., Suite 202, Atlanta GA 30350. (770)650-1102. **Fax:** (770)650-2848. **E-mail:** gwyn@ knowatlanta.com. **Website:** www.knowatlanta.com. **Contact:** Gwyn Herbein, editor. Estab. 1986. Circ. 48,000. Quarterly. Serves as a relocation guide to the Atlanta metro area with a corporate audience. Photography reflects regional and local material as well as corporate-style imagery.

NEEDS Buys more than 10 photos from freelancers/issue; more than 40 photos/year. Photos of cities/urban, events, performing arts, business concepts, medicine, technology/computers. Reviews photos with or without a manuscript. Model release required; property release preferred. Photo captions preferred.

SPECS Uses 8×10 glossy color prints; 35mm, transparencies. Accepts images in digital format. Send via CD, ZIP, e-mail as TIFF, EPS, JPEG files at 300 dpi.

MAKING CONTACT & TERMS Send query letter with photocopies. Provide résumé, business card, self-promotion piece to be kept on file for possible future assignments. Responds only if interested; send non-returnable samples. Pays $600 maximum for color cover; $300 maximum for color inside. Pays on publication. Credit line given. Buys first rights.

TIPS "Think like our readers. What would they want to know about or see in this magazine? Try to represent the relocated person if using subjects in photography."

◎ $ ○ LACROSSE MAGAZINE

113 W. University Pkwy., Baltimore MD 21210. (410)235-6882. **Fax:** (410)366-6735. **E-mail:** feedback@laxmagazine.com; mdasilva@uslacrosse.org. **Website:** www.laxmagazine.com; www.uslacrosse.org. **Contact:** Matt DaSilva, editor; Gabriella O'Brien, art director. Estab. 1978. Circ. 235,000. Publication of U.S. Lacrosse. Monthly. Emphasizes sport of lacrosse. Readers are male and female lacrosse enthusiasts of all ages. Sample copy free with general information pack.

NEEDS Buys 15-30 photos from freelancers/issue; 120-240 photos/year. Needs lacrosse action shots. Photo captions required; include rosters with numbers for identification.

SPECS Accepts images in digital format. Digital photographs should be submitted in the form of original, unedited JPEGs. Suggested captions are welcome. Photographs may be submitted via CD or e-mail. Prints also are accepted and are returned upon request. Photographer credit is published when supplied. Original RAW/NEF files or 300 dpi TIFFs.

MAKING CONTACT & TERMS Send unsolicited photos by mail with SASE for consideration. Provide résumé, business card, brochure, flyer, or tearsheets to be kept on file for possible future assignments. Responds in 3 weeks. Simultaneous submissions and previously published work OK. Pays $250 for color cover; $75-150 inside. Pays on publication. Credit line given. Buys one-time rights.

$ $ LADIES HOME JOURNAL

805 Third Ave., 26th Floor, New York NY 10022. (212)499-2087. **Website:** www.lhj.com. Circ. 6 million. Monthly. Features women's issues. Readership consists of women with children and working women in 30s age group.

NEEDS Uses 90 photos/issue; 100% supplied by freelancers. Needs photos of children, celebrities and women's lifestyles/situations. Reviews photos only without manuscript. Model release preferred. Photo captions preferred.

MAKING CONTACT & TERMS Provide résumé, business card, brochure, flier or tearsheet to be kept on file for possible assignment. "Do not send slides or original work; send only promo cards or disks." Responds in 3 weeks. **Pays on acceptance.** Credit line given. Buys one-time rights.

$ LAKELAND BOATING MAGAZINE

727 South Dearborn St., Suite 812, Chicago IL 60605. (312)276-0610. **Fax:** (312)276-0619. **E-mail:** cbauhs@lakelandboating.com; ljohnson@lakelandboating.com. **Website:** www.lakelandboating.com. **Contact:** Lindsay Johnson, editor. Estab. 1945. Circ. 60,000. Monthly magazine. Emphasizes powerboating in the Great Lakes. Readers are affluent professionals, predominantly men over age 35.

NEEDS Shots of particular Great Lakes ports and waterfront communities. Model release preferred. Photo captions preferred.

MAKING CONTACT & TERMS Send query letter with list of stock photo subjects. Provide résumé, business card, brochure, flyer or tearsheets to be kept on file for possible future assignments. Pays on publication. Credit line given.

$ ◐ LAKE SUPERIOR MAGAZINE

Lake Superior Port Cities, Inc., P.O. Box 16417, Duluth MN 55816-0417. (218)722-5002. **Fax:** (218)722-4096. **E-mail:** edit@lakesuperior.com. **Website:** www.lakesuperior.com. **Contact:** Konnie LeMay, editor. Estab. 1979. Circ. 20,000. Bimonthly. "Beautiful picture magazine about Lake Superior." Readers are male and female, ages 35-55, highly educated, upper-middle and upper-management level through working. Sample copy available for $4.95 plus $5.95 S&H. Photo guidelines free with SASE or via website.

NEEDS Buys 21 photos from freelancers/issue; 126 photos/year. Also buys photos for calendars and books. Needs photos of landscapes/scenics, travel, wildlife, personalities, boats, underwater—all Lake Superior related. Photo captions preferred.

SPECS Uses mainly images in digital format. Send via CD with at least thumbnails on a printout.

MAKING CONTACT & TERMS Send unsolicited photos by mail with SASE for consideration. Provide résumé, business card, brochure, flyer or tearsheets to be kept on file for possible future assignments. Responds in 2 months. Simultaneous submissions OK. Pays $150 for color cover; $50 for b&w or color inside. Pays on publication. Credit line given. Buys first North American serial rights; reserves second rights for future use.

TIPS "Be aware of the focus of our publication—Lake Superior. Photo features concern only that. Features with text can be related. We are known for our fine color photography and reproduction. It has to be tops. We try to use images large; therefore, detail quality and resolution must be good. We look for unique outlook on subject, not just snapshots. Must communicate emotionally. Some photographers send material we can keep in-house and refer to, and these will often get used."

🌑 LINCOLNSHIRE LIFE

9 Checkpoint Court, Sadler Rd., Lincoln LN6 3PW, United Kingdom. (44)(152)252-7127. **Fax:** (44)(152)228-2000. **E-mail:** editorial@lincolnshirelife.co.uk; studio@lincolnshirelife.co.uk. **Website:** www.lincolnshirelife.co.uk. Estab. 1961. Circ. 10,000. Monthly county magazine featuring the culture and history of Lincolnshire. Sample copy available for £2. Photo guidelines free.

NEEDS Buys 10 photos from freelancers/issue; 120 photos/year. Needs photos of Lincolnshire scenes, animals, people. Photo captions required.

SPECS Color transparencies with vertical orientation for cover. Accepts color prints for inside.

MAKING CONTACT & TERMS Send query letter with samples. Art director will contact photographer for portfolio review if interested. Portfolio should include slides or transparencies. Keeps samples on file. Responds in 1 month. Previously published work OK. Payment negotiable. Pays on publication. Credit line given. Buys first rights.

LION

Lions Clubs International, 300 W. 22nd St., Oak Brook IL 60523-8842. (630)468-6909. **Fax:** (630)571-1685. **E-mail:** magazine@lionsclubs.org. **Website:** www.lionsclubs.org. **Contact:** Jay Copp, senior editor. Estab. 1918. Circ. 490,000. Monthly magazine for members of the Lions Club and their families. Empha-

sizes Lions Club activities and membership. Sample copy and photo guidelines free.

NEEDS Uses 50-60 photos/issue. Needs photos of Lions Club service or fundraising projects. All photos must be as candid as possible, showing an activity in progress. Please, no award presentations, meetings, speeches, etc. Generally, photos are purchased with manuscript (300-1,500 words) and used as a photo story. We seldom purchase photos separately. Model release preferred for young or disabled children. Photo caption is required. Uses 5×7, 8×10 glossy color prints, 35mm transparencies, also accepts digital images in JPEG or TIFF format via e-mail at 300 dpi or larger.

MAKING CONTACT & TERMS Works with freelancers on assignment only. Provide résumé to be kept on file for possible future assignments. Query first with résumé of credits or story idea. Must accompany story on the service or fundraising project of the Lions Club. Pays on acceptance. Buys all rights, negotiable.

TIPS Query on specific project and photos to accompany ms.

💲 ⭕ LIVING FREE

P.O. Box 969, Winnisquam NH 03289. (603)455-7368. **E-mail:** free@natnh.com. **Website:** www.natnh.com/lf/mag.html. **Contact:** Tom Caldwell, editor-in-chief. Estab. 1987. Quarterly electronic magazine succeeding Naturist Life International's online e-zine. Emphasizes nudism/naturism. Readers are male and female nudists/naturists. Sample copy available on CD for $10. Photo guidelines free with SASE. We periodically organize naturist photo safaris to shoot nudes in nature.

NEEDS Buys 36 photos from freelancers/issue; 144 photos/year. Photos depicting family-oriented nudist/naturist work, recreational activity and travel. Reviews photos with or without a manuscript. Model release required (including Internet use) for recognizable nude subjects. Photo captions preferred.

SPECS Prefers digital images, minimum 1MB in size, submitted on CD or via e-mail.

MAKING CONTACT & TERMS Send query letter with résumé of credits. Send unsolicited photos by mail or e-mail for consideration; include SASE for return of material. Provide résumé, business card, brochure, flier or tearsheets to be kept on file for possible future assignments. Responds in 2 weeks. Pays $50 for color cover; $10-25 for others. Pays on publication. Credit line given. "Prefer to own all rights but sometimes agree to one-time publication rights."

TIPS "The ideal photo shows ordinary-looking people of all ages doing everyday activities, in the joy of nudism. We do not want 'cheesecake' glamour images or anything that emphasizes the erotic."

$$ ◐ LOG HOME LIVING

Home Buyer Publications, Inc., 4125 Lafayette Center Dr., Suite 100, Chantilly VA 20151. (703)222-9411; (800)826-3893. **Fax:** (703)222-3209. **E-mail:** editor@timberhomeliving.com. **Website:** www.loghome.com. Estab. 1989. Circ. 132,000. Monthly. Emphasizes planning, building and buying a log home. Sample copy available for $4. Photo guidelines available online.

NEEDS Buys 90 photos from freelancers/issue; 120 photos/year. Needs photos of homes—living room, dining room, kitchen, bedroom, bathroom, exterior, portrait of owners, design/decor—tile sunrooms, furniture, fireplaces, lighting, porch and deck, doors. Close-up shots of details (roof trusses, log stairs, railings, dormers, porches, window/door treatments) are appreciated. Model release required.

SPECS Prefers to use digital images or 4×5 color transparencies/Kodachrome or Ektachrome color slides; smaller color transparencies and 35mm color prints also acceptable.

MAKING CONTACT & TERMS Send unsolicited photos by mail for consideration. Keeps samples on file. Responds only if interested. Previously published work OK. Pays $2,000 maximum for color feature. Cover shot submissions also accepted; fee varies, negotiable. **Pays on acceptance.** Credit line given. Buys first world one-time stock serial rights; negotiable.

TIPS "Send photos of log homes, both interiors and exteriors."

LOST LAKE FOLK OPERA

Shipwreckt Books Publishing Company, 309 W. Stevens Ave., Rushford MN 55971. **E-mail:** contact@shipwrecktbooks.com. **Website:** www.shipwrecktbooks.com. **Contact:** Tom Driscoll, managing editor. Estab. 2013. Circ. 500. *Lost Lake Folk Opera* magazine is the arts heartbeat and journalistic pulse of rural mid-America. Currently accepting submissions of critical journalism, short fiction, poetry, and graphic art. Published three times, annually. Covers rural mid-American arts, politics, economics, and opinions.

MAKING CONTACT & TERMS Freelancers should query. Does not offer payment. Holds one-time rights.

$ LOYOLA MAGAZINE

820 N. Michigan Ave., Chicago IL 60611. (312)915-6930. **E-mail:** abusiek@luc.edu. **Website:** www.luc.edu/loyolamagazine. **Contact:** Anastasia Busiek, editor. Estab. 1971. Circ. 120,000. Loyola University alumni magazine. Quarterly. Emphasizes issues related to Loyola University Chicago. Readers are Loyola University Chicago alumni—professionals, ages 22 and up.

NEEDS Buys 20 photos from freelancers/issue; 60 photos/year. Needs Loyola-related or Loyola alumni-related photos only. Model release preferred. Photo captions preferred.

SPECS Uses 8×10 b&w and color prints; 35mm, 2¼×2¼ transparencies. Accepts high-res digital images. Query before submitting.

MAKING CONTACT & TERMS Best to query by mail before making any submissions. If interested, will ask for résumé, business card, brochure, flyer or tearsheets to be kept on file for possible future assignments. Simultaneous submissions and previously published work OK. **Pays on acceptance.** Credit line given.

TIPS "Send us information, but don't call."

◐ ○ LULLWATER REVIEW

P.O. Box 122036, Atlanta GA 30322. **E-mail:** emorylullwaterreview@gmail.com. **Website:** www.lullwaterreview.wordpress.com. **Contact:** Aneyn M. O'Grady, editor-in-chief; Gabriel Unger, managing editor. Estab. 1990. Circ. 2,000. "We're a small, student-run literary magazine published out of Emory University in Atlanta with 2 issues yearly—1 in the fall and 1 in the spring. You can find us in the *Index of American Periodical Verse*, the *American Humanities Index* and as a member of the Council of Literary Magazines and Presses. We welcome work that brings a fresh perspective, whether through language or the visual arts." Magazine: 6×9; 100 pages; 60-lb. paper; photos. "*Lullwater Review* seeks submissions that are strong and original. We require no specific genre or subject."

NEEDS Architecture, cities/urban, rural, landscapes, wildlife, alternative process, avant garde, fine art and historical/vintage photos.

MAKING CONTACT & TERMS Send an e-mail with photographs. Samples kept on file. Portfolio should include b&w, color, photographs and finished, original art. Credit line given when appropriate.

TIPS "Read our magazine. We welcome work of all different types, and we encourage submissions that bring a fresh or alternative perspective. Submit at least 5 works. We frequently accept 3-5 pieces from a single artist and like to see a selection."

⊕⊕ ◑ THE LUTHERAN

8765 W. Higgins Rd., 5th Floor, Chicago IL 60631-4183. (800)638-3522, ext. 2540. **Fax:** (773)380-2409. **E-mail:** michael.watson@thelutheran.org; lutheran@thelutheran.org. **Website:** www.thelutheran.org. **Contact:** Michael Watson, art director. Estab. 1988. Circ. 300,000. Monthly publication of Evangelical Lutheran Church in America. "Please send samples of your work that we can keep in our files. Though we prefer to review online portfolios, a small number of slides, prints or tearsheets, a brochure, or even a few photocopies are acceptable as long as you feel they represent you."

NEEDS Buys 10-15 photos from freelancers/issue; 120-180 photos/year. Current news, mood shots. Subjects include babies/children/teens, couples, multicultural, families, parents, senior citizens, disasters, landscapes/scenics, cities/urban, education, religious. Interested in fine art, seasonal. "We usually assign work with exception of 'Reflections' section." Model release required. Photo captions preferred.

SPECS Accepts images in digital format. Send via CD or e-mail as TIFF or JPEG files at 300 dpi.

MAKING CONTACT & TERMS Send query letter with list of stock photo subjects. Provide résumé, brochure, flyer or tearsheets to be kept on file for possible future assignments. Pays on publication. Credit line given. Buys one-time rights; credits the photographer.

TIPS Trend toward "more dramatic lighting; careful composition." In portfolio or samples, wants to see "candid shots of people active in church life, preferably Lutheran. Church-only photos have little chance of publication. Submit sharp, well-composed photos with borders for cropping. Send printed or duplicate samples to be kept on file; no originals. If we like your style, we will call you when we have a job in your area."

THE MACGUFFIN

18600 Haggerty Rd., Livonia MI 48152. (734)462-4400, ext 5327. **E-mail:** macguffin@schoolcraft.edu. **Website:** www.macguffin.org. **Contact:** Steven A. Dolgin, editor; Gordon Krupsky, managing editor;.

Estab. 1984. Magazine covering the best new work in contemporary poetry, prose and visual art. "Our purpose is to encourage, support and enhance the literary arts in the Schoolcraft College community, the region, the state, and the nation. We also sponsor annual literary events and give voice to deserving new writers as well as established writers."

NEEDS Reviews photos in TIFF, EPS, JPEG formats. Captions required.

MAKING CONTACT & TERMS Send an e-mail with samples. "Please submit name and contact information with your work, along with captions." Portfolio not required. Credit line given.

THE MAGAZINE ANTIQUES

Brant Publications, 110 Greene St., New York NY 10012. (212)941-2800. **Fax:** (212)941-2819. **E-mail:** tmaedit@brantpub.com (JavaScript required to view). **Website:** www.themagazineantiques.com. **Contact:** Editorial. Estab. 1922. Circ. 40,000. Bimonthly magazine. Emphasizes art, antiques, architecture. Readers are male and female collectors, curators, academics, interior designers, ages 40-70. Sample copy available for $12 plus shipping costs. Buys 24-48 photos from freelancers/issue; 288-576 photos/year. Needs photos of interiors, architectural exteriors, objects. Reviews photos with or without a ms. Uses 8×10 glossy prints; 4×5 transparencies; JPEGs at 300 dpi. Submit portfolio for review; phone ahead to arrange drop-off. Does not keep samples on file; include SASE for return of material. Responds in 6 weeks. Previously published work OK. Payment negotiable. Pays on publication. Credit line given.

MAKING CONTACT & TERMS E-mail: tmaedit@brantpub.com (JavaScript required to view).

⊕ ◐ MAISONNEUVE

E-mail: anna@maisonneuve.org. **Website:** www.maisonneuve.org. Estab. 2002. Circ. under 10,000. *Maisonneuve* has been described as a new *New Yorker* for a younger generation, or as *Harper's* meets *Vice*, or as *Vanity Fair* without the vanity—but *Maisonneuve* is its own creature. *Maisonneuve's* purpose is to keep its readers informed, alert, and entertained, and to dissolve artistic borders between regions, countries, languages, and genres. It does this by providing a diverse range of commentary across the arts, sciences, and daily and social life. The magazine has a balanced perspective and "brings the news" in a wide variety of ways.

MAKING CONTACT & TERMS Reviews GIF/JPEG files. Captions, identification of subjects, model releases required. Negotiates payment individually. Buys one-time rights.

🌑🌑 MARLIN

P.O. Box 8500, Winter Park FL 32790. (407)628-4802. **Fax:** (407)628-7061. **E-mail:** editor@marlinmag.com. **Website:** www.marlinmag.com. Estab. 1982. Circ. 50,000. Published 8 times/year. Emphasizes offshore big game fishing for billfish, tuna and other large pelagics. Readers are 94% male, 75% married, average age 43, very affluent businessmen. Sample copy free with 8×10 SASE. Photo guidelines free with SASE or online.

NEEDS Buys 45 photos from freelancers/issue; 270 photos/year. Photos of fish/action shots, scenics and how-to. Special photo needs include big game fishing action and scenics (marinas, landmarks, etc.). Model release preferred. Photo captions preferred.

SPECS Uses 35mm transparencies. Also accepts high-res images on CD or via FTP.

MAKING CONTACT & TERMS Contract required. Send unsolicited photos by mail with SASE for consideration. Responds in 1 month. Simultaneous submissions OK with notification. Pays $1,200 for color cover; $100-300 for color inside. Pays on publication. Buys first North American rights.

TIPS "Send sample material with SASE. No phone call necessary. Don't hesitate to call editor Dave Ferrel or managing editor Charlie Levine at (407)628-4802 anytime you have any general or specific questions about photo needs, submissions or payment."

🌑🌑 ⭕ METROSOURCE MAGAZINE

137 W. 19th St., 2nd Floor, New York NY 10011. (212)691-5127. **E-mail:** letters@metrosource.com. **Website:** www.metrosource.com. Estab. 1990. Circ. 145,000. Upscale, gay men's luxury lifestyle magazine published 6 times/year. Emphasizes fashion, travel, profiles, interiors, film, art. Sample copies free.

NEEDS Buys 10-15 photos from freelancers/issue; 50 photos/year. Photos of celebrities, architecture, interiors/decorating, adventure, food/drink, health/fitness, travel, product shots/still life. Interested in erotic, fashion/glamour, seasonal. Also needs still-life drink shots for spirits section. Reviews photos with or without a ms. Model/property release preferred. Photo captions preferred.

SPECS Uses 8×10 glossy or matte color and b&w prints; 2¼×2¼, 4×5 transparencies. Prefers images in digital format. Send via CD, ZIP, e-mail as TIFF, EPS, JPEG files at 300 dpi.

MAKING CONTACT & TERMS Send query letter with self-promo cards. "Please call first for portfolio drop-off." Provide self-promotion piece to be kept on file for possible future assignments. Responds only if interested; send nonreturnable samples. Simultaneous submissions and previously published work OK. Pays $500-800 for cover; up to $300 for inside. Pays on publication. Credit line given. Buys one-time rights.

TIPS "We work with creative established and newly-established photographers. Our budgets vary depending on the importance of story. Have an e-mail address on card so we can see more photos or whole portfolio online."

MICHIGAN OUT-OF-DOORS

P.O. Box 30235, Lansing MI 48912. (517)371-1041. **Fax:** (517)371-1505. **E-mail:** thansen@mucc.org; magazine@mucc.org. **Website:** www.michiganoutofdoors.com. **Contact:** Tony Hansen, editor. Estab. 1947. Circ. 40,000. Monthly. For people interested in "outdoor recreation, especially hunting and fishing; conservation; environmental affairs." Sample copy available for $3.50; editorial guidelines free.

NEEDS Buys 6-12 photos from freelancers/issue; 72-144 photos/year. Photos of animals/wildlife, nature, scenics, sports (hunting, fishing, backpacking, camping, cross-country skiing, other forms of noncompetitive outdoor recreation). Materials must have a Michigan slant. Photo captions preferred.

MAKING CONTACT & TERMS Digital photos only. Include SASE for return of material. Responds in 1 month. Pays $275 for cover; $20 minimum for b&w inside; $40 for color inside. Credit line given. Buys first North American serial rights.

🌑 ◎ 🌓 MINNESOTA GOLFER

Minnesota Golf Association, 6550 York Ave. S., Suite 211, Edina MN 55435. (952)927-4643; (800)642-4405. **Fax:** (952)927-9642. **E-mail:** editor@mngolf.org; wp@mngolf.org. **Website:** www.mngolf.org. **Contact:** W.P. Ryan, editor. Estab. 1970. Circ. 55,000. Quarterly association magazine covering Minnesota golf scene. Sample copies available online at mngolf.org/magazine.

NEEDS Works on assignment only. Buys 25 photos from freelancers/issue; 100 photos/year. Photos of golf, golfers, and golf courses only. Will accept exceptional photography that tells a story or takes specific point of view. Reviews photos with or without manuscript. Model/property release required. Photo captions required; include date, location, names and hometowns of all subjects.

SPECS Accepts images in digital format. Send via DVD or CD, e-mail as TIFF files.

MAKING CONTACT & TERMS Send query letter with digital medium. Provide business card or self-promotion piece to be kept on file for possible future assignments. Responds only if interested; send non-returnable samples. Pays on publication. Credit line given. Buys one-time rights. Will negotiate one-time or all rights, depending on needs of the magazine and the MGA.

TIPS "We use beautiful golf course photography to promote the game and Minnesota courses to our readers. We expect all submissions to be technically correct in terms of lighting, exposure, and color. We are interested in photos that portray the game and golf courses in new, unexpected ways. For assignments, submit work with invoice and all expenses. For unsolicited work, please include contact, fee, and rights terms submitted with photos; include captions where necessary."

MISSOURI LIFE

501 High St., Suite A, Boonville MO 65233. (660)882-9898. **Fax:** (660)882-9899. **E-mail:** dcawthon@missourilife.com. **Website:** www.missourilife.com. **Contact:** David Cawthon, associate editor. Estab. 1973. Circ. 96,800. Bimonthly. "*Missouri Life* celebrates Missouri people and places, past and present, and the unique qualities of our great state with interesting stories and bold, colorful photography." Sample copy available for $4.95 and SASE with $2.44 first-class postage. Photo guidelines available on website.

NEEDS Buys 80 photos from freelancers/issue; more than 500 photos/year. Needs photos of environmental, seasonal, landscapes/scenics, wildlife, architecture, cities/urban, rural, adventure, historical sites, entertainment, events, hobbies, performing arts, travel. Reviews photos with or without manuscript. Model/property release required. Photo captions required; include location, names and detailed identification (including any title and hometown) of subjects.

SPECS Prefers images in high-res digital format (minimum 300 ppi at 8×10). Send via e-mail, CD, ZIP as EPS, JPEG, TIFF files.

MAKING CONTACT & TERMS Send query letter with résumé, stock list. Provide self-promotion piece to be kept on file for possible future assignments. Responds in 1 month. Pays $100-150 for color cover; $50 for color inside. Pays on publication. Credit line given. Buys first rights, nonexclusive rights, limited rights.

TIPS "Be familiar with our magazine and the state of Missouri. Provide well-labeled images with detailed caption and credit information."

⊕ ◐ MONDAY MAGAZINE

Black Press Ltd., 818 Broughton St., Victoria British Columbia V8W 1E4, Canada. (250)382-6188. **Website:** www.mondaymag.com. **Contact:** Kyle Slovin, editor. Estab. 1975. Circ. 20,000. "*Monday Magazine* is Victoria's only alternative newsweekly. For more than 35 years, we have published fresh, informative, and alternative perspectives on local events."

MAKING CONTACT & TERMS Reviews GIF/JPEG files (300 dpi at 4x6). Captions, identification of subjects required. Offers no additional payment for photos accepted with ms. Buys one-time rights.

◕ ◎ ◑ ◐ MORPHEUS TALES

E-mail: morpheustales@blueyonder.co.uk. **Website:** www.morpheustales.com. **Contact:** Adam Bradley, publisher. Estab. 2008. Circ. 1,000. Publishes experimental fiction, fantasy, horror, and science fiction. Publishes 4-6 titles/year.

NEEDS "Look at magazine and website for style."

MAKING CONTACT & TERMS Portfolio should include b&w, color, finished and original art. Responds within 30 days. Model and property release are required.

MOTHER JONES

Foundation for National Progress, 222 Sutter St., Suite 600, San Francisco CA 94108. (415)321-1700. **E-mail:** mmurrmann@motherjones.com; query@motherjones.com. **Website:** www.motherjones.com. **Contact:** Mark Murrmann, photo editor; Ivylise Simones, creative director; Monika Bauerlein and Clara Jeffery, editors. Estab. 1976. Circ. 240,000. "Recognized worldwide for publishing groundbreaking work by some of the most talented photographers, *Mother Jones* is proud to include the likes of Antonin Kratochvil, Eugene Richards, Sebastião Salgado, Lana Šlezić, and Larry Sultan as past contributors. We remain committed to championing the best in photography and are always looking for exceptional photographers with a unique visual style. It's best to give us a URL for a portfolio website. For photo essays, describe the work that you've done or propose to do; and if possible, provide a link to view the project online. We will contact you if we are interested in seeing more work. Or you can mail non-returnable samples or discs to: Mark Murrmann."

TIPS "Please do not submit original artwork or any samples that will need to be returned. *Mother Jones* cannot be responsible for the return or loss of unsolicited artwork."

MOTORING & LEISURE

Britannia House, 21 Station St., Brighton BN1 4DE, United Kingdom. **E-mail:** magazine@csmaclub.co.uk. **Website:** www.csma.uk.com. Circ. 300,000. In-house magazine of CSMA (Civil Service Motoring Association); 144 pages printed 10 times/year (double issue July/August and November/December). Covers car reviews, worldwide travel features, lifestyle and leisure, gardening. Sample copy available.

NEEDS Innovative photos of cars and motorbikes, old and new, to give greater choice than usual stock shots; motoring components (tires, steering wheels, windscreens); car manufacturer logos; UK traffic signs, road markings, general traffic, minor roads and motorways; worldwide travel images; UK villages, towns and cities; families on UK outdoor holidays; caravans, motor homes, camping, picnics sites. Reviews photos with or without manuscript. Photo captions preferred; include location.

SPECS Prefers images in digital format. Send JPEG files via e-mail, 300 dpi where possible, or 72 dpi at the largest possible image size. Maximum limit per e-mail is 8MB so may need to send images in separate e-mails or compress byte size. Most file formats (EPS, TIFF, PDF, PSD) accepted for PC use. Unable to open Mac files. TIFFs and very large files should be sent on a CD.

MAKING CONTACT & TERMS Prefers to be contacted via e-mail. Simultaneous submissions and previously published work OK. Payment negotiated with individual photographers and image libraries. Credit line sometimes given if asked. Buys one-time rights.

MOUNTAIN LIVING

Wiesner Media Network Communications, Inc., 1780 S. Bellaire St., Suite 505, Denver CO 80222. (303)248-2060. **Fax:** (303)248-2066. **E-mail:** greatideas@mountainliving.com; hscott@mountainliving.com; cdeorio@mountainliving.com. **Website:** www.mountainliving.com. **Contact:** Holly Scott, publisher; Christine DeOrio, editor-in-chief. Estab. 1994. Circ. 40,000. Published 7 times/year covering architecture, interior design, and lifestyle issues for people who live in, visit, or hope to live in the mountains.

NEEDS Photos of home interiors, architecture. Model/property release required.

SPECS Prefers images in digital format. Send via CD as TIFF files at 300 dpi.

MAKING CONTACT & TERMS Submit portfolio for review. Send query letter with stock list. Provide résumé, business card, brochure, flyer or tearsheets to be kept on file for possible future assignments. Responds in 6-8 weeks. Pays $400/half day; $800/full day. **Pays on acceptance.** Credit line given. Buys one-time and first North American serial rights as well as rights to use photos on the *Mountain Living* website and in promotional materials; negotiable.

MUSCLEMAG INTERNATIONAL

Robert Kennedy Publishing, 400 Matheson Blvd. W., Mississauga Ontario L5R 3M1, Canada. (888)254-0767; (905)507-3545. **Fax:** (905)507-2372. **Website:** www.emusclemag.com. **Contact:** Art director. Estab. 1974. Circ. 300,000. Monthly. Emphasizes hardcore bodybuilding for men and women. Sample copy available for $6.

NEEDS Buys 3,000 photos/year; 50% assigned; 50% stock. Needs bodybuilding, celebrity/personality, swimsuit, how-to, special effects/experimental and spot news. "We require action exercise photos of bodybuilders and fitness enthusiasts training with sweat and strain." Wants on a regular basis "different" pics of top names, bodybuilders or film stars famous for their physiques (e.g., Schwarzenegger, The Hulk). No photos of mediocre bodybuilders. "They have to be among the top 100 in the world or top film stars exercising." Photos may be purchased with accompanying manuscript. Photo captions preferred.

SPECS Uses 8×10 glossy b&w prints; 35mm, 2¼×2¼ or 4×5 transparencies; high-resolution digital thumbnails; vertical format preferred for cover.

MAKING CONTACT & TERMS Send material by mail for consideration; send $3 for return postage. Send query letter with contact sheet. Responds in 1 month. Pays on publication. Credit line given. Buys all rights.

TIPS "We would like to see photographers take up the challenge of making exercise photos look like exercise motion. In samples we want to see sharp, color-balanced, attractive subjects, no grain, artistic eye. Someone who can glamorize bodybuilding on film. To break in get serious: read, ask questions, learn, experiment and try, try again. Keep trying for improvement—don't kid yourself that you are a good photographer when you don't even understand half the attachments on your camera. Immerse yourself in photography. Study the best; study how they use light, props, backgrounds, angles. Current biggest demand is for swimsuit-type photos of fitness men and women (splashing in waves, playing/posing in sand, etc.). Shots must be sexually attractive."

MUSHING MAGAZINE

P.O. Box 1195, Willow AK 99688. (907)495-2468. **E-mail:** editor@mushing.com. **Website:** www.mushing.com. **Contact:** Greg Sellentin, publisher and executive editor. Estab. 1987. Circ. 10,000.

NEEDS Uses 50 photos/issue; most supplied by freelancers. Needs action photos: all-season and wilderness; still and close-up photos: specific focus (sledding, carting, dog care, equipment, etc.). Special photo needs include skijoring, feeding, caring for dogs, summer carting or packing, 1- to 3-dog-sledding, and kids mushing. Model release preferred. Photo captions preferred.

SPECS Accepts images in digital format. Send via CD, ZIP, e-mail as JPEG files at 300 dpi.

MAKING CONTACT & TERMS Send unsolicited photos by mail for consideration. Responds in 6 months. Pays $175 maximum for color cover; $15-40 for b&w inside; $40-50 for color inside. Pays $10 extra for 1 year of electronic use rights on the Web. Pays within 60 days after publication. Credit line given. Buys first serial rights and second reprint rights.

TIPS Wants to see work that shows "the total mushing adventure/lifestyle from environment to dog house." To break in, one's work must show "simplicity, balance and harmony. Strive for unique, provocative shots that lure readers and publishers. Send 10-40 images for review. Allow for 2-6 months' review time for at least a screened selection of these."

MUSKY HUNTER MAGAZINE

P.O. Box 340, 7978 Hwy. 70 E., St. Germain WI 54558. (715)477-2178. **Fax:** (715)477-8858. **E-mail:** editor@muskyhunter.com. **Website:** www.muskyhunter.com. **Contact:** Jim Saric, editor. Estab. 1988. Circ. 37,000. Serves the vertical market of musky fishing enthusiasts. "We're interested in how-to, where-to articles."

MUZZLE BLASTS

P.O. Box 67, Friendship IN 47021. (812)667-5131. **Fax:** (812)667-5136. **E-mail:** ttrowbridge@nmlra.org. **Website:** www.nmlra.org. Estab. 1939. Circ. 17,500. Publication of the National Muzzle Loading Rifle Association. Monthly. Emphasizes muzzleloading. Sample copy free. Photo guidelines free with SASE.

NEEDS Interested in muzzleloading, muzzleloading hunting, primitive camping. "Ours is a specialized association magazine. We buy some big-game wildlife photos but are more interested in photos featuring muzzleloaders, hunting, powder horns and accoutrements." Model/property release required. Photo captions preferred.

SPECS Accepts images in digital format. Send via e-mail or on a CD in JPEG or TIFF format. Also accepts 3×5 color transparencies, quality color and b&w prints sharply contrasting 35mm color slides are acceptable.

MAKING CONTACT & TERMS Send query letter with stock list. Keeps samples on file; include SASE for return of material. Responds in 2 weeks. Simultaneous submissions OK. Pays $300 for color cover; $25-50 for b&w inside. Pays on publication. Credit line given. Buys one-time rights.

NA'AMAT WOMAN

505 Eighth Ave., Suite 1204, New York NY 10018. (212)563-5222. **E-mail:** naamat@naamat.org; judith@naamat.org. **Website:** www.naamat.org. **Contact:** Judith Sokoloff, editor. Estab. 1926. Circ. 12,000. Quarterly organization magazine focusing on issues of concern to contemporary Jewish families and women.

NEEDS Buys 5-10 photos from freelancers/issue; 50 photos/year. Photos of Jewish themes, Israel, women, babies/children/teens, families, parents, senior citizens, landscapes/scenics, architecture, religious, travel. Interested in documentary, fine art, historical/vintage, seasonal. Reviews photos with or without manuscript. Photo captions preferred.

SPECS Uses color and b&w prints. Accepts images in digital format. Contact editor before sending.

MAKING CONTACT & TERMS Provide résumé, business card, self-promotion piece or tearsheets to be kept on file for possible future assignments. Art director will contact photographer for portfolio review if interested. Keeps samples on file; include SASE for return of material. Responds in 6 weeks. Pays $200 maximum for cover; $35-75 for inside. Pays on publication. Credit line given. Buys one-time, first rights.

NATIONAL GEOGRAPHIC

P.O. Box 98199, Washington DC 20090-8199. **Fax:** (202)828-5460. **E-mail:** ngsforum@nationalgeographic.com. **Website:** www.nationalgeographic.com. **Contact:** Chris Johns, editor-in-chief. Estab. 1888. Circ. 9 million. Monthly publication of the National Geographic Society.

This is a premiere market that demands photographic excellence. *National Geographic* does not accept unsolicited work from freelance photographers. Photography internships and faculty fellowships are available. Contact Susan Smith, deputy director of photography, for application information.

NATIONAL PARKS MAGAZINE

National Parks Conservation Association, 777 Sixth St. NW, Suite 700, Washington DC 20001. (202)223-6722; (800)628-7275. **Fax:** (202)454-3333. **E-mail:** npmag@npca.org. **Website:** www.npca.org/magazine/. **Contact:** Scott Kirkwood, editor-in-chief. Estab. 1919. Circ. 340,000. Quarterly. Emphasizes the preservation of national parks and wildlife. Sample copy available for $3 and 8½×11 or larger SASE. Photo guidelines available online.

SPECS "Photographers who are new to *National Parks* may submit ONLY digitally for an initial review—we prefer links to clean, easily-navigable and searchable websites, or lightboxes with well-captioned images. We DO NOT accept and are not responsible for unsolicited slides, prints, or CDs."

MAKING CONTACT & TERMS "The best way to break in is to send a brief, concise e-mail message to Sarah Rutherford. See guidelines online. Less than 1 percent of our image needs are generated from unsolicited photographs, yet we receive dozens of submissions every week. Photographers are welcome to send postcards or other simple promotional materials that we do not have to return or respond to." Photographers who are regular contributors may submit images in the following forms: digitally, via CD, DVD, or e-mail (as in attachments or a link to a lightbox or FTP site) physically, as slides or prints, via courier mail. Pays within 30 days after publication. Buys one-time rights.

TIPS "When searching for photos, we frequently use www.agpix.com to find photographers who fit our needs. If you're interested in breaking into the magazine, we suggest setting up a profile and posting your absolute best parks images there."

NATIVE PEOPLES MAGAZINE

5333 N. Seventh St., Suite C-224, Phoenix AZ 85014. (602)265-4855. **Fax:** (602)265-3113. **E-mail:** dgibson@nativepeoples.com; kcoochwytewa@nativepeoples.com. **Website:** www.nativepeoples.com. **Contact:** Daniel Gibson, editor; Kevin Coochwytewa, art director. Estab. 1987. Circ. 40,000. Bimonthly. "Dedicated to the sensitive portrayal of the arts and lifeways of the native peoples of the Americas." Photo guidelines upon request.

NEEDS Buys 20-50 photos from freelancers/issue; 120-300 photos/year. Needs Native American lifeways photos (babies/children/teens, celebrities, couples, multicultural, families, parents, senior citizens, events). Also uses photos of entertainment, performing arts, travel. Interested in fine art. Model/property release preferred. Photo captions preferred; include names, location and circumstances.

SPECS Accepts images in digital format. Send via CD, ZIP, e-mail as TIFF, JPEG, EPS files at 300 dpi.

MAKING CONTACT & TERMS Submit portfolio for review. Responds in 1 month. Pays on publication. Buys one-time rights.

NATURAL HISTORY

P.O. Box 110623, Research Triangle Park NC 27709-5623. **E-mail:** nhmag@naturalhistorymag.com. **Website:** www.nhmag.com. Circ. 50,000. Printed 10 times/year. Readers are primarily well-educated people with interests in the sciences. Free photo guidelines available by request.

NEEDS Buys 400-450 photos/year. Subjects include animal behavior, photo essay, documentary, plant and landscape. "We are interested in photo essays that give an in-depth look at plants, animals, or people and that are visually superior. We are also looking for photos for our photographic feature, 'The Natural Moment.' This feature focuses on images that are both visually arresting and behaviorally interesting."

Photos used must relate to the social or natural sciences with an ecological framework. Accurate, detailed captions required.

SPECS Prefers digital submissions; Uses 35mm, 2¼×2¼, 4×5, 6×7, 8×10 color transparencies. Covers are always related to an article in the issue.

MAKING CONTACT & TERMS Send query letter with résumé of credits. "We prefer that you send digital images. Please don't send us any non-digital photographs without a query first, describing the work you would like to send. No submission should exceed 30 original transparencies or negatives. However, please let us know if you have additional images that we might consider. Potential liability for submissions that exceed 30 originals shall be no more than $100 per slide." Responds in 2 weeks if possible. Previously published work OK but must be indicated on delivery memo. Pays (for color and b&w) $400-600 for cover; $350-500 for spread; $300-400 for oversize; $250-350 for full-page; $200-300 for ¼ page; $175-250 for less than ¼ page. Pays $50 for usage on contents page. Pays on publication. Credit line given. Buys one-time rights (which includes rights for web reproduction accompanying magazine digital publication formats).

👤 $ ◐ NATURE FRIEND MAGAZINE

4253 Woodcock Lane, Dayton VA 22821. (540)867-0764. **E-mail:** info@naturefriendmagazine.com; editor@naturefriendmagazine.com; photos@naturefriendmagazine.com. **Website:** www.naturefriendmagazine.com. **Contact:** Kevin Shank, editor. Estab. 1982. Circ. 13,000.

NEEDS Buys 5-10 photos from freelancers/issue; 100 photos/year. Photos of wildlife, wildlife interacting with each other, humorous wildlife, all natural habitat appearance. Reviews photos with or without ms. Model/property release preferred. Photo captions preferred.

SPECS Prefers images in digital format. Send via CD or DVD as TIFF files at 300 dpi at 8×10 size; provide color thumbnails when submitting photos. "Transparencies are handled and stored carefully; however, we do not accept liability for them so discourage submissions of them."

MAKING CONTACT & TERMS Responds in 1 month to queries; 2 weeks to portfolios. "Label contact prints and digital media with your name, address, and phone number so we can easily know how to contact you if we select your photo for use. Please send articles rather than queries. We try to respond within 4-6 months." Simultaneous submissions and previously published work OK. Pays $75 for front cover; $50 for back cover; $15-25 for inside photos. Pays on publication. Credit line given. Buys one-time rights.

TIPS "We're always looking for photos of wild animals doing something unusual or humorous. Please label every sheet of paper or digital media with name, address, and phone number. We may need to contact you on short notice, and you do not want to miss a sale. Also, photos are selected on a monthly basis, after the articles. What this means to a photographer is that photos are secondary to writings and cannot be selected far in advance. High-res photos in our files the day we are making selections will stand the greatest chance of being published. "

$ NATURE PHOTOGRAPHER

P.O. Box 220, Lubec ME 04652. (207)733-4201. **E-mail:** nature_photographer@yahoo.com. **Website:** www.naturephotographermag.com. Estab. 1990. Circ. 41,000. Quarterly 4-color, high-quality magazine. Emphasizes "conservation-oriented, low-impact nature photography" with strong how-to focus. Readers are male and female nature photographers of all ages. Sample copy available with 10×13 SASE with 6 first-class stamps.

💬 *Nature Photographer* charges $80/year to be a "field contributor."

NEEDS Buys 90-120 photos from freelancers/issue; 400 photos/year. Needs nature shots of "all types—abstracts, animals/wildlife, flowers, plants, scenics, environmental images, etc. Shots must be in natural settings; no set-ups, zoo or captive animal shots accepted." Reviews photos (slides or digital images on CD) with or without ms 4 times/year: May (for fall issue); August (for winter issue); November (for spring issue); and January (for summer issue). Photo captions required; include description of subject, location, type of equipment, how photographed.

MAKING CONTACT & TERMS Contact by e-mail or with SASE for guidelines before submitting images. Prefers to see 35mm transparencies or CD of digital images. Send digital images via CD.

TIPS Recommends working with "the best lens you can afford and slow-speed slide film; or, if shooting digital, using the RAW mode." Suggests editing with a 4× or 8× loupe (magnifier) on a light board to check for sharpness, color saturation, etc. "Color prints are not normally used for publication in our magazine. When editing digital captured images, please enlarge to the point that you are certain that the focal point is tack sharp. Also avoid having grain in the final image."

⊖⊖ NEW MEXICO MAGAZINE

Lew Wallace Bldg., 495 Old Santa Fe Trail, Santa Fe NM 87501-2750. (505)827-7447. **E-mail:** artdirector@ nmmagazine.com. **Website:** www.nmmagazine.com. Estab. 1923. Circ. 100,000. Monthly. For affluent people ages 35-65 interested in the Southwest or who have lived in or visited New Mexico. Sample copy available for $4.95 with 9×12 SASE and 3 first-class stamps. Photo guidelines available online.

NEEDS Buys 10 photos from freelancers/issue; 120 photos/year. Needs New Mexico photos only—landscapes, people, events, architecture, etc. Model release preferred.

SPECS Uses 300 dpi digital files with contact sheets (8-12 per page). Photographers must be in photodata. Photo captions required; include who, what, where.

MAKING CONTACT & TERMS Submit portfolio; include SASE for return of material, or e-mail with web gallery link. Pays $450/day; $300 for color or b&w cover; $60-100 for color or b&w stock. Pays on publication. Credit line given. Buys one-time rights.

TIPS "New Mexico Magazine is the official magazine for the state of New Mexico. Photographers should know New Mexico. We are interested in the less common stock of the state. The magazine is editorial driven, and all photos directly relate to a story in the magazine." Cover photos usually relate to the main feature in the magazine.

NEWSWEEK

The Daily Beast, 251 W. 57th St., New York NY 10019. (212)445-4000. **Website:** www.newsweek.com. **Contact:** Kira Bindrim, managing editor. Estab. 1933. Circ. 3.2 million. Newsweek reports the week's developments on the newsfront of the world and the nation through news, commentary and analysis. News is divided into National Affairs; International; Business; Society; Science & Technology; and Arts & Entertainment. Relevant visuals, including photos, accompany most of the articles. Query before submitting.

⊖ ○ NEW YORK STATE CONSERVATIONIST MAGAZINE

NYSDEC, 625 Broadway, Albany NY 12233-4502. (518)402-8047. **E-mail:** magazine@gw.dec.state.ny.us. **Website:** www.dec.ny.gov. **Contact:** Eileen Stege-

mann, assistant editor. Estab. 1946. Circ. 100,000. Bimonthly nonprofit, New York State government publication. Emphasizes natural history, environmental and outdoor interests pertinent to New York State. Sample copy available for $3.50. Photo guidelines free with SASE or online.

NEEDS Uses 40 photos/issue; 80% supplied by freelancers. Needs wildlife shots, people in the environment, outdoor recreation, forest and land management, fisheries and fisheries management, environmental subjects. Also needs landscapes/scenics, cities, travel, historical/vintage, seasonal. Model release preferred. Photo captions required.

SPECS Accepts images in digital format. Send via CD as TIFF files at 300 dpi. Also uses 35mm, 2¼×2¼, 4×5, 8×10 transparencies.

MAKING CONTACT & TERMS Send material by mail for consideration, or submit portfolio for review. Provide résumé, bio, business card, brochure, flyer or tearsheets to be kept on file for possible future assignments. Responds in 3 weeks. Simultaneous submissions and previously published work OK. Pays $50 for cover photos; $15 for b&w or color inside. Pays on publication. Buys one-time rights.

TIPS Looks for "artistic interpretation of nature and the environment; unusual ways of picturing environmental subjects (even pollution, oil spills, trash, air pollution, etc.); wildlife and fishing subjects at all seasons. Try for unique composition, lighting. Technical excellence a must."

THE NEW YORK TIMES MAGAZINE

620 Eighth Ave., New York NY 10018. (212)556-1234. **Fax:** (212)556-3830. **E-mail:** magazine@nytimes.com; nytnews@nytimes.com; executive-editor@nytimes. com. **Website:** www.nytimes.com/pages/magazine. **Contact:** Margaret Editor, public editor. Circ. 1.8 million. The New York Times Magazine appears in the New York Times on Sunday. The 'Arts and Leisure' section appears during the week. The 'Op Ed' page appears daily.

NEEDS Number of freelance photos purchased varies. Model release required. Photo captions required.

MAKING CONTACT & TERMS "Please FedEx all submissions." Include SASE for return of material. Responds in 1 week. Pays $345 for full page; $260 for half page; $230 for quarter page; $400/job (day rates); $750 for color cover. **Pays on acceptance.** Credit line given. Buys one-time rights.

🔾 NITE-WRITER'S INTERNATIONAL LITERARY ARTS JOURNAL

158 Spencer Ave., Suite 100, Pittsburgh PA 15227. (412)668-0691. **E-mail:** nitewritersliteraryarts@gmail. com. **Website:** nitewritersinternational.webs.com. **Contact:** John Thompson. Estab. 1994. *Nite-Writer's International Literary Arts Journal* is an online literary arts journal. "We are 'dedicated to the emotional intellectual' with a creative perception of life."

NEEDS Wants artistic, botanical, landscape, nature (please include title of work).

MAKING CONTACT & TERMS Send at 800 pixels.

🔾 🔾 NORTH AMERICAN WHITETAIL

2250 Newmarket Pkwy., Suite 110, Marietta GA 30067. (678)589-2000. **Fax:** (678)279-7512. **E-mail:** patrick. hogan@imoutdoors.com; whitetail@imoutdoors.com. **Website:** www.northamericanwhitetail.com. Estab. 1982. Circ. 125,000. Published 7 times/year (July-February) by InterMedia Outdoors. Emphasizes trophy whitetail deer hunting. Sample copy available for $4. Photo guidelines free with SASE.

NEEDS Buys 5 photos from freelancers/issue; 35 photos/year. Needs photos of large, live whitetail deer, hunter posing with or approaching downed trophy deer, or hunter posing with mounted head. Also uses photos of deer habitats and signs. Model release preferred. Photo captions preferred; include when and where scene was photographed.

SPECS Accepts images in digital format. Send via CD at 300 dpi with output of 8×12 inches. Also uses 35mm transparencies.

MAKING CONTACT & TERMS Send query letter with résumé of credits and list of stock photo subjects. Will return unsolicited material in 1 month if accompanied by SASE. Simultaneous submissions not accepted. Tearsheets provided. Pays 60 days prior to publication. Credit line given. Buys one-time rights.

TIPS "In samples we look for extremely sharp, well-composed photos of whitetaile deer in natural settings. We also use photos depicting deer hunting scenes. Please study the photos we are using before making submission. We'll return photos we don't expect to use and hold the remainder for potential use. Please do not send dupes. Use an 8×10 envelope to ensure sharpness of images, and put name and identifying number on all slides and prints. Photos returned at time of publication or at photographer's request."

🔾 NORTH CAROLINA LITERARY REVIEW

East Carolina University, Mailstop 555 English, Greenville NC 27858-4353. (252)328-1537. **Fax:** (252)328-4889. **E-mail:** nclrsubmissions@ecu.edu. **Website:** www.nclr.ecu.edu. **Contact:** Margaret Bauer. Estab. 1992. Circ. 750. Annual literary magazine with North Carolina focus. *NCLR* publishes poetry, fiction and nonfiction by and interviews with NC writers, and articles and essays about NC literature, literary history and culture. Photographs must be NC-related. Sample copy available for $15. Photo guidelines available on website.

NEEDS Photo captions preferred.

SPECS Accepts images in digital format, 5×7 at 300 dpi. Inquire first; submit TIFF, GIF files at 300 dpi to nclrsubmissions@ecu.edu only after requested to.

MAKING CONTACT & TERMS Send query letter with website address to show sample of work. If selected, art acquisitions editor will be in touch.

TIPS *"Only NC photographers.* See our website."

🔾 🔾 🔾 NORTH DAKOTA HORIZONS

1605 E. Capitol Ave., Suite 101, Bismarck ND 58502. (866)462-0744. **Fax:** (701)223-4645. **E-mail:** ndho rizons@btinet.net. **Website:** www.ndhorizons.com. **Contact:** Angela Magstadt, editor. Estab. 1971. Quality regional magazine. Photos used in magazines, audiovisual, calendars.

NEEDS Buys 50 photos/year; offers 10 assignments/year. Scenics of North Dakota events, places and people. Also wildlife, cities/urban, rural, adventure, entertainment, events, hobbies, performing arts, travel, agriculture, industry. Interested in historical/vintage, seasonal. Model/property release preferred. Photo captions preferred.

SPECS Prefers images in digital format. Send via CD, as TIFF, EPS files at 600 dpi.

MAKING CONTACT & TERMS Prefers e-mail query letter. Pays by the project, varies ($125-300); negotiable. Pays on usage. Credit line given. Buys one-time rights; negotiable.

NORTHERN WOODLANDS MAGAZINE

Center for Woodlands Education, Inc., 1776 Center Rd., P.O. Box 471, Corinth VT 05039-0471. (802)439-6292; (800)290-5232. **Fax:** (802)368-1053. **E-mail:** dave@northernwoodlands.org. **Website:** www.north ernwoodlands.org. Estab. 1994. Circ. 15,000. Quarterly. "Created to inspire landowners' sense of stewardship by increasing their awareness of the natural history and the principles of conservation and forestry that are directly related to their land; to encourage loggers, foresters, and purchasers of raw materials to continually raise the standards by which they utilize the forest's resources; to increase the public's awareness and appreciation of the social, economic, and environmental benefits of a working forest; to raise the level of discussion about environmental and natural resource issues; and to educate a new generation of forest stewards." Sample copies available for $6. Photo guidelines available on website.

NEEDS Buys 10-50 photos from freelancers/year. Photos of forestry, environmental, landscapes/scenics, wildlife, rural, adventure, travel, agriculture, science. Interested in historical/vintage, seasonal. Other specific photo needs: vertical format, photos specific to assignments in northern New England and upstate New York. Reviews photos with or without a manuscript. Model release preferred. Photo captions required.

SPECS Prefers images in digital format. Send via CD, ZIP, e-mail as TIFF, JPEG, EPS files at 300 dpi maximum. No e-mails larger than 5MB.

MAKING CONTACT & TERMS Send cover photo submissions as either slides or digital photos. Digital photos, less than 1MB each, can be e-mailed in JPEG, PDF, or TIFF format. If yours is chosen, we will request a higher-res image. You may also mail us a CD of your images to Attn: Cover Photos. Send query letter with slides. We have an online e-mail form available. Provide self-promotion piece to be kept on file for possible future assignments. Responds only if interested; send nonreturnable samples. Previously published work OK. Pays $150 for color cover; $25-75. "We might pay upon receipt or as late as publication." Credit line given. Buys one-time rights. "We will hold your photos until publication of the magazine for which they are being considered, unless you ask otherwise. All materials will be returned by certified mail."

◎ ◑ ◐ NOTRE DAME MAGAZINE

University of Notre Dame, 500 Grace Hall, Notre Dame IN 46556-5612. (574)631-5335. **E-mail:** ndmag@nd.edu. **Website:** magazine.nd.edu. **Contact:** Kerry Temple, editor; Kerry Prugh, art director. Estab. 1972. Circ. 150,000. "We are a university magazine with a scope as broad as that found at a university, but we place our discussion in a moral, ethical, and spiritual context reflecting our Catholic heritage."

NEEDS People, cities, education, architecture, business, science, environmental and landscapes. Model and property releases are required. Photo captions are required.

MAKING CONTACT & TERMS E-mail (JPEG samples at 72 dpi) or send a postcard sample.

NOW & THEN: THE APPALACHIAN MAGAZINE

East Tennessee State University, Box 70556, Johnson City TN 37614-1707. (423)439-5348. **Fax:** (423)439-6340. **E-mail:** nowandthen@etsu.edu. **E-mail:** sandersr@etsu.edu. **Website:** www.etsu.edu/cass/nowandthen. **Contact:** Randy Sanders, managing editor; Wayne Winkler, music editor; Charlie Warden, photo editor. Estab. 1984. Circ. 1,000. Photo guidelines free with SASE to photo editor. Guidelines available online at www.etsu.edu/cass/nowandthen/guidelines/photographers.aspx.

MAKING CONTACT & TERMS Send query letter with résumé, photocopies. Provide self-promotion piece to be kept on file for possible future assignments. Responds only if interested; send nonreturnable samples. Simultaneous submissions OK. Credit line given along with a free issue of the magazine in which the photography is featured.

TIPS Know what our upcoming themes are. Keep in mind, we cover only the Appalachian region (see the website for a definition of the region).

OFF THE COAST

Resolute Bear Press, P.O. Box 14, Robbinston ME 04671. (207)454-8026. **E-mail:** poetrylane2@gmail.com. **Website:** www.off-the-coast.com. **Contact:** Valerie Lawson, editor/publisher. Estab. 1994. "The mission of *Off the Coast* is to become recognized around the world as Maine's international poetry journal, a publication that prizes quality, diversity and honesty in its publications and in its dealings with poets. *Off the Coast*, a quarterly journal, publishes poetry, artwork and reviews. Arranged much like an anthology, each issue bears a title drawn from a line or phrase from one of its poems."

MAKING CONTACT & TERMS "We accept b&w graphics and photos to grace the pages of *Off the Coast*, and color or b&w for the cover. Send 3-6 images in TIFF, PNG, or JPEG format, minimum 300 dpi resolution. We prefer you select and send images rather than send a link to your website."

OHIO MAGAZINE

Great Lakes Publishing Co., 1422 Euclid Ave., Suite 730, Cleveland OH 44115. (216)771-2833. **E-mail:** vpospisil@ohiomagazine.com. **Website:** www.ohio magazine.com. **Contact:** Vivian Pospisil, executive editor. Estab. 1978. Circ. 40,000. E-mail 5-10, low-resolution published samples to art director or a link to your online portfolio. Only qualified photographers from Ohio and bordering states will be considered. Slides and hard copies discouraged. Rates and policies outlined on Artist Guidelines on website. Pays on publication. 50% kill fee. Byline given for assignments, photo credit for submitted art. Submit seasonal material 6 months in advance. Freelance design work demands knowledge of InDesign, Photoshop, and Illustrator CS4 or higher.

TIPS "Please have a knowledge of the magazine and audience before submitting. Freelancers should send all queries electronically or through the mail. Telephone inquiries are strongly discouraged."

🟢🔵 ⓘ OKLAHOMA TODAY

P.O. Box 1468, Oklahoma City OK 73101-1468. (405)230-8450. **Fax:** (405)230-8650. **E-mail:** megan. rossman@travelok.com. **Website:** www.oklahomato day.com. **Contact:** Megan Rossman, photography editor. Estab. 1956. Circ. 45,000. Bimonthly. "We cover all aspects of Oklahoma, from history to people profiles, but we emphasize travel." Readers are "Oklahomans, whether they live in-state or are exiles. Studies show them to be above average in education and income." Sample copy available for $4.95. Photo guidelines free with SASE or online.

NEEDS Buys 45 photos from freelancers/issue; 270 photos/year. Needs photos of "Oklahoma subjects only; the greatest number are used to illustrate a specific story on a person, place or thing in the state. We are also interested in stock scenics of the state." Other areas of focus are adventure—sport/travel, reenactment, historical and cultural activities. Photo captions required.

SPECS Uses 8×10 glossy b&w prints; 35mm, 2¼×2¼, 4×5, 8×10 transparencies. "Strongly prefer images in digital format, though we can accept high-quality transparencies." Send via CD or e-mail.

MAKING CONTACT & TERMS Send query letter with samples; include SASE for return of material. Re-

sponds in 2 months. Simultaneous submissions and previously published work OK (on occasion). Pays $50-150 for b&w photos; $50-250 for color photos; $125-1,000/job. Pays on publication. Buys one-time rights with a 4-month from publication exclusive, plus right to reproduce photo in promotions for magazine and on oklahomatoday.com without additional payment with credit line.

TIPS To break in, "read the magazine. Subjects are normally activities or scenics (mostly the latter). I would like good composition and very good lighting. I look for photographs that evoke a sense of place, look extraordinary and say something only a good photographer could say about the image. Look at what Ansel Adams and Eliot Porter did and what Muench and others are producing, and send me that kind of quality. We want the best photographs available, and we give them the space and play such quality warrants."

ⓘ ONBOARD MEDIA

1691 Michigan Ave., Suite 600, Miami Beach FL 33139. (305)673-0400. **Fax:** (305)673-3575. **E-mail:** virginia. valls@onboardmedia.com. **Website:** www.onboard media.com. **Contact:** Virginia Valls, director design & production. Estab. 1990. Circ. 792,184. Close to 100 annual and quarterly publications. Emphasize travel in the Caribbean, Europe, Mexican Riviera, Bahamas, Alaska, Bermuda, Las Vegas. Custom in-cabin/in-room publications reach cruise vacationers and vacation/resort audience. Photo guidelines free with SASE.

NEEDS Photos of scenics, nature, prominent landmarks based in Caribbean, Mexican Riviera, Bahamas, Alaska, Europe and Las Vegas. Model/property release required. Photo captions required; include where the photo was taken and explain the subject matter. Credit line information requested.

SPECS Uses 35mm, 2¼×2¼, 4×5, 8×10 transparencies. Prefers images in digital format RAW data. Send via FTP at 300 dpi.

MAKING CONTACT & TERMS Send query letter with stock list. Provide résumé, business card, brochure, flyer or tearsheets to be kept on file for possible future assignments. Keeps samples on file. Responds in 3 weeks. Previously published work OK. Rates negotiable per project. Pays on publication. Credit line given.

ONE

Catholic Near East Welfare Association, 1011 First Ave., New York NY 10022-4195. (212)826-1480. **Fax:**

(212)838-1344. **E-mail:** cnewa@cnewa.org. **Website:** www.cnewa.org. **Contact:** Deacon Greg Kandra, executive editor. Estab. 1974. Circ. 100,000. Official publication of Catholic Near East Welfare Association, "a papal agency for humanitarian and pastoral support." *ONE* informs Americans about the traditions, faiths, cultures, and religious communities of the Middle East, Northeast Africa, India, and Eastern Europe. Sample copy and photo guidelines available for 7½×10½ SAE with 2 first-class stamps. Freelancers supply 80% of photos. Prefers to work with writer/photographer team.

NEEDS Looking for evocative photos of people—not posed—involved in activities: work, play, worship. Liturgical shots also welcome. Extensive captions required if text is not available.

MAKING CONTACT & TERMS Send query letter first. "Please do not send an inventory; rather, send a letter explaining your ideas." Include 8½×11 SASE. Responds in 3 weeks, acknowledges receipt of material immediately. Simultaneous submissions and previously published work OK, but "neither is preferred. If previously published, please tell us when and where." Pays on publication. Credit line given. "Credits appear on page 3 with masthead and table of contents." Buys first North American serial rights.

TIPS Stories should weave current lifestyles with issues and needs. Avoid political subjects, stick with ordinary people. Photo essays are welcome. Write requesting sample issue and guidelines, then send query. We rarely use stock photos but have used articles and photos submitted by a single photojournalist or writer/photographer team.

OREGON COAST

4969 Hwy. 101 N, Suite 2, Florence OR 97439. (800)348-8401. **E-mail:** Alicia@nwmags.com. **Website:** www.northwestmagazines.com. **Contact:** Alicia Spooner. Estab. 1982. Circ. 50,000. Bimonthly. Emphasizes Oregon coast life. Sample copy available for $6, including postage. Photo guidelines available with SASE or on website.

NEEDS Buys 3-5 photos from freelancers/issue; 18-30 photos/year. Needs scenics. Especially needs photos of typical subjects—waves, beaches, lighthouses—with a fresh perspective. Needs mostly vertical format. Model description in megadata and on caption sheet. "Now only accepting digital images. We recommend acquiring model releases for any photos that include

people, but we don't require releases except for photos used on covers or in advertising. Photos must be current, shot within the last five years."

MAKING CONTACT & TERMS Digital photos must be sent on CDs as high-res (300 dpi) TIFF, JPEG, or EPS files without compression. Images should be 8½×11. Include clear, color contact sheets of all images (no more than 8 per page). CDs are not returned. To be considered for calendars, photos must have horizontal formats. The annual deadline for calendars is August 15. Responds in 3 months. Pays $425 for color cover; $100 for calendar usage; $25-50 for b&w inside; $25-100 for color inside; $100-250 for photo/text package. Credit line given. Buys one-time rights. We do not sign for personal delivery. SASE or return postage required.

⊙ OUTDOOR CANADA MAGAZINE

54 St. Patrick St., Toronto Ontario M5T 1V1, Canada. (416)599-2000. **E-mail:** editorial@outdoorcanada.ca. **Website:** www.outdoorcanada.ca. Estab. 1972. Circ. 90,000. 4-color magazine for Canadian anglers and hunters. Stories on fishing, hunting and conservation. Readers are 81% male. Publishes 6 regular issues/year. "We are looking for strong, attention-grabbing images that capture the love our readers have for hunting and fishing. We're interested in finding and cultivating new Canadian talent and appreciate submissions from new photographers and illustrators to add to our list."

NEEDS Buys 200-300 photos/year. Needs photos of wildlife; fishing, hunting, ice-fishing; action shots. *Canadian content only.* Photo captions required; include location and identification of fish, bird or animal.

SPECS Digital images only.

TIPS "We get hundreds of promotional pieces each year, so we can't possibly respond to them all, but we'll do our best. If we'd like to see more of your portfolio or assign work to you, we'll contact you. Art guidelines are available."

⊙ ❶ OWL MAGAZINE

10 Lower Spadina Ave., Suite 400, Toronto Ontario M5V 2Z2, Canada. (416)340-2700. **Fax:** (416)340-9769. **E-mail:** tracey.jacklin@owlkids.com. **Website:** www.owlkids.com. **Contact:** Tracey Jacklin, photo editor. Estab. 1976. Circ. 80,000. Published 10 times/year. A discovery magazine for children ages 9-13. Sample copy available for $4.95 and 9×12 SAE with

$1.50 money order for postage. Photo guidelines free with SAE or via e-mail.

NEEDS Photo stories, photo puzzles, photos of children ages 12-14, extreme weather, wildlife, science, technology, environmental, pop culture, multicultural, events, adventure, hobbies, humor, sports, extreme sports. Interested in documentary, seasonal. Model/property release required. Photo captions required. Will buy story packages.

SPECS Accepts images in digital format. E-mail as JPEG files at 72 dpi. Requires 300 dpi for publication.

MAKING CONTACT & TERMS Accepts no responsibility for unsolicited material. Previously published work OK. Credit line given. Buys one-time rights.

TIPS "Photos should be sharply focused with good lighting, and engaging for kids. We are always on the lookout for humorous, action-packed shots; eye-catching, sports, animals, bloopers, etc. Photos with a 'wow' impact."

☺ OXYGEN

Robert Kennedy Publishing, 400 Matheson Blvd. W., Mississauga Ontario L5R 3M1, Canada. (905)507-3545; (888)254-0767. **Fax:** (905)507-2372. **Website:** www.oxygenmag.com. Estab. 1997. Circ. 340,000. Monthly. Emphasizes exercise and nutrition for women. Readers are women ages 20-39. Sample copy available for $5.

NEEDS Buys 720 photos from freelancers/issue. Needs photos of women weight training and exercising aerobically. Model release required. Photo captions preferred; include names of subjects.

SPECS Accepts high-res digital images. Uses 35mm, 2¼×2¼ transparencies. Prints occasionally acceptable.

MAKING CONTACT & TERMS Send unsolicited photos by mail for consideration. Does not keep samples on file; include SASE for return of material. Responds in 3 weeks. Pays $200-400/hour; $800-1,500/day; $500-1,500/job; $500-2,000 for color cover; $50-100 for color or b&w inside. **Pays on acceptance.** Credit line given. Buys all rights.

TIPS "We are looking for attractive, fit women working out on step machines, joggers, rowers, treadmills, ellipticals; with free weights; running for fitness; jumping, climbing. Professional pictures only, please. We particularly welcome photos of female celebrities who are into fitness; higher payments are made for these."

OYEZ REVIEW

Roosevelt University, Dept. of Literature & Languages, 430 S. Michigan Ave., Chicago IL 60605. **E-mail:** oyezreview@roosevelt.edu. **Website:** oyezreview.wordpress.com. Estab. 1965. Circ. 600 with an e-book available. Annual magazine of the Creative Writing Program at Roosevelt University, publishing fiction, creative nonfiction, poetry, and art. There are no restrictions on style, theme, or subject matter. Each issue has 100 pages: 92 pages of text and an 8-page b&w or color spread of 1 artist's work (usually drawing, painting, or photography) with the front and back covers totaling 10 pieces. Accepts outstanding work from beginning and established photographers. Expects a high level of professionalism from all photographers who make contact. Reviews photos with or without a manuscript.

NEEDS Accepts 10 photos from freelancers/issue; 10 photos/year. Needs babies/children/teens, senior citizens, cities/urban, pets, religious, rural, military, political, product shots/still life, disasters, environmental, landscapes/scenics, wildlife, adventure, automobiles, events, hobbies, humor, performing arts, sports, travel, avant garde, documentary, fine art, seasonal.

SPECS Submit in b&w or color.

MAKING CONTACT & TERMS Now accepting submissions through Submittable as well as regular mail. No longer accepting e-mail submissions. Model and property release is preferred. Photo captions are preferred.

PACIFICA LITERARY REVIEW

E-mail: pacificalitreview@gmail.com. **Website:** www.pacificareview.com. "*Pacifica Literary Review* is a small literary arts magazine based in Seattle. Our print editions are published biannually in winter and summer. *PLR* is now accepting submissions of poetry, fiction, creative nonfiction, author interview, and b&w photography. Submission period: September 15-May 7."

NEEDS Looking for quality b&w photography.

SPECS Guidelines available online.

MAKING CONTACT & TERMS See online submission form, accepts simultaneous submissions, acquires first North American rights.

☺ PACIFIC YACHTING

OP Publishing, Ltd., 1166 Alberni St., Suite 802, Vancouver British Columbia V6E 3Z3, Canada. (604)428-0259. **Fax:** (604)620-0425. **E-mail:** editor@pacific yachting.com; ayates@oppublishing.com. **Website:** www.pacificyachting.com. **Contact:** Dale Miller, editor; Arran Yates, art director. Estab. 1968. Circ. 19,000. Monthly. Emphasizes boating on West Coast. Readers are ages 35-60; boaters, power and sail. Sample copy available for $6.95 Canadian plus postage.

NEEDS Buys 75 photos from freelancers/issue; 900 photos/year. Photos of landscapes/scenics, adventure, sports. Interested in historical/vintage, seasonal. "All should be boating related. Reviews photos with accompanying manuscript only. Always looking for covers; must be shot in British Columbia."

MAKING CONTACT & TERMS Keeps samples on file. Simultaneous submissions and previously published work OK. Pays $400 Canadian for color cover. Payment negotiable. Credit line given. Buys one-time rights.

PAKN TREGER

National Yiddish Book Center, 1021 West St., Amherst MA 01002. (413)256-4900. **E-mail:** aatherley@bikher.org; pt@bikher.org;. **Website:** www.yiddish bookcenter.org. **Contact:** Anne Atherley, editor's assistant. Estab. 1980. Circ. 20,000.

NEEDS Photos of families, parents, senior citizens, education, religious, humor, historical/vintage, Jewish and Yiddish culture. Reviews photos with or without a manuscript. Captions required; include identification of subjects.

SPECS Accepts images in digital format. Send JPEG or GIF files.

MAKING CONTACT & TERMS Negotiates payment. Pays on publication. Credit line given. Buys one-time rights.

🌐🟢 PENNSYLVANIA ANGLER & BOATER

P.O. Box 67000, Harrisburg PA 17106-7000. (717)705-7835. **E-mail:** ra-pfbcmagazine@pa.gov. **Website:** www.fish.state.pa.us. Bimonthly. *"Pennsylvania Angler & Boater* is the Keystone State's official fishing and boating magazine, published by the Pennsylvania Fish & Boat Commission." Readers are anglers and boaters in Pennsylvania. Sample copy and photo guidelines free with 9×12 SASE and 9 oz. postage, or online.

NEEDS Buys 8 photos from freelancers/issue; 48 photos/year. Needs "action fishing and boating shots." Model release required. Photo captions required.

MAKING CONTACT & TERMS "Don't submit without first considering contributor guidelines, available

online. Then send query letter with résumé of credits. Send low-res images on CD; we'll later request high-res images of those shots that interest us." Responds in about 8 weeks. Pays $400 maximum for color cover; $30 minimum for color inside; $50-300 for text/photo package. Pays between acceptance and publication. Credit line given.

🟢 PENNSYLVANIA GAME NEWS

2001 Elmerton Ave., Harrisburg PA 17110-9797. (717)787-3745. **Website:** www.pgc.state.pa.us. Circ. 75,000. Monthly. Published by the Pennsylvania Game Commission. Readers are people interested in hunting, wildlife management and conservation in Pennsylvania. Sample copy available with 9×12 SASE. Editorial guidelines free.

NEEDS Considers photos of "any outdoor subject (Pennsylvania locale), except fishing and boating." Reviews photos with accompanying manuscript. Manuscript not required.

MAKING CONTACT & TERMS The agency expects all photos to be accompanied with a photo credit (e.g., Jake Dingel/PGC Photo). E-mail Robert Mitchell at robmitchel@state.pa.us with questions about images and policy. Send prints or slides. "No negatives, please." Include SASE for return of material. Will accept electronic images via CD only (no e-mail). Will also view photographer's website if available. Responds in 2 months. Pays $40-300. **Pays on acceptance.**

🟢 PENNSYLVANIA MAGAZINE

P.O. Box 755, Camp Hill PA 17001. (717)697-4660. **E-mail:** editor@pa-mag.com. **Website:** www.pa-mag. com. **Contact:** Matthew K. Holliday, editor. Circ. 30,000. Bimonthly. Emphasizes history, travel and contemporary topics. Readers are 40-70 years old, professional and retired. Samples available upon request. Photo guidelines free via e-mail or on the magazine's website.

NEEDS Uses about 25 photos/issue; most supplied by freelancers. Needs include history, travel, wildlife and scenic. All photos must be taken in Pennsylvania. Reviews photos with or without accompanying manuscript. Photo captions required.

MAKING CONTACT & TERMS Send query letter with samples. Send digital submissions for consideration. Sharpness is more important than pixel size. If your submitted images are of interest, the editor will communicate as to sizes needed. Responds in

1 month. Simultaneous submissions and previously published work OK with notification. Pays $100-150 for color cover; $35 for color inside; $50-500 for text/photo package and 15 to 20 cents per published word. Credit line given. Buys one-time, first use rights or other rights as arranged.

TIPS Look at several past issues and review guidelines before submitting.

⊘ PENTHOUSE

General Media Communications, 2 Penn Plaza, 11th Floor, New York NY 10121. (212)702-6000. **Fax:** (212)702-6279. **E-mail:** pbloch@pmgi.com. **Website:** www.penthouse.com. Estab. 1969. Circ. 640,000. Monthly. For the sophisticated male. Editorial scope ranges from outspoken contemporary comment to photography essays of beautiful women. Features interviews with personalities, sociological studies, humor, travel, food and wines, and fashion and grooming for men. Query before submitting.

⚫ ⊛ PERIOD IDEAS

21-23 Phoenix Court, Hawkins Rd., Colchester, Essex CO2 8JY, United Kingdom. (44)(1206)505976. **E-mail:** susan.dickerson@aceville.co.uk. **Website:** www.periodideas.com. **Contact:** Susan Dickerson. Circ. 38,000. Monthly home interest magazine for readers with period properties which they wish to renovate sympathetically.

NEEDS Photos of architecture, interiors/decorating, gardens. Reviews photos with or without ms.

SPECS Uses images in digital format. Send via CD as TIFF, JPEG files at 300 dpi.

MAKING CONTACT & TERMS Send query letter with prints or send low res images by e-mail with your query. Does not keep samples on file; include SASE for return of material. Responds only if interested; send nonreturnable samples. Accepts second rights work photos and copy; covers/packages/single shots negotiated one-on-one (please indicate expectations). Processes payment at the end of the cover-dated publication date and payment comes to contributors the following month. Credit line sometimes given. Buys one-time rights.

TIPS "Label each image with what it is, name and contact address/telephone number of photographer."

⊛⊛ ◑ PERSIMMON HILL

1700 NE 63rd St., Oklahoma City OK 73111. (405)478-2250, ext. 213. **Fax:** (405)478-4714. **E-mail:** editor@

nationalcowboymuseum.org. **Website:** www.nationalcowboymuseum.org. **Contact:** Judy Hilovsky. Estab. 1970. Circ. 7,500. Biannual publication of the National Cowboy and Western Heritage Museum. Emphasizes the West, both historical and contemporary views. Has diverse international audience with an interest in preservation of the West. Sample copy for $11.

◯ This magazine has received Outstanding Publication honors from the Oklahoma Museums Association, the International Association of Business Communicators, Ad Club and Public Relations Society of America.

NEEDS Buys 65 photos from freelancers/issue; 260 photos/year. "Photos must pertain to specific articles unless it is a photo essay on the West." Western subjects include celebrities, couples, families, landscapes, wildlife, architecture, interiors/decorating, rural, adventure, entertainment, events, hobbies, travel. Interested in documentary, fine art, historical/vintage, seasonal. Model release required for children's photos. Photo captions required; include location, names of people, action. Proper credit is required if photos are historic.

SPECS Accepts images in digital format. Send via CD.

MAKING CONTACT & TERMS Responds in 6 weeks. Pays $150-500 for color cover; $100-150 for b&w cover; $50-150 for color inside; $25-100 for b&w inside. Credit line given. Buys first North American serial rights.

TIPS "Make certain your photographs are high quality and have a story to tell. We are using more contemporary portraits of things that are currently happening in the West and using fewer historical photographs. Work must be high quality, original, innovative. Photographers can best present their work in a portfolio format and should keep in mind that we like to feature photo essays on the West in each issue. Study the magazine to understand its purpose. Show only the work that would be beneficial to us or pertain to the traditional Western subjects we cover."

PHOTOGRAPHER'S FORUM MAGAZINE

813 Reddick St., Santa Barbara CA 93103. (805)963-0439, ext. 240. **Fax:** (805)965-0496. **E-mail:** julie@serbin.com. **Website:** www.pfmagazine.com. **Contact:** Julie Simpson, managing editor. Quarterly magazine for the serious student and emerging professional photographer. Includes feature articles on historic

and contemporary photographers, interviews, book reviews, workshop listings, and new products.

☼ ⑥ ◎ ◑ PHOTO LIFE

Apex Publications, 171 St. Paul St., Suite 102, Quebec City Québec G1K 3W2, Canada. (418)-692-3392. **Fax:** (800)664-2739. **E-mail:** editor@photolife.com. **Website:** www.photolife.com. **Contact:** Editor. Circ. 30,000. Published 6 times/year. Readers are amateur, advanced amateur and professional photographers. Photo submission guidelines available on website. Priority is given to Canadian photographers.

NEEDS Needs landscape/wildlife shots, fashion, scenics, b&w images and so on.

SPECS Accepts images in digital format, must be TIFF or high-res JPEG. Send via CD at 300 dpi.

MAKING CONTACT & TERMS Send query letter with résumé of credits, SASE. Pays on publication. Buys one-time rights.

TIPS "Looking for good writers to cover any subject of interest to the amateur and advanced photographer. Fine art photos should be striking, innovative. General stock and outdoor photos should be presented with a strong technical theme."

PILOT GETAWAYS MAGAZINE

Airventure Publishing LLC, P.O. Box 550, Glendale CA 91209. (818)241-1890; (877)745-6849. **Fax:** (818)241-1895. **E-mail:** info@pilotgetaways.com; editor@pilotgetaways.com. **Website:** www.pilotgetaways.com. **Contact:** John T. Kounis, editor. Estab. 1999. Circ. 25,000. Bimonthly. Focuses on travel by private aircraft. Includes sections on back-country, bush and mountain flying. Emphasizes private pilot travel—weekend getaways, fly-in dining, bush flying, and complete flying vacations. Readers are mid-life males, affluent.

NEEDS Uses assignment photos. Needs photos of adventure, travel, product shots/still life. Model release required. Photo captions required.

SPECS Accepts medium-format and 35mm slides. Accepts images in digital format. Send via CD as TIFF files at 300 dpi.

MAKING CONTACT & TERMS Provide résumé, business card or tearsheets to be kept on file for possible future assignments; contact by e-mail. Simultaneous submissions OK. Prefers previously unpublished work. Pays 30 days after publication. Credit line given. Buys all rights; negotiable.

TIPS "Exciting, fresh and unusual photos of airplanes used for recreation. Aerial landscapes, fly-in destinations. Outdoor recreation: skiing, hiking, fishing and motor sports. Affluent back-country lifestyles: homes, hangars and private airstrips. Query first. Don't send originals—color copies or low-res digital OK for evaluation."

⑨ ⑥ PILOT MAGAZINE

Evolution House, 2-6 Easthampstead Road, Wokingham RG40 2EG, United Kingdom. +44(0)118 742 527. **Fax:** +44(0)7834 104843. **Website:** www.pilotweb.aero. Estab. 1966. Circ. 11,500. "The UK's best-selling monthly general aviation magazine."

NEEDS Photos of aviation. Reviews photos with or without a manuscript. Photo captions required.

SPECS Accepts images in digital format. Send via web or CD as JPEG files at 300 dpi.

MAKING CONTACT & TERMS Does not keep samples on file; include SAE for return of material. Previously published work OK. Pays from £25 for color inside. Pays on publication. Credit line given. Buys first UK publication rights.

TIPS "Read our magazine. Label all photos with name and address. Supply generous captions."

⑨ ⑥ ◑ PLANET

P.O. Box 44, Aberystwyth SY23 3ZZ, Wales. (44)(1970)611255. **Fax:** (44)(1970)611197. **E-mail:** planet.enquiries@planetmagazine.org.uk. **Website:** www.planetmagazine.org.uk. Estab. 1970. Circ. 1,400. Bimonthly cultural magazine devoted to Welsh culture, current affairs, the arts, the environment, but set in broader international context. Audience based mostly in Wales.

NEEDS Photos of environmental, performing arts, sports, agriculture, industry, political, science. Interested in fine art, historical/vintage. Reviews photos with or without manuscript. Model/property release preferred. Photo captions required; include subject, copyright holder.

SPECS Uses glossy color and b&w prints; 4×5 transparencies. Accepts images in digital format. Send as JPEG files at 300 dpi.

MAKING CONTACT & TERMS Send query letter with résumé, slides, prints, photocopies. Does not keep samples on file; include SASE for return of material. Simultaneous submissions and previously published work OK. Pays on publication. Credit line given. Buys first rights.

TIPS "Read the magazine first to get an idea of the kind of areas we cover so incompatible/unsuitable material is not submitted. Submission guidelines available online."

💲💲 ⬤ PLAYBOY MAGAZINE

9346 Civic Center Dr., #200, Beverly Hills CA 90210. (310)264-6600. **Fax:** (310)786-7440. **Website:** www. playboy.com. Estab. 1953. Monthly magazine and website with daily updates. Pay site: Playboy Cyber Club. This is a premier market that demands photographic excellence. *Playboy* frequently uses freelancers but only those with superior-quality work. *Playboy* accepts model submissions from all photographers, but copies of model photo ID showing they are at least 18 years of age must be included with submission. Playmate finder's fees are paid. Readers are 75% male, 25% female, ages 18-70; come from all economic, ethnic, and regional backgrounds.

NEEDS Photographic needs focus primarily on glamour/pretty girls with nudity. Also includes still life, fashion, food, personalities, travel.

SPECS Raw digital file preferred with a minimum of 40-50MB.

MAKING CONTACT & TERMS Pay is negotiable depending on job. Finder's fee for a published Playmate is $500. The modeling fee for a published Playmate is $25,000. **Pays on acceptance.** Buys all rights.

TIPS "Lighting and attention to detail is most important when photographing women, especially the ability to use strobes indoors. Refer to magazine for style and quality guidelines."

➕ POCKETS

The Upper Room, P.O. Box 340004, Nashville TN 37203. (615)340-7333. **E-mail:** pockets@upperroom. org. **Website:** pockets.upperroom.org. **Contact:** Lynn W. Gilliam, editor. Estab. 1981. Magazine published 11 times/year. "*Pockets* is a Christian devotional magazine for children ages 6-12. All submissions should address the broad theme of the magazine. Each issue is built around one theme with material which can be used by children in a variety of ways. Scripture stories, fiction, poetry, prayers, art, graphics, puzzles, and activities are included. Submissions do not need to be overtly religious. They should help children experience a Christian lifestyle that is not always a neatly-wrapped moral package, but is open to the continuing revelation of God's will. Seasonal material, both secular and liturgical, is desired."

○ Add name, address of photographer, and statement of parents' permission to use photos of all children appearing in the photos.

POINT

Converge Worldwide (Baptist General Conference), Mail Code 200, 11002 Lake Hart Dr., Orlando FL 32832. **Fax:** (866)990-8980. **E-mail:** bob.putman@ convergeww.org. **Website:** www.convergeworldwide. org. Circ. 45,000. *Point* is the official magazine of Converge Worldwide (BCG). Almost exclusively uses articles related to Converge, their churches, or by/about Converge people.

MAKING CONTACT & TERMS Reviews prints, some high-resolution digital. Captions, identification of subjects, model releases required. Offers $15-60/photo. Buys one-time rights.

🄳 POPULAR PHOTOGRAPHY & IMAGING

Bonnier Corporation, 460 N. Orlando Ave., Suite 200, Winter Park FL 32789. (407)628-4802. **Fax:** (407)628-7061. **E-mail:** mleuchter@hfmus.com; popeditor@hf mus.com. **Website:** www.popularphotography.com. **Contact:** Miriam Leuchter, managing editor. Estab. 1937. Circ. 450,000. Monthly. Readers are male and female photographers, amateurs to professionals of all ages. Photo guidelines free with SASE.

NEEDS "We are primarily interested in articles on new or unusual phases of photography which we have not covered recently or in recent years. We do not want general articles on photography which could just as easily be written by our staff. We reserve the right to rewrite, edit, or revise any material we are interested in publishing."

MAKING CONTACT & TERMS "Queries should be accompanied by a sampling of how-to pictures (particularly when equipment is to be constructed or a process is involved), or by photographs which support the text. Please send duplicates only; do not send negatives or original slides. We are not responsible for the loss of original work. The sender's name and address should be clearly written on the back of each print, on the mount of each slide, watermarked on digitally sent sample images, and on the first and last pages of all written material, including the accompanying letter. Technical data should accompany all pictures, including the camera used, lens, film (or image format if digital), shutter speed, aperture, lighting, and any other points of special interest on how the picture was made. Material mailed to us should be carefully wrapped or packaged to avoid damage. All submissions must be accompanied by a SASE. The rate of payment depends upon the importance of the feature, quality of the photographs, and our presentation of it. Upon acceptance, fees will be negotiated by the author/photographer and the editors of the magazine. We are unable to accept individual portfolios for review. However, we do welcome samples of your work in the form of promotional mailers, press kits, or tearsheets for our files. These should be sent to the attention of Miriam Leuchter, managing editor, at the above address or via e-mail at mleuchter@hfmus.com."

TIPS The Annual Reader's Picture Contest gives photographers the opportunity to have their work recognized in the largest photo magazine in the world, as well as on PopPhoto.com. See website for submission guidelines, or e-mail acooper@hfmus.com.

POWER & MOTORYACHT

10 Bokum Rd., Essex CT 06426. (860)767-3200. **E-mail:** jwood@aimmedia.com; cwhite@aimmedia.com. **Website:** www.powerandmotoryacht.com. Erin Kenney, creative director. **Contact:** Jason Y. Wood, editor-in-chief; Chris White, managing editor. Estab. 1985. Circ. 157,000. Monthly. Covers powerboats 24 feet and larger with special emphasis on the 35-foot-plus market. "Readers have an average of 33 years experience boating, and we give them accurate advice on how to choose, operate, and maintain their boats as well as what electronics and gear will help them pursue their favorite pastime. In addition, since powerboating is truly a lifestyle and not just a hobby for them, *Power & Motoryacht* reports on a host of other topics that affect their enjoyment of the water: chartering, sportfishing, and the environment, among others."

POZ

CDM Publishing, LLC, 462 Seventh Ave., 19th Floor, New York NY 10018. (212)242-2163. **Fax:** (212)675-8505. **E-mail:** website@poz.com; editor-in-chief@poz.com. **Website:** www.poz.com. **Contact:** Doriot Kim, art director. Estab. 1994. Circ. 125,000. Monthly. Focuses exclusively on HIV/AIDS news, research, and treatment.

NEEDS Buys 10-25 photos from freelancers/issue; 120-300 photos/year. Reviews photos with or without a ms. Model release preferred. Photo captions required.

SPECS Prefers online portfolios.

MAKING CONTACT & TERMS Send query letter with nonreturnable samples. Provide self-promotion piece to be kept on file for possible future assignments. Responds only if interested; send nonreturnable samples. Simultaneous submissions and previously published work OK. Pays $400-1,000 for color cover; $100-500 for color inside. Pays on publication. Credit line given.

THE PRAIRIE JOURNAL

P.O. Box 68073, 28 Crowfoot Terrace NW, Calgary Alberta Y3G 3N8, Canada. **E-mail:** editor@prairiejournal.org (queries only); prairiejournal@yahoo.com. **Website:** www.prairiejournal.org. **Contact:** A.E. Burke, literary editor. Estab. 1983. Circ. 650-750. Literary magazine published twice/year. Features mainly poetry and artwork. Sample copy available for $6 and 7×8½ SAE. Photo guidelines available for SAE and IRC.

NEEDS Buys 4 photos/year. Needs literary only, artistic.

SPECS Uses b&w prints. Accepts images in digital format. Send via e-mail "if your query is successful."

MAKING CONTACT & TERMS Send query letter with photocopies only (no originals) by mail. Provide self-promotion piece to be kept on file. Responds in 6 months, only if interested; send nonreturnable samples. Pays $10-50 for b&w cover or inside. Pays on publication. Credit line given. Buys first rights.

TIPS "Black & white literary, artistic work preferred; not commercial. We especially like newcomers. Read our publication or check out our website. You need to own copyright for your work and have permission to reproduce it. We are open to subjects that would be suitable for a literary arts magazine containing poetry, fiction, reviews, interviews. We do not commission but choose from your samples."

PRAIRIE MESSENGER

Benedictine Monks of St. Peter's Abbey, P.O. Box 190, Muenster Saskatchewan S0K 2Y0, Canada. (306)682-1772. **Fax:** (306)682-5285. **E-mail:** pm.canadian@stpeterspress.ca. **Website:** www.prairiemessenger.ca. **Contact:** Maureen Weber, associate editor. Estab. 1904. Circ. 5,000. Weekly Catholic publication published by the Benedictine Monks of St. Peter's Abbey in Muenster, Saskatchewan, Canada. Has a strong focus on ecumenism, social justice, interfaith relations, aboriginal issues, arts and culture.

NEEDS People, religious, agriculture, industry, military, environmental, entertainment, performing arts, lifestyle, seasonal photographs. Buys 50 photos/year. "I usually need photos to illustrate columns and occasionally use 'filler' feature photos with captions I either make up or seek quotations for. This means a range of themes is possible, including seasonal, environmental, religious, etc. Also, we carry a weekly poem submitted by freelancers, but I use stock photos to illustrate the poems."

MAKING CONTACT & TERMS Accepts photos as TIFF or JPEG format. E-mail with JPEG samples at 72 dpi. Credit line given.

PRICK OF THE SPINDLE

P.O. Box 17067, Birmingham AL 35217. **E-mail:** pseditor@prickofthespindle.com. **Website:** www.prickofthespindle.com. **Contact:** Cynthia Reeser, editor-in-chief. Estab. 2007. Circ. 6,200 hits/day. Literary magazine published quarterly online, biannually in print. We accept artwork that shows imagination and skill that covers a broad range of themes and subjects. Sample copy available for $10. Art/photo submission guidelines available on website.

MAKING CONTACT & TERMS Send query letter or e-mail with résumé, prints and SASE (regular mail) or JPEG samples at 72 dpi. Keeps samples on file, provide résumé, business card or self-promotion piece to be kept on file for future assignments. Samples only return with SASE. Responds in 7 days. Will contact artist for portfolio review if interested. Portfolio should include b&w, color, finished art, original art, photographs. Considers simultaneous submissions and previously published work. Credit line given. Buys first North American rights. Willing to negotiate. Finds freelancers through submissions.

PRINCETON ALUMNI WEEKLY

194 Nassau St., Suite 38, Princeton NJ 08542. (609)258-4722. **Fax:** (609)258-2247. **E-mail:** federici@princeton.edu; mnelson@princeton.edu. **Website:** www.princeton.edu/paw. **Contact:** Katherine Federici Greenwood, editor; Marianne Nelson, art director. Circ. 60,000. Published 15 times/year. Emphasizes Princeton University and higher education. Readers are alumni, faculty, students, staff and friends of Princeton University. Sample copy available for $2 with 9×12 SASE and 2 first-class stamps.

NEEDS Assigns local and out-of-state photographers and purchases stock. Needs photos of people, campus scenes; subjects vary greatly with content of each issue.

MAKING CONTACT & TERMS Arrange a personal interview to show portfolio. Provide sample card to be kept on file for possible future assignments. Payment varies according to usage, size, etc. Pays on publication. Buys one-time rights.

◎ ⊛ ○ THE PROGRESSIVE

409 E. Main St., Madison WI 53703. (608)257-4626. **Fax:** (608)257-3373. **E-mail:** editorial@progressive.org; mattr@progressive.org. **Website:** www.progressive.org. **Contact:** Matthew Rothschild, editor. Estab. 1909. Monthly political magazine. "Grassroots publication from a left perspective, interested in foreign and domestic issues of peace and social justice." Photo guidelines free and online.

NEEDS Buys 5-10 photos from freelancers/issue; 50-100 photos/year. Looking for images documenting the human condition and the social/political environments of contemporary society. Special photo needs include "labor activities, environmental issues and political movements." Photo captions required; include name, place, date, credit information.

SPECS Accepts low-res JPEGs via e-mail.

MAKING CONTACT & TERMS Send query letter with photocopies; include SASE. Provide stock list to be kept on file for possible future assignments. Art director will contact photographer for portfolio review if interested. Responds once every month. Simultaneous submissions and previously published work OK. Pays $50-150 for b&w inside. Pays on publication. Credit line given. Buys one-time rights. All material returned with SASE.

TIPS "Most of the photos we publish are of political actions. Interesting and well-composed photos of creative actions are the most likely to be published. We also use 2-3 short photo essays on political or social subjects per year." For detailed photo information, see the website.

✚ QST

(860)594-0200. **Fax:** (860)594-0259. **E-mail:** qst@arrl.org. **Website:** www.arrl.org. **Contact:** Steve Ford, editor. Estab. 1915. Circ. 150,000. "QST is the monthly membership journal of ARRL, the national association for amateur radio, covering subjects of interest to amateur ('ham') radio operators."

MAKING CONTACT & TERMS Reviews color prints, slides, GIF/JPEG files. Captions, identification of subjects required. Offers no additional payment for photos accepted with ms. Buys all rights.

💲 ◎ ◐ RACQUETBALL MAGAZINE

1685 W. Uintah, Suite 103, Colorado Springs CO 80904-2906. (719)635-5396. **Fax:** (719)635-0685. **E-mail:** jhiser@usra.org. **Website:** www.usaracquetball. com. **Contact:** Jim Hiser, program manager. Estab. 1990. Circ. 30,000. Bimonthly magazine of USA Racquetball. Emphasizes racquetball. Sample copy available for $4.50. Photo guidelines available.

NEEDS Buys 6-12 photos from freelancers/issue; 36-72 photos/year. Needs photos of action racquetball. Model/property release preferred. Photo captions required.

SPECS Accepts images in digital format. Send via CD as EPS files at 900 dpi.

MAKING CONTACT & TERMS Provide résumé, business card, brochure, flyer or tearsheets to be kept on file for possible future assignments. Responds in 1 month. Previously published work OK. Pays on publication. Credit line given. Buys all rights; negotiable.

RELOCATING TO THE LAKE OF THE OZARKS

Showcase Publishing, 2820 Bagnell Dam Blvd., #1B, Lake Ozark MO 65049. (573)365-2323, ext. 301. **Fax:** (573)365-2351. **E-mail:** spublishingco@msn.com. **Website:** www.relocatingtothelakeoftheozarks.com. **Contact:** Dave Leathers, publisher. Circ. 12,000. Semi-annual relocation guide; free for people moving to the area.

SPECS "Only digital images are accepted. Digital images must be submitted with resolutions of 300 dpi and can be submitted as JPEG, EPS, TIFF or PSD files. They must be submitted with physical width of 6 inches wide at the very least and should preferably be submitted as being set to CMYK mode."

REVOLUTIONARY WAR TRACKS

E-mail: revolutionarywartracks@yahoo.com. **Contact:** Shannon Bridget Murphy. Estab. 2005. Quarterly. "Bringing Revolutionary War history alive for children and teens." Photo guidelines available by e-mail request.

NEEDS Buys 12-24 photos/year. Photos of babies/children/teens, multicultural, families, parents, disasters, environmental, landscapes/scenics, wildlife, cities/urban, education, religious, rural, adventure, events, food/drink, sports, travel, agriculture, medicine, military, political, product shots/still life, science, technology—as related to Revolutionary War history. Interested in alternative process, avant garde, documentary, fashion/glamour, fine art, historical/vintage, seasonal. Reviews photos with or without a manuscript. Model/property release preferred.

SPECS Uses glossy or matte color and b&w prints.

MAKING CONTACT & TERMS Send query letter via e-mail. "If possible, please do not include photographs in files if they are sent through e-mail. A disc with your photographs is acceptable." Provide résumé, business card or self-promotion piece to be kept on file for possible future assignments. "Photographs sent with CDs are requested but not required." Responds within 1 month to queries; 1 week to portfolios. Simultaneous submissions and previously published work OK. **Pays on acceptance.** Credit line given. Buys one-time rights, first rights; negotiable.

THE ROANOKER

Leisure Publishing Co., 3424 Brambleton Ave., Roanoke VA 24018. (540)989-6138; (800)548-1672. **Fax:** (540)989-7603. **E-mail:** jwood@leisurepublishing. com; krheinheimer@leisurepublishing.com. **Website:** www.theroanoker.com. **Contact:** Kurt Rheinheimer, editor; Austin Clark, creative director; Patty Jackson, production director. Estab. 1974. Circ. 10,000. Bimonthly. Emphasizes Roanoke region and western Virginia. Readers are upper-income, educated people interested in their community. Sample copy available for $3.

NEEDS Buys 30 photos from freelancers/issue; 180 photos/year. Needs photos of couples, multicultural, families, parents, senior citizens, architecture, cities/urban, education, interiors/decorating, entertainment, events, food/drink, health/fitness/beauty, performing arts, sports, travel, business concepts, medicine, technology/computers, seasonal. Needs "travel and scenic photos in western Virginia; color photo essays on life in western Virginia." Model/property release preferred. Photo captions required.

MAKING CONTACT & TERMS Accepts digital format. Send via CD, e-mail as TIFF, EPS, JPEG files at 300 dpi, minimum print size 8×10 with cutlines and thumbnails. Responds in 1 month. Simultaneous submissions and previously published work OK. Pays $100-150 for color cover; $15-25 for b&w inside, $25-

100 for color inside; $100/day. Pays on publication. Credit line given. Rights purchased vary; negotiable.

⊕ ROBB REPORT

CurtCo Robb Media, LLC, 29160 Heathercliff Rd., Suite #200, Malibu CA 90265. (310)589-7700. **Fax:** (310)589-7701. **E-mail:** editorial@robbreport.com. **Website:** www.robbreport.com. Estab. 1976. Circ. 104,000. "For over 30 years, *Robb Report* magazine has served as the definitive authority on connoisseurship for ultra-affluent consumers. *Robb Report* not only showcases the products and services available from the most prestigious luxury brands around the globe, but it also provides its sophisticated readership with detailed insight into a range of these subjects, which include sports and luxury automobiles, yachts, real estate, travel, private aircraft, fashion, fine jewelry and watches, art, wine, state-of-the-art home electronics, and much more. For connoisseurs seeking the very best that life has to offer, *Robb Report* remains the essential luxury resource."

ROLLING STONE

Wenner Media, 1290 Avenue of the Americas, New York NY 10104. (212)484-1616. **Fax:** (212)484-1664. **E-mail:** rseditors@rollingstone.com. **Website:** www. rollingstone.com. **Contact:** Caryn Ganz, editorial director. Circ. 1.46 million. Monthly. Emphasizes film, CD reviews, music groups, celebrities, fashion. Readers are young adults interested in news of popular music, politics, and culture.

NEEDS Photos of celebrities, political, entertainment, events. Interested in alternative process, avant garde, documentary, fashion/glamour.

SPECS Accepts images in digital format. Send as TIFF, JPEG files at 300 dpi.

MAKING CONTACT & TERMS Portfolio may be dropped off every Wednesday and picked up on Friday afternoon. Provide business card, self-promotion piece to be kept on file for possible future assignments. Responds only if interested; send nonreturnable samples.

TIPS "It's not about a photographer's experience, it's about a photographer's talent and eye. Lots of photographers have years of professional experience, but their work isn't for us. Others might not have years of experience, but they have this amazing eye."

ROMANTIC HOMES

Y-Visionary Publishing, 22840 Savi Ranch Pkwy., Suite 200, Yorba Linda CA 92887. **E-mail:** jdemon

travel@beckett.com. **Website:** www.romantichomes. com. **Contact:** Jacqueline DeMontravel, editor. Estab. 1994. Circ. 200,000. Monthly. For women who want to create a warm, intimate and casually elegant home. Provides how-to advice, along with information on furniture, home decorating ideas, floor and window coverings, artwork, travel, etc. Sample copy available with SASE.

NEEDS Buys 20-30 photos from freelancers/issue; 240-360 photos/year. Needs photos of gardening, interiors/decorating, travel. Reviews photos with accompanying manuscripts only. Model/property release required. Photo captions preferred.

SPECS Uses 2¼×2¼ transparencies.

MAKING CONTACT & TERMS Send query letter with transparencies, stock list. Provide self-promotion piece to be kept on file for possible future assignments. Responds in 3 weeks. Simultaneous submissions OK. Pays net 30 days for images and on publication for articles. Credit line/byline given. Buys all rights; negotiable.

THE ROTARIAN

Rotary International, One Rotary Center, 1560 Sherman Ave., Evanston IL 60201. (847)866-3000. **Fax:** (847)328-8554. **E-mail:** rotarian@rotary.org. **Website:** www.rotary.org. Estab. 1911. Circ. 510,000. Monthly organization magazine for Rotarian business and professional men and women and their families. "Dedicated to business and professional ethics, community life, and international understanding and goodwill." Sample copy and photo guidelines free with SASE.

NEEDS Assigns photography to freelancers and staff photographers. Subject varies from studio to location, from environmental portraiture to photojournalism, but there is always a Rotary connection.

SPECS Digital images only. Prefers RAW files, but will accept high-res JPEG.

MAKING CONTACT & TERMS Send query e-mail, fee schedule and link to online portfolio. Clearly identify your location in the subject of your e-mail. Creative director will contact photographer. No calls please. Keeps e-mail, promotion samples on file. Do not send unsolicited originals. Responds in 3 weeks. Payment negotiable. **Pays on acceptance.** Credit line given. Buys one-time rights; occasionally all rights; negotiable.

TIPS "We prefer high-res digital images in most cases. The key words for the freelance photographer to keep in mind are *internationality* and *variety*. Study the magazine. Read the kinds of articles we publish. Think how your photographs could illustrate such articles in a dramatic, storytelling way."

RUNNING TIMES

Rodale, Inc., 400 S. 10th St., Emmaus PA 18098-0099. (610)967-5171. **Fax:** (610)967-8964. **E-mail:** editor@ runningtimes.com. **Website:** www.runningtimes. com. **Contact:** Jonathan Beverly, editor-in-chief. Estab. 1977. Circ. 125,000. Published 10 times/year. Covers distance running and racing. "*Running Times* is the national magazine for the experienced running participant and fan. Our audience is knowledgeable about the sport and active in running and racing. All editorial relates specifically to running: improving performance, enhancing enjoyment, or exploring events, places, and people in the sport."

MAKING CONTACT & TERMS Identification of subjects required. Negotiates payment individually. Buys one time rights.

RURAL HERITAGE

P.O. Box 2067, Cedar Rapids IA 52406. (319)362-3027. **E-mail:** info@ruralheritage.com. **Website:** www.rur alheritage.com. **Contact:** Joe Mischka, editor. Estab. 1976. Circ. 9,500. Bimonthly journal in support of modern-day farming and logging with draft animals (horses, mules, oxen). Sample copy available for $8 ($10 outside the US). Photo guidelines available online or via e-mail.

NEEDS "Quality photographs of draft animals working in harness."

SPECS "For interior pages we use glossy color prints, high-quality slides, or high-res images (300 dpi or greater) shot with a quality digital camera. For covers we use 5×7 glossy color prints, large-format transparencies, or high-res images shot with a quality digital camera. Digital images must be original (not resized, cropped, etc.) files from a digital camera; scans unacceptable."

MAKING CONTACT & TERMS Send query letter with samples. "Please include SASE for the return of your material, and put your name and address on the back of each piece." Pays $100 for color cover; $10-25 for b&w inside. Also provides 2 copies of issue in which work appears. Pays on publication.

TIPS "Animals usually look better from the side than from the front. We like to see all the animal's body parts, including hooves, ears and tail. For animals in harness, we want to see the entire implement or vehicle. We prefer action shots (plowing, harvesting hay, etc.). Watch out for shadows across animals and people. Please include the name of any human handlers involved, the farm, the town (or county), state, and the animals' names (if possible) and breeds. You'll find current guidelines in the 'Business Office' of our website."

RUSSIAN LIFE

RIS Publications, P.O. Box 567, Montpelier VT 05601. **Website:** www.russianlife.com. Estab. 1956. Circ. 15,000. Bimonthly. Uses 25-35 photos/issue. Offers 10-15 freelance assignments/year.

NEEDS Photojournalism related to Russian culture, art and history.

SPECS Send 35mm, 2¼×2¼, 4×5, 8×10 transparencies; digital format.

MAKING CONTACT & TERMS Send query letter. After inquiry and response, be prepared to send digital thumbnails or links to same online. We no longer accept submissions by mail. Responds in 1 month. Pays $20-50 (color photo with accompanying story), depending on placement in magazine. Pays on publication. Credit line given. Buys one-time and non-exclusive electronic rights.

TIPS "Our readers are informed Russophiles with an avid interest in all things Russian. But we do not publish personal travel journals or the like."

SAIL

180 Canal St., Suite 301, Boston MA 02114. (617)720-8600. **Fax:** (617)723-0912. **E-mail:** sailmail@sailmag azine.com. **Website:** www.sailmagazine.com. **Contact:** Peter Nielsen, editor-in-chief. Estab. 1970. Circ. 180,000. Monthly. Emphasizes all aspects of sailing. Readers are managers and professionals, average age 44. Photo guidelines free with SASE and on website.

NEEDS Buys 50-100 images/issue. Particularly interested in photos for cover and "pure sail" sections. Ideally, these photos would be digital files @300 dpi with a run size of approximately 9×12 for cover, 9×16 for "pure sail." Also accepts 35mm transparencies. Vertical cover shots also needed. Photo captions required.

SPECS Accepts images in digital format. Send high-res JPEG, TIFF and RAW files via CD, DVD or FTP (contact for FTP log-in info). Also accepts all forms of transparencies and prints with negatives.

MAKING CONTACT & TERMS Send unsolicited 35mm and 2¼×2¼ transparencies by mail with SASE for consideration. Pays $1,000 for color cover; $50-800 for color inside; also negotiates prices on a per day, per hour and per job basis. Pays on publication. Credit line given. Buys one-time North American rights. Photo shoots commissioned using half- or full-day rates.

SAILING MAGAZINE

125 E. Main St., P.O. Box 249, Port Washington WI 53074. (262)284-3494. **Fax:** (262)284-7764. **E-mail:** editorial@sailingmagazine.net. **Website:** www.sailingmagazine.net. **Contact:** Greta Schanen, managing editor. Estab. 1966. Circ. 45,000. Monthly. Emphasizes sailing. Readers are experienced sailors who race, cruise and daysail on all types of boats: dinghies, large and small mono and multihulls. Sample copy available with 11×15 SASE and 9 first-class stamps. Photo guidelines free with SASE.

NEEDS "We are a large-format journal, with a strong emphasis on top-notch photography backed by creative, insightful writing. Need photos of sailing, both long shots and on-deck. We encourage creativity; send me a sailing photograph I have not seen before." Photo captions required; include boat and people IDs, location, conditions, etc.

SPECS Uses 35mm and larger transparencies. Accepts images in digital format. Send via CD as TIFF, JPEG files at 300 dpi. Include printed thumbnails with CD. If photos are also being submitted by e-mail, they should be sent as low-res attachments, and under no circumstances be embedded in a Word document. Only submit photos via e-mail or ftp upon request.

MAKING CONTACT & TERMS Send query letter with samples; include SASE for return of material. Portfolios may be dropped off by appointment. Send submissions by mail; e-mail samples or portfolios will not be considered. Responds in 3 months. "Tell us of simultaneous submissions; previously published work OK if not with other sailing publications that compete with us." Pays $50-500. Pays 30 days after publication.

SAILING WORLD

Bonnier Corporation, 55 Hammarlund Way, Middletown RI 02842. (401)845-5100. **Fax:** (401)845-5180. **E-mail:** editor@sailingworld.com; dave.reed@sailingworld.com. **Website:** www.sailingworld.com.

Contact: Dave Reed, editor. Estab. 1962. Circ. 65,000. Monthly. Emphasizes performance sailing and racing for upper-income sailors. Readers are males ages 35-45, females ages 25-35 who are interested in sailing. Sample copy available for $7. Photo guidelines available online.

NEEDS Freelance photography in a given issue: 20% assignment and 80% freelance stock. Covers most sailing races. Needs photos of adventure, health/fitness, humor, sports. "We will send an updated e-mail listing our photo needs on request."

MAKING CONTACT & TERMS Responds in 1 month. Pays $650 for cover; $75-400 for inside. Pays on publication. Credit line given. Buys first North American serial rights.

TIPS "We look for photos that are unusual in composition, lighting, and/or color that feature performance sailing at its most exciting. We would like to emphasize speed, skill, fun, and action. Photos must be of high quality. We prefer Fuji Velvia film. We have a format that allows us to feature work of exceptional quality. A knowledge of sailing and experience with on-the-water photography is a requirement. We cover current events and generally only use photos taken in the past 30-60 days."

○ SALT HILL LITERARY JOURNAL

E-mail: salthillart@gmail.com. **Website:** www.salthilljournal.net. **Contact:** Art editor. Circ. 1,000. "*Salt Hill* seeks unpublished 2D art: drawings, paintings, photography, mixed media, documentation of 3D art, typographic art diagrams, maps, etc., for its semiannual publication. We offer all colors, shapes, and stripes."

NEEDS Seeking graphic novels, literary and experimental art. Sample copy available for $6. Responds in 3 months.

MAKING CONTACT & TERMS See website for specifications.

SALT WATER SPORTSMAN

Bonnier Corporation, 460 N. Orlando Ave., Suite 200, Winter Park FL 32789. (407)628-4802. **E-mail:** editor@saltwatersportsman.com. **Website:** www.saltwatersportsman.com. **Contact:** Glenn Law, editor. Circ. 170,000. Monthly. Emphasizes all phases of saltwater sport fishing for the avid beginner-to-professional saltwater angler. "No. 1 monthly marine sport fishing magazine in the U.S." Sample copy free with 9×12 SASE and 7 first-class stamps. Photo guidelines free.

NEEDS Buys photos (including covers) without ms; 20-30 photos/issue with ms. Needs saltwater fishing photos. "Think fishing action, scenery, mood, story-telling close-ups of anglers in action. Make it come alive—and don't bother us with the obviously posed 'dead fish and stupid fisherman' back at the dock." Wants, on a regular basis, cover shots (clean verticals depicting saltwater fishing action). For accompanying ms, needs fact/feature articles dealing with marine sport fishing in the U.S., Canada, Caribbean, Central and South America. Emphasis on how-to.

SPECS Send via CD, ZIP; format as 8-bit, unconverted, 300 dpi, RGB or TIFF. A confirming laser or proof of each image must accompany the media. A printed disk directory with each new name written next to each original name must be provided.

MAKING CONTACT & TERMS Send material by mail for consideration, or query with samples. Provide résumé or tearsheets to be kept on file for possible future assignments. Responds in 1 month. Pays $2,500 maximum for cover; $100-500 for color inside; $500 minimum for text-photo package. **Pays on acceptance.**

TIPS "Prefer to see a selection of fishing action and mood; must be sport fishing-oriented. Read the magazine! No horizontal cover images with suggestions it can be cropped. We're using more 'outside' photography—that is, photos not submitted with ms package. Take lots of verticals and experiment with lighting."

⑤ ◐ SANDLAPPER MAGAZINE

Sandlapper Society, Inc., 3007 Millwood Ave., Columbia SC 29205. (803)779-8763. **Fax:** (803)254-4833. **E-mail:** elaine@sandlapper.org. **Website:** www.sandlapper.org. **Contact:** Elaine Gillespie, executive director. Estab. 1969. Circ. 8,000. Quarterly. Emphasizes South Carolina topics only.

NEEDS Uses about 10 photographers/issue. Photos of anything related to South Carolina in any style, "as long as they're not in bad taste." Model release preferred. Photo captions required; include places and people.

SPECS Uses 8×10 color and b&w prints; 35mm, 2¼×2¼, 4×5, 8×10 transparencies. Accepts images in digital format. Send via CD, ZIP as TIFF, JPEG files at 300 dpi. "Do not format exclusively for PC. RGB preferred. Submit low- and high-res files, and label them as such."

MAKING CONTACT & TERMS Send query letter with samples. Keeps samples on file; include SASE for return of material. Responds in 1 month. Pays 1 month *after* publication. Credit line given. Buys first rights plus right to reprint.

TIPS "We see plenty of beach sunsets, mountain waterfalls, and shore birds. Would like fresh images of people working and playing in the Palmetto state."

SANTA BARBARA MAGAZINE

2064 Alameda Padre Serra, Suite 120, Santa Barbara CA 93103. (805)965-5999. **Fax:** (805)965-7627. **E-mail:** alisa@sbmag.com. **Website:** www.sbmag.com. **Contact:** Alisa Baur, art director; Gina Tolleson, editor. Estab. 1975. Circ. 40,000. Bimonthly. Emphasizes Santa Barbara community and culture. Sample copy available for $4.95 with 9×12 SASE.

NEEDS Buys 64-80 photos from freelancers/issue; 384-480 photos/year. Needs portrait, environmental, architectural, travel, celebrity, etc. Reviews photos with accompanying manuscript only. Model release required. Photo captions preferred.

MAKING CONTACT & TERMS Provide résumé, business card, brochure, flier or tearsheets to be kept on file for possible future assignments; "portfolio drop-off 24 hours." Cannot return unsolicited material. Pays $75-250 for b&w or color. Pays on publication. Credit line given. Buys first North American serial rights.

⑤ SCHOLASTIC MAGAZINES

557 Broadway, New York NY 10012. (212)343-7147. **Fax:** (212)389-3913. **E-mail:** sdiamond@scholastic.com. **Website:** www.scholastic.com. **Contact:** Steven Diamond, executive director of photography. Estab. 1920. Publication of magazines varies from weekly to monthly. "We publish 27 titles on topics from current events, science, math, fine art, literature and social studies. Interested in featuring high-quality, well-composed images of students of all ages and all ethnic backgrounds. We publish hundreds of books on all topics, educational programs, Internet products and new media."

NEEDS Photos of various subjects depending upon educational topics planned for academic year. Model release required. Photo captions required. "Images must be interesting, bright and lively!"

SPECS Accepts images in digital format. Send via CD, e-mail.

MAKING CONTACT & TERMS Send query letter with résumé, business card, brochure, flyer or tearsheets to be kept on file for possible future assignments. Material cannot be returned. Previously published work OK. Pays on publication.

TIPS Especially interested in good photography of all ages of student population. All images must have model/property releases.

SCIENTIFIC AMERICAN

75 Varick St., 9th Floor, New York NY 10013-1917. (212)451-8200. **E-mail:** editors@sciam.com. **Website:** www.sciam.com. **Contact:** Mariette DiChristina, editor-in-chief. Estab. 1845. Circ. 710,000. Emphasizes science, policy, technology and people involved in science. Seeking to broaden our 20-40 year-old readership.

NEEDS Buys 100 photos from freelancers/issue. Needs all kinds of photos. Model release required; property release preferred. Photo captions required.

MAKING CONTACT & TERMS Arrange a personal interview to show portfolio. "Do not send unsolicited photos." Provide résumé, business card, brochure, flyer or tearsheets to be kept on file for possible future assignments and note photo website. Cannot return material. Responds in 1 month. Pays $600/day; $1,000 for color cover. Pays on publication. Credit line given. Buys one-time rights and world rights. Frequently leads to re-use buying and develops relationships with scientists and writers needing photo work.

TIPS Wants to see strong natural and artificial lighting, location portraits and location shooting. Intelligent artistic photography and photo-illustration welcomed. Send business cards and promotional pieces frequently when dealing with magazine editors. Find a niche.

SCRAP

1615 L St. W, Suite 600, Washington DC 20036-5664. (202)662-8547. **Fax:** (202)626-0947. **E-mail:** kentkiser@scrap.org. **Website:** www.scrap.org. **Contact:** Kent Kiser, publisher. Estab. 1987. Circ. 9,600. Bimonthly magazine of the Institute of Scrap Recycling Industries. Emphasizes scrap recycling for owners and managers of recycling operations worldwide. Sample copy available for $8.

NEEDS Buys 0-15 photos from freelancers/issue; 15-70 photos/year. Needs operation shots of companies being profiled and studio concept shots. Model release required. Photo captions required.

SPECS Accepts images in digital format. Send via CD, ZIP, e-mail as JPEG or TIFF file at 300 dpi.

MAKING CONTACT & TERMS Provide résumé, business card, brochure, flyer or tearsheets to be kept on file for possible future assignments. Previously published work OK. Pays $800-1,500/day; $100-400 for b&w inside; $200-600 for color inside. Pays on delivery of images. Credit line given. Rights negotiable.

TIPS Photographers must possess "ability to photograph people in corporate atmosphere, as well as industrial operations; ability to work well with executives, as well as laborers. We are always looking for good color photographers to accompany our staff writers on visits to companies being profiled. We try to keep travel costs to a minimum by hiring photographers located in the general vicinity of the profiled company. Other photography (primarily studio work) is usually assigned through freelance art director."

$ [O] SEA

Duncan McIntosh Co., 17782 Cowan, Suite C, Irvine CA 92614. (949)660-6150. **Fax:** (949)660-6172. **E-mail:** editorial@seamag.com; mikew@seamag.com. **Website:** seamag.com. **Contact:** Mike Werling, managing editor. Circ. 50,000. Monthly. Emphasizes "recreational boating in 13 Western states (including some coverage of Mexico and British Columbia) for owners of recreational power boats." Sample copy and photo guidelines free with 10×13 SASE.

NEEDS Uses about 50-75 photos/issue; most supplied by freelancers; 10% assignment; 75% requested from freelancers, existing photo files, or submitted unsolicited. Needs "people enjoying boating activity (families, parents, senior citizens) and scenic shots (travel, regional); shots that include parts or all of a boat are preferred." Photos should have West Coast angle. Model release required. Photo captions required.

SPECS Accepts images in digital format. Send via CD, FTP, e-mail as TIFF, EPS, JPEG files at least 300 dpi. Contact via online form to query.

MAKING CONTACT & TERMS Send query letter with samples; include SASE for return of material. Responds in 1 month. Pay rate varies according to size published. Pays on publication. Credit line given. Buys one-time North American rights and retains reprint rights via print and electronic media.

TIPS "We are looking for sharp images with good composition showing pleasure boats in action, and people having fun aboard boats in a West Coast location. Digital shots are preferred; they must be at least 5" wide and a minimum of 300 dpi. We also use studio shots of marine products and do personality profiles. Send samples of work with a query letter and a résumé or clips of previously published photos. *Sea* does not pay for shipping; will hold photos up to 6 weeks."

SEVENTEEN MAGAZINE

300 W. 57th St., 17th Floor, New York NY 10019. (917)934-6500. **Fax:** (917)934-6574. **E-mail:** mail@seventeen.com. **Website:** www.seventeen.com. **Contact:** Consult masthead to contact appropriate editor. Estab. 1944. Circ. 2,000,000. *Seventeen* is a young women's fashion and beauty magazine. Tailored to young women in their teens and early 20s, *Seventeen* covers fashion, beauty, health, fitness, food, cars, college, careers, talent, entertainment, plus crucial personal and global issues. Photos purchased on assignment only. Query before submitting.

SHINE BRIGHTLY

GEMS Girls' Clubs, 1333 Alger St. SE, Grand Rapids MI 49507. (616)241-5616. **Fax:** (616)241-5558. **E-mail:** shinebrightly@gemsgc.org. **Website:** www.gemsgc.org. **Contact:** Kristine Palosaari, executive director; Kelli Gilmore, managing editor. Estab. 1970. Circ. 17,000. Monthly publication of GEMS Girls' Club. Emphasizes girls ages 9-14 in action. The magazine is a Christian girls' publication that inspires, motivates, and equips girls to become world changers. Sample copy and photo guidelines available for $1 with 9×12 SASE.

NEEDS Uses about 5-6 photos/issue. Photos suitable for illustrating stories and articles: photos of babies/children/teens, multicultural, religious, girls aged 9-14 from multicultural backgrounds, close-up shots with eye contact." Model/property release preferred.

SPECS Uses 5×7 glossy color prints. Accepts images in digital format. Send via ZIP, CD as TIFF, BMP files at 300 dpi.

MAKING CONTACT & TERMS Send 5×7 glossy color prints by mail (include SASE), electronic images by CD only (no e-mail) for consideration. Will view photographer's website if available. Responds in 2 months. Simultaneous submissions OK. Pays $50-75 for cover; $35 for color inside. Pays on publication. Credit line given. Buys one-time rights.

TIPS "Make the photos simple. We prefer to get a spec sheet or CDs rather than photos, and we'd really like to hold photos for our annual theme update and try to get photos to fit the theme of each issue." Recommends that photographers "be concerned about current trends in fashions, hair styles, and realize that all girls don't belong to 'families.' Please, no slides, no negatives and no e-mail submissions."

💲🕓 🌓 SHOOTING SPORTS USA

11250 Waples Mill Rd., Fairfax VA 22030. (703)267-1310. **E-mail:** shootingsportsusa@nrahq.org; publications@nrahq.org; clohman@nrahq.org. **Website:** www.nrapublications.org. **Contact:** Chip Lohman, editor. Monthly publication of the National Rifle Association of America. Emphasizes competitive shooting sports (rifle, pistol and shotgun). Readers range from beginner to high master. Past issues available online. Editorial guidelines free via e-mail.

NEEDS 15-25 photos from freelancers/issue; 180-300 photos/year. Needs photos of how-to, shooting positions, specific shooters. Quality photos preferred with accompanying manuscript. Model release required. Photo captions preferred.

SPECS Accepts images in digital format. Send via CD or e-mail as TIFF files at 300 dpi.

MAKING CONTACT & TERMS Send query letter with photo and editorial ideas by e-mail. Include SASE. Responds in 1 week. Previously published work OK when cleared with editor. Pays $150-400 for color cover; $50-150 for color inside; $250-500 for photo/text package; amount varies for photos alone. Pays on publication. Credit line given. Buys first North American serial rights.

TIPS Looks for "generic photos of shooters shooting, obeying all safety rules and using proper eye protection and hearing protection. If text concerns certain how-to advice, photos are needed to illuminate this. Always query first. We are in search of quality photos to interest both beginning and experienced shooters."

SHOTGUN SPORTS MAGAZINE

P.O. Box 6810, Auburn CA 95604. (530)889-2220. **Fax:** (530)889-9106. **E-mail:** shotgun@shotgunsportsmagazine.com. **Website:** www.shotgunsportsmagazine.com. **Contact:** Johnny Cantu, editor in chief.

SPECS On disc or e-mailed at least 5 inches and 300 dpi (contact graphics artist for details).

🌓 SHOTS

P.O. Box 27755, Minneapolis MN 55427-0755. **E-mail:** shots@shotsmag.com. **Website:** www.shotsmag.com. **Contact:** Russell Joslin, editor/publisher. Circ. 2,000. Quarterly fine art photography magazine. "We publish b&w fine art photography by photographers with an innate passion for personal, creative work." Sample copy available for $6.50. Photo guidelines free with SASE or on website.

NEEDS Fine art photography of all types accepted for consideration (but not bought). Reviews photos with or without a manuscript. Model/property release preferred. Photo captions preferred.

SPECS Uses 8×10 b&w prints. Accepts images in digital format. Send via CD as TIFF files at 300 dpi. "See website for further specifications."

MAKING CONTACT & TERMS Send query letter with prints. There is a $16 submission fee for nonsubscribers (free for subscribers). Include SASE for return of material. Responds in 3 months. Credit line given. Does not buy photographs/rights.

● SHOWBOATS INTERNATIONAL

Boat International Media, 41-47 Hartfield Rd., London SW19 3RQ, United Kingdom. (954)522-2628 (US number). **Fax:** (954)522-2240. **E-mail:** marilyn.mower@boatinternationalmedia.com. **Website:** www.boatinternational.com. **Contact:** Marilyn Mower, editorial director. Estab. 1995. Circ. 50,000. "Luxury yachting publication aimed at the world's discerning yachting audience. We provide the most exclusive coverage of super yachts over 100 feet worldwide."

SIERRA

Website: www.sierraclub.org. Estab. 1893. Bimonthly. Emphasizes conservation and environmental politics for people who are well educated, activist, outdoor-oriented, and politically well informed with a dedication to conservation.

◐ ◑◑ SKI CANADA

117 Indian Rd., Toronto Ontario M6R 2V5, Canada. (416)538-2293. **E-mail:** mac@skicanadamag.com; design@skicanadamag.com. **Website:** www.skicanadamag.com. **Contact:** Iain MacMillan, editor. Circ. 46,438. Published monthly, September-January. Readership is 65% male, ages 25-44, with high income. Sample copy free with SASE.

NEEDS Buys 80 photos from freelancers/issue; 480 photos/year. Needs photos of skiing—travel (within Canada and abroad), new school, competition, equipment, instruction, news and trends.

SPECS Accepts images in digital format. Send via e-mail to norm@k9designco.com.

MAKING CONTACT & TERMS "The publisher assumes no responsibility for the return of unsolicited

material." Provide résumé, business card, brochure, flyer, or tearsheets to be kept on file for possible future assignments. Responds in 1 month. Simultaneous submissions OK. Pays within 30 days of publication. Credit line given. Editorial lineup available online.

SKIING MAGAZINE

Bonnier Corp., 5720 Flatiron Pkwy., Boulder CO 80301. (303)253-6300. **Fax:** (303)448-7638. **E-mail:** editor@skiingmag.com. **Website:** www.skinet.com/skiing. Estab. 1936. Circ. 430,000. *Skiing Magazine* is an online ski-lifestyle publication written and edited for recreational skiers. Its content is intended to help them ski better (technique), buy better (equipment and skiwear), and introduce them to new experiences, people, and adventures.

◎ ◕ SKIPPING STONES: A MULTICULTURAL LITERARY MAGAZINE

P.O. Box 3939, Eugene OR 97403-0939. (541)342-4956. **E-mail:** editor@skippingstones.org. **Website:** www.skippingstones.org. **Contact:** Arun Toké, editor. Estab. 1988. Circ. 1,400 print, plus Web. "We promote multicultural awareness, international understanding, nature appreciation, and social responsibility. We suggest authors, artists and photographers not make stereotypical generalizations in their contributions. We like when they include their own experiences, or base their articles on their personal immersion experiences in a culture or country." Has featured Xuan Thu Pham, Soma Han, Jon Bush, Zarouhie Abdalian, Paul Dix, Elizabeth Zunon and Najah Clemmons.

NEEDS Buys /teens/children, celebrities, multicultural, families, disasters, environmental, landscapes, wildlife, cities, education, gardening, rural, events, health/fitness/beauty, travel, documentary and seasonal. Reviews 4×6 prints, low-res JPEG files. Captions required.

MAKING CONTACT & TERMS Send query letter or e-mail with photographs (digital JPEGs at 72 dpi).

TIPS "We are a multicultural magazine for youth and teens. We consider your work as a labor of love that contributes to the education of youth. We publish photoessays on various cultures and countries/regions of the world in each issue of the magazine to promote international and intercultural (and nature) understanding. Tell us a little bit about yourself, your motivation, goals, and mission."

◎ SMITHSONIAN MAGAZINE

Capital Gallery, Suite 6001, MRC 513, P.O. Box 37012, Washington DC 20013. (202)275-2000. **E-mail:** smithsonianmagazine@si.edu. **Website:** www.smithsonianmag.com. **Contact:** Molly Roberts, photo editor; Jeff Campagna, art services coordinator. Circ. 2.3 million. Monthly. *Smithsonian* chronicles the arts, environment, sciences and popular culture of the times for today's well-rounded individuals with diverse, general interests, providing its readers with information and knowledge in an entertaining way. Visit website for photo submission guidelines. *Does not accept unsolicited photos or portfolios.* Use online submission form. Query before submitting.

SOLDIER OF FORTUNE

2135 11th St., Boulder CO 80302. (303)443-0300. **E-mail:** editorsof@aol.com. **Website:** www.sofmag.com. **Contact:** Lt. Col. Robert A. Brown, editor/publisher. Estab. 1975. Circ. 60,000. Monthly. Covers military, paramilitary, police, combat subjects, and action/adventure.

MAKING CONTACT & TERMS Reviews contact sheets, transparencies. Captions, identification of subjects required. Pays $500 for cover photo. Buys one-time rights.

⊕ ❸❸ SOUTHERN BOATING

Southern Boating & Yachting, Inc., 330 N. Andrews Ave., Ft. Lauderdale FL 33301. (954)522-5515. **Fax:** (954)522-2260. **E-mail:** liz@southernboating.com; john@southernboating.com. **Website:** www.southernboating.com. **Contact:** Liz Pasch, editorial director; John Lambert, art director. Estab. 1972. Circ. 40,000. Monthly. Emphasizes "powerboating, sailing, and cruising in the southeastern and Gulf Coast US, Bahamas, and the Caribbean." Readers are "concentrated in 30-60 age group, mostly male, affluent, very experienced boat owners." Sample copy available for $7.

NEEDS Number of photos/issue varies; many supplied by freelancers. Seeks "boating lifestyle" cover shots. Buys stock only. No "assigned covers." Model release required. Photo captions required.

SPECS Accepts images in digital format. Send via CD or e-mail as JPEG, TIFF files, minimum 4×6 at 300 dpi.

MAKING CONTACT & TERMS Send query letter with list of stock photo subjects, SASE. Response time varies. Simultaneous submissions and previously published work OK. Pays within 30 days of publication. Credit line given. Buys one-time print and electronic/website rights.

TIPS "We want lifestyle shots of saltwater cruising, fishing or just relaxing on the water. Lifestyle or family boating shots are actively sought."

❸❸❸ ⓞ SOUTHWEST AIRLINES SPIRIT

Spirit Magazine Editorial Office, Pace Communications, Inc., 2811 McKinney Ave., Suite 360, Dallas TX 75204. (214)580-8070. **Fax:** (214)580-2491. **Website:** www.spiritmag.com. **Contact:** Emily Kimbro, art director. Circ. 350,000. Monthly in-flight magazine. "Reader is college-educated business person, median age of 45, median household income of $82,000. Spirit targets the flying affluent. Adventurous perspective on contemporary themes." Sample copy available for $3. Photo guidelines available.

NEEDS Buys 5-10 photos from freelancers/issue; 120 photos/year. Needs photos of celebrities, couples, multicultural, environmental, landscapes/scenics, wildlife, architecture, cities/urban, adventure, automobiles, entertainment, events, food/drink, health/fitness, hobbies, humor, performing arts, sports, travel, business concepts, industry, medicine, political, product shots/still life, science, technology. Interested in alternative process, avant garde, documentary, fashion/glamour. Reviews photos with or without a manuscript. Model/property release required. Photo captions required; include names of people in shot, location, names of buildings in shot.

SPECS Uses 35mm, 2¼×2¼, 4×5 transparencies. Accepts images in digital format. Send via CD as TIFF, EPS files at 300 dpi.

MAKING CONTACT & TERMS "Queries are accepted by mail only; e-mail and phone calls are strongly discouraged." Send query letter with slides, prints, photocopies, tearsheets, transparencies, SASE. Portfolio may be dropped off Monday through Friday. Provide self-promotion piece to be kept on file for possible future assignments. Responds only if interested; send nonreturnable samples. Pays $1,000-1,500 for cover; $900-2,500 for inside. **Pays on acceptance.** Credit line given. Buys one-time rights.

TIPS "Read our magazine. We have high standards set for ourselves and expect our freelancers to have the same or higher standards."

SPECIALIVING

P.O. Box 1000, Bloomington IL 61702. (309)962-2003. **E-mail:** gareeb@aol.com. **Website:** www.specialiving. com. Estab. 2001. Circ. 12,000. Quarterly. For physically disabled people. Emphasizes travel, home modifications, products, info, inspiration. Sample copy available for $5.

NEEDS Any events/settings that involve physically disabled people (who use wheelchairs), not developmentally disabled. Reviews photos with or without a manuscript. Model release preferred. Photo captions required.

SPECS Uses glossy or matte color and b&w prints. Accepts images in digital format. Send via CD, ZIP, e-mail as TIFF, JPEG files at 300 dpi.

MAKING CONTACT & TERMS Send query letter with prints. Online e-mail form available on website. Does not keep samples on file; include SASE for return of material. Responds in 3 weeks. Simultaneous submissions and previously published work OK. Pays $50 minimum for b&w cover; $100 maximum for color cover; $10 minimum for b&w or color inside. Pays on publication. Credit line given. Buys one-time rights.

TIPS "Need good-quality photos of someone in a wheelchair involved in an activity. Need caption and where I can contact subject to get story if wanted."

SPORT FISHING

Bonnier Corporation, 460 N. Orlando Ave., Suite 200, Winter Park FL 32789. (407)628-4802. **Fax:** (407)628-7061. **E-mail:** Editor@sportfishingmag.com. **Website:** www.sportfishingmag.com. Estab. 1985. Circ. 250,000. "*Sport Fishing*'s readers are middle-aged, affluent, mostly male, who are generally proficient in and very educated to their sport. We are about fishing from boats, not from surf or jetties." Emphasizes saltwater sport fishing. Sample copy available for $2.50, 9×12 SASE and 6 first-class stamps. Photo guidelines available on website, via e-mail or with SASE.

NEEDS Buys 50% or more photos from freelancers/issue. Needs photos of saltwater fish and fishing—especially good action shots. "Are working more from stock—good opportunities for extra sales on any given assignment." Model release not generally required.

SPECS Prefers images in RAW, unaltered/undoctored digital format, especially for the option to run images very large, with accompanying low-res JPEGs for quick review. Original 35mm (or larger) transparencies are accepted for smaller images, but no lon-

ger for the cover or 2-page spreads. All guidelines, rates, suggestions available online; click on "Editorial Guidelines" at bottom of home page.

MAKING CONTACT & TERMS Send query letter with samples. Send unsolicited photos by mail or low-res digitals by e-mail for consideration. Provide business card, brochure, flyer or tearsheets to be kept on file for possible future assignments. Responds in 3 weeks. Pays $1,000 for cover; $75–400 for inside. Buys one-time rights unless otherwise agreed upon.

TIPS "Sharp focus critical; avoid 'kill' shots of big game fish, sharks; avoid bloody fish in/at the boat. The best guideline is the magazine itself. Know your market. Get used to shooting on, in or under water using the RAW setting of your camera. Most of our needs are found in the magazine. If you have first-rate photos and questions, e-mail us."

SPORTS AFIELD

Field Sports Publishing, 15621 Chemical Lane, Huntington Beach CA 92649. (714)373-4910. **E-mail:** letters@sportsafield.com. **Website:** www.sportsafield. com. **Contact:** Jerry Gutierrez, art director. Estab. 1887. Circ. 50,000.

NEEDS Hunting/wildlife themes only. Considers all media.

SPECS Reviews 35mm slides transparencies, TIFF/JPEG files.

MAKING CONTACT & TERMS Captions, model releases required. Buys first time rights.

SPORTS ILLUSTRATED

Time, Inc., 1271 Avenue of the Americas, New York NY 10020. (212)522-1212. **E-mail:** story_queries@si mail.com. **Website:** www.si.com. Estab. 1954. Circ. 3.3 million. *Sports Illustrated* reports and interprets the world of sports, recreation and active leisure. It previews, analyzes and comments on major games and events, as well as those noteworthy for character and spirit alone. In addition, the magazine has articles on such subjects as fashion, physical fitness and conservation. Query before submitting.

💲 ⭕ STICKMAN REVIEW

E-mail: art@stickmanreview.com. **Website:** www. stickmanreview.com. **Contact:** Anthony Brown, editor. Estab. 2001. Biannual literary magazine publishing fiction, poetry, essays and art for a literary audience. Sample copies available on website.

NEEDS Accepts 1-2 photos from freelancers/issue; 4 photos/year. Interested in alternative process, avant garde, documentary, erotic, fine art. Reviews photos with or without a manuscript.

SPECS Accepts images in digital format. Send via e-mail as JPEG, GIF, TIFF, PSD files at 72 dpi (500K maximum).

MAKING CONTACT & TERMS Contact through e-mail only. Does not keep samples on file; cannot return material. Do not query, just submit the work you would like considered. Responds 2 months to portfolios. Simultaneous submissions OK. Credit line given.

TIPS "Please check out the magazine on our website. We are open to anything, so long as its intent is artistic expression."

STIRRING: A LITERARY COLLECTION

Dept. of English, 301 McClung Tower, University of Tennessee, Knoxville TN 37996. **E-mail:** eesmith81@gmail.com. **E-mail:** stirring.fiction@gmail.com; stirring.poetry@gmail.com; stirring.nonfiction@gmail.com. **Website:** www.sundresspublications.com/stirring. **Contact:** Erin Elizabeth Smith, managing editor. Estab. 1999.

MAKING CONTACT & TERMS For photography, send all submissions as JPEG attachments to stirring-photo@sundresspublications.com.

THE SUN

107 N. Roberson St., Chapel Hill NC 27516. (919)942-5282. **Fax:** (919)932-3101. **Website:** www.thesunmagazine.org. **Contact:** Sy Safransky, editor. Estab. 1974. Circ. 72,000. Needs b&w photos and photo essays. Sample copy available for $7. Photo guidelines free with SASE or on website.

NEEDS Buys 10-30 photos/issue; 200-300 photos/year. Needs photo essays and individual photographs that relate to political, spiritual, environmental, and social themes. "We're looking for artful and sensitive photographs that aren't overly sentimental. Most of our photos of people feature unrecognizable individuals, although we do run portraits in specific places, including the cover." Model/property release strongly preferred.

SPECS Uses 5×7 to 11×17 glossy or matte b&w prints. Slides are not accepted, and color photos are discouraged. "We began accepting digital photo submissions in early 2014. If you are submitting digital images, please send high-quality digital prints first. If we accept your images for publication, we will request the image files on CD or DVD media (Mac or PC) in uncompressed TIFF grayscale format at 300 dpi or greater."

MAKING CONTACT & TERMS Include SASE for return of material. Responds in 3-6 months. Simultaneous submissions and previously published work OK. "Submit no more than 30 of your best b&w prints. Pays $500 for b&w cover; $100-250 for b&w inside. Pays on publication. Credit line given. Buys one-time rights.

◎ ◐ SURFACE MAGAZINE

140 W. 26th St., Street Level W., New York NY 10001. (212)229-1500. **E-mail:** editorial@surfacemag.com. **Website:** www.surfacemag.com. Estab. 1994. Circ. 112,000. Published 6 times/year. "*Surface* is the definitive American source for engaging, curated content covering all that is inventive and compelling in the design world. Contains profiles of emerging designers and provocative projects that are reshaping the creative landscape."

NEEDS Buys 200 photos from freelancers/issue; 1,600 photos/year. Needs photos of environmental, landscapes/scenics, architecture, cities/urban, interiors/decorating, performing arts, travel, product shots/still life, technology. Interested in avant garde, fashion, portraits, fine art, seasonal.

SPECS Uses 11×17 glossy matte prints; 35mm, 2¼×2¼, 4×5, 8×10 transparencies. Accepts images in digital format. Send via CD, ZIP as TIFF, JPEG files at 300 dpi.

MAKING CONTACT & TERMS Contact through rep or send query letter with prints, photocopies, tearsheets. Provide self-promotion piece to be kept on file for possible future assignments. "Portfolios are reviewed on Friday each week. Submitted portfolios must be clearly labeled and include a shipping account number or postage for return. Please call for more details." Responds only if interested; send nonreturnable samples. Simultaneous submissions OK. Credit line given.

⊖⊖ ◐ SURFING MAGAZINE

E-mail: tony.perez@sorc.com; peter@surfingmagazine.com. **Website:** www.surfingthemag.com. **Contact:** Tony Perez, publisher; Peter Taras, photo editor. Circ. 180,000. Monthly. "Emphasizes surfing action and related aspects of beach lifestyle. Travel to new surfing areas covered as well. Average age of readers is 17 with 95% being male. Nearly all drawn to publication due to high-quality, action-packed photographs." Sample copy available with legal-size SASE and 9 first-class stamps. Photo guidelines free with SASE or via e-mail.

NEEDS Buys an average of 10 photos from freelancers/issue. Needs "in-tight, front-lit surfing action photos, as well as travel-related scenics. Beach lifestyle photos always in demand."

SPECS Uses 35mm transparencies. Accepts digital images via CD; contact for digital requirements before submitting digital images.

MAKING CONTACT & TERMS Send samples by mail for consideration; include SASE for return of material. Responds in 1 month. Pays on publication. Credit line given. Buys one-time rights.

TIPS Prefers to see "well-exposed, sharp images showing both the ability to capture peak action, as well as beach scenes depicting the surfing lifestyle. Color, lighting, composition and proper film usage are important. Ask for our photo guidelines prior to making any film/camera/lens choices."

TECHNICAL ANALYSIS OF STOCKS & COMMODITIES

4757 California Ave. SW, Seattle WA 98116. (206)938-0570. **E-mail:** editor@traders.com. **Website:** www.traders.com. Estab. 1982. Circ. 60,000. "Magazine covers methods of investing and trading stocks, bonds and commodities (futures), options, mutual funds, and precious metals using technical analysis."

TEXAS GARDENER

Suntex Communications, Inc., P.O. Box 9005, 10566 N. River Crossing, Waco TX 76714. (254)848-9393. **Fax:** (254)848-9779. **E-mail:** info@texasgardener.com. **Website:** www.texasgardener.com. Estab. 1981. Circ. 20,000. Bimonthly. Emphasizes gardening. Readers are "51% male, 49% female, home gardeners, 98% Texas residents." Sample copy available for $4.

NEEDS Buys 18-27 photos from freelancers/issue; 108-162 photos/year. Needs color photos of gardening activities in Texas. Special needs include cover photos shot in vertical format. Must be taken in Texas. Photo captions required.

SPECS Prefers high-res digital images. Send via e-mail as JPEG files at 300 dpi.

MAKING CONTACT & TERMS Send query letter with samples, SASE. Responds in 3 weeks. Pays $100-200 for color cover; $25-100 for color inside. Pays on publication. Credit line given. Buys one-time rights.

TIPS "Provide complete information on photos. For example, if you submit a photo of watermelons growing in a garden, we need to know what variety they are and when and where the picture was taken."

TEXAS HIGHWAYS

P.O. Box 141009, Austin TX 78714-1009. (800)839-4997. **Website:** www.texashighways.com. Estab. 1974. Circ. 250,000. Monthly. "*Texas Highways* interprets scenic, recreational, historical, cultural and ethnic treasures of the state and preserves the best of Texas heritage. Its purpose is to educate and entertain, to encourage recreational travel to and within the state, and to tell the Texas story to readers around the world." Readers are ages 45 and over (majority), $24,000 to $60,000/year salary bracket with a college education. Photo guidelines and online submission form available on website.

NEEDS Buys 30-60 photos from freelancers/issue; 360-420 photos/year. Needs "travel and scenic photos in Texas only." Special needs include "fall, winter, spring and summer scenic shots and wildflower shots (Texas only)." Photo captions required; include location, names, addresses and other useful information.

SPECS "We take only color originals, 35mm or larger transparencies. No negatives or prints." Accepts images in digital format. Prefers camera RAW files with tweaks and captions in sidecar files. Consult guidelines before submitting.

MAKING CONTACT & TERMS Send query letter with samples, SASE. Provide business card and tearsheets to be kept on file for possible future assignments. Responds in 1 month. Simultaneous submissions OK. Pays $400 for color cover; $60-170 for color inside. Pays $15 extra for electronic usage. Pays on publication. Credit line given. Buys one-time rights. Online feedback form is used for correspondence with all magazine staff.

TIPS "Look at our magazine and format. We accept only high-quality, professional-level work—no snapshots. Interested in a photographer's ability to edit own material and the breadth of a photographer's work. Look at 3-4 months of the magazine. Query not just for photos but with ideas for new/unusual topics."

TEXAS MONTHLY

Emmis Publishing LP, P.O. Box 1569, Austin TX 78767. (512)320-6900. **Fax:** (512)476-9007. **E-mail:** lbaldwin@texasmonthly.com. **Website:** www.texasmonthly.com. **Contact:** Brian D. Sweany, editor; Leslie Baldwin, photo editor; Andi Beierman, deputy art director. Estab. 1973. Circ. 300,000. *Texas Monthly* is edited for the urban Texas audience and covers the state's politics, sports, business, culture and changing lifestyles. It contains lengthy feature articles, reviews and interviews, and presents critical analysis of popular books, movies and plays.

NEEDS Uses about 50 photos/issue. Photos of celebrities, sports, travel.

MAKING CONTACT & TERMS "Please feel free to submit your photography or illustration portfolio to us. The best way to do this is by e-mailing us a link to your work. If you do not have a website, simply attaching a few images of your work in an e-mail is fine. Send samples or tearsheets. No preference on printed material—b&w or color. Responds only if interested. Keeps samples on file."

TIPS "Visit www.texasmonthly.com/artguide for information on sending portfolios."

THEMA

Thema Literary Society, P.O. Box 8747, Metairie LA 70011-8747. **E-mail:** thema@cox.net. **Website:** thema literarysociety.com. **Contact:** Gail Howard, poetry editor. Estab. 1988. Literary magazine published 3 times/year emphasizing theme-related short stories, poetry, creative nonfiction, photography, and art. Sample copy available for $10.

NEEDS Photo must relate to one of *THEMA*'s upcoming themes (indicate the target theme on submission of photo). See website for themes.

SPECS Uses 5×7 glossy color and/or b&w prints. Accepts images in digital format. Send via ZIP as TIFF files at 200 dpi.

MAKING CONTACT & TERMS Send query letter with prints, photocopies. Does not keep samples on file; include SASE for return of material. Responds in 1 week to queries; 3 months after deadline to submissions. Simultaneous submissions and previously published work OK. Pays $25 for cover; $10 for b&w inside. **Pays on acceptance.** Credit line given. Buys one-time rights.

TIPS "Submit only work that relates to one of *THEMA*'s upcoming themes. Be sure to specify target theme in cover letter. Contact by snail mail preferred."

THIN AIR MAGAZINE

English Department, Northern Arizona University, Bldg. 18, Room 133, Flagstaff AZ 86011. (928)523-0469. **E-mail:** editors@thinairmagazine.com; jmh522@nau.edu. **Website:** thinairmagazine.com. Estab. 1995. Circ. 400. Annual literary magazine.

Emphasizes arts and literature—poetry, fiction and essays. Readers are collegiate, academic, writerly adult males and females interested in arts and literature. Sample copy available for $6.

NEEDS Buys 2-4 photos from freelancers/issue; 4-8 photos/year. Needs scenic/wildlife shots and b&w photos that portray a statement or tell a story. Looking for b&w or color cover shots. Model/property release preferred. Photo captions preferred; include name of photographer, date of photo.

SPECS Uses 8×10 b&w prints.

MAKING CONTACT & TERMS Send unsolicited photos by mail with SASE for consideration. Photos accepted August through May only. Keeps samples on file. Responds in 3 months. Simultaneous submissions and previously published work OK. Pays 2 contributor's copies. Credit line given. Buys one-time rights.

TIDE MAGAZINE

6919 Portwest Dr., Suite 100, Houston TX 77024. (713)626-4234; (800)201-FISH. **Fax:** (713)626-5852. **E-mail:** ccantl@joincca.org. **Website:** www.joincca.org. Estab. 1979. Circ. 80,000. Bimonthly magazine of the Coastal Conservation Association. Emphasizes coastal fishing, conservation issues—exclusively along the Gulf and Atlantic Coasts. Readers are mostly male, ages 25-50, coastal anglers and professionals.

NEEDS Buys 12-16 photos from freelancers/issue; 72-96 photos/year. Needs photos of *only* Gulf and Atlantic coastal activity, recreational fishing and coastal scenics/habitat, tight shots of fish (saltwater only). Model/property release preferred. Photo captions not required, but include names, dates, places and specific equipment or other key information.

MAKING CONTACT & TERMS Send query letter with stock list. Responds in 1 month. Simultaneous submissions and previously published work OK. Pays on publication. Credit line given. Buys one-time rights; negotiable.

TIPS Wants to see "fresh twists on old themes—unique lighting, subjects of interest to my readers. Take time to discover new angles for fishing shots. Avoid the usual poses, i.e., 'grip-and-grin.' We see too much of that already."

TIKKUN

2342 Shattuck Ave., Suite 1200, Berkeley CA 94704. (510)644-1200. **Fax:** (510)644-1255. **E-mail:** magazine@tikkun.org. **Website:** www.tikkun.org. **Contact:** managing editor. Estab. 1986. Circ. 41,000.

Quarterly. Jewish and interfaith critique of politics, culture and society.

NEEDS Uses 70 photos/issue, mostly from the public domain; 5% supplied by freelancers. Needs political, social commentary; Middle East and US photos. "Looks for photos that show hope, suffering, oppression, poverty or struggle to change the world." Reviews photos with or without a manuscript.

SPECS Uses b&w and color prints. Accepts images in digital format for Mac.

MAKING CONTACT & TERMS Response time varies. "Turnaround is 4 months, unless artist specifies other." Previously published work OK. As a nonprofit publication with barely any image budget, we seek donation of most images. Pays on publication. Credit line given. Artists must agree to these terms: Nonexclusive worldwide publishing rights for use of the images in *Tikkun* is, in the whole or in part, distributed, displayed and archived, with no time restriction. Art guidelines are available online.

TIPS "Look at our magazine and suggest how your photos can enhance our articles and subject material. Send samples."

TIME

1271 Avenue of the Americas, New York NY 10020. **E-mail:** letters@time.com. **Website:** www.time.com. **Contact:** Nancy Gibbs, managing editor. Estab. 1923. Circ. 4 million. *TIME* is edited to report and analyze a complete and compelling picture of the world, including national and world affairs, news of business, science, society and the arts, and the people who make the news. Query before submitting.

TIMES OF THE ISLANDS

Times Publications, Ltd., P.O. Box 234, Lucille Lightbourne Bldg., #7, Providenciales Turks & Caicos Islands, British West Indies. (649)946-4788. **Fax:** (649)946-4788. **E-mail:** timespub@tciway.tc. **Website:** www.timespub.tc. Estab. 1988. Circ. 10,000. Quarterly. Focuses on in-depth topics specifically related to Turks and Caicos islands. Targeted beyond mass tourists to homeowners, investors, developers and others with strong interest in learning about these islands. Sample copy available for $6. Photo guidelines available on website.

NEEDS Buys 5 photos from freelancers/issue; 20 photos/year. Needs photos of environmental, landscapes/scenics, wildlife, architecture, adventure, travel. Interested in historical/vintage. Also scuba diving, islands in TCI beyond main island of Providenciales. Reviews photos with or without a manuscript. Photo captions required; include specific location, names of any people.

SPECS Prefers high resolution digital images. Send via CD or e-mail as JPEG files.

MAKING CONTACT & TERMS Send query e-mail with photo samples. Provide business card, self-promotion piece to be kept on file for possible future assignments. Responds in 6 weeks to queries. Simultaneous submissions and previously published work OK. Pays $150 for color cover; $15-50 for inside. Pays on publication. Credit line given. Buys one-time rights; negotiable.

TIPS "Make sure photo is specific to Turks & Caicos and location/subject accurately identified."

TRACK & FIELD NEWS

2570 El Camino Real, Suite 220, Mountain View CA 94040. (650)948-8188. **Fax:** (650)948-9445. **E-mail:** editorial@trackandfieldnews.com. **Website:** www.trackandfieldnews.com. **Contact:** Jon Hendershott, associate editor (features/photography). Estab. 1948. Circ. 18,000. Monthly. Emphasizes national and world-class track and field competition and participants at those levels for athletes, coaches, administrators and fans. Sample copy free with 9×12 SASE. Photo guidelines free.

NEEDS Buys 10-15 photos from freelancers/issue; 120-180 photos/year. Wants, on a regular basis, photos of national-class athletes, men and women, preferably in action. "We are always looking for quality pictures of track and field action, as well as offbeat and different feature photos. We also welcome shots from road and cross-country races for both men and women. Any photos may eventually be used to illustrate news stories in *T&FN*, feature stories in *T&FN*, or may be used in our other publications (books, technical journals, etc.). Any such editorial use will be paid for, regardless of whether material is used directly in *T&FN*. About all we don't want to see are pictures taken with someone's Instamatic. No shots of someone's child or grandparent running. Professional work only." Photo captions required; include subject name (last name first), meet date/name.

SPECS Images must be in digital format. Send via CD, e-mail; all files at 300 dpi.

MAKING CONTACT & TERMS Send query letter with samples, SASE. Responds in 10–14 days. Pays

$225 for color cover; $25 for b&w inside (rarely used); $50 for color inside ($100 for full-page interior color; $175 for interior 4-color poster). Payment is made monthly. Credit line given. Buys one-time rights.

TIPS "No photographer is going to get rich via *T&FN*. We can offer a credit line, nominal payment and, in some cases, credentials to major track and field meets. Also, we can offer the chance for competent photographers to shoot major competitions and competitors up close, as well as being the most highly regarded publication in the track world as a forum to display a photographer's talents."

➕ TRAIL & TIMBERLINE

The Colorado Mountain Club, 710 Tenth St., Suite 200, Golden CO 80401. (303)279-3080. **E-mail:** editor@cmc.org. **Website:** www.cmc.org/about/newsroom/trailandtimberline.aspx. **Contact:** Editor. Estab. 1918. Circ. 10,500. Official quarterly publication for the Colorado Mountain Club. "Articles in *Trail & Timberline* conform to the mission statement of the Colorado Mountain Club to unite the energy, interest, and knowledge of lovers of the Colorado mountains, to collect and disseminate information 'regarding the Colorado mountains in the areas of art, science, literature, and recreation,' to stimulate public interest, and to encourage preservation of the mountains of Colorado and the Rocky Mountain region."

MAKING CONTACT & TERMS Send images at 72 dpi, 5×7 in. "If possible, please post images on a website for us to view. Please do not send slides, prints, or other artwork. If photos or illustrations are required for your submission, we will request them when your work is accepted for publication. Typically, photo submissions must have been shot at 300 dpi, 11×17 to be considered for publication. Please, do not resize in Photoshop." Buys one-time rights.

TRAIL RUNNER

Big Stone Publishing, 2567 Dolores Way, Carbondale CO 81623. (970)704-1442. **Fax:** (970)963-4965. **E-mail:** pcunobooth@bigstonepub; mbenge@bigstonepub.com. **Website:** www.trailrunnermag.com. **Contact:** Michael Benge, editor; Yitka Winn, associate editor. Estab. 1999. Circ. 31,000. *Trail Runner* regularly features stunning photography of trail running destinations, races, adventures and faces of the sport.

NEEDS Buys 10-15 photos from freelancers/issue; 50-100 photos/year. Needs photos of landscapes/scenics, adventure, health/fitness, sports, travel. Interested in anything related to running on trails and the outdoors. Reviews photos with or without a manuscript. Model/property release preferred. Photo captions required.

SPECS Accepts images in digital format. E-mail as TIFF or JPEG files at 300 dpi.

MAKING CONTACT & TERMS Send query letter via e-mail to photos@bigstonepub.com. Contact art director, ad@bigstonepub.com, for appointment to drop off portfolio. Provide résumé, business card or self-promotion piece to be kept on file for possible future assignments. Responds in 4 weeks. Simultaneous submissions OK. Pays $500 for color cover; $50-250 for inside; $375 for spread. Pays 30 days from date of publication. Credit line given. Buys one-time rights, first rights; negotiable.

TIPS "Read our magazine. Stay away from model shots, or at least those with make-up and spandex clothing. No waving at the camera."

TRAVEL + LEISURE

1120 Avenue of the Americas, 9th Floor, New York NY 10036. (212)382-5600. **E-mail:** TLPhoto@aexp.com. **Website:** www.travelandleisure.com. Monthly magazine emphasizing travel, resorts, dining and entertainment.

MAKING CONTACT & TERMS "If mailing a portfolio, include a SASE package for its safe return. You may also send it by messenger Monday–Friday, 11-5. We accept work in book form exclusively—no transparencies, loose prints, nor scans on CD, disk or e-mail. Send photocopies or photo prints, not originals, as we are not responsible for lost or damaged images in unsolicited portfolios. We do not meet with photographers if we haven't seen their book. However, please include a promo card in your portfolio with contact information, so we may get in touch with you if necessary."

🔄 🌐 TRAVELLER MAGAZINE & PUBLISHING

3rd Floor, Dorset House, 27-45 Stamford St., London SE1 9NT, United Kingdom. (44)(207)838 5998. **E-mail:** traveller@and-publishing.co.uk. **Website:** www.wexas.com/traveller-magazine. **Contact:** Amy Sohanpaul, editor. Circ. 18,000. Quarterly. Readers are predominantly male, professional, ages 35 and older. Sample copy available for £6.95.

NEEDS Uses 75-100 photos/issue; all supplied by freelancers. Needs photos of travel, wildlife, tribes.

Reviews photos with or without a manuscript. Photo captions preferred.

MAKING CONTACT & TERMS Send at least 20 original color slides or b&w prints. Or send at least 20 low-res scans by e-mail or CD (include printout of thumbnails); high-res (300 dpi) scans will be required for final publication. Does not keep samples on file; include SASE for return of material. Responds in 3 months. Pays £150 for color cover; £80 for full page; from £40 for other sizes. Pays on publication. Buys one-time rights.

TIPS Look at guidelines for contributors on website.

⊕ ◑ TRAVELWORLD INTERNATIONAL MAGAZINE

3579 Foothill Blvd., #744, Pasadena CA 91107. (626)376-9754. **E-mail:** helen@natja.org. **Website:** www.natja.org, www.travelworldmagazine.com. **Contact:** Helen Hernandez, CEO. Estab. 1992. Circ. 75,000. Quarterly online magazine of the North American Travel Journalists Association (NATJA). Emphasizes travel, food, wine, and hospitality industries.

NEEDS Photos of food/drink, travel.

SPECS Uses color and b&w. Prefers digital images.

MAKING CONTACT & TERMS Send query via e-mail.

TIPS Only accepts submissions/queries from members.

TRICYCLE

89 5th Ave., Suite 301, New York NY 10013. (212)929-0320. **E-mail:** editorial@tricycle.com. **Website:** www.tricycle.com. **Contact:** Emma Varvaloucas, managing editor. Estab. 1991. Circ. 50,000. Quarterly magazine providing a unique and independent public forum for exploring Buddhist teachings and practices, establishing a dialogue between Buddhism and the broader culture, and introducing Buddhist thinking to Western disciplines.

NEEDS Buys 10 photos from freelancers/issue; 40 photos/year. Reviews photos with or without a ms. Model/property release preferred. Photo captions preferred.

SPECS Uses glossy b&w and color prints; 35mm transparencies. Accepts images in digital format. Send via CD, ZIP, e-mail as TIFF, EPS, BMP, GIF, JPEG files at 300 dpi.

MAKING CONTACT & TERMS "We prefer to receive copies or CDs of photographs or art, rather than originals, in both color and b&w. For the safety of your own work, please do not send anything which you would fear losing, as we cannot assume responsibility for the loss of unsolicited artwork. If you would like to receive a reply from us and wish your work returned, you must include a SASE with sufficient postage."

TIPS "Read the magazine to get a sense of the kind of work we publish. We don't only use Buddhist art; we select artwork depending on the content of the piece."

TURKEY COUNTRY

National Wild Turkey Federation, P.O. Box 530, Edgefield SC 29824-0530. (803)637-3106. **E-mail:** info@nwtf.net; klee@nwtf.net. **Website:** www.turkeycountrymagazine.com. **Contact:** Karen Lee, editor; Matt Lindler, photo editor. Estab. 1973. Circ. 180,000. Bimonthly. For members of the National Wild Turkey Federation—people interested in conserving the American wild turkey. Sample copy available for $5 with 9×12 SASE. Images may be submitted to accompany specific assignments or on speculation. See photograph submission information and send speculative images to the photo editor at the NWTF shipping address. Photo guidelines free with SASE or on website at www.turkeycountrymagazine.com/contributor_guidelines.html.

NEEDS Buys at least 100 photos/year. Needs photos of "wildlife, including wild turkeys, upland birds, North American Big Game; wild turkey hunting; wild turkey management techniques (planting food, trapping for relocation, releasing); wild turkey habitat; families, women, children, and people with disabilities hunting or enjoying the outdoors." Photo captions required.

SPECS Prefers images in digital format from 6mp or higher resolution cameras. Send via CD/DVD at 300 dpi with thumbnail page (see guidelines for more details).

MAKING CONTACT & TERMS Send copyrighted photos to editor for consideration; include SASE. Responds in 6 weeks. Purchases both print rights and for electronic usage on turkeycountrymagazine.com, which includes a digital version of the magazine. Additional usage on the website, other than in the digital magazine, will be negotiated. Pays on publication. Credit line given. Buys one-time rights.

TIPS "No poorly posed or restaged shots, no mounted turkeys representing live birds, no domestic animals representing wild animals. Photos of dead animals in a tasteful hunt setting are considered. Contributors must agree to the guidelines before submitting."

TV GUIDE

11 W. 42nd St., 16th Floor, New York NY 10036. (212)852-7500. **Fax:** (212)852-7470. **Website:** www.tvguide.com. **Contact:** Debra Birnbaum, editor-in-chief. Estab. 1953. Circ. 9 million. *TV Guide* watches television with an eye for how TV programming affects and reflects society. It looks at the shows and the stars, and covers the medium's impact on news, sports, politics, literature, the arts, science and social issues through reports, profiles, features, and commentaries. **MAKING CONTACT & TERMS** Works only with celebrity freelance photographers. "Photos are for one-time publication use. Mail self-promo cards to photo editor at above address. No calls, please."

☺ UP HERE

P.O. Box 1350, Yellowknife Northwest Territories X1A 2N9, Canada. (867)766-6710. **Fax:** (867)873-9876. **E-mail:** matthew@uphere.ca; angela@uphere.ca. **Website:** www.uphere.ca. **Contact:** Matthew Mallon, editor-in-chief; Angela Gzowski, photo editor;. Estab. 1984. Circ. 22,000. Published 8 times/year. Emphasizes Canada's North. Readers are educated, affluent men and women ages 30 to 60.

NEEDS Buys 18-27 photos from freelancers/issue; 144-216 photos/year. Needs photos of Northern Canada environmental, landscapes/scenics, wildlife, adventure, performing arts. Interested in documentary, seasonal. Purchases photos with or without accompanying manuscript. Photo captions required.

SPECS Accepts images in digital format. Send via CD, e-mail. Also uses color transparencies, not prints, labeled with the photographer's name, address, phone number, and caption.

MAKING CONTACT & TERMS Provide résumé, business card, brochure, flyer or tearsheets to be kept on file for possible future assignments. Pays $350-400 for color cover, up to $300 for color inside. Pays on publication. Credit line given. Buys one-time rights.

TIPS "We are a *people* magazine. We need stories that are uniquely Northern (people, places, etc.). Few scenics as such. We approach local freelancers for given subjects, but routinely complete commissioned photography with images from stock sources. Please let us know about Northern images you have." Wants to see "sharp, clear photos, good color and composition.

We always need verticals to consider for the cover, but they usually tie in with an article inside."

VELONEWS

Inside Communications, Inc., 3002 Sterling Circle, Suite 100, Boulder CO 80301. (303)440-0601. **Fax:** (303)444-6788. **E-mail:** webletters@competitorgroup.com; nrogers@competitorgroup.com. **Website:** www.velonews.com. **Contact:** Neal Rogers, editor-in-chief. Estab. 1972. Circ. 48,000.

○ Covers road racing, mountain biking and recreational riding. Sample copy free with 9×12 SASE.

NEEDS Uses photos of bicycle racing (road, mountain and track). "Looking for action and feature shots that show the emotion of cycling, not just finish-line photos with the winner's arms in the air." No bicycle touring. Photos purchased with or without accompanying manuscript. Uses news, features, profiles. Photo captions required.

SPECS Uses negatives and transparencies.

MAKING CONTACT & TERMS Send samples of work or tearsheets with assignment proposal. Query first. Pays on publication. Credit line given. Buys one-time rights.

TIPS "Photos must be timely."

⊕ VICTORIAN HOMES

Beckett Media, 22840 Savi Ranch Pkwy., Suite 200, Yorba Linda CA 92887. (714)939-9991. **Fax:** (714)939-9909. **E-mail:** ephillips@beckett.com. **Website:** www.victorianhomesmag.com. **Contact:** Elaine K. Phillips, editor; Jacqueline deMontravel, editorial director. Estab. 1981. Circ. 100,000. *Victorian Homes* is read by Victorian home owners, restorers, house museum management, and others interested in the Victorian revival. Feature articles cover home architecture, interior design, furnishings, and the home's history. Photography is very important to the feature.

MAKING CONTACT & TERMS Captions required. Send low-res photos with query. Final image specs 300 dpi, at least 5×7 inches. Negotiates payment individually. Buys both print and web rights.

THE WASHINGTON BLADE

P.O. Box 53352, Washington DC 20009. (202)747-2077. **Fax:** (202)747-2070. **E-mail:** knaff@washblade.com. **Website:** www.washblade.com. **Contact:** Kevin Naff, editor. Estab. 1969. Circ. 30,000. Weekly tabloid for and about the gay community. Readers are gay men and lesbians; moderate- to upper-level income; print readers primarily in Washington DC, metropolitan area, web audience is global. Sample copy free with 10×13 SASE plus 11 first-class stamps.

💬 *The Washington Blade* stores images on CD; manipulates size, contrast, etc.—but not content.

NEEDS Uses about 6–7 photos/issue. Needs "gay-related news, sports, entertainment, events; profiles of gay people in news, sports, entertainment, other fields." Photos purchased with or without accompanying manuscript. Model release preferred. Photo captions preferred.

SPECS Accepts images in digital format. Send via e-mail.

MAKING CONTACT & TERMS Send query letter with résumé of credits. Provide résumé, business card and tearsheets to be kept on file for possible future assignments. Responds in 1 month. Simultaneous submissions and previously published work OK. Pays $10 fee to go to location, $15/photo, $5/reprint of photo; negotiable. Pays within 30 days of publication. Credit line given. Buys all rights when on assignment, otherwise one-time rights.

TIPS "Be timely! Stay up-to-date on what we're covering in the news, and call if you know of a story about to happen in your city that you can cover. Also, be able to provide some basic details for a caption (*tell* us what's happening, too). It's especially important to avoid stereotypes."

WASHINGTON TRAILS

705 Second Ave., Suite 300, Seattle WA 98104. (206)625-1367. **E-mail:** eli@wta.org. **Website:** www.wta.org/trail-news/magazine. **Contact:** Eli Boschetto, editor. Estab. 1966. Circ. 9,000. Magazine of the Washington Trails Association. Published 6 times/year. Emphasizes "backpacking, hiking, cross-country skiing, all nonmotorized trail use, outdoor equipment and minimum-impact camping techniques." Readers are "people active in outdoor activities, primarily backpacking; residents of the Pacific Northwest, mostly Washington; age group: 9-90; family-oriented; interested in wilderness preservation, trail maintenance." Photo guidelines free with SASE or online.

NEEDS Uses 10–15 photos from volunteers/issue; 100–150 photos/year. Needs "wilderness/scenic; people involved in hiking, backpacking, skiing, snowshoeing, wildlife; outdoor equipment photos, all with Pacific Northwest emphasis." Photo captions required.

MAKING CONTACT & TERMS Send JPEGs by e-mail for consideration. Responds in 1–2 months. Simultaneous submissions and previously published work OK. No payment for photos. A 1-year subscription offered for use of color cover shot. Credit line given.

TIPS "Photos must have a Pacific Northwest slant. Photos that meet our cover specifications are always of interest to us. Familiarity with our magazine will greatly aid the photographer in submitting material to us. Contributing to *Washington Trails* won't help pay your bills, but sharing your photos with other backpackers and skiers has its own rewards."

$$ ○ WATERCRAFT WORLD

(805)667-4100. **Fax:** (805)667-4336. **E-mail:** gmansfield@affinitygroup.com. **Website:** www.watercraftworld.com. **Contact:** Gregg Mansfield, editorial director. Estab. 1987. Circ. 75,000. Published 6 times/year. Emphasizes personal watercraft (Jet Skis, Wave Runners, Sea-Doo). Readers are 95% male, average age 37, boaters, outdoor enthusiasts. Sample copy available for $4.

NEEDS Buys 7-12 photos from freelancers/issue; 42-72 photos/year. Needs photos of personal watercraft travel, race coverage. Model/property release required. Photo captions preferred.

SPECS Accepts images in digital format. Send via CD, ZIP, e-mail as TIFF, EPS, GIF, JPEG files at 300 dpi.

MAKING CONTACT & TERMS Send query letter with résumé of credits. Provide résumé, business card, brochure, flyer or tearsheets to be kept on file for possible future assignments. "Call with ideas." Responds in 1 month. Pays on publication. Credit line given. Rights negotiable.

TIPS "Call to discuss project. We take and use many travel photos from all over the United States (very little foreign). We also cover many regional events (e.g., charity rides, races)."

$$ WATERSKI

460 N. Orlando Ave., Suite 200, Winter Park FL 32789. (407)628-4802. **Fax:** (407)628-7061. **E-mail:** todd.ristorcelli@bonniercorp.com. **Website:** www.waterskimag.com. **Contact:** Todd Ristorcelli, editor. Estab. 1978. Circ. 105,000. Published 8 times/year. Emphasizes water skiing instruction, lifestyle, competition, travel. Readers are 36-year-old males, average house-

hold income $65,000. Sample copy available for $2.95. Photo guidelines free with SASE.

NEEDS Buys 20 photos from freelancers/issue; 160 photos/year. Needs photos of instruction, travel, personality. Model/property release preferred. Photo captions preferred; include person, trick described.

MAKING CONTACT & TERMS Query with good samples, SASE. Keeps samples on file. Responds within 2 months. Pays $200–500/day; $500 for color cover; $50–75 for b&w inside; $75–300 for color inside; $150/color page rate; $50–75/b&w page rate. Pays on publication. Credit line given. Buys first North American serial rights.

TIPS "Clean, clear, tight images. Plenty of vibrant action, colorful travel scenics and personality. Must be able to shoot action photography. Looking for photographers in other geographic regions for diverse coverage."

THE WATER SKIER

1251 Holy Cow Rd., Polk City FL 33868. (863)324-4341. **Fax:** (863)325-8259. **E-mail:** satkinson@usawaterski.org. **Website:** www.usawaterski.org. **Contact:** Scott Atkinson, editor. Estab. 1951. Circ. 20,000. Magazine of USA Water Ski. Published 6 times/year. Emphasizes water skiing. Readers are male and female professionals, ages 20-65. Sample copy available for $3.50. Photo guidelines available.

NEEDS Buys 1-5 photos from freelancers/issue; 9-45 photos/year. Needs photos of sports action. Model/property release required. Photo captions required.

MAKING CONTACT & TERMS Call first. Pays $50-150 for color photos. Pays on publication. Credit line given. Buys all rights.

WATERWAY GUIDE

P.O. Box 1125, 16273 General Puller Hwy., Deltaville VA 23043. (804)776-8999. **Fax:** (804)776-6111. **E-mail:** joan@waterwayguide.com. **Website:** www. waterwayguide.com. **Contact:** Tom Hale, editor. Estab. 1947. Circ. 30,000. Cruising guide with 6 annual regional editions. Emphasizes recreational boating. Readers are men and women ages 25-65, management or professional, with average income $138,000. Sample copy available for $39.95 and $3 shipping. Photo guidelines free with SASE.

NEEDS Buys 10-15 photos from freelancers/issue. Needs aerial photos of waterways. Expects to use more coastal shots from Maine to the Bahamas; also Hudson River, Great Lakes, Lake Champlain and Gulf of Mexico. Model release required. Photo captions required.

SPECS Accepts images in digital format. Send as EPS, TIFF files at 300 dpi.

MAKING CONTACT & TERMS Send unsolicited photos by mail with SASE for consideration. Responds in 4 months. Pay varies; negotiable. Pays on publication. Credit line given. Must sign contract for copyright purposes.

⊕⊕ ⓓ WESTERN OUTDOORS

185 Avenida La Pata, San Clemente CA 92673. (949)366-0030. **E-mail:** rich@wonews.com. **Website:** www.wonews.com. **Contact:** Rich Holland, editor. Estab. 1961. Circ. 100,000. Published 9 times/year. Emphasizes fishing and boating "for Far West states." Sample copy free. Editorial and photo guidelines free with SASE.

NEEDS Uses 80-85 photos/issue; 70% supplied by freelancers; 80% comes from assignments, 25% from stock. Needs photos of fishing in California, Oregon, Washington, Baja. Most photos purchased with accompanying manuscript. Model/property release preferred for women and men in brief attire. Photo captions required.

SPECS Prefers images in digital format.

MAKING CONTACT & TERMS Query or send photos with SASE for consideration. Responds in 3 weeks. **Pays on acceptance.** Buys one-time rights for photos only; first North American serial rights for articles; electronic rights are negotiable.

TIPS "Submissions should be of interest to Western fishermen, and should include a 1,120- to 1,500-word manuscript; a Trip Facts Box (where to stay, costs, special information); photos; captions; and a map of the area. Emphasis is on fishing how-to, somewhere-to-go. Submit seasonal material 6 months in advance. Query only; no unsolicited manuscripts. Make your photos tell the story, and don't depend on captions to explain what is pictured. Get action shots, live fish. In fishing, we seek individual action or underwater shots. For cover photos, use vertical format composed with action entering picture from right; leave enough left-hand margin for cover blurbs, space at top of frame for magazine logo. Add human element to scenics to lend scale. Get to know the magazine and its editors. Ask for the year's editorial schedule (available through advertising department), and offer cover photos to match the theme of an issue. In samples, looks for color saturation, pleasing use of color components; originality, creativity; attractiveness of human subjects, as well as fish; above all—sharp, sharp, sharp focus!"

WEST SUBURBAN LIVING MAGAZINE

C2 Publishing, Inc., P.O. Box 111, Elmhurst IL 60126. (630)834-4995. **Fax:** (630)834-4996. **E-mail:** wsl@westsuburbanliving.net. **Website:** www.westsuburbanliving.net. Estab. 1995. Circ. 25,000. Bimonthly regional magazine serving the western suburbs of Chicago. Sample copies available.

NEEDS Photos of babies/children/teens, couples, families, senior citizens, landscapes/scenics, architecture, gardening, interiors/decorating, entertainment, events, food/drink, health/fitness/beauty, performing arts, travel. Interested in seasonal. Model release required. Photo captions required.

MAKING CONTACT & TERMS Responds only if interested; send nonreturnable samples. Simultaneous submissions and previously published work OK. Credit line given. Buys one-time rights, first rights, all rights; negotiable.

WHISKEY ISLAND MAGAZINE

English Dept., Cleveland State University, Cleveland OH 44115. (216)687-3951. **E-mail:** whiskeyisland@csuohio.edu. **Website:** whiskeyislandmagazine.com. "This is a nonprofit literary magazine that has been published (in one form or another) by students of Cleveland State University for over 30 years." Biannual literary magazine publishing extremely contemporary writing. Sample copy: $6. Photo guidelines available with SASE.

NEEDS Uses 10 photos/issue; 20 photos/year. Interested in mixed media, alternative process, avant garde, fine art. Surreal and abstract are welcome. Do not send sentimental images, "rust-belt" scenes, photos of Cleveland, straight landscapes, or anything that can be viewed as "romantic." Model/property release preferred. Photo captions required; include title of work, photographer's name, address, phone number, e-mail, etc.

SPECS Accepts images in digital format. Send via e-mail attachment as individual, high-res JPEG files. No TIFFs. No disks.

MAKING CONTACT & TERMS E-mail with sample images. Do not just send your website link. Does not keep samples on file; responds in 3 months. Pays 2 contributor's copies and a one-year subscription.

Credit line given. Include as much contact information as possible.

WINE & SPIRITS

2 W. 32nd St., Suite 601, New York NY 10001. (212)695-4660, ext. 15. **E-mail:** elenab@wineandspiritsmagazine.com; info@wineandspiritsmagazine.com. **Website:** www.wineandspiritsmagazine.com. **Contact:** Elena Bessarabova-Leone, art director. Estab. 1985. Circ. 70,000. Bimonthly. Emphasizes wine. Readers are male, ages 39-60, married, parents, $70,000-plus income, wine consumers. Sample copy available for $4.95; Special issues are $4.95-6.50 each.

NEEDS Buys 0-30 photos from freelancers/issue; 0-180 photos/year. Needs photos of food, wine, travel, people. Photo captions preferred; include date, location.

SPECS Accepts images in digital format. Send via SyQuest, ZIP at 300 dpi.

MAKING CONTACT & TERMS Submit portfolio for review. Provide résumé, business card, brochure, flyer or tearsheets to be kept on file for possible future assignments. Responds in 2 weeks, if interested. Simultaneous submissions OK. Pays on publication. Credit line given. Buys one-time rights.

WISCONSIN SNOWMOBILE NEWS

P.O. Box 182, Rio WI 53960-0182. (920)992-6370. **Website:** www.sledder.net. **Contact:** Cathy Hanson, editor. Estab. 1969. Circ. 28,000. Published 7 times/year. Official publication of the Association of Wisconsin Snowmobile Clubs. Emphasizes snowmobiling. Sample copy free with 9×12 SASE and 5 first-class stamps.

NEEDS Buys very few stand-alone photos from freelancers. "Most photos are purchased in conjunction with a story (photo/text) package. Photos need to be Midwest region only!" Needs photos of family-oriented snowmobile action, travel. Model/property release preferred. Photo captions preferred; include where, what, when.

SPECS Uses 8×10 glossy color and b&w prints; 35mm, 2¼×2¼, 4×5, 8×10 transparencies. Digital files accepted at 300 dpi.

MAKING CONTACT & TERMS Submit portfolio for review. Send unsolicited photos by mail for consideration; include SASE for return of material. Provide résumé, business card, brochure, flyer or tearsheets to be kept on file for possible future assignments. Responds in 2 weeks. Pays on publication. Credit line given. Buys one-time rights, all rights; negotiable.

💲💲 WOODMEN LIVING

Woodmen Tower, 1700 Farnam St., Omaha NE 68102. (402)342-1890. **Fax:** (402)271-7269. **E-mail:** service@ woodmen.com. **Website:** www.woodmen.org. **Contact:** Billie Jo Foust, editor. Estab. 1890. Circ. 480,000. Quarterly magazine published by Woodmen of the World/Omaha Woodmen Life Insurance Society. Emphasizes American family life. Sample copy and photo guidelines free.

NEEDS Buys 10-12 photos/year. Needs photos of the following themes: historic, family, insurance, humorous, photo essay/photo feature, human interest and health. Model release required. Photo captions preferred.

SPECS Uses 8×10 glossy b&w prints on occasion; 35mm, 2¼×2¼, 4×5 transparencies; for cover: 4×5 transparencies, vertical format preferred. Accepts images in digital format. Send high-res scans via CD.

MAKING CONTACT & TERMS Send material by mail with SASE for consideration. Responds in 1 month. Previously published work OK. **Pays on acceptance.** Credit line given on request. Buys one-time rights.

TIPS "Submit good, sharp pictures that will reproduce well."

💲💲 📷 ● YANKEE MAGAZINE

1121 Main St., P.O. Box 520, Dublin NH 03444. (603)563-8111. **E-mail:** heatherm@yankeepub.com. **Website:** www.yankeemagazine.com. **Contact:** Heather Marcus, photo editor; Lori Pedrick, art director. Estab. 1935. Circ. 350,000. Monthly. Emphasizes general interest within New England, with national distribution. Readers are of all ages and backgrounds; majority are actually outside of New England. Sample copy may be viewed on our website. "We give assignments to experienced professionals. If you want to work with us, show us a portfolio of your best work. Contact our photo editor before sending any photography to our art department. Please do not send any unsolicited original photography or artwork."

NEEDS Buys 10-30 photos from freelancers/issue; 60–180 photos/year. Needs photos of landscapes/scenics, wildlife, gardening, interiors/decorating. "Always looking for outstanding photo essays or portfolios shot in New England." Model/property release preferred. Photo captions required; include name, locale, pertinent details.

MAKING CONTACT & TERMS Submit portfolio for review. Keeps samples on file; include SASE for return of material. Responds in 1 month. Simultaneous submissions and previously published work OK. Credit line given. Buys one–time rights; negotiable.

💲 YOUTH RUNNER MAGAZINE

P.O. Box 1156, Lake Oswego OR 97035. (503)236-2524. **Fax:** (503)620-3800. **E-mail:** photos@youthrunner. com. **Website:** www.youthrunner.com. Estab. 1996. Circ. 100,000. Publishes 10 issues per year. Features track, cross country and road racing for young athletes, ages 8-18. Photo guidelines available on website.

NEEDS Uses 30–50 photos/issue. Also uses photos on website daily. Needs action shots from track, cross country and indoor meets. Model release preferred; property release required. Photo captions preferred.

SPECS Accepts images in digital format only. Ask for Dropbox link. Only InDesign.

MAKING CONTACT & TERMS Send low-res photos via e-mail first or link to gallery for consideration. Responds to e-mail submissions immediately. Simultaneous submissions OK. Pays $25 minimum. Credit line given. Buys electronic rights, all rights.

NEWSPAPERS

When working with newspapers, always remember that time is of the essence. Newspapers have various deadlines for each of their sections. An interesting feature or news photo has a better chance of getting in the next edition if the subject is timely and has local appeal. Most of the markets in this section are interested in regional coverage. Find publications near you and contact editors to get an understanding of their deadline schedules.

More and more newspapers are accepting submissions in digital format. In fact, most newspapers prefer digital images. However, if you submit to a newspaper that still uses film, ask the editors if they prefer certain types of film or if they want color slides or black-and-white prints. Many smaller newspapers do not have the capability to run color images, so black-and-white prints are preferred. However, color slides and prints can be converted to black and white. Editors who have the option of running color or black-and-white photos often prefer color film because of its versatility.

Although most newspapers rely on staff photographers, some hire freelancers as stringers for certain stories. Act professionally and build an editor's confidence in you by supplying innovative images. For example, don't get caught in the trap of shooting "grip-and-grin" photos when a corporation executive is handing over a check to a nonprofit organization. Turn the scene into an interesting portrait. Capture some spontaneous interaction between the recipient and the donor. By planning ahead you can be creative.

When you receive assignments, think about the image before you snap your first photo. If you are scheduled to meet someone at a specific location, arrive early and scout around. Find a proper setting or locate some props to use in the shoot. Do whatever you can to show the editor you are willing to make that extra effort.

Always try to retain resale rights to shots of major news events. High news value means high resale value, and strong news photos can be resold repeatedly. If you have an image with national appeal, search for larger markets, possibly through the wire services. You also may find buyers among national news magazines such as *Time* or *Newsweek*.

While most newspapers offer low payment for images, they are willing to negotiate if the image will have a major impact. Front-page artwork often sells newspapers, so don't underestimate the worth of your images.

⊕⊖ ✱ AMERICAN SPORTS NETWORK

Box 6100, Rosemead CA 91770. (626)280-0000. **Fax:** (626)280-0001. **E-mail:** info@asntv.com. **Website:** www.fitnessamerica.com. Circ. 873,007. Publishes 4 newspapers covering "general collegiate, amateur and professional sports, e.g., football, baseball, basketball, wrestling, boxing, powerlifting and bodybuilding, fitness, health contests." Also publishes special bodybuilder annual calendar, collegiate and professional football pre-season and post-season editions.

NEEDS Buys 10–80 photos from freelancers/issue for various publications. Needs "sport action, hardhitting contact, emotion-filled photos." Model release preferred. Photo captions preferred.

MAKING CONTACT & TERMS Send 8×10 glossy b&w prints, 4×5 transparencies, video demo reel, or film work by mail for consideration. Include SASE for return of material. Provide résumé, business card, brochure, flyer or tearsheets to be kept on file for possible future assignments. Simultaneous submissions and previously published work OK. Negotiates rates by the job and hour. Pays on publication. Buys first North American serial rights.

⊘ THE ANGLICAN JOURNAL

(416)924-9192. **Fax:** (416)921-4452. **E-mail:** editor@anglicanjournal.com; story queries: jthomas@national.anglican.ca; editor@anglicanjournal.com; photography queries: sfielder@national.anglican.ca. **Website:** www.anglicanjournal.com. **Contact:** Janet Thomas; Saskia Rowley Fielder. Estab. 1875. Circ. 141,000. Covers news of interest to Anglicans in Canada and abroad.

SPECS Reviews GIF/JPEG files (high res at 300 dpi).

MAKING CONTACT & TERMS Identification of subjects required. Negotiates payment individually. Buys all rights.

⊙ O AQUARIUS

200 Market St., Suite 210, Roswell GA 30075. (770)641-9055. **E-mail:** donmartin@aquarius-atlanta.com. **Website:** www.aquarius-atlanta.com. **Contact:** Don Martin. Estab. 1991. Circ. 50,000; readership online: 110,000. Monthly. "Emphasizes New Age, metaphysical, holistic health, alternative religion; environmental audience primarily middle-aged, college-educated, computer-literate, open to exploring new ideas. Our mission is to publish a newspaper for the purpose of expanding awareness and supporting all those seeking spiritual growth. We are committed to excellence and integrity in an atmosphere of harmony and love." Sample copy available with SASE.

NEEDS "We use photos of authors, musicians, and photos that relate to our articles, but we have no budget to pay photographers at this time. We offer byline in paper, website, and copies." Needs photos of New Age and holistic health, celebrities, multicultural, environmental, religious, adventure, entertainment, events, health/fitness, performing arts, travel, medicine, technology, alternative healing processes. Interested in coverage on environmental issues, genetically altered foods, photos of "anything from Sufi Dancers to Zen Masters." Model/property release required. Photo captions required; include photographer's name, subject's name, and description of content.

SPECS Uses color and b&w photos. Accepts images in digital format. Send via ZIP, e-mail as JPEG files at 300 dpi.

MAKING CONTACT & TERMS Send e-mail samples with cover letter. Provide résumé, business card or self-promotion piece to be kept on file for possible future assignments. Pays in copies, byline with contact info (phone number, e-mail address published if photographer agrees).

⊚ ⊕ O CATHOLIC SENTINEL

P.O. Box 18030, Portland OR 97218. (503)281-1191 or (800)548-8749. **E-mail:** sentinel@catholicsentinel.org; bobp@ocp.org. **Website:** www.catholicsentinel.org. **Contact:** Robert Pfohman, editor. Estab. 1870. Circ. 20,000. Twice monthly. "We are the newspaper for the Catholic community in Oregon." Sample copies available with SASE. Photo guidelines available via e-mail.

NEEDS Buys 15 photos from freelancers/issue; 800 photos/year. Needs photos of religious and political subjects. Interested in seasonal. Model/property release preferred. Photo captions required; include names of people shown in photos, spelled correctly.

SPECS Prefers images in digital format. Send via e-mail or FTP as TIFF or JPEG files at 300 dpi.

MAKING CONTACT & TERMS Send query letter with résumé and tearsheets. Portfolio may be dropped off every Thursday. Keeps samples on file. Responds only if interested; send nonreturnable samples. Simultaneous submissions and previously published work OK. Pays on publication or on receipt of photographer's invoice. Credit line given. Buys first rights and electronic rights.

TIPS "We use photos to illustrate editorial material, so all photography is on assignment. Basic knowledge of Catholic Church (e.g., don't climb on the altar) is a big plus. Send accurately spelled cutlines. Prefer images in digital format."

$ CHILDREN'S DEFENSE FUND

25 E St. NW, Washington DC 20001. (800)233-1200. **E-mail:** cdfinfo@childrensdefense.org. **Website:** www.childrensdefense.org. Children's advocacy organization.

NEEDS Buys 20 photos/year. Buys stock and assigns work. Wants to see photos of children of all ages and ethnicity—serious, playful, poor, middle class, school setting, home setting and health setting. Subjects include babies/children/teens, families, education, health/fitness/beauty. Some location work. Domestic photos only. Model/property release required.

SPECS Uses b&w and some color prints. Accepts images in digital format. Send via e-mail as TIFF, EPS, JPEG files at 300 dpi or better.

MAKING CONTACT & TERMS Provide résumé, business card, self-promotion piece or tearsheets to be kept on file for possible future assignments. Keeps photocopy samples on file. Previously published work OK. Pays on usage. Credit line given. Buys one-time rights; occasionally buys all rights.

TIPS Looks for "good, clear focus, nice composition, variety of settings and good expressions on faces."

🌐 $ THE CHURCH OF ENGLAND NEWSPAPER

14 Great College St., London SW1P 3RX, United Kingdom. 44 20 7222 8700. **E-mail:** cen@churchnewspaper.com; colin.blakely@churchnewspaper.com. **Website:** www.churchnewspaper.com. **Contact:** Colin Blakely, editor; Peter May, graphic designer. Estab. 1828. Circ. 12,000. Weekly religious newspaper. Sample copies available.

NEEDS Buys 2-3 photos from freelancers/issue; 100 photos/year. Needs political photos. Reviews photos with or without a manuscript. Photo captions required.

SPECS Uses glossy color prints; 35mm transparencies.

MAKING CONTACT & TERMS Does not keep samples on file; include SASE for return of material. Responds only if interested; send nonreturnable samples. Pays on publication. Credit line given. Buys one-right rights.

$ THE CLARION-LEDGER

P.O. Box 40, Jackson MS 39205. (601)961-7000; (601)961-7175; (877)850-5343. **E-mail:** btolley@jackson.gannett.com. **Website:** www.clarionledger.com. **Contact:** Brian Tolley, executive editor. Circ. 95,000. Daily. Emphasizes photojournalism: news, sports, features, fashion, food and portraits. Readers are in a very broad age range of 18-70 years, male and female. Sample copies available.

NEEDS Buys 1-5 photos from freelancers/issue; 365-1,825 photos/year. Needs news, sports, features, portraits, fashion and food photos. Special photo needs include food and fashion. Model release required. Photo captions required.

SPECS Uses 8×10 matte b&w and color prints; 35mm slides/color negatives. Accepts images in digital format. Send via CD, e-mail as JPEG files at 200 dpi.

MAKING CONTACT & TERMS Provide résumé, business card, brochure, flyer or tearsheets to be kept on file for possible future assignments. Pays on publication. Credit line given. Buys one-time or all rights; negotiable.

$ 📷 ○ FULTON COUNTY DAILY REPORT

190 Pryor St. SW, Atlanta GA 30303. (404)521-1227. **Fax:** (404)659-4739. **E-mail:** jbennitt@alm.com. **Website:** www.dailyreportonline.com. **Contact:** Jason R. Bennitt, art director. Daily (5 times/week). Emphasizes legal news and business. Readers are male and female professionals, age 25+, involved in legal field, court system, legislature, etc. Sample copy available for $2 with 9¾×12¾ SASE and 6 first-class stamps.

NEEDS Buys approx. 50 photos from freelancers or wire per year. Needs informal environmental photographs of lawyers, judges and others involved in legal news and business. Some real estate, etc. Photo captions necessary; include complete name of subject and date shot, along with other pertinent information. Two or more people should be identified from left to right.

SPECS Accepts images in digital format. Send via CD or e-mail as JPEG files at 200–600 dpi.

MAKING CONTACT & TERMS Submit portfolio for review. Mail or e-mail samples. Keeps samples on file. Simultaneous submissions and previously published work OK. "Freelance work generally done on an assignment-only basis." Pays $75–125 for color cover; $50–75 for color inside. Credit line given.

TIPS Wants to see ability with "casual, environmental portraiture, people—especially in office settings, urban environment, courtrooms, etc.—and photojournalistic coverage of people in law or courtroom settings." In general, needs "competent, fast freelancers from time to time around the state of Georgia who can be called in at the last minute. We keep a list of them for reference. Good work keeps you on the list." Recommends that "when shooting for *FCDR*, it's best to avoid law-book-type photos if possible, along with other overused legal clichés."

◎ $ ◐ GRAND RAPIDS BUSINESS JOURNAL

549 Ottawa Ave. NW, Suite 201, Grand Rapids MI 49503-1444. (616)459-4545. **Fax:** (616)459-4800. **E-mail:** knugent@grbj.com; editorial@grbj.com. **Website:** www.grbj.com. Estab. 1983. Circ. 6,000. Weekly tabloid. Emphasizes West Michigan business community. Sample copy available for $1.

NEEDS Buys 5–10 photos from freelancers/issue; 520 photos/year. Needs photos of local community, manufacturing, world trade, stock market, etc. Model/property release required. Photo captions required.

MAKING CONTACT & TERMS Send query letter with résumé of credits, stock list. Responds in 1 month. Simultaneous submissions and previously published work OK. Pays on publication. Credit line given. Buys one-time rights and first North American serial rights; negotiable.

🍁 $ ◐ THE LAWYERS WEEKLY

123 Commerce Valley Dr. E., Suite 700, Markham Ontario L3T 7W8, Canada. (905)479-2665; (800)668-6481. **Fax:** (905)479-3758. **E-mail:** robert.kelly@lexisnexis.ca. **Website:** www.thelawyersweekly.ca. **Contact:** Rob Kelly, editor-in-chief. Estab. 1983. Circ. 20,300.

NEEDS Uses 12-20 photos/issue; 1 supplied by freelancers. Needs head shots of lawyers and judges mentioned in stories, as well as photos of legal events.

SPECS Accepts images in digital format. Send as JPEG, TIFF files.

MAKING CONTACT & TERMS Deadlines: 1- to 2-day turnaround time. Does not keep samples on file; include SASE for return of material. Responds only when interested. **Pays on acceptance.**

TIPS "We need photographers across Canada to shoot lawyers and judges on an as-needed basis. Send a résumé, and we will keep your name on file."

$ ◎ ◐ THE LOG NEWSPAPER

17782 Cowan, Suite C, Irvine CA 92614. (949)660-6150. **Fax:** (949)660-6172. **E-mail:** eston@thelog.com. **Website:** www.thelog.com. **Contact:** Eston Ellis, editor. Estab. 1971. Circ. 41,018.

NEEDS Buys 5-10 photos from freelancers/issue; 130-260 photos/year. Needs photos of marine-related, recreational sailing/powerboating in Southern California. Photo captions required; include location, name and type of boat, owner's name, race description if applicable.

SPECS Accepts images in digital format. Send via e-mail as TIFF, EPS, JPEG files at 300 dpi or greater.

MAKING CONTACT & TERMS Simultaneous submissions and previously published work OK. Pays on publication. Credit line given. Buys all rights; negotiable.

TIPS "We want timely and newsworthy photographs! We always need photographs of people enjoying boating, especially power boating. 95% of our images are of California subjects."

$ NATIONAL MASTERS NEWS

P.O. Box 1117, Orangevale CA 95662. (916)989-6667. **E-mail:** nminfo@nationalmastersnews.com. **Website:** www.nationalmastersnews.com. **Contact:** Randy Sturgeon. Estab. 1977. Circ. 8,000. Monthly tabloid. Official world and US publication for Masters (ages 30 and over) track and field, long distance running, and race walking.

NEEDS Uses 25 photos/issue; 30% assigned and 70% from freelance stock. Needs photos of Masters athletes (men and women over age 30) competing in track and field events, long distance running races or racewalking competitions. Photo captions required.

MAKING CONTACT & TERMS Send photos digitally by e-mail for consideration. Responds in 1 month. Simultaneous submissions and previously published work OK. Pays on publication. Credit line given. Buys one-time rights.

THE NEW YORK TIMES ON THE WEB

620 Eighth Ave., New York NY 10018. **E-mail:** generalmgr@nytimes.com; nytnews@nytimes.com; executive-editor@nytimes.com. **Website:** www.nytimes.com. Circ. 1.3 million. Daily newspaper. "Covers breaking news and general interest." Sample copy available with SASE or online.

NEEDS Photos of celebrities, architecture, cities/urban, gardening, interiors/decorating, industry, medicine, military, political, product shots/still life, science, technology/computers, disasters, environmental, landscapes/scenics, wildlife, automobiles, entertainment, events, food/drink, health/fitness/beauty, hobbies, performing arts, sports, travel, alternative process, avant garde, documentary, fashion/glamour, fine art, breaking news. Model release required. Photo captions required.

SPECS Accepts images in digital format. Send via CD, e-mail as TIFF, JPEG files.

MAKING CONTACT & TERMS E-mail query letter with link to photographer's website. Provide business card, self-promotion piece to be kept on file for possible future assignments. Simultaneous submissions OK. Pays on publication. Credit line given. Buys one-time rights and electronic rights.

💲 ⊚ ❶ STREETPEOPLES WEEKLY NEWS

P.O. Box 270942, Dallas TX 75227-0942. **E-mail:** sw_n@yahoo.com. **Contact:** Lon G. Dorsey, Jr., publisher. Estab. 1977. Sample copy no longer available temporarily. "Seeking help to launch homeless television show and photo gallery."

◯ Photographers needed in every metropolitan city in the US.

NEEDS Photos of babies/children/teens, celebrities, couples, multicultural, families, parents, senior citizens, cities/urban, education, pets, religious, rural, events, food/drink, health/fitness, hobbies, humor, political, technology/computers. Interested in alternative process, documentary, fine art, historical/vintage, seasonal. Subjects include: photojournalism on homeless or street people. Model/property release required. "All photos *must* be accompanied by *signed* model releases." Photo captions required.

SPECS Accepts images in digital format. Send via CD, e-mail as GIF, JPEG files. "Items to be considered for publishing must be in PDF from a *SWNews*-certified photographer. Write first to gain certification with publisher."

MAKING CONTACT & TERMS "Hundreds of photographers are needed to show national state of America's homeless." Do not send unsolicited materials. Responds promptly. Pay scale information provided to *SWNews*-certified photographers. Pays extra for electronic usage (negotiable). Pays on acceptance or publication. Credit line sometimes given. Buys all rights; negotiable.

🌐 💲 ❶ THE SUNDAY POST

80 Kingsway East, Dundee DD4 8SL, Scotland. (44) (1382)223131. **E-mail:** mail@sundaypost.com. **Website:** www.sundaypost.com. Estab. 1919. Circ. 328,129. Readership 901,000. Weekly family newspaper.

NEEDS Photos of "UK news and news involving Scots," sports. Other specific needs: exclusive news pictures from the UK, especially Scotland. Reviews photos with accompanying manuscript only. Model/property release preferred. Photo captions required; include contact details, subjects, date. "Save in the caption field of the file info metadata, so they can be viewed on our picture desk system. Mac users should ensure attachments are PC-compatible as we use PCs."

SPECS Prefers images in digital format. Send via e-mail as JPEG files. "We need a minimum 11MB file saved at quality level 9/70% or above, ideally at 200 ppi/dpi."

MAKING CONTACT & TERMS Send query letter with tearsheets, stock list. Does not keep samples on file; include SASE for return of material. Responds in 2 weeks to queries. Simultaneous submissions OK. Pays $150 (USD) for b&w or color cover; $100 (USD) for b&w or color inside. Pays on publication. Credit line not given. Buys single use, all editions, one date, worldwide rights; negotiable.

TIPS "Offer pictures by e-mail before sending: low-res only, please—72 ppi, 800 pixels on the widest side; no more than 10 at a time. Make sure the daily papers aren't running the story first and that it's not being covered by the Press Association (PA). We get their pictures on our contracted feed."

SYRACUSE NEW TIMES

Alltimes Publishing, LLC, 1415 W. Genesee St., Syracuse NY 13204. **E-mail:** ldietrich@syracusenewtimes.com; editorial@syracusenewtimes.com. **Website:** www.syracusenewtimes.com. **Contact:** Larry Dietrich. Estab. 1969. Circ. 40,000. *"Syracuse New Times* is an alternative weekly that is topical, provocative, irreverent, and intensely local." 50% freelance written. Publishes ms an average of 1 month after acceptance. Submit seasonal material 3 months in advance. Sample copy available with 8×10 SASE.

NEEDS Photos of performing arts. Interested in alternative process, fine art, seasonal. Reviews photos with or without a manuscript. Model/property release required. Photo captions required; include names of subjects.

SPECS Uses 5×7 b&w prints; 35mm transparencies.
MAKING CONTACT & TERMS Send query letter with résumé, stock list. Does not keep samples on file; include SASE for return of material. Responds in 6 weeks. Responds only if interested; send nonreturnable samples. Previously published work OK. Pays on publication. Credit line given. Buys one-time rights.
TIPS "Realize the editor is busy and responds as promptly as possible."

TORONTO SUN PUBLISHING

333 King St. E., Toronto Ontario M5A 3X5, Canada. (416)947-2399. **Fax:** (416)947-1664. **E-mail:** kevin. hann@sunmedia.ca; torsun.photoeditor@sunmedia. ca. **Website:** www.torontosun.com. **Contact:** Kevin Hann, deputy editor. Estab. 1971. Circ. 180,000. Daily. Emphasizes sports, news and entertainment. Sample copy free with SASE.
NEEDS Uses 30–50 photos/issue; occasionally uses freelancers (spot news pics only). Needs photos of Toronto personalities making news out of town. Also disasters, beauty, sports, fashion/glamour. Reviews photos with or without a manuscript. Photo captions preferred.
SPECS Accepts images in digital format. Send via CD or e-mail.
MAKING CONTACT & TERMS Arrange a personal interview to show portfolio. Send any size color prints; 35mm transparencies; press link digital format. Deadline: 11 p.m. daily. Does not keep samples on file. Responds in 1–2 weeks. Simultaneous submissions and previously published work OK. Pays on publication. Credit line given. Buys one-time and other negotiated rights.
TIPS "The squeaky wheel gets the grease when it delivers the goods. Don't try to oversell a questionable photo. Return calls promptly."

VENTURA COUNTY REPORTER

700 E. Main St., Ventura CA 93001. (805)648-2244. **E-mail:** editor@vcreporter.com. **Website:** www.vcreporter.com. Art director (artdirector@vcreporter.com). **Contact:** Michael Sullivan, editor. Circ. 35,000. Weekly tabloid covering local news (entertainment and environment).
NEEDS Uses 12-14 photos/issue; 40-45% supplied by freelancers. "We require locally slanted photos (Ventura County CA)." Model release required.
SPECS Accepts images in digital format. Send via e-mail or CD.

MAKING CONTACT & TERMS Send sample b&w or color original photos; include SASE for return of material. Simultaneous submissions OK. Pays on publication. Credit line given. Buys one-time rights.

WATERTOWN PUBLIC OPINION

120 Third Ave. NW, P.O. Box 10, Watertown SD 57201. (605)886-6901. **Fax:** (605)886-4280. **E-mail:** maryt@ thepublicopinion.com; rogerwhittle@thepublicopinion.com. **Website:** www.thepublicopinion.com. **Contact:** Mary Tuff, editorial assistant; Roger Whittle, managing editor. Estab. 1887. Circ. 15,000. Daily. Emphasizes general news of the region; state, national and international news.
NEEDS Uses up to 8 photos/issue. Reviews photos with or without a manuscript. Model release required. Photo captions required.
SPECS Uses b&w or color prints. Accepts images in digital format. Send via CD.
MAKING CONTACT & TERMS Send unsolicited photos by mail for consideration. Does not keep samples on file; include SASE for return of material. Responds in 1-2 weeks. Simultaneous submissions OK. Pays on publication. Credit line given. Buys one-time rights; negotiable.

THE WESTERN PRODUCER

P.O. Box 2500, 2310 Millar Ave., Saskatoon SK S7K 2C4, Canada. (306)665-3544. **Fax:** (306)934-2401. **E-mail:** newsroom@producer.com. **Website:** www.producer.com. Estab. 1923. Circ. 48,000. Weekly. Emphasizes agriculture and rural living in western Canada.
NEEDS Photos of various farm situations with people engaged in some activity—repairing equipment, feeding livestock, enjoying leisure time on the farm, etc., or of animals in natural behavior; are more appealing than horizons, antiques or derelict buildings.
SPECS Photos must be current (taken within the last month). Submissions should include as much cutline information as possible—who, what, where, when and why. Include the date when the picture was taken. Accepts digital images, at 200 dpi and at least 2MB. Save images in JPEG format. Send digital images to newsroom@producer.com. Photo guidelines mailed or e-mailed.
MAKING CONTACT & TERMS Address submissions sent by mail to the attention of the news editor; include SASE for return of material. Pays on publication. Credit line given. Buys one–time rights.

TRADE PUBLICATIONS

Most trade publications are directed toward the business community in an effort to keep readers abreast of the ever-changing trends and events in their specific professions. For photographers, shooting for these publications can be financially rewarding and can serve as a stepping stone toward acquiring future assignments.

As often happens with this category, the number of trade publications produced increases or decreases as professions develop or deteriorate. In recent years, for example, magazines involving new technology have flourished as the technology continues to grow and change.

Trade publication readers are usually very knowledgeable about their businesses or professions. The editors and photo editors, too, are often experts in their particular fields. So, with both the readers and the publications' staffs, you are dealing with a much more discriminating audience. To be taken seriously, your photos must not be merely technically good pictures, but also should communicate a solid understanding of the subject and reveal greater insights.

In particular, photographers who can communicate their knowledge in both verbal and visual form will often find their work more in demand. If you have such expertise, you may wish to query about submitting a photo/text package that highlights a unique aspect of working in a particular profession or that deals with a current issue of interest to that field.

Many photos purchased by these publications come from stock—both freelance inventories and stock photo agencies. Generally, these publications are more conservative with their freelance budgets and use stock as an economical alternative. For this reason, some listings in this section will advise sending a stock list as an initial method of contact. (See sample stock list in "Running Your Business.") Some of the more established publications with larger circulations and advertising bases will sometimes offer assignments as they become familiar with a particular photographer's work. For the most part, though, stock remains the primary means of breaking in and doing business with this market.

⑤ ❶ ❶ AAP NEWS

141 Northwest Point Blvd., Elk Grove Village IL 60007. (847)434-4755. **Fax:** (847)434-8000. **E-mail:** mhayes@aap.org. **Website:** www.aapnews.org. **Contact:** Michael Hayes, art director/production coordinator. Estab. 1985. Monthly tabloid newspaper. Publication of American Academy of Pediatrics.

NEEDS Uses 60 photos/year. Needs photos of babies/children/teens, families, health/fitness, sports, travel, medicine, pediatricians, health care providers—news magazine style. Interested in documentary. Model/property release required as needed. Photo captions required; include names, dates, locations and explanations of situations.

SPECS Accepts images in digital format. Send via CD or e-mail as TIFF, EPS or JPEG files at 300 dpi.

MAKING CONTACT & TERMS Provide résumé, business card or tearsheets to be kept on file (for 1 year) for possible future assignments. Cannot return material. Simultaneous submissions and previously published work OK. Pays $50–150 for one-time use of photo. Pays on publication. Buys one-time or all rights; negotiable.

TIPS "We want great photos of real children in real-life situations—the more diverse the better."

ACRES U.S.A.

P.O. Box 301209, Austin TX 78703. (512)892-4400. **Fax:** (512)892-4448. **E-mail:** editor@acresusa.com. **Website:** www.acresusa.com. Estab. 1970. Circ. 20,000. "Monthly trade journal written by people who have a sincere interest in the principles of organic and sustainable agriculture."

SPECS Reviews GIF/JPEG/TIFF files.

MAKING CONTACT & TERMS Captions, identification of subjects required. Negotiates payment individually. Buys one-time rights.

AG WEEKLY

Lee Agri-Media, P.O. Box 918, Bismarck ND 58501. (701)255-4905. **Fax:** (701)255-2312. **E-mail:** mark.conlon@lee.net. **Website:** www.agweekly.com. **Contact:** Mark Conlon, editor. *Ag Weekly* is an agricultural publication covering production, markets, regulation, politics.

SPECS Reviews GIF/JPEG files.

MAKING CONTACT & TERMS Captions required. Offers $10/photo. Buys one-time rights.

● AMERICAN BAR ASSOCIATION JOURNAL

321 N. Clark St., 20th Floor, Chicago IL 60654. (312)988-5822. **E-mail:** debora.clark@americanbar.org. **Website:** www.abajournal.com. **Contact:** Debora Clark, deputy design director. Estab. 1915. Circ. 330,000. Monthly membership magazine of the American Bar Association. Emphasizes law and the legal profession. Readers are lawyers.

NEEDS Buys 50 photos and illustrations/graphics from freelancers/issue; 1,00 photos/illustrations and graphics per year. Needs vary; mainly shots of lawyers and clients by assignment only.

SPECS Prefers digital images sent as TIFF files at 300 dpi.

MAKING CONTACT & TERMS "Send us your website address to view samples." Cannot return unsolicited material. Payment negotiable. Credit line given. Buys first-time world-wide rights.

⑤ AMERICAN BEE JOURNAL

51 S. Second St., Hamilton IL 62341. (217)847-3324. **Fax:** (217)847-3660. **E-mail:** editor@americanbeejournal.com. **Website:** www.americanbeejournal.com. **Contact:** Joe B. Graham, editor. Estab. 1861. Circ. 13,500. Monthly. Emphasizes beekeeping for hobby and professional beekeepers. Sample copy free with SASE.

NEEDS Buys 1–2 photos from freelancers/issue; 12–24 photos/year. Needs photos of beekeeping and related topics, beehive products, honey and cooking with honey. Special needs include color photos of seasonal beekeeping scenes. Model release preferred. Photo captions preferred.

MAKING CONTACT & TERMS Send query e-mail with samples. Send thumbnail samples to e-mail. Send 5×7 or 8½×11 color prints by mail for consideration; include SASE for return of material. Responds in 2 weeks. Pays on publication. Credit line given. Buys all rights. Submission guidelines available online.

⑤ ◎ ❶ AMERICAN POWER BOAT ASSOCIATION

17640 E. Nine Mile Rd., P.O. Box 377, Eastpointe MI 48021-0377. (586)773-9700. **Fax:** (586)773-6490. **E-mail:** apbahq@apba.org. **Website:** www.apba.org. Estab. 1903. Sanctioning body for US power boat racing; monthly online magazine printed quarterly. Majority of assignments made on annual basis. Photos used in monthly magazine, brochures, audiovisual presentations, press releases, programs and website.

NEEDS Photos of APBA boat racing—action and candid. Interested in documentary, historical/vintage. Photo captions or class/driver ID required.

SPECS Accepts images in digital format. Send via CD, e-mail as TIFF, EPS, JPEG files at 300 dpi.

MAKING CONTACT & TERMS Initial personal contact preferred. Suggests initial contact by e-mail; JPEG samples or link to website welcome. Responds in 2 weeks when needed. Payment varies. Standard is $25 for color cover; $15 for interior pages. Credit line given. Buys one-time rights; negotiable. Photo usage must be invoiced by photographer within the month incurred.

TIPS Prefers to see selection of shots of power boats in action or pit shots, candids, etc., (all identified). Must show ability to produce clear color action shots of racing events. "Send a few samples with e-mail, especially if related to boat racing."

ANGUS BEEF BULLETIN

Angus Productions, Inc., 3201 Frederick Ave., St. Joseph MO 64506-2997. (816)383-5270. **E-mail:** journal@angusjournal.com; shermel@angusjournal.com. **Website:** www.angusbeefbulletin.com. **Contact:** Shauna Rose Hermel, editor. Estab. 1985. Circ. 65,000-70,000. Mailed free to commercial cattlemen who have purchased an Angus bull and had the registration transferred to them, and to others who sign a request card.

ANGUS JOURNAL

Angus Productions, Inc., 3201 Frederick Ave., St. Joseph MO 64506-2997. (816)383-5270. **E-mail:** shermel@angusjournal.com. **Website:** www.angusjournal.com. Estab. 1919. Circ. 13,500. *Angus Journal* is the official magazine of the American Angus Association. Its primary function as such is to report to the membership association activities and information pertinent to raising Angus cattle.

SPECS Reviews 5×7 glossy prints.

MAKING CONTACT & TERMS Identification of subjects required. Offers $25-400/photo. Buys all rights.

🚫 🔴 ANIMAL SHELTERING

P.O. Box 15276, North Hollywood CA 91615. (800)565-9226. **E-mail:** asm@humanesociety.org. **Website:** www.animalsheltering.org. **Contact:** Shevaun Brannigan, production/marketing manager;

Carrie Allan, editor. Estab. 1978. Circ. 6,000. Published 6 times a year. Magazine of the Humane Society of the United States. Magazine for animal care professionals and volunteers, dealing with animal welfare issues faced by animal shelters, animal control agencies, and rescue groups. Emphasis on news for the field and professional, hands-on work. Readers are shelter and animal control directors, kennel staff, field officers, humane investigators, animal control officers, animal rescuers, foster care volunteers, general volunteers, shelter veterinarians, and anyone concerned with local animal welfare issues. Sample copy free.

NEEDS Buys about 2–10 photos from freelancers/issue; 30 photos/year. Needs photos of pets interacting with animal control and shelter workers; animals in shelters, including farm animals and wildlife; general public visiting shelters and adopting animals; humane society work, functions, and equipment. Photo captions preferred.

SPECS Accepts color images in digital or print format. Send via CD, ZIP, e-mail as TIFF, JPEG files at 300 dpi.

MAKING CONTACT & TERMS Provide samples of work to be kept on file for possible future use or assignments; include SASE for return of material. Responds in 1 month. Pays $150 for cover; $75 for inside. Pays on publication. Credit line given. Buys one-time and electronic rights.

TIPS "We almost always need good photos of people working with animals in an animal shelter or in the field. We do not use photos of individual dogs, cats and other companion animals as often as we use photos of people working to protect, rescue or care for dogs, cats, and other companion animals. Contact us for upcoming needs."

💲💲 🔴 AOPA PILOT

421 Aviation Way, Frederick MD 21701. (301)695-2371. **Fax:** (301)695-2375. **E-mail:** pilot@aopa.org; mike.kline@aopa.org. **Website:** www.aopa.org. **Contact:** Michael Kline, design director. Estab. 1958. Circ. 400,000. Monthly association magazine. "The world's largest aviation magazine. The audience is primarily pilot and aircraft owners of General Aviation airplanes." Sample copies and photo guidelines available online.

NEEDS Buys 5–25 photos from freelancers/issue; 60–300 photos/year. Photos of couples, adventure, travel, industry, technology. Interested in documentary. Reviews photos with or without a manuscript. Model/property release preferred. Photo captions preferred.

SPECS Uses images in digital format. Send via CD, DVD as TIFF, EPS, JPEG files at 300 dpi. *AOPA Pilot* prefers original 35mm color transparencies (or larger), although high-quality color enlargements sometimes can be used if they are clear, sharp, and properly exposed. (If prints are accepted, the original negatives should be made available.) Avoid the distortion inherent in wide-angle lenses. Most of the photographs used are made with lenses in the 85mm to 135mm focal length range. Frame the picture to the focal length rather than the other way around, and avoid the use of zoom lenses unless they are of professional optical quality. Slides should be sharp and properly exposed; slower-speed films (ISO 25 to ISO 100) generally provide the best results. We are not responsible for unsolicited original photographs; send duplicate slides and keep the original until we request it.

MAKING CONTACT & TERMS Send query letter. Provide self-promotion piece to be kept on file for possible future assignments. Responds only if interested; send nonreturnable samples. Pays $800–2,000 for color cover; $200–720 for color inside. **Pays on acceptance.** Credit line given. Buys one-time, all rights; negotiable.

TIPS "A knowledge of our subject matter, airplanes, is a plus. Show range of work and not just one image."

APA MONITOR

750 First St. NE, Washington DC 20002-4242. (202)336-5500; (800)374-2721. **Website:** www.apa.org/monitor. Circ. 150,000. Monthly. Emphasizes "news and features of interest to psychologists and other behavioral scientists and professionals, including legislation and agency action affecting science and health, and major issues facing psychology both as a science and a mental health profession." Sample copy available for $3 and 9×12 SASE envelope.

NEEDS Buys 60-90 photos/year. Photos purchased on assignment. Needs portraits, feature illustrations and spot news.

SPECS Prefers images in digital format; send TIFF files at 300 dpi via e-mail. Uses 5×7 and 8×10 glossy prints.

MAKING CONTACT & TERMS Arrange a personal interview to show portfolio or query with samples. Pays by the job. Pays on receipt of invoice. Credit line given. Buys first serial rights.

TIPS "Become good at developing ideas for illustrating abstract concepts and innovative approaches to clichés such as meetings and speeches. We look for quality in technical reproduction and innovative approaches to subjects."

$ $ AQUA MAGAZINE

22 E. Mifflin St., Suite 910, Madison WI 53703. (608)249-0186. **E-mail:** scott@aquamagazine.com. **Website:** www.aquamagazine.com. **Contact:** Scott Webb, executive editor; Eric Herman, senior editor; Cailley Hammel, associate editor; Scott Maurer, art director. Estab. 1976. Circ. 15,000. AB Media (formerly Athletic Business Publications). Business publication for spa and pool professionals. Monthly magazine. "*AQUA* serves spa dealers, swimming pool dealers and/or builders, spa/swimming pool maintenance and service, casual furniture/patio dealers, landscape architects/designers and others allied to the spa/swimming pool market. Readers are qualified owners, GM, sales directors, titled personnel."

NEEDS Photos of residential swimming pools and/or spas (hot tubs) that show all or part of pool/spa. "The images may include grills, furniture, gazebos, ponds, water features." Photo captions including architect/builder/designer preferred.

MAKING CONTACT & TERMS "OK to send promotional literature, and to e-mail contact sheets/web gallery or low-res samples, but do not send anything that has to be returned (e.g., slides, prints) unless asked for." Simultaneous submissions and previously published work OK, "but should be explained." Pays $400 for color cover (negotiable); $200 for color inside. Pays on publication. Credit line given. Buys all rights; negotiable.

TIPS Wants to see "visually arresting images, high-quality, multiple angles, day/night lighting situations. Photos including people are rarely published."

$ $ ARCHITECTURAL LIGHTING

One Thomas Circle NW, Suite 600, Washington DC 20005. (202)452-0800. **Fax:** (202)785-1974. **E-mail:** edonoff@hanleywood.com; rogle@hanleywood.com. **Website:** www.archlighting.com. **Contact:** Elizabeth Donoff, editor-in-chief; Robb Ogle, art director. Estab. 1981. Circ. 25,000. Published 7 times/year. Emphasizes architecture and architectural lighting. Readers are architects and lighting designers. Sample copy free.

NEEDS Buys 3-5 photos/feature story. Needs photos of architecture and architectural lighting.

SPECS Prefers images in digital format. Send via e-mail as TIFF files at 300 dpi, minimum 4×6 inches.

MAKING CONTACT & TERMS Query *first* by e-mail to obtain permission to e-mail digital samples. Keeps samples on file. Cannot return material. Responds in 1-2 weeks. Simultaneous submissions OK. Pays $300-400 for color cover; $50-125 for color inside. Pays net 40 days point of invoice submission. Credit line given. Buys all rights for all media, including electronic media.

TIPS "Looking for a strong combination of architecture and architectural lighting."

🟢 🔵 ⭕ ASIAN ENTERPRISE MAGAZINE

Asian Business Ventures, Inc., P.O. Box 1126, Walnut CA 91788. (909)896-2865; (909)319-2306. **E-mail:** wilyb@asianenterprise.com; alma.asianent@gmail.com; almag@asianenterprise.com. **Website:** www.asianenterprise.com. Estab. 1993. Circ. 100,000. Monthly trade magazine. "Largest Asian American small business focus magazine in US." Sample copy available with SASE and first-class postage. Editorial calendar available online.

NEEDS Buys 3-5 photos from freelancers/issue; 36-60 photos/year. Needs photos of multicultural, business concepts, senior citizens, environmental, architecture, cities/urban, education, travel, military, political, technology/computers. Reviews photos with or without a manuscript. Model/property release required.

SPECS Uses 4×6 matte b&w prints. Accepts images in digital format. Send via ZIP as TIFF, JPEG files at 300-700 dpi.

MAKING CONTACT & TERMS Send query letter with prints. Provide self-promotion piece to be kept on file for possible future assignments. Responds only if interested; send nonreturnable samples. Simultaneous submissions OK. Pays $50-200 for color cover; $25-100 for b&w inside. Pays on publication. Credit line given. Buys one-time rights.

♻ THE ATA MAGAZINE

11010 142nd St. NW, Edmonton Alberta T5N 2R1, Canada. (780)447-9400. **Fax:** (780)455-6481. **E-mail:** government@teachers.ab.ca. **Website:** www.teachers.ab.ca. Estab. 1920. Circ. 42,100. Quarterly magazine covering education.

SPECS Reviews 4×6 prints.

MAKING CONTACT & TERMS Captions required. Negotiates payment individually. Negotiates rights.

💲💲 ATHLETIC BUSINESS

Athletic Business Media, Inc., 22 E. Mifflin St., Suite 910, Madison WI 53703. (800)722-8764, ext. 119. **Fax:** (608)249-1153. **E-mail:** editors@athleticbusiness.com. **Website:** www.athleticbusiness.com. **Contact:** Sadye Ring, graphic designer. Estab. 1977. Circ. 42,000. The leading resource for athletic, fitness and recreation professionals. Monthly magazine. Emphasizes athletics, fitness and recreation. Readers are athletic, park and recreational directors and club managers, ages 30-65. Sample copy available for $8. The magazine can also be viewed digitally at www.athleticbusiness.com. Become a fan on Facebook or LinkedIn.

NEEDS Buys 2-3 photos from freelancers per issue; 24-26 photos/year. Needs photos of college and high school team sports, coaches, athletic equipment, recreational parks, and health club/multi-sport interiors." Model/property release preferred. Photo captions preferred.

MAKING CONTACT & TERMS Use online e-mail to contact. "Feel free to send promotional literature, but do not send anything that has to be returned (e.g., slides, prints) unless asked for." Simultaneous submissions and previously published work OK, "but should be explained." Pays $300 for color cover (negotiable); $100 for color inside. Pays on publication. Credit line given. Buys all rights; negotiable.

TIPS Wants to see "visually arresting images, ability with subject and high-quality photography." To break in, "shoot a quality and creative shot (that is part of our market) from more than one angle and at different depths."

💲 ATHLETIC MANAGEMENT

20 East Lake Rd., Ithaca NY 14850-9785. (607)257-6970. **Fax:** (607)257-7328. **E-mail:** ef@momentummedia.com. **Website:** www.athleticmanagement.com. **Contact:** Eleanor Frankel, editor-in-chief. Estab. 1989. Circ. 30,000. Bimonthly magazine. Emphasizes the management of athletics. Readers are managers of high school and college athletic programs.

NEEDS Uses 10–20 photos/issue; 50% supplied by freelancers. Needs photos of athletic events and athletic equipment/facility shots; college and high school sports action photos. Model release preferred.

MAKING CONTACT & TERMS Previously published work OK. Pays on publication. Credit line given. Buys first North American serial rights; negotiable.

AUTOINC.

Automotive Service Association, 8209 Mid Cities Blvd., North Richland Hills TX 76182. (817)514-2900, ext. 119. Direct line: (817)514-2919. **Fax:** (817)514-0770. **E-mail:** editor@asashop.org. **Website:** www.autoinc.org. Estab. 1952. Circ. 14,000. The mission of *AutoInc.*, ASA's official publication, is to be the informational authority for ASA and industry members nationwide. Its purpose is to enhance the professionalism of these members through management, technical and legislative articles, researched and written with the highest regard for accuracy, quality, and integrity.

SPECS Reviews 2×3 transparencies, 3×5 prints, high resolution digital images.

MAKING CONTACT & TERMS Captions, identification of subjects, model releases required. Negotiates payment individually. Buys one-time and electronic rights.

[O] AUTOMATED BUILDER

CMN Associates, Inc., 2401 Grapevine Dr., Oxnard CA 93036. (805)351-5931. **Fax:** (805)351-5755. **E-mail:** cms03@pacbell.net. **Website:** www.automatedbuilder.com. **Contact:** Don O. Carlson, editor/publisher. Estab. 1964. Circ. 75,000 when printed. Published bimonthly on the Internet. Emphasizes home, apartment and commercial in-plant construction. Each Automated Builder has 2 segments, In-Plant and At-Home.

NEEDS Needs in-plant and/or job site construction photos with the stories.

SPECS Photos may be 4/C prints or disks.

AUTOMOTIVE NEWS

1155 Gratiot Ave., Detroit MI 48207-2997. (313)446-0363. **E-mail:** mvanders@crain.com. **Website:** www.autonews.com. **Contact:** Mary Beth Vander Schaaf, managing editor. Estab. 1926. Circ. 77,000. Weekly tabloid. Emphasizes the global automotive industry. Readers are automotive industry executives, including people in manufacturing and retail. Sample copies available.

NEEDS Buys 5 photos from freelancers/issue; 260 photos/year. Needs photos of automotive executives (environmental portraits), auto plants, new vehicles, auto dealer features. Photo captions required; include identification of individuals and event details.

SPECS Uses 8×10 color prints; 35mm, 2¼×2¼, 4×5 transparencies. Accepts images in digital format. Send as JPEG files at 300 dpi (at least 6 inches wide).

MAKING CONTACT & TERMS Send unsolicited photos by mail with SASE for consideration. Provide résumé, business card, brochure, flyer or tearsheets to be kept on file for possible future assignments. Keeps samples on file. Responds in 2 weeks. Simultaneous submissions and previously published work OK. Pays on publication. Credit line given. Buys one-time rights, possible secondary rights for other Crain publications.

[O] AUTO RESTORER

BowTie, Inc., 3 Burroughs, Irvine CA 92618. (213)385-2222. **Fax:** (213)385-8565. **E-mail:** tkade@i5publishing.com. **Website:** www.autorestorermagazine.com. **Contact:** Ted Kade, editor. Estab. 1989. Circ. 60,000. Offers no additional payment for photos accepted with ms. "Interview the owner of a restored car. Present advice to others on how to do a similar restoration. Seek advice from experts. Go light on history and nonspecific details. Make it something that the magazine regularly uses. Do automotive how-tos."

NEEDS Photos of auto restoration projects and restored cars.

SPECS Prefers images in high-res digital format. Send via CD at 240 dpi with minimum width of 5 inches. Uses transparencies, mostly 35mm, 2¼×2¼.

MAKING CONTACT & TERMS Submit inquiry and portfolio for review. Provide résumé, business card, brochure, flyer, or tearsheets to be kept on file for possible future assignments. Responds in 1 month. Simultaneous submissions OK.

$$ ◐ AVIONICS MAGAZINE

(310) 354-1820. **E-mail:** mholmes@accessintel.com. **Website:** www.avionicsmagazine.com. **Contact:** Mark Holmes, editor. Estab. 1978. Circ. 20,000. Monthly magazine. Emphasizes aviation electronics. Readers are avionics and air traffic management engineers, technicians, executives. Sample copy free with 9×12 SASE.

NEEDS Buys 1–2 photos from freelancers/issue; 12–24 photos/year. Needs photos of travel, business concepts, industry, technology, aviation. Interested in alternative process, avant garde. Reviews photos with or without a manuscript. Photo captions required.

SPECS Prefers images in digital format. Send as JPEG files at 300 dpi minimum.

MAKING CONTACT & TERMS Query by e-mail. Provide résumé, business card, brochure, flyer or tearsheets to be kept on file for possible future assignments. Simultaneous submissions OK. Responds in 2 months. Pay varies; negotiable. **Pays on acceptance.** Credit line given. Rights negotiable.

BALLINGER PUBLISHING

41 N. Jefferson St., Suite 402, Pensacola FL 32502. (850)433-1166. **E-mail:** rita@ballingerpublishing.com. **Website:** www.ballingerpublishing.com. **Contact:** Rita Laymon, art director. Estab. 1990. Circ. 15,000. Monthly magazines. Emphasize business, lifestyle. Readers are executives, ages 35-54, with average annual income of $80,000. Sample copy available for $1.

NEEDS Photos of Florida topics: technology, government, ecology, global trade, finance, travel, regional and life shots. Model/property release required. Photo captions preferred.

SPECS Uses 5×7 b&w and color prints; 35mm. Prefers images in digital format. Send via CD, ZIP as TIFF, EPS files at 300 dpi.

MAKING CONTACT & TERMS Send unsolicited photos by mail or e-mail for consideration; include SASE for return of material sent by mail. Provide résumé, business card, brochure, flyer or tearsheets to be kept on file for possible future assignments. Pays on publication. Buys one-time rights.

BARTENDER MAGAZINE

Foley Publishing, P.O. Box 158, Liberty Corner NJ 07938. (908)766-6006. **Fax:** (908)766-6607. **E-mail:** barmag@aol.com. **Website:** www.bartender.com. **Contact:** Jackie Foley, editor. Estab. 1979. Circ. 150,000. Magazine published 4 times/year. *Bartender Magazine* serves full-service drinking establishments (full-service means able to serve liquor, beer and wine). "We serve single locations, including individual restaurants, hotels, motels, bars, taverns, lounges and all other full-service on-premises licensees." Sample copy available for $2.50. Number of photos/issue varies; number supplied by freelancers varies. Reviews photos with or without a ms.

NEEDS Photos of liquor-related topics, drinks, bars/bartenders

MAKING CONTACT & TERMS Model/property release required. Photo captions preferred. Provide résumé, business card, brochure, flyer or tearsheets

to be kept on file for possible future assignments; include SASE for return of material. Previously published work OK. Payment negotiable. Pays on publication. Credit line given. Buys all rights; negotiable.

BEDTIMES

501 Wythe St., Alexandria VA 22314-1917. (571)482-5442. **Fax:** (703)683-4503. **E-mail:** jkitchen@sleep products.org. **Website:** www.bedtimesmagazine.com. **Contact:** Jane Kitchen, editor-in-chief. Estab. 1917. Monthly association magazine; 40% of readership is overseas. Readers are manufacturers and suppliers in bedding industry. Sample copies available.

NEEDS Head shots, events, product shots/still life, conventions, shows, annual meetings. Reviews photos with or without a manuscript. Photo captions required; include correct spelling of name, title, company, return address for photos.

SPECS Prefers digital images sent as JPEGs via e-mail.

MAKING CONTACT & TERMS Send query letter with résumé, photocopies. Responds in 3 weeks to queries. Simultaneous submissions and previously published work may be OK—depends on type of assignment. Pays on publication. Credit line given. Buys one-time rights; negotiable.

BEE CULTURE

P.O. Box 706, Medina OH 44256-0706. (330)725-6677; (800)289-7668. **Fax:** (330)725-5624. **E-mail:** kim@beeculture.com. **Website:** www.beeculture. com. **Contact:** Mr. Kim Flottum, editor. Estab. 1873. Monthly trade magazine emphasizing beekeeping industry—how-to, politics, news and events. Sample copies available. Photo guidelines available on website. Buys 1-2 photos from freelancers/issue; 6-8 photos/year.

NEEDS Needs photos of honey bees and beekeeping, honey bees on flowers, etc.

SPECS Send via e-mail as TIFF, EPS, JPEG files at 300 dpi. Low-res for review encouraged.

MAKING CONTACT & TERMS Reviews photos with or without a manuscript. Accepts images in digital format. Does not keep samples on file; include SASE for return of material. E-mail contact preferred. Responds in 2 weeks to queries. Payment negotiable. **Pays on acceptance.** Credit line given.

TIPS "Read 2-3 issues for layout and topics. Think in vertical!"

BEEF TODAY

P.O. Box 958, Mexico MO 65265. (913)871-9066. **E-mail:** ghenderson@farmjournal.com. **Website:** www.beeftoday.com. **Contact:** Greg Henderson, editorial director. Circ. 220,000. Monthly magazine. Emphasizes American agriculture. Readers are active farmers, ranchers or agribusiness people. Sample copy and photo guidelines free with SASE.

NEEDS Buys 5–10 photos from freelancers/issue; 180–240 photos/year. "We use studio-type portraiture (environmental portraits), technical, details, scenics." Wants photos of environmental, livestock (feeding transporting, worming cattle), landscapes/scenics (from different regions of the US). Model release preferred. Photo captions required.

SPECS Accepts images in digital format. Send via CD or e-mail as TIFF, EPS, JPEG files, color RGB only.

MAKING CONTACT & TERMS Arrange a personal interview to show portfolio. Send query letter with résumé of credits along with business card, brochure, flyer or tearsheets to be kept on file for possible future assignments. Do not send originals! Responds in 2 weeks. Simultaneous submissions OK. Payment negotiable. "We pay a cover bonus." **Pays on acceptance.** Credit line given. Buys one-time rights.

TIPS In portfolio or samples, likes to see "about 20 images showing photographer's use of lighting and ability to work with people. Know your intended market. Familiarize yourself with the magazine and keep abreast of how photos are used in the general magazine field."

$$ BEVERAGE DYNAMICS

17 High St., 2nd Floor, Norwalk CT 06851. (203)855-8499. **E-mail:** alane@specialtyim.com; rbrandes@specialtyim.com. **Website:** www.adamsbevgroup.com. **Contact:** Adam Lane, art director; Richard Brandes, editor. Circ. 67,000. Quarterly. Emphasizes distilled spirits, wine and beer. Readers are retailers (liquor stores, supermarkets, etc.), wholesalers, distillers, vintners, brewers, ad agencies and media.

NEEDS Uses 5-10 photos/issue. Needs photos of retailers, products, concepts and profiles. Special needs include good retail environments, interesting store settings, special effect photos. Model/property release required. Photo captions required.

MAKING CONTACT & TERMS Send query letter with samples and list of stock photo subjects. Provide business card to be kept on file for possible future assignments. Keeps samples on file; send nonreturnable samples, slides, tearsheets, etc. Simultaneous submissions OK. Pays on publication. Credit line given. Buys one-time rights or all rights.

TIPS "We're looking for good location photographers who can style their own photo shoots or have staff stylists. It also helps if they are resourceful with props."

$ ○ BIZTIMES MILWAUKEE

BizTimes Media, 126 N. Jefferson St., Suite 403, Milwaukee WI 53202-6120. (414)277-8181. **Fax:** (414)277-8191. **E-mail:** shelly.tabor@biztimes.com. **Website:** www.biztimes.com. **Contact:** Shelly Tabor, art director. Estab. 1994. Circ. 13,500. Biweekly business news magazine covering southeastern Wisconsin region.

NEEDS Buys 2-3 photos from freelancers/issue; 200 photos/year; mostly by assignment. Needs photos of Milwaukee, including cities/urban, business men and women, business concepts. Interested in documentary/photo-journalistic style.

SPECS Accepts images in digital format only.

MAKING CONTACT & TERMS Provide résumé, business card, self-promotion piece to be kept on file for possible future assignments. Responds only if interested; send nonreturnable samples. Simultaneous submissions and previously published work OK. Pays $250 maximum for color cover; $100 maximum for inside. **Pays on publication.**

TIPS "Readers are owners/managers/CEOs. Cover stories and special reports often need conceptual images and portraits. Clean, modern and cutting edge with good composition. Covers have lots of possibility! Approximate 1-week turnaround. Most assignments are for the Milwaukee area."

$$ ◐ BOXOFFICE MAGAZINE

Boxoffice Media, LLC, 9107 Wilshire Blvd., Suite. 450, Beverly Hills CA 90210. (310) 876-9090. **E-mail:** ken@boxoffice.com. **Website:** www.BoxOffice.com. Estab. 1920. Circ. 6,000. Magazine about the motion picture industry for executives and managers working in the film business, including movie theater owners and operators, Hollywood studio personnel and leaders in allied industries.

NEEDS All photos must be of movie theaters and management. Reviews photos with accompanying manuscript only.

SPECS Send via CD, ZIP as TIFF files at 300 dpi.

MAKING CONTACT & TERMS Send query letter with résumé, tearsheets. Does not keep samples on file; cannot return material. Responds in 1 month to queries. Responds only if interested; send nonreturnable samples. Previously published work OK.

⊕ BRAND PACKAGING

BNP Media, 2401 W. Big Beaver Rd., Suite 700, Troy MI 48084. (248)205-6869. **E-mail:** zielinskil@bnpmedia.com. **Website:** www.brandpackaging.com. **Contact:** Laura Zielinski, editor-in-chief. Estab. 1997. Circ. 33,000. Publishes strategies and tactics to make products stand out on the shelf. Market is brand managers who are marketers but need to know something about packaging.

MAKING CONTACT & TERMS Identification of subjects required. Negotiates payment individually. Buys one-time rights.

⊕ CANADIAN GUERNSEY JOURNAL

5653 Hwy. 6 N, RR 5, Guelph Ontario N1H 6J2, Canada. (519)836-2141. **Fax:** (519)763-6582. **E-mail:** info@guernseycanada.ca. **Website:** www.guernseycanada.ca. **Contact:** Jessie Weir. Estab. 1927. Annual journal of the Canadian Guernsey Association. Emphasizes dairy cattle, purebred and grade Guernseys. Readers are dairy farmers and agriculture-related companies. Sample copy available for $15.

NEEDS Photos of Guernsey cattle: posed, informal, scenes. Photo captions preferred.

MAKING CONTACT & TERMS Contact through administration office. Keeps samples on file.

⊕ CASINO JOURNAL

BNP Media, 2401 W. Big Weaver Rd., Troy MI 48084. (248)786-1728. **Fax:** (248)362-0317. **E-mail:** gizickit@bnpmedia.com. **Website:** www.casinojournal.com. **Contact:** Tammie Gizicki, art director. Estab. 1985. Circ. 35,000. Monthly journal. Emphasizes casino operations. Readers are casino executives, employees and vendors. Sample copy free with 11×14 SASE. Ascend Media Gaming Group also publishes *IGWB*, *Slot Manager*, and *Indian Gaming Business*. Each magazine has its own photo needs.

NEEDS Buys 0-2 photos from freelancers/issue; 12-24 photos/year. Needs photos of gaming tables and slot machines, casinos and portraits of executives. Model release required for gamblers, employees. Photo captions required.

MAKING CONTACT & TERMS Send query letter with résumé of credits, stock list. Pays on publication. Credit line given. Buys all rights; negotiable.

TIPS "Read and study photos in current issues."

CATHOLIC LIBRARY WORLD

205 W. Monroe St., Suite 314, Chicago IL 60606. (312)739-1776. **Fax:** (312)739-1778. **E-mail:** mmccarthy@cathla.org; cla@cathla.org. **Website:** www.cathla.org/cathlibworld.html. **Contact:** Malachy R. McCarthy, acting executive director. Estab. 1929. Circ. 1,100. Quarterly magazine of the Catholic Library Association. Emphasizes libraries and librarians (community/school libraries; academic/research librarians; archivists). Readers are librarians who belong to the Catholic Library Association; other subscribers are generally employed in Catholic institutions or academic settings. Sample copy available for $25.

NEEDS Uses 2-5 photos/issue. Needs photos of authors of children's books, and librarians who have done something to contribute to the community at large. Special needs include photos of annual conferences. Model release preferred for photos of authors. Photo captions preferred.

MAKING CONTACT & TERMS Send electronically in high-res, 450 dpi or greater. Deadlines: January 2, April 1, July 1, October 1. Responds in 2 weeks. Credit line given. Acquires one-time rights.

⊕ CEA ADVISOR

Connecticut Education Association, Capitol Place, Suite 500, 21 Oak St., Hartford CT 06106. (860)525-5641; (800)842-4316. **Fax:** (860)725-6356; (860)725-6323. **E-mail:** kathyf@cea.org. **Website:** www.cea.org. **Contact:** Kathy Frega, director of communications; Michael Lydick, managing editor. Circ. 42,000. Monthly tabloid. Emphasizes education. Readers are public school teachers. Sample copy free with 6 first-class stamps.

NEEDS Buys 1-2 photos from freelancers/issue; 12-24 photos/year. Needs "classroom scenes, students, school buildings." Model release preferred. Photo captions preferred.

MAKING CONTACT & TERMS Send b&w contact sheet by mail for consideration. Provide résumé, business card, brochure, flyer or tearsheets to be kept on file for possible future assignments. Cannot return material. Responds in 1 month. Simultaneous submissions and previously published work OK. Pays $50 for b&w cover; $25 for b&w inside. Pays on publication. Credit line given. Buys all rights.

⊙ CHILDHOOD EDUCATION

1101 16th St. NW, Suite 300, Washington DC 20036. (202)372-9986; (800)423-3563. **Fax:** (202)372-9989. **E-mail:** editorial@acei.org. **Website:** www.acei.org. **Contact:** Anne Watson Bauer, editor/director of publications. Estab. 1924. Circ. 15,000. Bimonthly journal of the Association for Childhood Education International. Emphasizes the education of children from infancy through early adolescence. Readers include teachers, administrators, day-care workers, parents, psychologists, student teachers, etc. Sample copy free with 9×12 SASE and $1.44 postage. Submission guidelines available online.

NEEDS Uses 1 photos/issue; 2-3 supplied by freelance photographers. Uses freelancers mostly for covers. Subject matter includes children, infancy-14 years, in groups or alone, in or out of the classroom, at play, in study groups; boys and girls of all races and in all cities and countries. Wants close-ups of children, unposed. Reviews photos with or without accompanying manuscript. Special needs include photos of minority children; photos of children from different ethnic groups together in one shot; boys and girls together. Model release required.

SPECS Accepts images in digital format, 300 dpi.

MAKING CONTACT & TERMS Send unsolicited photos by e-mail to abauer@acei.org and bherzig@acei.org. Responds in 1 month. Simultaneous submissions and previously published work are discouraged but negotiable. Pays on publication. Credit line given. Buys one-time rights.

TIPS "Send pictures of unposed children in educational settings, please."

⊙ ● THE CHRONICLE OF PHILANTHROPY

1255 23rd St. NW, 7th Floor, Washington DC 20037. (202)466-1200. **Fax:** (202)452-1033. **E-mail:** creative@chronicle.com; editor@philanthropy.com. **Website:** philanthropy.com. **Contact:** Sue LaLumia, art director. Estab. 1988. Biweekly tabloid. Readers come from all aspects of the nonprofit world such as charities, foundations and relief agencies such as the Red Cross. Sample copy free.

NEEDS Buys 10-15 photos from freelancers/issue; 260-390 photos/year. Needs photos of people (profiles) making the news in philanthropy and environ-

mental shots related to person(s)/organization. Most shots arranged with freelancers are specific. Model release required. Photo caption required.

SPECS Accepts images in digital format. Send via CD, ZIP.

MAKING CONTACT & TERMS Arrange a personal interview to show portfolio. Send 35mm, 2¼×2¼ transparencies and prints by mail for consideration. Provide résumé, business card, brochure, flyer or tearsheets to be kept on file for possible future assignments. Responds in 2 days. Previously published work OK. Pays (color and b&w) $275 plus expenses/half day; $450 plus expenses/full day; $100 for web publication (2-week period). Pays on publication. Buys one-time rights.

⊙ ⊕ ◑ CIVITAN MAGAZINE

P.O. Box 130744, Birmingham AL 35213-0744. (205)591-8910. **E-mail:** civitan@civitan.org. **Website:** www.civitan.org. Estab. 1920. Circ. 24,000. Quarterly publication of Civitan International. Emphasizes work with mental retardation/developmental disabilities. Readers are men and women, college age to retirement, usually managers or owners of businesses. Sample copy free with 9×12 SASE and 2 first-class stamps.

NEEDS Buys 1-2 photos from freelancers/issue; 6-12 photos/year. Always looking for good cover shots (multicultural, travel, scenic, how-to), babies/children/teens, families, religious, disasters, environmental, landscapes/scenics. Model release required. Photo captions preferred.

SPECS Accepts images in digital format. Send via CD or e-mail at 300 dpi only.

MAKING CONTACT & TERMS Send sample of unsolicited 2¼×2¼ or 4×5 transparencies by mail for consideration. Provide résumé, business card, brochure, flyer or tearsheets to be kept on file for possible future assignments. Responds in 1 month. Simultaneous submissions and previously published work OK. Pays $50-200 for color cover; $20 for color inside. **Pays on acceptance.** Buys one-time rights.

⊙ CLASSICAL SINGER

P.O. Box 1710, Draper UT 84020. (801)254-1025; (877)515-9800. **Fax:** (801)254-3139. **E-mail:** info@classicalsinger.com. **Website:** www.classicalsinger.com. **Contact:** Blaine Hawkes. Estab. 1988. Circ. 9,000. Glossy monthly trade magazine for classical singers. Sample copy free.

NEEDS Looking for photos in opera or classical singing. E-mail for calendar and ideas. Photo captions preferred; include where, when, who.

SPECS Uses b&w and color prints or high-res digital photos.

MAKING CONTACT & TERMS Responds in 1 month to queries. Simultaneous submissions and previously published work OK. Pays honorarium plus 10 copies. Pays on publication. Credit line given. Buys one-time rights. Photo may be used in a reprint of an article on paper or website. "In an effort to reduce spam, we are no longer providing our e-mail addresses from our website. Please use the online form to contact individual staff members."

TIPS "Our publication is expanding rapidly. We want to make insightful photographs a big part of that expansion."

$ ◐ CLEANING & MAINTENANCE MANAGEMENT

NTP Media, 19 British American Blvd., W., Latham NY 12110. (518)783-1281, ext. 3137. **Fax:** (518)783-1386. **E-mail:** marty@grandviewmedia.com; rdipaolo@ntpmedia.com. **Website:** www.cmmonline.com. **Contact:** Marty Harris, art director. Estab. 1963. Circ. 38,300. Monthly. Emphasizes management of cleaning/custodial/housekeeping operations for commercial buildings, schools, hospitals, shopping malls, airports, etc. Readers are middle- to upper-level managers of in-house cleaning/custodial departments, and managers/owners of contract cleaning companies. Sample copy free (limited) with SASE.

NEEDS Uses 10-15 photos/issue. Needs photos of cleaning personnel working on carpets, hardwood floors, tile, windows, restrooms, large buildings, etc. Model release preferred. Photo captions required.

MAKING CONTACT & TERMS Provide résumé, business card, brochure, flyer or tearsheets to be kept on file for possible future assignments. "Send query letter with specific ideas for photos related to our field." Responds in 1-2 weeks. Simultaneous submissions and previously published work OK. Pays $25 for b&w inside. Credit line given. Rights negotiable.

TIPS "Query first and shoot what the publication needs."

⊘ COMMERCIAL CARRIER JOURNAL

3200 Rice Mine Rd., NE, Tuscaloosa AL 35406. (800)633-5953. **Fax:** (205)750-8070. **E-mail:** production@ccjdigital.com. **Website:** www.ccjmagazine.com. **Contact:** David Watson, art director. Estab. 1911. Circ. 105,000. Monthly magazine. Emphasizes truck and bus fleet maintenance operations and management.

NEEDS Spot news (of truck accidents, Teamster activities and highway scenes involving trucks). Photos purchased with or without accompanying manuscript, or on assignment. Model release required. Detailed captions required.

SPECS Prefers images in digital format. Send via e-mail as JPEG files at 300 dpi. For covers, uses medium-format transparencies (vertical only).

MAKING CONTACT & TERMS Does not accept unsolicited photos. Query first; send material by mail with SASE for consideration. Responds in 3 months. Pays on a per-job or per-photo basis. **Pays on acceptance.** Credit line given. Buys all rights.

TIPS Needs accompanying features on truck fleets and news features involving trucking companies.

CONSTRUCTION EQUIPMENT GUIDE

470 Maryland Dr., Ft. Washington PA 19034. (215)885-2900 or (800)523-2200. **E-mail:** production@cegltd.com; editorial@cegltd.com. **Website:** www.cegltd.com. **Contact:** Craig Mongeau, editor-in-chief. Estab. 1957. Circ. 120,000. Biweekly trade newspaper. Emphasizes construction equipment industry, including projects ongoing throughout the country. Readers are males and females of all ages; many are construction executives, contractors, dealers and manufacturers. Free sample copy.

NEEDS Buys 35 photos from freelancers/issue; 910 photos/year. Needs photos of construction job sites and special event coverage illustrating new equipment applications and interesting projects. Call to inquire about special photo needs for coming year. Model/property release preferred. Photo captions required for subject identification.

MAKING CONTACT & TERMS Send any size matte or glossy b&w prints by mail with SASE for consideration. Provide résumé, business card, brochure, flyer or tearsheets to be kept on file for possible future assignments. Responds in 3 weeks. Payment negotiable. Pays on publication. Credit line given. Buys all rights; negotiable.

THE COOLING JOURNAL

3000 Village Run Rd., Suite 103, #221, Wexford PA 15090. (724)799-8415. **Fax:** (724)799-8416. **E-mail:** info@narsa.org. **Website:** www.narsa.org. Estab. 1956.

Published 10 times a year. Magazine of NARSA—The International Heat Exchange Association. Emphasis on thermal management products and services for transportation, energy and industry.
NEEDS Buys photos, images, and stories about people, organizations, processes, technologies, and products in heat exchange industry which includes: automotive, heavy truck and mobile machinery engine and transmission cooling; automotive, heavy truck, and mobile machinery air conditioning and cabin heating; engine and transmission cooling for marine applications; engine and transmission cooling for vehicle high performance and racing; heat exchange for energy exploration and generation; construction, mining, agricultural applications for heat exchange products and services; metals joining including welding and brazing; heat exchange product fabrication, design and engineering.
MAKING CONTACT & TERMS Send inquiry for current story board, rates, and deadlines. Pays on publication.

COTTON GROWER MAGAZINE

Meister Media Worldwide, Cotton Media Group, 8000 Centerview Pkwy., Suite 114, Cordova TN 38018-4246. (901)756-8822. **E-mail:** mccue@meister media.com. **Website:** www.cotton247.com. **Contact:** Mike McCue, editor. Circ. 43,000. Monthly magazine. Emphasizes "cotton production; for cotton farmers." Sample copies and photo guidelines available.
NEEDS Photos of agriculture. "Our main photo needs are cover shots of growers. We write cover stories on each issue."
SPECS Prefers high-res digital images; send JPEGs at 300 dpi via e-mail or CD. Uses high-quality glossy prints from 35mm.
MAKING CONTACT & TERMS Send query letter with slides, prints, tearsheets. **Pays on acceptance.** Credit line given. Buys all rights.
TIPS Most photography hired is for cover shots of cotton growers.

☉☉ CROPLIFE

37733 Euclid Ave., Willoughby OH 44094. (440)942-2000. **E-mail:** erics@croplife.com. **Website:** www. croplife.com. Estab. 1894. Circ. 24,500. Monthly magazine. Serves the agricultural distribution channel delivering fertilizer, chemicals and seed from manufacturer to farmer. Sample copy and photo guidelines free with 9×12 SASE.

NEEDS Buys 6-7 photos/year; 5-30% supplied by freelancers. Needs photos of agricultural chemical and fertilizer application scenes (of commercial—not farmer—applicators), people shots of distribution channel executives and managers. Model release preferred. Photo captions required.
SPECS Uses 8×10 glossy b&w and color prints; 35mm slides, transparencies.
MAKING CONTACT & TERMS Send query letter first with résumé of credits. Simultaneous submissions and previously published work OK. **Pays on acceptance.** Buys one-time rights.

☉☉ DAIRY TODAY

P.O. Box 1167, 261 E. Broadway, Monticello MN 55362. (763)271-3363. **E-mail:** jdickrell@farmjournal.com. **Website:** www.agweb.com/livestock/dairy/. **Contact:** Jim Dickrell, editor. Circ. 20,000. Monthly magazine. Emphasizes American agriculture. Readers are active farmers, ranchers or agribusiness people. Sample copy and photo guidelines free with SASE.
NEEDS Buys 5-10 photos from freelancers/issue; 60-120 photos/year. "We use studio-type portraiture (environmental portraits), technical, details, scenics." Wants photos of environmental, landscapes/scenics, agriculture, business concepts. Model release preferred. Photo captions required.
MAKING CONTACT & TERMS Arrange a personal interview to show portfolio. Send query letter with résumé of credits along with business card, brochure, flyer or tearsheets to be kept on file for possible future assignments. "Portfolios may be submitted via CD." *Do not send originals!* Responds in 2 weeks. Simultaneous submissions OK. "We pay a cover bonus." **Pays on acceptance.** Credit line given, except in advertorials. Buys one-time rights.
TIPS In portfolio or samples, likes to see "about 40 slides showing photographer's use of lighting and ability to work with people. Know your intended market. Familiarize yourself with the magazine and keep abreast of how photos are used in the general magazine field."

➕ DERMASCOPE MAGAZINE

Aesthetics International Association, 310 E. Interstate 30, Suite B107, Garland TX 75043. (469)429-9300. **Fax:** (469)429-9301. **E-mail:** amanda@dermascope. com. **Website:** www.dermascope.com. **Contact:** Amanda Strunk-Miller, managing editor. Estab. 1978. Circ. 16,000. *Dermascope* is a source of practical advice and continuing education for skin care, body, and spa therapy professionals. Main readers are salon, day spa, and destination spa owners, managers, or technicians and aesthetics students.

MAKING CONTACT & TERMS Accepts disk submissions. Electronic images should be 300 dpi, CMYK, and either JPEG, TIFF, PSD, or EPS format. Photo credits, model releases, and identification of subjects or techniques shown in photos are required. Samples are not filed. Photos will not be returned; do not send original artwork. Responds only if interested. Rights purchased vary according to project. Pays on publication.

◎ ❶ DESIGN:RETAIL MAGAZINE

1145 Sanctuary Pkwy., Suite 355, Alpharetta GA 30009. (770)291-5520. **E-mail:** wendi.vaneldik@em eraldexpo.com. **Website:** www.designretailonline. com. **Contact:** Wendi Van Eldik, art director. Estab. 1988. Circ. 21,500. Monthly magazine. Emphasizes retail design, store planning, visual merchandising. Readers are retail architects, designers and retail executives. Sample copies available.

NEEDS Buys 7 or fewer photos from freelancers/issue; 84 or fewer photos/year. Needs photos of architecture, mostly interior. Property release preferred.

SPECS Prefers digital submissions. Send as TIFF or JPEG files at 300 dpi.

MAKING CONTACT & TERMS Send query letter with résumé of credits. Provide résumé, business card, brochure, flyer or tearsheets to be kept on file for possible future assignments. Responds in 3 weeks. Credit line given. Rights negotiable.

TIPS Looks for architectural interiors, ability to work with different lighting. "Send samples (photocopies OK) and résumé."

DM NEWS

Haymarket Media, Inc., 114 W. 26th St., New York NY 10001. (646)638-6186. **E-mail:** James.Jarnot@ dmnews.com; news@dmnews.com. **Website:** www. dmnews.com. Estab. 1979. Circ. 50,300. Company publication for Courtenay Communications Corporation. Weekly newspaper. Emphasizes direct, interactive and database marketing. Readers are decision makers and marketing executives, ages 25-55. Sample copy available for $2.

NEEDS Uses 20 photos/issue; 3-5 supplied by freelancers. Needs news head shots, product shots. Reviews photos purchased with accompanying manuscript only. Photo captions required.

MAKING CONTACT & TERMS Provide résumé, business card, brochure, flyer or tearsheets to be kept on file for possible future assignments. Responds in 1-2 weeks. Payment negotiable. **Pays on acceptance.** Buys worldwide rights.

TIPS "News and business background are a prerequisite."

ELECTRICAL APPARATUS

Barks Publications, Inc., Suite 901, 500 N. Michigan Ave., Chicago IL 60611. (312)321-9440. **Fax:** (312)321-1288. **E-mail:** eamagazine@barks.com. **Website:** www.barks.com/eacurr.html. **Contact:** Elizabeth Van Ness, publisher; Kevin N. Jones, senior editor. Estab. 1967. Circ. 16,000. Monthly magazine. Emphasizes industrial electrical machinery maintenance and repair for the electrical aftermarket. Readers are "persons engaged in the application, maintenance and servicing of industrial and commercial electrical and electronic equipment." Sample copies available.

NEEDS "Assigned materials only. We welcome innovative industrial photography, but most of our material is staff-prepared." Photos purchased with accompanying manuscript or on assignment. Model release required "when requested." Photo captions required.

MAKING CONTACT & TERMS Send query letter with résumé of credits. Contact sheet OK; include SASE for return of material. Responds in 3 weeks. Pays up to $200, digital format only. Pays on publication. Credit line given. Buys all rights, but exceptions are occasionally made.

❸ ❸ ❶ ELECTRIC PERSPECTIVES

701 Pennsylvania Ave. NW, Washington DC 20004. (202)508-5065. **E-mail:** bcannon@eei.org. **Website:** www.eei.org/magazine/Pages/ElectricPerspectivesIssues.aspx. **Contact:** Bruce Cannon, associate editor. Estab. 1976. Circ. 11,000. Bimonthly magazine of the Edison Electric Institute. Emphasizes issues and subjects related to shareholder-owned electric utilities. Sample copy available on request.

NEEDS Photos relating to the business and operational life of electric utilities—from customer service to engineering, from executive to blue collar. Model release required. Photo captions preferred.

SPECS Uses 8×10 glossy color prints; 35mm, 2¼×2¼, 4×5 transparencies. Accepts images in digital format. All high-res non-postscript formats accepted. Send via ZIP, e-mail as TIFF, JPEG files at 300 dpi and scanned at a large size, at least 4×5.

MAKING CONTACT & TERMS Send query letter with stock list or send unsolicited photos by mail for consideration. Provide electronic résumé, business card, or brochure to be kept on file for possible future assignments. Keeps samples on file. Pays on publication. Buys one-time rights; negotiable (for reprints).

TIPS "We're interested in annual-report-quality images in particular. Quality and creativity are often more important than subject."

EL RESTAURANTE

P.O. Box 2249, Oak Park IL 60303-2249. (708)267-0023. **E-mail:** kfurore@comcast.net. **Website:** www.restmex.com. **Contact:** Kathleen Furore, editor. Estab. 1997. Circ. 25,000. Formerly *El Restaurante Mexicano*. Bimonthly magazine for restaurants that serve Mexican, Tex-Mex, Southwestern and Latin cuisine. Sample copies available.

NEEDS Buys very few photos from freelancers. Needs photos of food/drink. Reviews photos with or without a manuscript.

SPECS Accepts digital submissions only. Send via e-mail as TIFF, JPEG files of at least 300 dpi.

MAKING CONTACT & TERMS Previously published work OK. Pays $450 maximum for color cover; $125 maximum for color inside. Pays on publication. Credit line given. Buys all rights; negotiable.

TIPS "We look for outstanding food photography; the more creatively styled, the better."

ESL TEACHER TODAY

E-mail: shannonaswriter@yahoo.com. **Contact:** Shannon Bridget Murphy. Quarterly magazine. Photo guildelines available via e-mail. Request photographer's sample copy for $3 sent through PayPal to scribblesbyshannon@yahoo.com.

NEEDS Buys 12-24 photos/year. Photos of babies/children/teens, multicultural, families, parents, disasters, environmental, landscapes/scenics, wildlife, cities/urban, education, religious, rural, adventure, events, food/drink, sports, travel, agriculture, medicine, military, political, product shots/still life, science, technology—as related to teaching ESL (English as a Second Language) around the globe. Interested in alternative process, avant garde, documentary, fashion/glamour, fine art, historical/vintage, seasonal. Reviews photos with or without a manuscript. Model/property release preferred.

SPECS Uses glossy or matte color and b&w prints.

MAKING CONTACT & TERMS Send query letter via e-mail. "If possible, please do not include photographs in files if they are sent through e-mail. A disc with your photographs sent to *ESL Teacher Today* is acceptable." Provide résumé, business card or self-promotion piece to be kept on file for possible future assignments. Responds within 1 month to queries; 1 week to portfolios. Simultaneous submissions and previously published work OK. **Pays on acceptance.** Credit line given. Buys one-time rights, first rights; negotiable.

⊘⊘ FARM JOURNAL

P.O. Box 958, Mexico MO 65265. **E-mail:** lbenne@farmjournal.com. **Website:** www.agweb.com/farm journal. Estab. 1877. Circ. 375,000. *Farm Journal*, the largest national US farm magazine, is a prime source of practical information on crops and livestock for farm families. Published 12 times a year, the magazine emphasizes agricultural production, technology and policy.

NEEDS Photos having to do with the basics of raising, harvesting and marketing of all the farm commodities (primarily corn, soybeans and wheat) and farm animals. All photos must relate to agriculture.

SPECS Accepts images in digital format.

MAKING CONTACT & TERMS Send online portfolios to the e-mail address above or send photo/thumbnails by mail.

TIPS Provide calling card and samples to be kept on file for possible future assignments.

FIRE CHIEF

Primedia Business, 330 N. Wabash Ave., Suite 2300, Chicago IL 60611. (312)595-1080. **Fax:** (312)595-0295. **E-mail:** lisa@firechief.com; sundee@firechief.com. **Website:** www.firechief.com. **Contact:** Lisa Allegretti, editor; Sundee Koffarnus; art director. Estab. 1956. Circ. 53,000. Monthly magazine. Focus on fire department management and operations. Readers are primarily fire officers and predominantly chiefs of departments. Sample copy free. Request photo guidelines via e-mail.

NEEDS Needs "fire and emergency response, especially leadership themes—if you do not have fire or EMS experience, please do not contact."

SPECS Digital format preferred, file name less than 15 characters. Send via e-mail, CD, ZIP as TIFF, EPS files at highest possible resolution.

MAKING CONTACT & TERMS Send JPEGs or TIFFs at no larger than 300 dpi for consideration along with caption, date, time, and location. Samples are kept on file. Expect confirmation/response within 1 month. Payment 90 days after publication. Buys first serial rights; negotiable.

TIPS "As the name *Fire Chief* implies, we prefer images showing a leading officer (white, yellow, or red helmet) in action—on scene of a fire, disaster, accident/rescue, hazmat, etc. Other subjects: administration, communications, decontamination, dispatch, EMS, foam, heavy rescue, incident command, live fire training, public education, SCBA, water rescue, wildland fire."

FIRE ENGINEERING

PennWell Corporation, 21-00 Rt. 208 S., Fair Lawn NJ 07410-2602. (973)251-5054. **E-mail:** dianer@pennwell.com. **Website:** www.fireengineering.com. **Contact:** Diane Rothschild, executive editor. Estab. 1877. Training magazine for firefighters. Photo guidelines free.

NEEDS Uses 400 photos/year. Needs action photos of disasters, firefighting, EMS, public safety, fire investigation and prevention, rescue. Photo captions required; include date, what is happening, location and fire department contact.

SPECS Accepts images in digital format. Send via e-mail or mail on CD as JPEG files at 300 dpi minimum.

MAKING CONTACT & TERMS Send unsolicited photos by mail for consideration. Pays on publication. Credit line given. "We retain copyright."

TIPS "Firefighters must be doing something. Our focus is on training and learning lessons from photos."

FIREHOUSE MAGAZINE

3 Huntington Quadrangle, Suite 301N, Melville NY 11747. (631)845-2700; (800)547-7377, ext. 6262. **E-mail:** marianne.mcintyre@cygnuspub.com. **Website:** www.firehouse.comin. **Contact:** Marianne McIntyre, art director. Estab. 1976. Circ. 90,000. Monthly. Emphasizes "firefighting—notable fires, techniques, dramatic fires and rescues, etc." Readers are "paid and volunteer firefighters, EMTs." Sample copy available for $5 with 9×12 SASE and 7 first-class stamps. Photo guidelines free with SASE or online.

NEEDS Buys 20 photos from freelancers/issue; 240 photos/year. Needs photos of fires, terrorism, firefighter training, natural disasters, highway incidents, hazardous materials, dramatic rescues. Model release preferred.

SPECS Uses 3×5, 5×7, 8×10 matte or glossy b&w or color prints; 35mm transparencies. Accepts images in digital format. Send via CD, e-mail as TIFF, EPS, JPEG files at 300 dpi.

MAKING CONTACT & TERMS "Photos must not be more than 30 days old." Include SASE. "Photos cannot be returned without SASE." Responds ASAP. Pays on publication. Credit line given. Buys one-time rights.

TIPS "Mostly we are looking for action-packed photos—the more fire, the better the shot. Show firefighters in full gear; do not show spectators. Fire safety is a big concern. Much of our photo work is freelance. Try to be in the right place at the right time as the fire occurs. Be sure that photos are clear, in focus, and show firefighters/EMTs at work. Firehouse encourages submissions of high-quality action photos that relate to the firefighting/EMS field. Please understand that while we encourage first-time photographers, a minimum waiting period of 3-6 months is not unusual. Although we are capable of receiving photos online, please be advised that there are color variations. Include captions. Photographers must include a SASE, and we cannot guarantee the return of unsolicited photos. Mark name and address on the back of each photo."

FIRERESCUE

4180 La Jolla Village Dr., Suite 260, La Jolla CA 92037. (800)266-5367. **E-mail:** frm.editor@pennwell.com. **Website:** www.firefighternation.com. **Contact:** Editor. Estab. 1997. Circ. 50,000. Monthly. Emphasizes techniques, equipment, action stories of fire and rescue incidents. Editorial slant: "Read it today, use it tomorrow."

NEEDS Photos of fires, fire ground scenes, commanders operating at fires, company officers/crews fighting fires, disasters, emergency medical services, rescue scenes, transport, injured victims, equipment and personnel, training, earthquake rescue operations. Special photo needs include strong color shots showing newsworthy rescue operations, including a unique or difficult firefighting, rescue/extrication, treatment, transport, personnel, etc.; b&w showing same. Photo captions required.

SPECS Accepts images in digital format. Prefers digital format submitted via e-mail or FTP (www.firefighternation.com/content/photographer-guide

lines). Send via ZIP, e-mail, CD as TIFF, EPS, JPEG files at 300 dpi.

MAKING CONTACT & TERMS Pays $300 for cover; $22-137 for color inside. Pays on publication. Credit line given. Buys one-time rights.

⊖⊖ ⊙ ◐ ⊛ FLORAL MANAGEMENT MAGAZINE

1601 Duke St., Alexandria VA 22314. (703)836-8700; (800) 336-4743. **Fax:** (703)836-8705. **E-mail:** kpenn@safnow.org. **Website:** www.safnow.org. **Contact:** Kate Penn, editor-in-chief. Estab. 1894. National trade association magazine representing growers, wholesalers and retailers of flowers and plants. Photos used in magazine and promotional materials.

NEEDS Offers 15-20 assignments/year. Needs photos of floral business owners, employees on location, and retail environmental portraits. Reviews stock photos. Model release required. Photo captions preferred.

SPECS Prefers images in digital format. Send via CD or e-mail as TIFF files at 300 dpi. Also uses b&w prints; transparencies.

MAKING CONTACT & TERMS Send query letter with samples. Provide résumé, business card, brochure, flyer or tearsheets to be kept on file for possible future assignments. Responds in 1 week. Credit line given. Buys one-time rights.

TIPS "We shoot a lot of tightly composed, dramatic shots of people, so we look for these skills. We also welcome input from the photographer on the concept of the shot. Our readers, as business owners, like to see photos of other business owners. Therefore, people photography, on location, is particularly popular." Photographers should approach magazine "via letter of introduction and sample. We'll keep name in file and use if we have a shoot near photographer's location."

⊖ ⊕ ○ FOREST LANDOWNER

900 Circle 75 Pkwy., Suite 205, Atlanta GA 30339. (800)325-2954; (404)325-2954. **Fax:** (404)325-2955. **E-mail:** info@forestlandowners.com. **Website:** www.forestlandowners.com. Estab. 1942. Circ. 10,000. Bimonthly magazine of the Forest Landowners Association. Emphasizes forest management and policy issues for private forest landowners. Readers are forest landowners and forest industry consultants; 94% male between the ages of 46 and 55. Sample copy available for $3 (magazine), $30 (manual).

NEEDS Uses 15-25 photos/issue; 3-4 supplied by freelancers. Needs photos of unique or interesting private southern forests. Other subjects: environmental, regional, wildlife, landscapes/scenics. Model/property release preferred. Photo captions preferred.

SPECS Accepts images in digital format. Send via CD, ZIP, e-mail as TIFF, EPS files at 300 dpi.

MAKING CONTACT & TERMS Send ZIP disk, color prints, negatives or transparencies by mail or e-mail for consideration. Send query letter with stock list. Keeps samples on file. SASE. Responds in 3 weeks. Simultaneous submissions and previously published work OK. Pays on publication. Credit line given. Buys one-time and all rights; negotiable.

TIPS "We most often use photos of timber management, seedlings, aerial shots of forests, and unique southern forest landscapes. Mail ZIP, CD or slides of sample images. Captions are important."

FRUIT GROWERS NEWS

Great American Publishing, P.O. Box 128, Sparta MI 49345. (616)887-9008. **Fax:** (616)887-2666. **E-mail:** fgnedit@fruitgrowersnews.com. **Website:** www.fruitgrowersnews.com. **Contact:** Matt Milkovich, managing editor; Lee Dean, editorial director. Estab. 1961. Circ. 16,429. Monthly. Emphasizes all aspects of tree fruit and small fruit growing as well as farm marketing. Readers are growers but include anybody associated with the field. Sample copy available.

NEEDS Buys 3 photos from freelancers/issue; 25 photos/year. Needs portraits of growers, harvesting, manufacturing, field shots for stock photography—anything associated with fruit growing. Photo captions required.

SPECS Accepts images in digital format. Send via CD as JPEG, TIFF or EPS files at 300 dpi, at least 4×6.

MAKING CONTACT & TERMS Query about prospective jobs. Simultaneous submissions and previously published work OK. Payment rates to be negotiated between editorial director and individual photographer. Pays on publication. Credit line given. Buys first North American rights.

TIPS "Learn about the field. Great American Publishing also publishes *The Vegetable Growers News*, *Spudman*, *Fresh Cut*, *Museums & More*, *Party & Paper Retailer and Stationery Trends*. Contact the editorial director for information on these publications."

GEOSYNTHETICS

1801 County Rd. B W., Roseville MN 55113. (651)222-2508 or (800)225-4324. **Fax:** (651)631-9334; (651)225-6966. **E-mail:** generalinfo@ifai.com; rwbygness@ifai.com. **Website:** www.geosyntheticsmagazine.com; www.ifai.com. **Contact:** Ron Bygness, editor. Estab. 1983. Circ. 18,000. Association magazine published 6 times/year. Emphasizes geosynthetics in civil engineering applications. Readers are civil engineers, professors and consulting engineers. Sample copies available.

NEEDS Uses 10-15 photos/issue; various number supplied by freelancers. Needs photos of finished applications using geosynthetics; photos of the application process. Reviews photos with accompanying manuscript only. Model release required. Photo captions required; include project, type of geosynthetics used and location.

SPECS Prefers images in high-res digital format.

MAKING CONTACT & TERMS "Please call before submitting samples!" Keeps samples on file. Responds in 1 month. Simultaneous submissions OK. Credit line given. Buys all rights; negotiable.

$ ◐ GOVERNMENT TECHNOLOGY

100 Blue Ravine Rd., Folsom CA 95630. (916)932-1300. **Fax:** (916)932-1470. **E-mail:** mhamm@govtech.com. **Website:** www.govtech.com. **Contact:** Michelle Hamm, creative director. Estab. 2001. Circ. 60,000. Monthly trade magazine. Emphasizes information technology as it applies to state and local government. Readers are government executives.

NEEDS Buys 2 photos from freelancers/issue; 20 photos/year. Needs photos of government officials, disasters, environmental, political, technology/computers. Reviews photos with accompanying manuscript only. Model release required; property release preferred. Photo captions required.

SPECS Accepts images in digital format only. Send via DVD, CD, ZIP, e-mail as TIFF, JPEG files at 300 dpi.

MAKING CONTACT & TERMS Send query letter with résumé, prints, tearsheets. Provide business card, self-promotion piece to be kept on file for possible future assignments. Responds only if interested; send nonreturnable samples. Simultaneous submissions and previously published work OK. Payment is dependent upon pre-publication agreement between photographer and *Government Technology*. Pays on publication. Credit line given. Buys one-time rights, electronic rights.

TIPS "View samples of magazines for style, available online at www.govtech.com/gt/magazines."

GRAIN JOURNAL

Country Journal Publishing Co., 3065 Pershing Court, Decatur IL 62526. (800)728-7511. **E-mail:** ed@grainnet.com. **Website:** www.grainnet.com. **Contact:** Ed Zdrojewski, editor. Estab. 1972. Circ. 12,000. Bimonthly magazine. Emphasizes grain industry. Readers are "elevator and feed mill managers primarily, as well as suppliers and others in the industry." Sample copy free with #10 SASE.

NEEDS Uses about 1-2 photos/issue. "We need photos concerning industry practices and activities. We look for clear, high-quality images without a lot of extraneous material." Photo captions preferred.

SPECS Accepts images in digital format minimum 300 dpi resolution. Send via e-mail, floppy disk, ZIP.

MAKING CONTACT & TERMS Send query letter with samples and list of stock photo subjects. Responds in 1 week. Pays $100 for color cover; $30 for b&w inside. Pays on publication. Credit line given. Buys all rights; negotiable.

HARD HAT NEWS

Lee Publications, Inc., P.O. Box 121, Palatine Bridge NY 13428. (518)673-3763; (800)218-5586. **Fax:** (518)673-2381. **E-mail:** jcasey@leepub.com. **Website:** www.hardhat.com. **Contact:** Jon Casey, editor. Estab. 1980. Circ. 15,000. Biweekly trade newspaper for heavy construction. "Our readers are contractors and heavy construction workers involved in excavation, highways, bridges, utility construction, and underground construction." Readership includes owners, managers, senior construction trades. Photo guidelines available via e-mail only.

NEEDS Buys 12 photos from freelancers/issue; 280 photos/year. Specific photo needs: heavy construction in progress, construction people. Reviews photos with accompanying mss only. Property release preferred. Photo captions required.

SPECS Only high-res digital photographs. Send via e-mail as JPEG files at 300 dpi.

MAKING CONTACT & TERMS E-mail only. Simultaneous submissions OK. Pays on publication. Credit line given. Buys first rights.

TIPS "Include caption and brief explanation of what picture is about."

$ HEARTH AND HOME

P.O. Box 1288, Laconia NH 03247. (800)258-3772; (603)528-4285. **Fax:** (888)873-3610; (603)527-3404. **E-mail:** production@villagewest.com. **Website:** hearthandhome.com. **Contact:** Erica Paquette, art director. Circ. 16,000. Monthly magazine. Emphasizes hearth, barbecue and patio news and industry trends for specialty retailers and manufacturers of solid fuel and gas appliances, barbeque grills, hearth appliances inside and outside and casual furnishings. Sample copy available for $5.

NEEDS Buys 3 photos from freelancers/issue; 36 photos/year. Photos of inside and outside fireplace and patio furnishings, gas grills, outdoor room shots emphasizing BBQs, furniture, and outdoor fireplaces. Assignments available for conferences." Model release required. Photo captions preferred.

SPECS Accepts digital images with color proof; high-res, 300 dpi preferred.

MAKING CONTACT & TERMS Contact before submitting material. Responds in 2 weeks. Simultaneous and photocopied submissions OK. Pays within 30 days after publication prints. Credit line given. Buys various rights.

TIPS "Call first and ask what we need. We're *always* on the lookout for gorgeous outdoor room material."

$ HEREFORD WORLD

Hereford Cattle Association, P.O. Box 014059, Kansas City MO 64101. (816)842-3757. **Fax:** (816)842-6931. **E-mail:** lgraber@hereford.org. **Website:** www.herefordworld.org. **Contact:** Lindsay Graber, creative services coordinator. Estab. 1947. Circ. 5,600. Monthly (11 issues with 7 glossy issues) association magazine. Emphasizes Hereford cattle for registered breeders, commercial cattle breeders and agribusinessmen in related fields. A tabloid-type issue is produced 4 times—January, February, August and October—and mailed to an additional 20,000 commercial cattlemen. "We also publish a commercial edition with a circulation of 20,000."

NEEDS "*Hereford World* includes timely articles and editorial columns that provide readers information to help them make sound management and marketing decisions. From basic how-to articles to in-depth reports on cutting-edge technologies, *Hereford World* offers its readers a solid package of beef industry information."

SPECS Uses b&w and color prints.

MAKING CONTACT & TERMS Query. Responds in 2 weeks. Pays on publication.

TIPS Wants to see "Hereford cattle in quantities, in seasonal and scenic settings."

🍁 HPAC: HEATING PLUMBING AIR CONDITIONING

(416)510-5218. **Fax:** (416)510-5140. **E-mail:** smacisaac@hpacmag.com; kturner@hpacmag.com. **Website:** www.hpacmag.com. **Contact:** Sandy MacIsaac, art director; Kerry Turner, editor. Estab. 1923. Circ. 19,500. Bimonthly magazine plus annual buyers guide. Emphasizes heating, plumbing, air conditioning, refrigeration. Readers are predominantly male mechanical contractors, ages 30-60. Sample copy available for $4.

NEEDS Photos of mechanical contractors at work, site shots, product shots. Model/property release preferred. Photo captions preferred.

SPECS Images in digital format. E-mail as TIFF, JPEG files at 300 dpi minimum.

MAKING CONTACT & TERMS Pays on publication. Credit line given. Buys one-time rights; negotiable.

$$ ◐ IEEE SPECTRUM

3 Park Ave., New York NY 10016. (212)419-7555. **E-mail:** r.silberman@ieee.org. **Website:** www.spectrum.ieee.org. **Contact:** Randi Silberman Klett, photo editor. Circ. 375,000. Monthly magazine of the Institute of Electrical and Electronics Engineers, Inc. (IEEE). Emphasizes electrical and electronics field and high technology for technology innovators, business leaders, and the intellectually curious. Spectrum explores future technology trends and the impact of those trends on society and business. Readers are technology professionals and senior executives worldwide in the high technology sectors of industry, government, and academia. Subscribers include engineering managers and corporate and financial executives, deans and provosts at every major engineering university and college throughout the world; males/females, educated, ages 20-70.

NEEDS Uses 20-30 photos/issue. Purchases stock photos in following areas: technology, energy, medicine, military, sciences and business concepts. Hires assignment photographers for location shots and portraiture, as well as product shots. Model/property release required. Photo captions required.

SPECS Accepts images in digital format. Send via CD as TIFF, JPEG files at 300 dpi.

MAKING CONTACT & TERMS Provide promos or tearsheets to be kept on file for possible future assignments. Pays $1,200 for color cover; $200-600 for inside. **Pays on acceptance.** Credit line given. Buys one-time rights.

TIPS Wants photographers who are consistent, have an ability to shoot color and b&w, display a unique vision, and are receptive to their subjects. "As our subject matter is varied, *Spectrum* uses a variety of imagemakers."

IGA GROCERGRAM

8745 W. Higgins Rd., Suite 350, Chicago IL 60631. (773)693-5902. **E-mail:** apage@igainc.com. **Website:** www.iga.com/igagrocergram.aspx. **Contact:** Ashley Page, communications. Quarterly magazine of the Independent Grocers Alliance. This comprehensive quarterly magazine—which evolved from the monthly that has chronicled the Alliance since its birth in 1926—is published in 4 seasonal editions each year and distributed to a worldwide audience. The glossy keep-sake issues profile IGA and its members through in-depth stories featuring stimulating interviews and informative analyses. Emphasizes food industry. Readers are IGA retailers. Sample copy available upon request.

NEEDS Needs in-store shots, food (appetite appeal). Prefers shots of IGA stores. Model/property release required. Photo captions required.

SPECS Accepts images in digital format. Send as TIFF files at 300 dpi.

MAKING CONTACT & TERMS Send samples by e-mail or link to website for consideration. Provide résumé, business card, brochure, flyer or tearsheets to be kept on file for possible future assignments. Keeps samples on file. Responds in 3 weeks. Simultaneous submissions and previously published work OK. Pay negotiable. **Pays on acceptance.** Credit line given. Buys one-time rights.

INDEPENDENT RESTAURATEUR

P.O. Box 917, Newark OH 43058. (740)345-5542. **Fax:** (740)345-5557. **E-mail:** editor@theindependentrestaurateur.com; jim@theindependentrestaurateur.com. **Website:** www.theindependentrestaurateur.com. **Contact:** Jim Young, publisher. Estab. 1986. Circ. 32,000.

NEEDS Upon request.

SPECS Accepts images in digital format only. Send via CD, e-mail as JPEG files at 300-800 dpi.

MAKING CONTACT & TERMS Send e-mail. Provide self-promotion piece to be kept on file for possible future assignments. Responds only if interested; send nonreturnable samples. Simultaneous submissions OK. Pay is based on experience. Pays on publication. Credit line given. Buys first rights.

JOURNAL OF ADVENTIST EDUCATION

12501 Old Columbia Pike, Silver Spring MD 20904-6600. (301)680-5069. **Fax:** (301)622-9627. **E-mail:** goffc@gc.adventist.org. **Website:** jae.adventist.org. **Contact:** Faith-Ann McGarrell, editor. Estab. 1939. Circ. 14,000 in English; 13,000 in other languages. Published 5 times/year in English, 2 times/year in French, Spanish and Portuguese. Emphasizes procedures, philosophy and subject matter of Christian education. Official professional organization of the Department of Education covering elementary, secondary and higher education for all Seventh-day Adventist educational personnel (worldwide).

NEEDS Buys 5-15 photos from freelancers/issue; up to 75 photos/year. Photos of children/teens, multicultural, parents, education, religious, health/fitness, technology/computers with people, committees, offices, school photos of teachers, students, parents, activities at all levels, elementary though graduate school. Reviews photos with or without a ms. Model release preferred. Photo captions preferred.

SPECS Uses mostly digital color images but also accepts color prints; 35mm, 2¼×2¼, 4×5 transparencies. Send digital photos via ZIP, CD or DVD (preferred); e-mail as TIFF, GIF, JPEG files at 300 dpi. Do not send large numbers of photos as e-mail attachments.

MAKING CONTACT & TERMS Send query letter with prints, photocopies, transparencies. Provide self-promotion piece to be kept on file for possible future assignments. Responds in 1 month to queries. Simultaneous submissions and previously published work OK. Pays $100-350 for color cover; $50-100 for color inside. Willing to negotiate on electronic usage of photos. Pays on publication. Credit line given. Buys one-time rights for use in magazine and on website.

TIPS "Get good-quality people shots—close-ups, verticals especially; use interesting props in classroom shots; include teacher and students together, teachers in groups, parents and teachers, cooperative learning and multiage, multicultural children. Pay attention to backgrounds (not too busy) and understand the need for high-res photos!"

JOURNAL OF PSYCHOACTIVE DRUGS

856 Stanyan St., San Francisco CA 94117. (415)752-7601. **E-mail:** hajpdeditor@comcast.net; hajournal@comcast.net. **Website:** www.hajpd.com. Estab. 1967. Circ. 1,400. Quarterly. Emphasizes "psychoactive substances (both legal and illegal)." Readers are "professionals (primarily health) in the drug abuse treatment field."

NEEDS Uses 1 photo/issue; supplied by freelancers. Needs "full-color abstract, surreal, avant garde or computer graphics."

MAKING CONTACT & TERMS Send query letter with 4×6 color prints or 35mm slides. Online and e-mail submissions are accepted. Include SASE for return of material. Responds in 2 weeks. Simultaneous submissions and previously published work OK. Pays $50 for color cover. Pays on publication. Credit line given. Buys one-time rights.

THE LAND

Free Press Co., P.O. Box 3169, Mankato MN 56002-3169. (507)345-4523. **E-mail:** editor@thelandonline.com. **Website:** www.thelandonline.com. Estab. 1976. Circ. 33,000. Weekly tabloid covering farming and rural life in Minnesota and Northern Iowa.

SPECS Reviews contact sheets.

MAKING CONTACT & TERMS Negotiates payment individually. Buys one-time rights.

LANDSCAPE ARCHITECTURE

636 Eye St. NW, Washington DC 20001-3736. (888)999-2752; (202)898-2444. **Fax:** (202)898-1185. **E-mail:** lspeckhardt@asla.org. **Website:** www.asla.org. Estab. 1910. Circ. 22,000. Monthly magazine of the American Society of Landscape Architects. Emphasizes "landscape architecture, urban design, parks and recreation, architecture, sculpture" for professional planners and designers.

NEEDS Buys 5-10 photos from freelancers/issue; 50-120 photos/year. Needs photos of landscape- and architecture-related subjects as described above. Special needs include aerial photography and environmental portraits. Model release required. Credit, caption information required.

MAKING CONTACT & TERMS Send query letter with samples or list of stock photo subjects. Provide brochure, flyer or tearsheets to be kept on file for possible future assignments. Response time varies. Previ-

ously published work OK. Pays on publication. Credit line given. Buys one-time rights.

THE MANITOBA TEACHER

191 Harcourt St., Winnipeg Manitoba R3J 3H2, Canada. (204)888-7961; (800)262-8803. **Fax:** (204)831-0877; (800)665-0584. **E-mail:** gstephenson@mbteach.org. **Website:** www.mbteach.org. **Contact:** George Stephenson, editor. Magazine of the Manitoba Teachers' Society published 7 times/year. Emphasizes education in Manitoba—specifically teachers' interests. Readers are teachers and others in education. Sample copy free with 10×12 SASE and Canadian stamps.

NEEDS Buys 3 photos from freelancers/issue; 21 photos/year. Needs action shots of students and teachers in education-related settings. Model release required.

MAKING CONTACT & TERMS Send 8×10 glossy b&w prints by mail for consideration; include SASE for return of material. Submit portfolio for review. Provide résumé, business card, brochure, flyer or tearsheets to be kept on file for possible future assignments. Responds in 1 month.

TIPS "Always submit action shots directly related to major subject matter of publication and interests of readership."

MANUFACTURING AUTOMATION

Annex Publishing and Printing, 222 Edward St., Aurora Ontario L4G 1W6, Canada. (905)727-0077 or (905)713-4378. **E-mail:** editor@automationmag.com. **Website:** www.automationmag.com. **Contact:** Mary Del Ciancio, editor. Estab. 1998. Circ. 19,020. Published seven times a year, providing a window into the world of advanced manufacturing and industrial automation. Sample copies available for SASE with first-class postage.

NEEDS Occasionally buys photos from freelancers. Subjects include industry and technology. Reviews photos with or without a manuscript. Model release required. Photo captions preferred.

SPECS Uses 5×7 color prints; 4×5 transparencies. "We prefer images in high-res digital format. Send as FTP files at a minimum of 300 dpi."

MAKING CONTACT & TERMS Send query letter with résumé, stock list. Provide self-promotion piece to be kept on file for possible future assignments. Responds only if interested. Simultaneous submissions and previously published work OK. Pays $400-600 for color cover and inside images. Pays 30-45 days after invoice date. Credit line given. Buys one-time rights, electronic rights; negotiable.

TIPS "Read our magazine. Put yourself in your clients' shoes. Meet their needs and you will excel. Understand your audience and the editors' needs. Meet deadlines, be reasonable and professional."

😊😊 🌓 MARKETING & TECHNOLOGY GROUP

1415 N. Dayton, Chicago IL 60622. (312)274-2216. **E-mail:** qburns@mtgmediagroup.com. **Website:** www.meatingplace.com. **Contact:** Queenie Burns, vice president of design and production. Estab. 1993. Circ. 18,000. Publishes magazines that emphasize meat and poultry processing. Readers are predominantly male, ages 35-65, generally conservative. Sample copy available for $4.

NEEDS Buys 1-6 photos from freelancers/issue. Needs photos of processing plant tours and product shots. Model/property release preferred. Photo captions preferred.

MAKING CONTACT & TERMS Provide résumé, business card, brochure, flyer or tearsheets to be kept on file for possible future assignments. Submit portfolio for review. Keeps samples on file. Responds in 1 month. Simultaneous submissions and previously published work OK. Payment negotiable. Pays on publication. Credit line given.

TIPS "Work quickly and meet deadlines. Follow directions when given; and when none are given, be creative while using your best judgment."

◑ 🌓 MEETINGS & INCENTIVE TRAVEL

(416)442-5600, ext. 3239; (416)764-1635. **E-mail:** lsmith@meetingscanada.com. **Website:** www.meetingscanada.com. **Contact:** Lori Smith, editor. Estab. 1970. Circ. 10,500. Bimonthly trade magazine emphasizing meetings and travel.

NEEDS Buys 1-5 photos from freelancers/issue; 7-30 photos/year. Needs photos of environmental, landscapes/scenics, cities/urban, interiors/decorating, events, food/drink, travel, business concepts, technology/computers. Reviews photos with or without a manuscript. Model/property release required. Photo captions required; include location and date.

SPECS Uses 8×12 prints depending on shoot and size of photo in magazine. Accepts images in digital format. Send via CD as TIFF files at 300 dpi.

MAKING CONTACT & TERMS Contact through rep or send query letter with tearsheets. Portfolio may be dropped off every Tuesday. Provide résumé, business card, self-promotion piece to be kept on file for possible future assignments. Responds only if interested; send nonreturnable samples. Simultaneous submissions and previously published work OK. "Payment depends on many factors." Credit line given. Buys one-time rights.

TIPS "Send samples to keep on file."

MIDWEST MEETINGS®

Hennen Publishing, 302 Sixth St. W, Brookings SD 57006. (605)692-9559. **Fax:** (605)692-9031. **E-mail:** info@midwestmeetings.com; editor@midwestmeetings.com. **Website:** www.midwestmeetings.com. **Contact:** Randy Hennen. Estab. 1996. Circ. 28,500. We provide information and resources to meeting/convention planners with a Midwest focus.

MAKING CONTACT & TERMS Reviews JPEG/EPS/TIF files (300 dpi). Captions, identification of subjects and permission statements/photo releases required. Offers no additional payment for photos accepted with ms. Buys one time rights.

💲 MILITARY OFFICER MAGAZINE

201 N. Washington St., Alexandria VA 22314. (800)234-6622. **E-mail:** editor@moaa.org. **Website:** www.moaa.org/militaryofficer. **Contact:** Jill Akers, photo editor. Estab. 1945. Circ. 400,000. Monthly publication of the Military Officers Association of America. Represents the interests of military officers from the 7 uniformed services: Army, Navy, Air Force, Marine Corps, Coast Guard, Public Health Service and National Oceanic and Atmospheric Administration. Emphasizes military history (particularly Vietnam and Korea), travel, health, second-career job opportunities, military family lifestyle and current military/political affairs. Readers are commissioned officers or warrant officers and their families. Sample copy available on request with 9×12 SASE.

NEEDS Buys 8 photos from freelancers/issue; 96 photos/year. "We're always looking for good color images of active-duty military people and healthy, active mature adults with a young 50s look—our readers are 55-65."

SPECS Uses digital images as well as 2¼×2¼ or 4×5 transparencies. Send digital images via e-mail as JPEG files at 300 dpi.

MAKING CONTACT & TERMS Send query letter with list of stock photo subjects. Provide résumé, brochure, flyer to be kept on file. "Do NOT send original photos unless requested to do so." Payment negotiated. "Photo rates vary with size and position." Pays on publication. Credit line given. Buys one-time rights. Pays $75 for ⅛ page; $125 for ¼ page; $175 for ½ page; $250 for full page. 5×7 or 8×10 b&w glossies occasionally acceptable. $20 for each b&w photo used. captions and credit lines should be on separate sheets of paper. Include SASE for return. Submission guidelines available online.

⊖⊛ ◑ NAILPRO

Creative Age Publications, 7628 Densmore Ave., Van Nuys CA 91406. (800)442-5667; (818)782-7328. **Fax:** (818)782-7450. **E-mail:** nailpro@creativeage. com. **Website:** www.nailpro.com. **Contact:** Stephanie Yaggy, executive editor. Estab. 1989. Circ. 65,000. Monthly magazine published by Creative Age Publications. Emphasizes topics for professional manicurists and nail salon owners. Readers are females of all ages. Sample copy available for $2 with 9×12 SASE.
NEEDS Buys 10-12 photos from freelancers/issue; 120-144 photos/year. Needs photos of beautiful nails illustrating all kinds of nail extensions and enhancements; photographs showing process of creating and decorating nails, both natural and artificial. Also needs salon interiors, health/fitness, fashion/glamour. Model release required. Photo captions required; identify people and process if applicable.
SPECS Accepts images in digital format. Send via ZIP, e-mail as TIFF, EPS files at 300 dpi or better.
MAKING CONTACT & TERMS Send query letter; responds only if interested. Call for portfolio review. "Art directors are rarely available, but photographers can leave materials and pick up later (or leave nonreturnable samples)." Send color prints; 35mm, 2¼×2¼, 4×5 transparencies. Keeps samples on file. Responds in 1 month. Previously published work OK. Pays $500 for color cover; $50-250 for color inside.
TIPS "Talk to the person in charge of choosing art about photo needs for the next issue and try to satisfy that immediate need; that often leads to assignments. Submit samples and portfolios with letter stating specialties or strong points."

⊛ NAILS MAGAZINE

Bobit Business Media, 3520 Challenger St., Torrance CA 90503. (310)533-2400 (main); (310)533-2537 (art director). **Fax:** (310)533-2507. **E-mail:** danielle.parisi@bobit.com. **Website:** www.nailsmag.com. **Contact:** Danielle Parisi, art director. Estab. 1982. Circ.

60,000. Monthly trade publication for nail technicians and beauty salon owners. Sample copies available.
NEEDS Buys up to 10 photos from freelancers/issue. Needs photos of celebrities, buildings, historical/vintage. Other specific photo needs: salon interiors, product shots, celebrity nail photos. Reviews photos with or without a ms. Model release required. Photo captions preferred.
SPECS Uses 35mm transparencies. Accepts images in digital format. Send via CD, Zip as TIFF, EPS files at 266 dpi.
MAKING CONTACT & TERMS Send query letter with résumé, slides, prints. Keep samples on file. Responds in 1 month on queries. **Pays on acceptance.** Credit line sometimes given if it's requested. Buys all rights.

⊖⊛ THE NATIONAL NOTARY

9350 De Soto Ave., Chatsworth CA 91311-4926. (800)876-6827. **E-mail:** publications@nationalnotary.org. **Website:** www.nationalnotary.org. Circ. 300,000+. Bimonthly association magazine. Emphasizes "Notaries Public and notarization—goal is to impart knowledge, understanding and unity among notaries nationwide and internationally." Readers are employed primarily in the following areas: law, government, finance and real estate.
NEEDS Number of photos purchased varies with each issue. "Photo subject depends on accompanying story/theme; some product shots used." Reviews photos with accompanying manuscript only. Model release required.
MAKING CONTACT & TERMS Send query letter with samples. Provide business card, tearsheets, résumé or samples to be kept on file for possible future assignments. Prefers to see prints as samples. Cannot return material. Previously published work OK. Pays on publication. Credit line given "with editor's approval of quality." Buys all rights.
TIPS "Since photography is often the art of a story, the photographer must understand the story to be able to produce the most useful photographs."

⊛ ⊕ ◑ NAVAL HISTORY

US Naval Institute, 291 Wood Rd., Annapolis MD 21402. (410)295-1048. **Fax:** (410)295-1049. **E-mail:** avoight@usni.org. **Website:** www.usni.org/magazines/navalhistory. **Contact:** Amy Voight, photo editor. Estab. 1873. Circ. 50,000. Bimonthly association publication. Emphasizes Navy, Marine Corps, Coast Guard. Readers are male and female naval officers (enlisted, retirees), civilians. Photo guidelines free with SASE.

NEEDS Needs 40 photos from freelancers/issue; 240 photos/year. Needs photos of foreign and US Naval, Coast Guard and Marine Corps vessels, industry, military, personnel and aircraft. Interested in historical/vintage. Photo captions required.

SPECS Uses 8×10 glossy or matte b&w and color prints (color preferred); transparencies. Accepts images in digital format. Send via CD, ZIP, e-mail as JPEG files at 300 dpi.

MAKING CONTACT & TERMS "We prefer to receive photo images digitally. We accept cross-platform (must be Mac and PC compatible) CDs with CMYK images at 300 dpi resolution (TIFF or JPEG). If e-mailing an image, send submissions to photo editor. We do not return prints or slides unless specified with a SASE, so please do not send original photographs. We negotiate fees with photographers who provide a volume of images for publication in books or as magazine pictorials. We sponsor 3 annual photo contests." For additional information please contact the photo editor. Responds in 1 month. Simultaneous submissions and previously published work OK. Pays on publication. Credit line given. Buys one-time and electronic rights.

$ NEVADA FARM BUREAU AGRICULTURE AND LIVESTOCK JOURNAL

2165 Green Vista Dr., Suite 205, Sparks NV 89431. (775)674-4000; (800)992-1106. **E-mail:** zacha@nvfb.org. **Website:** www.nvfb.org. **Contact:** Zach Allen, editor. Circ. 1,500. Monthly magazine. Emphasizes Nevada agriculture. Readers are primarily Nevada Farm Bureau members and their families; men, women and youth of various ages. Members are farmers and ranchers. Sample copy free with 10×13 SASE with 3 first-class stamps.

NEEDS Uses 5 photos/issue; 30% occasionally supplied by freelancers. Needs photos of Nevada agriculture people, scenes and events. Model release preferred. Photo captions required.

MAKING CONTACT & TERMS Send 3×5 and larger b&w or color prints, any format and finish, by mail with SASE for consideration. Responds in 1 week. Pays $10 for b&w cover, $50 for color cover; $5 for b&w inside. **Pays on acceptance.** Credit line given. Buys one-time rights.

TIPS In portfolio or samples, wants to see "newsworthiness, 50%; good composition, 20%; interesting action, 20%; photo contrast/resolution, 10%. Try for new angles on stock shots: awards, speakers, etc. We like 'Great Basin' agricultural scenery such as cows on the rangelands and high desert cropping. We pay little, but we offer credits for your résumé."

🌐 $ ◐ NEWDESIGN

Media Culture 46 Pure Offices, Plate Close Leamington Spa, Warwick, Warwickshire CV34 6WE, United Kingdom. +44 (0)1926 671338. **E-mail:** info@newdesignmagazine.co.uk; tanya@newdesignmagazine.co.uk. **Website:** www.newdesignmagazine.co.uk. Estab. 2000. Circ. 5,000. Published 10 times/year. Emphasizes product design for product designers: informative, inspirational. Sample copies available.

NEEDS Photos of product shots/still life, technology. Reviews photos with or without a manuscript.

SPECS Uses glossy color prints; 35mm transparencies. Accepts images in digital format. Send via CD as TIFF, JPEG files at 300 dpi.

MAKING CONTACT & TERMS Send query letter with résumé. Provide self-promotion piece to be kept on file for possible future assignments. Cannot return material. Responds only if interested; send nonreturnable samples. Pays on publication. Credit line given.

NFPA JOURNAL

1 Batterymarch Park, Quincy MA 02169-7471. (617) 770-3000; (617)984-7568. **E-mail:** ssutherland@nfpa.org. **Website:** www.nfpa.org. **Contact:** Scott Sutherland, executive editor. Circ. 85,000. Bimonthly magazine of the National Fire Protection Association. Emphasizes fire and life safety information. Readers are fire professionals, engineers, architects, building code officials, ages 20-65. Sample copy free with 9×12 SASE or via e-mail.

NEEDS Buys 5-7 photos from freelancers/issue; 30-42 photos/year. Needs photos of fires and fire-related incidents. Model release preferred. Photo captions preferred.

MAKING CONTACT & TERMS Send query letter with list of stock photo subjects. Provide résumé, business card, brochure, flyer or tearsheets to be kept on file for possible future assignments. Send color prints and 35mm transparencies in 3-ring slide sleeve with date. Responds in 3 weeks. Payment negotiated. Pays on publication. Credit line given.

TIPS "Send cover letter, 35mm color slides, preferably with manuscripts and photo captions."

☺ NORTHWEST TERRITORIES EXPLORER'S GUIDE

P.O. Box 610, Yellowknife Northwest Territories X1A 2N5, Canada. (867)873-5007; (800)661-0788. **Fax:** (867)873-4059. **E-mail:** info@spectacularnwt.com. **Website:** www.spectacularnwt.com. Estab. 1996. Circ. 90,000. Annual tourism publication for Northwest Territories. Sample copies available.

NEEDS Photos of babies/children/teens, couples, multicultural, families, senior citizens, landscapes/ scenics, wildlife, adventure, automobiles, events, travel. Interested in historical/vintage, seasonal. Also needs photos of Northwest Territories, winter and road touring.

SPECS Uses 35mm transparencies.

MAKING CONTACT & TERMS Send query letter with résumé, slides, prints, photocopies, tearsheets, transparencies, stock list. Portfolio may be dropped off Monday–Saturday. Provide résumé, business card, self-promotion piece to be kept on file for possible future assignments. Responds in 1 week to queries. Simultaneous submissions OK. **Pays on acceptance.**

☺ ⑤ THE ONTARIO TECHNOLOGIST

10 Four Seasons Place, Suite 404, Etobicoke Ontario M9B 6H7, Canada. (416)621-9621. **Fax:** (416)621-8694. **E-mail:** editor@oacett.org. **Website:** www.oacett.org. Circ. 24,000. Bimonthly publication of the Ontario Association of Certified Engineering Technicians and Technologists. Emphasizes engineering and applied science technology. Sample copy free with SASE and IRC.

NEEDS Uses 10-12 photos/issue. Needs how-to photos—"building and installation of equipment; similar technical subjects." Model release preferred. Photo captions preferred.

MAKING CONTACT & TERMS Prefers business card and brochure for files. Send high-res digital images at 300 dpi for consideration. Responds in 1 month. Previously published work OK. Credit line given.

⑤⑤ ☻ PEDIATRIC ANNALS

6900 Grove Rd., Thorofare NJ 08086. (856)848-1000. **Fax:** (856)848-6091. **E-mail:** pedann@healio.com. **Website:** www.healio.com/pediatrics/journals/Ped Ann. Monthly journal. Readers are practicing pediatricians. Sample copy free with SASE.

NEEDS Uses 5-7 photos/issue; primarily stock. Occasionally uses original photos of children in medical settings.

SPECS Color photos preferred. Accepts images in digital format. Send as EPS, JPEG files at 300 dpi.

MAKING CONTACT & TERMS Request editorial calendar for topic suggestions. E-mail query with links to samples. Simultaneous submissions and previously published work OK. Pays varies; negotiable. Pays on publication. Credit line given. Buys unlimited North American rights including any and all subsidiary forms of publication, such as electronic media and promotional pieces.

☻ ⑤ ◐ PEOPLE MANAGEMENT

151 The Broadway London, London SW19 1JQ, United Kingdom. **E-mail:** pmeditorial@haymarket.com. **Website:** www.peoplemanagement.co.uk. **Contact:** Rob MacLachlan, editor. Circ. 120,000. Official publication of the Chartered Institute of Personnel and Development. Biweekly trade journal for professionals in personnel, training and development.

NEEDS Photos of industry, medicine. Interested in alternative process, documentary. Reviews photos with or without a manuscript. Model release preferred. Photo captions preferred.

SPECS Accepts images in digital format. Send via CD, Jaz, ZIP, e-mail, ISDN as TIFF, EPS, JPEG files at 300 dpi.

MAKING CONTACT & TERMS Send query letter with samples. To show portfolio, photographer should follow-up with call. Portfolio should include b&w prints, slides, transparencies. Keeps samples on file. Responds only if interested; send nonreturnable samples. Pays on publication. Rights negotiable.

⑤ ◐ PET PRODUCT NEWS

BowTie, Inc., P.O. Box 6050, Mission Viejo CA 92690-6040. (949)855-8822. **Fax:** (949)855-3045. **E-mail:** erothrock@i5publishing.com. **Website:** www.pet productnews.com. **Contact:** Ellyce Rothrock, editor. Monthly B2B tabloid. Emphasizes pets and the pet retail business. Readers are pet store owners and managers. Sample copy available for $5. Photo guidelines upon request via e-mail.

NEEDS Buys 5-10 photos from freelancers/issue; 60-120 photos/year. Needs photos of retailers interacting with customers and pets, pet stores and pet product displays. Also needs wildlife, events, industry, product shots/still life. Interested in seasonal. Reviews photos with or without a manuscript. Model/property release preferred. "Enclose a shipment description with each set of photos detailing the type of animal, name of pet store, names of well-known subjects and any procedures being performed on an animal that are not self-explanatory."

SPECS Accepts images in digital format only. Send via CD, ZIP, e-mail as TIFF, EPS, JPEG files at 300 dpi.

MAKING CONTACT & TERMS "We cannot assume responsibility for submitted material, but care is taken with all work. Freelancers must include a SASE for returned work." Send sharp 35mm color slides or prints by mail for consideration. Responds in 2 months. Previously published work OK. Pays $75 for cover; $50 for inside. Pays on publication. Photographer also receives 1 complimentary copy of issue in which their work appears. Credit line given; name and identification of subject must appear on each image. Buys one-time rights.

TIPS Looks for "appropriate subjects, clarity and framing, sensitivity to the subject. No avant garde or special effects. We need clear, straight-forward photography. Definitely no 'staged' photos; keep it natural. Read the magazine before submission. We are a trade publication and need business-like, but not boring, photos that will add to our subjects."

THE PHOTO REVIEW

140 E. Richardson Ave., Suite 301, Langhorne PA 19047. (215)891-0214. **Fax:** (215)891-9358. **E-mail:** info@photoreview.org. **Website:** www.photoreview.org. Estab. 1976. Circ. 2,000. "*The Photo Review* publishes critical reviews of photography exhibitions and books, critical essays, and interviews. We do not publish how-to or technical articles."

MAKING CONTACT & TERMS Reviews electronic images. Captions required. Offers no additional payment for photos accepted with ms. Buys all rights.

⊖⊖ PLANNING

American Planning Association, 205 N. Michigan Ave., Suite 1200, Chicago IL 60601. (312)431-9100. **Fax:** (312)786-6700. **E-mail:** slewis@planning.org. **Website:** www.planning.org. **Contact:** Sylvia Lewis, editor; Joan Cairney, art director. Estab. 1972. Circ. 44,000. Monthly magazine. "We focus on urban and regional planning, reaching most of the nation's professional planners and others interested in the topic." Published 11 times a year.

NEEDS Buys 4-5 photos from freelancers/issue; 60 photos/year. Photos purchased with accompanying manuscript and on assignment. Photo essay/photo feature (architecture, neighborhoods, historic preservation, agriculture); scenic (mountains, wilderness, rivers, oceans, lakes); housing; transportation (cars, railroads, trolleys, highways). "No cheesecake; no sentimental shots of dogs, children, etc. High artistic quality is very important. We publish high-quality nonfiction stories on city planning and land use. Ours is an association magazine but not a house organ, and we use the standard journalistic techniques: interviews, anecdotes, quotes. Topics include energy, the environment, housing, transportation, land use, agriculture, neighborhoods and urban affairs." Photo captions required.

SPECS Accepts images in digital format. Send via ZIP, CD as TIFF, EPS, JPEG files at 300 dpi and around 5×7 in physical size.

MAKING CONTACT & TERMS Send query letter with samples; include SASE for return of material. Responds in 1 month. Previously published work OK. Pays on publication. Credit line given.

TIPS "Subject lists are only minimally useful. How the work looks is of paramount importance. Your best chance is to send addresses for your website showing samples of your work. We no longer keep paper on file. If we like your style we will commission work from you."

⊖ PLASTICS NEWS

1155 Gratiot, Detroit MI 48207-2997. (313)446-6000. **E-mail:** dloepp@crain.com. **Website:** www.plasticsnews.com. **Contact:** Don Loepp, editor. Estab. 1989. Circ. 45,000. Weekly tabloid. Emphasizes plastics industry business news. Readers are male and female executives of companies that manufacture a broad range of plastics products; suppliers and customers of the plastics processing industry. Sample copy available for $1.95.

NEEDS Buys 1-3 photos from freelancers/issue; 52-156 photos/year. Needs photos of technology related to use and manufacturing of plastic products. Model/property release preferred. Photo captions required.

MAKING CONTACT & TERMS Send unsolicited photos by mail for consideration. Provide résumé, business card, brochure, flyer or tearsheets to be kept on file for possible future assignments. Send query letter with stock list. Keeps samples on file; include SASE for return of material. Responds in 2 weeks. Simultaneous submissions and previously published work OK. Pays $125-175 for color cover; $100-150 for b&w inside; $125-175 for color inside. Pays on publication. Credit line given. Buys one-time and all rights.

🟢🟢🟢 🅾 PLASTICS TECHNOLOGY

6915 Valley Ave., Cincinnati OH 45244. (513)527-8800, (800)950-8020. **Fax:** (646)827-4859. **E-mail:** sbriggs@gardnerweb.com. **Website:** www.ptonline.com. **Contact:** Sheri Briggs, art director. Estab. 1954. Circ. 50,000. Monthly trade magazine. Sample copy available for first-class postage.

NEEDS Buys 1-3 photos/issue. Needs photos of agriculture, business concepts, industry, science, technology. Model release required. Photo captions required.
SPECS Accepts images in digital format. Send via e-mail as TIFF, EPS, JPEG files at 300 dpi.
MAKING CONTACT & TERMS Send query letter with résumé, photocopies, tearsheets. Provide business card, self-promotion piece to be kept on file for possible future assignments. Responds only if interested; send nonreturnable samples. Simultaneous submissions OK. Pays $1,000-1,300 for color cover; $300 minimum for color inside. Pays on publication. Credit line given. Buys one-time rights, all rights; negotiable.

POETS & WRITERS MAGAZINE

90 Broad St., Suite 2100, New York NY 10004. (212)226-3586. **E-mail:** editor@pw.org. **Website:** www.pw.org/magazine. **Contact:** Kevin Larimer, editor. Estab. 1987. Circ. 60,000. Bimonthly literary trade magazine. "We offer poets and literary prose writers in-depth information about the publishing industry, details about writers conferences and workshops, practical advice about how to get published, essays about the writing life, listings of grants and awards available to writers, as well as interviews and profiles of contemporary authors."

NEEDS Needs photos of contemporary writers: poets, fiction writers, writers of creative nonfiction. Photo captions required.
SPECS Digital format.
MAKING CONTACT & TERMS Provide URL, self-promotion piece or tearsheets to be kept on file for possible future assignments. Pays on publication. Credit line given.

POLICE AND SECURITY NEWS

DAYS Communications, Inc., 1208 Juniper St., Quakertown PA 18951-1520. (215)538-1240. **Fax:** (215)538-1208. **E-mail:** dyaw@policeandsecuritynews.com. **Website:** www.policeandsecuritynews.com. **Contact:** David Yaw, publisher. Estab. 1984. Circ. 24,000. Bimonthly trade journal. "*Police and Security News* is edited for middle and upper management and top administration. Editorial content is a combination of articles and columns ranging from the latest in technology, innovative managerial concepts, training, and industry news in the areas of both public law enforcement and Homeland security." Sample copy free with 13×10" SASE and $2.24 first-class postage.

NEEDS Buys 2 photos from freelancers/issue; 12 photos/year. Needs photos of law enforcement and security related. Reviews photos with or without a manuscript. Photo captions preferred.
SPECS Uses color and b&w prints.
MAKING CONTACT & TERMS Provide résumé, business card, self-promotion piece or tearsheets to be kept on file for possible future assignments. Art director will contact photographer for portfolio review if interested. Portfolio should include b&w and/or color prints or tearsheets. Keeps samples on file; include SASE for return of material. Simultaneous submissions and previously published work OK. Pays $20-40 for color inside. Pays on publication. Credit line given. Buys one-time rights; negotiable.

🟢 🅾 POLICE TIMES/CHIEF OF POLICE

6350 Horizon Dr., Titusville FL 32780. (321)264-0911. **E-mail:** peterc@aphf.org. **Website:** www.aphf.org. **Contact:** Peter Connolly, publications editor. Circ. *Police Times*: quarterly trade magazine (circ. 155,000); *Chief of Police*: bimonthly trade magazine (circ. 33,000). Readers are law enforcement officers at all levels. *Police Times* is the official journal of the American Federation of Police and Concerned Citizens. Sample copy available for $2.50. Photo guidelines free with SASE.

NEEDS Buys 60-90 photos/year. Needs photos of police officers in action, civilian volunteers working with the police, and group shots of police department personnel. Wants no photos that promote other associations. Police-oriented cartoons also accepted on spec. Model release preferred. Photo captions preferred.
MAKING CONTACT & TERMS Send glossy b&w and color prints for consideration; include SASE for

return of material. Responds in 3 weeks. Simultaneous submissions and previously published work OK. **Pays on acceptance.** Credit line given if requested; editor's option. Buys all rights, but may reassign to photographer after publication; includes online publication rights.

TIPS "We are open to new and unknowns in small communities where police are not given publicity."

PONDS USA AND WATER GARDENS

BowTie, Inc., P.O. Box 6050, Mission Viejo CA 92690. (949)855-8822. **Fax:** (949)855-3045. **E-mail:** ponds@bowtieinc.com. **Website:** www.pondsmagazine.com. **Contact:** Patricia Knight, editor. Estab. 1998. Annual consumer magazine. *Ponds USA* publishes articles about various subjects, focusing on setup and maintenance of ponds (including plants and fish) and the pondkeeping lifestyle (stress relief, water gardening, etc.). Photography submission guidelines are free with SASE or via e-mail. Buys stock photos only. Accepts outstanding work from beginning and established photographers; expects a high level of professionalism from all photographers who make contact. Purchases 60 photos a year.

SPECS Reviews photos with or without a manuscript. Accepts images in digital format on CD as TIFF or JPEG files as 300 dpi. Images must be at least 5×7 print size at 300 dpi. Please see our photo guidelines before submitting. Responds to queries in 1 week. Varies for submissions. Finds freelancers through submissions.

MAKING CONTACT & TERMS Send a query letter via SASE or e-mail.

TIPS "We prefer photos of ponds that are well-cared-for (not a lot of algae, etc.). We also take photos of water features (pondless). Please read our guidelines before submitting."

🔂 💲 ⭕ PROCEEDINGS

U.S. Naval Institute, 291 Wood Rd., Annapolis MD 21402-5034. (410)268-6110. **Fax:** (410)571-1703. **E-mail:** articlesubmissions@usni.org. **Website:** www.usni.org/magazines/proceedings. **Contact:** Paul M. Merzlak, editor in chief; Emily Martin, photo researcher. Estab. 1873. Circ. 60,000. Monthly trade magazine dedicated to providing an open forum for national defense. Sample copy available online. Photo guidelines on website.

NEEDS Buys 10 photos from freelancers/issue; 120 photos/year. Needs photos of industry, military, political. Model release preferred. Photo captions required;

include time, location, subject matter, service represented—if necessary.

SPECS Uses glossy color prints. Prefers images in digital format. Send via CD, ZIP as TIFF, JPEG files at 300 dpi.

MAKING CONTACT & TERMS Send query letter with résumé, prints. Does not keep samples on file; include SASE for return of material. Responds only if interested; send nonreturnable samples. Simultaneous submissions and previously published work OK. Pays $200 for color cover; $25-50 for color inside. Pays on publication. Credit line given. Buys one-time and sometimes electronic rights.

TIPS "We look for original work. The best place to get a feel for our imagery is to see our magazine or look at our website."

◎ 💲 PRODUCE RETAILER

Vance Publishing Corp., 10901 W. 84th Ter., Suite 200, Lenexa KS 66214. (913)438-0603; (512)906-0733. **E-mail:** pamelar@produceretailer.com; treyes@produceretailer.com. **Website:** produceretailer.com. **Contact:** Pamela Riemenschneider, editor; Tony Reyes, art director. Estab. 1988. Circ. 12,000. Monthly magazine, e-mail newsletters, and online. Emphasizes the retail end of the fresh produce industry. Readers are male and female executives who oversee produce operations in US and Canadian supermarkets as well as in-store produce department personnel. Sample copies available.

NEEDS Buys 2-5 photos from freelancers/issue; 24-60 photos/year. Needs in-store shots, environmental portraits for cover photos or display pictures. "Photo captions required; include subject's name, job title and company title—all verified and correctly spelled."

SPECS Accepts images in digital format. Send via e-mail as TIFF, JPEG files.

MAKING CONTACT & TERMS E-mail only. Response time "depends on when we will be in a specific photographer's area and have a need." Pays $500-750 for color cover; $25-50/color photo. **Pays on acceptance.** Credit line given. Buys all rights.

TIPS "We seek photographers who serve as our on-site 'art director' to ensure capture of creative angles and quality images."

PROFESSIONAL PHOTOGRAPHER

Professional Photographers of America, 229 Peachtree St. NE, Suite 2200, International Tower, Atlanta GA 30303. (404)522-8600, ext. 260. **Fax:** (404)614-6406.

E-mail: jgaboury@ppa.com. **Website:** www.ppmag. com. Debbie Todd, art director. Estab. 1907. Circ. 26,000. Monthly magazine. Emphasizes professional photography in the fields of portrait, wedding, editorial, photojournalism, travel, commercial/advertising, sports, corporate and industrial. Readers include professional photographers and photographic services and educators. Approximately half the circulation is Professional Photographers of America members. Sample copy available for $5 postpaid.

○　PPA members submit material unpaid to promote their photo businesses and obtain recognition. Images sent to *Professional Photographer* should be technically perfect, and photographers should include information about how the photo was produced.

NEEDS Reviews photos with accompanying manuscript only.

SPECS Accepts images in digital format only. Send via CD, e-mail as TIFF, EPS, JPEG files at 72 dpi minimum.

MAKING CONTACT & TERMS "We prefer a story query, or complete manuscript if writer feels subject fits our magazine. Photos will be part of manuscript package." Responds in 2 months. Credit line given.

◎　**PUBLIC POWER**

2451 Crystal Dr., Suite 1000, Arlington VA 22202-4804. (202)467-2900. **Fax:** (202)467-2910. **E-mail:** news@publicpower.org; ldalessandro@publicpower. org; rthomas@publicpower.org. **Website:** www.pub licpower.org. **Contact:** Laura D'Alessandro, editor; Robert Thomas, art director. Estab. 1942. Publication of the American Public Power Association, published 6 times a year. Emphasizes electric power provided by cities, towns, and utility districts. Sample copy and photo guidelines free.

NEEDS Buys photos on assignment only.

SPECS Prefers digital images; call art director (Robert Thomas) at (202)467-2983 to discuss.

MAKING CONTACT & TERMS Send query letter with samples. Provide résumé, business card, brochure, flyer or tearsheets to be kept on file for possible future assignments. **Pays on acceptance.** Credit line given. Buys one-time rights.

◉◑　**QSR**

101 Europa Dr., Suite 150, Durham NC 27707. (919) 945-0700. **Fax:** (919)489-4767. **E-mail:** mitch@qsr magazine.com. **Website:** www.qsrmagazine.com.

Contact: Mitch Avery, production manager. Estab. 1997. Trade magazine directed toward the business aspects of quick-service restaurants (fast food). "Our readership is primarily management level and above, usually franchisors and franchisees. Our goal is to cover the quick-service and fast, casual restaurant industries objectively, offering our readers the latest news and information pertinent to their business." Photo guidelines free.

NEEDS Buys 10-15 photos/year. Needs corporate identity portraits, images associated with fast food, general food images for feature illustration. Reviews photos with or without a ms. Model/property release preferred.

SPECS Prefers images in digital format. Send via CD/DVD, ZIP as TIFF, EPS files at 300 dpi.

MAKING CONTACT & TERMS Send query letter with samples, brochure, stock list, tearsheets. Art director will contact photographer for portfolio review if interested. Portfolio should include slides and digital sample files. Keeps samples on file. Responds only if interested; send nonreturnable samples. Simultaneous submissions and previously published work OK. Pays on publication. Publisher only interested in acquiring all rights unless otherwise specified.

TIPS "Willingness to work with subject and magazine deadlines essential. Willingness to follow artistic guidelines necessary but should be able to rely on one's own eye. Our covers always feature quick-service restaurant executives with some sort of name recognition (e.g., a location shot with signage in the background, use of product props which display company logo)."

◉◑　**QUICK FROZEN FOODS INTERNATIONAL**

2125 Center Ave., Suite 305, Fort Lee NJ 07024-5898. (201)592-7007. **Fax:** (201)592-7171. **E-mail:** JohnQF FI@aol.com. **Website:** www.qffintl.com. **Contact:** John M. Saulnier, chief editor/publisher. Circ. 15,000. Quarterly magazine. Emphasizes retailing, marketing, processing, packaging and distribution of frozen foods around the world. Readers are international executives involved in the frozen food industry: manufacturers, distributors, retailers, brokers, importers/exporters, warehousemen, etc. Sample copy available for $20.

NEEDS Buys 10-25 photos/year. Uses photos of agriculture, plant exterior shots, step-by-step in-plant processing shots, photos of retail store frozen food cases, head shots of industry executives, etc. Photo captions required.

SPECS Accepts digital images via CD at 300 dpi, CMYK. Also accepts 5×7 glossy b&w or color prints.

MAKING CONTACT & TERMS Send query letter with résumé of credits. Responds in 1 month. Payment negotiable. Pays on publication. Buys all rights but may reassign to photographer after publication.

TIPS A file of photographers' names is maintained; if an assignment comes up in an area close to a particular photographer, she/he may be contacted. "When submitting your name, inform us if you are capable of writing a story if needed."

RANGEFINDER

85 Broad St., 11th Floor, New York NY 10004. (646)654-4500. **Fax:** (310)481-8037. **E-mail:** adana. jimenez@emeraldexpo.com. **Website:** www.range findermag.com. Bill Hunter, editor. **Contact:** Adana Jimenez, creative director. Estab. 1952. Circ. 61,000. Monthly magazine. Emphasizes topics, developments and products of interest to the professional photographer. Readers are professionals in all phases of photography. Sample copy free with 11×14 SASE and 2 first-class stamps. Photo guidelines free with SASE.

NEEDS Buys very few photos from freelancers/issue. Needs all kinds of photos; almost always run in conjunction with articles. "We prefer photos accompanying 'how-to' or special interest stories from the photographer." No pictorials. Special needs include seasonal cover shots (vertical format only). Model release required; property release preferred. Photo captions preferred.

MAKING CONTACT & TERMS Send query letter with résumé of credits. Keeps samples on file; include SASE for return of material. Responds in 1 month. Previously published work occasionally OK; give details. Payment varies. Covers submitted gratis. Pays on publication. Credit line given. Buys first North American serial rights; negotiable.

⑤ ❶ RECOMMEND

Worth International Media Group, 5979 NW 151st St., Suite 120, Miami Lakes FL 33014. (305)828-0123; (800)447-0123. **Fax:** (305)826-6950. **E-mail:** paloma@ recommend.com. **Website:** www.recommend.com; www.worthit.com. **Contact:** Paloma de Rico, editor-in-chief. Estab. 1985. Circ. 55,000. Monthly. Empha-

sizes travel. Readers are travel agents, meeting planners, hoteliers, ad agencies.

NEEDS Buys 16 photos from freelancers/issue; 192 photos/year. "Our publication divides the world into 7 regions. Every month we use travel destination-oriented photos of animals, cities, resorts and cruise lines; feature all types of travel photography from all over the world." Model/property release required. Photo captions preferred; identification required on every photo.

SPECS Accepts images in digital format. Send via CD, ZIP as TIFF, EPS files at 300 dpi minimum. "We do not accept 35mm slides or transparencies."

MAKING CONTACT & TERMS "Contact via e-mail to view sample of photography." Simultaneous submissions and previously published work OK. Pays 30 days after publication. Credit line given. Buys one-time rights.

TIPS Prefers to see high-res digital files.

❶ ⑤ ❶ REFEREE

Referee Enterprises, Inc., 2017 Lathrop Ave., Racine WI 53405. (800)733-6100. **Fax:** (262)632-5460. **E-mail:** submissions@referee.com. **Website:** www.ref eree.com. **Contact:** Julie Sternberg, managing editor. Estab. 1976. Circ. 40,000. Monthly magazine. Readers are mostly male, ages 30-50. Sample copy free with 9×12 SASE and appropriate postage. Photo guidelines free with SASE.

NEEDS Buys 25-40 photos from freelancers/issue; 300-400 photos/year. Needs action officiating shots—all sports. Photo needs are ongoing. Photo captions required; include officials' names and hometowns.

SPECS Prefers to use digital files (minimum 300 dpi submitted on CD or DVDs).

MAKING CONTACT & TERMS Send unsolicited photos by mail or to submissions@referee.com for consideration. Responds in 2 weeks. Simultaneous submissions and previously published work OK. Pays $100 for color cover; $35 for color inside. Pays on publication. Credit line given. Rights purchased negotiable.

TIPS "Prefer photos that bring out the uniqueness of being a sports official. Need photos primarily of officials at or above the high school level in baseball, football, basketball, softball, volleyball and soccer in action. Other sports acceptable, but used less frequently. When at sporting events, take a few shots with the officials in mind, even though you may be on assignment for another reason. Don't be afraid to give it a try. We're receptive, always looking for new freelance contributors. We are constantly looking for pictures of officials/umpires. Our needs in this area have increased. Names and hometowns of officials are required."

RELAY MAGAZINE

P.O. Box 10114, Tallahassee FL 32302. (850)224-3314, ext. 4 or ext. 5. **Fax:** (850)224-2831. **E-mail:** gholmes@publicpower.com. **Website:** relaymagazine.org. **Contact:** Garnie Holmes, editor. Estab. 1957. Circ. 5,000. Quarterly industry magazine of the Florida Municipal Electric Association. Emphasizes energy, electric, utility and telecom industries in Florida. Readers are utility professionals, local elected officials, state and national legislators, and other state power associations.

NEEDS Number of photos/issue varies; various number supplied by freelancers. Needs photos of electric utilities in Florida (hurricane/storm damage to lines, utility workers, power plants, infrastructure, telecom, etc.); cityscapes of member utility cities. Model/property release preferred. Photo captions required.

SPECS Uses 3×5, 4×6, 5×7, 8×10 b&w and color prints. Accepts images in digital format.

MAKING CONTACT & TERMS Send query letter with description of photo or photocopy. Keeps samples on file. Simultaneous submissions and previously published work OK. Payment negotiable. Rates negotiable. Pays on use. Credit line given. Buys one-time rights, repeated use (stock); negotiable.

TIPS "Must relate to our industry. Clarity and contrast important. Always query first."

REMODELING

HanleyWood, LLC, One Thomas Circle NW, Suite 600, Washington DC 20005. (202)452-0800. **Fax:** (202)785-1974. **E-mail:** salfano@hanleywood.com; ibush@hanleywood.com; sbell@hanleywood.com. **Website:** www.remodelingmagazine.com. **Contact:** Sal Alfano, editorial director; Ingrid Bush, managing editor; Sarah Bell, art director. Estab. 1985. Circ. 80,000. Published 13 times/year. "Business magazine for remodeling contractors. Readers are small contractors involved in residential and commercial remodeling." Sample copy free with 8×11 SASE.

NEEDS Uses 10-15 photos/issue; number supplied by freelancers varies. Photos of remodeled residences, both before and after. Interior and exterior photos of residences that emphasize the architecture over the furnishings. Reviews photos with "short description of project, including architect's or contractor's name and phone number. We have 1 regular photo feature: 'Before and After' describes a whole-house remodel. Request editorial calendar to see upcoming design features."

SPECS Accepts images in digital format. Send via ZIP as TIFF, GIF, JPEG files at 300 dpi.

MAKING CONTACT & TERMS Provide résumé, business card, brochure, flyer or tearsheets to be kept on file for possible future assignments. Responds in 1 month. **Pays on acceptance.** Credit line given. Buys one-time rights; Web rights.

REP.

1166 Avenue of the Americas, 10th Floor, New York NY 10036. (212)204-4260. **E-mail:** sean.barrow@penton.com. **Website:** www.wealthmanagement.com. **Contact:** Sean Barrow, art director. Estab. 1976. Circ. 100,000. Monthly trade publication provides stockbrokers and investment advisors with industry news and financial trends. Emphasizes stock brokerage and financial services industries. Magazine is "requested and read by 90% of the nation's top financial advisors."

NEEDS Uses about 8 photos/issue—3 supplied by freelancers. Needs environmental portraits of financial and brokerage personalities, and conceptual shots of financial ideas—all by assignment only. Model/property release is photographer's responsibility. Photo captions required.

SPECS Prefers 100 ISO film or better. Accepts images in digital format. Send electronically, or via CD.

MAKING CONTACT & TERMS Provide brochure, flyer or tearsheets to be kept on file for possible future assignments. Cannot return material. Due to space limitations, please obtain permission *prior* to sending digital samples via e-mail. Simultaneous submissions and previously published work OK. Pays $500-1,500 for cover; $500-1,000 for inside. Pays 30 days after publication. Credit line given. Buys one-time rights. Publisher requires signed rights agreement.

TIPS "We're always looking for young talent. The focus of our magazine is on design, so talent and professionalism are key."

RESTAURANT HOSPITALITY

Penton Media, 1300 E. Ninth St., Cleveland OH 44114. (216)931-9942. **Fax:** (216)696-0836. **E-mail:** chris.roberto@penton.com. **Website:** www.restaurant-hos

pitality.com. **Contact:** Chris Roberto, group creative director; Michael Sanson, editor-in-chief. Estab. 1919. Circ. 100,000. Monthly. Emphasizes "ideas for full-service restaurants" including business strategies and industry menu trends. Readers are restaurant owners/operators and chefs for full-service independent and chain concepts.

NEEDS Assignment needs vary; 10-15 photos from freelancers/issue, plus stock; 120 photos/year. Needs "on-location portraits, restaurant interiors and details, and occasional project specific food photos." Special needs include subject-related photos: industry chefs, personalities and food trends. Model release preferred. Photo captions preferred.

SPECS Accepts images in digital format. Send via FTP, download link or e-mail.

MAKING CONTACT & TERMS Send postcard samples and e-mail with link to website. Previously published work OK. Pay varies; negotiable. Cover fees on per project basis. **Pays on acceptance.** Credit line given. Buys one-time rights plus usage in all media.

TIPS "Send a postcard that highlights your work and website."

☯ RETAILERS FORUM

383 E. Main St., Centerport NY 11721. (800)635-7654. **E-mail:** forumpublishing@aol.com. **Website:** www. forum123.com. **Contact:** Martin Stevens, publisher. Estab. 1981. Circ. 70,000. Monthly magazine. Readers are entrepreneurs and retail store owners. Sample copy available for $7.50.

NEEDS Buys 3-6 photos from freelancers/issue; 36-72 photos/year. "We publish trade magazines for retail variety goods stores and flea market vendors. Items include jewelry, cosmetics, novelties, toys, etc. (five-and-dime-type goods). We are interested in creative and abstract impressions—not straight-on product shots. Humor a plus." Model/property release required.

SPECS Uses color prints. Accepts images in digital format. Send via e-mail at 300 dpi.

MAKING CONTACT & TERMS Send unsolicited photos by mail or e-mail for consideration. Does not keep samples on file; include SASE for return of material. Responds in 2 weeks. Simultaneous submissions and previously published work OK. Pays $100 for color cover; $50 for color inside. **Pays on acceptance.** Buys one-time rights.

RTOHQ: THE MAGAZINE

1504 Robin Hood Trail, Austin TX 78703. (800)204-2776. **Fax:** (512)794-0097. **E-mail:** nferguson@rtohq.org; bkeese@rtohq.org. **Website:** www.rtohq.org. **Contact:** Neil Ferguson, art director; Bill Keese, executive editor. Estab. 1980. Circ. 5,500. Bimonthly magazine published by the Association of Progressive Rental Organizations. Emphasizes the rental-purchase industry. Readers are owners and managers of rental-purchase stores in North America, Canada, Great Britain, and Australia.

NEEDS Buys 1-2 photos from freelancers/issue; 6-12 photos/year. Needs "strongly conceptual, cutting-edge photos that relate to editorial articles on business/management issues. Also looking for photographers to capture unique and creative environmental portraits of our members." Model/property release preferred.

MAKING CONTACT & TERMS Provide brochure, flyer, or tearsheets to be kept on file for possible future assignments. Simultaneous submissions and previously published work OK. Pays $200-450/job; $350-450 for cover; $200-450 for inside. Pays on publication. Credit line given. Buys one-time and electronic rights.

TIPS "Understand the industry and the specific editorial needs of the publication, e.g., don't send beautiful still-life photography to a trade association publication."

☯ SCIENCE SCOPE

National Science Teachers Association, 1840 Wilson Blvd., Arlington VA 22201. (703)243-7100. **Fax:** (703)243-7177. **E-mail:** wthomas@nsta.org; scope@nsta.org. **Website:** www.nsta.org. **Contact:** Will Thomas, art director. Journal published 9 times/year during the school year. Emphasizes "activity-oriented ideas—ideas that teachers can take directly from articles." Readers are mostly middle school science teachers. Sample copy available for $6.25. Photo guidelines free with SASE.

NEEDS About half our photos are supplied by freelancers. Needs photos of classroom activities with students participating. "In some cases, say for interdisciplinary studies articles, we'll need a specialized photo." Model release required. Need for photo captions "depends on the type of photo."

SPECS Uses slides, negatives, prints. Accepts images in digital format. Send via CD, e-mail as TIFF, EPS files at 300 dpi minimum.

MAKING CONTACT & TERMS Arrange a personal interview to show portfolio. Send query letter with stock list. Provide résumé, business card, brochure, flyer or tearsheets to be kept on file for possible future assignments. Considers previously published work; "prefer not to, although in some cases there are exceptions." Pays on publication. Sometimes pays kill fee. Credit line given. Buys one-time rights; negotiable.

TIPS "We look for clear, crisp photos of middle-level students working in the classroom. Shots should be candid with students genuinely interested in their activity. (The activity is chosen to accompany manuscript.) Please send photocopies of sample shots along with listing of preferred subjects and/or listing of stock photo topics."

SECURITY DEALER & INTEGRATOR

Cygnus Business Media, 12735 Morris Rd., Bldg. 200, Suite 180, Alpharetta GA 30004. (800)547-7377, ext 2226. **E-mail:** paul.rothman@cygnus.com. **Website:** www.securityinfowatch.com/magazine. **Contact:** Paul Rothman, editor-in-chief. Circ. 25,000. Monthly. Emphasizes security subjects. Readers are business owners who install alarm, security, CCTV, home automation, and access control systems. Sample copy free with SASE. "*SD&I* seeks credible, reputable thought leaders to provide timely, original editorial content for our readers—security value-added resellers, integrators, systems designers, central station companies, electrical contractors, consultants and others—on rapidly morphing new communications and signaling technologies, networking, standards, business acumen, project information, and other topics to hone new skills and build business. Content must add value to our pages and provide thought-provoking insights on the industry and its future. In most cases, content must be vendor-neutral, unless the discussion is on a patented or proprietary technology."

"Photographs and graphics, drawings and white papers are encouraged."

NEEDS Uses 2-5 photos/issue; none at present supplied by freelance photographers. Photos of security-application-equipment. Model release preferred. Photo captions required.

SPECS Photos must be JPEG, TIFF or EPS form for any section of the magazine, including product sections (refer to the editorial calendar). "We require a 300 dpi image at a minimum 100% size of 2×3 for product submissions."

MAKING CONTACT & TERMS Send b&w and color prints by mail for consideration; include SASE for return of material. Responds "immediately." Simultaneous submissions and/or previously published work OK.

TIPS "Do not send originals; send dupes only, and only after discussion with editor."

SPECIALTY TRAVEL INDEX

Alpine Hansen, P.O. Box 458, San Anselmo CA 94979. (415)455-1643. **E-mail:** info@specialtytravel.com. **Website:** www.specialtytravel.com. Estab. 1980. Circ. 35,000. Biannual trade magazine. Directory of special interest travel. Readers are travel agents. Sample copy available for $6.

NEEDS Contact for want list. Buys photo/ms packages. Photo captions preferred.

SPECS Uses digital images. Send via CD or photographer's website. "No e-mails for photo submissions."

MAKING CONTACT & TERMS Send query letter with résumé, stock list and website link to view samples. Does not keep samples on file; include SASE for return of material. Responds in 2 months to queries. Simultaneous submissions and previously published work OK. Pays $25/photo. **Pays on acceptance.** Credit line given.

💲💲 SUCCESSFUL MEETINGS

Northstar Travel Media, 100 Lighting Way, Secaucus NJ 07094. (646)380-6247. **E-mail:** valonzo@ntmllc.com; jruf@ntmllc.com. **Website:** www.successfulmeetings.com. **Contact:** Vincent Alonzo, editor-in-chief; Jennifer Ruf, art director. Estab. 1955. Circ. 70,000. Monthly. Emphasizes business group travel for all sorts of meetings. Readers are business and association executives who plan meetings, exhibits, conventions and incentive travel. Sample copy available for $10.

NEEDS Special needs include high-quality corporate portraits; conceptual, out-of-state shoots.

MAKING CONTACT & TERMS Arrange a personal interview to show portfolio. Send query letter with résumé of credits and list of stock photo subjects. Responds in 2 weeks. Simultaneous submissions and previously published work OK, "only if you let us know." Pays $500-750 for color cover; $50-150 for b&w inside; $75-200 for color inside; $150-250/ b&w page; $200-300/color page; $50-100/hour; $175-350/3/4 day. **Pays on acceptance.** Credit line given. Buys one-time rights.

THE SURGICAL TECHNOLOGIST

6 W. Dry Creek Circle, Suite 200, Littleton CO 80120-8031. (303)694-9130. **Fax:** (303)694-9169. **E-mail:** kludwig@ast.org. **Website:** www.ast.org. **Contact:** Karen Ludwig, editor/publisher. Circ. 23,000. Monthly journal of the Association of Surgical Technologists. Emphasizes surgery. Readers are operating room professionals, well educated in surgical procedures, ages 20-60. Sample copy free with 9×12 SASE and 5 first-class stamps. Photo guidelines free with SASE.

NEEDS Needs "surgical, operating room photos that show members of the surgical team in action." Model release required.

MAKING CONTACT & TERMS Send low-res JPEGs with query via e-mail. Responds in 4 weeks after review by editorial board. Simultaneous submissions and previously published work OK. Payment negotiable. **Pays on acceptance.** Credit line given. Buys all rights.

$ ◐ TECHNIQUES

1410 King St., Alexandria VA 22314. (703)683-3111; 800-826-9972. **Fax:** (703)683-7424. **E-mail:** techniques@acteonline.org. **Website:** www.acteonline.org. **Contact:** Margaret Mitchell, managing editor. Estab. 1926. Circ. 25,000.

💬 This publication uses stock photography or artwork accompanying an article and offers no opportunity for freelance photography.

$$ TEXAS REALTOR MAGAZINE

P.O. Box 2246, Austin TX 78768. (800)873-9155; (512)370-2286. **Fax:** (512)370-2390. **E-mail:** jmathews@texasrealtors.com. **Website:** www.texasrealtors.com. **Contact:** Joel Mathews, art director; Brandi Alderetti. Estab. 1972. Circ. 50,000. Monthly magazine of the Texas Association of Realtors. Emphasizes real estate sales and related industries. Readers are male and female realtors, ages 20-70. Sample copy free with SASE.

NEEDS Buys 10 photos from freelancers/issue; 120 photos/year. Needs photos of architectural details, business, office management, telesales, real estate sales, commercial real estate, nature. Property release required.

MAKING CONTACT & TERMS Buys one-time rights; negotiable.

$ ◎ TEXTILE RENTAL MAGAZINE

1800 Diagonal Rd., Suite 200, Alexandria VA 22314. (703)519-0026; (877)770-9274. **Fax:** (703)519-0026. **E-mail:** jmorgan@trsa.org. **Website:** www.trsa.org. Monthly magazine of the Textile Rental Services Association of America. Emphasizes the linen supply, industrial and commercial textile rental and service industry. Readers are "heads of companies, general managers of facilities, predominantly male; national and international readers."

NEEDS Photos needed on assignment basis only. Model release preferred. Photo captions preferred or required "depending on subject."

MAKING CONTACT & TERMS "We contact photographers on an as-needed basis from a directory. We also welcome inquiries and submissions." Cannot return material. Previously published work OK. Pays $350 for color cover plus processing; "depends on the job." **Pays on acceptance.** Credit line given if requested. Buys all rights.

$ TOBACCO INTERNATIONAL

Lockwood Publications, Inc., 3743 Crescent St., 2nd Fl., Long Island City NY 11101. (212)391-2060. **Fax:** (212)827-0945. **E-mail:** editor@tobaccointernational.com. **Website:** www.tobaccointernational.com. **Contact:** Murdoch McBride. Estab. 1886. Circ. 5,000. Monthly international business magazine. Emphasizes cigarettes, tobacco products, tobacco machinery, supplies and services. Readers are executives, ages 35-60. Sample copy free with SASE.

NEEDS Uses 20-30 photos/issue. "Photography that represents tobacco industry activity, processing or growing tobacco products from all around the world, but any interesting newsworthy photos relevant to subject matter is considered." Model or property release preferred.

MAKING CONTACT & TERMS Send query letter with photocopies, transparencies, slides or prints. Does not keep samples on file; include SASE for return of material. Responds in 3 weeks. Simultaneous submissions OK (not if competing journal). Pays $50/color photo. Pays on publication. Credit line may be given.

● $$ ◐ TOBACCO JOURNAL INTERNATIONAL

Quartz Business Media, Westgate House, 120/130 Station Rd., Redhill, Surrey RH1 1ET, United Kingdom. +44(0)1737 855000. **Fax:** +44(0)1737 855327. **E-mail:**

joseph.mapother@konradin.de; anja.helk@konradin.de; william.mcewen@konradin.de. **Website:** www.worldtobacco.co.uk. **Contact:** Anja Helk, editor; William McEwen, editor. Circ. 4,300. Trade magazine. "Focuses on all aspects of the tobacco industry from international trends to national markets, offering news and views on the entire industry from leaf farming to primary and secondary manufacturing, to packaging, distribution and marketing." Sample copies available. Request photo guidelines via e-mail.

NEEDS Buys 5-10 photos from freelancers/issue; agriculture, product shots/still life. "Anything related to tobacco and smoking. Abstract smoking images considered, as well as international images."

SPECS Accepts almost all formats. Minimum resolution of 300 dpi at the size to be printed. Prefers TIFFs to JPEGs, but can accept either.

MAKING CONTACT & TERMS E-mail query letter with link to photographer's website, JPEG samples at 72 dpi. Provide self-promotion piece to be kept on file for possible future assignments. Pays £200 maximum for cover photo. **Pays on acceptance.** Credit line given.

TIPS "Check the features list on our website."

○ TODAY'S PHOTOGRAPHER

American Image Press, P.O. Box 42, Hamptonville NC 27020-0042. (336)468-1138. **Fax:** (336)468-1899. **E-mail:** homeoffice@ainewsservice.net. **Website:** www.aipress.com. **Contact:** Vonda H. Blackburn, editor-in-chief. Estab. 1986. Circ. 78,000. Published once a year in print, twice/year online. Magazine of the International Freelance Photographers Organization. Emphasizes making money with photography. Readers are 90% male photographers. Sample copy available for 9×12 SASE. Photo guidelines free with SASE.

NEEDS Buys 40 photos from freelancers/issue; 240 photos/year. Model release required. Photo captions preferred. Only buys content from members of IFPO ($74 membership fee, plus $7 shipping).

MAKING CONTACT & TERMS Send 35mm, 2¼×2¼, 4×5, 8×10 b&w and color prints or transparencies by mail for consideration; include SASE for return of material. Responds at end of quarter. Simultaneous submissions and previously published work OK. Payment negotiable. Credit line given. Buys one-time rights, per contract.

⊙⊙ TOP PRODUCER

383 N. Downey St., P.O. Box 958, Mexico MO 65265. (573)581-6387; (563)284-5054. **E-mail:** drafferty@

farmjournal.com. **Website:** www.agweb.com. **Contact:** Dana Rafferty, art director; Jeanne Bernick, editor. Circ. 120,000. Monthly. Emphasizes American agriculture. Readers are active farmers, ranchers or agribusiness people. Sample copy and photo guidelines free with SASE.

NEEDS Buys 5-10 photos from freelancers/issue; 60-100 photos/year. "We use studio-type portraiture (environmental portraits), technical, details and scenics." Model release preferred. Photo captions required.

MAKING CONTACT & TERMS Send query letter with résumé of credits along with business card, brochure, flyer or tearsheets to be kept on file for possible future assignments. "Do not send originals!" Please send information for online portfolios/websites, as we often search for stock images on such sites. Digital files and portfolios may be sent via CD to the address noted above." Simultaneous submissions and previously published work OK. **Pays on acceptance.** Credit line given. Buys one-time rights.

TIPS In portfolio or samples, likes to see "about 40 samples showing photographer's use of lighting and ability to work with people. Know your intended market. Familiarize yourself with the magazine and keep abreast of how photos are used in the general magazine field."

⊙ TRANSPORTATION MANAGEMENT & ENGINEERING

Scranton Gillette Communications, Inc., 3030 W. Salt Creek Lane, Suite 201, Arlington Heights IL 60005. (847)391-1029. **E-mail:** bwilson@sgcmail.com. **Website:** www.roadsbridges.com. **Contact:** Bill Wilson, editor. Estab. 1994. Circ. 18,000. Quarterly supplement. "*TM&E* is a controlled publication targeted toward 18,000 traffic/transit system planners, designers, engineers and managers in North America." Sample copies available.

NEEDS Buys 1-2 photos from freelancers/issue; 5-10 photos/year. Needs photos of landscapes/scenics, transportation-related, traffic, transit. Reviews photos with or without ms. Property release preferred. Photo captions preferred.

SPECS Uses 5×7 glossy prints; 35mm transparencies. Accepts images in digital format. Send via CD as TIFF, EPS files at 300 dpi.

MAKING CONTACT & TERMS Send query letter with prints. Portfolio may be dropped off every Monday. Responds in 3 weeks to queries. Responds only if interested; send nonreturnable samples. Pays on publication. Credit line sometimes given. Buys all rights; negotiable.

TIPS "Read our magazine."

TRANSPORT TOPICS

950 N. Glebe Rd., Suite 210, Arlington VA 22203. (703)838-1770. **Fax:** (703)838-7916. **E-mail:** gdively@ttnews.com. **Website:** www.ttnews.com. **Contact:** George Dively, art director. Estab. 1935. Circ. 31,000. Weekly tabloid. Publication of American Trucking Associations. Emphasizes the trucking industry and freight transportation. Readers are executives, ages 35-65.

NEEDS Uses approximately 12 photos/issue; amount supplied by freelancers "depends on need." Needs photos of truck transportation in all modes. Model/property release preferred. Photo captions preferred.

MAKING CONTACT & TERMS Send unsolicited JPEGs by e-mail for consideration. Provide résumé, business card, brochure, flyer or tearsheets to be kept on file for possible future assignments. Does not keep samples on file; include SASE for return of material. Responds in 1 month. Simultaneous submissions and previously published work OK. Payment negotiable. Pays standard "market rate" for color cover photo. **Pays on acceptance**. Credit line given. Buys one-time or permanent rights; negotiable.

TIPS "Trucks/trucking must be dominant element in the photograph—not an incidental part of an environmental scene."

TREE CARE INDUSTRY MAGAZINE

Tree Care Industry Association, 136 Harvey Rd., Suite 101, Londonderry NH 03053. (800)733-2622 or (603)314-5380. **Fax:** (603)314-5386. **E-mail:** editor@tcia.org. **Website:** www.tcia.org. **Contact:** Don Staruk, editor. Estab. 1990. Circ. 24,000. Monthly trade magazine for arborists, landscapers and golf course superintendents interested in professional tree care practices. Sample copy available for $5.

NEEDS Buys 3-6 photos/year. Needs photos of tree work, landscapes and gardening. Reviews photos with or without a ms.

SPECS Accepts images in digital format. Send via e-mail or FTP as JPEG or TIFF files at 300 dpi.

MAKING CONTACT & TERMS Send query letter with stock list. Does not keep samples on file; include SASE for return of material. Pays $100 maximum for color cover; $25 minimum for color inside. Pays on

publication. Credit line given. Buys one-time and online rights.

UNDERGROUND CONSTRUCTION

Oildom Publishing Company of Texas, Inc., P.O. Box 941669, Houston TX 77094-8669. (281)558-6930, ext. 220. **Fax:** (281)558-7029. **E-mail:** rcarpenter@oildom.com; efitzpatrick@oildom.com. **Website:** www.undergroundconstructionmagazine.com. **Contact:** Robert Carpenter, editor-in-chief; Oliver Klinger, publisher; Elizabeth Fitzpatrick, art director. Circ. 40,000. Monthly trade journal. Emphasizes construction and rehabilitation of sewer, water, gas, telecom, electric, and oil underground pipelines/conduit. Readers are contractors, utilities and engineers. Sample copy available for $3.

NEEDS Uses photos of underground construction and rehabilitation.

SPECS Uses high-resolution digital images (minimum 300 dpi); large-format negatives or transparencies.

MAKING CONTACT & TERMS Query before sending photos. Generally responds within 30 days. Pays $100-400 for color cover; $50-250 for color inside. Buys one-time rights.

TIPS "Freelancers are competing with staff as well as complimentary photos supplied by equipment manufacturers. Subject matter must be unique, striking and/or off the beaten track. People on the job are always desirable."

🟢 UNITED AUTO WORKERS (UAW)

UAW Solidarity House, 8000 E. Jefferson Ave., Detroit MI 48214. (313)926-5291. **E-mail:** uawsolidarity@uaw.net. **Website:** www.uaw.org. **Contact:** Vince Piscopo, editor. Trade union representing 650,000 workers in auto, aerospace, agricultural-implement industries, government and other areas. Publishes *Solidarity* magazine. Photos used for magazine, brochures, newsletters, posters and calendars.

NEEDS Buys 85 freelance photos/year; offers 12-18 freelance assignments/year. Needs photos of workers at their place of employment, and social issues for magazine story illustrations. Reviews stock photos. Model release preferred. Photo captions preferred.

SPECS Uses 8×10 prints.

MAKING CONTACT & TERMS Arrange a personal interview to show portfolio. In portfolio, prefers to see b&w and color workplace shots. Send query letter with samples and SASE by mail for consideration.

Prefers to see published photos as samples. Provide résumé or tearsheets to be kept on file for possible future assignments. Notifies photographer if future assignments can be expected. Responds in 2 weeks. Credit line given. Buys one-time rights and all rights; negotiable.

VETERINARY ECONOMICS

8033 Flint St., Lenexa KS 66214. (800)255-6864. **Fax:** (913)871-3808. **E-mail:** ve@advanstar.com. **Website:** veterinarybusiness.dvm360.com. Estab. 1960. Circ. 54,000. Monthly trade magazine emphasizing practice management for veterinarians.
NEEDS Photographers on an "as needed" basis for editorial portraits; must be willing to sign license agreement; 2-3 photo portraits/year. License agreement required. Photo captions preferred.
SPECS Prefers images in digital format. Send via FTP, e-mail as JPEG files at 300 dpi.
MAKING CONTACT & TERMS Send 1 e-mail with sample image less than 1 MB; repeat e-mails are deleted. Does not keep samples on file. **Pays on acceptance.** Credit line given.

WATER WELL JOURNAL

National Ground Water Association, 601 Dempsey Rd., Westerville OH 43081. **Fax:** (614)898-7786. **E-mail:** tplumley@ngwa.org. **Website:** www.waterwelljournal.org. **Contact:** Thad Plumley, director of publications; Mike Price, associate editor. Circ. 24,000. Monthly association publication. Emphasizes construction of water wells, development of ground water resources and ground water cleanup. Readers are water well drilling contractors, manufacturers, suppliers, and ground water scientists. Sample copy available for $15 US, $36 foreign.
NEEDS Buys 1-3 freelance photos/issue plus cover photos; 12-36 photos/year. Needs photos of installations and how-to illustrations. Model release preferred. Photo captions required.
SPECS Accepts images in digital format. Send via CD, ZIP as TIFF files at 300 dpi.
MAKING CONTACT & TERMS Send query letter with samples. "We'll contact you." Pays $250 for color cover; $50 for b&w or color inside; "flat rate for assignment." Pays on publication. Credit line given. Buys all rights.
TIPS "E-mail or send written inquiries; we'll reply if interested. Unsolicited materials will not be returned."

THE WHOLESALER

2615 Shermer Rd., Suite A, Northbrook IL 60062. (847)564-1127. **E-mail:** editor@thewholesaler.com. **Website:** www.thewholesaler.com. Estab. 1946. Circ. 35,000. Monthly news tabloid. Emphasizes wholesaling/distribution in the plumbing, heating, air conditioning, piping (including valves), fire protection industry. Readers are owners and managers of wholesale distribution businesses; manufacturer representatives. Sample copy free with 11×15¾ SASE and 5 first-class stamps.
NEEDS Buys 3 photos from freelancers/issue; 36 photos/year. Interested in field and action shots in the warehouse, on the loading dock, at the job site. Property release preferred. Photo captions preferred—"just give us the facts."
MAKING CONTACT & TERMS Send query letter with stock list. Send any size glossy color and b&w prints by mail with SASE for consideration. Responds in 2 weeks. Simultaneous submissions and previously published work OK. Pays on publication. Buys one-time rights.

WINES & VINES

Wine Communications Group, 65 Mitchell Blvd., Suite A, San Rafael CA 94903. (415)453-9700; (866)453-9701. **Fax:** (415)453-2517. **E-mail:** edit@winesandvines.com; info@winesandvines.com. **Website:** www.winesandvines.com. **Contact:** Jim Gordon, editor; Kate Lavin, managing editor. Estab. 1919. Circ. 5,000. Monthly. Emphasizes winemaking, grape growing, and marketing in North America and internationally for wine industry professionals, including winemakers, grape growers, wine merchants, and suppliers.
NEEDS Color cover subjects—on a regular basis.
SPECS Accepts images in digital format. Send via CD, ZIP, e-mail as TIFF, or JPEG files at 400 dpi.
MAKING CONTACT & TERMS Prefers e-mail query with link to portfolio; or send material by mail for consideration. Will e-mail if interested in reviewing photographer's portfolio. Provide business card to be kept on file for possible future assignments. Responds in 3 months. Previously published work considered. Pays $100-350 for color cover, or negotiable ad trade out. Pays on publication. Credit line given. Buys one-time rights.

🌎 WISCONSIN ARCHITECT

321 S. Hamilton St., Madison WI 53703-4000. (608)257-8477. **E-mail:** editor@aiaw.org. **Website:** www.aiaw.org. Estab. 1931. Circ. 3,700. Annual magazine of the American Institute of Architects Wisconsin. Emphasizes architecture. Readers are design/construction professionals.

NEEDS Uses approximately 100 photos/issue. "Photos are almost exclusively supplied by architects who are submitting projects for publication. Of these, approximately 65% are professional photographers hired by the architect."

MAKING CONTACT & TERMS "Contact us using online submission/contact form." Keeps samples on file. Responds when interested. Simultaneous submissions and previously published work OK. Pays on publication. Credit line given. Rights negotiable.

WOMAN ENGINEER

Equal Opportunity Publications, Inc., 445 Broad Hollow Rd., Suite 425, Melville NY 11747. (631)421-9421. **Fax:** (631)421-1352. **E-mail:** info@eop.com; jschneider@eop.com. **Website:** www.eop.com. **Contact:** James Schneider, editor. Estab. 1968. Circ. 16,000. Magazine published 3 times/year. Emphasizes career guidance for women engineers at the college and professional levels. Readers are college-age and professional women in engineering. Sample copy free with 9×12 SAE and 6 first-class stamps.

NEEDS Uses at least 1 photo/issue (cover); planning to use freelance work for covers and possibly editorial; most of the photos are submitted by freelance writers with their articles. Model release preferred. Photo captions required.

TIPS "We are looking for strong, sharply focused photos or slides of women engineers. The photo should show a woman engineer at work, but the background should be uncluttered. The photo subject should be dressed and groomed in a professional manner. Cover photo should represent a professional woman engineer at work and convey a positive and professional image. Read our magazine, and find actual women engineers to photograph. We're not against using cover models, but we prefer cover subjects to be women engineers working in the field."

WOODSHOP NEWS

Cruz Bay Publishing, Inc., 10 Bokum Rd., Essex CT 06426. (860)767-8227. **Fax:** (860)767-1048. **E-mail:** editorial@woodshopnews.com. **Website:** www.wood shopnews.com. **Contact:** Tod Riggio, editor. Estab. 1986. Circ. 60,000. Monthly trade magazine (tabloid format) covering all areas of professional woodworking. Sample copies available.

NEEDS Buys 12 sets of cover photos from freelancers/year. Photos of celebrities, architecture, interiors/decorating, industry, product shots/still life. Interested in documentary. "We assign our cover story, which is always a profile of a professional woodworker. These photo shoots are done in the subject's shop and feature working shots, portraits, and photos of subject's finished work." Photo captions required; include description of activity contained in shots. "Photo captions will be written in-house based on this information."

SPECS Prefers digital photos.

MAKING CONTACT & TERMS Send query letter with résumé, photocopies, tearsheets. Provide self-promotion piece to be kept on file for possible future assignments. Responds only if interested; send nonreturnable samples. Previously published work OK occasionally. Pays $600-800 for color cover. Note: "We want a cover photo 'package'—one shot for the cover, others for use inside with the cover story." **Pays on acceptance.** Credit line given. Buys "perpetual" rights, but will pay a lower fee for one-time rights.

TIPS "I need a list of photographers in every geographical region of the country—I never know where our next cover profile will be done, so I need to have options everywhere. Familiarity with woodworking is a definite plus. Listen to our instructions! We have very specific lighting and composition needs, but some photographers ignore instructions in favor of creating 'artsy' photos, which we do not use, or poorly lighted photos, which we cannot use."

BOOK PUBLISHERS

//

There are diverse needs for photography in the book publishing industry. Publishers need photos for the obvious (covers, jackets, text illustrations, and promotional materials), but they may also need them for use on CD-ROMs and websites. Generally, though, publishers either buy individual or groups of photos for text illustration, or they publish entire books of photography.

Those in need of text illustration use photos for cover art and interiors of textbooks, travel books, and nonfiction books. For illustration, photographs may be purchased from a stock agency or from a photographer's stock, or the publisher may make assignments. Publishers usually pay for photography used in book illustration or on covers on a per-image or per-project basis. Some pay photographers hourly or day rates, if on an assignment basis. No matter how payment is made, however, the competitive publishing market requires freelancers to remain flexible.

To approach book publishers for illustration jobs, send a cover letter with photographs or slides and a stock photo list with prices, if available. (See sample stock list in "Running Your Business.") If you have a website, provide a link to it. If you have published work, tearsheets are very helpful in showing publishers how your work translates to the printed page.

PHOTO BOOKS

Publishers who produce photography books usually publish books with a theme, featuring the work of one or several photographers. It is not always necessary to be well-known to publish your photographs as a book. What you do need, however, is a unique perspective, a salable idea, and quality work.

For entire books, publishers may pay in one lump sum or with an advance plus royalties (a percentage of the book sales). When approaching a publisher for your own book of photographs, query first with a brief letter describing the project, and include sample photographs. If the publisher is interested in seeing the complete proposal, you can send additional information in one of two ways depending on the complexity of the project.

Prints placed in sequence in a protective box, along with an outline, will do for easy-to-describe, straightforward book projects. For more complex projects, you may want to create a book dummy. A dummy is basically a book model with photographs and text arranged as they will appear in finished book form. Book dummies show exactly how a book will look, including the sequence, size, format and layout of photographs and accompanying text. The quality of the dummy is important, but keep in mind that the expense can be prohibitive.

To find the right publisher for your work, first check the Subject Index in the back of the book to help narrow your search, then read the appropriate listings carefully. Send for catalogs and guidelines for those publishers that interest you. You may find guidelines on publishers' websites as well. Also, become familiar with your local bookstore or visit the site of an online bookstore such as Amazon.com. By examining the books already published, you can find those publishers who produce your type of work. Check for both large and small publishers. While smaller firms may not have as much money to spend, they are often more willing to take risks, especially on the work of new photographers. Keep in mind that photo books are expensive to produce and may have a limited market.

🟡🟡 🌓 ALLYN & BACON PUBLISHERS

445 Hutchinson Ave., Columbus OH 43235. **Website:** www.allynbaconmerrill.com. Find local rep to submit materials via online rep locator. Publishes college textbooks. Photos used for text illustrations, book covers. Examples of recently published titles: *Criminal Justice; Including Students With Special Needs; Social Psychology* (text illustrations and promotional materials). Offers one assignment plus 80 stock projects/year.

NEEDS Photos of babies/children/teens, celebrities, couples, multicultural, families, parents, senior citizens, disasters, education, special education, science, technology/computers. Interested in fine art, historical/vintage. Also uses multi-ethnic photos in education, health and fitness, people with disabilities, business, social sciences, and good abstracts. Reviews stock photos. Model/property release required.

SPECS Uses b&w prints, any format; all transparencies. Accepts images in digital format.

MAKING CONTACT & TERMS Send via CD, ZIP, e-mail as TIFF, EPS, PICT, GIF, JPEG files at 72 dpi for review, 300 dpi for use. See photo and art specifications online.

TIPS "Send tearsheets and promotion pieces. Need bright, strong, clean abstracts and unstaged, nicely lit people photos."

🟡🟡 ◎ 🌓 APPALACHIAN MOUNTAIN CLUB BOOKS

5 Joy St., Boston MA 02108. (617)523-0636. **Fax:** (617)523-0722. **E-mail:** amcbooks@outdoors.org. **Website:** www.outdoors.org. Estab. 1876. Publishes hardcovers and trade paperbacks. Photos used for text illustrations, book covers. Examples of recently published titles: *Quiet Water* series, *Best Day Hikes* series, *Trail Guide* series. Model release required. Photo captions preferred; include location, description of subject, photographer's name and phone number. Uses print-quality color and gray-scale images.

NEEDS Looking for photos of nature, hiking, backpacking, biking, paddling, skiing in the Northeast.

MAKING CONTACT & TERMS E-mail light boxes. Art director will contact photographer if interested. Keeps samples on file. Responds only if interested.

◎ AUTONOMEDIA

P.O. Box 568, Williamsburg Station, Brooklyn NY 11211. **Website:** www.autonomedia.org. Estab. 1974. Publishes books on radical culture and politics. Photos used for text illustrations, book covers. Examples of recently published titles: *TAZ* (cover illustration); *Cracking the Movement* (cover illustration); *Zapatistas* (cover and photo essay).

NEEDS "The number of photos bought annually varies, as does the number of assignments offered." Model/property release preferred. Photo captions preferred.

MAKING CONTACT & TERMS Send query letter with samples. Does not keep samples on file; include SASE for return of material. Responds in 1 month. Works on assignment only. Payment negotiable. Pays on publication. Buys one-time and electronic rights.

BARBOUR PUBLISHING, INC.

1810 Barbour Dr., P.O. Box 719, Urichsville OH 44683. **E-mail:** editors@barbourbooks.com; aschrock@barbourbooks.com; fictionsubmit@barbourbooks.com. **Website:** www.barbourbooks.com. Estab. 1981. "Barbour Books publishes inspirational/devotional material that is nondenominational and evangelical in nature. We're a Christian evangelical publisher." Specializes in short, easy-to-read Christian bargain books. "Faithfulness to the Bible and Jesus Christ are the bedrock values behind every book Barbour's staff produces."

BEARMANOR MEDIA

P.O. Box 71426, Albany GA 31708. (800)755-4506. **Fax:** (814)690-1559. **E-mail:** books@benohmart.com. **Website:** www.bearmanormedia.com. **Contact:** Ben Ohmart, publisher. Estab. 2000. Publishes 70 titles/year. Payment negotiable. Responds only if interested. Catalog available online or free with a 8×10 SASE submission.

TIPS "Potential freelancers should be familiar with our catalog and be computer savvy."

◎ 🏳 BENTLEY PUBLISHERS

1734 Massachusetts Ave., Cambridge MA 02138. (617)547-4170. **Fax:** (617)876-9235. **Website:** www.bentleypublishers.com. **Contact:** Michael Bentley, president. Estab. 1950. Publishes professional, technical, consumer how-to books. Photos used for text illustrations, promotional materials, book covers, dust jackets. Examples of published titles: *Porsche: Genesis of Genius; Toyota Prius Repair and Maintenance Manual.*

NEEDS Buys 70-100 photos/year; offers 5-10 freelance assignments/year. Looking for motorsport, automotive technical and engineering photos. Reviews stock photos. Model/property release required. Photo captions required; include date and subject matter.

SPECS Uses 8×10 transparencies. Accepts images in digital format.

MAKING CONTACT & TERMS Send query letter with samples. Provide résumé, business card, brochure, flyer or tearsheets to be kept on file for possible future assignments. Keeps samples on file; cannot return material. Works on assignment only. Responds in 6 weeks. Simultaneous submissions and previously published work OK. Payment negotiable. Credit line given. Buys electronic and one-time rights.

TIPS "Bentley Publishers publishes books for automotive enthusiasts. We are interested in books that showcase good research, strong illustrations, and valuable technical information."

CAPSTONE PRESS

1710 Roe Crest Dr., North Mankato MN 56003. (800)747-4992. **Fax:** (888)262-0705. **E-mail:** nf.il.sub@capstonepub.com (nonfiction); il.sub@capstonepub.com (fiction). **Website:** www.capstonepress.com. **Contact:** Dede Barton, photo director. Estab. 1991. Publishes juvenile nonfiction and educational books. Subjects include animals, ethnic groups, vehicles, sports, history, scenics. Photos used for text illustrations, promotional materials, book covers. "To see examples of our products, please visit our website." Submission guidelines available online.

NEEDS Buys about 3,000 photos/year. "Our subject matter varies (usually 100 or more different subjects/year); editorial-type imagery preferable although always looking for new ways to show an overused subject or title (fresh)." Model/property release preferred. Photo captions preferred; include "basic description; if people of color, state ethnic group; if scenic, state location and date of image."

SPECS Accepts images in digital format for submissions as well as for use. Digital images must be at least 8×10 at 300 dpi for publishing quality (TIFF, EPS or original camera file format preferred).

MAKING CONTACT & TERMS Send query letter with stock list. E-mail résumé, sample artwork, and a list of previous publishing credits if applicable. Keeps samples on file. Responds in 6 months. Simultaneous submissions and previously published work OK. Pays after publication. Credit line given. Looking to buy worldwide all language rights for print and digital rights. Producing online projects (interactive websites and books); printed books may be bound up into binders.

TIPS "Be flexible. Book publishing usually takes at least 6 months. Capstone does not pay holding fees. Be prompt. The first photos in are considered for covers first."

CENTERSTREAM PUBLICATION LLC

P.O. Box 17878, Anaheim CA 92807. (714)779-9390. **E-mail:** centerstrm@aol.com. **Website:** www.centerstream-usa.com. **Contact:** Ron Middlebrook, owner. Estab. 1982. "Centerstream is known for its unique publications for a variety of instruments. From instructional and reference books and biographies, to fun song collections and DVDs, our products are created by experts who offer insight and invaluable information to players and collectors." Publishes music history, biographies, DVDs, music instruction (all instruments). Photos used for text illustrations, book covers. Examples of published titles: *Dobro Techniques*; *History of Leedy Drums*; *History of National Guitars*; *Blues Dobro*; *Jazz Guitar Christmas* (book covers).

NEEDS Reviews stock photos of music. Model release preferred. Photo captions preferred.

SPECS Uses color and b&w prints; 35mm, 2¼×2¼, 4×5 transparencies. Accepts images in digital format. Send via ZIP as TIFF files.

MAKING CONTACT & TERMS Send query letter with samples and stock list. Send unsolicited photos by mail for consideration. Provide résumé, business card, brochure, flyer or tearsheets to be kept on file for possible future assignments. Works on assignment only. Responds in 1 month. Simultaneous submissions and previously published work OK. Payment negotiable. Pays on receipt of invoice. Credit line given. Buys all rights.

CLEIS PRESS

Cleis Press & Viva Editions, 2246 Sixth St., Berkeley CA 94710. (510)845-8000 or (800)780-2279. **Fax:** (510)845-8001. **E-mail:** cleis@cleispress.com; bknight@cleispress.com. **Website:** www.cleispress.com. **Contact:** Brenda Knight, publisher. Estab. 1980. Cleis Press publishes provocative, intelligent books in the areas of sexuality, gay and lesbian studies, erotica, fiction, gender studies, and human rights. Publishes fiction, nonfiction, trade and gay/lesbian erotica. Photos used for book covers. Buys 20 photos/year. Reviews stock photos. Works with freelancers on assignment only. Keeps samples on file. Pays on publication.

NEEDS Fiction, nonfiction, trade and gay/lesbian erotica; photos used for book covers.

SPECS Uses color and/or b&w prints.

MAKING CONTACT & TERMS Query via e-mail only. Provide résumé, business card, brochure, flyer or tearsheets to be kept on file for possible future assignments.

🟢🟢 CONARI PRESS

Red Wheel/Weiser, LLC., 665 Third St., Suite 400, San Francisco CA 94107. **E-mail:** info@rwwbooks.com; submissions@rwwbooks.com. **Website:** www.red wheelweiser.com. **Contact:** Pat Bryce, acquisitions editor. Estab. 1987. Publishes hardcover and trade paperback originals and reprints. Subjects include women's studies, psychology, parenting, inspiration, home and relationships (all nonfiction titles). Photos used for text illustrations, book covers, dust jackets.

NEEDS Buys 5-10 freelance photos /year. Looking for artful photos; subject matter varies. Interested in reviewing stock photos of most anything except high-tech, corporate or industrial images. Model release required. Photo captions preferred; include photography copyright.

SPECS Prefers images in digital format.

MAKING CONTACT & TERMS Provide résumé, business card, self-promotion piece or tearsheets to be kept on file for possible future assignments. Art director will contact photographer for portfolio review if interested. Portfolio should include prints, tearsheets, slides, transparencies or thumbnails. Keeps samples on file. Simultaneous submissions and previously published work OK. Pays by the project: $400-1,000 for color cover; rates vary for color inside. Pays on publication. Credit line given on copyright page or back cover.

TIPS "Review our website to make sure your work is appropriate."

🟢 CRABTREE PUBLISHING COMPANY

PMB 59051, 350 Fifth Ave., 59th Floor, New York NY 10118. (212)496-5040; (800)387-7650. **Fax:** (800)355-7166. **Website:** www.crabtreebooks.com. Estab. 1978. Publishes juvenile nonfiction, library and trade. Subjects include science, cultural events, history, geography (including cultural geography), sports. Photos used for text illustrations, book covers. Examples of recently published titles: *The Mystery of the Bermuda Triangle, Environmental Activist, Paralympic Sports Events, Presidents' Day, Plant Cells, Bomb and Mine Disposal Officers.*

🖵 This publisher also has offices in Canada, United Kingdom and Australia.

NEEDS Buys 20-50 photos/year. Wants photos of cultural events around the world, animals (exotic and domestic). Model/property release required for children, photos of artwork, etc. Photo captions preferred; include place, name of subject, date photographed, animal behavior.

SPECS Uses high-res digital files (no compressed JPEG files).

MAKING CONTACT & TERMS *Does not accept unsolicited photos.* Provide résumé, business card, brochure, flyer or tearsheets to be kept on file for possible future assignments. Simultaneous submissions and previously published work OK. Pays $100 for color photos. Pays on publication. Credit line given. Buys non-exclusive, worldwide and electronic rights.

TIPS "Since our books are for younger readers, lively photos of children and animals are always excellent." Portfolio should be diverse and encompass several subjects, rather than just 1 or 2; depth of coverage of subject should be intense so that any publishing company could, conceivably, use all or many of a photographer's photos in a book on a particular subject."

CREATIVE WITH WORDS PUBLICATIONS (CWW)

P.O. Box 223226, Carmel CA 93922. **Fax:** (831)655-8627. **E-mail:** geltrich@mbay.net. **Website:** members.tripod.com/CreativeWithWords. Estab. 1975. Publishes 2 poetry and prose anthologies per year according to set themes. B&w photos used for text illustrations, book covers. Photo guidelines, theme list and submittal forms free with SASE.

NEEDS Needs theme-related b&w photos. Currently looking for spring and fall themes. Model/property release preferred.

SPECS Uses any size b&w photos. "We will reduce to fit the page."

MAKING CONTACT & TERMS Request theme list, then query with photos. Does not keep samples on file; include SASE for return of material. Responds 3 weeks after deadline if submitted for a specific theme. Payment for illustrations negotable. Pays on publication. Credit line given. Buys one-time rights.

DOWN THE SHORE PUBLISHING

P.O. Box 100, West Creek NJ 08092. **Fax:** (609)597-0422. **E-mail:** info@down-the-shore.com. **Website:** www.down-the-shore.com. Publishes regional calendars; seashore, coastal and regional books (specific to the mid-Atlantic shore and New Jersey). Photos used for text illustrations, scenic calendars (New Jersey and mid-Atlantic only). Examples of recently published titles include *Great Storms of the Jersey Shore* (text illustrations); *NJ Lighthouse Calendar* (illustrations, cover); *Shore Stories* (text illustrations, dust jacket). Photo guidelines free with SASE or on website.

NEEDS Buys 30-50 photos/year. For calendars, needs scenic coastal shots, photos of beaches and New Jersey lighthouses (New Jersey and mid-Atlantic region). Interested in seasonal. Reviews stock photos. Model release required, property release preferred. Photo captions preferred, specific location identification essential. Digital submissions via high-res files on DVD/CD. Provide reference prints. Accepts 35mm, 2¼×2¼, 4×5, transparencies.

MAKING CONTACT & TERMS Refer to guidelines before submitting. Send query letter with stock list. Provide résumé, business card, brochure, flyer or tearsheets to be kept on file for possible future requests. Responds in 6 weeks. Previously published work OK. Pays $100-200 for b&w or cover color; $10-100 for b&w or color inside. Pays 90 days from publication. Credit line given. Buys one-time or book rights, negotiable.

TIPS "We are looking for an honest depiction of familiar scenes from an unfamiliar and imaginative perspective. Images must be specific to our very regional needs. Limit your submissions to your best work. Edit your work very carefully."

🍁 $$ ◘ ◐ ECW PRESS

2120 Queen St. E., Suite 200, Toronto Ontario M4E 1E2, Canada. (416)694-3348. **Fax:** (416)698-9906. **E-mail:** info@ecwpress.com. **Website:** www.ecwpress.com. **Contact:** Jack David, publisher. Estab. 1974. Publishes hardcover and trade paperback originals. Subjects include entertainment, biography, sports, travel, fiction, poetry. Photos used for text illustrations, book covers, dust jackets.

NEEDS Buys hundreds of freelance photos/year. Looking for color, b&w, fan/backstage, paparazzi, action, original, rarely used. Reviews stock photos. Property release required for entertainment or star shots. Photo captions required; include identification of all people.

SPECS Accepts images in digital format only.

MAKING CONTACT & TERMS "It is best to contact us by e-mail and direct us to your work online. Please also describe what area(s) you specialize in. Since our projects vary in topic, we will keep you on file in case we publish something along the lines of your subject(s)." Pays by the project: $250-600 for color cover; $50-125 for color inside. Pays on publication. Credit line given. Buys one-time book rights (all markets).

FARCOUNTRY PRESS

P.O. Box 5630, Helena MT 59604. (800)821-3874. **Fax:** (406)443-5480. **E-mail:** will@farcountrypress.com. **Website:** www.farcountrypress.com. **Contact:** Will Harmon. Photographer guidelines are available on our website.

NEEDS Color photography of landscapes (including recreation), cityscapes, and wildlife in the US.

SPECS For digital photo submissions, please send 8- or 16-bit TIFF files (higher preferred), at least 350 dpi or higher, formatted for Mac, RGB profile. All images should be flattened—no channels or layers. Information, including watermarks, should not appear directly on the images. Include either a contact sheet or a folder with low-res files for quick editing. Include copyright and caption data. Model releases are required for all images featuring recognizable individuals. Note on the mount or in the metadata that a model release is available. Do not submit images that do not have model releases.

MAKING CONTACT & TERMS Send query letter with stock list. Unsolicited submissions of photography WILL NOT be accepted and WILL NOT be returned. Simultaneous submissions and previously published work OK.

🍁 $$ FIFTH HOUSE PUBLISHERS

Fitzhenry & Whiteside, 195 Allstate Pkwy., Markham Ontario L3R 4T8, Canada. (403)571-5230; (800)387-9776. **E-mail:** sfitz@fifthhousepublishers.ca. **Website:** www.fifthhousepublishers.ca. **Contact:** Sharon Fitzhenry, publisher. Estab. 1982. "Fifth House Publishers is committed to 'bringing the West to the rest' by publishing approximately 15 books a year about the land and people who make this region unique. We publish the acclaimed *Going Wild* series, Pierre Berton's *History for Young Canadians, Keepers of Life,* the *Western Canadian Classics* series, the *Prairie Gardening* series, and more. Our books are selected for their quality and contribution to the understanding of western-Canadian (and Canadian) history, culture and environment."

NEEDS Buys 15-20 photos/year. Looking for photos of Canadian weather. Model/property release preferred. Photo captions required; include location and identification.

MAKING CONTACT & TERMS Send query letter with samples and stock list. Keeps samples on file. Pays $400 Canadian/calendar image. Pays on publication. Credit line given. Buys one-time rights.

☺ FIREFLY BOOKS

50 Staples Ave., Unit 1, Richmond Hill Ontario L4B 0A7, Canada. (416)499-8412. **E-mail:** service@firefly books.com; valerie@fireflybooks.com. **Website:** www. fireflybooks.com. Estab. 1974. Publishes high-quality nonfiction. Photos used for text illustrations, book covers and dust jackets.

NEEDS "We're looking for book-length ideas, *not* stock. We pay a royalty on books sold, plus advance."

SPECS Prefers images in digital format, but will accept 35mm transparencies.

MAKING CONTACT & TERMS Send query letter with résumé of credits. Does not keep samples on file; include SAE/IRC for return of material. Simultaneous submissions OK. Payment negotiated with contract. Credit line given.

FLASHLIGHT PRESS

527 Empire Blvd., Brooklyn NY 11225. (718)288-8300. **Fax:** (718)972-6307. **E-mail:** editor@flashlightpress. com. **Website:** www.flashlightpress.com. **Contact:** Shari Dash Greenspan, editor. Estab. 2004.

MAKING CONTACT & TERMS Submission guidelines available at www.flashlightpress.com/submis sionguidelines.html. Buys all rights, accepts reprints.

● FOCAL PRESS

Taylor & Francis Group, 7625 Empire Dr., Florence KY 41042. (800)634-7064. **Fax:** (800)248-4724. **E-mail:** jessie.taylor@taylorandfrancis.com. **Website:** www.focalpress.com. Estab. 1938.

NEEDS "We publish professional reference titles, practical guides and student textbooks in all areas of media and communications technology, including photography and digital imaging. We are always looking for new proposals for book ideas. Send e-mail for proposal guidelines."

MAKING CONTACT & TERMS Simultaneous submissions and previously published work OK. Buys all rights; negotiable.

GRYPHON HOUSE, INC.

P.O. Box 10, 6848 Leon's Way, Lewisville NC 27023. **Website:** www.gryphonhouse.com. **Contact:** Kathy Charner, editor-in-chief. Estab. 1981.

NEEDS Model release required.

SPECS Uses 5×7 glossy color (cover only) and b&w prints. Accepts images in digital format. Send via CD, ZIP, e-mail as TIFF files at 300 dpi.

MAKING CONTACT & TERMS Send query letter with samples and stock list. Keeps samples on file. Simultaneous submissions OK. Payment negotiable. Pays on receipt of invoice. Credit line given. Buys book rights.

☺ GUERNICA EDITIONS

1569 Heritage Way, Oakville Ontario L6M 2Z7, Canada. (905)599-5304. **Fax:** (416)981-7606. **E-mail:** michaelmirolla@guernicaeditions.com. **Website:** www.guernicaeditions.com. **Contact:** Michael Mirolla, editor/publisher (poetry, nonfiction, short stories, novels). Estab. 1978. Publishes adult trade (literary). Photos used for book covers. Examples of recently published titles: *Untying the Apron: Daughters Remember Their Mothers of the 1950s*, edited by Lorri Neilsen Glenn (anthology); *Camerado & the Trial of Pius XII*, by Richard Gambino (plays); *Where the Sun Shines Best*, by Austin Clarke (poems); *Fatal Light Awareness*, by John O'Neill (novel).

SPECS Uses color or b&w prints. Accepts images in digital format. Send via CD, ZIP as TIFF, GIF files at 300 dpi minimum.

MAKING CONTACT & TERMS Manuscript queries by e-mail only (via online contact form). "Before inquiring, please check our website to determine the type of material that best fits our publishing house."

⊕ ◑ HARPERCOLLINS CHILDREN'S BOOKS/HARPERCOLLINS PUBLISHERS

195 Broadway, New York NY 10007. (212)207-7000. **Website:** www.harpercollins.com. **Contact:** Katherine Tegen, vice president and publisher; Anica Mrose Rissi, executive editor; Claudia Gabel, executive editor; Kathleen Duncan, general design assistant; Erica Dechavez, picture book assistant designer. Publishes hardcover originals and reprints, trade paperback originals and reprints, mass market paperback originals and reprints, and audiobooks. 500 titles/year.

NEEDS Babies/children/teens, couples, multicultural, pets, food/drink, fashion, lifestyle. Send links to work. No attachments, please. "We are interested in seeing samples of map illustrations, chapter spots, full page pieces, etc. We are open to half-tone and line art illustrations for our interiors." Negotiates a flat payment fee upon acceptance. Will contact if interested. Catalog available online.

MAKING CONTACT & TERMS Art only, no ms's. Submission of texts to editorial departments only; no attachments please. Send links to artwork only.

TIPS "Be flexible and responsive to comments and corrections. Hold to scheduled due dates for work. Show work that reflects the kinds of projects you *want* to get, be focused on your best technique and showcase the strongest, most successful examples."

$$ ◐ HOLT MCDOUGAL

1900 S. Batavia Ave., Geneva IL 60134. (800)462-6595. **Fax:** (888)872-8380. **E-mail:** k12orders@hmhpub.com. **Website:** www.hmhco.com. Estab. 1866. Publishes textbooks in multiple formats. Photos are used for text illustrations, promotional materials and book covers.

NEEDS Uses 6,500+ photos/year. Wants photos that illustrate content for mathematics, sciences, social studies, world languages and language arts. Model/property release preferred. Photo captions required; include scientific explanation, location and/or other detailed information.

SPECS Prefers images in digital format. Send via CD or broadband transmission.

MAKING CONTACT & TERMS Send a query letter with a sample of work (nonreturnable photocopies, tearsheets, printed promos) and a list of subjects in stock. Self-promotion pieces kept on file for future reference. Include promotional website link if available. "Do not call!" Will respond only if interested. Payment negotiable depending on format and number of uses. Credit line given.

TIPS "Our book image programs yield an emphasis on rights-managed stock imagery, with a focus on teens and a balanced ethnic mix. Though we commission assignment photography, we maintain an in-house studio with 2 full-time photographers. We are interested in natural-looking, uncluttered photographs labeled with exact descriptions that are technically correct and include no evidence of liquor, drugs, cigarettes or brand names."

$$ HUMAN KINETICS PUBLISHERS

E-mail: acquisitions@hkusa.com. **E-mail:** lauraaf@hkusa.com. **Website:** www.humankinetics.com. **Contact:** Laura Fitch, photo asset manager. Estab. 1979. Publishes consumer books and textbooks in various formats, online courses, websites and DVD. Subjects include sports, fitness, physical therapy, sports medicine, nutrition, physical activity. Photos used for text illustrations, promotional materials, catalogs, web content, book covers. Photo guidelines available via e-mail.

NEEDS Buys stock photography for many products. "We have an in-house photo studio with 1 full-time photographer but hire freelance photographers when needed." Stock subject matter varies but often includes: sports (all ages, abilities and levels, from elite to intramural), health and fitness, nutrition, K-12 education, active aging and dance. Emphasis on diversity. Model releases preferred.

SPECS Accepts digital submissions only. Prefers links to lightboxes but will accept JPEGs via FTP or CD. High resolution files should be available 9×12 inches @ 300 dpi if selected. Full guidelines available via e-mail.

MAKING CONTACT & TERMS Send query e-mail with URL to your work online for placement onto our photo research request mailing list or to be considered for future photo assignment work. Responds only if interested. Simultaneous submissions and previously published work OK. Pays on publication. Credit line given. Buys one-time rights. Prefers world rights, all languages, for one edition in both print and e-book formats; negotiable. Pay for covers ranges from $200-500; pay for interior photos ranges from $75-125.

TIPS " View our products at our website humankinetics.com or at your local bookstore to decide if your work matches our content. We lean toward editorial style photography focused on people and lifestyle. Photographs generally should be well composed and natural looking. Diversity in race, ethnicity, age and ability is important. Also note that book production is a lengthy process. A time frame of 6 months from photo selection to finished layout is typical. We request invoices once layout is final and ready for print. Changes to photo selections can and do happen within that time period."

⊚ ● HYPERION BOOKS FOR CHILDREN

44 S. Broadway, Floor 16, White Plains NY 10601. (914)288-4100. **Website:** www.disneybooks.com. Publishes children's books, including picture books and books for young readers. Subjects include adventure, animals, history, multicultural, sports. Catalog available with 9×12 SASE and 3 first-class stamps.

NEEDS Photos of multicultural subjects.

MAKING CONTACT & TERMS Provide résumé, business card, self-promotion piece to be kept on file for possible future assignments. Pays royalties based on retail price of book, or a flat fee.

🔁 💲 🌗 IMMEDIUM

P.O. Box 31846, San Francisco CA 94131. (415)452-8546. **Fax:** (360)937-6272. **Website:** www.immedium.com. Estab. 2005. "*Immedium* focuses on publishing eye-catching children's picture books, Asian American topics, and contemporary arts, popular culture, and multicultural issues."

NEEDS Babies/children/teens, multicultural, families, parents, entertainment, lifestyle. Photos for dust jackets, promotional materials and book covers.

MAKING CONTACT & TERMS Send query letter with résumé, samples and/or SASE. Photo captions and property releases are required. Rights are negotiated and will vary with project.

TIPS "Look at our catalog—it's colorful and a little edgy. Tailor your submission to our catalog. We need responsive workers."

💲💲 ⊚ 🌗 INNER TRADITIONS/BEAR & COMPANY

1 Park St., Rochester VT 05767. (802)767-3174. **Fax:** (802)767-3726. **E-mail:** peris@innertraditions.com. **Website:** www.innertraditions.com. **Contact:** Peri Ann Swan, art director. Estab. 1975. Publishes adult trade and teen self-help. Subjects include new age, health, self-help, esoteric philosophy. Photos used for text illustrations, book covers. Examples of recently published titles: *Tibetan Sacred Dance* (cover, interior); *Tutankhamun Prophecies* (cover); *Animal Voices* (cover, interior).

NEEDS Buys 10-50 photos/year; offers 5-10 freelance assignments/year. Photos of babies/children/teens, multicultural, families, parents, religious, alternative medicine, environmental, landscapes/scenics. Interested in fine art, historical/vintage. Reviews stock photos. Model/property release required. Photo captions preferred.

SPECS Prefers images in digital format. Send via CD, ZIP as TIFF, EPS, JPEG files at 300 dpi or provide comps via e-mail.

MAKING CONTACT & TERMS Provide résumé, business card, brochure, flyer or tearsheets to be kept on file for possible future assignments. Works with freelancers on assignment only. Simultaneous submissions OK. Pays $150-600 for color cover; $50-200 for b&w and color inside. Pays on publication. Credit line given. Buys book rights; negotiable.

LERNER PUBLISHING GROUP

1251 Washington Ave. N., Minneapolis MN 55401. (800)452-7236; (612)332-3344. **Fax:** (612)337-7615. **E-mail:** editorial@karben.com. **Website:** www.karben.com; www.lernerbooks.com. Estab. 1957. Publishes educational books for grades K-12. Subjects include animals, biography, history, geography, science, vehicles, and sports. Photos used for editorial purposes for text illustrations, promotional materials, book covers. Examples of recently published titles: *A Temperate Forest Food Chain—Follow That Food* (text illustrations, book cover); *Protecting Earth's Water Supply—Saving Our Living Earth* (text illustrations, book cover).

NEEDS Buys more than 6,000 photos/year; occasionally offers assignments. Photos of children/teens, celebrities, multicultural, families, disasters, environmental, landscapes/scenics, wildlife, cities/urban, education, pets, rural, hobbies, sports, agriculture, industry, political, science, vehicles, technology/computers. Model/property release preferred when photos are of social issues (e.g., the homeless). Photo captions required; include who, where, what and when.

SPECS Prefers images in digital format. Send via FTP, CD, or e-mail as TIFF or JPEG files at 300 dpi.

MAKING CONTACT & TERMS Send query letter with detailed stock list by mail, fax or e-mail. Provide current editorial use pricing. "No calls, please." Cannot return material. Responds only if interested. Previously published work OK. Pays by the project: $150-400 for cover; $50-150 for inside. Pays on receipt of invoice. Credit line given. Licenses images for book based on print-run rights, electronic rights, all language rights, worldwide territory rights. Submission guidelines available online.

TIPS Prefers crisp, clear images that can be used editorially. "Send in as detailed a stock list as you can (including fees for clearing additional rights), and be willing to negotiate price."

☺ MAGENTA PUBLISHING FOR THE ARTS

151 Winchester St., Toronto Ontario M4X 1B5, Canada. **E-mail:** info@magentafoundation.org. **Website:** www.magentafoundation.org. **Contact:** Submissions. Estab. 2004. "Established in 2004, The Magenta Foundation is Canada's pioneering non-profit, charitable arts publishing house. Magenta was created to organize promotional opportunities for artists, in an international context, through circulated exhibitions and publications. Projects mounted by Magenta are supported by credible international media coverage and critical reviews in all mainstream-media formats (radio, television and print). Magenta works with respected individuals and international organizations to help increase recognition for artists while uniting the global photography community."

○ Magenta works with key international organizations and individuals to help increase recognition for Canadian artists around the world, uniting the global photography community. Through its partnerships, Magenta sets a standard for community collaboration while developing both a domestic and international presence vital to the success of Canadian artists. Magenta's good reputation is growing with each project. The attention our artists receive reinforces our organization's mandate to remain dedicated to increasing Canada's visual arts profile around the world.

◎ MBI, INC.

47 Richards Ave., Norwalk CT 06857. (203)853-2000. **E-mail:** webmail@mbi-inc.com. **Website:** www.mbi-inc.com/publishing.asp. Estab. 1965.

○ Our Book Division is Easton Press. Maintains one of America's largest private archives of specially commissioned illustrations, book introductions, and literary criticism.

⑤⑤⑤ ❶ MCGRAW-HILL

1333 Burr Ridge Pkwy., Burr Ridge IL 60527. (630)789-4000. **Fax:** (800)634-3963. **E-mail:** cheryl_georgas@mcgraw-hill.com. **Website:** www.mheducation.com. Publishes hardcover originals, textbooks, CDs. Photos used for book covers.

NEEDS Buys 20 freelance photos/year. Needs photos of business concepts, industry, technology/computers.
SPECS Uses 8×10 glossy prints; 35mm, 2¼×2¼, 4×5 transparencies. Accepts images in digital format. Send via CD.
MAKING CONTACT & TERMS Contact through local sales rep (see submission guidelines online) or via online form. Provide business card, self-promotion piece to be kept on file for possible future assignments. Responds only if interested. Previously published work OK. Pays extra for electronic usage of photos. Pays on publication. Credit line given. Buys one-time rights.

❹ ⑤ MITCHELL LANE PUBLISHERS, INC.

P.O. Box 196, Hockessin DE 19707. (302)234-9426. **Fax:** (866)834-4164. **E-mail:** barbaramitchell@mitchelllane.com. **Website:** www.mitchelllane.com. **Contact:** Barbara Mitchell, publisher. Estab. 1993. Publishes hardcover originals for library market. Subjects include biography and other nonfiction for children and young adults. Photos used for text illustrations, book covers. Examples of recently published titles: *Your Land and My Land: Africa*; Abby Wambach and Kevin Durant (text illustrations, book cover).
NEEDS Photo captions required.
SPECS Accepts images in digital format. Send via CD as TIFF, JPEG files at 300 dpi.
MAKING CONTACT & TERMS Send query letter with stock list (stock photo agencies only). Does not keep samples on file; cannot return material. Responds only if interested. Pays on publication. Credit line given. Buys one-time editorial rights.

○ MONDIAL

203 W. 107th St., Suite 6C, New York NY 10025. (212)851-3252. **Fax:** (208)361-2863. **E-mail:** contact@mondialbooks.com. **Website:** www.mondialbooks.com; www.librejo.com. **Contact:** Andrew Moore, editor. Estab. 1996. Publishes mainstream fiction, romance, history and reference books. Specializes in linguistics.
NEEDS Landscapes, travel and erotic. Printing rights are negotiated according to project. Illustrations are used for text illustration, promotional materials and book covers. Publishes 20 titles/year. Responds only if interested.
MAKING CONTACT & TERMS Payment on acceptance.

MUSEUM OF NORTHERN ARIZONA

3101 N. Fort Valley Rd., Flagstaff AZ 86001. (928)774-5213. **E-mail:** publications@mna.mus.az.us. **Website:** www.musnaz.org. **Contact:** publications department. Estab. 1928. Subjects include biology, geology, archaeology, anthropology and history. Photos used for *Plateau: Land and People of the Colorado Plateau* magazine, published twice/year (May, October).

NEEDS Buys approximately 80 photos/year. Biology, geology, history, archaeology and anthropology—subjects on the Colorado Plateau. Reviews stock photos. Photo captions preferred; include location, description and context.

SPECS Uses 8×10 glossy b&w prints; 35mm, 2¼×2¼, 4×5 and 8×10 transparencies. Prefers 2¼×2¼ transparencies or larger. Possibly accepts images in digital format. Submit via ZIP.

MAKING CONTACT & TERMS Send query letter with samples, SASE. Responds in 1 month. Simultaneous submissions and previously published work OK. Credit line given. Buys one-time and all rights; negotiable. Offers internships for photographers.

TIPS Wants to see top-quality, natural history work. To break in, send only pre-edited photos.

MUSIC SALES GROUP

14-15 Berners St., London W1T 3LJ, United Kingdom. +44 (020) 7612 7400. **Fax:** +44 (020) 7612 7547. **E-mail:** chris.charlesworth@musicsales.co.uk; info@omnibuspress.com. **Website:** www.musicsales.com; www.omnibuspress.com. Publishes instructional music books, song collections and books on music. Photos used for covers and interiors. Examples of recently published titles: *Bob Dylan: 100 Songs and Photos*; *Paul Simon: Surprise*; *AC/DC: Backtracks*.

NEEDS Buys 200 photos/year. Model release required on acceptance of photo. Photo captions required.

SPECS Uses 8×10 glossy prints; 35mm, 2×2, 5×7 transparencies. High-res digital 3000 × 4000 pixels.

MAKING CONTACT & TERMS Send query letter first with résumé of credits. Provide business card, brochure, flyer or tearsheets to be kept on file for possible future assignments. Responds in 2 months. Simultaneous submissions and previously published work OK.

TIPS In samples, wants to see "the ability to capture the artist in motion with a sharp eye for framing the shot well. Portraits must reveal what makes the artist unique. We need rock, jazz, classical—onstage and impromptu shots. Please send us an inventory list of available stock photos of musicians. We rarely send photographers on assignment and buy mostly from material on hand. Send business card and tearsheets or prints stamped 'proof' across them. Due to the nature of record releases and concert events, we never know exactly when we may need a photo. We keep photos on permanent file for possible future use."

NICOLAS-HAYS, INC.

P.O. Box 540206, Lake Worth FL 33454-0206. **E-mail:** info@nicolashays.com; info@ibispress.net. **Website:** www.nicolashays.com. Estab. 1976. Publishes trade paperback originals and reprints. Subjects include Eastern philosophy, Jungian psychology, New Age how-to. Photos used for book covers. Example of recently published title: *Dervish Yoga for Health and Longevity: Samadeva Gestual Euphony—The Seven Major Arkanas* (book cover). Catalog available upon request.

NEEDS Buys 1 freelance photo/year. Needs photos of landscapes/scenics.

SPECS Uses color prints; 35mm, 2¼×2¼, 4×5 transparencies. Accepts images in digital format.

MAKING CONTACT & TERMS Send query letter with photocopies, tearsheets. Provide self-promotion piece to be kept on file for possible future assignments. Responds only if interested; send nonreturnable samples. Simultaneous submissions and previously published work OK. **Pays on acceptance.** Credit line given. Buys one-time rights.

TIPS "We are a small company and do not use many photos. We keep landscapes/seascapes/skyscapes on hand—images need to be inspirational."

W.W. NORTON & COMPANY, INC.

500 Fifth Ave., New York NY 10110. (212)354-5500. **Fax:** (212)869-0856. **Website:** www.wwnorton.com. Estab. 1923. Photos used for text illustrations, book covers, dust jackets.

NEEDS Variable. Photo captions preferred.

SPECS Accepts images in all formats; digital images at a minimum of 300 dpi for reproduction and archival work.

MAKING CONTACT & TERMS "Due to the workload of our editorial staff and the large volume of materials we receive, we are no longer able to accept unsolicited submissions. If you are seeking publication, we suggest working with a literary agent who will represent you to the house."

RICHARD C. OWEN PUBLISHERS, INC.

P.O. Box 585, Katonah NY 10536. (914)232-3903; (800)262-0787. **E-mail:** richardowen@rcowen.com. **Website:** www.rcowen.com. **Contact:** Richard Owen, publisher. Estab. 1982. Publishes picture/storybook fiction and nonfiction for 5- to 7-year-olds; author autobiographies for 7- to 12-year-olds; professional books for educators. Photos used for text illustrations, promotional materials, book covers. Check website for examples of titles.

NEEDS Number of photos bought annually varies; offers 3-10 freelance assignments/year. Needs unposed people shots and nature photos that suggest storyline. "For children's books, must be child-appealing with rich, bright colors and scenes, no distortions or special effects. For professional books, similar, but often of classroom scenes, including teachers. Nothing posed; should look natural and realistic." Reviews stock photos of children involved with books and classroom activities, ranging from kindergarten to 6th grade. Also wants photos of babies/children/teens, multicultural, families, environmental, landscapes/scenics, wildlife, architecture, cities/urban, pets, adventure, automobiles, sports, travel, science. Interested in documentary. (All must be of interest to children ages 5-9.) Model release required for children and adults. Children (under the age of 21) must have signature of legal guardian. Property release preferred. Photo captions required; include "any information we would need for acknowledgments, including if special permission was needed to use a location."

SPECS "For materials that are to be used, we need 35mm mounted transparencies or high-definition color prints. We usually use full-color photos."

MAKING CONTACT & TERMS Submit copies of samples by mail for review. Provide brochure, flyer or tearsheets to be kept on file for possible future assignments; no slides or disks. Include a brief cover letter with name, address, and daytime phone number, and indicate *Photographer's Market* as a source for correspondence. Works with freelancers on assignment only. "For samples, we like to see any size color prints (or color copies)." Keeps samples on file "if appropriate to our needs." Responds in 1 month. Simultaneous submissions OK. Pays $10-100 for color cover; $10-100 for color inside; $250-800 for multiple photo projects. "Each job has its own payment rate and arrangements." **Pays on acceptance.** Credit line sometimes given, depending on the project. "Photographers' credits appear in children's books and in professional books, but not in promotional materials for books or company." For children's books, publisher retains ownership, possession and world rights, which apply to first and all subsequent editions of a particular title and to all promotional materials. "After a project, (children's books) photos can be used by photographer for portfolio."

TIPS Wants to see "real people in natural, real life situations. No distortion or special effects. Bright, clear images with jewel tones and rich colors. Keep in mind what would appeal to children. Be familiar with what the publishing company has already done. Listen to the needs of the company. Send tearsheets, color photocopies with a mailer. No slides, please."

PELICAN PUBLISHING COMPANY

1000 Burmaster St., Gretna LA 70053. (504)368-1175. **Fax:** (504)368-1195. **E-mail:** editorial@pelicanpub.com. **Website:** www.pelicanpub.com. Estab. 1926. Publishes adult trade, cooking and art books.

NEEDS Buys 8 photos/year; offers 3 freelance assignments/year. Needs photos of cooking/food, business concepts, nature/inspirational. Reviews royalty-free stock photos of people, nature, etc. Model/property release required. Photo captions required. Specs Uses 8×10 glossy color prints; 35mm, 4×5 transparencies. Accepts images in digital format. Send via CD as TIFF files at 300 dpi or higher.

PRAKKEN PUBLICATIONS, INC.

P.O. Box 8623, Ann Arbor MI 48107. (734)975-2800. **Fax:** (734)975-2787. **E-mail:** pam@eddigest.com; susanne@eddigest.com. **Contact:** Susanne Peckham, book editor; Sharon K. Miller, art/design/production manager. Estab. 1934. "We publish books for educators in career/vocational and technology education, as well as books for the machine trades and machinists' education. Currently emphasizing machine trades." Publishes *The Education Digest* (magazine for teachers and administrators), *Tech Directions* (magazine for technology and career/technical educators), text and reference books for technology and career/technical education, and posters. Photos used for text illustrations, promotional materials, book covers, magazine covers and posters. Photo guidelines available at website.

NEEDS Wants photos of education "in action," especially technology, career/technical education and general education; prominent historical figures, technology/computers, industry. Photo captions required; include scene location, activity.

SPECS Uses all media; any size. Accepts images in digital format. Send via CD, or e-mail, TIFF, EPS, JPEG files at 300 dpi.

MAKING CONTACT & TERMS Send query letter with samples. Send unsolicited photos by mail for consideration. Keeps samples on file. Payment negotiable. Methods of payment to be arranged. Credit line given. Rights negotiable.

TIPS Wants to see "high-quality action shots in tech/career tech-ed and general education classrooms" when reviewing portfolios. Send inquiry with relevant samples to be kept on file. "We buy very few freelance photographs but would be delighted to see something relevant."

QUARTO PUBLISHING PLC.

The Old Brewery, 6 Blundell St., London N7 9BH, United Kingdom. +44 020 7700 6700. **Fax:** +44 020 7700 8066. **E-mail:** info@quarto.com. **Website:** www.quarto.com. Publishes nonfiction books on a wide variety of topics including arts, crafts, natural history, home and garden, reference. Photos used for text illustrations, book covers, dust jackets. Examples of recently published titles: *The Color Mixing Bible*; *Garden Birds*; *The Practical Geologist*. Contact for photo guidelines.

NEEDS Buys 1,000 photos/year. Subjects vary with current projects. Needs photos of multicultural, environmental, wildlife, architecture, gardening, interiors/decorating, pets, religious, adventure, food/drink, health/fitness, hobbies, performing arts, sports, travel, product shots/still life, science, technology/computers. Interested in fashion/glamour, fine art, historical/vintage. Special photo needs include arts, crafts, alternative therapies, New Age, natural history. Model/property release required. Photo captions required; include full details of subject and name of photographer.

SPECS Uses all types of prints. Accepts images in digital format. Send via CD, floppy disk, ZIP, e-mail as TIFF, EPS, JPEG files at 72 dpi for viewing, 300 dpi for reproduction.

MAKING CONTACT & TERMS Provide résumé, business card, samples, brochure, flyer or tearsheets to be kept on file for future reference. Arrange a personal interview to show portfolio. Simultaneous sub-

missions and previously published work OK. Pays on publication. Credit line given. Buys one-time rights; negotiable.

TIPS "Be prepared to negotiate!"

ROBERTS PRESS

False Bay Books, 685 Spring St., #PMB 161, 330 False Bay Dr., Harbor WA 98250. **E-mail:** submit-robertspress@falsebaybooks.com. **Website:** www.robertsbookpress.com. Estab. 2004. Publishes ebook originals and reprints, trade paperback originals and reprints, and audio books. Publishes fiction, including Christian fiction, fantasy, thrillers, mystery, women's fiction, family drama, juvenile fiction, mainstream fiction, science fiction, young adult and literary fiction, anthologies and multi-author collaborations. Recent titles include *The End of Law, Elemental, Drowning, Camouflage.*

RUNNING PRESS BOOK PUBLISHERS

2300 Chestnut St., Suite 200, Philadelphia PA 19103. (215)567-5080. **Fax:** (215)568-2919. **E-mail:** frances.soopingchow@perseusbooks.com; perseus.promos@perseusbooks.com. **Website:** www.runningpress.com. **Contact:** Frances Soo Ping Chow, design director. Estab. 1972. Publishes hardcover originals, trade paperback originals. Subjects include adult and children's fiction and nonfiction; cooking; crafts, lifestyle, kits; miniature editions used for text illustrations, promotional materials, book covers, dust jackets. Examples of recently published titles: *Skinny Bitch, Eat What You Love, The Ultimate Book of Gangster Movies, Fenway Park, The Speedy Sneaky Chef, Les Petits Macarons, New York Fashion Week, I Love Lucy: A Celebration of All Things Lucy, Upcycling.*

NEEDS Buys a few hundred freelance photos/year and lots of stock images. Photos for gift books; photos of wine, food, lifestyle, hobbies, and sports. Model/property release preferred. Photo captions preferred; include exact locations, names of pertinent items or buildings, names and dates for antiques or special items of interest.

SPECS Prefers images in digital format. Send via CD/DVD, via FTP/e-mail as TIFF, EPS files at 300 dpi.

MAKING CONTACT & TERMS Send URL and provide contact info. Do not send original art or anything that needs to be returned. Responds only if interested. Simultaneous submissions and previously published work OK. Pays $500-1000 for color cover; $100-250 for inside. Pays 45 days after receipt of invoice. Credits listed on separate copyright or credit pages. Buys one-time rights.

TIPS Submission guidelines available online.

SCHOLASTIC LIBRARY PUBLISHING

90 Old Sherman Turnpike, Danbury CT 06816. (203)797-3500. **Fax:** (203)797-3197. **E-mail:** slpservice@scholastic.com. **Website:** www.scholastic.com/librarypublishing. **Contact:** Phil Friedman, vice president/publisher; Kate Nunn, editor-in-chief; Marie O'Neil, art director. Estab. 1895. "Scholastic Library is a leading publisher of reference, educational, and children's books. We provide parents, teachers, and librarians with the tools they need to enlighten children to the pleasure of learning and prepare them for the road ahead." Publishes 7 encyclopedias plus specialty reference sets in print and online versions. Photos used for text illustrations. Examples of published titles: *The New Book of Knowledge*; *Encyclopedia Americana*.

NEEDS Buys 5,000 images/year. Needs excellent-quality editorial photographs of all subjects A-Z and current events worldwide. All images must have clear captions and specific dates and locations, and natural history subjects should carry Latin identification.

SPECS Uses 8×10 glossy b&w and/or color prints; 35mm, 4×5, 8×10 (reproduction-quality dupes preferred) transparencies. Accepts images in digital format. Send via photo CD, floppy disk, ZIP as JPEG files at requested resolution.

MAKING CONTACT & TERMS Send query letter, stock lists and printed examples of work. Cannot return unsolicited material and does not send guidelines. Include SASE only if you want material returned. Pricing to be discussed if/when you are contacted to submit images for specific project. Please note, encyclopedias are printed every year, but rights are requested for continuous usage until a major revision of the article in which an image is used (including online images).

TIPS "Send subject lists and small selection of samples. Printed samples *only*, please. In reviewing samples, we consider the quality of the photographs, range of subjects, and editorial approach. Keep in touch, but don't overdo it—quarterly e-mails are more than enough for updates on subject matter."

SCHOOL GUIDE PUBLICATIONS

606 Halstead Ave., Mamaroneck NY 10543. (800)433-7771. **E-mail:** mridder@schoolguides.com; info@schoolguides.com. **Website:** www.schoolguides.com. **Contact:** Myles Ridder, publisher. Estab. 1935. Publishes mass market paperback originals. Photos used for promotional materials, book covers.

NEEDS Needs photos of college students.

SPECS Accepts images in digital format; send via CD, ZIP, e-mail as TIFF or JPEG files.

MAKING CONTACT & TERMS E-mail query letter. **Pays on acceptance.**

TIGHTROPE BOOKS

#207-2 College St., Toronto Ontario M5G 1K3, Canada. (416)928-6666. **E-mail:** tightropeasst@gmail.com. **Website:** www.tightropebooks.com. **Contact:** Jim Nason, publisher. Estab. 2005.

NEEDS Publishes 12 titles/year. SASE returned. Responds only if interested. Catalog and guidelines free upon request and online.

MAKING CONTACT & TERMS Send an e-mail with résumé, digital images and artist's website, if available.

TILBURY HOUSE PUBLISHERS

WordSplice Studio, Inc., 12 Starr St., Thomaston ME 04861. (800)582-1899. **Fax:** (207)582-8772. **E-mail:** tilbury@tilburyhouse.com. **Website:** www.tilburyhouse.com. **Contact:** Audrey Maynard, children's book editor; Jonathan Eaton, publisher. Estab. 1990.

MAKING CONTACT & TERMS Send photocopies of photos/artwork.

VINTAGE BOOKS

1745 Broadway, New York NY 10019. (212)782-9000. **E-mail:** vintageanchorpublicity@randomhouse.com; jgall@randomhouse.com. **Website:** www.randomhouse.com. **Contact:** John Gall, art director. Publishes trade paperback reprints; fiction. Photos used for book covers. Examples of recently published titles: *Selected Stories* by Alice Munro (cover); *The Fight* by Norman Mailer (cover); *Bad Boy* by Jim Thompson (cover).

NEEDS Buys 100 freelance photos/year. Model/property release required. Photo captions preferred.

MAKING CONTACT & TERMS Send query letter with samples, stock list. Portfolios may be dropped off every Wednesday. Keeps samples on file. Responds only if interested; send nonreturnable samples. Pays by the project, per use negotiation. Pays on publication. Credit line given. Buys one-time and first North American serial rights.

TIPS "Show what you love. Include samples with name, address and phone number."

VISITOR'S CHOICE MAGAZINE

2151 Ontario St., Vancouver British Columbia V5T 2X1, Canada. (604)608-5180; (604)688-2398. **E-mail:** art@visitorschoice.com. **Website:** www.visitorschoice. com. Estab. 1977. Publishes full-color visitor guides for 16 communities and areas of British Columbia. Photos used for text illustrations, book covers, websites. Photo guidelines available via e-mail upon request.

NEEDS Looking for photos of attractions, mountains, lakes, views, lifestyle, architecture, festivals, people, sports and recreation—specific to British Columbia region. Specifically looking for people/activity shots. Model release required; property release preferred. Photo captions required—make them detailed but brief.

SPECS Uses color prints; 35mm transparencies. Prefers images in digital format.

MAKING CONTACT & TERMS Send query letter or e-mail with samples; include SASE for return of material. Works with Canadian photographers. Keeps digital images on file. Responds in 3 weeks. Previously published work OK. Payment varies with size of photo published. Pays in 30-60 days. Credit line given.

VOYAGEUR PRESS

Quayside Publishing Group, 400 First Ave. N., Suite 400, Minneapolis MN 55401. (800)458-0454. **Fax:** (612)344-8691. **Website:** voyageurpress.com. Estab. 1972. Publishes adult trade books, hardcover originals and reprints. Subjects include regional history, nature, popular culture, travel, wildlife, Americana, collectibles, lighthouses, quilts, tractors, barns and farms. Photos used for text illustrations, book covers, dust jackets, calendars. Examples of recently published titles: *Legendary Route 66: A Journey Through Time Along America's Mother Road*; *Illinois Central Railroad*; *Birds in Love: The Secret Courting & Mating Rituals of Extraordinary Birds*; *Backroads of New York*; *How to Raise Cattle*; *Knitknacks*; *Much Ado About Knitting*; *Farmall: The Red Tractor That Revolutionized Farming*; *Backroads of Ohio*; *Farmer's Wife Baking Cookbook*; *John Deere Two-Cylinder Tractor Encyclopedia* (text illustrations, book covers, dust jackets). Photo guidelines free with SASE.

Voyageur Press is an imprint of MBI Publishing Company (see separate listing in this section).

NEEDS Buys 500 photos/year. Wants photos of wildlife, Americana, environmental, landscapes/scenics, cities/urban, gardening, rural, hobbies, humor, travel, farm equipment, agricultural. Interested in fine art, historical/vintage, seasonal. "Artistic angle is crucial—books often emphasize high-quality photos." Model release required. Photo captions preferred; include location, species, "interesting nuggets," depending on situation.

MAKING CONTACT & TERMS "Photographic dupes must be of good quality for us to fairly evaluate your photography. We prefer 35mm and large format transparencies; will accept images in digital format for review only; prefers transparencies for production. Send via CD, ZIP, e-mail as TIFF, BMP, GIF, JPEG files at 300 dpi." Simultaneous submissions OK. Pays $300 for cover; $75-175 for inside. Pays on publication. Credit line given, "but photographer's website will not be listed." Buys all rights; negotiable.

TIPS "We are often looking for specific material (crocodiles in the Florida Keys; farm scenics in the Midwest; wolf research in Yellowstone), so subject matter is important. However, outstanding color and angles and interesting patterns and perspectives are strongly preferred whenever possible. If you have the capability and stock to put together an entire book, your chances with us are much better. Though we use some freelance material, we publish many more single-photographer works. Include detailed captioning info on the mounts."

WAVELAND PRESS, INC.

4180 Illinois Rt. 83, Suite 101, Long Grove IL 60047. (847)634-0081. **Fax:** (847)634-9501. **E-mail:** info@ waveland.com. **Website:** www.waveland.com. Estab. 1975. Publishes college-level textbooks and supplements. Photos used for text illustrations, book covers. Examples of recently published titles: *Our Global Environment: A Health Perspective*, 7th edition; *Juvenile Justice*, 2nd edition.

NEEDS Number of photos purchased varies depending on type of project and subject matter. Subject matter should relate to college disciplines: criminal justice, anthropology, speech/communication, sociology, archaeology, etc. Photos of multicultural, disasters, environmental, cities/urban, education, religious, rural, health/fitness, agriculture, political, technology. Interested in fine art, historical/vintage. Model/property release required. Photo captions preferred.

SPECS Accepts images in digital format. Send via CD, ZIP, e-mail as TIFF, EPS, JPEG files at 300 dpi.

MAKING CONTACT & TERMS Send query letter with stock list. Provide résumé, business card, brochure, flyer or tearsheets to be kept on file for possible future assignments. Simultaneous submissions and previously published work OK. Pays $100-200 for cover; $50-100 for inside. Pays on publication. Credit line given. Buys one-time and book rights.

WILLOW CREEK PRESS

P.O. Box 147, Minocqua WI 54548. (715)358-7010. **Fax:** (715)358-2807. **Website:** www.willowcreekpress.com. **Contact:** Managing Editor. Estab. 1986. Publishes hardcover, paperback and trade paperback originals; hardcover and paperback reprints and calendars. Subjects include pets, outdoor sports, gardening, cooking, birding, wildlife. Photos used for text illustrations, promotional materials, book covers, dust jackets, and calendars. Examples of recently published titles: *Pug Principles, Just Sons, It's a Dad Thing, Spirit of the Wolf*. Catalog free with No. 10 SASE. Photo guidelines free with No. 10 SASE or on website.

NEEDS Buys 2,000 freelance photos/year. Needs photos of gardening, pets, outdoors, recreation, landscapes/scenics, wildlife. Model/property release required. Photo captions required.

MAKING CONTACT & TERMS Send query letter with sample of work. Provide self-promotion piece to be kept on file. Responds only if interested. Simultaneous submissions and previously published work OK. Pays by the project. Pays on publication. Credit line given. Buys one-time rights.

TIPS "We specialize in nature, outdoor, and sporting topics, including gardening, wildlife, and animal books. Pets, cookbooks, and a few humor books and essays round out our titles. Currently emphasizing pets (mainly dogs and cats), wildlife, outdoor sports (hunting, fishing). De-emphasizing essays, fiction."

⑨ WOMEN'S HEALTH GROUP

Rodale, 400 S. Tenth St., Emmaus PA 18098. (212)573-0296. **Website:** www.rodaleinc.com. **Contact:** Yelena Nesbit, communications director. Publishes hardcover originals and reprints, trade paperback originals and reprints, one-shots. Subjects include healthy, active living for women, including diet, cooking, health, beauty, fitness and lifestyle.

NEEDS Photos of babies/children/teens, couples, multicultural, families, parents, senior citizens, food/drink, health/fitness/beauty, sports, travel, women, Spanish women, intimacy/sexuality, alternative medicine, herbs, home remedies. Model/property release preferred.

SPECS Uses color and b&w prints; 35mm, 2¼×2¼, 4×5 transparencies. Accepts images in digital format. Send via CD, ZIP, e-mail as TIFF, EPS, JPEG files at 300 dpi.

MAKING CONTACT & TERMS Send query letter with résumé, prints, photocopies, tearsheets, stock list. Provide résumé, business card, self-promotion piece to be kept on file for possible future assignments. Responds only if interested; send nonreturnable samples. Simultaneous submissions and previously published work OK. Pays additional 20% for electronic promotion of book cover and designs for retail of book. **Pays on acceptance.** Credit line given. Buys one-time rights, electronic rights; negotiable.

TIPS "Include your contact information on each item that is submitted."

GREETING CARDS, POSTERS, & RELATED PRODUCTS

The greeting card industry takes in more than $7.5 billion per year—the lion's share through the giants American Greetings and Hallmark Cards. Naturally, these big companies are difficult to break into, but there is plenty of opportunity to license your images to smaller companies.

There are more than 3,000 greeting card companies in the United States, many of which produce low-priced cards that fill a niche in the market, focusing on anything from the cute to the risqué to seasonal topics. A number of listings in this section produce items like calendars, mugs, and posters, as well as greeting cards.

Before approaching greeting card, poster, or calendar companies, it's important to research the industry to see what's being bought and sold. Start by checking out card, gift, and specialty stores that carry greeting cards and posters. Pay attention to the selections of calendars, especially the large seasonal displays during December. Studying what you see on store shelves will give you an idea of what types of photos are marketable.

Greetings etc., published by Edgell Publications, is a trade publication for marketers, publishers, designers, and retailers of greeting cards. The magazine offers industry news and information on trends, new products, and trade shows. Look for the magazine at your library or visit their website: www.greetingsmagazine.com. Also the National Stationery Show (www.nationalstationeryshow.com) is a large trade show held every year in New York City. It is the main event of the greeting card industry.

APPROACHING THE MARKET

After your initial research, query companies you are interested in working with and send a stock photo list. (See sample stock list in "Running Your Business.") You can help narrow your search by consulting the Subject Index in the back of this book. Check the index for companies interested in the subjects you shoot.

Since these companies receive large volumes of submissions, they often appreciate knowing what is available rather than actually receiving samples. This kind of query can lead to future sales even if your stock inventory doesn't meet their immediate needs. Buyers know they can request additional submissions as their needs change. Some listings in this section advise sending quality samples along with your query while others specifically request only a list. As you plan your queries, follow the instructions to establish a good rapport with companies from the start.

Some larger companies have staff photographers for routine assignments but also look for freelance images. Usually, this is in the form of stock, and images are especially desirable if they are of unusual subject matter or remote scenic areas for which assignments—even to staff shooters—would be too costly. Freelancers are usually offered assignments once they have established track records and demonstrated a flair for certain techniques, subject matter, or locations. Smaller companies are more receptive to working with freelancers, though they are less likely to assign work because of smaller budgets for photography.

The pay in this market can be quite lucrative if you provide the right image at the right time for a client in need of it, or if you develop a working relationship with one or a few of the better-paying markets. You should be aware, though, that one reason for higher rates of payment in this market is that these companies may want to buy all rights to images. But with changes in the copyright law, many companies are more willing to negotiate sales that specify all rights for limited time periods or exclusive product rights rather than complete surrender of copyright. Some companies pay royalties, which means you will earn the money over a period of time based on the sales of the product.

☺☺ ◑ ADVANCED GRAPHICS

466 N. Marshall Way, Layton UT 84041. (801)499-5000 or (800)488-4144. **Fax:** (801)499-5001. **E-mail:** info@advancedgraphics.com. **Website:** www.advancedgraphics.com. Estab. 1984. Specializes in life-size standups and cardboard displays, decorations and party supplies.

NEEDS Photos of celebrities (movie and TV stars, entertainers), babies/children/teens, couples, multicultural, families, parents, senior citizens, wildlife. Interested in seasonal. Reviews stock photos.

SPECS Uses 4×5, 8×10 transparencies. Accepts images in digital format. Send via CD, ZIP, e-mail.

MAKING CONTACT & TERMS Send query letter with stock list. Keeps samples on file. Responds in 1 month. Pays $400 maximum/image; royalties of 7-10%. Simultaneous submissions and previously published work OK. **Pays on acceptance.** Credit line given. Buys exclusive product rights; negotiable.

TIPS "We specialize in publishing life-size, standup cardboard displays of celebrities. Any pictures we use must show the entire person, head to toe. We must also obtain a license for each image that we use from the celebrity pictured or from that celebrity's estate. The image should be vertical and not too wide."

✪ ART IN MOTION

425-625 Agnes St., New Westminster British Columbia V3M 5Y4, Canada. (604)525-3900 or (800)663-1308. **Fax:** (604)525-6166 or (877)525-6166. **E-mail:** artistrelations@artinmotion.com. **Website:** www.artinmotion.com. **Contact:** Art relations. Specializes in open edition reproductions, framing prints, wall decor and licensing.

NEEDS "We are publishers of fine art reproductions, specializing in the decorative and gallery market. In photography, we often look for alternative techniques such as hand coloring, Polaroid transfer, or any process that gives the photograph a unique look."

SPECS Accepts unzipped digital images sent via e-mail as JPEG files at 72 dpi.

MAKING CONTACT & TERMS Submit portfolio for review. Pays royalties of 10%. Royalties paid monthly. "Art In Motion covers all associated costs to reproduce and promote your artwork."

TIPS "Contact us via e-mail, or direct us to your website; also send slides or color copies of your work (all submissions will be returned)."

⊘ ARTVISIONS: FINE ART LICENSING

12117 SE 26th St., Bellevue WA 98005-4118. **E-mail:** ee website for contact form. **Website:** www.artvisions.com. **Contact:** Neil Miller, president. Estab. 1993. Licenses "fashionable, decorative fine art photography and high-quality art to the commercial print, décor and puzzle/game markets."

NEEDS Handles fine art and photography licensing only.

MAKING CONTACT & TERMS "See website. Not currently seeking new talent. However, we are always willing to view the work of top-notch established artists and photographers. If you fit this category, please contact ArtVisions via e-mail and include a link to a website where your art can be seen." Exclusive worldwide representation for licensing is required. Written contract provided.

TIPS "To gain an idea of the type of art we license, please view our website. Animals, children, people and pretty places should be generic, rather than readily identifiable (this also prevents potential copyright issues and problems caused by not having personal releases for use of a 'likeness'). We prefer that your original work be in the form of high-resolution TIFF files from a 'pro-quality' digital camera. Note: scans/digital files are not to be interpolated or compressed in any way. We are firmly entrenched in the digital world; if you are not, then we cannot represent you. If you need advice about marketing your art, please visit: www.artistsconsult.com."

☺☺ ◑ AVANTI PRESS, INC.

6 W. 18th St., 6th Floor, New York NY 10011. (212)414-1025; (800)228-2684. **E-mail:** artsubmissions@avantipress.com. **Website:** www.avantipress.com. Estab. 1980. Specializes in photographic greeting cards. Photo guidelines free with SASE or on website.

NEEDS Buys approximately 200 images/year; all are supplied by freelancers. Interested in humorous, narrative, colorful, simple, to-the-point photos of babies, children (4 years old and younger), mature adults, human characters (not models), animals (in humorous situations) and exceptional florals. Has specific deadlines for seasonal material. Does not want travel, sunsets, landscapes, nudes, high-tech. Reviews stock photos. Model/property release required.

SPECS Accepts all mediums and formats. Accepts images in digital format. Send via CD as TIFF, JPEG files.

MAKING CONTACT & TERMS Please submit low-res JPEGs using the e-mail submission form at avantipress.com. Do not submit original material. Pays on license. Credit line given. Buys 5-year worldwide, exclusive card rights.

● BENTLEY PUBLISHING GROUP

11100 Metric Blvd., Suite 100, Austin TX 78758. (512)467-9400 or (888)456-2254. **Fax:** (512)467-9411. **E-mail:** artist@bentleyglobalarts.com; info@bentleyglobalarts.com. **Website:** www.bentleyglobalarts.com. Estab. 1986. Publishes posters.

NEEDS Interested in figurative, architecture, cities, urban, gardening, interiors/decorating, rural, food/drink, travel—b&w, color or hand-tinted photography. Interested in alternative process, avant garde, fine art, historical/vintage. Reviews stock photos and slides. Model/property release required. Include location, date, subject matter or special information.

SPECS Mainly uses 16×20, 22×28, 18×24, 24×30, 24×36 color and b&w prints; 4×5 transparencies from high-quality photos. Accepts images in digital format. Send via CD as TIFF or JPEG files.

MAKING CONTACT & TERMS Prefers digital submissions. But also accepts mail with the online artist submission form- include photos, printouts, transparencies, disks or other marketing materials. If you send a disk, please include a printout showing thumbnail images of the contents. Please do not include orginal artwork. You can also e-mail JPEGs, along with contact information, to artist@benteyglobalarts.com. All submissions will be considered. Due to the large volume of submissions received, we can only respond if interested. For mail, send to Bentley Global Arts Group at address listed, ATTN: Artist Submissions.

◎ ● BON ART

66 Fort Point St., Norwalk CT 06855. (203)845-8888. **E-mail:** sales@bonartique.com. **Website:** www.bonartique.com. **Contact:** Brett Bonnist. Estab. 1980. Art publisher, poster company, licensing and design studio. Publishes/distributes fine art prints, canvas transfers, unlimited editions, offset reproductions and posters. Clients: Internet purveyors of art, picture frame manufacturers, catalog companies, distributors.

NEEDS Licenses hundresds of images/year. Artistic/decorative photos (not stock photos) of landscapes/scenics, wildlife, architecture, cities/urban, gardening, interiors/decorating, rural, adventure, health/fitness, extreme sports. Interested in fine art, cutting edge b&w, sepia photography. Model release required. Photo captions preferred.

SPECS Uses high-res digital files.

MAKING CONTACT & TERMS Prefers e-mail but will accept website links. Works on assignment only. Responds in 3 months. Simultaneous submissions and previously published work OK. Pays advance against royalties—specific dollar amount is subjective to project. Pays on publication. Credit line given if required. Buys all rights; exclusive reproduction rights. Royalties are paid quarterly according to the agreement.

TIPS "Send us new and exciting material; subject matter with universal appeal. Submit color copies, slides, transparencies, actual photos of your work; if we feel the subject matter is relevant to the projects we are currently working on, we'll contact you."

● THE BOREALIS PRESS

35 Tenney Hill, Blue Hill ME 04614. (207)370-6020 or (800)669-6845. **E-mail:** art@borealispress.net. **Website:** www.borealispress.net. **Contact:** Mark Baldwin. Estab. 1989. Specializes in greeting cards, magnets and "other products for thoughtful people." Photo guidelines available for SASE.

NEEDS Buys more than 100 images/year; 90% are supplied by freelancers. Needs photos of humor, babies/children/teens, couples, families, parents, senior citizens, adventure, events, hobbies, pets/animals. Interested in documentary, historical/vintage, seasonal. Photos must tell a story. Model/property release preferred.

SPECS Low-res files are fine for review. Any media OK for finals. Uses 5×7 to 8×10 prints; 35mm, 2¼×2¼, 4×5, 8×10 transparencies. Accepts images in digital format. Send via CD. Send low-res files if e-mailing. Send images to art@borealispress.net.

MAKING CONTACT & TERMS Send query letter with slides (if necessary), prints, photocopies, SASE. Send no originals on initial submissions. "Artist's name must be on every image submitted." Responds in 2 weeks to queries; 3 weeks to portfolios. Previously published work OK. Pays by the project, royalties. **Pays on acceptance**, receipt of contract.

TIPS "Photos should have some sort of story, in the loosest sense. They can be in any form. We do not want multiple submissions to other card companies.

Include SASE, and put your name on every image you submit."

CENTRIC CORP.

6712 Melrose Ave., Los Angeles CA 90038. (323)936-2100. **Fax:** (323)936-2101. **E-mail:** centric@juno.com. **Website:** www.centriccorp.com. Estab. 1986. Specializes in products that have nostalgic, humorous, thought-provoking images or sayings on them and in the following product categories: T-shirts, watches, pens, clocks, pillows, and drinkware.

NEEDS Photos of cities' major landmarks, attractions and things for which areas are well-known, and humorous or thought-provoking images. Submit seasonal material 5 months in advance. Reviews stock photos.

SPECS Uses 8×12 color and/or b&w prints; 35mm transparencies. Accepts images in digital format. Send via CD as PDF or JPEG files.

MAKING CONTACT & TERMS Submit portfolio online for review or query with résumé of credits. Provide résumé, business card, self-promotion piece or tearsheets to be kept on file for possible future assignments. Responds in 2 weeks. Works mainly with local freelancers. Pays by the job; negotiable. **Pays on acceptance.** Rights negotiable.

TIPS "Research the demographics of buyers who purchase Elvis, Lucy, Marilyn Monroe, James Dean, Betty Boop and Bettie Page products to know how to 'communicate a message' to the buyer."

COMSTOCK CARDS

1344 Disc Dr. #185, Sparks NV 89436. (800)326-7825. **Fax:** (888)266-2610. **E-mail:** production@cmpmarket. com. **Website:** www.comstockmarketplace.com. Estab. 1986. Specializes in greeting cards, invitations, notepads, games, gift wrap. Photo guidelines free with SASE.

NEEDS Buys/assigns 30-40 images/year; all are supplied by freelancers. Wants wild, outrageous and shocking adult humor; seductive images of men or women. Definitely does not want to see traditional, sweet, cute, animals or scenics. "If it's appropriate to show your mother, we don't want it!" Frontal nudity in both men and women is OK and now being accepted as long as it is professionally done—no snapshots from home. Submit seasonal material 10 months in advance. Model/property release required. Photo captions preferred.

SPECS Uses 5×7 color prints. Accepts images in digital format.

MAKING CONTACT & TERMS Send query letter with samples, tearsheets, SASE. Responds in 2 months. Pays $150-250 on publication. Buys all rights; negotiable.

TIPS "Submit with SASE if you want material returned."

DELJOU ART GROUP

1616 Huber St., Atlanta GA 30318. (404)350-7190 or (800)237-4638. **Fax:** (404)350-7195. **E-mail:** submit@deljouartgroup.com. **Website:** www.deljouartgroup.com. Estab. 1980. Specializes in wall decor, fine art.

NEEDS All images supplied by freelancers. Specializes in artistic images for reproduction for high-end art market. Work sold through art galleries as photos or prints. Needs nature photos, architectural images or other subjects with artistic quality. Reviews stock photos of graphics, b&w photos. No tourist photos: only high-quality, artistic photos.

SPECS Uses color and/or b&w prints. Accepts images in digital format. Prefers initial digital submissions via e-mail, but will accept CDs. Final, accepted images must be high-res, of at least 300 dpi.

MAKING CONTACT & TERMS Submit portfolio for review; include SASE for return of material. Also send portfolio via e-mail. Simultaneous submissions and previously published work OK. Pays royalties on sales. Credit line sometimes given depending upon the product. Rights negotiable.

TIPS "Abstract-looking photographs OK. Digitally created images are OK. Hand-colored b&w photographs needed."

DESIGN DESIGN, INC.

19 La Grave Ave., Grand Rapids MI 49503. (616)771-8319; (866)935-2648. **E-mail:** susan.birnbaum@designdesign.us. **E-mail:** retailhelp@designdesign.us; tom.vituj@designdesign.us. **Website:** www.designdesign.us. Estab. 1986. Specializes in greeting cards and paper-related product development.

NEEDS Licenses stock images from freelancers and assigns work. Specializes in humorous topics. Submit seasonal material 1 year in advance. Model/property release required.

SPECS Uses 35mm transparencies. Accepts images in digital format. Send via ZIP.

MAKING CONTACT & TERMS Submit portfolio for review. Provide résumé, business card, self-promotion piece or tearsheets to be kept on file for possible future assignments. Do not send original work. Pays royalties. Pays upon sales. Credit line given.

FOTOFOLIO, INC.

561 Broadway, New York NY 10012. (212)226-0923. **E-mail:** contact@fotofolio.com; submissions@fotofolio. com. **Website:** www.fotofolio.com. **Contact:** Submissions department. Estab. 1976. Publishes art and photographic postcards, greeting cards, notebooks, books, T-shirts and postcard books.

NEEDS Buys 60-120 freelance designs and illustrations/year. Reproduces existing works. Primarily interested in photography and contemporary art. Produces material for Christmas, Valentine's Day, birthday and everyday. Submit seasonal material 8 months in advance. Art guidelines with SASE with first-class postage.

MAKING CONTACT & TERMS "Fotofolio, Inc. reviews color and b&w photography for publication in postcard, notecard, poster and T-shirt formats. To submit your work, please make a well-edited selection of no more than 40 images, attn: Submissions. Fotofolio will accept photocopies, laser copies and promotional pieces only. Fotofolio will not accept digital images via e-mail to be downloaded or digital files submitted on disk. You may e-mail a website address where your work may be viewed. You'll be contacted if we are interested in seeing further work. Please note that Fotofolio, Inc. is not responsible for any lost or damaged submissions."

TIPS "When submitting materials, present a variety of your work (no more than 40 images) rather than one subject/genre."

GALLANT GREETINGS CORP.

(800)621-4279; (847)671-6500. **Fax:** (847)671-7500. **E-mail:** info@gallantgreetings.com; custserv@gallant greetings.com. **Website:** www.gallantgreetings.com. Estab. 1966. Specializes in greeting cards.

NEEDS Buys vertical images; all are supplied by freelancers. Photos of landscapes/scenics, wildlife, gardening, pets, religious, automobiles, humor, sports, travel, product shots/still life. Interested in alternative process, avant garde, fine art. Submit seasonal material 1 year in advance. Model release required. Photo captions preferred.

SPECS Accepts images in digital format. Send via CD, e-mail as TIFF files at 300 dpi. No slides accepted.

MAKING CONTACT & TERMS Send query letter with photocopies. Provide self-promotion piece to be kept on file for possible future assignments. Send nonreturnable samples. Pays by the project. Buys US greeting card and allied product rights; negotiable.

➕ 💲💲 GLM CONSULTING

366 Amsterdam Avenue, #159, New York NY 10024. (212)683-5830. **Fax:** (212)779-8564. **E-mail:** george@ glmconsultart.com. **Website:** www.glmconsultart. com. Estab. 1967. Sells reproduction rights of designs to manufacturers of multiple products around the world. Represents artists in 50 different countries. "Our clients specialize in greeting cards, giftware, giftwrap, calendars, postcards, prints, posters, stationery, paper goods, food tins, playing cards, tabletop, bath and service ware and much more."

NEEDS Approached by several hundred artists/year. Seeking creative decorative art in traditional and computer media (Photoshop and Illustrator work accepted). Prefers artwork previously made with few or no rights pending. Graphics, sports, occasions (e.g., Christmas, baby, birthday, wedding), humorous, "soft touch," romantic themes, animals. Accepts seasonal/holiday material any time. Prefers artists/designers experienced in greeting cards, paper products, tabletop and giftware.

MAKING CONTACT & TERMS Please submit via e-mail, a link to your website or a sampling of your work, consisting of 6-10 designs which represent your collection as a whole. The sampling should show all range of subject matter, technique, style, and medium that may exist in your collection. Digital files should be submitted as e-mail attachments and in low-res. Low-res (LR) image files are typically 5×7, 72 dpi, CMYK, JPEG/TIFF/PDF format and are under 100 KB. "Once your art is accepted, we require original color art—Photoshop files on disc (TIFF, 300 dpi). We will respond only if interested." Pays on publication. No credit line given. Offers advance when appropriate. Sells one-time rights and exclusive product rights. Simultaneous submissions and previously published work OK. "Please state reserved rights, if any."

TIPS Recommends the annual New York SURTEX and Licensing shows. In photographer's portfolio samples, wants to see "a neat presentation, perhaps thematic in arrangement."

MARIAN HEATH GREETING CARDS

9 Kendrick Rd., Wareham MA 02571. **E-mail:** dreposa@marianheath.com; submissions@marianheath.com. **Website:** www.marianheath.com. **Contact:** Diane Reposa, licensing agent. Publishes greeting cards.
NEEDS Model and property release preferred. Art guidelines available with SASE.
MAKING CONTACT & TERMS Send color copies via e-mail or on CD as JPEG files. Submission should be clearly labeled with artists name and identifying number or title if available. Approached by 100 freelancers/year. Works with 35-45 freelancers/year. Buys 500 freelance designs and illustrations/year. Prefers freelancers with experience in social expression. Art guidelines free for SASE with first-class postage or e-mail requesting guidelines. Uses freelancers mainly for greeting cards. Considers all media and styles. Generally 5¼×7¼ unless otherwise directed. Will accept various sizes due to digital production/manipulation. 30% of freelance design and illustration work demands knowledge of Photoshop, Illustrator, QuarkXPress. Produces material for all holidays and seasons and everyday. Submit seasonal material 1 year in advance. "If you wish samples to be returned, please indicate so and include postage-paid packaging."

IMPACT PHOTOGRAPHICS

4961 Windplay Dr., El Dorado Hills CA 95762. (916)939-9333. **E-mail:** sandeea@impactphotographics.com. **Website:** www.impactphotographics.com. **Contact:** Sandee Ashley. Estab. 1975. Specializes in photographic souvenir products for the tourist industry. Photo guidelines and fee schedule available.
This company sells to specific tourist destinations; their products are not sold nationally. They need material that will be sold for at least a 5-year period.
NEEDS Photos of wildlife, scenics, US travel destinations, national parks, theme parks and animals. Buys stock. Buys 3,000+ photos/year. Submit seasonal material 4-5 months in advance. Model/property release required. Photo captions preferred.
SPECS Can print from digital or film. Accepts images in digital format (for initial review). Send via CD, ZIP (or Dropbox such as you send it) as TIFF, JPEG files at 120 dpi for review purposes. Please make sure they can print out nicely at 4×6 for final review purposes. Will need 300 dpi for final printing.

MAKING CONTACT & TERMS "Must have submissions request before submitting samples. No unsolicited submissions." Send query letter with stock list. Provide business card, self-promotion piece or tearsheets to be kept on file for possible future assignments. Simultaneous submissions and previously published work OK. Request fee schedule; rates vary by size. Pays on usage. Credit line and printed samples of work given. Buys one-time and nonexclusive product rights.

JILLSON & ROBERTS

3300 W. Castor St., Santa Ana CA 92704-3908. (714)424-0111. **Fax:** (714)424-0054. **E-mail:** sales@jillsonroberts.com. **Website:** www.jillsonroberts.com. **Contact:** art director. Estab. 1974. Specializes in gift wrap, totes, printed tissues, accessories. Photo guidelines free with SASE. Eco-friendly products.
NEEDS Specializes in everyday and holiday products. Themes include babies, sports, pets, seasonal, weddings. Submit seasonal material 3-6 months in advance.
MAKING CONTACT & TERMS Submit portfolio for review or query with samples. Provide résumé, business card, self-promotion piece or tearsheets to be kept on file for possible future assignments. The review process can take up to 4 months. Pays average flat fee of $250.
TIPS "Please follow our guidelines!"

LANTERN COURT, LLC

P.O. Box 61613, Irvine CA 92602. (800)454-4018; (714)798-2270. **Fax:** (714)798-2281. **E-mail:** art@lanterncourt.com; customerservice@lanterncourt.com. **Website:** www.lanterncourt.com. **Contact:** Seher Zaman, creative director. Estab. 2011. Lantern Court specializes in party supplies and paper goods for the Muslim community or anyone who appreciates Islamic art and design. Produces balloons, calendars, decorations, e-cards, giftbags, giftwrap/wrapping paper, greeting cards, paper tableware, and part supplies. Buys 10-30 freelance designs/illustrations each year. Prefers freelancers with experience in stationery design. Buys stock photos and offers assignments.
NEEDS Islamic themed and Muslim holiday-related designs. Seasonal material should be submitted 10-12 months in advance. 100% of freelance work demands computer skills. Artists should be familiar with Illustrator, Photoshop, InDesign, and QuarkXPress.

SPECS Accepts images in digital format on CD as TIFF files at 300dpi.

MAKING CONTACT & TERMS Guidelines available free online. Requires model and property release. Photo captions are preferred. E-mail query letter with link to photographer's website or with JPEG samples at 72 dpi. Keeps samples on file. Please provide a résumé. Responds only if interested. Buys one-time rights. Pays by the project. Maximum payment $750.

⊛⊛ ● MCGAW GRAPHICS, INC.

(888)426-2429 ext. 206. **Website:** www.mcgawgraphics.com. **Contact:** Katy Daly. Estab. 1979. Specializes in posters, framing prints, wall decor.

NEEDS Licenses over 500 images/year in a variety of media; 25% in photography. Interested in b&w: still life, floral, figurative, landscape; color: landscape, still life, floral. Also considers celebrities, environmental, wildlife, architecture, rural, fine art, historical/vintage. Does not want images that are too esoteric or too commercial. Model/property release required for figures, personalities, images including logos or copyrighted symbols. Photo captions required; include artist's name, title of image, year taken. Not interested in stock photos.

MAKING CONTACT & TERMS Submit 10-20 low resolution JPEGs or a link to your website to katy.daly@mcgawgraphics.com for review. Responds in 1 month. Pays royalties on sales. Pays quarterly following first sale. Credit line given. Buys exclusive product rights for all wall decor.

TIPS "Work must be accessible without being too commercial. Our posters/prints are sold to a mass audience worldwide who are buying art prints. Images that relate a story typically do well for us. The photographer should have some sort of unique style or look that separates him from the commercial market. It is important to take a look at our catalog or website before submitting work to get a sense of our aesthetic. We do not typically license traditional stock-type images—we are a decorative house appealing to a higher-end market."

● NEW YORK GRAPHIC SOCIETY PUBLISHING GROUP

129 Glover Ave., Norwalk CT 06850. (203)847-2000 or (800)677-6947. **Fax:** (203)757-5526. **Website:** www.nygs.com. Estab. 1925. Specializes in fine art reproductions, prints, posters, canvases.

NEEDS Buys 150 images/year; 125 are supplied by freelancers. "Looking for variety of images."

SPECS Prefers digital format. Send low-res JPEGs via e-mail; no ZIP files.

MAKING CONTACT & TERMS Send query letter with samples to Attn: Artist Submissions. Does not keep samples on file; include SASE for return of material. Responds in 3 months. Payment negotiable. Pays on usage. Credit line given. Buys exclusive product rights. No phone calls.

TIPS "Visit website to review artist submission guidelines and to see appropriate types of imagery for publication."

⊛ ● NOVA MEDIA, INC.

1724 N. State St., Big Rapids MI 49307-9073. (231)796-4637. **E-mail:** trund@netonecom.net. **Website:** www.novamediainc.com. **Contact:** Thomas J. Rundquist, chairman. Estab. 1981. Specializes in CDs, CDs/tapes, games, limited edition plates, posters, school supplies, T-shirts. Photo guidelines free with SASE.

NEEDS Buys 100 images/year; most are supplied by freelancers. Offers 20 assignments/year. Seeking art fantasy photos. Photos of children/teens, celebrities, multicultural, families, landscapes/scenics, education, religious, rural, entertainment, health/fitness/beauty, military, political, technology/computers. Interested in documentary, erotic, fashion/glamour, fine art, historical/vintage. Submit seasonal material 2 months in advance. Reviews stock photos. Model release required. Photo captions preferred.

SPECS Uses color and b&w prints. Accepts images in digital format. Send via CD.

MAKING CONTACT & TERMS Send query letter with samples. Accepts e-mail submissions. Responds in 1 month. Keeps samples on file; does not return material. Simultaneous submissions and previously published work OK. Payment negotiable. Pays extra for electronic usage of photos. Pays on usage. Credit line given. Buys electronic rights; negotiable.

TIPS "The most effective way to contact us is by e-mail or regular mail. Visit our website."

OHIO WHOLESALE, INC./KENNEDY'S COUNTRY COLLECTION

286 W. Greenwich Rd., Seville OH 44273. (330)769-5050. **Fax:** (330)769-5566. **E-mail:** annes@ohiowholesale.com; AnneV@ohiowholesale.com. **Website:** www.ohiowholesale.com. **Contact:** Anne Secoy, vice president of product development. Estab. 1978. Home dé-

cor, giftware, seasonal. Produces home décor, wall art, canvas, tabletop, seasonal decorations, gifts, ornaments and textiles.

MAKING CONTACT & TERMS Send an e-mail query with brochure, photographs and SASE. Samples not kept on file. Company will contact artist for portfolio if interested. Pays by the project. Rights negotiated.

TIPS "Be able to work independently with your own ideas—use your 'gift' and think outside the box. *Wow me!*"

◐ PAPER PRODUCTS DESIGN

60 Galli Dr., Suite 1, Novato CA 94949. (800)370-9998; (415)883-1888. **Fax:** (415)883-1999. **E-mail:** carol@ppd.co. **Website:** www.paperproductsdesign. com. **Contact:** Carol Florsheim. Estab. 1992. Specializes in napkins, plates, candles, porcelain.

NEEDS Buys 500 images/year; all are supplied by freelancers. Needs photos of babies/children/teens, architecture, gardening, pets, food/drink, humor, travel. Interested in avant garde, fashion/glamour, fine art, historical/vintage, seasonal. Submit seasonal material 6 months in advance. Model release required. Photo captions preferred.

SPECS Uses glossy color and b&w prints; 35mm, 2¼×2¼, 4×5, 8×10 transparencies. Accepts images in digital format. Send via ZIP, e-mail at 350 dpi.

MAKING CONTACT & TERMS Send query letter with photocopies, tearsheets. Responds in 1 month to queries, only if interested. Simultaneous submissions and previously published work OK.

♻ ◉◉ ◐ PI CREATIVE ART

1180 Caledonia Rd., Toronto Ontario M6A 2W5, Canada. (416)789-7156. **Fax:** (416)789-7159. **E-mail:** dow@pifineart.com; info@pifineart.com; anna@ picreativeart.com. **Website:** www.picreativeart.com. **Contact:** Darounny (Dow) Marcus, creative director. Estab. 1976. Specializes in posters/prints. Photo guidelines available.

NEEDS Photos of landscapes/scenics, floral, architecture, cities/urban, European, hobbies. Interested in alternative process, avant garde, fine art, historical/vintage. Interesting effects, Polaroids, painterly or hand-tinted submissions welcome. Submit seasonal material 2 months in advance. Model/property release preferred. Photo captions preferred; include date, title, artist, location.

SPECS Accepts images in digital format. Send via CD, ZIP, e-mail as low-res JPEG files for review. Images of interest will be requested in minimum 300 dpi TIFF files.

MAKING CONTACT & TERMS Send query letter with résumé, slides, prints, photocopies, tearsheets, transparencies, stock list. Provide business card, self-promotion piece to be kept on file for possible future assignments. Responds in 2 weeks to queries; 5 weeks to portfolios. Simultaneous submissions OK. Pays royalties of 10% minimum. Buys worldwide rights for approximately 4-5 years to publish in poster form.

TIPS "Keep all materials in contained unit. Provide easy access to contact information. Provide any information on previously published images. Submit a number of pieces. Develop a theme (we publish in series of 2, 4, 6, etc.). B&w performs very well. Vintage is also a key genre; sepia great, too. Catalog is published with supplement 2 times/year. We show our images in our ads, supporting materials and website."

⬛ ◐ PORTFOLIO GRAPHICS, INC.

(801)266-4844. **E-mail:** info@portfoliographics.com. **Website:** www.nygs.com. **Contact:** Kent Barton, creative director. Estab. 1986. Publishes and distributes prints, posters, and canvases (through contract framers, furniture stores, designers, as well as all major retailers), as well as images and designs on alternative substrates such as metal, wooden plaques and wall decals.

NEEDS Buys 100 images/year; nearly all are supplied by freelancers. "Seeking inspiring artists with unique vision and distinctive imagery. Our company leads the way in defining trends and inspiring fresh perspectives. We are a top resource to all buyers of art in the wall decor industry—selling to the trade only." Reviews stock photos.

SPECS High-res digital files recommended.

MAKING CONTACT & TERMS E-mail JPEGs, PDF, or website links. Will responds if interested. Pays royalties of 10%. Quarterly royalties paid per pieces sold. Credit line given. Buys exclusive wall decor product rights license per piece.

TIPS "We find artists through galleries, magazines, art exhibits and submissions.

◉◉ ◐ RECYCLED PAPER GREETINGS, INC.

111 N. Canal St., Suite 700, Chicago IL 60606-7206. (800)777-3331. **Website:** www.recycledpapergreetings. com. **Contact:** Art Director. Estab. 1971. "Since the beginning, we've always worked with independent

artists because we value the power of true individual expression. Together, we create the most productive (and awesome) greeting cards out there. We take great pride in our family of independent artists, a family we are always looking to grow. Want to join our family?" **MAKING CONTACT & TERMS** "Artwork should be designed to mimic a complete greeting card—message included (vertical 5×7). Please send up to 10 ideas (labeled with your name, address and phone number). Please do not send holiday-specific cards, as we work far in advance of holidays. Do not send slides, disks, tearsheets, or original artwork. Recycled Paper Greetings is not responsible for any damage to artwork submitted. We suggest submitting color copies or photographs of your art. Do not send previously published cards. The review process can take up to 2 months. Simultaneous submissions to other companies are perfectly acceptable. If your work is chosen, we will contact you to discuss all of the details. If your work is not selected, we will return it to you. Thank you for your interest in Recycled Paper Greetings. Send submissions to the Art Department. E-mail low-res files (less than 2MB total) of formatted designs or links to your portfolio to: newartistsubs@prgreetings.com."

🔾 🇸🇸 RIG

500 Paterson Plank Rd., Union City NJ 07087. (201)863-4500. **E-mail:** info@rightsinternational. com. **Website:** www.rightsinternational.com. Estab. 1996. Licensing agency specializing in the representation of photographers and artists to manufacturers for licensing purposes. Manufacturers include greeting card, calendar, poster and home furnishing companies.

NEEDS Photos of architecture, entertainment, humor, travel, floral, coastal. "Globally influenced—not specific to one culture. Moody feel." See website for up-to-date needs. Reviews stock photos. Model/property release required.

SPECS Uses prints, slides, transparencies. Accepts images in digital format. Send via CD, e-mail as JPEG files.

MAKING CONTACT & TERMS Submit portfolio for review. Keeps samples on file. Simultaneous submissions and previously published work OK. Payment negotiable. Pays on license deal. Credit line given. Buys exclusive product rights.

🔾 SANTORO LTD.

Rotunda Point, 11 Hartfield Crescent, Wimbledon, London SW19 3RL, United Kingdom. (44)(208)781-1100. **Fax:** (44)(208)781-1101. **E-mail:** submissions@ santrographics.com. **Website:** www.santoro-london. com. **Contact:** Submissions. Estab. 1983. Features landscapes/scenics, wildlife, humor and historical/vintage photography.

MAKING CONTACT & TERMS Model/property release required. E-mail query letter. Accepts EPS files at 300 dpi.

SPENCER'S

6826 Black Horse Pike, Egg Harbor Twp. NJ 08234-4197. **Website:** www.spencersonline.com. Estab. 1947. Specializes in packaging design, full-color art, novelty gifts, brochure design, poster design, logo design, promotional P-O-P.

🔾   Products offered by store chain include posters, T-shirts, games, mugs, novelty items, cards, 14K jewelry, neon art, novelty stationery. Spencer's is moving into a lot of different product lines, such as custom lava lights and Halloween costumes and products. Visit a store if you can to get a sense of what they offer.

NEEDS Photos of babies/children/teens, couples, party scenes (must have releases), jewelry (gold, sterling silver, body jewelry—earrings, chains, etc.). Interested in fashion/glamour. Model/property release required. Photo captions preferred.

SPECS Uses transparencies. Accepts images in digital format. Send via CD, DVD at 300 dpi. Contracts some illustrative artwork. All styles considered.

MAKING CONTACT & TERMS Send query letter with photocopies. Portfolio may be dropped off any weekday, 9-5. Provide self-promotion piece to be kept on file for possible future assignments. Responds only if interested; send *only* nonreturnable samples. Pays by the project, $250-850/image. Pays on receipt of invoice. Buys all rights; negotiable. Will respond upon need of services.

🔾 🇸 🔾 🔾 TELDON

Unit 100-12751 Vulcan Way, Richmond British Columbia V6V 3C8, Canada. **E-mail:** photos@teldon. com. **Website:** www.teldon.com. **Contact:** Photo editor. Estab. 1969. Publishes high-quality dated and nondated promotional products, including wall calendars, desk calendars, magnetic calendars, etc. E-mail for photo guidelines—waiting list applies.

NEEDS Buys over 1,000 images/year; 70% are supplied by freelancers. Photos of lifestyles (babies/children/teens, couples, multicultural, families, parents, senior citizens (all model released), wildlife (North American), architecture (exterior residential homes–property released only), gardening, interiors/decorating (property released only), adventure, sports, travel (world), motivational, inspirational, landscape/scenic. Reviews stock photos. Model/property release required for trademarked buildings, residential houses, people. Photo captions required; include complete detailed description of destination (e.g., Robson Square, Vancouver, British Columbia, Canada), month picture taken also helpful.

SPECS Accepts digital submissions only. Contact photo editor for details.

MAKING CONTACT & TERMS Send query letter or e-mail. "No submissions accepted unless photo guidelines have been received and reviewed." Responds in 1 month, depending on workload. Simultaneous submissions and previously published work OK. Works with freelancers and stock agencies. Pays $150 for one-time use, non-negotiable. Pays in September of publication year. Credit line and complementary calendar copies given. Photos used for one-time use in dated products, North American rights, unlimited print runs.

TIPS City shots should be no older than 1 year. "Examine our catalog on our website carefully, and you will see what we are looking for."

❸❸ ⌨ ◐ TIDE-MARK PRESS

22 Prestige Park Circle, East Hartford CT 06108. (860)310-3370. **E-mail:** scott@tide-mark.com. **Website:** www.tidemarkpress.com. **Contact:** Scott Kaeser, acquisitions editor. Estab. 1979. Specializes in calendars. Photo guidelines available on website.

NEEDS Buys 1,000 images/year; 800 are supplied by freelancers. Categories: landscapes/scenics, wildlife, architecture, pets, adventure, automobiles, health/fitness, hobbies, humor, performing arts, sports, travel. Interested in fine art, historical/vintage; African-American. Needs "complete calendar concepts that are unique but also have identifiable markets; groups of photos that could work as an entire calendar; ideas and approach must be visually appealing and innovative but also have a definable audience. No general nature or varied subjects without a single theme." Submit seasonal material 12 months in advance. Re-

views stock photos. Model release preferred. Photo captions required.

SPECS Uses film and digital images. Accepts low-res images in PDF or JPEG format for initial review; send high-res only on selection.

MAKING CONTACT & TERMS "Offer specific topic suggestions that reflect specific strengths of your stock." Send e-mail with sample images. Editor will contact photographer for portfolio review if interested. Responds in 3 weeks. Pays $100-150/color image for single photos; royalties on net sales if entire calendar supplied. Pays on publication or per agreement. Credit line given. Buys one-time rights.

TIPS "We tend to be a niche publisher and rely on photographers with strong stock to supply our needs. Check the website, then call or send a query suggesting a specific calendar concept based on your stock."

❸ ◐ TRAILS MEDIA GROUP

333 W. State St., Milwaukee WI 53201. **Fax:** (414)647-4723. **E-mail:** editor@wistrails.com; clewis@jrn.com. **Website:** www.wisconsintrails.com. Estab. 1960. Specializes in calendars (horizontal and vertical) portraying seasonal scenics. Also publishes regional books and magazines, including *Wisconsin Trails.*

NEEDS Buys 300 photos/year. Needs photos of nature, landscapes, wildlife and regional (Wisconsin, Michigan, Iowa, Minnesota, Indiana, Illinois) activities. Makes selections in January for calendars, 6 months ahead for magazine issues. Photo captions required.

SPECS No longer accepts film submissions, only digital.

MAKING CONTACT & TERMS Submit via e-mail. Send your contact information including address, phone, e-mail, and website to editor@wistrails.com. Information gets entered into our database and will be added to our "photo call" e-mail list. Photos are credited and the photographer retains all rights.

TIPS "Be sure to inform us how you want materials returned and include proper postage. Calendar scenes must be horizontal to fit 8¾×11 format, but we also want vertical formats for engagement calendars. See our magazine and books and be aware of our type of photography. E-mail for an appointment."

◎ ⌨ ◐ ZITI CARDS

601 S. Sixth St., St. Charles MO 63301. (800)497-5908. **Fax:** (636)352-2146. **E-mail:** mail@ziticards. com. **Website:** www.ziticards.com. **Contact:** Salva-

tore Ventura, owner. Estab. 2006. Produces greeting cards. Specializes in holiday cards for architects, construction businesses and medical professionals. Art guidelines available via e-mail.

NEEDS Buys 30+ freelance photographs per year. Produces material for greeting cards, mainly Christmas. Submit seasonal material at any time. Final art size should be proportional to and at least 5×7. "We purchase exclusive rights for the use of photographs on greeting cards and do not prevent photographers from using images on other non-greeting card items. Photographers retain all copyrights and can end the agreement for any reason." Pays $50 advance and 5% royalties at the end of the season. Finds freelancers through submissions. Accepts prints, transparencies, and digital formats.

MAKING CONTACT & TERMS E-mail query letter with résumé, link and samples or send a query letter with résumé slides, prints, tearsheets and/or transparencies. Samples not kept on file, include SASE for return of material.

TIPS "Pay attention to details, look at other work that publishers use, follow up on submissions, have good presentations. We need unusual and imaginative photographs for general greeting cards and especially the Christmas holiday season. Architecture plus snow, holiday decorations/colors/symbols, etc. Present your ideas for cards if your portfolio does not include such work."

THE ZOLAN COMPANY, LLC

32857 N. 74th Way, Scottsdale AZ 85266. (203)300-3290. **E-mail:** jenniferzolan@yahoo.com. **Website:** www.zolan.com. **Contact:** Jennifer Zolan, president/art director. Commercial and fine art business. Photos used for artist reference in oil paintings.

NEEDS Buys 8-10 images/year; works on assignment; looking for photographs of Farmall tractors, especially models M, C, H, 1066, 460, 1566, 1026, Farmall 1206, Farmall tractor models from the 1960s and 1970s. John Deere tractors are also needed. Looking for photos of puppies and dogs for paintings. Reviews stock photos.

SPECS Will only review images in digital format. Send via e-mail, PDF, GIF, JPEG files at 72 dpi for preview.

MAKING CONTACT & TERMS Request photo guidelines by e-mail. Will only review submissions in electronic files. If submissions are sent by mail or other shipping services, they will not be returned. Does not keep samples on file. Pays up to $100 per photo. **Pays on acceptance.**

TIPS "We are happy to work with amateur and professional photographers. Will work on assignment shoots with photographers who have access to Farmall tractors. Will also purchase what is in stock if it fits the needs."

STOCK PHOTO AGENCIES

If you are unfamiliar with how stock agencies work, the concept is easy to understand. Stock agencies house large files of images from contracted photographers and market the photos to potential clients. In exchange for licensing the images, agencies typically extract a 50-percent commission from each use. The photographer receives the other 50 percent.

In recent years, the stock industry has witnessed enormous growth, with agencies popping up worldwide. Many of these agencies, large and small, are listed in this section. However, as more and more agencies compete for sales, there has been a trend toward partnerships among some small to mid-size agencies. Other agencies have been acquired by larger agencies and essentially turned into subsidiaries. Often these subsidiaries are strategically located to cover different portions of the world. Typically, smaller agencies are bought if they have images that fill a need for the parent company. For example, a small agency might specialize in animal photographs and be purchased by a larger agency that needs those images but doesn't want to search for individual wildlife photographers.

The stock industry is extremely competitive, and if you intend to sell stock through an agency, you must know how they work. Below is a checklist that can help you land a contract with an agency.

- Build a solid base of quality images before contacting any agency. If you send an agency 50–100 images, they are going to want more if they're interested. You must have enough quality images in your files to withstand the initial review and get a contract.
- Be prepared to supply new images on a regular basis. Most contracts stipulate that photographers must send additional submissions periodically—perhaps quarterly, monthly, or annually. Unless you are committed to shooting regularly, or unless you have amassed a gigantic collection of images, don't pursue a stock agency.

- Make sure all of your work is properly cataloged and identified with a file number. Start this process early so that you're prepared when agencies ask for this information. They'll need to know what is contained in each photograph so that the images can be properly keyworded on websites.
- Research those agencies that might be interested in your work. Smaller agencies tend to be more receptive to newcomers because they need to build their image files. When larger agencies seek new photographers, they usually want to see specific subjects in which photographers specialize. If you specialize in a certain subject area, be sure to check out our Subject Index in the back of the book, which lists companies according to the types of images they need.
- Conduct reference checks on any agencies you plan to approach to make sure they conduct business in a professional manner. Talk to current clients and other contracted photographers to see if they are happy with the agency. Also, some stock agencies are run by photographers who market their own work through their own agencies. If you are interested in working with such an agency, be certain that your work will be given fair marketing treatment.
- Once you've selected a stock agency, contact them via e-mail or whatever means they have stipulated in their listing or on their website. Today, almost all stock agencies have websites and want images submitted in digital format. If the agency accepts slides, write a brief cover letter explaining that you are searching for an agency and that you would like to send some images for review. Wait to hear back from the agency before you send samples. Then send only duplicates for review so that important work won't get lost or damaged. Always include a SASE when sending samples by regular mail. It is best to send images in digital format; some agencies will only accept digital submissions.
- Finally, don't expect sales to roll in the minute a contract is signed. It usually takes a few years before initial sales are made.

SIGNING AN AGREEMENT

There are several points to consider when reviewing stock agency contracts. First, it's common practice among many agencies to charge photographers fees, such as catalog insertion rates or image duping fees. Don't be alarmed and think the agency is trying to cheat you when you see these clauses. Besides, it might be possible to reduce or eliminate these fees through negotiation.

Another important item in most contracts deals with exclusive rights to market your images. Some agencies require exclusivity to sales of images they are marketing for you. In other words, you can't market the same images they have on file. This prevents photographers from undercutting agencies on sales. Such clauses are fair to both sides as long as you can continue marketing images that are not in the agency's files.

An agency also may restrict your rights to sign with another stock agency. Usually such clauses are designed merely to keep you from signing with a competitor. Be certain your contract allows you to work with other agencies. This may mean limiting the area of distribution for each agency. For example, one agency may get to sell your work in the United States, while the other gets Europe. Or it could mean that one agency sells only to commercial clients, while the other handles editorial work. Before you sign any agency contract, make sure you can live with the conditions, including 40/60 fee splits favoring the agency.

Finally, be certain you understand the term limitations of your contract. Some agreements renew automatically with each submission of images. Others renew automatically after a period of time unless you terminate your contract in writing. This might be a problem if you and your agency are at odds for any reason. Make sure you understand the contractual language before signing anything.

REACHING CLIENTS

One thing to keep in mind when looking for a stock agent is how they plan to market your work. A combination of marketing methods seems the best way to attract buyers, and most large stock agencies are moving in that direction by offering catalogs, CDs, and websites.

But don't discount small, specialized agencies. Even if they don't have the marketing muscle of big companies, they do know their clients well and often offer personalized service and deep image files that can't be matched by more general agencies. If you specialize in regional or scientific imagery, you may want to consider a specialized agency.

MICROSTOCK

A relatively new force in the stock photography business is microstock. The term *microstock* comes from the "micro payments" that these agencies charge their clients—often as little as one dollar (the photographer gets only half of that), depending on the size of the image. Compare that to a traditional stock photo agency, where a rights-managed image could be licensed for hundreds of dollars, depending on the image and its use. Unlike the traditional stock agencies, microstock agencies are more willing to look at work from amateur photographers, and they consider their content "member generated." However, they do not accept all photos or all photographers; images must still be vetted by the microstock site before the photographer can upload his collection and begin selling. Microstock sites are looking for the lifestyle, people, and business images that their traditional counterparts often seek. Unlike most traditional stock agencies, microstock sites offer no rights-managed images; all images are royalty free.

So if photographers stand to make only fifty cents from licensing an image, how are they supposed to make money from this arrangement? The idea is to sell a huge quantity of photos at these low prices. Microstock agencies have tapped into a budget-minded client that the traditional agencies have not normally attracted—the small business, nonprofit organization, and even the individual who could not afford to spend $300 for a photo for their newsletter or brochure. There is currently a debate in the photography community about the viability of microstock as a business model for stock photographers. Some say it is driving down the value of all photography and making it harder for all photographers to make a living selling their stock photos. While others might agree that it is driving down the value of photography, they say that microstock is here to stay and photographers should find a way to make it work for them or find other revenue streams to counteract any loss of income due to the effects of microstock. Still others feel no pinch from microstock: They feel their clients would never purchase from a microstock site and that they are secure in knowing they can offer their clients something unique.

If you want to see how a microstock site works, see the following websites, which are some of the more prominent microstock sites. You'll find directions on how to open an account and start uploading photos.

- www.shutterstock.com
- www.istockphoto.com
- www.bigstockphoto.com
- www.fotolia.com
- www.dreamstime.com

DIGITAL IMAGING GUIDELINES AND SYSTEMS

The photography industry is in a state of flux as it grapples with the ongoing changes that digital imaging has brought. In an effort to identify and promote digital imaging standards, the Universal Photographic Digital Imaging Guidelines (UPDIG, www.updig.org) were established. The objectives of UPDIG are to:

- Make digital imaging practices more clear and reliable
- Develop an Internet resource for imaging professionals (including photo buyers, photographers, and nonprofit organizations related to the photography industry)
- Demonstrate the creative and economic benefits of the guidelines to clients
- Develop industry guidelines and workflows for various types of image reproduction, including RAW file delivery, batch-converted files, color-managed master files, and CMYK with proofs.

PLUS (Picture Licensing Universal System) is a cooperative, multi-industry initiative designed to define and categorize image usage around the world. It does not address pricing or negotiations, but deals solely with defining licensing language and managing license data so that photographers and those who license photography can work with the same systems and use the same language when licensing images. To learn more about PLUS, visit www.useplus.com.

MARKETING YOUR OWN STOCK

If you find the terms of traditional agencies unacceptable, there are alternatives available. Many photographers are turning to the Internet as a way to sell their stock images without an agent and are doing very well. Your other option is to join with other photographers sharing space on the Internet. Check out PhotoSource International at www.photosource .com and www.agpix.com.

If you want to market your own stock, it is not absolutely necessary that you have your own website, but it will help tremendously. Photo buyers often "google" the keyword they're searching for—that is, they use an Internet search engine, keying in the keyword plus "photo." Many photo buyers, from advertising firms to magazines, at one time or another, either have found the big stock agencies too unwieldy to deal with, or they simply did not have exactly what the photo buyer was looking for. Googling can lead a photo buyer straight to your site; be sure you have adequate contact information on your website so the photo buyer can contact you and possibly negotiate the use of your photos.

One of the best ways to get into stock is to sell outtakes from assignments. The use of stock images in advertising, design, and editorial work has risen in the last five years. As the quality of stock images continues to improve, even more creatives will embrace stock as an inexpensive and effective means of incorporating art into their designs. Retaining the rights to your assignment work will provide income even when you are no longer able to work as a photographer.

LEARN MORE ABOUT THE STOCK INDUSTRY

There are numerous resources available for photographers who want to learn about the stock industry. Here are a few of the best.

- **PhotoSource International**, (715)248-3800, website: www.photosource.com, e-mail: info@photosource.com. Owned by author/photographer Rohn Engh, this company produces several newsletters that can be extremely useful for stock photographers. A few of these include *PhotoStockNotes*, *PhotoDaily*, *PhotoLetter*, and *PhotoBulletin*. Engh's *Sell & Re-Sell Your Photos* (Writer's Digest Books) tells how to sell stock to book and magazine publishers.
- **Selling Stock**, (301)251-0720, website: www.pickphoto.com, e-mail: Jim@scphoto.com. This newsletter is published by one of the photo industry's leading insiders, Jim Pickerell. He gives plenty of behind-the-scenes information about agencies and is a huge advocate for stock photographers.
- **Negotiating Stock Photo Prices**, 5th edition, by Jim Pickerell and Cheryl Pickerell DiFrank, 110 Frederick Ave., Suite A, Rockville MD 20850, (301)251-0720. This is the most comprehensive and authoritative book on selling stock photography.

- **The Picture Archive Council of America**, (800)457-7222, website: www.pacaoffice.org. Anyone researching an American agency should check to see if the agency is a member of this organization. PACA members are required to practice certain standards of professionalism in order to maintain membership.
- **British Association of Picture Libraries and Agencies**, (44)(020)7713-1780, website: www.bapla.org.uk. This is PACA's counterpart in the United Kingdom and is a quick way to examine the track record of many foreign agencies.
- **Photo District News**, website: www.pdn-pix.com. This monthly trade magazine for the photography industry frequently features articles on the latest trends in stock photography, and publishes an annual stock photography issue.
- **Stock Artists Alliance**, website: www.stockartistsalliance.org. This trade organization focuses on protecting the rights of independent stock photographers.

✷ 911 PICTURES

P.O. Box 1679, Sag Harbor NY 11963. (631)804-4540. **E-mail:** info@911pictures.com. **Website:** www.911pictures.com. **Contact:** Michael Heller, president. Estab. 1996. Stock agency. Has 3,500 photos in files. Clients include: advertising agencies, public relations firms, audiovisual firms, businesses, book publishers, magazine publishers, calendar companies, insurance companies, public safety training facilities.

NEEDS Photos of disaster services, public safety/emergency services, fire, police, EMS, rescue, hazmat. Interested in documentary.

SPECS Accepts images in digital format on CD at minimum 300 dpi, 8 inches minimum short dimension. Images for review may be sent via e-mail, CD as BMP, GIF, JPEG files at 72 dpi.

PAYMENT & TERMS Pays 50% commission for b&w and color photos; 75% for film and videotape. Enforces minimum prices. Offers volume discounts to customers. Works with photographers on contract basis only. Offers nonexclusive contract. Charges any print fee (from negative or slide) or dupe fee (from slide). Statements issued/sale. Payment made/sale. Photographers allowed to review account records in cases of discrepancies only. Offers one-time rights. Informs photographers and allows them to negotiate when client requests all rights. Model release preferred. Photo captions preferred; include photographer's name and a short caption as to what is occurring in photo.

HOW TO CONTACT Send query letter with résumé, slides, prints, photocopies, tearsheets. "Photographers can also send e-mail with thumbnail (low-res) attachments." Does not keep samples on file; include SASE for return of material. Responds only if interested; send nonreturnable samples. Photo guidelines sheet free with SASE.

TIPS "Keep in mind that there are hundreds of photographers shooting hundreds of fires, car accidents, rescues, etc., every day. Take the time to edit your own material, so that you are only sending in your best work. We are especially in need of hazmat, police and natural disaster images. At this time, 911 Pictures is only soliciting work from those photographers who shoot professionally or who shoot public safety on a regular basis. We are not interested in occasional submissions of 1 or 2 images."

ACCENT ALASKA/KEN GRAHAM AGENCY

P.O. Box 272, Girdwood AK 99587. (907)561-5531; (800)661-6171. **Fax:** (907)783-3247. **E-mail:** info@accentalaska.com. **Website:** www.accentalaska.com; www.alaska-in-pictures.com. **Contact:** Ken Graham, owner. Estab. 1979. Stock agency. Has 80,000 photos online. Clients include: advertising agencies, public relations firms, audiovisual firms, businesses, book publishers, magazine publishers, newspapers, calendar companies, greeting card companies, postcard publishers.

NEEDS Modern stock images of Alaska, Antarctica. "Please do not submit material we already have in our files."

SPECS Uses images from digital cameras 10 megapixels or greater; no longer accepting film. Send via CD, ZIP, e-mail lightbox URL.

PAYMENT & TERMS Pays 50% commission. Negotiates fees at industry-standard prices. Works with photographers on contract basis only. Offers nonexclusive contract. Payment made quarterly. "We are a rights managed agency."

HOW TO CONTACT "See our website contact page. Any material must include SASE for returns." Expects minimum initial submission of 60 images. Prefers online web gallery for initial review.

TIPS "Realize we specialize in Alaska although we do accept images from Antarctica. The bulk of our sales are Alaska-related. We are always interested in seeing submissions of sharp, colorful and professional-quality images with model-released people when applicable. Do not want to see same material repeated in our library."

◗ ACE STOCK LIMITED

E-mail: web@acestock.com. **Website:** www.acestock.com. **Contact:** John Panton, director. Estab. 1980. Stock photo agency. Has approximately 500,000 photos on file; over 40,000 online. Clients include: ad agencies, audiovisual firms, businesses, book/encyclopedia publishers, magazine publishers, postcard companies, calendar companies, greeting card companies, design companies, direct mail companies.

NEEDS Photos of babies/children/teens, couples, multicultural, families, parents, senior citizens, environmental, landscapes/scenics, wildlife, pets, adventure, automobiles, food/drink, health/fitness, hobbies, humor, sports, travel, business concepts, industry, medicine, product shots/still life, science, technology/computers. Interested in alternative process, avant garde, documentary, fashion/glamour, seasonal. **SPECS** High-quality digital submissions only. Scanning resolutions for low-res at 72 dpi and high-res at 300 dpi with 30MB minimum size. Accepts online submissions only.

PAYMENT & TERMS Pays 50% commission on net receipts. Average price per image (to clients): $400. Works with photographers on contract basis only. Offers limited regional exclusivity. Contracts renew automatically for 2 years with each submission. No charges for scanning. Charges $200/image for catalog insertion. Statements issued quarterly. Payment made quarterly. Photographers permitted to review sales records with 1-month written notice. Offers one-time rights, first rights or mostly nonexclusive rights. Informs photographers when client requests to buy all rights, but agency negotiates for photographer. Model/property release required for people and buildings. Photo captions required; include place, date and function. "Prefer data as IPTC-embedded within Photoshop File Info 'caption' for each scanned image."

HOW TO CONTACT Send e-mail with low-res attachments or website link or FTP. Alternatively, arrange a personal interview to show portfolio or post 50 sample transparencies. Responds within 1 month. Photo guidelines sheet free with SASE. Online tips sheet for contracted photographers.

TIPS Prefers to see "definitive cross-section of your collection that typifies your style and prowess. Must show originality, command of color, composition and general rules of stock photography. All people must be mid-Atlantic to sell in UK. No dupes. Scanning and image manipulation is all done in-house. We market primarily via online search engines and e-mail promos. In addition, we distribute printed catalogs and CDs."

ACTION PLUS SPORTS IMAGES

30 Ashlands Road, Cheltenham Gloucestershire GL51 0DE, United Kingdom. (44)020 7403 1558. **Fax:** (44)020 7403 1558. **E-mail:** info@actionplus.co.uk. **Website:** www.actionplus.co.uk. **Contact:** Stephen Hearn. Estab. 1976. News/feature syndicate. Has 2.8 million photos on file; 2 million transparencies and 800,000 digital images. Branch office in Los Angeles (contact London office). Clients include: ad agencies, businesses, book publishers, magazine publishers, newspapers, calendar companies, greeting card companies.

NEEDS Photos of sports.

SPECS Submit images via ZIP or e-mail. Send as JPEG files.

PAYMENT & TERMS Pays commission: 50% for b&w photos. Average price per image (to clients): $10-10,000. Negotiates fees below stated minimums. Discount sales terms not negotiable. Works with photographers on contract basis only. Offers nonexclusive contract. Contracts renew automatically with additional submissions. Photographers permitted to review account records in cases of discrepancies only. Offers one-time rights. Informs photographers when client requests to buy all rights, but agency negotiates for photographer. Model/property release required for people and buildings (for commercial images only-not editorial). Photo captions required; include place, date and function. "Prefer data as IPTC-embedded within Photoshop File Info 'caption' for each scanned image."

HOW TO CONTACT E-mail query letter with link to your website. JPEG samples at 72 dpi. Does not keep samples on file; cannot return material. Responds in 1 week. Photo guidelines available.

A+E

9 Hochgernstr, Stein D-83371, Germany. (49)8621-61833. **Fax:** (49)8621-63875. **E-mail:** apluse@aol.com. **Website:** www.apluse.de. **Contact:** Elisabeth Pauli, director. Estab. 1987. Picture library. Has over 30,000 photos in files. Clients include newspapers, postcard publishers, book publishers, calendar companies, magazine publishers.

NEEDS Photos of nature/landscapes/scenics, pets, "only your best material."

SPECS Uses 35mm, 6×6 transparencies, digital. Accepts images in digital format. Send via CD as JPEG files at 100 dpi for referencing purposes only.

PAYMENT & TERMS Pays 50% commission. Offers volume discounts to customers. Works with photographers on contract basis only. Offers nonexclusive contract. Subject exclusivity may be negotiated. Statements issued annually. Payment made annually. Photographers allowed to review account records in cases of discrepancies only. Offers one-time rights. Model/property release required. Photo captions must include country, date, name of object (person, town, landmark, etc.).

HOW TO CONTACT Send query letter with your qualification, description of your equipment, transparencies or CD, stock list. Include SASE for return of material in Europe. Cannot return material outside Europe. Expects minimum initial submission of 100 images with annual submissions of at least 100 images. Responds in 1 month.

TIPS "Judge your work critically. Only technically perfect photos will attract a photo editor's attention! Sharp focus, high colors, creative views."

✪ AERIAL ARCHIVES

Petaluma Airport, 561 Sky Ranch Dr., Petaluma CA 94954. (415)771-2555. **Fax:** (707)769-7277. **E-mail:** www.aerialarchives.com/contact.htm; herb@aerialarchives.com. **Website:** www.aerialarchives.com. **Contact:** Herb Lingl. Estab. 1989. Has 100,000 photos in files. Has 2,000 hours of film, video footage. Clients include: advertising agencies, public relations firms, audiovisual firms, businesses, book publishers, magazine publishers, newspapers, calendar companies.

NEEDS Aerial photography only.

SPECS Accepts images in digital format only, unless they are historical. Uses 2¼×2¼, 4×5, 9×9 transparencies; 70mm, 5 inches and 9×9 (aerial film). Other media also accepted.

PAYMENT & TERMS Buys photos, film, videotape outright only in special situations where requested by submitting party. Pays on commission basis. Average price per image (to clients): $325. Enforces minimum prices. Offers volume discounts to customers. Photographers can choose not to sell images on discount terms. Works with photographers on contract basis only. Statements issued quarterly. Payment made monthly. Photographers allowed to review account records in cases of discrepancies only. Offers one-time rights, electronic media rights, agency promotion rights. Informs photographers and allows them to negotiate when client requests all rights. Property release preferred. Photo captions required; include date, location, and altitude if available.

HOW TO CONTACT Send query letter with stock list. Provide résumé, business card, self-promotion piece to be kept on file. Expects minimum initial submission of 100 images with quarterly submissions of at least 50 images. Responds only if interested; send nonreturnable samples. Photo guidelines sheet available via e-mail.

TIPS "Supply complete captions with date and location; aerial photography only."

🌐 AFLO FOTO AGENCY

7F Builnet 1, 6-16-9, Ginza, Chuo-ku Tokyo 104-0061, Japan. (81)3-5550-2120. **E-mail:** support@aflo.com. **Website:** www.aflo.com (Japanese); www.afloimages.com (English). Estab. 1980. Stock agency, picture library and news/feature syndicate. Japan's largest photo agency, employing over 120 staff based in Tokyo and Osaka. Clients include: advertising agencies, designers, public relations firms, new media, book publishers, magazine publishers, educational users and television. Member of the Picture Archive Council of America (PACA). Has 1 million photos in files. "We have other offices in Tokyo and Osaka."

NEEDS Photos of babies/children/teens, celebrities, couples, multicultural, families, parents, senior citizens, disasters, environmental, landscapes/scenics, wildlife, architecture, cities/urban, education, gardening, interiors/decorating, pets, religious, rural, adventure, automobiles, entertainment, events, food/drink, health/fitness, hobbies, humor, performing arts, sports, travel, agriculture, business concepts, industry, medicine, military, political, product shots/still life, science, technology/computers. Interested in alternative process, avant garde, documentary, erotic, fashion/glamour, fine art, historical/vintage, lifestyle, seasonal.

SPECS Uses 35mm, 2¼×2¼, 4×5, 8×10 transparencies. Accepts images in digital format. Send via CD, e-mail as TIFF, JPEG files. When making initial submission via e-mail, files should total less than 3MB.

PAYMENT & TERMS Pays commission. Average price per image (to clients): $195 minimum for b&w photos; $250 minimum for color photos, film, videotape. Offers volume discounts to customers; terms specified in photographers' contracts. Photographers can choose not to sell images on discount terms. Works with photographers with or without a contract; negotiable. Contract type varies. Statements issued quarterly. Payment made quarterly. Photographers allowed to review account records. Model/property release preferred. Photo captions required.

HOW TO CONTACT Send all inquiries regarding images or submissions to support@aflo.com. Any submission inquiries should be accompanied by gallery links or image sets.

AGE FOTOSTOCK

Zurbano 45, 1ª planta, Madrid 28010, Spain. (34)91 451 86 00. **Fax:** (34)91 451 86 01. **E-mail:** agemadrid@ agefotostock.com. **Website:** www.agefotostock.com. Estab. 1973. Stock agency. Photographers may submit their images to Barcelona directly. Clients include: advertising agencies, businesses, newspapers, postcard publishers, public relations firms, book publishers, calendar companies, audiovisual firms, magazine publishers, greeting card companies. See website for other locations.

NEEDS "We are a general stock agency and are constantly uploading images onto our website. Therefore, we constantly require creative new photos from all categories."

SPECS Accepts all formats. Details available upon request, or see website ("Photographers/submitting images").

PAYMENT & TERMS Pays 50% commission for all formats. Terms specified in photographer's contract. Works with photographers on contract basis only. Offers image exclusivity worldwide. Statements issued monthly. Payment made monthly. Photographers allowed to review account records. Model/property release required. Photo captions required.

HOW TO CONTACT "Send query letter with résumé and 100 images for selection. Download the photographer's info pack from our website."

AGSTOCK IMAGES

25315 Arriba del Mundo Dr., Carmel CA 93923. (831)624-8600. **Fax:** (831)626-3260. **E-mail:** anne@ agstockimages.com. **Website:** www.agstockimages. com. Estab. 1996. AgStockUSA was acquired by Design Pics, Inc. in the fall of 2013 and is now AgStock Images. AgStock Images is the leading, most comprehensive stock photography library of worldwide agricultural photography. Representing over 100 leading agriculture, produce, livestock, entomology, botany and plant photographers, professors and researchers in the US, Canada, Europe and South America. Clients include: ad agencies, graphic design firms, editorial, publishers, calendar, magazine, greeting card. Images should cover all aspects of agriculture worldwide; fruits, vegetables, grains at various stages of growth, aerials, harvesting, processing, irrigation, insects, weeds, farm life, equipment, livestock, plant damage and disease.

NEEDS Photos should cover all aspects of agriculture worldwide: fruits, vegetables and grains in various growth stages; studio work, aerials; harvesting, processing, irrigation, insects, weeds, farm life, agricultural equipment, livestock, plant damage and plant disease.

SPECS Accepts images in digital format only; final file requirements 62MB TIFF files; professional DSLR cameras only please.

PAYMENT & TERMS Commissions 40% on rights managed and royalty free, exclusive contract only. Model and property releases required for commercial looking imagery. Photo captions required, location and all technical information. Distribution: design pics distributes the AgStock Images collection worldwide through their agency network and directly from their design pics brand websites.

HOW TO CONTACT "Contact anne@agstockimages. com. We will direct you to a web delivery link to send us a submission of a minimum 30 low-res JPEGs (1000 pixels on the long side) as an initial review."

AKM IMAGES, INC.

109 Bushnell Place, Mooresville NC 28115. **E-mail:** anniekmimages@gmail.com. **Website:** www.anniek mimages.com. **Contact:** Annie-Ying Molander, president. Estab. 2002. Stock agency. Has over 130,000 photos in files (and still increasing). Clients include: advertising agencies, book publishers, magazine publishers, newspapers, calendar and greeting card companies, and postcard publishers.

NEEDS Photos of agriculture, city/urban, food/wine, gardening, multicultural, religious, rural, landscape/ scenic, birds, wildlife, wildflowers, butterflies, insects, cats, dogs, farm animals, fishing, outdoor activity, travel and underwater images. "We also need landscape and culture from Asian countries, Nordic countries (Sweden, Norway, Finland, Iceland), Alaska and Greenland. Also need culture about Sami and Laplander from Nordic countries and Native American."

SPECS Uses 35mm transparencies. Accepts images in digital format. Send via CD/DVD at JPEG or TIFF files at low and high-res files (300 dpi) printable size 12×14 and low resolution files for PC Windows 7 & 8 and XP or at a ZIP file through links.

PAYMENT & TERMS Pays 48% commission for color photos. Terms specified in photographers' submission guidelines. Works with photographers with a signed contract only. Offers nonexclusive contract. Contracts renew automatically every 5 years. Offers one-time rights. Model/property release required. Photo captions required.

HOW TO CONTACT Send query letter by e-mail with image samples and stock list. Does not keep samples on file. Include SASE for return of material. Expects minimum initial submission of 100 images. Responds in 1 month to samples. Photo submission guidelines available free with SASE or via e-mail.

ALAMUPHOTO.COM

12415 Archwood St., Suite 10, North Hollywood CA 91606-1350. (310)809-5929. **E-mail:** info@alamupho to.com; Bannerimage@yahoo.com. **Website:** alamu photo.com. **Contact:** Eric Jackson, art editor. Estab. 1989.

NEEDS Images with focus on people of African descent involved in work, play, and family events that suggest a storyline. Quality images of individuals and/or groups involved in business, leisure, travel, etc. A few examples are people involved with rural and urban communities—farms and cities, courts, law enforcement, transit, construction, aviation, military, formal balls, musicians, temples, churches, mosques, and synagogues. Sport images involving fencing, deep sea diving, sky diving, motorcycle clubs, marathons, chess clubs, etc. "Bottom line: give us something we have not seen within the communities of African-Americans, African-Europeans, African-South Americans." Buys 50 images annually; 95% are supplied by freelancers. Buys stock photos only. Specializes in calendars, posters, T-shirts, documentary books. Accepts outstanding work from beginner and established photographers; expects a high level of professionalism from all photographers who make contact. Guidelines: No nudity or pornographic.

PAYMENT & TERMS Credit line given upon use. Model release and property release are required. Photo captions preferred.

HOW TO CONTACT Contact website with 2 images that best represent your work and we will make contact if interested; JPEG samples at 72 dpi. Cannot return material, so please do not send samples. Responds only if interested. Considers simultaneous submissions or previously published work.

ALAMY

127 Olympic Ave., Milton Park, Abingdon Oxon OX14 4SA, United Kingdom. UK: 44 1235 844 600; US: (866)671-7305. **Fax:** 44 1235 844 650. **E-mail:** Con-

tributors: memberservices@alamy.com; Customers: sales@alamy.com. **Website:** www.alamy.com. Estab. 1999.

SPECS "Register at www.alamy.com. Upload digital files 17MB+ via the Alamy website. Comission is 50% for any sales you make. You will receive your own Alamy account, which shows sales figures and account details. Alamy's contract is non-exclusive. You can find more information at www.alamy.com/contributor/help/default.asp."

ALASKA STOCK

Design Pics, Inc., 135 Christensen Dr., 3B, Anchorage AK 99501. (800)487-4285; (907)268-2091. **Fax:** (780)451-8568. **E-mail:** rick@designpics.com; ann@alaskastock.com. **Website:** www.alaskastock.com. **Contact:** Rick Carlson, president; Ann Matchett, content and contributor manager. Estab. 1990. Stock photo agency. Has 80,000 photos in files. Clients include: international and national advertising agencies; businesses; magazines and newspapers; book/encyclopedia publishers; calendar, postcard and greeting card publishers.

NEEDS Photos of everything related to Alaska, including babies/children/teens, couples, multicultural, families, parents, senior citizens involved in winter activities and outdoor recreation, wildlife, environmental, landscapes/scenics, cities/urban, pets, adventure, travel, industry. Interested in alternative process, avant garde, documentary (images which were or could have been shot in Alaska), historical/vintage, seasonal, Christmas.

SPECS Accepts images in digital format only. Send via CD or FTP as JPEG files at 1,000 pixels on long side for review purposes or put together a gallery of low-res images on your website and send us the URL. Do not e-mail images. Accepted images must be 60MB minimum shot as raw originals.

PAYMENT & TERMS Pays commission for color and b&w photos based on photographer. Negotiates fees below stated minimums for preferred vendors. Offers volume discounts to customers. Works with photographers on contract basis only. Guaranteed subject exclusivity. Annual contract renewal after first 5 years. Statements issued monthly. Payment made monthly. Photographers allowed to review account records. Offers negotiable rights. Informs photographer and negotiates rights for photographer when client requests all rights. Model/property release required when applicable. Photo captions required; include who, what, when, where.

HOW TO CONTACT E-mail query letter with link to photographer's website or JPEG samples at 72 dpi. Expects minimum initial submission of 100 images with periodic submissions of at least 100 images 4 times/year. Responds in 1 month. Photo guidelines free on request through e-mail. Market tips sheet free via e-mail, distributed to those with contracts.

TIPS "Interested in high-quality digital files only from full-frame cameras. Provide links to collections, galleries and websites. Show a minimum of 200 images to represent the quality of your work."

AMANAIMAGES INC.

2-2-43 Higashi-Shinagawa, Shinagawa-ku, Tokyo 140-0002, Japan. +81-3-3740-1018. **Fax:** +81-3-3740-4036. **E-mail:** planet_info@amanaimages.com; a.ito@amanaimages.com. **Website:** amanaimages.com. **Contact:** Mr. Akihiko Ito, partner relations. Estab. 1979. Stock photo agency. Member of the Picture Archive Council of America (PACA). Has 2,500,000 digital files and continuously growing. Clients include: advertising agencies, public relations firms, businesses, book/encyclopedia publishers, magazine publishers, newspapers, postcard publishers, calendar companies, greeting card companies, and TV stations.

NEEDS Photos of babies/children/teens, celebrities, couples, multicultural, families, parents, senior citizens, disasters, environmental, landscapes/scenics, wildlife, architecture, cities/urban, education, gardening, interiors/decorating, pets, religious, rural, adventure, automobiles, entertainment, events, food/drink, health/fitness, hobbies, humor, performing arts, sports, travel, agriculture, business concepts, medicine, military, political, industry, product shots/still life, science, technology/computers. Interested in documentary, erotic, fashion/glamour, fine art, historical/vintage, seasonal.

SPECS Digital format by single-lens reflex camera, data size should be larger than 30MB with 8-bit, Adobe RGB, JPEG format. Digital high-res image size: larger than 48MB for CG, 3D, etc., using editing software, e.g., Photoshop or Shade, digital change made by scanning, composed images, collage images.

PAYMENT & TERMS Based on agreement.

HOW TO CONTACT Send 30-50 sample images (shorter side has to be 600 pixel as JPEG file) and your profile by e-mail. "After inspection of your images we may offer you an agreement. Submissions are accepted only after signing the agreement."

AMERICAN MUSEUM OF NATURAL HISTORY LIBRARY, PHOTOGRAPHIC COLLECTION

Library Services, Central Park West at 79th St., New York NY 10024. (212)769-5420. **Fax:** (212)769-5009. **E-mail:** speccol@amnh.org. **Website:** www.amnh.org; library.amnh.org/index.php. **Contact:** Gregory Raml, special collections librarian. Estab. 1869. Provides services for authors, film and TV producers, general public, government agencies, picture researchers, scholars, students, teachers and publishers.

NEEDS "We accept only donations with full rights (nonexclusive) to use; we offer visibility through credits." Model release required. Photo captions required.

PAYMENT & TERMS Credit line given. Buys all rights.

THE ANCIENT ART & ARCHITECTURE COLLECTION, LTD.

15 Heathfield Court, Heathfield Terrace, Chiswick, London W4 4LP, United Kingdom. +44 (0)20 8995 0895. **Fax:** +44 (0)20 8429 4646. **E-mail:** library@aaacollection.co.uk. **Website:** www.aaacollection.com. Picture library. Has 150,000 photos in files. Represents C.M. Dixon Collection. Clients include: advertising agencies, book/encyclopedia publishers, magazine publishers, newspapers.

NEEDS Photos of ancient/archaeological site, sculptures, objects, artifacts of historical nature. Interested in fine art, historical/vintage.

SPECS Digital images only. JPEG format; minimum 34MB file size.

PAYMENT & TERMS Pays commission on quarterly basis. Works with photographers on contract basis only. Non-exclusive contract. Contracts renew automatically with additional submissions. Statements issued quarterly. Payment made quarterly. Photographers allowed to review account records. Offers one-time rights. Detailed photo captions required.

HOW TO CONTACT Send query letter with samples, stock list, SASE.

TIPS "Material must be suitable for our specialist requirements. We cover historical and archeological periods from 25,000 B.C. to the 19th century A.D., worldwide. All civilizations, cultures, religions, objects and artifacts as well as art may be included. Pictures with tourists, cars, TV aerials, and other modern intrusions not accepted. Send us a submission of CD by mail with a list of other material that may be suitable for us."

ANDES PRESS AGENCY

26 Padbury Court, Shoreditch, London E2 7EH, United Kingdom. 44 (0)20 7613 5417. **Fax:** 44 (0)20 7739 3159. **E-mail:** apa@andespressagency.com; val@andes pressagency.com. **Website:** www.andespressagency. com. Picture library and news/feature syndicate. Has 300,000 photos in files. Clients include: magazine publishers, businesses, book publishers, non-governmental charities, newspapers.

NEEDS Photos of multicultural, senior citizens, disasters, environmental, landscapes/scenics, architecture, cities/urban, education, religious, rural, travel, agriculture, business, industry, political. "We have color and b&w photographs on social, political and economic aspects of Latin America, Africa, Asia and Britain, specializing in contemporary world religions."

SPECS Uses 35mm and digital files.

PAYMENT & TERMS Works with photographers on contract basis only. Offers nonexclusive contract. Contracts renew with additional submissions. Statements issued bimonthly. Payment made bimonthly. Offers one-time rights. "We never sell all rights; photographer has to negotiate if interested." Model/property release preferred. Photo captions required.

HOW TO CONTACT Send query via e-mail. Do not send unsolicited images.

TIPS "We want to see that the photographer has mastered one subject in depth. Also, we have a market for photo features as well as stock photos. Please write to us first via e-mail."

ANIMALS ANIMALS/EARTH SCENES

17 Railroad Ave., Chatham NY 12037. (518)392-5500. **Website:** www.animalsanimals.com. **Contact:** Nancy Carrizales. Member of PACA Digital Media Licensing Association. Has over 1.5 million images in its collection. Clients include: ad agencies, book publishers, magazine publishers, encyclopedia publishers, newspapers, postcard companies, calendar companies, greeting card companies.

NEEDS *"We are currently not reviewing any new portfolios."*

ANTHRO-PHOTO FILE

133 Washington St., Belmont MA 02478. (617)484-6490. **E-mail:** cdevore@anthrophoto.com. **Website:** www.anthrophoto.com. **Contact:** Claire DeVore. Es-

tab. 1969. Stock photo agency specializing in anthropology and behavioral biology. Has 10,000 photos in files (including scientists at work, tribal peoples, peasant societies, hunter-gatherers, archeology, animal behavior, natural history). Clients include: book publishers, magazine publishers.

NEEDS Photos of anthropologists at work.

SPECS Uses b&w prints; 35mm transparencies. Accepts images in digital format.

PAYMENT & TERMS Pays 50% commission. Average price per image (to clients): $200 minimum for b&w photos; $225 minimum for color photos. Offers volume discounts to customers; discount terms negotiable. Works with photographers with contract. Contracts renew automatically. Statements issued annually. Payment made annually. Photographers allowed to review account records. Offers one-time rights. Photo captions required.

HOW TO CONTACT Send query letter with stock list. Keeps samples on file; include SASE for return of material. See website for image delivery options.

TIPS Photographers should e-mail first.

APPALIGHT

230 Griffith Run Rd., Spencer WV 25276. (304)927-2978. **E-mail:** wyro@appalight.com. **Website:** www. appalight.com; www.wyrophoto.com. **Contact:** Chuck Wyrostok, director. Estab. 1988. Stock photo agency. Has over 30,000 photos in files. Clients include advertising agencies, public relations firms, businesses, book/encyclopedia publishers, magazine publishers, calendar companies, greeting card companies, graphic designers.

Currently not accepting submissions.

NEEDS General subject matter with emphasis on the people, natural history, culture, commerce, flora, fauna, and travel destinations of the Appalachian Mountain region.

SPECS Uses digital images.

PAYMENT & TERMS Pays 50% commission. Works with photographers on nonexclusive contract basis only. Contracts renew automatically for 2-year period with additional submissions. Payment made quarterly. Photographers allowed to review account records during regular business hours or by appointment. Offers one-time rights, electronic media rights. Model release preferred. Photo captions required.

HOW TO CONTACT AppaLight is not currently accepting submissions.

TIPS "We look for a solid blend of topnotch technical quality, style, content and impact. Images that portray metaphors applying to ideas, moods, business endeavors, risk-taking, teamwork and winning are especially desirable."

ARCHIVO CRIOLLO

Payamino e7-141, Av. 6 de Diciembre, Quito, Ecuador. (593 2) 60 38 748. **E-mail:** info@archivocriollo.com; info@archivocriollo.com.ec. **Website:** www.archivo criollo.com. **Contact:** Diana Santander, administrator. Estab. 1998. Picture library. Has 20,000 photos in files. Clients include: advertising agencies, businesses, newspapers, postcard publishers, calendar companies, magazine publishers, greeting card companies, travel agencies.

NEEDS Photos of multicultural, environmental, landscapes/scenics, wildlife, architecture, cities/urban, religious, rural, adventure, travel, art and culture, photo production, photo design, press photos. Interested in alternative process, documentary, fine art, historical/vintage.

SPECS Uses 35mm transparencies. Accepts images in digital format. Send via CD, ZIP, e-mail or FTP as JPEG files at 300 dpi, 11 inches.

PAYMENT & TERMS Enforces minimum prices. Offers volume discounts to customers; terms specified in photographers' contracts. Photographers can choose not to sell images on discount terms. Works with photographers with or without a contract; negotiable. Offers nonexclusive contract. Charges 50% sales fee. Payment made quarterly. Photographers allowed to review account records. Informs photographers and allows them to negotiate when client requests all rights. Photo captions preferred.

HOW TO CONTACT Send query letter with stock list. Responds only if interested. Catalog available.

ARGUS PHOTO, LTD. (APL)

Room 2007, Progress Commercial Bldg., 9 Irving St., Causeway Bay, Hong Kong. (852)2890 6970. **Fax:** (852)2881 6979. **E-mail:** argus@argusphoto.com. **Website:** www.argusphoto.com. **Contact:** Lydia Li, photo editor. Estab. 1992. Stock photo agency with branches in Beijing. Has over 1 million searchable photos online. Clients include: advertising agencies, graphic houses, corporations, real estate developers, book and magazine publishers, postcard, greeting card, calendar and paper product manufacturers.

NEEDS "We are a quality images provider specializing in high-end lifestyle, luxurious interiors/home decor, club scene, food and travel, model in fashion and/or jewelry, well-being, gardenscape and Asian/oriental images. High-quality features on home and garden, travel and leisure, fashion and accessories, and celebrities stories are welcome."

SPECS Accepts high-quality digital images only. Send 50MB JPEG files at 300 dpi via DVD or website link for review. English captions and keywords are required.

PAYMENT & TERMS Pays 50% commission. Average price per image (to US clients): $100-6,000. Offers volume discounts to customers. Works with photographers on contract basis only. Statement/payment made quarterly. Informs photographers and allows them to negotiate when client requests all rights. Model/property release may be required. Expects minimum initial submission of 200 images.

ART LICENSING INTERNATIONAL

P.O. Box 727, Nokomis FL 34274. (941)966-8912. **E-mail:** artlicensinginc@gmail.com. **Website:** wwwootblicensing.com. **Contact:** Michael Woodward, president; Jane Mason, licensing manager. Estab. 1986. "We represent artists, photographers and designers who wish to establish a licensing program for their work. We are particularly interested in photographic images that we can license internationally, particularly for fine art posters, canvas giclees for mass market retailers and interior design projects and home and office decor." We also want large scale pictorial photography for murals.

NEEDS "We prefer concepts that have a unique look or theme and that are distinctive from the generic designs produced in-house by publishers and manufacturers. Images for prints and posters must be in pairs or sets of 4 or more with a regard for trends and color palettes related to the home décor and interior design trends. Nature themes, florals, b&w picturesque images, transitional images, and landscapes are of particular interest. We need landscapes, cityscapes of New York and Paris, trees, poppies, roosters, Tuscany scenes, cafe scenes, as well as florals."

PAYMENT & TERMS "Our general commission rate is 50% with no expenses to the photographer. Photographer must provide high-resolution digital files at 300 dpi to print 30-36 inches."

HOW TO CONTACT E-mail JPEGs or details of your website. No postal submissions, please.

TIPS "We require substantial portfolios of work that can generate good incomes, or concepts that have wide commercial appeal."

ART RESOURCE

536 Broadway, 5th Floor, New York NY 10012. (212)505-8700. **Fax:** (212)505-2053. **E-mail:** requests@artres.com. **Website:** www.artres.com. **Contact:** Ryan Jensen. Estab. 1970. Stock photo agency specializing in fine arts. Member of the Picture Archive Council of America (PACA). Has access to 3 million photos. Clients include: advertising agencies, public relations firms, audiovisual firms, businesses, book/encyclopedia publishers, magazine publishers, newspapers, postcard publishers, calendar companies, greeting card companies, all other publishing.

NEEDS Photos of painting, sculpture, architecture *only.*

SPECS Digital photos at 300 dpi.

PAYMENT & TERMS Pays 50% commission. Average price per image (to client): $185-10,000 for color photos. Negotiates fees below standard minimum prices. Offers volume discounts to customers; terms specified in photographer's contract. Discount sales terms not negotiable. Offers one-time rights, electronic media rights, agency promotion and other negotiated rights. Photo captions required.

HOW TO CONTACT Send query letter with stock list.

TIPS "We represent European fine art archives and museums in the US and Europe but occasionally represent a photographer with a specialty in photographing fine art."

ARTWERKS STOCK PHOTOGRAPHY

5045 Brennan Bend, Idaho Falls ID 83406. (208)523-1545. **E-mail:** photojournalistjerry@msn.com. **Contact:** Jerry Sinkovec, owner. Estab. 1984. News/feature syndicate. Has 100,000 photos in files. Clients include: advertising agencies, public relations firms, businesses, book publishers, magazine publishers, calendar companies, postcard publishers.

NEEDS Photos of Native Americans, ski action, ballooning, British Isles, Europe, Southwest scenery, disasters, environmental, landscapes/scenics, wildlife, adventure, events, food/drink, hobbies, performing arts, sports, travel, business concepts, industry, product shots/still life, science, technology/computers. Interested in documentary, fine art, historical/vintage, lifestyle.

SPECS Uses 8×10 glossy color and/or b&w prints; 35mm, 2¼×2¼, 4×5 transparencies. Accepts images in digital format. Send via CD, ZIP as JPEG files.

PAYMENT & TERMS Pays 50% commission. Average price per image (to clients): $125-800 for b&w photos; $150-2,000 for color photos; $250-5,000 for film and videotape. Negotiates fees below stated minimums depending on number of photos being used. Offers volume discounts to customers; terms not specified in photographers' contracts. Discount sales terms not negotiable. Works with photographers with or without a contract, negotiable. Offers nonexclusive contract. Charges 100% duping fee. Statements issued quarterly. Payment made quarterly. Offers one-time rights. Does not inform photographers or allow them to negotiate when a client requests all rights. Model/property release preferred. Photo captions preferred.

HOW TO CONTACT Send query letter with brochure, stock list, tearsheets. Provide résumé, business card. Portfolios may be dropped off every Monday. Agency will contact photographer for portfolio review if interested. Portfolio should include slides, tearsheets, transparencies. Works with freelancers on assignment only. Does not keep samples on file; include SASE for return of material. Expects minimum initial submission of 20 images. Responds in 2 weeks.

ASIA IMAGES GROUP

15 Shaw Rd., #08-02, Teo Bldg., 367953, Singapore. (65)6288-2119. **Fax:** (65)6288-2117. **E-mail:** info@asiaimagesgroup.com. **Website:** www.asiapix.com. **Contact:** Alexander Mares-Manton, founder and creative director. Estab. 2001. Stock agency. We specialize in creating, distributing and licensing locally relevant Asian model-released lifestyle and business images. Our image collections reflect the visual trends, styles and issues that are current in Asia. We have 3 major collections: Asia Images (rights managed); AsiaPix (royalty free); and Picture India (royalty free). Clients include: advertising agencies, corporations, public relations firms, book publishers, calendar companies, magazine publishers.

NEEDS Photos of babies/children/teens, couples, families, parents, senior citizens, health/fitness/beauty, science, technology. "We are only interested in seeing images about or from Asia."

SPECS Accepts images in digital format. "We want to see 72 dpi JPEGs for editing and 300 dpi TIFF files for archiving and selling."

PAYMENT & TERMS "We have minimum prices that we stick to unless many sales are given to one photographer at the same time. Works with photographers on image-exclusive contract basis only. We need worldwide exclusivity for the images we represent, but photographers are encouraged to work with other agencies with other images. Statements issued monthly. Payment made monthly. Photographers allowed to review account records. Offers one-time rights, electronic media rights. Model and property releases are required for all images."

AURORA PHOTOS

45 York St., Portland ME 04101. (207)828-8787. **Fax:** (207)828-5524. **Website:** www.auroraphotos.com. **Contact:** José Azel, owner. Estab. 1993. 1.4 million digital photo archive. Clients include: advertising agencies, businesses, corporations, book publishers, magazine publishers, newspapers, calendar companies, and websites.

NEEDS Photos of outdoor adventure, travel, lifestyle, nature, landscape, wildlife, iPhone, culture, conceptual, environmental, portraits, sports, commercial, editorial, celebrities, news, multicultural, military, politics, agriculture, technology, extreme sports.

SPECS Accepts digital submissions only; contact for specs.

PAYMENT & TERMS Accepts digital submissions only; e-mail info@auroraphotos.com for specs. Offers volume discounts to customers. Statements issued monthly. Payment made monthly. Photographers allowed to review account records once/year. Offers one-time rights, electronic media rights. Model/property release preferred.

HOW TO CONTACT Aurora's Open Collection combines the user-friendliness of royalty-free licensing with a picture archive that captures the breadth of sports, recreation, and outdoor lifestyles. View Aurora's Open Collection online. If you are interested in having your images reviewed, please send a link to your website portfolio for review. Does not keep samples on file; does not return material. Responds in 1 month. Photo guidelines available after initial contact.

TIPS "Review our website closely. List area of photo expertise/interest and forward a personal website address where your photos can be found."

AUSCAPE INTERNATIONAL

P.O. Box 1024, Bowral NSW 2576, Australia. (612) 4885 2245. **E-mail:** sales@auscape.com.au. **Website:** www.auscape.com.au. **Contact:** Sarah Tahourdin, director. Has 250,000 photos in files. Clients include: advertising agencies, educational book publishers, magazine publishers, newspapers, calendar companies, greeting card companies, museums, tourism companies.

NEEDS Photos of environmental, landscapes/scenics, travel, wildlife, pets.

SPECS Uses 35mm, 6×6, 4×5 transparencies. Accepts images in digital format. Send via CD or DVD as TIFF files at 300 dpi.

PAYMENT & TERMS Pays 40% commission for color photos. Enforces minimum prices. Offers volume discounts to customers. Works with photographers on contract basis only. Requires exclusive contract. Statements issued quarterly. Payment made quarterly. Photographers allowed to review account records. Charges scan fees for all transparencies scanned in-house; all scans placed on website. Offers one-time rights. Photo captions required; include scientific names, common names, locations.

HOW TO CONTACT Does not keep samples on file. Expects minimum initial submission of 200 images with monthly submissions of at least 50 images. Responds in 3 weeks to samples. Photo guidelines sheet free.

TIPS "Send only informative, sharp, well-composed pictures. We are a specialist natural history agency and our clients mostly ask for pictures with content rather than empty-but-striking visual impact. There must be passion behind the images and a thorough knowledge of the subject."

AXIOM PHOTOGRAPHIC

Design Pics, Inc., 10 The Shaftesbury Centre, 85 Barlby Rd., London W10 6BN, United Kingdom. 44(0)20 8964 9970. **Fax:** 44(0)20 89648440. **E-mail:** sales@axiomphotographic.com. **Website:** www.axiomphotographic.com. **Contact:** Tim Hook, general manager/sales director Europe. Estab. 1996. Stock photo agency. Member of Picture Archive Council of America. Has 160,000 photos in files. Affiliated with Alaska Stock (alaskastock.com), First Light (firstlight.com), The Irish Image Collection (theirishimagecollection.com), Design Pics (designpics.com) and Pacific Stock (pacificstock.com). Does business with advertising agencies, public relations firms, businesses, book publishers, magazine publishers, newspapers, calendar companies, greeting card companies and postcard publishers.

SPECS Accepts images in digital format only. Submit samples first. Send via e-mail with link to photographer's own website or online gallery. Full specs can be found at www.axiomphotographic.com/bin/Axiom2.dll/go?a+disp&t+tp-loader.html&tpl+contactus-submit.html. Model release and property release are preferred. Photo captions are required.

PAYMENT & TERMS Pays on a commission basis. Rights managed and royalty free. Offers volume discounts to customers. Works with photographers on contract basis only, exclusive contract. Contract does not automatically renew. Statements of photographers' sales issued monthly.

HOW TO CONTACT E-mail query letter with link to photographer's website as per specs above. Contact must be through submissions@axiomphotographic.com. Keeps samples on file. Photo guidelines available online. A copy of our catalog is available on the website

TIPS Follow the guidelines as given on our website and above.

THE BERGMAN COLLECTION

134 Leabrook Lane, Princeton NJ 08540. (609)921-0749. **E-mail:** information@pmiprinceton.com. **Website:** pmiprinceton.com. **Contact:** Victoria B. Bergman, vice president. Estab. 1980. Collection established in the 1930s. Stock agency. Has 20,000 photos in files. Clients include: advertising agencies, book publishers, audiovisual firms, magazine publishers, other.

NEEDS "Specializes in medical, technical and scientific stock images of high quality and accuracy."

SPECS Uses digital formats.

PAYMENT & TERMS Pays on commission basis. Works with photographers on contract basis only. Offers one-time rights. Model/property release required. Photo captions required; must be medically, technically, scientifically accurate.

HOW TO CONTACT "Do not send unsolicited images. Please call, write, or e-mail if you have images that meet our criteria. Include a description of the field of medicine, technology or science in which you have images. We contact photographers when a specific need arises."

TIPS "Our needs are for very specific images that usually will have been taken by specialists in the field as part of their own research or professional practice."

BIOLOGICAL PHOTO SERVICE AND TERRAPHOTOGRAPHICS

P.O. Box 490, Moss Beach CA 94038. (650)359-6219. **E-mail:** bpsterra@pacbell.net. **Website:** www.agpix.com/biologicalphoto. **Contact:** Carl W. May, photo agent. Estab. 1980. Stock photo agency. Has 80,000 photos in files. Clients include: ad agencies, businesses, book/encyclopedia publishers, magazine publishers.

NEEDS All subjects in the pure and applied life and earth sciences. Stock photographers must be scientists. Subject needs include: electron micrographs of all sorts, b&w and skillfully colorized; modern research techniques in lab and field; light microscopy, especially fluorescence and other contemporary thechniques; modern medical imaging; marine and freshwater biology; diverse invertebrates; organisms used in research; tropical biology; and land and water conservation. All aspects of general and pathogenic microbiology, normal human biology, petrology, volcanology, seismology, paleontology, mining, petroleum industry, alternative energy sources, meteorology and the basic medical sciences, including anatomy, histology, medical microbiology, human embryology and human genetics.

SPECS Prefers digital but also uses 4×5 through 11×14 glossy, high-contrast b&w prints for EM's; 35mm, 2¼×2¼, 4×5, 8×10 transparencies. Images in digital format should be 45-100MB TIFF files.

PAYMENT & TERMS Pays 50% commission for b&w and color photos. General price range (for clients): $75-500, sometimes higher for advertising uses. Works with photographers with or without a contract, but only as an exclusive agency/distributor. Photographers may market directly on their own, but not through other agencies, distributors or online sites. Statements issued quarterly. Payment made quarterly; "one month after end of quarter." Photographers allowed to review account records to verify sales figures "by appointment at any time." Offers only rights-managed uses of all kinds; negotiable. Informs photographers and allows them veto authority when client requests a buyout. Model/property release required for photos used in advertising and other commercial areas. Thorough scientific photo captions required in IPTC metadata for digital images and on labels for analog; include complete identification of subject and location.

HOW TO CONTACT Interested in receiving work from scientific and medical photographers if they have the proper background. Send query letter or e-mail with stock list, résumé of scientific and photographic background; include SASE for return of material. Responds in 2 weeks. Photo guidelines free with query, résumé and SASE. Tips sheet distributed intermittently to stock photographers only. "Nonscientists should not apply."

TIPS "When samples are requested, we look for proper exposure, maximum depth of field, adequate visual information and composition, and adequate technical and general information in captions. Digital files should be in TIFF format have image information in IPTC and EXIF fields, and be clean and color-corrected. We avoid excessive overlap among our photographer/scientists. Our 3 greatest problems with potential photographers are: 1) inadequate captions/metadata; 2) inadequate quantities of *fresh* and *diverse* photos; 3) poor sharpness/depth of field/resolution/composition in photos."

BLEND IMAGES

501 E. Pine St., Suite 200, Seattle WA 98122. (888)721-8810, ext. 5. **Fax:** (206)749-9391. **E-mail:** jerome@blendimages.com. **Website:** www.blendimages.com. **Contact:** Jerome Montalto, submission and content manager. Estab. 2005. Stock agency. Clients include: advertising agencies, businesses, public relations firms, magazine publishers. Blend Images represents a "robust, high-quality collection of ethnically diverse lifestyle and business imagery.

NEEDS Photos of babies/children/teens, couples, multicultural, families, parents, senior citizens, business concepts; interested in lifestyle. Photos must be ethnically diverse.

SPECS Accepts images in digital format only. Images should be captured using professional-level SLRs of 11+ megapixels, pro digital backs, or high-end scanners that can deliver the required quality. Final media should be 48-52MB, 24-bit RGB (8 bits per channel), uncompressed TIFF files at 300 dpi. Images should be fully retouched, color-corrected, and free from dust, dirt, posterization, artifacing or other flaws. Files should be produced in a color-managed environment with Adobe RGB 1998 as the desired color space.

HOW TO CONTACT E-mail your photographic background and professional experience, along with 30-50 tightly edited, low-res JPEGs in one of the following ways: 1. URL with your personal website. 2. Web photo gallery. (Web galleries can be created using your imaging software. Reference your owner's manual for instructions.) 3. Spring-loaded hot link—a clickable link that provides downloadable JPEGs.

BRIDGEMAN IMAGES

274 Madison Ave., Suite 1604, New York NY 10016. (212)828-1238. **Fax:** (212)828-1255. **E-mail:** nyresearch@bridgemanimages.com; edward.whitley@bridgemanart.com. **Website:** www.bridgemanimages.com. **Contact:** Ed Whitley. Estab. 1972. Member of the Picture Archive Council of America (PACA). Has over 1 million photos in files and over 9,000 video/film clips online. Also offers vast offline collection for licensing. Has branch offices in London, Paris, and Berlin. Clients include: advertising agencies, public relations firms, TV and film production companies, audiovisual firms, product design, book publishers, magazine publishers, newspapers, calendar companies, greeting card companies, postcard publishers, on demand prints, museums and auction houses.

NEEDS Specifically fine artists working with photography

SPECS Uses 2¼×2¼, 4×5, 8×10 transparencies and 50MB+ digital files.

PAYMENT & TERMS Pays 50% commission for color photos, b&w photos, film and video. Enforces minimum prices. Offers volume discounts to customers; terms not specified in photographers' contracts. Discount sales terms not negotiable. Works with photographers on contract basis only; nonexclusive contract. Contract does not renew automatically. Charges 100% duping fee. Statements issued quarterly. Payments issued quarterly. Photographers allowed to review account records. Offers one-time rights, electronic media rights, agency promotion rights. Photo captions required.

HOW TO CONTACT E-mail query letter with link to website, JPEG samples at 72 dpi, transparencies, and stock list. Does not keep samples on file; cannot return material. Expects minimum initial submission of 50 images. Responds only if interested; send nonreturnable samples. Photo guidelines and catalog available online.

BSIP

36 rue Villiers-de-l'Isle-Adam, Paris 75020, France. 33(0)1 43 58 69 87. **Fax:** 33(0)1 43 58 62 14. **E-mail:** ex port@bsip.com; info@bsip.com. **Website:** www.bsip. com. Estab. 1990. Member of Coordination of European Picture Agencies Press Stock Heritage (CEPIC). Has 300,000 downloadable high-res images online. Clients include: advertising agencies, book publishers, magazine publishers, newspapers.

NEEDS Photos of environmental, food/drink, health/fitness, medicine, science, nature and animals.

SPECS Accepts images in digital format only. Send via CD, DVD, FTP as TIFF or JPEG files at 330 dpi, 3630×2420 pixels.

PAYMENT & TERMS Offers volume discounts to customers; terms specified in photographers' contracts. Discount sales terms not negotiable. Works with photographers with or without a contract; negotiable. Offers guaranteed subject exclusivity. Contracts renew automatically with additional submissions for 5 years. Statements issued monthly. Payment made monthly. Photographers allowed to review account records. Offers one-time rights, electronic media rights, agency promotion rights. Model release required. Photo captions required.

HOW TO CONTACT Send query letter. Portfolio may be dropped off Monday–Friday. Keeps samples on file. Expects minimum initial submission of 50 images with monthly submissions of at least 20 images. Photo guidelines sheet available on website. Catalog free with SASE. Market tips sheet available.

CALIFORNIA VIEWS/THE PAT HATHAWAY HISTORICAL PHOTO COLLECTION

469 Pacific St., Monterey CA 93940-2702. (831)373-3811. **E-mail:** hathaway@caviews.com. **Website:** www. caviews.com. **Contact:** Mr. Pat Hathaway, photo archivist. Estab. 1970. Picture library; historical collection. Has 80,000 b&w images; 10,000 35mm color images in files. Clients include: advertising agencies, public relations firms, audiovisual firms, book/encyclopedia publishers, magazine publishers, museums, postcard companies, calendar companies, television companies, interior decorators, film companies.

NEEDS Historical photos of California from 1855 to today, including disasters, landscapes/scenics, rural, agricultural, automobiles, travel, military, portraits, John Steinbeck and Edward F. Rickets.

PAYMENT & TERMS Payment negotiable. Offers volume discounts to customers.

HOW TO CONTACT "We accept donations of California photographic material in order to maintain our position as one of California's largest archives. Please do not send unsolicited images." Does not keep samples on file; cannot return material.

CAL SPORT MEDIA WIRE

35557 Trevino TRL, Beaumont CA 92223. (805)895-6726. **Fax:** (323)908-4100. **E-mail:** calsportmedia@verizon.net. **Website:** www.csmimages.com. **Contact:** John Pyle, editor. Estab. 2002. Stock agency. Has 750,000 photos in files. Clients include: magazine publishers, newspapers.

NEEDS Photos of sports.

SPECS Accepts images in digital format. Send as JPEG files.

PAYMENT & TERMS Payments made monthly. Photo captions required.

HOW TO CONTACT E-mail query letter JPEG samples at 72 dpi. Responds in 1 week.

TIPS "Please contact by e-mail only your best work (15-20 images), showing your ability to produce magazine quality images. We receive many submissions, please be sure to include what type of equipment you use and list your experience as a professional photographer."

CAMERA PRESS, LTD.

21 Queen Elizabeth St., London SE1 2PD, United Kingdom. 44 (0)20 7378 1300. **Fax:** 44 (0)20 7278 5126. **E-mail:** info@camerapress.com. **Website:** www.camerapress.com. Quality syndication service and picture library. Clients include: advertising agencies, public relations firms, audiovisual firms, book/encyclopedia publishers, magazine publishers, newspapers, postcard companies, calendar companies, greeting card companies and TV stations. Clients principally press but also advertising, publishers, etc.

Camera Press sends and receives images via ISDN, FTP, and e-mail. Has a fully operational electronic picture desk to receive/send digital images via modem/ISDN lines, FTP.

NEEDS Celebrities, world personalities (e.g., politics, sports, entertainment, arts), news/documentary, scientific, human interest, humor, women's features, stock.

SPECS Accepts images in digital format as TIFF, JPEG files, as long as they are a minimum of 300 dpi or 16MB.

PAYMENT & TERMS Standard payment term: 50% net commission. Statements issued every 2 months along with payments.

HOW TO CONTACT "Images should then be sent to us high resolution, either on CD, or via e-mail or FTP. For FTP transmission we will need to set you up with a username and password. Images should ideally be submitted in jpeg format, and should be no smaller than 25MB, up to 50MB for lifestyle and studio images."

TIPS "Camera Press, one of the oldest and most celebrated family-owned picture agencies, represents some of the top names in the photographic world but also welcome emerging talents and gifted newcomers. We seek quality celebrity images; lively, colorful features which tell a story; and individual portraits of world personalities, both established and up-and-coming. Accurate captions are essential. Remember there is a big worldwide demand for celebrity premieres and openings. Other needs include: scientific development and novelties; beauty, fashion, interiors, food and women's interests; humorous pictures featuring the weird, the wacky and the wonderful."

🌀 ⊛ CAPITAL PICTURES

85 Randolph Ave., London W9 1DL, United Kingdom. 44 (0)20 7193 3606. **E-mail:** sales@capitalpictures.com, phil@capitalpictures.com. **Website:** www.capitalpictures.com. Estab. 1980. Picture library. Has 500,000 photos on file. Clients include: advertising agencies, book publishers, magazine publishers, newspapers. Specializes in high-quality photographs of famous people (politics, royalty, music, fashion, film and television).

NEEDS "We have a lot of clients looking for 'pictures of the capital.' We need very high-quality images of London, postcard-type images for international sales. Not just large files, but great content; famous landmarks photographed at the best time, from the best angle, creating interesting and evocative images. Try looking online for pictures of London for some inspiration."

SPECS High-quality digital format only. Send via CD or e-mail as JPEG files.

PAYMENT & TERMS Pays 50% commission of money received. "We have our own price guide but will negotiate competitive fees for large quantity usage or supply agreements." Offers volume discounts to customers. Discount sales terms negotiable. Works with photographers with or without a contract; negotiable, whatever is most appropriate. No charges. Statements issued monthly. Payment made monthly. Photographers allowed to review account records. Offers any rights they wish to purchase. Informs photographers and allows them to negotiate when client requests all rights." Photo captions preferred; include date, place, event, name of subjects.

HOW TO CONTACT Send query letter with samples. Agency will contact photographer for portfolio review if interested. Keeps samples on file. Expects minimum initial submission of 24 images with monthly submissions of at least 24 images. Responds in 1 month to queries.

CATHOLIC NEWS SERVICE

3211 Fourth St. NE, Washington DC 20017. (202)541-3250. **Fax:** (202)541-3255. **E-mail:** cns@catholicnews.com; broller@catholicnews.com. **Website:** www.catholicnews.com. News service transmitting news, features, photos and graphics to Catholic newspapers and religious publishers.

NEEDS Timely news and feature photos related to the Catholic Church or Catholics, head shots of Catholic newsmakers or politicians, and other religions or religious activities, including those that illustrate spirituality. Also interested in photos of family life, modern lifestyles, teenagers, poverty and active seniors.

SPECS Prefers high-res JPEG files, 8×10 at 200 dpi. If sample images are available online, send URL via e-mail, or send samples via CD.

PAYMENT & TERMS Pays for unsolicited news or feature photos accepted for one-time editorial use in the CNS photo service. Include full-caption information. Unsolicited photos can be submitted via e-mail for consideration. Some assignments made, mostly in large US cities and abroad, to experienced photojournalists; inquire about assignment terms and rates.

HOW TO CONTACT Query by mail or e-mail; include samples of work. Calls are fine, but be prepared to follow up with letter and samples.

TIPS "See our website for an idea of the type and scope of news covered. No scenic, still-life, or composite images."

✿ CHARLTON PHOTOS, INC.

3605 Mountain Dr., Brookfield WI 53045. (262)781-9328; (888)242-7586. **Fax:** (262)781-9390. **E-mail:** jim@charltonphotos.com. **Website:** www.charltonphotos.com. **Contact:** James Charlton, director of research. Estab. 1981. Stock photo agency. Has 475,000 photos. Clients include: ad agencies, public relations firms, audiovisual firms, businesses, book/encyclopedia publishers, magazine publishers, newspapers, calendar companies.

NEEDS "We handle photos of agriculture, rural lifestyles and pets."

SPECS Uses color and b&w photos; digital only.

PAYMENT & TERMS Pays 60/40% commission. Average price per image (to clients): $500-650 for color photos. Offers volume discounts to customers; terms specified in photographers' contracts. Works with photographers on contract basis only. Prefers exclusive contract, but negotiable based on subject matter submitted. Contracts renew automatically with additional submissions for 3 years minimum. Charges duping fee, 50% catalog insertion fee and materials fee. Statements issued monthly. Payment made monthly. Photographers allowed to review account records that relate to their work. Model/property release required for identifiable people and places. Photo captions required; include who, what, when, where.

HOW TO CONTACT Query by e-mail before sending any material. Expects initial submission of 1,000 images. Responds in 2 weeks. Photo guidelines free with SASE. Market tips sheet distributed quarterly to contract freelance photographers; free with SASE.

TIPS "Provide our agency with images we request by shooting a self-directed assignment each month. Visit our website."

◑ CODY IMAGES

2 Reform St., Beith KA15 2AE, Scotland. (08)(45) 223-5451. **E-mail:** ted@codyimages.com; info@codyimages.com. **Website:** www.codyimages.com. **Contact:** Ted Nevill. Estab. 1989. Picture library. Has 100,000 photos in files. Clients include: advertising agencies, newspapers, book publishers, calendar companies, audiovisual firms, magazine publishers.

NEEDS Photos of historical and modern civil and military aviation and warfare, including weapons, warships, and personalities.

SPECS Accepts images in ditigal format.

PAYMENT & TERMS Pays commission. Average price per image (to clients): $40 minimum. Offers volume discounts to customers. Discount sales terms not negotiable. Works with photographers with or without a contract; negotiable. Offers nonexclusive contract. Contracts renew automatically with additional submissions. Statements issued quarterly. Payment made quarterly. Photographers allowed to review account records. Offers one-time rights, electronic media rights. Informs photographers and allows them to negotiate when a client requests all rights. Model/property release preferred. Photo captions preferred.

HOW TO CONTACT Send e-mail with examples and stock list. Provide résumé, business card, self-promotion piece to be kept on file. Expects minimum initial submission of 1,000 images. Responds in 1 month.

◑ EDUARDO COMESAÑA AGENCIA DE PRENSA/BANCO FOTOGRÁFICO

Av. Olleros 1850 4 to. "F", Buenos Aires C1426CRH, Argentina. (54-11)4771-9418. **E-mail:** info@comesana.com. **Website:** www.comesana.com. **Contact:** Eduardo Comesaña, managing director. Estab. 1977. Stock agency, news/feature syndicate. Has 500,000 photos in files. Clients include: advertising agencies, businesses, newspapers, postcard publishers, book publishers, calendar companies, magazine publishers.

NEEDS Photos of babies/children/teens, celebrities, couples, families, parents, disasters, environmental, landscapes/scenics, wildlife, education, adventure, entertainment, events, health/fitness, humor, performing arts, travel, agriculture, business concepts, industry, medicine, political, science, technology/computers. Interested in documentary, fine art, historical/vintage.

SPECS Accepts images in JPEG format only, minimum 300 dpi.

PAYMENT & TERMS Offers volume discounts to customers; terms specified in photographer's contracts. Photographers can choose not to sell images on discount terms. Works with photographers with or without a contract; negotiable. Offers limited regional exclusivity. Contracts renew automatically with additional submissions. Statements issued quarterly. Payment made quarterly. Photographers allowed to review account records in cases of discrepancies only. Offers one-time rights. Model release preferred; property release required.

HOW TO CONTACT Send query letter with tearsheets, stock list. Provide self-promotion piece to be kept on file. Expects minimum initial submission of 200 images in low-res files with monthly submissions of at least 200 images. Responds only if interested; send nonreturnable samples.

CORBIS

250 Hudson St., 4th Floor, New York NY 10013. (800)260-0444; (212)777-6200. **Fax:** (212)375-7700. **E-mail:** contributorrelations@corbis.com. **Website:** www.corbis.com. Estab. 1991. Stock agency, picture library, news/feature syndicate. Member of the Picture Archive Council of America (PACA). Corbis also has offices in London, Paris, Dusseldorf, Tokyo, Seattle, Chicago and Los Angeles. Clients include: advertising agencies, businesses, newspapers, public relations firms, book publishers, calendar companies, audiovisual firms, magazine publishers, greeting card companies, businesses/corporations, media companies.

HOW TO CONTACT "Please check 'About Corbis' on our website for current submission information."

◯ CRESTOCK CORPORATION

3 Concorde Gate, 4th Floor, Toronto Ontario M3C 3N7, Canada. **E-mail:** help@crestock.com. **Website:** www.crestock.com. "Crestock is a growing player in micropayment royalty-free stock photography, helping clients with small budgets find creative images for their projects. With a fast and reliable image upload system, Crestock gives photographers and illustrators a great platform for licensing their creative work. Over 1,700,000 photographs, illustrations and vectors are available for purchase and download online. Masterfile acquired the agency in 2010 and has since added the Crestock collection to www.masterfile.com. Crestock has a general collection of photographs, illustrations and vectors available in a wide-range of sizes. Crestock sells single images, as well offers a selection of subscription and credit packages. Clients include designers, advertising agencies, small business owners, corporations, newspapers, public relations firms, publishers as well as greeting card and calendar companies."

NEEDS Looking for model-released photographs, as well as illustrations and vectors on a wide-range of subjects, including business, finance, holidays, sports and leisure, travel, nature, animals, technology, education, health and beauty, shopping, green living, architecture, still-life as well as conceptual and general lifestyle themes.

SPECS Accepts images in digital format. Submissions must be uploaded for review via website or FTP as JPEG, EPS or AI. For full technical requirements, see www.crestock.com/technical-requirements.aspx.

PAYMENT & TERMS Pays contributors based on request, once a minimum amount is reached. Requires model and/or property releases on certain images. For more information, see: www.crestock.com/modelrelease.aspx. Artists are required to caption and keyword their own material in English before submission. In order to join Crestock, register at www.crestock.com and submit photos for approval. To see general information for artists, see www.crestock.com/information-for-contributors.aspx.

TIPS "Crestock is among the most selective microstock agencies, so be prepared for strict quality standards."

DDB STOCK PHOTOGRAPHY, LLC

P.O. Box 80155, Baton Rouge LA 70898. (225)763-6235. **Fax:** (225)763-6894. **E-mail:** info@ddbstock.com. **Website:** www.ddbstock.com. **Contact:** Douglas D. Bryant, president. Estab. 1970. Stock photo agency. Member of American Society of Picture Professionals. Rights managed stock only, no RF. Currently represents 105 professional photographers. Has 500,000 original color transparencies and 25,000 b&w prints in archive, and 125,000 high-res digital images with 45,000 available for download on website. Clients include: text-trade book/encyclopedia publishers, travel industry, museums, ad agencies, audiovisual firms, magazine publishers, CD publishers and many foreign publishers.

NEEDS Specializes in picture coverage of Latin America with emphasis on Mexico, Central America, South America, and the Caribbean. Needs photos of anthropology/archeology, art, commerce, crafts, secondary and university education, festivals and ritual, geography, history, indigenous people and culture, museums, parks, political figures, religion. Also uses teens 6th-12th grade/young adults college age, couples, multicultural, families, parents, senior citizens, architecture, rural, adventure, entertainment, events, food/drink, restaurants, health/fitness, performing arts, business concepts, industry, science, technology/computers.

SPECS Prefers images in TIFF digital format on DVD at 10 megapixels or higher. Prepare digital submissions filling IPTC values. Caption, copyright, and keywords per instructions at: www.ddbstock.com/submissionguidelines.html. Accepts uncompressed JPEGs, TIFFs, and original 35mm transparencies.

PAYMENT & TERMS "Rights to reproduction of color transparencies and b&w prints are sold on a 50% commission basis with remittance made to photographers within 2 weeks following receipt of payment. Exceptions to this include sales made through our affiliate offices around the world where we receive a 60% cut, leaving the photographer with 30%. DDB Stock negotiates only one-time use rights. The pictures on file remain the property of the photographer. The agency asks only that a photographer agree to place material in the files for at least 3 years. This ensures that the agency will have ample opportunity to recover the costs of placing a new photographer's material in the files. This also keeps the images in our files for the hottest selling period, which occurs from 12 to 36 months after they enter the files. It is important to have the images in the files when repeat interest is expressed by an editor. Photographers who want images returned from the files prior to the 3-year minimum must agree to pay a $15 hourly pull fee plus shipping charges for early return of pictures." Model/property release preferred for ad set-up shots. Photo captions required; include location and detailed description. "We have a geographic focus and need specific location info on captions (Geocode latitude/longitude if you carry a GPS unit, and include latitude/longitude in captions)."

HOW TO CONTACT Interested in receiving work from professional photographers who regularly visit Latin America. Send query letter with brochure, tearsheets, stock list. Expects minimum initial submission of 300 digital images/original transparencies and yearly submissions of at least 500 images. Responds in 6 weeks. Photo guidelines available on website.

TIPS "Speak Spanish and spend 1-6 months shooting in Latin America and the Caribbean every year. Follow our needs list closely. Call before leaving on assignment. Shoot digital TIFFs at 12 megapixels or larger. Shoot RAW/NEF/DNG adjust and convert to TIFF or Fuji professional transparency film if you have not converted to digital. Edit carefully. Eliminate images with focus, framing, excessive grain/noise, or exposure problems. The market is far too competitive for average pictures and amateur photographers. Review guidelines for photographers on our website. Include coverage from at least 3 Latin American countries or 5 Caribbean Islands. No one-time vacation shots! Shoot subjects in demand listed on website."

⊕ DANITA DELIMONT STOCK PHOTOGRAPHY

Delimont, Herbig & Assoc., LLC, 4911 Somerset Dr. SE, Bellevue WA 98006. (425)562-1563. **Fax:** (425)373-5316. **E-mail:** danita@danitadelimont.com. **Website:** www.danitadelimont.com. **Contact:** Danita Delimont, owner. Estab. 1980. Stock agency. Member of the Picture Archive Council of America. Has 900,000 photos in files; 6,000 film/video clips. Clients include: advertising agencies, budinesses, public relations firms, audiovisual firms, book publishers, magazine publishers, newspapers, calendar and greeting card companies, travel companies, and postcard publishers.

NEEDS Photos of landscapes/scenics, wildlife, adventure, travel, fine art, historical/vintage, seasonal, travel.

SPECS Accepts images in digital format. Send via CD or ZIP as JPEG files.

PAYMENT & TERMS Pays on commission. Offers volume discount to customers. Terms specified in contract. Works with photographers on contract basis only. Offers nonexclusive contract. Contracts renew automatically. Sales statements issued quarterly. Payments made quarterly. Model/property release preferred. Photo captions required.

HOW TO CONTACT E-mail query letter with link to website. Responds only if interested. Photo submission guidelines available.

TIPS "Present yourself in a professional manner, including cover letters and on-going documentation of submissions, metadata prep and whatever's necessary to help license your images."

☁ DESIGN PICS, INC.

#101, 10464-176 St., Edmonton Alberta T5S 1L3, Canada. (780)447-5433. **Fax:** (780)451-8568. **E-mail:** rick@designpics.com. **Website:** www.designpics.com. **Contact:** Rick Carlson, president. Estab. 2000. Stock photo agency. Member of PACA. Has 450,000 photos in files. Clients include: advertising agencies, businesses, newspapers, postcard publishers, book publishers, calendar companies, magazine publishers and greeting card companies.

SPECS Accepts images in digital format. Send via CD or FTP as TIFF files (60MB) at 300 dpi.

PAYMENT & TERMS Does not buy photos, film or video outright. Pays on a commission basis based on photographer. Average price varies. Negotiates fees below stated minimums, based on preferred vendor agreements. Offers volume discounts to costumers. Works with photographers on contract basis.

HOW TO CONTACT E-mail query letter with link to photographer's website or JPEG samples at 72 dpi. Expects minimum initial submission of 100 images with periodic submissions of at least 100 images 2 times/year. Responds in 1 month. Photo guidelines free on request through e-mail. Catalog available on website. Market tips sheet free via e-mail, distributed to those with contracts.

TIPS "Interested in high-quality digital files only from full-frame cameras. Provide links to collections, galleries and websites. Show a minimum of 200 images to represent the quality of your work."

● DINODIA PHOTO LIBRARY

66 Bajaj Bhawan, Nariman Point Mumbai 400 021, India. 91(22)2204 4016. **E-mail:** jagdish@dinodia.com; info@dinodia.com. **Website:** www.dinodia.com. **Contact:** Jagdish Agarwal, founder. Estab. 1987. Stock photo agency. Member Picture Archive Council of America. Has 10 million photos on website. Clients include: advertising agencies, public relations firms, audiovisual firms, businesses, book publishers, magazine publishers, newspapers, postcard publishers, calendar companies, greeting card companies.

NEEDS Photos of babies/children/teens, celebrities, couples, multicultural, families, parents, senior citizens, disasters, environmental, landscapes/scenics, wildlife, architecture, cities/urban, education, gardening, interiors/decorating, pets, religious, rural, adventure, automobiles, entertainment, events, food/drink, health/fitness/beauty, hobbies, humor, performing arts, sports, travel, agriculture, business concepts, industry, medicine, military, political, product shots/still life, science, technology/computers. Interested in alternative process, avant garde, documentary, erotic, fashion/glamour, fine art, historical/vintage, lifestyle, seasonal. Also need photos of India.

SPECS Accepts images in digital format via CD. Send JPEG files at 300 dpi. Accepts 8×10 prints in glossy,

matte, color, b&w. "At the moment we are only accepting digital. Initially it is better to send a link to your website for our review."

PAYMENT & TERMS Pays 50% commission for b&w and color photos. General price range (to clients): US $20-200. Negotiates fees below stated minimum prices for bulk orders. Offers volume discounts to customers; inquire about specific terms. Discount sales terms not negotiable. Works with photographers on contract basis only. Offers nonexclusive contract. Contracts renew automatically with additional submissions for 3 years. Statement issued monthly. Payment made monthly. Photographers permitted to review account records. Informs photographers and allows them to negotiate when client requests all rights. Offers one-time rights. Model release preferred. Photo captions required (what, where).

HOW TO CONTACT Send query e-mail with link to website. Send query letter with résumé and prints. Keeps samples on file; provide résumé, business card, self-promotion piece. Expects minimum initial submission of 100 images with yearly submissions of at least 100 images. Responds only if interested.

TIPS "See website for kind of photos already available."

DK STOCK, INC.

4531 Worthings Dr., Powder Springs GA 30127. (866)362-4705. **Fax:** (678)384-1883. **E-mail:** david@dkstock.com. **Website:** www.dkstock.com. **Contact:** David Deas, photo editor. Estab. 2000. "A multicultural stock photo company based in New York City. Prior to launching DK Stock, its founders worked for years in the advertising industry as a creative team specializing in connecting clients to the $1.6 trillion multicultural market. This market is growing, and DK Stock's goal is to service it with model-released, well composed, professional imagery." Member of the Picture Archive Council of America (PACA). Has 15,000 photos on file. Clients include: advertising agencies, public relations firms, graphic design businesses, book publishers, magazine publishers, newspapers, calendar companies, greeting card companies.

NEEDS "Looking for contemporary lifestyle images that reflect the black and Hispanic Diaspora." Wants photos of babies/children/teens, celebrities, couples, multicultural, families, parents, senior citizens, education, adventure, entertainment, health/fitness/beauty, hobbies, humor, performing arts, sports, travel, agriculture, business concepts, industry, medicine, military, political, science, technology/computers. Interested in historical/vintage, lifestyle. "Images should include models of Hispanics and/or people of African descent. Images of Caucasian models interacting with black people or Hispanic people can also be submitted. Be creative, selective and current. Visit website to get an idea of the style and range of representative work. E-mail for a current copy of 'needs list.'"

SPECS Accepts images in digital format. 50MB, 300 dpi.

PAYMENT & TERMS Pays 50% commission for b&w or color photos. Average price per image (to clients): $485. Enforces minimum prices. Offers volume discounts to customers; terms specified in photographers' contracts. Photographers can choose not to sell images on discount terms. Works with photographers on contract basis only. Offers non-exclusive contract. Contracts renew automatically with additional submissions for 5 years. Statements issued monthly. Payment made monthly. Photographers allowed to review account records. Model/property release required. Photo captions not necessary.

HOW TO CONTACT Send query letter with disc or DVD. Portfolio may be dropped off every Monday-Friday. Does not keep samples on file; include SASE for return of material. Expects minimum initial submission of 50 images with 5 times/year submissions of at least 200 images. Responds in 2 weeks to samples, portfolios. Photo guidelines free with SASE. Catalog free with SASE.

TIPS "We love working with talented people. If you have 10 incredible images, let's begin a relationship. Also, we're always looking for new and upcoming talent as well as photographers who can contribute often. There is an increasing demand for lifestyle photos of multicultural people. Our clients are based in the Americas, Europe, Asia and Africa. Be creative, original and technically proficient."

● DRK PHOTO

100 Starlight Way, Sedona AZ 86351. (928)284-9808. **E-mail:** info@drkphoto.com. **Website:** www.drkphoto.com. "We handle only the personal best of a select few photographers, not hundreds. This allows us to do a better job aggressively marketing the work of these photographers." Clients include: ad agencies; PR and AV firms; businesses; book, magazine and textbook publishers; newspapers; postcard, calendar and greet-

ing card companies; branches of the government; and nearly every facet of the publishing industry, both domestic and foreign.

NEEDS "Especially need marine and underwater coverage." Also interested in S.E.Ms, African, European and Far East wildlife, and good rainforest coverage.

SPECS Digital capture preferred, digital scans accepted.

PAYMENT & TERMS General price range (to clients): $100-"into thousands." Works with photographers on contract basis only. Contracts renew automatically. Statements issued quarterly. Payment made quarterly. Offers one-time rights; "other rights negotiable between agency/photographer and client." We are not interested in images being offered by anyone else as royalty-free images. We only accept and market rights-managed images. Model release preferred. Photo captions required.

HOW TO CONTACT "With the exception of established professional photographers shooting enough volume to support an agency relationship, we are not soliciting open submissions at this time. Those professionals wishing to contact us in regards to representation should query with a brief letter of introduction."

● DW STOCK PICTURE LIBRARY

108 Beecroft Rd., Beecroft NSW 2119, Australia. (61)2 9869 0717. **E-mail:** info@dwpicture.com.au; admin@dwpicture.com.au. **Website:** www.dwpicture.com.au. Estab. 1997. Has more than 200,000 photos on file and 30,000 online. "Strengths include historical images, marine life, African wildlife, Australia, travel, horticulture, agriculture, people and lifestyles." Clients include: advertising agencies, designers, printers, book publishers, magazine publishers, calendar companies.

NEEDS Photos of babies/children/teens, families, parents, senior citizens, disasters, gardening, pets, rural, health/fitness, travel, industry. Interested in lifestyle.

SPECS Accepts images in digital format. Send as lowres JPEG files via CD.

PAYMENT & TERMS Average price per image (to clients): $200 for color photos. Enforces minimum prices. Offers volume discounts to customers. Works with photographers on contract basis only. Statements issued quarterly. Photographers allowed to review account records in cases of discrepancies only. Offers one-time rights. Model release preferred. Photo captions required.

HOW TO CONTACT Send query letter with images; include SASE if sending by mail. Expects minimum initial submission of 200 images.

⚫ ECOSCENE

Empire Farm, Throop Rd., Templecombe, Somerset BA8 0HR, United Kingdom. 44(0)1963 371 700. **E-mail:** sally@ecoscene.com, pictures@ecoscene.com. **Website:** www.ecoscene.com. **Contact:** Sally Morgan, director. Estab. 1988. Picture library. Has 80,000 photos in files. Clients include: advertising agencies, businesses, book/encyclopedia publishers, magazine publishers, newspapers, online, multimedia.

NEEDS Photos of disasters, environmental, energy issues, sustainable development, wildlife, gardening, rural, agriculture, medicine, science, pollution, industry, energy, indigenous peoples.

SPECS Accepts digital submissions only. High-quality JPEG at 300 dpi, minimum file size when opened of 50MB.

PAYMENT & TERMS Pays 55% commission for color photos. Negotiates fees below stated minimum prices, depending on quantity reproduced by a single client. Offers volume discounts to customers. Discount sales terms not negotiable. Works with photographers on contract basis only. Offers nonexclusive contract. Contracts renew automatically with additional submissions, 4 years minimum. Statements issued quarterly. Payment made quarterly. Offers one-time and electronic media rights. Informs photographers and allows them to negotiate when client requests all rights. Model/property release required. Photo captions required; include location, subject matter, keywords and common and Latin names of wildlife and any behavior shown in pictures.

HOW TO CONTACT Send e-mail with résumé of credits. Digital submissions only. Keeps samples on file; include SASE for return of material. Expects minimum initial submission of 100 images with annual submissions of at least 100 images. Responds in 2 months. Photo guidelines free with SASE. Market tips sheets distributed quarterly to anybody who requests, and to all contributors.

TIPS "Photographers should carry out a tight EDT, no fillers, and be critical of their own work."

✣ ESTOCK PHOTO, LLC

27-28 Thomson Ave., Suite 628, Long Island City NY 11101. (800)284-3399. **Fax:** (212)545-1185. **E-mail:** submissions@estockphoto.com. **Website:** www.es

tockphoto.com. Member of Picture Archive Council of America (PACA). Specialties include: world travel, cultures, landmarks, leisure, nature and scenics. Has over 1 million photos in files. Clients include: ad agencies, public relations and AV firms; businesses; book, magazine and encyclopedia publishers; newspapers, calendar and greeting card companies; textile firms; travel agencies and poster companies.

NEEDS Exceptional travel-related imagery and people/leisure photography.

SPECS Submission guidelines available on our website under the "contact us" page.

HOW TO CONTACT Send query letter with samples, a list of stock photo subjects or submit portfolio for review. Response time depends; often the same day. Photo guidelines free with SASE.

TIPS "Photos should show what the photographer is all about. They should show technical competence—photos that are sharp, well-composed, have impact; if color, they should show color."

⚫ EYE UBIQUITOUS

P.O. Box 2190, Shoreham-by-Sea West Sussex BN43 9EZ, United Kingdom. 44(0)1243 864005. **Fax:** 44(0)1273 440116. **Website:** www.eyeubiquitous. com. Estab. 1988. Picture library. Has 300,000+ photos in files. Clients include: ad agencies, public relations firms, businesses, book/encyclopedia publishers, magazine publishers, newspapers, television companies.

NEEDS Photos of worldwide social documentary and general stock.

SPECS Transparencies and 50MB files at 300 dpi.

PAYMENT & TERMS Offers volume discounts to customers; inquire about specific terms. Discount sales terms not negotiable. Works with photographers on contract basis only. Offers exclusive, limited regional exclusivity and nonexclusive contracts. Contracts renew automatically with additional submissions. Charges to photographers "discussed on an individual basis." Payment made quarterly. Photographers allowed to review account records. Buys one-time, electronic media and agency promotion rights; negotiable. Does not inform photographers or allow them to negotiate when client requests all rights. Model/property release preferred for people, "particularly Americans." Photo captions required; include where, what, why, who.

HOW TO CONTACT Submit portfolio for review. Works with freelancers only. Keeps samples on file. Include SASE for return. No minimum number of images expected in initial submission, but "the more the better." Responds as time allows. Photo guidelines free with SASE. Catalog free with SASE. Market tips sheet distributed to contributors "when we can" free with SASE.

TIPS "Find out how picture libraries operate. This is the same for all libraries worldwide. Amateurs can be very good photographers, but very bad at understanding the industry after reading some irresponsible and misleading articles. Research the library requirements."

FAMOUS PICTURES & FEATURES AGENCY

13 Harwood Rd., London SW6 4QP, United Kingdom. +44(0)20 7731 9333. **Fax:** +44(0)20 7731 9330. **E-mail:** info@famous.uk.com; pictures@famous.uk.com. **Website:** www.famous.uk.com. Estab. 1985. Picture library, news/feature syndicate. Has more than 500,000 photos on database. Clients include: advertising agencies, book publishers, magazine publishers, newspapers, calendar companies, postcard publishers and poster publishers.

NEEDS Photos of music, film, TV personalities; international celebrities; live, studio, party shots (paparazzi) with stars of all types.

SPECS Prefers images in digital format. Send via FTP or e-mail as JPEG files at 300 dpi or higher.

PAYMENT & TERMS Offers volume discounts to customers. Photographers can choose not to sell images on discount terms. Works with photographers with or without a contract; contracts available for all photographers. Offers limited regional exclusivity. Statements issued monthly. Payment made monthly. Photographers allowed to review account records. Offers one-time rights. Photo captions preferred.

HOW TO CONTACT E-mail, phone or write, provide samples. Provide résumé, business card, self-promotion piece or tearsheets to be kept on file. Agency will contact photographer for portfolio review if interested. Keeps samples in online database. Will return material with SAE/IRC.

TIPS "We are solely marketing images via computer networks. Our fully searchable archive of new and old pictures is online. Send details via e-mail for more information. When submitting work, please caption pictures correctly."

FIRST LIGHT

Design Pics, Inc. 10464 176th St., #101, Edmonton Alberta T5S 1L3, Canada. (416)597-8625; toll free in Canada (800)668-2003. **Fax:** (416)597-2035. **E-mail:** anne@firstlight.com. **Website:** www.firstlight.com. **Contact:** Anne Bastarache, director, photography. Estab. 1984. First Light sales staff serves their clients through the e-commerce website, which includes over 9 million royalty-free and rights-managed images and video.

NEEDS Representing over 200 photographers, and in combination with Design Pics Canadian-based photographers, First Light has one of the most extensive collections of Canadian content available anywhere. In addition, the site has over 50 third-party providers.

SPECS "For initial review submission we require low-res JPEG files. Contact us if you are interested in submitting images. For final submissions we require clean 62MB high-res TIFF files, captured on professional grade cameras."

HOW TO CONTACT Send query letter via e-mail.

TIPS "We want to see tightly edited submissions. Well-produced, non-candid, commercial quality imagery."

THE FLIGHT COLLECTION

Quadrant House, The Quadrant, Oxford Rd., Sutton Surrey SM2 5AS, United Kingdom. 44(0)20 8652 8888. **E-mail:** flight@uniquedimension.com; flight@image-asset-management.com. **Website:** www.theflightcollection.com. Estab. 1983. Has 1 million+ photos in files. Clients include: advertising agencies, public relations firms, audiovisual firms, businesses, book publishers, magazine publishers, newspapers, calendar companies, greeting card companies, postcard publishers.

NEEDS Photos of aviation.

SPECS Accepts all transparency film sizes: Send a sample of 50 for viewing. Accepts images in digital format. Send via CD as TIFF files at 300 dpi.

PAYMENT & TERMS Enforces minimum prices. Offers volume discounts to customers. Discount sales terms not negotiable. Works with photographers on contract basis only. Offers nonexclusive contract. Contracts renew automatically with additional submissions, no specific time. Statements issued monthly. Payment made monthly. Offers one-time rights. Model/property release required. Photo captions required; include name, subject, location, date.

HOW TO CONTACT Send query letter with transparencies or CD. Does not keep samples on file; include SASE for return of material. Expects minimum initial submission of 50 images. Photo guidelines sheet free via e-mail.

TIPS "Caption slides/images properly. Provide a list of what's submitted."

🌀 FLOWERPHOTOS

P.O. Box 2190, Shoreham-by-Sea West Sussex BN43 9EZ, United Kingdom. +44(0)1243 864005. **E-mail:** stephen@flowerphotos.com. **Website:** www.flower photos.com. **Contact:** Stephen Rafferty, library manager. Estab. 1993. Stock photo agency. Has 30,000 photos in files. Clients include: ad agencies, businesses, book publishers, magazine publishers, postcard companies, calendar companies, greeting card companies, public relations firms, newspapers.

NEEDS Photos of gardening, rural, agriculture, business concepts, environmental, landscapes/scenics, wildlife.

SPECS Send via CD or Dropbox. Minimum 50 MB at 300 dpi size 12 JPEGs only, full captions and keywords embedded.

PAYMENT & TERMS Pays commission for color photos, film and video. Negotiates fees below stated minimums; various price agreements based on market forces. Works with photographers on contract basis only. Offers exclusive contract, limited regional exclusivity, nonexclusive contract and guaranteed subject exclusivity. Contracts renew automatically with each submission. Payment made quarterly. Photographers permitted to review sales records in cases of discrepancies only. Offers one-time rights, electronic media rights. Model/property release preferred. Photo captions required; include correct botanical and common names.

HOW TO CONTACT E-mail query letter with JPEG samples at 72 dpi. Does not keep samples on file; cannot return material. Expects minimum initial submission of 100 images with quarterly submissions of at least 100 images. Photo guidelines available online. Market tips sheet available free via e-mail.

TIPS "Look at our stock and gauge our style and range and supply images that complement and/or expand the collection."

FOODPIX

Getty Images, 605 Fifth Ave. S., Suite 400, Seattle WA 98104. (206)925-5000. **E-mail:** sales@gettyimages. com. **Website:** www.gettyimages.com. Estab. 1994. Stock agency. Member of the Picture Archive Council of America (PACA). Has 40,000 photos in files. Clients include: advertising agencies, businesses, newspapers, book publishers, calendar companies, design firms, magazine publishers.

NEEDS Food, beverage and food/lifestyle images.

SPECS Accepts analog and digital images. Review and complete the online submission questionnaire on the website before submitting work.

PAYMENT & TERMS Enforces minimum prices. Offers volume discounts to customers; terms specified in photographers' contracts. Works with photographers on contract basis only. Offers exclusive contract only. Statements issued monthly. Payment made quarterly. Offers one-time rights. Model/property release required. Photo captions required.

HOW TO CONTACT Send query e-mail with samples. Expects maximum initial submission of 50 images. Catalog available.

FOTOAGENT

E-mail: werner@fotoagent.com. **Website:** www.foto agent.com. **Contact:** Werner J. Bertsch, president. Estab. 1985. Stock photo agency. Has 1.5 million photos in files. Clients include: magazines, advertising agencies, newspapers, publishers.

NEEDS General worldwide travel, medical and industrial.

SPECS Uses digital files only. Upload your files on website.

PAYMENT & TERMS Pays 50% commission for b&w or color photos. Average price per image (to clients): $175 minimum for b&w or color photos. Works with photographers on contract basis only. Offers nonexclusive contract. Contracts renew automatically with each submission for 1 year. Statements issued monthly. Payment made monthly. Photographers allowed to review account records to verify sales figures. Offers one-time rights. Model release required. Photo captions required.

HOW TO CONTACT Use the "Contact Us" feature on website.

TIPS Wants to see "clear, bright colors and graphic style. Looking for photographs with people of all ages with good composition, lighting and color in any material for stock use."

◗ FOTO-PRESS TIMMERMANN

Speckweg 34A, Moehrendorf D-91096, Germany. 49(0)9131 42801. **Fax:** 49(0)9131 450528. **E-mail:** info@f-pt.com. **Website:** www.f-pt.com. **Contact:** Wolfgage Timmermann. Stock photo agency. Has 750,000 photos in files. Clients include: advertising agencies, audiovisual firms, businesses, book/encyclopedia publishers, magazine publishers, newspapers, calendar companies.

NEEDS Landscapes, countries, travel, tourism, towns, people, business, nature, babies/children/teens, couples, families, parents, senior citizens, adventure, entertainment, health/fitness/beauty, hobbies, industry, medicine, technology/computers. Interested in erotic, fine art, seasonal, lifestyle.

SPECS Uses 2¼×2¼, 4×5, 8×10 transparencies (no prints). Accepts images in digital format. Send via CD, ZIP as TIFF files.

PAYMENT & TERMS Pays 50% commission for color photos. Works on nonexclusive contract basis (limited regional exclusivity). First period: 3 years; contract automatically renewed for 1 year. Photographers allowed to review account records. Statements issued quarterly. Payment made quarterly. Offers one-time rights. Informs photographers and allows them to negotiate when a client requests to buy all rights. Model/property release preferred. Photo captions required; include state, country, city, subject, etc.

HOW TO CONTACT Send query letter with stock list. Send unsolicited photos by mail for consideration; include SAE/IRC for return of material. Responds in 1 month.

◗ FOTOSCOPIO

Roosevelt 3751, Piso 12, Depto. A, C1430AGJ, Capital Federal, Buenos Aires 1203AAQ, Argentina. (54)(114)544-2997. **Fax:** (54)(114)542-2997. **E-mail:** online contact form. **Website:** www.fotoscopio.com.ar. **Contact:** Gustavo Di Pace, director. Estab. 1999. Latin American stock photo agency. Has 50,000 photos in files. Clients include: advertising agencies, businesses, postcard publishers, book publishers, calendar companies, magazine publishers, greeting card companies.

NEEDS Photos of Hispanic people, Latin American countries, babies/children/teens, celebrities, couples, multicultural, families, senior citizens, disasters, environmental, landscapes/scenics, wildlife, architecture, cities/urban, interiors/decorating, pets, religious, adventure, automobiles, entertainment, health/fitness/beauty, hobbies, sports, travel, agriculture, business concepts, industry, product shots/still life, technology/computers. Interested in documentary, fine art, historical/vintage.

SPECS Uses 35mm, 2¼×2¼, 4×5, 8×10 transparencies. Accepts images in digital format. Send via CD, ZIP.

PAYMENT & TERMS Average price per image (to clients): $50-300 for b&w photos; $50-800 for color photos. Negotiates fees below stated minimums. Offers volume discounts to customers; terms specified in photographer's contracts. Discount sales terms not negotiable. Works with photographers on contract basis only. Offers nonexclusive contract. Contracts renew automatically with additional submissions for 1 year. Statements issued and payment made whenever one yields rights of reproduction of his photography. Photographers allowed to review account records in cases of discrepancies only. Offers one-time and electronic media rights. Model release required; property release preferred. Photo captions preferred.

HOW TO CONTACT Send query letter with résumé, slides, prints, photocopies, tearsheets, transparencies, stock list. Provide résumé, business card, self-promotion piece to be kept on file. Expects minimum initial submission of 100 images. Responds in 1 month to samples. Photo guidelines sheet free with SASE.

FUNDAMENTAL PHOTOGRAPHS

210 Forsyth St., Suite 2, New York NY 10002. (212)473-5770. **E-mail:** mail@fphoto.com. **Website:** www.fphoto.com. **Contact:** Kip Peticolas, partner. Estab. 1979. Stock photo agency. Applied for membership into the Picture Archive Council of America (PACA). Member of ASPP. Has 100,000 photos in files. Searchable online database. Clients include: textbook/encyclopedia publishers, advertising agencies, science magazine publishers, travel guide book publishers, corporate industrial.

NEEDS Photos of medicine, biology, microbiology, environmental, industry, weather, disasters, science-related business concepts, agriculture, technology/computers, optics, advances in science and industry, green technologies, pollution, physics and chemistry concepts.

SPECS Accepts 35mm and all large-format transparencies but digital is strongly preferred. Send digital as

RAW or TIFF unedited original files at 300 dpi, 11×14 or larger size. Please e-mail for current submission guidelines.

PAYMENT & TERMS Pays 50% commission for color photos. General price range (to clients): $100-500 for b&w photos; $150-1,200 for color photos; depends on rights needed. Enforces strict minimum prices. Offers volume discount to customers. Works with photographers on contract basis only. Offers guaranteed subject exclusivity. Contracts renew automatically with additional submissions for 2 or 3 years. Charges $5/image scanning fee; can increase to $15 if corrective Photoshop work required. Charges copyright registration fee (optional). Statements issued and payment made quarterly for any sales during previous quarter. Photographers allowed to review account records with written request submitted 2 months in advance. Offers one-time and electronic media rights. Gets photographer's approval when client requests all rights; negotiation conducted by the agency. Model release required. Photo captions required; include date and location.

HOW TO CONTACT E-mail request for current photo guidelines. Contact via e-mail to arrange digital submission. Submit link to web portfolio for review. Send query e-mail with résumé of credits, samples or list of stock photo subjects. Keeps samples on file; include SASE for return of material if sending by post. Expects minimum initial submission of 100 images. E-mail crucial for communicating current photo needs.

TIPS "Our primary market is science textbooks. Photographers should research the type of illustration used and tailor submissions to show awareness of salable material. We are looking for science subjects ranging from nature and rocks to industrials, medicine, chemistry and physics; macro photography, photomicrography, stroboscopic; well-lit still-life shots are desirable. The biggest trend that affects us is the need for images that document new discoveries in sciences and ecology. Please avoid images that appear dated, images with heavy branding, soft focus or poorly lit subjects."

GETTY IMAGES

605 Fifth Ave. S., Seattle WA 98104. (206)925-5000, (800)462-4379. **E-mail:** sales@gettyimages.com, editorialsubmissions@gettyimages.com. **Website:** www.gettyimages.com. "Getty Images is the world's leading imagery company, creating and distributing the largest and most relevant collection of still and moving images to communication professionals around the globe and supporting their work with asset management services. From news and sports photography to contemporary and archival imagery, Getty Images' products are found each day in newspapers, magazines, advertising, films, television, books and websites. Gettyimages.com is the first place customers turn to search, purchase, download and manage powerful imagery. Seattle-headquartered Getty Images is a global company with customers in more than 100 countries."

HOW TO CONTACT Visit www.gettyimages.com/contributors.

🌐 GLOBALEYE IMAGES

OzImages International Pty Ltd, P.O. Box 99, Yorkeys Knob, Qld 4878, Australia. +61 (0) 740 557 669. **Fax:** +61 (0) 740 557 669. **E-mail:** admin@globaleyeimages.com. **Website:** www.globaleyeimages.com. **Contact:** Matt Brading, owner. Estab. 1998. Stock photo agency. Has over 250,000 photos in files online; estimated 10 million in offline archives. Clients: advertising agencies, public relations firms, audiovisual firms, businesses, newspapers, magazine and book publishers, calendar companies, greeting card companies, postcard publishers.

NEEDS Photos of babies/children/teens, couples, multicultural, families, parents, senior citizens, architecture, education, religious, business concepts, industry, medicine, military, science, technology/computers, environmental, adventure, health/fitness/beauty, documentary, lifestyle, sports, travel.

PAYMENT & TERMS Pays 100% to photographer. Average price per image (to client): $100-1,500. Negotiates fees below stated minimum; "photographers always have final say. We encourage them to set minimums but it's their decision." Offers volume discount (photographer's decision; can choose not to sell images on discount terms). Works with photographers with or without contract; negotiable. Offers nonexclusive contract. Contracts renew automatically with additional submissions. A simple contributor agreement applies for the membership term, monthly, quarterly or annual. A flat rate membership fee is paid to cover costs and then no fees or agency commissions are deducted from the photographer's sales. Photographer keeps 100% of all sales. Photographers may cancel contract with 60 days written notice. Offers one-time rights, electronic media rights. Informs photographers when a client requests exclusive rights. Model/property release preferred. Photo captions required.

HOW TO CONTACT Does not keep samples on file. Cannot return material. Responds in 1-2 days to online applications. Photo guidelines available online. Copy of catalog available online. Market tips sheet available monthly to contributors. Prefer a minimum of 100 images as an initial submission with monthly submissions of at least 50 images.

TIPS "Show the same attention to detail to the written aspects of your application as you do to your photography. With our structure, the photographer deals directly with our clients, so communication and presentation is key. We are always reluctant to take on new photographers who come across as careless or unprofessional, no matter how good their work might be."

GRANATAIMAGES.COM

Milestone Media SRL, Via Giuseppe Saragat, 11, Milan 20128, Italy. (39)(02)26680702. **Fax:** (39)(02)26681126. **E-mail:** redazione@milestonemedia.it; info@milestonemedia.it. **Website:** www.milestonemedia.it. Estab. 1985. Stock and press agency. Member of CEPIC. Has 2 million photos in files and 800,000 images online. Clients include: advertising agencies, newspapers, book publishers, calendar companies, audiovisual firms, magazine publishers, production houses.

NEEDS Photos of celebrities, people.

SPECS Uses high-res digital files. Send via ZIP, FTP, e-mail as TIFF, JPEG files.

PAYMENT & TERMS Negotiates fees below stated minimums in cases of volume deals. Offers volume discounts to customers. Photographers can choose not to sell images on discount terms. Works with photographers on contract basis only. Offers exclusive contract only. Contracts renew automatically with additional submissions for 1 year. Statements issued monthly. Photographers allowed to review account records in cases of discrepancies only. Offers one-time rights. Model/property release preferred. Photo captions required; include location, country and any other relevant information.

HOW TO CONTACT Send query letter with digital files.

HERITAGE IMAGES

Clerks Court, 18-20 Farringdon Lane, London EC1R 3AU, United Kingdom. U.K.: 0800 436 867, US: (888)761-9293. **Fax:** 44(0) 20 7434 0673. **E-mail:** angela.davies@heritage-images.com. **Website:** www.heritage-images.com. Estab. 1998. Member of BAPLA (British Association of Picture Libraries and Agencies). Has 250,000+ images on file. Clients include: advertisers/designers, businesses, book publishers, magazine publishers, newspapers, calendar/card companies, merchandising, TV.

NEEDS Worldwide religion, faith, spiritual images, buildings, clergy, festivals, ceremony, objects, places, food, ritual, monks, nuns, stained glass, carvings, the unusual. Mormons, Shakers, all groups/sects, large or small. Death: burial, funerals, graves, gravediggers, green burial, commemorative. Ancient/heritage/Bible/lands/saints/eccentricities/festivals: curiosities, unusual oddities like follies, signs, symbols. Architecture, religious or secular. Manuscripts and illustrations, old and new, linked with any of the subjects above.

SPECS Accepts images in digital format. Send via CD, JPEG files in medium to high-res. Uses 35mm, 2¼×2¼, 4×5 transparencies.

PAYMENT & TERMS Average price per image (to clients): $140-200 for color photos. Offers volume discounts to customers. Works with photographers on contract basis for 5 years, offering exclusive/non-exclusive contract renewable automatically with additional submissions. Offers one-time rights. Model release where necessary. Photo captions very important and must be accurate; include what, where, any special features or connections, name, date (if possible), and religion.

HOW TO CONTACT Send query letter with slides, tearsheets, transparencies/CD. Expects minimum initial submission of 40 images. Photo guidelines sheet and "wants list" available via e-mail.

TIPS "Decide on exact subject of image. *Get in close and then closer.* Exclude all extraneous matter. Fill the frame. Dynamic shots. Interesting angles, light. No shadows or miniscule subject matter far away. Tell us what is important about the picture. No people in shot unless they have a role in the proceedings as in a festival or service, etc."

🌐 HUTCHISON PICTURE LIBRARY

P.O. Box 2190, Shoreham-by-Sea West Sussex BN43 9EZ, United Kingdom. **E-mail:** library@hutchison pictures.co.uk. **Website:** www.hutchisonpictures. co.uk. **Contact:** Stephen Rafferty, manager. Stock photo agency, picture library. Has around 500,000 photos in files. Clients include: ad agencies, public relations firms, audiovisual firms, businesses, book/encyclopedia publishers, magazine publishers, newspapers, postcard companies, calendar companies, television and film companies.

NEEDS "We are a general, documentary library (no news or personalities). We file mainly by country and aim to have coverage of every country in the world. Within each country we cover such subjects as industry, agriculture, people, customs, urban, landscapes, etc. We have special files on many subjects such as medical (traditional, alternative, hospital, etc.), energy, environmental issues, human relations (relationships, childbirth, young children, etc., but all real people, not models). We constantly require images of Spain and Spanish-speaking countries. Also interested in babies/children/teens, couples, multicultural, families, parents, senior citizens, disasters, architecture, education, gardening, interiors/decorating, religious, rural, health/fitness, travel, military, political, science, technology/computers. Interested in documentary, seasonal. We are a color library."

SPECS Uses 35mm transparencies. Accepts images in digital format: 50MB at 300 dpi, cleaned of dust and scratches at 100%, color corrected.

PAYMENT & TERMS Pays 40% commission for exclusive; 35% for nonexclusive. Statements issued semiannually. Payment made semiannually. Sends statement with check in June and January. Offers one-time rights. Model release preferred. Photo captions required.

HOW TO CONTACT Always willing to look at new material or collections. Arrange a personal interview to show portfolio. Send letter with brief description of collection and photographic intentions. Responds in about 2 weeks, depends on backlog of material to be reviewed. "We have letters outlining working practices and lists of particular needs (they change)." Distributes tips sheets to photographers who already have a relationship with the library.

TIPS Looks for "collections of reasonable size (rarely less than 1,000 transparencies) and variety; well captioned (or at least well indicated picture subjects; cap-

tions can be added to mounts later); sharp pictures, good color, composition; and informative pictures. Prettiness is rarely enough. Our clients want information, whether it is about what a landscape looks like or how people live, etc. The general rule of thumb is that we would consider a collection that has a subject we do not already have coverage of or a detailed and thorough specialist collection. Please do not send *any* photographs without prior agreement."

🌐 ✳ ICP DI ALESSANDRO MAROSA

Via Pico della Mirandola 8/A - 20151, Milano , Italy. Milan: 39-02-89605794; Rome: 39-06-452217748; Torino: 39-011-23413919. **Fax:** 39-02-700565601. **E-mail:** icp@icponline.it; alessandro@icponline.it. **Website:** www.icponline.it. **Contact:** Mr. Alessandro Marosa, CEO. Estab. 1970. Stock photo agency. Clients include: advertising agencies, public relations firms, audiovisual firms, businesses, book/encyclopedia publishers, magazine publishers, postcard publishers, calendar companies and greeting card companies.

SPECS High-res digital (A3-A4, 300 dpi), keyworded (English and, if possible, Italian).

PAYMENT & TERMS Pays 50% commission for color photos. Offers volume discounts to customers; terms specified in photographer's contract. Discount sales terms not negotiable. Contracts renew automatically with additional submissions, for 3 years. Statements issued monthly. Payment made monthly. Photographers permitted to review account records to verify sales figures or deductions. Offers one-time, first and sectorial exclusive rights. Model/property release required. Photo captions required.

HOW TO CONTACT Arrange a personal interview to show portfolio. Send query letter with samples and stock list. Works on assignment only. No fixed minimum for initial submission. Responds in 3 weeks, if interested.

🌐 IMAGES.DE FULFILLMENT

Potsdamer Str. 96, Berlin D-10785, Germany. +49(0)30-2579 28980. **Fax:** +49(0)30-2579 28999. **E-mail:** info@images.de. **Website:** www.images.de. Estab. 1997. News/feature syndicate. Has 50,000 photos in files. Clients include: advertising agencies, newspapers, public relations firms, book publishers, magazine publishers. "We are a service company with 10 years experience on the picture market. We offer fulfillment services to picture agencies, including translation, distribution into Fotofiner and APIS picture-maxx, customer communication, invoicing, media control, cash delivery, and usage control."

NEEDS Photos of babies/children/teens, couples, multicultural, families, parents, senior citizens, environment, entertainment, events, food/drink, health/fitness, hobbies, travel, agriculture, business concepts, industry, medicine, political, science, technology/computers.

SPECS Accepts images in digital format. Send via FTP, CD.

PAYMENT & TERMS Pays 50% commission for b&w photos; 50% for color photos. Average price per image (to clients): $50-1,000 for b&w photos or color photos. Offers volume discounts to customers. Discount sales terms not negotiable. Works with photographers with or without a contract; negotiable. Offers limited regional exclusivity. Statements issued monthly. Payment made monthly. Photographers allowed to review account records in cases of discrepancies only. Offers one-time rights, electronic media rights. Informs photographers and allows them to negotiate when client requests all rights. Model release preferred; property release required. Photo captions required.

HOW TO CONTACT Send query letter with CD or link to website. Expects minimum initial submission of 100 images.

THE IMAGE WORKS

P.O. Box 443, Woodstock NY 12498. (845)679-8500 or (800)475-8801. **Fax:** (845)679-0606. **E-mail:** info@theimageworks.com; mark@theimageworks.com. **Website:** www.theimageworks.com. **Contact:** Mark Antman, president. Estab. 1983. Stock photo agency. Member of Picture Archive Council of America (PACA). Has over 1 million photos in files. Clients include: ad agencies, book/encyclopedia publishers, magazine publishers, newspapers, postcard publishers, greeting card companies, documentary video.

NEEDS "We are always looking for excellent documentary photography. Our prime subjects are people-related subjects like family, education, health care, workplace issues, worldwide historical, technology, fine arts."

SPECS All images must be in digital format; contact for digital guidelines. Rarely accepts 35mm, 2¼×2¼ transparencies and prints.

PAYMENT & TERMS Works with photographers on contract basis only. Offers nonexclusive contract. Statements issued monthly. Payments made monthly.

Photographers allowed to review account records to verify sales figures by appointment. Offers one-time, agency promotion and electronic media rights. Informs photographers and allows them to negotiate when clients request all rights. Model release preferred. Photo captions required.

HOW TO CONTACT Send e-mail with description of stock photo archives. Expects minimum initial submission of 500 images.

TIPS "The Image Works was one of the first agencies to market images digitally. All digital images from photographers must be of reproduction quality. When making a new submission to us, be sure to include a variety of images that show your range as a photographer. We also want to see some depth in specialized subject areas. Thorough captions are a must. We will not look at uncaptioned images. Write or call first."

INMAGINE

315 Montgomery St., San Francisco CA 94104. (832)632-9299; (800)810-3888. **Fax:** (866)998-8383. **E-mail:** photo@inmagine.com. **Website:** www.inmagine.com. Estab. 2000. Stock agency, picture library. Member of the Picture Archive Council of America (PACA). Has 7 million photos in files. Branch offices in USA, Hong Kong, Australia, Malaysia, Thailand, Singapore, Indonesia, and China. Clients include: advertising agencies, businesses, newspapers, public relations firms, magazine publishers.

NEEDS Photos of babies, children, teens, couples, multicultural, families, parents, education, business concepts, industry, medicine, environmental and landscapes, adventure, entertainment, events, food and drink, health, fitness, beauty, hobbies, sports, travel, fashion/glamour, and lifestyle.

SPECS Accepts images in digital format. Submit online via submission.inmagine.com or send JPEG files at 300 dpi.

PAYMENT & TERMS Pays 50% commission for color photos. Average price per image (to clients): $100 minimum, maximum negotiable. Negotiates fees below stated minimums. Offers volume discounts to customers, terms specified in photographers' contracts. Works with photographers on a contract basis only. Offers nonexclusive contract. Payments made monthly. Photographers are allowed to view account records in cases of discrepancies only. Offers one-time rights. Model and property release required. Photo caption required.

HOW TO CONTACT Contact through website. Expects minimum initial submission of 5 images. Responds in 1 week to samples. Photo guidelines available online.

TIPS "Complete the steps as outlined in the IRIS submission pages. E-mail us if there are queries. Send only the best of your portfolio for submission, stock-oriented materials only. EXIF should reside in file with keywords and captions."

⊙ INTERNATIONAL PHOTO NEWS

2902 29th Way, West Palm Beach FL 33407. (561)313-1465. **E-mail:** jay@jaykravetz.com. **Contact:** Jay Kravetz, photo editor. News/feature syndicate. Has 50,000 photos in files. Clients include: newspapers, magazines, book publishers. Previous/current clients include: newspapers that need celebrity photos with story.

NEEDS Photos of celebrities, entertainment, events, health/fitness/beauty, performing arts, travel, politics, movies, music and television, at work or play. Interested in avant garde, fashion/glamour.

SPECS Accepts images in digital format. Send via CD, ZIP, e-mail as TIFF, JPEG files at 300 dpi. Uses 5×7, 8×10 glossy b&w prints.

PAYMENT & TERMS Pays $10 for b&w photos; $25 for color photos; 5-10% commission. Average price per image (to clients): $25-100 for b&w photos; $50-500 for color photos. Works with photographers on contract basis only. Offers nonexclusive contract. Contracts renew automatically with additional submissions; 1-year renewal. Photographers allowed to review account records. Statements issued monthly. Payment made monthly. Offers one-time rights. Model/property release preferred. Photo captions required.

HOW TO CONTACT Send query letter with résumé of credits. Solicits photos by assignment only. Responds in 1 week.

TIPS "We use celebrity photographs to coincide with our syndicated columns. Must be approved by the celebrity."

⊙ THE IRISH IMAGE COLLECTION

#101, 10464 - 176 St., Edmonton Alberta T5S 1L3, Canada. (780)447-5433. **E-mail:** kristi@theirishimagecollection.com. **Website:** www.theirishimagecollection.ie. **Contact:** Kristi Bennell, office manager. Stock photo agency and picture library. Has 50,000+

photos in files. Clients include: advertising agencies, public relations firms, businesses, book/encyclopedia publishers, magazine publishers, newspapers and designers.

NEEDS Consideration is given only to Irish or Irish-connected subjects.

SPECS Uses 35mm and all medium-format transparencies.

PAYMENT & TERMS Pays 40% commission for color photos. Average price per image (to client): $85-2,000. Works on contract basis only. Offers exclusive contracts and limited regional exclusivity. Contracts renew automatically with additional submissions. Statements issued quarterly. Payment made quarterly. Photographers allowed to review account records. Offers one-time and electronic media rights. Informs photographer when client requests all rights, but "we take care of negotiations." Model release required. Photo captions required.

HOW TO CONTACT Send query letter with list of stock photo subjects. Does not return unsolicited material. Expects minimum initial submission of 250 transparencies; 1,000 images annually. "A return shipping fee is required: important that all similars are submitted together. We keep our contributor numbers down and the quantity and quality of submissions high. Send for information first by e-mail."

TIPS "Our market is Ireland and the rest of the world. However, our continued sales of Irish-oriented pictures need to be kept supplied. Pictures of Irish-Americans in Irish bars, folk singing, Irish dancing, in Ireland or anywhere else would prove to be useful. They would be required to be beautifully lit, carefully composed with attractive, model-released people."

⊙ THE IRISH PICTURE LIBRARY

69b Heather Rd., Sandyford Industrial Estate, Dublin 18, Ireland. (353)1295 0799. **Fax:** (353)1295 0705. **E-mail:** info@davison.com; ipl@davisonphoto.com. **Website:** www.davisonphoto.com/ipl. Estab. 1990. Picture library. Has 60,000+ photos in files. Clients include: advertising agencies, businesses, book publishers, magazine publishers, newspapers, calendar companies.

NEEDS Photos of historic Irish material. Interested in alternative process, fine art, historical/vintage.

SPECS Uses any prints. Accepts images in digital format. Send via CD as TIFF, JPEG files at 400 dpi.

PAYMENT & TERMS Enforces minimum prices. Offers volume discounts to customers. Photographers can choose not to sell images on discount terms. Works with photographers on contract basis only. Statements issued quarterly. Payment made quarterly. Photographers allowed to review account records. Offers one-time rights, electronic media rights. Property release required. Photo captions required.

HOW TO CONTACT Send query letter with photocopies. Does not keep samples on file; include SAE/IRC for return of material.

ISOPIX

Werkhuizenstraat 7-9 Rue des Ateliers, Brussel-Bruxelles 1080, Belgium. 32 2 420 30 50. **Fax:** 32 2 420 41 22. **E-mail:** isopix@isopix.be. **Website:** www.isopix.be. Estab. 1984. News/feature syndicate. Has 2.5 million photos on website, including press (celebrities, royalty, portraits, news sports, archival), stock (contemporary and creative photography) and royalty-free. Clients include: advertising agencies, public relations firms, businesses, book publishers, magazine publishers, newspapers, calendar companies, postcard publishers.

NEEDS Photos of teens, celebrities, couples, families, parents, senior citizens, disasters, environmental, landscapes/scenics, wildlife, education, religious, events, food/drink, health/fitness, hobbies, humor, agriculture, business concepts, industry, medicine, science, technology/computers. Interested in alternative process, avant garde, documentary, fashion/glamour, fine art, historical/vintage, seasonal.

SPECS Accepts images in digital format; JPEG files only.

PAYMENT & TERMS Enforces strict minimum prices. Works with photographers with or without a contract; negotiable. Offers limited regional exclusivity. Contracts renew automatically with additional submissions. Statements issued monthly. Payment made monthly. Photographers allowed to review account records in cases of discrepancies only. Model/property release preferred. Photo captions required.

HOW TO CONTACT Contact through rep. Does not keep samples on file; include SAE/IRC for return of material. Expects minimum initial submission of 1,000 images with quarterly submissions of at least 500 images.

ISRAELIMAGES.COM

POB 60, Kammon 20112, Israel. (972)3-6320374. **Fax:** 972-153-4-9082023. **E-mail:** israel@israelimages. com; info@israelimages.com. **Website:** www.israel images.com. **Contact:** Israel Talby, managing director. Estab. 1991. Has 650,000 photos in files. Clients include: advertising agencies, web designers, businesses, book publishers, magazine publishers, newspapers, calendar companies, greeting card and postcard publishers, multimedia producers, schools and universities, etc.

NEEDS "We are interested in everything about Israel, Judaism (worldwide) and The Holy Land."

SPECS Uses digital material only, minimum accepted size 2000×3000 pixels. Simply upload your pictures directly to the site. "When accepted, we need TIFF or JPEG files at 300 dpi, RGB, saved at quality '11' in Photoshop."

PAYMENT & TERMS Average price per image (to clients): $50-3,000/picture. Negotiates fees below standard minimum against considerable volume that justifies it. Offers volume discounts to customers. Works with photographers on contract basis only. Offers limited regional exclusivity, nonexclusive contract. Contracts renew automatically with additional submissions. Sales reports are displayed on the site at the Contributor's personal account. Payments are constantly made. Photographers allowed to review account records. Offers one-time rights, electronic media rights, agency promotion rights. Informs photographers and allows them to negotiate when a client requests all rights. Model/property release preferred. Photo captions required (what, who, when, where).

HOW TO CONTACT E-mail any query to: Israel@israelimages.com. No minimum submission. Responds within 1-2 days.

TIPS "We strongly encourage everyone to send us images to review. When sending material, a strong edit is a must. We don't like to get 100 pictures with 50 similars. Last, don't overload our e-mail with submissions. Make an e-mail query, or better yet, view our submission guidelines on the website. Good luck and welcome!"

JAYTRAVELPHOTOS

7A Napier Rd., Wembley, Middlesex HA0 4UA, United Kingdom. (44)(208)795-3581. **Fax:** (44)(202)975-4083. **E-mail:** jaytravelphotos@aol.com. **Website:** www.jaytravelphotos.co.uk; www.jaylondonphotos. co.uk. **Contact:** Rohith or Franco, partners. Estab. 1992. Stock photo agency and picture library. Has 250,000 photos in files. Clients include: advertising agencies, businesses, book/encyclopedia publishers, magazine publishers, newspapers, postcard publishers, tour operators/travel companies.

NEEDS Travel and tourism-related images worldwide.

SPECS Accepts digital, minimum 12 megapixel SLR (see website for guidelines). Uses 35mm up to 6×7cm original transparencies.

PAYMENT & TERMS Pays 60% commission for digital images and 50% for transparencies. Average price per image (to clients): $125-1,000. Enforces minimum prices of $125, "but negotiable on quantity purchases." Offers volume discounts to customers; inquire about specific terms. Discount sales terms not negotiable. Works with photographers on contract basis only. Offers limited regional exclusivity contract. Statements issued quarterly. Payment made quarterly, within 30 days of payment received from client. Offers one-time and exclusive rights for fixed periods. Does not inform photographers or allow them to negotiate when client requests all rights. Model/property release preferred. Photo captions required; include country, city/location, subject description.

HOW TO CONTACT Send e-mail with stock list, or call. Expects a minimum initial submission of 300 images with quarterly submissions of at least 100 images. Responds in 3 weeks.

TIPS "Study our guidelines on our website on what to submit. If you're planning a photo shoot anywhere, you need to give us an itinerary, with as much detail as possible, so we can brief you on what kind of pictures the library may need."

JEROBOAM

120 27th St., San Francisco CA 94110. (415)312-0198. **E-mail:** jeroboamster@gmail.com. **Contact:** Ellen Bunning, owner. Estab. 1972. Has 200,000 b&w photos, 200,000 color slides in files. Clients include: text and trade book, magazine and encyclopedia publishers, editorial (mostly textbooks), greeting cards, and calendars.

NEEDS "We want people interacting, relating photos, comic, artistic/documentary/photojournalistic images, especially ethnic and handicapped. Images must have excellent print quality—contextually interesting and exciting and artistically stimulating." Photos of babies/children/teens, couples, multicultural, families, parents, senior citizens, disasters, environmental, cities/urban, education, gardening, pets, religious, rural, adventure, health/fitness, humor, performing arts, sports, travel, agriculture, industry, medicine, military, political, science, technology/computers. Interested in documentary, historical/vintage, seasonal. Needs shots of school, family, career and other living situations. Child development, growth and therapy, medical situations. No nature or studio shots.

SPECS Uses 35mm transparencies.

PAYMENT & TERMS Works on consignment only; pays 50% commission. Average price per image (to clients): $150 minimum for b&w and color photos. Works with photographers without a signed contract. Statements issued monthly. Payment made monthly. Photographers allowed to review account records to verify sales figures. Offers one-time and electronic media rights. Informs photographers and allows them to negotiate when client requests all rights. Model/property release preferred for people in contexts of special education, sexuality, etc. Photo captions preferred; include "age of subject, location, etc."

HOW TO CONTACT "Call if in the Bay Area; if not, query with samples and list of stock photo subjects; send material by mail for consideration or submit portfolio for review. Let us know how long you've been shooting." Responds in 2 weeks.

TIPS "The Jeroboam photographers have shot professionally a minimum of 5 years, have experienced some success in marketing their talent, and care about their craft excellence and their own creative vision. New trends are toward more intimate, action shots; more ethnic images needed."

KIMBALL STOCK

1960 Colony St., Mountain View CA 94043. (650)969-0682; (888)562-5522. **Fax:** (650)969-0485. **E-mail:** sales@kimballstock.com; submissions@kimballstock.com. **Website:** www.kimballstock.com. Estab. 1970. Has 1 million photos in files. Clients include: advertising agencies, businesses, newspapers, postcard publishers, public relations firms, book publishers, calendar companies, magazine publishers, greeting card companies. "Kimball Stock strives to provide automotive and animal photographers with the best medium possible to sell their images. In addition, we work to give every photographer a safe, reliable, and pleasant experience."

NEEDS Photos of dogs, cats, lifestyle with cars and domestic animals, landscapes/scenics, wildlife (outside of North America). Interested in seasonal.

SPECS Prefers images in digital format, minimum of 12-megapixel digital camera, although 16-megapixel is preferred. Send via e-mail as JPEG files or send CD to mailing address. Uses 35mm, 120mm, 4×5 transparencies.

PAYMENT & TERMS Works with photographers with a contract; negotiable. Offers nonexclusive contract. Statements issued quarterly. Payments made quarterly. Photographers allowed to review account records. Offers one-time rights, electronic media rights. Model/property release required. Photo captions required.

HOW TO CONTACT Send query letter with transparencies, digital files, stock list. Provide self-promotion piece to be kept on file. Please limit your initial submission to no more than 200 images (with at least 100 images) showing the range and variety of your work. Responds only if interested in 5-6 weeks or 3 months during busy seasons; send nonreturnable samples. Photo guidelines available online at www.kimballstock.com/submissions.asp.

JOAN KRAMER AND ASSOCIATES, INC.

10490 Wilshire Blvd., Suite 1701, Los Angeles CA 90024. (310)446-1866. **Fax:** (310)446-1856. **E-mail:** erwin@erwinkramer.com. **Website:** www.erwinkramer.com. Joan Kramer, president. **Contact:** Erwin Kramer. Member of Picture Archive Council of America (PACA). Has 1 million photos in files. Clients include: ad agencies, magazines, recording companies, photo researchers, book publishers, greeting card companies, promotional companies, AV producers.

NEEDS "We use any and all subjects! Stock slides must be of professional quality." Subjects on file include travel, cities, personalities, animals, flowers, lifestyles, underwater, scenics, sports and couples.

SPECS Uses 8×10 glossy b&w prints; any size transparencies.

PAYMENT & TERMS Pays 50% commission. Offers all rights. Model release required.

HOW TO CONTACT Send query letter or call to arrange an appointment. Do not send photos before calling.

LAND OF THE BIBLE PHOTO ARCHIVE

P.O. Box 8441, Jerusalem 91084, Israel. (972)(2)566-2167. **Fax:** (972)(2)566-3451. **E-mail:** radovan@netvision.net.il. **Website:** www.biblelandpictures.com. **Contact:** Zev Radovan. Estab. 1975. Picture library. Has 50,000 photos in files. Clients include: book publishers, magazine publishers, newspapers, calendar companies, postcard publishers.

NEEDS Photos of museum objects, archaeological sites. Also multicultural, landscapes/scenics, architecture, religious, travel. Interested in documentary, fine art, historical/vintage.

SPECS Uses high-res digital system.

PAYMENT & TERMS Average price per image (to clients): $80-700 for b&w, color photos. Offers volume discounts to customers; terms specified in photographers' contracts.

TIPS "Our archives contain tens of thousands of color slides covering a wide range of subjects: historical and archaeological sites, aerial and close-up views, museum objects, mosaics, coins, inscriptions, the myriad ethnic and religious groups individually portrayed in their daily activities, colorful ceremonies, etc. Upon request, we accept assignments for in-field photography."

LATITUDE STOCK

Home Farm, Stratfield Saye, Hampshire RG7 2BT, United Kingdom. 44 (0)845 0940546. **E-mail:** stuart@latitudestock.com. **Website:** www.latitudestock.com. Has over 115,000 photos in files. Clients include: advertising agencies, businesses, newspapers, public relations firms, book publishers, calendar companies, audiovisual firms, magazine publishers, greeting card companies.

NEEDS Photos of multicultural, environmental, landscapes/scenics, wildlife, architecture, cities/urban, gardening, religious, rural, adventure, events, food/drink, health/fitness/beauty, hobbies, sports, travel.

SPECS Uses 35mm and medium-format transparencies. Accepts images in digital format. See website for details.

PAYMENT & TERMS Pays on a commission basis. Enforces minimum prices. Offers volume discounts to customers. Works with photographers on contract basis only. Offers exclusive contract only. Statements issued quarterly. Payment made quarterly. Photographers allowed to review account records. Offers one-time rights. Model/property release required. Photo captions required.

HOW TO CONTACT "Please e-mail first."

LEBRECHT MUSIC & ARTS PHOTO LIBRARY

3 Bolton Rd., London NW8 0RJ, United Kingdom. +44 207 625 5341; (866)833-1793. **E-mail:** pictures@lebrecht.co.uk. **Website:** www.lebrecht.co.uk. **Contact:** Ms. E. Lebrecht. Estab. 1992. Picture library has 300,000 high-res images online—musicians, artists, authors, politicians, scientists. Clients include: newspapers, public relations firms, book publishers, calendar companies, magazine publishers, greeting card companies.

NEEDS Photos of arts personalities, performing arts, instruments, musicians, dance (ballet, comtemporary and folk), orchestras, opera, concert halls, jazz, blues, rock, authors, artists, theater, comedy, art, writers, historians, plays, playwrights, philosophers, etc. Interested in historical/vintage.

SPECS Accepts images in digital format only.

PAYMENT & TERMS Pays 50% commission for b&w and color photos. Offers volume discounts to customers. Works with photographers on contract basis only. Offers limited regional exclusivity. Statements issued quarterly. Offers one-time rights. Informs photographers and allows them to negotiate when a client requests all rights. Model release preferred. Photo captions required; include who is in photo, location, date.

HOW TO CONTACT Send e-mail to pictures@lebrecht.co.uk.

LIGHTWAVE PHOTOGRAPHY

(781)354-7747. **E-mail:** paul@lightwavephoto.com. **Website:** www.lightwavephoto.com. **Contact:** Paul Light. Has 250,000 photos in files. Clients include: advertising agencies, textbook publishers.

NEEDS Candid photos of people in school, work and leisure activities, lifestyle.

SPECS Uses digital photographs.

PAYMENT & TERMS Pays $210/photo; 50% commission. Works with photographers on contract basis only. Offers nonexclusive contract. Contracts renew automatically each year. Statements issued annually. Payments made "after each usage." Offers one-time rights. Informs photographers and allows them to negotiate when client requests all rights. Model/property release preferred. Photo captions preferred.

HOW TO CONTACT "Create a small website and send us the URL."

TIPS "Photographers should enjoy photographing people in everyday activities. Work should be carefully edited before submission. Shoot constantly and watch what is being published. We are looking for photographers who can photograph daily life with compassion and originality."

LINEAIR FOTOARCHIEF BV

Raapopseweg 66, Arnhem 6824DT, Netherlands. (31)(26)4456713. **E-mail:** info@lineairfoto.nl. **Website:** www.lineairfoto.nl. **Contact:** Ron Giling, manager. Estab. 1990. Stock photo agency and since 2001 also an image-research department as service to publishers and other customers. Has nearly 2 million downloadable images available through the website. Clients include advertising agencies, public relations firms, book/encyclopedia publishers, magazine publishers. Library specializes in images from Asia, Africa, Latin America, Eastern Europe and nature in all forms on all continents. Member of WEA, a group of international libraries that use the same server to market each other's images, uploading only once.

NEEDS Photos of disasters, environment, landscapes/scenics, wildlife, cities/urban, education, religious, adventure, travel, agriculture, business concepts, industry, political, science, technology/computers, health, education. Interested in everything that has to do with the development of countries all over the world, especially in Asia, Africa and Latin America.

SPECS Accepts images in digital format only. Send via CD, DVD (or use our FTP) as high-quality JPEG files at 300 dpi. "Photo files need to have IPTC information!"

PAYMENT & TERMS Pays 50% commission. Average price per image (to clients): $100-500. Enforces minimum prices. Offers volume discounts to customers; inquire about specific terms. Photographers can choose not to sell images on discount terms. Works with or without a signed contract; negotiable. Offers limited regional exclusivity. Statements issued quarterly. Payments made quarterly. Photographers allowed to review account records. "They can review bills to clients involved." Offers one-time rights. Informs photographers and allows them to negotiate when client requests all rights. Photo captions required; include country, city or region, description of the image.

HOW TO CONTACT Submit portfolio or e-mail thumbnails (20KB files) for review. There is no minimum for initial submissions. Responds in 3 weeks.

Market tips sheet available upon request. View website to see subject matter and quality.

TIPS "We like to see high-quality pictures in all aspects of photography. So we'd rather see 50 good ones than 500 for us to select the 50 out of. Send contact sheets upon our request. We will mark the selected pictures for you to send as high-res, including the very important IPTC (caption and keywords)."

LIVED IN IMAGES

1401 N. El Camino Real, Suite 203, San Clemente CA 92672. (949)361-3959. **Fax:** (949)492-1370. **E-mail:** jonathan@livedinimages.com. **Website:** www.lived inimages.com. **Contact:** Jonathan Thomas, president. Estab. 2004. Stock agency and news/feature syndicate. Member of the Picture Archive Council of America. Has 500,000+ photos on file. Clients include: advertising agencies, businesses, book publishers, magazine publishers, newspapers.

SPECS Accepts images in digital format. Send via CD, ZIP as TIFF or JPEG files at 300 dpi.

PAYMENT & TERMS Pays 50% commission for b&w photos; 50% for color photos; 50% for film; 50% for video. Offers volume discount to customers. Discount sales terms not negotiable. Works with photographers on contract basis only. Offers exclusive contract. Statements issued monthly. Payment made monthly. Photographers allowed to review account records. Offers one-time rights, electronic media and agency promotion rights. Model/property release required.

HOW TO CONTACT E-mail query letter with link to photographer's website. Samples not kept on file. Materials cannot be returned. Expects minimum initial submission of 100 images with monthly submissions of at least 50 images. Photo guidelines available online. Market tips sheet distributed monthly to contributors under contract (also available online or free via e-mail).

TIPS "Think about your submission and why you are submitting to the agency. Who is the end user? We receive a great deal of work that has absolutely no value. Also, continue to submit! To make a decent monthly income, photographers need to continually submit their work. It's a numbers game. The more you have, the better you will do!"

🌑 LONELY PLANET IMAGES

Getty Images, 6300 Wilshire Blvd., 16th Floor, Los Angeles CA 90048. (510)250-6400; (800)275-8555. **Fax:** (510)893-8572. **Website:** www.lonelyplanetim ages.com; www.lonelyplanet.com. International stock photo agency with offices in Oakland, London and Footscray (outside Melbourne). Clients include: advertising agencies, public relations firms, book/encyclopedia publishers, magazine publishers, newspapers, calendar companies, greeting card companies, design firms.

NEEDS Photos of international travel destinations.

SPECS Uses original color transparencies in all formats; digital images from 10-megapixel and higher DSLRs.

PAYMENT & TERMS Pays 40% commission. Works with photographers on contract basis only. Offers image exclusive contract. Contract renews automatically. Model/property release preferred. Photo captions required.

HOW TO CONTACT Download submission guidelines from website—click on "work for us" at the bottom of www.lonelyplanet.com page.

TIPS "Photographers must be technically proficient, productive, and show interest and involvement in their work."

♻ 🞈 LONE PINE PHOTO

22 Robinson Crescent, Saskatoon Saskatchewan S7L 6N9, Canada. (306)683-0889. **Fax:** (306)242-1892. **E-mail:** lonepinephoto@shaw.ca. **Website:** www.lone pinephoto.ca. **Contact:** Clarence W. Norris. Estab. 1991. "Lone Pine Photo is a photo stock agency specializing in well-edited images of Canada. Our library consists of: 60,000+ 35mm slides, 20,000+ digital images. All images are rights managed. A licensing fee is required for the use of all of our images. All images provided are copyrighted to the photographers that we represent. We have updated our website on which clients may browse through a variety of galleries. Each gallery bears a gallery description summarizing the contents and useful search tips. Full caption information is displayed. Click on a thumbnail for larger image and more image info. Keywords allow clients to refine their searches."

SPECS "We are seeking stock photographers who have the following attributes: Excellent technical and creative skills to produce top-quality images based on our submission guidelines, subject want lists and on their specific photographic interests and travels. The ability to carefully edit their own work and to send us only the very best with detailed captions. An existing image file to provide us with 500+ images to start.

The time and resources to photograph regularly and to submit 500+ images annually for our review. The ability to work together as part of a team to develop a top-quality Canadian stock photo agency." All rights managed. Credit line.

LUCKYPIX

1132 W. Fulton Market, Chicago IL 60607. (773)235-2000. **E-mail:** info@luckypix.com; mmoore@lucky pix.com. **Website:** www.luckypix.com. **Contact:** Megan Moore. Estab. 2001. Stock agency. Has 9,000 photos in files (adding constantly). Clients include: advertising agencies, businesses, book publishers, design companies, magazine publishers.

NEEDS Outstanding people/lifestyle images.

SPECS 50+MB TIFFs, 300 dpi, 8-bit files. Photos for review: upload to website or e-mail info@luckypix. com. Final: CD/DVD as TIFF files.

PAYMENT & TERMS Enforces minimum prices. Offers exclusivity by image and similars. Contracts renew automatically annually. Statements and payments issued quarterly. Model/property release required.

HOW TO CONTACT Call or upload sample from website (preferred). Responds in 1 week. See website for guidelines.

TIPS "Have fun shooting. Search the archives before deciding what pictures to send."

☼ ✪ ♫ MASTERFILE

3 Concorde Gate, 4th Floor, Toronto Ontario M3C 3N7, Canada. (800)387-9010. **E-mail:** info@masterfile. com. **Website:** www.masterfile.com. General stock agency offering photos, illustrations and vectors under different licenses, including rights-managed, royalty-free, budget royalty-free and a subscription model. The combined online collection exceeds 5 million images. Clients include: major advertising agencies, broadcasters, graphic designers, public relations firms, book and magazine publishers, producers of greeting cards, calendars and packaging.

SPECS Accepts images in digital format only, in accordance with submission guidelines.

PAYMENT & TERMS Contributor terms outlined in photographer's contract, which is image-exclusive. Photographer sales statements and royalty payments issued monthly.

HOW TO CONTACT Refer to www.masterfile.com/info/artists/submissions.html for submission guidelines.

TIPS "Do not send transparencies, prints or discs as a first-time submission. If we like what we see, you will be contacted by Artist Recruitment to submit additional work, and high resolution files for a technical review. Due to the large volume of submissions, we contact only those artists we are interested in."

✪ MICHELE MATTEI PHOTOGRAPHY

1714 Wilton Place, Los Angeles CA 90028. (323)462-6342. **Fax:** (323)462-7568. **E-mail:** michele@michele mattei.com. **Website:** michelemattei.net. **Contact:** Michele Mattei, director. Estab. 1974. Stock photo agency. Clients include: book/encyclopedia publishers, magazine publishers, television, film.

TIPS "Shots of celebrities and home/family stories are frequently requested." In samples, looking for "high-quality, recognizable personalities and current news-making material. We are interested mostly in celebrity photography. Written material on personality or event helps us to distribute material faster and more efficiently."

♺ ✪ MAXX IMAGES, INC.

P.O. Box 30064, North Vancouver British Columbia V7H 2Y8, Canada. (888)511-3939. **E-mail:** new submissions@maxximages.com; info@maxximag es.com. **Website:** www.maxximages.com. **Contact:** Dave Maquignaz, president. Estab. 1994. Stock agency. Member of the Picture Archive Council of America (PACA). Has 19 million images online. Has 30,000+ video clips. Clients include: advertising agencies, public relations firms, audiovisual firms, businesses, book publishers, magazine publishers, newspapers, calendar companies, postcard publishers, video production, graphic design studios.

NEEDS Photos of people, lifestyle, business, recreation, leisure.

SPECS Uses all formats.

HOW TO CONTACT Send e-mail.

THE MEDICAL FILE, INC.

279 E. 44th St., 21st Floor, New York NY 10017. (212)883-0820 or (917)215-6301. **E-mail:** themedical file@gmail.com. **Website:** www.themedicalfile.com. **Contact:** Barbara Gottlieb, president. Estab. 2005. Clients include: advertising agencies, public relations firms, businesses, book/encyclopedia publishers, magazine publishers, postcard companies, calendar companies, greeting card companies.

NEEDS Any medically related imagery including fitness and food in relation to health care.

SPECS Accepts digital format images only on CD or hard drive. Images can be uploaded to an FTP site.

PAYMENT & TERMS Average price per image (for clients): $250 and up. Accepted work will be distributed through our partner agents worldwide. Works on exclusive and nonexclusive contract basis. Contracts renew automatically with each submission for length of original contract. Payments made quarterly. Offers one-time rights. Informs photographers when clients request all rights or exclusivity. Model release required. Photo captions required.

HOW TO CONTACT Arrange a personal interview to show portfolio. Submit portfolio or samples for review. Tip sheets distributed as needed to contract photographers only.

TIPS Wants to see a cross-section of images for style and subject. "Photographers should not photograph people *before* getting a model release. The day of the 'grab shot' is over. We only accept digital submissions."

MEDISCAN

2nd Floor Patman House, 23-27 Electric Parade, George Lane South Woodford, London E18 2LS, United Kingdom. 44(0)20 8530 7589. **Fax:** 44(0)20 8989 7795. **E-mail:** info@mediscan.co.uk. **Website:** www.mediscan.co.uk. Estab. 2001. Picture library. Has over 1 million photos and over 2,000 hours of film/video footage on file. Subject matter includes medical personnel and environment, diseases and medical conditions, surgical procedures, microscopic, scientific, ultrasound/CT/MRI scans and x-rays. Online catalog on website. Clients include: advertising and design agencies, business-to-business, newspapers, public relations, book and magazine publishers in the health care, medical and science arenas.

NEEDS Photos of babies/children/teens/senior citizens; health/lifestyle/fitness/beauty; medicine, especially plastic surgery, rare medical conditions; model-released images; science, including microscopic imagery, botanical and natural history.

SPECS Accepts negatives; 35mm and medium format transparencies; digital images (make contact before submitting samples).

PAYMENT & TERMS Pays up to 50% commission. Statements issued quarterly. Payment made quarterly. Model/property release required, where necessary.

HOW TO CONTACT E-mail or call.

MEGAPRESS IMAGES

1751 Richardson, Suite 2205, Montreal Québec H3K 1G6, Canada. (514)279-9859. **Fax:** (514)279-9859. **E-mail:** info@megapress.ca. **Website:** www.megapress.ca. Estab. 1992. Stock photo agency. Has 500,000 photos in files. Has 2 branch offices. Clients include: book/encyclopedia publishers, magazine publishers, postcard publishers, calendar companies, greeting card companies, advertising agencies.

NEEDS Photos of people (babies/children/teens, couples, people at work, medical); animals including puppies in studio; industries; celebrities and general stock. Also needs families, parents, senior citizens, disasters, environmental, landscapes/scenics, wildlife, gardening, pets, religious, adventure, automobile, food/drink, health/fitness/beauty, sports, travel, business concepts, still life, science. "Looking only for the latest trends in photography and very high-quality images. A part of our market is Quebec's local French market."

SPECS Accepts images in digital format only. Send via CD, floppy disk, ZIP as JPEG files at 300 dpi.

PAYMENT & TERMS Pays 50% commission for color photos. Average price per image (to client): $100. Enforces minimum prices. Will not negotiate below $60. Works with photographers with or without a contract. Statements issued semiannually. Payments made semiannually. Offers one-time rights. Model release required for people and controversial news.

HOW TO CONTACT Submit link first by e-mail. "If interested, we'll get back to you." Does not keep samples on file; include SAE/IRC for return of material. Expects minimum initial submission of 250 images with periodic submission of at least 1,000 digital pictures per year. Make first contact by e-mail. Accepts digital submissions only.

TIPS "Pictures must be very sharp. Work must be consistent. We also like photographers who are specialized in particular subjects. We are always interested in Canadian content. Lots of our clients are based in Canada."

MIRA

716 Iron Post Rd., Moorestown NJ 08057. (856)231-0594. **E-mail:** mira@mira.com. **Website:** library.mira.com/gallery-list. "Mira is the stock photo agency of the Creative Eye, a photographers cooperative. Mira seeks premium rights-protected images and contributors who are committed to building the Mira archive into a first-choice buyer resource. Mira offers a broad

and deep online collection where buyers can search, price, purchase and download on a 24/7 basis. Mira sales and research support are also available via phone and e-mail. "Our commitment to customer care is something we take very seriously and is a distinguishing trait." Client industries include: advertising, publishing, corporate, marketing, education.

NEEDS Mira features premium stock photo images depicting a wide variety of subjects including travel, Americana, business, underwater, food, landscape, cityscapes, lifestyle, education, wildlife, conceptual and adventure sports, among many others.

SPECS "We require you to use the enhanced version of the Online Captioning software or to embed your captions and keywords using the Photoshop File Info feature, or an application such as Extensis Portfolio 7 or iView MediaPro 2.6 to embed this info in the IPTC metadata fields. Please read over the Mira Keywording Guidelines (download PDF) before preparing your submission. For additional suggestions on Captioning and Keywording see the Metalogging section of the Controlled Vocabulary site."

HOW TO CONTACT "E-mail, call or visit our websites to learn more about participation in Mira."

TIPS "Review the submission guidelines completely. Failure to follow the submission guidelines will result in the return of your submission for appropriate corrections."

MPTV

16735 Saticoy St., Suite 109, Van Nuys CA 91406. (818)997-8292. **Fax:** (818)997-3998. **E-mail:** sales@mptvimages.com. **Website:** www.mptvimages.com. Estab. 1988. "Established over 20 years ago, mptv is a unique stock photo agency that is passionate about preserving the memory of some of the greatest legends of our time through the art of still photography. We offer one of the largest and continually expanding collections of entertainment photography in the world—images from Hollywood's Golden Age and all the way up to the present day. Our unbelievable collection includes some 1 million celebrity and entertainment-related images taken by more than 60 photographers from around the world. Many of these photographers are represented exclusively through mptv and can't be found anywhere else. While mptv is located in Los Angeles, our images are used worldwide and can be seen in galleries, magazines, books, advertising, online and in various products."

HOW TO CONTACT If interested in representation, send an e-mail to photographers@mptvimages.com.

NATURIMAGES

8 rue de l'Auditoire, Charenton du Cher 18210, France. **E-mail:** annelaure.robert@naturimages.com. **Website:** www.naturimages.com. **Contact:** Annelaure Robert. Estab. 2007. Picture library with 300,000 photos in files. Clients include: advertising agencies, public relations firms, book publishers, magazine publishers, newspapers, calendar companies, postcard publishers.

NEEDS Photos of cities/urban, gardening, pets, agriculture, environmental, landscapes/scenics, wildlife, science.

SPECS Accepts images in digital format only. Send via CD, ZIP or e-mail as JPEG files at 300 dpi.

PAYMENT & TERMS Pays on commission. 50% b&w; 50% color. Average price to clients for photos: $10-1,000. Offers volume discounts to customers. Discount sales terms not negotiable. Works with photographers with or without a contract; negotiable. Offers exclusivity on French agency. Statements issued semiannually. Payment made semiannually. Photographers allowed to review account records by request. Offers one-time rights. Model release and property release preferred. Photo captions required. Include location, species.

HOW TO CONTACT E-mail query letter with JPEG samples at 72 dpi. Expects minimum initial submission of 30 images. Responds in 4 weeks.

NOVASTOCK

1306 Matthews Plantation Dr., Matthews NC 28105-2463. **E-mail:** Novastock@aol.com. **Website:** www.portfolios.com/novastock. **Contact:** Anne Clark, submission department. Estab. 1993. Stock agency. Clients include: advertising agencies, businesses, postcard publishers, public relations firms, book publishers, calendar companies, magazine publishers, greeting card companies, and large international network of subagents.

NEEDS "We need commercial stock subjects such as lifestyles, fitness, business, science, medical, family, etc. We also are looking for unique and unusual imagery. Wants photos of babies/children/teens, couples, multicultural, families, parents, senior citizens, disasters, environmental, wildlife, rural, adventure, health/fitness, travel, business concepts, military, science, technology/computers.

SPECS Prefers images in digital format as follows: (1) Original digital camera files. (2) Scanned images in the 30-50MB range. "When sending files for editing, please send small files only. Once we make our picks, you can supply larger files. Final large files should be JPEGs. *Never* sharpen or use contrast and saturation filters. Always flatten layers. Files and disks must be readable on Windows PC."

PAYMENT & TERMS Pays 50% commission for b&w and color photos. "We never charge the photographer for any expenses whatsoever." Works with photographers on contract basis only. "We need exclusivity only for images accepted, and similars." Photographer is allowed to market work not represented by Novastock. Statements and payments are made in the month following receipt of income from sales. Informs photographers and discusses with photographer when client requests all rights. Model/property release required. Photo captions required; include who, what and where. "Science and technology need detailed and accurate captions. Model releases must be cross-referenced with the appropriate images."

HOW TO CONTACT Contact by e-mail or send query letter with digital files, tearsheets.

TIPS "Digital files on CD/DVD are preferred. All images must be labeled with caption and marked with model release information and your name and copyright. We market agency material through more than 50 agencies in our international subagency network. The photographer is permitted to freely market non-similar work any way he/she wishes."

● ONASIA

30 Cecil St., Prudential Tower Level 15, 049712, Singapore. (66)2-714-3968. **Fax:** (66)2655 4682. **E-mail:** info@onasia.com; sales@onasia.com. **Website:** www.onasia.com. **Contact:** Peter Charlesworth or Yvan Cohen, directors. An Asia-specialized agency offering rights-managed stock, features and assignment services. Represents over 180 photographers. Has over 180,000 high-res images available online and 400,000 photos in files. Offices in Singapore and Bangkok. Clients include: advertising and graphic design agencies, newspapers, magazines, book publishers, calendar and gift card companies.

NEEDS Model-released Asia-related conceptual, lifestyle and business imagery as well as a broad range of nonreleased editorial imagery including current affairs, historical collections, travel and leisure, eco-nomics as well as social and political trends. Please note: "We only accept images from or relating to Asia."

SPECS Accepts images in digital format. Send via CD or to our FTP site as 12×18 JPEG files at 300 dpi. All files must be retouched to remove dust and dirt. Photo captions required; include dates, location, country and a detailed description of image, including names where possible.

PAYMENT & TERMS Pays 50% commission to photographers. Terms specified in photographer contracts. Photographers are required to submit on an image-exclusive basis. Statements issued monthly.

HOW TO CONTACT E-mail queries with low-res JPEG samples or a link to photographer's website. Does not keep samples on file; cannot return material. Expects minimum initial submission of 150 images. Photo guidelines available via e-mail.

TIPS "Provide a well-edited low-res portfolio for initial evaluation. Ensure that subsequent submissions are tightly edited, sized to Onasia's specs, retouched and submitted with full captions."

ONREQUEST IMAGES

1415 Western Ave., Suite 300, Seattle WA 98101. **Website:** www.onrequestimages.com. "OnRequest Images is the leading provider of powerful, custom imagery and photo production services for the Global 2000. Having the world's largest photo production services network enables our clients to utilize the best fully vested resources the world has to offer, including photographers, stylists, locations and crews. Combined with OnPro™, our collaborative workflow system which underpins every detail of a production, OnRequest Images delivers brand-aligned, cost effective, fast photography solutions for marketers, brand leaders and creative teams. We have the talent, tenacity and technology to make things happen even on the grandest scale. OnRequest Images is headquartered in Seattle, with offices in New York, Chicago, Denver, Los Angeles, Miami, San Francisco, London, Paris and Barcelona."

NEEDS Photos of babies, multicultural, families, parents, senior citizens, environmental, landscapes/scenics, architecture, education, interiors/decorating, pets, rural, adventure, food/drink, health/fitness/beauty, travel, agriculture, business concepts, science, technology/computers. Interested in lifestyle, seasonal.

SPECS Accepts images in digital format as TIFF files at 300 dpi. Send via e-mail or upload.

PAYMENT & TERMS Offers volume discounts to customers; terms specified in photographers' contracts. Photographers can choose not to sell images on discount terms. Works with photographers on contract basis only. Offers nonexclusive contract; guaranteed subject exclusivity (within files). Statements issued quarterly. Payments made within 45 days. Rights offered depend on contract. Informs photographers and allows them to negotiate when a client requests all rights. Model release/property release required. Captions required.

HOW TO CONTACT E-mail query letter with link to photographer's website. Provide self-promotion piece to be kept on file. Expects minimum initial submission of 15 images. Photo guidelines sheet available.

TIPS "Be honest about what you specialize in."

☻ OPÇÃO BRASIL IMAGENS

Rua Barata Ribeiro, No. 370 Gr. 215/216, Copacabana, Rio de Janeiro 22040-901, Brazil. 55 21 2256-9007. **Fax:** 55 21 2256-9007. **E-mail:** pesquisa@opcaobrasil.com.br. **Website:** www.opcaobrasil.com.br. Estab. 1993. Has 600,000+ photos in files. Clients include: advertising agencies, book publishers, magazine publishers, calendar companies, postcard publishers, publishing houses.

NEEDS Photos of babies/children/teens, couples, families, parents, wildlife, health/fitness, beauty, education, hobbies, sports, industry, medicine. "We need photos of wild animals, mostly from the Brazilian fauna. We are looking for photographers who have images of people who live in tropical countries and must be brunette."

SPECS Accepts images in digital format.

PAYMENT & TERMS Pays 50% commission for b&w or color photos. Negotiates fees below standard minimum prices only in cases of renting at least 20 images. Offers volume discounts to customers. Works with photographers on contract basis only. Offers limited regional exclusivity. Contracts renew automatically with additional submissions for 3 years. Charges $200/image for catalog insertion. Statements issued quarterly. Payment made quarterly. Photographers allowed to review account records in cases of discrepancies only. Offers one-time rights, electronic media rights, agency promotion rights. Model release required; property release preferred. Photo captions required.

HOW TO CONTACT Initial contact should be by e-mail or fax. Explain what kind of material you have. Provide business card, self-promotion piece to be kept on file. "If not interested, we return the samples." Expects minimum initial submission of 500 images with quarterly submissions of at least 300 images.

TIPS "We need creative photos presenting the unique look of the photographer on active and healthy people in everyday life at home, at work, etc., showing modern and up-to-date individuals. We are looking for photographers who have images of people with the characteristics of Latin American citizens."

☻ OUTDOORIA OUTDOOR IMAGE AGENCY

Valfiskengata 800, Haninge 13664, Sweden. 46 707833785. **E-mail:** info@outdooria.com contributor@outdooria.com. **Website:** www.outdooria.com. **Contact:** Patrik Lindqvist, CEO. Estab. 2009. Stock agency and picture library. Has over 6,500 photos on file. Clients include advertising agencies, businesses, newspapers, postcard publishers, public relations firms, book publishers, calendar companies, magazine publishers, and greeting card companies.

SPECS Model and property release preferred. Photo captions required.

PAYMENT & TERMS Does not offer volume discounts to customers. Works with photographers on a contract basis only. Agency contracts review automatically with additional submissions.

HOW TO CONTACT E-mail query letter with link to photographer's website or JPEG samples at 72 dpi. Accepts images in digital format. Please send via CD, or ZIP as a TIFF or JPEG file. Expects minimum initial submission of 40 images. Responds in 1 week to samples and portfolios. Guidelines available online.

OUTSIDE IMAGERY LLC

Boulder CO 80301. (303)530-3357. **E-mail:** John@outsideimagery.com. **Website:** www.outsideimagery.com. **Contact:** John Kieffer, president. Estab. 1986. Outside Imagery has a new website featuring auto-downloads and payment, plus expanded print sales. Clients include: advertising agencies, businesses, multimedia, greeting card and postcard publishers, book publishers, graphic design firms, magazine publishers.

NEEDS Photos showing a diversity of people participating in an active and healthy lifestyle in natural and urban settings, plus landscapes and cityscapes. Photos of people enjoying the outdoors.

SPECS Requires images in high-res digital format. No film. Send low-res files via CD or e-mail in JPEG format at 72 dpi.

PAYMENT & TERMS Pays 50% commission for all imagery. Offers nonexclusive contract. Payments made quarterly. Model release required; property release preferred. Photo captions and keywords required.

HOW TO CONTACT "First review our website. Then send a query e-mail, and include a stock list or an active link to your website. If you don't hear from us in 3 weeks, send a reminder e-mail."

PACIFIC STOCK/PRINTSCAPES.COM

(808)394-5100. **Fax:** (780)451-8568. **E-mail:** info@pacificstock.com; ashlee@pacificstock.com. **Website:** www.pacificstock.com. **Contact:** Ann Matchett, content and contributor manager. Member of Picture Archive Council of America (PACA). 25,000 digital images online. "Pacific Stock specializes exclusively in imagery from throughout the Pacific, Asia and Hawaii." Clients include: advertising agencies, public relations firms, book/encyclopedia publishers, magazine publishers, postcard companies, calendar companies, greeting card companies. "Printscapes caters to the professional interior design market at our new fine art website, www.printscapes.com."

NEEDS Photos and fine art of Hawaii, Pacific Islands, and Asia. Subjects for both companies include: people (women, babies/children/teens, couples, multicultural, families, parents, senior citizens), culture, marine science, environmental, landscapes, wildlife, adventure, food/drink, health/fitness, sports, travel, agriculture, business concepts." We also have an extensive vintage Hawaii file as well as fine art throughout the Pacific Rim."

PAYMENT & TERMS Pays commission for color and b&w photos based on the photographer. Negotiates fees below stated minimums for preferred vendors. Offers volume discounts to customers. Works with photographers on contract basis only. Guaranteed subject exclusivity. Annual contract renewal after first 5 years. Statements issued monthly. Photographers allowed to review account records. Offers negotiable rights.

HOW TO CONTACT Accepts images in digital format only. Send via CD or FTP as JPEG files at 1,000

pixels on long side for review purposes or put together a gallery of low-res images on your website and send us the URL. Do not e-mail images. Accepted images must be 60MB minimum shot as raw originals. Model/property release required when applicable. Photo captions required; include who, what, when, where. E-mail query letter with link to photographer's website or JPEG samples at 72 dpi. Expects minimum initial submission of 100 images with periodic submissions of at least 100 images 4 times/year. Responds in 1 month. Photo guidelines free on request through e-mail. Market tips sheet free via e-mail, distributed to those with contracts. Interested in high-quality digital files only from full-frame cameras. Provide links to collections, galleries and websites. Show a minimum of 200 images to represent the quality of your work.

PANORAMIC IMAGES

2302 Main St., Evanston IL 60202. (847)324-7000 or (800)543-5250. **Fax:** (847)324-7004. **Website:** www.panoramicimages.com. Estab. 1987. Stock photo agency. Member of ASPP, NANPA and IAPP. Clients include: design firms, graphic designers, advertising agencies, corporate art consultants, postcard companies, magazine publishers, newspapers and calendar companies.

NEEDS Photos of landscapes/scenics, wildlife, architecture, cities/urban, cityscapes and skylines, gardens, rural, adventure, health/fitness, sports, travel, business concepts, industry, science, technology/computers. Interested in alternative process, avant garde, documentary, fine art, historical/vintage, seasonal. Works only with *panoramic formats* (2:1 aspect ratio or greater). Subjects include: cityscapes/skylines, international travel, nature, backgrounds, conceptual.

SPECS "E-mail for digital and film submission guidelines or see website."

PAYMENT & TERMS Pays 40% commission for photos. Average price per image (to clients): $300. No charge for scanning, metadata or inclusion on website. Statements issued quarterly. Payments made quarterly. Offers one-time, electronic rights and limited exclusive usage. Model release preferred "and property release, if necessary." Photo captions required. See website for submission guidelines before submitting.

HOW TO CONTACT Send e-mail with stock list or low-res scans/lightbox. Specific want lists created for contributing photographers. Photographer's work is represented on full e-commerce website and distributed worldwide through image distribution partnerships with Getty Images, National Geographic Society Image Collection, Amana, etc. See website for more detailed submission guidelines.

TIPS Wants to see "well-exposed chromes or very high-res stitched pans. Panoramic views of well-known locations nationwide and worldwide. Also, generic beauty panoramics."

◉ PAPILIO

155 Station Rd., Herne Bay, Kent CT6 5QA, United Kingdom. (44)(122)736-0996. **E-mail:** library@papiliophotos.com. **Website:** www.papiliophotos.com. **Contact:** Justine Pickett. Estab. 1984. Has 120,000 photos in files. Clients include: advertising agencies, book publishers, magazine publishers, newspapers, calendar companies, greeting card companies, postcard publishers.

NEEDS Photos of wildlife.

SPECS Prefers digital submissions. Uses digital shot in-camera as RAW and converted to TIFF for submission, minimum file size 17MB. See webpage for further details or contact for a full information sheet about shooting and supplying digital photos.

PAYMENT & TERMS Works with photographers on contract basis only. Offers nonexclusive contract. Statements issued quarterly. Payment made quarterly. Offers one-time rights, electronic media rights. Photo captions required; include Latin names and behavioral information and keywords.

HOW TO CONTACT Send query letter with résumé. Does not keep samples on file. Expects minimum initial submission of 150 images. Responds in 1 month to samples. Returns all unsuitable material with letter. Photo guidelines sheet free with SASE.

TIPS "Contact first for information about digital. Send digitial submissions on either CD or DVD. Supply full caption listing for all images. Wildlife photography is very competitive. Photographers are advised to send only top-quality images."

PHOTO AGORA

3711 Hidden Meadow Lane, Keezletown VA 22832. (540)269-8283. **Fax:** (540)269-8283. **E-mail:** photoagora@aol.com. **Website:** www.photoagora.com. **Contact:** Robert Maust. Estab. 1972. Stock photo agency. Has over 65,000 photos in files. Clients include: businesses, book/encyclopedia and textbook publishers, magazine publishers, calendar companies.

NEEDS Photos of families, children, students, Virginia, Africa and other Third World areas, work situations, etc. Also needs babies/children/teens, couples, multicultural, parents, senior citizens, disasters, environmental, landscapes/scenics, wildlife, cities/urban, education, gardening, pets, religious, rural, health/fitness, travel, agriculture, industry, medicine, science, technology/computers.

SPECS Send high-res digital images. Ask for password to download agreement and submission guidelines from website.

PAYMENT & TERMS Pays 50% commission for b&w and color photos. Average price per image (to clients): $40 minimum for b&w photos; $100 minimum for color photos. Negotiates fees below standard minimum prices. Offers volume discounts to customers; inquire about specific terms. Photographers can choose not to sell images on discount terms. Works with photographers with or without a contract. Offers nonexclusive contract. Payment made quarterly. Photographers allowed to review account records. Offers one-time rights. Informs photographers and allows them to negotiate when client requests all rights. Model/property release preferred. Embedded photo captions required; include location, important dates, scientific names, etc.

HOW TO CONTACT Call, write or e-mail. No minimum number of images required in initial submission. Responds in 3 weeks. Photo guidelines free with SASE or download from website.

PHOTOEDIT, INC.

3505 Cadillac Ave., Suite P-101, Costa Mesa CA 92626. (800)860-2098. **Fax:** (714)434-5937. **E-mail:** submissions@photoeditinc.com. **Website:** www.photoeditinc.com. Estab. 1987. Stock photo agency. Member of Picture Archive Council of America (PACA). Has 600,000 photos. Clients include: textbook/encyclopedia publishers, magazine publishers, advertising agencies, government agencies. "PhotoEdit Inc. is a leading multiethnic and multicultural stock agency specializing in diverse, culturally relevant imagery. Whether our images are used commercially, or as positive education tools, we keep in mind all of our clients' unique needs when selecting images for our 100% digital rights-managed collection. Our images capture real life as it happens all over the globe. We're in search of photographers who have access to models of every ethnicity who will shoot actively and on spec."

SPECS Uses digital images only.

PAYMENT & TERMS Pays 40% commission for color images. Works on contract basis only. Offers non-exclusive contract. Payments and statements issued monthly. Model release preferred.

HOW TO CONTACT Submit digital portfolio for review. Photo guidelines available on website.

THE PHOTOLIBRARY GROUP

Getty Images, 75 Varick St., New York NY 10013. (646)613-4000; (800)462-4379. **Fax:** (212)633-1914. **E-mail:** sales@gettyimages.com. **Website:** www.gettyimages.com/photolibrary. "The Photolibrary Group represents the world's leading stock brands and the finest photographers around the world, to bring memorable, workable content to the creative communities in America, Europe, Asia, and the Pacific. We provide customers with access to over 5 million images and thousands of hours of footage and full composition music. The Photolibrary Group was founded in 1967 and, 40 years on has a global presence with offices in the United Kingdom (London), the USA (New York), Australia (Sydney and Melbourne), Singapore, India, Malaysia, the Philippines, Thailand, New Zealand and the United Arab Emirates. Photolibrary is always on the lookout for new and innovative photographers and footage producers. Due to the highly competitive market for stock imagery we are very selective about the types of work that we choose to take on. We specialize in high quality, creative imagery primarily orientated to advertising, business-to-business and the editorial and publishing markets. Interested contributors should go to the website and click on the Artists tab for submission information. For additional information regarding our house brands, follow the 'About Us' link."

🌀 PHOTOLIFE CORPORATION, LTD.

513 Hennessy Rd., 20/F Wellable Commercial Bldg., Causeway Bay , Hong Kong. (852)2808 0012. **Fax:** (852)3511 9002. **E-mail:** info@aimageworks.com. **Website:** www.photolife.com.hk. Estab. 1994. Stock photo library. Has over 1.6 million photos in files. Clients include: advertising agencies, newspapers, book publishers, calendar companies, magazine publishers, greeting card companies, corporations, production houses, graphic design firms.

NEEDS Contemporary images of architecture, interiors, garden, infrastructure, concepts, business, finance, sports, lifestyle, nature, travel, animal, marine life, foods, medical.

SPECS Accepts images in digital format only. "Use only professional digital cameras (capable of producing 24MB+ images) with high-quality interchangeable lenses; or images from high-end scanners producing a file up to 50 MB."

PAYMENT & TERMS Pays 50% commission for b&w and color photos. Average price per image (to clients): $105-1,550 for b&w photos; $105-10,000 for color photos. Offers volume discounts to customers; terms specified in photographers' contracts. Works with photographers on contract basis only. Contract can be initiated with minimum 300 selected images. Quarterly submissions needed. Informs photographers and allows them to negotiate when client requests all rights. Model release required; property release preferred. Photo captions required; include destination and country.

HOW TO CONTACT E-mail 50 low-res images (1,000 pixels or less), or send CD with 50 images.

TIPS "Visit our website. Edit your work tightly. Send images that can keep up with current trends in advertising and print photography."

PHOTO RESOURCE HAWAII

111 Hekili St., #241, Kailua HI 96734. (808)599-7773. **E-mail:** prh@photoresourcehawaii.com. **Website:** www.PhotoResourceHawaii.com. **Contact:** Tami Kauakea Winston, owner. Estab. 1983. Stock photo agency. Has e-commerce website with electronic delivery of over 20,000 images. Clients include: ad agencies, audiovisual firms, businesses, book/encyclopedia publishers, magazine publishers, calendar companies, greeting card companies, postcard publishers.

NEEDS Photos of Hawaii and the South Pacific.

SPECS Accepts images online only via website submission in digital format only; 48 MB or larger; JPEG files from RAW files preferred.

PAYMENT & TERMS Pays 40% commission. Enforces minimum prices. Offers volume discounts to customers. Discount sales terms not negotiable. Works with photographers on contract basis only. Offers nonexclusive contract. Contracts renew automatically with additional submissions. Statements issued bimonthly. Payment made bimonthly. Offers royalty-free and rights-managed images. Model/property release preferred. Photo captions and keywording online required.

HOW TO CONTACT Send query e-mail with samples. Expects minimum initial submission of 100 images with periodic submissions at least 3 times/year. Responds in 2 weeks. Offers photographer retreats in Hawaii to learn how to become a contributor and enjoy a healthy Hawaiian vacation.

PIX INTERNATIONAL

(773)975-0158. **E-mail:** lmatlow@yahoo.com. **Website:** www.pixintl.com. **Contact:** Linda Matlow, president. Estab. 1978. Stock agency, news/feature syndicate. Has 200,000 photos in files. Clients include: advertising agencies, public relations firms, businesses, book publishers, magazine publishers, newspapers.

NEEDS Photos of celebrities, entertainment, performing arts.

SPECS Accepts images in digital format only. E-mail link to website. "Do not e-mail any images. Do not send any unsolicited digital files. Make contact first to see if we're interested."

PAYMENT & TERMS Enforces minimum prices. Offers volume discounts to customers; terms specified in photographers' contracts. Discount sales terms not negotiable. Works with photographers with or without a contract; negotiable. Statements issued monthly. Payments made monthly. Photographers allowed to review account records in cases of discrepancies only. Offers one-time rights. Informs photographers and allows them to negotiate when client requests all rights. Model release not required for general editorial. Photo captions required; include who, what, when, where, why.

HOW TO CONTACT "Only accept e-mail queries. E-mail us your URL with thumbnail examples of your work that can be clicked for a larger viewable image." Responds in 2 weeks to samples, only if interested.

TIPS "We are looking for razor-sharp images that stand up on their own without needing a long caption. Let us know by e-mail what types of photos you have, your experience, and cameras used. We do not take images from the lower-end consumer cameras—digital or film. They just don't look very good in publications. For photographers we do accept, we would only consider high-res 300 dpi at 6×9 or higher scans submitted on CD. Please direct us to samples on your website."

PLANS, LTD. (PHOTO LIBRARIES AND NEWS SERVICES)

5-17-2 Inamura, Kamakura 248-0024, Japan. 81-467-31-0330. **Fax:** 81-467-31-0330. **E-mail:** yoshida@plans.jp. **Website:** www.plans.jp. **Contact:** Takashi Yoshida, president. Estab. 1982. Was a stock agency. Now representing ProImageExperts as ProImageExperts Japan as a joint project such as scanning, keywording, dust busting, or color correction for photographers in the stock photo market. Has 100,000 photos in files. Clients include: photo agencies, newspapers, book publishers, magazine publishers, advertising agencies.

NEEDS "We do consulting for photo agencies for the Japanese market."

HOW TO CONTACT Send query e-mail. Responds only if interested.

PONKAWONKA, INC.

(416)638-2475. **E-mail:** contact@ponkawonka.com. **Website:** www.ponkawonka.com. Estab. 2002. Stock agency. Has 60,000+ photos in files. Clients include: advertising agencies, businesses, newspapers, public relations firms, book publishers, calendar companies, magazine publishers.

NEEDS Photos of religious events and holy places. Interested in avant garde, documentary, historical/vintage. "Interested in images of a religious or spiritual nature. Looking for photos of ritual, places of worship, families, religious leaders, ritual objects, historical, archaeological, anything religious, especially in North America."

SPECS Accepts images in digital format. Send via CD or DVD as TIFF or JPEG files.

PAYMENT & TERMS Pays 50% commission for any images. Offers volume discounts to customers. Works with photographers on contract basis only. Charges only apply if negatives or transparencies have to be scanned. Statements issued quarterly. Payments made quarterly. Offers one-time rights. Informs photographers and allows them to negotiate when client requests all rights. Model/property release preferred. Photo captions required; include complete description and cutline for editorial images.

HOW TO CONTACT Send query e-mail. Does not keep samples on file; cannot return material. Expects minimum initial submission of 200 images with annual submissions of at least 100 images. Responds only if interested; send 30-40 low-res samples by e-mail. Photo guidelines available on website.

TIPS "We are always looking for good, quality images of religions of the world. We are also looking for photos of people, scenics and holy places of all religions. Send us sample images. First send us an e-mail introducing yourself, and tell us about your work. Let us know how many images you have that fit our niche and what cameras you are using. If it looks promising, we will ask you to e-mail us 30-40 low-res images (72 dpi, no larger than 6 inches on the long side). We will review them and decide if a contract will be offered. Make sure the images are technically and aesthetically salable. Images must be well-exposed and a large file size. We are an all-digital agency and expect scans to be high-quality files. Tell us if you are shooting digitally with a professional DSLR or if scanning from negatives with a professional slide scanner."

✛ POSITIVE IMAGES

53 Wingate St., Haverhill MA 01832. (978)556-9366. **Fax:** (978)556-9448. **E-mail:** pat@positiveimages photo.com. **Website:** www.agpix.com/positiveimages. **Contact:** Patricia Bruno, owner. Stock photo agency and fine art gallery. Member of ASPP, GWAA. Clients include: advertising agencies, public relations firms, book/encyclopedia publishers, magazine publishers, greeting card and calendar companies, sales/promotion firms, design firms.

NEEDS Horticultural images showing technique and lifestyle, photo essays on property-released homes and gardens, travel images from around the globe, classy and funky pet photography, health and nutrition, sensitive and thought-provoking images suitable for high-end greeting cards, calendar-quality landscapes, castles, lighthouses, country churches. Model/property releases preferred.

PAYMENT & TERMS Pays 50% commission for stock photos; 60% commision for fine art. Average price per image (to clients): $250. Works with photographers on contract basis only. Offers limited regional exclusivity. Payments made quarterly. Offers one-time and electronic media rights. "We never sell all rights."

HOW TO CONTACT "Positive Images Stock is accepting limited new collections; however, if your images are unique and well organized digitally, we will be happy to review online after making e-mail contact. Our gallery will review fine art photography portfolios online as well and will consider exhibiting non-members' work."

TIPS "Positive Images has taken on more of a boutique approach, limiting our number of photographers so that we can better service them and offer a more in-depth and unique collection to our clients. The gallery is a storefront in a small historic arts district. Our plan is to evolve this into an online gallery as well. We are always in search of new talent, so we welcome anyone with a fresh approach to contact us!"

◐ PRESS ASSOCIATION IMAGES

Pearl House, Friar Lane, Nottingham NG1 6BT, United Kingdom. 44(0)20 7963 7000. **Fax:** 44(0)115 844 7448. **E-mail:** joel.tegerdine@pressassociation.com. **Website:** www.pressassociation.com. Formerly Empics Sports Photo Agency. Picture library. Has over 3 million news, sports and entertainment photos (from around the world, past and present) online. Clients include: advertising agencies, newspapers, public relations firms, book publishers, magazine publishers, web publishers, television broadcasters, sporting bodies, rights holders.

NEEDS Photos of news, sports and entertainment.

SPECS Uses glossy or matte color and b&w prints; 35mm transparencies. Accepts the majority of images in digital format.

PAYMENT & TERMS Negotiates fees below stated minimums. Offers volume discounts to customers. Works with photographers on contract basis only. Rights offered varies.

HOW TO CONTACT Send query letter or e-mail. Does not keep samples on file; cannot return material.

PURESTOCK

6622 Southpoint Dr. S., Suite 240, Jacksonville FL 32216. (904)565-0066; (800)828-4545. **Fax:** (904)565-1620. **E-mail:** yourfriends@superstock.com. **Website:** www.purestock.com. "The Purestock royalty-free brand is designed to provide the professional creative community with high-quality images at high resolution and very competitive pricing. Purestock offers CDs and single-image downloads in a wide range of categories including lifestyle, business, education and sports to distributors in over 100 countries. Bold and fresh beyond the usual stock images."

NEEDS "A variety of categories including lifestyle, business, education, medical, industry, etc."

SPECS "Digital files which are capable of being output at 80MB with minimal interpolation. File must be 300 dpi, RGB, TIFF at 8-bit color."

PAYMENT & TERMS Statements issued monthly to contracted image providers. Model release required. Photo captions required.

HOW TO CONTACT Submit a portfolio including a subject-focused collection of 300+ images. Photo guidelines available on website at www.superstock.com/submissions.asp.

TIPS "Please review our website to see the style and quality of our imagery before submitting."

🌀 RAILPHOTOLIBRARY.COM

(44)(116)259-2068. **Website:** www.railphotolibrary.com. Estab. 1969. Has 400,000 photos in files relating to railways worldwide. Clients include: advertising agencies, businesses, newspapers, postcard publishers, public relations firms, book publishers, calendar companies, audiovisual firms, magazine publishers, greeting card companies.

NEEDS Photos of railways.

SPECS Uses digital images; glossy b&w prints; 35mm, 2¼×2¼ transparencies.

PAYMENT & TERMS Buys photos, film or videotape outright depending on subject; negotiable. Pays 50% commission for b&w and color photos. Average price per image (to clients): $125 maximum for b&w and color photos. Works with photographers with or without a contract; negotiable. Statements issued quarterly. Photographers allowed to review account records in cases of discrepancies only. Photo captions preferred.

HOW TO CONTACT Send query letter with slides, prints. Portfolio may be dropped off Monday-Saturday. Does not keep samples on file; include SAE/IRC for return of material. Unlimited initial submission.

TIPS "Submit well-composed pictures of all aspects of railways worldwide: past, present and future; captioned digital files, prints or slides. We are the world's leading railway picture library, and photographers to the railway industry."

REX USA

1133 Broadway, Suite 1626, New York NY 10010. (212)586-4432. **E-mail:** requests@rexusa.com; or derdesk@berlinerphotography.com. **Website:** www.rexusa.com. Estab. 1935. Stock photo agency, news/feature syndicate. Affiliated with Rex Features in London. Member of Picture Archive Council of America (PACA). Has 1.5 million photos. Clients include: advertising agencies, public relations firms, audiovisual firms, businesses, book/encyclopedia publishers, magazine publishers, newspapers, postcard compa-nies, calendar companies, greeting card companies, TV, film and record companies.

NEEDS Primarily editorial material: celebrities, personalities (studio portraits, candid, paparazzi), human interest, news features, movie stills, glamour, historical, geographic, general stock, sports and scientific.

SPECS Digital only.

PAYMENT & TERMS Payment varies depending on quality of subject matter and exclusivity. "We obtain highest possible prices, starting at $100-100,000 for one-time sale." Works with or without contract. Offers nonexclusive contract. Statements issued monthly. Payments made monthly. Photographers allowed to review account records. Offers one-time, first and all rights. Informs photographers and allows them to negotiate when client requests all rights. Model release required. Photo captions required.

HOW TO CONTACT E-mail query letter with samples and list of stock photo subjects. Or fill out online submission form to offer material and discuss terms for representation.

ROBERTSTOCK/CLASSICSTOCK

4203 Locust St., Philadelphia PA 19104. **E-mail:** info@robertstock.com; robertag@classicstock.com. **Website:** www.robertstock.com, www.classicstock.com. **Contact:** Roberta Groves, vice-president, creative. Estab. 1920. Stock photo agency. Member of the Picture Archive Council of America (PACA). Has 2 different websites: Robertstock offers contemporary rights-managed and some royalty-free images; ClassicStock offers retro and vintage images. Clients include: advertising agencies, public relations firms, design firms, businesses, book publishers, magazine publishers, newspapers, postcard publishers, calendar companies, greeting card companies, website designers. Only accepts digital submissions.

NEEDS Offers images on all subjects in depth.

🌀 SCIENCE PHOTO LIBRARY, LTD.

327-329 Harrow Rd., London W9 3RB, United Kingdom. +44(0)20 7432 1100. **Fax:** +44(0)20 7286 8668. **E-mail:** info@sciencephoto.com. **Website:** www.sciencephoto.com. Stock photo agency. Clients include: book publishers, magazines, newspapers, medical journals, advertising, design, TV and online in the U.K. and abroad. "We currently work with agents in over 30 countries, including America, Japan, and in Europe."

NEEDS Specializes in all aspects of science, medicine and technology.

SPECS Digital only via CD/DVD. File sizes at least 38MB with no interpolation. Captions, model, and property releases required.

PAYMENT & TERMS Pays 50% commission. Works on contract basis only. Agreement made for 5 years; general continuation is assured unless otherwise advised. Offers exclusivity. Statements issued quarterly. Payments made quarterly. Photographers allowed to review account records to verify sales figures; fully computerized accounts/commission handling system. Model and property release required. Photo captions required. "Detailed captions can also increase sales so please provide us with as much information as possible."

HOW TO CONTACT "Please complete the inquiry form on our website so that we are better able to advise you on the salability of your work for our market. You may e-mail us low-res examples of your work. Once you have provided us with information, the editing team will be in contact within 2-3 business weeks. Full photo guidelines available on website."

SCIENCE SOURCE/PHOTO RESEARCHERS, INC.

307 Fifth Ave., New York NY 10016. (212)758-3420 or (800)833-9033. **E-mail:** info@sciencesource.com. **Website:** www.sciencesource.com. Stock agency. Has over 1 million photos and illustrations in files, with 250,000 images in a searchable online database. Clients include: advertising agencies; graphic designers; publishers of textbooks, encyclopedias, trade books, magazines, newspapers, calendars, greeting cards; foreign markets.

NEEDS Images of all aspects of science, astronomy, medicine, people (especially contemporary shots of teens, couples and seniors). Particularly needs model-released people, European wildlife, up-to-date travel and scientific subjects. Lifestyle images must be no older than 2 years; travel images must be no older than 5 years.

SPECS Prefers images in digital format.

PAYMENT & TERMS Rarely buys outright; pays 50% commission on stock sales. General price range (to clients): $150-7,500. Works with photographers on contract basis only. Offers limited regional exclusivity. Contracts renew automatically with additional submissions for 5 years (initial term; 1 year thereafter). Photographers allowed to review account records

upon reasonable notice during normal business hours. Statements issued monthly, bimonthly or quarterly, depending on volume. Informs photographers and allows them to negotiate when a client requests to buy all rights, but does not allow direct negotiation with customer. Model/property release required for advertising; preferred for editorial. Photo captions required; include who, what, where, when. Indicate model release.

HOW TO CONTACT See submission guidelines on website.

TIPS "We seek the photographer who is highly imaginative or into a specialty (particularly in the scientific or medical fields). We are looking for serious contributors who have many hundreds of images to offer for a first submission and who are able to contribute often."

SILVER IMAGE® PHOTO AGENCY AND WEDDINGS

4104 NW 70th Terrace, Gainesville FL 32606. (352)373-5771. **E-mail:** carla@silverimagephotoagen cy.com. **Website:** www.silverimagephotoagency.com; www.facebook.com/silverimagefloridalink. **Contact:** Carla Hotvedt, president/owner. Estab. 1987. Stock photo agency and rep for award-winning photojournalists. Assignments in Florida/southern Georgia. Photographers are based in Florida, but available for worldwide travel. Has 5,000 photos in files. Clients include: public relations firms, brides and grooms, magazine publishers, newspapers, rebranding campaigns, and convention coverage.

NEEDS Stock photos from Florida only: nature, travel, tourism, news, people.

SPECS Accepts images in digital format only. No longer accepting new photographers.

PAYMENT & TERMS Pays 50% commission for image licensing fees. Average price per image (to clients): $150-600. Works with photographers on contract basis only. Offers non-exclusive contract. Payment made monthly. Statements provided when payment is made. Photographers allowed to review account records. Offers one-time rights. Informs photographer and allows them to be involved when client requests all rights. Model release preferred. Photo captions required; include name, year shot, city, state, etc.

HOW TO CONTACT Communication via e-mail is preferred.

SKYSCAN PHOTOLIBRARY

Oak House, Toddington, Cheltenham, Gloucestershire GL54 5BY, United Kingdom. (44)(124)262-1357. **Fax:** (44)(124)262-1343. **E-mail:** info@skyscan.co.uk. **Website:** www.skyscan.co.uk. **Contact:** Brenda Marks, library manager. Estab. 1984. Picture library. Member of the British Association of Picture Libraries and Agencies (BAPLA) and the National Association of Aerial Photographic Libraries (NAPLIB). Has more than 450,000 photos in files. Clients include: advertising agencies, public relations firms, businesses, book publishers, magazine publishers, newspapers, calendar companies, postcard publishers.

NEEDS "Air-to-ground photos of U.K. and worldwide. As well as holding images ourselves, we also wish to make contact with holders of other aerial collections worldwide to exchange information."

SPECS Uses color and b&w prints; any format transparencies. Accepts images in digital format. Send via CD, e-mail.

PAYMENT & TERMS Pays 50% commission for b&w and color photos. Average price per image (to clients): $100 minimum. Enforces strict minimum prices. Offers volume discounts to customers. Photographers can choose not to sell images on discount terms. Works with photographers with or without a contract; negotiable. Offers guaranteed subject exclusivity (within files); negotiable to suit both parties. Statements issued quarterly. Payment made quarterly. Photographers allowed to review account records in cases of discrepancies only. Offers one-time, electronic media and agency promotion rights. Informs photographers and allows them to negotiate when a client requests all rights. Will inform photographers and act with photographer's agreement. Model/property release preferred for "air-to-ground of famous buildings (some now insist they have copyright to their building)." Photo captions required; include subject matter, date of photography, location, interesting features/notes.

HOW TO CONTACT Send query letter or e-mail. Provide résumé, business card, self-promotion piece or tearsheets to be kept on file. Agency will contact photographer for portfolio review if interested. No minimum submissions. Photo guidelines sheet and catalog both free with SASE. Market tips sheet free quarterly to contributors only.

TIPS "We have invested heavily in suitable technology and training for in-house scanning, color management, and keywording, which are essential skills in today's market. Contact first by letter or e-mail with résumé of material held and subjects covered."

SOVFOTO/EASTFOTO, INC.

263 W. 20th St. #3, New York NY 10011. (212)727-8170. **Fax:** (212)727-8228. **E-mail:** info@sovfoto.com. **Website:** sovfoto.com. Estab. 1935. Stock photo agency. Has 500,000+ photos in files. Clients include: advertising firms, audiovisual firms, book/encyclopedia publishers, magazine publishers, newspapers.

NEEDS All subjects acceptable as long as they pertain to Russia, Eastern European countries, Central Asian countries or China.

SPECS Uses b&w historical; color prints; 35mm transparencies. Digital submissions preferred.

PAYMENT & TERMS Pays 50% commission. Statements issued quarterly. Payment made quarterly. Photographers allowed to review account records to verify sales figures or account for various deductions. Offers one-time print, electronic media, and nonexclusive rights. Model/property release preferred. Photo captions required.

TOM STACK & ASSOCIATES, INC.

154 Tequesta St., Tavernier FL 33070. (305)852-5520. **E-mail:** tomstack@earthlink.net. **Website:** tomstackassociates.photoshelter.com. **Contact:** Therisa Stack. Has 500,000 photos in files. Clients include: advertising agencies, public relations firms, businesses, audiovisual firms, book publishers, magazine publishers, encyclopedia publishers, postcard companies, calendar companies, greeting card companies.

NEEDS Photos of wildlife, endangered species, marine life, landscapes; foreign geography; photomicrography; scientific research; whales; solar heating; mammals such as weasels, moles, shrews, fisher, marten, etc.; extremely rare endangered wildlife; wildlife behavior photos; lightning and tornadoes; hurricane damage; dramatic and unusual angles and approaches to composition, creative and original photography with impact. Especially needs photos on life science, flora and fauna and photomicrography. No run-of-the-mill travel or vacation shots. Special needs include photos of energy-related topics—solar and wind generators, recycling, nuclear power and coal burning plants, waste disposal and landfills, oil and gas drilling, supertankers, electric cars, geo-thermal energy.

SPECS Only accepts images in digital format. Send sample JPEGs or link to website where your images can be viewed.

PAYMENT & TERMS Pays 50% commission. Works with photographers on contract basis only. Contracts renew automatically with additional submissions for 2 years. Statements issued quarterly. Payments made quarterly. Offers one-time and electronic media rights. Informs photographers and allows them to negotiate when client requests all rights. Model release preferred. Photo captions preferred.

HOW TO CONTACT E-mail: tomstack@earthlink. net.

TIPS "Strive to be original, creative and take an unusual approach to the commonplace; do it in a different and fresh way. We take on only the best so we can continue to give more effective service."

STILL MEDIA

714 Mission Park Dr., Santa Barbara CA 93105. (805)682-2868. **Fax:** (805)682-2659. **E-mail:** info@ stillmedia.com; images@stillmedia.com. **Website:** www.stillmedia.com. Photojournalism and stock photography agency. Has 500,000 photos in files. Clients include: advertising agencies, public relations firms, businesses, book/encyclopedia publishers, magazine publishers, newspapers, calendar companies.

NEEDS Reportage, world events, travel, cultures, business, the environment, sports, people, industry.

SPECS Accepts images in digital format only. Contact via e-mail.

PAYMENT & TERMS Pays 50% commission for color photos. Works with photographers on contract basis only. Offers nonexclusive and guaranteed subject exclusivity contracts. Statements issued quarterly. Payment made quarterly. Photographers allowed to review account records. Offers one-time and electronic media rights. Model/property release preferred. Photo captions required.

STOCK CONNECTION

10319 Westlake Dr., Suite 162, Bethesda MD 20817. (301)530-8518. **Fax:** Please call first. **E-mail:** photos@ scphotos.com. **Website:** www.scphotos.com. **Contact:** Cheryl DiFrank, president and photographer relations. Stock photo agency. Member of the Picture Archive Council of America (PACA). Has over 220,000 photos in files. Clients: advertising agencies, graphic design firms, magazine and textbook publishers, greeting card companies.

NEEDS "We handle many subject categories including lifestyles, business, concepts, sports and recreation, travel, landscapes and wildlife. We will help photographers place their images into our extensive network of over 35 distributors throughout the world. We specialize in placing images where photo buyers can find them."

SPECS Accepts images in digital format (high-res JPEG), minimum 50MB uncompressed, 300 dpi, Adobe RGB.

PAYMENT & TERMS Pays 65% commission. Average price per image (to client): $450-500. Works with photographers on contract basis only. Offers nonexclusive contract. Contracts renew automatically with additional submissions. Photographers may cancel contract with 60 days written notice. Charges for keywording average $2 per image, depending on volume. If photographer provides acceptable scans and keywords, no upload charges apply. Statements issued monthly. Photographers allowed to review account records. Offers rights-managed and royalty-free. Informs photographers when a client requests exclusive rights. Model/property release required. Photo captions required.

HOW TO CONTACT Please e-mail for submission guidelines. Prefer a minimum of 100 images as an initial submission.

TIPS "The key to success in today's market is wide distribution of your images. We offer an extensive network reaching a large variety of buyers all over the world. Increase your sales by increasing your exposure."

STOCKFOOD

109 Lafayette Center, Kennebunk ME 04043. (800)967-0229. **Website:** www.stockfood.com. Estab. 1979. Stock agency, picture library. Member of the Picture Archive Council of America (PACA). Has over 500,000 photos in files. Clients include: advertising agencies, businesses, newspapers, postcard publishers, public relations firms, book publishers, calendar companies, magazine publishers, greeting card companies.

NEEDS Photos and video clips of food/drink, health/ fitness/food, wellness/spa, people eating and drinking, interiors, nice flowers and garden images, eating and drinking outside, table settings.

SPECS Accepts only digital format. Submission guidelines on our website.

PAYMENT & TERMS Enforces minimum prices. Works with photographers on contract basis only. Offers limited regional exclusivity, guaranteed subject exclusivity (within files). Contracts renew automatically. Statements issued quarterly. Photographers allowed to review account records. Offers one-time rights. Model release required; photo captions required.

HOW TO CONTACT Send e-mail with new examples of your work as JPEG files.

○ ⊛ STOCK FOUNDRY IMAGES

Artzooks Multimedia Inc., P.O. Box 78089, Ottawa Ontario K2E 1B1, Canada. (613)258-1551; (866)644-1644. **E-mail:** info@stockfoundry.com; submissions@stockfoundry.com; sales@stockfoundry.com. **Website:** www.stockfoundry.com. Estab. 2006. Stock agency. Clients include: advertising agencies, businesses, newspapers, public relations firms, book publishers, audiovisual firms, magazine publishers.

NEEDS Photos of babies/children/teens, celebrities, couples, multicultural, families, parents, senior citizens, architecture, cities/urban, education, gardening, interiors/decorating, pets, religious, rural, agriculture, business concepts, industry, medicine, military, political, product shots/still life, science, technology/computers, disasters, environmental, landscapes/scenics, wildlife, adventure, automobiles, entertainment, events, food/drink, health/fitness/beauty, hobbies, humor, performing arts, sports, travel. Interested in alternative process, avant garde, documentary, erotic, fashion/glamour, fine art, historical/vintage, lifestyle, seasonal.

SPECS Accepts images in digital format. Send via CD. Save as EPS, JPEG files at 300 dpi. For film and video: .MOV.

PAYMENT & TERMS Buys photos/film/video outright. Pays 50% commission. Average price per image (to clients): $60 minimum for all photos, film and videotape. Negotiates fees below stated minimums. Offers volume discounts to customers. Terms specified in photographer's contracts. Works with photographers on contract basis only. Offers guaranteed subject exclusivity (within files). Contracts renew automatically with additional submissions. "Term lengths are set on each submission from the time new image submissions are received and accepted. There is no formal obligation for photographers to pay for inclusion into catalogs, advertising, etc.; however, we do plan to make this an optional item." Statements issued monthly or in real time online. Payment made monthly. Photographers allowed to review account records in cases of discrepancies only. Informs photographers and allows them to negotiate when a client requests all rights. Negotiates fees below stated minimums. "Volume discounts sometimes apply for preferred customers." Model/property release required. Captions preferred: include actions, location, event, and date (if relevant to the images, such as in the case of vintage collections).

HOW TO CONTACT E-mail query letter with link to photographer's website. Send query letter with tearsheets, stocklist. Portfolio may be dropped off Monday–Friday. Expects initial submission of 100 images with monthly submission of at least 25 images. Responds only if interested; send nonreturnable samples. Provide résumé to be kept on file. Photo guidelines sheet available online. Market tips sheet is free annually via e-mail to all contributors.

TIPS "Submit to us contemporary work that is at once compelling and suitable for advertising. We prefer sets of images that are linked stylistically and by subject matter (better for campaigns). It is acceptable to shoot variations of the same scene (orientation, different angles, with copy space and without, etc.); in fact, we encourage it. Please try to provide us with accurate descriptions, especially as they pertain to specific locations, places, dates, etc. Our wish list for the submission process would be to receive a PDF tearsheet containing small thumbnails of all the high-res images. This would save us time, and speed up the evaluation process."

STOCK OPTIONS

P.O. Box 1048, Fort Davis TX 79734. (432)426-2777. **Fax:** (432)426-2779. **E-mail:** stockoptions@sbcglobal.net. **Contact:** Karen Hughes, owner. Estab. 1985. Stock photo agency. Member of Picture Archive Council of America (PACA). Has 75,000 photos in files. Clients include: advertising agencies, public relations firms, audiovisual firms, corporations, book/encyclopedia and magazine publishers, newspapers, postcard companies, calendar companies, greeting card companies.

NEEDS Emphasizes the southern US. Files include Gulf Coast scenics, wildlife, fishing, festivals, food, industry, business, people, etc. Also western folklore and the Southwest.

SPECS Uses 35mm, 2¼×2¼, 4×5 transparencies.

PAYMENT & TERMS Pays 50% commission for color photos. Average price per image (to client): $300-3,000. Works with photographers on contract basis only. Offers nonexclusive contract. Contracts renew automatically with each submission for 5 years from expiration date. When contract ends photographer must renew within 60 days. Charges catalog insertion fee of $300/image and marketing fee of $15/hour. Statements issued upon receipt of payment from client. Payment made immediately. Photographers allowed to review account records to verify sales figures. Offers one-time and electronic media rights. "We will inform photographers for their consent only when a client requests all rights, but we will handle all negotiations." Model/property release preferred for people, some properties, all models. Photo captions required; include subject and location.

HOW TO CONTACT Interested in receiving work from full-time commercial photographers. Arrange a personal interview to show portfolio. Send query letter with stock list. Contact by phone and submit 200 sample photos. Tips sheet distributed annually to all photographers.

TIPS Wants to see "clean, in-focus, relevant and current materials." Current stock requests include industry, environmental subjects, people in up-beat situations, minorities, food, cityscapes and rural scenics.

STOCKYARD PHOTOS

1520 Center St. #2, Houston TX 77007. (713)520-0898. **Fax:** (713)820-6965. **E-mail:** jim@stockyard.com. **Website:** www.stockyard.com. Estab. 1992. Stock agency. Niche agency specializing in images of Houston and China. Has thousands of photos in files. Clients include: advertising agencies, businesses, newspapers, postcard publishers, public relations firms, book publishers, calendar companies, audiovisual firms, magazine publishers, greeting card companies, real estate firms, interior designers, retail catalogs.

NEEDS Photos relating to Houston and the Gulf Coast. Energy stock including oil & gas, wind, solar

SPECS Accepts images in digital format only. To be considered, e-mail link to photographer's website, showing a sample of 20 images for review.

PAYMENT & TERMS Average price per image (to clients): $250-1,500 for color photos. Offers volume discounts to customers. Photographers can choose not to sell images on discount terms.

STSIMAGES

225, Neha Industrial Estate, Off Dattapada Rd., Borivali (East) Mumbai 400 066, India. (91)(22)2870-1586. **Fax:** (91)(22)2870-1609. **E-mail:** info@stsimages.com; images@stsimages.com; pawan@stsimages.com. **Website:** www.stsimages.com. **Contact:** Mr. Pawan Tikku. Estab. 1993. Has over 200,000 photos on website. Clients include: advertising agencies, businesses, postcard publishers, public relations firms, book publishers, calendar companies, freelance web designers, audiovisual firms, magazine publishers, greeting card companies.

NEEDS Royalty-free and rights-managed images of babies/children/teens, celebrities, couples, multicultural, families, parents, senior citizens, disasters, environmental, landscapes/scenics, wildlife, architecture, cities/urban, education, gardening, interiors/decorating, pets, religious, rural, adventure, automobiles, entertainment, events, food/drink, health/fitness, hobbies, humor, performing arts, sports, travel, agriculture, business concepts, industry, medicine, military, political, product shots/still life, science, technology/computers. Interested in alternative process, avant garde, documentary, fashion/glamour, fine art, historical/vintage, seasonal. Also needs vector images.

SPECS Accepts images in digital format only. Send via DVD or direct upload to website, JPEG files at 300 dpi. Minimum file size 25MB, preferred 50MB or more. Image submissions should be made separately for royalty-free and rights-managed images

PAYMENT & TERMS Pays 50% commission. Enforces minimum prices. Offers to customers. Works with photographers on contract basis only. Offers nonexclusive contract, limited regional exclusivity. Contracts renew automatically with additional submissions for 3 years. Statements issued quarterly. Payment made monthly. Photographers allowed to review account records. Offers royalty-free images as well as one-time rights. Model release required; property release preferred. Photo captions and keyword are mandatory in the file info area of the image. Include names, description, location.

HOW TO CONTACT Send e-mail with image thumbnails. Expects minimum initial submission of 200 images with regular submissions of at least some images every month. Responds in 1 month to queries. Ask for photo guidelines by e-mail. Market tips available to regular contributors only.

TIPS 1) Strict self-editing of images for technical faults. 2) Proper keywording is essential. 3) All images should have the photographer's name in the IPTC(XMP) area. 4) All digital images must contain necessary keywords and caption information within the "file info" section of the image file. 5) Send images in both vertical and horizontal formats.

SUGAR DADDY PHOTOS

Website: www.sugardaddyphotos.com; www.face book.com/sugardaddyphotos; www.twitter.com/sugardaddyphoto. **Contact:** Henry Salazar, editor-in-chief. Estab. 2000. Art collector and stock agency. Target audience includes advertising agencies, businesses, newspapers, postcard publishers, public relations firms, book publishers, calendar companies, audiovisual firms, magazine publishers and greeting card companies.

NEEDS Photos of babies/children/teens, celebrities, couples, multicultural, families, parents, senior citizens, architecture, cities/urban, education, gardening, interiors/decorating, pets, religious, rural, agriculture, business concepts, industry, medicine, military, political, product shots/still life, science, technology/computers, disasters, environmental, landscapes/scenics, wildlife, adventure, automobiles, entertainment, events, food/drink, health/fitness/beauty, hobbies, humor, performing arts, sports (football, baseball, soccer, basketball, hockey), travel/family travel, hotels, beaches, exotic locations. Interested in alternative process, avant garde, documentary, erotic, fashion/glamour, fine art, historical/vintage, lifestyle, seasonal.

SPECS Accepts images in digital format. Send RAW, TIFF or JPEG files at minimum 300 dpi. Pay 15% commission level. Average price per image (to clients): $100-1,000 for photos and streaming video. Enforces strict minimum prices. "We have set prices; however, they are subject to change without notice." Negotiable. Offers nonexclusive contract. Payments made monthly. Offers one-time rights. Informs photographers and allows them to negotiate when a client requests all rights. Model/property release required. Photo captions required; include location, city, state, country, full description, related keywords, date image was taken.

HOW TO CONTACT "All prospects are to submit work from agencies or a person via any online social media (Facebook, Twitter, etc.), including websites."

TIPS "Arrange your work in categories to view. Clients expect the very best in professional-quality material."

SUPERSTOCK, INC.

6622 Southpoint Dr. S., Suite 240, Jacksonville FL 32216. (904)565-0066; (800)828-4545. **Fax:** (904)565-1620. **E-mail:** yourfriends@superstock.com. **Website:** www.superstock.com. International stock photo agency represented in 192 countries. Offices in Jacksonville, New York and London. Extensive rights-managed, royalty-free content within 3 unique collections: contemporary, vintage and fine art. Clients include: advertising agencies, businesses, book and magazine publishers, newspapers, greeting card and calendar companies.

NEEDS "SuperStock is looking for dynamic lifestyle, travel, sports and business imagery, as well as fine art content and vintage images with releases."

SPECS Accepts images in digital format only. Digital files must be a minimum of 50MB (up-sized), 300 dpi, 8-bit color, RGB, JPEG format.

PAYMENT & TERMS Statements issued monthly to contracted contributors. "Rights offered vary, depending on image quality, type of content, and experience." Informs photographers when client requests all rights. Model release required. Photo captions required.

TIPS "Please review our website to see the style and quality of our imagery before submitting."

⬤ ULLSTEIN BILD

Schützenstr. 15-17, Berlin 10117, Germany. +49 30 2591 72547. **Fax:** +49 30 2591 73896. **E-mail:** ramer shoven@ullsteinbild.de. **Website:** www.ullsteinbild. de. Estab. 1900. Stock agency, picture library and news/feature syndicate. Has approximately 12 million photos in files. Clients include: advertising agencies, public relations firms, audiovisual firms, businesses, book publishers, magazine publishers, newspapers, calendar companies, greeting card companies, postcard publishers, TV companies.

NEEDS Photos of celebrities, couples, multicultural, families, parents, senior citizens, wildlife, disasters, environmental, landscapes/scenics, architecture, cities/urban, education, pets, religious, rural, adventure, automobiles, entertainment, events, health/fitness, hobbies, humor, performing arts, sports, travel, agriculture, buildings, computers, industry, medicine, military, political, portraits, science, technology/computers. Interested in digital, documentary, fashion/glamour, historical/vintage, regional, seasonal. Other specific photo needs: German history.

SPECS Accepts images in digital format only. Send via FTP, CD, e-mail as TIFF, JPEG files at minimum 25MB decompressed.

PAYMENT & TERMS Pays on commission basis. Works with photographers on contract basis only. Offers nonexclusive contract for 5 years minimum. Statements issued monthly, quarterly, annually. Payments made monthly, quarterly, annually. Photographers allowed to review account records in cases of discrepancies only. Offers one-time rights. Photo captions required; include date, names, events, place.

HOW TO CONTACT "Please contact Mr. Ulrich Ramershoven (ramershoven@ullsteinbild.de) before sending pictures."

VIEWFINDERS STOCK PHOTOGRAPHY

3245 SE Ankeny St., Portland OR 97214. (503)222-5222. **Fax:** (503)274-7995. **E-mail:** studio@viewfindersnw.com. **Website:** www.viewfindersnw.com. **Contact:** Bruce Forster, owner. Estab. 1996. Stock agency. Member of the Picture Archive Council of America (PACA). Has 70,000 photos in files. Clients include: advertising agencies, public relations firms, businesses, book publishers, magazine publishers, design agencies.

NEEDS "We are a stock photography agency providing images of the Pacific Northwest. Founded by Bruce Forster in 1996, our image collection has content from over 10 locally known photographers. whether you're looking for landscapes and landmarks, aerials, cityscapes, urban living, industry, recreation, agriculture or green energy images, our photography collection covers it all. Contact us for your image needs."

VIREO (VISUAL RESOURCES FOR ORNITHOLOGY)

The Academy of Natural Sciences of Drexel University, 1900 Ben Franklin Pkwy., Philadelphia PA 19103. (215)299-1069. **E-mail:** vireo@ansp.org. **Website:** vireo.ansp.org. **Contact:** Doug Wechsler, director. Estab. 1979. Picture library. "We specialize in birds only." Has 180,000 photos in files. Clients include: advertising agencies, businesses, book publishers, magazine

publishers, newspapers, calendar companies, CD publishers.

NEEDS High-quality photographs of birds from around the world with special emphasis on behavior. All photos must be related to birds or ornithology.

SPECS Uses digital format. See website for specs.

PAYMENT & TERMS Pays 50% commission for b&w and color photos. Average price per image (to clients): $125. Negotiates fees below stated minimums; "we deal with many small nonprofits as well as commercial clients." Offers volume discounts to customers. Discount sales terms negotiable. Works with photographers on contract basis only. Offers nonexclusive contract. Statements issued semiannually. Payments made semiannually. Offers one-time rights. Model release preferred for people. Photo captions required; include location.

HOW TO CONTACT Read guidelines on website. To show portfolio, photographer should send 10 JPEGs or a link to web pages with the images. Follow up with a call. Responds in 1 month to queries.

TIPS "Study our website and show us some bird photos we don't have or better images than those we do have. Write to us describing the types of bird photographs you have, the type of equipment you use, and where you do most of your bird photography. Please send us a web link to a portfolio of your work if you have one. Edit work carefully."

VWPICS.COM

Luis Bermejo 8, 7-B, Zaragoza 50009, Spain. (203)606-8794 (US office). **E-mail:** vwpics.office@gmail.com; Spanish office: vwpics.office3@gmail.com. **Website:** www.vwpics.com. **Contact:** Reyes, office manager; Nano Calvo, director; Kike Calvo, director. Estab. 1997. Digital and news stock agency. Has 750,000 photos in files. Has branch office in New York. Clients include: advertising agencies, businesses, newspapers, postcard publishers, public relations firms, book publishers, calendar companies, audiovisual firms, magazine publishers, greeting card companies, zoos, aquariums.

NEEDS Wants photos of babies/children/teens, celebrities, couples, multicultural, families, parents, senior citizens, disasters, environmental, landscapes/scenics, wildlife, architecture, cities/urban, education, pets, religious, rural, adventure, travel, agriculture, business concepts, industry, science, technology/computers. Interested in documentary, erotic, fashion/glamour, fine art. Also needs underwater imagery: reefs, sharks, whales, dolphins and colorful creatures, divers and anything related to oceans. Images that show the human impact on the environment. Very interested in people images with model releases.

SPECS Accepts images in digital format. Send an e-mail with portfolio or website. Once accepted, the photographers submit images via FTP.

PAYMENT & TERMS Pays 50% commission for photos. Enforces minimum prices. Works with photographers with or without contract; negotiable. "E-mail us to be added to our mailing list. You will get almost daily requests from our current photo needs." Offers nonexclusive contract. Statements issued quarterly. Payment made quarterly. Any deductions are itemized. Offers one-time rights. Informs photographers and allows them to negotiate when client requests all rights. Model release required. Photo caption required. Photo essays should include location, Latin name, what, why, when, how, who.

HOW TO CONTACT "The best way is to send an e-mail with your website." Send query letter with résumé, tearsheets, stock list. Expects minimum initial submission of 100 images with periodic submissions of at least 50 images.

TIPS "Interested in reaching Spanish-speaking countries? We might be able to help you. We look for composition, color, and a unique approach. Images that have a mood or feeling. Tight, quality editing. We send a want list via e-mail."

⚫ WESTEND61

Schwanthalerstr. 86, Munich 80336, Germany. +49 (0) 89 4524426-0. **Fax:** +49 (0) 89 4524426-20. **E-mail:** service@westend61.de. **Website:** www.westend61.de. **Contact:** Oliver Marquardt, contributor relations. Estab. 2003. Stock photo agency. Has 150,000 photos on file. Clients include: ad agencies, businesses, book publishers, magazine publishers, newspapers, postcard companies, calendar companies, greeting card companies.

NEEDS Photos of babies/children/teens, couples, multicultural, families, parents, senior citizens, environmental, disasters, landscapes/scenics, wildlife, architecture, cities/urban, education, gardening, interiors/decorating, pets, rural, adventure, agriculture, food/drink, health/fitness/beauty, hobbies, sports, travel, business concepts, industry, medicine, product shots/still life, science, technology/computers, alternative process, avant garde, documentary, erotic, lifestyle, seasonal.

SPECS Accepts images in digital format; upload on website. Send as JPEGs at 300 dpi.

PAYMENT & TERMS Pays commission: 40-50% for b&w photos; 40-50% for color photos. Average price per image (to clients): $75-500. Negotiates fees below stated minimums. Offers volume discounts to customers; discount sales terms not negotiable. Works with photographers on contract basis only. Offers guaranteed subject exclusivity. Contracts renew automatically (initial 5-year term, 7-year terms afterwards) with submissions. Statements issued quarterly. Payment made quarterly. Photographers permitted to review account records in cases of discrepancies only. Offers one-time rights and royalty-free rights. Informs photographers when client requests to buy all rights. Model/property release required. Photo captions required.

HOW TO CONTACT E-mail query letter with link to your website. Does not keep files on sample; cannot return material. Responds in 7 weeks. Photo guidelines available online. Market tips sheet available on website.

ADVERTISING, DESIGN, & RELATED MARKETS

///

Advertising photography is always "commercial" in the sense that it is used to sell a product or service. Assignments from ad agencies and graphic design firms can be some of the most creative, exciting, and lucrative that you'll ever receive.

Prospective clients want to see your most creative work—not necessarily your advertising work. Mary Virginia Swanson, an expert in the field of licensing and marketing fine art photography, says that the portfolio you take to the Museum of Modern Art is also the portfolio that Nike would like to see. Your clients in advertising and design will certainly expect your work to show, at the least, your technical proficiency. They may also expect you to be able to develop a concept or to execute one of their concepts to their satisfaction. Of course, it depends on the client and their needs: Read the tips given in many of the listings on the following pages to learn what a particular client expects.

When you're beginning your career in advertising photography, it is usually best to start close to home. That way, you can make appointments to show your portfolio to art directors. Meeting the photo buyers in person can show them that you are not only a great photographer but that you'll be easy to work with as well. This section is organized by region to make it easy to find agencies close to home.

When you're just starting out, you should also look closely at the agency descriptions at the beginning of each listing. Agencies with smaller annual billings and fewer employees are more likely to work with newcomers. On the flip side, if you have a sizable list of ad and design credits, larger firms may be more receptive to your work and be able to pay what you're worth.

Trade magazines such as *HOW*, *Print*, *Communication Arts*, and *Graphis* are good places to start when learning about design firms. These magazines not only provide information about how designers operate, but they also explain how creatives use photography. For ad agencies, try *Adweek* and *Advertising Age*. These magazines are more business oriented, but they reveal facts about the top agencies and about specific successful campaigns. (See Publications in the Resources section for ordering information.) The website of American Photographic Artists (APA) contains information on business practices and standards for advertising photographers (www.apanational.org).

☺ ○ ✿ THE AMERICAN YOUTH PHILHARMONIC ORCHESTRAS

4026 Hummer Rd., Annandale VA 22003. (703)642-8051, ext. 25. **Fax:** (703)642-8054. **E-mail:** exec@aypo.org. **Website:** www.aypo.org. **Contact:** Dr. Graham Elliott, executive director. Estab. 1964. Nonprofit organization that promotes and sponsors 4 youth orchestras. Photos used in newsletters, posters, audiovisual and other forms of promotion.

NEEDS Photographers usually donate their talents. Offers 8 assignments/year. Photos taken of orchestras, conductors and soloists. Photo captions preferred.

AUDIOVISUAL NEEDS Uses slides and videotape.

SPECS Uses 5×7 glossy color and b&w prints.

MAKING CONTACT & TERMS Arrange a personal interview to show portfolio. Works with local freelancers on assignment only. Keeps samples on file. Payment negotiable. "We're a résumé-builder, a nonprofit that can cover expenses but not service fees." **Pays on acceptance.** Credit line given. Rights negotiable.

AMPM, INC.

P.O. Box 1887, Midland MI 48641. (989)837-8800. **E-mail:** solutions@ampminc.com. **Website:** www.ampminc.com. Estab. 1969. Member of Art Directors Club, Illustrators Club, National Association of Advertising Agencies and Type Directors Club. Ad agency. Approximate annual billing: $125 million. Number of employees: 265. Firm specializes in display design, direct mail, magazine ads, packaging. Types of clients: food, industrial, retail, pharmaceutical, health and beauty and entertainment. Examples of recent clients: Cadillac (ads for TV); Oxford (ads for magazines).

NEEDS Works with 6 photographers/month. Uses photos for consumer and trade magazines, direct mail, P-O-P displays, catalogs, posters, newspapers and audiovisual. Subjects include: landscapes/scenics, wildlife, commercials, celebrities, couples, architecture, gardening, interiors/decorating, pets, adventure, automobiles, entertainment, events, food/drink, health/fitness, humor, performing arts, agriculture, business concepts, industry, medicine, product shots/still life. Interested in avant garde, erotic, fashion/glamour, historical/vintage, seasonal. Reviews stock photos of food and beauty products. Model release required. Photo caption preferred.

AUDIOVISUAL NEEDS "We use multimedia slide shows and multimedia video shows."

SPECS Uses 8×10 color and/or b&w prints; 35mm, 2¼×2¼, 4×5, 8×10 transparencies; 8×10 film; broadcast videotape. Accepts images in digital format. Send via e-mail.

MAKING CONTACT & TERMS Arrange personal interview to show portfolio. Send unsolicited photos by mail for consideration. Provide résumé, business card, brochure, flyer or tearsheets to be kept on file. Keeps samples on file. Responds in 2 weeks. Pays $50-250/hour; $500-2,000/day; $2,000-5,000/job; $50-300 for b&w photos; $50-300 for color photos; $50-300 for film; $250-1,000 for videotape. Pays on receipt of invoice. Credit line sometimes given, depending upon client and use. Buys one-time, exclusive product, electronic and all rights; negotiable.

TIPS Wants to see originality in portfolio or samples. Sees trend toward more use of special lighting. Photographers should "show their work with the time it took and the fee."

BERSON, DEAN, STEVENS

P.O. Box 3997, Westlake Village CA 91359. (877)447-0134, ext. 111. **E-mail:** info@bersondeanstevens.com. **Website:** www.bersondeanstevens.com. **Contact:** Lori Berson, owner. Estab. 1981. Specializes in branding, website design and development, content marketing, e-mail marketing, social media marketing, video production, collateral, direct mail, exhibits, signage, promotions and packaging.

NEEDS Works with 4 photographers/month. Uses photos for billboards, trade magazines, direct mail, P-O-P displays, catalogs, posters, packaging, signage and web. Subjects include: product shots and food. Reviews stock photos. Model/property release required.

SPECS Accepts images in digital format only. Send via CD, DVD as TIFF, EPS, JPEG files at 300 dpi.

MAKING CONTACT & TERMS Provide résumé, business card, brochure, flyer or tearsheets to be kept on file. Works on assignment only. Responds in 1-2 weeks. Payment negotiable. Pays within 30 days after receipt of invoice. Credit line not given. Rights negotiable.

☺ ✪ ◑ BOB BOEBERITZ DESIGN

247 Charlotte St., Asheville NC 28801. (828)258-0316. **E-mail:** bob@bobboeberitzdesign.com. **Website:** www.bobboeberitzdesign.com. **Contact:** Bob Boeberitz, owner. Estab. 1984. Member of American Advertising Federation—Asheville Chapter, Asheville Freelance Network and Asheville Creative Services

Group. Graphic design studio. Approximate annual billing: $100,000. Number of employees: 1. Firm specializes in annual reports, collateral, direct mail, magazine ads, packaging, publication design, signage, websites. Types of clients: management consultants, retail, recording artists, mail-order firms, industrial, nonprofit, restaurants, hotels, book publishers.

NEEDS Works with 1 freelance photographer "every 6 months or so." Uses photos for consumer and trade magazines, direct mail, brochures, catalogs, posters. Subjects include: babies/children/teens, couples, multicultural, families, parents, senior citizens, environmental, landscapes/scenics, wildlife, architecture, cities/urban, education, pets, rural, adventure, entertainment, events, food/drink, health/fitness/beauty, hobbies, performing arts, sports, travel, business concepts, industry, medicine, product shots/still life, science, technology/computers; some location, some stock photos. Interested in fashion/glamour, seasonal. Model/property release required.

SPECS Accepts images in digital format. Send via CD, e-mail as TIFF, BMP, JPEG, GIF files at 300 dpi. E-mail samples at 72 dpi. No EPS attachments.

MAKING CONTACT & TERMS Provide résumé, business card, brochure, flier or postcard to be kept on file. Cannot return unsolicited material. Responds "when there is a need." Pays $75-200 for b&w photos; $100-500 for color photos; $75-150/hour; $500-1,500/day. Pays on per-job basis. Buys all rights; negotiable.

TIPS "Send promotional piece to keep on file. Do not send anything that has to be returned. I usually look for a specific specialty; no photographer is good at everything. I also consider studio space and equipment. Show me something different, unusual, something that sets you apart from any average local photographer. If I'm going out of town for something, it has to be for something I can't get done locally. I keep and file direct mail pieces (especially postcards). I do not keep anything sent by e-mail. If you want me to remember your website, send a postcard."

⊕ ⊚ BRAGAW PUBLIC RELATIONS SERVICES

3093 Epstein Circle, Mundelein IL 60060. (847)997-3876. **E-mail:** info@bragawpr.com; rbragaw@bragaw pr.com. **Website:** bragawpr.com. **Contact:** Richard Bragaw, president. Estab. 1981. Member of Publicity Club of Chicago.

NEEDS Uses photos for trade magazines, direct mail, brochures, newspapers, newsletters/news releases. Subjects include: "products and people." Model release preferred. Photo captions preferred.

SPECS Uses 3×5, 5×7, 8×10 glossy prints.

MAKING CONTACT & TERMS Provide résumé, business card, brochure, flyer or tearsheets to be kept on file. Works with freelance photographers on assignment basis only. Payment is negotiated at the time of the assignment. Pays on receipt of invoice. Credit line "possible." Buys all rights; negotiable.

TIPS "Execute an assignment well, at reasonable costs, with speedy delivery."

⊛ ⊚ BRAMSON + ASSOCIATES

7400 Beverly Blvd., Los Angeles CA 90036. (323)938-3595. **E-mail:** gene@bramson-associates.com. **Website:** www.bramson-associates.com. **Contact:** Gene Bramson, principal. Estab. 1970. Ad agency. Approximate annual billing: $2 million. Number of employees: 7. Types of clients: industrial, financial, food, retail, health care. Examples of recent clients: Sumitomo Metal and Mining: Biotech, Japan; Lawry's Restaurants, Inc.; AF Growlabs, Division of Hairraising Personal Care Products, Inc.

NEEDS Works with 1-2 photographers/month. Uses photos for trade magazines, direct mail, posters, newspapers, signage, websites, corporate brochures, and collateral. Subject matter varies; includes babies/children/teens, couples, multicultural, families, architecture, cities/urban, gardening, interiors/decorating, pets, automobiles, food/drink, health/fitness/beauty, business concepts, medicine, science. Interested in avant garde, documentary, erotic, fashion/glamour, historical/vintage. Reviews stock photos. Model/property release required. Photo captions preferred.

AUDIOVISUAL NEEDS Works with 1 videographer/month. Uses videotape for industrial, product.

SPECS Mostly DVD and digital format.

MAKING CONTACT & TERMS Submit portfolio for review. Send unsolicited photos by mail for consideration; include SASE for return of material. Works with local freelancers on assignment only. Provide résumé, business card, brochure, flyer or tearsheet to be kept on file. Responds in 3 weeks. Payment negotiable, depending on budget for each project. Pays on receipt of invoice. Credit line not given. Buys one-time and all rights.

TIPS "Innovative, crisp, dynamic, unique style–otherwise we'll stick with our photographers. If it's not great work, don't bother."

◎ ✪ BRIGHT LIGHT VISUAL COMMUNICATIONS

602 Main St., Suite 810, Cincinnati OH 45202. (513)721-2574. **Fax:** (513)721-3329. **E-mail:** info@brightlightusa.com. **Website:** www.brightlightusa.com. **Contact:** Linda Spalazzi, CEO. Visual communication company. Types of clients: national, regional and local companies in the governmental, educational, industrial and commercial categories. Examples of recent clients: Procter & Gamble; US Grains Council; Convergys.

NEEDS Model/property release required. Photo captions preferred.

AUDIOVISUAL NEEDS "Hires crews around the world using a variety of formats."

MAKING CONTACT & TERMS Provide résumé, flyer and brochure to be kept on file. Call to arrange appointment or send query letter with résumé of credits. Works on assignment only. Pays $100 minimum/day for grip; payment negotiable based on photographer's previous experience/reputation and day rate (10 hours). Pays within 30 days of completion of job. Buys all rights.

TIPS Sample assignments include camera assistant, gaffer or grip. Wants to see sample reels or samples of still work. Looking for sensitivity to subject matter and lighting. "Show a willingness to work hard. Every client wants us to work smarter and provide quality at a good value."

✪ ❸ ❶ BYNUMS MARKETING AND COMMUNICATIONS, INC.

301 Grant St., Suite 4300, Pittsburgh PA 15219. (412)471-4332. **Fax:** (412)471-1383. **E-mail:** rbynum2124@earthlink.net; russell@bynums.com. **Website:** www.bynums.com. Estab. 1985. Ad agency. Number of employees: 8-10. Firm specializes in annual reports, collateral, direct mail, magazine ads, packaging, publication design, signage. Types of clients: financial, health care, consumer goods, nonprofit.

NEEDS Works with 1 photographer/month. Uses photos for billboards, brochures, direct mail, newspapers, posters. Subjects include: babies/children/teens, couples, multicultural, families, parents, senior citizens, environmental, wildlife, cities/urban, education, religious, adventure, automobiles, events, food/drink, health/fitness, performing arts, sports, medicine, product shots/still life, science, technology/computers. Interested in fine art, seasonal. Model/property release required. Photo captions preferred.

AUDIOVISUAL NEEDS Works with 1 videographer and 1 filmmaker/year. Uses slides, film, videotape.

SPECS Uses 8×10 glossy or matte color and b&w prints; 35mm, 4×5 transparencies. Accepts images in digital format. Send via ZIP, e-mail as TIFF files.

MAKING CONTACT & TERMS Send query letter with résumé, prints, tearsheets, stock list. Provide business card, self-promotion piece to be kept on file. Responds only if interested, send nonreturnable samples. Pays $150-300 for b&w and color photos. "Payment may depend on quote and assignment requirements." Buys electronic rights.

❸❸❸ ✪ CARMICHAEL LYNCH

110 N. Fifth St., Minneapolis MN 55403. (612)334-6000. **Fax:** (612)334-6090. **E-mail:** portfolio@clynch.com. **Website:** www.carmichaellynch.com. **Contact:** Sandy Boss Febbo, executive art producer; Bonnie Brown, Jill Kahn, Jenny Barnes, art producers. Member of American Association of Advertising Agencies. Ad agency. Number of employees: 250. Firm specializes in collateral, direct mail, magazine ads, packaging. Types of clients: finance, health care, sports and recreation, beverage, outdoor recreational. Examples of recent clients: Harley-Davidson, Porsche, Northwest Airlines, American Standard.

NEEDS Uses many photographers/month. Uses photos for billboards, consumer and trade magazines, direct mail, P-O-P displays, brochures, posters, newspapers and other media as needs arise. Subjects include: environmental, landscapes/scenics, architecture, interiors/decorating, rural, adventure, automobiles, travel, product shots/still life. Model/property release required for all visually recognizable subjects.

SPECS Uses all print formats. Accepts images in digital format. Send TIFF, GIF, JPEG files at 72 dpi or higher.

MAKING CONTACT & TERMS Submit portfolio for review. Provide résumé, business card, brochure, flyer or tearsheets to be kept on file. Payment negotiable. Pay depends on contract. Buys all, one-time or exclusive product rights, "depending on agreement."

TIPS "No 'babes on bikes'! In a portfolio, we prefer to see the photographer's most creative work—not necessarily ads. Show only your most technically, artistically satisfying work."

✪ CONCORD DIRECT

92 Old Turnpike Rd., Concord NH 03301-7305. (603)410-1205. **Fax:** (603)224-5503. **E-mail:** dchristiansen@concord-direct.com. **Website:** www.directconcord.com. **Contact:** Deidre Christiansen, art resource coordinator. Estab. 1958. Number of employees: 50. Integrated marketing communications, printer with in-house design department. Specializes in direct mail, greeting cards. Clients: non-profit.
NEEDS Approached by 20 illustrators/year. Work with 3 illustrators/year. Prefers illustrators with experience in watercolor, gouache, oil, acrylic. Buys stock photos. Pays $150-750. Works with beginning an established photographers. Uses photos for direct mail, greeting cards, calendars.
SPECS Accepts images in digital format (e-mail) as JPEG files at 72 dpi (300 dpi if artwork is licensed).
MAKING CONTACT & TERMS E-mail query letter with website and JPEG samples at 72 dpi. No Flickr or Facebook sites. Does not keep samples on file. Responds in 1 month. Illustration: pays by the project, $200-700. Licensing fee per project or term. Photography: Pays by the project, $150-700. Pays on receipt of invoice. Credit line given. Buys one time rights, reprint rights; rights purchased vary according to project. Finds illustrators/photographers through agents, internet and Surtex.
TIPS "Have a website withe keyword images and a search option. It's easier to forward to members of a design team, who need to quickly select from a variety of art styles. Use scans of artwork (never photographs) and have high resolution scans available when the image is licensed."

⊛ ⊚ DYKEMAN ASSOCIATES, INC.

4115 Rawlins St., Dallas TX 75219. (214)587-2995. **E-mail:** info@dykemanassociates.com. **Website:** www.dykemanassociates.com. Estab. 1974. Member of Public Relations Society of America. PR, marketing, video production firm. Firm specializes in website creation and promotion, crisis communication plans, media training, collateral, direct marketing. Types of clients: industrial, financial, sports, technology.
NEEDS Works with 4-5 photographers and videographers. Uses photos for publicity, consumer and trade magazines, direct mail, catalogs, posters, newspapers, signage, websites.

AUDIOVISUAL NEEDS "We produce and direct video. Just need crew with good equipment and people and ability to do their part."
MAKING CONTACT & TERMS Arrange a personal interview to show portfolio. Pays $800-1,200/day; $250-400/1-2 days. "Currently we work only with photographers who are willing to be part of our trade dollar network. Call if you don't understand this term." Pays up to 30 days after receipt of invoice.
TIPS Reviews portfolios with current needs in mind. "If video, we would want to see examples. If for news story, we would need to see photojournalism capabilities."

🌐 🌗 ⊛ FLINT COMMUNICATIONS

101 Tenth St. N., Suite 300, Fargo ND 58102. (701)237-4850. **Fax:** (701)234-9680. **E-mail:** gerril@flintcom.com, dawnk@flintcom.com. **Website:** www.flintcom.com. **Contact:** Gerri Lien, creative director; Dawn Koranda, creative director. Estab. 1946. Ad agency. Approximate annual billing: $9 million. Number of employees: 30. Firm specializes in display design, direct mail, magazine ads, publication design, signage, annual reports. Types of clients: industrial, financial, agriculture, health care and tourism.
NEEDS Works with 2-3 photographers/month. Uses photos for direct mail, P-O-P displays, posters and audiovisual. Subjects include: babies/children/teens, couples, parents, senior citizens, architecture, rural, adventure, automobiles, events, food/drink, health/fitness, sports, travel, agriculture, industry, medicine, political, product shots/still life, science, technology, manufacturing, finance, health care, business. Interested in documentary, historical/vintage, seasonal. Reviews stock photos. Model release preferred.
AUDIOVISUAL NEEDS Works with 1-2 filmmakers and 1-2 videographers/month. Uses slides and film.
SPECS Uses 35mm, 2¼×2¼, 4×5 transparencies. Accepts images in digital format. Send via CD, ZIP as TIFF, EPS, JPEG files.
MAKING CONTACT & TERMS Send query letter with stock list. Submit portfolio for review. Provide résumé, business card, brochure, flier or tearsheets to be kept on file. Responds in 1-2 weeks. Pays $50-150 for b&w photos; $50-1,500 for color photos; $50-130/hour; $400-1,200/day; $100-2,000/job. Pays on receipt of invoice. Buys one-time rights.

⬤ ◐ ❀ FRIEDENTAG PHOTOGRAPHICS

314 S. Niagara St., Denver CO 80224-1324. (303)333-0570. **E-mail:** harveyfriedentag@msn.com. Estab. 1957. AV firm. Approximate annual billing: $500,000. Number of employees: 3. Firm specializes in direct mail, annual reports, publication design, magazine ads. Types of clients: business, industry, financial, publishing, government, trade and union organizations. Produces slide sets, motion pictures and videotape. Examples of recent clients: Perry Realtors annual report (advertising, mailing); Lighting Unlimited catalog (illustrations).

NEEDS Works with 5-10 photographers/month on assignment only. Buys 1,000 photos and 25 films/year. Reviews stock photos of business, training, public relations, and industrial plants showing people and equipment or products in use. Other subjects include agriculture, business concepts, industry, medicine, military, political, science, technology/computers. Interested in avant garde, documentary, erotic, fashion/glamour. Model release required.

AUDIOVISUAL NEEDS Uses freelance photos in color slide sets and motion pictures. "No posed looks." Also produces mostly 16mm Ektachrome and some 16mm × ¾" and VHS videotape. Length requirement: 3-30 minutes. Interested in stock footage on business, industry, education and unusual information. "No scenics, please!"

SPECS Uses 8×10 glossy b&w and color prints; 35mm, 2¼×2¼, 4×5 color transparencies. Accepts images in digital format. Send via CD as JPEG files.

MAKING CONTACT & TERMS Send material by mail for consideration. Provide flyer, business card, brochure and nonreturnable samples to show clients. Responds in 3 weeks. Pays $500/day for still; $700/day for motion picture plus expenses; $100 maximum for b&w photos; $200 maximum for color photos; $700 maximum for film; $700 maximum for videotape. **Pays on acceptance.** Buys rights as required by clients.

TIPS "More imagination needed—be different; *no scenics, pets or portraits.* Above all, technical quality is a must. There are more opportunities now than ever, especially for new people. We are looking to strengthen our file of talent across the nation."

⬤ ◎ ❀ GIBSON ADVERTISING

P.O. Box 20735, Billings MT 59104. (406)670-3412. **E-mail:** mike@gibsonad.com. **Website:** www.gibsonad.

com. **Contact:** Mike Curtis, president. Estab. 1984. Ad agency. Number of employees: 2. Types of clients: industrial, financial, retail, food, medical.

NEEDS Works with 1-3 freelance photographers and 1-2 videographers/month. Uses photos for direct mail, P-O-P displays, catalogs, posters, newspapers, signage, audiovisual. Subjects vary with job. Reviews stock photos. "We would like to see more Western photos." Model release required. Property release preferred.

AUDIOVISUAL NEEDS Uses slides and videotape.

SPECS Uses color and b&w prints; 35mm, 2¼×2¼, 4×5, 8×10 transparencies; 16mm, VHS, Betacam videotape; and digital formats.

MAKING CONTACT & TERMS Send query letter with résumé of credits or samples. Provide résumé, business card, brochure, flyer or tearsheets to be kept on file. Works with local freelancers on assignment only. Keeps samples on file. Cannot return material. Responds in 2 weeks. Pays $75-150/job; $150-250 for color photo; $75-150 for b&w photo; $100-150/hour for video. Pays on receipt of invoice, net 30 days. Credit line sometimes given. Buys one-time and electronic rights. Rights negotiable.

❀ HALLOWES PRODUCTIONS & ADVERTISING

750 W. 15th Ave., Escondido CA 92925. (310)390-4767. **E-mail:** Jim@HallowesProductions.com; adjim@aol.com. **Website:** www.jimhallowes.com; www.hallowesproductions.com. **Contact:** Jim Hallowes, creative director/producer-director. Estab. 1984. Creates and produces TV commercials, corporate films and videos, and print and electronic advertising.

NEEDS Buys 8-10 photos/year. Uses photos for magazines, posters, newspapers and brochures. Reviews stock photos; subjects vary.

AUDIOVISUAL NEEDS Uses film and video for TV commercials and corporate films.

SPECS Uses 35mm, 4×5 transparencies; 35mm/16mm film; Beta SP videotape; all digital formats.

MAKING CONTACT & TERMS Send query letter with résumé of credits. "Do not fax unless requested." Keeps samples on file. Responds if interested. Payment negotiable. Pays on usage. Credit line sometimes given, depending upon usage, usually not. Buys first and all rights; rights vary depending on client.

$$$ ◐ HAMPTON DESIGN GROUP

(610)821-0963. **E-mail:** wendy@hamptondesigngroup.com. **Website:** www.hamptondesigngroup.com. **Contact:** Wendy Ronga, creative director. Estab. 1997. Member of Type Director Club, Society of Illustrators, Art Directors Club, Society for Publication Designers. Design firm. Approximate annual billing: $450,000. Number of employees: 3. Firm specializes in annual reports, magazine and book design, editorial packaging, advertising, collateral, direct mail. Examples of recent clients: Conference for the Aging, Duke University/Templeton Foundation (photo shoot/5 images); Religion and Science, UCSB University (9 images for conference brochure).

NEEDS Works with 2 photographers/month. Uses photos for billboards, brochures, catalogs, consumer magazines, direct mail, newspapers, posters, trade magazines. Subjects include: babies/children/teens, multicultural, senior citizens, environmental, landscapes/scenics, wildlife, pets, religious, health/fitness/beauty, business concepts, medicine, science. Interested in alternative process, avant garde, fine art, historical/vintage, seasonal. Model/property release required. Photo captions preferred.

SPECS Prefers images in digital format. Send via CD as TIFF, EPS, JPEG files at 300 dpi.

MAKING CONTACT & TERMS Send query letter. Keeps samples on file. Responds only if interested; send nonreturnable samples or web address to see examples. Pays $150-1,500 for color photos; $75-1,000 for b&w photos. Pays extra for electronic usage of photos, varies depending on usage. Price is determined by size, how long the image is used and if it is on the home page. **Pays on receipt of invoice.** Credit line given. Buys one-time rights, all rights, electronic rights; negotiable.

TIPS "Use different angles and perspectives, a new way to view the same old boring subject. Try different films and processes."

$ ◐ HOWARD/MERRELL, INC.

4800 Falls Neuse Rd., Suite 300, Raleigh NC 27609. (919)848-2400. **Fax:** (919)845-9845. **Website:** www.howardmerrell.com. **Contact:** Lori Kramerson. Estab. 1945. Number of employees: 25.

NEEDS Works with approximately 1 photographer/month. Uses photos for consumer and trade magazines, newspapers, collateral, outdoor boards and websites. Purchases stock images. Model/property release required.

MAKING CONTACT & TERMS Works on assignment and buys stock photos. Pays on receipt of invoice. Buys one-time and all rights.

$$$ ◐ HUTCHINSON ASSOCIATES, INC.

822 Linden Ave., Suite 200, Oak Park IL 60302. (312)455-9191. **Fax:** (312)455-9190. **E-mail:** hutch@hutchinson.com. **Website:** www.hutchinson.com. **Contact:** Jerry Hutchinson, president. Estab. 1988. Member of American Institute of Graphic Arts. Design firm. Number of employees: 3. Firm specializes in brand identity design, website design and development, annual reports, collateral, advertising, publication design, marketing brochures. Types of clients: industrial, financial, real estate, retail, publishing, nonprofit and medical. Recent clients: Magenta Corp, Taylor Group Insurance, Hadley Capital, Crains Chicago Business.

NEEDS Works with 1 photographer/month. Uses photographs for websites and marketing materials. Subjects include: still life, real estate. Reviews stock photos.

SPECS Accepts images in digital format.

MAKING CONTACT & TERMS Send query letter with samples. Keeps samples on file. Responds "when the right project comes along." Payment rates depend on the client. Pays within 30-45 days. Credit line sometimes given. Buys one-time, exclusive product and all rights; negotiable.

TIPS In samples, "print quality and composition count."

🎞 ◎ $ IDEA BANK MARKETING

P.O. Box 2117, Hastings NE 68902. (402)463-0588. **Fax:** (402)463-2187. **Website:** www.ideabankmarketing.com. **Contact:** Sherma Jones, vice president/creative director. Estab. 1982. Member of Lincoln Ad Federation. Ad agency. Approximate annual billing: $1.5 million. Number of employees: 14. Types of clients: industrial, financial, tourism and retail.

NEEDS Works with 1-2 photographers/quarter. Uses photos for direct mail, catalogs, posters and newspapers. Subjects include people and products. Reviews stock photos. Model release required; property release preferred.

AUDIOVISUAL NEEDS Works with 1 videographer/quarter. Uses slides and videotape for presentations.

SPECS Uses digital images.

MAKING CONTACT & TERMS Provide résumé, business card, brochure, flyer or tearsheets to be kept on file. Works with freelancers on assignment only. Responds in 2 weeks. Pays $75-125/hour; $650-1,000/day. Pays on acceptance with receipt of invoice. Credit line sometimes given depending on client and project. Buys all rights; negotiable.

✹ IMAGE INTEGRATION

2619 Benvenue Ave. #A, Berkeley CA 94704. (510)504-2605. **E-mail:** vincesail@aol.com. **Contact:** Vince Casalaina, owner. Estab. 1971. Firm specializes in material for TV productions and Internet sites. Approximate annual billing: $100,000. Examples of recent clients: "Internet coverage of Melges 32 World Championship, 505 World Championship, Snipe World Championship, Snipe Women's World Championship. 30-Minute Documentary on the Snipe Class as it turns 80 in 2011."

NEEDS Works with 1 photographer/month. Reviews stock photos of sailing only. Property release preferred. Photo captions required; include regatta name, regatta location, date.

AUDIOVISUAL NEEDS Works with 1 videographer/month. Uses videotape. Subjects include: sailing only.

SPECS Uses 4×5 or larger matte color and b&w prints; 35mm transparencies; 16mm film and Betacam videotape. Prefers images in digital format. Send via e-mail, ZIP, CD (preferred).

MAKING CONTACT & TERMS Send unsolicited photos of sailing by mail with SASE for consideration. Keeps samples on file. Responds in 2 weeks. Payment depends on distribution. Pays on publication. Credit line sometimes given, depending upon whether any credits included. Buys nonexclusive rights; negotiable.

◐ JUDE STUDIOS

8000 Research Forest, Suite 115-266, The Woodlands TX 77382. (281)364-9366. **E-mail:** frontdesk@judestudios.com. **Contact:** Judith Dollar, art director. Estab. 1994. Number of employees: 2. Firm specializes in collateral, direct mail, packaging. Types of clients: nonprofits, builder, retail, destination marketing, event marketing, service. Examples of recent clients: home builder; festivals and events; corporate collateral; banking.

NEEDS Works with 1 photographer/month. Uses photos for newsletters, brochures, catalogs, direct mail, trade and trade show graphics. Needs photos of families, active adults, shopping, recreation, concert, music, education, business concepts, industry, product shots/still life. Stock photos also used. Model release required; property release preferred.

SPECS Accepts images in digital format. Do not e-mail attachments.

MAKING CONTACT & TERMS Send e-mail with link to website, blog, or portfolio. Provide business card, self-promotion piece to be kept on file. Responds only if interested; send nonreturnable samples. Pays by the project. Pays on receipt of invoice.

💲💲 LOHRE & ASSOCIATES, INC.

126A W. 14th St., 2nd Floor, Cincinnati OH 45202-7535. (513)961-1174. **Website:** www.lohre.com. **Contact:** Chuck Lohre, president. Ad agency. Types of clients: industrial.

NEEDS Uses photos for trade magazines, direct mail, catalogs and prints. Subjects include: machine-industrial themes and various eye-catchers.

SPECS Uses high-res digital images.

MAKING CONTACT & TERMS Send query letter with résumé of credits. Provide business card, brochure, flyer or tearsheets to be kept on file.

💲💲💲 ⊘ THE MILLER GROUP

1516 Bundy Dr., Suite 200, Los Angeles CA 90025. **E-mail:** gary@millergroupmarketing.com. **Website:** www.millergroupmarketing.com. **Contact:** Gary Bettman, vice president. Estab. 1990. Member of WSAAA. Approximate annual billing: $12 million. Number of employees: 10. Firm specializes in print advertising. Types of clients: consumer.

NEEDS Uses photos for billboards, brochures, consumer magazines, direct mail, newspapers. Model release required.

MAKING CONTACT & TERMS Contact through rep or send digital submissions. Provide self-promotion piece to be kept on file. Buys all rights; negotiable.

TIPS "Please, no calls!"

◐ MONDERER DESIGN, INC.

2067 Massachusetts Ave., 3rd Floor, Cambridge MA 02140. (617)661-6125. **Fax:** (617)661-6126. **E-mail:** info@monderer.com. **Website:** www.monderer.com. stewart@monderer.com. **Contact:** Stewart Monderer, president. Estab. 1981. Specializes in corporate identity, branding, print collateral, website, event and interactive solutions. Clients: corporations (technology, education, consulting and life science). Current clients include Solidworks, Thermo Scientific, MIT Sloan, Northeastern University, Progress Software, Kronos, Greenlight Fund, and Canaccord Genuity.

NEEDS Works with 2 photographers/month. Uses photos for adverstising, catalogs, posters and brochures. Subjects include: environmental, architecture, cities/urban, education, adventure, automobiles, entertainment, events, performing arts, sports, travel, business concepts, industry, medicine, product shots/still life, science, technology/computers, conceptual, site specific, people on location. Interested in alternative process, avant garde, documentary. Model release preferred; property release sometimes required.

SPECS Accepts images in digital format. Send TIFF, EPS files at 300 dpi.

MAKING CONTACT & TERMS Send unsolicited photos by mail for consideration. Keeps samples on file. Follow up from photographers recommended. Payment negotiable. Pays on receipt of invoice. Credit line sometimes given depending upon client. Rights always negotiated depending on use.

◎ ◐ MYRIAD PRODUCTIONS

415 Barlow Court, Johns Creek GA 30022. (678)417-0043. **E-mail:** myriad@mindspring.com. **Contact:** Ed Harris, president. Estab. 1965. Primarily involved with entertainment productions and sporting events. Types of clients: publishing, nonprofit.

NEEDS Works with photographers on assignment-only basis. Uses photos for portraits, live-action and studio shots, special effects, advertising, illustrations, brochures, TV and film graphics, theatrical and production stills. Subjects include: celebrities, entertainment, sports. Model/property release required. Photo captions preferred; include names, location, date, description.

SPECS Uses 8×10 b&w and color prints; 2¼×2¼ transparencies. Accepts images in digital format. Send "Mac-compatible CD or DVD. No floppy disks or ZIPs!"

MAKING CONTACT & TERMS Provide brochure, résumé or samples to be kept on file. Send material by mail for consideration. "No telephone or fax inquiries, please!" Cannot return material. Response time "depends on urgency of job or production." Payment negotiable. Credit line sometimes given. Buys all rights.

TIPS "We look for an imaginative photographer—one who captures all the subtle nuances. Working with us depends almost entirely on the photographer's skill and creative sensitivity with the subject. All materials submitted will be placed on file and not returned, pending future assignments. Photographers should not send us their only prints, transparencies, etc., for this reason."

$$ ◎ ◐ ⊛ NOVUS VISUAL COMMUNICATIONS

59 Page Ave., Suite 300, Tower One, Yonkers NY 10704. (212)473-1377. **E-mail:** novuscom@aol.com. **Website:** www.novuscommunications.com. **Contact:** Robert Antonik, managing director. Estab. 1988. Integrated marketing company. Lectures on new marketingtools & techniques. Clients include B2B, B2C and nonprofits. Uses the services of music houses, independent songwriters/composers and lyricists for scoring, background music for documentaries, commercials, multimedia applications, website, film shorts, and commercials for radio and TV. Commissions 2 composers and 4 lyricists/year. Pay varies per job. Buys one-time rights.

NEEDS Works with 1 photographer/month. Uses photos for integrated campaigns, business-to-business, B2C, direct mail, digital displays, online and print catalogs, posters, packaging and signage. Subjects include: babies/children/teens, couples, multicultural, families, parents, senior citizens, environmental, landscapes/scenics, wildlife, architecture, cities/urban, education, gardening, interiors/decorating, pets, religious, rural, adventure, automobiles, entertainment, events, food/drink, health/fitness, hobbies, humor, performing arts, sports, travel, agriculture, business concepts, industry, medicine, military, political, product shots/still life, science, technology/computers. Interested in alternative process, avant garde, documentary, fashion/glamour, fine art, historical/vintage, seasonal. Reviews stock photos. Model/property release required. Photo captions preferred.

SPECS Digital and film, videotape, DVD. Prefers links to websites to review content.

MAKING CONTACT & TERMS Works on assignment only. Keeps samples on file. Cannot return material. Responds in 1-2 weeks. Pays $150-200 for b&w photos; $275-800 for color photos; $500-1,500 for digital film; $500-1,500 for videotape. Pays upon client's payment. Credit line given. Rights negotiable.

TIPS "The marriage of photos and illustrations continues to evolve. Being knowledgeable in Photoshop is very important. It helps shape the vision and enhances the visual. More illustrators and photographers add stock usage as part of their creative business plan. E-mail with link to website. Send a sample postcard; follow up with phone call. Use low-tech marketing like direct mail, it works."

OMNI PRODUCTIONS

P.O. Box 302, Carmel IN 46082-0302. (317)846-2345. **Fax:** (317)846-6664. **E-mail:** omni@omniproductions.com. **Website:** www.omniproductions.com. **Contact:** Winston Long, president. Estab. 1984. AV firm. Types of clients: industrial, corporate, educational, government, medical.

NEEDS Works with 6-12 photographers/month. Uses photos for AV presentations. Subject matter varies. Also works with freelance filmmakers to produce training films and commercials. Model release required.

SPECS Uses b&w and color prints; 35mm transparencies; 16mm and 35mm film and videotape. Accepts images in digital format.

MAKING CONTACT & TERMS Provide complete contact info, rates, business card, brochure, flyer, digital samples or tearsheets to be kept on file. Works with freelance photographers on assignment basis only. Cannot return unsolicited material. Payment negotiable. **Pays on acceptance.** Credit line given "sometimes, as specified in production agreement with client." Buys all rights on most work; will purchase one-time use on some projects.

POINTBLANK AGENCY

(818)539-2282. **Fax:** (818)551-9681. **E-mail:** valn@pointblankagency.com. **Website:** www.pointblankagency.com. **Contact:** Valod Nazarian. Ad and design agency. Serves travel, high-technology and consumer-technology clients.

NEEDS Uses photos for trade show graphics, websites, consumer and trade magazines, direct mail, P-O-P displays, newspapers. Subject matter of photography purchased includes: conceptual shots of people and table top (tight shots of electronics products). Model release required. Photo captions preferred.

SPECS Uses 8×10 matte b&w and color prints; 35mm, 2¼×2¼, 4×5, 8×10 transparencies. Accepts images in digital format. Send via CD.

MAKING CONTACT & TERMS Arrange a personal interview to show portfolio. Provide résumé, business card, brochure, flyer or tearsheets to be kept on file. Works on assignment basis only. Does not return

unsolicited material. Responds in 3 weeks. Pay is negotiable. Pays on receipt of invoice. Buys one-time, exclusive product, electronic, buy-outs, and all rights (work-for-hire); negotiable.

TIPS Prefers to see "originality, creativity, uniqueness, technical expertise" in work submitted. There is more use of "photo composites, dramatic lighting and more attention to detail" in photography.

POSEY SCHOOL

57 Main St., Northport NY 11768. (631)757-2700. **E-mail:** PoseySchoolOfDance@gmail.com; msposey@optonline.net. **Website:** www.poseyschool.com. **Contact:** Elsa Posey, president. Estab. 1953. Sponsors a school of dance, art, music, drama; regional dance company and acting company. Uses photos for brochures, news releases, newspapers.

NEEDS Buys 12-15 photos/year; offers 4 assignments/year. Special subject needs include children dancing, ballet, modern dance, jazz/tap (theater dance) and "photos showing class situations in any subjects we offer. Photos must include girls and boys, women and men." Interested in documentary, fine art, historical/vintage. Reviews stock photos. Model release required.

SPECS Uses 8×10 glossy b&w prints. Accepts images in digital format. Send via CD, e-mail.

MAKING CONTACT & TERMS "Call us." Responds in 1 week. Pays $35-50 for most photos, b&w or color. Credit line given if requested. Buys one-time rights; negotiable.

TIPS "We are small but interested in quality (professional) work. Capture the joy of dance in a photo of children or adults. Show artists, actors or musicians at work. We prefer informal action photos, not posed pictures. We need photos of *real* dancers dancing. Call first. Be prepared to send photos on request."

QUALLY & CO., INC.

(312)280-1898. **E-mail:** iva@quallycompany.com; michael@quallycompany.com. **Website:** www.quallycompany.com. **Contact:** Michael Iva, creative director. Estab. 1979. Ad agency. Types of clients: new product development and launches.

NEEDS Uses photos for every media. "Subject matter varies, but it must always be a 'quality image' regardless of what it portrays." Model/property release required. Photo captions preferred.

SPECS Uses b&w and color prints; 35mm, 4×5, 8×10 transparencies. Accepts images in digital format.

MAKING CONTACT & TERMS Send query letter with photocopies, tearsheets. Provide résumé, business card, brochure, flyer or tearsheets to be kept on file. Responds only if interested; send nonreturnable samples. Payment negotiable. Pays net 30 days from receipt of invoice. Credit line sometimes given, depending on client's cooperation. Rights purchased depend on circumstances.

◐ QUON DESIGN

543 River Rd., Fair Haven NJ 07704-3227. (732)212-9200. **E-mail:** studio@quondesign.com. **Website:** www.quondesign.com; www.quonart.com. **Contact:** Mike Quon, president/creative director. Specializes in corporate identity, brand image, publications and web design. Types of clients: industrial, financial, retail, publishers, nonprofit.

NEEDS Limited use of stock photography. Works with 1-3 photographers/year.

SPECS Uses color and b&w digital images.

MAKING CONTACT & TERMS Contact through mail or e-mail only. Pays net 30 days. Buys first rights, one-time rights; negotiable.

◒◒ ◑ TED ROGGEN ADVERTISING AND PUBLIC RELATIONS

101 Westcott St., Unit 306, Houston TX 77007. (713)426-2314. **Fax:** (713)869-3563. **E-mail:** ted@tedroggen-advertising.com. **Website:** www.tedroggen-advertising.com. **Contact:** Ted Roggen. Estab. 1945. Ad agency and PR firm. Number of employees: 3. Firm specializes in magazine ads, direct mail. Types of clients: construction, entertainment, food, finance, publishing, travel.

NEEDS Buys 25-50 photos/year; offers 50-75 assignments/year. Uses photos for billboards, direct mail, radio, TV, P-O-P displays, brochures, annual reports, PR releases, sales literature and trade magazines. Subjects include adventure, health/fitness, sports, travel. Interested in fashion/glamour. Model release required. Photo captions required.

SPECS Uses 5×7 glossy or matte b&w and color prints; 4×5 transparencies. "Contact sheet OK."

MAKING CONTACT & TERMS Provide résumé to be kept on file. Pays $75-250 for b&w photos; $125-300 for color photos; $150/hour. **Pays on acceptance.** Rights negotiable.

◒◒◒ ✷ SIDES & ASSOCIATES

222 Jefferson St., Suite B, Lafayette LA 70501. (337)233-6473. **E-mail:** info@sides.com. **Website:** www.sides.com. **Contact:** Larry Sides, agency president. Estab. 1976. Member of AAAA, PRSA, Association for Strategic Planning, Chamber of Commerce, Better Business Bureau. Ad agency. Number of employees: 13. Firm specializes in publication design, display design, signage, video and radio production. Types of clients: governmental, healthcare, financial, retail, nonprofit. Examples of recent clients: US Dept of Homeland Security, ESF #14 (web, brochure, and special event planning); Lafayette Regional Airport (signs, brochures), Our Lady of Lourdes Regional Medical Center (TV, outdoor, print ads, brochures).

NEEDS Works with 2 photographers/month. Uses photos for billboards, brochures, newspapers, P-O-P displays, posters, signage. Subjects include: setup shots of people. Reviews stock photos of everything. Model/property release required.

AUDIOVISUAL NEEDS Works with 2 filmmakers and 2 videographers/month. Uses slides and/or film or video for broadcast, TV, newspaper.

SPECS Uses 35mm, 2¼×2¼, 4×5 transparencies.

MAKING CONTACT & TERMS Provide résumé, business card, self-promotion piece or tearsheets to be kept on file. Works with local freelancers only. Responds only if interested; send nonreturnable samples. Payment determined by client and usage. Pays "when paid by our client." Rights negotiable.

◒ ◐ ✤ SOUNDLIGHT

5438 Tennessee Ave., New Port Richey FL 34652. (727)842-6788. **E-mail:** keth@soundlight.org. **Website:** www.soundlight.org. **Contact:** Keth Luke. Estab. 1972. Approximate annual billing: $150,000. Number of employees: 2. Firm specializes in websites, direct mail, magazine ads, model portfolios, publication design. Types of clients: businesses, astrological and spiritual workshops, books, calendars, fashion, magazines, models, special events, products, nonprofit, web pages. Examples of recent clients: Sensual Women of Hawaii (calendars, postcards).

NEEDS Works with 1 freelance photographer every 7 months. Subjects include: women, celebrities, couples, Goddess, people in activities, landscapes/scenics, animals, religious, adventure, health/fitness/beauty, humor, alternative medicine, spiritual, travel sites and activities, exotic dance and models (art, glamour, lingerie, nude). Interested in alternative process, avant garde, erotic, fine art. Reviews stock photos, slides, computer images. Model release preferred for models and advertising people. Photo captions preferred; include who, what, where.

AUDIOVISUAL NEEDS Uses freelance photographers for slide sets, multimedia productions, videotapes, websites.

SPECS Accepts images in digital format. Send via CD, floppy disk, Dropbox, e-mail as TIFF, GIF, JPEG files at 70-100 dpi.

MAKING CONTACT & TERMS Send query letter with résumé, stock list. Provide prints, slides, business card, computer disk, CD, contact sheets, self-promotion piece or tearsheets to be kept on file. Works on assignment; sometimes buys stock nude model photos. May not return unsolicited material. Responds in 3 weeks. Pays $100 maximum for b&w and color photos; $10-1,800 for videotape; $10-100/hour; $50-750/day; $2,000 maximum/job; sometimes also pays in "trades." Pays on publication. Credit line sometimes given. Buys one-time, all rights; various negotiable rights depending on use.

TIPS "In portfolios or demos, we look for unique lighting, style, emotional involvement; beautiful, artistic, sensual, erotic viewpoints. We see a trend toward manipulated computer images. Send query about what you have to show, to see what we can use at that time."

○ ❸ ◎ ⊛ SUN.ERGOS

130 Sunset Way, Priddis Alberta T0L 1W0, Canada. (403)931-1527. **Fax:** (403)931-1534. **E-mail:** walter moke@sunergos.com. **Website:** www.sunergos.com. **Contact:** Robert Greenwood, artistic and managing director. Estab. 1977. "A unique, professional, two-man company of theater and dance, touring nationally and internationally as cultural ambassadors to urban and rural communities."

NEEDS Buys 10-30 photos/year; offers 3-5 assignments/year. Uses photos for brochures, newsletters, posters, newspapers, annual reports, magazines, press releases, audiovisual uses, catalogs. Reviews theater and dance stock photos. Property release required for performance photos for media use. Photo captions required; include subject, date, city, performance title.

AUDIOVISUAL NEEDS Uses digital images, slides, film and videotape for media usage, showcases and international conferences. Subjects include performance pieces/showcase materials.

SPECS Uses 8×10, 8½×11 color and b&w prints; 35mm, 2¼×2¼ transparencies; 16mm film; NTSC/PAL/SECAM videotape.

MAKING CONTACT & TERMS Arrange a personal interview to show portfolio. Send query letter with résumé of credits. Provide résumé, business card, self-promotion piece or tearsheets to be kept on file. Works on assignment only. Response time depends on project. Pays $100-150/day; $150-300/job; $2.50-10 for color or b&w photos. Pays on usage. Credit line given. Buys all rights.

TIPS "You must have experience shooting dance and *live* theater performances."

◎ ⊛ VIDEO I-D, TELEPRODUCTIONS

105 Muller Rd., Washington IL 61571. (309)444-4323. **E-mail:** videoid@videoid.com. **Website:** www.videoid.com. **Contact:** Sam B. Wagner, president. Estab. 1977. Number of employees: 10. Types of clients: health, education, industry, service, cable and broadcast.

NEEDS Works with 2 photographers/month to shoot digital stills, multimedia backgrounds and materials, films and videotapes. Subjects "vary from commercial to industrial—always high quality." Somewhat interested in stock photos/footage. Model release required.

AUDIOVISUAL NEEDS Uses digital stills, videotape, DVD, CD.

SPECS Uses digital still extension, Beta SP, HDV and HD. Accepts images in digital format. Send via DVD, CD, e-mail, FTP.

MAKING CONTACT & TERMS Provide résumé, business card, self-promotion piece or tearsheets to be kept on file. Also send video sample reel. Include SASE for return of material. Works with freelancers on assignment only. Responds in 3 weeks. Pays $10-65/hour; $160-650/day. Usually pays by the job; negotiable. **Pays on acceptance.** Credit line sometimes given. Buys all rights; negotiable.

TIPS "Sample reel—indicate goal for specific pieces. Show good lighting and visualization skills. Show me you can communicate what I need to see, and have a willingness to put out effort to get top quality."

○ WORCESTER POLYTECHNIC INSTITUTE

100 Institute Rd., Worcester MA 01609-2280. (508)831-6715; (508)831-5099. **Fax:** (508)831-5820. **E-mail:** mdeiana@wpi.edu. **Website:** www.wpi.edu. **Contact:** Maureen Deiana, director of marketing programs. Estab. 1865. Publishes periodicals; pro-

motional, recruiting and fund-raising printed materials. Photos used in brochures, newsletters, posters, audiovisual presentations, annual reports, catalogs, magazines, press releases, online.

NEEDS On-campus, comprehensive and specific views of all elements of the WPI experience.

SPECS Prefers images in digital format, but will use 5×7 (minimum) glossy b&w and color prints.

MAKING CONTACT & TERMS Arrange a personal interview to show portfolio or query with website link. Provide résumé, business card, brochure, flyer or tearsheets to be kept on file. "No phone calls." Responds in 6 weeks. Payment negotiable. Credit line given in some publications. Buys one-time or all rights; negotiable.

GALLERIES

The popularity of photography as a collectible art form has improved the market for fine art photographs over the last decade. Collectors now recognize the investment value of prints by Ansel Adams, Irving Penn, and Henri Cartier-Bresson, and therefore frequently turn to galleries for photographs to place in their private collections.

The gallery/fine art market can make money for many photographers. However, unlike commercial and editorial markets, galleries seldom generate quick income for artists. Galleries should be considered venues for important, thought-provoking imagery, rather than markets through which you can make a substantial living.

More than any other market, this area is filled with photographers who are interested in delivering a message. Many photography exhibits focus on one theme by a single artist. Group exhibits feature the work of several artists, and they often explore a theme from many perspectives, though not always. These group exhibits may be juried (i.e., the photographs in the exhibit are selected by a committee of judges who are knowledgeable about photography). Some group exhibits also may include other mediums such as painting, drawing, or sculpture. In any case, galleries want artists who can excite viewers and make them think about important subjects. They, of course, also hope that viewers will buy the photographs shown in their galleries.

As with picture buyers and art directors, gallery directors love to see strong, well-organized portfolios. Limit your portfolio to twenty top-notch images. When putting together your portfolio, focus on one overriding theme. A director wants to be certain you have enough quality work to carry an entire show. After the portfolio review, if the director likes your style, then you might discuss future projects or past work that you've done. Directors who see promise in your work, but don't think you're ready for a solo exhibition, may place your photographs in a group exhibition.

HOW GALLERIES OPERATE

In exchange for brokering images, a gallery often receives a commission of 40–50 percent. They usually exhibit work for a month, sometimes longer, and hold openings to kick off new shows. They also frequently provide pre-exhibition publicity. Some smaller galleries require exhibiting photographers to help with opening night reception expenses. Galleries also may require photographers to appear during the show or opening. Be certain that such policies are put in writing before you allow them to show your work.

Gallery directors who foresee a bright future for you might want exclusive rights to represent your work. This type of arrangement forces buyers to get your images directly from the gallery that represents you. Such contracts are quite common, usually limiting the exclusive rights to specified distances. For example, a gallery in Tulsa, Oklahoma, may have exclusive rights to distribute your work within a 200-mile radius of the gallery. This would allow you to sign similar contracts with galleries outside the 200-mile range.

FIND THE RIGHT FIT

As you search for the perfect gallery, it's important to understand the different types of exhibition spaces and how they operate. The route you choose depends on your needs, the type of work you do, your long-term goals, and the audience you're trying to reach.

- **Retail or commercial galleries.** The goal of the retail gallery is to sell and promote artists while turning a profit. Retail galleries take a commission of 40–50 percent of all sales.
- **Co-op galleries.** Co-ops exist to sell and promote artists' work, but they are run by artists. Members exhibit their own work in exchange for a fee, which covers the gallery's overhead. Some co-ops also take a commission of 20–30 percent to cover expenses. Members share the responsibilities of gallery-sitting, sales, housekeeping, and maintenance.
- **Rental galleries.** The rental gallery makes its profit primarily through renting space to artists and consequently may not take a commission on sales (or will take only a very small commission). Some rental spaces provide publicity for artists, while others do not. Showing in this type of gallery is risky. Rental galleries are sometimes thought of as "vanity galleries," and, consequently, they do not have the credibility other galleries enjoy.
- **Nonprofit galleries.** Nonprofit spaces will provide you with an opportunity to sell work and gain publicity, but will not market your work aggressively, because their goals are not necessarily sales-oriented. Nonprofits normally take a commission of 20–30 percent.

- **Museums.** Don't approach museums unless you have already exhibited in galleries. The work in museums is by established artists and is usually donated by collectors or purchased through art dealers.
- **Art consultancies.** Generally, art consultants act as liaisons between fine artists and buyers. Most take a commission on sales (as would a gallery). Some maintain small gallery spaces and show work to clients by appointment.

If you've never exhibited your work in a traditional gallery space before, you may want to start with a less traditional kind of show. Alternative spaces are becoming a viable way to help the public see your work. Try bookstores (even large chains), restaurants, coffee shops, upscale home furnishings stores, and boutiques. The art will help give their business a more pleasant, interesting environment at no cost to them, and you may generate a few fans or even a few sales.

Think carefully about what you take pictures of and what kinds of businesses might benefit from displaying them. If you shoot flowers and other plant life, perhaps you could approach a nursery about hanging your work in their sales office. If you shoot landscapes of exotic locations, maybe a travel agent would like to take you on. Think creatively and don't be afraid to approach a business person with a proposal. Just make sure the final agreement is spelled out in writing so there will be no misunderstandings, especially about who gets what money from sales.

COMPOSING AN ARTIST'S STATEMENT

When you approach a gallery about a solo exhibition, they will usually expect your body of work to be organized around a theme. To present your work and its theme to the public, the gallery will expect you to write an artist's statement, a brief essay about how and why you make photographic images. There are several things to keep in mind when writing your statement: Be brief. Most statements should be 100–300 words long. You shouldn't try to tell your life's story leading up to this moment. Write as you speak. There is no reason to make up complicated motivations for your work if there aren't any. Just be honest about why you shoot the way you do. Stay focused. Limit your thoughts to those that deal directly with the specific exhibit for which you're preparing.

Before you start writing your statement, consider your answers to the following questions: Why do you make photographs (as opposed to using some other medium)? What are your photographs about? What are the subjects in your photographs? What are you trying to communicate through your work?

440 GALLERY

440 Sixth Ave., Brooklyn NY 11215. (718)499-3844. **E-mail:** gallery440@verizon.net. **Website:** www.440gallery.com. **Contact:** Nancy Lunsford, co-founder and director. Estab. 2005. 440 is a Cooperative gallery. We maintain our membership at approximately 14 artists and occasionally seek a new member when an individual moves or leaves the collective. There is a co-op membership fee plus a donation of time. All prospective members must submit a portfolio and be interviewed. In addition to members' solo exhibitions, we host 2 national juried exhibitions each year, in the summer and winter, with an outside curator making selections. Located in Park Slope (Brooklyn), the gallery is approximately 400 sq. ft. with two exhibition areas (the solo gallery in the front and Project Space in the back). Open Tuesday-Friday, 4-7; weekends 11-7. Patrons are primarily from the New York regions, especially Brooklyn. Due to our proximity to popular Brooklyn destinations, we are visited often by tourists interested in culture and art. Overall price range $100-12,000 with prices set by the artist. Average length of an exhibition is 5 weeks.

EXHIBITS Our artists most frequently exhibit painting, collage/assemblage, photography and sculpture.

MAKING CONTACT & TERMS Artwork is accepted on consignment and there is a 20% commission on sales for members and 30-40% on juried shows. Gallery provides promotion.

SUBMISSIONS For consideration as a member, please e-mail a query including a link to your website, which should include a résumé. For an application to our juried shows, visit our website and find the "Call for Entry" link.

ADDISON/RIPLEY FINE ART

1670 Wisconsin Ave. NW, Washington DC 20007. (202)338-5180. **Fax:** (202)338-2341. **E-mail:** addisonrip@aol.com. **Website:** www.addisonripleyfineart.com. **Contact:** Christopher Addison, owner. Estab. 1981. Art consultancy, for-profit gallery. Approached by 100 artists/year; represents or exhibits 25 artists. Average display time 6 weeks. Gallery open Tuesday–Saturday, 11-5:30 and by appointment. Closed end of summer. Located in Georgetown in a large, open, light-filled gallery space. Overall price range $500-80,000. Most work sold at $2,500-10,000.

EXHIBITS Works of all media.

MAKING CONTACT & TERMS Gallery provides insurance, promotion, contract. Accepted work should be framed, mounted, matted.

SUBMISSIONS Mail portfolio for review. Send query letter with artist's statement, bio, photocopies, résumé, SASE. Responds in 1 month.

TIPS "Submit organized, professional-looking materials."

ADIRONDACK LAKES CENTER FOR THE ARTS

3446 St. Rt. 28, Blue Mountain Lake NY 12812. (518)752-7715; (518)352-7715. **Fax:** (518)352-7333. **E-mail:** office@adirondackarts.org. **Website:** www.adirondackarts.org. **Contact:** Stephen Svodoba, executive director. Estab. 1967. "ALCA is a 501c, nonprofit organization showing national and international work of emerging to established artists. A tourist and second-home market, demographics profile our client as highly educated, moderately affluent, environmentally oriented and well-traveled. In addition to its public programs, the Arts Center also administers the New York State Decentralization Regrant Program for Hamilton County. This program provides grants to local nonprofit organizations to sponsor art and cultural events, including concerts, workshops, and lectures in their own communities. The area served by the Arts Center includes Hamilton County, and parts of Essex, Franklin, Warren, and Herkimer counties. Our intent, with this diversity, is to enrich and unite the entire Adirondacks via the arts. The busy season is June through September."

EXHIBITS Solo, group, call for entry exhibits of color and b&w work. Sponsors 15-20 exhibits/year. Average display time 1 month. Overall price range $100-2,000. Most work sold at $250.

MAKING CONTACT & TERMS Consignment gallery, fee structure on request. Payment for sales follows within 30 days of close of exhibit. White mat and black frame required, except under prior agreement. ALCA pays return shipping only or cover work in transit.

SUBMISSIONS Apply by CD or slides, résumé and bio. Must include SASE for return of materials. Upon acceptance notification, price sheet and artist statement required.

TIPS "ALCA offers a residency program, maintains a fully equipped darkroom with 24-hour access."

⊘ AKRON ART MUSEUM

1 S. High St., Akron OH 44308. (330)376-9185. **Fax:** (330)376-1180. **E-mail:** mail@akronartmuseum.org. **Website:** www.akronartmuseum.org. Located on the corner of East Market and South High Streets in the heart of downtown Akron. Open Wednesday–Sunday, 11-5; Thursday, 11-9. Closed Monday and Tuesday. Closed holidays.

○ Annually awards the Knight Purchase Award to a living artist working with photographic media.

EXHIBITS To exhibit, photographers must possess "a notable record of exhibitions, inclusion in publications, and/or a role in the historical development of photography. We also feature area photographers (northeast Ohio)." Interested in innovative works by contemporary photographers; any subject matter. Interested in alternative process, documentary, fine art, historical/vintage.

MAKING CONTACT & TERMS Payment negotiable. Buys photography outright.

SUBMISSIONS "Please submit a brief letter of interest, résumé, and 20-25 representative images (slides, snapshots, JPEGs on CD, DVDs or website links). Do not send original artworks. If you would like your material returned, please include a SASE." Allow 2-3 months for review.

TIPS "Send professional-looking materials with high-quality images, a résumé and an artist's statement. Never send original prints."

ALASKA STATE MUSEUM

395 Whittier St., Juneau AK 99801-1718. (907)465-2901. **Fax:** (907)465-2151. **E-mail:** jackie.manning@alaska.gov. **Website:** www.museums.alaska.gov. **Contact:** Jackie Manning, curator of exhibitions. Estab. 1900. Approached by 80 artists/year. Sponsors at least 1 photography exhibit every 2 years. Average display time 10 weeks. Exhibit travels statewide. Next call for submissions in spring 2016. Downtown location.

EXHIBITS Interested in historical and fine art.

SUBMISSIONS Finds Alaskan artists through submissions and portfolio reviews every 2 years.

ALBUQUERQUE MUSEUM

2000 Mountain Rd., NW, Albuquerque NM 87104. (505)243-7255. **Website:** www.cabq.gov/museum. Glenn Fye, photo archivist. **Contact:** Andrew Connors, curator of art. Estab. 1967.

SUBMISSIONS Submit portfolio of slides, photos, or disk for review. Responds in 2 months.

CHARLES ALLIS ART MUSEUM

1801 N. Prospect Ave., Milwaukee WI 53202. (414)278-8295. **E-mail:** jsterr@cavtmuseums.org. **Website:** www.charlesallis.org. **Contact:** John Sterr, executive director. Estab. 1947. The Charles Allis Art Museum exhibits emerging, mid-career and established artists that have lived or studied in Wisconsin. Exhibited artists include Anne Miotke (watercolor); Evelyn Patricia Terry (pastel, acrylic, multi-media). Sponsors 3 exhibits/year. Average display time: 3 months. Open all year; Wednesday–Sunday, 1-5. Located in an urban area, historical home, 3 galleries. Clients include local community, students and tourists. 10% of sales are to corporate collectors. Overall price range: $200-6,000.

EXHIBITS Considers acrylic, collage, drawing, installation, mixed media, oil, pastel, pen & ink, sculpture, watercolor and photography. Print types include engravings, etchings, linocuts, lithographs, serigraphs and woodcuts.

MAKING CONTACT & TERMS Artwork can be purchased during run of an exhibition; a 30% commission fee applies. Retail price set by the artist. Museum provides insurance, promotion and contract. Accepted work should be framed. Does not require exclusive representation locally. Accepts only artists from or with a connection to Wisconsin.

SUBMISSIONS Finds artists through submissions to Request for Proposals which can be found at www.charlesallis.org/news.html.

AMERICAN PRINT ALLIANCE

302 Larkspur Turn, Peachtree City GA 30269-2210. **E-mail:** director@printalliance.org. **Website:** www.printalliance.org. **Contact:** Carol Pulin, director. Estab. 1992.

EXHIBITS "We only exhibit original prints, artists' books and paperworks." Usually sponsors 2 traveling exhibits/year—all prints, paperworks and artists' books; photography within printmaking processes but not as a separate medium. Most exhibits travel for 2 years. Hours depend on the host gallery/museum/arts center. "We travel exhibits throughout the US and occasionally to Canada." Overall price range for Print Bin: $150-3,200; most work sold at $300-500. "We accept all styles, genres and subjects; the decisions are made on quality of work." Individual subscription: $32-39. Print Bin is free with subscription."

MAKING CONTACT & TERMS Subscribe to journal, *Contemporary Impressions* (www.printalliance.org/alliance/al_subform.html), send one slide and signed permission form (www.printalliance.org/gallery/printbin_info.html). Returns slide if requested with SASE. Usually does not respond to queries from nonsubscribers. Files slides and permission forms. Finds artists through submissions to the gallery or Print Bin, and especially portfolio reviews at printmakers conferences.

AMERICAN SOCIETY OF ARTISTS

P.O. Box 1326, Palatine IL 60078. (847)991-4748 or (312)751-2500. **E-mail:** asoaartists@aol.com. **Website:** www.americansocietyofartists.org. **Contact:** Helen Del Valle, membership chairman. American Society of Artists. Fine arts & fine selected crafts shows held annually May–September. Outdoors. Event(s) held in various locations in Illinois. Accepts photography, paintings, sculpture, glass works, jewelry and more. Juried. Exhibition space is approximately 100 sq. ft. for single space; other sizes available.

EXHIBITS Members and nonmembers may exhibit. "Our members range from internationally known artists to unknown artists—quality of work is the important factor. We have numerous shows throughout the year that accept photographic art.

MAKING CONTACT & TERMS Accepted work should be framed, mounted or matted.

SUBMISSIONS Send SASE and 4 slides/photos representative of your work or 1 slide or photo of your display, #10 SASE, a résumé or show listing is helpful. Number of exhibitors: varies according to show. To jury via e-mail: submit only to: Asoaartists@aol.com. If you pass jury you will receive a non-member jury/approval number. Deadline for entry is approximately 2 months prior or earlier if spaces fill. Entry fee: varies depending upon show and space size. For more information artists should send jury first and when you pass jury, you will receive a nonmember jury/approval number and be sent information you requested.

TIPS "Remember that when you are at work in your studio, you are an artist. But when you are at a show, you are a business person selling your work."

THE ANN ARBOR ART CENTER GALLERY SHOP

117 W. Liberty St., Ann Arbor MI 48104. (734)994-8004. **Fax:** (734)994-3610. **E-mail:** nrice@annarbor artcenter.org; sbingham@annarborartcenter.org. **Website:** www.annarborartcenter.org. **Contact:** Nathan Rice, gallery curator; Samantha Bingham, gallery curator. Estab. 1909. Represents over 350 artists, primarily Michigan and regional. Gallery shop purchases support the Art Center's community outreach programs. "We are the only organization in Ann Arbor that offers hands-on art education, art appreciation programs and exhibitions all in one facility." Open Monday–Friday, 10-7; Saturday, 10-6; Sunday, 12-5.

○ The Ann Arbor Art Center also has exhibition opportunities for Michigan artists in its exhibition gallery and art consulting program.

EXHIBITS Considers original work in virtually all 2D and 3D media, including jewelry, prints and etchings, ceramics, glass, fiber, wood, photography and painting.

MAKING CONTACT & TERMS Submission guidelines available online. Accepts work on consignment. Retail price set by artist. Offers member discounts and payment by installments. Exclusive area representation not required. Gallery provides contract; artist pays for shipping.

SUBMISSIONS "The Art Center seeks out artists through the exhibition visitation, wholesale and retail craft shows, networking with graduate and undergraduate schools, word of mouth, in addition to artist referral and submissions."

ARC GALLERY

Attn: Exhibition Committee, 2156 N. Damen Ave., Chicago IL 60647. (773)252-2232. **E-mail:** info@arc gallery.org. **Website:** www.arcgallery.org. **Contact:** Iris Goldstein, president. Estab. 1973. Sponsors 5-8 exhibits/year. Average display time 1 month. Overall price range $100-1,200.

○ "ARC Gallery and Educational Foundation is a not-for-profit gallery and foundation whose mission is to bring innovative, experimental visual art to a wide range of viewers, and to provide an atmosphere for the continued development of artistic potential, experimentation and dialogue. ARC serves to educate the public on various community-based issues by presenting exhibits, workshops, discussion groups and programs for, and by, underserved populations."

EXHIBITS All styles considered. Contemporary fine art photography, documentary and journalism.

MAKING CONTACT & TERMS Charges no commission, but there is a space rental fee.

SUBMISSIONS Must send slides, résumé and statement to gallery for review; include SASE. Reviews JPEGs. Responds in 1 month.

TIPS Photographers "should have a consistent body of work. Show emerging and experimental work."

ARIZONA STATE UNIVERSITY ART MUSEUM

P.O. Box 872911, Tenth St. and Mill Ave., Tempe AZ 85287-2911. (480)965-2787. **Fax:** (480)965-5254. **Website:** asuartmuseum.asu.edu. **Contact:** Gordon Knox, director. Estab. 1950. Has 3 facilities and approximately 8 galleries of 2,500 square feet each; mounts approximately 15 exhibitions/year. Average display time: 3-4 months.

EXHIBITS Proposals are reviewed by curatorial staff.

MAKING CONTACT & TERMS Accepted work should be framed, mounted, matted.

SUBMISSIONS E-mail or send query letter with résumé, reviews, images of current work and SASE for return of materials. "Allow several months for a response since we receive many proposals and review monthly."

ARNOLD ART

210 Thames St., Newport RI 02840. (401)847-2273; (800)352-2234. **Fax:** (401)848-0156. **E-mail:** info@arnoldart.com. **Website:** www.arnoldart.com. **Contact:** William Rommel, owner. Estab. 1870. For-profit gallery. Represents or exhibits 40 artists. Average display time 1 month. Gallery open Monday–Saturday, 9:30-5:30; Sunday, 12-5. Closed Christmas, Thanksgiving, Easter. Art gallery is 17×50 ft., open gallery space (3rd floor). Overall price range $100-35,000. Most work sold at $300.

EXHIBITS Marine (sailing), classic yachts, America's Cup, wooden boats, sailing/racing. Artwork is accepted on consignment, and there is a 45% commission. Gallery provides promotion. Accepted work should be framed.

MAKING CONTACT & TERMS E-mail to arrange personal interview to show portfolio.

THE ARSENAL GALLERY

The Arsenal Bldg., Room 20, Central Park, 830 Fifth Ave., New York NY 10065. (212)360-8163. **Fax:** (212)360-1329. **E-mail:** artandantiquities@parks.nyc.gov; jennifer.lantzas@parks.nyc.gov. **Website:** www.nycgovparks.org/art. Jennifer Lantzas, public art coordinator. Estab. 1971.

EXHIBITS Exhibits photos of environmental, landscapes/scenics, wildlife, architecture, cities/urban, adventure, NYC parks. Interested in alternative process, avant garde, documentary, fine art, historical/vintage. Artwork is accepted on consignment, and there is a 15% commission. Gallery provides promotion. Contact parks for submission deadlines.

MAKING CONTACT & TERMS Mail portfolio for review. Send query letter with artist's statement, bio, brochure, business card, photocopies, résumé, reviews, SASE. Responds within 6 months, only if interested. Finds artists through word of mouth, portfolio reviews, art exhibits, referrals by other artists.

ART@NET INTERNATIONAL GALLERY

E-mail: artnetg@yahoo.com. **Website:** www.artnet.com. **Contact:** Yavor Shopov-Bulgari, director. Estab. 1998. Artwork is accepted on consignment; there is a 10% commission and a rental fee for space of $1/image per month or $5/image per year. First 6 images are displayed free of rental fee. Gallery provides promotion. Accepted work should be matted. Main usage of all works exhibited in our gallery is for limited edition (photos) or original (paintings) wall decoration of offices and homes, so photos must have quality of paintings.

EXHIBITS Photos of creative photography including: travel, landscapes/scenics, fashion/glamour, erotic, figure landscapes, beauty, abstracts, avant garde, fine art, silhouettes, architecture, buildings, cities/urban, science, astronomy, education, seasonal, wildlife, sports, adventure, caves, crystals, minerals and luminescence.

MAKING CONTACT & TERMS "We accept computer scans only; no slides, please. E-mail attached scans, 900×1200 pixels (300 dpi for prints or 900 dpi for 36mm slides), as JPEG files for PCs." E-mail query letter with artist's statement, bio, résumé. Responds in 6 weeks. Finds artists through submissions, portfolio reviews, art exhibits, art fairs, referrals by other artists." E-mail a tightly edited selection of less than 20 scans of your best work. All work must force any person to look over it again and again.

TIPS "We like to see strong artistic sense of mood, composition, light, color and strong graphic impact or expression of emotions. For us, only quality of work is important, so newer, lesser-known artists are welcome."

ART 3 GALLERY

44 W. Brook St., Manchester NH 03101. (603)668-6650; (800)668-9983. **Fax:** (603)668-5136. **E-mail:** info@art3gallery.com. **Website:** www.art3gallery.com. **Contact:** Joni Taube, owner. Estab. 1980. For-profit gallery and art consultancy. Exhibits emerging, mid-career, and established artists. Approached by 50+ artists a year; exhibits 180+ artists. Exhibited artists include James Aponorich (oil painting) and Stan Moeller (oil painting). Sponsors 4 exhibits/year. Average display time 2-3 months. Open Monday-Friday 9-4. Located in downtown Manchester in a two-story, 2,000-sq.-ft. exhibit space. Clients include local community, tourists, and upscale clients. Overall price range $150-20,000. Most work sold at $1,000.

MAKING CONTACT & TERMS Artwork is accepted on consignment and there is a 50% commission. Retail price set by the gallery and artist. Gallery provides insurance, promotion, and contract. Accepted artwork should be framed, mounted, and matted. Does not require exclusive local representation.

SUBMISSIONS E-mail query letter with link to artist's website or JPEG samples at 72 dpi. Materials returned with SASE. Responds if interested in 4 weeks. Finds artists through word of mouth, submissions, art exhibits, art fairs, and referrals by other artists.

ARTEFACT/ROBERT PARDO GALLERY

805 Lake Ave., Lake Worth FL 33460. (561)329-6264. **E-mail:** robert@theartefactgallery.com. **Website:** www.theartefactgallery.com. **Contact:** Robert Pardo. Estab. 1986. Approached by 500 artists/year; represents or exhibits 18 artists. Sponsors 3 photography exhibits/year. Average display time 4-5 weeks. Gallery open 7 days a week until 6.

EXHIBITS Interested in avant garde, fashion/glamour, fine art.

SUBMISSIONS Arrange personal interview to show portfolio of slides, transparencies. Responds in 1 month.

ARTISTS' COOPERATIVE GALLERY

405 S. 11th St., Omaha NE 68102. (402)342-9617. **E-mail:** artistscoopgallery@gmail.com. **Website:** www.artistsco-opgallery.com. Estab. 1974. Gallery sponsors all-member exhibits and outreach exhibits; individual artists sponsor their own small group exhibits throughout the year. Overall price range $100-5,000.

"Artist must be willing to work 13 days per year at the gallery. Sponsors 12 exhibits/year. Average display time 1 month. Fine art photography only. We are a member-owned-and-operated cooperative. Artist must also serve on one committee. Write for membership application. Membership committee screens applicants August 1-15 each year. Responds by September 1. New membership year begins October 1. Members must pay annual fee of $400. Our community outreach exhibits include local high school photographers and art from local elementary schools." Open Tuesday–Thursday, 11-5; Friday-Saturday, 11-10; Sunday, 12-6. Thursdays during holiday season and summer hours until 10 p.m.

EXHIBITS Interested in all types, styles and subject matter. Charges no commission. Reviews transparencies. Accepted work should be framed work only.

SUBMISSIONS Send query letter with résumé, SASE. Responds in 2 months.

ARTPROJECTA

P.O. Box 597, Ketchum ID 883340. (208)726-3036; (208)841-9200. **E-mail:** info@artprojecta.com. **Website:** www.artprojecta.com. **Contact:** Barbi Reed (barbi@annereedgallery.com). Estab. 1912. Represents emerging talent and mid-career artists. Barbi Reed, Claudia Aulum, co-founders. Exhibited artists include: Kirk Anderson, Gary Mankus, Owen Mortensen, Andrew Romanoff, Andrew Saftel, Ruth Silverman, Bob Smith, Larry Stephenson, Maggie Hasbrouck, Lisa Holley, among others. All art retails from $65-4500. Clientele: 70% private collectors, 30% corporate collectors, art consultants, designers.

EXHIBITS Most frequently exhibits photographs, paintings, fine art prints. Exhibits expressionism, abstraction, conceptualism, photorealism, realism, landscape. Prefers contemporary. Established to provide carefully curated fine art at affordable prices. Independent consulting available to achieve the most exciting, appropriate and tasteful art to complement and enhance residential, commercial, institutional settings.

MAKING CONTACT & TERMS Retail price set by gallery and artist. Sometimes we offer client discounts. Gallery provides promotion, networking on artist's behalf, shipping costs to clients. ARTprojectA is not responsible for materials sent that are unsolicited.

SUBMISSIONS E-mail your work and include your artist website's URL. Make sure the latest work and an updated résumé are on your site.

TIPS Spend time on our website www.artprojecta.com prior to contacting us.

THE ARTS COMPANY

215 Fifth Ave., Nashville TN 37219. (615)254-2040; (877)694-2040. **Fax:** (615)254-9289. **E-mail:** art@theartscompany.com. **Website:** www.theartscompany.com. **Contact:** Anne Brown, owner. Estab. 1996. Art consultancy, for-profit gallery. Sponsors 6-10 photography exhibits/year. Average display time 1 month. Open Tuesday-Saturday, 11-5. Located in downtown Nashville, the gallery has 6,000 sq. ft. of contemporary space in a historic building. Overall price range $10-35,000. Most work sold at $300-3,000.

EXHIBITS Photos of celebrities, architecture, cities/urban, rural, environmental, landscapes/scenics, entertainment, performing arts. Interested in documentary, fine art, historical/vintage.

MAKING CONTACT & TERMS "We prefer an initial info packet via e-mail." Send query letter with artist's statement, bio, brochure, business card, photocopies, résumé, reviews, SASE, CD. Returns material with SASE.

SUBMISSIONS "Provide professional images on a CD along with a professional bio, résumé." Artwork is accepted on consignment. Gallery provides insurance, contract. Accepted work should be framed.

TIPS Finds artists through word of mouth, art fairs, art exhibits, submissions, referrals by other artists.

ARTS ON DOUGLAS

123 Douglas St., New Smyrna Beach FL 32168. (386)428-1133. **Fax:** (386)428-5008. **E-mail:** mmartin@artsondouglas.net. **Website:** www.artsondouglas.net. **Contact:** Meghan Martin, gallery director. Estab. 1996. For-profit gallery. Represents 50 Florida artists in ongoing group exhibits and features 8 artists/year in solo exhibitions. Average display time 1 month. Gallery open Tuesday-Friday, 10-5; Saturday, 11-3; by appointment. Location has 5,000 sq. ft. of exhibition space. Overall price range varies.

EXHIBITS Interested in alternative process, documentary, fine art.

MAKING CONTACT & TERMS Artwork is accepted on consignment, and there is a 50% commission. Gallery provides insurance, promotion. Accepted work

should be framed. Requires exclusive representation locally. *Accepts only professional artists from Florida.*

SUBMISSIONS Call in advance to inquire about submissions/reviews. Send a query letter and include a CD with 6 current images, bio, CV and artist's statement. Finds artists through referrals by other artists.

ART SOURCE L.A., INC.

2801 Ocean Park Blvd., #7, Santa Monica CA 90405. (310)452-4411; (800)721-8477. **Fax:** (310)452-0300. **E-mail:** info@artsourcela.com. **Website:** www.artsourcela.com. **Contact:** Francine Ellman, president. Estab. 1980. Overall price range $300-15,000. Most work sold at $600.

EXHIBITS Photos of multicultural, environmental, landscapes/scenics, wildlife, architecture, cities/urban, gardening, interiors/decorating, rural, automobiles, food/drink, travel, technology/computers. Interested in alternative process, avant garde, fine art, historical/vintage, seasonal. "We do projects worldwide, putting together fine art for corporations, health care, hospitality, government and public space. We use a lot of photography."

MAKING CONTACT & TERMS Interested in receiving work from emerging and established photographers. Charges 50% commission.

SUBMISSIONS Digital submissions only via e-mail to info@artsourcela.com.

TIPS "Show a consistent body of work, well marked and presented so it may be viewed to see its merits."

[ARTSPACE] AT UNTITLED

1 NE Third St., Oklahoma City OK 73104. (405)815-9995. **Fax:** (405)813-2070. **E-mail:** info@artspaceatuntitled.org. **Website:** www.artspaceatuntitled.org. Estab. 2003. Alternative space, nonprofit art center. Contemporary art center. Average display time: 6-12 weeks. Gallery is open to the public Wednesday–Saturday, 10-6; and Sunday, 12-6. Closed Monday–Tuesday. The [Press] at Untitled, an open printmaking studio, located within Artspace, offers memberships for artists and other creatives. The [Press] also engages photographers through demo sessions and workshops on how to create their works as hand-pulled prints. The [Press] at Untitled is open Wednesday, 10-6; Thursday-Saturday 10-10; Sunday 12-6. "Located in a reclaimed industrial space abandoned by decades of urban flight. Damaged in the 1995 Murrah Federal Building bombing, Artspace at Untitled has emerged as a force for creative thought. As part of the Deep

Deuce historic district in downtown Oklahoma City, Artspace at Untitled brings together visual arts, performance, music, film, design and architecture with a focus on innovation, works on paper and new media art. Our mission is to stimulate creative thought and new ideas through contemporary art. We are committed to providing access to quality exhibitions, educational programs, performances, publications, and to engaging the community in collaborative outreach efforts." Most work sold at $500-2,500, but not primarily a sales gallery.

MAKING CONTACT & TERMS There is a 50% commission for any works sold.

SUBMISSIONS Mail portfolio for review. Send query letter with artist's statement, bio, résumé, slides, or CD of images. Prefers 10-15 images on a CD. Include SASE for return of materials or permission to file the portfolio. Reviews occur twice annually, in January and July. Finds artists through submissions and portfolio reviews. Responds to queries within 3 months.

TIPS "Review our previous programming to evaluate if your work is along the lines of our mission. Take the time to type and proof all written submissions. Make sure your best work is represented in the images you choose to show. Nothing takes away from the review like poorly scanned or photographed work."

THE ART STORE

233 Hale St., Charleston WV 25301. (304)345-1038. **Fax:** (304)345-1858. **E-mail:** gallery@theartstorewv.com. **Website:** www.theartstorewv.com. "The Art Store is dedicated to showing original 20th-century and contemporary American art by leading local, regional and nationally recognized artists. Professional integrity, commitment and vision are the criteria for artist selection, with many artists having a history of exhibitions and museum placement. Painting, sculpture, photography, fine art prints and ceramics are among the disciplines presented. A diverse series of solo, group and invitational shows are exhibited throughout the year in the gallery." Retail gallery. Represents 50 mid-career and established artists. Sponsors 11 shows/year. Average display time 4 weeks. Open Tuesday–Friday, 10-5:30; Saturday, 10-5; anytime by appointment. Located in a upscale shopping area; 2,000 sq. ft.; 50% of space for special exhibitions. Clientele: professionals, executives, decorators. 80% private collectors, 20% corporate collectors. Overall price range $200-8,000; most work sold at $2,000.

MAKING CONTACT & TERMS Accepts artwork on consignment (50% commission). Retail price set by gallery and artist. Gallery provides insurance, promotion and shipping costs from gallery. Prefers artwork unframed.

TIPS Send query e-mail.

ASIAN AMERICAN ARTS CENTRE

111 Norfolk St., New York NY 10002. **Fax:** (360)283-2154. **E-mail:** aaacinfo@artspiral.org. **Website:** www.artspiral.org. Estab. 1974. "Our mission is to promote the preservation and creative vitality of Asian-American cultural growth through the arts, and its historical and aesthetic linkage to other communities." Exhibits should be Asian American or significantly influenced by Asian culture and should be entered into the archive-a historical record of the presence of Asia in the US. Interested in "creative art pieces." Average display time 6 weeks. Open Monday–Friday, 12:30-6:30 (by appointment).

MAKING CONTACT & TERMS To be considered for the AAAC Artist Archive and artasiamerica.org, please submit 20 images either as 35mm slides (labeled with artist's name, title, date, materials, techniques and dimensions) or digital images of work as TIFF or JPEG on CD or DVD, at minimum 2,000 pixel width with resolution of 300 dpi; corresponding artwork list with artist's name, title, date, materials, techniques and dimensions; 1 page artist statement (to be dated); artists not of Asian descent should mention specifically how they consider themselves influenced by Asia; artist bio and résumé (to be dated); other support materials (catalogs, newspaper/journal articles, reviews, announcement cards, press releases, project plans, etc.); completed AAAC information form located at www.artspiral.org/archive_submission.

ATELIER GALLERY

153 King St., Charleston SC 29401. **E-mail:** gabrielle@theateliergalleries.com. **Website:** www.theateliergalleries.com. **Contact:** Gabrielle Egan, curator and owner. Estab. 2008. Fine art gallery. Exhibits mid-career, and established artists. Represents or exhibits 60 artists. For exhibited artists, see website at www.theatelilergalleries.com. Open Monday-Friday, 10-6; Sundays, by chance. Closed Holidays. Clients include local community, students, tourists, upscale, and artists and designers. Overall price range: $50-15,000. Most work sold in the $2,500-5,000 range.

MAKING CONTACT & TERMS Artwork is accepted on consignment with a 50% commission. Retail price set by the gallery and artist. Gallery provides insurance, promotion, and contract. Atelier requires exclusive representation within 250 miles of the gallery in downtown Charleston SC.

SUBMISSIONS E-mail query letter along with 6 images of the most current body of work. Please include medium, dimensions, framing specifications, pricing. Also provide all artist contact information to include website, e-mail and telephone number. Atelier Gallery will contact each artist via e-mail once the submission has been reviewed. If more information is needed, the gallery will request it directly.

ATLANTIC GALLERY

548 W. 28th St., Suite 540, New York NY 10001. (212)219-3183. **E-mail:** info@atlanticgallery.org. **Website:** www.atlanticgallery.org. **Contact:** Jeff Miller, president. Estab. 1974. Cooperative gallery. There is a co-op membership plus a donation of time required. Approached by 50 artists/year; represents 24 emerging, mid-career and established artists. Exhibited artists include Ragnar Naess (sculptor), Sally Brody (oil, acrylic), and Whitney Hansen (oil). Average display time 4 weeks. Gallery open Tuesday, Wednesday, Friday, Saturday, 12-6; Thursday, 12-9. Closed August. Located in Chelsea. Has kitchenette. Clients include local community, tourists and upscale clients. 2% of sales are to corporate collectors. Overall price range $100-13,000. Most work sold at $1,500-5,000. Finds artists through word of mouth, submissions, art exhibits, referrals by other artists.

EXHIBITS Interested in fine art.

MAKING CONTACT & TERMS Call or write to arrange a personal interview.

SUBMISSIONS "Submit an organized folder with slides, CD, bio, and 3 pieces of actual work. If we respond with interest, we then review again." Responds in 1 month. Views submitted works monthly.

AXIS GALLERY

71 Burnett Terrace, West Orange NJ 07052. (212)741-2582. **E-mail:** info@axisgallery.com. **Website:** www.axisgallery.com. **Contact:** Lisa Brittan, director. Estab. 1997. For-profit gallery. Approached by 30 African artists/year; representative of 20 artists. Check gallery hours and show locations online; other times by appointment. Closed during summer. Overall price range $500-50,000.

EXHIBITS Interested in alternative process, avant garde, documentary, erotic, fine art, historical/vintage. Also interested in photojournalism, resistance.

MAKING CONTACT & TERMS Artwork is accepted on consignment, and there is a 50% commission. Gallery provides insurance, promotion, contract. *Only accepts artists from Africa.*

SUBMISSIONS Send digital submission with letter, résumé, reviews and images via e-mail. Responds in 3 months. Finds artists through research, recommendations, submissions, portfolio reviews, art exhibits, referrals by other artists.

TIPS "Photographers should research gallery first to check if their work fits the gallery program. Avoid bulk mailings."

BAKER ARTS CENTER

624 N. Pershing Ave., Liberal KS 67901. (620)624-2810. **Fax:** (620)624-7726. **E-mail:** dianemarsh@bakerartscenter.org. **Website:** www.bakerartscenter.org. **Contact:** Diane Marsh, art director. Estab. 1986. Nonprofit gallery. Exhibits emerging, mid-career, and established artists. Approached by 6-10 artists a year. Represents of exhibits 6-10 artists. Exhibited artists include J. McDonald (glass) and J. Gustafson (assorted). Sponsors 5 total exhibits/year. 1 photography exhibit/year. Model and property release are preferred. Average display time 40-50 days. Open Tuesday-Friday, 9-5; Saturdays, 2-5. Closed Christmas, Thanksgiving and New Year's Eve. Clients include local community, students, and tourists. Overall price range $10-1,000. Most work sold at $400.

MAKING CONTACT & TERMS Artwork is accepted on consignment and there is a 30% commission fee. Retail price set by the artist. Gallery provides insurance, promotion, and contract. Accepted work should be framed, mounted, and matted.

SUBMISSIONS Write to arrange personal interview to show portfolio or e-mail query letter with link to artist's website or JPEG samples at 72 dpi. Returns material with SASE. Responds in 2-4 weeks. Finds artists through word of mouth, submissions, art exhibits, and referrals by other artists.

BALZEKAS MUSEUM OF LITHUANIAN CULTURE ART GALLERY

6500 S. Pulaski Rd., Chicago IL 60629. (773)582-6500. **Fax:** (773)582-5133. **E-mail:** info@balzekasmuseum.org. **Website:** www.balzekasmuseum.org. **Contact:** Stanley Balzekas, Jr., president. Estab. 1996. Museum,

museum retail shop, nonprofit gallery, rental gallery. Approached by 20 artists/year. Sponsors 2 photography exhibits/year. Average display time 6 weeks. Open daily, 10-4. Closed Christmas, Easter and New Year's Day. Overall price range $150-6,000. Most work sold at $545.

EXHIBITS Photos of babies/children/teens, celebrities, couples, multicultural, families, parents, senior citizens, disasters, environmental, landscapes/scenics, wildlife, architecture, cities/urban, education, gardening, interiors/decorating, pets, religious, rural, adventure, automobiles, entertainment, events, food/drink, health/fitness, hobbies, humor, performing arts, sports, travel, agriculture, buildings, business concepts, industry, medicine, military, political, product shots/still life, science, technology/computers. Interested in alternative process, avant garde, documentary, erotic, fashion/glamour, fine art, historical/vintage, seasonal.

MAKING CONTACT & TERMS Artwork is accepted on consignment, and there is a 33⅓% commission. Gallery provides promotion. Accepted work should be framed.

SUBMISSIONS Write to arrange personal interview to show portfolio. Responds in 2 months. Finds artists through word of mouth, art exhibits, referrals by other artists.

BARRON ARTS CENTER

582 Rahway Ave., Woodbridge NJ 07095. (732)634-0413. **E-mail:** barronarts@twp.woodbridge.nj.us. **Website:** www.twp.woodbridge.nj.us/Departments/BarronArtsCenter/tabid/251/Default.aspx. **Contact:** Cynthia Knight, director. Estab. 1977. The Barron Arts Center serves as a center for the arts for residents of Woodbridge Township and Central New Jersey. Overall price range $150-400. Most work sold at $150. Charges 20% commission.

○   "In terms of the market, we tend to hear that there are not enough galleries that will exhibit photography."

SUBMISSIONS Reviews transparencies but prefers portfolio. Submit portfolio for review; include SASE for return. Responds "depending upon date of review, but generally within a month of receiving materials." CDs of photos acceptable for review. "Make a professional presentation of work with all pieces matted or treated in a like manner."

BELIAN ART CENTER

5980 Rochester Rd., Troy MI 48085. (248)828-1001. **E-mail:** zabelbelian@gmail.com. **Website:** www.belianart.com. **Contact:** Zabel Belian, gallery director. Estab. 1985. Sponsors 1-2 exhibits/year. Average display time 3 weeks. Sponsors openings. Average price range $200-2,000.

EXHIBITS Looks for originality, capturing the intended mood, perfect copy, mostly original editions. Subjects include landscapes, cities, rural, events, agriculture, buildings, still life.

MAKING CONTACT & TERMS Charges 40-50% commission. Buys photos outright. Reviews transparencies. Requires exclusive representation locally. Arrange a personal interview to show portfolio. Send query letter with résumé and SASE.

CECELIA COKER BELL GALLERY

Coker College Art Dept., 300 E. College Ave., Hartsville SC 29550. (843)383-8150. **E-mail:** artgallery@coker.edu. **Website:** www.ceceliacokerbellgallery.com. **Contact:** Jean Grosser, gallery director & department chair. "A campus-located teaching gallery that exhibits a variety of media and styles to expose students and the community to the breadth of possibility for expression in art. Exhibits include regional, national and international artists with an emphasis on quality and originality. Shows include work from emerging, mid, and late career artists." Sponsors 5 solo shows/year, with a 4-week run for each show. Open Monday–Friday, 10-4 (when classes are in session).

EXHIBITS Considers all media including installation and graphic design. Most frequently exhibits painting, photography, sculpture/installation and mixed media.

MAKING CONTACT & TERMS Retail price set by artist (sales are not common). Exclusive area representation not required. Gallery provides insurance, promotion and contract; shipping costs are shared.

SUBMISSIONS Send résumé, 15-20 JPEG files on CD (or upload them to a Dropbox account) with a list of images, statement, résumé, and SASE. Reviews, web pages, and catalogues are welcome, though not required. If you would like response, but not your submission items returned, simply include an e-mail address. Visits by artists are welcome; however, the exhibition committee will review and select all shows from the JPEGs submitted by the artists.

BENNETT GALLERIES AND COMPANY

5308 Kingston Pike, Knoxville TN 37919. (865)584-6791. **Fax:** (865)588-6130. **E-mail:** info@bennettgalleries.com. **Website:** www.bennettgalleries.com. Estab. 1985. For-profit gallery. Represents or exhibits 40 artists/year. Sponsors 1-2 photography exhibits/year. Average display time 1 month. Gallery open Monday–Thursday, 10-6; Friday–Saturday, 10-5:30. Conveniently located a few miles from downtown Knoxville in the Bearden area. The formal art gallery has over 2,000 sq. ft. and 20,000 sq. ft. of additional space. Overall price range $100-12,000. Most work sold at $400-600.

EXHIBITS Photos of landscapes/scenics, architecture, cities/urban, humor, sports, travel. Interested in alternative process, fine art, historical/vintage.

MAKING CONTACT & TERMS Artwork is accepted on consignment, and there is a 50% commission. Gallery provides insurance, promotion, contract. Accepted work should be framed. Requires exclusive representation locally.

SUBMISSIONS Mail portfolio for review. Send query letter with artist's statement, bio, photographs, SASE, CD. Responds within 1 month, only if interested. Finds artists through word of mouth, submissions, art exhibits, referrals by other artists.

TIPS When submitting material to a gallery for review, the package should include information about the artist (neatly written or typed), photographic material, and SASE if you want your materials back.

BENRUBI GALLERY

521 W. 26th Street, 2nd Floor, New York NY 10001. (212)888-6007. **Fax:** (212)751-0819. **E-mail:** info@benrubigallery.com. **Website:** www.benrubigallery.com. Estab. 1987. Sponsors 7-8 exhibits/year. Average display time 6 weeks. Overall price range $500-50,000.

EXHIBITS Interested in 19th- and 20th-century photography, mainly contemporary.

MAKING CONTACT & TERMS Charges commission. Buys photos outright. Accepted work should be matted. Requires exclusive representation locally. No manipulated work.

SUBMISSIONS Not currently accepting submissions. Submit portfolio for review; include SASE. Responds in 2 weeks. Portfolio review is the first Thursday of every month. Out-of-towners can send slides with SASE, and work will be returned.

MONA BERMAN FINE ARTS

78 Lyon St., New Haven CT 06511. (203)562-4720. **E-mail:** info@monabermanfinearts.com. **Website:** www.monabermanfinearts.com. **Contact:** Mona Berman, director. Estab. 1979. Overall price range $500-20,000.

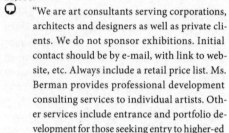 "We are art consultants serving corporations, architects and designers as well as private clients. We do not sponsor exhibitions. Initial contact should be by e-mail, with link to website, etc. Always include a retail price list. Ms. Berman provides professional development consulting services to individual artists. Other services include entrance and portfolio development for those seeking entry to higher-ed fine art and interior design programs. Ms. Berman also provides post-secondary curriculum development for higher education programs in fine arts and interior design."

EXHIBITS "Interested in all except figurative, although we do use some portrait work."

MAKING CONTACT & TERMS Charges 50% commission. "Payment to artist 30 days after receipt of payment from client."

SUBMISSIONS "E-mail digital images or web links. Inquire by e-mail; no calls, please. Always include retail prices." Unsolicited mailings will not be returned. Responds in 1 month.

TIPS "Looking for new perspectives, new images, new ideas, excellent print quality, ability to print in *very* large sizes, consistency of vision. Digital prints must be archival. Not interested in giclée prints."

BIRMINGHAM BLOOMFIELD ART CENTER

1516 S. Cranbrook Rd., Birmingham MI 48009. (248)644-0866. **E-mail:** annievangelderen@bbartcenter.org. **Website:** www.bbartcenter.org. **Contact:** Annie VanGelderen, president and CEO. Estab. 1962. Nonprofit gallery shop and gallery exhibit space. Represents emerging, mid-career and established artists. Presents ongoing exhibitions in 4 galleries. Open all year; Monday-Thursday, 9-6; Friday-Saturday, 9-5; second Sundays, 1-4. Suburban location. 70% of space for gallery artists. Clientele upscale, local. 100% private collectors. Overall price range $50-25,000.

EXHIBITS Considers 2D and 3D fine art in all media. Most frequently exhibits 3D work: jewelry, glass, ceramics, fiber, mixed media sculpture; and 2D work:

painting, printmaking, drawing, mixed media and video.

MAKING CONTACT & TERMS Accepts work on consignment (45% commission). Retail price set by the artist. Gallery provides contract and some promotion; artist pays for shipping costs to gallery.

SUBMISSIONS Send query letter with résumé, website address, digital images (preferred), photographs, review, artist's statement and bio.

TIPS "We consider conceptual content, technique, media, presentation and condition of work as well as professionalism of the artist."

BLOUNT-BRIDGERS HOUSE/HOBSON PITTMAN MEMORIAL GALLERY

130 Bridgers St., Tarboro NC 27886. (252)823-4159. **E-mail:** edgecombearts@embarqmail.com. **Website:** www.edgecombearts.org. Estab. 1982. Museum. Gallery hours vary by time of year, see website for details. Closed major holidays, Christmas-New Year. Located in historic house in residential area of small town. Gallery is approximately 48×20 ft. Overall price range $250-5,000. Most work sold at $500.

◯   Interested in fine art, historical/vintage.

EXHIBITS Photos of landscapes/scenics, wildlife. Approached by 1-2 artists/year; represents or exhibits 6 artists. Sponsors 1 exhibit/year. Average display time 6 weeks.

MAKING CONTACT & TERMS Artwork is accepted on consignment, and there is a 30% commission. Gallery provides insurance, limited promotion. Accepted work should be framed. Accepts artists from the Southeast and Pennsylvania. Finds artists through word of mouth, submissions, art exhibits, referrals by other artists.

SUBMISSIONS Mail portfolio review. Send query letter with artist's statement, bio, SASE, slides. Responds in 3 months.

BLUE GALLERY

118 Southwest Blvd., Kansas City MO 64108. (816)527-0823. **E-mail:** kellyk@bluegalleryonline.com. **Website:** www.bluegalleryonline.com. **Contact:** Kelly Kuhn, owner/director. Estab. 2000. A for-profit gallery. Exhibits emerging, mid-career, and established artists. Approached by hundreds of artists a year; represents or exhibits 45 artists a year. Sponsors 12 total exhibits/year. Average display time 30 days. Open Tuesday-Saturday, 10-5:30 or by appointment. Clients include local community, tourists, and upscale estab-

lishments among others. A large percentage is sold to corporate collectors. Overall price range $50-80,000. Finds artists through word of mouth, submissions, portfolio reviews, art exhibits, art fairs, and referrals by other artists.

MAKING CONTACT & TERMS Artwork is accepted on consignment. Retail price set by the artist. Gallery provides insurance, promotion, and contract. Accepted work should be framed. Requires exclusive representation locally.

SUBMISSIONS E-mail query letter with link to artist's website and JPEG samples at 72 dpi. Mail portfolio for review. Send query letter with artist's statement, bio, brochure, business card, photocopies, résumé, reviews, and SASE. Returns material with SASE. Responds in 3 months.

BLUE SKY/OREGON CENTER FOR THE PHOTOGRAPHIC ARTS

122 NW Eighth Ave., Portland OR 97209. (503)225-0210. **Website:** www.blueskygallery.org. **Contact:** Zemie Barr, exhibitions manager. Estab. 1975.

EXHIBITS All photography and videography considered. Exhibits documentary, photojournalism, and conceptual art. Considers all genres.

MAKING CONTACT & TERMS Artwork is accepted on consignment and there is a 50% commission. Retail price set by the artist. Gallery provides insurance, promotion, and contract. Does not require exclusive local representation.

SUBMISSIONS Submit CD of JPEG samples at 72 dpi. Include artist's statement, bio, and résumé. Returns materials with SASE. Responds in 6 weeks. Finds artists through submissions, portfolio reviews, and art fairs.

TIPS "Follow website instructions."

BOOK BEAT GALLERY

26010 Greenfield, Oak Park MI 48237. (248)968-1190. **Fax:** (248)968-3102. **E-mail:** info@thebookbeat.com; bookbeat@aol.com. **Website:** www.thebookbeat.com. **Contact:** Cary Loren, director. Estab. 1982. Sponsors 6 exhibits/year. Average display time 6-8 weeks. Overall price range $300-5,000. Most work sold at $600.

EXHIBITS "Book Beat is a bookstore specializing in fine art and photography. We have a backroom gallery devoted to photography and folk art. Our inventory includes vintage work from 19th- to 20th-century, rare books, issues of *Camerawork*, and artist books. Book Beat Gallery is looking for courageous and as-

tonishing image makers, high-quality digital work is acceptable. Artists are welcome to submit a handwritten or typed proposal for an exhibition, include artist bio, statement, and website, book or CD with sample images. We are especially interested in photographers who have published book works or work with originals in the book format, also those who work in 'dead media' and extinct processes."
SUBMISSIONS Responds in 6 weeks.

RENA BRANSTEN GALLERY

1639 Market St., San Francisco CA 94103. (415)982-3292. **Fax:** (415)982-1807. **E-mail:** info@renabrans tengallery.com; calvert@renabranstengallery.com; rena@renabranstengallery.com. **Website:** www.ren-abranstengallery.com. **Contact:** Rena Bransten, owner. Estab. 1974. For-profit gallery. Approached by 200 artists/year; represents or exhibits 12-15 artists. Average display time: 4-5 weeks. Open Tuesday–Friday, 11-5; Saturday, 11-4. Usually closed the last week of August and the first week of September. Retail price(s) set by the gallery and the artist.
SUBMISSIONS E-mail JPEG samples at 72 dpi. Finds artists through word of mouth, art exhibits, submissions, art fairs, portfolio reviews, referrals by other artists.

J.J. BROOKINGS GALLERY

330 Commercial St., San Jose CA 95112. (408)287-3311. **Fax:** (408)275-1777. **E-mail:** info@jjbrookings.com. **Website:** www.jjbrookings.com. Sponsors rotating group exhibits. Sponsors openings. Overall price range $500-30,000.
EXHIBITS Interested in photography created with a "painterly eye."
MAKING CONTACT & TERMS Charges 50% commission.
SUBMISSIONS Send material by mail for consideration. Responds in 3-5 weeks if interested; immediately if not acceptable.
TIPS Wants to see "professional presentation, realistic pricing, numerous quality images. We're interested in whatever the artist thinks will impress us the most. 'Painterly' work is best. No documentary or politically oriented work."

THE CAROLE CALO GALLERY

320 Washington St., Easton MA 02357. **Contact:** Candice Smith Corby, gallery director. Nonprofit, college gallery (formerly the Cushing-Martin Gallery). Approached by 4-8 artists/year, represents/exhibits 10-20 artists/year. Closed during the summer when school is not in session. Clients include local community and students.
MAKING CONTACT & TERMS Proceeds of sales go to the artist; sales are not common. Price set by the artist. Gallery provides insurance and promotion. Accepted work should be framed and mounted.
SUBMISSIONS Mail portfolio for review. Include artist's statement, bio, résumé, SASE, and CD. Returns material with SASE. Responds in 6 months. Files "interesting" materials. Finds artists through word of mouth, submissions, art exhibits, and referrals by other artists.

WILLIAM CAMPBELL CONTEMPORARY ART

4935 Byers Ave., Ft. Worth TX 76107. (817)737-9566. **Fax:** (817)737-5466. **E-mail:** wcca@flash.net. **Website:** www.williamcampbellcontemporaryart.com. **Contact:** William Campbell, owner/director. Estab. 1974. Sponsors 8-10 exhibits/year. Average display time 5 weeks. Sponsors openings; provides announcements, press releases, installation of work, insurance, cost of exhibition. Overall price range $500-20,000.
MAKING CONTACT & TERMS Charges 50% commission. Reviews transparencies. Accepted work should be mounted. Requires exclusive representation within metropolitan area.
SUBMISSIONS Send CD (preferred) and résumé by mail with SASE. Responds in 1 month.

CAPITOL COMPLEX EXHIBITIONS

500 S. Bronough St., R.A. Gray Bldg., Department of State, The Capitol, Tallahassee FL 32399-0250. (850)245-6490. **Fax:** (850)245-6454. **E-mail:** rachelle. ashmore@dos.myflorida.com. **Website:** www.flori da-arts.org. Average display time: 3 months. Overall price range: $200-1,000. Most work sold at $400.
EXHIBITS "The Capitol Complex Exhibitions Program is designed to showcase Florida artists and art organizations. Exhibitions are displayed in the Capitol Gallery (22nd floor) and the Cabinet Meeting Room in Florida's capitol. Exhibitions are selected based on quality, diversity of media, and regional representation."
MAKING CONTACT & TERMS Does not charge commission. Accepted work should be framed. *Interested only in Florida artists or arts organizations.*

SUBMISSIONS Download application from website, complete and send with image CD. Responds in 3 weeks.

CENTER FOR CREATIVE PHOTOGRAPHY

University of Arizona, P.O. Box 210103, 1030 North Olive Rd., Tucson AZ 85721-0103. (520)621-7968. **Fax:** (520)621-9444. **E-mail:** info@ccp.library.arizona.edu. **Website:** www.creativephotography.org. Estab. 1975. Museum/archive, research center, museum retail shop. Sponsors 3-4 photography exhibits/year. Average display time 3-4 months. Gallery open Monday–Friday, 9-5; weekends, 1-4. Closed most holidays. 5,500 sq. ft.

CENTER FOR DIVERSIFIED ART

P.O. Box 641062, Beverly Hills FL 34465. **E-mail:** diversifiedart101@gmail.com. **Website:** www.diversifiedart.org. **Contact:** Anita Walker, founder and director. Estab. 2010. Nonprofit gallery. Exhibits emerging, mid-career and established artists. Approached by 12 artists/year; represents or exhibits about 24 artists currently. Exhibited artists include David Kontra (acrylics) and Linda Litteral (sculptor). We specialize in visual art that has a social and/or environmental theme that raises awareness. Sponsors 1 exhibit/year, photography is included in our annual exhibit. One piece from each of our artists is shown indefinitely in our online gallery and publications. We are a web-based gallery and sponsor 1 brick and mortar exhibition a year. We also use visual art to go with educational material that we produce and publish. Many of our artists have a strong commitment to raising awareness. Clients include the local community and students. Overall price range: $150-4,000.

EXHIBITS Considers all media and all types of prints (prints must be a limited edition and include a certificate of authenticity).

MAKING CONTACT & TERMS Artwork is accepted on consignment and there is a 20% commission. Retail price set by the artist. Gallery provides promotion. Accepted work should be framed.

SUBMISSIONS Please make sure your work has a social and/or environmental theme that raises awareness before submitting. E-mail query letter with link to artist's website, 3 JPEG samples at 72 dpi, résumé and how your work relates to raising awareness on social and/or environmental issues. Responds only if interested within 1 month. Finds artists through word of mouth, art exhibits, submissions, portfolio reviews and referrals by other artists.

TIPS Follow the directions above.

⊛ CENTER FOR EXPLORATORY AND PERCEPTUAL ART

617 Main St., Suite 201, Buffalo NY 14203. (716)856-2717. **Fax:** (716)270-0184. **E-mail:** info@cepagallery.com. **Website:** www.cepagallery.org. **Contact:** Sean J. Donaher, executive director. Estab. 1974. "CEPA is an artist-run space dedicated to presenting photographically based work that is under-represented in tradiional cultural institutions." Sponsors 5-6 exhibits/year. Average display time 6 weeks. Call or see website for hours. Total gallery space is approximately 6,500 sq. ft. Overall price range $200-3,500.

○ CEPA conducts an annual Emerging Artist Exhibition for its members. You must join the gallery in order to participate.

EXHIBITS Interested in political, digital, video, culturally diverse, contemporary and conceptual works. Extremely interested in exhibiting work of newer, lesser-known photographers.

MAKING CONTACT & TERMS Sponsors openings; reception with lecture. Accepted work should be framed or unframed, mounted or unmounted, matted or unmatted.

SUBMISSIONS Send query letter with artist's statement, résumé that will give insight into your work. "Up to 20 numbered slides with a separate checklist (work will not be considered without a complete checklist). Each slide must have your name, a number, and an indication of 'top.' The checklist must have your name, address, phone/fax/e-mail, title of the work, date, image size, process, and presentation size. Do not send prints or original works. CDs running on a MAC platform may be submitted." Include SASE for return of material. Responds in 3 months.

TIPS "We review CD portfolios and encourage digital imagery. We will be showcasing work on our website."

CENTER FOR PHOTOGRAPHIC ART

Sunset Cultural Center, P.O. Box 1100, Carmel CA 93921. (831)625-5181. **Fax:** (831)625-5199. **E-mail:** info@photography.org. **Website:** www.photography.org. Estab. 1988. Nonprofit gallery. Sponsors 7-8 exhibits/year. Average display time 5-7 weeks. Hours: Wednesday-Saturday, 12-4.

EXHIBITS Interested in fine art photography.

SUBMISSIONS "Currently not accepting unsolicited submissions. Please e-mail the center and ask to be added to our submissions contact list if you are not a member." Photographers should see website for more information.

THE CENTER FOR PHOTOGRAPHY AT WOODSTOCK

59 Tinker St., Woodstock NY 12498. (845)679-9957. **Fax:** (845)679-6337. **E-mail:** info@cpw.org. **Website:** www.cpw.org. **Contact:** Ariel Shanberg, executive director. Estab. 1977. Alternative space, nonprofit arts and education center. Approached by more than 500 artists/year. Hosts 10 photography exhibits/year. Average display time 7 weeks. Gallery open all year; Wednesday–Sunday, 12-5.

EXHIBITS Interested in presenting all aspects of contemporary creative photography including digital media, film, video, and installation by emerging and under-recognized artists. "We host 5 group exhibitions and 5 solo exhibitions annually. Group exhibitions are curated by guest jurors, curators, and CPW staff. Solo exhibition artists are selected by CPW staff. Visit the exhibition archives on our website to learn more."

MAKING CONTACT & TERMS CPW hosts exhibition and opening reception; provides insurance, promotion, a percentage of shipping costs, installation and de-installation, and honorariaum for solo exhibition artists who give gallery talks. CPW receives 25% commission on exhibition-related sales. Accepted work should be framed and ready for hanging.

SUBMISSIONS Send introductory letter with samples, résumé, artist's statement, SASE. Responds in 4 months. Finds artists through word of mouth, art exhibits, open calls, portfolio reviews, referrals by other artists.

TIPS "CPW accepts submissions on thumbdrives, CD-ROMs and accepts video works in DVD format. Please send 10-20 digital work samples on CD (3×5 no larger than 300 dpi) by mail (include an image script with your name, telephone number, image title, image media, size). Include a current résumé, statement, SASE for return. We are not responsible for unlabeled submission. We *do not* welcome solicitations to visit websites. We *do* advise artists to visit our website and become familiar with our offerings."

CENTRAL MICHIGAN UNIVERSITY ART GALLERY

University Art Gallery, Wightman 132, Central Michigan University, Mt. Pleasant MI 48859. (989)774-3800. **E-mail:** gochelas@cmich.edu. **Website:** www.uag.cmich.edu. **Contact:** Anne Gochenour, gallery director. Estab. 1970. Nonprofit academic gallery. Exhibits emerging, mid-career and established contemporary artists. Past artists include Sandy Skoglund, Michael Ferris, Blake Williams, John Richardson, Valerie Allen, Randal Crawford, Jane Gilmor, Denise Whitebread Fanning, Alynn Guerra, Dylan Miner, Mark Menjivar, Jason DeMarte, Paho Mann, Al Wildey, Hillerbrand and Magsamen, Susana Raab, Peter Menzel. Sponsors 12 exhibits/year (2-4 curated). Average display time: 1 month. Open August-May whileexhibits are present; Tuesday–Friday, 11-6; Saturday, 11-3. Clients include local community, students and tourists.

EXHIBITS Considers all media and all types of prints. Most frequently exhibits sculpture, prints, ceramics, painting and photography.

MAKING CONTACT & TERMS Buyers are referred to the artist. Gallery provides insurance, promotion and contract. Accepted work should be framed. Does not require exclusive representation locally.

SUBMISSIONS Send query letter with artist's statement, bio, résumé, reviews, and images on CD. Responds within 2 months, only if interested. Finds artists through word of mouth, submissions, portfolio reviews, art exhibits, and referrals by other artists.

CHABOT FINE ART GALLERY

Chabot Fine Art Gallery, P.O. Box 623, Greenville RI 02828. (401)432-7783. **Fax:** (401)432-7783. **E-mail:** chris@chabotgallery.com. **Website:** www.chabotgallery.com. **Contact:** Chris Chabot, director. Estab. 2007. Fine art rental gallery. Approached by 50 artists/year; represents 30 emerging, mid-career and established artists. Exhibited artists include Lee Chabot (owner of the gallery). Sponsors 12 total exhibits/year; 1 photography exhibit/year. Average display time 30 days. Open Tuesday-Saturday, 12-6, or by appointment or chance. The gallery is located on Historic Federal Hill in Providence. It has over 1,000 sq. ft. of exhibition space and a courtyard sculpture garden that is open in the warmer months. Clients include local community, tourists, upscale. 10% corporate collectors. Overall price range: $1,200-10,000. Most work sold at $3,500.

EXHIBITS Considers all media except craft. Most frequently exhibits oil, acrylics and watercolor. Considers all styles and genres. Most frequently exhibits abstract, impressionism, abstract expressionism.

MAKING CONTACT & TERMS Artwork is accepted on consignment with a 50% commission. Retail price is set by the gallery and artist. Gallery provides insurance, promotion, and contract. Accepted work should be framed, mounted, and matted.

SUBMISSIONS Mail portfolio for review. Send query letter with artist's statement, bio, résumé, CD with images, and SASE. Returns material with SASE. Responds in 1 month. Files all submitted material. Finds artist through word of mouth, submissions, portfolio reviews, art exhibits, and referrals by other artists. "We are not taking submissions at this time. We will announce when we are looking for artists to display their works on the new site."

TIPS Be professional in your presentation, have good images in your portfolio, and submit all necessary information.

○ THE CHAIT GALLERIES DOWNTOWN

218 E. Washington St., Iowa City IA 52240. (319)338-4442. **Fax:** (319)338-3380. **E-mail:** attendant@thegalleriesdowntown.com; terri@thegalleriesdowntown.com; bpchait@aol.com. **Website:** www.chaitgalleries.com. **Contact:** Benjamin Chait, director. Estab. 2003. For-profit gallery. Approached by 100 artists/year; represents or exhibits 150 artists. Open Monday–Friday, 10-6; Saturday, 10-5; Sunday, 12-4. Located in a downtown building renovated to its original look of 1883 with 14-ft.-high molded ceiling and original 9-ft. front door. Professional museum lighting and Scamozzi-capped columns complete the elegant gallery. Overall price range: $50-10,000.

EXHIBITS Landscapes, oil and acrylic paintings, sculpture, fused glass wall pieces, jewelry, all types of prints.

MAKING CONTACT & TERMS Artwork is accepted on consignment, and there is a 50% commission. Gallery provides insurance, promotion and contract. Accepted work should be framed.

SUBMISSIONS Call; mail portfolio for review. Responds to queries in 2 weeks. Or, stop in anytime during normal business hours with a couple samples.

Finds artists through art fairs, art exhibits, portfolio reviews and referrals by other artists.

CHAPMAN FRIEDMAN GALLERY

1835 Hampden Court, Louisville KY 40205. (502)584-7954. **E-mail:** friedman@imagesol.com. **Website:** www.imagesol.com. **Contact:** Julius Friedman, owner. Estab. 1992. For-profit gallery. Approached by 100 or more artists/year; represents or exhibits 25 artists. Sponsors 1 photography exhibit/year. Average display time 1 month. Open by appointment only. Located downtown; approximately 3,500 sq. ft. with 15-ft. ceilings and white walls. Overall price range: $75-10,000. Most work sold at more than $1,000.

EXHIBITS Photos of landscapes/scenics, architecture. Interested in alternative process, avant garde, erotic, fine art.

MAKING CONTACT & TERMS Artwork is accepted on consignment, and there is a 50% commission. Gallery provides insurance, promotion and contract. Accepted work should be framed. Requires exclusive representation locally.

SUBMISSIONS Send query letter with artist's statement, bio, brochure, photographs, résumé, slides and SASE. Responds to queries within 1 month, only if interested. Finds artists through portfolio reviews and referrals by other artists.

CLAMPART

531 W. 25th St., Ground Floor, New York NY 10001. (646)230-0020. **E-mail:** info@clampart.com; portfolioreview@clampart.com. **Website:** www.clampart.com. **Contact:** Brian Paul Clamp, director. Estab. 2000. For-profit gallery. Specializes in modern and contemporary paintings and photographs. Approached by 1,200 artists/year; represents 15 emerging, mid-career and established artists. Exhibited artists include Jill Greenberg (photography), Lori Nix (photography) and Mark Beard (painting). See portfolio review guidelines at www.clampart.com/portfolio.html.

EXHIBITS Photos of couples, disasters, environmental, landscapes/scenics, architecture, cities/urban, humor, performing arts, travel, science, technology/computers. Interested in alternative process, avant garde, documentary, erotic, fashion/glamour, fine art, historical/vintage.

MAKING CONTACT & TERMS Artwork is accepted on consignment, and there is a 50% commission. Gal-

lery provides insurance, promotion and contract. Accepted work should be framed, mounted and matted.
SUBMISSIONS E-mail query letter with artist's statement, bio and JPEGs (JPEGs larger than 72 dpi at 8×8 will not be accepted). Responds to queries in 2 weeks. Finds artists through portfolio reviews, submissions and referrals by other artists.
TIPS "Include a bio and well-written artist's statement. Do not submit work to a gallery that does not handle the general kind of work you produce."

CATHARINE CLARK GALLERY

248 Utah St., San Francisco CA 94103. (415)399-1439. **Fax:** (415)543-1338. **E-mail:** info@cclarkgallery.com. **Website:** www.cclarkgallery.com. **Contact:** Catherine Clark, owner/director. Estab. 1991. For-profit gallery. Approached by 1,000 artists/year; represents or exhibits 28 artists. Sponsors 1-3 photography exhibits/year. Average display time 4-6 weeks. Overall price range $200-150,000. Most work sold at $5,000. Charges 50% commission. Gallery provides insurance, promotion.
SUBMISSIONS Accepted work should be ready to hang. Requires exclusive representation locally. "Do not call." No unsolicited submissions. Finds artists through word of mouth, art exhibits, art fairs, referrals by other artists and colleagues.
TIPS Interested in alternative process, avant garde. "The work shown tends to be vanguard with respect to medium, concept and process."

STEPHEN COHEN GALLERY

7354 Beverly Blvd., Los Angeles CA 90036. (323)937-5525. **Fax:** (323)937-5523. **E-mail:** info@stephencohengallery.com; claudia@stephencohengallery.com. **Website:** www.stephencohengallery.com. Estab. 1992. Photography, photo-related art, works on paper gallery. Exhibits vintage and contemporary photography and photo-based art from the US, Europe, Asia, and Latin America. The gallery is also able to locate work by photographers not represented in the gallery. The Cohen Gallery works with contemporary artists/photographers and has a large inventory of classic photography. Average display time 7-8 weeks. Open Tuesday-Saturday, 11-6. Overall price range $500-20,000. Most work sold at $2,000.
EXHIBITS All styles of photography and photo-based art. "The Gallery has exhibited vintage and contemporary photography and photo-based art from the United States, Europe and Latin America. The gallery is also able to locate work by photographers not

represented by the gallery. As host gallery for Photo LA, the gallery has helped to expand the awareness of photography as an art form to be appreciated by the serious collector."
SUBMISSIONS Send query letter, or e-mail, with artist's statement, bio, brochure, photographs, résumé, reviews, SASE. Responds within 3 months, only if interested. Finds artists through word of mouth, published work.
TIPS "Photography is still the best bargain in 20th-century art. There are more people collecting photography now, increasingly sophisticated and knowledgeable people aware of the beauty and variety of the medium."

THE CONTEMPORARY ARTS CENTER (CINCINNATI)

44 E. Sixth St., Cincinnati OH 45202. (513)345-8400. **Fax:** (513)721-7418. **E-mail:** jludwig@contemporaryartscenter.org. **Website:** www.contemporaryartscenter.org. **Contact:** Justine Ludwig, adjunct curator. Nonprofit arts center. Without a permanent collection, all exhibitions on view are temporary and ever-changing. Sponsors 9 exhibits/year. Average display time 6-12 weeks. Sponsors openings; provides printed invitations, music, refreshments, cash bar. Open Saturday-Monday, 10-4; Wednesday–Friday, 10-9. Closed Thanksgiving, Christmas and New Year's Day.
EXHIBITS Photographer must be selected by the curator and approved by the board. Exhibits photos of multicultural, disasters, environmental, landscapes/scenics, gardening, technology/computers. Interested in avant garde, innovative photography, fine art.
MAKING CONTACT & TERMS Photography sometimes sold in gallery. Charges 15% commission.
SUBMISSIONS Send query with résumé, slides, SASE. Responds in 2 months.

CONTEMPORARY ARTS CENTER (LAS VEGAS)

CAC @ Emergency Arts, 6th and Fremont, Suite 154, P.O. Box 582, Las Vegas NV 89125. (702)496-0569. **E-mail:** info@lasvegascac.org. **Website:** www.lasvegascac.org. Estab. 1989. "The CAC is a nonprofit 501(c)3 art organization dedicated to presenting new, high-quality, visual, and performing art, while striving to build, educate, and sustain audiences for contemporary art." Sponsors more than 9 exhibits/year. Average display time: 1 month. Gallery open Thursday-Friday, 3-7; Saturday-Sunday, 2-7, and by appointment. Preview Thursday, 6-9; 1st Friday, 6-8. Closed Thanksgiving, Christmas, New Year's Day. 1,200 sq. ft. Overall price range $200-4,000. Most work sold at $400.

○ "The CAC is accepting submissions of work for East Side Projects, a series of monthly projects in the gallery's front window space facing Charleston Blvd. This ongoing call is open to all contemporary artists working in any media. Artists must be current CAC members (defined as dues-paying members starting at the $25 level) in order to be eligible for consideration. To become a member go to lasvegascac.org/support/join. Site-specific work for the space is encouraged. We encourage artists to visit or e-mail the gallery to see the space."

MAKING CONTACT & TERMS Artwork is accepted through annual call for proposals of individual or group shows. Gallery provides insurance, promotion, contract.

SUBMISSIONS Finds artists through annual call for proposals, membership, word of mouth, submissions, portfolio reviews, art exhibits, art fairs, referrals by other artists and walk-ins. Check website for dates and submission guidelines. Submissions must include a proposal, current CV/résumé, artist bio/statement, disc with JPEG images of original artwork (300 dpi) and image reference sheet (including artist, title, media, dimensions, and filename). Send SASE for return.

TIPS Submitted slides should be "well labeled and properly exposed with correct color balance."

CONTEMPORARY ARTS CENTER (NEW ORLEANS)

900 Camp St., New Orleans LA 70130. (504)528-3805. **Fax:** (504)528-3828. **E-mail:** jfrancino@cacno.org; info@cacno.org. **Website:** www.cacno.org. **Contact:** Jennifer Francino, visual arts manager. Estab. 1976.

EXHIBITS Interested in alternative process, avant garde, fine art. Cutting-edge contemporary preferred.

MAKING CONTACT & TERMS Send query letter with bio, SASE, slides or CD. Responds in 4 months. Finds artists through word of mouth, submissions, art exhibits, art fairs, referrals by other artists, professional contacts, art periodicals.

TIPS Submit only 1 slide sheet with proper labels (title, date, media, dimensions) or CD-ROM with the same information.

CORCORAN FINE ARTS LIMITED, INC.

12610 Larchmere Blvd., Cleveland OH 44120. (216)767-0770. **Fax:** (216)767-0774. **E-mail:** corcoranfinearts@gmail.com; gallery@corcoranfinearts.com. **Website:** www.corcoranfinearts.com. **Contact:** James Corcoran, director/owner. Estab. 1986. 36 years of gallery and certified appraisal expertise. Represents 30 artists, many Cleveland School 1900-2013 paintings, drawings, prints and graphics. 18th-, 19th- and 20th-century American, Canadian and European art. Open Monday-Friday, 12-6; Saturday, 12-5 and by appointment.

EXHIBITS Interested in fine art. Specializes in representing high-quality 19th- and 20th-century work.

MAKING CONTACT & TERMS Gallery receives 50% commission. Requires exclusive representation. Few contemporary artists represented locally.

SUBMISSIONS For first contact, send a query letter, résumé, bio, slides, JPEGs and catalog details, SASE. Responds within 1 month. After initial contact, drop-off or mail-in appropriate materials for review by gallery director Gary Marshall and owner James Corcoran. Portfolio should include photographs/slides. Additionally finds artists through solicitation.

CO|SO: COPLEY SOCIETY OF ART

158 Newbury St., Boston MA 02116. (617)536-5049. **Fax:** (617)267-9396. **E-mail:** info@copleysociety.org. **Website:** www.copleysociety.org. **Contact:** Suzan Redgate, executive director. Estab. 1879. Co|So is the oldest nonprofit art association in the US. Sponsors 20-30 exhibits/year, including solo exhibitions, thematic group shows, juried competitions and fundraising events. Average display time: 4-6 weeks. Open Tuesday–Saturday, 11-6; Sunday, 12-5, Monday by appointment. Overall price range: $100-10,000. Most work sold at $700.

EXHIBITS Interested in all styles.

MAKING CONTACT & TERMS Must apply and be accepted as an artist member. "Once accepted, artists are eligible to compete in juried competitions. Artists can also display or show smaller works in the lower gallery throughout the year." Guaranteed showing in annual Small Works Show. There is a possibility of group or individual show, on an invitational basis, if merit exists. Charges 40% commission. Reviews digital images only with application. Preliminary application available via website. "If invited to apply to membership committee, a date would be agreed upon."

SUBMISSIONS Digital images must be saved on CD as JPEG files of 300 dpi resolution (approx. size: 4×6) with file names in the format: "LastName_FirstName_Title_Number" (for example: Doe_John_TitleofFirst Piece_1). Three views of each 3D artwork are recommended. All images must be professionally presented: frames should not be visible, and colors should match those of the original piece as closely as possible.

TIPS Wants to see "professional, concise and informative completion of application. The weight of the judgment for admission is based on quality of work. Only the strongest work is accepted.

COURTHOUSE GALLERY, LAKE GEORGE ARTS PROJECT

1 Amherst St., Lake George NY 12845. (518)668-2616. **E-mail:** mail@lakegeorgearts.org. **Website:** www.lakegeorgearts.org. **Contact:** Laura Von Rosk, gallery director. Estab. 1986. Nonprofit gallery. Approached by more than 200 artists/year; represents or exhibits 10-15 artists. Sponsors 1-2 photography exhibits/year. Average display time 5-6 weeks. Gallery open Tuesday-Friday, 12-5; weekends, 12-4. Closed mid-December to mid-January. Overall price range $100-5,000. Most work sold at $500.

MAKING CONTACT & TERMS Artwork is accepted on consignment and there is a 25% commission. Gallery provides insurance, promotion, contract. Accepted work should be framed, mounted, matted.

SUBMISSIONS Mail portfolio for review. Deadline: January 31. Send query letter with artist's statement, bio, résumé, 10-12 JPEG images (approximately 4-6 inches and no more than 1200×1200 pixels) on a CD, SASE. Responds in 4 months. Finds artists through word of mouth, submissions, portfolio reviews, art exhibits, art fairs, referrals by other artists.

CATHERINE COUTURIER GALLERY

2635 Colquitt St., Houston TX 77098. (713)524-5070. **E-mail:** gallery@catherinecouturier.com. **Website:** www.catherinecouturier.com. Estab. 1996. Fine art photography. Average display time 5 weeks. Open Tuesday–Saturday, 10-5 and by appointment. Located in upper Kirby District of Houston, Texas. Overall price range $500-40,000. Most work sold at $1,000-2,500.

EXHIBITS Photos of babies/children/teens, celebrities, couples, multicultural, families, parents, senior citizens, landscapes/scenics, wildlife, architecture, cities/urban, education, pets, religious, rural, adventure, automobiles, entertainment, events, humor, performing arts, travel, agriculture, industry, military, political, portraits, product shots/still life, science, technology/computers. Interested in alternative process, documentary, fashion/glamour, fine art, historical/vintage.

MAKING CONTACT & TERMS Artwork is bought outright or accepted on consignment with a 50% commission. Gallery provides insurance, promotion, contract.

SUBMISSIONS Call to show portfolio of photographs. Finds artists through submissions, art exhibits. Due to the volume of submissions, only able to review work once or twice a year. We only accept submissions via mail. E-mailed submissions will not be viewed. Send at least one printed sample of your work so that we may judge the quality of print you produce. Enclose a SASE with your submission so we may return the work to you if we decide it is not suited for Catherine Couturier Gallery. Any unsolicited work sent without return postage will not be returned.

○ CREALDÉ SCHOOL OF ART

600 St. Andrews Blvd., Winter Park FL 32792. (407)671-1886. **Fax:** (407)671-0311. **E-mail:** btiffany2000@yahoo.com. **Website:** www.crealde.org. **Contact:** Barbara Tiffany, director of painting & drawing. Estab. 1975. "The school's gallery holds 6-7 exhibitions/year, representing artists from regional/national stature." Open Monday–Thursday, 9-4; Friday–Saturday, 9-1.

EXHIBITS All media.

MAKING CONTACT & TERMS Send 20 slides or digital images, résumé, statement and return postage.

CROSSMAN GALLERY

950 W. Main St., Whitewater WI 53190. (262)472-5708 (office); (262)472-1207 (gallery). **E-mail:** flanagam@uww.edu. **Website:** blogs.uww.edu/crossman. **Contact:** Michael Flanagan, director. Estab. 1971. Photography is regularly featured in thematic exhibits at the gallery. Average display time: 1 month. Overall price range: $250-3,000. Located on the 1st floor of the Center of the Arts on the campus of the University of Wisconsin-Whitewater. Open Monday–Friday, 10-5; Monday–Thursday evening, 6-8; Saturday, 1-4. Special hours may apply when classes are not in session. Please call before visiting to insure access.

EXHIBITS "We primarily exhibit artists from the Midwest but do include some from national and international venues. Works by Latino artists are also featured in a regular series of ongoing exhibits." Interested in all types of innovative approaches to photography. Sponsors openings; provides food, beverage, show announcement, mailing, shipping (partial) and possible visiting artist lecture/demo.

SUBMISSIONS Submit 10-20 images on CD, artist's statement, résumé, SASE.

TIPS "The Crossman Gallery operates within a university environment. The focus is on exhibits that have the potential to educate viewers about processes and techniques and have interesting thematic content."

DARKROOM GALLERY

12 Main St., Essex Junction VT 05452. (802)777-3686. **E-mail:** info@darkroomgallery.com; submissions@darkroomgallery.com. **Website:** www.darkroomgallery.com. **Contact:** Ken Signorello, owner. Estab. 2010. For-profit and rental gallery. Exhibits 300 emerging, mid-career and established artists. Sponsors 14 photography exhibits/year. Average display time 3½ weeks. Open Monday-Sunday, 11-4; closed on major holidays. The gallery is a freshly renovated 1300-sq.-ft. first floor store front air conditioned space with hardwood floors and an 11-ft. ceiling. Our lighting system uses 3,000 LED flood lights. Nearly every image has a dedicated light and hangs from a fully adjustable hanging system. We are located at the "Five Corners" right next to Martone's Market and Café. The Village of Essex Junction is located within 10 miles of the University of Vermont and 3 other colleges, downtown Burlington and Burlington International Airport. Clients include local community, students, tourists and upscale. Overall price range $50-300. Most work sold at $200.

EXHIBITS Most frequently exhibits photography. Considers all styles.

MAKING CONTACT & TERMS Artwork is accepted on consignment and there is a 34-66% commission. Retail price of the art is set by the artist. Accepted work should be framed, mounted and matted.

SUBMISSIONS Returns material with SASE. Responds in 1 week. Files prints up to 13×19. Finds artists through submissions.

THE DAYTON ART INSTITUTE

456 Belmonte Park N., Dayton OH 45405-4700. (937)223-5277. **Fax:** (937)223-3140. **E-mail:** info@daytonart.org. **Website:** www.daytonartinstitute.org. Es-

tab. 1919. Museum. Galleries open Tuesday-Saturday, 11-5; Thursday, 11-8; Sunday, 12-5.

EXHIBITS Interested in fine art.

DELAWARE CENTER FOR THE CONTEMPORARY ARTS

200 S. Madison St., Wilmington DE 19801. (302)656-6466. **E-mail:** alaszczkowska@thedcca.org. **Website:** www.thedcca.org. **Contact:** Annette Laszczkowska, curatorial assistant. Alternative space, museum retail shop, nonprofit gallery. Approached by more than 800 artists/year; exhibits 50 artists. Sponsors 30 total exhibits/year. Average display time: 6 weeks. Gallery open Tuesday, Thursday, Friday, and Saturday, 10-5; Wednesday and Sunday, 12-5. Closed on Monday and major holidays. Seven galleries located along rejuvenated Wilmington riverfront.

EXHIBITS Interested in alternative process, avant garde.

MAKING CONTACT & TERMS Gallery provides PR and contract. Accepted work should be framed, mounted, matted. Prefers only contemporary art.

SUBMISSIONS Send query letter with artist's statement, bio, SASE, 10 digital images. Returns material with SASE. Does not accept original artwork or slides for consideration. Responds within 6 months. Finds artists through calls for entry, word of mouth, submissions, portfolio reviews, art exhibits, referrals by other artists.

DEMUTH MUSEUM

120 E. King St., Lancaster PA 17602. (717)299-9940. **E-mail:** information@demuth.org. **Website:** www.demuth.org. **Contact:** Gallery director. Estab. 1981. Museum. Average display time 2 months. Open Tuesday–Saturday, 10-4; Sunday, 1-4. Located in the home and studio of Modernist artist Charles Demuth (1883-1935). Exhibitions feature the museum's permanent collection of Demuth's works with changing, temporary exhibitions.

DETROIT FOCUS

P.O. Box 843, Royal Oak MI 48068-0843. (248)541-2210. **E-mail:** michael@sarnacki.com. **Website:** www.detroitfocus.org. Estab. 1978. Artist alliance. Approached by 100 artists/year; represents or exhibits 100 artists. Sponsors 1 or more photography exhibit/year.

EXHIBITS Interested in photojournalism, avant garde, documentary, erotic, fashion/glamour, fine art.

MAKING CONTACT & TERMS No charge or commission.

SUBMISSIONS Call or e-mail. Responds in 1 week. Finds artists through word of mouth, submissions, art exhibits, referrals by other artists.

SAMUEL DORSKY MUSEUM OF ART

1 Hawk Dr., New Paltz NY 12561. (845)257-3844. **Fax:** (845)257-3854. **E-mail:** sdma@newpaltz.edu. **Website:** www.newpaltz.edu/museum. **Contact:** Committee. Estab. 1964. Sponsors ongoing photography exhibits throughout the year. Average display time: 4 months. Museum open Wednesday–Sunday, 11-5. Closed legal and school holidays and during intersession; check website to confirm your visit.

EXHIBITS Interested in alternative process, avant garde, documentary, fine art, historical/vintage.

SUBMISSIONS "If you are an artist or a curator and you would like to submit a proposal, please review our mission statement and past and upcoming exhibitions web pages. If you feel that your exhibition is relevant to our mission and programming and wish to propose an exhibition, please submit a proposal that includes the following: Cover letter with contact information, exhibition proposal detailing the themes and artist(s) included in the exhibit, and the exhibition's relevance to the mission of The Dorsky MuseumOrganizer's CV, illustrated checklist with artist name, date, medium, and dimensions for each entry, images/videos on disk, high-resolution prints, or link to Dropbox or targeted website, a SASE for materials to be returned. Please mail submissions to: Curator, Samuel Dorsky Museum of Art State University of New York at New Paltz, 1 Hawk Drive, New Paltz, NY 12561. Submissions can also be emailed, Attn: Curator, to sdma@newpaltz.edu. Attachments may not exceed 10 MB in total. Exhibition proposals are reviewed by the staff on an ongoing basis. Materials sent without a SASE will not be returned." Finds artists through art exhibits.

○ DOT FIFTYONE GALLERY

187 NW 27th St., Miami FL 33127. (305)573-9994, ext. 450. **E-mail:** info@dotfiftyone.com; dot@dotfiftyone.com. **Website:** www.dotfiftyone.com. Estab. 2003. Sponsors 6 photography exhibits per year. Average display time: 30 days. Clients include the local community, tourists, and upscale corporate collectors. Art sold for $1,000-20,000 (avg. $5,000) with a 50% commission. Prices are set by the gallery and the artist. Gallery provides insurance, promotion and contract.

Work should be framed, mounted and matted. Will respond within 1 month if interested.

MAKING CONTACT & TERMS E-mail 5 JPEG samples at 72 dpi.

GEORGE EASTMAN HOUSE

900 East Ave., Rochester NY 14607. (585)271-3361. **Website:** www.eastmanhouse.org. Estab. 1947. Museum. "As the world's preeminent museum of photography, Eastman House cares for and interprets hundreds of thousands of photographs encompassing the full history of this medium. We are also one of the oldest film archives in the US and now considered to be among the top cinematic collections worldwide." Approached by more than 400 artists/year. Sponsors more than 12 photography exhibits/year. Average display time 3 months. Gallery open Tuesday-Saturday, 10-5; Sunday, 11-5. Closed Thanksgiving and Christmas. Museum has 7 galleries that host exhibitions, ranging from 50- to 300-print displays.

EXHIBITS GEH is a museum that exhibits the vast subjects, themes and processes of historical and contemporary photography.

SUBMISSIONS See website for detailed information: eastmanhouse.org/inc/collections/submissions.php. Mail portfolio for review. Send query letter with artist's statement, résumé, SASE, slides, digital prints. Responds in 3 months. Finds artists through word of mouth, art exhibits, referrals by other artists, books, catalogs, conferences, etc.

TIPS "Consider as if you are applying for a job. You must have succinct, well-written documents; a well-selected number of visual treats that speak well with written document provided; an easel for reviewer to use."

CATHERINE EDELMAN GALLERY

300 W. Superior St., Lower Level, Chicago IL 60654. (312)266-2350. **Fax:** (312)266-1967. **E-mail:** tim@edelmangallery.com. **Website:** www.edelmangallery.com. **Contact:** Tim Campos, gallery manager. Estab. 1987. Sponsors 7 exhibits/year. Average display time 8-10 weeks. Open Tuesday–Saturday, 10-5:30. Overall price range $1,500-25,000.

EXHIBITS "We exhibit works ranging from traditional photography to mixed media photo-based work."

MAKING CONTACT & TERMS Charges 50% commission. Requires exclusive representation in the Midwest.

SUBMISSIONS Currently not accepting unsolicited submissions. Submissions policy on the website.

TIPS Looks for "consistency, dedication and honesty. Try to not be overly eager and realize that the process of arranging an exhibition takes a long time. The relationship between gallery and photographer is a partnership."

PAUL EDELSTEIN STUDIO AND GALLERY

540 Hawthorne St., Memphis TN 38112-5029. (901)496-8122. **E-mail:** henrygrove@yahoo.com. **Website:** www.pauledelsteinstudioandgallery.com. **Contact:** Paul R. Edelstein, director/owner. Estab. 1985. "Shows are presented continually throughout the year." Overall price range: $300-10,000. Most work sold at $1,000.

EXHIBITS Photos of celebrities, children, multicultural, families. Interested in avant garde, historical/vintage, C-print, dye transfer, ever color, fine art and 20th-century photography that intrigues the viewer—figurative still life, landscape, abstract—by upcoming and established photographers.

MAKING CONTACT & TERMS Charges 50% commission. Buys photos outright. Reviews transparencies. Accepted work should be framed or unframed, mounted or unmounted, matted or unmatted work. There are no size limitations. Submit portfolio for review. Send query letter with samples. Cannot return material. Responds in 3 months.

TIPS "Looking for figurative and abstract figurative work."

THOMAS ERBEN GALLERY

526 W. 26th St., Floor 4, New York NY 10001. (212)645-8701. **Fax:** (212)645-9630. **E-mail:** info@thomaserben.com. **Website:** www.thomaserben.com. Estab. 1996. For-profit gallery. Approached by 100 artists/year; represents or exhibits 15 artists. Average display time 5-6 weeks. Gallery open Tuesday–Saturday, 10-6 (Monday–Friday in July). Closed Christmas/New Year's Day and August.

SUBMISSIONS Mail portfolio for review. Responds in 1 month.

ETHERTON GALLERY

135 S. Sixth Ave., Tucson AZ 85701. (520)624-7370. **Fax:** (520)792-4569. **E-mail:** info@ethertongallery.com. **Website:** www.ethertongallery.com. **Contact:** Terry Etherton. Estab. 1981. Retail gallery and art consultancy. Specializes in vintage, modern and contemporary photography. Represents 50+ emerging, mid-career and established artists. Exhibited artists include Kate Breakey, Harry Callahan, Jack Dykinga, Elliott Erwitt, Mark Klett, Danny Lyon, Rodrigo Moya, Luis Gonzalez Palma, Lisa M. Robinson, Frederick Sommer, Joel-Peter Witkin and Alex Webb. Sponsors 3-5 shows/year. Average display time: 8 weeks. Open year round. Located in downtown Tucson; 3,000-sq.-ft. gallery in historic building with wood floors and 16-ft. ceilings. Clientele: 50% private collectors, 25% corporate collectors, 25% museums. Overall price range: $800-50,000; most work sold at $2,000-5,000. Media: Considers all types of photography, painting, works on paper. Etherton Gallery purchases 19th-century, vintage, and classic photography; occasionally purchases contemporary photography and artwork. Interested in seeing work that is "well-crafted, cutting-edge, contemporary, issue-oriented."

MAKING CONTACT & TERMS Usually accepts work on consignment (50% commission). Retail price set by gallery and artist. Gallery provides insurance and promotion; shipping costs are shared; prefers framed artwork.

SUBMISSIONS Send 10-20 JPEGs, artist statement, résumé, reviews, bio. Materials not returned. No unprepared, incomplete or unfocused work. Responds in 6 weeks if interested.

TIPS "Become familiar with the style of our gallery and with contemporary art scene in general."

EVERSON MUSEUM OF ART

401 Harrison St., Syracuse NY 13202. (315)474-6064. **Fax:** (315)474-6943. **E-mail:** everson@everson.org; smassett@everson.org. **Website:** www.everson.org. **Contact:** Sarah Massett, assistant director. Estab. 1897. "In fitting with the works it houses, the Everson Museum building is a sculptural work of art in its own right. Designed by renowned architect I.M. Pei, the building itself is internationally acclaimed for its uniqueness. Within its walls, Everson houses roughly 11,000 pieces of art; American paintings, sculpture, drawings, graphics and one of the largest holdings of American ceramics in the nation." Open all year; Wednesday, Friday & Sunday, noon-5; Thursday noon-8; Saturday 10-5; closed Monday & Tuesday. The museum features 4 large galleries with 24-ft. ceilings, back lighting and oak hardwood, a sculpture court, Art Zone for children, a ceramic study center and 5 smaller gallery spaces.

EVOLVE THE GALLERY

P.O. Box 5944, Sacramento CA 95817. **E-mail:** info@ evolvethegallery.com. **Website:** www.evolvethegallery.com. **Contact:** A. Michelle Blakeley, co-owner. Estab. 2010. For-profit and art consultancy gallery. Approached by 250+ artists/year. Represents emerging, mid-career and established artists. Exhibited artists include Richard Mayhew (master fine artist, watercolor), Corinne Whitaker (pioneer digital painter), Ben F. Jones (prominent international artist). Sponsors 12+ exhibits/year. Model and property release required. Average display time: 1 month. Open Thursday-Saturday, by appointment. Clients include local community, students, tourists, upscale. 1% of sales are to corporate collectors. Overall price range: $1-10,000. Most work sold at $3,000.

EXHIBITS Considers all media (except craft), all types of prints, conceptualism, geometric abstraction, neo-expressionism, postmodernism and painterly abstraction.

MAKING CONTACT & TERMS Artwork is accepted on consignment and there is a 50% commission. Retail price of the art set by the artist; reviewed by the gallery. Gallery provides insurance, promotion, contract. Accepted work should be framed, mounted.

SUBMISSIONS E-mail with link to artist's website, JPEG samples at 72 dpi. Must include artist statement and CV. Materials returned with SASE. Responds only if interested (within weeks). Finds artists through word of mouth, submissions, portfolio reviews, art exhibits, art fairs, referrals by other artists.

FAHEY/KLEIN GALLERY

148 N. La Brea Ave., Los Angeles CA 90036. (323)934-2250. **Fax:** (323)934-4243. **E-mail:** contact@faheykleingallery.com. **Website:** www.faheykleingallery.com. **Contact:** David Fahey or Ken Devlin, co-owners. Estab. 1986. For-profit gallery. "Devoted to the enhancement of the public's appreciation of the medium of photography through the exhibition and sale of 20th-century and contemporary fine art photography. The gallery, with over 8,000 photographs in stock, deals extensively in photographs as works of art in all genres including portraits, nudes, landscapes, still-life, reportage and contemporary photography. The website contains a broad range of over 10,000 images." Approached by 200 artists/year; represents or exhibits 60 artists. Sponsors 10 exhibits/year. Average display time 5-6 weeks. Open Tuesday–Saturday, 10-6. Closed on all major holidays. Sponsors openings; provides announcements and beverages served at reception. Overall price range $500-500,000. Most work sold at $2,500. Located in Hollywood; gallery features 2 exhibition spaces with extensive work in back presentation room.

EXHIBITS Interested in established work; photos of celebrities, landscapes/scenics, wildlife, architecture, entertainment, humor, performing arts, sports. Interested in alternative process, avant garde, documentary, erotic, fashion/glamour, fine art, historical/vintage. Specific photo needs include iconic photographs, Hollywood celebrities, photojournalism, music-related, reportage and still life.

MAKING CONTACT & TERMS Artwork is accepted on consignment, and the commission is negotiated. Gallery provides insurance, promotion, contract. Accepted work should be unframed, unmounted and unmatted. Requires exclusive representation within metropolitan area. Photographer must be established for a minimum of 5 years; preferably published.

SUBMISSIONS Prefers website URLs for initial contact, or send material (CD, reproductions, no originals) by mail with SASE for consideration. Responds in 2 months. Finds artists through art fairs, exhibits, portfolio reviews, submissions, word of mouth, referrals by other artists.

TIPS "Please be professional and organized. Have a comprehensive sample of innovative work. Interested in seeing mature work with resolved photographic ideas and viewing complete portfolios addressing one idea."

FALKIRK CULTURAL CENTER

1408 Mission Ave. at E St., San Rafael CA 94901. (415)485-3328. **E-mail:** Beth.Goldberg@cityofsanrafael.org. **Website:** www.falkirkculturalcenter.org. **Contact:** Beth Goldberg, curator. Estab. 1974. Nonprofit gallery and national historic place (1888 Victorian) converted to multi-use cultural center. Approached by 500 artists/year; exhibits 300 artists. Sponsors 2 photography exhibits/year. Average display time: 2 months. Open Tuesday–Friday, 1-5; Saturday, 10-1; by appointment.

MAKING CONTACT & TERMS Gallery provides insurance.

SUBMISSIONS Submit digital entries only. Limit of 3 digital images per artist. Label each digital image with your LAST NAME, FIRST NAME, and TITLE

OF WORK. E-mail images to: beth.goldberg@cityof sanrafael.org. Send images as JPEGs at 72 dpi with approximately 2,500 ppi as largest dimension. Not to exceed 2.0 MB for each image submitted. Finds artists through word of mouth, submissions, portfolio reviews, art exhibits, art fairs, referrals by other artists.

FAVA (FIRELANDS ASSOCIATION FOR THE VISUAL ARTS)

New Union Center for the Arts, 39 S. Main St., Oberlin OH 44074. (440)774-7158. **Fax:** (440)775-1107. **E-mail:** favagallery@oberlin.net. **Website:** www.fava gallery.org. Estab. 1979. Nonprofit gallery. Features changing exhibits of high-quality artwork in a variety of styles and media. Sponsors 1 photography exhibit/year. Average display time 1 month. Open Tuesday–Saturday, 11-5; Sunday, 1-5. Overall price range $75-3,000. Most work sold at $200.

EXHIBITS Open to all media, including photography. Exhibits a variety of subject matter and styles.

MAKING CONTACT & TERMS Charges 30% commission. Accepted work should be framed or matted. Sponsors 1 regional juried photo exhibit/year: Six-State Photography, open to residents of Ohio, Kentucky, West Virginia, Pennsylvania, Indiana, Michigan. Deadline for applications: March. Send annual application for 6 invitational shows by mid-December of each year; include 15-20 slides, slide list, résumé.

SUBMISSIONS Interested artists should send a proposal to the attention of the Gallery Coordinator by December 15 to be considered by the Exhibitions Committee for the following year's season (Sept.-Aug.). Include: cover letter with complete contact information (address, phone, e-mail, website if available), current résumé with your background and exhibition experience, 15-20 professional quality high-res digital images on a CD of your recent work; additional images may be included to show essential detail or installation information; images should be numbered, list of works—list the number, title, medium, and size (H"×W"×D" of each image; designate detail and installation images if provided, artist statement/exhibition concept with past reviews. Application materials will only be returned if prepaid return mailer is included with the application.

TIPS "As a nonprofit gallery, we do not represent artists except during the juried show. Present the work in a professional format; the work, frame and/or mounting should be clean, undamaged, and (in cases of more complicated work) well organized."

FINE ARTS CENTER GALLERY

P.O. Box 1920, Jonesboro AR 72467. (870)972-3050. **Fax:** (870)972-3932. **Website:** www.astate.edu/col lege/fine-arts/art. Estab. 1968. Represents/exhibits 3-4 emerging, mid-career and established artists/year. Sponsors 3-4 shows/year. Average display time: 1 month. Open fall, winter and spring, Monday-Friday 10-5. Located on Arkansas State University campus; 1,868 sq. ft.; 60% of time devoted to special exhibitions, 40% to student work. Clientele include students and community.

EXHIBITS Considers all media and prints. Most frequently exhibits painting, sculpture and photography.

MAKING CONTACT & TERMS Exhibition space only, artist responsible for sales. Retail price set by the artist. Gallery provides promotion and contract; shipping costs are shared. Prefers artwork framed.

SUBMISSIONS Send query letter with résumé, CD/DVD and SASE to: FAC Gallery Director, c/o Department of Art, Arkansas State University, P.O. Box 1920, State University AR 72467. Portfolio should be submitted on CD/DVD only. Responds only if interested within 2 months. Files résumé. Finds artists through call for artists published in regional and national art journals.

TIPS Show us 20 digital images of your best work. Don't overload us with lots of collateral materials (reprints of reviews, articles, etc.). Make your vita as clear as possible.

HOWARD FINSTER VISION HOUSE

177 Greeson St., Summerville GA 30747. (706)857-2926. **E-mail:** david@dlg-gallery.com. **Website:** www.howardfinstervisionhouse.com. **Contact:** David Leonardis, owner. Estab. 1992. For-profit gallery. Approached by 100 artists/year; represents or exhibits 12 artists. Average display time 30 days. Gallery open Tuesday–Saturday, 12-7; Sunday, 12-6. "One big room, four big walls." Overall price range $50-5,000. Most work sold at $500.

EXHIBITS Photos of celebrities. Interested in fine art.

MAKING CONTACT & TERMS Artwork is accepted on consignment, and there is a 50% commission. Gallery provides promotion. Accepted work should be framed.

SUBMISSIONS E-mail to arrange a personal interview to show portfolio. Mail portfolio for review. Send query letter via e-mail. Responds only if interested.

Finds artists through word of mouth, art exhibits, referrals by other artists.

TIPS "Artists should be professional and easy to deal with."

FLORIDA STATE UNIVERSITY MUSEUM OF FINE ARTS

530 W. Call St., Room 250, Fine Arts Bldg., Tallahassee FL 32306-1140. (850)644-6836. **Fax:** (850)644-7229. **E-mail:** apalladinocraig@fsu.edu. **Website:** www.mofa.fsu.edu. Estab. 1970. Shows work by over 100 artists/year; emerging, mid-career and established. Sponsors 12-22 shows/year. Average display time: 3-4 weeks. Located on the university campus; 16,000 sq. ft. 50% for special exhibitions.

EXHIBITS Considers all media, including electronic imaging and performance art. Most frequently exhibits painting, sculpture and photography.

MAKING CONTACT & TERMS "Interested collectors are placed into direct contact with the artists; the museum takes no commission." Retail price set by the artist. Museum provides promotion and shipping costs to and from the museum for invited artists.

TIPS "The museum offers a yearly international competition and catalog: The Tallahassee International. Visit website for more information."

FOCAL POINT GALLERY

321 City Island Ave., City Island NY 10464. (718)885-1403. **E-mail:** ronterner@gmail.com. **Website:** www.focalpointgallery.net. **Contact:** Ron Terner, photographer/director. Estab. 1974. Overall price range $175-750. Most work sold at $300-500.

EXHIBITS All mediums and subjects accepted.

MAKING CONTACT & TERMS Retail gallery and alternative space. Interested in emerging and mid-career artists. Sponsors 12 group shows/year. Average display time: 3-4 weeks. Clients include locals and tourists. Overall price range: $175-750; most work sold at $300-500. Charges 30% commission.

FREEPORT ART MUSEUM

121 N. Harlem Ave., Freeport IL 61032. (815)235-9755. **Fax:** (815)235-6015. **E-mail:** info@freeportartmuseum.org. **Website:** www.freeportartmuseum.org. **Contact:** Jessica J. Modica, director. Formerly Freeport Arts Center. Sponsors approx. 6 exhibits/year. Average display time: 8 weeks.

EXHIBITS All artists are eligible to submit exhibition proposals. Exhibits contemporary, abstract, avant garde, multicultural, families, landscapes/scenics, architecture, cities/urban, rural, performing arts, travel, agriculture. Interested in fine art.

MAKING CONTACT & TERMS Charges 30% commission. Accepted work should be ready to hang.

SUBMISSIONS Visit FAM's website for directions on sending exhibition proposal materials. Retains exhibition proposal on file for future inquiries.

⊘ THE G2 GALLERY

1503 Abbot Kinney Blvd., Venice CA 90291. (310)452-2842. **Fax:** (310)452-0915. **E-mail:** info@theg2gallery.com. **Website:** www.theg2gallery.com. **Contact:** Jolene Hanson, gallery director. Estab. 2008. For-profit gallery exhibiting emerging, mid-career, and established artists. Approached by 150+ artists/year; represents or exhibits 45 artists. Exhibited photography by Ansel Adams and Robert Glenn Ketchum. Average display time is 6 weeks. Open Monday-Saturday, 10-7; Sunday, 10-6. "The G2 Gallery is a green art space. The first floor features a gift shop and some additional exhibition space. In 2008, before the gallery opened, the building was renovated to be as eco-friendly as possible. The space is rich in natural light with high ceilings and there are large-screen televisions and monitors for exhibition-related media. The G2 Gallery donates 100% of all proceeds to environmental causes and partners with conservation organizations related to exhibition themes. Our motto is 'Supporting Art and the Environment.'" Clients include local community, tourists, upscale. Price range of work: $150-15,000.

EXHIBITS Photography featuring environmental, landscapes/scenics, wildlife, alternative process, documentary, fine art, historical/vintage.

MAKING CONTACT & TERMS Art is accepted on consignment with a 40% commission. Retail price of the art is set by the artist. Gallery provides insurance, promotion, and contract. Accepted work should be framed, mounted, matted. Accepts photography only.

SUBMISSIONS All prospective artists are vetted through a juried application process. Please e-mail to request an application or download the application from website. Responds only if interested. "The G2 Gallery will contact artist with a confirmation that application materials have been received." Accepts only electronic materials. Physical portfolios are not accepted. Finds artists through word of mouth, submissions.

TIPS "Preferred applicants have a website with images of their work, inventory list, and pricing. Please do not contact the gallery once we have confirmed that your application has been received."

GALLERY 72

1806 Vinton St., Omaha NE 68108. (402)496-4797. E-mail: info@gallery72.com. **Website:** www.gallery72.com. **Contact:** John A. Rogers, owner. Estab. 1972. Represents or exhibits 20 artists. Sponsors 6 solo and 4 group shows/year. Average display time: 4-5 weeks. Gallery open Wednesday-Saturday, 10-6, by appointment and for special events. 1,800 sq. ft. of gallery space, 160 ft. of wall space.

EXHIBITS Photos of senior citizens, landscapes/scenics, cities/urban, interiors/decorating, rural, performing arts, travel.

MAKING CONTACT & TERMS Artwork is accepted on consignment, and there is a 50% commission. Gallery provides insurance, promotion. Requires exclusive representation locally. "No Western art."

SUBMISSIONS "Please consider making your submission of works to Gallery 72 as easy as possible to view and to be considered. We can and will accept information images that (1.) are mailed via the US postal service, (2.) are e-mailed, but be aware of possible limits for total size of e-mail messages, and (3.) are delivered by personal contact. If you plan to visit Gallery 72 please contact the gallery or director for an appointment prior to stopping in. Please include a brief artist's biography, statement and resume with your submission of images or artwork. Send images in the following format: lastname, firstname_title. jpg." Finds artists through word of mouth, submissions, art exhibits.

GALLERY 110 COLLECTIVE

110 Third Ave. S., Seattle WA 98104. (206)624-9336. **E-mail:** director@gallery110.com. **Website:** www.gallery110.com. **Contact:** Paula Maratea Fuld, director. Estab. 2002. "Gallery 110 is a 501(c)(3), established in 2002, as a space dedicated to providing dynamic opportunities for established and emerging professional artists. Gallery 110 plays an important role in Seattle's Pioneer Square Art district by connecting artists to curators, collectors and other artists with a valuable alternative space to exhibit their work. Hundreds of artists in the Northwest and throughout the country have participated in Gallery 110 programming, through juried exhibitions, artist talks, workshops, membership, as special guests and more. Our artists are emerging and established professionals, actively engaged in their artistic careers. We aspire to present fresh exhibitions of the highest professional caliber. The exhibitions change monthly and consist of solo, group and/or thematic shows." Open Wednesday-Saturday, 12-5; hosts receptions every first Thursday of the month, 6-8. Overall price range: $125-3,000; most work sold at $500-800.

MAKING CONTACT & TERMS Yearly active membership with dues, art on consignment, or available for rent.

TIPS "The artist should research the gallery to confirm it is a good fit for their work. The artist should be interested in being an active member, collaborating with other artists and participating in the success of the gallery. The work should challenge the viewer through concept, a high sense of craftsmanship, artistry, and expressed understanding of contemporary art culture and history. Artists should be emerging or established individuals with a serious focus on their work and participation in the field."

GALLERY 218

207 E. Buffalo St., Suite 218, Milwaukee WI 53202. (414)643-1732. **E-mail:** director@gallery218.com. **Website:** www.gallery218.com. **Contact:** Judith Hooks, president/director. Estab. 1990. Located in the Marshall Building of Milwaukee's historic Third Ward. Sponsors 12 exhibits/year. Average display time: 1 month. Sponsors openings. "If a group show, we make arrangements and all artists contribute. If a solo show, artist provides everything." Overall price range: $200-5,000. Most work sold at $200-600.

EXHIBITS Interested in alternative process, avant garde, abstract, fine art. Membership dues: $55/year plus $55/month rent. Artists help run the gallery. Group and solo shows. Photography is shown alongside fine arts painting, printmaking, sculpture, etc.

MAKING CONTACT & TERMS Charges 25% commission. There is an entry fee for each month. Fee covers the rent for 1 month. Accepted work must be framed.

SUBMISSIONS Send SASE for an application. "This is a cooperative space. A fee is required."

TIPS "Get involved in the process if the gallery will let you. We require artists to help promote their show so that they learn what and why certain things are required. Have inventory ready. Read and follow instructions on entry forms; be aware of deadlines. Attend openings for shows you are accepted into locally."

GALLERY 400

University of Illinois, Chicago, 400 S. Peoria St. (MC 034), Chicago IL 60607. (312)996-6114. **Fax:** (312)355-3444. **Website:** gallery400.uic.edu. **Contact:** Lorelei Stewart, director. Estab. 1983. Nonprofit gallery. Approached by 500 artists/year; exhibits 80 artists. Sponsors 1 photography exhibit/year. Average display time 6 weeks. Gallery open Tuesday–Friday, 10-6; Saturday, 12-6. Clients include local community, students, tourists and upscale.

MAKING CONTACT & TERMS Gallery provides insurance and promotion.

SUBMISSIONS Interact, propose an exhibition. Check info section of website for guidelines (gallery400.uic.edu/interact-page/propose-an-exhibition--2). Responds in 4 months. Finds artists through word of mouth, art exhibits, referrals by other artists.

TIPS "Follow the proposal guidelines on the website. We do not respond to e-mail submissions that do not follow the guidelines."

GALLERY 825

Los Angeles Art Association, 825 N. La Cienega Blvd., Los Angeles CA 90069. (310)652-8272. **E-mail:** peter@laaa.org. **Website:** www.laaa.org. **Contact:** Peter Mays, executive director. Estab. 1925. Holds approximately 1 exhibition/month. Average display time: 4-5 weeks. Fine art only. Exhibits all media.

MAKING CONTACT & TERMS Gallery provides promotion, exhibition venues and resources.

SUBMISSIONS To become an LAAA Artist member, visit website for screening dates and submission requirements.

○ THE GALLERY AT PETERS VALLEY SCHOOL OF CRAFT

19 Kuhn Rd., Layton NJ 07851. (973)948-5202. **Fax:** (973)948-0011. **E-mail:** gallery@petersvalley.org. **Website:** www.petersvalley.org. **Contact:** Brienne Rosner, gallery manager. Estab. 1977. "National Delaware Water Gap Recreation Area in the Historic Village of Bevans, Peters Valley School of Craft hosts a large variety of workshops in the spring and summer. The Gallery is located in an old general store; first floor retail space and second floor rotating exhibition gallery."

GALLERY FIFTY SIX

2231 Central Ave., Memphis TN 38104. (901)276-1251. **E-mail:** rollin@galleryfiftysix.com. **Website:** www.galleryfiftysix.com. Blog: www.galleryfiftysix. blogspot.com. **Contact:** Rollin Kocsis, director. Estab. 2008. For-profit gallery. Approached by 35 artists/year; represents or exhibits 24 emerging, mid-career and established artists. Exhibited artists include John Armistead (oil on canvas), Bryan Blankenship (painting and ceramics), Terry Kenney and Joseph Morzuch (painting). Sponsors 12 exhibits/year. Model and property release are preferred. Average display time: 1 month. Open Monday-Saturday, 10-5. Contains 1 large room with 1 level. Clients include local community, students, tourists and upscale. Overall price range: $200-3,000. Most work sold at $750.

EXHIBITS Considers acrylic, ceramics, collage, drawing, fiber, glass, mixed media, oil, pastel, sculpture. Most frequently exhibits oil on canvas, acrylic on canvas, assemblages. Considers engravings, etchings, linocuts, serigraphs, woodcuts. Considers color field, expressionism, geometric abstraction, imagism, impressionism, pattern painting, postmodernism, primitivism realism, surrealism, painterly abstraction. Most frequently exhibits realism, abstract, expressionism. Considers all genres. No nudes.

MAKING CONTACT & TERMS Artwork is accepted on consignment and there is a 50% commission. Gallery provides promotion and contract. Accepted work should be gallery wrapped or frames with black or natural wood finish. Requires exclusive representation locally.

SUBMISSIONS E-mail 8-12 JPEGs. Write to arrange personal interview to show portfolio of photographs, e-mail JPEG samples at 72 dpi or send query letter with artist's statement, bio, brochure, business card, photographs, résumé, reviews and SASE. Material returned with SASE. Responds in 2 weeks. Files JPEGs, CDs, photos. Finds artists through word of mouth, submissions, portfolio reviews, art exhibits and referrals by other artists.

TIPS "Send good quality photos, by e-mail, with all important information included. Not interested in installations or subject matter that is offensive, political, sexual or religious."

GALLERY NORTH

90 N. Country Rd., Setauket NY 11733. (631)751-2676. **E-mail:** info@gallerynorth.org. **Website:** www.galle

rynorth.org. **Contact:** Judith Levy, director. Regional arts center. "Our mission is to present exhibitions of exceptional contemporary artists and artisans, especially those from Long Island and the nearby regions; to assist and encourage artists by bringing their work to the attention of the public; and to stimulate interest in the arts by presenting innovative educational programs. Exhibits the work of emerging, mid-career and established artists from Long Island and throughout the Northeast. The Gallery North community involves regional and local artists, collectors, art dealers, corporate sponsors, art consultants, businesses and schools, ranging from local elementary students to the faculty and staff at Long Island's many colleges and universities including our neighbor, Stony Brook University and the Stony Brook Medical Center. With our proximity to New York City and the East End, our region attracts a wealth of talent and interest in the arts." Located in the Historic District of Setauket, Long Island NY, in an 1840s farm house, 1 mile from the State University at Stony Brook. Open year-round; Tuesday–Saturday, 10-5; Sunday, 12-5; closed Monday. **EXHIBITS** "Works to be exhibited are selected by our director, Judith Levy, with input from our Artist Advisory Board. We encourage artist dialogue and participation in gallery events and community activities and many artists associated with our gallery offer ArTrips and ArTalks, as well as teaching in our education programs. Along with monthly exhibitions in our 1,000-sq.-ft. space, our Gallery Shop strives to present the finest handmade jewelry and craft by local and nationally recognized artisans."
SUBMISSIONS To present work to the gallery, send an e-mail with 2-5 medium-sized images, price list (indicating title, size, medium, and date), artist's statement, biography and link to website. "We encourage artists to visit the gallery and interact with our exhibitions." Visit the website for more information.

⊘ SANDRA GERING , INC.

14 E. 64th St., New York NY 10065. (646)336-7183. **E-mail:** info@geringlopez.com; laura@geringlopez.com. **Website:** www.geringlopez.com. **Contact:** Laura Bloom, director. Estab. 1991. For-profit gallery. Approached by 240 artists/year; represents or exhibits 12 artists. Sponsors 1 photography exhibit/year. Average display time 5 weeks. Gallery open Tuesday–Friday, 10-6; Saturday, 11-5.

EXHIBITS Interested in alternative process, avant garde; digital, computer-based art.
MAKING CONTACT & TERMS Artwork is accepted on consignment.
SUBMISSIONS E-mail with link to website or send postcard with image. Responds within 6 months, only if interested. Finds artists through word of mouth, art exhibits, art fairs, referrals by other artists. *Sandra Gering, Inc. is currently NOT accepting unsolicited submissions.*
TIPS "Most important is to research the galleries and only submit to those that are appropriate. Visit websites if you don't have access to galleries."

GIERTZ GALLERY AT PARKLAND COLLEGE

2400 W. Bradley Ave., Champaign IL 61821. (217)351-2485. **Fax:** (217)373-3899. **E-mail:** parklandartgallery@parkland.edu. **Website:** www.parkland.edu/gallery. **Contact:** Lisa Costello, director. Estab. 1980. Nonprofit gallery. Approached by 130 artists/year; 7 exhibitions per year. Average display time 4- 6 weeks. Open Monday–Thursday, 10-7; Friday. 10-3; Saturday, 12-2 (fall and spring semesters). Summer: Monday-Thursday, 10-7. Parkland Art Gallery at Parkland College seeks exhibition proposals in all genres of contemporary approaches to art making by single artists, collaborative groups, or curators. Parkland Art Gallery is a professionally designed gallery devoted primarily to education through contemporary art. Parkland Art Gallery hosts 7 exhibitions per year including 2 student exhibitions, one art and design faculty show, and a Biennial Watercolor Invitational that alternates with a National Ceramics Invitational. Other shows vary depending on applications and the vision of the Art Gallery Advisory Board. Exhibits are scheduled on a 4- to 6-week rotation. Closed college and official holidays. Overall price range $100-5,000. Most work sold at $900.
EXHIBITS Interested in alternative process, avant garde, documentary, fine art, historical/vintage.
MAKING CONTACT & TERMS Gallery provides insurance, promotion. Accepted work should be framed.
SUBMISSIONS Send 20 slides or a CD containing 20 images; an identifying list with titles, sizes, dates, and media; a résumé; an artist statement; and a SASE (if necessary) to attention of the Director, Parkland Art Gallery, Parkland College. Only complete proposal packages including all information listed on the Proposal Guidelines will be reviewed. Responds in 4

months. No online proposals accepted. Finds artists through word of mouth, portfolio reviews, art exhibits, referrals by other artists. Call for entry.

GLOUCESTER ARTS ON MAIN

6580-B Main St., Gloucester VA 23061. (804)824-9464. **Fax:** (804)824-9469. **E-mail:** curator@gloucesterarts.org. **Website:** www.gloucesterarts.org. **Contact:** Kay Van Dyke, curator. Estab. 2010. Nonprofit, rental gallery. Alternative space. Exhibits emerging, mid-career and established artists. Approached by 15 artists/year; represents or exhibits 60 artists currently. Exhibited artists include Harriett McGee (repoussé and mixed media) and Victoria Watson (animal drawings). Sponsors 12 exhibits/year, 1-2 photography exhibits/year. There are always photos on exhibit. Average display time: 1 month or length of rental contract. Open Tuesday-Saturday, 12-6; weekend events, 6-9. Located on walkable Main Street near restaurants and other shops, small town near major cities in Eastern Virginia. Very flexible gallery space with 120+ ft. of perimeter exhibition space and 96 ft. of movable walls. 4,000 sq. ft. total exhibition space. Clients include the local community, students, tourists and upscale clients. 10% of sales are to corporate collectors. Overall price range: $20-7,500; most work sold at $300.

EXHIBITS Considers all media. Most frequently exhibits paintings (oil, acrylic and watercolor), 2D and 3D metal work, and photography. Considers all types of prints except posters.

MAKING CONTACT & TERMS Artwork is accepted on consignment and there is a 30% commission with a rental fee for wall or shelf space. The fee covers 6 months and there is a 30% commission. Retail price set by the artist. Gallery provides promotion and contract. Accepted work should be framed, matted and mounted. Prefers to represent artists from Eastern Virginia.

SUBMISSIONS E-mail query letter with link to artist's website, JPEG samples at 72 dpi, résumé, artist's statement and bio; or call for appointment to show portfolio. Jury system responds within 2 weeks. Finds artists through word of mouth, art exhibits, submissions, portfolio reviews and referrals by other artists.

TIPS Work should be presented for jury ready to exhibit, i.e., framed or mounted appropriately. Digital images presented for review should be clear, cropped and professional in appearance at high resolution.

GRAND RAPIDS ART MUSEUM

101 Monroe Center St. NW, Grand Rapids MI 49503. (616)831-1000. **E-mail:** rplatt@artmuseumgr.org. **Website:** www.artmuseumgr.org. Estab. 1910. Museum. Usually sponsors 1 photography exhibit/year. Average display time: 4 months. Open all year; Tuesday, Wednesday, Friday, Saturday, 10-5; Thursday, 10-9; Sunday, 12-5; closed Mondays and major holidays. Located in the heart of downtown Grand Rapids, the Grand Rapids Art Museum presents exhibitions of national caliber and regional distinction.

EXHIBITS Interested in fine art, historical/vintage.

ANTON HAARDT GALLERY

2858 Magazine St., New Orleans LA 70130. (504)891-9080. **E-mail:** anton3@earthlink.net. **Website:** www.antonart.com. Estab. 2001. For profit gallery. Represents or exhibits 25 artists. Overall price range $500-5,000. Most work sold at $1,000.

EXHIBITS Exhibits photos of celebrities. Mainly photographs (portraits of folk artists).

MAKING CONTACT & TERMS Prefers only artists from the South. Self-taught artists who are original and pure, specifically art created from 1945 to 1980. "I rarely take on new artists, but I am interested in buying estates of deceased artist's work or an entire body of work by artist."

SUBMISSIONS Send query letter with artist's statement.

TIPS "I am only interested in a very short description if the artist has work from early in his or her career."

CARRIE HADDAD GALLERY

622 Warren St., Hudson NY 12534. (518)828-1915. **Fax:** (518)828-3341. **E-mail:** carrie.haddad@carriehaddadgallery.com. **Website:** www.carriehaddadgallery.com. **Contact:** Carrie Haddad, owner. Estab. 1990. Art consultancy, for-profit gallery. "Hailed as the premier gallery of the Hudson Valley, the Carrie Haddad Gallery presents 8 large exhibits/year and includes all types of painting, both large and small sculpture, works on paper and a variety of techniques in photography." Approached by 50 artists/year; represents or exhibits 60 artists. Open daily, 11-5; Sunday, 12-5. Overall price range $350-6,000. Most work sold at $1,000.

EXHIBITS Photos of nudes, landscapes/scenics, architecture, pets, rural, product shots/still life.

MAKING CONTACT & TERMS Artwork is accepted on consignment, and there is a 50% commission. Gallery provides insurance, promotion. Requires exclusive representation locally.

SUBMISSIONS Send query letter with bio, photocopies, photographs, price list, SASE. Responds in 1 month. Finds artists through word of mouth, submissions, art exhibits, referrals by other artists.

THE HALSTED GALLERY INC.

P.O. Box 250321, Franklin MI 48025. (248)895-0204; (248)894-0353. **E-mail:** tomhalsted@hotmail.com. **Website:** www.halstedgallery.com. **Contact:** Wendy or Thomas Halsted. Sponsors 3 exhibits/year. Average display time 2 months. Sponsors openings. Overall price range $500-25,000.

EXHIBITS Interested in 19th- and 20th-century photographs.

SUBMISSIONS Call to arrange a personal interview to show portfolio only. Prefers to see scans. Send no slides or samples. Unframed work only.

TIPS No limitations on subjects. Wants to see creativity, consistency, depth and emotional work.

LEE HANSLEY GALLERY

225 Glenwood Ave., Raleigh NC 27603. (919)828-7557. **Fax:** (919)828-7550. **Website:** www.leehansley gallery.com. **Contact:** Lee Hansley, gallery director. Estab. 1993. "Located in Raleigh's bustling Glenwood South, we are dedicated to showcasing quality fine art through a series of changing exhibitions, both group and solo shows, featuring works from professional artists from North Carolina, the Southeast and the nation. There are 35 artists in the gallery whose works are shown on a rotating basis. The gallery also hosts invitational exhibitions in which non-gallery artists show alongside stable artists. The gallery organizes at least 1 historical exhibition annually exploring the work of a single artist or group of stylistically related artists." Sponsors 3 exhibits/year. Average display time 4-6 weeks. Overall price range $250-1,600. Most work sold at $400. Open Tuesday–Saturday, 11-6; 1st Friday, 11-10; or by appointment.

EXHIBITS Photos of environmental, landscapes/scenics, architecture, cities/urban, gardening, rural, performing arts. Interested in alternative process, avant garde, erotic, fine art. Interested in new images using the camera as a tool of manipulation; also wants minimalist works. Looks for top-quality work with an artistic vision.

MAKING CONTACT & TERMS Charges 50% commission. Payment within 1 month of sale.

SUBMISSIONS Send material by mail for consideration; include SASE. May be on CD. Does not accept e-mails. Responds in 2 months.

TIPS "Looks for originality and creativity—someone who sees with the camera and uses the parameters of the format to extract slices of life, architecture and nature."

JOEL AND LILA HARNETT MUSEUM OF ART AND PRINT STUDY CENTER

University of Richmond Museums, 28 Westhampton Way, Richmond VA 23173. (804)289-8276. **Fax:** (804)287-1894. **E-mail:** rwaller@richmond.edu; mu seums@richmond.edu. **Website:** museums.richmond. edu. **Contact:** Richard Waller, executive director. Estab. 1968. Represents emerging, mid-career and established artists. Sponsors 6 exhibitions/year. Average display time: 6 weeks. Open academic year; limited summer hours May-August. Located on university campus; 5,000 sq. ft. 100% of space for special exhibitions.

EXHIBITS Considers all media and all types of prints. Most frequently exhibits painting, sculpture, prints, photography and drawing.

MAKING CONTACT & TERMS Work accepted on loan for duration of special exhibition. Retail price set by the artist. Museum provides insurance, promotion, contract and shipping costs. Prefers artwork framed.

SUBMISSIONS Send query letter with résumé, 8-12 images on CD, brochure, SASE, reviews and printed material if available. Write for appointment to show portfolio of "whatever is appropriate to understanding the artist's work." Responds in 1 month. Files résumé and other materials the artist does not want returned (printed material, CD, reviews, etc.).

WILLIAM HAVU GALLERY

1040 Cherokee St., Denver CO 80204. (303)893-2360. **Fax:** (303)893-2813. **E-mail:** info@williamhavugal lery.com. **Website:** www.williamhavugallery.com. **Contact:** Bill Havu, owner and director; Nick Ryan, gallery administrator. For-profit gallery. "Engaged in an ongoing dialogue through its 7 exhibitions a year with regionalism as it affects and is affected by both national and international trends in realism and abstraction. Strong emphasis on mid-career and established artists." Approached by 120 artists/year; represents or exhibits 50 artists. Sponsors 1 photography exhibit/year. Average display time: 6-8 weeks. Open Tuesday–Friday, 10-6; Saturday, 11-5; 1st Friday of each month, 10-8; Sundays and Mondays by appointment; closed Christmas and New Year's Day. Overall price range: $250-15,000; most work sold at $1,000-4,000.

EXHIBITS Photos of multicultural, landscapes/scenics, religious, rural. Interested in alternative process, documentary, fine art.

MAKING CONTACT & TERMS Gallery provides insurance, promotion, contract. Accepted work should be framed. Requires exclusive representation locally. Accepts only artists from Rocky Mountain, Southwestern region.

SUBMISSIONS "Please submit a representative sampling of your current body of work. We prefer to receive digital printouts, printed cards and invitations, or other easily reviewed formats. If you prefer, you may submit CDs, e-mail a link to your website or include these materials in an e-mail. Mailed materials will only be returned if you have provided a SASE. Please also include: A current résumé listing your contact information, education, exhibition history, collections, and awards. An artist statement. Any other supporting materials (reviews, articles, etc.). A SASE for the return of your materials. (If you do not provide a SASE, your materials will not be returned to you.) We ask that you please not contact the gallery regarding the status of your portfolio review. Portfolios are reviewed only periodically, so it may be many months before the gallery reviews your materials. If, after evaluating your materials, we have an interest, we will be in touch with you to discuss next steps."

TIPS "Always mail a portfolio packet. We do not accept walk-ins or phone calls to review work. Explore website or visit gallery to make sure work would fit with the gallery's objective. We only frame work with archival quality materials and feel its inclusion in work can 'make' the sale."

⊘ HEMPHILL

1515 14th St. NW, Suite 300, Washington DC 20005. (202)234-5601. **Fax:** (202)234-5607. **E-mail:** gallery@hemphillfinearts.com. **Website:** www.hemphillfinearts.com. Estab. 1993. Art consultancy and for-profit gallery. Represents or exhibits 30 artists/year. Hemphill is a member of the Association of International Photography Art Dealers (AIPAD). Gallery open Tuesday–Saturday, 10-5, and by appointment. Overall price range $900-300,000.

EXHIBITS Photos of landscapes/scenics, architecture, cities/urban, rural. Interested in alternative process, fine art, historical/vintage.

SUBMISSIONS Gallery does not accept or review portfolio submissions.

HENRY ART GALLERY

University of Washington, 15th Ave. NE and NE 41st St., Seattle WA 98195. (206)543-2280. **Fax:** (206)685-3123. **E-mail:** press@henryart.org. **Website:** www.henryart.org. **Contact:** Luis Croquer, deputy director of exhibitions, collections and programs. Estab. 1927. Contemporary Art Museum. Exhibits emerging, mid-career, and established domestic and international artists. Presents approx. 20 exhibitions/year. Open Wednesday, Saturday, Sunday 11-4; Thursday-Friday, 11-9. Located on the University of Washington campus. Visitors include local community, students, and tourists.

EXHIBITS Considers all media. Most frequently exhibits photography, video, and installation work. Exhibits all types of prints.

MAKING CONTACT & TERMS Does not require exclusive representation locally.

SUBMISSIONS Send query letter with artist statement, résumé, SASE, 10-15 images. Returns material with SASE. Finds artists through art exhibitions, exhibition announcements, individualized research, periodicals, portfolio reviews, referrals by other artists, submissions, and word of mouth.

HENRY STREET SETTLEMENT/ABRONS ART CENTER

466 Grand St., New York NY 10002. (212)598-0400; (212)766-9200. **E-mail:** info@henrystreet.org; jdurham@henrystreet.org. **Website:** www.abronsartscenter.org. **Contact:** Jonathan Durham, director of exhibitions and AIRspace. Alternative space, nonprofit gallery, community center. "The Abrons Art Center brings innovative artistic excellence to Manhattan's Lower East Side through diverse performances, exhibitions, residencies, classes and workshops for all ages and arts-in-education programming at public schools. Holds 9 solo photography exhibits/year. Open Tuesday–Friday, 10-10; Saturday, 9-10; Sunday, 11-6; closed major holidays.

EXHIBITS Photos of multicultural, environmental, landscapes/scenics, architecture, cities/urban, rural. Interested in alternative process, avant garde, documentary, fine art, historical/vintage.

MAKING CONTACT & TERMS Artwork is accepted on consignment, and there is a 20% commission. Gallery provides insurance, space, contract.

SUBMISSIONS Send query letter with artist's statement, SASE. Finds artists through word of mouth, submissions, referrals by other artists.

HERA EDUCATIONAL FOUNDATION AND ART GALLERY

P.O. Box 336, Wakefield RI 02880. (401)789-1488. **E-mail:** info@heragallery.org. **Website:** www.heragallery.org. Estab. 1974. Cooperative gallery. "Hera Gallery/Hera Educational Foundation was a pioneer in the development of alternative exhibition spaces across the US. in the 1970s and one of the earliest women's cooperative galleries. Although many of these galleries no longer exist, Hera is proud to have not only continued, but also expanded our programs, exhibitions and events." The number of photo exhibits varies each year. Average display time: 6 weeks. Open Wednesday-Friday, 1-5; Saturday, 10-4; or by appointment; closed during the month of January. Sponsors openings; provides refreshments and entertainment or lectures, demonstrations and symposia for some exhibits. Call for information on exhibitions. Overall price range: $100-10,000.

EXHIBITS Photos of disasters, environmental, landscapes/scenics. Interested in all types of innovative contemporary art that explores social and artistic issues. Interested in fine art.

MAKING CONTACT & TERMS Charges 25% commission. Works must fit inside a 6'6"×2'6" door. Photographer must show a portfolio before attaining membership.

SUBMISSIONS Inquire about membership and shows. Membership guidelines and application available on website or mailed on request.

TIPS "Hera exhibits a culturally diverse range of visual and emerging artists. Please follow the application procedure listed in the Membership Guidelines. Applications are welcome at any time of the year."

GERTRUDE HERBERT INSTITUTE OF ART

506 Telfair St., Augusta GA 30901-2310. (706)722-5495. **Fax:** (706)722-3670. **E-mail:** ghia@ghia.org. **Website:** www.ghia.org. **Contact:** Rebekah Henry, executive director. Estab. 1937. Nonprofit gallery. Has 5 solo or group shows annually; exhibits approximately 40 artists annually. Average display time: 6-8 weeks. Open Monday–Friday, 10-5; weekends by appointment only. Closed 1st week in August, and December 17-31. Located in historic 1818 Ware's Folly mansion.

MAKING CONTACT & TERMS Artwork is accepted on consignment, and there is a 35% commission.

SUBMISSIONS Send query letter with artist's statement, bio, brochure, résumé, reviews, slides or CD of work, SASE. Responds to queries in 1-3 months. Finds artists through art exhibits, submissions, referrals by other artists.

HEUSER ART CENTER GALLERY & HARTMANN CENTER ART GALLERY

Bradley University Galleries, 1400 W. Bradley Ave., Peoria IL 61625. (309)677-2989. **Website:** art.bradley.edu/bug. **Contact:** Erin Buczynski, director of galleries, exhibitions and collections. Estab. 1984. Alternative space, nonprofit gallery, educational. "We have 2 formal exhibition spaces, one in the Heuser Art Center, where the art department is located, and one in the Hartmann Center, where the theater department is housed." Approached by 260 artists/year; represents or exhibits 50 artists. Sponsors 1 photography exhibit/year. Average display time: 4-6 weeks. Heuser Art Gallery hours: Monday–Thursday, 9-7; Friday, 9-5; and by appointment. Hartmann Center Gallery hours: Monday–Friday, 9-5; and by appointment. See website for more information.

EXHIBITS Photos of babies/children/teens, celebrities, couples, multicultural, families, parents, senior citizens, disasters, environmental, landscapes/scenics, wildlife, architecture, cities/urban, education, rural, entertainment, events, performing arts, travel, agriculture, business concepts, industry, medicine, military, political, product shots/still life, science, technology/computers. Interested in alternative process, avant garde, documentary, fashion/glamour, fine art, historical/vintage, large-format Polaroid.

MAKING CONTACT & TERMS Artwork is accepted on consignment, and there is a 30% commission. Gallery provides promotion and contract. Accepted work should be framed or glazed with Plexiglas. "We consider all professional artists."

SUBMISSIONS Mail portfolio of 20 slides for review. Send query letter with artist's statement, bio, brochure, business card, photocopies, photographs, résumé, reviews, SASE, slides and CD. Finds artists through art exhibits, portfolio reviews, referrals by other artists and critics, submissions and national calls.

TIPS "No handwritten letters. Print or type slide labels. Send only 20 slides total."

EDWARD HOPPER HOUSE ART CENTER

82 N. Broadway, Nyack NY 10960. (845)358-0774. **E-mail:** info@hopperhouse.org; caroleperry@edwardhopperhouse.org. **Website:** www.edwardhopperhouse.org. **Contact:** Carole Perry, director. Estab. 1971. Nonprofit gallery and historic house. Approached by 200 artists/year; exhibits 100 artists. Sponsors 1-2 photography exhibits/year. Average display time: 1 month. Also offers an annual summer jazz concert series. Open Thursday–Sunday, 1-5; or by appointment. The house was built in 1858; there are 4 gallery rooms on the 1st floor. Overall price range: $100-12,000. Most work sold at $750.

EXHIBITS Photos of all subjects. Interested in alternative process, avant garde, documentary, fine art, historical/vintage, seasonal.

MAKING CONTACT & TERMS Artwork is accepted on consignment, and there is a 35% commission. Gallery provides insurance, promotion and contract. Accepted work should be framed, mounted and matted.

SUBMISSIONS "Exhibits are scheduled 18 months to 2 years in advance. E-mail 10 images identifying each image with your name, title of work, medium and dimensions, as well as a résumé/bio and artist statement."

EDWYNN HOUK GALLERY

745 Fifth Ave., Suite 407, New York NY 10151. (212)750-7070. **Fax:** (212)688-4848. **E-mail:** info@houkgallery.com; julie@houkgallery.com; tess@houkgallery.com. **Website:** www.houkgallery.com. **Contact:** Julie Castellano, director; Tess Vinnedge, assistant director. For-profit gallery. The gallery is a member of the Art Dealers Association of America and Association of International Photography Art Dealers. The gallery represents the Estates of Ilse Bing, Bill Brandt, Brassaï and Dorothea Lange, and is the representative for such major contemporary photographers as Robert Polidori, Joel Meyerowitz, Sally Mann, Herb Ritts, Bettina Rheims, Lalla Essaydi, Hannes Schmid, Sebastiaan Bremer, Danny Lyon and Elliott Erwitt. Open Tuesday–Saturday, 11-6.

EXHIBITS Specializes in masters of 20th-century photography with an emphasis on the 1920s and 1930s and contemporary photography.

HUDSON GALLERY

5645 N. Main St., Sylvania OH 43560. (419)885-8381. **Fax:** (419)885-8381. **E-mail:** info@hudsongallery.net. **Website:** www.hudsongallery.net. **Contact:** Scott Hudson, director. Estab. 2003. For-profit gallery. Approached by 30 artists/year; represents or exhibits 90 emerging, mid-career and established artists. Sponsors 10 exhibits/year. Average display time: 1 month. Open Tuesday-Friday, 10-6; Saturday, 10-3. This street-level gallery has over 2,000 sq. ft. of primary exhibition space. Clients include local community, tourists and upscale. 5% of sales are to corporate collectors. Overall price range: $50-10,000.

EXHIBITS Considers acrylic, ceramics, collage, drawing, fiber, glass, mixed media, oil, paper, pastel, sculpture, watercolor, engravings, etchings, linocuts, lithographs, mezzotints, serigraphs, woodcuts. Most frequently exhibits acrylic, oil, ceramics; considers all styles and genres.

MAKING CONTACT & TERMS Artwork is accepted on consignment and there is a 40% commission. Retail price of the art set by the gallery and artist. Gallery provides insurance, promotion and contract.

SUBMISSIONS Call, e-mail, write or send query letter with artist's statement, bio, JPEGs; include SASE. Material returned with SASE. Responds within 4 months. Finds artists through word of mouth, submissions, portfolio reviews and referrals by other artists.

TIPS Follow guidelines on our website.

HUNTSVILLE MUSEUM OF ART

300 Church St. S, Huntsville AL 35801-4910. (256)535-4350. **E-mail:** cmadkour@hsvmuseum.org. **Website:** www.hsvmuseum.org. **Contact:** Christopher Madkour, executive director. Estab. 1970. This nationally-accredited museum fills its 13 galleries with a variety of exhibitions throughout the year, including prestigious traveling exhibits and the work of nationally and regionally acclaimed artists. The museum's own 2,522-piece permanent collection also forms the basis for several exhibitions each year. Sponsors 1-2 exhibits/year. Average display time 2-3 months. Open Sunday, noon-5; Tuesday, Wednesday, Friday, Saturday, 11-5; Thursday, 11-8; Closed Monday.

EXHIBITS No specific stylistic or thematic criteria. Interested in alternative process, avant garde, documentary, fine art, historical/vintage.

MAKING CONTACT & TERMS Buys photos outright. Accepted work may be framed or unframed, mounted or unmounted, matted or unmatted. Must have professional track record and résumé, slides, critical reviews in package (for curatorial review).

SUBMISSIONS Regional connection strongly preferred. Send material by mail with SASE for consideration.

ICEBOX QUALITY FRAMING & GALLERY

1500 Jackson St. NE, Suite #443, Minneapolis MN 55413. (612)788-1790. **E-mail:** icebox@bitstream. net. **Website:** www.iceboxminnesota.com. Estab. 1988. Exhibition, promotion and sales gallery. Represents photographers and fine artists in all media, predominantly photography. "A sole proprietorship gallery, Icebox sponsors installations and exhibits in the gallery's 1,700 sq. ft. space in the Minneapolis Arts District." Overall price range $200-1,500. Most work sold at $200-800. Open Thursday and Friday, 10-6; Saturday, 12-5; Tuesday and Wednesday, by appointment only.

EXHIBITS Photos of multicultural, environmental, landscapes/scenics, rural, adventure, travel. Interested in alternative process, documentary, erotic, fine art, historical/vintage. Specifically wants "fine art photographs from artists with serious, thought-provoking work."

MAKING CONTACT & TERMS Charges 50% commission.

SUBMISSIONS "Send letter of interest telling why and what you would like to exhibit at Icebox. Include only materials that can be kept at the gallery and updated as needed. Check website for more details about entry and gallery history."

TIPS "We are experienced with the out-of-town artist's needs."

ILLINOIS STATE MUSEUM CHICAGO GALLERY

100 W. Randolph, Suite 2-100, Chicago IL 60601. (312)814-5322. **E-mail:** jstevens@museum.state.il.us. **Website:** www.museum.state.il.us./ismsites/chicago/ exhibitions.html. **Contact:** Jane Stevens, gallery administrator. Estab. 1985. Sponsors 2-3 exhibits/year. Average display time 4 months. Sponsors openings; provides refreshments at reception and sends out announcement cards for exhibitions.

EXHIBITS *Must be an Illinois photographer.* Interested in contemporary and historical/vintage, alternative process, fine art.

SUBMISSIONS Send résumé, artist's statement, 2-20 JPEGS or slides, SASE. Responds in 6 months.

INDIANAPOLIS ART CENTER

820 E. 67th St., Indianapolis IN 46220. (317)255-2464. **E-mail:** kyleh@indplsartcenter.org. **Website:** www. indplsartcenter.org. **Contact:** Kyle Herrington, director of exhibitions. Estab. 1934. "The Indianapolis Art Center is one of the largest community art facilities in the United States not connected with a university, welcoming more than 250,000 visitors a year. The mission of the Indianapolis Art Center is to engage, enlighten and inspire our community by providing interactive art education, outreach to underserved audiences, support of artists and exposure to the visual arts. The Art Center's campus includes the Marilyn K. Glick School of Art, a 40,000-sq.-ft. facility designed by renowned architect Michael Graves. The building houses 11 state-of-the-art studios, 5 public art galleries, a 224-seat auditorium and a library. It also features ArtsPark, a 9-acre outdoor creativity and sculpture garden that includes public art and is located in one of Indianapolis' most popular and diverse neighborhoods. The park is connected to one of the city's most utilized greenway trail systems, the Monan Trail."

MAKING CONTACT & TERMS "The Indianapolis Art Center Exhibitions Department accepts proposals for gallery and ArtsPark exhibits from June–December each year. Generally we are looking for exhibits to book 2 years out or more. Proposals will be accepted starting June 1–December 31. All works insured while on site and a stipend may be available in curated exhibitions. For further information about the gallery sizes and contract terms, please contact us."

SUBMISSIONS "Any artist may submit a proposal to be considered for a solo or group exhibition by sending a complete artist's packet to: Indianapolis Art Center, ATTN: Exhibits Department, 820 E. 67th St., Indianapolis, IN 46220. Your proposal should include the following items on a CD or DVD: an artist statement, not to exceed 1 page; a résumé or biography, not to exceed 3 pages; 12-15 images of individual works (details may be included); a list with title, medium, size, and year completed for each image. Videos may also be submitted, as well as videos of interactive and/

or performance work. NOTE: your proposal materials WILL NOT be returned to you. While all proposals will be given equal consideration, artists living or working within 250 miles of Indianapolis are especially encouraged to apply. All proposals collected during the year will be reviewed on a rolling basis. Proposals may be kept for upwards of 3 years by the exhibitions department for future consideration."

INDIVIDUAL ARTISTS OF OKLAHOMA

P.O. Box 60824, Oklahoma City OK 73146. (405)232-6060. **Fax:** (405)232-6061. **E-mail:** kbrown@iaogallery.org. **Website:** www.iaogallery.org. **Contact:** Kendall Brown. Estab. 1979. Alternative space. "IAO creates opportunities for Oklahoma artists by curating and developing socially relevant exhibitions in one of the finest gallery spaces in the region." Approached by 60 artists/year; represents or exhibits 30 artists. Sponsors 10 photography exhibits/year. Average display time: 3-4 weeks. Open Tuesday–Saturday, 12-6. Gallery is located in downtown art district, 3,500 sq. ft. with 10-ft. ceilings and track lighting. Overall price range: $100-2,000; most work sold at $400.

EXHIBITS Interested in alternative process, avant garde, documentary, fine art, historical/vintage photography. Other specific subjects/processes: contemporary approach to variety of subjects.

MAKING CONTACT & TERMS Charges 30% commission. Gallery provides insurance, promotion, contract. Accepted work must be framed.

SUBMISSIONS Mail portfolio for review with artist's statement, bio, photocopies or slides, résumé, SASE. Reviews quarterly. Finds artists through word of mouth, art exhibits, referrals by other artists.

INTERNATIONAL CENTER OF PHOTOGRAPHY

1133 Avenue of the Americas, New York NY 10036. (212)857-0000; (212)857-9707. **E-mail:** portfolio@icp.org; kheisler@icp.org. **Website:** www.icp.org. **Contact:** Department of Exhibitions & Collections. Estab. 1974.

SUBMISSIONS "Due to the volume of work submitted, we are only able to accept portfolios in the form of CDs or e-mail attachments. JPEG files are preferable; each image file should be a maximum of 1000 pixels at the longest dimension, at 72 dpi. CDs must be labeled with a name and address. Submissions must be limited to no more than 20 images. All files should be accompanied by a list of titles and dates. Portfolios of more than 20 images will not be accepted. Photographers may also wish to include the following information: cover letter, rèsumè or curriculum vitae, artist's statement and/or project description. ICP can only accept portfolio submissions via e-mail with "portfolio review" in the subject line or mail (or FedEx, etc.). Please include a SASE for the return of materials. ICP cannot return portfolios submitted without return postage."

INTERNATIONAL VISIONS GALLERY

2629 Connecticut Ave. NW, Washington DC 20008. **E-mail:** intvisionsgallery@gmail.com. **Website:** www.inter-visions.com. **Contact:** Timothy Davis, owner/director. Estab. 1997. Private art gallery and consulting firm. Overall price range: $500-8,000. Most work sold at $2,500.

EXHIBITS Photos of babies/children/teens, multicultural.

MAKING CONTACT & TERMS Interested photographers may send images or web address to intvisions2@gmail.com

JACKSON FINE ART

3115 E. Shadowlawn Ave., Atlanta GA 30305. (404)233-3739. **Fax:** (404)233-1205. **Website:** www.jacksonfineart.com. **Contact:** Sarah Durning, director. Estab. 1990. Specializes in 20th-century and contemporary photography. Exhibitions are rotated every 2 months. Gallery open Tuesday-Saturday, 10-5. Overall price range $600-500,000. Most work sold at $5,000.

EXHIBITS Interested in innovative photography, avant garde, fine art.

MAKING CONTACT & TERMS Only buys vintage photos outright. Requires exclusive representation locally. Exhibits only nationally known artists and emerging artists who show long-term potential. "Photographers must be established, preferably published in books or national art publications. They must also have a strong biography, preferably museum exhibitions, national grants."

SUBMISSIONS Send JPEG files via e-mail. Responds in 3 months, only if interested. Unsolicited original work is not accepted.

ELAINE L. JACOB GALLERY AND ART DEPARTMENT GALLERY

480 W. Hancock St., Detroit MI 48202. (313)577-2423; (313)993-7813. **E-mail:** tpyrzewski@wayne.edu. **Website:** www.art.wayne.edu. **Contact:** Tom Pyrzewski.

Estab. 1995. "The Elaine L. Jacob Gallery serves as a forum for the display of national and international contemporary art. The Art Department Gallery serves as an exhibition venue for the Department of Art and Art History's faculty, students, alumni and community-based groups."

JADITE GALLERIES

413 W. 50th St., New York NY 10019. (212)315-2740. **Fax:** (212)315-2793. **Website:** www.jadite.com. **Contact:** Roland Sainz, director. Estab. 1985. "Exhibitions cover the spectrum of art form created by a myriad of talented artists from the US, Europe, Latin America and Asia. With 3 exhibition spaces, we have fostered a number of promising artists and attracted many serious collectors over the years." Sponsors 3-4 exhibits/year. Average display time 1 month. Open Tuesday–Saturday, 12-6. Overall price range $300-5,000. Most work sold at $1500.

EXHIBITS Photos of landscapes/scenics, architecture, cities/urban, travel. Interested in avant garde, documentary and b&w, color and mixed media.

MAKING CONTACT & TERMS Gallery receives 40% commission. There is a rental fee for space (50/50 split of expenses such as invitations, advertising, opening reception, etc.). Accepted work should be framed.

SUBMISSIONS Arrange a personal interview to show portfolio. Responds in 5 weeks.

ALICE AND WILLIAM JENKINS GALLERY

600 St. Andrews Blvd., Winter Park FL 32792. (407)671-1886. **Fax:** (407)671-0311. **E-mail:** btif fany2000@yahoo.com. **Website:** www.crealde.org. **Contact:** Barbara Tiffany, director of painting and drawing department. Estab. 1980. "The Jenkins Gallery mission is to exhibit the work of noted and established Florida artists, as well as to introduce national and international artists to the Central Florida region." Each of the four to six annual exhibitions are professionally curated by a member of the Crealdé Gallery Committee or a guest curator.

JHB GALLERY

26 Grove St., Suite #4C, New York NY 10014. (212)255-9286. **Fax:** (212)229-8998. **E-mail:** info@jhbgallery. com. **Website:** www.jhbgallery.com. **Contact:** Jayne Baum. Estab. 1982. Private art dealer and consultant. Gallery open by appointment only. Overall price range $1,500-40,000. Most work sold at $1,500-100,000.

MAKING CONTACT & TERMS Artwork is accepted on consignment, and there is a 50% commission. Gallery provides promotion.

SUBMISSIONS Accepts online submissions. Send query letter with résumé, CD, slides, artist's statement, reviews, SASE. Finds artists through submissions, portfolio reviews, art exhibits, art fairs, referrals by other curators.

STELLA JONES GALLERY

201 St. Charles Ave., New Orleans LA 70170. (504)568-9050. **E-mail:** stellajonesgallery.manalia@gmail.com. **Website:** www.stellajonesgallery.com. **Contact:** Stella Jones. Estab. 1996. For-profit gallery. "The gallery provides a venue for artists of the African diaspora to exhibit superior works of art. The gallery fulfills its educational goals through lectures, panel discussions, intimate gallery talks and exhibitions with artists in attendance." Approached by 40 artists/year; represents or exhibits 45 artists. Sponsors 1 photography exhibit/year. Average display time: 6-8 weeks. Open Monday–Saturday, 12-5. Located on 1st floor of corporate 53-story office building downtown, 1 block from French Quarter. Overall price range: $500-150,000. Most work sold at $5,000.

EXHIBITS Photos of babies/children/teens, multicultural, families, cities/urban, education, religious, rural.

MAKING CONTACT & TERMS Artwork is accepted on consignment, and there is a 50% commission. Gallery provides insurance, promotion, contract. Accepted work should be framed. Requires exclusive representation locally.

SUBMISSIONS Call to show portfolio of photographs, slides, transparencies. Mail portfolio for review. Send query letter with artist's statement, bio, brochure, business card, photocopies, photographs, résumé, reviews, slides, SASE. Responds in 1 month. Finds artists through word of mouth, submissions, portfolio reviews, art exhibits, referrals by other artists.

TIPS "Photographers should be organized with good visuals."

JRB ART AT THE ELMS

2810 North Walker, Oklahoma City OK 73103. (405)528-6336. **Fax:** (405)528-6337. **E-mail:** jreed belt@jrbartgallery.com. **Website:** www.jrbartgallery. com. **Contact:** Joy Reed Belt, director. Estab. 2003. "JRB Art at the Elms presents a diverse roster of emerging, established and internationally-exhibited artists who create in a wide range of media, including paintings, drawings, sculpture, ceramics, glass, fine crafts, functional objects, fiber art, fine art prints and photographs. This award-winning gallery in Oklahoma City's Paseo Arts District, with its historic 8,000-sq.-ft. exhibition space, changes its exhibits monthly in a gracious environment that fosters a dialogue between the arts and the larger community while providing quality art for first-time buyers as well as individual, corporate and museum collections."

KENT STATE UNIVERSITY SCHOOL OF ART GALLERIES

P.O. Box 5190, Kent OH 44242. (330)672-1379. E-mail: haturner@kent.edu. **Website:** galleries.kent.edu. **Contact:** Anderson Turner, director of galleries. Located in six locations throughout northeast Ohio, please see website for location and hours. Sponsors at least 6 photography exhibits/year. Average display time 4 weeks.

EXHIBITS Interested in all types, styles and subject matter of photography. Photographer must present quality work.

MAKING CONTACT & TERMS Photography can be sold in gallery. Charges 40% commission. Buys photography outright.

SUBMISSIONS Send proposal, résumé, and a CD of 10-20 digital images of work to be included in the exhibition. Send material by mail for consideration; include SASE. Responds "usually in 4 months, but it depends on time submitted."

KIRCHMAN GALLERY

P.O. Box 115, 213 N. Nugent St., Johnson City TX 78636. (830)868-9290. **E-mail:** susan@kirchmangallery.com. **Website:** www.kirchmangallery.com. **Contact:** Susan Kirchman, owner/director. Estab. 2005. Art consultancy and for-profit gallery. Represents or exhibits 25 artists. Average display time 1 month. Sponsors 4 photography exhibits/year. Open Sunday, 12-5; Monday 11-5; Thursday 12-6; Friday & Saturday, 11-6; anytime by appointment. Located across from Johnson City's historic Courthouse Square in the heart of Texas hill country. Overall price range $250-25,000. Most work sold at $500-1,000.

EXHIBITS Photos of landscapes/scenics. Interested in alternative process, avant garde, fine art.

MAKING CONTACT & TERMS Artwork is accepted on consignment, and there is a 50% commission.

SUBMISSIONS "Send 20 digital-format examples of your work, along with a résumé and artist's statement."

ROBERT KLEIN GALLERY

38 Newbury St., 4th Floor, Boston MA 02116. (617)267-7997. **Fax:** (617)267-5567. **E-mail:** inquiry@robertkleingallery.com. **Website:** www.robertkleingallery.com. **Contact:** Robert L. Klein, owner; Eunice Hurd, director. Estab. 1980. Devoted exclusively to fine art photography, specifically 19th and 20th century and contemporary. Sponsors 10 exhibits/year. Average display time 5 weeks. Overall price range $1,000-200,000. Open Tuesday–Friday, 10-5:30; Saturday, 11-5 and by appointment.

EXHIBITS Interested in fashion, documentary, nudes, portraiture, and work that has been fabricated to be photographs.

MAKING CONTACT & TERMS Charges 50% commission. Buys photos outright. Accepted work should be unframed, unmatted, unmounted. Requires exclusive representation locally. Must be established a minimum of 5 years; preferably published.

SUBMISSIONS "The Robert Klein Gallery is not accepting any unsolicited submissions. Unsolicited submissions will not be reviewed or returned."

ROBERT KOCH GALLERY

49 Geary St., 5th Floor, San Francisco CA 94108. (415)421-0122. **Fax:** (415)421-6306. **E-mail:** info@kochgallery.com. **Website:** www.kochgallery.com. Estab. 1979. "Our gallery has exhibited and offered a wide range of museum quality photography that spans the history of the medium from the 19th century to the present. Our extensive inventory emphasizes Modernist and experimental work from the 1920s and 1930s, 19th-century and contemporary photography." Sponsors 6-8 photography exhibits/year. Average display time 2 months. Located in the heart of San Francisco's downtown Union Square. Open Tuesday–Saturday, 11-5:30.

MAKING CONTACT & TERMS Artwork is accepted on consignment. "E-mail artist, title or description of subject matter, date, medium, dimensions and any other pertinent information with a low-res JPEG. Also include your name, e-mail address, phone number and the best time to reach you." Gallery provides insurance, promotion, contract. Requires West Coast or national representation.

SUBMISSIONS Finds artists through publications, art exhibits, art fairs, referrals by other artists and curators, collectors, critics.

LANDING GALLERY

8 Elm St., Rockland ME 04841. (207)594-4544. E-mail: landinggallery@gmail.com. **Website:** www.landingart.com. **Contact:** Bruce Busko, president. Estab. 1985. For-profit gallery. Approached by 40 artists/year. Exhibits 35 emerging, mid-career and established artists.

EXHIBITS Photos of landscapes/scenics, architecture, cities/urban, rural, adventure, automobiles, entertainment. Interested in alternative process, avant garde, erotic, fine art, historical/vintage. Seeking photos "with hand color or embellishment."

MAKING CONTACT & TERMS Artwork is accepted on consignment, and there is a 50% commission. Gallery provides insurance, promotion, contract. Accepted work should be framed. Requires exclusive representation locally.

SUBMISSIONS Call to show portfolio. Mail portfolio for review. Send query letter with artist's statement, bio, brochure, business card, photocopies, photographs, résumé, reviews, slides, SASE. Responds in 2 weeks. Finds artists through word of mouth, submissions, portfolio reviews, art exhibits, art fairs, referrals by other artists.

⊕ LAWNDALE ART CENTER

4912 Main St., Houston TX 77002. (713)528-5858. **Fax:** (713)528-4140. **E-mail:** askus@lawndaleartcenter.org. **Website:** www.lawndaleartcenter.org. **Contact:** Dennis Nance, exhibitions & programming director. Estab. 1979. Nonprofit gallery, museum, alternative space. Exhibits emerging, mid-career and established artists. Approached by 1,200 artists/year. Exhibits 150 artists. Sponsors 25 exhibits/year; approx. 5 photography exhibits/year. Model/property release preferred. Average display time: 5 weeks. Open Monday—Friday, 10–5; Saturday, 12–5; closed Sunday, Christmas Eve until New Year's Day, Presiden'ts Day, Memorial Day, Independence Day, Labor Day, Columbus Day and Thanksgiving. "Located at the edge of Downtown in the Museum District, Lawndale includes 4 museum-quality galleries, 3 artist studios, an outdoor sculpture garden and annual rotating mural wall." Clients include: local community, students, tourists, upscale, artists, collectors, art enthusiasts, volunteers, young professionals.

EXHIBITS Considers all media. Gallery provides insurance, promotion, contract. Prefers artists from Houston TX and surrounding area.

MAKING CONTACT & TERMS "Visit the proposal section of our website: www.lawndaleartcenter.org/exhibitions/proposals.shtml." Does not accept mailed proposals. All proposals must be made online.

SUBMISSIONS Finds artists through word of mouth, submissions, referrals by other artists.

TIPS "Please visit us or our website to learn about what type of work we exhibit and how we accept submissions to artists before contacting."

LAW WARSCHAW GALLERY

Macalester College, Janet Wallace Fine Arts Center, 1600 Grand Ave., St. Paul MN 55105. (651)696-6416. **Fax:** (651)696-6266. **E-mail:** gallery@macalester.edu. **Website:** www.macalester.edu/gallery. **Contact:** Gregory Fitz, curator. Estab. 1964. Nonprofit gallery. Approached by 15 artists/year; represents or exhibits 3 artists. Sponsors 1 photography exhibit/year. Average display time 4-5 weeks. Gallery open Monday-Friday, 10-4; Thursdays, 12-8; weekends, 12-4. Closed major holidays, summer and school holidays. Located in the core of the Janet Wallace Fine Arts Center on the campus of Macalester College. While emphasizing contemporary, the gallery also hosts exhibitions on a wide-range of historical and sociological topics. Gallery is approx. 1,100 sq. ft. and newly renovated. Overall price range: $200-1,000. Most work sold at $350.

EXHIBITS Photos of multicultural, environmental, landscapes/scenics, architecture, rural. Interested in avant garde, documentary, fine art, historical/vintage.

MAKING CONTACT & TERMS Gallery provides insurance. Accepted work should be framed, mounted, matted.

SUBMISSIONS Send query letter with artist's statement, bio, brochure, business card, photocopies, photographs, résumé, reviews, SASE, slides. Finds artists through word of mouth, portfolio reviews, referrals by other artists.

TIPS "Photographers should present quality slides which are clearly labeled. Include a concise artist's statement. Always include a SASE. No form letters or mass mailings."

⊘ ELIZABETH LEACH GALLERY

417 NW Ninth Ave., Portland OR 97209-3308. (503)224-0521. **Fax:** (503)224-0844. **Website:** www.elizabethleach.com. Currently not accepted unsolic-

ited submissions. Sponsors 3-4 exhibits/year. Average display time 1 month. "The gallery has extended hours every first Thursday of the month for our openings." Overall price range $300-5,000.

EXHIBITS Photographers must meet museum conservation standards. Interested in "high-quality concept and fine craftmanship."

MAKING CONTACT & TERMS Charges 50% commission. Accepted work should be framed or unframed, matted. Requires exclusive representation locally.

SUBMISSIONS Not accepting submissions at this time.

SHERRY LEEDY CONTEMPORARY ART

2004 Baltimore Ave., Kansas City MO 64108. (816)221-2626. **Fax:** (816)221-8689. **E-mail:** sherryleedy@sherryleedy.com. **Website:** www.sherryleedy.com. **Contact:** Sherry Leedy, director. Estab. 1985. Retail gallery. Represents 50 mid-career and established artists. Exhibited artists include Jun Kaneko, Mike Schultz, Vera Mercer, and more. Sponsors 6 shows/year. Average display time: 6 weeks. Open Tuesday–Saturday, 11-5, and by appointment. 5,000 sq. ft. of exhibit area in 3 galleries. Clients include established and beginning collectors. 50% of sales are to private collectors, 50% corporate clients. Overall price range: $50-100,000; most work sold at $3,500-35,000.

EXHIBITS Considers all media and one-of-a-kind or limited-edition prints; no posters. Most frequently exhibits painting, photography, ceramic sculpture and glass.

MAKING CONTACT & TERMS Accepts work on consignment (50% commission). Retail price set by gallery in counsultation with the artist. Sometimes offers customer discounts and payment by installment. Exclusive area representation required. Gallery provides insurance, promotion; shipping costs are shared. Prefers artwork framed.

SUBMISSIONS E-mail query letter, résumé, artist's statement, and digital images or link to website. No work will be reviewed in person without a prior appointment.

TIPS "Please allow 3 months for gallery to review submissions."

LEEPA-RATTNER MUSEUM OF ART

P.O. Box 1545, Tarpon Springs FL 34688. (727)712-5762. **E-mail:** lrma@spcollege.edu. **Website:** www.spcollege.edu/museum. **Contact:** R. Lynn Whitelaw, curator. "The museum's 20th-century collection is made up of art from Abraham Rattner's estate, donated by Allen and Isabelle Leepa, and a large donation made by the Tampa Museum of Art. The museum is filled with Rattner's retrospective works: lithographs, tapestries, sculptures, paintings and stained glass." Open Tuesday, Wednesday, Saturday, 10-5; Thursday, 10-8; Friday, 10-4; Sunday, 1-5; closed Mondays and national holidays. Located on the Tarpon Springs campus of St. Petersburg College.

EXHIBITS Photos of babies/children/teens, celebrities, couples, multicultural, families, parents, senior citizens, architecture, cities/urban, education, gardening, interiors/decorating, pets, religious, rural, agriculture, business concepts, industry, medicine, military, political, product shots/still life, science, technology/computers, disasters, environmental, landscapes/scenics, wildlife, adventure, automobiles, entertainment, events, food/drink, health/fitness/beauty, hobbies, humor, performing arts, sports, travel. Interested in alternative process, avant garde, documentary, erotic, fashion/glamour, fine art, historical/vintage, seasonal.

LEGION ARTS

1103 Third St. SE, Cedar Rapids IA 52401-2305. (319)364-1580. **Fax:** (319)362-9156. **E-mail:** info@legionarts.org. **Website:** www.legionarts.org. **Contact:** Mel Andringa, producing director. Estab. 1991. Alternative space. Approached by 50 artists/year; represents or exhibits 15 artists. Sponsors 4 photography exhibits/year. Average display time: 2 months. Open Wednesday–Sunday, 11-6; closed July and August. Overall price range: $50-500. Most work sold at $200.

EXHIBITS Interested in alternative process, avant garde, documentary, fine art.

MAKING CONTACT & TERMS Artwork is accepted on consignment and there is a 30% commission. Gallery provides insurance, promotion. Accepted work should be framed.

SUBMISSIONS Send query letter with artist's statement, bio, slides, SASE. Responds in 6 months. Finds artists through word of mouth, art exhibits, referrals by other artists, art trade magazine.

LEHIGH UNIVERSITY ART GALLERIES

420 E. Packer Ave., Bethlehem PA 18015. (610)758-3619; (610)758-3615. **Fax:** (610)758-4580. **E-mail:** rv02@lehigh.edu. **Website:** www.luag.org. **Contact:** Ricardo Viera, director/curator. Sponsors 5-8 exhib-

its/year. Average display time 6-12 weeks. Sponsors openings.

EXHIBITS Fine art/multicultural, Latin American. Interested in all types of works. The photographer should "preferably be an established professional."

MAKING CONTACT & TERMS Reviews transparencies. Arrange a personal interview to show portfolio. Send query letter with SASE. Responds in 1 month.

TIPS "Don't send more than 10 slides or a CD."

DAVID LEONARDIS GALLERY

1346 N. Paulina St., Chicago IL 60622. (312)863-9045. **E-mail:** david@dlg-gallery.com. **Website:** www.dlg-gallery.com. **Contact:** David Leonardis, owner. Estab. 1992. For-profit gallery. Approached by 100 artists/year. Represents 12 emerging, mid-career and established artists. Average display time: 30 days. Open by appointment. Clients include local community, tourists, upscale. 10% of sales are to corporate collectors. Overall price range: $50-5,000; most work sold at $500.

EXHIBITS Photos of celebrities. Interested in fine art.

MAKING CONTACT & TERMS Artwork is accepted on consignment, and there is a 50% commission. Gallery provides promotion. Accepted work should be framed.

SUBMISSIONS E-mail to arrange a personal interview to show portfolio. Mail portfolio for review. Send query letter via e-mail. Responds only if interested. Finds artists through word of mouth, art exhibits, referrals by other artists.

TIPS "Artists should be professional and easy to deal with."

LEOPOLD GALLERY

324 W. 63rd St., Kansas City MO 64113. (816)333-3111. **Fax:** (816)333-3616. **E-mail:** email@leopoldgallery.com. **Website:** www.leopoldgallery.com. **Contact:** Paula Busser, assistant director. Estab. 1991. For-profit gallery. Approached by 100+ artists/year; represents 40 artists/year. Sponsors 8 exhibits/year. Average display time 4 weeks. Open Monday–Friday, 10-6; Saturday, 10-5. Closed holidays. The gallery has two levels of exhibition space. Clients include H&R Block, Warner Bros., Kansas City Royals, local community, tourists. 65% of sales are to corporate collectors. Overall price range: $50-25,000; most work sold at $1,500. "We are located in Brookside, a charming retail district built in 1920 with more than 70 shops and restaurants. The gallery has 2 levels of exhibition space, with the upper level dedicated to artist openings/exhibitions."

EXHIBITS Photos of architecture, cities/urban, rural, environmental, landscapes/scenics, wildlife, entertainment, performing arts. Interested in alternative process, avant garde, documentary, fine art.

MAKING CONTACT & TERMS Artwork is accepted on consignment; there is a 50% commission. Gallery provides insurance, promotion, contract. Accepted work should be framed, mounted, matted. **Accepts artists from Kansas City area only.** Send query letter with artist's statement, bio, brochure, business card, résumé, reviews, SASE, disk with images. Responds in 2 weeks. Finds artists through word of mouth, art exhibitions, submissions, art fairs, portfolio reviews, referrals by other artists.

SUBMISSIONS E-mail 5-10 JPEG images of your body of work to email@leopoldgallery.com. Before sending, please scan your e-mail for viruses, as any viral e-mails will be deleted upon receipt. Images should be saved at 72 dpi, approximately 5×7 and compressed to level 3 JPEG. Please save for Windows. Or, send e-mail query letter with link to artist's website.

LICHTENSTEIN CENTER FOR THE ARTS

28 Renne Ave., Pittsfield MA 01201. (413)499-9348. **Fax:** (413)442-8043. **Website:** www.discoverpittsfield.com. **Contact:** Dan Gigliotti, gallery manager. Estab. 1975. Sponsors 10 exhibits/year. Open Wednesday–Saturday, 12-5. Overall price range $50+

MAKING CONTACT & TERMS Charges 20% commission. Will review transparencies of photographic work. Accepted work should be framed, mounted, matted.

SUBMISSIONS "Photographer should send SASE with 20 slides or prints, résumé and statement by mail only to gallery."

TIPS "To break in, send portfolio, slides and SASE. We accept all art photography. Work must be professionally presented and framed. Send in by July 1 each year. Expect exhibition 2-3 years from submission date. We have a professional juror look at slide entries once a year (usually July-September). Expect that work to be tied up for 2-3 months in jury."

LIMITED EDITIONS & COLLECTIBLES

697 Haddon Ave., Collingswood NJ 08108. (856)869-5228. **Fax:** (856)869-5228. **E-mail:** jdl697ltd@juno.com. **Website:** www.ltdeditions.net. **Contact:** John Daniel Lynch, Sr., owner. Estab. 1997. For-profit on-

line gallery. Approached by 24 artists/year; represents or exhibits 70 artists. Sponsors 20 photography exhibits/year. Overall price range $100-3,000. Most work sold at $450.

EXHIBITS Photos of landscapes/scenics, wildlife, adventure, automobiles, entertainment, events, food/drink, health/fitness/beauty, hobbies, humor, performing arts, sports, travel. Interested in alternative process, documentary, erotic, fashion/glamour, historical/vintage, seasonal.

MAKING CONTACT & TERMS Artwork is accepted on consignment, and there is a 30% commission. Gallery provides insurance, promotion, contract.

SUBMISSIONS Call or write to show portfolio. Send query letter with bio, business card, résumé. Responds in 1 month. Finds artists through word of mouth, portfolio reviews, art exhibits, referrals by other artists.

LIMNER GALLERY

123 Warren St., Hudson NY 12534. (518)828-2343. **E-mail:** thelimner@aol.com. **Website:** www.slowart. com. **Contact:** Tim Slowinski, director. Estab. 1987. Alternative space. Established in Manhattan's East Village. Approached by 200-250 artists/year; represents or exhibits 90-100 artists. Sponsors 2 photography exhibits/year. Average display time: 4 weeks. Open Thursday-Saturday, 12-5; Sunday, 12-4. Closed January, July-August (weekends only). Located in the art and antiques center of the Hudson Valley. Exhibition space is 1,000 sq. ft.

EXHIBITS Interested in alternative process, avant garde, documentary, erotic, fine art, historical/vintage.

SUBMISSIONS Artists should e-mail a link to their website; or download exhibition application at www. slowart.com/prospectus; or send query letter with artist's statement, bio, brochure or photographs/slides, SASE. Finds artists through submissions.

TIPS "Artist's website should be simple and easy to view. Complicated animations and scripted design should be avoided, as it is a distraction and prevents direct viewing of the work. Not all galleries and art buyers have cable modems. The website should either work on a telephone line connection or 2 versions of the site should be offered—one for telephone, one for cable/high-speed Internet access."

LIZARDI/HARP GALLERY

P.O. Box 91895, Pasadena CA 91109. (626)791-8123. **Fax:** (626)791-8887. **E-mail:** lizardiharp@earthlink.net. **Contact:** Grady Harp, director. Estab. 1981. Sponsors 3-4 exhibits/year. Average display time 4-6 weeks. Overall price range $250-1,500. Most work sold at $500.

EXHIBITS Primarily interested in the figure. Also exhibits photos of celebrities, couples, performing arts. Must have more than one portfolio of subject, unique slant and professional manner. Interested in avant garde, erotic, fine art, figurative, nudes, "maybe" manipulated work, documentary and mood landscapes, both b&w and color.

MAKING CONTACT & TERMS Charges 50% commission. Accepted work should be unframed, unmounted; matted or unmatted.

SUBMISSIONS Submit portfolio for review. E-mail query letter with résumé, samples. Responds in 1 month.

TIPS Include 20 labeled slides, résumé and artist's statement with submission. "Submit at least 20 images that represent bodies of work. I mix photography of figures, especially nudes, with shows on painting."

ANNE LLOYD GALLERY

125 N. Water St., Decatur IL 62523-1025. **E-mail:** sue@decaturarts.org. **Website:** www.decaturarts. org. **Contact:** Sue Powell, gallery director. Estab. 2004. Nonprofit gallery. Approached by 10 artists/year. Represents 20 artists. Exhibits emerging, midcareer and established artists. Exhibited artists include Seth Casteel (photographer) and Rob O'Dell (watercolor). Sponsors 8 exhibits/year, 1 photography exhibit. Average display time: 1 month. Open Monday–Friday, 8:30-4:30; Saturday, 10-2. Closed major holidays. Located within the Madden Arts Center (community arts center owned/operated by Decatur Area Arts Council) in downtown Decatur IL. Approx. 1,500 sq. ft. space with 113 linear feet wall space; 14 ft. ceilings; 10 ft. high gallery cloth walls. Excellent track/grid lighting. Clients include local community, students and tourists. 1% of sales are to corporate collectors. Overall price range: $100-5,000. Most work sold at $100-500.

EXHIBITS Considers alternative process, avant garde, fine art. Most frequently exhibits acrylic, oil, and watercolor. Considers all media except installation. Considers all types of prints. Considers all styles. Considers all genres. Most frequently exhibits painting, mixed media, sculpture.

MAKING CONTACT & TERMS Artwork is accepted on consignment and there is a 35% commission. Retail price set by the artist. Museum provides insurance, promotion, and contract. Accepted work should be framed or mounted. Does not require exclusive representation locally. Art must be appropriate for a family-type venue.

SUBMISSIONS Call; e-mail query letter with link to website and JPEG samples at 72 dpi; or send query letter with artist's statement, bio, CD with images. Can also mail portfolio for review. Material is returned with SASE. Responds in 4 weeks. Files bio, statement, images, contact info. Finds artists through art exhibits, referrals by other artists, portfolio reviews, art fairs, research online, submissions, and word of mouth.

TIPS "Please include 6-10 images on a CD. This is important."

LOS ANGELES MUNICIPAL ART GALLERY

4800 Hollywood Blvd., Los Angeles CA 90027. **Website:** www.lamag.org. **Contact:** Scott Canty, curator. Estab. gallery 1971; support group LAMAGA 1954. City-run, municipally-owned gallery. Nonprofit. Exhibits emerging, mid-career, and established artists. Sponsors 8 total exhibits/year. Average display time: 8 weeks. Open Thursday-Sunday, 12-5. 10,000 sq. ft. city-run facility located in Barnsdall Park in Hollywood, CA. Clients include local community, students, tourists, and upscale clientele.

EXHIBITS Accepts all media.

SUBMISSIONS "Visit our website at lamag.org for upcoming show opportunities." Files artists and proposals of interests. Finds artists through word of mouth, submissions, portfolio review, art exhibits, art fairs, referrals by other artists and the DCA Slide Registry.

BILL LOWE GALLERY

764 Miami Circle, Suite 210, Atlanta GA 30324. (404)352-8114. **Fax:** (404)352-0564. **E-mail:** contact@lowegallery.com; alexis@lowegallery.com. **Website:** www.lowegallery.com. For-profit gallery. Approached by 300 artists/year; represents or exhibits approximately 67 artists. Average display time: 4-6 weeks. Open Tuesday–Friday, 10-5:30; Saturday, 11-5:30; Sunday by appointment. Exhibition space is 6,000 sq. ft. with great architectural details, such as 22-ft.-high ceilings. Exhibition spaces range from monumental to intimate.

EXHIBITS Photos of babies/children/teens, multicultural. Interested in alternative process, mixed media.

MAKING CONTACT & TERMS Artwork is accepted on consignment, and there is a 50% commission. Requires exclusive representation locally.

SUBMISSIONS Send query letter with artists's statement, bio, images on CD (including titles, media, dimensions, retail price), résumé, reviews, SASE. Prefers mail to e-mail. If submitting through e-mail, it should not exceed 2MB. Include contact information website link, biographical information, exhibition history, artist statement, reviews or any other supplemental material (within reason). Response time approximately 6 weeks. Finds artists through word of mouth, art exhibits, submissions, art fairs, portfolio reviews, referrals by other artists. Submission guidelines available online.

TIPS "Look at the type of work that the gallery already represents, and make sure your work is an aesthetic fit first! Send lots of great images with dimensions and pricing."

LUX CENTER FOR THE ARTS

2601 N. 48th St., Lincoln NE 68504. (402)466-8692. **Fax:** (402)466-3786. **E-mail:** info@luxcenter.org. **Website:** www.luxcenter.org. Estab. 1978. Nonprofit gallery. Over 450 fine arts prints collected by the art center's benefactor are preserved in the Gladys M. Lux Historical Gallery. Exhibited artists include Guy Pene DuBois, Joseph Hirsch, Doris Emrick Lee, Fletcher Martin, Georges Schreiber, Marguerite Zorach and many more. Represents or exhibits 60+ artists. Sponsors 3-4 photography exhibits/year. Average display time 1 month. Open Tuesday–Friday, 11-5; Saturday, 10-5; 1st Friday, 11-8.

EXHIBITS Photos of landscapes/scenics. Interested in alternative process, avant garde, fine art.

MAKING CONTACT & TERMS Artwork is accepted on consignment, and there is a 50% commission.

SUBMISSIONS Mail current résumé, artist's statement, biography, 10-20 digital images of your work, and accompanying image identification information.

TIPS "To make your submission professional, you should have high-quality images (either slides or high-res digital images), cover letter, bio, résumé, artist's statement and SASE."

MACNIDER ART MUSEUM

303 Second St. SE, Mason City IA 50401. (641)421-3666. **Fax:** (641)422-9612. **E-mail:** eblanchard@masoncity.net; macniderinformation@masoncity.net. **Website:** www.macniderart.org. Estab. 1966. Nonprofit gallery. Represents or exhibits 1-10 artists. Sponsors 2-5 photography exhibits/year (1 is competitive for the county). Average display time: 2 months. Gallery open Wednesday, Friday and Saturday, 9-5; Tuesday and Thursday, 9-8; closed Sunday and Monday. Overall price range: $50-2,500. Most work sold at $200.

MAKING CONTACT & TERMS Artwork is accepted on consignment, and there is a 40% commission. Gallery provides insurance, promotion, contract. Accepted work should be framed.

SUBMISSIONS Mail portfolio for review. Responds within 3 months, only if interested. Finds artists through word of mouth, submissions, portfolio reviews, art exhibits, art fairs, referrals by other artists. Exhibition opportunities: exhibition in galleries, presence in museum shop on consignment or booth at Festival Art Market in June.

MAIN STREET GALLERY

330 Main St., Ketchikan AK 99901. (907)225-2211. **E-mail:** info@ketchikanarts.org. **Website:** www.ketchikanarts.org. **Contact:** Marni Rickelmann, program director. Estab. 1953. Nonprofit gallery. Exhibits emerging, mid-career and established artists. Number of artists represented or exhibited varies based on applications. Applications annually accepted for March 1 deadline. Sponsors 11 total exhibits/year. Model and property release are preferred. Average display time: 20 days-1 month. Open Monday-Friday, 9-5; Saturday, 11-3; closed last 2 weeks of December. Located in downtown Ketchikan, housed in renovated church. 800 sq. ft. Clients include local community, students, tourists, upscale. Overall price range: $20-4,000; most work sold at $150.

MAKING CONTACT & TERMS There is a membership fee plus a donation of time. There is a 25% commission. Retail price set by the artist. Gallery provides insurance, promotion and contract. Accepted work should be framed and mounted.

SUBMISSIONS E-mail query letter with link to artist's website, 10 JPEG samples at 72 dpi or résumé and proposal. March 1 gallery exhibit deadline for September-August season. Returns material with SASE.

Responds in 2 months from March 1 deadline. Files all application materials. Finds artists through word of mouth, submissions, art exhibits and referrals from other artists.

TIPS Respond clearly to application.

BEN MALTZ GALLERY

Otis College of Art & Design, Ground Floor, Bronya and Andy Galef Center for Fine Arts, 9045 Lincoln Blvd., Los Angeles CA 90045. (310)665-6905. **E-mail:** galleryinfo@otis.edu. **Website:** www.otis.edu/benmaltzgallery. Estab. 1957. Nonprofit gallery. Exhibits local, national and international emerging, mid-career and established artists. Sponsors 4-6 exhibits/year. Average display time: 1-2 months. Open Tuesday–Friday, 10-5 (Thursday, 10-9); Saturday-Sunday, 12-4; closed Mondays and major holidays. Located near Los Angeles International Airport (LAX); approximately 3,520 sq. ft.; 14-ft. walls. Clients include students, Otis community, local and city community, regional art community, artists, collectors and tourists.

EXHIBITS Fine art/design. Considers all media, most frequently exhibits paintings, drawings, mixed media, sculpture and video.

SUBMISSIONS Submission guidelines available online. Submissions via internet only. Do not send other materials unless requested by the gallery after your initial submission has been reviewed.

TIPS "Follow submission guidelines and be patient. Attend opening receptions when possible to familiarize yourself with the gallery, director, curators and artists."

MANITOU ART CENTER

513 Manitou Ave., Manitou Springs CO 80829. (719)685-1861. **E-mail:** director@thebac.org. **Website:** www.thebac.org. Estab. 1988. The MAC is a nonprofit gallery situated in 2 renovated landmark buildings in the Manitou Springs National Historic District, located at 513 and 515 Manitou Ave. Art studios are available for rent and often include equipment. The Manitou Art Center sponsors 16 exhibits/year in our 5 galleries. Average display time: 6 weeks-2 months. Gallery open most days, 8-8; closed Tuesday. Overall price range $50-3,000. Most work sold at $300.

EXHIBITS Photos of environmental, landscapes/scenics, wildlife, gardening, rural, adventure, health/fitness, performing arts, travel. Interested in alternative process, avant garde, documentary, fashion/glamour, fine art.

MAKING CONTACT & TERMS "Artwork is accepted for our open submission and shows and there is a 30% commission." The gallery provides insurance, promotion and a basic contract. Accepted work should be framed and ready to hang.

SUBMISSIONS Write to arrange a personal interview to show portfolio. "We often find artists through word of mouth, submissions, art exhibits and referrals by other artists."

MARIN MUSEUM OF CONTEMPORARY ART

500 Palm Dr., Novato CA 94949. (415)506-0137. **Fax:** (415)506-0139. **E-mail:** info@marinmoca.org. **Website:** www.marinmoca.org. **Contact:** Heidi LaGrasta, executive director. Estab. 2007. Nonprofit gallery. Exhibits emerging, mid-career and established artists. Sponsors 15+ exhibits/year. Model and property release is preferred. Average display time: 5 weeks. Open Wednesday-Sunday, 11-4; closed Thanksgiving, Christmas, New Year's Day. MarinMOCA is located in historic Hamilton Field, a former Army Air Base. The Spanish-inspired architecture makes for a unique and inviting exterior and interior space. Houses 2 exhibition spaces—the Main Gallery (1,633 sq. ft.) and the Ron Collins Gallery (750 sq. ft.). Part of the Novato Arts Center, which also contains approximately 50 artist studios and a classroom (offers adult classes and a summer camp for children). Clients include local community, students, tourists, upscale. Overall price range: $200-20,000; most work sold at $500-1,000.

EXHIBITS Considers all media except video. Most frequently exhibits acrylic, oil, sculpture/installation. Considers all prints, styles and genres.

MAKING CONTACT & TERMS Artwork is accepted on consignment and there is a 40% commission. Retail price of the art set by the artist. Gallery provides insurance, promotion (for single exhibition only, not representation), contract (for consignment only, not representation). Accepted work should be framed (canvas can be unframed, but prints/collage/photos should be framed). "We do not have exclusive contracts with, nor do we represent artists."

SUBMISSIONS "We are currently not accepting portfolio submissions at this time. Please visit our website for updates. If you are interested in gallery rental, please contact Heidi LaGrasta." Finds artists through word of mouth and portfolio reviews.

TIPS "Keep everything clean and concise. Avoid lengthy, flowery language and choose clear explanations instead. Submit only what is requested and shoot for a confident, yet humble tone. Make sure images are good quality (300 dpi) and easily identifiable regarding title, size, medium."

MARKEIM ARTS CENTER

104 Walnut St., Haddonfield NJ 08033. (856)429-8585. **E-mail:** markeim@verizon.net. **Website:** www.markeimartcenter.org. **Contact:** Elizabeth H. Madden, executive director. Estab. 1956. Sponsors 10-11 exhibits/year. Average display time: 4 weeks. The exhibiting artist is responsible for all details of the opening. Overall price range: $75-1,000. Most work sold at $350.

EXHIBITS Interested in all types work. Exhibits photos of babies/children/teens, celebrities, couples, multicultural, families, parents, senior citizens, environmental, landscapes/scenics, wildlife, architecture, cities/urban, education, rural, adventure, automobiles, entertainment, performing arts, sports, travel, agriculture, product shots/still life. Interested in alternative process, avant garde, documentary, fine art, historical/vintage, seasonal.

MAKING CONTACT & TERMS Charges 30% commission. Accepted work should be framed and wired, ready to hang, mounted or unmounted, matted or unmatted. Artists from New Jersey and Delaware Valley region are preferred. Work must be professional and high quality.

SUBMISSIONS Send slides by mail or e-mail for consideration. Include SASE, résumé and letter of intent. Responds in 1 month.

TIPS "Be patient and flexible with scheduling. Look not only for one-time shows, but for opportunities to develop working relationships with a gallery. Establish yourself locally and market yourself outward."

MARLBORO GALLERY

Prince George's Community College, 301 Largo Rd., Largo MD 20477. (301)322-0965. **E-mail:** beraulta@pgcc.edu. **Website:** academic.pgcc.edu/art/gallery. **Contact:** Tom Berault, curator-director. Estab. 1976. Average display time 5 weeks. Overall price range $50-4,000. Most work sells at $300-2,500.

EXHIBITS Fine art, photos of celebrities, portraiture, landscapes/scenics, wildlife/adventure, entertainment, events and travel. Also interested in alternative processes, experimental/manipulated, avant garde photographs. Not interested in commercial work.

MAKING CONTACT & TERMS "We do not take commission on artwork sold." Accepted work must be framed and suitable for hanging.

SUBMISSIONS "We are most interested in fine art photos and need 15-20 examples to make assessment. Reviews are done on an ongoing basis. We prefer to receive submissions February through April." Please send cover letter with résumé, CD or digital media with 15 to 20 JPEGs (approx. 1,200×800 pixels), image list with titles, media and dimensions, artist's statement, and SASE to return. Responds in 1 month.

TIPS "Send examples of what you wish to display, and explanations if photos do not meet normal standards (e.g., out of focus, experimental subject matter)."

MASUR MUSEUM OF ART

1400 S. Grand St., Monroe LA 71202. (318)329-2237. **Fax:** (318)329-2847. **E-mail:** info@masurmuseum. org; evelyn.stewart@ci.monroe.la.us. **Website:** www. masurmuseum.org. **Contact:** Evelyn Stewart, director. Estab. 1963. Approached by 500 artists/year; represents or exhibits 150 artists. Sponsors 2 photography exhibits/year. Average display time 2 months. Museum open Tuesday–Friday, 9-5; Saturday, 12-5. Closed Mondays, between exhibitions and on major holidays. Located in historic home, 3,000 sq. ft. Overall price range $100-12,000. Most work sold at $300.

EXHIBITS Photos of babies/children/teens, celebrities, environmental, landscapes/scenics. Interested in alternative process, avant garde, documentary, fine art, historical/vintage.

MAKING CONTACT & TERMS Artwork is accepted on consignment, and there is a 20% commission. Gallery provides insurance, promotion. Accepted work should be framed.

SUBMISSIONS Send query letter with artist's statement, bio, résumé, reviews, slides, SASE. Responds in 6 months. Finds artists through word of mouth, submissions, art exhibits, referrals by other artists.

MAUI HANDS

P.O. Box 974, Makawao, HI 96768 (808)573-2021. **Fax:** (808)573-2022. **E-mail:** panna@mauihands. com. **Website:** www.mauihands.com. **Contact:** Panna Cappelli, owner. Estab. 1992. For-profit gallery. Approached by 50-60 artists/year. Continuously exhibits 300 emerging, mid-career and established artists. Exhibited artists include Linda Whittemore (abstract

monotypes) and Steven Smeltzer (ceramic sculpture). Sponsors 15-20 exhibits/year; 2 photography exhibits/ year. Average display time: 1 month. Open Monday-Sunday, 10-7; weekends, 10-6; closed on Christmas and Thanksgiving. Four spaces: #1 on Main Highway, 1,200-sq.-ft. gallery, 165-sq.-ft. exhibition; #2 on Main Highway, 1,000-sq.-ft. gallery, 80-sq.-ft. exhibition; #3 in resort, 900-sq.-ft. gallery, 50-sq.-ft. exhibition; #4 1169 Makawao Ave., Makawao HI 96768. Clients include local community, tourists and upscale. 3% of sales are to corporate collectors. Overall price range: $10-7,000. Most work sold at $350.

EXHIBITS Considers all media. Most frequently exhibits oils, pastels, and mixed media. Considers engravings, etchings, linocuts, lithographs, and serigraphs. Styles considered are painterly abstraction, impressionism and primitivism realism. Most frequently exhibits impressionism and painterly abstraction. Genres include figurative work, florals, landscapes and portraits.

MAKING CONTACT & TERMS Artwork accepted on consignment with a 55% commission. Retail price of the art set by the gallery and artist. Gallery provides insurance and promotion. Artwork should be framed, mounted and matted, as applicable. Only accepts artists from Hawaii.

SUBMISSIONS Artists should call, write to arrange personal interview to show portfolio of original pieces, e-mail query letter with link to artist's website (JPEG samples at 72 dpi) or send query letter with artist's statement, bio, brochure, photographs, résumé, business cards and reviews. Responds in days. All materials filed. Finds artists through word of mouth, submissions, portfolio reviews, art exhibits, art fairs and referrals by other artists.

TIPS "Best to submit your work via e-mail."

ERNESTO MAYANS GALLERY

601 Canyon Rd., Santa Fe NM 87501. (505)983-8068. **E-mail:** arte2@aol.com. **Website:** ernestomayansgal lery.com. **Contact:** Ernesto Mayans, director. Estab. 1977. Publishers, retail gallery and art consultancy. Publishes books, catalogs and portfolios. Overall price range: $200-$5,000. Considers oil, acrylic, watercolor, pastel, pen & ink, drawings, mixed media, sculpture, photography, and original, handpulled prints. Most frequently exhibits oil, photography and lithographs. Exhibits 20th-century American and Latin American art. Genres include landscapes and

figurative work. "We exhibit Digital Chromogenic prints on Metallic Paper by Sibylle Szaggars-Redford, Photogravures by Unai San Martin; Pigment prints by Pablo Mayans, Digital prints by Eric Olson, Silver Gelatin prints by Richard Faller (Vintage Southwest Works) and Johanna Saretzki and Sean McGann (Nudes)."

MAKING CONTACT & TERMS Accepts work on consignment (50% commission). Retail price set by gallery and artist. Requires exclusive representation within area. "Please call before submitting." Arrange a personal interview to show portfolio. Send query by mail with SASE for consideration. Size limited to 11×20 maximum. Responds in 2 weeks.

MCDONOUGH MUSEUM OF ART

525 Wick Ave., Youngstown OH 44502. (330)941-1400. **E-mail:** mcdonoughmuseumofart@gmail.com. **Website:** mcdonoughmuseum.ysu.edu. **Contact:** Leslie Brothers, director. Estab. 1991. A center for contemporary art, education and community, the museum offers exhibitions in all media, experimental installation, performance, and regional outreach programs to the public. The museum is also the public outreach facility for the Department of Art and supports student and faculty work through exhibitions, collaborations, courses and ongoing discussion. Open Tuesday-Saturday, 11-4.

SUBMISSIONS Send exhibition proposal.

MESA CONTEMPORARY ARTS AT MESA ARTS CENTER

P.O. Box 1466, Mesa AZ 85211. (480)644-6561; (480)644-6567. **E-mail:** patty.haberman@mesaartscenter.com. **Website:** www.mesaartscenter.com. **Contact:** Patty Haberman, curator. Estab. 1980. Not-for-profit art space. "Mesa Contemporary Arts is the dynamic visual art exhibition space at Mesa Arts Center. In 5 stunning galleries, Mesa Contemporary Arts showcases curated and juried exhibitions of contemporary art by emerging and internationally recognized artists. We also offer lectures by significant artists and arts professionals, art workshops and a volunteer docent program." Public admission: $3.50; free for children ages 7 and under; free on Thursdays (sponsored by Salt River Project); free on the first Sunday of each month, via the "3 for Free" program sponsored by Target (also includes free admission to the Arizona Museum for Youth and the Arizona Museum of Natural History). "Currently not accepting unsolicited proposals. Artists who do not follow the guidelines outlined in the Prospectus and were not contracted directly by Mesa Contemporary Arts staff about participating in an exhibition are considered unsolicited artists. Artists who apply for an opportunity and follow the guidelines in the Prospectus are not considered unsolicited. Unsolicited materials will be returned without comment."

EXHIBITS Photos of babies/children/teens, celebrities, couples, multicultural, families, parents, senior citizens, disasters, environmental, landscapes/scenics, wildlife, architecture, cities/urban, interiors/decorating, rural, adventure, automobiles, entertainment, events, performing arts, travel, industry, political, science, technology/computers. Interested in alternative process, avant garde, documentary, fine art, historical/vintage, seasonal, and contemporary photography.

MAKING CONTACT & TERMS Charges $25 entry fee, 25% commission.

TIPS "We do invitational or national juried exhibits. Submit professional-quality slides."

⊘ R. MICHELSON GALLERIES

132 Main St., Northampton MA 01060. (413)586-3964. **Fax:** (413)587-9811. **E-mail:** RM@rmichelson.com. **Website:** www.rmichelson.com. **Contact:** Richard Michelson, owner and president. Estab. 1976. Retail gallery. Sponsors 1 exhibit/year. Average display time: 6 weeks. Open all year; Monday-Wednesday, 10-6; Thursday-Saturday, 10-9; Sunday, 12-5. Located downtown; Northampton gallery has 5,500 sq. ft.; 50% of space for special exhibitions. Clientele 80% private collectors, 20% corporate collectors. Sponsors openings. Overall price range: $1,200-25,000.

EXHIBITS Interested in contemporary, landscape and/or figure work.

MAKING CONTACT & TERMS Sometimes buys photos outright. Accepted work can be framed or unframed, mounted or unmounted, matted or unmatted. Requires exclusive representation. Not taking on new photographers at this time. Represents the photography of Jeanne Birdsall and Leonard Nimoy.

MILL BROOK GALLERY & SCULPTURE GARDEN

236 Hopkinton Rd., Concord NH 03301. (603)226-2046. **E-mail:** artsculpt@mindspring.com. **Website:** www.themillbrookgallery.com. Estab. 1996. Exhibits 70 artists. Sponsors 1 photography exhibit/year. Average display time 6 weeks. Gallery open Tuesday–Sun-

day, 11-5, April 1–December 24; and by appointment. Outdoor juried sculpture exhibit. Three rooms inside for exhibitions, 1,800 sq. ft. Overall price range $8-30,000. Most work sold at $500-1,000.

MAKING CONTACT & TERMS Artwork is accepted on consignment, and there is a 50% commission. Gallery provides insurance, promotion, contract. Accepted work should be framed, matted.

SUBMISSIONS Write to arrange a personal interview to show portfolio of photographs, slides. Send query letter with artist's statement, bio, photocopies, photographs, résumé, slides, SASE. Responds within 1 month, only if interested. Finds artists through word of mouth, submissions, art exhibits, referrals by other artists.

MILLS POND HOUSE GALLERY

Smithtown Township Arts Council, 660 Rt. 25 A, St. James NY 11780. **E-mail:** gallery@stacarts.org. **Website:** www.stacarts.org. **Contact:** Gallery coordinator. Nonprofit gallery. Sponsors 9 exhibits/year (1-2 photography). Average display time: 4 weeks. Open Monday–Friday, 10-4; weekends, 12-4. Considers all types of prints, media and styles. Prices set by the artist. Gallery provides insurance and promotion. Work should be framed. Clients: local and national community. Digital entries.

MOBILE MUSEUM OF ART

4850 Museum Dr., Mobile AL 36608-1917. (251)208-5200; (251)208-5221. **E-mail:** dklooz@mobilemuseumofart.com. **Website:** www.mobilemuseumofart.com. **Contact:** Donan Klooz, curator of exhibitions. Sponsors 4 exhibits/year. Average display time: 3 months. Sponsors openings; provides light hors d'oeuvres and cash bar.

EXHIBITS Open to all types and styles.

MAKING CONTACT & TERMS Photography sold in gallery. Charges 20% commission. Occasionally buys photos outright. Accepted work should be framed.

SUBMISSIONS Arrange a personal interview to show portfolio; send material by mail for consideration. Returns material when SASE is provided "unless photographer specifically points out that it's not required."

TIPS "We look for personal point of view beyond technical mastery."

MONTEREY MUSEUM OF ART

559 Pacific St., Monterey CA 93940. (831)372-5477. **Fax:** (831)372-5680. **E-mail:** info@montereyart.org.

Website: www.montereyart.org. Estab. 1959. Additional location at 720 Via Mirada, Monterey CA 93940. Featuring special exhibitions and presentations of the Museum's collection. Open Thursday-Monday, 11-5. Closed Thanksgiving, Christmas, New Year's, and July 4. Check website for location details, exhibition schedule and calendar of events including free-admission days, family day activities and programs for children and more.

MULTIPLE EXPOSURES GALLERY

Torpedo Factory Art Center, 105 N. Union St. #312, Alexandria VA 22314. (703)683-2205. **E-mail:** info@multipleexposuresgallery.com. **Website:** www.multipleexposuresgallery.com. Estab. 1986. Cooperative gallery. Represents or exhibits 15 artists. Sponsors 12 photography exhibits/year. Average display time 1-2 months. Open daily, 11-5; Thursday 2-8. Closed on 5 major holidays throughout the year. Located in Torpedo Factory Art Center; 10-ft. walls with about 40 ft. of running wall space; 1 bin for each artist's matted photos, up to 20×24 in size with space for 25 pieces.

EXHIBITS Photos of landscapes/scenics, architecture, beauty, cities/urban, religious, rural, adventure, automobiles, events, travel, buildings. Interested in alternative process, documentary, fine art. Other specific subjects/processes: "We have on display roughly 300 images that run the gamut from platinum and older alternative processes through digital capture and output."

MAKING CONTACT & TERMS There is a co-op membership fee, a time requirement, a rental fee and a 15% commission. Accepted work should be matted. *Accepts only artists from Washington DC region.* Accepts only photography. "Membership is by jury of active current members. Membership is limited. Jurying for membership is only done when a space becomes available; on average, 1 member is brought in about every 2 years."

SUBMISSIONS Send query letter with SASE to arrange a personal interview to show portfolio of photographs, slides. Responds in 2 months. Finds artists through word of mouth, referrals by other artists, ads in local art/photography publications.

TIPS "Have a unified portfolio of images mounted and matted to archival standards."

MICHAEL MURPHY GALLERY M

2701 S. MacDill Ave., Tampa FL 33629. (813)902-1414. **Fax:** (813)835-5526. **Website:** www.michaelmur

phygallery.com. **Contact:** Michael Murphy. Estab. 1988. (Formerly Michael Murphy Gallery, Inc.) For-profit gallery. Approached by 100 artists/year; exhibits 35 artists. Sponsors 1 photography exhibit/year. Average display time: 1 month. See website for current gallery hours. Overall price range: $500-15,000; most work sold at less than $1,000. "We provide elegant, timeless artwork for our clients' home and office environment as well as unique and classic framing design. We strongly believe in the preservation of art through the latest technology in archival framing."

EXHIBITS Photos of babies/children/teens, celebrities, couples, multicultural, families, parents, senior citizens, disasters, environmental, landscapes/scenics, wildlife, architecture, cities/urban, education, gardening, interiors/decorating, pets, religious, rural, agriculture, business concepts, industry, medicine, military, political, product shots/still life, science, technology/computers. Interested in alternative process, avant garde, documentary, erotic, fashion/glamour, fine art, historical/vintage, seasonal.

MAKING CONTACT & TERMS Artwork is accepted on consignment, and there is a 50% commission. Accepted work should be framed. Requires exclusive representation locally.

SUBMISSIONS Send query with artist's statement, bio, brochure, business card, photocopies, photographs, résumé, reviews, slides and SASE. Responds to queries in 1 month, only if interested.

🌀 MUSEO DE ARTE DE PONCE

2325 Blvd. Luis A. Ferre, Ponce Puerto Rico 00717-0776. (787)840-1510. **Fax:** (787)841-7309. **E-mail:** info@museoarteponce.org. **Website:** www.museoarteponce.org. **Contact:** Curatorial department. Estab. 1959. Museum. Approached by 50 artists/year; mounts 3 exhibitions/year. Open Wednesday-Monday, 10-5; Sunday, 12-5. Closed New Year's Day, January 6, Good Friday, Thanksgiving and Christmas Day. Admission: $6 for adults, $3 for senior citizens, students with an ID card, and children.

EXHIBITS Interested in avant garde, fine art, European and Old Masters.

SUBMISSIONS Send query letter with artist's statement, résumé, images, reviews, publications. Responds in 3 months. Finds artists through research, art exhibits, studio and gallery visits, word of mouth, referrals by other artists.

MUSEO ITALOAMERICANO

Fort Mason Center, Bldg. C, San Francisco CA 94123. (415)673-2200. **Fax:** (415)673-2292. **E-mail:** sfmuseo@sbcglobal.net. **Website:** www.museoitaloamericano.org. Estab. 1978. Museum. "The first museum in the US devoted exclusively to Italian and Italian-American art and culture." Approached by 80 artists/year; exhibits 15 artists. Sponsors 1 photography exhibit/year (depending on the year). Average display time: 2-3 months. Open Tuesday–Sunday, 12-4; Monday by appointment; closed major holidays. Gallery is located in the San Francisco Marina District, with a beautiful view of the Golden Gate Bridge, Sausalito, Tiburon and Alcatraz; 3,500 sq. ft. of exhibition space.

EXHIBITS Photos of babies/children/teens, celebrities, couples, multicultural, families, parents, senior citizens, environmental, landscapes/scenics, architecture, cities/urban, education, religious, rural, entertainment, events, food/drink, hobbies, humor, performing arts, sports, travel, product shots/still life. Interested in alternative process, avant garde, documentary, fine art, historical/vintage.

MAKING CONTACT & TERMS "The museum rarely sells pieces. If it does, it takes 20% of the sale." Museum provides insurance, promotion. Accepted work should be framed, mounted, matted. *Accepts only Italian or Italian-American artists.*

SUBMISSIONS Call or write to arrange a personal interview to show portfolio of photographs, slides, catalogs. Send query letter with artist's statement, bio, brochure, photographs, résumé, reviews, slides, SASE. Responds in 2 months. Finds artists through word of mouth, submissions.

TIPS "Photographers should have good, quality reproduction of their work with slides, and clarity in writing their statements and résumés. Be concise."

MUSEUM OF CONTEMPORARY ART SAN DIEGO

700 Prospect St., La Jolla CA 92037-4291. (858)454-3541. **E-mail:** info@mcasd.org. **Website:** www.mcasd.org. Estab. 1941. Located in the heart of downtown San Diego and in the coastal community of La Jolla, MCASD provides an unprecedented variety of exhibition spaces and experiences for the community. With two locations, the Museum of Contemporary Art San Diego (MCASD) is the region's foremost forum devoted to the exploration and presentation of the art of our time, presenting works across all media since

1950. Open daily, 11–5; closed Wednesdays and during installation.

EXHIBITS Interested in avant garde, documentary, fine art.

SUBMISSIONS See artist proposal guidelines at mcasd.org/about/artist-proposals.

MUSEUM OF CONTEMPORARY PHOTOGRAPHY, COLUMBIA COLLEGE CHICAGO

600 S. Michigan Ave., Chicago IL 60605. (312)663-5554. **Fax:** (312)369-8067. **E-mail:** curatorialcommittee@colum.edu. **Website:** www.mocp.org. **Contact:** Portfolio review coordinator. Estab. 1976. The Museum of Contemporary Photography (MoCP) is a stimulating and innovative forum for the collection, creation and examination of contemporary image-making in its camera tradition and in its expanded vocabulary of digital processes. "We present approx. 4 exhibits/year." Average display time: 2-3 months. Open Monday–Friday, 10-5; Thursday, 10-8; Saturday, 10-5; Sunday 12-5.

EXHIBITS Exhibits and collects national and international works including portraits, environment, architecture, urban, rural, performance art, political issues, journalism, social documentary, mixed media, video. Primarily interested in experimental work of the past ten years.

SUBMISSIONS Reviews of portfolios for purchase and/or exhibition held monthly. Submission protocols on website. Responds in 2-3 months. No critical review guaranteed.

TIPS "Professional standards apply; only very high-quality work considered."

MUSEUM OF PHOTOGRAPHIC ARTS

1649 El Prado, San Diego CA 92101. (619)238-7559. **Fax:** (619)238-8777. **E-mail:** curate@mopa.org. **Website:** www.mopa.org. **Contact:** Debra Klochko, executive director. Estab. 1983. "The Museum of Photographic Arts (MOPA) is one of the leading museums in the United States devoted exclusively to photography, film and video. Since its founding, MOPA has been dedicated to collecting, preserving and exhibiting the entire spectrum of the photographic medium. The museum's endeavors consistently address cultural, historical and social issues through its exhibitions and educational programs." Sponsors 8-10 exhibits/year. Average display time: 3 months.

EXHIBITS Interested in the history of photography, from the 19th century to the present.

MAKING CONTACT & TERMS "The criteria is simply that the photography be of advanced artistic caliber, relative to other fine art photography. MOPA is a museum and therefore does not sell works in exhibitions." Exhibition schedules planned 2-3 years in advance. Holds a private members' opening reception each exhibition cycle.

SUBMISSIONS Portfolios can be submitted by e-mail to curate@mopa.org or direct mail to the above address. Materials are not accepted at the museum admission desk. All artist submissions should include: website, digital or print portfolio, additional materials, such as press reviews, exhibition catalogs or print-on-demand books. Please include résumé, artist's statement and other supporting materials with your submission. If materials require return, please include postage and appropriate packaging. Submissions sent without return postage are considered property of the museum, and will be held or disposed of at will. All submitted materials must be no larger than 8½×11. Learn more at mopa.org/content/artist-submissions.

TIPS "Exhibitions presented by the museum represent the full range of artistic and journalistic photographic works. There are no specific requirements. The executive director and curator make all decisions on works that will be included in exhibitions. There is an enormous stylistic diversity in the photographic arts. The museum does not place an emphasis on one style or technique over another."

MUSEUM OF PRINTING HISTORY

1324 W. Clay, Houston TX 77019. (713)522-4652, ext. 207. **E-mail:** kburrows@printingmuseum.org. **Website:** www.printingmuseum.org. **Contact:** Keelin Burrows, curator. Estab. 1982. "The mission of the museum is to promote, preserve and share the knowledge of printed communication and art as the greatest contributors to the development of the civilized world and the continuing advancement of freedom and literacy." Represents or exhibits approximately 12 exhibitions/year. Sponsors 1 photography exhibit/year. Average display time 12 weeks. Open Tuesday–Saturday, 10-5. Closed 4th of July, Thanksgiving, Christmas Eve, Christmas, New Year's Eve/Day.

MUSEUM OF THE PLAINS INDIAN

P.O. Box 410, Browning MT 59417. (406)338-2230. **Fax:** (406)338-7404. **E-mail:** mpi@3rivers.net; mpi@

ios.doi.gov. **Website:** www.doi.gov/iacb/museums/museum_plains.html. Estab. 1941. Open Tuesday-Saturday, 9-4:45 (June-September); Monday–Friday, 10-4:30 (October-May). Admission is free of charge October–May. Contact for additional information.

M.G. NELSON FAMILY GALLERY AT THE SAA

700 N. Fourth St., Springfield IL 62702. (217)523-2631. **Fax:** (217)523-3866. **E-mail:** director@springfieldart.org. **Website:** www.springfieldart.org. **Contact:** Betsy Dollar, executive director. Estab. 1913. Nonprofit gallery. Exhibits emerging, mid-career and established artists. Sponsors 13 total exhibits/year, including theme-based shows 2-3 times/year. 1 exclusive photo show every couple of years. Average display time: 1 month. Open Monday-Friday, 9-5; Saturday, 10-3; closed Sundays and Christmas-New Year's Day. Located at the Springfield Art Association, campus includes a historic house, museum and community art school. Clients include local community, students, tourists and upscale clients. 5% of sales are to corporate collectors. Overall price range: $10-5,000; most work sold under $100.

EXHIBITS Considers all media.

MAKING CONTACT & TERMS Model and property release are required. Artwork is accepted on consignment and there is a 30% commission. Retail price set by the artist. Gallery provides insurance, promotion and contract. Accepted work should be framed, mounted and matted—ready to hang.

SUBMISSIONS Call or e-mail query letter with link to artist's website or JPEG samples at 72 dpi. Responds in 2 weeks. Will return material with SASE. Files CV, résumé, printed samples and business cards. Find artists through word of mouth, submissions, portfolio reviews, art exhibits, art fairs and referrals by other artists.

TIPS "Good quality images with artist's name included in file name."

NEVADA MUSEUM OF ART

160 W. Liberty St., Reno NV 89501. (775)329-3333. **Fax:** (775)329-1541. **Website:** www.nevadaart.org. **Contact:** Ann Wolfe, senior curator and deputy director. Estab. 1931. Sponsors 12-15 exhibits/year in various media. Average display time: 4-5 months.

SUBMISSIONS See website for detailed submission instructions. No phone calls, please."

TIPS "We are a museum of ideas. While building upon our founding collections and values, we cultivate meaningful art and societal experiences, and foster new knowledge in the visual arts by encouraging interdisciplinary investigation. The Nevada Museum of Art serves as a cultural and educational resource for everyone."

NEW MEXICO STATE UNIVERSITY ART GALLERY

P.O. Box 30001, Las Cruces NM 88003-8001. (575)646-2545. **Fax:** (575)646-8036. **E-mail:** artglry@nmsu.edu. **Website:** www.uag.nmsu.edu. **Contact:** director. Estab. 1969. Museum. Average display time 2-3 months. Gallery open Tuesday–Saturday, 10-4. Closed Christmas through New Year's Day and university holidays. See website for summer hours. Located on university campus, 3,900 sq. ft. of exhibit space.

NEW ORLEANS MUSEUM OF ART

P.O. Box 19123, New Orleans LA 70179-0123. (504)658-4100. **Fax:** (504)658-4199. **E-mail:** staylor@noma.org. **Website:** www.noma.org. **Contact:** Susan Taylor, director. Estab. 1973. "The city's oldest fine arts institution, NOMA has a magnificent permanent collection of more than 40,000 objects. The collection, noted for its extraordinary strengths in French and American art, photography, glass, African and Japanese works, continues to grow." Sponsors exhibits continuously. Average display time 1-3 months. Open Tuesday–Thursday, 10-6; Friday, 10-9; Saturday and Sunday, 11-5.

EXHIBITS Interested in all types of photography.

MAKING CONTACT & TERMS Buys photography outright; payment negotiable. "Current budget for purchasing contemporary photography is very small." Sometimes accepts donations from established artists, collectors or dealers.

SUBMISSIONS Send query letter with color photocopies (preferred) or slides, résumé, SASE. Accepts images in digital format; submit via website. Responds in 3 months.

TIPS "Send thought-out images with originality and expertise. Do not send commercial-looking images."

NEXUS/FOUNDATION FOR TODAY'S ART

1400 N. American St., Philadelphia PA 19122. **E-mail:** info@nexusphiladelphia.org. **Website:** www.nexusphiladelphia.org. Estab. 1975. Alternative space; co-operative, nonprofit gallery. Approached by 40 artists/year; represents or exhibits 20 artists. Sponsors

2 photography exhibits/year. Average display time: 1 month. Open Wednesday–Sunday, 12-6; closed July and August. Located in Fishtown, Philadelphia; 2 gallery spaces, approximately 750 sq. ft. each. Overall price range: $75-1,200; most work sold at $200-400.

EXHIBITS Photos of multicultural, families, environmental, architecture, rural, entertainment, humor, performing arts, industry, political. Interested in alternative process, documentary, fine art.

SUBMISSIONS Send query letter with artist's statement, bio, photocopies, photographs, slides, SASE. Finds artists through portfolio reviews, referrals by other artists, submissions, and juried reviews 2 times/year. "Please visit our website for submission dates."

TIPS "Learn how to write a cohesive artist's statement."

NICOLAYSEN ART MUSEUM

400 E. Collins St., Casper WY 82601. (307)235-5247. **E-mail:** info@thenic.org. **Website:** www.thenic.org. **Contact:** Brooks Joyner, executive director. Estab. 1967. Regional contemporary art museum. Average display time: 3-4 months. Interested in emerging, mid-career and established artists. Sponsors 10 solo and 10 group shows/year. Open all year. Clientele 90% private collectors, 10% corporate clients.

EXHIBITS Considers all media with special attention to regional art.

SUBMISSIONS Send résumé, statement and biography as well as images in digital format. "Due to the volume of correspondence we receive, we may not be able to respond directly to each and every submission and we cannot assume responsibility for or guarantee the return of any materials that are submitted."

NICOLET COLLEGE ART GALLERY

5355 College Dr., P.O. Box 518, Rhinelander WI 54501. (715)365-4556. **E-mail:** kralph@nicoletcollege.edu. **Website:** www.nicoletcollege.edu/about/creative-arts-series/art-gallery/index.html. **Contact:** Katy Ralph, gallery director. Exhibits 9-11 different shows each year including the Northern National Art Competition. The deadline for the annual competition is in May. For a prospectus, or more information, contact gallery director, Katy Ralph.

MAKING CONTACT & TERMS Call or e-mail for further information.

NKU GALLERY

Northern Kentucky University, Art Galleries, Nunn Dr., Highland Heights KY 41099. (859)572-5148. **Fax:** (859)572-6501. **E-mail:** knight@nku.edu. **Website:** artscience.nku.edu/departments/art/galleries.html. **Contact:** David Knight, director of collections and exhibitions. Estab. 1970. The NKU Art Department Galleries are located on the 3rd floor of the Fine Arts Center. There are 2 gallery spaces: The Main Gallery and the Third Floor Gallery. Approached by 30 artists/year; represents or exhibits 5-6 artists. Average display time 1 month. Open Monday–Friday, 9-9; closed weekends and major holidays. Main Gallery is 2,500 sq. ft.; Third Floor Gallery is 600 sq. ft. Overall price range $25-3,000. Most work sold at $500.

MAKING CONTACT & TERMS Gallery provides insurance, promotion, contract. Accepted work should be framed, mounted, matted.

SUBMISSIONS Finds artists through word of mouth, art exhibits, referrals by other faculty.

TIPS "Submission guidelines, current exhibitions and complete information available on our website."

NORTHWEST ART CENTER

Minot State University, 500 University Ave. W., Minot ND 58707. (701)858-3264. **Fax:** (701)858-3894. **E-mail:** nac@minotstateu.edu. **Website:** www.minotstateu.edu/nac. Estab. 1969. Nonprofit gallery. Represents emerging, mid-career and established artists. Represents 20 artists. Sponsors 20 total exhibits/year; 2 photography exhibits/year. Model and property release preferred. Average display time: 4 weeks. Open Monday-Friday, 9-4. Two galleries located on university campus, each gallery approximately 100 linear feet. Clients include local community and students. 50% of sales are to corporate collectors. Overall price range: $100-1,000; most work sold at $350.

EXHIBITS Special interest in printmaking, works on paper, contemporary art and drawings.

MAKING CONTACT & TERMS Accepted work should be framed and mounted. Artwork is accepted on consignment with a 30% commission. Retail price set by the artist. Gallery provides insurance, promotion and contract.

SUBMISSIONS Send query letter with artist's statement, photocopies bio, résumé and reviews. Returns material with SASE. Responds, if interested, within 3 months. Finds artists through art exhibits, submissions, referrals by other artists and entries in our juried competitions.

NORTHWESTERN UNIVERSITY DITTMAR MEMORIAL GALLERY

1999 Campus Dr., Norris University Center, Evanston IL 60208. (847)491-2348. **E-mail:** dittmargallery@u.northwestern.edu. **Website:** www.dittmar.northwestern.edu. **Contact:** Gallery Coordinator. Estab. 1972. Nonprofit, student-operated gallery. Approached by over 100 artists/year, including 10-15 photographers; represents or exhibits more than 10 artists. Sponsors 1-2 photography exhibits/year. Average display time 6 weeks. Open daily 10-10. Closed in December during winter break. The gallery is located within the Norris Student Center on the main floor behind the information desk.

EXHIBITS Photos of babies/children/teens, couples, multicultural, families, parents, disasters, environmental, landscapes/scenics, wildlife, architecture, cities/urban, education, gardening, adventure, automobiles, entertainment, events, food/drink, health/fitness, hobbies, humor, performing arts, sports, travel. Interested in avant garde, fashion/glamour, fine art, historical/vintage, seasonal.

MAKING CONTACT & TERMS Artwork is accepted on consignment, and there is a 20% commission. Gallery provides promotion, contract. Accepted work should be mounted.

SUBMISSIONS Mail portfolio for review. Send query letter with 5 images that "demonstrate the work you are proposing for a show" or previous work with proposal for a new show, work list for the images including title, medium, size and year, artist's statement, résumé, and any available contact information. Responds in 3 months. Finds artists through word of mouth, submissions, referrals by other artists.

TIPS "Do not send photocopies. Send a typed letter and good photos, images need to be high resolution. Send résumé of past exhibits, or if emerging, a typed statement."

THE NOYES MUSEUM OF ART

733 Lily Lake Rd., Oceanville NJ 08231. (609)652-8848. **Fax:** (609)652-6166. **E-mail:** info@noyesmuseum.org. **Website:** www.noyesmuseum.org. **Contact:** Michael Cagno, executive director; Dorrie Papademetriou, director of exhibitions. Estab. 1983. Sponsors 10-12 exhibits/year. Average display time 12 weeks. The Noyes Museum of Art of The Richard Stockton College of New Jersey presents exhibitions and events that benefit students and enthusiasts of the arts, as well as the entire southern New Jersey community. In 2010, Stockton partnered with the Noyes Museum, bringing an expanded array of educational opportunities, events, exhibits and performances to the nearby off-campus facility. Stockton is also home to one of the area's top performing arts centers, and its own art gallery.

EXHIBITS Interested in alternative process, avant garde, fine art, historical/vintage.

MAKING CONTACT & TERMS Charges commission. Accepted work must be ready for hanging, preferably framed. Infrequently buys photos for permanent collection.

SUBMISSIONS Any format OK for initial review; most desirable is a challenging, cohesive body of work. Send material by mail for consideration; include résumé, artist's statement, slide samples or CD, handwritten proposals not accepted. May include photography and mixed media. See website for further details.

TIPS "Send a challenging, cohesive body of work."

OAKLAND UNIVERSITY ART GALLERY

2200 N. Squirrel Rd./208 Wilson Hall, Oakland University, Rochester MI 48309-4401. (248)370-3005. **E-mail:** jaleow@oakland.edu. **Website:** www.oakland.edu/ouag. Estab. 1962. Nonprofit gallery. Represents 10-25 artists/year. Sponsors 4-6 exhibits/year. Open September–May: Tuesday–Sunday, 12-5; evenings during special events and theater performances (Wednesday–Friday, 7 p.m. through 1st intermission, weekends, 5 p.m. through 1st intermission). Closed Monday and holidays. Located on the campus of Oakland University; exhibition space is approximately 2,350 sq. ft. of floor space, 301-ft. linear wall space, with 10-ft. 7-in. ceiling. The gallery is situated across the hall from the Meadow Brook Theatre. "We do not sell work, but do make available price lists for visitors with contact information noted for inquiries."

EXHIBITS Considers all styles and all types of prints and media.

MAKING CONTACT & TERMS Charges no commission. Gallery provides insurance, promotion and contract. Accepted work should be framed, mounted, matted. No restrictions on representation; however, prefers emerging Detroit artists.

SUBMISSIONS E-mail bio, education, artist's statement and JPEG images. Mail portfolio for review. Send query letter with artist's statement, bio, photocopies, curriculum vitae. Returns material with

SASE. Responds to queries in 1-2 months. Finds artists through referrals by other artists, word of mouth, art community, advisory board and other arts organizations.

OPALKA GALLERY

The Sage Colleges, 140 New Scotland Ave., Albany NY 12208. (518)292-7742. **E-mail:** opalka@sage.edu; lynchj2@sage.edu. **Website:** www.sage.edu/opalka. **Contact:** Jacqueline Lynch, assistant to the director and gallery operations. Estab. 2002. Nonprofit gallery. Approached by 90-120 artists/year; mounts 3-4 exhibitions per academic calendar year. Average display time 5 weeks. Open Tuesday-Friday, 10-8; weekends, 12-5; June-July, 10-4 and by appointment only during installations and when classes are not in session. Closed July 4. Located on the Sage Albany campus, The gallery's primary concentration is on work by professional artists from outside the region. The gallery frequently features multidisciplinary projects and hosts poetry readings, recitals and symposia in conjunction with exhibitions. The 7,400-sq.-ft. facility includes a vaulted gallery and a 75-seat lecture/presentation hall with Internet connectivity.

EXHIBITS Interested in fine art.

MAKING CONTACT & TERMS Reviews work by artists from outside the region and those who have ties to the Sage Colleges, a local photography regional is hosted every 3 years requiring artists to have exclusive local representation.

SUBMISSIONS Under terms of an exhibition loan agreement, artwork may be sold by the artist while on exhibit. The gallery does not take commissions or sell artwork.

TIPS "Contact the gallery by e-mail or phone to inquire about submission policy."

OPENING NIGHT GALLERY

2836 Lyndale Ave. S., Minneapolis MN 55408-2108. (612)872-2325. **Fax:** (612)872-2385. **E-mail:** deen@onframe-art.com; info@onframe-art.com. **Website:** www.onframe-art.com. **Contact:** Deen Braathen. Estab. 1975. Rental gallery. Approached by 40 artists/year; represents or exhibits 15 artists. Sponsors 1 photography exhibit/year. Average display time: 6-10 weeks. Gallery open Monday–Friday, 8:30-5; Saturday, 10:30-4. Overall price range: $300-12,000; most work sold at $2,500.

EXHIBITS Photos of landscapes/scenics, architecture, cities/urban.

MAKING CONTACT & TERMS Artwork is accepted on consignment, and there is a 50% commission. Gallery provides insurance, promotion, contract. "Accepted work should be framed by our frame shop." Requires exclusive representation locally.

SUBMISSIONS Mail slides for review. Send query letter with artist's statement, bio, résumé, slides, SASE. Responds in 2 months. Finds artists through word of mouth, submissions, portfolio reviews.

PALO ALTO ART CENTER

1313 Newell Rd., Palo Alto CA 94303. (650)329-2366. **Fax:** (650)326-6165. **E-mail:** artcenter@cityofpaloalto.org. **Website:** www.cityofpaloalto.org/artcenter. **Contact:** exhibitions department. Estab. 1971. Average display time: 1-3 months. Hours: Tuesday, Wednesday, Friday, Saturday, 10-5; Thursday, 10-9; Sunday, 1-5. Sponsors openings.

EXHIBITS "Exhibit needs vary according to curatorial context." Seeks "imagery unique to individual artist. No standard policy. Photography may be integrated in group exhibits." Interested in alternative process, avant garde, fine art; emphasis on art of the Bay Area.

SUBMISSIONS Send slides/CD, bio, artist's statement, SASE.

LEONARD PEARLSTEIN GALLERY

Drexel University, 3401 Filbert St., Philadelphia PA 19104. (215)895-1029; (215)895-2548. **E-mail:** gallery@drexel.edu; degroff@drexel.edu. **Contact:** Jacqueline DeGroff, curator. Estab. 1986. Nonprofit gallery. Located in Nesbitt Hall in the Antoinette Westphal College of Media Arts and Design at Drexel. Committed to exhibiting the work of local, national and international contemporary artists and designers. Sponsors 8 total exhibits/year; 1 or 2 photography exhibits/year. Average display time 1 month. Open Monday–Saturday, 11-5. Closed during summer.

MAKING CONTACT & TERMS Artwork is bought outright. Gallery takes 20% commission. Gallery provides insurance, promotion. Accepted work should be framed, mounted, matted. "We will not pay transport fees."

SUBMISSIONS Write to arrange a personal interview to show portfolio. Send query letter with artist's statement, bio, résumé, SASE. Returns material with SASE. Responds by February, only if interested. Finds artists through referrals by other artists, academic instructors.

PETERS VALLEY SCHOOL OF CRAFT

19 Kuhn Rd., Layton NJ 07851. (973)948-5202. **Fax:** (973)948-0011. **E-mail:** store@petersvalley.org. **Website:** www.petersvalley.org. **Contact:** Brienne Rosner, gallery manager. Estab. 1970. Nonprofit gallery and store. Approached by about 100 artists/year; represents about 350 artists. Average display time varies for store items. Gallery exhibitions approx. 1 month. Open year round; call for hours. Located in northwestern New Jersey in Delaware Water Gap National Recreation Area; 2 floors, approximately 3,000 sq. ft. Overall price range: $5-3,000. Most work sold at $100-300. "Focuses its programs on fine contemporary crafts in mediums such as ceramics, metals (both fine and forged), glass, wood, photography, fibers (surface design and structural), print."

EXHIBITS Considers all media and all types of prints. Also exhibits non-referential, mixed media, collage and sculpture.

MAKING CONTACT & TERMS Artwork is accepted on consignment, and there is a 60% commission to artist. "Retail price set by the gallery in conjunction with artist." Gallery provides insurance and promotion. Accepted work should be framed, mounted and matted.

SUBMISSIONS Submissions reviewed on an ongoing basis. Send query letter with artist's statement, bio, résumé and images. Responds in 2 months. Finds artists through submissions, art exhibits, art fairs, referrals by other artists.

TIPS "Submissions must be neat and well-organized throughout."

PHILLIPS GALLERY

444 E. 200 S., Salt Lake City UT 84111. (801)364-8284. **Fax:** (801)364-8293. **Website:** www.phillips-gallery. com. **Contact:** Meri DeCaria, director/curator. Estab. 1965. Commercial gallery. We represent artists working in a variety of media including painting, drawing, sculpture, photography, ceramics, printmaking, jewelry, and mixed media. Our artists, many of whom have been with us since 1965, are primarily from Utah or the surrounding area. Phillips Gallery also represents national and international artists who have an association with Utah. You will discover a full range of subject matter from traditional to contemporary. Average display time: 4 weeks. Sponsors openings; provides refreshments, advertisement, and half of mailing costs. Overall price range: $100-18,000; most work sold at $600.

EXHIBITS Accepts all types and styles.

MAKING CONTACT & TERMS Charges 50% commission. Accepted work should be matted. Requires exclusive representation locally. *Photographers must have Utah connection.* Must be actively pursuing photography.

SUBMISSIONS Submit portfolio for review digitally; include SASE. Responds in 2 weeks.

PHOTO-EYE GALLERY

541 S. Guadalupe St., Santa Fe NM 87501. (505)988-5152, ext. 202; (505)988-5159, ext. 121; (800)227-6941. **Fax:** (505)988-4487. **E-mail:** gallery@photoeye.com. **Website:** www.photoeye.com. **Contact:** Anne Kelly, gallery director. Estab. 1991. Approached by 40+ artists/year. Exhibits 30 established artists/year. Exhibited artists include Nick Brandt, Julie Blackmon, Tom Chambers (all fine-art photographers). Sponsors 6 photography exhibits/year. Average display time: 6 weeks. Open Tuesday–Saturday, 10-5:30. Closed Sunday and Monday. The gallery is located approximately 1 mile from The Plaza; approximately 1,000 sq. ft. Clients include: local community, tourists, upscale and collectors. 30% of sales are to corporate collectors. Overall price range: $900-50,000. Most work sold at $2,500.

EXHIBITS Photography only. Fine-art photographs using only archival methods. Considers all styles. Most frequently exhibits contemporary photography projects and bodies of work.

MAKING CONTACT & TERMS Retail price of the art set by the artist. Gallery provides insurance, promotion and contract. Accepted work should be matted. "Prefers fine-art photography with exciting, fresh projects that are cohesive and growing."

SUBMISSIONS "Submit your work via 'The Photographer's Showcase' on our website." Material cannot be returned. Responds in 2 weeks if dropped off at gallery, but prefers online submissions. Finds artists through word of mouth, art fairs, portfolio review and online through "The Photographer's Showcase."

TIPS "Be consistent, professional and only submit approximately 20 images. Call or e-mail gallery to find out the submission policy."

PHOTOGRAPHIC RESOURCE CENTER

832 Commonwealth Ave., Boston MA 02215. (617)975-0600. **Fax:** (617)975-0606. **E-mail:** info@

prcboston.org. **Website:** www.prcboston.org. "The PRC is a nonprofit arts organization founded to facilitate the study and dissemination of information relating to photography." The PRC brings in nationally recognized artists to lecture to large audiences and host workshops on photography. Please check our website for the current exhibition schedule and hours. Offers monthly portfolio reviews for PRC members. "Due to overwhelming numbers, we do not review unsolicited submissions for exhibitions on the web or through the mail. Please do not send materials unless they are specifically requested; please do not expect a response to unrequested submissions."

PIERRO GALLERY OF SOUTH ORANGE

Baird Center, 5 Mead St., South Orange NJ 07079. (973)378-7754. **Fax:** (973)378-7833. **E-mail:** pierro gallery@southorange.org; smartiny@southorange. org. **Website:** www.pierrogallery.org. **Contact:** Sandy Martiny, gallery director. Estab. 1994. Nonprofit gallery. Approached by 75-185 artists/year; represents or exhibits 25-50 artists. Average display time: 5 weeks. Open Wednesday and Thursday, 2-7; Friday, 2-5; Saturday, 1-4, and by appointment; closed July-August. Overall price range: $100-10,000; most work sold at $800.

EXHIBITS Interested in fine art, "which can be inclusive of any subject matter."

MAKING CONTACT & TERMS Artwork is accepted on consignment, and there is a 15% commission. Gallery provides insurance, promotion, contract. Accepted work should be framed.

SUBMISSIONS Mail portfolio for review. Send cover letter, biography and/or résumé, brief artist statement, up to 3 reviews/press clippings, representation of work in either CD or DVD format; no more than 10 labeled representative images up to 72 dpi. "Portfolios must be received by the first week of February, June or October to be included in that month's review." Finds artists through word of mouth, submissions, portfolio reviews, referrals by other artists.

POLK MUSEUM OF ART

800 E. Palmetto St., Lakeland FL 33801-5529. (863)688-7743, ext. 241 or 289. **Fax:** (863)688-2611. **E-mail:** kpope@polkmuseumofart.org. **Website:** www.polkmuseumofart.org. **Contact:** Kalisa Pope, curatorial assistant. Estab. 1966. Approached by 75 artists/year; represents or exhibits 3 artists. Sponsors 1-3 photography exhibits/year. Galleries open Tues-

day–Saturday, 10-5; Sunday, 1-5; closed Mondays and major holidays. Four different galleries of various sizes and configurations.

EXHIBITS Interested in alternative process, avant garde, documentary, fine art, historical/vintage.

MAKING CONTACT & TERMS Museum provides insurance, promotion, contract. Accepted work should be framed.

SUBMISSIONS Mail portfolio for review. Send query letter with artist's statement, bio, résumé, slides or CD, SASE.

THE PRINT CENTER

1614 Latimer St., Philadelphia PA 19103. (215)735-6090. **Fax:** (215)735-5511. **E-mail:** info@printcen ter.org. **Website:** www.printcenter.org. Estab. 1915. Nonprofit gallery and Gallery Store. Represents over 75 artists from around the world in Gallery Store. Sponsors 5 photography exhibits/year. Average display time 2 months. Open all year Tuesday-Saturday, 11-6; closed Christmas Eve to New Year's Day. Three galleries. Overall price range $15-15,000. Most work sold at $200.

EXHIBITS Contemporary prints and photographs of all processes. Accepts original artwork only—no reproductions.

MAKING CONTACT & TERMS Accepts artwork on consignment (50%). Gallery provides insurance, promotion, contract. Artists must be printmakers or photographers.

SUBMISSIONS Must be member to submit work. Member's work is reviewed by curator and gallery store manager. See website for membership application. Finds artists through submissions, art exhibits and membership.

PUCKER GALLERY, INC.

240 Newbury St., 3rd Floor, Boston MA 02116. (617)267-9473. **Fax:** (617)424-9759. **E-mail:** contact us@puckergallery.com; destiny@puckergallery.com. **Website:** www.puckergallery.com. **Contact:** Bernard H. Pucker, owner/director; Destiny M. Barletta, director. Estab. 1967. For-profit gallery. Pucker Gallery is always willing to review artist's slides and submissions. Approached by 100 artists/year; represents or exhibits 50 artists. Sponsors 2 photography exhibits/year. Average display time: 1 month. Open Monday–Saturday, 10-5:30; Sunday, 10:30-5. Five floors of exhibition space. Overall price range: $500-75,000.

EXHIBITS Photos of multicultural, environmental, landscapes/scenics, architecture, cities/urban, religious, rural. Interested in fine art, abstracts, seasonal.
MAKING CONTACT & TERMS Gallery provides promotion.
SUBMISSIONS Send query letter with artist's statement, bio, slides/CD, SASE. Maximum 20 images (slides, prints or hi-res digital files on a disc). "We do not accept e-mail submissions nor do we visit artists' websites." Finds artists through submissions, referrals by other artists.

PUMP HOUSE CENTER FOR THE ARTS

P.O. Box 1613, Chillicothe OH 45601. **E-mail:** pumphouseartgallery@aol.com. **Website:** www.pumphouseartgallery.com. **Contact:** Priscilla V. Smith, director. Estab. 1991. Nonprofit gallery. Approached by 6 artists/year; represents or exhibits more than 50 artists. Average display time 6 weeks. Open Tuesday-Saturday, 11-4; Sunday, 1-4. Overall price range $150-600. Most work sold at $300. Facility is also available for rent (business, meetings, reunions, weddings, receptions or rehearsals, etc.).
EXHIBITS Photos of landscapes/scenics, wildlife, architecture, gardening, travel, agriculture. Interested in fine art, historical/vintage.
MAKING CONTACT & TERMS Artwork is accepted on consignment, and there is a 30% commission. Gallery provides insurance, promotion. Accepted work should be framed, matted, wired for hanging. Call or stop in to show portfolio of photographs, slides. Send query letter with bio, photographs, slides, SASE. Responds in 1 month. Finds artists through word of mouth, submissions, portfolio reviews, art exhibits, art fairs, referrals by other artists.
TIPS "All artwork must be original designs, framed, ready to hang (wired—no sawtooth hangers)."

QUEENS COLLEGE ART CENTER

Benjamin S. Rosenthal Library, Flushing NY 11367. (718)997-3770. **Fax:** (718)997-3753. **E-mail:** tara.mathison@qc.cuny.edu; artcenter@qc.cuny.edu. **Website:** www.queenscollegeartcenter.org. **Contact:** Tara Tye Mathison, director and curator. Estab. 1955. Queens College Art Center is a successor since 1987 of the Klapper Library Art Center that was based in the Queens College Art Library's gallery founded in 1960. Focuses on modern and contemporary art, presenting the works of both emerging and established artists in diverse media, in programming expressive of

the best of the art of our time. Open Monday–Friday, 9-5; closed weekends and holidays. Average display time approximately 6-8 weeks. Overall price range $100-3,000.
EXHIBITS Open to all types, styles, subject matter; decisive factor is quality.
MAKING CONTACT & TERMS Charges 40% commission. Accepted work can be framed or unframed, mounted or unmounted, matted or unmatted. Sponsors openings. Photographer is responsible for providing/arranging refreshments and cleanup.
SUBMISSIONS Online preferred, or send query letter with résumé, samples and SASE, as appropriate. Responds within 1-2 months.

☺ MARCIA RAFELMAN FINE ARTS

10 Clarendon Ave., Toronto Ontario M4V 1H9, Canada. (416)920-4468. **Fax:** (416)968-6715. **E-mail:** info@mrfinearts.com. **Website:** www.mrfinearts.com. **Contact:** Marcia Rafelman, president; Meghan Richardson, gallery director. Estab. 1984. Semiprivate gallery. Average display time 1 month. Gallery is centrally located in Toronto; 2,000 sq. ft. on 2 floors. Overall price range $800-25,000. Most work sold at $1,500.
EXHIBITS Photos of environmental, landscapes. Interested in alternative process, documentary, fine art, historical/vintage.
MAKING CONTACT & TERMS Charges 50% commission. Gallery provides insurance, promotion, contract. Requires exclusive representation locally.
SUBMISSIONS Mail (must include SASE) or e-mail portfolio (preferred) for review; include bio, photographs, reviews. Responds only if interested. Finds artists through word of mouth, submissions, art fairs, referrals by other artists.
TIPS "We only accept work that is archival."

ELLA WALTON RICHARDSON FINE ART

58 Broad St., Charleston SC 29401. (843)722-3660. **Fax:** (843)722-4330. **E-mail:** ella@ellarichardson.com. **Website:** www.ellarichardson.com. **Contact:** Ella Richardson, owner. Estab. 2001. For-profit gallery. Exhibits established artists. Approached by 100s of artists a year; represents or exhibits 28 artists. Exhibited artists include Aleksander and Lyuba Titovets, Lindsay Goodwin, the Baranovs, Jeff Jamison, and Michael Coleman. Model and property release are required. Open Monday-Saturday, 10-5. Located in historic downtown Charleston, the gallery has 3 rooms

of artwork. The gallery is in the heart of the gallery district. It is an elegant and inviting space with hardwood floors, granite counters, and dual fireplaces. Clients included local community, students, tourists, and upscale. 5% of sales are to corporate collectors. Overall price range: $500-16,000.

MAKING CONTACT & TERMS Artwork is accepted on consignment and there is a 50% commission. Retail price set by the gallery and artist. gallery provides insurance and promotion. Accepted artwork should be framed. Requires exclusive representation locally.

SUBMISSIONS Mail or e-mail query letter with link to artist's website, JPEG samples at 72 dpi. Include artist's statement, bio, brochure, business card, photocopies, photographs, résumé, and reviews. Materials returned with SASE.

TIPS "Address the gallery individually. Sound knowledgeable about our space and artists. Organization and preparation."

RIVER GALLERY

400 E. Second St., Chattanooga TN 37403. (423)265-5033, ext. 5. **E-mail:** art@river-gallery.com; details@river-gallery.com. **Website:** www.river-gallery.com. **Contact:** Mary R. Portera, owner/director. Estab. 1992. Retail gallery. Represents 100 emerging, mid-career and established artists/year. Exhibited artists include Michael Kessler and Scott E. Hill. Sponsors 12 shows/year. Open Monday–Saturday, 10-5; Sunday, 1-5; and by appointment. Located in Bluff View Art District in downtown area; 2,500 sq. ft.; restored early New Orleans-style 1900s home; arched openings into rooms. 20% of space for special exhibitions; 80% of space for gallery artists. Clients include upscale tourists, local community. 95% of sales are to private collectors, 5% corporate collectors. Overall price range $5-10,000; most work sold at $200-2,000.

EXHIBITS Considers all media. Most frequently exhibits oil, original prints, photography, watercolor, mixed media, fiber, clay, jewelry, wood, glass and sculpture.

MAKING CONTACT & TERMS Accepts work on consignment (50% commission). Retail price set by the gallery. Gallery provides free gift wrap, insurance, promotion and contract; shipping costs are shared. Prefers artwork framed.

SUBMISSIONS Send query letter with résumé, slides, bio, photographs, SASE, reviews and artist's statement. Call or e-mail for appointment to show portfolio of photographs and slides. Files all material unless we are not interested then we return all information. Can also submit via form on website. Finds artists through word of mouth, referrals by other artists, visiting art fairs and exhibitions, submissions, ads in art publications.

ROCHESTER CONTEMPORARY

137 East Ave., Rochester NY 14604. (585)461-2222. **Fax:** (585)461-2223. **E-mail:** info@rochestercontemporary.org; bleu@rochestercontemporary.org. **Website:** www.rochestercontemporary.org. **Contact:** Bleu Cease, executive director. Estab. 1977. Located in Rochester's downtown "East End" cultural district. The 4,500-sq.-ft. space is handicap-accessible. Sponsors 10-12 exhibits/year. Average display time 4-6 weeks. Gallery open Wednesday–Sunday, 1-5; Friday, 1-10. Overall price range $100-500.

MAKING CONTACT & TERMS Charges 25% commission.

SUBMISSIONS Send up to 20 images via CD/DVD. Discs "must be labeled with your name and contact information. The checklist must have your name, address, phone number, e-mail address, and website (if available) at the top, followed by the title of the work, date, materials, and presentation size for each image submitted. Do not send prints or original works." Also include letter of intent, résumé, and statement.

ROCKPORT CENTER FOR THE ARTS

902 Navigation Circle, Rockport TX 78382. (361)729-5519. **Fax:** (361)729-3551. **E-mail:** info@rockportartcenter.com. **Website:** www.rockportartcenter.com. Estab. 1969. Rockport Center for the Arts is a hub of creative activity on the Texas Gulf Coast. Two parlor galleries are dedicated entirely to the works of its member artists, while the main gallery allows the center to host local, regional, national, and internationally acclaimed artists in both solo and group exhibitions. In 2000, the Garden Gallery was added, allowing the center for the first time to simultaneously feature 3 distinct exhibitions, at times displaying over 100 original works of art. Today, the building also houses 2 visual arts classrooms and an outdoor sculpture garden featuring works by internationally acclaimed artists. A well-furnished pottery studio is always active, and includes a kiln room which hosts daily firings. Visitors enjoy the exhibitions, education programs and gift shop, as well as the Annual Rockport Art Festival every July 4th weekend. Gal-

lery hours vary. Call, e-mail or visit website for more information.

THE ROTUNDA GALLERY

647 Fulton St., Brooklyn NY 11217. (718)683-5600. **E-mail:** bric@bricartsmedia.org. **Website:** www.bricon line.org/rotunda. Estab. 1981. Nonprofit gallery. Average display time 6 weeks. Open Tuesday–Saturday, 12-6.

EXHIBITS Interested in contemporary works.

MAKING CONTACT & TERMS Gallery provides photographer's contact information to prospective buyers. Shows are limited by walls that are 22 feet high.

SUBMISSIONS Send material by mail for consideration; include SASE. "View our website for guidelines and artist registry form."

SAN DIEGO ART INSTITUTE

1439 El Prado, San Diego CA 92101. (619)236-0011. **Fax:** (619)236-1974. **E-mail:** director@sandiego-art. org; admin@sandiego-art.org. **Website:** www.sandi ego-art.org. **Contact:** Ginger Shulick Porcella, executive director. Estab. 1941. Nonprofit gallery. SDAI's most visible activity focuses on showcasing the work of San Diego's emerging area visual artists through a program of over 30 juried shows a year. Different art professionals are selected as jurors for each show assuring exhibitions of high quality and great variety. Jurors' Choice and Honorable Mention certificates are awarded at monthly public receptions. Represents or exhibits 500 member artists. Overall price range: $50-3,000; most work sold at $700. Open Tuesday–Saturday, 10-4; Sunday, 12-4.

EXHIBITS Photos of babies/children/teens, couples, multicultural, families, parents, senior citizens, disasters, environmental, landscapes/scenics, wildlife, architecture, cities/urban, education, gardening, pets, rural, adventure, entertainment, events, food/drink, health/fitness/beauty, hobbies, humor, performing arts, sports, travel, agriculture, political, product shots/still life, science, technology. Interested in alternative process, avant garde, documentary, erotic, fine art, historical/vintage, seasonal.

MAKING CONTACT & TERMS Artwork is accepted on consignment with a 40% commission. Membership fee: $125. Accepted work should be framed. Work must be carried in by hand for each monthly show except for annual international show, JPEG online submission.

SUBMISSIONS Membership not required for submission in monthly juried shows, but fee required. Artists interested in membership should request membership packet. Finds artists through referrals by other artists.

TIPS "All work submitted must go through jury process for each monthly exhibition. Work must be framed in professional manner. No glass—Plexiglas or acrylic only."

⊘ THE JOSEPH SAXTON GALLERY OF PHOTOGRAPHY

520 Cleveland Ave. NW, Canton OH 44702. (330)438-0030. **Fax:** (330)456-9566. **E-mail:** maria@josephsax ton.com; gallery@josephsaxton.com. **Website:** www. josephsaxton.com. **Contact:** Maria Hadjian, acting manager. Estab. 2009. A premier photography gallery with nearly 7,000 sq. ft. of display space. "We house over 200 pieces by more than 160 master photographers and represented artists. Predominantly, we serve upscale clients, but welcome the general public. Prices range from $69-20,000, with the average piece selling for $1,500. Approached by numerous artists each year, new shows vary in number and length." Exhibited artists include: Steve McCurry, Art Wolfe, Lewis Wickes Hine, Eddie Adams, Annie Leibovitz, Sally Mann, Edward Weston, Berenice Abbott, Lisa Law and more. In addition to books, our Book Nook offers magazines, DVDs, apparel, novelty cameras and accessories. Open Wednesday–Saturday, 12-5. Tim Belden, owner. The gallery considers and exhibits various styles and genres of photography.

EXHIBITS "Our subject matter is inclusive by exhibiting photographs of celebrities, families, architecture, cities/urban life, agriculture, industry, military, political figures, product shots/still life, disasters, landscapes, wildlife, automobiles, entertainment, events, performing arts, sports, travel, fashion/glamour, fine art and those of historical content/vintage."

MAKING CONTACT & TERMS Artwork is accepted on consignment with a commission fee. The retail price of the art is set by the artist. The Gallery provides insurance and promotion ALONG with a contract. We require exclusive representation locally. Model and property releases are preferred.

SUBMISSIONS Accepted work should be matted and framed. "Please e-mail inquiry letter along with link to artists website. We will respond to all, but may request a nonreturnable disc (or will return materials with a SASE). We locate artists through word of mouth, portfolio reviews, referrals and by other means."

⊕ SCHLUMBERGER GALLERY

Website: www.schlumbergergallery.com. P.O. Box 2864, Santa Rosa CA 95405. (707)544-8356. **Fax:** (707)538-1953. **E-mail:** sande@schlumberger.org. **Contact:** Sande Schlumberger, owner. Estab. 1986. Art publisher/distributor and gallery. Publishes and distributes limited editions, posters, original paintings and sculpture. Specializes in decorative and museum-quality art and photographs.

EXHIBITS Interested in fine art.

MAKING CONTACT & TERMS Send query letter with tearsheets and photographs. Samples are not filed and are returned by SASE if requested by artist. Publisher/distributor will contact artist for portfolio review if interested. Portfolio should include color photographs and transparencies. Negotiates payment. Offers advance when appropriate. Rights purchased vary according to project. Provides advertising, in-transit insurance, insurance while work is at firm, promotion, shipping to and from firm, written contract and shows. Finds artists through exhibits, referrals, submissions and "pure blind luck."

TIPS "Strive for quality, clarity, clean lines and light. Bring spirit into your images. It translates!"

WILLIAM & FLORENCE SCHMIDT ART CENTER

Southwestern Illinois College, 2500 Carlyle Ave., Belleville IL 62221. (618)222-5278. **Website:** www.swic.edu/sac. Estab. 2002. Nonprofit gallery. Sponsors 1-2 photography exhibits/year.

EXHIBITS Interested in fine art and historical/vintage photography.

SUBMISSIONS Mail portfolio for review. Send query letter with artist's statement, bio and 12-20 digital images on a CD with image list. Finds artists through art fairs and exhibits, portfolio reviews, referrals by other artists, submissions and word of mouth.

SCHMIDT/DEAN

1719 Chestnut St., Philadelphia PA 19103. (215)569-9433. **Fax:** (215)569-9434. **E-mail:** schmidtdean@netzero.com. **Website:** www.schmidtdean.com. **Contact:** Christopher Schmidt, director. Estab. 1988. For-profit gallery. Houses eclectic art. Sponsors 4 photography exhibits/year. Average display time 6 weeks. Gallery open Tuesday–Saturday, 10:30-6. Au-

gust hours are Tuesday–Friday, 10:30-6. Overall price range $1,000-70,000.

EXHIBITS Interested in alternative process, documentary, fine art.

MAKING CONTACT & TERMS Charges 50% commission. Gallery provides insurance, promotion. Accepted work should be framed, mounted, matted. Requires exclusive representation locally.

SUBMISSIONS Call/write to arrange a personal interview to show portfolio. Send query letter with SASE. "Send digital images on CD and a résumé that gives a sense of your working history. Include a SASE."

SIOUX CITY ART CENTER

225 Nebraska St., Sioux City IA 51101-1712. (712)279-6272. **Fax:** (712)255-2921. **E-mail:** siouxcityartcenter@sioux-city.org. **Website:** www.siouxcityartcenter.org. **Contact:** Todd Behrens, curator. Estab. 1938. Museum. Exhibits emerging, mid-career and established artists. Approached by 50 artists/year; represents or exhibits 2-3 artists. Sponsors 15 total exhibits/year. Average display time: 10-12 weeks. Gallery open Tuesday, Wednesday, Friday, Saturday, 10-4; Thursday, 10-9; Sunday, 1-4. Closed on Mondays and municipal holidays. Located in downtown Sioux City; 2 galleries, each 40×80 ft. Clients include local community, students and tourists.

EXHIBITS Considers all media and types of prints. Most frequently exhibits paintings, sculpture and mixed media.

MAKING CONTACT & TERMS Artwork is accepted on consignment with a 30% commission. "However, the purpose of our exhibitions is not sales." Retail price of the art set by the artist. Gallery provides insurance, promotion and contract.

SUBMISSIONS Artwork should be framed. Only accepts artwork from upper-Midwestern states. E-mail query letter with link to artist's website; 15-20 JPEG samples at 72 dpi. Or send query letter with artist's statement, résumé and digital images. Returns materials if SASE is enclosed. Do not send original works. Responds, only if interested, within 6 months. Files résumé, statement and images if artist is suitable. Finds artists through word of mouth, art exhibits, submissions, art fairs, portfolio reviews and referrals by other artists.

TIPS "Submit good photography with an honest and clear statement."

SOHN FINE ART—GALLERY & GICLÉE PRINTING

69 Church St., Lenox MA 01240. (413)551-7353. **E-mail:** info@sohnfineart.com. **Website:** www. sohnfineart.com. **Contact:** Cassandra Sohn, owner. Estab. 2011. Alternative space and for-profit gallery. Approached by 25-50 artists/year; represents or exhibits 12-20 emerging, mid-career and established artists. Exhibited artists include Greg Gorman, Matchuska, Fran Forman, John Atchley, Seth Resnick, Savannah Spirit, Bruce Checefsky, Cassandra Sohn, etc. Average display time: 1-3 months. Open Thursday-Monday, 11-5. Located in the Berkshires of Western Massachusetts. The area is known for arts and culture and full of tourists. 80% of the population are 2nd-home owners from New York and Boston. Clients include local community, tourists and upscale. Overall price range: $300-6,000; most work sold for $300-2,500.

EXHIBITS Considers photography and sculpture. Considers all styles and genres.

MAKING CONTACT & TERMS Artwork is accepted on consignment and there is a 50% commission. Retail price of the art set by the artist. Gallery provides insurance, promotion and contract. Accepted work should be framed, mounted and matted. Requires exclusive representation locally.

SUBMISSIONS E-mail query letter with link to artist's website and JPEG samples at 72 dpi. Material cannot be returned. Responds only if interested. Finds artists through word of mouth, art exhibits, submissions, art fairs, portfolio reviews and referrals by other artists.

SOHO MYRIAD

1250 Menlo Dr., Atlanta GA 30318. (404)351-5656. **Fax:** (404)351-8284. **E-mail:** info@sohomyriad.com. **Website:** www.sohomyriad.com. Estab. 1977. Art consulting firm and for-profit gallery. Represents and/or exhibits over 2,000 artists. Sponsors 1 photography exhibit/year. Average display time: 2 months. Overall price range $500-20,000. Most work sold at $500-5,000.

○ Additional offices in Los Angeles and London. See website for contact information.

EXHIBITS Photos of landscapes/scenics, architecture, floral/botanical and abstracts. Interested in alternative process, avant garde, fine art, historical/vintage.

MAKING CONTACT & TERMS Artwork is accepted on consignment, and there is a 50% commission. Gallery provides insurance.

SOUTH DAKOTA ART MUSEUM

South Dakota State University, Medary Ave. and Harvey Dunn St., P.O. Box 2250, Brookings SD 57007. (605)688-5423. **Fax:** (605)688-4445. **Website:** www. southdakotaartmuseum.com. Sponsors 1-2 photography exhibits/year. Average display time: 4 months. Gallery open Monday-Friday, 10-5; Saturday, 10-4; Sunday, 12-4; closed state holidays and Sundays, January–March. Seven galleries offer 26,000 sq. ft. of exhibition space.

EXHIBITS Interested in alternative process, documentary, fine art.

MAKING CONTACT & TERMS Please visit website for additional details.

SOUTHSIDE GALLERY

150 Courthouse Square, Oxford MS 38655. (662)234-9090. **E-mail:** southside@southsideartgallery.com. **Website:** www.southsideartgallery.com. **Contact:** Duncan Bass, director. Estab. 1993. For-profit gallery. Average display time 4 weeks. Gallery open Tuesday–Saturday, 10-6. Overall price range $300-20,000. Most work sold at $425.

EXHIBITS Photos of landscapes/scenics, architecture, cities/urban, rural, entertainment, events, performing arts, sports, travel, agriculture, political. Interested in avant garde, fine art.

MAKING CONTACT & TERMS Artwork is accepted on consignment, and there is a 55% commission. Gallery provides promotion. Accepted work should be framed.

SUBMISSIONS Mail between 10 and 25 slides that reflect current work with SASE for review. CDs are also accepted with images in JPEG or TIFF format. Include artist statement, biography, and résumé. Responds within 4-6 months. Finds artists through submissions.

B.J. SPOKE GALLERY

299 Main St., Huntington NY 11743. (631)549-5106. **E-mail:** manager@bjspokegallery.com. **Website:** www.bjspokegallery.com. **Contact:** Marilyn Lavi, gallery manager. Estab. 1978.

MAKING CONTACT & TERMS Arrange a personal interview to show portfolio. Send query letter with SASE.

SUBMISSIONS Charges 35% commission. Photographer sets price.

SRO PHOTO GALLERY AT LANDMARK ARTS

School of Art, Texas Tech University, Box 42081, Lubbock TX 79409-2081. (806)742-1947. **Fax:** (806)742-1971. **E-mail:** srophotogallery.art@ttu.edu. **Website:** www.landmarkarts.org. **Contact:** Joe R. Arredondo, director. Estab. 1984. Nonprofit gallery. Hosts an annual competition to fill 8 solo photography exhibition slots each year. Average display time 4 weeks. Open Monday–Friday, 8-5; Saturday, 10-5; Sunday, 12-4. Closed university holidays.

EXHIBITS Interested in art utilizing photographic processes.

MAKING CONTACT & TERMS "Exhibits are for scholarly purposes. Gallery will provide artist's contact information to potential buyers." Gallery provides insurance, promotion, contract. Accepted work should be matted.

SUBMISSIONS Exhibitions are determined by juried process. See website for details (under call for entries). Deadline for submissions is end of March.

THE STATE MUSEUM OF PENNSYLVANIA

300 North St., Harrisburg PA 17120. (717)787-4980. **E-mail:** bhager@state.pa.us. **Website:** www.statemuseumpa.org. Offers visitors 4 floors representing Pennsylvania's story, from Earth's beginning to the present. Features archaeological artifacts, minerals, paintings, decorative arts, animal dioramas, industrial and technological innovations, and military objects representing the Commonwealth's heritage. Number of exhibits varies. Average display time: 3 months. Open Wednesday–Saturday, 9-5; Sunday 12-5.

EXHIBITS Fine art photography is a new area of endeavor for The State Museum, both collecting and exhibiting. Interested in works produced with experimental techniques.

MAKING CONTACT & TERMS Artwork is sold in gallery as part of annual Art of the State exhibition only. Overall price range: $50-3,000. Connects artists with interested buyers. Art must be created by a native or resident of Pennsylvania to be considered for Art of the State, and/or contain subject matter relevant to Pennsylvania to be considered for permanent collection. Send material by mail for consideration; include SASE. Responds in 1 month.

STATE OF THE ART GALLERY

120 W. State St., Ithaca NY 14850. (607)277-1626. **E-mail:** gallery@soag.org. **Website:** www.soag.org. Estab. 1989. Cooperative gallery. Sponsors 2 juried exhibits/year. Average display time 1 month. Gallery open Wednesday–Friday, 12-6; weekends, 12-5. Located in downtown Ithaca, 2 rooms about 1,100 sq. ft. Overall price range $100-6,000. Most work sold at $200-500.

EXHIBITS Photos in all media and subjects. Interested in alternative process, avant garde, fine art, computer-assisted photographic processes.

MAKING CONTACT & TERMS There is a co-op membership fee plus a donation of time. There is a 10% commission for members, 30% for nonmembers. Gallery provides promotion, contract. Accepted work must be ready to hang. Write for membership application. See website for further details.

STATE STREET GALLERY

1804 State St., La Crosse WI 54601. (608)782-0101. **Contact:** Ellen Kallies, president. Estab. 2000. Wholesale, retail and trade gallery. Approached by 15 artists/year; exhibits 12-14 artists/quarter in gallery. Average display time: 4-6 months. Open Tuesday, Thursday and Friday, 10-4, Saturday, 10-2; other times by chance or appointment. Located across from the University of Wisconsin/La Crosse. Overall price range: $50-12,000; most work sold at $500-1,200 and above.

EXHIBITS Photos of environmental, landscapes/scenics, architecture, cities/urban, gardening, rural, travel, medicine.

MAKING CONTACT & TERMS Artwork is accepted on consignment, and there is a 40% commission. Gallery provides insurance, promotion, contract. Accepted work should be framed, matted.

SUBMISSIONS Call or mail portfolio for review. Send query letter with artist's statement, photographs, slides, SASE. Responds in 1 month. Finds artists through word of mouth, art exhibits, art fairs, referrals by other artists.

TIPS "Be organized, professional in presentation, flexible."

PHILIP J. STEELE GALLERY

Rocky Mt. College of Art + Design, 1600 Pierce St., Denver CO 80214. (303)753-6046. **Fax:** (303)759-4970. **Website:** www.rmcad.edu/gallery-exhibitions/philip-j-steele-gallery. **Contact:** Lisa Spivak, director. Estab. 1962. Located in the Mary Harris Auditorium building on the southeast corner of the quad. Approached by 25 artists/year; represents or exhibits 6-9 artists. Sponsors 1 photography exhibit/year. Average display time 1 month. Open Monday-Friday, 11-4. Photographers should call or visit website for more information.

EXHIBITS No restrictions on subject matter.

MAKING CONTACT & TERMS No fee or percentage taken. Gallery provides insurance, promotion. Accepted work should be framed.

SUBMISSIONS Send query letter with artist's statement, bio, slides, résumé, reviews, SASE. Reviews in May, deadline April 15. Finds artists through word of mouth, submissions, referrals by other artists.

STEVENSON UNIVERSITY ART GALLERY

1525 Greenspring Valley Rd., Stevenson MD 21153. (443)352-4491. **Fax:** (410)352-4500. **E-mail:** exhibitions@stevenson.edu. **Website:** www.stevenson.edu/stuarteffects. **Contact:** Matt Laumann, cultural programs manager. Estab. 1997. Sponsors 10 exhibits/year across 3 museum quality gallery spaces, University Art Gallery, St. Paul Companies Pavilion, and the new School of Design Gallery. Average display time: 6 weeks. Gallery open Monday, Tuesday, Wednesday, Friday, 11-5; Thursday, 11-8; Saturday, 1-4. "Since its 1997 inaugural season, the Stevenson University Art Gallery has presented a dynamic series of substantive exhibitions in diverse media and has achieved the reputation as a significant venue for regional artists and collectors. The museum quality space was designed to support the Baltimore arts community, provide greater opportunities for artists, and be integral to the educational experience of Stevenson students."

EXHIBITS Interested in alternative process, avant garde, documentary, fine art, historical/vintage. "We are looking for artwork of substance by artists from the mid-Atlantic region."

MAKING CONTACT & TERMS "We facilitate inquiries directly to the artist." Gallery provides insurance. *Accepts artists from mid-Atlantic states only; emphasis on Baltimore artists.*

SUBMISSIONS Write to show portfolio. Send artist's statement, bio, résumé, reviews, portfolio link or CD. Responds in 3 months. Finds artists through word of mouth, submissions, portfolio reviews, referrals by other artists.

TIPS "Be clear, concise. Have good representation of your images."

STILL POINT ART GALLERY

193 Hillside Rd., Brunswick ME 04011. (207)837-5760. **Website:** www.stillpointartgallery.com. **Contact:** Christine Cote, owner/director. Estab. 2009. For-profit online gallery. Exhibits emerging, mid-career and established artists. Approached by 300 artists/year. Represents 25 artists. Sponsors 4 juried shows/year. Distinguished artists earn representation and publication in gallery's art journal, *Still Point Arts Quarterly*. Model and property release preferred. Average display time: 14 months. Overall price range: $200-5,000.

EXHIBITS Considers all media and styles. Most frequently exhibits painting and photography. Considers engravings, etchings, serigraphs, linocuts, woodcuts, lithographs and mezzotints. Considers all genres.

MAKING CONTACT & TERMS Retail price set by the artist. Gallery takes no commission from sales. Gallery provides promotion. Respond to calls for artists posted on website.

TIPS "Follow the instructions posted on our website."

SYNCHRONICITY FINE ARTS

106 W. 13th St., New York NY 10011. (646)230-8199. **E-mail:** jsa@synchroncityspace.com; contact@synchroncityspace.com. **Website:** www.synchronicityspace.com. **Contact:** John Amato, director. Estab. 1989. Nonprofit gallery. Approached by hundreds of artists/year; represents or exhibits over 60 artists. Sponsors 2-3 photography exhibits/year. Gallery open Wednesday-Saturday, 1-7. Closed 2 weeks in August. Overall price range $1,500-20,000. Most work sold at $3,000.

EXHIBITS Photos of multicultural, environmental, landscapes/scenics, architecture, cities/urban, education, rural, events, agriculture, industry, medicine, political. Interested in avant garde, documentary, fine art, historical/vintage.

MAKING CONTACT & TERMS Gallery provides insurance, promotion, contract. Accepted work should be framed, mounted, matted.

SUBMISSIONS Submissions may be made via electronic or e-mail as JPEG small files as well as the other means. Write to arrange a personal interview to show portfolio of photographs, transparencies, slides. Send query letter with photocopies, SASE, photographs, slides, résumé. Responds in 3 weeks. Finds artists through art exhibits, submissions, portfolio reviews, referrals by other artists.

LILLIAN & COLEMAN TAUBE MUSEUM OF ART

2 N. Main St., Minot ND 58703. (701)838-4445. **E-mail:** taube@srt.com. **Website:** www.taubemuseum.

org. **Contact:** Nancy Walter, executive director. Estab. 1970. Established nonprofit organization. Sponsors 1-2 photography exhibits/year. Average display time: 4-6 weeks. Located in a renovated historic landmark building with room to show 2 exhibits simultaneously. Overall price range: $15-225. Most work sold at $40-100.

EXHIBITS Photos of babies/children/teens, couples, multicultural, families, parents, senior citizens, disasters, landscapes/scenics, wildlife, beauty, rural, travel, agriculture, buildings, military, portraits. Interested in avant garde, fine art.

MAKING CONTACT & TERMS Charges 30% commission for members; 40% for nonmembers. Sponsors openings.

SUBMISSIONS Submit portfolio along with a minimum of 6 examples of work in digital format for review. Responds in 3 months.

TIPS "Wildlife, landscapes and floral pieces seem to be the trend in North Dakota. We get many portfolios to review for our photography exhibits each year. We also appreciate figurative, unusual and creative photography work."

NATALIE AND JAMES THOMPSON ART GALLERY

Department of Art & Art History, San Jose State University, San Jose CA 95192-0089. (408)924-4723. **Fax:** (408)924-4326. **E-mail:** thompsongallery@sjsu.edu. **Website:** www.sjsu.edu. **Contact:** Jo Farb Hernandez, director. Nonprofit gallery. Approached by 100 artists/year. Sponsors 1-2 photography exhibits/year. Average display time: 1 month. Gallery open Monday, Wednesday-Friday, 10-4; Tuesday, 10-4 and 6-7:30.

EXHIBITS All genres, aesthetics and techniques.

MAKING CONTACT & TERMS Works not generally for sale. Gallery provides insurance, promotion. Accepted work should be framed or ready to hang.

SUBMISSIONS Send query letter with artist's statement, bio, résumé, reviews, slides, SASE. Responds as soon as possible. Finds artists through word of mouth, submissions, portfolio reviews, art exhibits, art fairs, referrals by other artists.

THROCKMORTON FINE ART

145 E. 57th St., 3rd Floor, New York NY 10022. (212)223-1059. **Fax:** (212)223-1937. **E-mail:** info@throckmorton-nyc.com. **Website:** www.throck morton-nyc.com. **Contact:** Spencer Throckmorton, owner; Norberto Rivera, photography. Estab. 1993.

For-profit gallery. A New York-based gallery specializing in vintage and contemporary photography of the Americas for over 25 years. Its primary focus is Latin American photographers. The gallery also specializes in Chinese jades and antiquities, as well as pre-Columbian art. Located in the Hammacher Schlemmer Building; 4,000 sq. ft.; 1,000 sq. ft. exhibition space. Clients include local community and upscale. Approached by 50 artists/year; represents or exhibits 20 artists. Sponsors 5 photography exhibits/year. Average display time: 2 months. Open Tuesday–Saturday, 11-5. Overall price range: $1,000-10,000; most work sold at $2,500.

EXHIBITS Photos of babies/children/teens, landscapes/scenics, architecture, cities/urban, rural. Interested in erotic, fine art, historical/vintage, Latin American photography.

MAKING CONTACT & TERMS Charges 50% commission. Gallery provides insurance, promotion.

SUBMISSIONS Write to arrange a personal interview to show portfolio of photographs/slides/CD, or send query letter with artist's statement, bio, photocopies, slides, CD, SASE. Responds in 3 weeks. Finds artists through word of mouth, portfolio reviews.

TIPS "Present your work nice and clean."

TILT GALLERY

7077 E. Main St., Suite 14, Scottsdale AZ 85251. (602)716-5667. **E-mail:** info@tiltgallery.com. **E-mail:** melanie@tiltgallery.com. **Website:** www.tiltgallery. com. **Contact:** Melanie Craven, gallery owner. Estab. 2005. For-profit gallery. "A contemporary fine art gallery specializing in hand applied photographic processes and mixed media projects." Represents or exhibits 30 emerging and established artists. Exhibited artists include France Scully Osterman and Mark Osterman, Aline Smithson, Jill Enfield, Anna Strickland. Sponsors 8 exhibits/year; 7 photography exhibits/year. Average display time: 1 month. Open Tuesday-Saturday, 10:30-5:30; Thursday (night art walk), 7-9; and by appointment.

TOUCHSTONE GALLERY

901 New York Ave. NW, Washington DC 20001-2217. (202)347-2787. **E-mail:** info@touchstonegallery.com. **Website:** www.touchstonegallery.com. Estab. 1976. Contemporary fine art gallery featuring 50 artists working in a variety of original art in all media—oil, acrylic, sculpture, photography, printing, engraving, etc.—exhibiting a new show monthly. This brand new

1,000+ sq.-ft. space features tall ceilings, great lighting, and polished flooring. The gallery is available for rent for brunch meetings, rehearsal dinners, cocktail parties, and life celebrations of all kinds. Located near the heart of the bustling Penn Quarter district in downtown Washington DC one block from the Washington Convention Center, the gallery is easily accessible at street level. Open Wednesday-Friday, 11-6; Saturday-Sunday, 12-5. Overall price range: $100-20,000. Visit the website or contact the gallery directly for further information.

UAB VISUAL ARTS GALLERY

Abroms-Engel Institute for the Visual Arts, 1221 10th Ave. S, Birmingham AL 35205. (205)975-6436. **Fax:** (205)975-2836. **E-mail:** aeiva@uab.edu. **Website:** www.uab.edu/cas/aeiva. Nonprofit university gallery. Sponsors 1-3 photography exhibits/year. Average display time: 3-4 weeks. Gallery open Monday–Friday, 10-6; Saturday, 12-6; closed major holidays and last 2 weeks of December.

EXHIBITS Photos of multicultural. Interested in alternative process, avant garde, fine art, historical/vintage.

MAKING CONTACT & TERMS Gallery provides insurance, promotion. Accepted work should be framed.

SUBMISSIONS Does not accept unsolicited exhibition proposals. Write to arrange a personal interview to show portfolio of slides. Send query letter with artist's statement, bio, brochure, photographs, résumé, reviews, slides, SASE.

UCR/CALIFORNIA MUSEUM OF PHOTOGRAPHY

University of California, 3824 Main St., Riverside CA 92501. **E-mail:** cmpcollections@ucr.edu; cmppress@ucr.edu; jonathan.green@ucr.edu. **Website:** www.cmp.ucr.edu. **Contact:** Jonathan Green, executive director. Sponsors 10-15 exhibits/year. Average display time 8-14 weeks. Open Tuesday–Saturday, 12-5. Located in a renovated 23,000-sq.-ft. building. "It is the largest exhibition space devoted to photography in the West."

EXHIBITS Interested in technology/computers, alternative process, avant garde, documentary, fine art, historical/vintage.

MAKING CONTACT & TERMS Curatorial committee reviews CDs, slides and/or matted or unmatted work. Photographer must have highest-quality work.

SUBMISSIONS Exhibition proposals should include a project description, cover letter, résumé, and selection of images. Artists can send either a link to a website or e-mail up to 10MB of digital files for consideration by the curatorial committee. These proposals will be reviewed as they are received. The museum's curators will actively solicit submissions for individuals whose work they would like to consider for future projects.

TIPS "This museum attempts to balance exhibitions among historical, technological, contemporary, etc. We do not sell photos but provide photographers with exposure. The museum is always interested in newer, lesser-known photographers who are producing interesting work. We're especially interested in work relevant to underserved communities. We can show only a small percent of what we see in a year."

UNI GALLERY OF ART

University of Northern Iowa, 104 Kamerick Art Bldg., Cedar Falls IA 50614-0362. (319)273-6134. **Fax:** (319)273-7333. **E-mail:** galleryofart@uni.edu. **Website:** www.uni.edu/artdept/gallery/Home.html. **Contact:** Darrell Taylor, director. Estab. 1978. Sponsors 9 exhibits/year. Average display time 1 month. Approximately 4,000 sq. ft. of space and 350 ft. of usable wall space. Interested in all styles of high-quality contemporary artwork.

MAKING CONTACT & TERMS "We do not sell work."

SUBMISSIONS Please provide a cover letter and proposal as well as an artist's statement, CV, and samples. Send material by mail for consideration or submit portfolio for review; include SASE for return of material. Response time varies.

UNION STREET GALLERY

1527 Otto Blvd., Chicago Heights IL 60411. (708)754-2601. **E-mail:** unionstreetart@gmail.com. **Website:** www.unionstreetgallery.org. **Contact:** Jessica Segal, gallery director. Estab. 1995. Nonprofit gallery. Represents or exhibits more than 100 artists. "We offer group invitations and juried exhibits every year." Average display time 5 weeks. Hours: Wednesday and Thursday, 12-5; Friday, 12-6; Saturday, 11-4. Overall price range $30-3,000. Most work sold at $300-500.

SUBMISSIONS Finds artists through submissions, referrals by other artists and juried exhibits at the gallery. "To receive prospectus for all juried events, call, write or e-mail to be added to our mailing list. Prospectus also available on website. Artists interested in studio space or solo/group exhibitions should contact the gallery to request information packets."

UNIVERSITY OF KENTUCKY ART MUSEUM

405 Rose St., Lexington KY 40506. (859)257-5716. **Fax:** (859)323-1994. **E-mail:** jwelk3@email.uky.edu. **Website:** www.uky.edu/artmuseum. **Contact:** Janie Welker, curator. Estab. 1979. Museum. In addition to the university community, the Art Museum serves the greater Lexington area and Central and Eastern Kentucky through art exhibitions, educational outreach, and other special events including lectures, symposia and family festivals.

EXHIBITS Annual photography lecture series and exhibits.

SUBMISSIONS Prefers e-mail query with digital images. Responds in 6 months.

UNIVERSITY OF RICHMOND MUSEUMS

28 Westhampton Way, Richmond VA 23173. (804)289-8276. **Fax:** (804)287-1894. **E-mail:** rwaller@richmond.edu; museums@richmond.edu. **Website:** museums.richmond.edu. **Contact:** Richard Waller, director. Estab. 1968. University Museums comprises Joel and Lila Harnett Museum of Art, Joel and Lila Harnett Print Study Center, and Lora Robins Gallery of Design from Nature. The museums are home to diverse collections and exhibitions of art, artifacts and natural history specimens. Sponsors 14-18 exhibits/year. Average display time: 8-10 weeks. See website for hours for each gallery.

EXHIBITS Interested in all subjects.

MAKING CONTACT & TERMS Charges 10% commission. Work must be framed for exhibition.

SUBMISSIONS Send query letter with résumé, samples. Send material by e-mail for consideration. Responds in 1 month.

TIPS "We are a nonprofit university museum interested in presenting contemporary art as well as historical exhibitions."

UPSTREAM GALLERY

8 Main St, Hastings-on-Hudson NY 10706. (914)674-8548. **E-mail:** upstreamgallery26@gmail.com. **Website:** www.upstreamgallery.com. Estab. 1990. "Upstream Gallery is a cooperative with up to 25 members practicing various disciplines including sculpture, painting, printmaking, photography, digital imagery and more." Requires membership to exhibit. Annual dues reflect an equal sharing of the yearly expenses of maintaining the gallery. Applicants can apply for a full (includes a 1 person show in 1 of the 2 galleries, rotating between the two every 18 or 24 months) or associate membership (sharing one of the galleries with another artist every 18-24 months and rotating similar to full membership). See website for more details.

EXHIBITS Only fine art. Accepts all subject matters and genres for jurying.

MAKING CONTACT & TERMS There is a co-op membership fee plus a donation of time. There is a 20% commission. Gallery provides insurance. Accepted work should be framed, mounted and matted.

SUBMISSIONS Write to arrange a personal interview to show portfolio of photographs and slides. Send query letter with artist's statement, bio, brochure, business card, photographs, résumé, reviews, slides and SASE. Responds to queries within 2 months, only if interested. Finds artists through referrals by other artists and submissions.

UPSTREAM PEOPLE GALLERY

5607 Howard St., Omaha NE 68106-1257. (402)991-4741. **E-mail:** shows@upstreampeoplegallery.com. **Website:** www.upstreampeoplegallery.com. **Contact:** Laurence Bradshaw, curator. Estab. 1998. Exclusive online virtual gallery with over 40 international exhibitions in the archives section of the website. Represents mid-career and established artists. Approached by approximately 1,500 artists/year; represents or exhibits 20,000 artists. Sponsors 12 total exhibits/year and 7 photography exhibits/year. Average display time: 12 months to 4 years. Overall price range: $100-60,000; most work sold at $300. 15% of sales are to corporate collectors.

EXHIBITS Considers all media except video and film. Most frequently exhibits oil, acrylic and ceramics. Considers all prints, styles and genres. Most frequently exhibits Neo-Expressionism, Realism and Surrealism.

MAKING CONTACT & TERMS Artwork is accepted on consignment; there is no commission if the artists sells, but a 20% commission if the gallery sells. Retail price set by the artist. Gallery provides promotion and contract.

SUBMISSIONS Accepted work should be photographed. Call or write to arrange personal interview to show portfolio, e-mail query letter with link to website and JPEG samples at 72 dpi or send query letter with artist's statement and CD/DVD. Returns material with SASE. Responds to queries within 1 week. Files résumés. Finds artists through art exhibits, referrals and online and magazine advertising.

TIPS "Make sure all photographs of works are in focus."

URBAN INSTITUTE FOR CONTEMPORARY ARTS

2 W. Fulton St., Grand Rapids MI 49503. (616)454-7000. **E-mail:** curator@uica.org. **Website:** www.uica. org. Estab. 1977. Alternative space and nonprofit gallery. Approached by 250 artists/year; represents or exhibits 20 artists. Sponsors 3-4 photography exhibits/year. Average display time: 6 weeks. Gallery open Tuesday-Saturday, 12-9; Sunday, 12-6.

EXHIBITS Most frequently exhibits mixed media, avant garde, and nontraditional work. Style of exhibits is conceptual and postmodern.

SUBMISSIONS Please check our website for gallery descriptions and how to apply. Artists should visit the website, go to Exhibitions, then Apply for a Show and follow the instructions. UICA exhibits artists through submissions.

VIRIDIAN ARTISTS, INC.

548 W. 28th St., Suite 632, New York NY 10001. (212)414-4040. **Website:** www.viridianartists.com. **Contact:** Vernita Nemec, director. Estab. 1968. Artist-owned gallery. Approached by 200 artists/year. Exhibits 25-30 emerging, mid-career and established artists/year. Sponsors 15 total exhibits/year; 2-4 photography exhibits/year. Average display time: 3 weeks. Open Tuesday–Saturday, 12-6; closed in August. "Classic gallery space with 3 columns, hardwood floor, white walls and track lights, approximately 1,100 sq. ft. The gallery is located in Chelsea, the prime area of contemporary art galleries in New York City." Clients include: local community, students, tourists, upscale and artists. 15% of sales are to corporate collectors. Overall price range: $100-8,000; most work sold at $1,500.

EXHIBITS Considers all media except craft, traditional glass and ceramic, unless it is sculpture. Most frequently exhibits paintings, photography and sculpture. Considers engravings, etchings, linocuts, lithographs, mezzotints, serigraphs, woodcuts and monoprints/limited edition digital prints. Considers all styles (mostly contemporary). Most frequently exhibits painterly abstraction, imagism and neo-expressionism. "We are not interested in particular styles, but in professionally conceived and professionally executed contemporary art. Eclecticism is our policy. The only unifying factor is quality. Work must be of the highest technical and aesthetic standards."

MAKING CONTACT & TERMS Artwork accepted on consignment with a 30% commission. There is a co-op membership fee plus a donation of time with a 30% commission. Retail price of the art is set by the gallery and artist. Gallery provides promotion and contract. "Viridian is an artist-owned gallery with a director and gallery assistant. Artists pay gallery expenses through monthly dues, but the staff takes care of running the gallery and selling the art. The director writes the press releases, helps install exhibits and advises artists on all aspects of their career. We try to take care of everything but making the art and framing it." Prefers artists who are familiar with the NYC art world and are working professionally in a contemporary mode which can range from realistic to abstract to conceptual and anything in between.

SUBMISSIONS Submitting art for consideration is a 2-step process: first through website or JPEGs, then if accepted at that level, by seeing 4-6 samples of the actual art. Artists should call, e-mail query letter with link to artist's website or JPEG samples at 72 dpi (include image list) or send query letter with artist's statement, bio, reviews, CD with images and SASE. Materials returned with SASE. Responds in 2-4 weeks. Files materials of artists who become members. Finds artists through word of mouth, submissions, art exhibits, portfolio reviews or referrals by other artists.

TIPS "Present current art completed within the last 2 years. Our submission procedure is in 2 stages: first we look at websites, JPEGs that have been e-mailed, or CDs that have been mailed to the gallery. When e-mailing JPEGs, include an image list with title, date of execution, size, media. Also, include a bio and artist's statement. Reviews about your work are helpful if you have them, but not necessary. If you make it through the first level, then you will be asked to submit 4-6 actual artworks. These should be framed or matted, and similar to the work you want to show. Realize it is important to present a consistency in your vision. If you do more than one kind of art, select what you feel best represents you, for the art you show will be a reflection of who you are."

VISUAL ARTS CENTER OF NORTHWEST FLORIDA

19 E. Fourth St., Panama City FL 32401. (850)769-4451. **E-mail:** vacoffice@knology.net. **Website:** www.vacnwf.org. **Contact:** Exhibition manager. Estab. 1988. Approached by 20 artists/year; represents local and national artists. Sponsors 1-2 photography exhibits/year. Average display time 6 weeks. Open Tuesday and Thursday, 10-8; Wednesday, Friday and Saturday, 10-6; closed Sunday and Monday. The Center features a large gallery (200 running ft.) upstairs and a smaller gallery (80 running ft.) downstairs. Overall price range $50-1,500.

EXHIBITS Photos of all subject matter, including babies/children/teens, couples, families, parents, senior citizens, environmental, landscapes/scenics, wildlife, architecture, product shots/still life. Interested in alternative process, avant garde, documentary, fashion/glamour, fine art, historical/vintage, seasonal, digital, underwater.

MAKING CONTACT & TERMS Artwork is accepted on consignment, and there is a 30% commission. Gallery provides promotion, contract, insurance. Accepted work must be framed, mounted, matted.

SUBMISSIONS Send query letter with artist's statement, bio, résumé, SASE, 10-12 slides or images on CD. Responds within 4 months. Finds artists through word of mouth, submissions, art exhibits.

WASHINGTON COUNTY MUSEUM OF FINE ARTS

401 Museum Dr., Hagerstown MD 21741. (301)739-5727. **Fax:** (301)745-3741. **E-mail:** info@wcmfa.org; kpalmateer@wcmfa.org. **Website:** www.wcmfa.org. **Contact:** Kay Palmateer, manager of collections & exhibitions. Estab. 1929. The museum has a long tradition of cultural leadership in the Cumberland Valley region, providing residents and visitors with access to a permanent collection and an active schedule of exhibitions, musical concerts, lectures, film, art classes and special events for children and adults. Typically sponsors 2 juried exhibitions per year. Average display time: 8-10 weeks. Open Tuesday-Friday, 9-5; Saturday, 9-4; Sunday, 1-5; closed Mondays and major holidays. Overall price range: under $1,500.

EXHIBITS Photos of babies/children/teens, celebrities, couples, multicultural, families, parents, senior citizens, disasters, environmental, landscapes/scenics, wildlife, architecture, cities/urban, education, gardening, interiors/decorating, pets, religious, rural, adventure, automobiles, entertainment, events, food/drink, health/fitness/beauty, hobbies, humor, performing arts, sports, travel, agriculture, business concepts, industry, medicine, military, political, product shots/still life, science, technology/computers. Interested in alternative process, avant garde, documentary, fashion/glamour, fine art, historical/vintage, seasonal. Most frequently exhibits oil, watercolor, ceramics, photographs and all types of prints except posters.

MAKING CONTACT & TERMS Museum is a nonprofit and does not provide honoraria. Retail prices set by the artist. If applicable, museum handles sale of works and assumes 40% commission.

SUBMISSIONS Write or e-mail to initiate submission process. Mail portfolio for review. Usually responds within 3 months. Finds artists through word of mouth, portfolio reviews, art exhibits, referrals by other artists.

TIPS "Please send name and address to be placed on mailing list for notification of annual juried shows."

WASHINGTON PROJECT FOR THE ARTS

10 I St. SW, Washington DC 20024. (202)234-7103. **Fax:** (202)234-7106. **E-mail:** info@wpadc.org. **Website:** www.wpadc.org. **Contact:** Christopher Cunetto, membership manager. Estab. 1975. Alternative space that exhibits emerging, mid-career and established artists. Approached by 1,500 artists/year, exhibits 800 artists. Sponsors 12 exhibits/year. Average display time: 4 weeks. WPA is located in the Capitol Skyline Hotel. We exhibit throughout the hotel and in various museums and venues throughout the region. Clients include local community, students, tourists and upscale. 5% of sales are to corporate collectors. Overall price range: $100-5,000; most work sold at $500-1,000.

EXHIBITS Considers all media. Most frequently exhibits performance, painting, drawing and photography.

MAKING CONTACT & TERMS Artwork is accepted on consignment and there is a 50% commission. Retail price set by the artist. Gallery provides insurance, promotion and contract. Accepted work should be framed.

SUBMISSIONS E-mail query letter with link to artist's website. Responds in 2 months. Finds artists through word of mouth, submissions, portfolio reviews, art exhibits and referrals by other artists.

TIPS Use correct spelling, make sure packages/submissions are tidy.

⊘ WEINSTEIN GALLERY

908 W. 46th St., Minneapolis MN 55419. (612)822-1722. **Fax:** (612)822-1745. **E-mail:** weinsteingallery@gmail.com. **Website:** www.weinstein-gallery.com. **Contact:** Leslie Hammons, director. Estab. 1996. For-profit gallery. Approached by hundreds of artists/year; represents or exhibits 12 artists. Average display time 6 weeks. Open Tuesday–Saturday, 12-5, or by appointment. Overall price range $4,000-250,000.

EXHIBITS Interested in fine art. Most frequently exhibits contemporary photography.

SUBMISSIONS "We do not accept unsolicited submissions."

WISCONSIN UNION GALLERIES

WUD Art Committee, 1308 W. Dayton St., Room 235, Madison WI 53715. (608)890-4432; (608)262-7592. **Fax:** (608)890-4411. **E-mail:** art@union.wisc.edu; schmoldt@wisc.edu. **Website:** www.union.wisc.edu/wud/art-events.htm. **Contact:** Robin Schmoldt, art collection manager. Estab. 1928. Nonprofit gallery. Estab. 1928. Approached by 100 artists/year; exhibits 30 shows/year. Average display time 4-6 weeks. Open 10-8 daily. Gallery 1308 in Union South is open 7 a.m.-10 p.m. weekdays and 8 a.m.-10 p.m. weekends. Closed during winter break and when gallery exhibitions turn over. Visit the website for the gallery's features.

EXHIBITS Interested in fine art. "Photography exhibitions vary based on the artist proposals submitted."

MAKING CONTACT & TERMS All sales through gallery during exhibition only.

SUBMISSIONS Current submission guidelines available at www.union.wisc.edu/wud/art-submissions.htm. Finds artists through art fairs, art exhibits, referrals by other artists, submissions, word of mouth.

WOMEN & THEIR WORK ART SPACE

1710 Lavaca St., Austin TX 78701. (512)477-1064. **Fax:** (512)477-1090. **Website:** www.womenandtheirwork.org. **Contact:** Chris Cowden, executive director. Estab. 1978. Alternative space, nonprofit gallery. Approached by more than 400 artists/year; represents or exhibits 6 solo exhibitions from Texas artists and 1 show/year for artists outside of Texas. Encourages the creation of new work. Types of media vary. Average display time: 6 weeks. Open Monday–Friday, 10-6; Saturday, 12-5; closed December 24–January 2, and other major holidays. Exhibition space is 2,000 sq. ft.

Overall price range: $500-5,000; most work sold at $800-2,000.

EXHIBITS Interested in contemporary, alternative process, avant garde, fine art.

MAKING CONTACT & TERMS "We select artists through a juried process and pay them to exhibit. We take 25% commission if something is sold." Gallery provides catalog, insurance, promotion, contract. Texas women in majority of solo shows. "Online Artist Slide Registry on website."

SUBMISSIONS Finds artists through nomination by art professional.

TIPS "Provide quality images, typed résumé and a clear statement of artistic intent."

WORLD FINE ART GALLERY

179 E. Third St., Suite 16, New York NY 10009-7705. (646)539-9622. **Fax:** (646)478-9361. **E-mail:** info@worldfineart.com. **Website:** www.worldfineart.com. **Contact:** O'Delle Abney, director. Estab. 1992. Online gallery since 2010. Services include online websites (www.worldfineart.com/join.html) and personal marketing. Group exhibitions around the New York City area.

SUBMISSIONS Responds to queries in 1 week. Non-exclusive agent to 12 current portfolio artists. Finds artists online.

TIPS "Have website available or send JPEG images for review."

YESHIVA UNIVERSITY MUSEUM

15 W. 16th St., New York NY 10011. (212)294-8330. **Fax:** (212)294-8335. **E-mail:** info@yum.cjh.org. **Website:** www.yumuseum.org. Estab. 1973. The museum's changing exhibits celebrate the culturally diverse intellectual and artistic achievements of 3,000 years of Jewish experience. Sponsors 6-8 exhibits/year; at least 1 photography exhibit/year. Average display time 4-6 months. The museum occupies 4 galleries and several exhibition arcades. All galleries are handicapped accessible. Open Sunday, Tuesday and Thursday, 11-5; Monday and Wednesday, 11-8; Friday, 11-2:30.

EXHIBITS Seeks "individual or group exhibits focusing on Jewish themes and interests; exhibition-ready work essential."

MAKING CONTACT & TERMS Accepts images in digital format. Send CD and accompanying text with SASE for return. Send color slide portfolio of 10-12 slides or photos, exhibition proposal, résumé

GALLERIES

with SASE for consideration. Reviews take place 3 times/year.

TIPS "We exhibit contemporary art and photography based on Jewish themes. We look for excellent quality, individuality, and work that reveals a connection to Jewish identity and/or spirituality."

MIKHAIL ZAKIN GALLERY

561 Piermont Rd., Demarest NJ 07627. (201)767-7160. **Fax:** (201)767-0497. **E-mail:** maria@tasoc.org; exhibitions@tasoc.org. **Website:** www.tasoc.org. **Contact:** Maria Danziger, executive director. Estab. 1974. Nonprofit gallery associated with the Art School at Old Church. "Ten-exhibition season includes contemporary, emerging, and established regional artists, NJ Annual Small Works show, student and faculty group exhibitions, among others." Open Monday–Friday, 9:30-5; call for weekend and evening hours. Exhibitions are mainly curated by invitation. However, unsolicited materials are reviewed. The gallery does not review artist websites, e-mail attachments or portfolios in the presence of the artist. Please follow the submission guidelines on website.

EXHIBITS All styles and genres are considered.

MAKING CONTACT & TERMS Charges 35% commission fee on all gallery sales. Gallery provides promotion and contract. Accepted work should be framed, mounted.

SUBMISSIONS Guidelines are available on gallery's website. Small Works prospectus is available online. Mainly finds artists through referrals by other artists and artist registries.

TIPS "Follow guidelines available online."

ZENITH GALLERY

1429 Iris St. NW, Washington DC 20012. (202)783-2963. **Fax:** (202)783-0050. **E-mail:** margery@zenithgallery.com; art@zenithgallery.com. **Website:** www.zenithgallery.com. **Contact:** Margery E. Goldberg, founder/owner/director. Estab. 1978. For-profit gallery. Open Friday and Saturday, 12-6, and by appointment. Curates The Gallery at 1111 Pennsylvania Ave. NW, Washington DC, open Monday–Friday, 8-7; Saturday and Sunday, by appointment. Overall price range: $500-15,000.

EXHIBITS Photos of landscapes/scenics and other. Interested in avant garde, fine art.

SUBMISSIONS E-mail or mail portfolio for review. Send query e-mail or letter with artist's statement, bio, brochure, business card, résumé, reviews, photocopies, photographs, CD, SASE. Responds to queries within 1 year, only if interested. Finds artists through art fairs and exhibits, portfolio reviews, referrals by other artists, submissions and word of mouth.

GALLERIES

ART FAIRS

//

How would you like to sell your art from New York to California, showcasing it to thousands of eager art collectors? Art fairs (also called art festivals or art shows) are not only a good source of income for artists but an opportunity to see how people react to their work. If you like to travel, enjoy meeting people, and can do your own matting and framing, this could be a great market for you.

Many outdoor fairs occur during the spring, summer, and fall months to take advantage of warmer temperatures. However, depending on the region, temperatures could be hot and humid, and not all that pleasant! And, of course, there is always the chance of rain. Indoor art fairs held in November and December are popular because they capitalize on the holiday shopping season.

To start selling at art fairs, you will need an inventory of work—some framed, some unframed. Even if customers do not buy the framed paintings or prints, having some framed work displayed in your booth will give buyers an idea of how your work looks framed, which could spur sales of your unframed prints. The most successful art fair exhibitors try to show a range of sizes and prices for customers to choose from.

When looking at the art fairs listed in this section, first consider local shows and shows in your neighboring cities and states. Once you find a show you'd like to enter, visit its website or contact the appropriate person for a more detailed prospectus. A prospectus is an application that will offer additional information not provided in the art fair's listing.

Ideally, most of your prints should be matted and stored in protective wraps or bags so that customers can look through your inventory without damaging prints and mats. You will also need a canopy or tent to protect yourself and your wares from the elements as well as some bins in which to store the prints. A display wall will allow you to show off your best framed prints. Generally, artists will have 100 square feet of space in which to set up their tents and canopies. Most listings will specify the dimensions of the exhibition space for each artist.

If you see the ☯ icon before a listing in this section, it means that the art fair is a juried event. In other words, there is a selection process artists must go through to be admitted into the fair. Many art fairs have quotas for the categories of exhibitors. For example, one art fair may accept the mediums of photography, sculpture, painting, metal work, and jewelry. Once each category fills with qualified exhibitors, no more will be admitted to the show that year. The jurying process also ensures that the artists who sell their work at the fair meet the sponsor's criteria for quality. So, overall, a juried art fair is good for artists because it means they will be exhibiting their work along with other artists of equal caliber.

Be aware there are fees associated with entering art fairs. Most fairs have an application fee or a space fee, or sometimes both. The space fee is essentially a rental fee for the space your booth will occupy for the art fair's duration. These fees can vary greatly from show to show, so be sure to check this information in each listing before you apply to any art fair.

Most art fair sponsors want to exhibit only work that is handmade by the artist, no matter what medium. Unfortunately, some people try to sell work that they purchased elsewhere as their own original artwork. In the art fair trade, this is known as "buy/sell." It is an undesirable situation because it tends to bring down the quality of the whole show. Some listings will make a point to say "no buy/sell" or "no manufactured work."

For more information on art fairs, pick up a copy of *Sunshine Artist* (www.sunshine artist.com) or *Professional Artist* (www.artcalendar.com), and consult online sources such as www.artfairsource.com.

🔊 4 BRIDGES ARTS FESTIVAL

30 Frazier Ave., Chattanooga TN 37405. (423)265-4282, ext. 106. **Fax:** (423)265-5233. **E-mail:** katdunn@avarts.org. **Website:** www.4bridgesartsfestival.org. **Contact:** Kat Dunn. Estab. 2000. Two-day fine arts & crafts show held annually in mid-April. Held in a covered, open-air pavilion. Accepts photography and 24 different mediums. Juried by 3 different art professionals each year. Awards: $10,000 in artist merit awards; the on-site jurying for merit awards will take place Saturday morning. Number of exhibitors: 150. Public attendance: 13,000. Public admission: $7/day or a 2-day pass for $10; children under 18 are free. Artists should apply at www.zapplication.org. Deadline for entry: early November (see website for details). Application fee: $40. Space fee: $450-550 for 10×12 ft.; $900-1,000 for 20×12 ft. Average gross sales/exhibitor: $2,923. For more information, e-mail, visit website or call. The event is held at First Tennessee Pavilion.

🎧 AKRON ARTS EXPO

220 Balch St., Akron OH 44302. (330)375-2836. **Fax:** (330)375-2883. **E-mail:** PBomba@akronohio.gov. **Website:** www.akronartsexpo.org. **Contact:** Penny Bomba, artist coordinator. Estab. 1979. Held in late July. "The Akron Arts Expo is a nationally recognized juried fine arts & crafts show held outside with over 160 artists, ribbon and cash awards, great food, an interactive children's area, and entertainment for the entire family. Participants in this festival present quality fine arts and crafts that are offered for sale at reasonable prices. For more information, see the website." Application fee $5. Booth fee: $200. Event held in Hardesty Park.

➕ 🎧 ALEXANDRIA KING STREET ART FESTIVAL

270 Central Blvd., Suite 107B, Jupiter FL 33458. (561)746-6615. **Fax:** (561)746-6528. **E-mail:** info@artfestival.com. **Website:** www.artfestival.com. **Contact:** Malinda Ratliff, communications manager. Estab. 2003. Fine art & craft fair held annually in late September. Outdoors. Accepts photography, jewelry, mixed media, sculpture, wood, ceramic, glass, painting, digital, fiber, metal. Juried. Number exhibitors: 230. Number attendees: 150,000. Free to public. Apply online via www.zapplication.org. Deadline: see website. Application fee: $35. Space fee: $575. Exhibition space: 10×10 and 10×20.

🔊 For more information, artists should e-mail, call, or visit website.

🔊 ALLEN PARK ARTS & CRAFTS STREET FAIR

16850 Southfield Rd., Allen Park MI 48101-2599. (734)258-7720. **E-mail:** applications@allenparkstreetfair.org. **Website:** www.allenparkstreetfair.org. **Contact:** Allen Park Festivities Commission. Estab. 1981. Arts & crafts show held annually the 1st Friday and Saturday in August. Outdoors. Accepts photography, sculpture, ceramics, jewelry, glass, wood, prints, drawings, paintings. All work must be of fine quality and original work of entrant. Such items as imports, velvet paintings, manufactured or kit jewelry and any commercially produced merchandise are not eligible for exhibit or sale. Juried by 5 photos (no slides) of work. Number of exhibitors: 200. Free to the public. Deadline: May 1. Application fee: $25. Space fee: $175-$200. Exhibition space: 10×10 ft. Apply via www.zapplication.org. Artists should call or see website for more information.

🎧 ALLENTOWN ART FESTIVAL

P.O. Box 1566, Buffalo NY 14205. (716)881-4269. **E-mail:** allentownartfestival@verizon.net. **Website:** www.allentownartfestival.com. **Contact:** Mary Myszkiewicz, president. Estab. 1958. Fine arts & crafts show held annually 2nd full weekend in June. Outdoors. Accepts photography, painting, watercolor, drawing, graphics, sculpture, mixed media, clay, glass, acrylic, jewelry, creative craft (hard/soft). Slides juried by hired professionals that change yearly. Awards/prizes: 41 cash prizes totaling over $20,000; includes Best of Show awarding $1,000. Number of exhibitors: 450. Public attendance: 300,000. Free to public. Artists should apply by downloading application from website. Deadline for entry: late January. Exhibition space: 10×13 ft. Application fee: $15. Booth fee $275. For more information, artists should e-mail, visit website, call or send SASE. Show held in Allentown Historic Preservation District.

TIPS "Artists must have attractive booth and interact with the public."

🔊 ALTON ARTS & CRAFTS EXPRESSIONS

P.O. Box 1326, Palatine IL 60078. (312)751-2500; (847)991-4748. **E-mail:** Asoaartists@aol.com. **Website:** www.americansocietyofartists.org. **Contact:** Office personnel. Estab. 1979. Fine arts & crafts show held annually indoors in Alton, Illinois, in spring and fall, usually March and September. Accepts quilting, fabric crafts, artwear, photography, sculpture, jewelry, glass works, woodworking and more. Please submit 4 images representative of your work you wish to exhibit, 1 of your display set-up, your first/last name, physical address, daytime telephone number—résumé/show listing helpful. "See our website for online jury information." Number of exhibitors: 50. Free to the public. Artists should apply by submitting jury materials. Submit to: Asoartists@aol.com. If juried in, you will receive a jury/approval number. Deadline for entry: 2 months prior to show or earlier if spaces fill. Space fee: to be announced. Exhibition space: approximately 100 sq. ft. for single space; other sizes available. For more information, artsits should send SASE, submit jury material and submit jury material to ASA, PO Box 1326, Palatine IL 60078.

TIPS "Remember that when you are at work in your studio, you are an artist. But when you are at a show, you are a business person selling your work."

AMERICAN ARTISAN FESTIVAL

P.O. Box 41743, Nashville TN 37204. (615)429-7708. **E-mail:** americanartisanfestival@gmail.com. **Website:** www.facebook.com/theamericanartisanfestival. Estab. 1971. Fine arts & crafts show held annually mid-June, Father's Day weekend. Outdoors. Accepts photography and 21 different medium categories. Juried by 3 different art professionals each year. 3 cash awards presented. Number of exhibitors: 165. Public attendance: 30,000. No admission fee for the public. Artists should apply online at www.zapplication.org. Deadline for entry: early March (see website for details). For more information, e-mail or visit the website. Festival held at Centennial Park, Nashville, TN.

AMISH ACRES ARTS & CRAFTS FESTIVAL

1600 W. Market St., Nappanee IN 46550. (574)773-4188 or (800)800-4942. **E-mail:** amishacres@amishacres.com; jenniwysong@amishacres.com; beckymaust@amishacres.com. **Website:** www.amishacres.com. **Contact:** Jenni Pletcher Wysong and Becky Maust Cappert, contact coordinators. Estab. 1962. Arts & crafts show held annually first weekend in August. Outdoors. Accepts photography, crafts, floral, folk, jewelry, oil, acrylic, sculpture, textiles, watercolors, wearable, wood. Juried by 5 images, either 35mm slides or e-mailed digital images. Awards/prizes: $5,000 Cash including Best of Show and $1,000 Purchase Prizes. Number of exhibitors: 300. Public attendance: 60,000. Children under 12 free. Artists should apply by sending SASE or printing application from website. Deadline for entry: April 1. Exhibition space: 10×12, 15×12, 20×12 or 30×12 ft.; optional stable fee, with tent, also available. For more information, artists should e-mail, visit website, call or send SASE.

TIPS "Create a vibrant, open display that beckons to passing customers. Interact with potential buyers. Sell the romance of the purchase."

ANACORTES ARTS FESTIVAL

505 O Ave., Anacortes WA 98221. (360)293-6211. **Fax:** (360)299-0722. **E-mail:** staff@anacortesartsfestival.com. **Website:** www.anacortesartsfestival.com. Fine arts & crafts show held annually 1st full weekend in August. Accepts photography, painting, drawings, prints, ceramics, fiber art, paper art, glass, jewelry, sculpture, yard art, woodworking. Juried by projecting 3 images on a large screen. Works are evaluated on originality, quality and marketability. Each applicant must provide 5 high-quality digital images, including a booth shot. Awards/prizes: festival offers awards totaling $3,600. Number of exhibitors: 250. We only accept online applications through Zapplication.org. Application fee: $30. Deadline for entry: early March. Space fee: $325. Exhibition space: 10×10 ft. For more information, artists should see website. Show is located on Commercial Ave. from 4th to 10th St.

ANN ARBOR STREET ART FAIR

721 E. Huron, Suite 200, Ann Arbor MI 48104. (734)994-5260. **Fax:** (734)994-0504. **E-mail:** production@artfair.org; mriley@artfair.org. **Website:** www.artfair.org. Estab. 1958. Fine arts & crafts show held annually 3rd Saturday in July. Outdoors. Accepts photography, fiber, glass, digital art, jewelry, metals, 2D and 3D mixed media, sculpture, clay, painting, drawing, printmaking, pastels, wood. Juried based on originality, creativity, technique, craftsmanship and production. Awards/prizes: cash prizes for outstanding work in any media. Number of exhibitors: 200. Public attendance: 500,000. Free to the public. Artists should apply through www.zapplication.org. Deadline for entry: January 13. Application fee: $35/40. Space fee: $650. Exhibition space: 10×12 ft. Average gross sales/exhibitor: $7,000. For more information, artists should e-mail, visit website, call.

ANN ARBOR SUMMER ART FAIR

118 N. Fourth Ave., Ann Arbor MI 48104. (734)662-3382. **Fax:** (734)662-0339. **E-mail:** info@theguild.org; nicole@theguild.org. **Website:** www.theguild.org. Estab. 1970. Fine arts and craft show held annually on the third Wednesday through Saturday in July. Outdoors. Accepts all fine art categories. Juried. Number of exhibitors: 325. Attendance: 500,000-750,000. Free to public. Deadline for entry is January; enter online at www.juriedartservices.com. Exhibition space: 10×10, 10×13, 10×17 ft. For information, artists should visit the website, call, or e-mail. Show is located on University of Michigan campus and in downtown Ann Arbor.

APPLE ANNIE CRAFTS & ARTS SHOW

4905 Roswell Rd., Marietta GA 30062. **Fax:** (770)552-6420. **E-mail:** sagw4905@gmail.com. **Website:** www.st-ann.org/womens-guild/apple-annie. Estab. 1981. Handmade arts & crafts show held annually the 1st weekend in December. Juried. Indoors. Accepts handmade arts and crafts like photography, woodworking, ceramics, pottery, painting, fabrics, glass, etc. Number of exhibitors: 120. Public attendance: 4,000. Artists should apply by visiting website to print application form. Deadline: March 1 (see website for details). Application fee: $20, nonrefundable. Booth fee $200. Exhibition space: 80 sq. ft. minimum, may be more. For more information, artists may visit website.

TIPS "We are looking for vendors with an open, welcoming booth, who are accessible and friendly to customers."

ARLINGTON FESTIVAL OF THE ARTS

270 Central Blvd., Suite 107B, Jupiter FL 33458. (561)746-6615. **Fax:** (561)746-6528. **E-mail:** info@artfestival.com. **Website:** www.artfestival.com. **Contact:** Malinda Ratliff, communications manager. Estab. 2013. Fine art & craft fair held annually in mid-April. Outdoors. Accepts photography, jewelry, mixed media, sculpture, wood, ceramic, glass, painting, digital, fiber, metal. Juried. Number exhibitors: 140. Number attendees: 50,000. Free to public. Apply online via zapplication.org. Deadline: see website. Application fee: $25. Space fee: $395. Exhibition space: 10×10 and 10×20. For more information, artists should e-mail, call, or visit website.

Festival located at Highland St. in the Clarendon district of Arlington VA.

ART-A-FAIR

P.O. Box 547, Laguna Beach CA 92652. (949)494-4514. **E-mail:** marketing@art-a-fair.com. **Website:** www.art-a-fair.com. Estab. 1967. Fine arts show held annually in June-August. Outoors. Accepts painting, sculpture, ceramics, jewelry, printmaking, photography, master crafts, digital art, fiber, glass, pencil, wood. Juried. Exhibitors: 125. Number of attendees: see website. Admission: $7.50 adults; $4.50 seniors; children 12 & under free. Apply online. Deadline for entry: see website. Application fee: $40 (per medium). Space fee: $200 + $35 membership fee. Exhibition space: see website. For more information, e-mail, visit website or call.

ART FAIR AT LAUMEIER SCULPTURE PARK

(314)615-5278. **E-mail:** artfair@laumeier.org. **Website:** www.laumeir.org. **Contact:** Sara Matthew, special events manager. Estab. 1987. Arts & crafts show held annually in May during Mother's Day weekend. Outdoors. Accepts fine handmade crafts, ceramics, fiber/textiles, glass, jewelry, mixed media 2D, printmaking/drawing, painting, photography/digital, sculpture, wood. Features regional food vendors, a wine garden, and live music. Juried. Awards/prizes: $5,000 in cash awards. Number of exhibitors: 150. Number of attendees: 15,000. Admission: $10 adults 12+; $5 children 6-11; children under 5 free. Apply via www.zapplication.org or visit www.laumeiersculpturepark.org/programs_events/art_fair/artists. Deadline for entry: January 10. Application fee: $35 (per category). Space fee: $350 (open booth); $450 (tented booth). Exhibition space: 10×10. Average sales: $5,000. For more information, see website.

ART FAIR ON THE COURTHOUSE LAWN

P.O. Box 795, Rhinelander WI 54501. (715)365-7460. **E-mail:** assistant@rhinelanderchamber.com. **Website:** www.explorerhinelander.com. **Contact:** Events Coordinator. Estab. 1985. Arts & crafts show held annually in June. Outdoors. Accepts woodworking (includes furniture), jewelry, glass items, metal, paintings and photography. Number of exhibitors: 150. Public attendance: 3,000. Free to the public. Space fee: $75-300. Exhibit space: 10×10 to 10×30 ft. For more information, artists should e-mail, call, or visit website. Show located at Oneida County Courthouse.

TIPS "We accept only items handmade by the exhibitor."

⊕ ◯ ART FAIR ON THE SQUARE

227 State St., Madison WI 53703. (608)257-0158, ext 229. **E-mail:** artfair@mmoca.org. **Website:** www.mmoca.org. **Contact:** Annik Dupaty. Estab. 1958. Arts & crafts show held annually in July. Outoors. Accepts handmade crafts, ceramics, fiber, leather, furniture, jewelry, glass, digital art, metal, sculpture, 2D/3D mixed media, painting, photography, printmaking/graphics/drawing, wood. Juried. Awards/prizes: Best of Show; Invitational Award. Exhibitors: varies. Number of attendees: 150,000+. Free to public. Apply via www.zapplication.org. Deadline for entry: see website. Application fee: $35. Space fee: $495 (single); $1,050 (double). Exhibition space: 10×10 (single); 10×10 (double). For more information, e-mail, visit website or call.

⊕ ◯ ART FEST BY THE SEA

270 Central Blvd., Suite 107B, Jupiter FL 33458. (561)746-6615. **Fax:** (561)746-6528. **E-mail:** info@artfestival.com. **Website:** www.artfestival.com. **Contact:** Malinda Ratliff, communications manager. Estab. 1989. Fine art & craft fair held annually in early March. Outdoors. Accepts photography, jewelry, mixed media, sculpture, wood, ceramic, glass, painting, digital, fiber, metal. Juried. Number exhibitors: 340. Number attendees: 125,000. Free to public. Apply online via zapplication.org. Deadline: see website. Application fee: $25. Space fee: $415. Exhibition space: 10×10 and 10×20. For more information, artists should e-mail, call, or visit website.

◖ Fair located along A1A Between Donald Ross Rd. and Marcinski in Juno Beach FL.

⊕ ◯ ARTFEST MIDWEST—"THE OTHER SHOW"

Stookey Companies, P.O. Box 31083, Des Moines IA 50310. (515)278-6200. **Fax:** (515)276-7513. **E-mail:** suestookey@att.net. **Website:** www.artfestmidwest.com. Fine art fair held annually in June. Indoors & outdoors. Accepts handmade fine art, ceramic, fiber, drawing, glass, jewelry, metal, 2D/3D mixed media, painting, photography, wood. Juried. Exhibitors: 240. Number of attendees: 30,000. Free to public. Apply via www.zapplication.org. Deadline for entry: March. Application fee: $30. Space fee: varies. Exhibition space: see website. For more information, e-mail

suestookey@att.net, visit website at www.artfestmidwest.com or call 515-278-6200.

◯ ART FESTIVAL BETH-EL

400 Pasadena Ave. S, St. Petersburg FL 33707. (727)347-6136. **Fax:** (727)343-8982. **E-mail:** info@artfestivalbethel.com. **Website:** www.artfestivalbethel.com. Estab. 1972. Fine arts & crafts show held annually the last weekend in January. Indoors. Accepts photography, painting, jewelry, sculpture, woodworking, glass. Juried by special committee on-site or through slides. Awards/prizes: over $7,000 prize money. Number of exhibitors: over 170. Public attendance: 8,000-10,000. Free to the public. Artists should apply by application with photos or slides; show is invitational. Deadline for entry: September. For more information, artists should call or visit website. A commission is taken.

TIPS "Don't crowd display panels with artwork. Make sure your prices are on your pictures. Speak to customers about your work."

◯ ARTIGRAS FINE ARTS FESTIVAL

5520 PGA Boulevard, Suite 200, Palm Beach Gardens FL 33418. (561)746-7111. **E-mail:** info@artigras.org. **Website:** www.artigras.org. **Contact:** Hannah Sosa, director of special events. Estab. 2008. Annual fine arts festival held in February during Presidents' Day weekend. Outdoors. Accepts all fine art (including photography). Juried. $17,000 in cash awards and prizes. Average number of exhibitors: 300. Average number of attendees: 85,000. Admission: $10. Artists should apply by enclosing a copy of prospectus or by application form, if available; can also apply via Zapplication.org. Deadline: September. Application fee: $40. Space fee: $450. Space is 12×12. For more information artists should e-mail or visit website.

◯ ART IN THE PARK (ARIZONA)

P.O. Box 748, Sierra Vista AZ 85636-0247. (520)803-0584. **E-mail:** edieartist@cox.net. **Website:** www.artintheparksierravista.com. Estab. 1972. Oldest longest running Arts & crafts fair in Southern Arizona. Fine arts & crafts show held annually 1st full weekend in October. Outdoors. Accepts photography, all fine arts and crafts created by vendor. No resale retail strictly applied. Juried by Huachaca Art Association Board. Artists submit 5 photos. Returnable with SASE. Number of exhibitors: 203. Public attendance: 15,000. Free to public. Artists should apply by downloading the ap-

ART FAIRS

plication www.artintheparksierravista.com. Deadline for entry: postmarked by late June. Last minute/late entries always considered. No application fee. Space fee: $200-275, includes jury fee. Exhibition space: 15×30 ft. Some electrical; additional cost of $25. Some RV space available at $15/night. For more information, artists should see website, e-mail, call or send SASE. Show located in Veteran's Memorial Park.

ART IN THE PARK FALL FOLIAGE FESTIVAL

P.O. Box 1447, Rutland VT 05701. (802)775-0356. **E-mail:** info@chaffeeartcenter.org; mbarros@chaffee artcenter.org. **Website:** www.chaffeeartcenter.org. Estab. 1961. A fine arts & crafts show held at Main Street Park in Rutland VT annually in October over Columbus Day weekend. Accepts fine art, specialty foods, fiber, jewelry, glass, metal, wood, photography, clay, floral, etc. All applications will be juried by a panel of experts. The Art in the Park Festivals are dedicated to high-quality art and craft products. Number of exhibitors: 100. Public attendance: 9,000-10,000. Public admission: voluntary donation. Artists should apply online and either e-mail or submit a CD with 3 photos of work and 1 of booth (photos upon preapproval). Deadline for entry: early bird discount of $25 per show for applications received by March 31. Space fee: $200-350. Exhibit space: 10×12 or 20×12 ft. For more information, artists should e-mail, visit website, or call. Show located in Main Street Park.

TIPS "Have a good presentation, variety, if possible (in pricing also), to appeal to a large group of people. Apply early, as there may be a limited amount of accepted vendors per category. Applications will be juried on a first come, first served basis until the category is determined to be filled."

ART IN THE PARK—FINE ARTS FESTIVAL

Swartz Creek Kiwanis, 5023 Holland Dr., Swartz Creek MI 48473. (810)635-2717. **E-mail:** aitp@hsaa. com. **Website:** www.swartzcreekkiwanis.org/art. Estab. 2008. Annual outdoor fine art festival held in August. Accepts all fine art. Juried by art professionals hired by the committee, monetary prizes given. Average number of exhibitors: 50. Average number of attendees: 2,500-3,000. Free admission. Artists should apply by accessing the website. Deadline: early July. Space fee of $125; $175 for late applications. Space is 144 sq. ft. For more information artists should e-mail or visit the website. Festival held at Elms Park.

TIPS "Bring unique products."

ART IN THE PARK (GEORGIA)

P.O. Box 1540, Thomasville GA 31799. (229)227-7020. **Fax:** (229)227-3320. **E-mail:** roseshowfest@rose.net; laura@thomasville.org. **Website:** www.downtown thomasville.com. **Contact:** Laura Beggs. Estab. 1998-1999. Art in the Park (an event of Thomasville's Rose Show and Festival) is a one-day arts & crafts show held annually in April. Outdoors. Accepts photography, handcrafted items, oils, acrylics, woodworking, stained glass, other varieties. Juried by a selection committee. Number of exhibitors: 60. Public attendance: 2,500. Free to public. Artists should apply by submitting official application. Deadline for entry: early February. Space fee varies by year. Exhibition space: 20×20 ft. For more information, artists should e-mail, call, or visit website. Show located in Paradise Park.

TIPS "Most important, be friendly to the public and have an attractive booth display."

ART IN THE PARK (MICHIGAN)

Holland Friends of Art, P.O. Box 1052, Holland MI 49422. **E-mail:** info@hollandfriendsofart.com. **Website:** www.hollandfriendsofart.com. **Contact:** Sarah Johnson, art fair chairperson. This annual fine arts and crafts fair is held on the first Saturday of August in Holland. The event draws one of the largest influx of visitors to the city on a single day, second only to Tulip Time. More than 300 fine artists and artisans from 8 states will be on hand to display and sell their work. Juried. All items for sale must be original. Public attendance: 10,000+. Entry fee: $90 (HFA members $80); includes a $20 application fee. Deadline: late March. Space fee: $160 for a double-wide space; $150 for a double-deep space. Exhibition space: 12×12 ft. Details of the jury and entry process are explained on the application. Application available online. Call, e-mail or visit website for more information. Event held in Centennial Park.

TIPS "Create an inviting and neat booth. Offer well-made quality artwork and crafts at a variety of prices."

ART IN THE PARK (VIRGINIA)

20 S. New St., Staunton VA 24401. (540)885-2028. **E-mail:** info@saartcenter.org; director@saartcenter.org. **Website:** www.saartcenter.org. **Contact:** Beth Hodges,

exec. director. Estab. 1961. Fine arts & crafts show held annually every Memorial Day weekend. Outdoors. Juried by submitting 4 photos representative of the work to be sold. Award/prizes: $1,500. Number of exhibitors: 60. Public attendance: 3,000-4,000. Free to public. Artists should apply by sending in application. Exhibition space: 10×10 ft. For more information, artists should e-mail, call, or visit website. Show located at Gypsy Hill Park.

⊕ ☋ ART IN THE VILLAGE WITH CRAFT MARKETPLACE

270 Central Blvd., Suite 107B, Jupiter FL 33458. (561)746-6615. **Fax:** (561)746-6528. **E-mail:** info@art festival.com. **Website:** www.artfestival.com. **Contact:** Malinda Ratliff, communications manager. Estab. 1991. Fine art & craft fair held annually in early June. Outdoors. Accepts photography, jewelry, mixed media, sculpture, wood, ceramic, glass, painting, digital, fiber, metal. Juried. Number exhibitors: 150. Number attendees: 70,000. Free to public. Apply online via zapplication.org. Deadline: see website. Application fee: $25. Space fee: $450. Exhibition space: 10×10 and 10×20. For more information, artists should e-mail, call, or visit website.

☋ Show located at Legacy Village in Cleveland, OH.

ARTISPHERE

16 Augusta St., Greenville SC 29601. (864)271-9355. **Fax:** (864)467-3133. **E-mail:** liz@greenvillearts.com. **Website:** www.artisphere.us. **Contact:** Liz Rundorff, program director; Kerry Murphy, executive director. Fine arts & crafts show held annually in early May (see website for details). Showcases local artists and top regional galleries in a gallery row at various venues along Main Street. Accepts digital art and photography. Apply via www.zapplication.org. Free to public. E-mail, call, or visit website for more information and to display your work.

☋ ART ON THE LAWN

Village Artisans, 100 Corry St., Yellow Springs OH 45387. (937)767-1209. **E-mail:** villageartisans.email@ yahoo.com. **Website:** www.villageartisans.blogspot. com. Blog: www.villageartisans.blogspot.com. **Contact:** Village Artisans. Estab. 1983. Fine arts & crafts show held annually the 2nd Saturday in August. Outdoors. Accepts photography, all hand-made media and original artwork. Juried, as received, from photos accompanying the application. Awards: "Best of

Show" receives a free booth space at next year's event. Number of exhibitors: 90-100. Free to public. Request an application by calling or e-mailing, or download an application from the website. Deadline for entry: July 31; however, the sooner received, the better the chances of acceptance. Jury fee: $15. Space fee: $75 before May; $85 until late July; $105 thereafter. Exhibition space: 10×10 ft. Average gross sales vary. For more information, artists should visit website, e-mail, call, send SASE or stop by Village Artisans at above address.

⊕ ☋ ART RAPIDS!

P.O. Box 301, Elk Rapids MI 49629. (231)264-6660. **E-mail:** art@mullalys128.com. **Website:** www.artrapids. org. **Contact:** Barb Mullaly. Arts & crafts fair held annually last Saturday in June. Outdoors. Accepts handmade crafts, ceramic, drawing, fiber, glass, jewelry, painting, photography, printmaking, sculpture, wood, metal, paper, or mixed media. Juried. Awards/ prizes: Best of Show, Honorable Mention, People's Choice. Exhibitors: 70. Number of attendees: 4,000. Free to public. Apply online. Deadline for entry: early April. Application fee: $20. Space fee: varies. Exhibition space: 10×10. For more information, e-mail, visit website or call.

☋ ARTS & CRAFTS ADVENTURE

P.O. Box 1326, Palatine IL 60078. (312)751-2500. **Fax:** (847)221-5853. **E-mail:** asoaartists@aol.com. **Website:** www.americansocietyofartists.org. **Contact:** Office personnel. Estab. 1991. Fine arts & crafts show held annually in early May and mid-September. Outdoors. Event held in Park Ridge IL. Accepts photography, pottery, paintings, sculpture, glass, wood, woodcarving, and more. Juried by 4 slides or photos of work and 1 slide or photo of display; a résumé or show listing is helpful. See our website for online jury. To jury via e-mail: asoaartists@aol.com. Number of exhibitors: 75. Free to the public. Artists should apply by submitting jury materials. Submit to asoaartists@ aol.com. If juried in, you will receive a jury/approval number. Deadline for entry: 2 months prior to show or earlier if spaces fill. Space fee: to be announced. Exhibition space: approximately 100 sq. ft. for single space; other sizes available. For more information, artists should send SASE, submit jury material. Show located in Hodges Park.

TIPS "Remember that when you are at work in your studio, you are an artist. But when you are at a show, you are a business person selling your work."

AN ARTS & CRAFTS AFFAIR, AUTUMN & SPRING TOURS

P.O. Box 655, Antioch IL 60002. (402)331-2889. E-mail: hpifestivals@cox.net. **Website:** www.hpifesti vals.com. **Contact:** Huffman Productions. Estab. 1983. An arts & crafts show that tours different cities and states. The Autumn Festival tours annually October-November; Spring Festival tours annually in March & April. Artists should visit website to see list of states and schedule. Indoors. Accepts photography, pottery, stained glass, jewelry, clothing, wood, baskets. All artwork must be handcrafted by the actual artist exhibiting at the show. Juried by sending in 2 photos of work and 1 of display. Awards/prizes: 4 $30 show gift certificates; $50, $100 and $150 certificates off future booth fees. Number of exhibitors: 300-500 depending on location. Public attendance: 15,000-35,000. Public admission: $8-9/adults; $7-8/seniors; 10 & under, free. Artists should apply by calling to request an application. Deadline for entry: varies for date and location. Space fee: $350-1,350. Exhibition space: 8×11 ft. up to 8×22 ft. For more information, artists should e-mail, call, or visit website.

TIPS "Have a nice display, make sure business name is visible, dress professionally, have different price points, and be willing to talk to your customers."

ARTS & CRAFTS FESTIVAL

Simsbury Woman's Club, P.O. Box 903, Simsbury CT 06070. (860)658-2684. **E-mail:** simsburywomans club@hotmail.com; swc_artsandcrafts@yahoo.com. **Website:** www.simsburywomansclub.org. **Contact:** Shirley Barsness, co-chairman. Estab. 1978. Arts & crafts show held in mid-September. Juried event. Outdoors rain or shine. Original artwork, photography, clothing, accessories, jewelry, toys, wood objects and floral arrangements accepted. Manufactured items or items made from kits not accepted. Individuals should apply by submitting completed application, 4 photos or JPEG files, including 1 of display booth. Exhibition space: 11×14 ft. or 15×14 ft. frontage. Space fee: $160-175; late applications $170-185. Number of exhibitors: 120. Public attendance: 5,000-7,000. Free to public. Deadline for entry: August 15. For more information, artists should e-mail swc_artsandcrafts@ yahoo.com or call Jean at (860)658-4490 or Shirley

at (860)658-2684. Applications available on website. Show located in Simsbury Center.

TIPS "Display artwork in an attractive setting."

ARTS ADVENTURE

P.O. Box 1326, Palatine IL 60078. (312)571-2500 or (847)991-4748. **Fax:** (847)221-5853. **E-mail:** asoaartists@aol.com. **Website:** www.americansoci etyofartists.org. Estab. 2001. American Society of Artists. Fine arts & crafts show held annually the end of July. Event held in Chicago. Outdoors. Accepts photography, paintings, pottery, sculpture, jewelry and more. Juried. Please submit 4 images representative of your work you wish to exhibit, 1 of your display set-up, your first/last name, physical address, daytime telephone number (résumé/show listing helpful). See our website for online jury. To jury: submit via e-mail to asoaartists@aol.com or to the above address. Include a business-size (#10) SASE please. Number of exhibitors: 50. Free to the public. If juried in, you will receive a jury/approval number. Deadline for entry: 2 months prior to show or earlier if spaces fill. Entry fee: TBA. Exhibition space: approximately 100 sq. ft. for single space; other sizes available. For more information, artists should send SASE.

TIPS "Remember that when you are at work in your studio, you are an artist. But when you are at a show, you are a business person selling your work."

ART'S ALIVE

200 125th St., Ocean City MD 21842. (410)250-0125. **Website:** oceancitymd.gov/recreation_and_parks/ specialevents.html. **Contact:** Brenda Moore, event coordinator. Estab. 2000. Fine art show held annually in mid-June. Outdoors. Accepts photography, ceramics, drawing, fiber, furniture, glass, printmaking, jewelry, mixed media, painting, sculpture, fine wood. Juried. Awards/prizes: $5,250 in cash prizes. Number of exhibitors: 100. Public attendance: 10,000. Free to public. Artists should apply by downloading application from website or call. Deadline for entry: February 28. Space fee: $200. Jury Fee: $25. Exhibition space: 10×10 ft. For more information, artists should visit website, call or send SASE. Show located in Northside Park.

TIPS Apply early.

ARTS EXPERIENCE

P.O. Box 1326, Palatine IL 60078. (312)751-2500 or (847)991-4748. **E-mail:** asoaartists@aol.com. **Website:** www.americansocietyofartists.org. Estab. 1979.

Fine arts & crafts show held in summer in Chicago. Outdoors. Accepts photography, paintings, graphics, sculpture, quilting, woodworking, fiber art, hand-crafted candles, glass works, jewelry and more. Juried by 4 images representative of work being exhibited; 1 image of display set-up, résumé with show listings helpful. Submit to asoaartists@aol.com. Number of exhibitors: 50. Free to public. Artists should apply by submitting jury material and indicate you are interested in this particular show. When you pass the jury, you will receive jury approval number and application you requested. You may also submit to ASA, P.O. Box 1326, Palatine IL 60078. Include a SASE (business size, #10). Deadline for entry: 2 months prior to show or earlier if space is filled. Space fee: to be announced. Exhibition space: 100 sq. ft. for single space; other sizes are available. For more information, artists should send SASE to submit jury material.

TIPS "Remember that at work in your studio, you are an artist. When you are at a show, you are a business person selling your work."

⊙ ARTS IN THE PARK

302 Second Ave. E., Kalispell MT 59901. (406)755-5268. **E-mail:** information@hockadaymuseum.com. **Website:** www.hockadaymuseum.org. Estab. 1968. Fine arts & crafts show held annually 4th weekend in July (see website for details). Outdoors. Accepts photography, jewelry, clothing, paintings, pottery, glass, wood, furniture, baskets. Juried by a panel of 5 members. Artwork is evaluated for quality, creativity and originality. Jurors attempt to achieve a balance of mediums in the show. Number of exhibitors: 100. Public attendance: 10,000. Artists should apply by completing the online application form and sending 5 images in JPEG format; 4 images of work and 1 of booth. Application fee: $25. Exhibition space: 10×10 or 10×20 ft. Booth fees: $170-435. For more information, artists should e-mail, call, or visit website. Show located in Depot Park.

⊙ ARTS ON THE GREEN

Arts Association of Oldham County, 104 E. Main St., LaGrange KY 40031. (502)222-3822. **Fax:** (502)222-3823. **E-mail:** maryklausing@bellsouth.net. **Website:** www.aaooc.org. **Contact:** Mary Klausing, director. Estab. 1999. Fine arts & crafts festival held annually 1st weekend in June. Outdoors. Accepts photography, painting, clay, sculpture, metal, wood, fabric, glass, jewelry. Juried by a panel. Awards/prizes: cash prizes for Best of Show and category awards. Number of exhibitors: 100. Public attendance: 7,500. Free to the public. Artists should apply online or call. Deadline for entry: April 15. Jury fee: $25. Space fee: $180. Electricity fee: $15. Exhibition space: 10×10 or 10×12 ft. For more information, artists should e-mail, visit website, call. Show located on the lawn of the Oldham County Courthouse Square.

TIPS "Make potential customers feel welcome in your space. Don't overcrowd your work. Smile!"

⊙ ⊙ ARTSPLOSURE

313 S. Blount St., #200B, Raleigh NC 27601. (919)832-8699. **Fax:** (919)832-0890. **E-mail:** sarah@artsplosure.org. **Website:** www.artsplosure.org. **Contact:** Sarah Wolfe, art market coordinator. Estab. 1979. Annual outdoor art/craft fair held the 3rd weekend of May. Accepts ceramics, glass, fiber art, jewelry, metal, painting, photography, wood, 2D and 3D artwork. Juried event. Awards: 6 totaling $3,500 cash. Number of exhibitors: up to 170. Public attendance: 75,000. Free admission to the public. Applications available in October, deadline is late January. Application fee: $32. Space fee: $330 for 12×12 ft.; $660 for a double space. Average sales: $2,500. To apply, visit www.artsplosure.org.

⊙ ARTWORKS OF EAU GALLIE FINE ARTS FESTIVAL

1490 Highland Ave., Suite A, Melbourne FL 32935. (321)242-1456. **E-mail:** artworksfestival@gmail.com. **Website:** www.artworksofeaugallie.org. **Contact:** Link Johnsten, president. Estab. 1996. Fine art & fine crafts show held annually in November the weekend before Thanksgiving. Outdoors. Accepts photography, various mediums—original artists' works only. Juried. Awards/prizes: Art Awards, Demonstrators' Awards, Sponsor Purchase Program. Number of exhibitors: 80-100. Public attendance: 15,000-20,000. Free to public. Artists should apply online. Applications accepted beginning March 1. Deadline for entry: September 1. Space fee: $160. Exhibition space: 12×12 ft. Average gross sales/exhibitor varies. For more information, artists should visit website.

TIPS "Artists must be prepared to demonstrate their methods of work by creating works of art in their booths."

⊕ ⊙ BEAVER CREEK ART FESTIVAL

270 Central Blvd., Suite 107B, Jupiter FL 33458. (561)746-6615. **Fax:** (561)746-6528. **E-mail:** info@

artfestival.com. **Website:** www.artfestival.com. **Contact:** Malinda Ratliff, communications manager. Estab. 1988. Fine arts & crafts fair held annually in August. Outdoors. Accepts handmade crafts, clay, digital, fiber, glass, jewelry, mixed media, painting, photography, printmaking/drawing, sculpture, wood. Juried. Awards/prizes: announced after jury. Exhibitors: 150. Number of attendees: varies. Free to public. Apply online. Deadline for entry: see website. Application fee: $35. Space fee: $475. Exhibition space: 10×10 and 10×20. For more information, artists should send e-mail, visit website or call.

○   Festival located at Beaver Creek Village in Avon, CO.

BEVERLY HILLS ART SHOW

Beverly Gardens Park, 9450 N. Santa Monica Blvd., Beverly Hills CA 90210. (310)285-6836. **E-mail:** kmclean@beverlyhills.org. **Website:** www.beverlyhills.org/artshow. Estab. 1973. Fine arts & crafts show held biannually 3rd weekend in May and 3rd weekend in October. Outdoors, 4 blocks in the center of Beverly Hills. Accepts photography, painting, sculpture, ceramics, jewelry, glass, traditional printmaking and digital media. Juried. Awards/prizes: 1st place in category, cash awards, Best in Show cash award; Mayor's Purchase Award in May show. Number of exhibitors: 230-250. Public attendance: 30,000-50,000. Free to public. Deadline for entry: mid-February for the May show; mid-July for the October show. For more information, artists should e-mail, visit website, call or send SASE. Show located at historic Beverley Gardens. **TIPS** "Art fairs tend to be commercially oriented. It usually pays off to think in somewhat commercial terms. Personally, I like risky and unusual art, but the artists who produce esoteric art sometimes go hungry! Be nice and have a clean presentation."

BLACK SWAMP ARTS FESTIVAL

P.O. Box 532, Bowling Green OH 43402. (419)354-2723. **E-mail:** info@blackswamparts.org. **Website:** www.blackswamparts.org. The Black Swamp Arts Festival (BSAF), held early September, connects art and the community by presenting an annual arts festival and by promoting the arts in the Bowling Green community. Awards: Best in Show ($1,500); Best 2D ($1,000); Best 3D ($1,000); 2nd ($750); 3rd ($500); Honorable Mentions (3 awards, $200 each). Apply online at www.zapplication.org. Call, e-mail, or visit website for more information. Application fee: $35.

Single booth fee: $275. Double booth fee: $550. Show located in downtown Bowling Green.

BOCA FEST

270 Central Blvd., Suite 107B, Jupiter FL 33458. (561)746-6615. **Fax:** (561)746-6528. **E-mail:** info@artfestival.com. **Website:** www.artfestivalc.com. **Contact:** Malinda Ratliff, communications manager. Estab. 1988. Fine art & craft fair held annually in January. Outdoors. Accepts photography, jewelry, mixed media, sculpture, wood, ceramic, glass, painting, digital, fiber, metal. Juried. Number exhibitors: 210. Number attendees: 80,000. Free to public. Apply online via www.zapplication.org. Deadline: see website. Application fee: $25. Space fee: $395. Exhibition space: 10×10 and 10×20. For more information, artists should e-mail, call, or visit website.

○   Festival located at The Shops at Boca Center in Boca Raton, FL.

BOCA RATON FINE ART SHOW

Hot Works, P.O. Box 1425, Sarasota FL 34230. (941)755-3088. **E-mail:** info@hotworks.org; patty@hotworks.org. **Website:** www.hotworks.org. **Contact:** Patty Naronzny. Estab. 2008. The annual Boca Raton Fine Art Show brings high-quality juried artists to sell their artworks in the heart of downtown Boca Raton. "The event takes place in a premium location on Federal Highway/US-1 at Palmetto Park Road. In its 3rd year, the Boca Raton Fine Art Show was voted no. 68 in the country by *Art Fair Source Book*." All work is original and personally handmade by the artist. We offer awards to attract the nation's best artists. Our goal is to create an atmosphere that enhances the artwork and creates a relaxing environment for art lovers. All types of disciplines for sale including sculpture, paintings, clay, glass, printmaking, fiber, wood, jewelry, photography, and more. Art show also has artist demonstrations, live entertainment, and food. Awards: 2 $500 Juror's Awards and 5 $100 Awards of Excellence. "In addition to the professional artists, as part of our commitment to bring art education into the event, there is a Budding Artists Art Competition, sponsored by the Institute for the Arts & Education, Inc., the 501(c)(3) nonprofit organization behind the event." For more information, see www.hotworks.org.

BRICK STREET MARKET

E-mail: info@zionsvillechamber.org. **Website:** www.zionsvillechamber.org. **Contact:** Dusky Loebel. Estab.

1985. Fine art, antique & craft show held annually the Saturday after Mother's Day. Outdoors. In collaboration with area merchants, this annual event is held on Main Street in the Historic Downtown of Zionsville IN. Please submit application found on line at www.zionsvillechamber.org and 3 JPEG images. All mediums are welcome. Artists are encouraged to perform demonstrations of their work and talk with visitors during the event. Tents will be provided. Artists may use their own white 10×10 ft. tents if space is available. Artists must supply display equipment. Committee will not accept catalog or mass-produced products. Number of exhibitors: 150-180. Public attendance: 8,000-10,000. Free to public. Space fee: see website.

BY HAND FINE ART & CRAFT FAIR

1 I-X Center Dr., Cleveland OH 44135. (216)265-2663. **E-mail:** rattewell@ixcenter.com. **Website:** www.clevelandbyhand.com. **Contact:** Rob Attewell, show manager. Estab. 2004. Fine arts & crafts show held annually in November. Indoors. Accepts photography, 2D, 3D, clay, digital, fiber, furniture, glass, jewelry, leather, metal, oil/acrylics, printmaking, sculpture, watercolor, wood, wearable art. Juried; group reviews applications and photos. Awards/prizes: ribbons, booths. Number of exhibitors: 150-200. Number of attendees: 20,000. Admission: free. Artists should apply via www.zapplication.org. Deadline: June 15. Application fee: $25. Space fee: $399 (8×10); $425 (10×10). Exhibition space: 10×10, 15×10, 20×10 ft. For more information, artists should e-mail or go to www.zapplication.org.

CAIN PARK ARTS FESTIVAL

40 Severance Circle, Cleveland Heights OH 44118-9988. (216)291-3669. **Fax:** (216)291-3705. **E-mail:** jhoffman@clvhts.com; artsfestival@clvhts.com. **Website:** www.cainpark.com. Estab. 1976. Fine arts & crafts show held annually 2nd weekend in July (3 day event). Outdoors. Accepts photography, painting, clay, sculpture, wood, jewelry, leather, glass, ceramics, clothes and other fiber, paper, block printing. Juried by a panel of professional artists; submit digital images online or mail CD. Awards/prizes: Artist to Artist Award, $450; also Judges' Selection, Director's Choice and Artists' Award. Number of exhibitors: 150. Public attendance: 15,000. Fee for public: $5; Free on Friday. "Applications are available online at our website www.cainpark.com." Artists should apply by requesting an application by mail, visiting website to

download application or by calling. Deadline for entry: early March. Application fee: $50. Space fee: $450. Exhibition space: 10×10 ft. Average gross sales/exhibitor: $4,000. For more information, artists should e-mail, call, or visit website. Show located in Cain Park. **TIPS** "Have an attractive booth to display your work. Have a variety of prices. Be available to answer questions about your work."

CALABASAS FINE ARTS FESTIVAL

100 Civic Center Way, Calabasas CA 91302. (818)224-1657. **E-mail:** artscouncil@cityofcalabasas.com. **Website:** www.calabasasartscouncil.com. Estab. 1997. Fine arts & crafts show held annually in late April/early May. Outdoors. Accepts photography, painting, sculpture, jewelry, mixed media. Juried. Number of exhibitors: 150. Public attendance: 10,000+. Free to public. Application fee: $25. Artists should apply online through www.zapplication.org; must include 3 photos of work and 1 photo of booth display. For more information, artists should call, e-mail or visit website. Show located at the Commons at Calabasas & the Calabasas Civic Center.

CAREFREE FINE ART & WINE FESTIVAL

15648 Eagles Nest Dr., Fountain Hills AZ 85268. (480)837-5637. **Fax:** (480)837-2355. **E-mail:** info@thunderbirdartists.com. **Website:** www.thunderbirdartists.com. **Contact:** Denise Colter, president. Estab. 1993. Fine arts & crafts show held annually 3 times a year (January, March, November). Outdoors. Accepts photography, paintings, bronzes, baskets, jewelry, stone, pottery. Juried; CEO blind juries by medium. Number of exhibitors: 175. Attendance: 30,000. Admission: $3. Applications available online at www.zapplication.org. Deadline for entry: mid-June (see website for specifics). Application fee: $30. Space fee: $430-$1,240. Exhibition space: 10×10 to 10×30 ft. For more information, artists should e-mail, call, or visit website. **TIPS** "A clean gallery-type presentation is very important."

CEDARHURST CRAFT FAIR

P.O. Box 923, 2600 Richview Rd., Mt. Vernon IL 62864. (618)242-1236, ext. 234. **Fax:** (618)242-9530. **E-mail:** linda@cedarhurst.org; sarah@cedarhurst.org. **Website:** www.cedarhurst.org. **Contact:** Linda Wheeler, staff coordinator. Estab. 1977. Arts & crafts show held annually on the 1st weekend after Labor

Day each September. Outdoors. Accepts photography, paper, glass, metal, clay, wood, leather, jewelry, fiber, baskets, 2D art. Juried. Awards/prizes: Best of most category. Number of exhibitors: 125+. Public attendance: 12,000. Public admission: $5. Artists should apply by filling out online application form. Deadline for entry: March. Application fee: $25. Exhibition space: 10×15 ft. For more information, artists should e-mail, call, or visit website.

CENTERVILLE–WASHINGTON TOWNSHIP AMERICANA FESTIVAL

P.O. Box 41794, Centerville OH 45441-0794. (937)433-5898. **Fax:** (937)433-5898. **E-mail:** ameri canafestival@sbcglobal.net. **Website:** www.ameri canafestival.org. Estab. 1972. Arts, crafts and antiques show held annually on the 4th of July, except when the 4th falls on a Sunday and then festival is held on Monday the 5th. Festival includes entertainment, parade, food, car show and other activities. Accepts arts, crafts, antiques, photography and all mediums. "No factory-made items accepted." Awards/prizes: 1st, 2nd, 3rd places; certificates and ribbons for most attractive displays. Number of exhibitors: 275-300. Public attendance: 75,000. Free to the public. Exhibitors should send SASE for application form, or apply online. Deadline for entry: early June (see website for details). Space fee: $40-55 site specific. Exhibition space: 12×10 ft. For more information, artists should e-mail, call, or visit website. Arts & crafts booths located on N. Main St., in Benham's Grove and limited spots in teh Children's Activity area.

TIPS "Moderately priced products sell best. Bring business cards and have an eye-catching display."

CHAMBER SOUTH'S ANNUAL SOUTH MIAMI ART FESTIVAL

Sunset Dr. (SW 72nd St.) from US 1 to Red Rd. (SW 57th Ave.), South Miami FL 33143. (305)661-1621. **Fax:** (305)666-0508. **E-mail:** art@chambersouth.com. **Website:** www.chambersouth.com/events/south-mi ami-art-festival. **Contact:** Arelis Ferro, art festival coordinator. Estab. 1971. Annual. Fine art & craft show held the 1st weekend in November. Outdoors. Accepts 2D & 3D mixed media, ceramics, clay, digital art, glass, jewelry, metalwork, painting (oil, acrylic, watercolor), printmaking, drawing, sculpture, textiles, wood. Juried by panel of jurors who meet to review work; includes artists and board members. Cash prizes, ribbons to display during event, exemption from jury in the following year's show. Average number of exhibitors: 130. Average number of attendees: 50,000. Admission: free. Artists should apply by www. zap plication.org. Deadline: July 31. Application fee: $25. Space fee: standard, $325; corner $375. Space is 10×10 (10×20 also available). For more information artists should e-mail, call, or visit the website.

TIPS "Good, clean displays; interact with customers without hounding."

CHARDON SQUARE ARTS FESTIVAL

P.O. Box 1063, Chardon OH 44024. (440)285-8686; (440)285-3519. **E-mail:** sgipson@aol.com. **Website:** www.chardonsquareassociation.org. **Contact:** Jan Gipson, chairman. Estab. 1980. Fine arts & crafts show held annually in early August (see website for details). Outdoors. Accepts photography, pottery, weaving, wood, paintings, jewelry. Juried. Number of exhibitors: 105. Public attendance: 4,000. Free to public. Artists can find application on website. Exhibition space: 12×12 ft. For more information, artists should call, or visit website.

TIPS "Make your booth attractive; be friendly and offer quality work."

CHATSWORTH CRANBERRY FESTIVAL

P.O. Box 286, Chatsworth NJ 08019. (609)726-9237. **Fax:** (609)726-1459. **E-mail:** lgiamalis@aol.com. **Website:** www.cranfest.org. **Contact:** Lynn Giamalis. Estab. 1983. Arts & crafts show held annually in mid-October (see website for details). Outdoors. The festival is a celebration of New Jersey's cranberry harvest, the 3rd largest in the country, and offers a tribute to the Pine Barrens and local culture. Accepts photography. Juried. Number of exhibitors: 200. Public attendance: 75,000-100,000. Free to public. Artists should apply by sending SASE to above address (application form online). Requires 3 pictures of products and 1 of display. Deadline: September 1. Space fee: $225 for 2 days. Exhibition space: 15×15 ft. For more information, artists should visit website. Show located in downtown Chatsworth.

CHUN CAPITOL HILL PEOPLE'S FAIR

1290 Williams St., Suite 102, Denver CO 80218. (303)830-1651. **Fax:** (303)830-1782. **E-mail:** nicole anderson@chundenver.org. **Website:** www.peoples fair.com; www.chundenver.org. **Contact:** Nicole Anderson, operations manager. Estab. 1972. Arts & music festival held annually 1st full weekend in June.

Outdoors. Accepts photography, ceramics, jewelry, paintings, wearable art, glass, sculpture, wood, paper, fiber, children's items, and more. Juried by professional artisans representing a variety of mediums and selected members of fair management. The jury process is based on originality, quality and expression. Awards/prizes: Best of Show. Number of exhibitors: 300. Public attendance: 200,000. Free to public. Artists should apply by downloading application from website. Deadline for entry: March. Application fee: $35. Space fee: $300-400, depending on type of art. Exhibition space: 10×10 ft. For more information, artists should e-mail, visit website or call. Festival located at Civic Center Park.

CHURCH STREET ART & CRAFT SHOW

Downtown Waynesville Association, P.O. Box 1409, Waynesville NC 28786. (828)456-3517. **E-mail:** info@downtownwaynesville.com; downtownwaynesville@charter.net. **Website:** www.downtownwaynesville.com. Estab. 1983. Fine arts & crafts show held annually 2nd Saturday in October. Outdoors. Accepts photography, paintings, fiber, pottery, wood, jewelry. Juried by committee: submit 4 slides or digital photos of work and 1 of booth display. Prizes: $100-400 Number of exhibitors: 100. Public attendance: 15,000-18,000. Free to public. Entry fee: $25. Space fee: $110 ($200 for 2 booths). Exhibition space: 10×12 ft. (option of 2 booths for 12×20 space). For more information and application, see website. Deadline: mid-August. Show located in downtown Waynesville on Main St. **TIPS** Recommends "quality in work and display."

CITY OF FAIRFAX FALL FESTIVAL

10455 Armstrong St., Fairfax VA 22030. (703)385-7949. **Fax:** (703)246-6321. **E-mail:** leslie.herman@fairfaxva.gov; mitzi.taylor@fairfaxva.gov. **Website:** www.fairfaxva.gov. **Contact:** Mitzi Taylor, special event coordinator. Estab. 1985. Arts & crafts festival held annually the 2nd weekend in October. Outdoors. Accepts photography, jewelry, glass, pottery, clay, wood, mixed media. Juried by a panel of 5 independent jurors. Number of exhibitors: 400. Public attendance: 25,000. Free to the public. Deadline for entry: mid-March. Artists should apply by contacting Mitzi Taylor for an application. Application fee: $12. Space fee: $160 10×10 ft. For more information, artists should e-mail. Festival located in historic downtown Fairfax.

CITY OF FAIRFAX HOLIDAY CRAFT SHOW

10455 Armstrong St., Fairfax VA 22030. (703)385-7949. **Fax:** (703)246-6321. **E-mail:** mitzi.taylor@fairfaxva.gov; leslie.herman@fairfaxva.gov. **Website:** www.fairfaxva.gov. **Contact:** Mitzi Taylor, event coordinator. Estab. 1985. Arts & crafts show held annually 3rd weekend in November. Indoors. Accepts photography, jewelry, glass, pottery, clay, wood, mixed media. Juried by a panel of 5 independent jurors. Number of exhibitors: 247. Public attendance: 5,000. Public admission: $5 for age 18 and older. $8 for 2 day pass. Artists should apply by contacting Mitzi Taylor for an application. Deadline for entry: early March (see website for details). Application fee: $12. Space fee: 10×6 ft. $195; 11×9 ft. $245; 10×10 ft. $270. For more information, artists should e-mail.

CITYPLACE ART FAIR

270 Central Blvd., Suite 107B, Jupiter FL 33458. (561)746-6615. **Fax:** (561)746-6528. **E-mail:** info@artfestival.com. **Website:** www.artfestival.com. **Contact:** Malinda Ratliff, communications manager. Estab. 2011. Fine art & craft fair held annually in early March. Outdoors. Accepts photography, jewelry, mixed media, sculpture, wood, ceramic, glass, painting, digital, fiber, metal. Juried. Number exhibitors: 200. Number attendees: 40,000. Free to public. Apply online via www.zapplication.org. Deadline: see website. Application fee: $25. Space fee: $395. Exhibition space: 10×10 and 10×20. For more information, artists should e-mail, call, or visit website.

Fair located in CityPlace in downtown West Palm Beach, FL.

COCONUT POINT ART FESTIVAL

270 Central Blvd., Suite 107B, Jupiter FL 33458. (561)746-6615. **Fax:** (561)746-6528. **E-mail:** info@artfestival.com. **Website:** www.artfestival.com. **Contact:** Malinda Ratliff, communications manager. Estab. 2007. Fine art & craft fair held annually in late December/early January & February. Outdoors. Accepts photography, jewelry, mixed media, sculpture, wood, ceramic, glass, painting, digital, fiber, metal. Juried. Number exhibitors: 200-280. Number attendees: 90,000. Free to public. Apply online via www.zapplication.org. Deadline: see website. Application fee: $25. Space fee: $395-425. Exhibition space: 10×10 and 10×20. For more information, artists should e-mail, call, or visit website.

🎧 Festival held at Coconut Point in Estero FL.

🎧 COLORSCAPE CHENANGO ARTS FESTIVAL

P.O. Box 624, Norwich NY 13815. (607)336-3378. **E-mail:** info@colorscape.org. **Website:** www.colorscape.org. Estab. 1995. A juried exhibition of art & fine crafts held annually the weekend after Labor Day. Outdoors. Accepts photography and all types of media. Juried. Awards/prizes: $6,000. Number of exhibitors: 115. Public attendance: 10,000-12,000. Free to public. Deadline for entry: see website for details. Application fee: $15 jury fee. Space fee: $175. Exhibition space: 12×12 ft. For more information, artists should e-mail, visit website, call or send SASE. Show located in downtown Norwich.

TIPS "Interact with your audience. Talk to them about your work and how it is created. People like to be involved in the art they buy and are more likely to buy if you involve them."

🎧 CONYERS CHERRY BLOSSOM FESTIVAL

1996 Centennial Olympic Pkwy., Conyers GA 30013. (770)860-4190; (770)860-4194. **E-mail:** rebecca.hill@conyersga.com. **Website:** www.conyerscherryblossomfest.com. **Contact:** Jill Miller. Estab. 1981. Arts & crafts show held annually in late March (see website for details). Outdoors. The festival is held at the Georgia International Horse Park at the Grand Prix Plaza overlooking the Grand Prix Stadium used during the 1996 Centennial Olympic Games. Accepts photography, paintings and any other handmade or original art. Juried. Submit 5 images: 1 picture must represent your work as it is displayed; 1 must represent a workshop photo of the artist creating their work; the other 3 need to represent your items as an accurate representation in size, style, and quality of work. Number of exhibitors: 300. Public attendance: 40,000. Free to public. Space fee: $135. Exhibition space: 10×10 ft. Electricity fee: $30. Application fee: $10; apply online. For more information, artists should e-mail, call, or visit website. Show located at the Georgia International Horse Park.

🎧 CRAFT FAIR AT THE BAY

38 Charles St., Rochester NH 03867. (603)332-2616. **Fax:** (603)332-8413. **E-mail:** info@castleberryfairs.com. **Website:** www.castleberryfairs.com. Estab. 1988. Arts & crafts show held annually in July in Alton Bay NH. Outdoors. Accepts photography and all other mediums. Juried by photo, slide or sample. Number of exhibitors: 85. Public attendance: 7,500. Free to the public. Artists should apply by downloading application from website. Deadline for entry: until full. Exhibition space: 100 sq. ft. For more information, artists should visit call, e-mail or visit website.

TIPS "Do not bring a book; do not bring a chair. Smile and make eye contact with everyone who enters your booth. Have them sign your guest book; get their e-mail address so you can let them know when you are in the area again. And, finally, make the sale—they are at the fair to shop, after all."

➕ 🎧 CRAFTS AT PURCHASE

P.O. Box 28, Woodstock NY 12498. (845)331-7900. **Fax:** (845)331-7484. **E-mail:** crafts@artrider.com. **Website:** www.artrider.com. **Contact:** Stacey Jarit. Estab. 2012. Boutique show of fine contemporary craft held annually in late October or early November. 100 indoors. Accepts photography, fine art, ceramics, wood, mixed media, leather, glass, metal, fiber, jewelry. Juried. Submit 5 images of work and 1 of booth. Attendance: 4,000. Admission: $10. Artists should apply online at www.artrider.com or www.zapplication.org. Deadline for entry: end of May. Application fee: $45. Space fee: $545. Exhibition space: 10×10. For more information, artists should e-mail, visit website, call.

🎧 CRAFTWESTPORT

P.O. Box 28, Woodstock NY 12498. (845)331-7484. **Fax:** (845)331-7484. **E-mail:** crafts@artrider.com. **Website:** www.craftwestport.com. Estab. 1975. Fine arts & craft show held annually in the 3rd weekend before Thanksgiving. Indoors. Accepts photography, wearable and nonwearable fiber, jewelry, clay, leather, wood, glass, painting, drawing, prints, mixed media. Juried by 5 images of work and 1 of booth, viewed sequentially. Number of exhibitors: 160. Public attendance: 5,000. Public admission: $10. Artists should apply online at www.artrider.com or at www.zapplication.org. Deadline for entry: end of May. Application fee: $45. Space fee: $525. Exhibition space: 10×10 ft. For more information, artists should e-mail, visit website, call.

➕ 🎧 CROCKER PARK FINE ART FAIR WITH CRAFT MARKETPLACE

270 Central Blvd., Suite 107B, Jupiter FL 33458. (561)746-6615. **Fax:** (561)746-6528. **E-mail:** info@artfestival.com. **Website:** www.artfestival.com.

Contact: Malinda Ratliff, communications officer. Estab. 2006. Fine art & craft fair held annually in mid-June. Outdoors. Accepts photography, jewelry, mixed media, sculpture, wood, ceramic, glass, painting, digital, fiber, metal. Juried. Number exhibitors: 125. Number attendees: 50,000. Free to public. Apply online via www. zapplication.org. Deadline: see website. Application fee: $25. Space fee: $395. Exhibition space: 10×10 and 10×20. For more information, artists should e-mail, call, or visit website.

◯ Fair located in Crocker Park in Westlake/ Cleveland OH.

✺ ◯ CUSTER FAIR

P.O. Box 6013, Evanston IL 60204. (847)328-2204. **Fax:** (847)328-2295. **E-mail:** office@custerfair.com. **Website:** www.custerfair.com. Estab. 1972. Outdoor fine art craft show held in June. Accepts photography and all mediums. Number of exhibitors: 400. Public attendance: 70,000. Free to the public. Application fee: $10. Booth fee: $250-400. Deadline for entry: early May. Space fee varies, e-mail, call, or visit website for more details.

TIPS "Be prepared to speak with patrons; invite them to look at your work and discuss."

A DAY IN TOWNE

Boalsburg Memorial Day Committee, 163 Boal Estate Dr., Boalsburg PA 16827. (814)466-6210. **E-mail:** office@boalmuseum.com. **Website:** www.boalsburgvillage.com. Arts & crafts show held annually the last Monday in May/Memorial Day weekend. Outdoors. Accepts photography, country fabric & wood, wool knit, soap, jewelry, dried flowers, children, pottery, blown glass. Vendor must make own work. Number of exhibitors: 125-135. Public attendance: 20,000. Artists should apply by writing an inquiry letter and sending 2-3 photos; 1 of booth and 2 of the craft. Deadline for entry: January 1–February 1. Space fee: $75. Exhibition space: 10×15 ft.

TIPS "Please do not send fees until you receive an official contract. Have a neat booth and nice smile. Have fair prices—if too high, product will not sell here."

◉ DEERFIELD FINE ARTS FESTIVAL

3417 R.F.D., Long Grove IL 60047. (847)726-8669. **E-mail:** dwevents@comcast.net. **Website:** www.dwevents.org. **Contact:** D&W Events, Inc. Estab. 2003. Fine art show held annually end of May/beginning of June. Outdoors. Accepts photography, fiber, oil, acrylic, watercolor, mixed media, jewelry, sculpture, metal, paper, ceramics, painting. Juried by 3 jurors. Awards/prizes: Best of Show; 1st Place, awards of excellence. Number of exhibitors: 120-150. Public attendance: 20,000. Free to public. Free parking. Artists should apply via www.zapplication.com or our promoter website: www.dwevents.org. Exhibition space: 100 sq. ft. For more information artists should e-mail, visit website, call. Show located at Park Avenue and Deerfield Road adjacent to Jewett Park in Deerfield, Illinois.

TIPS "Artists should display professionally and attractively, and interact positively with everyone."

◉ DELAWARE ARTS FESTIVAL

P.O. Box 589, Delaware OH 43015. **E-mail:** info@delawareartsfestival.org. **Website:** www.delawareartsfestival.org. Estab. 1973. Fine arts & crafts show held annually the Saturday and Sunday after Mother's Day. Outdoors. Accepts photography; all mediums, but no buy/sell. Juried by category panels who are also artists. Awards/prizes: Ribbons, cash awards, free booth for Best of Show the following year. Number of exhibitors: 160. Public attendance: 50,000. Free to the public. Submit 3 photographs per category that best represent your work. Your work will be juried in accordance with our guidelines. Photos (no slides) will be returned only if you provide a SASE. Artists should apply by visiting website for application. Jury fee: $10 per category, payable to the Delaware Arts Festival. Space fee: $140. Exhibition space: 120 sq. ft. For more information, artists should e-mail or visit website. Show located in historic downtown Delaware OH, just 2 blocks from the heart of Ohio Wesleyan University Campus.

TIPS "Have high-quality, original stuff. Engage the public. Applications will be screened according to originality, technique, craftsmanship and design. Unaffiliated professional judges are hired to make all prize award decisions. The Delaware Arts Festival, Inc. will exercise the right to reject items during the show that are not the quality of the media submitted with the applications. No commercial buy and resell merchandise permitted. Set up a good booth."

✚ ◉ DELRAY MARKETPLACE ART & CRAFT FESTIVAL

270 Central Blvd., Suite 107B, Jupiter FL 33458. (561)746-6615. **Fax:** (561)746-6528. **E-mail:** info@artfestival.com. **Website:** www.artfestival.com. **Contact:** Malinda Ratliff, communications manager. Estab. 2013. Fine art & craft fair held annually in November.

Outdoors. Accepts photography, jewelry, mixed media, sculpture, wood, ceramic, glass, painting, digital, fiber, metal. Juried. Number exhibitors: 100. Number attendees: 40,000. Free to public. Apply online via zapplication.org. Deadline: see website. Application fee: $25. Space fee: $350. Exhibition space: 10×10 and 10×20. For more information, artists should e-mail, call, or visit website.

⊙ Festival located at Delray Marketplace off West Atlantic Ave. in Delray Beach FL.

DICKENS CHRISTMAS SHOW & FESTIVAL
2101 N. Oak St., Myrtle Beach SC 29577. (843)448-9483. **Fax:** (843)626-1513. **E-mail:** dickensshow@sc.rr.com. **Website:** www.dickenschristmasshow.com. **Contact:** Samantha Bower, manager. Estab. 1981. Annual arts & crafts, seasonal/holiday show held in November. Indoors. Accepts all fine art. Average number of exhibitors: 350. Average number of attendees: 16,000. Admission: $8.50 (plus tax). Artists should apply by application. Deadline: see website. Space fee: $300-800. Space is 10×10. For more information artists should e-mail, call, or visit the website. Show held at Myrtle Beach Convention Center.

TIPS "Make sure your products are good and your display is good."

⊙ ALDEN B. DOW MUSEUM SUMMER ART FAIR
1801 W. St. Andrews Rd., Midland MI 48640. **Fax:** (989)631-7890. **E-mail:** mills@mcfta.org. **Website:** www.mcfta.org. **Contact:** Emmy Mills, business manager/art fair coordinator. Estab. 1966. Fine art & crafts show held annually in early June. Outdoors. Accepts photography, ceramics, fibers, jewelry, mixed media 3D, painting, wood, drawing, glass, leather, sculpture, basket, furniture. Juried by a panel. Awards: $500 1st Place, $300 2nd Place, $100 3rd Place. Average number of exhibitors: 150. Public attendance: 5,000-8,000. Free to public. Artists should apply at www.mcfta.org/specialevents.html. Deadline for entry: late March; see website for details. Application fee: jury $25, second medium $5/each. Space fee: $195/single booth, $365/double booth. Exhibition space: approximately 12×12 ft. Average gross sales/exhibitor: $1,500. Artists should e-mail or visit website for more information. Event takes place at Midland Center for the Arts.

⊕ ⊙ DOWNTOWN ASPEN ART FESTIVAL
270 Central Blvd., Suite 107B, Jupiter FL 33458. (561)746-6615. **Fax:** (561)746-6528. **E-mail:** info@artfestival.com. **Website:** www.artfestival.com. **Contact:** Malinda Ratliff, communications manager. Estab. 2003. Fine art & craft fair held annually in July. Outdoors. Accepts photography, jewelry, mixed media, sculpture, wood, ceramic, glass, painting, digital, fiber, metal. Juried. Number exhibitors: 150. Number attendees: 80,000. Free to public. Apply online via www.zapplication.org. Deadline: see website. Application fee: $35. Space fee: $475. Exhibition space: 10×10 and 10×20. For more information, artists should e-mail, call, or visit website.

⊙ Festival located at Monarch Street in Aspen CO.

⊕ ⊙ DOWNTOWN DELRAY BEACH FESTIVAL OF THE ARTS
207 Central Blvd., Suite 107B, Jupiter FL 33458. (561)746-6615. **Fax:** (561)746-6528. **E-mail:** info@artfestival.com. **Website:** www.artfestival.com. **Contact:** Malinda Ratliff, communications manager. Estab. 2000. Fine art & craft fair held annually in mid-January. Outdoors. Accepts photography, jewelry, mixed media, sculpture, wood, ceramic, glass, painting, digital, fiber, metal. Juried. Number exhibitors: 305. Number attendees: 100,000. Free to public. Apply online via www.zapplication.org. Deadline: see website. Application fee: $25. Space fee: $395. Exhibition space: 10×10 and 10×20. For more information, artists should e-mail, call, or visit website.

⊙ Festival located at Atlantic Ave. in downtown Delray Beach, FL.

⊕ DOWNTOWN DELRAY BEACH THANKSGIVING WEEKEND ART FESTIVAL
207 Central Blvd., Suite 107B, Jupiter FL 33458. (561)746-6615. **Fax:** (561)746-6528. **E-mail:** info@artfestival.com. **Website:** www.artfestival.com. **Contact:** Malinda Ratliff, communications manager. Estab. 2000. Fine art & craft fair held annually in November. Outdoors. Accepts photography, jewelry, mixed media, sculpture, wood, ceramic, glass, painting, digital, fiber, metal. Juried. Number exhibitors: 150. Number attendees: 80,000. Free to public. Apply online via www.zapplication.org. Deadline: see website. Application fee: $25. Space fee: $395. Exhibition

space: 10×10 and 10×20. For more information, artists should e-mail, call, or visit website.

🎧 Festival located at 4th Ave. & Atlantic Ave. in downtown Delray Beach FL.

➕ 🎧 DOWNTOWN DUNEDIN ART FESTIVAL

270 Central Blvd., Suite 107B, Jupiter FL 33458. (561)746-6615. **Fax:** (561)746-6528. **E-mail:** info@artfestival.com. **Website:** www.arfestival.com. **Contact:** Malinda Ratliff, communications manager. Estab. 1997. Fine art & craft fair held annually in January. Outdoors. Accepts photography, jewelry, mixed media, sculpture, wood, ceramic, glass, painting, digital, fiber, metal. Juried. Number exhibitors: 130. Number attendees: 40,000. Free to public. Apply online via www.zapplication.org. Deadline: see website. Application fee: $25. Space fee: $395. Exhibition space: 10×10 and 10×20. For more information, artists should e-mail, call, or visit website.

🎧 Festival located at Main St. in downtown Dunedin FL.

🎧 DOWNTOWN FESTIVAL & ART SHOW

P.O. Box 490, Gainesville FL 32627. (352)393-8536. **Fax:** (352)334-2249. **E-mail:** piperlr@cityofgainesville.org. **Website:** www.gvlculturalaffairs.org. **Contact:** Linda Piper, events coordinator. Estab. 1981. Fine arts & crafts show held annually in November (see website for more details). Outdoors. Accepts photography, wood, ceramic, fiber, glass, and all mediums. Juried by 3 digital images of artwork and 1 digital image of booth. Awards/prizes: $15,000 in cash awards; $3,000 in purchase awards. Number of exhibitors: 250. Public attendance: 100,000. Free to the public. Artists should apply by mailing 4 digital images. Deadline for entry: May. Space fee: $235, competitive, $215 noncompetitive. Exhibition space: 12×12 ft. Average gross sales/exhibitor: $6,000. For more information, artists should e-mail, visit website, call.

TIPS "Submit the highest quality digital images. A proper booth image is very important."

➕ 🎧 DOWNTOWN SARASOTA CRAFT FAIR

270 Central Blvd., Suite 107B, Jupiter FL 33458. (561)746-6615. **Fax:** (561)746-6528. **E-mail:** info@ArtFestival.com. **Website:** www.artfestival.com. **Contact:** Malinda Ratliff, communications manager. "This popular annual craft festival has garnered crowds of fine craft lovers each year. Behold contemporary crafts from more than 100 of the nation's most talented artisans. A variety of jewelry, pottery, ceramics, photography, painting, clothing and much more—all handmade in America—will be on display, ranging from $15 to $3,000. An expansive Green Market with plants, orchids, exotic flora, handmade soaps, gourmet spices and freshly popped kettle corn further complements the weekend, blending nature with nurture."

➕ 🎧 DOWNTOWN SARASOTA FESTIVAL OF THE ARTS

270 Central Blvd., Suite 107B, Jupiter FL 33458. (561)746-6615. **Fax:** (561)746-6528. **E-mail:** info@artfestival.com. **Website:** www.artfestival.com. Fine art & craft fair held annually in mid-February. Outdoors. Accepts photography, jewelry, mixed media, sculpture, wood, ceramic, glass, painting, digital, fiber, metal. Juried. Number exhibitors: 305. Number attendees: 80,000. Free to public. Apply online via zapplication.org. Deadline: see website. Application fee: $25. Space fee: $395. Exhibition space: 10×10 and 10×20. For more information, artists should e-mail, call, or visit website. Festival located at Main St. at Orange Ave. heading east and ending at Links Ave. in Downtown Sarasota FL.

➕ 🎧 DOWNTOWN STEAMBOAT SPRINGS ART FESTIVAL ON YAMPA STREET, THE YAMPA ART STROLL

270 Central Blvd., Suite 107B, Jupiter FL 33458. (561)746-6615. **Fax:** (561)746-6528. **E-mail:** info@artfestival.com. **Website:** www.artfestival.com. **Contact:** Malinda Ratliff, communications manager. Estab. 2015. Fine art & craft fair held annually in August. Outdoors. Accepts photography, jewelry, mixed media, sculpture, wood, ceramic, glass, painting, digital, fiber, metal. Juried. Number exhibitors: see website. Number attendees: see website. Free to public. Apply online via www.zapplication.org. Deadline: see website. Application fee: $35. Space fee: $350. Exhibition space: 10×10 and 10×20. For more information, artists should e-mail, call, or visit website.

🎧 Festival located at Yampa Ave. in Steamboat Springs CO.

➕ 🎧 DOWNTOWN STUART ART FESTIVAL

270 Central Blvd., Suite 107B, Jupiter FL 34458. (561)746-6615. **Fax:** (561)746-6528. **E-mail:** info@artfestival.com. **Website:** www.artfestival.com.

Contact: Malinda Ratliff, communications manager. Estab. 1991. Fine art & craft fair held annually in February. Outdoors. Accepts photography, jewelry, mixed media, sculpture, wood, ceramic, glass, painting, digital, fiber, metal. Juried. Number exhibitors: 200. Number attendees: 50,000. Free to public. Apply online via www.zapplication.org. Deadline: see website. Application fee: $25. Space fee: $395. Exhibition space: 10×10 and 10×20. For more information, artists should e-mail, call, or visit website.

Festival located at Osceola St. in Stuart FL.

⊕ ☺ DOWNTOWN VENICE ART FESTIVAL

270 Central Blvd., Suite 107B, Jupiter FL 33458. (561)746-6615. **Fax:** (561)746-6528. **E-mail:** info@artfestival.com. **Website:** www.artfestival.com. **Contact:** Malinda Ratliff, communications manager. Estab. 1987. Fine art & craft fair held annually in early March & mid-November. Outdoors. Accepts photography, jewelry, mixed media, sculpture, wood, ceramic, glass, painting, digital, fiber, metal. Juried. Number exhibitors: 130-200. Number attendees: 50,000. Free to public. Apply online via www.zapplication.org. Deadline: see website. Application fee: $25. Space fee: $350-395. Exhibition space: 10×10 and 10×20. For more information, artists should e-mail, call, or visit website.

Festival located at W. Venice Ave. in downtown Venice FL.

☺ DURANGO AUTUMN ARTS FESTIVAL

802 E. Second Ave., Durango CO 81301. (970)422-8566. **Fax:** (970)259-6571. **E-mail:** daaf@durangoarts.org. **Website:** www.durangoarts.org/programs. Estab. 1994. Fine arts & crafts show. Third weekend in September. Outdoors. Accepts photography and all mediums. Juried. Number of exhibitors: 90. Public attendance: 6,500. Free to public. Exhibition space: 10×10 ft. & 10×20 ft. Space fee $325 & $625. Application fee of $30. Apply via www.zapplication.org. For more information, artists should visit website.

☺ EDENS ART FAIR

P.O. Box 1326, Palatine IL 60078. (312)751-2500. **E-mail:** asoa@webtv.net; asoaartists@aol.com. **Website:** www.americansocietyofartists.com. **Contact:** Office personnel. Estab. 1995 (after renovation of location; held many years prior to renovation). American Society of Artists. Fine arts & fine selected crafts show held annually in mid-July. Outdoors. Event held in Wilmette, Illinois. Accepts photography, paintings, sculpture, glass works, jewelry and more. Juried. Send 4 slides or photos of your work and 1 slide or photo of your display; #10 SASE; a résumé or show listing is helpful. Number of exhibitors: 50. Free to the public. Artists should apply by submitting jury materials. Please jury by submitting 4 images representative of your work you wish to exhibit, one of your display set-up, your first/last name, physical address, daytime telephone number—résumé/show listing helpful. Submit to: asoaartists@aol.com. If you pass jury you will receive a nonmember jury approval number. If juried in, you will receive a jury/approval number. Deadline for entry: 2 months prior to show or earlier if spaces fill. Entry fee: to be announced. Exhibition space: approximately 100 sq. ft. for single space; other sizes available. For more information, artists should send SASE, submit jury material.

TIPS "Remember that when you are at work in your studio, you are an artist. But when you are at a show, you are a business person selling your work."

EL DORADO COUNTY FAIR

100 Placerville Dr., Placerville CA 95667. (530)621-5860. **Fax:** (530)295-2566. **E-mail:** fair@eldoradocountyfair.org. **Website:** www.eldoradocountyfair.org. Estab. 1859. County fair held annually in June. Indoors. Accepts photography, fine arts and handicrafts. Awards/prizes given, see entry guide on website for details. Number of exhibitors: 350-450. Average number of attendees: 55,000. Admission fee: $9. Deadline: mid-May. Application fee: varies by class, see entry guide. For more information, visit website. Fair held at El Dorado County Fairgrounds in Placerville CA.

TIPS "Not a lot of selling at fair shows, competition mostly."

☺ ELMWOOD AVENUE FESTIVAL OF THE ARTS, INC.

P.O. Box 786, Buffalo NY 14213-0786. (716)830-2484. **E-mail:** directoreafa@aol.com. **Website:** www.elmwoodartfest.org. Estab. 2000. Arts & crafts show held annually in late August, the weekend before Labor Day weekend. Outdoors. Accepts photography, metal, fiber, ceramics, glass, wood, jewelry, basketry, 2D media. Juried. Awards/prizes: to be determined. Number of exhibitors: 170. Public attendance: 80,000-120,000. Free to the public. Artists should apply by e-mailing their contact information or by downloading application from website. Deadline for entry: April. Application fee: $25. Space fee: $295. Exhibition space: 10×15 ft. Average gross sales/exhibitor: $3,000. For more information, artists should e-mail, call, or visit website. Show located on Elmwood Ave.

TIPS "Make sure your display is well designed, with clean lines that highlight your work. Have a variety of price points—even wealthy people don't always want to spend $500 at a booth where they may like the work."

ESTERO FINE ART SHOW

Hot Works, LLC, Miromar Outlets, 10801 Corkscrew Rd., Estero FL 33928. (941)755-3088. **E-mail:** patty@hotworks.org. **Website:** www.hotworks.org. **Contact:** Patty Narozny, executive director. Estab. 2008. Biannual fine art show held for 2 days in early January and early November. Outdoors. "This event showcases artists from around the globe. Art includes glass, clay, wood, fiber, jewelry, sculpture, painting, photography, and metal. There is artwork for every budget. Focus is on technique/execution, quality and originality." Juried by art professionals in the industry. 3 images of work, 1 of booth. Awards: $1,500 distributed as follows; 2 $500 Juror's Award of Excellence (purchase awards) and 5 $100 Awards of Excellence. Number of exhibitors: 110. Average number of attendees: 10,000. Free admission and free parking. Application fee: $30. Space fee: $385. Space: 11×11. For more information, artists should e-mail, call, see website or visit www.zapplication.org for details. Show located at Miromar Design Center, 10800 Corkscrew Road, Estero FL 33928.

TIPS "Bring enough work to sell that people want to see—original work! Stay positive."

EVERGREEN FINE ARTS FESTIVAL

Evergreen Artists Association, 22528 Blue Jay Rd., Morrison CO 80465. (303)618-9834. **E-mail:** joshtrefethen@gmail.com. **Website:** www.evergreenfineartsfestival.com; www.evergreenartists.org. **Contact:** Josh Trefethen, festival director. Estab. 1966. Fine arts show held annually the 4th weekend in August. Outdoors in Historic Heritage Grove Venue, next to Hiwan Homestead. Accepts both 2D and 3D media, including photography, fiber, oil, acrylic, pottery, jewelry, mixed media, ceramics, wood, watercolor. Juried event with jurors that change yearly. Artists should submit online 3 views of work and 1 of booth display by digital photograph high-res. Awards/prizes: Best of Show in 2D and 3D and 6 awards of excellence, monetary plus jury exempt next year. Number of ex-

hibitors: 100. Public attendance: 6,000-8,000. Free to public. Deadline for entry: March 15. Application fee: $30. Space: $350 (upon acceptance). Exhibition space: 10×10 ft. Submissions only on www.zapplication.org begin in December and jurying completed in early April. "Currently ranked in the top 100 by Art Fair Source Book." For more information, artists should call or send SASE.

FAIRE ON THE SQUARE

117 W. Goodwin St., Prescott AZ 86303. (928)445-2000, ext. 112. **Fax:** (928)445-0068. **E-mail:** chamber@prescott.org; scott@prescott.org. **Website:** www.prescott.org. Estab. 1985. Arts & crafts show held annually Labor Day weekend. Outdoors. Accepts photography, ceramics, painting, sculpture, clothing, woodworking, metal art, glass, floral, home décor. No resale. Juried. Photos of work and artist creating work are required. Number of exhibitors: 170. Public attendance: 10,000-12,000. Free to public. Application can be printed from website or obtained by phone request. Deadline: spaces are sold until show is full. Exhibition space: $425; $460 for food booth; 10×15 ft. For more information, artist should e-mail, visit website, or call.

A FAIR IN THE PARK

6300 Fifth Ave., Pittsburgh PA 15232. **E-mail:** fairdirector@craftsmensguild.org. **Website:** www.afairinthepark.org. Estab. 1969. Contemporary fine arts & crafts show held annually the weekend after Labor Day outdoors. Accepts photography, clay, fiber, jewelry, metal, mixed media, wood, glass, 2D visual arts. Juried. Awards/prizes: 1 Best of Show and 4 Craftsmen's Guild Awards. Number of exhibitors: 105. Public attendance: 25,000+. Free to public. Submit 5 JPEG images; 4 of artwork, 1 of booth display. Application fee: $25. Booth fee: $350 or $400 for corner booth. Deadline for entry: see website. Exhibition space: 10×10 ft. Average gross sales/exhibitor: $1,000 and up. For more information artists should e-mail or visit website. Show located in Mellon Park.

TIPS "It is very important for artists to present their work to the public, to concentrate on the business aspect of their artist career. They will find that they can build a strong customer/collector base by exhibiting their work and by educating the public about their artistic process and passion for creativity."

FALL CRAFTS AT LYNDHURST

P.O. Box 28, Woodstock NY 12498. (845)331-7900. **Fax:** (845)331-7484. **E-mail:** crafts@artrider.com.

Website: www.artrider.com. Estab. 1984. Fine arts & crafts show held annually in early to mid September. Outdoors. Accepts photography, wearable and nonwearable fiber, jewelry, clay, leather, wood, glass, painting, drawing, prints, mixed media. Juried by 5 images of work and 1 of booth, viewed sequentially. Number of exhibitors: 275. Attendance: 14,000. Admission: $10. Artists should apply at www.artrider. com or www.zapplication.org. Deadline for entry: end of May. Application fee: $45. Space fee: $795-895. Exhibition space: 10×10 ft. For more information, artists should e-mail, visit website, call.

FALL FEST IN THE PARK
117 W. Goodwin St., Prescott AZ 86303. (928)445-2000 or (800)266-7534. **E-mail:** chamber@prescott. org; scott@prescott.org. **Website:** www.prescott.org. Estab. 1981. Arts & crafts show held annually in mid-October. Outdoors. Accepts photography, ceramics, painting, sculpture, clothing, woodworking, metal art, glass, floral, home décor. No resale. Juried. Photos of work, booth, and artist creating work are required. Number of exhibitors: 150. Public attendance: 6,000-7,000. Free to public. Application can be printed from website or obtained by phone request. Deposit: $50, nonrefundable. Electricity is limited and has a fee of $15. Deadline: Spaces are sold until show is full. Exhibition space: $250; $275 for food booth; 10×15 ft. For more information, artists should e-mail, visit website or call.

FALL FESTIVAL OF ART AT QUEENY PARK
P.O. Box 31265, St. Louis MO 63131. (314)889-0433. **E-mail:** info@gslaa.org. **Website:** artfairatqueeny park.com. Estab. 1976. Fine arts & crafts show held annually Labor Day weekend at Queeny Park. Indoors. Accepts photography, all fine art and fine craft categories. Juried by 4 jurors; 5 slides shown simultaneously. Awards/prizes: 3 levels, ribbons, $4,000+ total prizes. Number of exhibitors: 130-140. Public attendance: 4,000-6,000. Admission: $5. Artists should apply online. Application fee: $25. Booth fee: $225; $250 for corner booth. Deadline for entry: mid-June, see website for specific date. Exhibition space: 80 sq. ft. (8×10) For more information, artists should e-mail or visit website.
TIPS "Excellent, professional slides; neat, interesting booth. But most important—exciting, vibrant, eye-catching artwork."

FALL FINE ART & CRAFTS AT BROOKDALE PARK
473 Watchung Ave., Bloomfield NJ 07003. (908)874-5247. **Fax:** (908)874-7098. **E-mail:** info@rosesquared. com. **Website:** www.rosesquared.com. **Contact:** Howard Rose, vice president. Estab. 1998. Fine arts & crafts show held annually in mid-October. Outdoors. Accepts photography and all other mediums. Juried. Number of exhibitors: 160. Public attendance: 12,000. Free to public. Artists should apply on the website. Deadline for entry: mid-September. Application fee: $25. Space fee: varies by booth size. Exhibitor space: 120 sq. ft. See application form on website for details. For more information, artists should visit the website. **TIPS** "Have a range of products and prices."

FARGO'S DOWNTOWN STREET FAIR
Downtown Community Partnership, 210 Broadway N., #202, Fargo ND 58102. (701)241-1570; (701)451-9062. **Fax:** (701)241-8275. **E-mail:** fargostreetfair@ downtownfargo.com. **Website:** www.downtownfar go.com. **Contact:** Stephanie Holland, street fair consultant. Estab. 1975. "This juried event is located in historic Downtown Fargo on Broadway in July. It is a street fair that successfully combines arts & crafts, food, marketplace, music and entertainment. It attracts a large number of visitors from the tri-state region/Winnepeg and many vacationers. The locals also look forward to it every year! The show is largely made up of traditional crafts, jewelry, clothing and is focused on increasing its fine arts entries each year." Outdoors. Accepts food/culinary, mixed media, pottery/ceramic, wood furniture, glass, music, printmaking, wood other, jewelry, naturals/floral, recycled/found object/green, leather, painting, sculpture, metal, photography, textiles/fibers/clothing. Number of exhibitors: 300. Public attendance: 130,000-150,000. Free to public. "Artists should apply online and submit 3 photos for the jury: 3 images of your work, 1 image of booth, and 4 images of process." All JPEG photos must be 300 dpi and be at least 1,800×1,200 pixels. Deadline for entry: mid-February. Space fee: $325-700 depending on size and/or corner. Exhibition space: 11×11. For more information, artists should visit www.downtownfargo.com. Fair located in downtown Fargo.

FAUST HERITAGE FESTIVAL
15185 Olive Blvd., St. Louis MO 63017. (314)615-8328. **E-mail:** lritchey@stlouisco.com. **Website:** www.

stlouisco.com/parks. **Contact:** Lori Ritchey, museum educator. Historic arts & crafts festival held annually in September. Outdoors. Accepts historic arts & crafts, watercolor, jewelry, wood , floral, baskets, prints, drawing, mixed media, folk art. Must be approved by staff to attend festival. Number exhibitors: 20-30. Number of attendees: 4,000. Admission: $5 adults; $2 children ages 4-12, 3 & under free. Apply by contacting festival coordinator. Deadline for entry: August. Space fee: 15% of gross sales. Exhibition space: varies; set up must be historically accurate with no plastic tents. For more information, artists should e-mail.

FESTIVAL IN THE PARK

(704)338-1060. **E-mail:** festival@festivalinthepark. org. **Website:** www.festivalinthepark.org. Estab. 1964. Fine arts & crafts show held annually in late September (3rd Friday after Labor Day). Outdoors. Accepts photography and all arts mediums. Awards/prizes: $4,000 in cash awards. Number of exhibitors: 180. Public attendance: 100,000. Free to the public. Artists should apply by visiting website for application. Application/space fee: $390. Exhibition space: 10×10 ft. For more information, artists should e-mail, visit website, call.

FILLMORE JAZZ FESTIVAL

Steven Restivo Event Services, LLC, P.O. Box 151017, San Rafael CA 94915. (800)310-6563. **Fax:** (415)456-6436. **Website:** www.fillmorejazzfestival.com. Estab. 1984. Fine arts & crafts show and jazz festival held annually 1st weekend of July in San Francisco, between Jackson & Eddy Streets. Outdoors. Accepts photography, ceramics, glass, jewelry, paintings, sculpture, metal clay, wood, clothing. Juried by prescreened panel. Number of exhibitors: 250. Public attendance: 100,000. Free to public. Deadline for entry: ongoing; apply online. Exhibition space: 8×10 ft. or 10×10 ft. Average gross sales/exhibitor: $800-11,000. For more information, artists should visit website or call.

FINE ART & CRAFTS AT ANDERSON PARK

274 Bellevue Ave., Upper Montclair NJ 07043. (908)874-5247. **Fax:** (908)874-7098. **E-mail:** info@rosesquared.com. **Website:** www.rosesquared.com. Estab. 1984. Fine art & craft show held annually in mid-September. Outdoors. Accepts photography and all other mediums. Juried. Number of exhibitors: 160. Public attendance: 12,000. Free to the public. Artists should apply on the website. Deadline for entry: mid-

August. Application fee: $25. Space fee varies by booth size; see application form on website for details. For more information, artists should visit the website.
TIPS "Create a range of sizes and prices."

FINE ART & CRAFTS AT VERONA PARK

542 Bloomfield Ave., Verona NJ 07044. (908)874-5247. **Fax:** (908)874-7098. **E-mail:** info@rosesquared.com. **Website:** www.rosesquared.com. **Contact:** Howard Rose, vice president. Estab. 1986. Fine arts & crafts show held annually in mid-May. Outdoors. Accepts photography and all other mediums. Juried. Number of exhibitors: 140. Public attendance: 10,000. Free to public. Artists should apply on the website. Deadline for entry: mid-April. Application fee: $25. Space fee varies by booth size; see application form on website for details. For more information, artists should visit the website.
TIPS "Have a range of sizes and price ranges."

FOOTHILLS ARTS & CRAFTS FAIR

2753 Lynn Rd., Suite A, Tryon NC 28782-7870. (828)859-7427. **E-mail:** info@blueridgebbqfestival.com. **Website:** www.blueridgebbqfestival.com. Estab. 1994. Fine arts & crafts show and Blue Ridge BBQ Festival/Championship held annually the 2nd Friday and Saturday in June. Outdoors. Accepts contemporary, traditional and fine art by artist only; nothing manufactured or imported. Juried. Number of exhibitors: 50. Public attendance: 15,000+. Public admission: $8; 12 and under free. Artists should apply by downloading application from website or sending personal information to e-mail or mailing address. See website for deadline for entry. Jury fee: $25, nonrefundable. Space fee: $175. Exhibition space: 10×10 ft. For more information, artists should e-mail or visit website.
TIPS "Have an attractive booth, unique items, and reasonable prices."

FOUNTAIN HILLS FINE ART & WINE AFFAIRE

15648 N. Eagles Nest Dr., Fountain Hills AZ 85268. (480)837-5637. **Fax:** (480)837-2355. **E-mail:** info@thunderbirdartists.com. **Website:** www.thunderbirdartists.com. **Contact:** Denise Colter, president. Estab. 2005. Fine arts & crafts show held annually in March. Outdoors. Accepts photography, paintings, bronzes, baskets, jewelry, stone, pottery. Juried; CEO blind juries by medium. Number of exhibitors: 125. Public attendance: 20,000. Public admission: $3. Apply online at www.zapplication.org. Deadline for entry:

November (see website for specifics). Application fee: $30. Space fee: $430-1,240. Exhibition space: 10×10 to 10×30 ft. For more information, artists should e-mail, call or see website.

TIPS "A clean, gallery-type presentation is very important."

FOURTH AVENUE STREET FAIR

434 E. Ninth St., Tucson AZ 85705. (520)624-5004 or (800)933-2477. **Fax:** (520)624-5933. **E-mail:** kurt@ fourthavenue.org. **Website:** www.fourthavenue.org. **Contact:** Kurt. Estab. 1970. Arts & crafts fair held annually in late March/early April and December (see website for details). Outdoors. Accepts photography, drawing, painting, sculpture, arts & crafts. Juried by 5 jurors. Awards/prizes: Best of Show. Number of exhibitors: 400. Public attendance: 300,000. Free to the public. Artists should apply by completing the online application at www.zapplication.org. Requires 4 photos of art/craft and 1 booth photo. $35 application fee. Booth fee $505, additional $150 for corner booth. Deadline for entry: see website for details. Exhibition space: 10×10 ft. Average gross sales/exhibitor: $3,000. For more information, artists should e-mail, visit website, call, send SASE. Fair located on 4th Ave., between 9th St. and University Ave.

FOURTH STREET FESTIVAL FOR THE ARTS & CRAFTS

P.O. Box 1257, Bloomington IN 47402. (812)575-0484; (812)335-3814. **E-mail:** info@4thstreet.org. **Website:** www.4thstreet.org. Estab. 1976. Fine arts & crafts show held annually Labor Day weekend. Outdoors. Accepts photography, clay, glass, fiber, jewelry, painting, graphic, mixed media, wood. Juried by a 4-member panel. Awards/prizes: Best of Show ($750), 1st, 2nd, 3rd in 2D and 3D. Number of exhibitors: 105. Public attendance: 25,000. Free to public. Artists should apply by sending requests by mail, e-mail or download application from website at www.zapplication.org. Exhibition space: 10×10 ft. Average gross sales/exhibitor: $2,700. For more information, artists should e-mail, visit website, call or send for information with SASE. Show located at 4th St. and Grant St. adjacent to Indiana University.

TIPS Be professional.

FRANKFORT ART FAIR

P.O. Box 566, Frankfort MI 49635. (231)352-7251. **Fax:** (231)352-6750. **E-mail:** fcofc@frankfort-elberta. com. **Website:** www.frankfort-elberta.com. **Contact:**

Joanne Bartley, executive director. Fine art fair held annually in August. Outdoors. Accepts photography, clay, glass, jewelry, textiles, wood, drawing/graphic arts, painting, sculpture, baskets, mixed media. Juried by 3 photos of work, 1 photo of booth display and 1 photo of work in progress. Prior exhibitors are not automatically accepted. No buy/sell allowed. Artists should apply online website, e-mailing or calling. Deadline for entry: May 1 ($50 late fee). Jury fee: $25. Space fee: $125 for Friday and Saturday. Exhibition space: 12×12 ft. For more information, artists should e-mail or visit website. Fair located in Market Square Park.

FREDERICK FESTIVAL OF THE ARTS

22 S. Market St., Suite 3, Frederick MD 21701. (301)662-4190. **Fax:** (301)663-3084. **E-mail:** info@ frederickartscouncil.org. **Website:** www.frederick artscouncil.org. Juried 2-day fine arts festival held annually the 1st weekend of June along Carroll Creek Linear Park in downtown Frederick. Features approximately 110 artists from across the country, 2 stages of musical performances, children's crafts and activities, artist demonstrations, as well as interactive classical theater performances. For more information, including application deadlines and fees, visit website. Festival takes place in Carroll Creek Linear Park in downtown Frederick.

FUNKY FERNDALE ART SHOW

Integrity Shows, P.O. Box 1070, Ann Arbor MI 48106. **E-mail:** info@integrityshows.com. **Website:** www. funkyferndaleartfair.com. **Contact:** Mark Loeb. Estab. 2004. Fine arts & crafts show held annually in September. Outdoors. Accepts photography and all fine art and craft mediums; emphasis on fun, funky work. Juried by 3 independent jurors. Awards/prizes: purchase and merit awards. Number of exhibitors: 120. Public attendance: 30,000. Free to the public. Application fee: $25. Booth fee: $295. Electricity limited; fee: $100. For more information, artists should visit our website.

TIPS "Show enthusiasm. Keep a mailing list. Develop collectors."

GAITHERSBURG-KENTLANDS DOWNTOWN ART FESTIVAL

270 Central Blvd., Suite 107B, Jupiter FL 33458. (561)746-6615. **Fax:** (561)746-6528. **E-mail:** info@ artfestival.com. **Website:** www.artfestival.com. **Contact:** Malinda Ratliff, communications manag-

er. Estab. 2015. Fine art & craft fair held annually in September. Outdoors. Accepts photography, jewelry, mixed media, sculpture, wood, ceramic, glass, painting, digital, fiber, metal. Juried. Number exhibitors: see website. Number attendees: see website. Free to public. Apply online via zapplication.org. Deadline: see website. Application fee: $25. Space fee: $450. Exhibition space: 10×10 and 10×20. For more information, artists should e-mail, call, or visit website.

○ Festival located at The Streets of Market and Main at Kentlands Downtown.

○ GARRISON ART CENTER'S JURIED FINE CRAFTS FAIR

23 Garrison's Landing, P.O. Box 4, Garrison NY 10524. (845)424-3960. **E-mail:** info@garrisonart center.org. **Website:** www.garrisonartcenter.org. Outdoor, riverside fine crafts show held annually on the third weekend in August. 85 exhibitors are selected to exhibit and sell handmade original work. Entries are judged based on creativity, originality and quality. Annual visitors 4,000-5,000. Visit our website for information, prospectus, and application. Fair located at Garrison's Landing.

TIPS "Have an inviting booth and be pleasant and accessible. Don't hide behind your product—engage the audience."

○ GENEVA ARTS FAIR

8 S. Third St., Geneva IL 60134. (630)232-6060. **E-mail:** chamberinfo@genevachamber.com. **Website:** www.genevachamber.com. Fine arts show held annually in late-July (see website for details). Outdoors. Juried. "The unprecedented Geneva Arts Fair transforms downtown Geneva into a venue for over 150 esteemed artists and draws a crowd of more than 20,000. The juried show was voted a Top 200 Fine Craft Fair by *Art Fair SourceBook* and a previous winner of 'Best Craft or Art Show' by *West Suburban Living* magazine." Accepts photography, ceramics, fiber, printmaking, mixed media, watercolor, wood, sculpture and jewelry. Application deadline: early February. Please visit www.emevents.com to apply.

GERMANTOWN FESTIVAL

P.O. Box 381741, Germantown TN 38183. (901)757-9212. **Website:** www.germantownfest.com. Estab. 1971. Arts & crafts show held annually the weekend after Labor Day. Outdoors. Accepts photography, all arts & crafts mediums. Number of exhibitors: 400+. Public attendance: 65,000. Free to public. Artists should apply by sending applications by mail. Deadline for entry: until filled. Application/space fee: $200-250. Exhibition space: 10×10 ft. For more information, artists should e-mail, call or send SASE. Show located atGermantown Civic Club Complex 7745 Poplar Pike.

TIPS "Display and promote to the public. Price attractively."

○ GLOUCESTER WATERFRONT FESTIVAL

38 Charles St., Rochester NH 03867. (603)332-2616. **E-mail:** info@castleberryfairs.com; terrym@world path.net. **Website:** www.castleberryfairs.com. **Contact:** Terry Mullen, events coordinator. Estab. 1971. Arts & crafts show held the 3rd weekend in August in Gloucester MA. Outdoors in Stage Fort Park. Accepts photography and all other mediums. Juried by photo, slide or sample. Number of exhibitors: 225. Public attendance: 50,000. Free to the public. Artists should apply by downloading application from website. Deadline for entry: until full. Space fee: $375. Exhibition space: 10×10 ft. Average gross sales/exhibitor: "Generally, this is considered an 'excellent' show, so I would guess most exhibitors sell ten times their booth fee, or in this case, at least $3,500 in sales." For more information, artists should visit website. Show located in Stage Fort Park, Hough Ave., Gloucester NH.

TIPS "Do not bring a book; do not bring a chair. Smile and make eye contact with everyone who enters your booth. Have them sign your guest book; get their e-mail address so you can let them know when you are in the area again. And, finally, make the sale—they are at the fair to shop, after all."

GOLD RUSH DAYS

P.O. Box 774, Dahlonega GA 30533. **E-mail:** DahlonegaJayceesFestival@gmail.com. **Website:** www.dahlonegajaycees.com. Arts & crafts show held annually the 3rd full week in October. Accepts photography, paintings and homemade, handcrafted items. No digitally originated artwork. Outdoors. Number of exhibitors: 300. Public attendance: 200,000. Application fee of $25. Free to the public. Artists should apply online under "Gold Rush," or send SASE to request application. Deadline: March. Exhibition space: 10×10 ft. Artists should e-mail, visit website for more information. Show located at the public square and historic district.

TIPS "Talk to other artists who have done other shows and festivals. Get tips and advice from those in the same line of work."

GOOD OLD SUMMERTIME ART FAIR

P.O. Box 1753, Kenosha WI 53141. (262)654-0065. **E-mail:** info@kenoshaartassociation.org. **Website:** www.kenoshaartassociation.org. Estab. 1975. Fine arts show held annually the 1st Sunday in June. Outdoors. Accepts photography, paintings, drawings, mosaics, ceramics, pottery, sculpture, wood, stained glass. Juried by a panel. Photos or slides required with application. Number of exhibitors: 100. Public attendance: 3,000. Free to public. Artists should apply by completing application form, and including fees and SASE. Deadline for entry: early April. Exhibition space: 12×12 ft. For more information, artists should e-mail, visit website or send SASE.

TIPS "Have a professional display, and be friendly."

GRAND FESTIVAL OF THE ARTS & CRAFTS

P.O. Box 429, Grand Lake CO 80447-0429. (970)627-3402. **Fax:** (970)627-8007. **E-mail:** glinfo@grandlakechamber.com. **Website:** www.grandlakechamber.com. Fine arts & crafts show held annually in June and September. Outdoors. Accepts photography, jewelry, leather, mixed media, painting, paper, sculpture, wearable art. Juried by chamber committee. Awards/prizes: Best in Show and People's Choice. Number of exhibitors: 60-75. Public attendance: 1,000+. Free to public. Artists should apply by submitting slides or photos. Deadline for entry: early June and early September. Application fee: $175; includes space fee and business license. No electricity available. Exhibition space: 10×10 ft. For more information, artists should e-mail or call. Show held at Town Square Park on Grand Ave.

GREAT LAKES ART FAIR

46100 Grand River Ave., Novi MI 48374. (248)348-5600, ext. 208. **Fax:** (248)347-7720. **E-mail:** info@greatlakesartfair.com. **Website:** www.greatlakesartfair.com. **Contact:** Andrea Picklo, event manager. Estab. 2009. Held in April. Accepts paintings, sculptures, metal and fiber work, jewelry, 2D and 3D art, ceramics and glass. Cash prizes are given. Number of exhibitors: 150-200. Public attendance: 12,000-15,000. Application fee: $30. Space fee: $400-800. Exhibition space: 10×12 ft.

TIPS E-mail, call, or visit website for more information.

GREAT NECK STREET FAIR

Showtiques Crafts, Inc., 1 Orient Way, Suite F, #127, Rutherford NJ 07070. (201)869-0406. **E-mail:** showtiques@gmail.com. **Website:** www.showtiques.com. Estab. 1978. Fine arts & crafts show held annually in early May (see website for details) in the Village of Great Neck. "Welcomes professional artists, craftspeople and vendors of upscale giftware." Outdoors. Accepts photography, all arts & crafts made by the exhibitor. Juried. Number of exhibitors: 250. Public attendance: 50,000. Free to public. Deadline for entry: until full. Space fee: $150-250. Exhibition space: 10×10 ft. For more information, artists should e-mail, visit website or call.

GREENWICH VILLAGE ART FAIR

711 N. Main St., Rockford IL 61103. (815)968-2787. **Fax:** (815)316-2179. **E-mail:** nsauer@rockfordartmuseum.org. **Website:** www.rockfordartmuseum.org/gvaf.html. **Contact:** Nancy Sauer. Estab. 1948. Juried. 2-day Outdoor fine art fair held annually in September. $4,500 in Best of Show and Judges' Choice Awards. Number of exhibitors: 155. Public attendance: 7,000. Application fee $30. Booth fee: $225. Deadline for entry: April 30. Exhibition space: 10×10 ft. Apply online through www.zapplication.org.

GUILFORD CRAFT EXPO

P.O. Box 589, Guilford CT 06437. (203)453-5947. **E-mail:** expo@guilfordartcenter.org. **Website:** www.guilfordartcenter.org. Estab. 1957. Fine craft & art show held annually in mid-July. Outdoors. Accepts photography, wearable and nonwearable fiber, metal and nonmetal jewelry, clay, leather, wood, glass, painting, drawing, prints, mixed media, sculpture. Juried by 5 images of work, viewed sequentially. Number of exhibitors: 180. Public attendance: 9,000. Public admission: $7 and $9. Artists should apply online at www.zapplication.org (preferred) or by downloading an application at www.guilfordartcenter.org. Deadline for entry: early January. Application fee: $40. Space fee: $680. Exhibition space: 10×10 ft. For more information, artists should e-mail, visit website, call.

HALIFAX ART FESTIVAL

P.O. Box 2038, Ormond Beach FL 32175-2038. (386)304-7247; (407)701-1184. **E-mail:** patabernathy2012@hotmail.com. **Website:** www.halifaxartfestival.com. Estab. 1962. Fine arts & crafts fair held annually in November. Outdoors. Accepts handmade crafts, ceramics, fiber, glass, jewelry, mixed media, 2D, painting, photography, and sculpture. Juried. Awards/prizes: Best of Show, Judges' Choice, Awards of Excellence, Awards of Distinction, Awards of Honor, Awards of Merit, Student Art Awards, Purchase Award, Patron Purchase Award. Number exhibitors: 200. Number attendees: 45,000. Free to public. Apply online. Deadline for entry: August. Application fee: $30. Space fee: $225 (competitive); $125 (non competitive). Exhibition space: see website. For more information, artists should e-mail, call, or visit website.

⊕ HERKIMER COUNTY ARTS & CRAFTS FAIR

100 Reservoir Rd., Herkimer NY 13350. (315)866-0300, ext. 8459. **Fax:** (315)866-1706. **E-mail:** fuhrerjm@herkimer.edu. **Website:** www.herkimer.edu/ac. **Contact:** Jan Fuhrer, coordinator. Estab. 1976. Fine art & craft show held annually in mid-November on Veterans Day weekend. Indoors. Accepts photography and all handcrafted artwork. Juried by a committee. Awards/prizes: ribbons. Number of exhibitors: 120+. Public attendance: 4,000. Admission: $4. Deadline: May 1 or until filled. Application fee: $10. Exhibition space: 10×6 ft. Space fee: $155. For more information, artists should call, e-mail, or send SASE.

⊕ HIGHLAND MAPLE FESTIVAL

P.O. Box 223, Monterey VA 24465. (540)468-2550. **Fax:** (540)468-2551. **E-mail:** highcc@cfw.com; info@highlandcounty.org. **Website:** www.highlandcounty.org. Estab. 1958. Fine arts & crafts show held annually the 2nd and 3rd weekends in March. Indoors and outdoors. Accepts photography, pottery, weaving, jewelry, painting, wood crafts, furniture. Juried by 5 photos or slides. Photos need to include one of setup and your workshop. Number of exhibitors: 150. Public attendance: 35,000-50,000. "Vendors accepted until show is full." Exhibition space: 10×10 ft. For more information, artists should e-mail, visit website, or call.
TIPS "Have quality work and good salesmanship."

⊕ HIGHLANDS ART LEAGUE'S ANNUAL FINE ARTS & CRAFTS FESTIVAL

1989 Lakeview Dr., Sebring FL 33870. (863)385-5312. **E-mail:** director@highlandsartleague.org. **Website:** www.highlandsartleague.org. **Contact:** Martile Blackman, festival director. Estab. 1966. Fine arts & crafts show held annually first Saturday in November. Outdoors. Accepts photography, pottery, painting, jewelry, fabric. Juried based on quality of work.

Awards/prizes: monetary awards. Number of exhibitors: 100+. Public attendance: more than 15,000. Free to the public. Artists should apply by calling or visiting website for application form. Deadline for entry: September 1. Exhibition space: 10×14 and 10×28 ft. Artists should e-mail for more information. Festival held in Circle Park in downtown Sebring.

⊕ ⊕ HILTON HEAD ISLAND ART FESTIVAL WITH CRAFT MARKETPLACE

270 Central Blvd., Suite 107B, Jupiter FL 33458. (561)746-6615. **Fax:** (561)746-6528. **E-mail:** info@artfestival.com. **Website:** www.artfestival.com. **Contact:** Malinda Ratliff, communications manager. Estab. 2009. Fine art & craft fair held annually in late May. Outdoors. Accepts photography, jewelry, mixed media, sculpture, wood, ceramic, glass, painting, digital, fiber, metal. Juried. Number exhibitors: 100. Number attendees: 60,000. Free to public. Apply online via www.zapplication.org. Deadline: see website. Application fee: $25. Space fee: $375. Exhibition space: 10×10 and 10×20. For more information, artists should e-mail, call, or visit website.
⊕   Festival located at Shelter Cove Harbour and Marina on Hilton Head Island.

⊕ HINSDALE FINE ARTS FESTIVAL

22 E. First St., Hinsdale IL 60521. (630)323-3952. **Fax:** (630)323-3953. **E-mail:** info@hinsdalechamber.com. **Website:** www.hinsdalechamber.com. Fine arts show held annually in mid-June. Outdoors. Accepts photography, ceramics, painting, sculpture, fiber arts, mixed media, jewelry. Juried by 3 images. Awards/prizes: Best in Show, President's Award and 1st, 2nd and 3rd place in 2D and 3D categories. Number of exhibitors: 140. Public attendance: 2,000-3,000. Free to public. Artists should apply online at www.zapplication.org. Deadline for entry: First week in March. Application fee: $30. Space fee: $275. Exhibition space: 10×10 ft. For more information, artists should e-mail or visit website.
TIPS "Original artwork sold by artist."

⊕ ⊕ HOBE SOUND FESTIVAL OF THE ARTS & CRAFT SHOW

270 Central Blvd., Suite 107B, Jupiter FL 33458. (561)746-6615. **Fax:** (561)746-6528. **E-mail:** info@artfestival.com. **Website:** www.artfestival.com. **Contact:** Malinda Ratliff, communications manager. Estab. 2006. Fine art & craft fair held annually in February. Outdoors. Accepts photography, jewelry, mixed me-

dia, sculpture, wood, ceramic, glass, painting, digital, fiber, metal. Juried. Number exhibitors: 130. Number attendees: 70,000. Free to public. Apply online via zapplication.org. Deadline: see website. Application fee: $25. Space fee: $395. Exhibition space: 10×10 and 10×20. For more information, artists should e-mail, call, or visit website.

○ Show located at A1A/Dixie Highway where the street intersects with Bridge Road in Hobe Sound FL.

♦ HOLIDAY CRAFTMORRISTOWN

P.O. Box 28, Woodstock NY 12498. (845)331-7900. **Fax:** (845)331-7484. **E-mail:** crafts@artrider.com. **Website:** www.artrider.com. Estab. 1990. Fine arts & crafts show held annually in early December. Indoors. Accepts photography, wearable and nonwearable fiber, jewelry, clay, leather, wood, glass, painting, drawing, prints, mixed media. Juried by 5 images of work and 1 of booth, viewed sequentially. Number of exhibitors: 165. Public attendance: 5,000. Public admission: $9. Artists should apply online at www.artrider.com or www.zapplication.org. Deadline for entry: end of May. Application fee: $45. Space fee: $545. Exhibition space: 10×10 ft. For more information, artists should e-mail, visit website, call.

♦ HOLIDAY FINE ARTS & CRAFTS SHOW

60 Ida Lee Dr., Leesburg VA 20176. (703)777-1368. **Fax:** (703)737-7165. **E-mail:** lfountain@leesburgva. gov. **Website:** www.idalee.org. Estab. 1990. Arts & crafts show held annually the 1st full weekend in December. Indoors. Accepts handcrafted items only, including but not limited to: photography, jewelry, pottery, baskets, clothing, gourmet food products, wood work, fine art, accessories, pet items, soaps/lotions and florals. Juried. Number of exhibitors: 95. Public attendance: 2,500. Free to public. Artists should apply by downloading application from website. Deadline for entry: August 31. Space fee: $110-150. Exhibition space: 10×7 ft. and 10×10 ft. For more information, artists should e-mail or visit website.

♦ HOLLY ARTS & CRAFTS FESTIVAL

P.O. Box 64, Pinehurst NC 28370. (910)295-7462. **E-mail:** info@pinehurstbusinessguild.com. **Website:** www.pinehurstbusinessguild.com. Estab. 1978. Annual arts & crafts show held 3rd Saturday in October. Outdoors. Accepts quality photography, arts and crafts. Juried based on uniqueness, quality of product and overall display. Number of exhibitors: 200. Public attendance: 7,000. Free to the public. Submit 3 color photos, 2 of work to be exhibited, 1 of booth. Deadline : Late March. Application fee: $25 by separate check. Space fee: $75. Electricity fee: $5 Exhibition space: 10×10 ft. For more information, artists should call or visit website.

HOME, CONDO AND OUTDOOR ART & CRAFT FAIR

P.O. Box 486, Ocean City MD 21843. (410)213-8090. **Fax:** (410)213-8092. **E-mail:** events@oceanpromotions.info. **Website:** www.oceanpromotions.info. Estab. 1984. Fine arts & crafts show held annually in March. Indoors. Accepts photography, carvings, pottery, ceramics, glass work, floral, watercolor, sculpture, prints, oils, pen and ink. Number of exhibitors: 50. Public attendance: 9,000. Public admission: $7/adults; $6/seniors & students; 13 and under free; military, fire and police free. Artists should apply by e-mailing request for info and application. Deadline for entry: until full. Space fee: $250. Exhibition space: 10×10 ft. For more information, artists should e-mail, visit website or call. Show held in the R.E. Powell Ocean City Convention Center.

HOME DECORATING & REMODELING SHOW

P.O. Box 230699, Las Vegas NV 89105-0699. (702)450-7984; (800)343-8344. **Fax:** (702)451-7305. **E-mail:** showprosadmin@cox.net. **Website:** www.nashville homeshow.com. Estab. 1983. Home show held annually in early September (see website for details). Indoors. Accepts photography, sculpture, watercolor, oils, mixed media, pottery. Awards/prizes: Outstanding Booth Award. Number of exhibitors: 350-400. Public attendance: 20,000. Public admission: $10 (discount coupon available on website); Seniors 62+ free on Friday; children 12 & under free with adult. Artists should apply by calling. Marketing is directed to middle and above income brackets. Deadline for entry: open until filled. Space fee: starts at $950. Exhibition space: 10×10 ft. or complements of 10×10 ft. For more information, artists should call or visit website.

♦ HOT SPRINGS ARTS & CRAFTS FAIR

308 Pullman, Hot Springs AR 71901. (501)623-9592. **E-mail:** sephpipkin@aol.com. **Website:** www. hotspringsartsandcraftsfair.com. **Contact:** Peggy Barnett. Estab. 1968. Fine arts & crafts show held annually the 1st full weekend in October at the Garland

County Fairgrounds. Indoors and outdoors. Accepts photography and varied mediums ranging from heritage, crafts, jewelry, furniture. Juried by a committee of 12 volunteers. Number of exhibitors: 350+. Public attendance: 50,000+. Free to public. Deadline for entry: August. Space fee: $125 (single); $250 (double). Exhibition space: 10×10 or 10×20 ft. For more information, and to apply, artists should e-mail, call, or visit website. Fair located at Garland County Fairgrounds.

☺ HYDE PARK ARTS & CRAFTS ADVENTURE

P.O. Box 1326, Palatine IL 60078. (312)751-2500, (847)991-4748. **Fax:** (847)221-5853. **E-mail:** asoaartists@aol.com. **Website:** www.americansocietyofartists.org. Estab. 2006. Arts & crafts show held once a year in late September. Event held in Chicago. Outdoors. Accepts photography, painting, glass, wood, fiber arts, hand-crafted candles, quilts, sculpture and more. Juried. Please submit 4 images representative of your work you wish to exhibit, 1 of your display set-up, your first/last name, physical address, daytime telephone number—résumé/show listing helpful. Number of exhibitors: 50. Free to the public. Artists should apply by submitting jury materials. Please submit to: asoaartists@aol.com. If juried in, you will receive a jury/approval number. See website for jurying online. Deadline for entry: 2 months prior to show or earlier if available. Entry fee: to be announced. Exhibition space: approximately 100 sq. ft. for single space; other sizes are available. For more information, artists should send SASE, submit jury material. Show located at University of Chicago's Hyde Park Shopping Center.
TIPS "Remember that when you are at work in your studio, you are an artist. But when you are at a show, you are a business person selling your work."

☺ STAN HYWET HALL & GARDENS OHIO MART

714 N. Portage Path, Akron OH 44303. (330)315-3255. **E-mail:** ohiomart@stanhywet.org. **Website:** www.stanhywet.org. Estab. 1966. Artisan crafts show held annually 1st full weekend in October. Outdoors. Accepts photography and all mediums. Juried via mail application. Awards/prizes: Best Booth Display. Number of exhibitors: 150. Public attendance: 15,000-20,000. Deadline varies. Application fee: $25, non-refundable. Application available online. Exhibition

space: 10×10 or 10×15 ft. For more information, artists should visit website or call.

☺ INDIANA ART FAIR

650 W. Washington St., Indianapolis IN 46204. (317)233-9348. **Fax:** (317)233-8268. **E-mail:** cmiller@indianamuseum.org. **Website:** www.indianamuseum.org. Estab. 2004. Annual art/craft show held the 2nd weekend of February. Indoors. Juried event; 5-6 judges award points in 3 categories. 60 exhibitors; 3,000 attendees. $13 admission for the public. Application fee $25. Space fee $165; 80 sq. ft. Accepts ceramics, glass, fiber, jewelry, painting, sculpture, mixed media, drawing/pastels, garden, leather, surface decoration, wood, metal, printmaking, and photography.
TIPS "Make sure that your booth space complements your product and presents well. Good photography can be key for juried shows."

☺ INDIAN WELLS ARTS FESTIVAL

78-200 Miles Ave., Indian Wells CA 92210. (760)346-0042. **Fax:** (760)346-0042. **E-mail:** info@indianwellsartsfestival.com. **Website:** www.indianwellsartsfestival.com. **Contact:** Dianne Funk, producer. "A premier fine arts festival attracting thousands annually. The Indian Wells Arts Festival brings a splash of color to the beautiful grass concourse of the Indian Wells Tennis Garden. This spectacular venue transforms into an artisan village featuring 200 judged and juried artists and hundreds of pieces of one-of-a-kind artwork available for sale. Enjoy special exhibits and demonstrations. Watch glass blowing, monumental rock sculpting, wood carving, pottery wheel, weaving and painting. Wine tasting, gourmet market, children's activities, entertainment and refreshments add to the festival atmosphere." Apply online at indianwellsartsfestival.com/artists.html. See website for more information.

⊕ INDIE SOUTH FAIR

660 N. Chase St., Athens GA 30601. **E-mail:** indiesouthfair@gmail.com. **Website:** www.indiesouthfair.com. **Contact:** Serra Ferguson, organizer. Estab. 2007. Arts & Crafts show held annually the 1st weekends of May & December. Outdoors. Accepts handmade crafts and all other mediums. Exhibitors: 100. Number of attendees: 3,000. Free to public. Apply via website. Deadline for entry: March 2nd for Spring show; September 28 for holiday market. Application fee: $15. Space fee: $175 (10×10); $90 (6×4). Exhibition space:

10×10; 6×4. Average sales: $800-1,200. For more information send e-mail.

🎧 INTERNATIONAL FOLK FESTIVAL

301 Hay St., Fayetteville NC 28302. (910)323-1776. **Fax:** (910)323-1727. **E-mail:** bobp@theartscouncil. com. **Website:** www.theartscouncil.com. Estab. 1978. Fine arts & crafts show held annually the last weekend in September. Outdoors. Accepts photography, painting of all mediums, pottery, woodworking, sculptures. Work must be original. Number of exhibitors: 120+. Public attendance: 85,000-100,000 over 2 days. Free to public. Artists should apply on the website. Exhibition space: 10×10 ft. For more information, artists should e-mail or visit website. Festival held in Festival Park/downtown Fayetteville.

TIPS "Have reasonable prices."

🎧 ISLE OF EIGHT FLAGS SHRIMP FESTIVAL

P.O. Box 17251, Fernandina Beach FL 32035. (904)701-2786. **Website:** www.islandart.org. Estab. 1963. Fine arts & crafts show and community celebration held annually the 1st weekend in May. Outdoors. Accepts all mediums. Juried. Awards: $9,000 in cash prizes. Number of exhibitors: 300. Public attendance: 150,000. Free to public. Artists should apply by downloading application from website. Slides are not accepted. Digital images in JPEG format only must be submitted on a CD/DVD with application. Deadline for entry: January 31. Application fee: $30 (non-refundable). Space fee: $225. Exhibition space: 10×12 ft. Average gross sales/exhibitor: $1,500+. For more information, artists should visit website.

🎧 JOHNS HOPKINS UNIVERSITY SPRING FAIR

3400 N. Charles St., Mattin Suite 210, Baltimore MD 21218. (410)516-7692. **Fax:** (410)516-6185. **E-mail:** info@jhuspringfair.com; springfair.artsandcrafts@ gmail.com. **Website:** www.jhuspringfair.com. Estab. 1972. Fine arts & crafts, campus-wide festival held annually in April. Outdoors. Accepts photography and all mediums. Juried. Number of exhibitors: 80. Public attendance: 20,000+. Free to public. Artists should apply via website. Deadline for entry: early March. Application and space fee: $200. Exhibition space: 10×10 ft. For more information, artists should e-mail, visit website, or call. Fair located on Johns Hopkins Homewood Campus.

TIPS "Artists should have fun displays, good prices, good variety and quality pieces."

🎧 JUBILEE FESTIVAL

Eastern Shore Chamber of Commerce, P.O. Drawer 310, Daphne AL 36526. (251)621-8222; (251)928-6387. **Fax:** (251)621-8001. **E-mail:** lroberts@eschamber. com; office@eschamber.com. **Website:** www.eschamber.com. **Contact:** Liz Roberts. Estab. 1952. Fine arts & crafts show held in late September in Olde Towne of Daphne AL. Outdoors. Accepts photography and fine arts and crafts. Juried. Awards/prizes: ribbons and cash prizes total $4,300 with Best of Show $750. Number of exhibitors: 258. Free to the public. Jury fee: $20. Space fee: $100 for single; $200 for double. Exhibition space: 10×10 ft. or 10×20 ft. For more information, and application form, artists should e-mail, call, see website. Festival located in "Olde Towne" Daphne on Main St.

🎧 KALAMAZOO INSTITUTE OF ARTS FAIR

Kalamazoo Institute of Arts,, 314 S. Park St., Kalamazoo MI 49007. (269)349-7775. **Fax:** (269)349-9313. **E-mail:** joeb@kiarts.org. **Website:** www.kiarts.org/artfair. **Contact:** Joe Bower. Estab. 1951. Fine jurored art fair held annually in June. Outdoors. "The KIA's annual art fair has been going strong for 64 years. Still staged in shady, historic Bronson Park, the fair boasts more hours, more artists and more activities. It now spans 2 full days. The art fair provides patrons with more time to visit and artists with an insurance day in case of rain. Some 190 artists will be invited to set up colorful booths. Numerous festivities are planned, including public art activities, musical performances, a beer garden and an artist dinner. For more information, visit www.kiarts.org/artfair." Apply via www.zapplication.org. Application fee: $30. Booth fee: $275.

🎧 KENTUCK FESTIVAL OF THE ARTS

503 Main Ave., Northport AL 35476. (205)758-1257. **Fax:** (205)758-1258. **E-mail:** kentuck@kentuck.org. **Website:** www.kentuck.org. **Contact:** Amy Echols, executive director. Call or e-mail for more information. General information about the festival available on the website. "Celebrates a variety of artistic styles ranging from folk to contemporary arts as well as traditional crafts. Each of the 250+ artists participating in the festival is either invited as a guest artist or is juried based on the quality and originality of their work. The guest artists are nationally recognized folk and

visionary artists whose powerful visual images continue to capture national and international acclaim." Festival held at Kentuck Park.

🎧 KETNER'S MILL COUNTY ARTS FAIR

P.O. Box 322, Lookout Mountain TN 37350. (423)267-5702. **E-mail:** contact@ketnersmill.org. **Website:** www.ketnersmill.org. **Contact:** Dee Nash, event coordinator. Estab. 1977. Arts & crafts show held annually the 3rd weekend in October held on the grounds of the historic Ketner's Mills, in Whitwell TN, and the banks of the Sequatchie River. Outdoors. Accepts photography, painting, prints, dolls, fiber arts, baskets, folk art, wood crafts, jewelry, musical instruments, sculpture, pottery, glass. Juried. Number of exhibitors: 170. Number of attendees: 10,000/day, depending on weather. Artists should apply online. Space fee: $125. Electricity: $10 limited to light use. Exhibition space: 15×15 ft. Average gross sales/exhibitor: $1,500. Fair held at Ketner's Mill.

TIPS "Display your best and most expensive work, framed. But also have smaller unframed items to sell. Never underestimate a show: Someone may come forward and buy a large item."

➕ 🎧 KEY BISCAYNE ART FESTIVAL

270 Central Blvd., Suite 107B, Jupiter FL 33458. (561)746-6615. **Fax:** (561)746-6528. **E-mail:** info@art festival.com. **Website:** www.artfestivalc.com. **Contact:** Malinda Ratliff, communications manager. Estab. 1964. Fine art & craft fair held annually in March. Outdoors. Accepts photography, jewelry, mixed media, sculpture, wood, ceramic, glass, painting, digital, fiber, metal. Juried. Number exhibitors: 125. Number attendees: 50,000. Free to public. Apply online via zapplication.org. Deadline: see website. Application fee: $25. Space fee: $395. Exhibition space: 10×10 and 10×20. For more information, artists should e-mail, call, or visit website.

🎧 Festival located at Village Green Park in Key Biscayne FL.

🎧 KINGS DRIVE ART WALK

Little Sugar Creek Greenway, Charlotte NC 28203. (704)338-1060. **E-mail:** festival@festivalinthepark.org. **Website:** www.festivalinthepark.org. **Contact:** Julie Whitney Austin, executive director. Estab. 1964. Fine art & craft show held annually in late April. Outdoors. Accepts photography. Juried. Number of exhibitors: 75. Public attendance: 25,000+. Free to public.

Artists should apply online at www.festivalinthepark.org/kingsdrive.asp. Deadline for entry: March 1. Application/space fee: $260. Exhibition space: 10×10 ft. For more information, artists should e-mail, call, or visit website.

🎧 KINGS MOUNTAIN ART FAIR

13106 Skyline Blvd., Woodside CA 94062. (650)851-2710. **E-mail:** kmafsecty@aol.com. **Website:** www.kingsmountainartfair.org. **Contact:** Carrie German, administrative assistant. Estab. 1963. Fine arts & crafts show held annually Labor Day weekend. Fundraiser for volunteer fire dept. Accepts photography, ceramics, clothing, 2D, painting, glass, jewelry, leather, sculpture, textile/fiber, wood. Juried. Number of exhibitors: 138. Public attendance: 10,000. Free to public. Deadline for entry: January 30. Application fee: $20 (online). Exhibition space: 10×10 ft. Average gross sales/exhibitor: $3,500. For more information, artists should e-mail or visit website.

TIPS "Located in Redwood Forest South of San Francisco. Keep an open mind and be flexible."

➕ 🎧 KPFA CRAFT FAIR

1929 MLK Jr. Way, Berkeley CA 94704. (510)848-6767 ext. 243. **E-mail:** events@kpfa.org. **Website:** www.kpfa.org/craftsfair/. **Contact:** Jan Etre, coordinator. Fine arts & crafts fair held annually in December. Indoors. Accepts handmade crafts, ceramics, fiber, glass, jewelry, mixed media, 2D, painting, photography, and sculpture. Juried. Number exhibitors: 200. Number attendees: see website. Admission: $10; disabled, 65+ and children under 17 free. Apply online. Deadline for entry: see website. Application fee: $20. Space fee: varies. Exhibition space: 10×10. For more information, artists should email, call, or visit website.

🎧 KRASL ART FAIR ON THE BLUFF

707 Lake Blvd., St. Joseph MI 49085. (269)983-0271. **Fax:** (269)983-0275. **E-mail:** info1@krasl.org. **Website:** www.krasl.org. **Contact:** Sara Shambarger; Colleen Villa. Estab. 1962. Fine arts & fine craft show held annually the 2nd weekend of July (see website for details). Outdoors. Accepts art in 19 media categories including photography, painting (oils, acrylics & watercolors), digital art, drawing, pastels, fibers (wearable and decorative), clay (functional and nonfunctional), glass, jewelry (precious and nonprecious), sculpture, printmaking and graphics, metals (mixed media 2D and 3D) and woods. Number of exhibitors:

200. Number of attendees: thousands. Free to public. Application fee: $30. Applications are available online through www.zapplication.org. Deadline for entry: early January. There is on-site jurying the same day of the fair and approximately 30% are invited back without having to pay the $30 application fee. Space fee: $275. Exhibition space: 10×10 to 15×15 ft. or $300 for 20×20 ft. (limited). "Krasl Art Fair on the Bluff is ranked: #10 in the *Sunshine Artist Magazine's* 200 Best for 2014; #8 on the Art Fair Calendar's new Best Art Shows List from their 2014 survey; #48 in the *Art Fair Source Book's* Top 100 shows." For more information, artists should e-mail or visit website.

🌐 LAKE CITY ARTS & CRAFTS FESTIVAL

P.O. Box 1147, Lake City CO 81235. (817)343-3305. E-mail: info@lakecityarts.org; kerrycoy@aol.com. Website: www.lakecityarts.org. Estab. 1975. Fine arts/arts & craft show held annually 3rd Tuesday in July. One-day event. Outdoors. Accepts photography, jewelry, metal work, woodworking, painting, handmade items. Juried by 3-5 undisclosed jurors. Prize: Winners are entered in a drawing for a free booth space in the following year's show. Number of exhibitors: 85. Public attendance: 500. Free to the public. Space fee: $75. Jury fee: $10. Exhibition space: 12×12 ft. Deadline for submission: mid April. Average gross sales/exhibitor: $500-$1,000. For more information, and application form, artists should visit website. Festival located at the Lake City Town Park and along Silver St.

TIPS "Repeat vendors draw repeat customers. People like to see their favorite vendors each year or every other year. If you come every year, have new things as well as your best-selling products."

🌐 LA QUINTA ARTS FESTIVAL

78150 Calle Tampico #215, La Quinta CA 92253. (760)564-1244. **Fax:** (760)564-6884. **E-mail:** helpline@lqaf.com. **Website:** www.lqaf.com. **Contact:** artists: Kathleen Hughes, events manager; photographers: Christi Salamone, executive director. Estab. 1983. Fine arts & crafts festival held annually. Outdoors. Accepts mixed-media 2D/3D, printmaking, photography, drawing and pastel, painting, jewelry, ceramics, fiber, sculpture, glass, wood. Juried over 3 days online by 5 jury members per each of the 11 media categories. Awards/prizes: cash, automatic acceptance into future show, gift cards from premier local restaurants, hotel package, ad in *SW Art*. Number of exhibitors: 230. Public attendance: 28,000+. Admis-

sion: $15-day pass; $20 multiday pass. Artists should apply via www.zapplication.org only. Deadline for entry: September 30. Jury fee: $50. Space fee: $275. Exhibition space: 12×12 ft. Average exhibitor sales: $13,450. For more information, artists should visit website.

TIPS "Make sure that booth image looks like an art gallery! Less is more."

➕ 🌐 LAS OLAS ART FAIR

270 Central Blvd., Suite 107B, Jupiter FL 33458. (561)746-6615. **Fax:** (561)746-6528. **E-mail:** info@artfestival.com. **Website:** www.artfestival.com. **Contact:** Malinda Ratliff, communications manager. Estab. 1988. Fine art & craft fair held annually in January, March and mid-October. Outdoors. Accepts photography, jewelry, mixed media, sculpture, wood, ceramic, glass, painting, digital, fiber, metal. Juried. Number exhibitors: 150. Number attendees: 70,000. Free to public. Apply online via www.zapplication.org. Deadline: see website. Application fee: $25. Space fee: $395. Exhibition space: 10×10 and 10×20. For more information, artists should e-mail, call, or visit website.

💬 Fair located on Las Olas Blvd. in Ft. Lauderdale FL.

🌐 LEEPER PARK ART FAIR

22180 Sundancer Court, #504, Estero FL 33928. (574)276-2942. **Fax:** (574)272-8598. **E-mail:** Studio266@aol.com. **Website:** www.leeperparkartfair.org. **Contact:** Judy Ladd, director. Estab. 1968. Fine arts & crafts show held annually in June. Outdoors. Accepts photography and all areas of fine art. Juried. Awards/prizes: $3,700. Number of exhibitors: 120. Public attendance: 10,000. Free to public. Artists should apply by going to the website and clicking on "To Apply." Deadline for entry: early March. Space fee: $330. Exhibition space: 12×12 ft. Average gross sales/exhibitor: $5,000. For more information, artists should e-mail, call, or visit website.

TIPS "Make sure your booth display is well presented and, when applying, slides are top notch!"

🌐 LES CHENEAUX FESTIVAL OF ARTS

P.O. Box 147, Cedarville MI 49719. (517)282-4950. **E-mail:** lcifoa@gmail.com. **Website:** www.lescheneaux.net/?annualevents. **Contact:** Rick Sapero. Estab. 1976. Fine arts & crafts show held annually 2nd Saturday in August. Outdoors. Accepts photography and all other media; original work and design only; no kits or commercially manufactured goods. Juried by a committee of 10. Submit 4 slides (3 of the artwork; 1 of booth display). Awards: monetary prizes for excellent and original work. Number of exhibitors: 70. Public attendance: 8,000. Public admission: $7. Artists should fill out application form to apply. Deadline for entry: March 15. Booth fee: $75; Jury fee: $5. Exhibition space: 10×10 ft. Average gross sales/exhibitor: $5-500. For more information, artists should call, send SASE, or visit website.

○ ☺ LIBERTY ARTS SQUARED

P.O. Box 302, Liberty MO 64069. **E-mail:** staff@ libertyartssquared.org. **Website:** www.liberty artssquared.org. Estab. 2010. Outdoor fine art/craft show held annually. Accepts all mediums. Awards: prizes totaling $4,000; Visual Arts for Awards $1,500; Folk Art for Awards $1,500; Overall Best of Show Award $500. Free admission to the public; free parking. Application fee: $25. Space fee: $200. Exhibition space: 10×10 ft. For more information, e-mail, or visit website.

☺ LILAC FESTIVAL ARTS & CRAFTS SHOWS

26 Goodman St., Rochester NY 14607. (585)244-0951. **E-mail:** lyn@rochesterevents.com. **Website:** www.rochesterevents.com. Estab. 1985. Arts & crafts shows held annually in mid-May (see website for details). Outdoors. Accepts photography, painting, ceramics, woodworking, metal sculpture, fiber. Juried by a panel. Number of exhibitors: 120. Public attendance: 25,000. Free to public. Exhibition space: 10×10 ft. Space fee: $200. For more information, and to apply, artists should e-mail or visit website. Festival held at Highland Park in Rochester NY.

➕ LIONS CLUB ARTS & CRAFTS FESTIVAL

Henderson Lions Club, P.O. Box 842, Henderson KY 42419. **E-mail:** lionsartsandcrafts@gmail.com. **Website:** www.lionsartsandcrafts.com. Estab. 1972. Formerly Gradd Arts & Crafts Festival. Arts & crafts show held annually 1st full weekend in October. Outdoors. Accepts photography taken by crafter only. Number of exhibitors: 100-150. Public attendance: 10,000+. Artists should apply by calling to be put on mailing list. Space fee: $100. Exhibition space: 15×15 ft. For more information, artists should e-mail, visit website, or call. Festival located at John James Audubon State Park.

TIPS "Be sure that only hand-crafted items are sold. No buy/sell items will be allowed."

☺ LOMPOC FLOWER FESTIVAL

414 W. Ocean Ave., Lompoc CA 93436. (805)735-8511. **E-mail:** lompocvalle1@verizon.net. **Website:** www.lompocvalleyartassociation.com. **Contact:** Kathy Badrak. Estab. 1942. Sponsored by Lompoc Valley Art Association, Cyprus Gallery. Show held annually last week in June. Festival event includes a parade, food booths, entertainment, beer garden and commercial center, which is not located near arts & crafts area. Outdoors. Accepts photography, fine art, woodworking, pottery, stained glass, fine jewelry. Juried by 5 members of the LVAA. Vendor must submit 3 photos of their work and a description on how they make their art. Artists should apply by downloading application from website. Deadline for entry: early May. Space fee: $375 (single); $575 (double); $100 cleaning deposit (to be refunded after show-see application for details). Exhibition space: 12×16 ft. For more information, artists should visit website.

➕ ☺ LOUISVILLE FESTIVAL OF THE ARTS WITH CRAFT MARKETPLACE AT PADDOCK SHOPS

270 Central Blvd., Suite 107B, Jupiter FL 33458. (561)746-6615. **Fax:** (561)746-6528. **E-mail:** info@artfestival.com. **Website:** www.artfestival.com. **Contact:** Malinda Ratliff, communications manager. Estab. 2008. Fine art & craft fair held annually in mid-June. Outdoors. Accepts photography, jewelry, mixed media, sculpture, wood, ceramic, glass, painting, digital, fiber, metal. Juried. Number exhibitors: 130. Number attendees: 50,000. Free to public. Apply online via www.zapplication.org. Deadline: see website. Application fee: $25. Space fee: $375. Exhibition space: 10×10 and 10×20. For more information, artists should e-mail, call, or visit website.

〇 Show located at Paddock Shops on Summit Plaza Dr. in Louisville KY.

☺ LUTZ ARTS & CRAFTS FESTIVAL

(813)949-7060; (813)949-1937. Estab. 1979. Fine arts & crafts show held annually in December in Lutz FL. Outdoors. Accepts fine arts, jewelry, painting, photography, sculpture, crafts. Juried. Number of exhibitors: 250. Public attendance: 35,000. Admission fee: $2 per car (for parking). Deadline for entry: September 1 or until category is full. Exhibition space: 12×12 ft. For more information, artists should e-mail fsincich@gmail.com or call. Festival takes place at Lake Park.

MADISON CHAUTAUQUA FESTIVAL OF ART

601 W. First St., Madison IN 47250. (812)265-6100. **Fax:** (812)273-3694. **E-mail:** georgie@madisonchautauqua.com. **Website:** www.madisonchautauqua.com. **Contact:** Georgie Kelly, coordinator. Estab. 1971. Premier juried fine arts & crafts show, featuring painting, photography, stained glass, jewelry, textiles pottery and more, amid the tree-lined streets of Madison's historic district. Held annually the last weekend in September. Stop by the Riverfront FoodFest for a variety of foods to enjoy. Relax and listen to the live performances on the Lanier Mansion lawn, on the plaza and along the riverfront. Takes place in late September. Painting (2D artists may sell prints, but must include originals as well), photography, pottery, sculpture, wearable, jewelry, fiber, wood, baskets, glass, paper, leather. The number of artists in each category is limited to protect the integrity of the show. Festival held in Madison's National Landmark Historic District.

➕ ⊕ MAIN STREET TO THE ROCKIES ART FESTIVAL

270 Central Blvd., Suite 107B, Jupiter FL 33458. (561)746-6615. **Fax:** (561)746-6528. **E-mail:** info@artfestival.com. **Website:** www.artfestival.com. **Contact:** Malinda Ratliff, communications manager. Estab. 2007. Fine art & craft fair held annually in mid-August. Outdoors. Accepts photography, jewelry, mixed media, sculpture, wood, ceramic, glass, painting, digital, fiber, metal. Juried. Number exhibitors: 100. Number attendees: 60,000. Free to public. Apply online via www.zapplication.org. Deadline: see website. Application fee: $35. Space fee: $475. Exhibition space: 10×10 and 10×20. For more information, artists should e-mail, call, or visit website.

◒ Festival located at Main St. in Downtown Frisco CO.

➕ ⊕ MARCO ISLAND FESTIVAL OF THE ARTS

270 Central Blvd., Suite 107B, Jupiter FL 33458. (561)746-6615. **Fax:** (561)746-6528. **E-mail:** info@artfestival.com. **Website:** www.artfestival.com. **Contact:** Malinda Ratliff, communications manager. Estab. 2014. Fine art & craft fair held annually in mid-March. Outdoors. Accepts photography, jewelry, mixed media, sculpture, wood, ceramic, glass, painting, digital, fiber, metal. Juried. Number exhibitors: 175. Number attendees: 40,000. Free to public. Apply online via www.zapplication.org. Deadline: see website. Application fee: $25. Space fee: $415. Exhibition space: 10×10 and 10×20. For more information, artists should e-mail, call, or visit website.

◒ Festival located at Veteran's Park off N. Collier Blvd. in Marco Island FL.

⊕ MASON ARTS FESTIVAL

Mason-Deerfield Arts Alliance, P.O. Box 381, Mason OH 45040. (513)309-8585. **E-mail:** masonarts@gmail.com; info@the-arts-alliance.org. **Website:** www.masonarts.org. Fine arts & crafts show held annually in mid-September (see website for details). Indoors and outdoors. Accepts photography, graphics, printmaking, mixed media; painting and drawing; ceramics, metal sculpture; fiber, glass, jewelry, wood, leather. Juried. Awards/prizes: $3,000+. Number of exhibitors: 75-100. Public attendance: 3,000-5,000. Free to the public. Artists should apply by visiting website for application, e-mailing or calling. Deadline for entry: see website. Jury fee: $25. Space fee: $75. Exhibition space: 12×12 ft.; artist must provide 10×10 ft. pop-up tent.

◒ City Gallery show is held indoors; these artists are not permitted to participate outdoors and vice versa. City Gallery is a juried show featuring approximately 30-50 artists who may show up to 2 pieces.

⊕ MEMORIAL WEEKEND ARTS & CRAFTS FESTIVAL

38 Charles St., Rochester NH 03867. (603)332-2616. **Fax:** (603)332-8413. **E-mail:** info@castleberryfairs.com. **Website:** www.castleberryfairs.com. **Contact:** Sherry Mullen. Estab. 1989. Arts & crafts show held annually on Memorial Day weekend in Meredith NH. Outdoors. Accepts photography and all other mediums. Juried by photo, slide or sample. Number of exhibitors: 85. Public attendance: 7,500. Free to the public. Artists should apply by downloading application from website. Deadline for entry: until full. Space fee: $225. Exhibition space: 10×10 ft. For more information, artists should visit website. Festival held at Mill Falls Marketplace.

TIPS "Do not bring a book; do not bring a chair. Smile and make eye contact with everyone who enters your booth. Have them sign your guest book; get their e-mail address so you can let them know when you are in the area again. And, finally, make the sale—they are at the fair to shop, after all."

🌐 MICHIGAN STATE UNIVERSITY HOLIDAY ARTS & CRAFTS SHOW

49 Abbot Rd., Room 26, MSU Union, East Lansing MI 48824. (517)355-3354. **E-mail:** uab@rhs.msu.edu; artsandcrafts@uabevents.com. **Website:** www.uabevents.com. **Contact:** Stephanie Bierlein. Estab. 1963. Arts & crafts show held annually the 1st weekend in December. Indoors. Accepts photography, basketry, candles, ceramics, clothing, sculpture, soaps, drawings, floral, fibers, glass, jewelry, metals, painting, graphics, pottery, wood. Selected by a committee using photographs submitted by each vendor to eliminate commercial products. They will evaluate on quality, creativity and crowd appeal. Number of exhibitors: 171. Public attendance: 15,000. Free to public. Artists should apply online. Exhibition space: 8×5 ft. For more information, artists should visit website or call.

🌐 MICHIGAN STATE UNIVERSITY SPRING ARTS & CRAFTS SHOW

49 Abbot Rd., Room 26, MSU Union, East Lansing MI 48824. (517)355-3354. **Fax:** (517)432-2448. **E-mail:** artsandcrafts@uabevents.com. **Website:** www.uabevents.com. **Contact:** Stephanie Bierlein. Estab. 1963. Arts & crafts show held annually the weekend before Memorial Day weekend in mid-May in conjunction with the East Lansing Art Festival. Both shows are free for the public to attend. Outdoors. Accepts photography, basketry, candles, ceramics, clothing, sculpture, soaps, drawings, floral, fibers, glass, jewelry, metals, painting, graphics, pottery, wood. Juried by a committee using photographs submitted by each vendor to eliminate commercial products. They will evaluate on quality, creativity and crowd appeal. Number of exhibitors: 329. Public attendance: 30,000. Free to public. Artists can apply online beginning in February. Online applications will be accepted until show is filled. Application fee: $310 ($290 if apply online). Exhibition space: 10×10 ft. (double booth available, $600 or $580 online). For more information, artists should visit website or call.

🌐 MID-MISSOURI ARTISTS CHRISTMAS ARTS & CRAFTS SALE

P.O. Box 116, Warrensburg MO 64093. (660)747-6092. **E-mail:** rlimback@iland.net. Estab. 1970. Holiday arts & crafts show held annually in November. Indoors. Accepts photography and all original arts and crafts. Juried by 3 good-quality color photos (2 of the artwork, 1 of the display). Number of exhibitors: 50.

Public attendance: 1,200. Free to the public. Artists should apply by e-mailing or calling for an application form. Entry form also available at www.midmissouriartists.webs.com. Deadline for entry: early November. Space fee: $50. Exhibition space: 10×10 ft. For more information, artists should e-mail or call.

TIPS "Items under $100 are most popular."

➕ 🌐 MISSION FEDERAL ARTWALK

2210 Columbia St., San Diego CA 92101. (619)615-1090. **Fax:** (619)615-1099. **E-mail:** info@artwalksandiego.org. **Website:** www.artwalksandiego.org. Fine arts & crafts fair held annually in April. Outdoors. Accepts handmade crafts, jewelry, ceramics, painting, photography, digital, printmaking and more. Juried. Number exhibitors: 350. Number attendees: 90,000. Free to public. Apply online. Deadline for entry: January. Application fee: none. Space fee: varies. Exhibition space: varies. For more information, artists should e-mail, call, or visit website.

MONTAUK ARTISTS' ASSOCIATION, INC.

P.O. Box 2751, Montauk NY 11954. (631)668-5336. **E-mail:** montaukart@aol.com. **Website:** montaukartistsassociation.org; www.montaukchamber.com. **Contact:** Anne Weissman. Estab. 1970. 501(c)(3). Arts & crafts show held annually Memorial Day weekend; 3rd weekend in August. Outdoors. Accepts photography, paintings, prints (numbered and signed in bins), sculpture, limited fine art, jewelry and ceramics. Number of exhibitors: 90. Public attendance: 8-10,000. Free to public. Exhibition space: 12×12. For more information, artists should call or visit website.

MOUNTAIN STATE FOREST FESTIVAL

P.O. Box 388, 101 Lough St., Elkins WV 26241. (304)636-1824. **Fax:** (304)636-4020. **E-mail:** msff@forestfestival.com; mwileman@forestfestival.com. **Website:** www.forestfestival.com. **Contact:** Cindy Nucilli, executive director. Estab. 1930. Arts, crafts & photography show held annually in early October. Accepts photography and homemade crafts. Awards/prizes: cash awards for photography only. Number of exhibitors: 50+. Public attendance: 75,000. Free to the public. Artists should apply by requesting an application form. For more information, artists should visit website, call, or visit Facebook page (search "Mountain State Forest Festival").

MOUNT GRETNA OUTDOOR ART SHOW

P.O. Box 637, Mount Gretna PA 17064. (717)964-3270. **Fax:** (717)964-3054. **E-mail:** mtgretnaart@comcast. net. **Website:** www.mtgretnaarts.com. Estab. 1974. Fine arts & crafts show held annually 3rd full weekend in August. Outdoors. Accepts photography, oils, acrylics, watercolors, mixed media, jewelry, wood, paper, graphics, sculpture, leather, clay/porcelain. Juried by 4 professional artists who assign each applicant a numeric score. The highest scores in each medium are accepted. Awards/prizes: Judges' Choice Awards: 30 artists are invited to return the following year, jury exempt; the top 10 are given a monetary award of $250. Number of exhibitors: 250. Public attendance: 15,000-19,000. Public admission: $10; children under 12 free. Artists should apply via www.zapplication.org. Deadline for entry: April 1. Application fee: $25. Space fee: $350 per 10×12 ft. space; $700 per 10×24 ft. double space. For more information, artists should e-mail, visit website, call.

NAPERVILLE WOMAN'S CLUB ART FAIR

(630)209-1246. **E-mail:** naperartfair@comcast.net. **Website:** www.napervillewomansclub.org. **Contact:** Roxanne Lang. "Over 100 local and national artists will be displaying original artwork in clay, fiber, glass, jewelry, mixed media, metal, painting, photography, sculpture and wood. Ribbons and cash prizes are awarded to winning artists by local judges and NWC. The Naperville Woman's Club Art Fair is the longest continuously running art fair in Illinois. Activities at this event include entertainment, a silent auction, artist demonstrations, the Empty Bowl Fundraiser to benefit local food pantries, and the Petite Picassos children's activities tent. This is the largest fundraiser of the year for the Naperville Woman's Club. Proceeds from the event help fund a local art scholarship and local charities. Admission and parking are free. For more information please email us at: naperartfair@ comcast.net."

NEW ENGLAND CRAFT & SPECIALTY FOOD FAIR

38 Charles St., Rochester NH 03867. (603)332-2616. **Fax:** (603)332-8413. **E-mail:** info@castleberryfairs. com. **Website:** www.castleberryfairs.com. Estab. 1995. Arts & crafts show held annually on Veterans Day weekend in Salem NH. Indoors. Accepts photog-

raphy and all other mediums. Juried by photo, slide or sample. Number of exhibitors: 200. Public attendance: 15,000. Artists should apply by downloading application from website. Deadline for entry: until full. Space fee: $350-450. Exhibition space: 10×6 or 10×10 ft. Average gross sales/exhibitor: "Generally, this is considered an 'excellent' show, so I would guess most exhibitors sell 10times their booth fee, or in this case, at least $3,000 in sales." For more information, artists should visit website. Fair is held at Rockingham Park Racetrack.

TIPS "Do not bring a book; do not bring a chair. Smile and make eye contact with everyone who enters your booth. Have them sign your guest book; get their e-mail address so you can let them know when you are in the area again. And, finally, make the sale—they are at the fair to shop, after all."

NEW MEXICO ARTS AND CRAFTS FAIR

2501 San Pedro St. NE, Suite 110, Albuquerque NM 87110. (505)884-9043. **E-mail:** info@nmartsand craftsfair.org. **Website:** www.nmartsandcraftsfair.org. Estab. 1962. Fine arts & craft show held annually in June. Indoors. Accepts decorative and functional ceramics, digital art, drawing, fiber, precious and non-precious jewelry, photography, paintings, printmaking, mixed media, metal, sculpture and wood. *Only New Mexico residents 18 years and older are eligible.* See website for more details.

NEW ORLEANS JAZZ & HERITAGE FESTIVAL

336 Camp St., Suite 250, New Orleans LA 70130. (504)410-4100. **Fax:** (504)558-6121. **Website:** www. nojazzfest.com. **Contact:** Mandy Dillon. Estab. 1970. This festival showcases music, cuisine, arts and crafts from the region and around the world. The Louisiana Heritage Fair is held at the Fair Grounds Race Course over the course of 2 weekends (late April/early May; see website for details). Apply online via www.zappli cation.org. Must submit 5 images, 4 of artwork, 1 of booth. Application fee: $30. Deadline: late December (see website for details). Call or visit website for more information.

NEW SMYRNA BEACH ART FIESTA

City of New Smyrna Beach, 210 Sams Ave., New Smyrna Beach FL 32168. (386)424-2175. **Fax:** (386)424-2177. **E-mail:** kshelton@cityofnsb.com. **Website:** www. cityofnsb.com; nsbfla.com/index.cfm. **Contact:** Kimla Shelton. Estab. 1952. Arts & crafts show held annually in February. Outdoors. Accepts photography, oil, acrylics, pastel, drawings, graphics, sculpture, crafts, watercolor. Awards/prizes: $15,000 prize money; $1,600/category; Best of Show. Number of exhibitors: 250. Public attendance: 14,000. Free to public. Artists should apply by calling to get on mailing list. Applications are always mailed out the day before Thanksgiving. Deadline for entry: until full. Exhibition space: 10×10 ft. For more information, artists should call. Show held in the Old Fort Park area.

☻ NEW WORLD FESTIVAL OF THE ARTS

P.O. Box 2300, Manteo NC 27954. (252)473-2838; (252)473-2133. **E-mail:** dareartsinfo@gmail.com. **Website:** www.townofmanteo.com. **Contact:** Edward Greene. Estab. 1963. Fine arts & crafts show held annually in mid-August (see website for details). Outdoors. Juried. Location is the Waterfront in downtown Manteo. Features 80 selected artists from Vermont to Florida exhibiting and selling their works. Application fee: $15. Space fee: $85.

NORTH CONGREGATIONAL PEACH & CRAFT FAIR

17 Church St., New Hartford CT 06057. (860)379-2466. **Website:** www.northchurchucc.com. **Contact:** K.T. "Sully" Sullivan. Estab. 1966. Arts & crafts show held annually in mid-August. Outdoors on the Green at Pine Meadow. Accepts photography, most arts and crafts. Number of exhibitors: 50. Public attendance: 500-2,000. Free to public. Artists should call for application form. Deadline for entry: August. Application fee: $60. Exhibition space: 11×11 ft.
TIPS "Be prepared for all kinds of weather."

☻ OAK PARK AVENUE-LAKE ARTS & CRAFTS SHOW

P.O. Box 1326, Palatine IL 60078. (312)751-2500; (847)991-4748. **E-mail:** asoaartists@aol.com. **Website:** www.americansocietyofartists.org. Estab. 1974. Fine arts & crafts show held annually in mid-August. Event held in Oak Park IL. Outdoors. Accepts photography, painting, graphics, sculpture, glass, wood, paper, fiber arts, mosaics and more. Juried. Please submit 4 images representative of your work you wish to exhibit, 1 of your display set-up, your first/last name, physical address, daytime telephone number—résumé/show listing helpful. Number of exhibitors: 150. Free to the public. Artists should apply by submitting jury materials. To jury online, submit to: asoaartists@aol.com. If juried in, you will receive a

jury/approval number. Deadline for entry: 2 months prior to show or earlier if spaces fill. Entry fee: $195. Exhibition space: approximately 100 sq. ft. for single space; other sizes available. For more information, artists should send SASE with jury material to the above address. Show takes place in Scoville Park (located in Oak Park).
TIPS "Remember that when you are at work in your studio, you are an artist. But when you are at a show, you are a business person selling your work."

☻ OC FAIR VISUAL ARTS COMPETITION

88 Fair Dr., Costa Mesa CA 92626. (714)708-1718. **E-mail:** visualarts@ocfair.com. **Website:** www.ocfair.com/competitions. **Contact:** Barbara Thompson, program coordinator, visual arts. Annual fine art and craft show held from mid-July to mid-August. Indoors. Accepted media includes: photography, 2D media, sculpture, ceramics, graphic arts, fine woodworking and film. Juried event with cash and purchase awards. Digital submissions only. Over 2,000 exhibitors each year. 1.3 million attendees. 20,000 sq. ft. exhibition space. Fair admission fee: $12. Artists should apply online at www.ocfair.com/competitions after April 1. Deadline for entry: June 1. Application fee of $10 per entry. Open to California residents 19 and older; young adults 13-18. E-mail or visit website for more information.

☻ OHIO SAUERKRAUT FESTIVAL

P.O. Box 281, Waynesville OH 45068. (513)897-8855, ext. 2. **Fax:** (513)897-9833. **E-mail:** waynesville@aol.com. **Website:** www.sauerkrautfestival.com. **Contact:** Barb Lindsay, office and event coordinator. Estab. 1969. Arts & crafts show held annually 2nd full weekend in October. Outdoors. Accepts photography and handcrafted items only. Juried by jury team. Number of exhibitors: 458. Public attendance: 350,000. Jury fee: $20. Space fee: $200 + $25 processing fee. Exhibition space: 10×10 ft. For more information, artists should visit website or call.
TIPS "Have reasonably priced items."

OLD TOWN ART FAIR

1763 N. North Park Ave., Chicago IL 60614. (312)337-1938. **E-mail:** info@oldtowntriangle.com. **Website:** www.oldtownartfair.com. Fine art festival held annually in early June (see website for details). Located in the city's historic Old Town Triangle District. Artists featured are chosen by an independent jury of professional artists, gallery owners and museum curators.

Features a wide range of art mediums, including 2D and 3D mixed media, drawing, painting, photography, printmaking, ceramics, fiber, glass, jewelry and works in metal, stone and wood. Apply online at www.zappplication.org. For more information, call, e-mail, or visit website. Fair located in Old Town Triangle District.

🎧 ON THE GREEN FINE ART & CRAFT SHOW

P.O. Box 304, Glastonbury CT 06033. (860)659-1196. **Fax:** (860)633-4301. **E-mail:** info@glastonburyarts.org. **Website:** www.glastonburyarts.org. **Contact:** Jane Fox, administrator. Estab. 1961. Fine art & craft show held annually 2nd week of September. Outdoors. Accepts photography, pastel, prints, pottery, jewelry, drawing, sculpture, mixed media, oil, acrylic, glass, watercolor, graphic, wood, fiber, etc. Juried (with 3 photos of work, 1 photo of booth). Awards/prizes: $3,000 total prize money in different categories. Number of exhibitors: 200. Public attendance: 15,000. Free to public. Artists should apply online. Deadline for entry: early June. Jury fee: $15. Space fee: $275. Exhibition space: 12×15 ft. Average gross sales/exhibitor varies. For more information, artists should visit website. Show located at Hubbard Green.

🎧 ORCHARD LAKE FINE ART SHOW

P.O. Box 79, Milford MI 48381-0079. (248)684-2613. **E-mail:** info@hotworks.org. **Website:** www.hotworks.org. **Contact:** Patty Narozny, executive director & producer. Estab. 2003. Voted in the top 100 art fairs nationwide the last 8 years in the row by *Sunshine Magazine* out of more than 4,000 art fairs. "The Orchard Lake Fine Art Show takes place in the heart of West Bloomfield, located on a street with high visibility from Orchard Lake Road, south of Maple Road, in an area that provides plenty of free parking for patrons and weekend access for local businesses. West Bloomfield MI is located adjacent to Bloomfiled Hills, listed as the #2 highest income city in the US, according to Wikipedia.org, and hoome of Cranbrook Art Institute. West Bloomfield has been voted one of *Money Magazine*'s 'Best Places to Live,' and is an upscale community with rolilng hills that provide a tranquil setting for beautiful and lavish homes. $5 admission helps support the Institute for the Arts & Education, Inc., a 501(c)(3) nonprofit organization whose focus is visual arts and community enrichment. 12 & under free. This event follows Ann Arbor, has great event hours and provides ease of move-in and move-out. All work must be original and personally handmade by the artist. There is $2,500 in professional artist awards. We accept all disciplines including sculpture, paintings, clay, glass, wood, fiber, jewelry, photography and more." Professional applications are accepted 'manual' or via www.zapplication.org. Please include 3 images of your most compelling work, plus one of your booth presentation as you would set up at the show. Space fee: $375, 10×10; 10×15, $525; 10×20, $650; add $75 for corner. "Generators are permitted as long as they do not bother anyone for any reason." Deadline to apply is March 15. "No buy/sell/import permitted. As part of our commitment to bring art education into the community, there is the Chadwick Accounting Group's Youth Art Competition for grades K-8 or ages 5-12, in which we encourage budding artists to create their original and personally handmade artwork that is publicly displayed in the show the entire weekend." $250 in youth art awards. The deadline to apply for youth art is July 1. More information can be found on the web at www.hotworks.org.

🎧 PANOPLY ARTS FESTIVAL

The Arts Council, Inc., 700 Monroe St. SW, Suite. 2, Huntsville AL 35801. (256)519-2787. **Fax:** (256)533-3811. **E-mail:** info@artshuntsville.org; vhinton@artshuntsville.org. **Website:** www.panoply.org. Estab. 1982. Fine arts show held annually the last weekend in April. Also features music and dance. Outdoors. Accepts photography, painting, sculpture, drawing, printmaking, mixed media, glass, fiber. Juried by a panel of judges chosen for their in-depth knowledge and experience in multiple mediums, and who jury from slides or disks in January. During the festival 1 judge awards various prizes. Number of exhibitors: 60-80. Public attendance: 140,000+. Public admission: $5/day or $10/weekend (children 12 and under free). Artists should e-mail, call, or go online for an application form. Deadline for entry: January. Space fee: $185. Exhibition space: 10×10 ft. (tent available, space fee $390). Average gross sales/exhibitor: $2,500. For more information, artists should e-mail or visit website. The festival is held in Big Spring International Park.

🎧 PARADISE CITY ARTS FESTIVALS

30 Industrial Dr. E, Northampton MA 01060. (800)511-9725. **Fax:** (413)587-0966. **E-mail:** artist@paradisecityarts.com. **Website:** www.paradisecityarts.com. Estab. 1995. 4 fine arts & crafts shows held

annually in March, May, October, and November. Indoors. Accepts photography, all original art and fine craft media. Juried by 5 digital images of work and an independent board of jury advisors. Number of exhibitors: 150-275. Public attendance: 5,000-20,000. Public admission: $12. Artists should apply by submitting name and address to be added to mailing list or print application from website. Deadlines for entry: April 1 (fall shows); September 9 (spring shows). Application fee: $30-45. Space fee: $855-1,365. Exhibition space varies by show, see website for more details . For more information, artists should e-mail, visit website, or call.

⊕ PARK FOREST ART FAIR

367 Artists Walk, Park Forest IL 60466. (708)748-3377. **Fax:** (708)748-9132. **E-mail:** tallgrass367@sbcglobal.net; jmuchnik@sbcglobal.net. **Website:** www.tallgrassarts.org. **Contact:** Janet Muchnik, president. Estab. 1955. Fine arts & crafts festival held annually 3rd weekend in September. Outdoors. Accepts photography and any media that would fit the criteria and meet the standards of fine art or craft. Juried by professional artists (representing several media). Jurying opens in January when "call for artists" is posted on website; closes at end of June. Jurying is done on a monthly basis so successful applicants can make plans to participate. Juried artists may also exhibit in the Tall Grass Gallery and Gift Shop. Awards/prizes: Best 2D work: $750; Best 3D work: $750; Best Jewelry: $750; 2 director's prizes: $100 each; Judge's Choice (any media); several purchase awards and 1 Purchase Prize for the Tall Grass Permanent Collection. Number of exhibitors: 70-100. Public attendance: 3,000-4,000. Free to the public. Artists should apply online. Submit 6 photographs of work by CD or e-mail. Deadline for entry: June 28. Jury fee: $35. Space fee: $175. Exhibition space: 12×10 ft. tent with space around it. "Some spaces are under an awning and do not require the use of a tent but should be requested early." For more information, artists should e-mail or visit website.

TIPS "A good display is a large key to sales; however, in recent years, fair attendees have also looked for a range of prices. This includes prints or smaller-size artworks. Exhibitors should be prepared (and willing) to talk about their artworks and techniques."

⊕ ◯ PARK POINT ART FAIR

(218)428-1916. **E-mail:** coordinator@parkpointartfair.org. **Website:** www.parkpointartfair.org. **Contact:** Carla Tamburro, art fair coordinator. Estab. 1970. Fine arts & crafts fair held annually in June. Outdoors. Accepts handmade crafts, jewelry, ceramics, painting, photography, digital, printmaking and more. Juried. Awards/prizes: $1,300 in awards. Number exhibitors: 120. Number attendees: 10,000. Free to public. Apply online. Deadline for entry: March. Application fee: $15. Space fee: $185. Exhibition space: 10×10. For more information, artists should e-mail, call, or visit website.

◯ PATTERSON APRICOT FIESTA

P.O. Box 442, Patterson CA 95363. (209)892-3118. **Fax:** (209)892-3388. **E-mail:** patterson_apricot_fiesta@hotmail.com. **Website:** www.apricotfiesta.com. **Contact:** Jaclyn Camara, chairperson. Estab. 1984. Arts & crafts show held annually in May/June. Outdoors. Accepts photography, oils, leather, various handcrafts. Juried by type of product. Number of exhibitors: 140-150. Public attendance: 30,000. Free to the public. Deadline for entry: mid-April. Application fee/space fee: $225/craft, $275/commerical. Exhibition space: 12×12 ft. For more information, artists should call, send SASE. Event held at Center Circle Plaza in downtown Patterson.

TIPS "Please get your applications in early!"

◯ PEND OREILLE ARTS COUNCIL

P.O. Box 1694, Sandpoint ID 83864. (208)263-6139; (208)255-1869. **E-mail:** art@sandpoint.net. **Website:** www.artinsandpoint.org. Estab. 1978. Arts & crafts show held annually, second week in August. Outdoors. Accepts photography and all handmade, noncommercial works. Juried by 8-member jury. Number of exhibitors: 120. Public attendance: 5,000. Free to public. Artists should apply by sending in application, available in February, along with 4 images (3 of your work, 1 of your booth space). Deadline for entry: April. Application fee: $15. Space fee: $185-280, no commission taken. Electricity: $50. Exhibition space: 10×10 ft. or 10×15 ft. (shared booths available). For more information, artists should e-mail, call, or visit website. Show located in downtown Sandpoint.

◯ PETERS VALLEY FINE CRAFT FAIR

19 Kuhn Rd., Layton NJ 07851. (973)948-5200. **E-mail:** craftfair@petersvalley.org; info@petersvalley.

org. **Website:** www.petersvalley.org. Estab. 1970. Fine craft show held annually in late September at the Sussex County Fairgrounds in Augusta NJ. Indoors/enclosed spaces. Accepts photography, ceramics, fiber, glass, basketry, metal, jewelry, sculpture, printmaking, paper, drawing, painting. Juried. Awards. Number of exhibitors: 150. Public attendance: 7,000-8,000. Public admission: $9. Artists should apply via www.zapplication.org. Deadline for entry: April 1. Application fee: $35. Space fee: $455 (includes electricity). Exhibition space: 10×10 ft. Average gross sales/exhibitor: $2,000-5,000. For more information artists should e-mail, visit website, or call.

PRAIRIE ARTS FESTIVAL

201 Schaumburg Court, Schaumburg IL 60193. (847)923-3605. **Fax:** (847)923-2458. **E-mail:** rben venuti@villageofschaumburg.com. **Website:** www.prairiecenter.org. **Contact:** Roxane Benvenuti, special events coordinator. Outdoor fine art & craft exhibition and sale featuring artists, food truck vendors, live entertainment and children's activities. Held over Saturday-Sunday of Memorial Day weekend. Located in the Robert O. Atcher Municipal Center grounds, adjacent to the Schaumburg Prairie Center for the Arts. Artist applications available in mid-January; due online or postmarked by March 6. 155 spaces available. Application fee: $110 (for 15×10 space); $220 (30×10 space). No jury fee. "With thousands of patrons in attendance, an ad in the Prairie Arts Festival program is a great way to get your business noticed. Rates are reasonable, and an ad in the program gives you access to a select regional market. Sponsorship opportunities are also available." For more information, call, e-mail or visit the website.

TIPS "Submit your best work for the jury since these images are selling your work."

PUNGO STRAWBERRY FESTIVAL

P.O. Box 6158, Virginia Beach VA 23456. (757)721-6001. **Fax:** (757)721-9335. **E-mail:** pungofestival@aol.com. **Website:** www.pungostrawberryfestival.info. Estab. 1983. Arts & crafts show held annually on Memorial Day weekend. Outdoors. Accepts photography and all media. Number of exhibitors: 60. Public attendance: 120,000. Free to public; $5 parking fee. Artists should apply by calling for application or downloading a copy from the website and mail in. Deadline for entry: early March; applications accepted from that point until all spaces are full. Notice of acceptance or denial by early April. Application fee: $50 refundable deposit. Space fee: $200 (off road location); $500 (on road location). Exhibition space: 10×10 ft. For more information, artists should e-mail, visit website or call.

PYRAMID HILL ANNUAL ART FAIR

1763 Hamilton Cleves Rd., Hamilton OH 45013. (513)868-8336. **Fax:** (513)868-3585. **E-mail:** pyramid@pyramidhill.org. **Website:** www.pyramidhill.org. Art fair held the last Saturday and Sunday of September. Application fee: $25. Booth fee: $100 for a single, $200 for a double. Call, e-mail or visit website for more information. Fair located at Pyramid Hill Sculpture Park and Museum.

TIPS "Make items affordable! Quality work at affordable prices will produce profit."

QUAKER ARTS FESTIVAL

P.O. Box 202, Orchard Park NY 14127. (716)667-2787. **E-mail:** opjaycees@aol.com; kelly@opjaycees.com. **Website:** www.opjaycees.com. Estab. 1961. Fine arts & crafts show held annually in mid-September (see website for details). 80% Outdoors, 20% indoors. Accepts photography, painting, graphics, sculpture, crafts. Juried by 4 panelists during event. Awards/prizes: over $10,000 total cash prizes, ribbons and trophies. Number of exhibitors: up to 300. Public attendance: 75,000. Free to the public. Artists can obtain applications online or by sending SASE. Deadline for entry: May 31 for returning exhibitors and then first come, first serve up to festival date (see website for details). Space fee: Before September 1: $185 (single) or $370 (double); after September 1: $210 (single) or $420 (double). Exhibition space: 10×12 ft. (outdoor), 10×6 ft. (indoor). For more information, artists should visit website or send e-mail.

TIPS "Have an inviting booth with a variety of work at various price levels."

RATTLESNAKE AND WILDLIFE FESTIVAL

P.O. Box 292, Claxton GA 30417. (912)739-3820. **E-mail:** rattlesnakewildlifefestival@yahoo.com; thall@claxtonevanschamber.com. **Website:** www.claxtonevanschamber.com; Facebook page: Rattlesnake & Wildlife Festival. Estab. 1968. Arts & crafts show held annually 2nd weekend in March. Outdoors. Accepts photography and various mediums. Number of exhibitors: 150-200. Public attendance: 15,000-20,000. Artists should apply by filling out an application. Click on the "Registration Tab" located on the Rattlesnake &

Wildlife Festival home page. Deadline for entry: late February/early March (see website for details). Space fee: $100 (outdoor); $200 (indoor). Exhibition space: 10×16 (indoor); 10×10 (outdoor). For more information, artists should e-mail, visit website or call.

TIPS "Your display is a major factor in whether people will stop to browse when passing by. Offer a variety."

⊕ ⌾ RHINEBECK ARTS FESTIVAL

P.O. Box 28, Woodstock NY 12498. (845)331-7900. **Fax:** (845)331-7484. **E-mail:** crafts@artrider.com. **Website:** www.artrider.com. **Contact:** Stacey Jarit. Estab. 2013. Festival of fine contemporary craft and art held annually in late September or early October. 150 indoors and 40 outdoors. Accepts photography, fine art, ceramics, wood, mixed media, leather, glass, metal, fiber, jewelry, sculpture. Juried. Submit 5 images of your work and 1 of your booth. Public attendance: 10,000. Public admission: $10. Artists should apply online at www.artrider.com or www.zapplication.org. Deadline for entry: first Monday in January. Application fee: $45. For more information, artists should e-mail, visit website, or call. Application fees: $0 first time Artrider applicant, $40 mailed in or online, $65 late. Space fee: $495-545. Exhibition space: 10×10 and 10×20 ft. For more information, artists should e-mail, visit website, or call.

⌾ RILEY FESTIVAL

312 E. Main St., Suite C, Greenfield IN 46140. (317)462-2141. **Fax:** (317)467-1449. **E-mail:** info@rileyfestival.com. **Website:** www.rileyfestival.com. **Contact:** Sarah Kesterson, public relations. Estab. 1970. Fine arts & crafts festival held in October. Outdoors. Accepts photography, fine arts, home arts, quilts. Juried. Awards/prizes: small monetary awards and ribbons. Number of exhibitors: 450. Public attendance: 75,000. Free to public. Artists should apply by downloading application on website. Deadline for entry: mid-September. Space fee: $185. Exhibition space: 10×10 ft. For more information, artists should visit website.

TIPS "Keep arts priced for middle-class viewers."

⌾ RIVERBANK CHEESE & WINE EXPOSITION

6618 Third St., Riverbank CA 95367-2317. (209)863-9600. **Fax:** (209)863-9601. **E-mail:** events@riverbankcheeseandwine.org. **Website:** www.riverbankcheeseandwine.org. **Contact:** Chris Elswick, event coordinator. Estab. 1977. Arts & crafts show and food show held annually 2nd weekend in October. Outdoors. Accepts photography, other mediums depends on the product. Juried by pictures and information about the artists. Number of exhibitors: 250. Public attendance: 60,000. Free to public. Artists should apply by calling and requesting an application. Applications also available on website. Deadline for entry: early September. Space fee: $300-500. Exhibition space: 12×12 ft. For more information, artists should e-mail, visit website, call or send SASE. Show located at Santa Fe & 3rd St., Riverbank CA.

TIPS Make sure your display is pleasing to the eye.

⊕ ⌾ ROTARY KEY BISCAYNE ART FESTIVAL

270 Central Blvd, Suite 107B, Jupiter FL 33458. (561)746-6615. **Fax:** (561)746-6528. **E-mail:** info@artfestival.com. **Website:** www.artfestival.com. Estab. 1963. "The annual Key Biscayne Art Fair benefits our partner and co producer, the Rotary Club of Key Biscayne. Held in Key Biscayne, an affluent island community in Miami-Dade County, just south of downtown Miami, the annual Key Biscayne Art Festival is one not to be missed! In fact, visitors plan their springtime vacations to South Florida around this terrific outdoor festival that brings together longtime favorites and the newest names in the contemporary art scene. Life-size sculptures, spectacular paintings, one-of-a-kind jewels, photography, ceramics, and much more make for one fabulous weekend." See website for more information.

⌾ ROYAL OAK OUTDOOR ART FAIR

211 Williams St., P.O. Box 64, Royal Oak MI 48068. (248)246-3180. **E-mail:** mail@royaloakartscouncil.com. **E-mail:** todg@ci.royal-oak.mi.us. **Website:** www.ci.royal-oak.mi.us. **Contact:** Recreation office staff. Estab. 1970. Fine arts & crafts show held annually in July. Outdoors. Accepts photography, collage, jewelry, clay, drawing, painting, glass, fiber, wood, metal, leather, soft sculpture. Juried. Number of exhibitors: 125. Public attendance: 25,000. Free to public. Free adjacent parking. Artists should apply with online application form at www.royaloakarts.com and 3 slides of current work. Space fee: $260 (plus a $30 nonrefundable processing fee per medium). Exhibition space: 15×15 ft. For more information, artists should e-mail, call, or visit website. Fair located at Memorial Park.

TIPS "Be sure to label your slides on the front with name, size of work and 'top.'"

SACO SIDEWALK ART FESTIVAL

P.O. Box 336, 12½ Pepperell Square, Suite 2A, Saco ME 04072. (207)286-3546. **E-mail:** sacospirit@hot mail.com. **Website:** www.sacospirit.com. Estab. 1970. Event held in late June. Annual event organized and managed by Saco Spirit, Inc., a nonprofit organization committed to making Saco a better place to live and work by enhancing the vitality of our downtown. Dedicated to promoting art and culture in our community. Space fee: $75. Exhibition space: 10×10 ft. See website for more details. Festival located in historic downtown Saco.

TIPS "Offer a variety of pieces priced at various levels."

ST. ARMANDS CIRCLE CRAFT FESTIVAL

270 Central Blvd., Suite 107B, Jupiter FL 33458. (561)746-6615. **Fax:** (561)746-6528. **E-mail:** info@art festival.com. **Website:** www.artfestival.com. **Contact:** Malinda Ratliff, communications manager. Estab. 2004. Fine art & craft fair held annually in January & November. Outdoors. Accepts photography, jewelry, mixed media, sculpture, wood, ceramic, glass, painting, digital, fiber, metal. Juried. Number exhibitors: 180-210. Number attendees: 80,000-100,000. Free to public. Apply online via www.zapplication.org. Deadline: see website. Application fee: $25. Space fee: $415-435. Exhibition space: 10×10 and 10×20. For more information, artists should e-mail, call, or visit website. Fair held in St. Armands Circle in Sarasota FL.

ST. CHARLES FINE ART SHOW

2 E. Main St., St. Charles IL 60174. (630)443-3967. **E-mail:** info@downtownstcharles.org. **Website:** www.downtownstcharles.org/fineartshow. **Contact:** Jamie Blair. Fine art show held annually in May during Memorial Day weekend. Outdoors. Accepts photography, painting, sculpture, glass, ceramics, jewelry, nonwearable fiber art. Juried by committee: submit 4 slides of art and 1 slide of booth/display. Awards/prizes: Cash awards in several categories. Free to the public. Artists can apply via website. Deadline for entry: early January. Jury fee: $35. Space fee: $375. Exhibition space: 10×10 ft. For more information, artists should e-mail or visit website.

ST. GEORGE ART FESTIVAL

50 S. Main, St. George UT 84770. (435)627-4500. **E-mail:** artadmn@sgcity.org; gary.sanders@sgcity.org; leisure@sgcity.org. **Website:** www.sgcity.org/artfes tival. **Contact:** Gary Sanders. Estab. 1979. Fine arts & crafts show held annually Easter weekend in either March or April. Outdoors. Accepts photography, painting, wood, jewelry, ceramics, sculpture, drawing, 3D mixed media, glass, metal, digital. Juried from digital submissions. Awards/prizes: $5,000 Purchase Awards. Art pieces selected will be placed in the city's permanent collections. Number of exhibitors: 110. Public attendance: 20,000/day. Free to public. Artists should apply by completing application form via EntryThingy, nonrefundable application fee, slides or digital format of 4 current works in each category and 1 of booth, and SASE. Deadline for entry: January 9. Exhibition space: 10×11 ft. For more information, artists should check website or e-mail.

TIPS "Artists should have more than 50% originals. Have quality booths and set-up to display art in best possible manner. Be outgoing and friendly with buyers."

ST. JAMES COURT ART SHOW

P.O. Box 3804, Louisville KY 40201. (502)635-1842. **Fax:** (502)635-1296. **E-mail:** mesrock@stjamescourt artshow.com. **Website:** www.sjcas.com. Estab. 1957. Annual fine arts & crafts show held the first full weekend in October. Accepts photography; has 17 medium categories. Juried in April; there is also a street jury held during the art show. Number of exhibitors: 270. Public attendance: 200,000. Free to the public. Artists should apply by visiting website and printing out an application or via www.zapplication.org. Deadline for entry: March 31 (see website for details). Application fee: $30. Space fee: $550. Exhibition space: 10×12 ft. For more information, artists should visit website.

TIPS "Have a variety of price points."

ST. LOUIS ART FAIR

225 S. Meramec Ave., Suite 105, St. Louis MO 63105. **E-mail:** info@culturalfestivals.com. **Website:** www.culturalfestivals.com. **Contact:** Laura Miller, director of operations. Estab. 1994. Fine art/craft show held annually in September, the weekend after Labor Day. Outdoors. Accepts photography, ceramics, drawings, digital, glass, fiber, jewelry, mixed-media, metalwork, printmaking, paintings, sculpture and wood. Juried event, uses 5 jurors using 3 rounds, digital app. Total

prize money available: $21,000—26 awards ranging from $500-1,000. Number of exhibitors: 180. Average attendance: 130,000. Admission free to the public. 2014 Deadline for applications: March 22. $40 application fee. Space fee: $625-725. 100 sq. ft. space. Average gross sales for exhibitor: $8.500. Apply at www.zapplication.org. For more information, call, e-mail or visit website. Fair held in the central business district of Clayton MO.

TIPS "Look at shows and get a feel for what it is."

ST. PATRICK'S DAY CRAFT SALE & FALL CRAFT SALE

P.O. Box 461, Maple Lake MN 55358-0461. **Website:** www.maplelakechamber.com. **Contact:** Kathy. Estab. 1988. Arts & crafts show held biannually in March and early November. Indoors. Number of exhibitors: 30-40. Public attendance: 300-600. Free to public. Deadline for entry: 2 weeks before the event. Exhibition space: 10×10 ft. For more information or an application, artists should visit website.

TIPS "Don't charge an arm and a leg for the items. Don't overcrowd your items. Be helpful, but not pushy."

☺ SANDY SPRINGS FESTIVAL

P.O. Box 422571, Atlanta GA 30342. (404)851-9111; (404)845-0793. **E-mail:** info@sandyspringsfestival.org; rmurphy@heritagesandysprings.org; patrick@affps.com; randall@affps.com. **Website:** www.sandyspringsfestival.com. Estab. 1985. Annual arts & crafts show held annually in mid-September. See website for details. Outdoors. Accepts photography, painting, sculpture, jewelry, furniture, clothing. Juried by artist committee. Awards/prizes: ribbons for Best in Show, 2nd Place, 3rd Place and Best Booth. Number of exhibitors: 135 maximum. Public attendance: 20,000. Public admission $5. Artists may apply via application on website or online at www.zapplication.org. Application fee: $25. Space fee: $250 for 10×10, $500 for 10×20. Average gross sales per exhibitor: $1,000. For more information, artists should e-mail or visit website.

TIPS "Many of the purchases made at Sandy Springs Festival are priced under $100. The look of the booth and its general attractiveness are very important, especially to those who might not know art."

☺ SANTA CALI GON DAYS FESTIVAL

210 W. Truman Rd., Independence MO 64050. (816)252-4745. **E-mail:** lois@ichamber.biz. **Website:** www.santacaligon.com. Estab. 1973. Market vendors 4-day show held annually Labor Day weekend. Outdoors. Ranked in top 20 for vendor profitability. Accepts handmade arts & crafts, photography, and other mediums. Juried by committee. Number of exhibitors: 250. Public attendance: 300,000. Free to public. Artists should apply online. Application requirements include completed application, full booth fee, $20 jury fee (via seperate check), 4 photos of product/art and 1 photo of display. Exhibition space: 10×10 ft. For more information, artists should e-mail, visit website or call.

SANTA FE COLLEGE SPRING ARTS FESTIVAL

3000 NW 83rd St., Gainesville FL 32606. (352)395-5355. **Fax:** (352)336-2715. **E-mail:** kathryn.lehman@sfcollege.edu. **Website:** www.springartsfestival.com. **Contact:** Kathryn Lehman, cultural programs coordinator. Fine arts and crafts festival held in mid-April (see website for details). "The festival is one of the 3 largest annual events in Gainesville and is known for its high-quality, unique artwork." Held in the downtown historic district. Public attendance: 130,000+. Call, e-mail or visit website for more information.

➕ ☺ SARASOTA CRAFT FAIR

270 Central Blvd., Suite 107B, Jupiter FL 33458. (561)746-6615. **Fax:** (561)746-6528. **E-mail:** info@artfestival.com. **Website:** www.artfestival.com. **Contact:** Malinda Ratliff, communications manager. "Behold contemporary crafts from more than 100 of the nation's most talented artisans. A variety of jewelry, pottery, ceramics, photography, painting, clothing and much more—all handmade in America—will be on display, ranging from $15-3,000. An expansive Green Market with plants, orchids, exotic flora, handmade soaps, gourmet spices and freshly popped kettle corn further compliments the weekend, blending nature with nurture." See website for more information.

☺ SAUSALITO ART FESTIVAL

P.O. Box 10, Sausalito CA 94966. (415)332-3555. **Fax:** (415)331-1340. **E-mail:** info@sausalitoartfestival.org. **Website:** www.sausalitoartfestival.org. Estab. 1952. Premiere fine art festival held annually Labor Day weekend. Outdoors. Accepts painting, photography, 2D and 3D mixed media, ceramics, drawing, fiber, functional art, glass, jewelry, printmaking, sculpture, watercolor, woodwork. Juried. Jurors are elected by their peers from the previous year's show (1 from each category). They meet for a weekend at the end of March and give scores of 1, 2, 4 or 5 to each applicant (5 being the highest). 5 images must be submitted, 4 of art and 1 of booth. Number of exhibitors: 280. Public attendance: 40,000. Artists should apply by visiting website for instructions and application. Applications are through Juried Art Services. Deadline for entry: March. Exhibition space: 100 or 200 sq. ft. Application fee: $50; $100 for late applications. Booth fees range from $1,425-3,125. Average gross sales/exhibitor: $7,700. For more information, artists should visit website. Festival located in Marinship Park.

SCOTTSDALE ARTS FESTIVAL

7380 E. Second St., Scottsdale AZ 85251. (480)874-2787; (480)994-2787. **Fax:** (480)874-4699. **Website:** www.scottsdaleartsfestival.org. Estab. 1970. Fine arts & crafts show held annually in March. Outdoors. Accepts photography, jewelry, ceramics, sculpture, metal, glass, drawings, fiber, paintings, printmaking, mixed media, wood. Juried. Awards/prizes: 1st, 2nd, 3rd places in each category and Best of Show. Number of exhibitors: 200. Public attendance: 40,000. Public admission: $10/single day; $15/2-day pass. Artists should apply through www.zapplication.org. Deadline for entry: October. Exhibition space: 100 sq. ft. For more information, artists should visit website.

SHADYSIDE ART & CRAFT FESTIVAL

270 Central Blvd., Suite 107B, Jupiter FL 33458. (561)746-6615. **Fax:** (561)746-6528. **E-mail:** info@ artfestival.com. **Website:** www.artfestival.com. **Contact:** Malinda Ratliff, communications manager. Estab. 1996. Fine art & craft fair held annually in late May. Outdoors. Accepts photography, jewelry, mixed media, sculpture, wood, ceramic, glass, painting, digital, fiber, metal. Juried. Number exhibitors: 125. Number attendees: 60,000. Free to public. Apply online via www.zapplication.org. Deadline: see website. Application fee: $25. Space fee: $395. Exhibition space: 10×10 and 10×20. For more information, artists should e-mail, call, or visit website.

Festival located at Walnut St. in Shadyside (Pittsburgh PA).

SHADYSIDE...THE ART FESTIVAL ON WALNUT STREET

270 Central Blvd., Suite 107B, Jupiter FL 33458. (561)746-6615. **Fax:** (561)746-6528. **E-mail:** info@ artfestival.com. **Website:** www.artfestival.com. **Con-**tact: Malinda Ratliff, communications manager. Estab. 1996. Fine art & craft fair held annually in late August. Outdoors. Accepts photography, jewelry, mixed media, sculpture, wood, ceramic, glass, painting, digital, fiber, metal. Juried. Number exhibitors: 125. Number attendees: 100,000. Free to public. Apply online via www.zapplication.org. Deadline: see website. Application fee: $25. Space fee: $450. Exhibition space: 10×10 and 10×20. For more information, artists should e-mail, call, or visit website.

Festival located at Walnut St. in Shadyside (Pittsburgh PA).

SIDEWALK ART MART

Downtown Helena, Inc., Mount Helena Music Festival, 225 Cruse Ave., Suite B, Helena MT 59601. (406)447-1535. **Fax:** (406)447-1533. **E-mail:** jmc hugh@mt.net. **Website:** www.downtownhelena.com. **Contact:** Jim McHugh. Estab. 1974. Arts, crafts and music festival held annually in June. Outdoors. Accepts photography. No restrictions except to display appropriate work for all ages. Number of exhibitors: 50+. Public attendance: 5,000. Free to public. Artists should apply by visiting website to download application. Space fee: $100-125. Exhibition space: 10×10 ft. For more information, artists should e-mail, visit website, or call. Festival held at Women's Park in Helena MT.

TIPS "Greet people walking by and have an eye-catching product in front of booth. We have found that high-end artists or expensively priced art booths that had business cards with e-mail or website information received many contacts after the festival."

SIERRA MADRE WISTARIA FESTIVAL

19 Suffolk Ave., Unit A, Sierra Madre CA 91024. (626)355-5111; (626)233-5524. **Fax:** (626)306-1150. **E-mail:** smadrecc@gmail.com. **Website:** www.sierra madrechamber.com/wistaria/photos.htm. Fine arts, crafts and garden show held annually in March. Outdoors. Accepts photography, anything handcrafted. Juried. Craft vendors send in application and photos to be juried. Most appropriate are selected. Awards/prizes: Number of exhibitors: 175. Public attendance: 12,000. Free to public. Artists should apply by sending completed and signed application, 3-5 photographs of their work, application fee, license application, space fee and 2 SASEs. Deadline for entry: late December. Application fee: $25. Public Safety Fee (nonrefundable) $25. Space fee: $185. Exhibition space: 10×10

ft. For more information, artists should e-mail, visit website or call. Applications can be found on chamber website.

TIPS "Have a clear and simple application. Be nice."

⊕ 🎧 SIESTA FIESTA

270 Central Blvd., Suite 107B, Jupiter FL 33458. (561)746-6615. **Fax:** (561)746-6528. **E-mail:** info@art-festival.com. **Website:** www.artfestival.com. **Contact:** Malinda Ratliff, communications manager. Estab. 1978. Fine art & craft fair held annually in April. Outdoors. Accepts photography, jewelry, mixed media, sculpture, wood, ceramic, glass, painting, digital, fiber, metal. Juried. Number exhibitors: 85. Number attendees: 40,000. Free to public. Apply online via www.zapplication.org. Deadline: see website. Application fee: $25. Space fee: $350. Exhibition space: 10×10 and 10×20. For more information, artists should e-mail, call, or visit website.

🎧 Festival located at Ocean Blvd. in Siesta Key Village.

SKOKIE ART GUILD FINE ART EXPO

Devonshire Cultural Center, 4400 Greenwood St., Skokie IL 60077. (847)677-8163. **E-mail:** info@skok ieartguild.org; skokieart@aol.com. **Website:** www.skokieartguild.org. Outdoor fine art/craft show open to all artists (18+) in the Chicagoland area. Held in mid-May. Entrance fee: $20 (members); $30 (non-members). Awards: 1st, 2nd, 3rd place ribbons, Purchase Awards. Deadline for application: early May. Event held at Oakton Park.

TIPS Display your work in a professional manner: matted, framed, etc.

🎧 SMITHVILLE FIDDLERS' JAMBOREE AND CRAFT FESTIVAL

P.O. Box 83, Smithville TN 37166. (615)597-8500. **E-mail:** eadkins@smithvillejamboree.com. **Website:** www.smithvillejamboree.com. **Contact:** Emma Adkins, craft coordinator. Estab. 1971. Arts & crafts show held annually the weekend nearest the Fourth of July holiday. Indoors. Juried by photos and personally talking with crafters. Awards/prizes: ribbons and free booth for following year for Best of Show, Best of Appalachian Craft, Best Display, Best New Comer. Number of exhibitors: 235. Public attendance: 130,000. Free to public. Artists should apply online. Deadline: May 1. Space fee: $125. Exhibition space: 12×12 ft. Average gross sales/exhibitors: $1,200+. For

more information, artists should call or visit website. Festival held in downton Smithville.

🎧 SOLANO AVENUE STROLL

1563 Solano Ave., #101, Berkeley CA 94707. (510)527-5358. **E-mail:** info@solanostroll.org. **Website:** www.solanostroll.org. **Contact:** Allen Cain. Estab. 1974. Fine arts & crafts show held annually 2nd Sunday in September. Outdoors. "Since 1974, the merchants, restaurants, and professionals, as well as the twin cities of Albany and Berkeley have hosted the Solano Avenue Stroll, the East Bay's largest street festival." Accepts photography and all other mediums. Juried by board of directors. Number of exhibitors: 150 spaces for crafts; 600 spaces total. Public attendance: 250,000. Free to the public. Artists should apply online in April, or send SASE. Space fee: $150. Exhibition space: 10×10 ft. For more information, artists should e-mail, visit website, send SASE. Event takes place on Solano Ave. in Berkeley and Albany CA.

TIPS "Artists should have a clean presentation; small-ticket items as well as large-ticket items; great customer service; enjoy themselves."

THE SOUTHWEST ARTS FESTIVAL

Indio Chamber of Commerce, 82921 Indio Blvd., Indio CA 92201. (760)347-0676. **Fax:** (763)347-6069. **E-mail:** jonathan@indiochamber.org; swaf@indio chamber.org. **Website:** www.southwestartsfest.com. Estab. 1986. Featuring over 275 acclaimed artists showing traditional, contemporary and abstract fine works of art and quality crafts, the festival is a major, internationally recognized cultural event attended by nearly 10,000 people. The event features a wide selection of clay, crafts, drawings, glass work, jewelry, metal works, paintings, photographs, printmaking, sculpture and textiles. Application fee: $55. Easy check-in and check-out procedures with safe and secure access to festival grounds for setup and breakdown. Allow advance set-up for artists with special requirements (very large art requiring the use of cranes, forklifts, etc., or artists with special needs). Artist parking is free. Disabled artist parking is available. Apply online. For more information, artists should call, e-mail, or visit website. Show takes place in January.

🎧 SPRING CRAFTMORRISTOWN

P.O. Box 28, Woodstock NY 12498. (845)331-7900. **Fax:** (845)331-7484. **E-mail:** crafts@artrider.com. **Website:** www.artrider.com. Estab. 1990. Fine arts & crafts show held annually in March. Indoors. Accepts photography, wearable and nonwearable fiber, jewelry, clay, leather, wood, glass, painting, drawing, prints, mixed media. Juried by 5 images of work and 1 of booth, viewed sequentially. Number of exhibitors: 150. Public attendance: 5,000. Public admission: $9. Artists should apply online at www.artrider.com or at www.zapplication.org. Deadline for entry: January 1. Application fee: $45. Space fee: $495. Exhibition space: 10×10 ft. For more information, artists should e-mail, visit website, or call.

🎧 SPRING CRAFTS AT LYNDHURST

P.O. Box 28, Woodstock NY 12498. (845)331-7900. **Fax:** (845)331-7484. **E-mail:** crafts@artrider.com. **Website:** www.artrider.com. Estab. 1984. Fine arts & crafts show held annually in early May. Outdoors. Accepts photography, wearable and nonwearable fiber, jewelry, clay, leather, wood, glass, painting, drawing, prints, mixed media. Juried by 5 images of work and 1 of booth, viewed sequentially. Number of exhibitors: 275. Public attendance: 14,000. Public admission: $10. Artists should apply at www.artrider.com or can apply online at www.zapplication.org. Deadline for entry: January 1. Application fee: $45. Space fee: $775-875. Exhibition space: 10×10 ft. For more information, artists should e-mail, visit website, or call.

SPRINGFEST

Southern Pines Business Association, P.O. Box 831, Southern Pines NC 28388. (910)315-6508. **E-mail:** spbainfo@southernpines.biz. **Website:** www.south ernpines.biz. **Contact:** Susan Harris. Estab. 1979. Arts & crafts show held annually last Saturday in April. Outdoors. Accepts photography and crafts. We host over 160 vendors from all around North Carolina and the country. Enjoy beautiful artwork and crafts including paintings, jewelry, metal art, photography, woodwork, designs from nature and other amazing creations. Event is held in conjunction with Tour de Moore, an annual bicycle race in Moore County, and is co-sponsored by the town of Southern Pines. Public attendance: 8,000. Free to the public. Deadline: March (see website for more details). Space fee: $75. Exhibition space: 10×12 ft. For more information, artists should e-mail, visit website, call, send SASE. Apply online. Event held in historic downtown Southern Pines on Broad St.

🎧 SPRING FINE ART & CRAFTS AT BROOKDALE PARK

473 Watchung Ave., Bloomfield NJ 07003. (908)874-5247. **Fax:** (908)874-7098. **E-mail:** info@rosesquared. com. **Website:** www.rosesquared.com. Estab. 1988. Fine arts & craft show held annually at Brookdale Park on the border of Bloomfield and Montclair NJ. Event takes place in mid-June on Father's Day weekend. Outdoors. Accepts photography and all other mediums. Juried. Number of exhibitors: 180. Public attendance: 16,000. Free to the public. Artists should apply by downloading application from website or call for application. Deadline: 1 month before show date. Application fee: $25. Space fee: varies by booth size. Exhibition space: 120 sq. ft. For more information, artists should e-mail, visit website, or call.

TIPS "Create a professional booth that is comfortable for the customer to enter. Be informative, friendly and outgoing. People come to meet the artist."

STEPPIN' OUT

Downtown Blacksburg, Inc., P.O. Box 233, Blacksburg VA 24063. (540)951-0454. **E-mail:** dbi@down townblacksburg.com; events@downtownblacksburg. com. **Website:** www.blacksburgsteppinout.com. Estab. 1981. Arts & crafts show held annually 1st Friday and Saturday in August. Outdoors. Accepts photography, pottery, painting, drawing, fiber arts, jewelry, general crafts. All arts and crafts must be handmade. Number of exhibitors: 170. Public attendance: 45,000. Free to public. Space fee: $175. An additional $10 is required for electricity. Exhibition space: 10×16 ft. Artists should apply by e-mailing, calling or downloading an application on website. Deadline for entry: early May.

TIPS "Visit shows and consider the booth aesthetic—what appeals to you. Put the time, thought, energy and money into your booth to draw people in to see your work."

🎧 STILLWATER ARTS FESTIVAL

P.O. Box 1449, Stillwater OK 74076. (405)747-8070. **E-mail:** stillwaterartsfestival@stillwater.org; rjanway@ stillwater.org. **Website:** www.stillwater.org/stillwater_ arts_festival/index.php. **Contact:** Rachel Janway. Estab. 1977. Fine art show held annually in April. Outdoors. Accepts photography, oil, acrylic, watercolor and multi media paintings, pottery, pastel work, fiber arts, jewelry, sculpture, glass art, wood and other. Juried. Awards are based on entry acceptance on quality, distribution and various media entries. Awards/prizes: Best of Show, $500; 1st Place, $200; 2nd Place, $150; 3rd Place, $100. Number of exhibitors: 80. Public attendance: 7,500-10,000. Free to public. Artists should apply via www.zapplication.org. Deadline for entry: early spring (visit website for details). Jury fee: $20. Booth fee $140; $240 for 2 booths. Exhibition space: 10×10 ft. For more information, artists should e-mail or call. Festival held at 8th & Husband Streets.

☺ STOCKLEY GARDENS FALL ARTS FESTIVAL

801 Boush St., Suite 302, Norfolk VA 23510. (757)625-6161. **Fax:** (757)625-7775. **E-mail:** aknox@hopehouse.org. **Website:** www.stockleygardens.com. **Contact:** Anne Knox, development coordinator. Estab. 1984. Fine arts & crafts show held biannually in the 3rd weekends in May and October. Outdoors. Accepts photography and all major fine art mediums. Juried. Number of exhibitors: 135. Public attendance: 25,000. Free to the public. Artists should apply by submitting application, jury and booth fees, 5 slides. Deadline for entry: February and July. Exhibition space: 10×10 ft. For more information, artists should visit the website.

☺ STONE ARCH BRIDGE FESTIVAL

(651)398-0590. **E-mail:** stacy@weimarketing.com; heatherwmpls@gmail.com. **Website:** www.stonearchbridgefestival.com. **Contact:** Sara Collins, manager. Estab. 1994. Fine arts & crafts and culinary arts show held annually on Father's Day weekend in the Riverfront District of Minneapolis. Outdoors. Accepts drawing/pastels, printmaking, ceramics, jewelry (metals/stone), mixed media, painting, photography, sculpture metal works, bead work (jewelry or sculpture), glass, fine craft, special consideration. Juried by committee. Awards/prizes: free booth the following year; $100 cash prize. Number of exhibitors: 250+. Public attendance: 80,000. Free to public. Artists should apply by application found on website or through www.zapplication.org. Application fee: $25. Deadline for entry: early April. Space fee: depends on booth location (see website for details). Exhibition space: 10×10 ft. For more information, artists should call (651)228-1664 or e-mail Stacy De Young at stacy@weimarketing.com.
TIPS "Have an attractive display and variety of prices."

☺ STRAWBERRY FESTIVAL

2815 Second Ave. N., Billings MT 59101. (406)294-5060. **Fax:** (406)294-5061. **E-mail:** info@strawberryfun.com; natashap@downtownbillings.com. **Website:** www.downtownbillings.com. **Contact:** Natasha. Estab. 1991. Fine arts & crafts show held annually 2nd Saturday in June. Outdoors. Accepts photography and only finely crafted work. Handcrafted works by the selling artist will be given priority. Requires photographs of booth set up and 2-3 of work. Juried. Public attendance: 15,000. Free to public. Artists should apply online. Deadline for entry: April. Space fee: $155. Exhibition space: 10×10 ft. For more information, artists should e-mail or visit website. Show located at N. Broadway & 2nd Ave. N in downtown Billings.

☺ SUMMER ART IN THE PARK FESTIVAL

16 S. Main St., Rutland VT 05701. (802)775-0356. **E-mail:** info@chaffeeartcenter.org. **Website:** www.chaffeeartcenter.org. Estab. 1961. A fine arts & crafts show held at Main Street Park in Rutland VT annually in mid-August. Accepts fine art, specialty foods, fiber, jewelry, glass, metal, wood, photography, clay, floral, etc. All applications will be juried by a panel of experts. The Art in the Park Festivals are dedicated to high-quality art and craft products. Number of exhibitors: 100. Public attendance: 9,000-10,000. Public admission: voluntary donation. Artists should apply online and either e-mail or submit a CD with 3 photos of work and 1 of booth (photos upon preapproval). Deadline for entry: early bird discount of $25 per show for applications received by March 31. Space fee: $200-350. Exhibit space: 10×12 or 20×12 ft. For more information, artists should e-mail, visit website, or call. Festival held in Main Street Park.
TIPS "Have a good presentation, variety if possible (in price ranges, too) to appeal to a large group of people. Apply early as there may be a limited amount of accepted vendors per category. Applications will be juried on a first come, first served basis until the category is determined to be filled."

☺ SUMMER ARTS & CRAFTS FESTIVAL

38 Charles St., Rochester NH 03867. **E-mail:** info@castleberryfairs.com. **Website:** www.castleberryfairs.com. Estab. 1992. Arts & crafts show held annually 2nd weekend in August in Lincoln NH. Outdoors. Accepts photography and all other mediums. Juried by photo, slide or sample. Number of exhibitors: 100. Public attendance: 7,500. Free to the public. Artists should apply by downloading application from website. Application fee: $50. Space fee: $225. Exhibition space: 10×10 ft. For more information, artists should

visit website. Festival held at Village Shops & Town Green, Main Street.

TIPS "Do not bring a book; do not bring a chair. Smile and make eye contact with everyone who enters your booth. Have them sign your guest book; get their e-mail address so you can let them know when you are in the area again. And, finally, make the sale—they are at the fair to shop, after all."

SUMMERFAIR

7850 Five Mile Rd., Cincinnati OH 45230. (513)531-0050. **Fax:** (513)531-0377. **E-mail:** exhibitors@summerfair.org. **Website:** www.summerfair.org. Estab. 1968. Fine arts & crafts show held annually the weekend after Memorial Day. Outdoors. Accepts photography, ceramics, drawing, printmaking, fiber, leather, glass, jewelry, painting, sculpture, metal, wood and mixed media. Juried by a panel of judges selected by Summerfair, including artists and art educators with expertise in the categories offered at Summerfair. Submit application with 5 digital images (no booth image) through www.zapplication.org. Awards/prizes: $11,000 in cash awards. Number of exhibitors: 300. Public attendance: 20,000. Public admission: $10. Deadline: February. Application fee: $30. Space fee: $375, single; $750, double space; $75 canopy fee (optional—exhibitors can rent a canopy for all days of the fair). Exhibition space: 10×10 ft. for single space; 10×20 ft. for double space. For more information, artists should e-mail, visit website, call. Fair held at Cincinnati's historic Coney Island.

SUN FEST, INC.

P.O. Box 2404, Bartlesville OK 74005. (918)331-0456. **Fax:** (918)331-3217. **E-mail:** sunfestbville@gmail.com. **Website:** www.bartlesvillesunfest.org. Estab. 1982. Fine arts & crafts show held annually in early June. Outdoors. Accepts photography, painting and other arts and crafts. Juried. Awards: $2,000 in cash awards along with a ribbon/award to be displayed. Number of exhibitors: 95-100. Number of attendees: 25,000-30,000. Free to the public. Artists should apply by e-mailing or calling for an entry form, or completing online, along with 3-5 photos showing your work and booth display. Deadline: April. Space fee: $125. An extra $20 is charged for use of electricity. Exhibition space: 10×10 ft. For more information, artists should e-mail, call, or visit website.

SURPRISE FINE ART & WINE FESTIVAL

15648 N. Eagles Nest Dr., Fountain Hills AZ 85268. (480)837-5637. **Fax:** (480)837-2355. **E-mail:** info@thunderbirdartists.com. **Website:** www.thunderbirdartists.com. **Contact:** Denise Colter, president. Estab. 2013. Fine arts & crafts show held annually in the winter. Outdoors. Accepts photography, paintings, bronzes, baskets, jewelry, stone, pottery. Juried; CEO blind juries by medium. Number of exhibitors: 100. Public attendance: 10,000. Public admission: $3. Apply online at www.zapplication.org. Deadline for entry: mid-June (see website for specifics). Application fee: $30. Space fee: $430-1,240. Exhibition space: 10×10 to 10×30 ft. For more information, artists should e-mail, call, or see website.

TIPS "A clean, gallery-type presentation is very important."

SYRACUSE ARTS & CRAFTS FESTIVAL

115 W. Fayette St., Syracuse NY 13202. (315)422-8284. **Fax:** (315)471-4503. **E-mail:** lreed@downtownsyracuse.com. **Website:** www.syracuseartsandcraftsfestival.com. **Contact:** Laurie Reed, director. Estab. 1970. Fine arts & crafts show held annually in late July. Outdoors. Accepts photography, ceramics, fabric/fiber, glass, jewelry, leather, metal, wood, computer art, drawing, printmaking, painting. Juried by 4 independent jurors. Jurors review 4 digital images of work and 1 digital image of booth display. Number of exhibitors: 165. Public attendance: 50,000. Free to public. Artists should apply online through www.zapplication.org. Application fee: $25. Space fee: $280. Exhibition space: 10×10 ft. For more information, artists should e-mail, visit website, or call.

TARPON SPRINGS FINE ARTS FESTIVAL

111 E. Tarpon Ave., Tarpon Springs FL 34689. (727)937-6109. **Fax:** (727)937-2879. **E-mail:** scottie@tarponspringschamber.org. **Website:** www.tarponspringschamber.com. Estab. 1974. Fine arts & crafts show held annually in late March. Outdoors. Accepts photography, acrylic, oil, ceramics, digital, fiber, glass, graphics, drawings, pastels, jewelry, leather, metal, mixed media, sculpture, watercolor, wood. Juried by CD or images e-mailed. Awards/prizes: cash, ribbons and Patron Awards. Number of exhibitors: 200. Public attendance: 20,000. Public admission: $5 (includes free drink ticket: wine, beer, soda or water); free-age 12 and under and active duty military. Artists should apply by submitting signed application,

CD or e-mailed images, fees and SASE. Deadline for entry: late December. Jury fee: $30. Space fee: $230. Exhibition space: 10×12 ft. For more information, artists should e-mail, call or send SASE.

TIPS "Produce good CDs for jurors."

THREE RIVERS ARTS FESTIVAL

803 Liberty Ave., Pittsburgh PA 15222. (412)456-6666. **Fax:** (412)471-6917. **Website:** www.3riversartsfest.org. **Contact:** Sonja Sweterlitsch, director. Estab. 1960. "Three Rivers Arts Festival has presented, during its vast and varied history, more than 10,000 visual and performing artists and entertained millions of residents and visitors. Three Rivers Arts Festival faces a new turning point in its history as a division of The Pittsburgh Cultural Trust, further advancing the shared mission of each organization to foster economic development through the arts and to enhance the quality of life in the region." Application fee: $35. Booth fee: $340-410. See website for more information. Festival located at Point State Park in downtown Pittsburgh.

TUBAC FESTIVAL OF THE ARTS

P.O. Box 1866, Tubac AZ 85646. (520)398-2704. **Fax:** (520)398-3287. **E-mail:** assistance@tubacaz.com. **Website:** www.tubacaz.com. Estab. 1959. Fine arts & crafts show held annually in early February (see website for details). Outdoors. Accepts photography and considers all fine arts and crafts. Juried. A 7-member panel reviews digital images and artist statement. Names are withheld from the jurists. Number of exhibitors: 170. Public attendance: 65,000. Free to the public; parking: $6. Deadline for entry: late October (see website for details). Application fee: $30. Artists should apply online and provide images on a labeled CD (see website for requirements). Space fee: $575. Electrical fee: $50. Exhibition space: 10×10 ft. (a limited number of double booths are available). For more information, artists should e-mail, call, or visit website.

TULIP FESTIVAL STREET FAIR

(425)321-7433. **Fax:** (360)428-6753. **E-mail:** mvstreet faircoordinator@gmail.com. **Website:** www.mount vernondowntown.org. Estab. 1984. Arts & crafts show held annually 3rd weekend in April. Outdoors. Accepts photography and original artists' work only. No manufactured work. Juried by a board. Jury fee: $10 with application and prospectus. Number of exhibitors: 220. Public attendance: 30,000-35,000. Free

to public. Artists should apply by downloading the prospectus (new vendors) or returning vendor application at www.mountvernondowntown.org/events/tulipfest. Deadline for entry: mid December. Application fee: none. Space fee: $300. Exhibition space: 10×10 ft. Average gross sales/exhibitor: $2,500-4,000. For more information, artists should e-mail, visit website, call or send SASE.

TIPS "Keep records of your street fair attendance and sales for your résumé. Network with other artists about which street fairs are better to return to or apply for."

TULSA INTERNATIONAL MAYFEST

2210 S. Main St., Tulsa OK 74114. (918)582-6435. **Fax:** (918)517-3518. **E-mail:** comments@tulsamayfest.org. **Website:** www.tulsamayfest.org. Estab. 1972. Fine arts & crafts show annually held in May. Outdoors. Accepts photography, clay, leather/fiber, mixed media, drawing, pastels, graphics, printmaking, jewelry, glass, metal, wood, painting. Juried by a blind jurying process. Artists should apply online at www.zapplication.org and submit 4 images of work and 1 photo of booth set-up. Awards/prizes: Best in Category and Best in Show. Number of exhibitors: 125. Public attendance: 350,000. Free to public. Artists should apply by downloading application in the fall. See website for deadline entry. Application fee: $35. Space fee: $350. Exhibition space: 10×10 ft. For more information, artists should e-mail or visit website.

UPTOWN ART FAIR

1406 W. Lake St., Lower Level C, Minneapolis MN 55408. (612)823-4581. **Fax:** (612)823-3158. **E-mail:** maude@uptownminneapolis.com; info@uptown minneapolis.com; jessica@uptownminneapolis.com; hannah@uptownminneapolis.com. **Website:** www. uptownartfair.com. Estab. 1963. Fine arts & crafts show held annually 1st full weekend in August. Outdoors. Accepts photography, painting, printmaking, drawing, 2D and 3D mixed media, ceramics, fiber, sculpture, jewelry, wood and glass. Juried by 4 images of artwork and 1 of booth display. Awards/prizes: Best in Show in each category; Best Artist. Number of exhibitors: 350. Public attendance: 375,000. Free to the public. The Uptown Art Fair uses www.zapplica tion.org. Each artist must submit 5 images of his or her work. All artwork must be in a high-quality digital format. Five highly qualified artists, instructors, and critics handpick Uptown Art Fair exhibitors after previewing projections of the images on 6-ft. screens. The identities of the artists remain anonymous during the entire review process. All submitted images must be free of signatures, headshots or other identifying marks. Three rounds of scoring determine the final selection and waitlist for the show. Artists will be notified shortly after of their acceptance. For additional information, see the links on website. Deadline for entry: early March. Application fee: $40. Space fee: $550 for 10×10 space; $1,100 for 10×20 space. For more information, artists should call or visit website. Fair located at Lake St. and Hennepin Ave. and "The Mall" in Southwest Minneapolis.

A VICTORIAN CHAUTAUQUA

1101 E. Market St., Jeffersonville IN 47130. (812)283-3728 or (888)472-0606. **Fax:** (812)283-6049. **E-mail:** hsmsteam@aol.com. **Website:** www.steamboatmuseum.org. **Contact:** Roger Fisher, festival chairman. Estab. 1993. Fine arts & crafts show held annually 3rd weekend in May. Outdoors. Accepts photography, all mediums. Juried by a committee of 5. Number of exhibitors: 80. Public attendance: 3,000. Exhibition space: 12×12 ft. For more information, artists should e-mail, call, or visit website.

VILLAGE SQUARE ARTS & CRAFTS FAIR

P.O. Box 176, Saugatuck MI 49453. **E-mail:** artclub@saugatuckdouglasartclub.org. **Website:** www.saugatuckdouglasartclub.org. Estab. 2004. The art club offers 2 fairs each summer. See website for upcoming dates. This fair has some fine artists as well as crafters. Both fairs take place on the 2 busiest weekends in the resort town of Saugatuck's summer season. Both are extremely well attended. Generally the vendors do very well. Booth fee: $95-140. Fair located at corner of Butler and Main Streets, Saugatuck MI.
TIPS "Create an inviting booth. Offer well-made artwork and crafts for a variety of prices."

VIRGINIA BEACH DOWNTOWN ART FAIR

270 Central Blvd., Suite 107B, Jupiter FL 33458. (561)746-6615. **Fax:** (561)746-6528. **E-mail:** info@artfestival.com. **Website:** www.artfestivalc.com. **Contact:** Malinda Ratliff, communications manager. Estab. 2015. Fine art & craft fair held annually in April. Outdoors. Accepts photography, jewelry, mixed media, sculpture, wood, ceramic, glass, painting, digital, fiber, metal. Juried. Number exhibitors: 80. Number attendees: see website. Free to public. Apply online

via www.zapplication.org. Deadline: see website. Application fee: $25. Space fee: $395. Exhibition space: 10×10 and 10×20. For more information, artists should e-mail, call, or visit website.

Festival located Main St. between Central Park Ave. and Constitution Dr.

VIRGINIA CHRISTMAS MARKET

The Exhibition Center at Meadow Event Park, 13111 Dawn Blvd., Doswell VA 23047. (804)253-6284. **Fax:** (804)253-6285. **E-mail:** bill.wagstaff@virginiashows.com. **Website:** www.virginiashows.com. Indoors. Virginia Christmas Market is held the last weekend in October at the Exhibition Center at Meadow Event Park. Virginia Christmas Market will showcase up to 300 quality artisans, crafters, boutiques and specialty food shops. Features porcelain, pottery, quilts, folk art, fine art, reproduction furniture, flags, ironwork, carvings, leather, toys, tinware, candles, dollcraft, wovenwares, book authors, musicians, jewelry, basketry, gourmet foods—all set amid festive Christmas displays. Accepts photography and other arts and crafts. Juried by 3 photos of artwork and 1 of display. Attendance: 15,000. Public admission: $7; children FREE (under 10). Artists should apply by calling, e-mailing or downloading application from website. Space fee: $335. Exhibit spaces: 10×10 ft. For more information, artists should call, e-mail, or contact through website.
TIPS If possible, attend the show before you apply.

VIRGINIA SPRING MARKET

11050 Branch Rd., Glen Allen VA 23059. (804)253-6284. **Fax:** (804)253-6285. **E-mail:** bill.wagstaff@virginiashows.com. **Website:** www.virginiashows.com. **Contact:** Bill Wagstaff. Estab. 1988. Holiday arts & crafts show held annually 1st weekend in March at The Exhibition Center at Meadow Event Park, 13111 Dawn Blvd., Doswell VA. Virginia Spring Market will showcase up to 300 quality artisans, crafters, boutiques and specialty food shops. Features porcelain, pottery, quilts, folk art, fine art, reproduction furniture, flags, ironwork, carvings, leather, toys, tinware, candles, dollcraft, wovenwares, book authors, musicians, jewelry, basketry and gourmet foods, all set amid festive spring displays. Accepts photography and other arts and crafts. Juried by 3 images of artwork and 1 of display. Public attendance: 12,000. Public admission: $7; children free (under 10). Artists should apply by calling, e-mailing, or downloading application from website. Space fee: $335. Exhibition space: 10×10 ft.

For more information, artists should call, e-mail, or contact through website.

TIPS "If possible, attend the show before you apply."

◯ WASHINGTON SQUARE OUTDOOR ART EXHIBIT

P.O. Box 1045, New York NY 10276. (212)982-6255. **Fax:** (212)982-6256. **E-mail:** jrm.wsoae@gmail.com. **Website:** www.wsoae.org. Estab. 1931. Fine arts & crafts show held semiannually Memorial Day weekend and Labor Day weekend. Outdoors. Accepts photography, oil, watercolor, graphics, mixed media, sculpture, crafts. Juried by submitting 5 slides of work and 1 of booth. Awards/prizes: certificates, ribbons and cash prizes. Number of exhibitors: 150. Public attendance: 100,000. Free to public. Artists should apply by sending a SASE or downloading application from website. Deadline for entry: March, spring show; July, fall show. Exhibition space: 5×10 ft. up to 10×10 ft., double spaces available. Jury fee of $20. First show weekend (3 days) fee of $410. Second show weekend (2 days) $310. Both weekends (all 5 days) fee of $525. For more information, artists should call or send SASE.

TIPS "Price work sensibly."

◯ WATERFRONT FINE ART & WINE FESTIVAL

15648 N. Eagles Nest Dr., Fountain Hills AZ 85268. (480)837-5637. **Fax:** (480)837-2355. **E-mail:** info@thunderbirdartists.com. **Website:** www.thunderbirdartists.com. **Contact:** Denise Colter, President. Estab. 2012. Fine art/craft show held annually the 1st weekend in December. Outdoors. Accepts photography, paintings, bronzes, baskets, jewelry, stone, pottery. Juried; blind jury by CEO. Number of exhibitors: 125. Public attendance: 20,000. Public admission: $3. Apply online at www.zapplication.org. Deadline for entry: mid-August (see website for specifics). Application fee: $30. Space fee: $430-1,240. Exhibition space: 10×10 to 10×30 ft. For more information, artists should e-mail, call, or visit website.

TIPS "A clean, gallery-type presentation is very important."

◯ WATERFRONT FINE ART FAIR

P.O. Box 176, Saugatuck MI 49453. **E-mail:** artclub@saugatuckdouglasartclub.org. **Website:** www.saugatuckdouglassartclub.org. Fee is $135. This includes application fee, booth fee, and city license. Applications juried in early April. For information, e-mail, call, or visit the website. Fair held at Cook Park.

TIPS "Create a pleasing, inviting booth. Offer well-made, top-quality fine art."

◯ WESTMORELAND ART NATIONALS

252 Twin Lakes Rd., Latrobe PA 15650-3554. (724)834-7474. **E-mail:** info@artsandheritage.com. **E-mail:** adam@artsandheritage.com. **Website:** www.artsandheritage.com. **Contact:** Adam Shaffer, executive director. Estab. 1975. Juried fine art exhibition & crafts show held annually in early July (see website for details). Juried art exhibition is indoors. Photography displays are indoors. Accepts photography, all handmade mediums. Juried by 2 jurors. Awards/prizes: $5,700 in prizes. Number of exhibitors: 190. Public attendance: 160,000. Free to public. Artists should apply by downloading application from website. Application fee: $25/craft show vendors; $35/art nationals exhibitors. Deadline for entry: early March. Space fee: $375-750. Exhibition space: 10×10 or 10×20 ft. For more information, artists should visit e-mail, call, or visit website. Please direct questions to our executive director.

◯ WHITEFISH ARTS FESTIVAL

P.O. Box 131, Whitefish MT 59937. (406)862-5875. **E-mail:** wafdirector@gmail.com. **Website:** www.whitefishartsfestival.org. Estab. 1979. High-quality art show held annually the 1st full weekend in July. Outdoors. Accepts photography, pottery, jewelry, sculpture, paintings, woodworking. Juried. Art must be original and handcrafted. Work is evaluated for creativity, quality and originality. Awards/prizes: Best of Show awarded $100 off booth fee for following year with no application fee. Number of exhibitors: 120. Public attendance: 3,000–5,000. Free to public. Entry fee: $29. Deadline: see website for details. Space fee: $215. Exhibition space: 10×10 ft. For more information, and to apply, artists should visit website.

TIPS Recommends "variety of price range, professional display, early application for special requests."

◯ WHITE OAK CRAFTS FAIR

P.O. Box 111, Woodbury TN 37190. (615)563-2787 or (800)235-9073. **E-mail:** mary@artscenterofcc.com. **E-mail:** carol@artscenterofcc.com. **Website:** www.artscenterofcc.com. Estab. 1985. Arts & crafts show held annually in early September (see website for details) featuring the traditional and contemporary craft arts of Cannon County and Middle Tennessee. Outdoors. Accepts photography; all handmade crafts, traditional and contemporary. Must be handcrafted displaying excellence in concept and technique. Juried by committee. Send 3 slides or photos. Awards/prizes: more than $1,000 cash in merit awards. Number of exhibitors: 80. Public attendance: 6,000. Free to public. Applications can be downloaded from website. Deadline: early July. Space fee: $120 ($90 for Artisan member) for a 10×10 ft. under tent; $95 ($65 for Artisan member) for a 12×12 ft. outside. For more information, artists should e-mail, call, or visit website. Fair takes place along the banks of the East Fork Stones River just down from the Arts Center.

☺ WILD WIND FOLK ART & CRAFT FESTIVAL

P.O. Box 719, Long Lake NY 12847. (814)723-0707; (814)688-1516. **E-mail:** wildwindcraftshow@yahoo. com. **Website:** www.wildwindfestival.com. **Contact:** Liz Allen and Carol Jilk, directors. Estab. 1979. Traditional crafts show held annually the weekend after Labor Day at the Warren County Fairgrounds in Pittsfield PA. Barn locations and outdoors. Accepts traditional country crafts, photography, paintings, pottery, jewelry, traditional crafts, prints, stained glass. Juried by promoters. Need 3 photos or slides of work plus 1 of booth, if available. Number of exhibitors: 160. Public attendance: 9,000. Artists should apply by visiting website and filling out application request, calling or sending a written request. Festival held at the Warren County Fairgrounds, Pittsfield, PA.

☺ WINNEBAGOLAND ART FAIR

South Park Ave., Oshkosh WI 54902. **E-mail:** oshkoshfaa@gmail.com. Estab. 1957. Fine arts show held annually the second Sunday in June. Outdoors. Accepts painting, wood or stone, ceramics, metal sculpture, jewelry, glass, fabric, drawing, photography, wall hangings, basketry. Artwork must be the original work of the artist in concept and execution. Juried. Applicants send in photographs to be reviewed. Awards/prizes: monetary awards, purchase, merit and Best of Show awards. Number of exhibitors: 125-160. Public attendance: 5,000-8,000. Free to public. Deadline for entry: Previous exhibitors due mid-March; new exhibitors due late March. $25 late entry fee after March. Exhibition space: 20×20 ft. For more information, artists should e-mail or see website. The updated entry form will be added to the website in early January.

TIPS "Artists should send clear, uncluttered photos of their current work which they intend to show in their booth as well as a photo of their booth setup."

☺ WYANDOTTE STREET ART FAIR

2624 Biddle Ave., Wyandotte MI 48192. (734)324-4502. **Fax:** (734)324-7283. **E-mail:** hthiede@wyan.org. **Website:** www.wyandottestreetartfair.org. **Contact:** Heather Thiede, special events coordinator. Estab. 1961. Fine arts & crafts show held annually 2nd week in July. Outdoors. Accepts photography, 2D mixed media, 3D mixed media, painting, pottery, basketry, sculpture, fiber, leather, digital cartoons, clothing, stitchery, metal, glass, wood, toys, prints, drawing. Juried. Awards/prizes: Best New Artist $500; Best Booth Design Award $500; Best of Show $1,200. Number of exhibitors: 300. Public attendance: 200,000. Free to the public. Artists may apply online or request application. Deadline for entry: early February. Application fee: $20 jury fee. Space fee: $250/single space; $475/double space. Exhibition space: 10×12 ft. Average gross sales/exhibitor: $2,000-$4,000. For more information, and to apply, artists should e-mail, visit website, call, or send SASE.

CONTESTS

Whether you're a seasoned veteran or a newcomer still cutting your teeth, you should consider entering contests to see how your work compares to that of other photographers. The contests in this section range in scope from tiny juried county fairs to massive international competitions. When possible, we've included entry fees and other pertinent information in our limited space. Contact sponsors for entry forms and more details.

Once you receive rules and entry forms, pay particular attention to the sections describing rights. Some sponsors retain all rights to winning entries or even *submitted* images. Be wary of these. While you can benefit from the publicity and awards connected with winning prestigious competitions, you shouldn't unknowingly forfeit copyright. Granting limited rights for publicity is reasonable, but you should never assign rights of any kind without adequate financial compensation or a written agreement. If such terms are not stated in contest rules, ask sponsors for clarification.

If you're satisfied with the contest's copyright rules, check with contest officials to see what types of images won in previous years. By scrutinizing former winners, you might notice a trend in judging that could help when choosing your entries. If you can't view the images, ask what styles and subject matters have been popular.

440 GALLERY ANNUAL SMALL WORKS SHOW

440 Sixth Ave., Brooklyn NY 11215. (718)499-3844. E-mail: gallery440@verizon.net. **Website:** www.440gallery.com. **Contact:** Nancy Lunsford, director. Annual juried exhibition hosted by 440 Gallery, a cooperative run by member artists. An exhibition opportunity for US artists whose work is selected by a different curator each year. All work, including frames and mounting materials must be less than 12 inches in all directions. Open to all 2D and 3D media. Videos are considered if the monitor provided is also under 12 inches. Three prizes awarded with small cash awards: The Curator's Choice Award (decided by the juror), the 440 Award (decided by the members of the cooperative), the People's Choice Award (decided by "liking" images posted on our Facebook page). Deadline: early November. For more information about entering submissions, visit website in late September/early October, go to "Call for Entry" page.

440 GALLERY ANNUAL THEMED SHOW

440 Sixth Ave., Brooklyn NY 11215. (718)449-3844. **E-mail:** gallery440@verizon.net. **Website:** www.440gallery.com. **Contact:** Nancy Lunsford. National juried exhibition with a stated theme, and the subject varies from year to year. Past themes have been: animals, Brooklyn, text. An outside curator is invited to judge entries. All media and styles welcome. There is no size limitation, but extremely large work is unlikely to be chosen. Open to all US artists ages 18 and over. Deadline: mid-May. Interested artists should see website for more information.

⬤ AESTHETICA ART PRIZE

P.O. Box 371, York YO23 1WL, United Kingdom. **E-mail:** info@aestheticamagazine.com; artprize@aestheticamagazine.com. **Website:** www.aesthetica magazine.com. There are 4 categories: Photograpic & Digital Art, Three Dimensional Design & Sculpture, Painting & Drawing, Video Installation & Performance. See guidelines at Artwork & Photography, Fiction, and Poetry. See guidelines at www.aestheti camagazine.com.

AFI FEST

2021 N. Western Ave., Los Angeles CA 90027. (323)856-7707; (323)856-7600. **E-mail:** programming@afi.com. **Website:** www.afi.com/afifest. **Contact:** Director of festivals. Cost: $50 shorts; $70 features. "LA's most prominent annual film festival."

Various cash and product prizes are awarded. Open to filmmakers of all skill levels. Deadline: August (see website for details). Photographers should write, call or e-mail for more information.

ALEXIA COMPETITION

S.I. Newhouse School of Communications, 215 University Place, Syracuse NY 13244-2100. (315)443-7388. **E-mail:** trkenned@syr.edul; mdavis@syr.edu. **Website:** www.alexiafoundation.org. **Contact:** Tom Kennedy. Annual contest. Provides financial ability for students to study photojournalism in England, and for professionals to produce a photo project promoting world peace and cultural understanding. Students win cash grants plus scholarships to study at workshops offered by Mediastorm: 1st Place and Momenta Workshops; 2nd Place and Award of Excellence—see website for updated description. Awards vary by year, $1,000–16,000. Photographers should e-mail or see website for more information.

⊕ APERTURE PORTFOLIO PRIZE

547 W. 27th St., 4th Floor, New York NY 10001. (212)505-5555. **Fax:** (212)979-7759. **E-mail:** aper tureprize@aperture.org. **Website:** www.aperture.org/portfolio-prize. **Contact:** Ashley Strazzinski, education & public programs assistant. Cost: see website or e-mail for cost info. Annual photography contest. The goal of this international photography competition is to identify trends in contemporary photography and highlight artists whose work deserves greater recognition. Awards: $3,000 and an exhibition at Aperture in New York. Open to all skill levels. See website for deadline and more information.

⊕ APERTURE SUMMER OPEN

547 W. 27th St., 4th Floor, New York NY 10001. (212)505-5555. **Fax:** (212)979-7759. **E-mail:** summer open@aperture.org. **Website:** www.aperture.org/summer-open. **Contact:** Ashley Strazzinski, education & public programs assistant. Cost: see website or e-mail for cost info. Annual photography contest. This contest is an open-submission exhibition for which all photographers are eligible to enter. Awards: Work will be displayed at Aperture Gallery in New York. Open to all skill levels. See website for deadline and for more information.

ARC AWARDS

500 Executive Blvd., Ossining-on-Hudson NY 10562. (914)923-9400. **Fax:** (914)923-9484. **E-mail:** info@

CONTESTS

mercommawards.com. **Website:** www.mercomm awards.com. Cost: $210-330. Annual contest. The International ARC Awards, is the "Academy Awards of Annual Reports," according to the financial media. It is the largest international competition honoring excellence in annual reports. The competition is open to corporations, small companies, government agencies, nonprofit organizations, and associations, as well as agencies and individuals involved in producing annual reports. The purpose of the contest is to honor outstanding achievement in annual reports. Major category for photography of annual report covers and interiors. "Best of Show" receives a personalized trophy. Grand Award winners receive personalized award plaques. Gold, silver, bronze and finalists receive a personalized award certificate. Every entrant receives complete judge score sheets and comments. Deadline is May. Please see website, write, call, or e-mail for more information.

ARTIST FELLOWSHIP GRANTS

Oregon Arts Commission, 775 Summer St. NE, Suite 200, Salem OR 97301-1280. (503)986-0082. **Fax:** (503)986-0260. **E-mail:** oregon.artscomm@state. or.us. **Website:** www.oregonartscommission.org. A highly competitive juried grant process offering $3,000 in cash awards to Oregon visual artists, awarded annually. Deadline: October. See website for more information.

ARTIST FELLOWSHIPS/VIRGINIA COMMISSION FOR THE ARTS

1001 E. Broad St., Suite 330, Richmond VA 23219. (804)225-3132. **Fax:** (804)225-4327. **E-mail:** arts@ arts.virginia.gov; tiffany.ferreira@vca.virginia.gov. **Website:** www.arts.virginia.gov. The purpose of the Artist Fellowship program is to encourage significant development in the work of individual artists, to support the realization of specific artistic ideas, and to recognize the central contribution professional artists make to the creative environment of Virginia. Grant amounts: $5,000. Emerging and established artists are eligible. Open only to artists who are legal residents of Virginia and are at least 18 years of age. Applications are available in July. See Guidelines for Funding and application forms on the website or write for more information.

ARTISTS ALPINE HOLIDAY

Ouray County Arts Association, P.O. Box 167, Ouray CO 81427. (970)626-5513. **E-mail:** jbhazen@yahoo.

com. **Website:** www.ourayarts.org. **Contact:** DeAnn McDaniel, registrar. Cost: $30, includes up to 2 entries. Annual fine arts show. Juried. Cash awards for 1st, 2nd and 3rd prizes in all categories total $7,200. Best of Show: $750; People's Choice Award: $50. Open to all skill levels. Photographers and artists should call or see website for more information.

ART OF PHOTOGRAPHY SHOW

1439 El Prado, San Diego CA 92101. (619)825-5575. **E-mail:** steven@artofphotographyshow.com. **Website:** www.artofphotographyshow.com. **Contact:** Steven Churchill, producer. Cost: $25 for 1st entry, $10 for each additional entry. Deadline: mid-June. International exhibition of photographic art which occurs each fall at the San Diego Art Institute in San Diego's beautiful Balboa Park. One of the distinguishing characteristics of this competition and exhibition is that the judge is always a highly acclaimed museum curator. "The Art of Photography Show is an established and critical force in the world of contemporary photography. The show provides tangible benefits to artists trying to break into the public eye. This well thought-out exhibition provides value to artists at every turn, from first-rate viewing in the judging process, to exhibition and publication opportunities, well-attended exhibitions and lectures, photo industry connections, and monetary awards." This competition accepts for consideration images created via any form of photography (e.g., shot on film, shot digitally, unaltered shots, alternative process, mixed media, digital manipulations, montages, photograms), so long as part of the image is photographically created. Upload via the website (preferred) or e-mail to entries@artofphotographyshow.com or mail a CD. Award: 1st Place $2,000; 2nd Place $1,600; 3rd Place $1,200; 4th Place $800; Honorable Mention $400 (11 HM awards). Photographers should e-mail or visit the website for more information.

ASTRID AWARDS

500 Executive Blvd., Ossining-on-Hudson NY 10562. (914)923-9400. **Fax:** (914)923-9484. **E-mail:** info@ mercommawards.com; contacts@mercommawards. com. **Website:** www.mercommawards.com. Annual contest. Cost: $330/classification; there is a multiple entry discount. The purpose of the contest is to honor outstanding achievement in design communications. Major category for photography, including books, brochures and publications. "Best of Show" receives

a personalized trophy. Grand Award winners receive personalized award plaques. Gold, silver, bronze and finalists receive a personalized award certificate. Every entrant receives complete judge score sheets and comments. Deadline: late February (see website for details). Photographers should see website, write, call or e-mail for more information.

ATLANTA PHOTOJOURNALISM SEMINAR CONTEST

PMB 420, 5579-B Chamblee Dunwoody Rd., Dunwoody GA 30338. **E-mail:** contest@photojournalism.org; info@photojournalism.org; erik@photojournalism.org. **Website:** www.photojournalism.org. **Contact:** Jeremy Brooks. Annual contest. This is an all-digital contest with several different categories (all related to news and photojournalism). Photographs may have been originally shot on film or with a digital camera, but the entries must be submitted in digital form. Photographs do not have to be published to qualify. No slide or print entries are accepted. Video frame grabs are not eligible. Rules are very specific. See website for official rules. Prizes start at $100, including $1,000 and Nikon camera gear for Best Portfolio. Open to all skill levels. Deadline: November (see website for more details).

☼ BANFF MOUNTAIN PHOTOGRAPHY COMPETITION

P.O. Box 1020, 107 Tunnel Mountain Dr., Banff Alberta T1L 1H5, Canada. (403)762-6347. **Fax:** (403)762-6277. **E-mail:** BanffMountainPhotos@banffcentre.ca. **Website:** www.banffcentre.ca/mountainfestival/. **Contact:** Competition coordinator. Annual contest. Maximum of 5 images (digital) in photo essay format. Entry fee: $10/essay. Entry form and regulations available on website. Approximately $5,000 in cash and prizes to be awarded. Open to all skill levels. Photographers should write, e-mail, or fax for more information.

➕ BUCKTOWN ARTS FEST POSTER CONTEST

2200 N. Oakley, Chicago IL 60647. **E-mail:** poster contest@bucktownartsfest.com. **Website:** www.bucktownartsfest.com/posters. **Contact:** Amy Waldon, committee member. Annual contest. "We hope you wil share your creativity and passion for the Bucktown Arts Fest by entering our Poster Contest! The purpose of the contest is to design a poster promoting the Bucktown Arts Fest. Just create an original

artwork in your media that you think best exemplefies the Bucktown Arts Fest and submit it in JEPG format. The deadline for entries is March 31. There is no fee to enter. Winners will receive a prize and complimentary admission into the festival. Plus, your artwork will be used to promote the Fest, including the Bucktown Arts Fest website, festival merchandise (posters, t-shirts, hangtags, postcards, program), collateral, press releases and signage." One winner will be selected. Winner will be announced May 31 via an e-mail blast.

➕ CAMERA USA: NATIONAL PHOTOGRAPHY EXHIBITION AND AWARD

585 Park St., Naples FL 34102-6611. (239)262-6517. **Fax:** (239)262-5404. **E-mail:** jack.obrien@napleart.org. **Website:** www.naplesart.org/callforartistcat/exhibit-opportunities. **Contact:** Jack O'Brien, curator. Cost: $32 entry fee. Annual competition. All photographers residing in the US are invited to submit one photograph taken in the US after January 1, 2012 for the Camera USA competition with a bricks & mortar exhibition held at the von Liebig Art Center in Naples FL from June 20-July 29, 2016. A maximum of 50 photographers will be included in the exhibition. Three art professionals will review and select photographs online and nominate the National Photography Award Winner. In addition to the $5,000 National Photography Award, the winning photographer will receive 2 nights hotel accomodations in Naples and round-trip economy class airfare. A winning photographer residing in Florida will receive a $300 travel stipend in lieu of airfare. Photographs must be exhibit ready and not exceed 40×40 in size, including frame if a frame is used." Open to all skill levels. Prize/Award: The National Photography Award-$5,000. Deadline for submissions: early March. Contestants should see website for more information.

THE CENTER FOR FINE ART PHOTOGRAPHY

400 North College Ave., Fort Collins CO 80524. (970)224-1010. **E-mail:** contact@c4fap.org. **Website:** www.c4fap.org. Cost: typically $35 for first 3 entries; $10 for each additional entry. Competitions held 10 times/year. "The Center's competitions are designed to attract and exhibit quality fine art photography created by emerging and established artists working in traditional, digital and mixed-media photography. The themes for each exhibition vary greatly. The

themes, rules, details and entry forms for each call for entry are posted on the Center's website." All accepted work is exhibited in the Center gallery. Additionally, the Center offers monetary awards, scholarships, solo exhibitions and other awards. Awards are stated with each call for entry. Open to all skill levels and to all domestic and international photographers working with digital or traditional photography or combinations of both. Photographers should see website for deadlines and more information.

COLLEGE & HIGH SCHOOL PHOTOGRAPHY CONTEST

Serbin Communications, 813 Reddick St., Santa Barbara CA 93103. (805)963-0439 or (800)876-6425. **Fax:** (805)965-0496. **E-mail:** admin@serbin.com; julie@serbin.com. **Website:** www.pfmagazine.com. **Contact:** Julie Simpson, managing editor. Annual student contest; runs September through mid-November. Sponsored by *Photographer's Forum Magazine* and Nikon. Winners and finalists have their photos published in the hardcover book *Best of College & High School Photography.* See website for entry form.

COLLEGE PHOTOGRAPHER OF THE YEAR

101B Lee Hills Hall, University of Missouri, Columbia MO 65211-1370. (573)884-2188. **E-mail:** info@cpoy. org. **Website:** www.cpoy.org. **Contact:** Rita Reed, director. Annual contest to recognize excellent photography by currently enrolled college students. Portfolio winner receives a plaque, cash and camera products. Other category winners receive cash and camera products. Open to beginning and intermediate photographers. Photographers should see website for more information.

COMMUNICATION ARTS ANNUAL PHOTOGRAPHY COMPETITION

110 Constitution Dr., Menlo Park CA 94025-1107. (650)326-6040. **E-mail:** competition@commarts.com. **Website:** www.commarts.com/competitions/photography. Entries must be entered on website. "Entries may originate from any country but a description in English is very important to the judges. The work will be chosen on the basis of its creative excellence by a nationally representative jury of designers, art directors and photographers." Cost: $40 single entry; $80 series. Categories include advertising, books, editorial, for sale, institutional, multimedia, self-promotion, unpublished and student work. Deadline: March 13. See website for more information.

CREATIVE QUARTERLY CALL FOR ENTRIES

244 Fifth Ave., Suite F269, New York NY 10001-7604. (718)775-3943. **E-mail:** coordinator@cqjournal. com. **Website:** www.cqjournal.com. Entry fee: varies. Quarterly contest. "Our publication is all about inspiration. Open to all art directors, graphic designers, photographers, illustrators and fine artists in all countries. Separate categories for professionals and students. We accept both commissioned and uncommissioned entries. Work is judged on the uniqueness of the image and how it best solves a marketing problem. Winners will be requested to submit an image of a person, place or thing that inspires their work. We will reprint these in the issue and select one for our cover image. *Creative Quarterly* has the rights to promote the work through our publications and website. Complete rights and copyright belong to the individual artist, designer or photographer who enters their work. Enter online or by sending a disc. Winners will be featured in the next issue of *Creative Quarterly* corresponding with the call for entries and will be displayed in our online gallery. Runners-up will be displayed online only. Winners and runners-up both receive a complimentary copy of the publication." Open to all skill levels. Deadline: Last Friday of January, April, July and October. See website for more information.

CURATOR'S CHOICE AWARDS

P.O. Box 2483, Santa Fe NM 87504. (505)984-8353. **E-mail:** programs@visitcenter.org. **Website:** www. visitcenter.org. **Contact:** Laura Pressley, executive director. Annual contest. Center's Choice Awards are in three different categories with different jurors and prizes. "You can submit to one, two or all categories. Our jurors are some of the most important and influential people in the business. Photographers are invited to submit their most compelling images. Open to all skill levels." Prizes include exhibition and more. Photographers should see submissions guidelines at: visitcenter.org.

DIRECT ART MAGAZINE

SlowArt Productions, 123 Warren St., Hudson NY 12534. (518)828-2343. **E-mail:** slowart@aol.com. **Website:** www.slowart.com. **Contact:** Tim Slowinski, director. Cost: $35. Annual contest. "This contest is to select artists for publication in the annual edition of *Direct Art Magazine.*" Open to all skill levels. Awards: publication in *Direct Art Magazine*, front and back covers; 4-to-6 page coverage; full-page display awards. Value of awards: $22,000. Deadline: March 31, annually. E-mail or see website for more information.

DIRECT ART MAGAZINE PUBLICATION COMPETITION

SlowArt Productions, 123 Warren St., Hudson NY 12534. **E-mail:** slowart@aol.com; limnerentry@aol.com. **Website:** www.slowart.com. **Contact:** Tim Slowinski, director. Cost: $35. Annual contest. National magazine publication of new and emerging art in all medias. Cover and feature article awards. Open to all skill levels. Send SASE or see website for more information. SlowArt Productions presents the annual group thematic exhibition. Open to all artists, national and international, working in all media. All forms of art are eligible. *Entrants must be 18 years of age or older to apply.* 96 inch maximum for wall hung work, 72 inch for free-standing sculpture.

THE DIRECTOR'S CHOICE AWARDS

P.O. Box 2483, Santa Fe NM 87504. (505)984-8353. **E-mail:** programs@visitcenter.org. **Website:** www.visitcenter.org. Recognizes outstanding photographers through the dealer's perspective. Cost: $30/members $40/non-members. Annual contest. Photographers are invited to submit their most compelling images. Open to all skill levels. Prizes include exhibition and more. Deadline: February (see website for details). Photographers should see website for more information.

THE EDITOR'S CHOICE AWARDS

P.O. Box 2483, Santa Fe NM 87504. (505)984-8353. **E-mail:** programs@visitcenter.org. **Website:** www.visitcenter.org. Annual contest. This award recognizes outstanding photographers working in all processes and subject matter. Open to all skill levels. Awards/prizes: 1st, 2nd, 3rd prizes and Honorable Mention awarded; 1st Prize includes exhibition at Center space, publication in *Lenscratch* magazine and online exhibition at VisitCenter.org; see website for listing of prizes. Photographers should see website for more information.

EMERGING ARTISTS

SlowArt Productions, 123 Warren St., Hudson NY 12534. (518)828-2343. **E-mail:** slowart@aol.com. **Website:** www.slowart.com. **Contact:** Tim Slowinski, director. Cost: $35. Annual contest. "This contest is dedicated to the exhibition, publication and promotion of emerging artists." Open to all skill levels. Awards: exhibition at the Limner Gallery; $1,000 cash; $2,200 in publication awards. Deadline: November 30, annually. E-mail or see website for more information.

✪ ENERGY GALLERY ART CALL

E-mail: info@energygallery.com. **Website:** www.energygallery.com. Cost: $35 for 5 images; additional images $10/each. Energy Gallery is an arts organization operated by professional artists, art instructors and curators for promoting emerging and established artists globally. Energy Gallery is a virtual gallery as well as a physical gallery that organizes exhibitions at art galleries, trade shows and public institutions. A jury selects artworks for the online exhibition at Energy Gallery's website for a period of 3 months and archived in Energy Gallery's website permanently. Selected artists also qualify to participate in Energy Gallery's annual exhibit. Photographers should visit website for submission form, current art calls and more information. Deadline: late August.

EXHIBITIONS WITHOUT WALLS FOR PHOTOGRAPHERS AND DIGITAL ARTISTS

130 SW 20th Street, Cape Coral FL 33991. (239)223-6824. **E-mail:** ewedman@exhibitionswithoutwalls.com. **Website:** www.exhibitionswithoutwalls.com. **Contact:** Ed Wedman, co-founder. Cost: $25 for up to 5 images, each additional image up to 10 is an additional charge of $4. Contest is held quarterly. Online international juried competitions for photographers and digital artists. Prizes vary, but a minimum of $900 in cash awards and additional prizes. Open to all skill levels. Deadline: 30 days after submissions open. Contestants should see website for more information.

FIRELANDS ASSOCIATION FOR THE VISUAL ARTS

39 S. Main St., Oberlin OH 44074. (440)774-7158. **Fax:** (440)775-1107. **E-mail:** favagallery@oberlin.net. **Website:** www.favagallery.org. Cost: $15/photographer; $12 for FAVA members. Biennial juried photography contest (odd-numbered years) for residents of OH, KY, IN, MI, PA and WV. Both traditional and experimental techniques welcome. Photographers may submit up to 3 works completed in the last 3 years. Annual entry deadline: March-April (date varies, see website for details). Photographers should call, e-mail or see website for entry form and more details.

HUMANITY PHOTO AWARD (HPA)

World Folklore Photographers Association, Suite 1605, Shangzuo Building, Yi 97 Xuanwumen Xi-dajie, Beijing Xicheng District 100031, China. (86)(10)62252175. **Fax:** (86)(10)62252175. **E-mail:** hpa@worldfpa.org; link@hpa.org.cn. **Website:** www.world-fpa.org;. **Contact:** Organizing Committee HPA. Cost: free. Biennial contest. Open to all skill levels. See website for more information and entry forms.

INFOCUS JURIED EXHIBITION

Palm Beach Photographic Centre, 415 Clematis St., West Palm Beach FL 33401. (561)253-2600. **E-mail:** info@workshop.org. **Website:** www.workshop.org. **Contact:** Fatima NeJame, CEO. Cost: $20/image, up to 5 images. Annual photography contest. Awards: Best of Show: $950. Two merit awards: free tuition for a Fotofusion passport or a master photography workshop of your choice. Open to members of the Palm Beach Photographic Center. Interested parties can obtain an individual membership for $95. The Centre invites photographers working in all mediums and styles to participate. Experimental and mixed techniques are welcome. Photographers should call or visit website for more information.

KENTUCKY ARCHAEOLOGY MONTH POSTER CONTEST

109-A W. Poplar St., Elizabethtown KY 42701. (270)855-9780. **E-mail:** christywpritchard@gmail.com. **Website:** www.kyopa-org.org/kentucky_archaeology_month.html. **Contact:** Christy Pritchard, chair. Estab. 2014. Winning artwork and design will be used as the official poster for the first annual Kentucky Archaeology Month, "Celebrating Kentucky Archaeology." Calling all artists and graphic designers to submit poster designs that reflect their interpretation of Kentucky's rich heritage. The KAM steering committee will select 3 finalists from the designs submitted. Finalists will be e-mailed to the KyOPA membership and the winner will be selected by a membership vote. The official Kentucky Archaeology Month poster will be distributed to the Governor's office, members of Kentucky House, Kentucky Senate, as well as Kentucky libraries, schools, and various parks within the state. See website for submission deadline. Artists should submit proposed artwork in electronic, camera-ready format. Submitting artists must also complete the entry form. Submission must be original artwork. Submissions must be 2-dimensional artwork. No syndicated, copyrighted or clip art images may be submitted. Reproducibility will be a factor in the committee's decision. High contrast and bright colors are recommended, the estimated size of the poster will be 18×24. Selected artwork for the poster will be artistic, positive in approach and informative for use as a teaching tool. Selected artwork for the poster will commemorate Kentucky Archaeology Month celebrating the long history of archaeology and heritage studies in Kentucky. Selected artwork for the poster will have broad appeal to Kentuckians, educators, students, those considering Kentucky for travel and vacation, historians, artists and the general public. A committee will select 3 finalists from the artwork submitted. The selection committee will consist of members from KyOPA, the Kentucky Heritage Council, and the Office of State Archaeology. Artwork will be judged based upon: quality of artwork, creativity and originality of artwork, positive and thematically appropriate artwork, reproducibility. The winner will be selected by electronic vote, via e-mail, from the KyOPA membership. The Kentucky Organization of Professional Archaeologists will retain rights of ownership for all final artwork commissioned via this solicitation. The committee reserves the right to use the artwork for additional purposes, such as websites and print materials.

LAKE CHAMPLAIN MARITIME MUSEUM'S ANNUAL JURIED PHOTOGRAPHY EXHIBIT

4472 Basin Harbor Rd., Vergennes VT 05491. (802)475-2022. **E-mail:** eloiseb@lcmm.org. **Website:** www.lcmm.org. **Contact:** Eloise Beil. Annual exhibition. Lake Champlain Through the Lens, images of Lake Champlain. "Amateur and professional photographers are invited to submit framed prints in color or b&w. Professional photographers will judge and comment on the work." Additional prints of work accepted for exhibition can be placed on consignment at museum store. Call for entries begins in June, photograph delivery in August, on view September and October. Photographers should call, e-mail, or visit website for registration form.

LAKE SUPERIOR MAGAZINE PHOTO CONTEST

P.O. Box 16417, Duluth MN 55816-0417. (888)244-5253; (218)722-5002. **Fax:** (218)722-4096. **E-mail:** lsmphotosubmission@lakesuperior.com. **Website:** www.lakesuperior.com. **Contact:** Konnie LeMay, editor. Annual contest. Photos must be taken in the Lake Superior region and should be labeled for categories: lake/landscapes, nature, people/humor, artsy/altered. Accepts up to 10 b&w and color digital images. Images can be submitted as thumbnails with accompanying CD or online. Grand Prize: $200 prize package, plus a 1-year subscription to *Lake Superior Magazine* and a Lake Superior wall calendar. Other prizes include subscriptions and calendars; all prize winners, including honorable mentions and finalists, receive a Certificate of Honor. Although there is no cost to enter, entries will not be returned without a SASE. See website for more information.

☮ LARSON GALLERY JURIED BIENNUAL PHOTOGRAPHY EXHIBITION

Yakima Valley Community College, P.O. Box 22520, Yakima WA 98907. (509)574-4875. **E-mail:** gallery@yvcc.edu. **Website:** www.larsongallery.org. **Contact:** Denise Olsen, assistant director. Cost: $20/entry (limit 4 entries). National juried competition. Awards: Approximately $3,000 in prize money. Held odd years in April. First jurying held in February. Photographers should write, fax, e-mail or visit the website for prospectus.

⊕ LONG ISLAND ARTISTS EXHIBITION

107 E. Deer Park Rd., Dix Hills NY 11746. (631)462-5400. **Website:** www.artleagueli.org. Cost: 2 images, $40; $5 each additional image up to 3. Total maximum 5 images; non-members: First 2 images , $50; $5 each additional image up to 3. Total maximum 5 images. Open to artists residing in Suffolk, Nassau, Brooklyn and Queens. 2D and 3D work in any medium may be submitted, including photography and fine craft. Prize/Award: $500 Awards of Excellence and Honorable Mentions of one year memberships in ALLI will be given at the discretion of the judge. Deadline for submissions: late February. Contestants should call or see website for more information.

☮ LOS ANGELES CENTER FOR DIGITAL JURIED COMPETITION

1515 Wilcox Ave., Los Angeles CA 90028. (323)646-9427. **E-mail:** info@lacphoto.org. **Website:** www.lacphoto.org. The Los Angeles Center of Photography (LACP) is dedicated to supporting photographers and the phtographic arts. LACP provides high-caliber classes, local and travel workshops, exhibitions, screenings, lectures, and community outreach efforts, including grants, need-based scholarships, and fo-cused programming for youth and low-income families.

LOVE UNLIMITED FILM FESTIVAL & ART EXHIBITION

100 Cooper Point Rd., Suite 140-136, Olympia WA 98502. **E-mail:** entries1@loveanddiversity.org; volunteers@loveanddiversity.org. **Website:** www.communitygardenlove.org. **Contact:** submissions administrator. Accepts art (ceramics, drawings, fiber, functional, furniture, jewelry, metal, painting, printmaking, digital or graphics, mixed media 2D, mixed media 3D, sculpture, watercolor, wood, other or beyond categorization (specify), photography, music, writing, photos and all types of designs, as well as film and scripts. Accepts poetry, hip-hop, spoken word and zine excerpts, autobiography/memoir, children's, fiction, horror, humor, journalism, mystery, nature, novels, short stories, nonfiction, poetry, romance, science fiction/fantasy, screenwriting, travel, young adult and other topic areas. We accept writing in all these topic areas provided these topic areas are directly, indirectly, literally or symbolically related to love. Awards: over $30,000 in cash and prizes and 120 given out during a red carpet gala event in Los Angeles and in Austin TX. Photos and videos of past events are online. Open to all skill levels. Deadlines: October for art, November for all other categories. See website for more information.

◗ THE MACQUARIE PHOTOGRAPHY PRIZE

P.O. Box 4689, Dubbo NSW 2830, Australia. +(61) 0412638210. **E-mail:** mike.coward@australianartsales.com.au. **Website:** www.australianartsales.com.au/MacquariePrize/Macquariephotographyprize.html. **Contact:** Mike Coward, owner/director. Cost: $8AUD per photograph. The Macquarie Prize is a global photography competition open to anyone from any country. The aim of the competition is to capture the world's best images. Each year the contest is divided into 4 categories and there is no limit to the number of photographs one person can enter. The winner is decided by public voting of 100 finalists both at exhibitions and online. The 100 finalists will be printed and exhibited in South East Australia. $20,000AUD in prizes. Open to all skill levels. Deadline: August. Contestants should see website for more information.

MERCURY EXCELLENCE AWARDS

500 Executive Blvd., Ossining-on-Hudson NY 10562. (914)923-9400. **Fax:** (914)923-9484. **E-mail:** info@ mercommawards.com. **Website:** www.mercomm awards.com. **Contact:** Ms. Reni L. Witt, president. Cost: $280-345/entry (depending on category). Annual contest. The purpose of the contest is to honor outstanding achievement in public relations and corporate communications. Major category for photography, including ads, brochures, magazines, etc. "Best of Show" receives a personalized trophy. Grand Award winners receive award plaques (personalized). Gold, silver, bronze and honors receive a personalized award certificate. All nominators receive complete judge score sheets and evaluation comments. Deadline: mid-November. Please write, call, or e-mail for more information.

✪ MICHIGAN ANNUAL XLIII (ART COMPETITION & EXHIBITION)

125 Macomb Place, Mt. Clemons MI 48043. (586)469-8666. **Fax:** (586)469-4529. **E-mail:** exhibitions@ theartcenter.org. **Website:** www.theartcenter.org. **Contact:** Stephanie Szmiot, exhibition manager. Cost: $35.00 per artist for up to two entries to be juried. Annual statewide juried art competition. Open to resident Michigan artists ages 18 and older. No size or media restrictions. Featuring new guest juror each year. Up to 50 selected artworks are on display for about 4 weeks in main gallery. Prize/Award: 1st Place $1,000, 2nd Place $600, 3rd Place $400, in addition to five Honorable Mention Awards. Deadline for submissions: late December-early January. Contestants should write, send SASE, call, e-mail, and see website for more information.

✪ THE MOBIUS AWARDS FOR ADVERTISING

713 S. Pacific Coast Hwy., Suite B, Redondo Beach CA 90277-4233. (310)540-0959. **Fax:** (310)316-8905. **E-mail:** KristenSzabo@mobiusawards.com; mobius info@mobiusawards.com. **Website:** www.mobius awards.com. **Contact:** Kristen Szabo, manger entrant relations & operations. Annual international awards competition founded in 1971 for TV, cinema/in-flight and radio commercials, print, outdoor, new media, direct, logo/trademark, online, mixed media campaigns and package design. Student and spec work welcome. Deadline: October 1. Late entries accepted. "Entries are judged by an international jury on their effectiveness and creativity. Mobius Awards reflects the most current trends in the advertising industry by updating the competition regularly, such as adding new media types and categories. We are dedicated to consistently providing a fair competition with integrity."

MYRON THE CAMERA BUG & THE SHUTTERBUGS FAMILY

E-mail: cambug8480@aol.com. **Website:** www. shutterbugstv.com. **Contact:** Len Friedman, director. Open to all photography students, educators and snapshooters. Photographers should e-mail for details or questions.

NEW YORK STATE FAIR PHOTOGRAPHY COMPETITION AND SHOW

581 State Fair Blvd., Syracuse NY 13209. (315)487-7711, ext. 1337. **Website:** www.nysfair.org/competi tions. You may enter by downloading and mailing in the entry form, or directly online (any competition marked "N/A" is not available for online entry). All entry forms and fees must be received in person at the entry department office at the State Fairgrounds by 4:30 p.m. or online by midnight on the specified competition deadline date. See website for complete details, and to enter.

✪ PARIS PHOTO-APERTURE FOUNDATION PHOTOBOOK AWARDS, THE

547 W. 27th St., 4th Fl., New York NY 10001. (212)505-5555. **Fax:** (212)979-7759. **E-mail:** bookawards@ap erture.org. **Website:** www.aperture.org/photobook awards. **Contact:** Katie Clifford, executive assistant. Cost: First PhotoBook, $30/book; PhotoBook of the Year, $60/book; Photography Catalouge of the Year, $60/book. Annual photography contest. The purpose of this competition is to celebrate the book's contribution to the evolving narrative of photography. Awards: First PhotoBook $10,000, book included in Photo-Book Review and exhibition; PhotoBook of the Year-book included in PhotoBook Review, exhibition and the Catalogue category. Open to all skill levels. See website for deadline and for more information.

THE GORDON PARKS PHOTOGRAPHY COMPETITION

Fort Scott Community College, 2108 S. Horton, Fort Scott KS 66701-3140. (620)223-2700; (800)874-3722, ext. 5850. **Fax:** (620)223-4927. **E-mail:** gordonparks center@fortscott.edu. **Website:** www.gordonparks center.org. **Contact:** Jill Warford. The annual Gordon Parks Photography Competition is in tribute to Fort

Scott KS native Gordon Parks. This competition is open to anyone. Photographs submitted should have been taken within the last 5 years. "I used my camera as a weapon against all I disliked about America—poverty, racism, discrimination," Parks said. Each photographer may submit up to 4 photographs which will be judged as an individual entry. Each photo entry is $15. Awards: $350 1st Place, $200 2nd Place, $100 3rd Place will be awarded and up to 3 Honorable Mentions will receive $50 each. See complete details and access entry forms online. Submission deadline: see website.

PERKINS CENTER FOR THE ARTS JURIED PHOTOGRAPHY EXHIBITION

395 Kings Hwy., Moorestown NJ 08057. (856)235-6488 or (800)387-5226. **Fax:** (856)235-6624. **E-mail:** create@perkinscenter.org. **Website:** www.perkinscenter.org; www.perkinsarts.org/artist-opportunities-2. Cost: $10/entry; up to 3 entries. Regional juried photography exhibition. Works from the exhibition are considered for inclusion in the permanent collection of the Philadelphia Museum of Art and the Woodmere Art Museum. Past jurors include Merry Foresta, former curator of photography at the Smithsonian American Art Museum; Katherine Ware, curator of photographs at the Philadelphia Museum of Art; and photographers Emmett Gowin, Ruth Thorne-Thomsen, Matthew Pillsbury, and Vik Muniz. All work must be framed with wiring in back and hand-delivered to Perkins Center. Prospectus must be downloaded from the Perkins site. Photographers should call, e-mail or see website for more information.

PHOTOGRAPHY NOW

Center for Photography at Woodstock, 59 Tinker St., Woodstock NY 12498. (845)679-9957. **Fax:** (845)679-6337. **E-mail:** info@cpw.org. **Website:** www.cpw.org. **Contact:** Ariel Shanberg, executive director. Annual contest for exhibitions. Juried annually by renowned photographers, critics, museum and gallery curators. Deadline: January. General submission is ongoing. Photographers must call or write for guidelines.

THE PHOTO REVIEW ANNUAL PHOTOGRAPHY COMPETITION

140 E. Richardson Ave., Suite 301, Langhorne PA 19047. (215)891-0214. **E-mail:** info@photoreview.org. **Website:** www.photoreview.org. **Contact:** Stephen Perloff, editor. Cost: $35 for up to 3 images; $8 each for each additional image. International annual contest. All types of photographs are eligible—b&w, color, nonsilver, computer-manipulated, etc. Submit images to smarterentry.com or prints unmatted, unframed, 17×22 or smaller. All entries must be labeled. Awards include an Olympus camera, SilverFast software from LaserSoft Imaging ($499), a 24×50 roll of Museo Silver Rag, a 20×24 silver gelatin fiber print from Digital Silver Imaging, camera bags, etc. All winners reproduced in the competition issue of *Photo Review* magazine and online and prizewinners exhibited at photography gallery of The University of Arts/Philadelphia. Open to all skill levels. Deadline: May 30. Photographers should see www.photoreview.org for more information.

PHOTOSPIVA

222 W. Third St., Joplin MO 64801. (417)623-0183. **Fax:** (417)623-3805. **E-mail:** spiva@spivaarts.org. **Website:** www.spivaarts.org; www.photospiva.org. **Contact:** Jo Mueller, director. Annual national fine art photography competition. Awards: $3,000 cash. Open to all photographers in the US and its territories; any photographic process welcome. Enter online. See website for updates on deadlines and exhibition dates.

PICTURES OF THE YEAR INTERNATIONAL

University of Missouri, 315 Reynolds Journalism Institute, Columbia MO 65211. (573)884-7351; (573)884-2188. **E-mail:** info@poyi.org. **Website:** www.poyi.org. **Contact:** Rick Shaw. Cost: $50/entrant. Annual contest to reward and recognize excellence in photojournalism, sponsored by the Missouri School of Journalism and the Donald W. Reynolds Journalism Institute. Over $20,000 in cash and product awards. Open to all skill levels. January deadline. Photographers should write, call, e-mail or see website for more information.

The Missouri School of Journalism also sponsors College Photographer of the Year. See website for details.

PROFESSIONAL WOMEN PHOTOGRAPHERS INTERNATIONAL WOMEN'S CALL FOR ENTRY

119 W. 72nd St., #223, New York NY 10023. (212)410-4388. **E-mail:** open.calls@pwponline.org. **Website:** www.pwponline.org. **Contact:** Terry Berenson, development director. Contest held annually. "Professional Women Photographers (PWP) helps fulfill its mission of advancing women in photography by hosting international Calls for Entry open to all women photographers around the world." Awards: "1st Prize:

One photographer will receive $600 and her selected image will appear in the Spring/Summer issue of *Imprints* magazine. Her image will be exhibited in the Soho Photo Gallery show and the online exhibition. 2nd Prize: One photographer will receive $500 and her image will appear in *Imprints* Spring/Summer issue. Her image will be exhibited in the SohoPhoto Gallery show and the online exhibition. 3rd Prize: One photographer will receive $400 and her image will appear in the Spring/Summer issue of *Imprints*. Her image will be exhibited in the SohoPhoto Gallery show and the online exhibition." Deadlines vary; see website for details.

PROJECT LAUNCH

P.O. Box 2483, Santa Fe NM 87504. (505)984-8353. **Website:** www.visitcenter.org. Annual contest. Project Launch honors committed photographers working on documentary projects and fine-art series. Three jurors reach a consensus on the 1st Prize and 10-25 Honorable Mentions. Each individual juror also selects a project to receive 1 of the 3 Juror's Choice Awards. Prizes include $5,000, 2 exhibitions and reception during Review Santa Fe, a year-long Photographer's Showcase at Photoeye.com, publication in *Lenscratch*, workshop tuition vouchers and an online exhibition at VisitCenter.org. Photographers should see website for more information.

RHODE ISLAND STATE COUNCIL ON THE ARTS FELLOWSHIPS

One Capitol Hill, Third Floor, Providence RI 02908. (401)222-3880. **Fax:** (401)222-3018. **Website:** www.arts.ri.gov/grants/guidelines/fellow.php. Rhode Island residents only. Cost: free. Annual contest "to encourage the creative development of Rhode Island artists by enabling them to set aside time to pursue their work and achieve specific career goals." Awards $5,000 fellowship; $1,000 merit award. Open to advanced photographers. Deadline: April 1. Photographers should go to www.arts.ri.gov/grants/guidelines/fellow.php for more information.

THE MANUEL RIVERA-ORTIZ FOUNDATION FOR DOCUMENTARY PHOTOGRAPHY & FILM

1110 Park Ave., Rochester NY 14610-1729. (917)720-5769. **Fax:** (585)256-6462. **E-mail:** submissions@mrofoundation.org. **Website:** www.mrofoundation.org. **Contact:** competition coordinator, annual contest. "Our mission is to support underrepresented photographers in communities throughout the developing and developed world. We encourage emerging and established photographers and filmmakers in the fields of Photojournalism/Photo Reportage and Documentary Film to submit their work on topics such as the plight of the poor, the forgotten, and the disenfranchised. Each year, shortlisted entries in two categories (selected from international submissions) in the genres of 'Documentary-Still Photography' and 'Documentary Short-Short Film,' will vie for our grant. Call is open to all skill levels. For more information, please see our website. There are no entry fees."

SAN DIEGO COUNTY FAIR ANNUAL EXHIBITION OF PHOTOGRAPHY

2260 Jimmy Durante Blvd., Del Mar CA 92014. (858)792-4207. **E-mail:** entry@sdfair.com; photo@sdfair.com. **Website:** www.sdfair.com. **Contact:** Entry office. Sponsor: San Diego County Fair (22nd District Agricultural Association). Annual event for still photos/prints. This is a juried competition open to individual photographers. Entry information is posted on the website as it becomes available in February and March. Pre-registration deadline: April/May. Access the dates and specifications for entry on website. Entry form can be submitted online.

A SHOW OF HEADS

SlowArt Productions, 123 Warren St., Hudson NY 12534. (518)828-2343. **E-mail:** slowart@aol.com. **Website:** www.slowart.com. **Contact:** Tim Slowinski, director. Cost: $35. Annual contest. "This contest is to select artists for exhibition in The Show of Heads at Limner Gallery. The show features work based on the portrayal and interpretation of the human head." Open to all skill levels. Awards: exhibition at Limner Gallery; 3 artists receive publication in *Direct Art Magazine*; 1 artist receives 2 full pages; 2 artists receive 1 page. Value of awards: $2,200. Deadline: August 31, annually. E-mail or see website for more information.

SPRING PHOTOGRAPHY CONTEST

Serbin Communications, 813 Reddick St., Santa Barbara CA 93103. (805)963-0439 or (800)876-6425. **Fax:** (805)965-0496. **E-mail:** julie@serbin.com. **Website:** www.pfmagazine.com. Annual amateur contest, runs January thru mid-May. Sponsored by *Photographer's Forum Magazine*. Winners and finalists have their photos published in the hardcover book, *Best of Pho-*

tography. Entry fee: $4.95-5.95 per photo. See website for entry form.

⊕ ◯ TALLAHASSEE INTERNATIONAL JURIED COMPETITION

530 W. Call St., Rm. 250FAB, Tallahassee FL 32306-1140. (850)644-3906. **Fax:** (850)644-7229. **E-mail:** tallahasseeinternational@fsu.edu. **Website:** www.mofa.cfa.fsu.edu/participate/tallahassee-international. **Contact:** Jean D. Young, coordinator. Cost: $20/2 images. Annual art contest. Artists worldwide, 18+ are eligible. All media and subject matter eligible for consideration. Juried by panel of FSU College of Fine Arts faculty. One entry/person. Awards: 1st- $1,000; 2nd- $500. Color catalog is produced. Open to all skill levels. Deadline: February 15, 2016. Photographers should e-mail or visit website for more information.

TAYLOR COUNTY PHOTOGRAPHY CLUB MEMORIAL DAY CONTEST

P.O. Box 613, Grafton WV 26354-0613. (304)265-5405. **E-mail:** bowtie1008@comcast.net. **Website:** tcphotoclub.webplus.net. **Contact:** Don Sapp, club secretary. Cost: $4/print (maximum of 10). Annual juried contest (nationally judged) held in observance of Memorial Day in Grafton WV. Color and b&w, all subject matter except nudes. All prints must be mounted or matted, with a minimum overall size of 8×10 and maximum overall size of 16×20. No framed prints or slides. No signed prints or mats. All prints must be identified on the back as follows: name, address, phone number, title, and entry number of print (e.g., 1 of 6). Entries need to have hangers on the back for display purposes. All entries must be delivered in a reusable container. Entrant's name, address and number of prints must appear on the outside of the container. Open to amateur photographers only. Six award categories. E-mail hsw123@comcast.net to receive an entry form.

● ◯ UNLIMITED EDITIONS INTERNATIONAL JURIED PHOTOGRAPHY COMPETITIONS

198 Brittany Place Dr., Suite V, Hendersonville NC 28792. (828)489-9609. **E-mail:** gregoryleng@aol.com; ultdeditionsIntl@aol.com. **Contact:** Gregory Hugh Leng, president/owner. Sponsors juried photography competitions several times yearly offering cash, award certificates and prizes. Photography accepted from amateurs and professionals. Open to all skill levels and ages. Prizes awarded in different categories or divisions such as commercial, portraiture, journalism, landscape, digital imaging, and retouching. We accept formats in print film, transparencies and digital images. B&w, color, and digital imaging CDs or DVDs may be submitted for consideration. Prints and large transparencies may be in mats, no frames. All entries must be delivered in a reusable container with prepaid postage to insure photography is returned. Unlimited Editions International also offers the unique opportunity to purchase photography from those photographers who wish to sell their work. All images submitted in competition remain the property of the photographer/entrants unless an offer to purchase their work is accepted by the photographer. All photographers must send SASE (with $1.44 postage) for entry forms, contest dates, and detailed information on how to participate in our International juried photography competitions.

YOUR BEST SHOT

Website: www.popphoto.com. Monthly contest. "Every month, we choose 3 images submitted by our readers to feature in the pages of *Popular Photography.* There are no category restrictions, we just want to see your most creative and well-done work. A gallery of the judges' picks will appear online and the overall winner will be revealed in an upcoming issue of the magazine." Awards/prizes: 1st Place $300; 2nd Place $200; 3rd Place $100. See website for complete details and submission deadlines.

CONTESTS

PHOTO REPRESENTATIVES

Many photographers are good at promoting themselves and seeking out new clients, and they actually enjoy that part of the business. Other photographers are not comfortable promoting themselves and would rather dedicate their time and energy solely to producing their photographs. Regardless of which camp you're in, you may need a photo rep.

Finding the rep who is right for you is vitally important. Think of your relationship with a rep as a partnership. Your goals should mesh. Treat your search for a rep much as you would your search for a client. Try to understand the rep's business, who they already represent, etc., before you approach them. Show you've done your homework.

When you sign with a photo rep, you basically hire someone to get your portfolio in front of art directors, make cold calls in search of new clients, and develop promotional ideas to market your talents. The main goal is to find assignment work for you with corporations, advertising firms, or design studios. And, unlike stock agencies or galleries, a photo rep is interested in marketing your talents rather than your images.

Most reps charge a 20- to 30-percent commission. They handle more than one photographer at a time, usually making certain that each shooter specializes in a different area. For example, a rep may have contracts to promote three different photographers—one who handles product shots, another who shoots interiors, and a third who photographs food.

DO YOU NEED A REP?

Before you decide to seek out a photo representative, consider these questions:

- Do you already have enough work, but want to expand your client base?
- Are you motivated to maximize your profits? Remember that a rep is interested in working with photographers who can do what is necessary to expand their businesses.

- Do you have a tightly edited portfolio with pieces showing the kind of work you want to do?
- Are you willing to do what it takes to help the rep promote you, including having a budget to help pay for self-promotional materials?
- Do you have a clear idea of where you want your career to go, but need assistance in getting there?
- Do you have a specialty or a unique style that makes you stand out?

If you answered yes to most of these questions, perhaps you would profit from the expertise of a rep. If you feel you are not ready for a rep or that you don't need one, but you still want some help, you might consider a consultation with an expert in marketing and/or self-promotion.

As you search for a rep, there are numerous points to consider. First, how established is the rep you plan to approach? Established reps have an edge over newcomers in that they know the territory. They've built up contacts in ad agencies, magazines, and elsewhere. This is essential since most art directors and picture editors do not stay in their positions for long periods of time. Therefore, established reps will have an easier time helping you penetrate new markets.

If you decide to go with a new rep, consider paying an advance against commission in order to help the rep financially during an equitable trial period. Usually it takes a year to see returns on portfolio reviews and other marketing efforts, and a rep who is relying on income from sales might go hungry if he doesn't have a base income from which to live.

Whatever you agree upon, always have a written contract. Handshake deals won't cut it. You must know the tasks that each of you is required to complete, and having your roles discussed in a contract will guarantee there are no misunderstandings. For example, spell out in your contract what happens with clients that you had before hiring the rep. Most photographers refuse to pay commissions for these "house" accounts, unless the rep handles them completely and continues to bring in new clients.

Also, it's likely that some costs, such as promotional fees, will be shared. For example, photographers often pay 75 percent of any advertising fees (such as sourcebook ads and direct mail pieces).

ROBERT BACALL REPRESENTATIVES INC.

4 Springwood Dr., Princeton Junction NJ 08550. (917)763-6554. **E-mail:** rob@bacall.com. **Website:** www.bacall.com. **Contact:** Robert Bacall. Estab. 1988. "We represent commercial photographers, CGI and motion content providers for both print and video animation needs." Agency specializes in digital imaging, healthcare, food, still life, fashion, beauty, kids, corporate, environmental, portrait, lifestyle, location, landscape. Markets include advertising agencies, corporations/clients direct, design firms, editorial/magazines, publishing/books, sales/promotion firms.

TERMS Rep receives 30-35% commission. Exclusive area representation required. For promotional purposes, talent must provide portfolios, cases, tearsheets, prints, etc. Advertises in *Found Folios*, *Workbook*, *Le Book*, *At-Edge* and all of their respective websites. Bacall reps can also be found on Facebook, Twitter and LinkedIn.

HOW TO CONTACT Send query letter/e-mail, direct mail flier/brochure. Responds only if interested. After initial contact, drop off or mail materials for review.

TIPS "Seek representation when you feel your portfolio is unique and can bring in new business." Also offering consulting services to photographers that are not represented but are looking to improve their business potential.

MARIANNE CAMPBELL ASSOCIATES

136 Bella Vista Ave., Belvedere CA 94920. (415)433-0353. **E-mail:** marianne@mariannecampbell.com; quinci@mariannecampbell.com. **Website:** www.mariannecampbell.com. **Contact:** Marianne Campbell or Quinci Kelly (149 Madison Ave.,#1102, New York NY 10016). Estab. 1989. Commercial photography representative. Member of APA, SPAR, Western Art Directors Club. Represents 7 photographers. Markets include advertising agencies, corporations/clients direct, design firms, editorial/magazines.

HANDLES Photography.

TERMS Negotiated individually with each photographer.

CASEY

20 W. 22nd St., #1605, New York NY 10010. (212)858-3757; (212)929-3757. **E-mail:** info@wearecasey.com. **Website:** www.wearecasey.com. Represents photographers. Agency specializes in representing commercial photographers. Markets include advertising agencies, corporate/client direct, design firms, editorial/magazines, direct mail firms.

HANDLES Photography.

HOW TO CONTACT Send brochure, promo cards. Responds only if interested. Portfolios may be dropped off Monday through Friday. To show portfolio, photographer should follow up with call. Rep will contact photographer for portfolio review if interested.

TIPS Finds new talent through submission, recommendations from other artists.

RANDY COLE REPRESENTS LLC

153 W. 27th St., Suite 200, New York NY 10001. (212)760-1212. **E-mail:** randy@randycole.com. **Website:** www.randycole.com. Estab. 1989. Commercial photography, video, and CGI representative. Member of SPAR. Represents 11 photographers and CGI artists. Staff includes an assistant. Markets include advertising agencies, corporate clients, design firms, magazine, newspaper and book publishers as well as entertainment and music companies.

HANDLES Photography.

TERMS Agent receives commission on the creative fees, dependent upon specific negotiation. Advertises in *At Edge*, *Archive* and *Le Book* as well as online creative directories. Social media includes Facebook, LinkedIn, and Twitter. Randy Cole Represents is certified by Women's Business Enterprise National Council as a woman owned, operated, and controlled business meeting the criteria of diversity supplies status.

HOW TO CONTACT To contact the agency about representation, please send an e-mail or promo piece and follow up with a call.

TIPS Finds new talent through submissions and referrals.

MICHAEL GINSBURG & ASSOCIATES INC.

250 White Plains Rd., Tarrytown NY 10591. (212)369-3594. **E-mail:** mg@michaelginsburg.com. **Website:** www.michaelginsburg.com. **Contact:** Michael Ginsburg. Estab. 1978. Commercial photography representative. Represents 9 photographers. Agency specializes in advertising and editorial photographers. Markets include advertising agencies, corporations/clients direct, design firms, editorial/magazines, sales/promotion firms.

HANDLES Photography.

TERMS Rep receives 30% commission. Charges for messenger costs, FedEx expenses. Exclusive area representation required. Advertising costs are paid 100% by talent. For promotional purposes, talent must provide a minimum of 5 portfolios—direct mail pieces 2 times per year—and at least 1 sourcebook per year. Advertises in *Workbook*, source books and online source books.

HOW TO CONTACT Send query letter, direct mail flier/brochure, or e-mail. Responds only if interested within 2 weeks. After initial contact, call for appointment to show portfolio of tearsheets, slides, photographs.

TIPS Obtains new talent through personal referrals and solicitation.

CAROL GUENZI AGENTS, INC.

865 Delaware St., Denver CO 80204. (303)820-2599; (800)417-5120. **E-mail:** art@artagent.com. **Website:** www.artagent.com. **Contact:** Carol Guenzi, president. Estab. 1984. Commercial and advertising photography, illustration, new media, video film/animation representative. Member of Art Directors Club of Denver, AIGA and ASMP. Represents 28 illustrators, 8 photographers, 6 computer multimedia designers, 4 film/video production companies. Agency specializes in a "worldwide selection of talent in all areas of visual communications." Markets include advertising agencies, corporations/clients direct, design firms, editorial/magazine, paper products/greeting cards, sales/promotions firms.

HANDLES Illustration, photography, new media, film and animation. Looking for unique styles and applications and digital imaging.

TERMS Rep receives 25-30% commission. Exclusive area representation required. Advertising costs are split: 70-75% paid by talent; 25-30% paid by representative. For promotional purposes, talent must provide "promotional material after 6 months, some restrictions on portfolios." Advertises in *Directory of Illustration* and *Workbook*.

HOW TO CONTACT E-mail JPEGs or send direct mail piece, tearsheets. Responds in 2-3 weeks, only if interested. After initial contact, call or e-mail for appointment or to drop off or ship materials for review. Portfolio should include tearsheets, prints, samples and a list of current clients.

TIPS Obtains new talent through solicitation, art directors' referrals and active pursuit by individual.

"Show your strongest style and have at least 12 samples of that style before introducing all your capabilities. Be prepared to add additional work to your portfolio to help round out your style. We do a large percentage of computer manipulation and accessing on network. All our portfolios are both electronic and prints."

CRISTOPHER LAPP PHOTOGRAPHY

1211 Sunset Plaza Dr., Suite 413, Los Angeles CA 90069. (310)612-0040. **E-mail:** cristopherlapp.photo@gmail.com. **Website:** www.cristopherlapp.com. **Contact:** Cristopher Lapp. Estab. 1994. Specializes in fine art prints, hand-pulled originals, limited edition, monoprints, monotypes, offset reproduction, unlimited edition, posters.

HANDLES Decorative art, fashionable art, commercial and designer marketing. Clients include: Posner Fine Art, Gilanyi Inc., Jordan Designs.

TERMS Keeps samples on file.

HOW TO CONTACT Send an e-mail inquiry.

LEE + LOU PRODUCTIONS INC.

12 Juniper Creek Blvd., Pinehurst NC 28374. (310)480-5475. **E-mail:** leelou@earthlink.net. **Website:** www.leelou.com. **Contact:** Lee Pisarski. Estab. 1981. Commercial illustration and photography representative, digital and traditional photo retouching. Represents 2 retouchers, 5 photographers, 5 film directors, 2 visual effects companies, 1 CGI company. Specializes in automotive. Markets include advertising agencies.

HANDLES Photography, commercial film, CGI, visual effects.

TERMS Rep receives 25% commission. Charges for shipping, entertainment. Exclusive area representation required. Advertising costs are paid by talent. For promotional purposes, talent must provide direct mail advertising material. Advertises in *Creative Black Book*, *Workbook* and *Single Image, Shoot, Boards*.

HOW TO CONTACT Send direct mail flyer/brochure, tearsheets. Responds in 1 week. After initial contact, call for appointment to show portfolio of photographs.

TIPS Obtains new talent through recommendations from others, some solicitation.

THE BRUCE LEVIN GROUP

305 Seventh Ave., Suite 1101, New York NY 10001. (212)627-2281. **E-mail:** brucelevin@mac.com. **Website:** www.brucelevingroup.com. **Contact:** Bruce Levin, president. Estab. 1983. Commercial photography representative. Member of SPAR and ASMP.

Represents 6 photographers. Specializes in advertising, editorial and catalog; heavy emphasis on fashion, lifestyle and computer graphics.

HANDLES Photography.

TERMS Rep receives 25% commission. Exclusive area representation required. Advertising costs are paid by talent. Advertises in *Workbook* and other sourcebooks.

HOW TO CONTACT Send brochure, photos; call. Portfolios may be dropped off every Monday–Friday.

TIPS Obtains new talent through recommendations, research, word of mouth, solicitation.

NORMAN MASLOV AGENT INTERNATIONALE

3200 Genesee St., Seattle WA 98118. (415)641-4376. **E-mail:** maslov@maslov.com. **Website:** maslov.com. Estab. 1986. Member of APA. Represents 10 photographers. Markets include advertising agencies, corporations/clients direct, design firms, editorial/magazines, paper products/greeting cards, publishing/books, private collections.

HANDLES Photography. Looking for "original work not derivative of other artists. Artist must have developed style."

TERMS Rep receives 30% commission. Exclusive US national representation required. Advertising costs split varies. For promotional purposes, talent must provide 3-4 direct mail pieces/year. Advertises in *Archive*, *Workbook* and *At Edge*.

HOW TO CONTACT Send query letter, direct mail flier/brochure, tearsheets. Do not send original work. Responds in 2-3 weeks, only if interested. After initial contact, call to schedule an appointment, or drop off or mail materials for review. Individual and group consulting available in person or via phone or website.

TIPS Obtains new talent through suggestions from art buyers and recommendations from designers, art directors, other agents, sourcebooks and industry magazines and social networks. "We prefer to follow our own leads rather than receive unsolicited promotions and inquiries. It's best to have represented yourself for several years to know your strengths and be realistic about your marketplace. The same is true of having experience with direct mail pieces, developing client lists, and having a system of follow up. We want our talent to have experience with all this so they can properly value our contribution to their growth and success—otherwise that 30% becomes a burden and point of resentment. Enter your best work into competitions such as *Communication Arts* and *Graphis* photo annuals. Create a distinctive promotion mailer if your concepts and executions are strong."

JUDITH MCGRATH

P.O. Box 133, 32W040 Army Trail Rd., Wayne IL 60184. (312)945-8450. **Fax:** (312)465-1638. **E-mail:** judy@judymcgrath.net. **Website:** www.judymcgrath. net. Estab. 1980. Commercial photography/videography representative. Represents photographers and videographers. Markets include advertising agencies, corporate/client direct, design firms, editorial/magazines, paper products/greeting cards, publishing/books, direct mail firms.

HANDLES Photography, videography.

TERMS Rep receives 25% commission. Exclusive area representation required. Advertising costs paid by talent. Advertises in *Workbook*.

HOW TO CONTACT Send query letter, bio, tearsheets, photocopies. Rep will contact artist for portfolio review if interested.

MUNRO CAMPAGNA ARTISTS REPRESENTATIVES

630 N. State St., #2109, Chicago IL 60654. (312)335-8925. **E-mail:** steve@munrocampagna.com. **Website:** www.munrocampagna.com. **Contact:** Steve Munro, president. Estab. 1987. Commercial photography and illustration representative. Member of SPAR, CAR (Chicago Artist Representatives). Represents 1 photographer, 30 illustrators. Markets include advertising agencies, corporations/clients direct, design firms, publishing/books.

HANDLES Illustration, photography.

TERMS Rep receives 30% commission. Exclusive national representation required. Advertising costs are paid by talent. For promotional purposes, talent must provide 2 portfolios, leave-behinds, several promos. Advertises in *Workbook*, other sourcebooks.

HOW TO CONTACT Send query letter, bio, tearsheets, SASE. Responds within 2 weeks, only if interested. After initial contact, write to schedule an appointment.

JACKIE PAGE

219 E. 69th St., New York NY 10021. (212)772-0346. **E-mail:** jackiepage@pobox.com. Estab. 1985. Commercial photography representative. Represents 6 photographers. Markets include advertising agencies.

HANDLES Photography. "I have represented many photographers for 20+ years in the New York City

Advertising industry. I now prefer to do consulting for photographers wanting to obtain major campaign work in the national market."

TERMS "Details given at a personal interview." Advertises in *Workbook*.

HOW TO CONTACT Send direct mail, promo pieces or e-mail with 2-3 sample pictures in JPEG format (under 200kb total). After initial contact, call for appointment to show portfolio of tearsheets, prints, chromes.

TIPS Obtains new talent through recommendations from others and mailings.

PHOTOKUNST

725 Argyle Ave., Friday Harbor WA 98250. (360)378-1028. **Fax:** (360)370-5061. **E-mail:** info@photokunst.com. **Website:** www.photokunst.com. **Contact:** Barbara Cox, principal. Estab. 1998. Consulting and marketing of photography archives and fine art photography, nationally and internationally. "Accepting select number of photographers on our website. Working with artists on licensing, marketing prints, curating and traveling gallery and museum exhibitions; development of photography books, act as agent to the publishing industry."

HANDLES Emphasis on cause-oriented photography, photojournalism, documentary and ethnographic photography.

TERMS Charges for consultation, per project rate or annual for full representation; for representation, percentage of sales and licensing apply.

HOW TO CONTACT Send website information. Responds in 2-3 months. Finds new talent through submissions, recommendations, publications, art fairs, portfolio reviews.

TIPS "In order to be placed in important galleries and museums, a book and/or exhibition project must be either in place or in serious planning stage."

PHOTOTHERAPY CONSULTANTS

11977 Kiowa Ave., Los Angeles CA 90049-6119. **E-mail:** rhoni@phototherapists.com. **Website:** www.phototherapists.com. **Contact:** Rhoni Epstein, acquisitions. Estab. 1983. Commercial and fine art photography consultant. "Consulting with a knowledgeable and well-respected industry insider is a valuable way to get focused and advance your career in a creative and cost-efficient manner. You will see how to differentiate yourself from other photographers. Inexpensive ways to customize your portfolio, marketing program, branding materials and websites will show the market who you are and why they need you. You will be guided to embrace your point of view and learn how to focus your images on making money!" Rhoni Epstein is an Adjunct Assistant Professor at Art Center College of Design, a panel moderator, portfolio reviewer, lecturer and contest judge.

HOW TO CONTACT Via e-mail.

TIPS "Work smart, remain persistent and enthusiastic; there is always a market for creative and talented people."

PICTURE MATTERS

(323)464-2492. **Fax:** (323)465-7013. **E-mail:** info@picturematters.com. **Website:** www.picturematters.com. Estab. 1985. Commercial photography representative. Member of APA. Represents 12 photographers. Staff: Sherwin Taghdiri, sales rep. Agency specializes in photography. Markets include advertising agencies, design firms.

HANDLES Photography.

TERMS Rep receives 25% commission. Charges shipping expenses. Exclusive representation required. No geographic restrictions. Advertising costs are paid by talent. For promotional purposes, talent must provide promos, advertising and a quality portfolio. Advertises in various source books.

HOW TO CONTACT Send direct mail flyer/brochure.

MARIA PISCOPO

1684 Decoto Rd., #271, Union City CA 94587. (714)356-4260. **E-mail:** maria@mpiscopo.com. **Website:** www.mpiscopo.com. **Contact:** Maria Piscopo. Estab. 1978. Commercial photography representative. Member of SPAR, Women in Photography, Society of Illustrative Photographers. Markets include advertising agencies, design firms, corporations.

HANDLES Photography. Looking for "unique, unusual styles; established photographers only."

TERMS Rep receives 25% commission. Exclusive area representation required. No geographic restrictions. Advertising costs are split: 50% paid by talent; 50% paid by representative. For promotional purposes, talent must have a website and provide 3 traveling portfolios, leave-behinds and at least 6 new promo pieces per year. Plans web, advertising and direct mail campaigns.

HOW TO CONTACT Send query letter and samples via PDF to maria@mpiscopo.com. Do not call. Responds within 2 weeks, only if interested.

TIPS Obtains new talent through personal referral and photo magazine articles. "Do lots of research. Be very businesslike, organized, professional and follow the above instructions!"

ALYSSA PIZER

13121 Garden Land Rd., Los Angeles CA 90049. (310)440-3930. **Fax:** (310)440-3830. **E-mail:** alyssa@alyssapizer.com. **Website:** www.alyssapizer.com. Estab. 1990. Represents 11 photographers. Agency specializes in fashion, beauty and lifestyle (catalog, image campaign, department store, beauty and lifestyle awards). Markets include advertising agencies, corporations/clients direct, design firms, editorial/magazines.

HANDLES Established photographers only.

HOW TO CONTACT Send query letter or direct mail flier/brochure or e-mail website address. Responds in a couple of days. After initial contact, call to schedule an appointment or drop off or mail materials for review.

VICKI SANDER/FOLIO FORUMS

48 Gramercy Park N., Suite 5, New York NY 10010. (212)420-1333. **E-mail:** vicki@vickisander.com. **Website:** www.vickisander.com. **Contact:** Vicki Sander. Estab. 1985. Commercial photography representative. Member of The One Club for Art and Copy, The New York Art Directors Club. Represents photographers. Markets include advertising agencies, corporate/client direct, design firms. "Folio Forums is a company that promotes photographers by presenting portfolios at agency conference rooms in catered breakfast reviews. Accepting submissions for consideration on a monthly basis."

HANDLES Photography, fine art. Looking for lifestyle, fashion, food.

TERMS Rep receives 30% commission. Consulting available.

HOW TO CONTACT Responds in 1 month. To show portfolio, photographer should follow up with a call and/or letter after initial query.

TIPS Finds new talent through recommendation from other artists, referrals. Have a portfolio put together and have promo cards to leave behind, as well as mailing out to rep prior to appointment.

WALTER SCHUPFER MANAGEMENT CORPORATION

401 Broadway, Suite 14, New York NY 10013. (212)366-4675. **Fax:** (212)255-9726. **E-mail:** mail@wschupfer.com. **Website:** www.wschupfer.com. **Contact:** Walter Schupfer, president. Estab. 1996. Commercial photography representative. Represents photographers, stylists, designers. Staff includes producers, art department, syndication. Agency specializes in photography. Markets include advertising agencies, corporate/client direct, design firms, editorial/magazines, record labels, galleries.

HANDLES Photography, design, stylists, make-up artists, specializing in complete creative management.

TERMS Charges for messenger service. Exclusive area representation required. For promotional purposes, talent must provide several commercial and editorial portfolios. Advertises in *Le Book*.

HOW TO CONTACT Send promo cards, "then give us a call." To show portfolio, photographer should follow up with call.

TIPS Finds new talent through submissions, recommendations from other artists. "Do research to see if your work fits our agency."

FREDA SCOTT, INC.

302 Costa Rica Ave., San Mateo CA 94402. (650)548-2446. **E-mail:** freda@fredascott.com. **Website:** www.fredascott.com. **Contact:** Freda Scott, rep/president. Estab. 1980. Commercial photography, illustration or photography, commercial illustration representative and licensing agent. Represents 12 photographers, 8 illustrators. Licenses photographers and illustrators. Markets include advertising agencies, architects, corporate/client direct, designer firms, developers, direct mail firms, paper products/greeting cards.

HANDLES Illustration, photography.

TERMS Rep receives 25% as standard commission. Advertising costs paid entirely by talent. For promotional purposes, talent must provide mailers/postcards. Advertises in *The Workbook* and *American Showcase/Illustrators*.

HOW TO CONTACT Send link to website. Responds, only if interested, within 2 weeks. Rep will contact the talent for portfolio review, if interested.

TIPS Obtains new talent through submissions and recommendations from other artists, art directors and designers.

☼ TAENDEM AGENCY

P.O. Box 47054, 15-555 W. 12th Ave., Vancouver British Columbia V5Z 4L6, Canada. (604)569-6544. **E-mail:** talent@taendem.com. **Website:** www.taendem.com. **Contact:** Corwin Hiebert, principal. Estab.

2006. International management agency. Represents a handful of photographers and videographers. Specializes in consulting with freelancers and assisting them with building and growing a successful small creative business. Also full-service business administration and marketing management for creative entrepreneurs. Offerings include: business planning, branding, marketing strategy, portfolio development, website development, social media planning, contract management, client management, project management, proposal writing, estimates and invoicing, itinerate speaking engagements, travel logistics, and production.

HANDLES Illustration, photography, fine art, design and videography.

TERMS Upon acceptance, we charge a minimum monthly retainer of $200 for access and management rights; for specific tasks we use project costing—quoted and applied upon talent's approval. Additional work is quoted and billed upon talent request/approval. Itinerate speaking commission rate is negotiated on a case-by-case basis. Management representation is nonexclusive. Business development consultation available to qualified talent only; full-service management representation is selectively offered at the discretion of the agency. 100% of advertising costs paid by talent. Standard offering includes no paid advertising. Talent must provide full contact information, current headshot, website link and a sample of their work. For photographers, we require 10 select portfolio images.

HOW TO CONTACT Send link to website and full contact information and a brief business description. Portfolio should include large thumbnails, videographers should provide demo reel (Vimeo or YouTube). A business manager will be in contact within 1 week.

TIPS Obtains new talent through submissions and recommendations from other artists. Keep e-mails short and friendly. No phone calls. "Creatives are more likely to generate demand when their business is well-organized and their marketing efforts elicit curiosity instead of trying to stand out in a crowd of talented peers. Growing your business network and developing your portfolio through personal and collaborative projects makes you more attractive to both reps and buyers. If you need help growing your creative small business, just remember: You are Batman. We are Robin."

 TM ENTERPRISES

Rua Firmino Barbosa, 147 Boqueirao, Santos 11045-400 SP, Brazil. **E-mail:** tmarques1@hotmail.com. **Contact:** Tony Marques. Estab. 1985. Commercial photography representative and photography broker. Member of Beverly Hills Chamber of Commerce. Represents 50 photographers. Agency specializes in photography of women only: high fashion, swimsuit, lingerie, glamour and fine (good taste) *Playboy*-style pictures, erotic. Markets include advertising agencies, corporations/clients direct, editorial/magazines, paper products/greeting cards, publishing/books, sales/promotion firms, medical magazines.

HANDLES Photography.

TERMS Rep receives 50% commission. Advertising costs are paid by representative. "We promote the standard material the photographer has available, unless our clients request something else." Advertises in Europe, South and Central America, and magazines not known in the US.

HOW TO CONTACT Send everything available. Responds in 2 days. After initial contact, drop off or mail appropriate materials for review. Portfolio should include slides, photographs, transparencies, printed work.

TIPS Obtains new talent through worldwide famous fashion shows in Paris, Rome, London and Tokyo; by participating in well-known international beauty contests; recommendations from others. "Send your material clean and organized. Do not borrow other photographers' work in order to get representation. Always protect yourself by copyrighting your material. Get releases from everybody who is in the picture (or who owns something in the picture)."

DOUG TRUPPE

121 E. 31st St., Suite 10A, New York NY 10016. (212)685-1223. **E-mail:** doug@dougtruppe.com. **Website:** www.dougtruppe.com. **Contact:** Doug Truppe, artist representative. Estab. 1998. Commercial photography representative. Represents 10 photographers. Agency specializes in lifestyle, food, sports, still life, portrait and children's photography. Markets include advertising agencies, corporate, design firms, editorial/magazines, publishing/books, direct mail firms.

HANDLES Photography. "Always looking for great commercial work." Established, working photographers only.

TERMS Rep receives 25% commission. Exclusive area representation required. Advertising costs are paid by talent. For promotional purposes, talent must provide directory ad (at least 1 directory per year), direct mail promo cards every 3 months, e-mail promos every month, website. Advertises in *Workbook*.

HOW TO CONTACT Send e-mail with website address. Responds within 1 month, only if interested. To show portfolio, photographer should follow up with call.

TIPS Finds artists through recommendations from other artists, source books, art buyers. "Please be willing to show some new work every 6 months. Have 2-3 portfolios available for representative. Have website and be willing to do direct mail every 3 months. Be professional and organized."

✪ V PRODUCTIONS

81 N. Roosevelt Ave., Apt. 11, Pasadena CA 91107. **E-mail:** workshopsonlocation@gmail.com. **Website:** www.workshopsonlocation.com. **Contact:** Gina Vriens, principal producer. Estab. 2014. Workshop & event organizer. Represents photographers, illustrators, designers, fine artists. "V Productions allows creative individuals to focus on their craft, while leaving the rest to us. We not only produce workshops, but also provide on-site workshop support and marketing consulting." Markets include corporate/client direct, festival/conference.

HOW TO CONTACT E-mail link to website and bio. Responds in 1 week.

WORKSHOPS & PHOTO TOURS

//

Taking a photography workshop or photo tour is one of the best ways to improve your photographic skills. There is no substitute for the hands-on experience and one-on-one instruction you can receive at a workshop. Besides, where else can you go and spend several days with people who share your passion for photography?

Photography is headed in a new direction. Digital imaging is here to stay and is becoming part of every photographer's life. Even if you haven't invested a lot of money into digital cameras, computers or software, you should understand what you're up against if you plan to succeed as a professional photographer. Taking a digital imaging workshop can help you on your way.

Outdoor and nature photography are perennial workshop favorites. Creativity is another popular workshop topic. You'll also find highly specialized workshops, such as underwater photography. Many photo tours specialize in a specific location and the great photo opportunities that location affords.

As you peruse these pages, take a good look at the quality of workshops and the skill level of photographers the sponsors want to attract. It is important to know if a workshop is for beginners, advanced amateurs, or professionals. Information from a workshop organizer can help you make that determination.

These workshop listings contain only the basic information needed to make contact with sponsors, and a brief description of the styles or media covered in the programs. We also include information on costs when possible. Write, call, or e-mail the workshop/photo tour sponsors for complete information. Most have websites with extensive information about their programs, when they're offered, and how much they cost.

A workshop or photo tour can be whatever the photographer wishes—a holiday from the normal working routine, or an exciting introduction to new skills and perspectives on the craft. Whatever you desire, you're sure to find in these pages a workshop or tour that fulfills your expectations.

EDDIE ADAMS WORKSHOP

(646)263-8596. **E-mail:** producer@eddieadamswork shop.com; info@eddieadamsworkshop.com; eaw staff@gmail.com. **Website:** www.eddieadamswork shop.com. **Contact:** Miriam Evers, workshop producer. Annual, tuition-free photojournalism workshop. The Eddie Adams Workshop brings together 100 promising young photographers with over 150 of the most influential picture journalists, picture editors, managing editors and writers from prestigious organizations such as the Associated Press, CNN, the White House, *Life, National Geographic, Newsweek, Time, Parade, Entertainment Weekly, Sports Illustrated,* the *New York Times,* the *Los Angeles Times* and the *Washington Post.* Pulitzer-prize winning photographer Eddie Adams created this program to allow young photographers to learn from experienced professionals about the story-telling power and social importance of photography. Participants are divided into 10 teams, each headed by a photographer, editor, producer, or multimedia person. Daily editing and critiquing help each student to hone skills and learn about the visual, technical, and emotional components of creating strong journalistic images. Open to photography students and professional photographers with 3 years or less of experience. Photographers should e-mail for more information.

ADVENTURE SAFARI NETWORK

(312)470-6704. **E-mail:** info@adventuresafarinet work.com. **Website:** www.adventuresafarinetwork. com. **Contact:** Gary Gullett, president. "Photography workshops are combined with adventure and unique venue access to not only maximize the personal experience, but also give stunning photographic opportunities. These are hands-on workshops with participants learning camera controls and concepts of photography. Popular adventure opportunities include Africa, India and Alaska, with many trips per year." See the website or call the office for more details. Open to all skill levels and types of cameras.

ANCHELL PHOTOGRAPHY WORKSHOPS

216 Whitman St. S, Monmouth OR 97361. (503)884-3882. **Fax:** (503)588-4003. **E-mail:** info@anchell workshops.com. **Website:** www.anchellworkshops. com. **Contact:** Steve Anchell. Film or digital, group or private workshops held throughout the year, including large-format, 35mm, studio lighting, figure,

darkroom, both color and b&w. Open to all skill levels. Since 2001, Steve has been leading successful humanitarian missions for photographers to Cuba. On each visit, the photographers deliver medicine to a community clinic in Havana and then have time to explore Havana and the Vinales tobacco region. This is a legal visit with each member possessing a US Treasury license allowing them to travel for humanitarian reasons. Though we will be in Cuba for humanitarian reasons, there will be discussion and informal instruction on street photography. See website for more information.

ANDERSON RANCH ARTS CENTER

P.O. Box 5598, Snowmass Village CO 81615. (970)923-3181. **Fax:** (970)923-3871. **E-mail:** info@anderson ranch.org. **Website:** www.andersonranch.org. Photography and new media workshops featuring distinguished artists and educators from around the world. Classes range from traditional silver and alternative photographic processes to digital formats and use of the computer as a tool for time-based and interactive works of art. Program includes video, animation, sound and installations.

ANIMALS OF MONTANA, INC.

170 Nixon Peak Rd., Bozeman MT 59715. (406)686-4224. **Fax:** (406)686-4224. **E-mail:** animals@animal sofmontana.com. **Website:** www.animalsofmontana. com. See website for pricing information. Held annually. Workshops held year round. "Whether you're a professional/amateur photographer or artist, or just looking for a Montana Wildlife experience, grab your camera and leave the rest to us! Visit our tour page for a complete listing of tours." Open to all skill levels. Photographers should call, e-mail, or see website for more information.

APOGEE PHOTO WORKSHOP

(904)619-2010. **Website:** www.apogeephoto.com. **Contact:** Marla Meier, editor/manager. To take our online photography class, visit our website for details.

SEAN ARBABI

508 Old Farm Rd., Danville CA 94526-4134. (925)855-8060. **Fax:** (925)855-8060. **E-mail:** work shops@seanarbabi.com. **Website:** www.seanarbabi. com/workshops. **Contact:** Sean Arbabi, commercial photographer/instructor. Online and seasonal workshops held in spring, summer, fall, winter. Taught around the world—online with PPSOP.com, and on

location with Calumet, Camera West, Tamron, Workshops on the Farm, as well as places and companies around the world. Sean Arbabi teaches through live presentations, software demonstrations, field shoots and hands-on instruction. All levels of workshops are offered from beginner to advanced. Subjects include digital photography, nature, composition, exposure, personal vision, high-dynamic range imagery, how to run a photo business, lighting, panoramas, utilizing equipment, and a philosophical approach to the art.

○ ◑ ● ARIZONA HIGHWAYS PHOTO WORKSHOPS

2039 W. Lewis Ave., Phoenix AZ 85009. (888)790-7042. **Fax:** (602)256-2873. **E-mail:** info@ahpw.org. **Website:** www.ahpw.org. **Contact:** Roberta Lites, executive director. AHPW is a nonprofit, full-service provider of photographic education from capture to print, taught by premier instructors at inspirational locations throughout the Southwest and beyond.

○ ◑ ARROWMONT SCHOOL OF ARTS AND CRAFTS

556 Pkwy., Gatlinburg TN 37738. (865)436-5860. **Fax:** (865)430-4101. **E-mail:** bmay@arrowmont.org; info@arrowmont.org. **Website:** www.arrowmont.org. Offers weekend, 1- and 2-week workshops in photography, drawing, painting, clay, metals/enamels, kiln glass, fibers, surface design, wood turning and furniture. Residencies, studio assistantships, work-study, and scholarships are available. See individual course descriptions for pricing.

○ ◑ ● ART IMMERSION TRIP WITH WORKSHOP IN NEW MEXICO

P.O. Box 1473, Cullowhee NC 28723. (828)342-6913. **E-mail:** contact@cullowheemountainarts.org. **Website:** www.cullowheemountainarts.org. **Contact:** Norma Hendrix, director. Cost: $1,379-$1,579 (includes lodging, 2-4 day workshop, breakfasts, 1 dinner, some transportation and museums). "Cullowhee Mountain Arts offers exceptional summer artist workshops in painting, drawing, printmaking, book arts, ceramics, photography and mixed media. Our distinguished faculty with national and international reputations will provide a week-long immersion in their topic supplemented with lectures, demonstrations or portfolio talks. Cullowhee Mountain Arts is committed to supporting the personal and professional development of every artist, whatever their level, by providing the setting and facilities for intense learning and art

making, shared in community. We believe that are enlivens community life and that in a supportive community, art thrives best. Our studios are located on Western Carolina University's campus, surrounded by the natural beauty of the Blue Ridge Mountains in North Carolina." Upcoming workshops in New Mexico include: Debra Fitts (Ceramic Sculpture: Intermediate to Advanced), "The Spirit & The Figure"; Ron Pokrasso (Printmaking: All Levels), "Monotype and More: Mixed Media Printmaking"; Nancy Reyner (Acrylic: Intermediate, Advanced, Masters), "Acrylic Innovation: Inventing New Painting Techniques & Styles"; and Sandra Wilson (Painting: All Levels), "Acrylic Textures, Transfers and Layers." Call, e-mail, or see website for more detailed information including exact dates and locations.

○ ◑ ● ART OF NATURE PHOTOGRAPHY WORKSHOPS

211 Kirkland Ave., Suite 503, Kirkland WA 98033-6408. (425)968-2884. **E-mail:** charles@charlesneedlephoto.com. **Website:** www.charlesneedlephoto.com. **Contact:** Charles Needle, founder/instructor. US and international locations such as Monet's Garden (France); Keukenhof Gardens (Holland), and Butchart Gardens (Canada); includes private access with personalized one-on-one field and classroom instruction and supportive image evaluations. Emphasis on creative camera techniques in the field and digital darkroom, allowing students to express "the art of nature" with unique personal vision. Topics include: creative macro, flower/garden photography, multiple-exposure impressionism, intimate landscapes and scenics, dynamic composition and lighting, etc. Open to all skill levels. Upcoming workshops include: Monet's Garden with private access in summertime, Great Gardens of Southern England, Atlanta Botanical Garden, Georgia Aquarium with private access, The Palouse, and Seattle Japanese Garden in Autumn. See website for more information and all upcoming workshops. Cost: $125-4,000 depending on workshop.

ART WORKSHOPS IN GUATEMALA

4758 Lyndale Ave. S., Minneapolis MN 55419-5304. (612)825-0747. **E-mail:** info@artguat.org. **Website:** www.artguat.org. **Contact:** Liza Fourre, director. Estab. 1995. Art & cultural workshops held in Antigua, Guatemala. See website for a list of upcoming workshops.

○ ◐ ● BACHMANN TOUR OVERDRIVE

P.O. Box 950833, Lake Mary FL 32746. (407)333-9988. **E-mail:** Bill@Billbachmann.com. **Website:** www.billbachmann.com. **Contact:** Bill Bachmann, owner. "Bill Bachmann shares his knowledge and adventures with small groups several times a year. Past trips have been to China, Tibet, South Africa, Antarctica, India, Nepal, Australia, New Zealand, New Guinea, Greece, Vietnam, Laos, Cambodia, Malaysia, Singapore, Guatemala, Honduras, Kenya, Tanzania, Greece and Cuba. Future trips will be back to Cuba, Antarctica, Eastern Canada, Italy, Eastern Europe, Peru, Argentina, Brazil and many other destinations. Programs are designed for adventure travelers who love photography and want to learn stock photography from a top stock photographer." Open to all skill levels.

○ ◐ ● NOELLA BALLENGER & ASSOCIATES PHOTO WORKSHOPS

P.O. Box 457, La Canada CA 91012. (818)954-0933. **Fax:** (818)954-0910. **E-mail:** Noella1B@aol.com. **Website:** www.noellaballenger.com. **Contact:** Noella Ballenger. A variety of online photo classes are offered through www.apogeephoto.com. Work at your own speed. Small class sizes. Emphasize visual awareness, composition and techniques. One-on-one evaluations and comments on all images submitted in class. Articles available at www.apogeephoto.com.

◐ ● FRANK BALTHIS PHOTOGRAPHY WORKSHOPS

P.O. Box 255, Davenport CA 95017. (831)426-8205. **E-mail:** frankbalthis@yahoo.com. **Website:** pa.photoshelter.com/c/frankbalthis. **Contact:** Frank S. Balthis, photographer/owner. "Workshops emphasize natural history, wildlife and travel photography, often providing opportunities to photograph marine mammals." Worldwide locations range from Baja California to Alaska. Frank Balthis runs a stock photo business and is the publisher of the Nature's Design line of cards and other publications.

BEGINNING DIGITAL PHOTOGRAPHY WORKSHOP

P.O. Box 5219, St. Marys GA 31558. (912)580-5308. **E-mail:** jackie@debuskphoto.com. **Website:** www.debuskphoto.com. **Contact:** Jackie DeBusk, photographer. $59 for 4-hour individual workshop at mutually-agreed location within 50 miles of St. Marys GA; 51-100 miles, $79; 101-150 miles, $99. Public workshops have varying fees and are announced on website. Instructor and participants are each responsible for any meals, parking or entrance fees (parks, zoos, etc.). Private workshops by request and public workshops announced throughout the year on website. Please see website for dates of upcoming workshops. Participants will learn how to take their SLR and bridge or prosumer cameras off of auto and begin to creatively apply exposure, metering and white balance settings, as well as learn about focus area, histograms and principles of sound composition. Workshop emphasis is on outdoor photography. Private workshops are conducted at mutually-agreed locations, public workshops are typically held at state parks or other public venues that offer excellent photography opportunities. Open to beginners. Interested parties should call, e-mail or see website for more information.

○ ◐ ● BETTERPHOTO.COM ONLINE PHOTOGRAPHY COURSES

23515 NE Novelty Hill Rd., Suite B221, #183, Redmond WA 98052. **E-mail:** course.sales@betterphoto.com; kerry@betterphoto.com. **Website:** www.betterphoto.com. **Contact:** Kerry Drager, course advisor. BetterPhoto is the worldwide leader in online photography education, offering an approachable resource for photographers who want to improve their skills, share their photos, and learn more about the art and technique of photography. BetterPhoto offers over 100 photography courses that are taught by top professional photographers. Courses begin the 1st Wednesday of every month. Courses range in skill level from beginner to advanced and consist of inspiring weekly lessons and personal feedback on students' photos from the instructors. "We provide websites for photographers, photo sharing solutions, free online newsletters, lively Q&A and photo discussions, a monthly contest, helpful articles and online photography courses." Open to all skill levels.

◐ BIRDS AS ART/INSTRUCTIONAL PHOTO-TOURS

P.O. Box 7245, 4041 Granada Dr., Indian Lake Estates FL 33855. (863)692-0906. **E-mail:** birdsasart@verizon.net; samandmayasgrandpa@att.net. **Website:** www.birdsasart-blog.com. **Contact:** Arthur Morris, instructor. The tours, which visit the top bird photography hot spots in North America and the world, feature in-classroom lectures, lunch, in-the-field instruction, 6 or more hours of photography, and most importantly, easily approachable yet free and wild subjects. See the complete IPT schedule here: www.birdsasart.com/include-pages/ipt-updates.

○ ◑ ● BLUE PLANET PHOTOGRAPHY WORKSHOPS AND TOURS

1526 W. Charlotte Ct., Nampa ID 83687. (208)466-9340. **Website:** www.blueplanetphoto.com. Professional photographer and former wildlife biologist Mike Shipman conducts small group workshops/tours emphasizing individual expression and exploration using all your senses & perception. Workshops and tours are held away from crowds in beautiful and inspiring locations in the US and worldwide, such as Maine, Yosemite, Vancouver Island, Iceland and Scotland. Group feedback sessions and digital presentations are available whenever possible. On-site transportation and lodging during workshop usually included; meals included on some trips. Specific fees, optional activities and gear list outlined in tour materials. Workshops and tours range from 2 to 12 days, sometimes longer; average is 9 days. Custom tours and workshops available upon request. Open to all skill levels. Photographers should see website and online contact form for more information.

BLUE RIDGE WORKSHOPS

4831 Keswick Court, Montclair VA 22025. (571)294-1383. **E-mail:** elliot@blueridgeworkshops.com; brian@blueridgeworkshops.com. **Website:** www.blueridgeworkshops.com. **Contact:** Elliot Stern, owner/photographer. These workshops sell out, so book early. See website for more information and a list of all upcoming workshops.

○ ◑ ● NANCY BROWN HANDS-ON WORKSHOPS

3100 NW Boca Raton Blvd., Suite 403, Boca Raton FL 33431. (561)347-1243. **Fax:** (561)988-1791. **E-mail:** nbrown50@bellsouth.net. **Website:** www.nancybrown.com. **Contact:** Nancy Brown. Offers one-on-one intensive workshops all year long in studio and on location in Florida. "You work with Nancy, the models and the crew to create your images." Photographers should call, fax, e-mail, or see website for more information.

⊕ ● ⟨$⟩⟨$⟩ ○ ◑ ● BURMA

111 Bank Street #218, Grass Valley CA 95945. (916)520-8574. **E-mail:** workshops@jenniferwu.com. **Website:** www.jenniferwu.com. **Contact:** Jennifer

Wu, owner/tour leader/photographer. Cost: $8,100 double occupancy; $9,650 single occupancy. Fee Includes: Lodging, meals, transportation in Burma including in-country flights and boat rides. "From the largest temple in the world, to home of many monks and the longest teak bridge in the world, to a variety of other photogenic temples and opportunities, this photographic tour is in for a treat. Life is changing fast in Myanmar (Burma) as this Southeast Asian country is in their first stages of development where much of its past remains alive and visible and is simultaneously transforming into the 21st century. After decades of suppression under a military junta, the first stirrings of democracy have been seen in the last few years. Join top photographers Jim Martin and Jennifer Wu on this picturesque trip as they lead you through Myanmar, capturing an endlessly fascinating country with unique history, people and culture. Your tour leaders know where to get the best shots, and will also give you in the field demos and compositional guidance to enhance the way you see and shoot. This tour is intended for intermediate and advanced photographers. However, any skill level is welcome and will enjoy Myanmar's photographic opportunities. Participants should have a working knowledge of their equipment. Jennifer Wu and James Martin have led dozens of photo tours and workshops domestically and around the world. Jennifer is a Canon Explorer of Light and James has produced more than 20 books. Together they collaborated on *Photography Night Sky* (Mountaineer Books), one of Amazon's most popular books on landscape photography." E-mail or see website for more information.

⟲ ○ ◑ ● BURREN COLLEGE OF ART WORKSHOPS

(353)65-7077200. **Fax:** (353)65-7077201. **E-mail:** julia@burrencollege.ie. **Website:** www.burrencollege.ie/programmes. **Contact:** Julia Long, photography. "Working with Photographs with Robert Ellis-Digital Photography, Photoshop & Printing"—This intensive 5 day workshop will guide photographers, both amateurs and advanced, towards making beautiful photographic prints. Over the course of 5 days, participants will learn about optimizing their camera for producing the best quality image and get a chance to make new work on field trips around the inspiring Burren landscape. Participants will then have the opportunity to enhance their image with post-production using

Adobe Bridge, Lightroom and Photoshop and finally they will get to produce beautiful photographic prints. An accommodation pakage has been arranged in the new BCA housing to facilitate participants. See website for the full range on offer.

CAMARGO FOUNDATION VISUAL ARTS FELLOWSHIP

1, Avenue Jermini, Cassis 13260, France. **E-mail:** apply@camargofoundation.org. **Website:** www.camargofoundation.org. Cross disciplinary residencies awarded to writers, playwrights, visual artists, photographers, video artists, filmmakers, media artists, choreographers, composers and academics. Artists may work on a specific project, develop a body of work, etc. Fellows must live on-site at foundation headquarters for the duration of the fellowship. Apartments with kitchens provided. Open to photographers of any nationality. Stipend of US $1,500 available. See website for deadline. Photographers should visit website to apply. If you are interested in applying for future fellowships, please check the website for announcements.

JOHN C. CAMPBELL FOLK SCHOOL

One Folk School Rd., Brasstown NC 28902. (828)837-2775 or (800)365-5724. **Fax:** (828)837-8637. **Website:** www.folkschool.org. The Folk School offers year-round weekend and weeklong courses in photography. Please call for free catalog or see website for more information and upcoming workshops.

THE CENTER FOR PHOTOGRAPHY AT WOODSTOCK

59 Tinker St., Woodstock NY 12498. (845)679-9957. **E-mail:** info@cpw.org. **Website:** www.cpw.org. **Contact:** Lindsay Stern, education coordinator. Woodstock Photography Workshops & Lecture Series. Held at CPW in Woodstock NY, our hands-on workshops allow you to expand your craft, skills and vision under the mentorship of a leading image-maker. Workshops are kept intimate by limited enrollment and taught by highly qualified support staff. Photographers should call, e-mail, or see website for more information and a list of upcoming workshops.

CHICAGO PHOTO SAFARIS

(312)470-6704. **E-mail:** info@chicagophotosafaris.com; gary@photosafarinetwork.com **Website:** www.chicagophotosafaris.com. **Contact:** Gary Gullett, president. Held daily. "Local travel photography workshops are held daily in iconic venues in Chicago. These are 'hands-on' workshops with participants learning the camera controls and concepts of photography in easy-to-understand language. There are also regional, national and worldwide safaris for the more adventurous. Popular adventure opportunities include Africa and Alaska, with many trips per year. Check the website or call the office for details." Open to photographers of all skill levels and types of cameras (film or digital).

CATHY CHURCH PERSONAL UNDERWATER PHOTOGRAPHY COURSES

P.O. Box 479, GT, Grand Cayman KY1 1106, Cayman Islands. (345)949-7415 or (607)330-3504 (US callers). **Fax:** (345)949-9770 or (607)330-3509 (US). **E-mail:** cathy@cathychurch.com. **Website:** www.cathychurch.com. **Contact:** Cathy Church. Hotel/dive package available at Sunset House Hotel. Private and group lessons available for all levels throughout the year; classroom and shore diving can be arranged. Lessons available for professional photographers expanding to underwater work. Photographers should e-mail for more information.

KATHY ADAMS CLARK NATURE PHOTOGRAPHY

P.O. Box 8674, The Woodlands TX 77387. (281)367-2042. **E-mail:** info@kathyadamsclark.com. **Website:** www.kathyadamsclark.com. **Contact:** Kathy Adams Clark, owner. "I am a wildlife photographer with over 20 years of experience in the editorial and calendar market. I've also been teaching photography for over 20 years with an emphasis on teaching basic to advanced technical skills. Anyone can photograph anything if they understand the basic components of photography. I am also an ever-curious naturalist and explorer. Technical photography and curiosity about the natural world are brought into every workshop, tour and safari. Workshops are held in several locations in the United States, including Big Bend National Park and private ranches in Texas and Arizona. International photo tours are coordinated through Strabo Tours to various locations including Tanzania, Morocco, Peru, Costa Rica, Ecuador, Iceland and Greece." Cost: varies. Open to all skill levels. If interested, call, e-mail, or see website for more information.

○ ◑ ● CLICKERS & FLICKERS PHOTOGRAPHY NETWORK—LECTURES & WORKSHOPS

P.O. Box 60508, Pasadena CA 91116-6508. (310)457-6130. **E-mail:** dawnhope@clickersandflickers.com; dawn5palms@yahoo.com. **Website:** www.clickersandflickers.com. **Contact:** Dawn Hope Stevens, organizer. Estab. 1985. Monthly networking dinners with outstanding guest speakers (many award winners, including the Pulitzer Prize), events and free activities for members. "Clickers & Flickers Photography Network, Inc., was created to provide people with an interest and passion for photography (cinematography, filmmaking, image making) the opportunity to meet others with similar interests for networking and camaraderie. It creates an environment in which photography issues, styles, techniques, enjoyment and appreciation can be discussed and viewed as well as experienced with people from many fields and levels of expertise (beginners, students, amateur, hobbyist, or professionals, gallery owners and museum curators). We publish a bimonthly color magazine listing thousands of activities for photographers and lovers of images." Most of its content is not on our website for a reason. Membership and magazine subscriptions help support this organization. Clickers & Flickers Photography Network, Inc. is a 21-year-old professional photography network association that promotes information and offers promotional marketing opportunities for photographers, cinematographers, individuals, organizations, businesses, and events. "C&F also provides referrals for photographers. Our membership includes photographers, videographers, and cinematographers who are skilled in the following types of photography: outdoor and nature, wedding, headshots, fine art, sports, events, products, news, glamour, fashion, macro, commercial, landscape, advertising, architectural, wildlife, candid, photojournalism, marquis gothic—fetish, aerial and underwater; using the following types of equipment: motion picture cameras (Imax, 70mm, 65mm, 35mm, 16mm, 8mm), steadicam systems, video, high-definition, digital, still photography—large format, medium format and 35mm." Open to all skill levels. Photographers should call or e-mail for more information.

⊕ ○ ◑ ● COLORADO PHOTOGRAPHIC ARTS CENTER

(303)837-1341. **E-mail:** info@cpacphoto.org. **Website:** www.cpacphoto.org. Offers monthly workshops on film & darkroom, digital, alternative process, portraiture, landscape, creativity, studio lighting, portfolio development and more. Open to all skill levels. Also have a gallery with changing juried photo exhibits. Photographers should call, e-mail, see website for more information and a list of upcoming workshops.

◑ ● COMMUNITY DARKROOM

Genesse Center for the Arts, 713 Monroe Ave., Rochester NY 14607. (585)271-5920. **E-mail:** darkroom@geneseearts.org. **Website:** www.geneseearts.org. "The Genesee Center for the Arts & Education offers programs in all of our visual arts areas: Community Darkroom, Genesee Pottery, and the Printing and Book Arts Center. We offer youth programs, classes and workshops, rent studio space to individuals and exhibit work in our galleries. Anyone may take classes, though you must be a member to use some of the facilities." See website for more information and upcoming workshops.

○ ◑ ● CONE EDITIONS WORKSHOPS

P.O. Box 51, East Topsham VT 05076. (802)439-5751, ext. 101. **E-mail:** cathy@cone-editions.com. **Website:** www.cone-editions.com. **Contact:** Cathy Cone. See website for details on workshop dates and prices. Cone Editions digital printmaking workshops are hands-on and cover a wide range of techniques, equipment and materials. The workshops take place in the studios of Cone Editions Press and offer attendees the unique opportunity to learn workflow and procedures from the masters. These workshops are an excellent opportunity to learn proven workflow in a fully equipped digital printmaking studio immersed in the latest technologies. Open to all skill levels. See website for more information and upcoming workshops.

◑ ● ◕ THE CORTONA CENTER OF PHOTOGRAPHY, ITALY

(404)876-6341. **E-mail:** workshop.inquiry@cortonacenter.com. **Website:** www.cortonacenter.com. Robin Davis leads personal, small-group photography workshops in the ancient city of Cortona, Italy, centrally located in Tuscany, once the heart of the Renaissance. Dramatic landscapes; Etruscan relics; Roman, Medieval and Renaissance architecture; and the wonderful and photogenic people of Tuscany await. "Photographers should e-mail or see our website for more information."

○ ◑ ● **CORY NATURE AND TRAVEL WORKSHOPS**

P.O. Box 42, Signal Mountain TN 37377. (423)886-1004. **E-mail:** tompatcory@aol.com. **Website:** www.tomandpatcory.com. **Contact:** Tom or Pat Cory. "Our emphasis is on nature and travel photography. We offer several short, small workshops (8-12 maximum participants) throughout the year in and around Chattanooga TN. Since we tailor our instruction to each ndividual's interests, our workshops are suitable for all experience levels. Cost and length vary by workshop. We also offer individual instruction and custom-designed workshops for groups. Participants are welcome to use digital or film cameras or even video." Photographers should write, call, e-mail or see our website for more information.

○ ◑ **CREALDÉ SCHOOL OF ART**

600 St. Andrews Blvd., Winter Park FL 32792. (407)671-1886. **E-mail:** pschreyer@crealde.org; rberrie@crealde.org. **Website:** www.crealde.org. **Contact:** Peter Schreyer, executive director; Robin Berrie, marketing manager. Crealdé School of Art is a community-based nonprofit arts organization established in 1975. It features a year-round curriculum of over 100 visual arts classes for students of all ages, taught by a faculty of over 40 working artists; a renowned summer art camp for children and teens; a visiting artist workshop series, 3 galleries, the contemporary sculpture garden, and award-winning outreach programs. Offers classes covering traditional and digital photography; b&w darkroom techniques; landscape, portrait, documentary, travel, wildlife and abstract photography; and educational tours. See website for more information and upcoming workshops.

○ ◑ ● **CREATIVE ARTS WORKSHOP**

80 Audubon St., New Haven CT 06511. (203)562-4927. **E-mail:** haroldshapirophoto@gmail.com. **Website:** www.creativeartsworkshop.org. **Contact:** Harold Shapiro, photography department head. A nonprofit regional center for education in the visual arts that has served the Greater New Haven area since 1961. Located in the heart of the award-winning Audubon Arts District, CAW offers a wide-range of classes in the visual arts in its own 3-story building with fully equipped studios and an active exhibition schedule in its well-known Hilles Gallery. Offers exciting classes and advanced workshops. Digital and traditional b&w darkroom. See website for more information and upcoming workshops.

○ ◑ ● **CULLOWHEE MOUNTAIN ARTS SUMMER WORKSHOP SERIES**

598 W. Main St., Sylva NC 28779. (828)342-6913. **E-mail:** contact@cullowheemountainarts.org. **Website:** www.cullowheemountainarts.org. **Contact:** Norma Hendrix, director (norma@cullowheemountainarts.org). Cost: $525-875 for 5-day tuition, lab fees and Sunday wine reception (housing and partial meal plans are available at an additional cost, ranging from $500-775 a week. Two catered meals can be purchased a la carte with prior registration). "Cullowhee Mountain Arts offers exceptional summer artist workshops in painting, ceramics, mixed media, encaustic, printmaking and book arts. The distinguished faculty with national and international reputations will provide an immersion in their topic supplemented with lectures, demonstrations or portfolio talks. Cullowhee Mountain Arts is committed to supporting the personal and professional development of every artist, whatever their level, by providing the setting and facilities for intense learning and art making, shared in community. Upcoming workshops on the WCU campus include: Building Books & Imagery (book arts), Alice Austin; Contemporary Dinnerware (ceramics), Jeff Oestreich and Pat Burns; Advanced Cold Wax and Oil Painting (painting), Rebecca Crowell; Introduction to Cold Wax (painting), Janice Mason Steeves; Encaustic Collagraphs (printmaking), Jane Nodine; Poetry, Plein Air and Otherwise (Creative Writing), Lola Haskins. Also offering workshops, trips and retreats to Santa Fe and Taos NM and spring and fall artist retreats at Lake Logan NC.

○ **CULTURAL PHOTO TOURS WITH PHOTO ENRICHMENT PROGRAMS, INC.**

4007 Landstrom Rd, Rockford IL 61114. (949)698-2859; (888)974-6869. **E-mail:** ralph@ralphvelasco.com; info@photoenrichment.com. **Website:** ralphvelasco.com. **Contact:** Ralph Velasco, president. Trips are custom designed to provide a unique opportunity for hands-on experience with a professional travel photography instructor. Learn to see like a photographer, develop skills that will allow you to readily notice and take advantage of more and better photo opportunities and begin to "think outside the camera!"

Includes: domestic (Chicago) and international photo tours that are fully scouted in advance and led by an award-winning travel photography instructor, author and international guide Ralph Velasco and/or other highly qualified guest photographers. Tours concentrate on international destinations including Morocco, Mexico's Copper Canyon, Cambodia, Central Europe, Romania, Turkey, Vietnam, Iceland, Spain, Egypt, and the Adriatic, as well as fully licensed People-to-People Exchange programs to Cuba (other destinations are added frequently). Costs: varies depending on location and length of trip. Payments accepted: personal check, bank transfer, online invoice or credit card. Open to all levels of photographers and non-photographers alike, with any equipment. Interested participants should e-mail or visit the website for more information and to register.

◑ ❈ ◑ ◐ ● DAWSON COLLEGE CENTRE FOR TRAINING AND DEVELOPMENT

4001 de Maisonneuve Blvd. W., Suite 2G.1, Montreal Quebec H3Z 3G4, Canada. (514)933-0047. **Fax:** (514)937-3832. **E-mail:** ctd@dawsoncollege.qc.ca. **Website:** www.dawsoncollege.qc.ca/ciait. Workshop subjects include imaging arts and technologies, computer animation, photography, digital imaging, desktop publishing, multimedia, and web publishing and design. See website for course and workshop information.

◑ ● CYNTHIA DELANEY PHOTO WORKSHOPS

168 Maple St., Elko NV 89801. (775)750-4501. **Fax:** (775)753-5833. **E-mail:** cynthia@cynthiadelaney.com; cynthiadelaney@frontiernet.net. **Website:** www.cynthiadelaney.com. **Contact:** Cynthia Delaney. "In addition to her photography classes, Cynthia offers outdoor photography workshops held in many outstanding locations. It is our hope to bring photographers to new and unusual places where inspiration comes naturally." See website for more information and upcoming workshops.

✚ ⬤ ⬤⬤⬤ ◑ ● ∅ EAGLES, WHALES, AND GLACIERS...OH MY!

111 Bank Street #218, Grass Valley CA 95945. (916)520-8574. **E-mail:** workshops@jenniferwu.com. **Website:** www.jenniferwu.com. **Contact:** Jennifer Wu, owner/tour leader/photographer. Cost: $7,395 (double, two people per room) or $8,195. "Prepare for a life changing experience when you join Jennifer Wu and Hal Schmitt with LIGHT Photographic Workshops for an Alaskan photography immersion. The sheer volume and quality of amazing subjects and opportunities are unrivaled by any other photo adventure; whether shooting wildlife, landscapes, and creating a panoramic or HDR, get ready to photograph in a "target rich environment." This adventure is based almost entirely on a yacht. The boat is not of a large cruise ship size, but is small and stable. The advantages of the Northern Song yacht, is that we can get closer to water level images and to our subjects than on larger vessel for photography unmatched anywhere else in Alaska. Our yacht is ideal for photography. To ensure each person reaches the best level of photography, this trip is limited to 6 participants. With a client to leader ratio of 3:1, as a photographer you will always have the guidance, technical and artistic support needed to make the best images." E-mail or see website for more information.

◯ ◑ ELOQUENT LIGHT PHOTOGRAPHY WORKSHOPS

903 W. Alameda St., #115, Santa Fe NM 87501. (505)983-2934. **E-mail:** cindylane@eloquentlight.com. **Website:** www.eloquentlight.com. **Contact:** Cindy Lane, managing director. Estab. 1986. "Eloquent Light Photography Workshops was founded in 1986 to provide exceptional educational photographic workshop experiences based on the history, character and beauty of the American West. We pride ourselves on offering real photographic education that helps participants become better photographers. We keep our group sizes small in order to address participants' needs. Open to all skill levels. In our Traditional workshops, you are encouraged to bring your own images with you for informal comment by the instructor and fellow participants. Photographs made during the week of your workshop will also be reviewed. The instructor and assistant are available to look at digital captures on participants' laptops during our adventure workshops when requested. For our Adventure workshops, these are shooting-intensive workshops providing hands-on, one-on-one guidance in the field as needed. Visit White Sands National Monument, Grand Teton National Park, Yosemite or the California Coast. See website for the current workshop schedule, more information and registration. Mentoring and private workshops also available.

Join us for a fun-filled adventure with your camera!" "The experience just got better. The workshop itself was packed with information and activity. The instructors and staff were always available, ready to instruct and answer questions, but careful to let each student work at their own pace."—Mary E., Texas. "It was a wonderful and very pleasant workshop. I learned a lot of things for the handling of my digital camera. I wish to express my hearty thanks."—Shiro T., Japan.

JOE ENGLANDER PHOTOGRAPHY WORKSHOPS & TOURS

P.O. Box 1261, Manchaca TX 78652. (512)922-8686. **E-mail:** info@englander-workshops.com. **Contact:** Joe Englander. Instruction in beautiful locations throughout the world, all formats and media, color/b&w/digital, Photoshop instruction. Locations include Europe, Asia with special emphasis on Bhutan and the Himalayas and the US. See website for more information.

EUROPA PHOTOGENICA PHOTO TOURS TO EUROPE

3920 W. 231st Place, Torrance CA 90505. (310)621-0914. **Fax:** (310)378-2821. **E-mail:** fraphoto@aol.com. **Website:** www.europaphotogenica.com. **Contact:** Barbara Van Zanten-Stolarski, owner. (Formerly France Photogenique/Europa Photogenica Photo Tours to Europe). Tuition provided for beginners/intermediate and advanced level. Workshops held in spring (1-2) and fall (1-2). 5- to 11-day photo tours of the most beautiful regions of Europe. Shoot landscapes, villages, churches, cathedrals, vineyards, outdoor markets, cafes and people in France, Paris, Provence, England, Italy, Greece, etc. Tours change every year. Open to all skill levels. Photographers should call or e-mail for more information.

EXPOSURE36 PHOTOGRAPHY

P.O. Box 964, Caldwell ID 83605. (503)707-5293. **E-mail:** workshop@exposure36.com. **Website:** www.exposure36.com. **Contact:** Jim Altengarten. Open to all skill levels. Workshops offered at prime locations in the US and Canada, including Nova Scotia, Smoky Mountains, Acadia and the bears in Alaska. International workshops include Russia, Southeast Asia, Guatemala and the Northern Lights in Finland. Also offers classes on the basics of photography in Seattle, Washington (through the Experimental College of the University of Washington). Photographers should write, call, e-mail, see website for more information and upcoming workshops.

FINDING & KEEPING CLIENTS

1684 Decoto Rd. #271, Union City CA 94587. (714)356-4260. **E-mail:** maria@mpiscopo.com. **Website:** www.mpiscopo.com. **Contact:** Maria Piscopo, instructor. "How to find new photo assignment clients and get paid what you're worth!" Maria Piscopo is the author of *The Photographer's Guide to Marketing & Self-Promotion*, 4th edition (Allworth Press). See website for more information and upcoming workshops.

FINE ARTS WORK CENTER

24 Pearl St., Provincetown MA 02657. (508)487-9960, ext. 103. **Fax:** (508)487-8873. **E-mail:** workshops@fawc.org. **Website:** www.fawc.org. Estab. 1968. Faculty includes Connie Imboden, David Hilliard, Pam Houston, Nick Flynn, Shellburne Thurber, Salvatore Scibona, John Murillo, Joanne Dugan, Rob Swainston and many more.

PETER FINGER PHOTOGRAPHER

1143 Blakeway St., Daniel Island SC 29492. (843)377-8652. **E-mail:** images@peterfinger.com. **Website:** www.peterfinger.com. **Contact:** Peter Finger, president. Offers over 20 weekend and week-long photo workshops, held in various locations. Workshops planned include Charleston, Savannah, Carolina Coast, Outer Banks, and the Islands of Georgia. "Group instruction from dawn till dusk." Write or visit website for more information.

FIRST LIGHT PHOTOGRAPHIC WORKSHOPS AND SAFARIS

10 Roslyn, Islip Terrace NY 11752. (516)769-2549' (516)965-3097. **E-mail:** info@firstlightphotography.com. **Website:** www.firstlightphotography.com. **Contact:** Bill Rudock, president. Photo workshops and photo safaris for all skill levels, specializing in landscape and wildlife photography. "We will personally teach you through our workshops and safaris, the techniques necessary to go from *taking pictures* to *creating* those unique, magical images while experiencing some of life's greatest adventures through the eye of your camera." See website for more information, pricing and registration.

FOCUS ADVENTURES

P.O. Box 771640, Steamboat Springs CO 80477. (970)879-2244. **E-mail:** karen@focusadventures.com. **Website:** www.focusadventures.com. **Contact:**

Karen Gordon Schulman, owner. "Photo workshops and tours emphasize photography and the creative spirit and self-discovery through photography. Summer photo workshops in Steamboat Springs, Colorado and at Focus Ranch, a private guest and cattle ranch in NW Colorado. Customized individual and small-group photo instruction available year-round. Karen is an experienced photographic artist and educator based out of Steamboat Springs, CO. Her current passion is the new and exciting world of iPhoneography. Karen leads international photo tours in conjunction with Strabo Photo Tour Collection to various destinations including Ecuador, Bali, Morocco, Bhutan and Western Ireland." Accommodations, most meals, photo instruction included in all of the above programs. See website for more details and registration information.

○ ◑ ● FOTOFUSION

Palm Beach Photographic Centre, 415 Clematis St., West Palm Beach FL 33401. (561)253-2600. **E-mail:** info@workshop.org. **Website:** www.fotofusion.org. America's foremost festival of photography and digital imaging is held each January. Learn from more than 90 master photographers, picture editors, picture agencies, gallery directors, and technical experts, over 5 days of field trips, seminars, lectures and Photoshop workshops. Open to all skill levels interested in nature, landscape, documentary, portraiture, photojournalism, digital, fine art, commercial, etc. Details available online.

◑ ● GALÁPAGOS TRAVEL

783 Rio Del Mar Blvd., Suite 49, Aptos CA 95003. (831)689-9192 or (800)969-9014. **E-mail:** info@galapagostravel.com. **Website:** www.galapagostravel.com. **Contact:** Mark Grantham. Landscape and wildlife photography tours of the islands with an emphasis on natural history. Spend either 11 or 15 days aboard the yacht in Galápagos, plus three nights in a first-class hotel in Quito, Ecuador. 25+ departures annually see website for additional information and registration.

○ ◑ ● GERLACH NATURE PHOTOGRAPHY WORKSHOPS & TOURS

P.O. Box 258, Macks Inn ID 83433. (208)244-1887. **E-mail:** michele@gerlachnaturephoto.com. **Website:** www.gerlachnaturephoto.com; www.facebook.com/gerlachnaturephotographyworkshops. **Contact:** Barbara Gerlach, office manager. Professional nature photographers John and Barbara Gerlach conduct intensive field workshops in the beautiful Upper Peninsula of Michigan in August and during October's fall color period. They lead a photo safari to the best game parks in Kenya each year. They also lead winter photo tours of Yellowstone National Park and conduct high-speed flash hummingbird photo workshops in British Columbia in late May and early June. They conduct inspirational one-day seminars on how to shoot beautiful nature images in major cities each year. Their 4 best-selling books, *Digital Nature Photography: The Art and the Science*, *Digital Wildlife Photography*, *Digital Landscape Photography*, and *Close Up Photography in Nature*, have helped thousands master the art of nature photography. Visit www.gerlachnaturephoto.com for more information.

○ ◑ ● GLOBAL PRESERVATION PROJECTS

P.O. Box 30866, Santa Barbara CA 93130. (805)682-3398 or (805)455-2790. **E-mail:** timorse@aol.com. **Website:** www.globalpreservationprojects.com. **Contact:** Thomas I. Morse, director. Offers photographic workshops and expeditions promoting the preservation of environmental and historic treasures. Produces international photographic exhibitions and publications. Workshops and expeditions in order normally done: Arches & Canyonlands, Winter Train Durango, Big Sur, Slot Canyons, Monument Valley, Eastern Sierra, Northern California & Oregon coasts, Colorado Fall Color, Death Valley and Alabama Hills. See website for details.

● ⊘ GOLDEN GATE SCHOOL OF PROFESSIONAL PHOTOGRAPHY

P.O. Box 5583, San Mateo CA 94402. (650)367-1265. **E-mail:** julie@ppgba.org. **Website:** www.goldengateschool.org. **Contact:** Julie Olson, director. Offers 1-2 day photography workshops and evening meetings for established and aspiring professional photographers in the San Francisco Bay Area.

○ ◑ ● ROB GOLDMAN CREATIVE PHOTOGRAPHY WORKSHOPS

R. Goldman, Inc., 755 Park Ave., Suite 190, Huntington NY 11743. (631)424-1650. **E-mail:** rob@rgoldman.com. **Website:** www.rgoldman.com. **Contact:** Rob Goldman, photographer. 1-on-1 private instruction for photographers of all levels, customized to each student's needs. "For over 15 years, beginner photographers through seasoned pros have received priceless instruction and support from Rob Goldman's private sessions. He possesses an uncanny ability to inspire and draw out a photographer's absolute best! Whether you're brand new to photography or looking to refine your vision or your craft, Rob's private lessons are the way to go!"

○ ◑ GREAT SMOKY MOUNTAINS INSTITUTE AT TREMONT

9275 Tremont Rd., Townsend TN 37882. (865)448-6709. **Fax:** (865)448-9250. **E-mail:** mail@gsmit.org; heather@gsmit.org. **Website:** www.gsmit.org. **Contact:** Registrar. Workshop instructors: Bill Lea, Will Clay and others. Emphasizes the use of natural light in creating quality scenic, wildflower and wildlife images.

◑ ● HALLMARK INSTITUTE OF PHOTOGRAPHY

241 Millers Falls Rd., Turners Falls MA 01376. (413)863-2478. **E-mail:** info@hallmark.edu. **Website:** www.hallmark.edu. Andy Vecellio, vice president for enrollment. **Contact:** Ed Martin, school president. Offers an intensive 10-month resident program teaching the technical, artistic and business aspects of professional photography for the career-minded individual.

JOHN HART PORTRAIT SEMINARS

344 W. 72nd St., New York NY 10023. (212)877-0516. **E-mail:** johnhartstudio1@mac.com. **Website:** www. headshotsbyjohnhart.com. Mr. Hart is a professor of photography at New York University. His photography sessions concentrate on "1-on-1" instruction that emphasizes advanced portrait techniques—concentrating mainly on lighting the subject in a truly professional manner, whether inside the studio or outside in natural lighting. He is the author of *50 Portrait Lighting Techniques* (Amazon.com; Barnes and Noble), *Professional Headshots*, *Lighting for Action*, and *The Art of the Storyboard* (Nook; eBook). His portrait seminars place a new emphasis on digital portrait photography, the subject of a new book he is working on.

○ ◑ ● HAWAII WORKSHOPS, RETREATS, PRIVATE PHOTO TOURS, INSTRUCTION & FINE ART PRINT SALES

P.O. Box 335, Honaunau HI 96726. (808)328-2162. **E-mail:** workshops@kathleencarr.com; kcarr@kathleencarr.com. **Website:** www.kathleentcarr.com; www.kathleencarr.com. **Contact:** Kathleen T. Carr. Pho-

tographing special places, digital infrared, model shoots, Photoshop, Polaroid/Fuji transfers, hand coloring and more. Location is Tropical Hideaway, South Kona, Big Island of Hawaii. See website for more information and registration.

○ ◑ ● HEART OF NATURE PHOTOGRAPHY WORKSHOPS & PHOTO TOURS

P.O. Box 1033, Volcano HI 96785. (808)345-7179. **E-mail:** rfphoto@jps.net. **Website:** www.hawaiiphototours.org. **Contact:** Robert Frutos. Be inspired, be amazed, be creative. Capture the beauty and spirit of the Big Island. Adventure, excitement and the experience of a lifetime await you on the breathtaking big island of Hawaii! Explore the majestic beauty. Discover the unique splendor. Experience exotic photo ops as well as little known awe-inspiring locations. Photograph and capture that potential once-in-a-lifetime image. Photographers can e-mail or see website for more information.

○ ◑ ● HORIZONS: ARTISTIC TRAVEL

P.O. Box 634, Leverett MA 01054. (413)367-9200. **Fax:** (413)367-9522. **E-mail:** horizons@horizons-art.com. **Website:** www.horizons-art.com. **Contact:** Jane Sinauer, director. "Horizons offers one-of-a-kind small-group travel adventures in Southern Africa: Sea to Safari; Peru: the Inca Heartland; Ecuador: Andes to the Amazon; Southeast Asia: Burma and Laos (2014); and new for 2013, A Foodie's Italy: Parma and Bologna. As of 2013, our catalog will solely be online to ensure that you always have the most up-to-date information. If you would like a detailed itinerary for any trip or have specific questions, please let us know."

○ ◑ ● HUI HO'OLANA

P.O. Box 280, Kualapùu, Molokài HI 96757. (808)567-6430. **E-mail:** hui@huiho.org; huihoolana@gmail.com. **Website:** www.huiho.org. **Contact:** Rik Cooke. "Hui Ho'olana is a nonprofit organization on the island of Molokai HI. We are dedicated to the fine art of teaching. Through workshops and volunteer residencies, our mission is to create a self-sustaining facility that supports educational programs and native Hawaiian reforestation projects. Our goal is to provide an environment for inspiration, a safe haven for the growth and nurturing of the creative spirit." Photographers should e-mail, call or visit website for more information, including the current workshop schedule.

➕ ◑ ⬤⬤⬤ ◯ ◑ ⬤ ICELAND'S BREATHTAKING LANDSCAPES

111 Bank St. #218, Grass Valley CA 95945. (916)520-8574. **E-mail:** workshops@jenniferwu.com. **Website:** www.jenniferwu.com. **Contact:** Jennifer Wu, owner/tour leader/photographer. Cost: $7,395 (double, two people per room) or $8,195. Included: hotel for nine nights and ten days, all ground transportation, all meals, non-alcoholic beverages and a boat ride through the ice lagoon, weather permitting. "Feel the spray from explosive geysers and iconic waterfalls. This is a special trip. Canon Explorer of Light and professional photographer Jennifer Wu, will be by your side at each location to help expand your techniques with in the field demos and will give compositional guidance to enhance the way you see and shoot. Photograph icebergs that are stranded on a black sand beach. Dine on farm fresh local cuisine. Travel in comfort. Hold a chunk of ice older than civilization. This workshop will give you the opportunity to capture highlights of the Great Circle, the best of the southern coast including the waterfalls, the ice lagoon, and the pastel hills of the interior. This tour is intended for intermediate and advanced photographers; however, any skill level is welcome and will enjoy Iceland's photographic opportunities. Participants should have a working knowledge of their equipment. Jennifer Wu has led dozens of photo tours and workshops domestically and around the world. Jennifer is the co-author of *Photography Night Sky* (Mountaineer Books), one of Amazon's most popular books on landscape photography." E-mail or see website for more information.

◑ IN FOCUS WITH MICHELE BURGESS

20741 Catamaran Lane, Huntington Beach CA 92646. (714)536-6104. **E-mail:** maburg5820@aol.com. **Website:** www.infocustravel.com. **Contact:** Michele Burgess, president. Offers overseas tours to photogenic areas with expert photography consultation at a leisurely pace and in small groups (maximum group size: 20).

◯ ◑ ⬤ INTERNATIONAL EXPEDITIONS

One Environs Park, Helena AL 35080. (855)232-1998; (205)428-1700. **Fax:** (205)428-1714. **E-mail:** nature@ietravel.com. **Website:** www.ietravel.com. **Contact:** Charlie Weaver, photo tour coordinator. Includes scheduled ground transportation; extensive pre-travel information; services of experienced English-speaking local guides; daily educational briefings; all excursions, entrance fees and permits; all accommodations; meals as specified in the respective itineraries; transfer and luggage handling when taking group flights. Guided nature expeditions all over the world: Amazon, Costa Rica, Machu Picchu, Galapagos, Laos & Vietnam, Borneo, Kenya, Patagonia and many more. Open to all skill levels. Photographers should write, call, e-mail, see website for more information.

◯ ◑ ⬤ JIVIDEN'S NATURALLY WILD PHOTO ADVENTURES

P.O. Box 333, Chillicothe OH 45601. (800)866-8655 or (740)774-6243. **Fax:** (740)774-6243 (call first). **E-mail:** mail@naturallywild.net. **Website:** www.naturallywild.net. **Contact:** Jerry or Barbara Jividen. "Experienced instructors with international photography publication credits. Photography workshops ranging from one-day digital bootcamps for $129 to week-long excursions in a variety of diverse North American locations (prices vary). Open to all skill levels. All workshops feature comprehensive instruction, guide service, pro tips to advanced photographers, editing tips, and portfolio reviews upon request. Workshops longer than two days normally include lodging, meals, ground transportation, entry permits if required and special group rates, as well as non-photographer guest rates for travel companions. Subject emphasis is on photographing nature, wildlife and natural history. Instruction focused on equipment use and techniques, proper exposure and equivalent options, composition and artistic merit, flash and lighting, and post-processing support. Free information available upon request, by phone or e-mail."

◑ ⬤ JORDAHL PHOTO WORKSHOPS

P.O. Box 3998, Hayward CA 94540. (510)909-4026. **E-mail:** kate@jordahlphoto.com. **Website:** www.jordahlphoto.com. **Contact:** Kate or Geir Jordahl, directors. Intensive 1- to 5-day workshops dedicated to inspiring creativity and community among artists through critique, field sessions and exhibitions.

BOB KORN IMAGING

46 Main St., P.O. Box 1687, Orleans MA 02653. (508)255-5202. **E-mail:** bob@bobkornimaging.com. **Website:** www.bobkornimaging.com. **Contact:** Bob Korn, director. The workshops at Bob Korn Imaging are for photographers and artists who are looking for one-on-one instruction in the Digital Darkroom. We will create workshops that meet your specific needs

from technical to creative and enable you to control the time and cost. Please call, e-mail, or see website for more information.

⊛ ○ ◐ ● THE LIGHT FACTORY

1817 Central Ave., Suite C200, Charlotte NC 28205. (704)333-9755. **E-mail:** info@lightfactory.org. **Website:** www.lightfactory.org. **Contact:** Dennis Kiel, chief curator. Estab. 1972. The Light Factory is a non-profit arts center dedicated to exhibition and education programs promoting the power of photography and film. From classes in basic point-and-shoot to portraiture, Photoshop, and more, TLF offers 3-8 week-long courses that meet once a week in our uptown Charlotte location. Classes are taught by professional instructors and cater to different expertise levels: introductory, intermediate and advanced in both photography and filmmaking. See website for a listing of classes and registration.

LIGHT PHOTOGRAPHIC WORKSHOPS

1060 Los Osos Valley Rd., Los Osos CA 93402. (805)528-7385. **Fax:** (888)254-6211. **E-mail:** info@lightworkshops.com. **Website:** www.lightworkshops.com. "LIGHT Photographic Workshops is located on the beautiful coast of California in the small town of Los Osos. We are halfway between Los Angeles and San Francisco near the Paso Robles wine area. It's a fantastic location for all sorts of photography! Offers small group workshops, private tutoring, Alaska and worldwide photography instruction cruises and tours, printing and canvas gallery wrap services, Canon gear rental, studio and classroom rental. New focus on digital tools to optimize photography, make the most of your images and improve your photography skills at the premier digital imaging school on the West Coast."

◒ ○ ◑ PETER LLEWELLYN PHOTOGRAPHY WORKSHOPS & PHOTO TOURS

645 Rollo Rd., Gabriola British Columbia VOR 1X3, Canada. (250)247-9109. **E-mail:** peter@peterllewellyn.com. **Website:** www.peterllewellyn.com. **Contact:** Peter Llewellyn. "Sports and wildlife photography workshops and photo tours at locations worldwide. Sports photography workshops feature instruction by some of the best sports photographers in the world. Workshops include photography, Photoshop skills, and digital workflow. Photo Tours are design to provide maximum photographic opportunities to participants with the assistance of a professional photographer. Trips include Brazil, Africa, Canada, and US. New destinations coming soon." Open to all skill levels. For further information, e-mail or see website. Costs vary.

○ ◐ ● C.C. LOCKWOOD WILDLIFE PHOTOGRAPHY WORKSHOP

P.O. Box 14876, Baton Rouge LA 70898. (225)769-4766. **E-mail:** cactusclyd@aol.com. **Website:** www.cclockwood.com. **Contact:** C.C. Lockwood, photographer. Lockwood periodically teaches hands-on photography workshops in the Grand Canyon, Colorado, Alaska, Louisiana marshes and rookeries, and the Atchafalaya Basin Swamp. Informative slide show lectures precede field trips into these great photo habitats. Call, write, e-mail or see website for a list of upcoming workshops.

○ ◐ ● ANDY LONG'S FIRST LIGHT PHOTOGRAPHY WORKSHOPS TOURS

P.O. Box 280952, Lakewood CO 80228. (303)601-2828. **E-mail:** andy@firstlighttours.com. **Website:** www.firstlighttours.com. **Contact:** Andy Long, owner. Tours cover a variety of locations and topics, including: Penguins of Falkland Islands, Alaskan northern lights, birds of Florida, south Texas birds, France, Iceland, eagles of southwest Alaska, Mt. Rainier National Park, Colorado wildflowers, Alaska bears, and more. See website for more information on locations, dates and prices. Open to all skill levels. See website for more details, schedule, detailed pricing information and registration.

○ ◐ ● LOS ANGELES CENTER OF PHOTOGRAPHY

755 Seward St., Los Angeles CA 90038. (323)464-0909. **Fax:** (323)464-0906. **E-mail:** workshops@juliadean.com. **Website:** www.juliadean.com. **Contact:** Brandon Gannon, director. The Julia Dean Photo Workshops (JDPW) is a practical education school of photography devoted to advancing the skills and increasing the personal enrichment of photographers of all experience levels and ages. Photography workshops of all kinds held throughout the year, including alternative and fine art, photography & digital camera fundamentals, lighting & portraiture, specialized photography, Photoshop and printing, photo safaris, and travel workshops. Open to all skill levels. Photographers should call, e-mail, or see website for more information.

◑ THE MACDOWELL COLONY

100 High St., Peterborough NH 03458. (603)924-3886. **Fax:** (603)924-9142. **E-mail:** admissions@macdowell colony.org. **Website:** www.macdowellcolony.org. Estab. 1907. Provides creative artists with uninterrupted time and seclusion to work and enjoy the experience of living in a community of gifted artists. Residencies of up to 8 weeks for writers, playwrights, composers, film/video makers, visual artists, architects and interdisciplinary artists. Artists in residence receive room, board and exclusive use of a studio. Average length of residency is 5 weeks. Ability to pay for residency is not a factor; there are no residency fees. Limited funds available for travel reimbursement and artist grants based on need. Application deadlines: January 15: summer (June-September); April 15: fall/winter (October-January); September 15: winter/spring (February-May). Visit website for online application and guidelines. Questions should be directed to the admissions director.

MADELINE ISLAND SCHOOL OF THE ARTS

978 Middle Rd., P.O. Box 536, LaPointe WI 54850. (715)747-2054. **E-mail:** misa@cheqnet.net. **Website:** www.madelineschool.com. **Contact:** Jenna J. Erickson, director of programs. Workshop tuition $425-760 for 5-day workshops. Lodging and meals are separate, both are provided on-site. Workshops held annually between May-October. Workshops offered in writing, painting, quilting, photography and yoga. Open to all skill levels. Interested parties should call, e-mail or see website for more information.

○ ◑ ● MAINE MEDIA WORKSHOPS

70 Camden St., P.O. Box 200, Rockport ME 04856. (207)236-8581 or (877)577-7700. **Fax:** (207)236-2558. **E-mail:** info@mainemedia.edu. **Website:** www. mainemedia.edu. "Maine Media Workshops is a nonprofit educational organization offering year-round workshops for photographers, filmmakers and media artists. Students from across the country and around the world attend courses at all levels, from absolute beginner and serious amateur to working professional; also high school and college students. Professional certificate and low-residency MFA degree programs are available through Maine Media College." See website for the fall calendar.

○ ◑ ● WILLIAM MANNING PHOTOGRAPHY

6396 Birchdale Court, Cincinnati OH 45236. (513)624-8148. **E-mail:** william@williammanning. com. **Website:** www.williammanning.com. Digital photography workshops worldwide with emphasis on travel, nature, and architecture. Offers small group tours. Participants will learn how to photograph with an open mind and shoot with post-production in mind and all of its possibilities. Participants should have a basic knowledge of Adobe Photoshop and own 1 or more plug-ins such as Topaz Adjust, Nik software and/or Auto FX (Mystical Lighting and Ambiance) software. See website for more information and registration.

○ ◑ ● JOE & MARY ANN MCDONALD WILDLIFE PHOTOGRAPHY WORKSHOPS AND TOURS

73 Loht Rd., McClure PA 17841-9340. (717)543-6423. **Fax:** (717)543-5342. **E-mail:** info@hoothollow.com. **Website:** www.hoothollow.com. **Contact:** Joe McDonald, owner. "We are wildlife photographers who not only maintain a huge inventory of stock images for editorial and advertising use, but who have dedicated ourselves to the sharing of photographic and natural history information through our various courses, tours, workshops, and safaris." Offers small group, quality instruction with emphasis on nature and wildlife photography. See website for more information and a list of upcoming workshops.

○ ◑ ● MENTOR SERIES ULTIMATE PHOTO ADVENTURE

Bonnier Technology Group, 2 Park Ave., 9th Floor, New York NY 10016. (888)676-6468; (212)779-5473. **Fax:** (212)779-5508. **E-mail:** michelle.cast@bonnier corp.com. **Website:** www.mentorseries.com. **Contact:** Michelle Cast, director of events. "For the past 17 years the Mentor Series program has taken photo enthusiasts to destinations across the country and around the world. With top Nikon professional photographers accompanying participants every day and giving advice on how and what to shoot, there is nothing like a Mentor Series trek. You and your photography will never be the same!" Designed to cater to all skill levels. Upcoming locations include: Croatia, Venice, Tampa Sports Video, Nevada Lighting, Costa Rica, Long Island NY, California, Ohio, Grand Tetons, Iceland, Olympic National Park, Quebec and

Vermont). Photographers should call, e-mail or see website for more information.

⊕ ○ ◑ ● MEXICO PHOTOGRAPHY WORKSHOPS

(304)478-3586. **E-mail:** ottercreekphotography@yahoo.com. **Contact:** John Warner. Intensive week-long, hands-on workshops held throughout the year in the most visually rich, and safest, regions of Mexico. Photograph snow-capped volcanoes, thundering waterfalls, pre-Columbian ruins, botanical gardens, vibrant street life, fascinating people, markets and colonial churches in jungle, mountain, desert and alpine environments. Photographers should call or e-mail for more information.

○ ◑ ● MID-ATLANTIC REGIONAL SCHOOL OF PHOTOGRAPHY

121 Webster Ave., Stratford NJ 08084. (888)267-MARS (6277). **E-mail:** registrar@marsschool.com; john@marsschool.com. **Website:** www.marsschool.com. One week continuing education classes. Covers many aspects of professional photography from digital to portrait to wedding. Open to photographers of all skill levels. Check website for information on the next workshop dates and online webinar mini courses .

○ ◑ ● MIDWEST PHOTOGRAPHIC WORKSHOPS

28830 W. Eight Mile Rd., Farmington Hills MI 48336. (248)471-7299. **E-mail:** officemanager@mpw.com; bryce@mpw.com. **Website:** www.mpw.com. **Contact:** Bryce Denison, owner. "One-day weekend and week-long photo workshops, small group sizes and hands-on shooting seminars by professional photographers/instructors on topics such as portraiture, landscapes, nudes, digital, nature, weddings, product advertising and photojournalism." Workshops held regularly. See website for more information and registration.

MISSOURI PHOTOJOURNALISM WORKSHOP

109 Lee Hills Hall, Columbia MO 65211. (573)882-4882. **Fax:** (573)884-4999. **E-mail:** reesd@missouri.edu. **Website:** www.mophotoworkshop.org. **Contact:** Photojournalism department. Workshop for photojournalists. Participants learn the fundamentals of documentary photo research, shooting, and editing. Held in a different Missouri town each year.

MIXED MEDIA PHOTOGRAPHY

498 Ripka St., Philadelphia PA 19128. (610)247-9964. **E-mail:** leahwax@aol.com; info@blissbooks.net. **Website:** www.blissbooks.net; www.leahmacdonald.net. **Contact:** Leah Macdonald. Quarterly 2-day workshop; and held via personal appointment. Also conducts one-on-one workshops with students. "The purpose of the workshop is to alter the surface of the photograph, using organic beeswax and oil paints in multiple forms and techniques to create surface textures and color enhancements that personalize and intensify the photographic image. My mixed-media techniques are used with both traditional darkroom papers and inkjet papers. I encourage creativity and self-expression through image surface enhancement and mixed media techniques to create original one-of-a-kind artwork." Cost: $600; lunch is included, lodging is not. Instructor is available hourly, as well as part-time, for private instruction. Open to all skill levels. Photographers should call, e-mail, or see website for more information.

● ⊘ MOUNTAIN WORKSHOPS

Western Kentucky University, 1906 College Heights, MMTH 131, Bowling Green KY 42101-1070. (270)745-8927. **E-mail:** mountainworkshops@wku.edu. **Website:** www.mountainworkshops.org. **Contact:** Jim Bye, workshop coordinator. Annual documentary photojournalism workshop held in October. Open to intermediate and advanced shooters. See website for upcoming dates.

○ TOM MURPHY PHOTOGRAPHY

402 S. Fifth St., Livingston MT 59047. (406)222-2302; (406)222-2986. **E-mail:** tom@tmurphywild.com. **Website:** tmurphywild.com. **Contact:** Tom Murphy, president. Offers programs in wildlife and landscape photography in Yellowstone National Park and special destinations.

◑ NATURAL HABITAT ADVENTURES

P.O. Box 3065, Boulder CO 80307. (303)449-3711 or (800)543-8917. **Fax:** (303)449-3712. **E-mail:** info@nathab.com. **Website:** www.nathab.com. Guided photo tours for wildlife photographers. Tours last 7-14 days. Destinations include North America, Latin America, Canada, Galápagos Islands, Africa, and Asia. See website for more information.

○ ◐ ● **NEVERSINK PHOTO WORKSHOP**

P.O. Box 641, Woodbourne NY 12788. (212)929-0009. **E-mail:** lhj3@mac.com. **Website:** www.neversinkphotoworkshop.com. **Contact:** Louis Jawitz, owner. "Neversink photo workshops concentrate on scenic and nature photography with supervised field trip shooting, as well as portfolio review and critique, discussions related to composition and perspective, technical skills, visual design, using color for impact, exposure control, basic digital workflow and developing a personal style. Individual or group workshops will be held any day during the summer months, with a possibility of an additional 'Fall Foliage' weekend in October (dates to be determined). See Application page to schedule dates. There will be no private/individual workshops scheduled any day that group workshops are in session." Call, e-mail, or see website for more detailed pricing information and specifics on what all is included in the registration fees.

◐ ● **NEW ENGLAND SCHOOL OF PHOTOGRAPHY**

537 Commonwealth Ave., Boston MA 02215. (617)437-1868 or (800)676-3767. **E-mail:** info@nesop.com. **Website:** www.nesop.com. Instruction in professional and creative photography in the form of workshops or a professional photography program. See website for details on individual workshops.

○ ◐ ● **NEW JERSEY HERITAGE PHOTOGRAPHY WORKSHOPS**

124 Diamond Hill Rd., Berkeley Heights NJ 07922. (908)790-8820. **E-mail:** nancyori@comcast.net. **Website:** www.nancyoriworkshops.com. **Contact:** Nancy Ori, director. Estab. 1990. Workshops held every spring. Nancy Ori, well-known instructor, freelance photographer and fine art exhibitor of landscape and architecture photography, teaches how to use available light and proper metering techniques to document the man-made and natural environments of Cape May. A variety of film and digital workshops taught by guest instructors are available each year and are open to all skill levels, especially beginners. Topics include hand coloring of photographs, creative camera techniques with Polaroid materials, intermediate and advanced digital, landscape and architecture with alternative cameras, environmental portraits with lighting techniques, street photography; as well as pastel, watercolor and oil painting workshops. All workshops include an historic walking tour of town, location shooting or painting, demonstrations and critiques.

○ ◐ ● **NEW JERSEY MEDIA CENTER LLC WORKSHOPS AND PRIVATE TUTORING**

124 Diamond Hill Rd., Berkeley Heights NJ 07922. (908)790-8820. **E-mail:** nancyori@comcast.net. **Website:** www.nancyoriworkshops.com. **Contact:** Nancy Ori. 1. Italy Photography Workshop: Delicious Photography in Italy with Nancy Ori. Explore the Italian countryside, cities and small villages, with emphasis on architecture, documentary, portrait and landscape photography. The group will venture in non-tourist areas to explore the culture with cooking lessons and visits to small shops and industrial locations to see how the real people live and eat. Significant others welcome and will have plenty to see and do while you photograph, sketch or paint. Cost: call for this year's price; includes tuition, accommodations at a 15th-century fully renovated hilltop retreat with all the modern amenities, breakfasts and some dinners. Open to all skill levels. 2. Private Photography Tutoring with Nancy Ori in Berkeley Heights NJ. This unique and personalized approach to learning photography is designed for the beginning or intermediate student who wants to expand his/her understanding of the craft and work more creatively with the camera, develop a portfolio and create an exhibit. The goal is to refine individual style while exploring the skills necessary to make expressive photographs. The content will be tailored to individual needs and interests. Cost: $350 for a total of 8 hours. 3. Capturing the Light of the Southwest, a painting, sketching and photography workshop with Nancy Ori, held every other year in October, will focus on the natural landscape and man-made structures of the area around Santa Fe and Taos. Participants can be at any level in their media. All will be encouraged to produce a substantial body of work worthy of portfolio or gallery presentation. Features special evening guest lecturers from the photography community in the Santa Fe area. Artists should e-mail for more information. 4. Cape May Photography Workshops are held annually in April and May. Also, a variety of subjects such as photojournalism, environmental portraiture, landscape, alternative cameras, Polaroid techniques, creative digital techniques, on-location wedding photography, large-format, and how to photograph birds

in the landscape are offered by several well-known East Coast instructors. Open to all skill levels. Includes critiques, demonstrations, location shooting of Victorian architecture, gardens, seascapes, and, in some cases, models in either film or digital. E-mail for dates, fees and more information. Workshops are either 3 or 4 days. 5: Capture the Light and Color of New England will emphasize time for careful study of the relationship between the natural environment, light, color and simple country architecture, which may effectively lead to paintings or photographs with insight and emotional value.

○ ◑ ● **NIKON SCHOOL | EDUCATE + INSPIRE**

1300 Walt Whitman Rd., Melville NY 11747. (631)547-8666. **Fax:** (631)547-0309. **E-mail:** nikonschool@nikon.net. **Website:** www.nikonschool.com. Photo education classes located in 25 major US cities with a variety of half-day ($99) and full-day ($159) classes, including: Action & People Photography, Elements of Photography, Landscape and Travel Photography, Creative Lighting, and SSLR Video-Gaming Control. For more information and to register, visit www.nikonschool.com, call (800)645-6687, or e-mail nikonschool@nikon.net.

◑ ● **NORTHERN EXPOSURES**

5129 Evergreen Way #D383, Everett WA 98203. (425)347-7650. **E-mail:** abenteuerbc@yahoo.com. **Contact:** Linda Moore, director. Offers 3- to 8-day intermediate to advanced nature photography workshops in several locations in Pacific Northwest and western Canada; spectacular settings including coast, alpine, badlands, desert and rain forest. Also, 1- to 2-week Canadian Wildlife and Wildlands Photo Adventures and nature photo tours to extraordinary remote wildlands of British Columbia, Alberta, Saskatchewan and Yukon.

○ ◑ ● **NYU TISCH SCHOOL OF THE ARTS**

Department of Photography & Imaging, 721 Broadway, Eighth Floor, New York NY 10003. (212)998-1930. **E-mail:** photo.tsoa@nyu.edu. **Website:** www.photo.tisch.nyu.edu. **Contact:** Department of Photography and Imaging. Summer classes offered for credit and noncredit covering digital imaging, career development, basic to advanced photography, darkroom techniques, photojournalism, and human rights & photography. Open to all skill levels.

○ ◑ ● **OREGON COLLEGE OF ART AND CRAFT**

8245 SW Barnes Rd., Portland OR 97225. (503)297-5544 or (800)390-0632. **Fax:** (503)297-9651. **E-mail:** admissions@ocac.edu; lradford@ocac.edu. **Website:** www.ocac.edu. Offering MFA, BFA and Post Baccalaureate in Craft, MFA in Applied Craft + Design (a joint program of OCAC and PNCA), continuing education for adults and children. For schedule information, call or visit website.

○ ◑ ● **PACIFIC NORTHWEST ART SCHOOL/PHOTOGRAPHY**

15 NW Birch St., Coupeville WA 98239. (360)678-3396. **E-mail:** info@pacificnorthwestartschool.org. **Website:** www.pacificnorthwestartschool.org. **Contact:** Registrar. "Join us on beautiful Whidbey Island and enjoy high-quality photography instruction from our renowned visiting faculty including Sam Abell, Sean Kernan, Arthur Meyerson and many more. Workshops held April-October, 2-6 days in duration.

○ ◑ ● **PALM BEACH PHOTOGRAPHIC CENTRE**

415 Clematis St., West Palm Beach FL 33401. (561)253-2600. **Fax:** (561)253-2604. **E-mail:** info@workshop.org. **Website:** www.workshop.org. The Centre is an innovative learning facility offering photography classes, workshops and seminars and digital imaging year round. Also offered are travel workshops to cultural destinations such as South Africa, Bhutan, Myanmar, Peru, and India. Emphasis is on photographing the indigenous cultures of each country. Also hosts the annual Fotofusion event (see separate listing in this section). Photographers should call for details.

○ ◑ ● **RALPH PAONESSA PHOTOGRAPHY WORKSHOPS**

509 W. Ward Ave., Suite B-108, Ridgecrest CA 93555-2542. (760)384-8666. **E-mail:** ralph@rpphoto.com. **Website:** www.rpphoto.com. **Contact:** Ralph Paonessa, director. Various workshops repeated annually. Nature, bird and landscape trips to the Eastern Sierra, Death Valley, Falkland Islands, Alaska, Costa Rica, Ecuador, and many other locations. Open to all skill levels. Upcoming workshop: "Ecuador Hummingbirds," September 23-October 6 in Quito. See website for more information.

◐ ○ ◑ ● **FREEMAN PATTERSON**
PHOTO WORKSHOPS

Shamper's Cove Limited, 3487 Rt. 845, Long Reach NB E5S 1X4, Canada. (506)763-2189. **Fax:** (506)763-2035. **E-mail:** freepatt@nbnet.nb.ca. **Website:** www.freemanpatterson.com. Freeman made several visits to Africa between 1967 and 1983, three of them at the request of the Photographic Society of Southern Africa. As a result of these contacts and others, he co-founded (with Colla Swart) the Namaqualand Photographic Workshops in 1984, and travels to the desert village of Kamieskroon once or twice a year to teach three or four week-long workshops. This project has expanded so rapidly that Freeman now works with several other instructors and no longer participates in every program. Freeman has also given numerous, week-long workshops in the US, New Zealand, and Israel and has completed lecture tours in the United Kingdom, South Africa and Australia. See website for more information and a list of upcoming workshops.

○ ◑ ● **PETERS VALLEY SCHOOL OF CRAFT**

19 Kuhn Rd., Layton NJ 07851. (973)948-5200. **Fax:** (973)948-0011. **E-mail:** info@petersvalley.org. **Website:** www.petersvalley.org. Offers workshops May, June, July, August and September; 2-5 days long. Offers instruction by talented photographers in a wide range of photographic disciplines—from daguereotypes to digital and everything in between. Also offers classes in blacksmithing/metals, ceramics, fibers, fine metals, weaving and woodworking. Located in northwest New Jersey in the Delaware Water Gap National Recreation Area, 70 miles west of New York. Artists and photographers should call for catalog or visit website for more information.

○ ◑ ● **PHOTO EXPLORER TOURS**

2506 Country Village, Ann Arbor MI 48103-6500. (800)315-4462 or (734)996-1440. **E-mail:** decoxphoto@gmail.com. **Website:** www.photoexplorertours.com. **Contact:** Dennis Cox, director. Scheduled group photographic explorations of Turkey and other select destinations to be announced.

○ ◑ ● **PHOTOGRAPHERS'**
FORMULARY

P.O. Box 950, 7079 Hwy. 83 N., Condon MT 59826-0950. (800)922-5255. **Fax:** (406)754-2896. **E-mail:** lynnw@blackfoot.net; formulary@blackfoot.net.

Website: www.photoformulary.com; www.workshopsinmt.com. **Contact:** Lynn Wilson, workshop program director. Photographers' Formulary workshops include a wide variety of alternative processes, and many focus on the traditional darkroom. Located in Montana's Swan Valley, some of the best wilderness lands in the Rocky Mountains. See website for details on costs and lodging. Open to all skill levels. Workshops held frequently throughout the year. See website for listing of dates and registration.

○ ◑ **PHOTOGRAPHIC ARTS**
WORKSHOPS

P.O. Box 1791, Granite Falls WA 98252. (360)691-4105. **Fax:** (360)691-4105. **E-mail:** PhotoArtsWrkshps@aol.com; barnbaum@aol.com. **Website:** www.barnbaum.com. **Contact:** Bruce Barnbaum. Offers a wide range of workshops across the US, Latin America and Europe. Instructors include masters of both traditional and digital imagery. Workshops feature instruction in the understanding and use of light, composition, exposure, development, printing, photographic goals and philosophy. All workshops include reviews of student portfolios. Sessions are intense but highly enjoyable, held in field, darkroom and classroom with outstanding photographer/instructors. Ratio of students to instructors is always 8:1 or fewer, with detailed attention to problems students want solved. All camera formats, color and b&w. The deposit for each workshop is $150, except the Escalante backpack, which is $200. Final payment is requested 5 weeks prior to the start of the workshop. The deposit is non-refundable. If a workshop is canceled for any reason, your deposit will be returned in full. Upcoming workshops: "Autumn Complete Photographic Process Workshop" (Granite Falls WA), cost: $1,125 (includes complete lab fees); "The High Sierra to Death Valley: The Highs and Lows of the American West," cost: $1,125. See website for latest info, dates and workshop descriptions: www.barnbaum.

PHOTOGRAPHIC CENTER NORTHWEST

900 12th Ave., Seattle WA 98122. (206)720-7222. **E-mail:** pcnw@pcnw.org; jbrendicke@pcnw.org. **Website:** www.pcnw.org. **Contact:** Rafael Soldi, marketing director. Frequent day and evening classes and workshops in fine art photography (b&w, color, digital) for photographers of all skill levels; accredited certificate program. See website for more information and a listing of upcoming workshops. We also have a

renowned photography gallery, photographic rental facilities for the public and professionals, and artist support programs.

◐ ● PHOTOGRAPHY AT THE SUMMIT: JACKSON HOLE

Clarkson Creative, 1553 Platte St., Suite 300, Denver CO 80302. (303)295-7770 or (800)745-3211. **Fax:** (303)295-7771. **E-mail:** workshops@clarkson-creative.com. **Website:** www.photographyatthesummit.com. **Contact:** Brett Wilhelm, administrator. Annual workshops held in the fall. Weeklong workshops with top journalistic, nature and illustrative photographers and editors. See website for more information.

⦿ ○ ◐ ● PHOTOGRAPHY IN PROVENCE

La Maison Claire, Rue du Buis, Ansouis 84240, France. **E-mail:** andrew@photography-provence.com. **Website:** www.photography-provence.com. **Contact:** Andrew Squires, M.A. Workshops May to October. Theme: What to Photograph and Why? Designed for people who are looking for a subject and an approach they can call their own. Explore photography of the real world, the universe of human imagination, or simply let yourself discover what touches you. Explore Provence and photograph on location. Possibility to extend your stay and explore Provence if arranged in advance. Open to all skill levels. E-mail for workshop dates and more information.

○ ◐ PRAGUE SUMMER SEMINARS

Division of International Education, 2000 Lakeshore Dr., International Center 124, University of New Orleans, New Orleans LA 70148. (504)280-6388. **E-mail:** prague@uno.edu. **Website:** inst.uno.edu/Prague. **Contact:** Mary I. Hicks, program director. Challenging courses which involve studio visits, culture series, excursions within Prague and field trips to Vienna, Austria, and Cesky Krumlov, Bohemia. Open to beginners and intermediate photographers. Photographers should call, e-mail, or see website for more information.

● ⊘ PROFESSIONAL PHOTOGRAPHERS' SOCIETY OF NEW YORK STATE PHOTO WORKSHOPS

2175 Stuyvesant St., Niskayuna NY 12309. (518)377-5935. **E-mail:** tmmack7@gmail.com; linda@ppsnysworkshop.com. **Website:** www.ppsnysworkshop.com. **Contact:** Tom Mack, director. Weeklong, specialized,

hands-on workshops for professional photographers in mid-July. See website for more information.

⤺ ○ ◐ ● PYRENEES EXPOSURES

Laroque des Albères, Pyrénées-Orientales, France. **E-mail:** explorerimages@yahoo.com. **Website:** www.explorerimages.com. **Contact:** Martin N. Johansen, director. Workshops held year-round. Offers 1- to 5-day workshops and photo expeditions in the French and Spanish Pyrenees mountains and along the Mediterranean Sea in northern Catalonia, with emphasis on landscapes, wildlife and culture. Workshops and tours are limited to small groups. Open to all skill levels. Photographers should e-mail or see website for more information.

◐ ● JEFFREY RICH WILDLIFE PHOTOGRAPHY TOURS

P.O. Box 1265, Cottonwood CA 96022. (530)410-8428. **E-mail:** jrich@jeffrichphoto.com. **Website:** www.jeffrichphoto.com. **Contact:** Jeffrey Rich. Estab. 1990. Leading wildlife photo tours in Alaska and western US—bald eagles, whales, birds, Montana babies and predators, Brazil's Pantanal, Borneo, and Japan's winter wildlife. Photographers should call or e-mail for brochure. Books are available for purchase through the website as well.

○ ◐ ● ROCKY MOUNTAIN CONSERVANCY-FIELD INSTITUTE

1895 Fall River Rd., Estes Park CO 80517. (970)586-3262. **E-mail:** fieldinstitute@rmconservancy.org; rachel.balduzzi@rmconservancy.org. **Website:** www.rmconservancy.org. Rachel Balduzzi, education director and NGF manager. **Contact:** Rachel Balduzzi. Day and weekend classes covering photographic techniques for wildlife and scenics in Rocky Mountain National Park. Professional instructors include W. Perry Conway, Don Mammoser, Glenn Randall, Eli Vega, John Fielder and Lee Kline. Call or e-mail for a free class catalog listing over 200 classes.

○ ◐ ● ROCKY MOUNTAIN SCHOOL OF PHOTOGRAPHY

216 N. Higgins, Missoula MT 59802. (406)543-0171 or (800)394-7677. **Fax:** (406)721-9133. **E-mail:** rmsp@rmsp.com. **Website:** www.rmsp.com. "RMSP offers three types of photography programs: Career Training, Workshops and Photo Weekend events. There are varied learning opportunities for students according to their individual goals and educational needs. In a

noncompetitive learning environment, we strive to instill confidence, foster creativity and build technical skills."

◯ ◑ ● SANTA FE PHOTOGRAPHIC WORKSHOPS

Santa Fe Photographic Workshops, 50 Mt. Carmel Rd., Fatima Hall, Santa Fe NM 87505. (505)983-1400. **Fax:** (505)989-8604. **E-mail:** info@santafeworkshops.com; carrie@santafeworkshops.com. **Website:** www.santafeworkshops.com. Over 120 week-long workshops encompassing all levels of photography and more than 35 digital lab workshops and 12 week-long workshops in Mexico—all led by top professional photographers. The workshops campus is located near the historic center of Santa Fe. Call or e-mail to request a free catalog.

⊕ SANTORINI BOUDOIR AND FASHION PHOTOGRAPHY WORKSHOPS

Fyra Santorini Island 84700, Greece. (0030) 6944 257 125. **E-mail:** giannisangelou@gmail.com. **Website:** www.santoriniboudoir.com; www.santoriniworkshops.com. **Contact:** John G. Angelou. See website for details on workshop dates and prices. Workshops held year-round. Offers boudoir photography workshops, from small groups (mainly 3-5 participants). Fashion and portrait, family, couples photography whorkshops also available. Custom photography workshops available upon request. See website for more information.

◯ ◑ ● SELLING YOUR PHOTOGRAPHY

1684 Decoto Rd., #271, Union City CA 94587. (714) 356-4260. **E-mail:** maria@mpiscopo.com. **Website:** www.mpiscopo.com. **Contact:** Maria Piscopo. One-day workshops cover techniques for pricing, marketing and selling art and photography services. Open to photographers and creative professionals of all skill levels. See website for dates and locations. Maria Piscopo is the author of *Photographer's Guide to Marketing & Self-Promotion*, 4th edition (Allworth Press).

◑ ● JOHN SEXTON PHOTOGRAPHY WORKSHOPS

P.O. Box 30, Carmel Valley CA 93924. (831)659-3130. **Fax:** (831)659-5509. **E-mail:** info@johnsexton.com. **Website:** www.johnsexton.com. Director: John Sexton. **Contact:** Anne Larsen, associate director. Offers a selection of intensive workshops with master pho-

tographers in scenic locations throughout the US. All workshops offer a combination of instruction in the aesthetic and technical considerations involved in making expressive b&w prints. Instructors include John Sexton, Charles Cramer, Ray McSavaney, Anne Larsen and others.

◯ ◑ THE SHOWCASE SCHOOL OF PHOTOGRAPHY

1135 Sheridan Rd., Atlanta GA 30324. (404)965-2205. **E-mail:** staff@theshowcaseschool.com; jan@theshowcaseschool.com. **Website:** www.theshowcaseschool.com. Offers photography classes to the general public, including beginning digital camera, people photography, nature photography and Photoshop. Open to beginner and intermediate amateur photographers. Classes offered frequently throughout the year; see website for upcoming dates.

◐ ◯ ◑ ● SINGING SANDS WORKSHOPS

207 Millbank, London Ontario N6C 4V1, Canada. (519)984-6329. **E-mail:** donmartelca@yahoo.ca. **Website:** www.singingsandsworkshops.com. Digital photography workshops. Semiannual workshops held in June and October. Creative photo techniques in the rugged coastline of Georgian Bay and the flats of Lake Huron taught by Don Martel. Open to all skill levels. Photographers should send SASE, call, e-mail, or see website for more information.

⬤ SKELLIG PHOTO TOURS

00353 66 9479022. **E-mail:** michaelherrmann@email.de. **Website:** www.skelligphototours.com. **Contact:** Michael Herrmann. Several photography workshops held throughout the year and on demand. Learn new, or improve, your photography skills through landscape photography in the magic scenery of Kerry. Exposure, composition, low-light photography and a variety of technical and artistic aspects of photography will be covered according to your needs; Also, photo editing in Photoshop and Lightroom. Open to all skill levels. If you are in the mood for the Irish experience, e-mail or see website for more information.

SOHN FINE ART—MASTER ARTIST WORKSHOPS

6 Elm St., 1B-C, Stockbridge MA 01230. (413)298-1025. **E-mail:** info@sohnfineart.com. **Website:** www.sohnfineart.com. **Contact:** Cassandra Sohn, owner. Workshops held every 1-3 months, taught by our rep-

resented master artists. Cost: $100-500, depending on the workshop (meals and lodging not included). Frequent areas of concentration are unique workshops within the photographic field. This includes all levels of students: beginner, intermediate and advanced, as well as Photoshop and Lightroom courses, alternative process courses and many varieties of traditional and digital photography courses. Interested parties should call, e-mail, or see the website for more information.

○ ◑ ● **SOUTH SHORE ART CENTER**

119 Ripley Rd., Cohasset MA 02025. (781)383-2787. **Fax:** (781)383-2964. **E-mail:** info@ssac.org. **Website:** www.ssac.org. South Shore Art Center is a non-profit organization based in the coastal area south of Boston. The facility features appealing galleries and teaching studios. Offers exhibitions and gallery programs, sales of fine art and studio crafts, courses and workshops, school outreach and special events. See website for more information and a list of upcoming workshops and events.

◑ ● **SPORTS PHOTOGRAPHY WORKSHOP: COLORADO SPRINGS, COLORADO**

Clarkson Creative, 1553 Platte St., Suite 300, Denver CO 80302. (303)295-7770 or (800)745-3211. **Fax:** (303)295-7771. **E-mail:** workshops@clarkson-creative. com. **Website:** www.sportsphotographyworkshop. com. **Contact:** Brett Wilhelm, administrator. Annual workshop held in midsummer. Weeklong workshop in sports photography at the US Olympic Training Center with *Sports Illustrated* and Associated Press photographers and editors. See website for more information.

◑ ● **SUPERIOR/GUNFLINT PHOTOGRAPHY WORKSHOPS**

E-mail: lk@laynekennedy.com. **Website:** www. laynekennedy.com. **Contact:** Layne Kennedy, director. Workshops & Photo Tours Worldwide. Schedule includes Iceland, Italy, Costa Rica, Ireland, Dogsledding, North Shore Lake Superior and Minneapolis. For all levels, experienced to beginner. Visit website for prices and description of specific workshops.

○ ◑ ● **SYNERGISTIC VISIONS WORKSHOPS**

623 Main St., Grand Junction CO 81501. (970)314-2054. **E-mail:** steve@synvis.com. **Website:** www.ccgal. com. **Contact:** Steve Traudt, director. Through Colo-

rado Canyons Gallery offers a variety of digital photography, Lightroom and Photoshop classes at various venues in Grand Junction, Moab, Ouray, and others. "Steve is also available to present day-long photo seminars to your group." See website for more information and upcoming workshops.

○ ◑ ● **TEXAS SCHOOL OF PROFESSIONAL PHOTOGRAPHY**

(806)296-2276. **Fax:** (979)272-5201. **E-mail:** don@ texasschool.org. **Website:** texasschool.org. **Contact:** Don Dickson, director. Twenty-five different classes offered, including portrait, wedding, marketing, background painting and video. See website for more information and a list of upcoming workshops.

○ ◑ ● **THE THIRD EYE PHOTOGRAPHIC ADVENTURES AND WORKSHOPS**

(404)876-6341. **E-mail:** workshop.inquiry@thethird eyephoto.com. **Website:** www.thethirdeyephoto.com. **Contact:** Robin Davis, instructor; Kathryn Kolb, instructor. "Workshops held year-round; check our online schedule. Concentrates on inspirational places, memorable experiences, personal instruction. Our purpose is to empower the connection between in-camera decisions and the personal creative goals of our students, while having a great time in amazing and, often, mysterious locations. Costs vary depending on the locations and number of days, and cover unique personalized instruction, and typically do not include meals or lodging. Open to all skill levels. Interested parties should call, e-mail, or see our website for more information."

○ ◑ ● **TRAVEL IMAGES**

P.O. Box 2434, Eagle ID 83616. (208)559-8248. **E-mail:** phototours@travelimages.com. **Website:** www. travelimages.com. **Contact:** John Baker, owner/guide. Small-group photo tours. Locations include US, Canada, Wales, Scotland, Ireland, England, Iceland, New Zealand, Tasmania, Galapagos Islands, Machu Picchu, Patagonia, Provence, Paris, Burgundy, Normandy/ Brittany/Loire valley, Tuscany, Cinque Terre, Venice, Austria, Switzerland, Germany and polar bears of Manitoba.

TRIPLE D GAME FARM

P.O. Box 5072, Kalispell MT 59903. (406)755-9653. **Fax:** (406)755-9021. **E-mail:** info@tripledgamefarm. com. **Website:** www.tripledgamefarm.com. **Contact:**

Kathleen O'Neil, assistant manager. We raise wildlife and train our species for photographers, artists, and cinema. Wolves, bears, mountain lions, bobcats, lynx, tigers, snow leopards, coyotes, fox, fisher, otter, porcupine and more are available. Open to all skill levels. Interested parties should write, call, e-mail, or see website for more information.

○ ◐ ● JOSEPH VAN OS PHOTO SAFARIS, INC.

P.O. Box 655, Vashon Island WA 98070. (206)463-5383. **Fax:** (206)463-5484. **E-mail:** info@photosafaris.com. **Website:** www.photosafaris.com. **Contact:** Joseph Van Os, director. Offers over 50 different photo tours and workshops worldwide. At least 1 tour offered each month; several tours already planned. See website for more details and a list of all upcoming tours.

○ ◐ ● VIRGINIA CENTER FOR THE CREATIVE ARTS (VCCA)

154 San Angelo Dr., Amherst VA 24521. (434)946-7236. **Fax:** (434)946-7239. **E-mail:** vcca@vcca.com. **Website:** www.vcca.com. VCCA (Virginia Center for the Creative Arts) is an international working retreat for writers, artists and composers. Nestled on 450 acres in the foothills of the Blue Ridge Mountains of central Virginia, VCCA offers residential fellowships ranging from 2 weeks to 2 months. VCCA can accommodate 25 fellows at a time and provides private working and living quarters and all meals. There is one fully equipped b&w darkroom at VCCA. Artists provide their own materials. VCCA application and work samples required. Call or see website for more information. Application deadlines are January 15, May 15, and September 15 each year.

○ ◐ ● VISION QUEST PHOTO WORKSHOPS

2370 Hendon Ave., St. Paul MN 55108-1453. (651)644-1400. **E-mail:** info@douglasbeasley.com. **Website:** www.vqphoto.com. **Contact:** Doug Beasley, director. Annual workshops held January through November. Hands-on photo workshops that emphasize content, vision and creativity over technique or gimmicks. Workshops held in a variety of national and international locations. Open to all skill levels. Upcoming workshops: Zen and the Art of Photography in Rockport ME; Breitenbush Hot Springs OR; Woodstock NY; Renewing Your Creative Spirit, Trade River Retreat Center WI. Photographers should e-mail or visit website for more information.

◐ ● VISUAL ARTISTRY WORKSHOP SERIES

P.O. Box 963, Eldersburg MD 21784. (410)552-4664. **Fax:** (410)552-3332. **E-mail:** tony@tonysweet.com. **Website:** tonysweet.com. **Contact:** Tony Sweet or Susan Milestone, susan@tonysweet.com. 5-day workshops, limit 5-10 participants. Extensive personal attention and instructional slide shows. Post-workshop support and image critiques for 6 months after the workshop (for an additional fee). Frequent attendees discounts and inclement weather discounts on subsequent workshops. Dealer discounts available from major vendors. "The emphasis is to create in the participant a greater awareness of composition, subject selection, and artistic rendering of the natural world using the raw materials of nature: color, form and line." Open to intermediate and advanced photographers. See website for more information.

○ ◐ ● WILDLIFE PHOTOGRAPHY WORKSHOPS AND LECTURES

Len Rue Enterprises, LLC, 138 Millbrook Rd., Blairstown NJ 07825. (908)362-6616. **E-mail:** rue@rue.com. **Website:** www.rue.com; www.rueimages.com. **Contact:** Len Rue, Jr. Taught by Len Rue, Jr., who has over 35 years experience in outdoor photography by shooting photographic stock for the publishing industry. Also leads tours and teaches photography.

⊕ ◑ [$][$][$] ○ ◐ ● WILD MADAGASCAR

111 Bank St. #218, Grass Valley CA 95945. (916)520-8574. **E-mail:** workshops@jenniferwu.com. **Website:** www.jenniferwu.com. **Contact:** Jennifer Wu, owner/tour leader/photographer. Cost: $9,900 double; $11,700 single. "Madagascar is one of the wonders of the world and home to an amazing variety of strange and beautiful endemic animals in surroundings that are close to being other worldly. Join top photographers Jim Martin and Jennifer Wu on this exceptionally special trip as they lead you through the country capturing an amazing variety of strange and beautiful endemic animals. Your tour leaders know where to get the best shots, and will also give you in the field demos and compositional guidance to enhance the way you see and shoot. This workshop will focus on landscapes and animals in both the wild and contained environments. These animals are not your typical zoo collec-

tion. In the land of the indri we will have the opportunities to photograph animals such as the lemur, which resembles a panda that sounds like a humpback whale. We will also photograph thumbnail-sized ground-dwelling Brookesia, to meter-long species that pluck birds out of the air with their tongues, to a collection of thousands of chameleons, and even leaf-tailed geckos and white sifaka lemurs. The photographic opportunities are endless on this exceptional workshop. This tour is intended for intermediate and advanced photographers. However, any skill level is welcome and will enjoy Madagascar's photographic opportunities. Participants should have a working knowledge of their equipment. Jennifer Wu and James Martin have led dozens of photo tours and workshops domestically and around the world. Jennifer is a Canon Explorer of Light and James has produced more than 20 books. Together they collaborated on *Photography Night Sky* (Mountaineer Books), one of Amazon's most popular books on landscape photography." E-mail or see website for more information.

○ ◑ ● WILD PHOTO ADVENTURES TV SHOW

2035 Buchanan Rd., Manning SC 29102. (803)460-7705. **E-mail:** doug@totallyoutdoorsimaging.com. **Website:** www.wildphotoadventures.com. **Contact:** Doug Gardner, host/photographer/cinematographer. "*Wild Photo Adventures* is the only wildlife and nature photography television show of its kind to ever be aired. Join us each week as we travel around the globe to great locations to photograph wildlife, its behavior and its environment. Each week, we will show you where to go, how to find wild subjects and how to photograph them in new and creative ways. *Wild Photo Adventures* delivers exciting and educational entertainment for anyone who has a love for the great outdoors or photography. Tag along with host Doug Gardner through adverse conditions and terrain in search of that one great photograph. Take a look behind the scenes at what it takes to be a professional nature photographer. Learn new tips and techniques that will bring life back into your photographs. Contact your local PBS station for air dates/times, or watch all the episodes online at www.wildphotoadventures.com/watchshow.html."

THE HELENE WURLITZER FOUNDATION

P.O. Box 1891, Taos NM 87571. (575)758-2413. **Fax:** (575)758-2559. **E-mail:** hwf@taosnet.com. **Website:** www.wurlitzerfoundation.org. **Contact:** Michael A. Knight, executive director. Estab. 1954. The foundation offers residencies to artists in the following creative fields: visual and literary arts and music composition. There are 2 12-week sessions from mid-January through mid-April, early September-early December, and 1-10 week session from early June to mid-August. Application deadline: January 18 for following year. For application, request by e-mail or visit website to download.

◑ ● YADDO

The Corporation of Yaddo Residencies, P.O. Box 395, 312 Union Ave., Saratoga Springs NY 12866-0395. (518)584-0746. **Fax:** (518)584-1312. **E-mail:** chwait@yaddo.org. **Website:** www.yaddo.org. **Contact:** Candace Wait, program director. Estab. 1900. Two seasons: large season is May-August; small season is October-May (stays from 2 weeks to 2 months; average stay is 5 weeks). Accepts 230 artists/year. Accommodates approximately 35 artists in large season. Those qualified for invitations to Yaddo are highly qualified writers, visual artists (including photographers), composers, choreographers, performance artists and film and video artists who are working at the professional level in their fields. Artists who wish to work collaboratively are encouraged to apply. An abiding principle at Yaddo is that applications for residencies are judged on the quality of the artists' work and professional promise. Site includes four small lakes, a rose garden, woodland, swimming pool, tennis courts. Yaddo's nonrefundable application fee is $30, to which is added a fee for media uploads ranging from $5-10 depending on the discipline. Application fees must be paid by credit card. Two letters of recommendation are requested. All application materials, including contact information, résumé, work sample, and reference letter, must be submitted online. Applications are considered by the Admissions Committee and invitations are issued by March 15 (deadline: January 1) and October 1 (deadline: August 1). Information available on website.

○ ◑ ● YELLOWSTONE ASSOCIATION INSTITUTE

P.O. Box 117, Yellowstone National Park WY 82190. (406)848-2400. **Fax:** (406)848-2847. **E-mail:** Registrar@yellowstoneassociation.org. **Website:** www.yellowstoneassociation.org. Offers workshops in nature and wildlife photography during the summer, fall and winter. Custom courses can be arranged. Photographers should see website for more information.

○ ◑ ● YOSEMITE CONSERVANCY OUTDOOR ADVENTURES

P.O. Box 230, El Portal CA 95318. (209)379-2646. **Fax:** (209)379-2486. **E-mail:** info@yosemiteconservancy.org; kchappell@yosemiteconservancy.org. **Website:** www.yosemiteconservancy.org. Offers workshops year round in Yosemite National Park with programs ranging from birding, snowshoeing, family programs, natural history, backpack treks, photography workshops and cultural programs. Please see our website for our full schedule along with information on our custom trips.

STOCK PHOTOGRAPHY PORTALS

//

These sites market and distribute images from multiple agencies and photographers.

AGPix www.agpix.com
Alamy www.alamy.com
Digital Railroad www.digitalrailroad.net
Find a Photographer www.asmp.org/find-a-photographer
Independent Photography Network (IPNStock) www.ipnstock.com
PhotoServe www.pdnonline.com/PhotoServe328.shtml
PhotoSource International www.photosource.com
Shutterpoint Photography www.shutterpoint.com
Veer www.veer.com
Workbook Stock www.workbook.com

PORTFOLIO REVIEW EVENTS

//

Portfolio review events provide photographers the opportunity to show their work to a variety of photo buyers, including photo editors, publishers, art directors, gallery representatives, curators, and collectors.

Art Directors Club, International Annual Awards Exhibition, New York City, www.adc global.org

Atlanta Celebrates Photography, held annually in October, Atlanta GA, www.acpinfo. org

The Center for Photography at Woodstock, New York City, www.cpw.org

Festival of Light, an international collaboration of twenty photography festivals, www. festivaloflight.net

Fotofest, March, biennial—held in even-numbered years, Houston TX, www.fotofest.org

FOTOfusion, January, West Palm Beach FL, www.fotofusion.org

The North American Nature Photography Association, annual summit held in January. Location varies. www.nanpa.org

Photo LA, January, Los Angeles CA, www.photola.com

Photolucida, March, biennial—held in odd-numbered years, Portland OR, www.photo lucida.org

The Print Center, events held throughout the year, Philadelphia PA, www.printcenter.org

Review Santa Fe, Summer, the only juried portfolio review event, Santa Fe NM, visitcen ter.org

Society for Photographic Education National Conference, March, different location each year, www.spenational.org

GRANTS

State, Provincial, & Regional

//

Arts councils in the United States and Canada provide assistance to artists (including photographers) in the form of fellowships or grants. These grants can be substantial and confer prestige upon recipients; however, only state or province residents are eligible. Because deadlines and available support vary annually, query first (with a SASE) or check websites for guidelines.

UNITED STATES ARTS AGENCIES

Alabama State Council on the Arts, 201 Monroe St., Montgomery AL 36130-1800. (334)242-4076. E-mail: staff@arts.alabama.gov. Website: alabamaarts.egrant.net.

Alaska State Council on the Arts, 161 S. Klevin St., Suite 102, Anchorage AK 99508-1506. (907)269-6610 or (888)278-7424. E-mail: aksca.info@alaska.gov. Website: www.eed.state.ak.us/aksca.

Arizona Commission on the Arts, 417 W. Roosevelt St., Phoenix AZ 85003-1326. (602)771-6501. E-mail: info@azarts.gov. Website: www.azarts.gov.

Arkansas Arts Council, 1500 Tower Bldg., 323 Center St., Little Rock AR 72201-2606. (501)324-9766. E-mail: info@arkansasarts.com. Website: www.arkansasarts.org.

California Arts Council, 1300 I St., Suite 930, Sacramento CA 95814. (916)322-6555 or (800)201-6201. E-mail: info@arts.ca.gov. Website: www.cac.ca.gov.

Colorado Creative Industries, 1625 Broadway, Suite 2700, Denver CO 80202. (303)892-3802. E-mail: online form. Website: www.coloradocreativeindustries.org.

Connecticut Office of Culture & Tourism, One Constitution Plaza, 2nd Floor, Hartford CT 06103. (860)256-2800. Website: www.cultureandtourism.org.

Delaware Division of the Arts, Carvel State Office Bldg., 4th Floor, 820 N. French St., Wilmington DE 19801. (302)577-8278 (New Castle County) or (302)739-5304 (Kent or Sussex Counties). E-mail: delarts@state.de.us. Website: www.artsdel.org.

District of Columbia Commission on the Arts and Humanities, 200 I St. SE, Washington DC 20003. (202)724-5613. E-mail: cah@dc.gov. Website: www.dcarts.dc.gov.

Florida Division of Cultural Affairs, R.A. Gray Building, 3rd Floor, 500 S. Bronough St., Tallahassee FL 32399-0250. (850)245-6470. E-mail: info@florida-arts.org. Website: www.florida-arts.org.

Georgia Council for the Arts, 75 Fifth St. NW, Suite 1200, Atlanta GA 30308. (404)685-2787. E-mail: gaarts@gaarts.org. Website: www.gaarts.org.

Guam Council on the Arts & Humanities Agency, P.O. Box 2950, Hagatna, Guam 96932. (671)300-1204/1205/1206/1207/1208. E-mail: info@caha.guam.gov. Website: www.guamcaha.org.

Hawai'i State Foundation on Culture and the Arts, 250 S. Hotel St., 2nd Floor, Honolulu HI 96813. (808)586-0300. Website: www.state.hi.us/sfca.

Idaho Commission on the Arts, P.O. Box 83720, Boise ID 83720-0008. (208)334-2119 or (800)278-3863. E-mail: info@arts.idaho.gov. Website: www.arts.idaho.gov.

Illinois Arts Council Agency, James R. Thompson Center, 100 W. Randolph St., Suite 10-500, Chicago IL 60601-3230. (312)814-6750 or (800)237-6994. E-mail: iac.info@illinois.gov. Website: www.arts.illinois.gov.

Indiana Arts Commission, 100 N. Senate Ave., Room N505, Indianapolis IN 46204. (317)232-1268. E-mail: IndianaArtsCommission@iac.in.gov. Website: www.in.gov/arts.

Iowa Arts Council, 600 E. Locust, Des Moines IA 50319-0290. (515)242-6194. Website: www.iowaartscouncil.org.

Kansas Arts Foundation, P.O. Box 1806, Manhattan KS 66505. (785)727-4537. E-mail: executivedirector@kansasartsfoundation.com. Website: www.kansasartsfoundation.com.

Kansas Creative Arts Industries Commission, 1000 Jackson St., Suite 100, Topeda KS 66612. (785)296-2178. E-mail: pjasso@kansascommerce.com. Website: www.kansascommerce.com/caic.

Kentucky Arts Council, Capital Plaza Tower, 21st Floor, 500 Mero St., Frankfort KY 40601-1987. (502)564-3757 or (888)833-2787. E-mail: kyarts@ky.gov. Website: www.artscouncil.ky.gov.

Louisiana Division of the Arts, P.O. Box 44247, Baton Rouge LA 70804-4247. (225)342-8180. Website: www.crt.state.la.us/cultural-development/arts.

Maine Arts Commission, 193 State St., 25 State House Station, Augusta ME 04333-0025. (207)287-2724. E-mail: MaineArts.info@maine.gov. Website: mainearts.maine.gov.

Maryland State Arts Council, 175 W. Ostend St., Suite E, Baltimore MD 21230. (410)767-6555. E-mail: msac@msac.org. Website: www.msac.org.

Massachusetts Cultural Council, 10 St. James Ave., 3rd Floor, Boston MA 02116-3803. (617)727-3668. E-mail: mcc@art.state.ma.us. Website: www.massculturalcouncil.org.

Michigan Council for Arts and Cultural Affairs, 300 N. Washington Square, Lansing MI 48913. (888)522-0103. Website: www.themedc.org/Arts.

Minnesota State Arts Board, Park Square Court, Suite 200, 400 Sibley St., St. Paul MN 55101-1928. (651)215-1600 or (800)866-2787. E-mail: msab@arts.state.mn.us. Website: www.arts.state.mn.us.

Mississippi Arts Commission, 501 N. West St., Suite 1101A, Woolfolk Bldg., Jackson MS 39201. (601)359-6030 or (800)582-2233. Website: www.arts.state.ms.us.

Missouri Arts Council, 815 Olive St., Suite 16, St. Louis MO 63101-1503. (314)340-6845 or (866)407-4752. E-mail: moarts@ded.mo.gov. Website: www.missouriartscouncil.org.

Montana Arts Council, P.O. Box 202201, Helena MT 59620-2201. (406)444-6430. E-mail: mac@mt.gov. Website: art.mt.gov.

National Assembly of State Arts Agencies, 1200 18th St. NW, Suite 1100, Washington DC 20036. (202)347-6352. E-mail: nasaa@nasaa-arts.org. Website: www.nasaa-arts.org.

Nebraska Arts Council, 1004 Farnam St., Burlington Bldg., Plaza Level, Omaha NE 68102. (402)595-2122 or (800)341-4067. E-mail: nac.info@nebraska.gov. Website: www.artscouncil.nebraska.gov.

Nevada Arts Council, 716 N. Carson St., Suite A, Carson City NV 89701. (775)687-6680. E-mail: infonvartscouncil@nevadaculture.org. Website: nac.nevadaculture.org.

New Hampshire State Council on the Arts, 19 Pillsbury St., 1st Floor, Concord NH 03301. (603)271-3584. Website: www.nh.gov/nharts.

New Jersey State Council on the Arts, P.O. Box 306, Trenton NJ 08608. (609)292-6130. Website: artscouncil.nj.gov.

New Mexico Arts, Bataan Memorial Building, 407 Galisteo St., Suite 270, Santa Fe NM 87501. (505)827-6490 or (800)879-4278. Website: www.nmarts.org.

New York State Council on the Arts, 300 Park Ave. S., 10th Floor, New York NY 10010. (212)459-8800. Website: www.nysca.org.

North Carolina Arts Council, 109 E. Jones St., Cultural Resources Building, Raleigh NC 27601. (919)807-6500. E-mail: ncarts@ncdcr.gov. Website: www.ncarts.org.

North Dakota Council on the Arts, 1600 E. Century Ave., Suite 6, Bismarck ND 58503-0649. (701)328-7590. Website: www.state.nd.us/arts.

Ohio Arts Council, 30 E. Broad St., 33rd Floor, Columbus OH 43215-3414. (614)466-2613. Website: www.oac.state.oh.us.

Oklahoma Arts Council, Jim Thorpe Building, 2101 N. Lincoln Blvd., Suite 640, Oklahoma City OK 73152-2001. (405)521-2931. E-mail: okarts@arts.ok.gov. Website: www.arts.ok.gov.

Oregon Arts Commission, 775 Summer St. NE, Suite 200, Salem OR 97301-1280. (503)986-0082. E-mail: oregon.artscomm@state.or.us. Website: www.oregonartscommission.org.

Pennsylvania Council on the Arts, 216 Finance Bldg., Commonwealth and North Streets, Harrisburg PA 17120. (717)787-6883. Website: www.arts.pa.gov.

Institute of Puerto Rican Culture, P.O. Box 9024184, San Juan, Puerto Rico 00902-4184. (787)724-0700. E-mail: mgarcia@icp.gobierno.pr. Website: www.icp.gobierno.pr.

Rhode Island State Council on the Arts, One Capitol Hill, 3rd Floor, Providence RI 02908. (401)222-3880. E-mail: info@arts.ri.gov. Website: www.arts.ri.gov.

American Samoa Arts Council, P.O. Box 1540, Pago Pago, American Samoa 96799. (684)633-4347. E-mail: cach@as.gov. Website: americansamoa.gov.

South Carolina Arts Commission, 1026 Sumter St., Suite 200, Columbia SC 29201. (803)734-8696. Website: www.southcarolinaarts.com.

South Dakota Arts Council, 711 E. Wells Ave., Pierre SD 57501-3369. (605)773-3301. E-mail: sdac@state.sd.us. Website: www.artscouncil.sd.gov.

Tennessee Arts Commission, 401 Charlotte Ave., Nashville TN 37243-0780. (615)741-1701. Website: tnartscommission.org.

Texas Commission on the Arts, E.O. Thompson Office Bldg., 920 Colorado, Suite 501, Austin TX 78701. (512)463-5535. E-mail: front.desk@arts.texas.gov. Website: www.arts.texas.gov.

Utah Division of Arts & Museums, 617 E. South Temple, Salt Lake City UT 84102-1177. (801)236-7555. Website: heritage.utah.gov/arts-and-museums/ops-grants.

Vermont Arts Council, 136 State St., Montpelier VT 05633-6001. (802)828-3291. E-mail: online form. Website: www.vermontartscouncil.org.

Virgin Islands Council on the Arts, 5070 Norre Gade, Suite 1, St. Thomas, Virgin Islands 00802-6876. (340)774-5984. Website: vicouncilonarts.org.

Virginia Commission for the Arts, 1001 E. Broad St., Richmond VA 23219. (804)225-3132. E-mail: arts@vca.virginia.gov. Website: www.arts.virginia.gov.

Washington State Arts Commission, 711 Capitol Way S., Suite 600, P.O. Box 42675, Olympia WA 98504-2675. (360)753-3860. E-mail: online form. Website: www.arts.wa.gov.

West Virginia Commission on the Arts, The Cultural Center, Capitol Complex, 1900 Kanawha Blvd. E., Charleston WV 25305-0300. (304)558-0240. Website: www.wvculture.org/arts.

Wisconsin Arts Board, Tommy G. Thompson Commerce Bldg., 201 W. Washington Ave., Madison WI 53708. (608)266-0190. E-mail: artsboard@wisconsin.gov. Website: artsboard.wisconsin.gov.

Wyoming Arts Council, 2301 Central Ave., Barrett Bldg., 2nd Floor, Cheyenne WY 82002. (307)777-7742. E-mail: online form. Website: wyoarts.state.wy.us.

CANADIAN PROVINCES ARTS AGENCIES

Alberta Foundation for the Arts, 10708 - 105 Ave., Edmonton Alberta T5H 0A1. (780)427-9968. E-mail: online form. Website: www.affta.ab.ca.

British Columbia Arts Council, P.O. Box 9819, Stn. Prov. Govt., Victoria British Columbia V8W 9W3. (250)356-1718. E-mail: BCArtsCouncil@gov.bc.ca. Website: www.bcartscouncil.ca.

Canada Council for the Arts, 150 Elgin St., P.O. Box 1047, Ottawa Ontario K1P 5V8. (613)566-4414 or (800)263-5588 (within Canada). E-mail: info@canadacouncil.ca. Website: www.canadacouncil.ca.

Manitoba Arts Council, 525-93 Lombard Ave., Winnipeg Manitoba R3B 3B1. (204)945-2237 or (866)994-2787 (within Manitoba). E-mail: info@artscouncil.mb.ca. Website: www.artscouncil.mb.ca.

New Brunswick Arts Board, 649 Queen St., 2nd Floor, Fredericton NB E3B 1C3. (506)444-4444 or (866)460-2787. E-mail: online form. Website: www.artsnb.ca.

Newfoundland and Labrador Arts Council, P.O. Box 98, St. John's Newfoundland A1C 5H5. (709)726-2212 or (866)726-2212 (within Newfoundland). E-mail: nlacmail@nlac.ca. Website: www.nlac.ca.

Nova Scotia Department of Communities, Culture, and Heritage, 1741 Brunswick St., 3rd Floor, P.O. Box 456, Stn. Central, Halifax Nova Scotia B3J 2R5. (902)424-4510. E-mail: cch@gov.ns.ca. Website: www.gov.ns.ca/cch.

Ontario Arts Council, 151 Bloor St. W., 5th Floor, Toronto Ontario M5S 1T6. (416)961-1660 or (800)387-0058 (within Ontario). E-mail: info@arts.on.ca. Website: www.arts.on.ca.

The Prince Edward Island Council of the Arts, 115 Richmond St., Charlottetown Prince Edward Island C1A 1H7. (902)368-4410 or (888)734-2784. E-mail: info@peica.ca. Website: www.peiartscouncil.com.

Québec Council for Arts & Literature, 79 boul. René-Lévesque Est, 3e étage, Québec G1R 5N5. (418)643-1707 or (800)897-1707. E-mail: info@calq.gouv.qc.ca. Website: www.calq.gouv.qc.ca.

Saskatchewan Arts Board, 1355 Broad St., Regina Saskatchewan S4P 7V1. (306)787-4056 or (800)667-7526 (within Saskatchewan). E-mail: info@artsboard.sk.ca. Website: www.artsboard.sk.ca.

Yukon Arts Section, Cultural Services Branch, Dept. of Tourism & Culture, Government of Yukon, Box 2703, Whitehorse Yukon Y1A 2C6. (867)667-8589 or (800)661-0408 (within Yukon). E-mail: arts@gov.yk.ca. Website: www.tc.gov.yk.ca/arts.html.

REGIONAL GRANTS & AWARDS

The following opportunities are arranged by state since most of them grant money to artists in a particular geographic region. Because deadlines vary annually, check websites or call for the most up-to-date information.

California

Flintridge Foundation Awards for Visual Artists, 236 W. Mountain St., Suite 106, Pasadena CA 91103. (626)449-0839 or (800)303-2139. Website: www.flintridge.org. For artists in California, Oregon, and Washington only.

James D. Phelan Art Awards, Kala Art Institute, Don Porcella, 1060 Heinz Ave., Berkeley CA 94710. (510)549-2977. E-mail: kala@kala.org. Website: www.kala.org. For artists born in California only.

Connecticut

Martha Boschen Porter Fund, Inc., 145 White Hallow Rd., Sharon CT 06064. E-mail: grants@berkshiretaconic.org. Website: www.berkshiretaconic.org/bReceivebNonprofitsIndividuals/SearchApplyforGrants/MarthaBoschenPorterFund.aspx. For artists in northwestern Connecticut, western Massachusetts, and adjacent areas of New York (except New York City).

Idaho

Betty Bowen Memorial Award, c/o Seattle Art Museum 1300 First Ave., Seattle, WA 98101. (206)654-3131. E-mail: bettybowen@seattleartmuseum.org. Website: www.seattleartmuseum.org/about-sam/art/submissions#bet. For artists in Washington, Oregon and Idaho only.

Illinois

Illinois Arts Council, Individual Artists Support Initiative, James R. Thompson Center, 100 W. Randolph, Suite 10-500, Chicago IL 60601. (312)814-6750. E-mail: iac.info@illinois.gov. Website: www.arts.illinois.gov/grants-programs/funding-programs/individual-artist-support. For Illinois artists only.

Kentucky

Kentucky Foundation for Women Grants Program, 1215 Heyburn Bldg., 332 W. Broadway, Louisville KY 40202. (502)562-0045 or (866)654-7564. E-mail: team@kfw.org. Website: www.kfw.org/grants. For female artists living in Kentucky only.

Massachusetts

See **Martha Boschen Porter Fund, Inc.,** under Connecticut.

Minnesota

McKnight Artist Fellowships for Photographers, University of Minnesota Dept. of Art, Regis Center for Art, E-201, 405 21st Ave. S., Minneapolis MN 55455. (612)626-9640. E-mail: gallery@mcad.edu. Website: www.mcknightphoto.org. For Minnesota artists only.

New York

A.I.R. Gallery Fellowship Program, 155 Plymouth St., Brooklyn NY 11201. (212)255-6651. E-mail: info@airgallery.org. Website: www.airgallery.org. For female artists from New York City metro area only.

Arts & Cultural Council for Greater Rochester, 200 W. Ridge St., Suite 214, Rochester NY 14615. (585)473-4000. E-mail: artsandculturalcouncil@artsrochester.org. Website: www.artsrochester.org.

Constance Saltonstall Foundation for the Arts Grants and Fellowships, 435 Ellis Hollow Creek Rd., Ithaca NY 14850. (607)539-3146. E-mail: artscolony@saltonstall.org. Website: www.saltonstall.org. For artists in the central and western counties of New York.

See **Martha Boschen Porter Fund, Inc.,** under Connecticut.

New York Foundation for the Arts: Artists' Fellowships, 20 Jay St., 7th Floor, Brooklyn NY 11201. (212)366-6900. E-mail: fellowships@nyfa.org. Website: www.nyfa.org. For New York artists only.

Oregon

See **Betty Bowen Memorial Award,** under Idaho.

See **Flintridge Foundation Awards for Visual Artists,** under California.

Pennsylvania

Leeway Foundation—Philadelphia, Pennsylvania Region, The Philadelphia Building, 1315 Walnut St., Suite 832, Philadelphia PA 19107. (215)545-4078. E-mail: info@leeway. org. Website: www.leeway.org. For female artists in Philadelphia only.

Texas

Individual Artist Grant Program—Houston, Texas, Houston Arts Alliance, 3201 Allen Pkwy., Suite 250, Houston TX 77019-1800. (713)527-9330. E-mail: online form. Website: www.houstonartsalliance.com. For Houston artists only.

Washington

See **Betty Bowen Memorial Award,** under Idaho.
See **Flintridge Foundation Awards for Visual Artists,** under California.

PROFESSIONAL ORGANIZATIONS

American Photographic Artists, National, 369 Montezuma Ave., #567, Santa Fe NM 87501. Membership office: 2055 Bryant St., San Francisco, CA 94110. E-mail: membershiprep@apanational.com. Website: www.apanational.com

American Photographic Artists, Atlanta, 2221-D Peachtree Rd. NE, Suite #553, Atlanta GA 30309. (888)889-7190, ext. 50. E-mail: info@apaatlanta.com. Website: www.apaatlanta.com

American Photographic Artists, Chicago, 1901 Grove Ave., Berwyn IL 60402. (312)834-4563. E-mail: apamidwest@gmail.com. Website: www.chicago.apanational.org

American Photographic Artists, Los Angeles, 9190 W. Olympic Blvd., #212, Beverly Hills CA, 90212. (323)933-1631. E-mail: director@apa-la.org. Website: www.apa-la.org

American Photographic Artists, New York, 419 Lafayette, 2nd Floor, New York NY 10011. (212)807-0399. E-mail: jocelyn@apany.com. Website: www.apany.com

American Photographic Artists, San Diego, E-mail: membershiprep@apanational.com. Website: apasd.org

American Photographic Artists, San Francisco, 2055 Bryant St., San Francisco CA 94110. (415)882-9780. E-mail: info@apasf.com. Website: sf.apanational.org

American Society of Media Photographers (ASMP), 150 N. Second St., Philadelphia, PA 19106. (215)451-2767. Website: www.asmp.org

American Society of Picture Professionals (ASPP), 201 E. 25th St., #11c, New York NY 10010. (516)500-3686. Website: www.aspp.com

The Association of Photographers, 49/50 Eagle Wharf Rd., London N1 7ED, United Kingdom. (44) (020) 7739-6669. E-mail: info@aophoto.co.uk. Website: www.the-aop.org

British Association of Picture Libraries and Agencies, 59 Tranquil Vale, Blackheath, London SE3 OBS, United Kingdom. (44) (0) 20 8297 1198. Fax: (44) (020) 8852-7211. E-mail: online form. Website: www.bapla.org.uk

British Institute of Professional Photography (BIPP), The Coach House, The Firs, High St., Whitchurch, Aylesbury, Buckinghamshire, HP22 4SJ, United Kingdom. (44) (012) 9671-8530. Fax: (44) (012) 9633-6367. E-mail: membership@bipp.com. Website: www.bipp.com

Canadian Association for Photographic Art, Box 357, Logan Lake British Columbia V0K 1W0, Canada. E-mail: capa@capacanada.ca. Website: www.capacanada.ca

Canadian Association of Journalists, Box 745, Cornwall Ontario K6H 5T5 Canada. E-mail: online form. Website: www.caj.ca

The Canadian Association of Professional Image Creators, 720 Spadina Ave., Suite 202, Toronto Ontario M5S 2T9, Canada. (416)462-3677 or (888)252-2742. Fax: (416)929-5256. E-mail: info@capic.org. Website: www.capic.org

The Center for Photography at Woodstock (CPW), 59 Tinker St., Woodstock NY 12498. (845)679-9957. Fax: (845)679-6337. E-mail: info@cpw.org. Website: www.cpw.org

Evidence Photographers International Council, Inc. (EPIC), 229 Peachtree St. NE, Suite 2200, Atlanta GA 30303. (866)868-3742. Fax: (404)614-6406. E-mail: csc@evidence photographers.com. Website: www.evidencephotographers.com

International Association of Panoramic Photographers, E-mail: online form. Website: www.panoramicassociation.org

International Center of Photography (ICP), 1114 Avenue of the Americas, New York NY 10036. (212)857-0003. E-mail: membership@icp.org. Website: www.icp.org

The Light Factory (TLF), 1817 Central Ave., Charlotte NC 28205. (704)333-9755. E-mail: info@lightfactory.org. Website: www.lightfactory.org

National Association of Photoshop Professionals (NAPP), 333 Douglas Rd. E., Oldsmar FL 34677. (813)433-5000 or (800)201-7323. E-mail: online form. Website: www.photoshopuser.com

National Press Photographers Association (NPPA), 3200 Croasdaile Dr., Suite 306, Durham NC 27705. (919)383-7246. Fax: (919)383-7261. E-mail: info@nppa.org. Website: www.nppa.org

The North American Nature Photography Association (NANPA), 6382 Charleston Rd., Alma IL 62807. (618)547-7616. Fax: (618)547-7438. E-mail: info@nanpa.org. Website: www.nanpa.org

Photographic Society of America (PSA), 8241 S. Walker Ave., Suite 104, Oklahoma City OK 73139. (405)843-1437. E-mail: online form. Website: www.psa-photo.org

Picture Archive Council of America (PACA), Digital Media Licensing Association, 3165 S. Alma School Rd., #29-261, Chandler AZ 85248-3760. (714)815-8427. Fax: (949)679-8224. E-mail: execdirector@pacoffice.org. Website: www.pacaoffice.org

PMA—The Worldwide Community of Imaging Association, 7918 Jonas Brand Dr., Suite 300, McLean VA 22102. (703)665-4416 Fax: (703)506-3266. Website: www.pmai.org

Professional Photographers of America (PPA), 229 Peachtree St. NE, Suite 2200, Atlanta GA 30303. (404)522-8600 or (800)786-6277. Fax: (404)614-6400. E-mail: online form. Website: www.ppa.com

Professional Photographers of Canada (PPOC), 209 Light St., Woodstock Ontario N45 6H6. (519)537-2555 or (888)643-7762. Fax: (888)831-4036. Website: www.ppoc.ca

The Royal Photographic Society, Fenton House, 122 Wells Rd., Bath BA2 3AH, United Kingdom. (44) (012) 2532-5733. E-mail: reception@rps.org. Website: www.rps.org

Society for Photographic Education, 2530 Superior Ave., #403, Cleveland OH 44114. (216)622-2733. Fax: (216)622-2712. E-mail: online form. Website: www.spenational.org

Volunteer Lawyers for the Arts, 1 E. 53rd St., 6th Floor, New York NY 10022. (212)319-2787, ext. 1. Fax: (212)752-6575. E-mail: vlany@vlany.org. Website: www.vlany.org

Wedding & Portrait Photographers International (WPPI), 85 Broad St. 11th Floor, New York NY 10004. Website: www.wppionline.com

The White House News Photographers Association (WHNPA), 7119 Ben Franklin Station, Washington DC 20044-7119. Website: www.whnpa.org

PUBLICATIONS

PERIODICALS

Advertising Age: www.adage.com
> Weekly magazine covering marketing, media and advertising.

Adweek: www.adweek.com
> Weekly magazine covering advertising agencies.

American Photo: www.americanphotomag.com
> Monthly magazine emphasizing the craft and philosophy of photography.

ASMP Bulletin: www.asmp.org
> Newsletter of the American Society of Media Photographers published five times/year. Subscription with membership.

Communication Arts: www.commarts.com
> Trade journal for visual communications.

Editor & Publisher: www.editorandpublisher.com
> Monthly magazine covering latest developments in journalism and newspaper production. Publishes an annual directory issue listing syndicates and another directory listing newspapers.

Folio: www.foliomag.com
> Monthly magazine featuring trends in magazine circulation, production, and editorial.

Graphis: www.graphis.com
> Magazine for the visual arts.

HOW: www.howdesign.com

Bimonthly magazine for the design industry.

News Photographer: www.nppa.org

Monthly news tabloid published by the National Press Photographers Association. Subscription with membership.

Outdoor Photographer: www.outdoorphotographer.com

Monthly magazine emphasizing equipment and techniques for shooting in outdoor conditions.

Photo District News: www.pdnonline.com

Monthly magazine for the professional photographer.

PhotoSource International: www.photosource.com

This company publishes several helpful newsletters, including PhotoLetter, Photo-Daily, and PhotoStockNotes.

Popular Photography: www.popphoto.com

Monthly magazine specializing in technical information for photography.

Print: www.printmag.com

Bimonthly magazine focusing on creative trends and technological advances in illustration, design, photography, and printing.

Professional Artist: www.professionalartistmag.com

Monthly magazine listing galleries reviewing portfolios, juried shows, percent-for-art programs, scholarships, and art colonies.

Professional Photographer: www.ppmag.com

Professional Photographers of America's monthly magazine emphasizing technique and equipment for working photographers.

Publishers Weekly: www.publishersweekly.com

Weekly magazine covering industry trends and news in book publishing; includes book reviews and interviews.

Rangefinder: www.rangefinderonline.com

Monthly magazine covering photography technique, products, and business practices.

Selling Stock: www.selling-stock.com

Newsletter for stock photographers; includes coverage of trends in business practices such as pricing and contract terms.

Shutterbug: www.shutterbug.com

Monthly magazine of photography news and equipment reviews.

BOOKS & DIRECTORIES

ASMP Professional Business Practices in Photography, 7th edition, American Society of Media Photographers. Handbook covering all aspects of running a photography business.

Bacon's Media Directory, Cision. Contains information on all daily and community newspapers in the U.S. and Canada, and 24,000 trade and consumer magazines, newsletters, and journals.

The Big Picture: The Professional Photographer's Guide to Rights, Rates & Negotiation by Lou Jacobs Jr., Writer's Digest Books, F+W, a Content + eCommerce Company. Essential information on understanding contracts, copyrights, pricing, licensing and negotiation.

Blogging for Creatives: How Designers, Artists, Crafters and Writers Can Blog to Make Contacts, Win Business, and Build Success by Robin Houghton, HOW Books, F+W, a Content + eCommerce Company. Approachable guide to the blogosphere, complete with hundreds of tips, tricks and motivational stories from artistic bloggers.

Business and Legal Forms for Photographers, 4th edition by Tad Crawford, Allworth Press. Negotiation book with thirty-four forms for photographers.

The Business of Photography: Principles and Practices by Mary Virginia Swanson, available through her website (www.mvswanson.com) or by e-mailing Lisa@mvswanson.com.

The Business of Studio Photography: How to Start and Run a Successful Photography Studio, 3rd edition by Edward R. Lilley, Allworth Press. A complete guide to starting and running a successful photography studio.

Children's Writer's & Illustrator's Market, Writer's Digest Books, F+W, a Content + eCommerce Company. Annual directory including photo needs of book publishers, magazines and multimedia producers in the children's publishing industry.

Color Confidence: The Digital Photographer's Guide to Color Management by Tim Grey, Sybex.

Color Management for Photographers: Hands-On Techniques for Photoshop Users by Andrew Rodney, Focal Press.

Creative Careers in Photography: Making a Living With or Without a Camera by Michal Heron, Allworth Press.

Digital Stock Photography: How to Shoot and Sell by Michal Heron, Allworth Press.

How to Grow as a Photographer: Reinventing Your Career by Tony Luna, Allworth Press.

How to Succeed in Commercial Photography: Insights From a Leading Consultant by Selina Maitreya, Allworth Press.

LA 411, 411 Publishing. Music industry guide, including record labels.

Legal Guide for the Visual Artist, 5th Edition by Tad Crawford, Allworth Press. The author, an attorney, offers legal advice for artists and includes forms dealing with copyright, sales, taxes, etc.

Licensing Photography by Richard Weisgrau and Victor S. Perlman, Allworth Press.

Literary Market Place, Information Today. Directory that lists book publishers and other book publishing industry contacts.

O'Dwyer's Directory of Public Relations Firms, J.R. O'Dwyer Company, available through website (www.odwyerpr.com). Annual directory listing public relations firms, indexed by specialties.

The Photographer's Guide to Copyright, American Society of Media Photographers.

The Photographer's Guide to Marketing and Self-Promotion, 4th edition by Maria Piscopo, Allworth Press. Marketing guide for photographers.

The Photographer's Market Guide to Building Your Photography Business, 2nd edition by Vic Orenstein, Writer's Digest Books, F+W, a Content + eCommerce Company. Practical advice for running a profitable photography business.

Photo Portfolio Success: A Guide to Submitting and Selling Your Photographs by John Kaplan, Writer's Digest Books, F+W, a Content + eCommerce Company.

Pricing Photography: The Complete Guide to Assignment & Stock Prices by Michal Heron and David MacTavish, Allworth Press.

The Professional Photographer's Legal Handbook by Nancy E. Wolff, Allworth Press.

Profitable Photography in the Digital Age: Strategies for Success by Dan Heller, Allworth Press. By explaining how business is done now, this book helps photographers understand what it takes to sell, deliver, and compete in today's market.

Real World Color Management: Industrial-Strength Production Techniques, 2nd edition by Bruce Fraser, Chris Murphy, and Fred Bunting, Peachpit Press.

Sell & Resell Your Photos, 5th edition by Rohn Engh, Writer's Digest Books, F+W, a Content + eCommerce Company. Revised edition of the classic volume on marketing your own stock.

Selling Your Photography: How to Make Money in New and Traditional Markets by Richard Weisgrau, Allworth Press.

Shooting & Selling Your Photos by Jim Zuckerman, Writer's Digest Books, F+W, a Content + eCommerce Company.

Songwriter's Market, Writer's Digest Books, F+W, a Content + eCommerce Company. Annual directory listing record labels.

Standard Rate and Data Service (SRDS), Kantar Media. Directory listing magazines and their advertising rates.

Starting Your Career as a Freelance Photographer by Tad Crawford, Allworth Press.

Starting Your Career as a Photo Stylist by Susan Linnet Cox, Allworth Press. This invaluable career manual explores the numerous directions a career in photo styling can take.

Workbook, Scott & Daughters Publishing. Numerous resources for the graphic arts industry.

Writer's Market, Writer's Digest Books, F+W, a Content + eCommerce Company. Annual directory listing markets for freelance writers. Many listings include photo needs and payment rates.

WEBSITES

///

PHOTOGRAPHY BUSINESS

The Alternative Pick www.altpick.com
Copyright Website www.benedict.com
APA/EP: Editorial Photographers www.editorialphoto.com
Learnhybrid.pro www.learnhybrid.pro
MacTribe www.mactribe.com
Photographers Black Book www.photographersblackbook.com
Small Business Administration www.sba.gov

MAGAZINE AND BOOK PUBLISHING

American Journalism Review's News Links www.ajr.org
Bookwire www.bookwire.com

STOCK PHOTOGRAPHY

Global Photographers Search www.photographers.com
PhotoSource International www.photosource.com
Selling Stock www.selling-stock.com
The Stockphoto Network www.stockphoto.net
Stock Photo Price Calculator www.photographersindex.com/stockprice.htm

ADVERTISING PHOTOGRAPHY

Advertising Age www.adage.com
Adweek, Mediaweek and Brandweek www.adweek.com
Communication Arts Magazine www.commarts.com

FINE ART PHOTOGRAPHY

Art Deadlines List www.artdeadlineslist.com
TheArtList.com www.theartlist.com
Art-Support www.art-support.com
Mary Virginia Swanson www.mvswanson.com

PHOTOJOURNALISM

The Digital Journalist www.digitaljournalist.org
Foto8 www.foto8.com
National Press Photographers Association www.nppa.org

MAGAZINES

Afterimage www.vsw.org
Aperture www.aperture.org
Black & White www.bandwmag.com
Blind Spot www.blindspot.com
British Journal of Photography www.bjp-online.com
LensWork www.lenswork.com
Photo District News www.pdnonline.com
Photograph Magazine photographmag.com
The Photo Review www.photoreview.org
Popular Photography www.popphoto.com
Professional Artist www.professionalartistmag.com
Shots Magazine www.shotsmag.com
View Camera www.viewcamera.com

E-ZINES

The following publications exist online only. Some offer opportunities for photographers to post their personal work.
The American Museum of Photography www.photographymuseum.com
Apogee Photo www.apogeephoto.com

Art Business News www.artbusinessnews.com

Art in Context www.artincontext.org

Art-Support www.art-support.com

Artists Register artistsregister.com

The Digital Journalist www.digitaljournalist.org

En Foco www.enfoco.org

Fabfotos www.fabfotos.com

Foto8 www.foto8.com

Fotophile www.fotophile.com

Musarium www.musarium.com

One World Journeys www.oneworldjourneys.com

PhotoArts www.photoarts.com

PhotoLinks www.photolinks.com

Photoworkshop.com www.photoworkshop.com

Picture Projects www.pictureprojects.com

PixelPress www.pixelpress.org

TakeGreatPictures.com www.takegreatpictures.com

Zone Zero www.zonezero.com

TECHNICAL

About.com www.photography.about.com

BetterPhoto.com® www.betterphoto.com

Learnhybrid.pro www.learnhybrid.pro

Photo.net www.photo.net

PhotoflexLightingSchool® www.photoflex.com/pls

Wilhelm Imaging Research www.wilhelm-research.com

HOW-TO

Adobe Tutorials www.adobe.com/designcenter.html

Digital Photography Review www.dpreview.com

Fred Miranda www.fredmiranda.com/forum/index.php

Imaging Resource www.imaging-resource.com

Lone Star Digital www.lonestardigital.com

National Association of Photoshop Professionals www.photoshopuser.com

Photography Review www.photographyreview.com

Steve's Digicams www.steves-digicams.com

GLOSSARY

Absolute-released images. Any images for which signed model or property releases are on file and immediately available. For working with stock photo agencies that deal with advertising agencies, corporations and other commercial clients, such images are absolutely necessary to sell usage of images. Also see *Model release, Property release.*

Acceptance (payment on). The buyer pays for certain rights to publish a picture at the time it is accepted, prior to its publication.

Agency promotion rights. Stock agencies request these rights in order to reproduce a photographer's images in promotional materials such as catalogs, brochures and advertising.

Agent. A person who calls on potential buyers to present and sell existing work or obtain assignments for a client. A commission is usually charged. Such a person may also be called a photographer's rep.

All rights. A form of rights often confused with work for hire. Identical to a buyout, this typically applies when the client buys all rights or claim to ownership of copyright, usually for a lump sum payment. This entitles the client to unlimited, exclusive usage and usually with no further compensation to the creator. Unlike work for hire, the transfer of copyright is not permanent. A time limit can be negotiated, or the copyright ownership can run to the maximum of 35 years.

Alternative processes. Printing processes that do not depend on the sensitivity of silver to form an image. These processes include cyanotype and platinum printing.

Archival. The storage and display of photographic negatives and prints in materials that are harmless to them and prevent fading and deterioration.

Artist's statement. A short essay, no more than a paragraph or two, describing a photographer's mission and creative process. Most galleries require photographers to provide an artist's statement.

Assign (designated recipient). A third-party person or business to which a client assigns or designates ownership of copyrights that the client purchased originally from a creator such as a photographer. This term commonly appears on model and property releases.

Assignment. A definite OK to take photos for a specific client with mutual understanding as to the provisions and terms involved.

Assignment of copyright, rights. The photographer transfers claim to ownership of copyright over to another party in a written contract signed by both parties.

Audiovisual (AV). Materials such as filmstrips, motion pictures and overhead transparencies which use audio backup for visual material.

Automatic renewal clause. In contracts with stock photo agencies, this clause works on the concept that every time the photographer delivers an image, the contract is automatically renewed for a specified number of years. The drawback is that a photographer can be bound by the contract terms beyond the contract's termination and be blocked from marketing the same images to other clients for an extended period of time.

Avant garde. Photography that is innovative in form, style or subject matter.

Biannual. Occurring twice a year. Also see *Semiannual*.

Biennial. Occurring once every two years.

Bimonthly. Occurring once every two months.

Bio. A sentence or brief paragraph about a photographer's life and work, sometimes published along with photos.

Biweekly. Occurring once every two weeks.

Blurb. Written material appearing on a magazine's cover describing its contents.

Buyout. A form of work for hire where the client buys all rights or claim to ownership of copyright, usually for a lump sum payment. Also see *All rights*, *Work for hire*.

Caption. The words printed with a photo (usually directly beneath it), describing the scene or action.

CCD. Charged coupled device. A type of light detection device, made up of pixels, that generates an electrical signal in direct relation to how much light strikes the sensor.

CD-ROM. Compact disc read-only memory. Non-erasable electronic medium used for digitized image and document storage and retrieval on computers.

Chrome. A color transparency, usually called a slide.

Cibachrome. A photo printing process that produces fade-resistant color prints directly from color slides.

Clips. See *Tearsheet*.

CMYK. Cyan, magenta, yellow and black. Refers to four-color process printing.

Color correction. Adjusting an image to compensate for digital input and output characteristics.

Commission. The fee (usually a percentage of the total price received for a picture) charged by a photo agency, agent or gallery for finding a buyer and attending to the details of billing, collecting, etc.

Composition. The visual arrangement of all elements in a photograph.

Compression. The process of reducing the size of a digital file, usually through software. This speeds processing, transmission times and reduces storage requirements.

Consumer publications. Magazines sold on newsstands and by subscription that cover information of general interest to the public, as opposed to trade magazines, which cover information specific to a particular trade or profession. See *Trade magazine*.

Contact sheet. A sheet of negative-size images made by placing negatives in direct contact with the printing paper during exposure. They are used to view an entire roll of film on one piece of paper.

Contributor's copies. Copies of the issue of a magazine sent to photographers in which their work appears.

Copyright. The exclusive legal right to reproduce, publish and sell the matter and form of an artistic work.

Cover letter. A brief business letter introducing a photographer to a potential buyer. A cover letter may be used to sell stock images or solicit a portfolio review. Do not confuse cover letter with query letter.

C-print. Any enlargement printed from a negative.

Credit line. The byline of a photographer or organization that appears below or beside a published photo.

Cutline. See *Caption*.

Day rate. A minimum fee that many photographers charge for a day's work, whether a full day is spent on a shoot or not. Some photographers offer a half-day rate for projects involving up to a half-day of work.

Demo. A sample reel of film or sample videocassette that includes excerpts of a filmmaker's or videographer's production work for clients.

Density. The blackness of an image area on a negative or print. On a negative, the denser the black, the less light that can pass through.

Digital camera. A filmless camera system that converts an image into a digital signal or file.

DPI. Dots per inch. The unit of measure used to describe the resolution of image files, scanners and output devices. How many pixels a device can produce in one inch.

DSLR. Digital single-lens reflex camera. Combines the parts of a single-lens reflex camera (SLR) and a digital camera back, replacing the photographic film. The reflex design scheme differentiates a DSLR from other digital cameras.

Electronic submission. A submission made by modem or on computer disk, CD-ROM or other removable media.

Emulsion. The light-sensitive layer of film or photographic paper.

Enlargement. An image that is larger than its negative, made by projecting the image of the negative onto sensitized paper.

Exclusive property rights. A type of exclusive rights in which the client owns the physical image, such as a print, slide, film reel or videotape. A good example is when a portrait is shot for a person to keep, while the photographer retains the copyright.

Exclusive rights. A type of rights in which the client purchases exclusive usage of the image for a negotiated time period, such as one, three or five years. May also be permanent. Also see *All rights*, *Work for hire*.

Fee-plus basis. An arrangement whereby a photographer is given a certain fee for an assignment—plus reimbursement for travel costs, model fees, props and other related expenses incurred in completing the assignment.

File format. The particular way digital information is recorded. Common formats are TIFF and JPEG.

First rights. The photographer gives the purchaser the right to reproduce the work for the first time. The photographer agrees not to permit any publication of the work for a specified amount of time.

Format. The size or shape of a negative or print.

Four-color printing, four-color process. A printing process in which four primary printing inks are run in four separate passes on the press to create the visual effect of a full-color photo, as in magazines, posters and various other print media. Four separate negatives of the color photo—shot through filters—are placed identically (stripped) and exposed onto printing plates, and the images are printed from the plates in four ink colors.

GIF. Graphics interchange format. A graphics file format common to the Internet.

Glossy. Printing paper with a great deal of surface sheen. The opposite of matte.

Hard copy. Any kind of printed output, as opposed to display on a monitor.

Honorarium. Token payment—small amount of money and/or a credit line and copies of the publication.

Image resolution. An indication of the amount of detail an image holds. Usually expressed as the dimension of the image in pixels and the color depth each pixel has. Example: a 640×480, 24-bit image has higher resolution than a 640×480, 16-bit image.

IRC. International reply coupon. IRCs are used with self-addressed envelopes instead of stamps when submitting material to buyers located outside a photographer's home country.

JPEG. Joint photographic experts group. One of the more common digital compression methods that reduces file size without a great loss of detail.

Licensing/leasing. A term used in reference to the repeated selling of one-time rights to a photo.

Manuscript. A typewritten document to be published in a magazine or book.

Matte. Printing paper with a dull, nonreflective surface. The opposite of glossy.

Metadata. Information written into a digital photo file to identify who owns it, copyright and contact information, what camera created the file, exposure information and descriptive keywords, making the file searchable on the Internet.

Model release. Written permission to use a person's photo in publications or for commercial use.

Multi-image. A type of slide show that uses more than one projector to create greater visual impact with the subject. In more sophisticated multi-image shows, the projectors can be programmed to run by computer for split-second timing and animated effects.

Multimedia. A generic term used by advertising, public relations and audiovisual firms to describe productions using more than one medium together—such as slides and full-motion, color video—to create a variety of visual effects.

News release. See *Press release*.

No right of reversion. A term in business contracts that specifies once a photographer sells the copyright to an image, a claim of ownership is surrendered. This may be unenforceable, though, in light of the 1989 Supreme Court decision on copyright law. Also see *All rights, Work for hire*.

On spec. Abbreviation for "on speculation." Also see *Speculation*.

One-time rights. The photographer sells the right to use a photo one time only in any medium. The rights transfer back to the photographer on request after the photo's use.

Page rate. An arrangement in which a photographer is paid at a standard rate per page in a publication.

Photo CD. A trademarked, Eastman Kodak-designed digital storage system for photographic images on a CD.

PICT. The saving format for bit-mapped and object-oriented images.

Picture Library. See *Stock photo agency*.

Pixels. The individual light-sensitive elements that make up a CCD array. Pixels respond in a linear fashion. Doubling the light intensity doubles the electrical output of the pixel.

Point-of-purchase (P-O-P), point-of-sale (P-O-S). A term used in the advertising industry to describe in-store marketing displays that promote a product. Typically, these highly-illustrated displays are placed near checkout lanes or counters, and offer tear-off discount coupons or trial samples of the product.

Portfolio. A group of photographs assembled to demonstrate a photographer's talent and abilities, often presented to buyers.

PPI. Pixels per inch. Often used interchangeably with DPI, PPI refers to the number of pixels per inch in an image. See *DPI*.

Press release. A form of publicity announcement that public relations agencies and corporate communications staff people send out to newspapers and TV stations to generate news coverage. Usually this is sent with accompanying photos or videotape materials.

Property release. Written permission to use a photo of private property or public or government facilities in publications or for commercial use.

Public domain. A photograph whose copyright term has expired is considered to be "in the public domain" and can be used for any purpose without payment.

Publication (payment on). The buyer does not pay for rights to publish a photo until it is actually published, as opposed to payment on acceptance.

Query. A letter of inquiry to a potential buyer soliciting interest in a possible photo assignment.

Raw image file. A file format that contains minimally processed data from the digital camera image sensor. Also called digital negatives, raw files save, with minimum loss of information, data obtained from the sensor and the metadata.

Rep. Trade jargon for sales representative. Also see *Agent*.

Resolution. The particular pixel density of an image, or the number of dots per inch a device is capable of recognizing or reproducing.

Résumé. A short written account of one's career, qualifications and accomplishments.

RGB. An additive color model in which red, green, and blue light are combined to create a variety of colors. Used for the sensing, representation, and display of images on televisions, computers and other electronic systems.

Royalty. A percentage payment made to a photographer/filmmaker for each copy of work sold.

R-print. Any enlargement made from a transparency.

SAE. Self-addressed envelope.

SASE. Self-addressed, stamped envelope. (Most buyers require a SASE if a photographer wishes unused photos returned to him, especially unsolicited materials.)

Self-assignment. Any project photographers shoot to show their abilities to prospective clients. This can be used by beginning photographers who want to build a portfolio or by photographers wanting to make a transition into a new market.

Self-promotion piece. A printed piece photographers use for advertising and promoting their businesses. These pieces generally use one or more examples of the photographer's best work, and are professionally designed and printed to make the best impression.

Semiannual. Occurring twice a year. Also see *Biannual.*

Semigloss. A paper surface with a texture between glossy and matte, but closer to glossy.

Semimonthly. Occurring twice a month.

Serial rights. The photographer sells the right to use a photo in a periodical. Rights usually transfer back to the photographer on request after the photo's use.

Simultaneous submissions. Submission of the same photo or group of photos to more than one potential buyer at the same time.

Speculation. The photographer takes photos with no assurance that the buyer will either purchase them or reimburse expenses in any way, as opposed to taking photos on assignment.

Stock photo agency. A business that maintains a large collection of photos it makes available to a variety of clients such as advertising agencies, calendar firms and periodicals. Agencies usually retain 40-60 percent of the sales price they collect, and remit the balance to the photographers whose photo rights they've sold.

Stock photography. Primarily the selling of reprint rights to existing photographs rather than shooting on assignment for a client. Some stock photos are sold outright, but most are rented for a limited time period. Individuals can market and sell stock images to individual clients from their personal inventory, or stock photo agencies can market photographers' work for them. Many stock agencies hire photographers to shoot new work on assignment, which then becomes the inventory of the stock agency.

Subsidiary agent. In stock photography, this is a stock photo agency that handles marketing of stock images for a primary stock agency in certain U.S. or foreign markets. These are usually affiliated with the primary agency by a contractual agreement rather than by direct ownership, as in the case of an agency that has its own branch offices.

SVHS. Super VHS. Videotape that is a step above regular VHS tape. The number of lines of resolution in a SVHS picture is greater, thereby producing a sharper picture.

Tabloid. A newspaper about half the page size of an ordinary newspaper that contains many photos and news in condensed form.

Tearsheet. An actual sample of a published work from a publication.

TIFF. Tagged image file format. A common bitmap image format developed by Aldus.

Trade magazine. A publication devoted strictly to the interests of readers involved in a specific trade or profession, such as beekeepers, pilots or manicurists, and generally available only by subscription.

Transparency. Color film with a positive image, also referred to as a slide.

Unlimited use. A type of rights in which the client has total control over both how and how many times an image will be used. Also see All rights, Exclusive rights, Work for hire.

Unsolicited submission. A photograph or photographs sent through the mail that a buyer did not specifically ask to see.

Work for hire. Any work that is assigned by an employer who becomes the owner of the copyright. Stock images cannot be purchased under work-for-hire terms.

World rights. A type of rights in which the client buys usage of an image in the international marketplace. Also see *All rights*.

Worldwide exclusive rights. A form of world rights in which the client buys exclusive usage of an image in the international marketplace. Also see *All rights*.

GEOGRAPHIC INDEX

GEORGIA

INTERNATIONAL INDEX

SUBJECT INDEX

ALTERNATIVE PROCESS

BABIES/CHILDREN/TEEN

BUSINESS CONCEPTS

CITIES/URBAN

DISASTERS

ENTERTAINMENT

ENVIRONMENTAL

FOOD/DRINK

GARDENING

HISTORICAL/VINTAGE

HOBBIES

INTERIORS/DECORATING

LANDSCAPES/SCENICS

MULTICULTURAL

PERFORMING ARTS

PORTRAITS

PRODUCT SHOTS/STILL LIFE

RELIGIOUS

SCIENCE

SENIOR CITIZENS

TECHNOLOGY/COMPUTERS

GENERAL INDEX

GENERAL INDEX

Ideas. Instruction. Inspiration.

Find the latest issues of *The Artist's Magazine* on newsstands, or visit artistsnetwork.com.

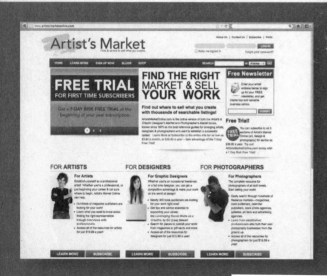

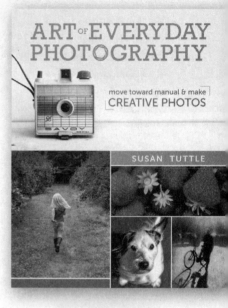

Receive **FREE** downloadable materials when you sign up for our free newsletter at artistsnetwork.com/Newsletter_Thanks.